Cyber Crime and
Digital Evidence

Cyber Crime and Digital Evidence

Materials and Cases

THIRD EDITION

Thomas K. Clancy

PROFESSOR EMERITUS
UNIVERSITY OF MISSISSIPPI SCHOOL OF LAW

CAROLINA ACADEMIC PRESS
Durham, North Carolina

ISBN 978-1-5310-0961-8
eISBN 978-1-5310-0962-5
LCCN 2018959085

Carolina Academic Press, LLC
700 Kent Street
Durham, North Carolina 27701
Telephone (919) 489-7486
Fax (919) 493-5668
www.cap-press.com

Printed in the United States of America

To my Family: Sally, Kevin, and Brian

Contents

Preface to the Third Edition

As stated in the second edition, the rapidity of change required publishing a new edition of this book. New cases continue to add clarity and needed guidance to the acquisition of digital evidence procedures required of law enforcement. New technology and case law discussing the impact of that technology have been added throughout the book. Of particular note, this third edition was delayed until *Carpenter v. United States*, 585 U.S. __ (2018), was decided. That case has the potential to revolutionize the Fourth Amendment's role in the acquisition of digital evidence. Also included in this edition are significant new cases on social media, the use of forensic software to execute a warrant, sexting, the Computer Fraud and Abuse Act, the regulation of threats, and sentencing.

This book is entitled "Cyber Crime and Digital Evidence" for one fundamental reason. In law practice, it is more likely that a lawyer or judge will now encounter digital evidence in almost every case and situation, given its ubiquity in modern life. Hence, about half of this book is devoted to the government's acquisition of digital evidence, regardless of the underlying crime. The balance of the book is devoted to various aspects of the criminal law that have been modified to address the variety of new forms of bad behavior that are facilitated by digital devices and networks.

Thomas K. Clancy
July 2018

Preface to the Second Edition

The rapidity of change required publishing a new edition of this book rather than supplementing the first edition. New cases, particularly United States Supreme Court cases on searching cell phones, have begun to add clarity and needed guidance to the acquisition of digital evidence procedures required of law enforcement. New technology and case law discussing the impact of that technology have been added throughout the book.

Thomas K. Clancy
December 2014

Preface to the First Edition

This book is designed to be an accessible introduction to Cyber Crime and Digital Evidence. The title is consciously styled: *Cyber Crime and Digital Evidence: Materials and Cases.* The title illuminates two significant aspects of this book. First, cyber crime is only a subset of a much broader trend in the criminal area, which is the use of digital evidence in virtually all criminal cases. Hence, it is important to understand the legal framework that regulates obtaining that increasingly used and important evidence. Second, by listing "materials *and* cases" (in that order) the title signals that this book attempts to provide a broader framework than an endless stream of cases offers. Law students deserve the broader context and, hopefully, will get some of it with this book.

This book is the product of numerous influences, ranging from many years of teaching law students, studying the Fourth Amendment and Cyber Crime, and witnessing the explosion of the use of digital evidence in criminal cases. Most immediately, I thank those who provided comments and insights on various aspects of the book. Those individuals include Don Mason, Will Wilkins, and Priscilla Grantham. I received invaluable editorial assistance from Andrew Coffman. For the past decade, I have had the privilege of serving as Director of the National Center for Justice and the Rule of Law and Research Professor at the University of Mississippi School of Law, where I created and developed national programs on Cyber Crime and the Fourth Amendment. Through those programs, the Center offers educational opportunities to judges, prosecutors, and law enforcement on search and seizure, including in emerging areas such as computer searches and seizures, and on broad areas concerning cyber crime. The conferences, lectures, and associations developed at the Center have brought many of the best minds in the country to Oxford, Mississippi to examine the new trends in the criminal law involving new forms of criminal activity and new forms of evidence. The thousands of judges, assistant attorneys general, and other attendees of the Center's events contributed many insights about actual litigation and law enforcement practices, as well as other challenges involved in adapting criminal law, procedure, and practice to the digital age. From each of those participants I have learned much and I deeply appreciate their contributions.

Thomas K. Clancy
December 1, 2011

A Note on Editing

The cases and materials in this book are extensively edited and most changes are done without acknowledgment of omissions of text or other material. Footnotes may be omitted or numbering changed. Capitalization and formatting are often changed based on omissions to the text. The reader should always consult the original source before citing or quoting material herein.

Table of Cases

Cyber Crime and
Digital Evidence

Chapter 1

Introduction

There is no standard definition for the term "Cyber Crime." It is sometimes referred to as, *inter alia*, Computer Crime, High Tech Crime, Internet Crime, and Information Age Crime.[1] There are a host of legislative responses to the use of computer technology from Congress and legislatures in individual states. The Computer Fraud and Abuse Act, 18 U.S.C. § 1030, is the primary federal statute aimed at combating computer-based criminal behavior. Aside from that statute, there are numerous other federal statutes that can be used to prosecute computer-related crimes.[2] As technology has evolved, all states have adopted responses, creating technology-specific laws, even when existing criminal prohibitions may also apply. For example, in *People v. Rice*,[3] the defendant used a computerized phone system to make biweekly claims for unemployment benefits. When the system asked if she had worked during the week for which she was claiming benefits, she entered "9" for "no," even though she had been working. Rice was convicted under Colorado's computer crime statute.[4] Although her act (calling into the system for the purpose of obtaining money to which she was not entitled) fit within the language of the statute, Rice's conduct could have been prosecuted as ordinary fraud.

The types of "Cyber Crimes" in the United States are not easily categorized. There has not been a "systematic approach to cybercrime":

---

1. *See, e.g.,* NAT'L INST. OF JUSTICE, DEPT. OF JUSTICE, COMPUTER CRIME: CRIMINAL JUSTICE RESOURCE MANUAL 2 (1989) (defining computer crime as "any violations of criminal law that involve a knowledge of computer technology for their perpetration, investigation, or prosecution"); BLACK'S LAW DICTIONARY (8th ed. 2004) (defining computer crime as "[a] crime involving the use of a computer"); Jo-Ann M. Adams, Comment, *Controlling Cyberspace: Applying the Computer Fraud and Abuse Act to the Internet*, 12 SANTA CLARA COMPUTER & HIGH TECH. L.J. 403, 409 (1996) (defining computer crime as "those crimes where knowledge of a computer system is essential to commit the crime").

2. *E.g.,* Ryan P. Wallace, *et al., Computer Crimes*, 42 AM. CRIM. L. REV. 223, 237 (2005).

3. People v. Rice, 198 P.3d 1241 (Colo. Ct. App. 2008).

4. COLO. REV. STAT. § 18-5-5-102(c)–(d) (2007), provided in part that "a person commits computer crime if the person knowingly"

> (c) Accesses any computer, computer network, or computer system, or any part thereof to obtain, by means of false or fraudulent pretenses, representations, or promises, money; property; . . . or other thing of value; or
> (d) Accesses any computer, computer network, or computer system, or any part therein to commit theft.

As cybercrime encompasses both general preexisting crime that is extended onto the Internet, as well as crimes that are specific to a twenty-first century world of networked computers, legal responses include the application of laws of general applicability as well as specific enactments aimed at crime on the Internet. To date, American efforts at dealing with Internet crime continue to be dominated by reactive legislation and responsive recasting of existing criminal law actions to deal with crimes such as unauthorized access, fraud, obscenity, child pornography, and copyright infringement.[5]

Functionally, it may be useful to think of Cyber Crime as any crime in which a computer or any other digital device is involved. Viewed from that perspective, Cyber Crime can be defined by reference to the three ways in which computers and other digital devices are involved in crime: Either as a *Target, Tool,* or *Container.* These are rough—but helpful—categorizations and any given statute may have multiple purposes. Notice that this book uses the words "computer" and "digital device" interchangeably, given the proliferation of numerous types of devices that utilize computer technology, including everything from cell phones, desk top computers, refrigerators, water meters, digital personal assistants in homes, to an ever expanding list of other devices. Cyber crime can involve any of those devices.

1. Computer as Target

Crimes in which computers are the target are sometimes thought of as true computer crimes. These are crimes that did not exist before the spread of computer technology and computer networks.

Examples of crimes that involve a computer as a target include various forms of unauthorized access, including hacking (gaining unauthorized access to a computer), cracking (aggravated hacking), or gaining unauthorized access to a computer to commit another crime, such as theft or vandalism. The Computer Fraud and Abuse Act, 18 U.S.C. § 1030, addresses these forms of criminal behavior. It has broad applicability to any computer connected to the Internet. Additionally, many states have statutes that seek to protect computers. In many states, simple hacking and aggravated hacking are treated as distinct crimes, with simple hacking often classified as a misdemeanor and aggravated hacking as a felony.[6] However, variations among states statutes abound. Depending on the jurisdiction, an act may be referred to as unauthorized access,[7] computer trespass,[8] unauthorized use,[9] or computer tampering.[10]

---

5. Salil K. Mehra, *Law and Cybercrime in the United States Today*, 58 Am. J. Comp. L. 659 (2010).

6. *E.g.*, Alaska Stat. §§ 11.46.484 & 11.46.740 (2000); Del. Code Ann. tit. 11, §§ 932 & 933 (1995); Md. Code Ann., Crim Law § 7-302 (1996).

7. *E.g.*, Cal. Penal Code § 502 (Supp. 2004); Vt. Stat. Ann. tit. 13, § 4102 (Supp. 2004).

8. *E.g.*, Ark. Code Ann. § 5-41-103 (1997); N.Y. Penal Law § 156.10 (1998).

9. *E.g.*, Cal. Penal Code § 502 (Supp. 2004).

10. *E.g.*, Ariz. Rev. Stat. Ann. § 13-2316 (2000).

Computer attacks often involve the release of malicious programs (malware) in the form of viruses, worms, or Trojans

> that cause an unexpected and frequently undesirable action on the victim's system. A virus is an executable file designed to spread to other computers without detection. It can be transmitted as an attachment to e-mail, as a download, or be present on a diskette or CD. A worm is a type of virus that self-replicates across a network, consuming system resources and slowing or halting the system. A Trojan is a malicious code concealed within an apparently harmless program that hides its true function.[11]

Some of the most destructive programs launch denial of service attacks by flooding a network with so many requests that regular traffic to the targeted website is interrupted. A number of states criminalize the dissemination of malware.[12] Many states have specific statutes criminalizing denial of service attacks[13] and attempted denial of service attacks,[14] although other states include denial of service in statutes prohibiting distribution of malware.[15] At the time this edition was written, according to the 2017 version of Symantec's Internet Security Threat Report, ransomware was a rapidly increasing threat:

> Ransomware continues to plague businesses and consumers, with indiscriminate campaigns pushing out massive volumes of malicious emails. In some cases, organizations can be overwhelmed by the sheer volume of ransomware-laden emails they receive. Attackers are demanding more and more from victims with the average ransom demand in 2016 rising to $1,077, up from $294 a year earlier. Attackers have honed a business model that usually involves malware hidden in innocuous emails, unbreakable encryption, and anonymous ransom payment involving cryptocurrencies. The success of this business model has seen a growing number of attackers jump on the bandwagon. The number of new ransomware families uncovered during 2016 more than tripled to 101 and Symantec logged a 36 percent increase in ransomware infections.

2. Computer as Tool

Almost any kind of traditional crime can be assisted through the use of computers or the Internet. While some offenses are unique to computers and require prosecution under statutes specific to computer operation and related activities, traditional

---

11. NAT'L INST. OF JUSTICE, DEPT. OF JUSTICE, INVESTIGATIONS INVOLVING THE INTERNET AND COMPUTER NETWORKS 55 (2007).

12. *E.g.*, MICH. COMP. LAWS ANN. § 752.795 (2004); Neb. Rev. Stat. § 28-1345 (1995); N.C. GEN. STAT. § 14-455 (Supp. 2004).

13. *E.g.*, CONN. GEN. STAT. § 53a-251(d) (2003); MISS. CODE. ANN. § 97-45-5 (1994).

14. *E.g.*, R.I. GEN. LAWS § 11-52-1 (2002); VA. CODE ANN. § 18.2-152.2 (Supp. 2004).

15. *E.g.*, S.C. CODE ANN. § 16-16-10(k)(3) (Supp. 2004).

statutes of general applicability are used to prosecute many computer related offenses. The Computer Fraud and Abuse Act and similar state computer statutes address certain criminal acts that are facilitated by the use of a computer. Some states specifically criminalize the use of a computer to engage in other criminal acts.[16]

In a case that made national news and ended in the suicide of a teenage girl, Lori Drew allegedly set up a profile as a young boy on Myspace and, pretending to be the boy, chatted with Megan Meier over a period of time. Putting aside the details of the alleged chats, Ms. Drew was charged under the Federal Computer Fraud and Abuse Act with intentionally and without authorization accessing a computer used in interstate commerce and, by means of an interstate communication, obtaining information from that computer to further a tortious act — the intentional infliction of emotional distress. A jury convicted her of three misdemeanor charges but the federal district judge overturned the guilty verdicts and acquitted her. That case is discussed later in this book.

The panoply of criminal activity that can be facilitated by use of a computer is limited only by the human imagination. This book looks at a disturbingly prevalent crime in which a computer is being used as a tool, trading child pornography. Other forms of child exploitation are also examined. Other crimes that fit within the "computer as a tool" category are copyright violations, bullying, stalking, and harassment. Various forms of fraud, some involving identity theft and others involving scams perpetrated via phishing and spoofing, also fit into this category.

3. Computer as Container

The most common way a computer is involved in criminal activity is as a container of evidence. If it had been used in one of the other ways — as a target or a tool — it will most likely have evidence of that activity. More generally, however, because of the ubiquity of digital devices, those devices are increasingly examined by law enforcement because of the evidence stored in the device's memory. For example, business records of a criminal enterprise may be stored in computer files. Email exchanges, driving directions, and search engine queries may all be important evidence. Because of the increasing use and importance of digital data in all criminal cases, a substantial portion of this book is devoted to the legal framework that regulates the acquisition of digital data.

There are two forms of digital evidence: user created; and computer created. Thus, for example, when a person takes a picture with a modern digital camera, not only is the picture stored in the digital memory, but embedded within that file is metadata created by the device. Depending on the camera, that metadata may include the GPS coordinates of where the picture was taken, the time and date it was

---

16. *E.g.*, Ark. Code Ann. § 5-41-103 (1997); Del. Code Ann. tit. 11 § 2738 (2004); Idaho Code Ann. § 18-2202 (1997).

taken, the serial number of the device used, focal information, and other information. Such information may be crucial in any given case.

As an example of the increasing importance of digital evidence in all criminal cases, consider the facts of *Riley v. California*, 573 U.S. ___, 134 S. Ct. 2473 (2014), which was a prosecution of an alleged gang member for a variety of firearms and violent offenses—not typically thought of as a "cyber crimes."

> David Riley was stopped by a police officer for driving with expired registration tags. In the course of the stop, the officer also learned that Riley's license had been suspended. The officer impounded Riley's car, pursuant to department policy, and another officer conducted an inventory search of the car. Riley was arrested for possession of concealed and loaded firearms when that search turned up two handguns under the car's hood. An officer searched Riley incident to the arrest and found items associated with the "Bloods" street gang. He also seized a cell phone from Riley's pants pocket. According to Riley's uncontradicted assertion, the phone was a "smart phone," a cell phone with a broad range of other functions based on advanced computing capability, large storage capacity, and Internet connectivity. The officer accessed information on the phone and noticed that some words (presumably in text messages or a contacts list) were preceded by the letters "CK"—a label that, he believed, stood for "Crip Killers," a slang term for members of the Bloods gang.
>
> At the police station about two hours after the arrest, a detective specializing in gangs further examined the contents of the phone. The detective testified that he "went through" Riley's phone "looking for evidence, because . . . gang members will often video themselves with guns or take pictures of themselves with the guns." Although there was "a lot of stuff" on the phone, particular files that "caught [the detective's] eye" included videos of young men sparring while someone yelled encouragement using the moniker "Blood." The police also found photographs of Riley standing in front of a car they suspected had been involved in a shooting a few weeks earlier.
>
> Riley was ultimately charged, in connection with that earlier shooting, with firing at an occupied vehicle, assault with a semiautomatic firearm, and attempted murder. The State alleged that Riley had committed those crimes for the benefit of a criminal street gang, an aggravating factor that carries an enhanced sentence. Prior to trial, Riley moved to suppress all evidence that the police had obtained from his cell phone.

The cell phone's memory thus yielded powerful evidence of guilt. Was that evidence properly seized? Was the cell phone permissibly searched? Did the fact that the item was a digital device change the analysis? Should it? Under what circumstances a cell phone may be searched is discussed later in this book.

Digital devices are not only containers—if that is indeed an accurate character-ization of data stored on them. They are also portals to access data stored elsewhere, such as on network servers or sites such as Drop Box, Instagram, or iCloud. If the container analogy has any merit, those other storage sites for digital information can also be viewed as containers but owned, serviced, and controlled by some entity other than the user. Under what circumstances those sites can be searched and who can object to the search is also considered in this book.

The challenges posed by digital evidence are enormous. The total amount of dig-itally stored information, which comprises every electronically stored piece of data or file, was estimated to be 1.2 million petabytes in 2010, according to estimates by IDC, a research and consulting firm. This was a 62 percent increase, up from 800,000 petabytes, over 2009. The IDC noted that most of the data is not unique, estimating that 75 percent of it is a copy of some other piece of electronic informa-tion. At the time the second edition of this book was drafted in 2014, the world's information was doubling every two years. Now, at the time of this third edition, the numbers are so large and ever increasing that it is not worth displaying here what was current at the time this book was drafted.

Chapter 2

Obtaining Digital Evidence: An Introduction

This chapter offers an overview of Fourth Amendment considerations and an introduction to statutory regulation. The Fourth Amendment regulates the acquisition of data stored on computers and other digital devices. What is less clear is the scope of its application to the acquisition of data in networks or in transit. Government acquisition of that data is largely regulated by statutes and the statutory requirements are generally more stringent than what the Fourth Amendment has been construed to require, resulting in statutory analysis often superseding Fourth Amendment analysis.

This book uses some informal terms to distinguish between the two situations. Issues involving the propriety of obtaining data on a computer or stored on any other digital device are referred to as *Inside the Box* issues. As to the proper methods to obtain data in transit and at its intended destination, such issues are referred to as *Outside the Box* considerations. The perspective from which this informal framework is measured is the individual user. She has her own device and may store data on that device—inside her box. She may also click send and transmit data somewhere else—outside her box. The distinction between *inside the box* and *outside the box* is solely designed to emphasize that much different legal regimes predominate in each of those situations.

Many investigations involve a combination of regulatory regimes. Hence, it is not uncommon for information about criminal activity to be brought to law enforcement's attention based on some Internet activity. For example, that activity could be in the form of an email, a conversation in a chat room, or an intrusion into a company's network. Law enforcement often must utilize the statutory framework to trace the source of the activity and then operate within the Fourth Amendment framework to seize evidence on the digital device that was the source of the activity. The *Perrine* case is included in this chapter to offer an overview of that process.

Some aspects of an investigation do not implicate any regulatory regime and law enforcement may, just like any private citizen, utilize the numerous ways that the Internet now offers to learn something to facilitate the investigation. For example, search engines such as Google, public web sites, and chat rooms offer a host of information to anyone who chooses to use them.

Many of the reported appellate decisions involving the search or seizure of digital evidence are concerned with the recovery of child pornography. The alcohol prohibition era had a significant influence on Fourth Amendment analysis in the 1920s and 1930s. The drug wars of the last 50 years have also impacted the structure of search and seizure jurisprudence. Now, during the digital age, governmental investigations designed to locate child pornography are having a similar influence.

§ 2.1 Analytical Structure of Fourth Amendment Questions[1]

The Fourth Amendment provides:

> The right of the people to be secure in their persons, houses, papers, and effects, against unreasonable searches and seizures, shall not be violated, and no Warrants shall issue, but upon probable cause, supported by Oath or affirmation, and particularly describing the place to be searched, and the persons or things to be seized.

In analyzing any criminal case involving a Fourth Amendment claim, three separate questions must be answered. First, is the Amendment applicable? The applicability question, in turn, is a two-sided inquiry: (a) does the governmental activity—which must be either a search or a seizure—invade (b) an individual interest protected by the Amendment? If the Amendment does not apply, that ends the inquiry; it does not matter if the governmental actions are reasonable or not. Second, if the Amendment does apply, is it satisfied? There are two aspects of the satisfaction question: the first clause of the Amendment requires that the search or seizure be reasonable; the second clause specifies the requirements for a warrant to issue. If it is found that the Amendment is applicable but not satisfied, a third question must be answered: what is the remedy, if any, for the violation? That third question is *not* a Fourth Amendment issue, given that the Supreme Court has held that the exclusionary rule is not constitutionally mandated.

1. Applicability

Defining a search or a seizure is a two-sided inquiry: governmental actions must invade a protected interest of the individual. If the individual does not have a protected interest, actions that might otherwise be labeled a search or seizure do not implicate the Fourth Amendment. If a person has a protected interest, then the applicability question turns on whether the governmental techniques used to obtain tangible things or information are considered searches or seizures. The Fourth Amendment is applicable only to governmental activity; it does not regulate private

---

1. This discussion is derived in part from Chapter 1 of Thomas K. Clancy, The Fourth Amendment: Its History and Interpretation (Carolina Academic Press 3rd ed. 2017).

searches and seizures. As a consequence, a rather complex jurisprudence has developed to distinguish between governmental searches and private party searches. Also, the Amendment applies to only two types of governmental activity: searches and seizures.

Search. The word "search" is a term of art in Fourth Amendment jurisprudence and is not used in its ordinary sense. The conclusion that a search has occurred varies depending on the type of governmental activity utilized to obtain the evidence. That activity may include physical manipulation, visual observation, or other use of the senses, as well as the employment of instrumentalities such as a dog's nose or technological devices. In Supreme Court jurisprudence, physical manipulation by the police comes closest to a common sense understanding of what is a search. That literal view must be contrasted with other situations, particularly those involving sense-enhancing devices, where the legal definition is divorced from the ordinary meaning of the term, thus permitting the Court to conclude that no search has occurred. The use of technological devices to learn something that otherwise would not be discovered is so rapidly expanding that it is difficult to grasp the myriad ways the government can obtain tangible evidence or information. Unfortunately, the Court has not provided a comprehensive definition of the concept of a search to ascertain when the Amendment is implicated by a device that the government employs.

Seizure. To determine if a seizure of property has occurred, the nature of the governmental conduct and the nature and scope of the individual's interest are examined. The Court has often repeated the following definition: a "'seizure' of property occurs when there is some meaningful interference with an individual's possessory interests in that property."[2] It has sometimes also stated that a seizure "deprives the individual of dominion over his or her property."[3] One could question whether such definitions adequately convey the full nature of the individual's interests implicated by a seizure. Nonetheless, the Court's inquiry has focused on possession and lower court opinions relentlessly reflect that focus. Unlike seizures of persons, seizures of property have generated comparatively little Supreme Court case law and the definition has been relatively stable. Most seizures of property are obvious takings of physical possession and require little analysis. There are some situations where a property seizure is not so patent, including those in which the property is in transit and unaccompanied by the owner. Of particular note, there is a conceptual problem using the Supreme Court's definition of a seizure of property in cases involving the acquisition of digital evidence.

Protected Interests. Governmental activity that would otherwise constitute a search or a seizure must invade an interest of a person protected by the Amendment in order for the Amendment to be applicable. The Fourth Amendment protects "[t]he right of the people to be secure in their persons, houses, papers, and effects."

---

2. United States v. Jacobsen, 466 U.S. 109, 114 (1984).
3. Horton v. California, 496 U.S. 128, 133 (1990).

There are two aspects to the analysis of this provision: what objects are protected; and to what extent is each object protected? Grammatically, there is a relational aspect to the right set forth in the Amendment, which speaks of certain objects protected—people, houses, papers, and effects. But those objects are not absolutely shielded. Instead, the right to be "secure" is protected. If one does not know what is protected by the Amendment, then it cannot be determined what the government can do without implicating it. If one does know what is protected, governmental intrusions of that protected interest must be analyzed to determine whether they are considered a search or seizure and accordingly justified as reasonable. As one distinguished commentator has observed: "The key to the Amendment is the question of what interests it protects."[4]

Currently, according to the Supreme Court, "[e]xpectations of privacy and property interests govern the analysis of Fourth Amendment search and seizure claims."[5] Following that command, one must distinguish between searches and seizures. Seizures of property implicate a person's right to possess it; seizures of persons implicate that person's liberty and freedom of movement; and searches implicate a person's reasonable expectation of privacy or physically invade the person's property. As a consequence, it must be determined which individual interest has been affected by the governmental action.

The Court in the last third of the twentieth century adopted and generally still employs the reasonable expectation of privacy test to define, in large part, the right to be secure. To have a protected interest, that two-pronged test requires that a person exhibit a subjective expectation of privacy, which must be recognized by society as reasonable. Pursuant to that test, the Court has created a hierarchy of expectations, with long lists of situations where it has found either no reasonable expectation of privacy or a reduced one. If no reasonable expectation of privacy is found (and no other protected interest is present), the Amendment is inapplicable to regulate the government action. If the Court finds a reduced expectation of privacy, the governmental intrusion has been almost uniformly upheld, with the Court utilizing a test for reasonableness favorable to the government.

As to effects, the Court has clearly distinguished one other protected interest in addition to privacy, that is, the individual's possessory interest in an object.[6] This has occurred in the context of distinguishing between searches and seizures: although a search typically implicates privacy concerns, a seizure implicates the person's interest in retaining possession of his or her property.[7]

---

4. Anthony G. Amsterdam, *Perspectives on the Fourth Amendment*, 58 MINN. L. REV. 349, 385 (1974).

5. United States v. Padilla, 508 U.S. 77, 82 (1993).

6. *See* Horton v. California, 496 U.S. 128, 134 (1990) (seizure of article in plain view does not involve invasion of privacy but does invade owner's possessory interest).

7. United States v. Jacobsen, 466 U.S. 109, 113 (1984).

In today's world, the concept of "papers" has assumed new meaning, with many courts viewing data in computer storage as forms of documents. Hence, many courts believe that a warrant that authorizes a search for "writings" or "records" permits a search of computer files.[8] This is to say that the government need not know the exact "form that records may take."[9] This view asserts that there is "no principled distinction between records kept electronically and those in paper form"[10] and, hence, there is "no justification for favoring those who are capable of storing their records on computer over those who keep hard copies of their records."[11] Other courts and some commentators view data stored on a computer much differently and have developed a "special approach" to digital data, creating new Fourth Amendment rules to search and seize that data.[12]

2. Satisfaction

The first clause of the Fourth Amendment requires that a search or seizure not be "unreasonable." This is the "fundamental command"[13] of the Amendment and this "imprecise and flexible term" reflects the Framers' recognition "that searches and seizures were too valuable to law enforcement to prohibit them entirely" but that "they should be slowed down."[14] Reasonableness is the measure of both the permissibility of the initial decision to search and seize and the permissible scope of those intrusions.[15] The wide scope of the Amendment's applicability continually creates new and unprecedented challenges to traditional notions of reasonableness. In the

---

8. *See* United States v. Hunter, 13 F. Supp. 2d 574, 581 (D. Vt. 1998) (warrant authorizing search for "records" permitted search of "computers, disks, and similar property"); United States v. Musson, 650 F. Supp. 525, 531 (D. Colo. 1986) (seizure of computer diskettes approved under a warrant authorizing the seizure of "any records or writings of whatsoever nature showing any business or financial transactions"); Frasier v. State, 794 N.E.2d 449, 454, 460 (Ind. Ct. App. 2003) (warrant that authorized search of "notes and or records" of marijuana sales permitted police to examine computer files); People v. Gall, 30 P.3d 145, 153 (Colo. 2001) (when warrant authorized seizure of "written and printed material" indicating an intent to do physical harm to a person or building pursuant to an investigation of a conspiracy to murder and use explosives against a facility, seizure of computers permissible because they were "reasonably likely to serve as 'containers' for writings, or the functional equivalent of 'written or printed material'"); People v. Loorie, 165 Misc. 2d 877, 877–881 (N.Y. County Ct. 1995) (warrant authorizing search for "records" permitted search of computer files). *Cf.* United States v. Harding, 273 F. Supp. 2d 411, 425 (S.D.N.Y. 2003) (because photographs may be taken by digital or film cameras and can be scanned if initially captured by film, a warrant authorizing the police to search for "photographs" allowed agents to open and inspect graphical image files on a zip disk).

9. United States v. Gawrysiak, 972 F. Supp. 853, 861 (D.N.J. 1997) (approving warrant to search business office for evidence of fraud), *aff'd*, 178 F.3d 1281 (3d Cir. 1999). *Accord* United States v. Henson, 848 F.2d 1374, 1383 (6th Cir. 1988).

10. United States v. Lievertz, 247 F. Supp. 2d 1052, 1063 (S.D. Ind. 2002).

11. United States v. Hunter, 13 F. Supp. 2d 574, 583 (D. Vt. 1998).

12. *See, e.g.*, United States v. Carey, 172 F.3d 1268 (10th Cir. 1999).

13. New Jersey v. T.L.O., 469 U.S. 325, 340 (1985).

14. Berger v. New York, 388 U.S. 41, 75 (1967) (Black, J., dissenting).

15. *E.g.*, New Jersey v. T.L.O., 469 U.S. 325, 341 (1985); Terry v. Ohio, 392 U.S. 1, 20 (1968).

context of obtaining digital evidence, there are a variety of views on what the Fourth Amendment requires.

The second clause of the Amendment sets forth the criteria for a warrant to issue: "and no Warrants shall issue, but upon probable cause, supported by Oath or affirmation, and particularly describing the place to be searched, and the persons or things to be seized." Regardless of whether a warrant is *required* by a particular view of reasonableness, it is still the *preferred* manner of searching and seizing. Hence, the standards by which courts review a magistrate's decision to issue a warrant are quite deferential. The good faith doctrine has significantly influenced this review. As a linguistic matter, the Warrant Clause of Fourth Amendment regulates when a warrant may issue but says nothing about the execution of a warrant.[16] Arguably, warrant execution issues are regulated by the Reasonableness Clause. In the digital age, however, some courts are creating special rules for warrants to issue that include regulation of the manner in which the warrant is executed.

3. Remedies

The chief enforcement mechanism to insure compliance with the Fourth Amendment is the exclusionary rule, which prohibits the introduction of illegally obtained evidence in the government's case-in-chief.[17] Although the rule was for some time considered constitutionally mandated, the Court now believes that the exclusionary sanction is a judicially created remedy designed to deter future police misconduct. It is not "'a personal constitutional right of the party aggrieved'" and it "is neither intended nor able to 'cure the invasion of the defendant's rights which he has already suffered.'"[18] To date, there are no cases involving digital evidence that have created unusual rules related to remedies or peculiar application of established rules.

4. Independent State Grounds

State search and seizure provisions vary significantly.[19] State courts have increasingly turned to analysis of their own search and seizure provisions to afford broader protections to individuals than the Fourth Amendment offers.[20] States can afford more protection to individuals than the Fourth Amendment does but if the state

---

16. *E.g.*, United States v. Grubbs, 547 U.S. 90 (2006); Dalia v. United States, 441 U.S. 238 (1979).

17. *E.g.*, Terry v. Ohio, 392 U.S. 1, 12–13 (1968).

18. United States v. Leon, 468 U.S. 897, 906 (1984).

19. The provisions are ably analyzed in Michael Gorman, *Survey: State Search and Seizure Analogs*, 77 Miss. L.J. 417 (2007); Stephen E. Henderson, *Learning from All Fifty States: How to Apply the Fourth Amendment and Its State Analogs to Protect Third Party Information from Unreasonable Search*, 55 Cath. U. L. Rev. 373 (2006).

20. For commentary on this question, see generally Symposium, *Independent State Grounds: Should State Courts Depart from the Fourth Amendment in Construing Their Own Constitutions, and if so, on What Basis Beyond Simple Disagreement with the U.S. Supreme Court's Result?*, 77 Miss. L.J. 1 (2007).

constitution is construed to offer less, the Fourth Amendment serves as a floor. Hence, for state judges, the question is whether the state constitution should be construed to afford more protection to individuals than the Fourth Amendment. Some courts have begun to do so for digital evidence cases. It is important for any litigator to determine if his or her state court departs from Fourth Amendment analysis. To date, there are a few significant departures from federal analysis by state courts regarding the acquisition of digital evidence and some of those departures are highlighted in later chapters.

In 2014, Missouri adopted the following modified version of Section 15, Article 1, of the Constitution of Missouri:

> That the people shall be secure in their persons, papers, homes [and], effects, **and electronic communications and data**, from unreasonable searches and seizures; and no warrant to search any place, or seize any person or thing, **or access electronic data or communication**, shall issue without describing the place to be searched, or the person or thing to be seized, **or the data or communication to be accessed**, as nearly as may be; nor without probable cause, supported by written oath or affirmation.

Would you vote for such a provision? Note the new language, in bold, above. Is it necessary? What are the consequences of each of the three new phrases? In *State ex rel. Koster v. Charter Communications, Inc.*, 461 S.W.3d 851 (Mo. Ct. App. 2015), an intermediate appellate court interpreted that amendment as having no effect on search and seizure law. The court held that "article I, section 15, even as amended, is not currently measurably more restrictive on the government than is the Fourth Amendment." Would you reach the same conclusion?

§ 2.2 Introduction to the Statutory Framework

Three federal statutes offer a partial framework to regulate government interception of Internet communications. The statutes are:

- The Wiretap Act, 18 U.S.C. §§ 2510–22, which governs interception of the contents of communications in real time.

- The Pen Register and Trap and Trace Devices statute ("Pen/Trap"), 18 U.S.C. §§ 3121–27, which governs interception of the noncontent aspects of communications in real time.

- The Stored Communications Act, 18 U.S.C. §§ 2701–11, which regulates access to the content and noncontent of records held in electronic storage by certain entities.

These statutes are examined in later chapters. They are in large part a reaction to Supreme Court decisions interpreting the Fourth Amendment and are, broadly speaking, designed to provide more protections to individuals. In *Olmstead v. United States*, 277 U.S. 438 (1928), the Court held that the Amendment did not regulate wiretapping but observed that Congress had the power to do so if it so chose. Congress responded by enacting the predecessor of the current statute regulating wiretapping phone calls; after numerous revisions,[21] the Wiretap Act now includes the interception of oral, electronic, and wire communications, including Internet communications. In *Smith v. Maryland*, 442 U.S. 735 (1979), the Court concluded that the Amendment did not regulate the capture of the numbers dialed from a telephone; the opinion created a distinction between content (which is protected by the Fourth Amendment) and non-content (which is not protected). In reaction, the predecessor of the current version of the Pen Register statute, which governs the interception of the noncontent aspects of communications in real time, was passed in 1986 as part of the broader Electronic Communications Privacy Act (ECPA). ECPA addressed gaps in the existing regulatory regime and responded to the advent of computer networks. Under ECPA, two important statutory considerations are whether the government is seeking the contents of the communication or merely non-content; and whether the interception occurs as the communication occurs ("real time" interception) or whether the communication is in electronic storage.[22]

§ 2.3 A Case Study: Major Steps in a Typical Internet Investigation

United States v. Steven C. Perrine

518 F.3d 1196 (10th Cir. 2008)

ANDERSON, CIRCUIT JUDGE.

Steven C. Perrine appeals the denial of his motion to suppress evidence following his conviction by a jury on three counts relating to the distribution, receipt and/or possession of child pornography, one count of possession of a firearm by a convicted felon, and two counts of criminal forfeiture.

On September 2, 2005, James Vanlandingham reported to local police that, while in a Yahoo! chat room and while using the screen name "dana_hotlips05," he began chatting with a person with the screen name "stevedragonslayer." "stevedragonslayer"

---

21. A substantial revision occurred in 1968 as Title III of the Omnibus Crime Control and Safe Streets Act of 1968 (and often referred to thereafter as "Title III"); it was again updated by ECPA in 1986.

22. In Zurcher v. The Stanford Daily, 436 U.S. 547 (1978), the Court refused to require authorities to first seek to obtain evidence held by a newspaper by means of a subpoena prior to resorting to a search warrant; the Court stated: "The Fourth Amendment has itself struck the balance between privacy and public need, and there is no occasion or justification for a court to revise the Amendment and strike a new balance by denying the search warrant in the circumstances present here and by insisting that the investigation proceed by subpoena *duces tecum*." The Privacy Protection Act, 42 § U.S.C. 2000aa, which regulates government searches and seizures of material that agents have reason to believe may be related to First Amendment activities such as publishing or posting materials on the Internet, is not covered in this book.

invited Vanlandingham/"dana_hotlips05" to watch a web cam video depicting two nude six-to-nine-year-old girls. While waiting for the police to arrive, Vanlandingham stayed on the line with "stevedragonslayer" and continued to chat. Vanlandingham asked if "stevedragonslayer" had any more videos, to which "stevedragonslayer" replied he did not know what might offend "dana_hotlips05." After Vanlandingham informed "stevedragonslayer" that he liked "the young hard stuff," "stevedragonslayer" played several videos depicting young girls in various explicit sexual acts.

"stevedragonslayer" stopped sending video clips to "dana_hotlips05" prior to the arrival of police officers at Vanlandingham's house, but Vanlandingham was able to preserve a copy of the chat room conversation. One of the Pennsylvania law enforcement authorities interviewed Vanlandingham and viewed the saved chat room conversation.

Based upon Vanlandingham's account of these events, Pennsylvania law enforcement personnel obtained a disclosure order dated October 14, 2005, pursuant to 18 U.S.C. § 2703(d) and 18 Pa. C.S.A. § 5743(d),[n.1][23] directing Yahoo! to provide the subscriber information for the screen name "stevedragonslayer." Yahoo!'s records indicated that "stevedragonslayer" logged on to the Yahoo! website from the IP address 68.103.177.146 on October 9, 2005, October 22, 2005, October 29, 2005, October 30, 2005, November 1, 2005, and November 6, 2005.[n.2][24]

Further investigation revealed that this IP address was maintained by Cox Communications, Inc. Pennsylvania authorities obtained another disclosure order requiring Cox to provide the subscriber information for that IP address. Cox reported that the Yahoo! logins from this particular IP address at the times reported by Yahoo! were associated with an account belonging to Steve Perrine, 11944 Rolling Hills Court, Wichita, Kansas.

Pennsylvania authorities then contacted Kansas authorities, who discovered that Steve Perrine had a prior state conviction for sexual exploitation of a child, for which he was still on probation. Wichita police obtained a search warrant for Perrine's house, which was executed on December 22, 2005. In addition to seizing Perrine's computer, the police also found firearms and drug paraphernalia. They accordingly amended the search warrant to authorize seizure of those items as well. A forensic examination of Perrine's computer revealed thousands of images of child pornography.

The district court held a motions hearing, at which Perrine testified that he was "stevedragonslayer." Perrine further testified that he had enabled peer-to-peer file sharing on his computer, thereby giving anyone with internet access and certain software the ability to gain entrance to certain files on his computer.

---

23. [n.1] 18 U.S.C. § 2703(d) is part of the Electronic Communications Privacy Act ("ECPA"), which regulates the disclosure of electronic communications and subscriber information.

24. [n.2] "The IP, or Internet Protocol, address is unique to a specific computer. Only one computer would be assigned a particular IP address."

The case proceeded to a jury trial. A Wichita Police Department Computer Forensics detective, Detective Stone, testified that he found in excess of 16,000 images of child pornography on Perrine's computer. Detective Stone also found Kazaa, a peer-to-peer file sharing program, installed on Perrine's computer. Stone further testified that Kazaa is a program which allows individual users like Perrine to identify folders that are available to share with others, search other computers with Kazaa for specific topics, and download files from other computers, while allowing other computers to download files from Perrine's computer.[n.3][25]

Additionally, Annie Cheung, the senior compliance paralegal at Yahoo!, testified that Yahoo! tracks dates, times, and IP addresses for log-in attempts on a Yahoo! account and maintains that information for approximately thirty days. She further testified that Yahoo! records showed that the IP addresses 68.103.177.226 and 68.103.177.146 belonged to "stevedragonslayer."

Perla Rodriguez, the Cox Communications Customer Escalations Coordinator, testified that residential account IP addresses can change because they are leased for twenty-four hours at a time. Cox Communications residential account IP addresses release and renew every twenty-four hours; when an IP address releases, if the same IP address is available, it reattaches within a few seconds. Rodriguez further testified that only one IP address is assigned to a user at a time and that it is the customer's address on the internet when he or she is online. She stated that the IP address 68.103.177.146 was used by Perrine.

I. ECPA/State Law and Fourth Amendment

Section 2703 is the core provision of the ECPA, and it authorizes the government to require disclosure of stored communications and transaction records by third-party service providers. Under 18 U.S.C. § 2703(c)(2), "[a] provider of electronic communication service or remote computing service shall disclose to a governmental entity the . . . name; . . . address; . . . telephone or instrument number or other subscriber number or identity, including any temporarily assigned network address . . . of a subscriber to or customer of such service. . . ." Section 2703(d) specifies that "[a] court order for disclosure under subsection . . . (c) . . . shall issue only

---

25. [n.3] Another court has recently described Kazaa as follows:
Kazaa is a computer program that connects a computer to other computers on which the Kazaa program is also running. Kazaa's purpose is to allow users to download each other's shared files. The Kazaa program allows the user to designate which folders—and therefore which files—on his computer are shared with other Kazaa users. Each shared file has several descriptive fields that are viewable by other Kazaa users. These fields generally describe the file's contents and can be edited by a file's possessor. Kazaa makes each user's shared files discoverable to other users by allowing any user to perform a keyword search of the descriptive fields of all shared files. Files with descriptive fields containing the search term are listed for the searcher, who can then see all the descriptive fields for each file on the list. Based on these descriptions, the searcher decides which of the available files to download onto his computer. The searcher is likewise free to refrain from downloading a file in which, based on its descriptive fields, the searcher is uninterested.

if the governmental entity offers specific and articulable facts showing that there are reasonable grounds to believe that the . . . records or other information sought[] are relevant and material to an ongoing criminal investigation."

Perrine argues that suppression is an available remedy for a violation of the ECPA. However, section 2708 of the ECPA specifically states that "[t]he remedies and sanctions described in this chapter are the only judicial remedies and sanctions for nonconstitutional violations of this chapter." Section 2707, in turn, describes remedies for violations of the Act as including civil actions for violators other than the United States and administrative discipline against federal employees in certain circumstances. Thus, violations of the ECPA do not warrant exclusion of evidence.

Perrine next argues that, in any event, the government violated the ECPA by failing to present "specific and articulable" facts in support of its applications for court orders requiring Yahoo! and Cox to reveal Perrine's IP address and name, and that the government therefore used illegally obtained information in support of its search warrants.

The affidavit attached to the October 14, 2005, application for a disclosure order for Yahoo! stated as follows:

> Officer Humbert received information from Leetsdale Police Officer Wayne Drish indicating that a resident of his jurisdiction had received what appeared to be child pornography via his computer while in a Yahoo! Inc messaging chat room.

> Officer Humbert interviewed the resident, James Vanlandingham, and learned that he was logged into Yahoo Messaging Chat on September 2, 2005 at approximately 2:00 PM EDT. He received a message from an individual logged in Yahoo Messaging Chat as "stevedragonslayer." This individual invited James Vanlandingham to view his web cam. When James Vanlandingham viewed the cam he was presented with images of a young female he describes as between 6 and 9 years of age performing oral sex on an adult male, images of a young female he describes as between 6 and 9 years of age having oral sex performed on her by an adult female and images of two young females he describes as between 6 and 9 years of age walking around in a bathroom unclothed. James Vanlandingham immediately reported the incident to law enforcement. I did view that chat log of this session between James Vanlandingham and "stevedragonslayer."

The affidavit attached to the December 8, 2005, application for a disclosure order for Cox recited the same information as above, and added at the bottom:

> On 11/22/05 I received a response from Yahoo! Inc. which provided the IP login address of 68.103.177.146 for the screenname "stevedragonslayer" on 10/09/05, 10/22/05, 10/29/05, 10/30/05, 11/01/05, and 11/06/05.

The statutory standard requires that "the governmental entity offers specific and articulable facts showing that there are reasonable grounds to believe that the . . .

records or other information sought, are relevant and material to an ongoing criminal investigation." 18 U.S.C. § 2703(d). The affidavits above satisfy that standard. There is no reason to doubt Vanlandingham's account of what happened; indeed, he immediately contacted the police, which suggests he was simply a concerned citizen. Further, the officer stated that he had personally read the chat log between Vanlandingham and "stevedragonslayer." The details provided are specific and certainly would lead to a reasonable suspicion that "stevedragonslayer" was involved in child pornography.

Perrine also alleges that the application for the order was deficient because it failed to show that "stevedragonslayer" was on line with Vanlandingham on September 2, 2005, at 2 PM. The district court dismissed this as "of no moment" because Yahoo!'s logs simply did not go back that far. As indicated above, Yahoo! employee Annie Cheung testified that Yahoo! tracks dates, times, and IP addresses for login attempts on a Yahoo! account and maintains that information for approximately thirty days. Both Cheung's testimony and the actual document turned over by Yahoo! to law enforcement pursuant to the court's order revealed that "stevedragonslayer" had IP addresses of both 68.103.177.226 and 68.103.177.146. Yahoo!'s records also revealed that "stevedragonslayer" with IP address 68.103.177.146 had logged on to Yahoo! a number of times in October and November 2005.

We agree with the district court that the absence of a specific record of "stevedragonslayer" with IP address 68.103.177.226 or 68.103.177.146 being logged on at 2 PM on September 2, 2005, does not undermine the adequacy of the affidavit. The reason for that absence is simply that Yahoo! fails to maintain records for more than thirty days. Perrine admitted he was "stevedragonslayer" and gives no explanation for who else could have been logged on to Yahoo! on September 2, 2005, with the name "stevedragonslayer," when every other login for "stevedragonslayer" matches the IP address of Perrine's computer.[n.7][26] In sum, we conclude that the affidavits submitted in the application for an order under the ECPA contained "specific and articulable facts showing that there are reasonable grounds to believe that the . . . information sought [is] relevant and material to an ongoing criminal investigation."

Perrine also appears to make a broader Fourth Amendment challenge to the government's acquisition of his subscriber information from Yahoo! and Cox. The district court held:

---

26. [n.7] It is widely known that any single service provider, like Yahoo!, does not permit more than one subscriber to have the same screen name. Thus, there would have been only one "stevedragonslayer" as a Yahoo! subscriber during the period of time relevant to this case. Since Perrine admitted he was "stevedragonslayer" and both Vanlandingham and Officer Humbert observed the chat session with "stevedragonslayer," there can be little doubt that the individual chatting with Vanlandingham on September 2, 2005, and showing pornographic videos was, in fact, Perrine. Furthermore, despite his wholly speculative arguments to the contrary, Perrine presents no evidence that anyone else "hijacked" his computer and went on line using the name "stevedragonslayer."

the identifying information at issue here—defendant's name, address, etc.—was information that he voluntarily transmitted to the third-party internet providers, Cox and Yahoo!. Indeed, defendant also admitted at the hearing that he had enabled peer-to-peer file sharing on his computer, thereby giving anyone with internet access the ability to gain entrance to his computer. Under such a scenario, a defendant holds no reasonable expectation of privacy that the Fourth Amendment will protect.

We agree with the district court.

Every federal court to address this issue has held that subscriber information provided to an internet provider is not protected by the Fourth Amendment's privacy expectation.

Furthermore, he had peer-to-peer software on his computer, which permitted anyone else on the internet to access at least certain folders in his computer. To the extent such access could expose his subscriber information to outsiders, that additionally vitiates any expectation of privacy he might have in his computer and its contents. Thus, Perrine has no Fourth Amendment privacy expectation in the subscriber information he gave to Yahoo! and Cox.

II. Search of His House

Perrine also challenges the search of his house. In particular, he argues "[t]he affidavits in support of the search warrants do not establish probable cause as the facts revealed therein were not particularized as to [Perrine], contained stale information of alleged criminal activity relating to [Perrine], and materially omitted facts vitiating probable cause."

"[P]robable cause exists where attending circumstances 'would lead a prudent person to believe there is a fair probability that contraband or evidence of a crime will be found in a particular place.'" In assessing whether there is probable cause for a warrant, "we assess the sufficiency of a supporting affidavit based on the totality of the circumstances." Further, a magistrate's or judge's determination that a warrant is supported by probable cause is entitled to "great deference." On review, our task is to "ensur[e] 'that the magistrate had a substantial basis for concluding probable cause existed.'"

The affidavits in support of the search warrants in this case provided sufficient information for the judge to conclude that probable cause existed. They recited essentially the same facts as in the applications for the disclosure orders, quoted above, with the addition of a description of the information obtained from Yahoo! and Cox, which identified Perrine as "stevedragonslayer." They also recited the fact that Wichita police officer Shawn Bostick, after further investigation of Perrine/"stevedragonslayer," discovered that he had been previously convicted in Kansas state court of exploitation of a child, was still on probation for that offense, and that the prior case involved Perrine sending images of child pornography and showing videos containing child pornography via Yahoo! Messenger using a web cam.

Perrine argues they were not "particularized to" him because they did not state that Yahoo!'s records showed that "stevedragonslayer" was in fact logged on to Yahoo! on September 2, 2005. For the same reasons we found that this omission did not undermine the sufficiency of the applications for the disclosure orders, we find it does not undermine the sufficiency of the affidavits in support of the search warrants.

Perrine next argues that the affidavits contained stale information. Perrine asserts that 111 days had passed between the chat between "stevedragonslayer" and Vanlandingham and the submission of the affidavits. Whether information is stale depends on "the nature of the criminal activity, the length of the activity, and the nature of the property to be seized." We have explained:

> The observation that images of child pornography are likely to be hoarded by persons interested in those materials in the privacy of their homes is supported by common sense and the cases. Since the materials are illegal to distribute and possess, initial collection is difficult. Having succeeded in obtaining images, collectors are unlikely to destroy them. Because of their illegality and the imprimatur of severe social stigma such images carry, collectors will want to secret them in secure places, like a private residence. This proposition is not novel in either state or federal court: pedophiles, preferential child molesters, and child pornography collectors maintain their materials for significant periods of time.

The district court correctly found that the information in the affidavits was not stale.

Finally, Perrine argues the affidavits omitted information that would have vitiated probable cause. Essentially, he reiterates the argument that the affidavits did not state that none of the log ons by the IP address connected to "stevedragonslayer" occurred on September 2, nor did they attach the Yahoo! Login Tracker, which revealed that fact. He argues that the judge, had he known those facts, would not have found probable cause. For the reasons already stated, we reject this argument.

Even were we to conclude that probable cause was not established, we would affirm the denial of Perrine's motion to suppress under the good faith exception of *United States v. Leon*, 468 U.S. 897, 920–24 (1984). In *Leon*, "the Supreme Court adopted a good-faith exception to the application of the exclusionary rule and specifically applied that exception where 'an officer acting with objective good faith has obtained a search warrant from a judge or magistrate and acted within its scope,' even though the search warrant was later deemed to be invalid."

In this case, law enforcement personnel searched Perrine's house in reliance on warrants issued by a state judge. The *Leon* Court recognized four situations in which an officer would not have reasonable grounds for believing that a search warrant had been properly issued. In any of those situations, the good-faith exception to the exclusionary rule does not apply. Thus, if the issuing judge was misled by an affidavit containing false information or information that the affiant would have known was false but for his "reckless disregard of the truth," the evidence should be suppressed. Or suppression is required when the affidavit supporting the warrant is "so lacking in indicia of probable cause as to render official belief in its existence entirely unreasonable." Additionally, the exception does not apply "when a warrant is so facially deficient that the executing officer could not reasonably believe it was valid." None of those situations is present in this case.

Notes

1. **Tracing an Internet Address to a Source**. A helpful overview is contained in National Institute for Justice, Investigations Involving the Internet and Computer Networks Ch. 2 (2007).

2. **IP Addresses.** Internet protocol (IP) numbers are owned by Internet service providers; each number is unique to each computer while it is online. Terrence Berg, *Practical Issues in Searching and Seizing Computers*, 7 T.M. Cooley J. Prac. & Clinical L. 27, 37 n.22 (2004). However, IP numbers can be either "dynamic" or "static." A dynamic number, typically used by persons who have dial-up Internet service, changes each time the user goes online: "it is only good for that transaction, and then returns to the pool of numbers after the transaction is over." *Id.* On the other hand, a static IP number, which is more commonly used today, is permanently assigned to a customer. *Id.* Some aspects of *Perrine* seem quite dated—chatrooms and desk top computers, for example. Many of the "early" computer search and seizure cases (until around 2010) involved desk top computers and methods of communicating on line that have been largely superseded by mobile devices and a proliferation of communication platforms. Nonetheless, the essential steps in an investigation that *Perrine* illustrates still persist, that is, tracing a communication and/or data through networks back to its source. And the legal framework that regulates that investigation is still grounded in statutes and constitutional law. For more on IP addresses and search and seizure, see Chapter 13.

3. Identify each of the steps in the investigation of the *Perrine* case. For each step, what regulatory regime, if any, did the police have to comply with to obtain information?

Chapter 3

Fourth Amendment Applicability: "Inside the Box"

§ 3.1 Expectation of Privacy Analysis

1. Introduction

A person seeking to challenge the propriety of a governmental search must establish that the individual has a protected interest, which the Supreme Court typically measures by ascertaining whether the individual has a legitimate expectation of privacy that has been invaded by the government.[1] This expectation of privacy inquiry is two pronged: the individual must show that he or she has a subjective expectation of privacy; and that that subjective expectation of privacy is one that society is prepared to recognize as reasonable.[2] If either prong is missing, no protected interest is established. The application of this doctrine in the computer context is not without critics;[3] nonetheless, it remains the framework to assess a person's ability to challenge the propriety of governmental searches. The following sections discuss common situations where the reasonable expectation of privacy analysis has been applied in the computer context.

---

1. The Court returned to also using property interests as a measure of a person's interest implicated by a search in United States v. Jones, 565 U.S. 400 (2012). To the extent that a government agent physically intrudes into a computer to seek information, *Jones* would offer protection. However, a typical search would not involve a physical invasion but rather an electronic search for data. *See generally* Thomas K. Clancy, The Fourth Amendment: Its History and Interpretation § 3.4.3. (2d ed. 2014) (discussing re-emergence of the physical trespass theory and constitutionally protected areas).

2. *See, e.g.*, Smith v. Maryland, 442 U.S. 735, 740 (1979). *See also* United States v. Caymen, 404 F.3d 1196, 1200–01 (9th Cir. 2005) (no reasonable expectation of privacy in the contents of computers the person has stolen or obtained by fraud).

3. *See, e.g.*, United States v. Hambrick, 55 F. Supp. 2d 504, 508 (W.D. Va. 1999) ("Cyberspace is a nonphysical 'place' and its very structure, a computer and telephone network that connects millions of users, defies traditional Fourth Amendment analysis. So long as the risk-analysis approach of *Katz* remains valid, however, this court is compelled to apply traditional legal principles to this new and continually evolving technology."); Thomas K. Clancy, The Fourth Amendment: Its History and Interpretation § 3.3. (3d ed. 2017).

2. The Location of the Computer

It is important to distinguish between the exterior of the computer (including what is visible on the screen) and its contents. As to locating a computer, the person seeking to challenge plain view observations made upon observing the computer must establish an expectation of privacy in the place where the computer is stored.[4] Thus, for example, when a computer is located in a common storage area accessible to hotel employees and tenants, a person does not have a reasonable expectation of privacy as to observations of the physical components of that computer.[5] In contrast, homeowners have a reasonable expectation of privacy in their belongings, including computers and other digital devices, in their home.[6] Equally true, however, is the principle that persons with no expectation of privacy in someone else's home or that home's contents cannot challenge observation of, or the search or seizure of, another's computer in that home.[7]

3. Data on Work Computers — The Basics

Government employees may have a legitimate expectation of privacy in their offices or parts of their offices.[8] However, office policies, practices, or regulations may reduce or eliminate that expectation of privacy.[9] In the context of government computers used by employees, the assessment whether an employee has standing to challenge a search is made "'in the context of the employment relation,' after considering what access other employees or the public had to [the employee's] office"[10] and is done on a case-by-case basis.[11]

When the employer has no policy notifying employees that their computer use could be monitored and there is no indication that the employer directs others to routinely access the employees' computers, the employees' subjective beliefs that their computer files are private may be objectively reasonable.[12] Thus, for example,

---

4. *See, e.g.,* United States v. Poulsen, 41 F.3d 1330, 1334–37 (9th Cir. 1994) (person who failed to pay rent had no reasonable expectation of privacy in the contents of storage locker, including computer tapes).

5. United States v. Nettles, 175 F. Supp. 2d 1089, 1093–94 (N.D. Ill. 2001).

6. Guest v. Leis, 255 F.3d 325, 333 (6th Cir. 2001). *See also* People v. O'Brien, 769 N.Y.S.2d 654, 656 (N.Y.A.D. 2003) (defendant had reasonable expectation of privacy in computer in his bedroom).

7. Guest v. Leis, 255 F.3d 325, 333 (6th Cir. 2001).

8. O'Connor v. Ortega, 480 U.S. 709, 716–18 (1987) (plurality opinion).

9. *Id.* at 717.

10. Leventhal v. Knapek, 266 F.3d 64, 73 (2nd Cir. 2001). *Cf.* Voyles v. State, 133 S.W.3d 303, 306 (Tex. App. 2004) (teacher had no reasonable expectation of privacy in computer owned by school district that had been placed on teacher's desk in computer laboratory to teach students about computers).

11. O'Connor v. Ortega, 480 U.S. 709, 718 (1987) (plurality opinion).

12. United States v. Slanina, 283 F.3d 670, 676–77 (5th Cir.), *remanded on other grounds,* 537 U.S. 802 (2002), *on appeal after remand,* 359 F.3d 356 (5th Cir. 2004).

in *Leventhal v. Knapek*,[13] the court held that Leventhal had a reasonable expectation of privacy in a computer in a private office that he occupied. He had exclusive use of the computer. The agency did not have a general practice of routinely conducting searches of office computers nor had it placed Leventhal on notice that he should have no expectation of privacy in the contents of his office computer. Although agency technical support staff had access to all computers in the agency's offices, their maintenance of the computers was normally announced; the one unannounced visit to Leventhal's computer was only to change the name of a server. Further, although agency "personnel might also need, at times, to search for a document in an unattended computer," those searches were not so frequent, widespread, or extensive as to constitute an atmosphere "'so open to fellow employees or the public that no expectation of privacy is reasonable.'" The *Leventhal* court concluded that the "'[c]onstitutional protection against *unreasonable* searches by the government does not disappear merely because the government has the right to make reasonable intrusions in its capacity as employer.'"

On the other hand, agency policies and notices indicating that computer use is not private or is subject to inspection or audit have routinely served to defeat expectation of privacy claims.[14] For example, a public employee had no reasonable expectation of privacy in the contents of his government computer based on his written acknowledgment of the agency's policy, which prohibited personal use, expressly stated that employees had no privacy rights, and that the employee consented to inspection and audit of the computer.[15]

4. The Supreme Court Avoids the Issue

In *City of Ontario v. Quon*, 560 U.S. 746 (2010), the Court had its first opportunity to examine when a person had a reasonable expectation of privacy in electronically stored information. The case arose when Sergeant Jeff Quon was employed by the Ontario Police Department as member of the Special Weapons and Tactics

---

13. 266 F.3d 64 (2d Cir. 2001).

14. *See* United States v. Angevine, 281 F.3d 1130, 1134–35 (10th Cir. 2002) (university policies and procedures, which *inter alia* reserved the right to randomly audit Internet use and to monitor individuals suspected of computer misuse, prevented employees from having reasonable expectation of privacy in data downloaded from the Internet and stored on university computers); United States v. Simons, 206 F.3d 392, 398–99 (4th Cir. 2000) (in light of agency's policy that permitted it to "audit, inspect, and/or monitor" employees' use of Internet, employee did not have reasonable expectation of privacy in files he transferred from the Internet or in the hard drive of computer he used); Wasson v. Sonoma County Junior College District, 4 F. Supp. 2d 893, 905–06 (N.D. Cal. 1997) (no legitimate expectation of privacy in computer files by employee based on school district's policy that reserved right to "access all information stored on district computers"). *But see* United States v. Long, 61 M.J. 539, 545–47 (N-M. Ct. Crim. App. 2005) (despite banner warning user of possible monitoring of computer network system, holding that defendant had reasonable expectation in privacy of email on her computer because the system administrator discovered the evidence as a result of a request by law enforcement to locate evidence rather than as a result of routine monitoring).

15. United States v. Thorn, 375 F.3d 679 (8th Cir. 2004).

(SWAT) Team. The City of Ontario had a written policy advising employees that use of city owned computer-related services for personal purposes was forbidden, that the city reserved the right to monitor "all network activity including e-mail and Internet use, with or without notice," and that "[u]sers should have no expectation of privacy or confidentiality when using these resources." Quon signed a statement acknowledging that he had read and understood the policy.

In October 2001, the City acquired 20 alphanumeric pagers capable of sending and receiving text messages. Arch Wireless Operating Company provided wireless service for the pagers. Under the City's service contract with Arch Wireless, each pager was allotted a limited number of characters sent or received each month. Excess usage resulted in an additional fee. The City issued pagers to Quon and other SWAT Team members to facilitate responses to emergencies. When the police department obtained the pagers, it informed the officers that the e-mail policy applied to pager messages. The Court described how the pager service operated:

> [A] text message sent on one of the City's pagers was transmitted using wireless radio frequencies from an individual pager to a receiving station owned by Arch Wireless. It was routed through Arch Wireless' computer network, where it remained until the recipient's pager or cellular telephone was ready to receive the message, at which point Arch Wireless transmitted the message from the transmitting station nearest to the recipient. After delivery, Arch Wireless retained a copy on its computer servers. The message did not pass through computers owned by the City.

The officer in charge of the administration of the pagers, Lieutenant Steve Duke, informed the SWAT team members that he would not audit pagers that went above the monthly limit if the officers agreed to pay for any overages. Eventually, Duke tired of collecting bills and the chief of police ordered a review of the pager transcripts for the two officers with the highest overages to determine whether the monthly character limit was insufficient to cover business-related messages. "At Duke's request, an administrative assistant employed by OPD contacted Arch Wireless. After verifying that the City was the subscriber on the accounts, Arch Wireless provided the desired transcripts. Duke reviewed the transcripts and discovered that many of the messages sent and received on Quon's pager were not work related, and some were sexually explicit. Duke reported his findings to [Police Chief] Scharf, who, along with Quon's immediate supervisor, reviewed the transcripts himself." The matter was referred to internal affairs to determine whether Quon was wasting time with personal matters while on duty. Sergeant McMahon of internal affairs first redacted all messages sent by Quon while off duty. McMahon then determined that, during the month under review, Quon sent or received 456 messages during work hours, of which no more than 57 were work related; he sent as many as 80 messages during a single day at work; and on an average workday, Quon sent or received 28 messages, of which only 3 were related to police business. Some of the messages were to his wife, some to his mistress, and many were sexually explicit. Quon, his wife, and mistress filed a § 1983 action against the City, the police department, and others, alleging Fourth Amendment violations.

A jury found that the chief of police's purpose in ordering review of the transcripts was to determine the character limit's efficacy. The District Court ruled that that action was reasonable under *O'Connor v. Ortega*, 480 U.S. 709 (1987). The Ninth Circuit reversed, holding that Quon possessed a reasonable expectation of privacy in his text messages and reasoning that the City's general policy was overridden by Lieutenant Duke's informal policy. The appellate court also held that the other respondents had a reasonable expectation of privacy in messages they had sent to Quon's pager by analogizing text messages to e-mail messages, regular mail, and telephone communications. The Ninth Circuit further held that the search was unreasonable in scope because the government could have accomplished its objectives through "a host of simple ways" without intruding on respondents' Fourth Amendment rights. Those methods included "warning Quon that for the month of September he was forbidden from using his pager for personal communications," "ask[ing] Quon to count the characters himself," or "ask[ing] him to redact personal messages and grant permission to the Department to review the redacted transcript."

The Supreme Court reversed the Ninth Circuit decision but did so in an opinion that was written to avoid the more important aspects of the case. Justice Kennedy wrote the opinion for the Court, which was joined in full by seven members of the Court and in part by Justice Scalia, who wrote a separate concurring opinion. Justice Stevens also filed a concurring opinion.[16]

Kennedy began his opinion by narrowing its focus (and importance): "Though the case touches issues of farreaching significance, the Court concludes it can be resolved by settled principles determining when a search is reasonable." Kennedy asserted:

> A broad holding concerning employees' privacy expectations vis-à-vis employer-provided technological equipment might have implications for future cases that cannot be predicted. It is preferable to dispose of this case on narrower grounds. For present purposes we assume several propositions *arguendo:* First, Quon had a reasonable expectation of privacy in the text messages sent on the pager provided to him by the City; second, petitioners' review of the transcript constituted a search within the meaning of the Fourth Amendment; and third, the principles applicable to a government

16. Justice Stevens, although joining the Court's opinion, wrote separately to suggest that Justice Blackmun's dissenting opinion in *O'Connor* remained a viable possible standard; Blackmun had advocated a cases-by-case approach to the assessment of reasonableness regarding public employee workplace searches. Stevens also emphasized that Quon "had only a limited expectation of privacy in relation to this particular audit of his pager messages." He believed that the result would be the same under any of the standards set forth in *O'Connor.*

employer's search of an employee's physical office apply with at least the same force when the employer intrudes on the employee's privacy in the electronic sphere.

The Court viewed the decision in *O'Connor* as dispositive. In *O'Connor*, the plurality concluded that the measure of reasonableness "'for noninvestigatory, work-related purposes, as well as for investigations of work-related misconduct, should be judged by the standard of reasonableness under all the circumstances.'" In contrast, Justice Scalia in a concurring opinion in *O'Connor* had maintained "'that government searches to retrieve work-related materials or to investigate violations of workplace rules — searches of the sort that are regarded as reasonable and normal in the private-employer context — do not violate the Fourth Amendment.'" Kennedy in *Quon* stated that it was unnecessary to determine which approach was proper and, instead, ruled that, under either approach, the search in *Quon* was reasonable.

Focusing on the *O'Connor* plurality standard, the Court found the search justified at its inception "because there were 'reasonable grounds for suspecting that the search [was] necessary for a noninvestigatory work-related purpose.'" The Court pointed out that Chief Scharf ordered the search to determine whether the character limit on the City's contract with Arch Wireless was sufficient to meet the City's needs. "The City and OPD had a legitimate interest in ensuring that employees were not being forced to pay out of their own pockets for work-related expenses, or on the other hand that the City was not paying for extensive personal communications."

Turning to the scope of the search, the Court believed that the review of the transcripts was reasonable as "an efficient and expedient way to determine whether Quon's overages were the result of work-related messaging or personal use." The Court believed that the review was not "excessively intrusive:"

> Quon had gone over his monthly allotment a number of times [and] OPD requested transcripts for only the months of August and September 2002. While it may have been reasonable as well for OPD to review transcripts of all the months in which Quon exceeded his allowance, it was certainly reasonable for OPD to review messages for just two months in order to obtain a large enough sample to decide whether the character limits were efficacious. And it is worth noting that during his internal affairs investigation, McMahon redacted all messages Quon sent while off duty, a measure which reduced the intrusiveness of any further review of the transcripts.

Moreover, the Court asserted that the extent of Quon's expectation of privacy was "relevant to assessing whether the search was too intrusive." Characterizing Quon's privacy expectation as "limited," Kennedy continued:

> [I]t would not have been reasonable for Quon to conclude that his messages were in all circumstances immune from scrutiny. Quon was told that his messages were subject to auditing. As a law enforcement officer, he would or should have known that his actions were likely to come under legal scrutiny, and that this might entail an analysis of his on-the-job communications.

Under the circumstances, a reasonable employee would be aware that sound management principles might require the audit of messages to determine whether the pager was being appropriately used. Given that the City issued the pagers to Quon and other SWAT Team members in order to help them more quickly respond to crises—and given that Quon had received no assurances of privacy—Quon could have anticipated that it might be necessary for the City to audit pager messages to assess the SWAT Team's performance in particular emergency situations.

[Quon's limited expectation of privacy] lessened the risk that the review would intrude on highly private details of Quon's life. OPD's audit of messages on Quon's employer-provided pager was not nearly as intrusive as a search of his personal e-mail account or pager, or a wiretap on his home phone line, would have been. That the search did reveal intimate details of Quon's life does not make it unreasonable, for under the circumstances a reasonable employer would not expect that such a review would intrude on such matters.

The Court rejected the Ninth Circuit's employment of a lesser intrusive means analysis, noting sharply that that "approach was inconsistent with controlling precedents." It also rejected the argument that the search was unreasonable because Arch had violated the Stored Communications Act. Assuming that Arch had violated the Act and again citing precedent, the Court noted that a mere statutory violation does not translate into a Fourth Amendment violation. It also noted that no "OPD employee either violated the law him—or herself or knew or should have known that Arch Wireless, by turning over the transcript, would have violated the law."

After disposing of Quon's claims, the Court turned to the claims of the other respondents, including the two women who sent and received messages from Quon. The Court stated:

Petitioners and respondents disagree whether a sender of a text message can have a reasonable expectation of privacy in a message he knowingly sends to someone's employer-provided pager. It is not necessary to resolve this question in order to dispose of the case, however. Respondents argue that because "the search was unreasonable as to Sergeant Quon, it was also unreasonable as to his correspondents." They make no corollary argument that the search, if reasonable as to Quon, could nonetheless be unreasonable as to Quon's correspondents. In light of this litigating position and the Court's conclusion that the search was reasonable as to Jeff Quon, it necessarily follows that these other respondents cannot prevail.

Finally, Kennedy, in Section III A of his opinion for the Court, noted "the parties' disagreement over whether Quon had a reasonable expectation of privacy." He pointed to the City's formal policy and to Duke's statements and observed that, if the Court were to address the threshold question whether the Fourth Amendment was applicable, "it would be necessary to ask whether Duke's statements could be taken as announcing a change in OPD policy, and if so, whether he had, in fact or appearance, the authority to make such a change and to guarantee the privacy of text messaging." Kennedy added:

> It would also be necessary to consider whether a review of messages sent on police pagers, particularly those sent while officers are on duty, might be justified for other reasons, including performance evaluations, litigation concerning the lawfulness of police actions, and perhaps compliance with state open records laws. These matters would all bear on the legitimacy of an employee's privacy expectation.

> The Court must proceed with care when considering the whole concept of privacy expectations in communications made on electronic equipment owned by a government employer. The judiciary risks error by elaborating too fully on the Fourth Amendment implications of emerging technology before its role in society has become clear. In [*Katz v. United States*, 389 U.S. 347 (1967)], the Court relied on its own knowledge and experience to conclude that there is a reasonable expectation of privacy in a telephone booth. It is not so clear that courts at present are on so sure a ground. Prudence counsels caution before the facts in the instant case are used to establish far-reaching premises that define the existence, and extent, of privacy expectations enjoyed by employees when using employer-provided communication devices.

> Rapid changes in the dynamics of communication and information transmission are evident not just in the technology itself but in what society accepts as proper behavior. As one *amici* brief notes, many employers expect or at least tolerate personal use of such equipment by employees because it often increases worker efficiency. Another *amicus* points out that the law is beginning to respond to these developments, as some States have recently passed statutes requiring employers to notify employees when monitoring their electronic communications. At present, it is uncertain how workplace norms, and the law's treatment of them, will evolve.

> Even if the Court were certain that the *O'Connor* plurality's approach were the right one, the Court would have difficulty predicting how employees' privacy expectations will be shaped by those changes or the degree to which society will be prepared to recognize those expectations as reasonable. Cell phone and text message communications are so pervasive that some persons may consider them to be essential means or necessary instruments for self-expression, even self-identification. That might strengthen the case for an expectation of privacy. On the other hand, the ubiquity of those devices has made them generally affordable, so one could counter that employees who need cell phones or similar devices for personal matters can purchase and pay for their own. And employer policies concerning communications will of course shape the reasonable expectations of their employees, especially to the extent that such policies are clearly communicated.

Section III A prompted Justice Scalia to write a concurring opinion, refusing to join that section. Finding the search reasonable, Scalia saw no need to address the threshold question whether the respondents had a reasonable expectation of privacy. Yet, Scalia maintained that the "proper threshold inquiry should be not whether the Fourth Amendment applies to messages on *public* employees' employer-issued pagers, but whether it applies *in general* to such messages on employer-issued pagers." He viewed Section III A as an "unnecessary" and "exaggerated" "excursus on the complexity and consequences of answering[] that admittedly irrelevant threshold question." Scalia stated:

> Applying the Fourth Amendment to new technologies may sometimes be difficult, but when it is necessary to decide a case we have no choice. The Court's implication that where electronic privacy is concerned we should decide less than we otherwise would (that is, less than the principle of law necessary to resolve the case and guide private action)—or that we should hedge our bets by concocting case-specific standards or issuing opaque opinions—is in my view indefensible. The-times-they-are-a-changin' is a feeble excuse for disregard of duty.

> Worse still, the digression is self-defeating. Despite the Court's insistence that it is agnostic about the proper test, lower courts will likely read the Court's self-described "instructive" expatiation on how the *O'Connor* plurality's approach would apply here (if it applied), as a heavy-handed hint about how *they* should proceed. Litigants will do likewise, using the threshold question whether the Fourth Amendment is even implicated as a basis for bombarding lower courts with arguments about employer policies, how they were communicated, and whether they were authorized, as well as the latest trends in employees' use of electronic media. In short, in saying why it is not saying more, the Court says much more than it should.

> The Court's inadvertent boosting of the *O'Connor* plurality's standard is all the more ironic because, in fleshing out its fears that applying that test to new technologies will be too hard, the Court underscores the unworkability of that standard. Any rule that requires evaluating whether a given gadget is a "necessary instrumen[t] for self-expression, even self-identification," on top of assessing the degree to which "the law's treatment of [workplace norms has] evolve[d]," is (to put it mildly) unlikely to yield objective answers.

Notes

1. *Quon* is arguably distinguishable from the other situations in this chapter because the information was obtained from a third party and not from either Quon's pager or from his correspondents. The other situations focus on when a person has a reasonable expectation of privacy in the particular digital device from which the

information was obtained. *Quon* is included here because of the Court's "excursus" regarding the Fourth Amendment's threshold question: when does a person have a reasonable expectation of privacy in a device owned by the government or by that person's employer? Is the Court's discussion of that question helpful?

2. *Quon* declined to distinguish between Quon and his two female correspondents as to the reasonableness of the search. But what about the threshold question: is there or should there be a distinction between Quon and the women as to the reasonableness of their expectations of privacy in the information?

---

5. Data on Work Computers — Illustrations

An analysis similar to government employees has been applied to work computers owned by a private employer. For example, it has been held that there is no reasonable expectation of privacy in a laptop provided by an employer based on the employer's reserving the right to inspect.[17] Also, a person who has no ownership in a computer that has been assigned by a company to another user has no standing to challenge its search.[18]

Robin Brown-Criscuolo v. Robert K. Wolfe

601 F. Supp. 2d 441 (D. Conn. 2009)

Dominic J. Squatrito, District Judge.

In 1998, the Plaintiff became the principal of the Jerome Harrison School in North Branford, Connecticut. Her responsibilities included not only the day-to-day duties of a principal, but also the supervision of the special education program. It was the Plaintiff's responsibility to ensure that special education laws and procedures were implemented and followed.

The Defendant became the Superintendent of Schools in North Branford in March of 2001. As North Branford's Superintendent of Schools, the Defendant was the Plaintiff's supervisor.

[The court detailed a list of disagreements between the plaintiff and defendant regarding the handling of the special education referral and evaluation process.]

The Plaintiff went out on an extended medical leave on January 31, 2005. Beginning on April 1, 2005, the Defendant assumed the role of acting principal, and

---

17. Muick v. Glenayre Electronics, 280 F.3d 741, 743 (7th Cir. 2002). *Cf.* United States v. Bailey, 272 F. Supp. 2d 822, 824, 835–37 (D. Neb. 2003) (no reasonable expectation of privacy in work computer owned by employee's company when company required employee to assent to search every time employee accessed computer).

18. United States v. Triumph Capital Group, Inc., 211 F.R.D. 31, 54 (D. Conn. 2002). *Cf.* United States v. Wong, 334 F.3d 831, 839 (9th Cir. 2003) (defendant had no standing to challenge search of former employer's laptop computer).

remained in that position until the Plaintiff returned to work. The Plaintiff alleges that the Defendant used the Plaintiff's work computer and looked at her emails without her permission. The Plaintiff further alleges that the Defendant forwarded to his own email account an email containing a letter, dated January 25, 2005, the Plaintiff had sent to her attorney, Howard Klebanoff. In this letter to Attorney Klebanoff, the Plaintiff described certain work-related problems she was having with the Defendant.

The Defendant maintains that he accessed the Plaintiff's email account to review school-related messages, and he did not view any emails that were clearly identifiable as personal. The Defendant further maintains that he thought the email to Attorney Klebanoff was school-related because it was his belief that Attorney Klebanoff was a special education lawyer. The parties agree that on April 11, 2005, the email (with the letter attachment) was forwarded to the Defendant's email account, and opened and saved on the Defendant's computer.

The Plaintiff filed this action alleging that the Defendant's conduct violated her rights in several respects.

The Court must first look at whether the Defendant's conduct infringed an expectation of privacy that society would consider reasonable because "[w]ithout a reasonable expectation of privacy, a workplace search by a public employer will not violate the Fourth Amendment, regardless of the search's nature and scope." In determining whether an employee had an expectation of privacy in emails sent or received on her employer's computer or email system, the Court should consider the following four factors:

> (1) does the corporation maintain a policy banning personal or other objectionable use, (2) does the company monitor the use of the employee's computer or e-mail, (3) do third parties have a right of access to the computer or e-mails, and (4) did the corporation notify the employee, or was the employee aware, of the use and monitoring policies?

The North Branford School District had an Acceptable Use Policy, which controlled the use of the North Branford School District's computer system. Under the AUP, the Plaintiff was provided with her own individual email account. It is undisputed that the Plaintiff had a password to her account, and that this password was not widely known, as apparently only the Plaintiff and the computer system's administrator had it. In addition, the terms of the AUP do not grant total privacy to users, nor do they abrogate all privacy. Instead, the AUP states that "[s]ystem users have a limited privacy expectation in the contents of their personal files on the District system." Thus, "[r]outine maintenance and monitoring of the system may lead to discovery that the user has or is violating the District [AUP], the district disciplinary code, or the law." In addition, "[a]n individual search will be conducted if there is reasonable suspicion that a user has violated the law or the district disciplinary code." Furthermore, the AUP puts employees on notice that "their personal files may be discoverable under CT State public records laws." Nonetheless, the AUP prohibits users from "attempt[ing] to gain unauthorized access to the [system] or . . . go[ing] beyond their authorized access[,]. . . . includ[ing] attempting to log in through another person's account or using an open account (not logged off) to access a computer or access another person's files."

In the Court's view, the Plaintiff did have a reasonable expectation of privacy in her emails at work. The Defendant argues that the computer system was to be used for educational and professional or career development activities. This is a correct reading of the AUP. The email and letter attachment in question, however, appear to relate to these types of activities, as they constitute communications to her lawyer expressing the Plaintiff's concerns and worries about certain aspects of her job.

The Defendant also argues that, because the AUP allows for "routine maintenance and monitoring" of the system, the Plaintiff, who was aware of this policy, could not have had a reasonable expectation of privacy in her email account. The Court is not persuaded by this argument, though, because the record does not indicate that it was actually the practice of the North Branford School District to routinely monitor system users' email accounts. The Court also does not see any evidence showing that it would be the duty of the superintendent (i.e., the Defendant), rather than the computer system's administrator, to conduct such routine maintenance and monitoring. Moreover, the Defendant does not claim that he accessed the Plaintiff's email account pursuant to his normal routine of maintaining and monitoring the computer system. The Defendant instead alleges that he accessed the email account because of a specific, particular circumstance, namely, the Plaintiff's medical leave. Indeed, it appears that the Defendant had some difficulty in accessing the Plaintiff's email account because it was protected by a password and not generally accessible to people other than the Plaintiff. In light of this, the Court fails to see how the Defendant's conduct was part of a routine of maintenance and monitoring the computer system.

The Defendant further argues that because the AUP advised employees that their personal files were potentially discoverable under public records laws, the Plaintiff could not have had a reasonable expectation of privacy in her email account. There is nothing in the record indicating that a request was made under any public records law to search the Plaintiff's personal files, let alone that the Defendant was acting pursuant to such a request. Therefore, given these circumstances, the Court concludes that the Plaintiff did have a reasonable expectation of privacy in her email account.

State v. Eric M. Young

974 So. 2d 601 (Fla. Dist. Ct. App. 2008)

Lewis, J.

Young was the pastor of Ft. Caroline United Methodist Church, a local church under the supervision of the larger United Methodist Church. Richard Neal, a district superintendent of the Church, testified regarding the Church's structure, as it related to Young's employment. The Church is divided into geographical sections known as conferences, and a bishop presides over each conference. Neal explained that bishops appoint pastors after consulting with district superintendents, who supervise the pastors and local churches within their districts.

Young's church was relatively small, with only three full-time staff members: the pastor, a custodian, and a person who served as both the church administrator and the pastor's secretary. Additionally, there was a body within the church known as the staff parish. Although the record is unclear as to the role or authority of the staff parish, the chairperson of staff parish relations testified via deposition that he was not Young's boss or supervisor.

The church provided Young with a desktop computer and a private office. Although the computer was provided to Young for use in connection with his duties at the church, there was no official policy regarding the use of the computer or others' access to it. Young's computer was not networked to any other computer, and it was kept in his private office. This office had a special lock that could not be opened with the Church's master key. Three keys to Young's office existed. Young kept two of the keys, and the church administrator kept the third key, which she stored in a locked credenza drawer in her office.

The church administrator testified that she regularly opened the door to Young's office for the custodian and visiting pastors, who occasionally used the office to prepare sermons. However, the church administrator acknowledged that no one was permitted to enter the office without Young's permission. Young testified to this fact and added that when he was absent from the office, even the church administrator's access was limited to reasonable business purposes, such as "deliver[ing] paperwork for [him] to sign." Young further testified that the church administrator was not permitted to log on to his computer when he was not physically present.

The church administrator received a call from the church's Internet service provider. A representative from that company informed the church administrator that spam had been linked to the church's Internet protocol address. In response to this call, the church administrator ran a "spybot" program on the church's computers. She testified that when she ran the program on Young's computer, she saw "some very questionable [w]eb site addresses." The church administrator then contacted a member of the staff parish and an information technology person to set up a time to have the computer examined.

Later, the chairperson of staff parish relations, Kenneth Moreland, contacted Neal to inform him of the situation. After discussing the matter with the bishop and getting approval for the decision, Neal instructed Moreland to contact law enforcement officials and allow them to see the computer. When officers arrived at the church, Moreland unlocked Young's office and signed "consent to search" forms for the office and computer.

To invoke the protection of the Fourth Amendment, a criminal defendant must establish standing by demonstrating a legitimate expectation of privacy in the area searched or the item seized. The likelihood that a person has an objectively reasonable expectation of privacy in an office setting is increased where the area or item searched is "reserved for [the defendant's] exclusive personal use." Other factors that have been considered in determining the legitimacy of an expectation of privacy in an item seized from an office include the employee's relationship to the item, whether the item was in the employee's immediate control when it was seized, and whether the employee took actions to maintain a sense of privacy in the item.

When a computer is involved, relevant factors include whether the office has a policy regarding the employer's ability to inspect the computer, whether the computer is networked to other computers, and whether the employer (or a department within the agency) regularly monitors computer use. For example, in *United States v. Angevine*, 281 F.3d 1130 (10th Cir. 2002), the court held that a university professor had no legitimate expectation of privacy in his office computer, partly because the university had an extensive policy regarding computer use and provided explicit warnings that the computer would be inspected by university officials. Similarly, in *Muick v. Glenayre Electronics*, 280 F.3d 741, 742 (7th Cir. 2002), the court observed that an employee had "no right of privacy" in the laptop computer his employer had "lent him for use in the workplace" because the employer had announced that it could inspect the laptop. We agree with these courts that where an employer has a clear policy allowing others to monitor a workplace computer, an employee who uses the computer has no reasonable expectation of privacy in it. In the absence of such a policy, the legitimacy of an expectation of privacy depends on the other circumstances of the workplace.

We conclude that Young had a subjective expectation of privacy in the office and computer. Young kept his office locked when he was away, thus taking specific measures to ensure his privacy in the office. When others used the office, the use was for limited purposes. The testimony at the suppression hearing indicated that Young expected no one to peruse his personal belongings in the office or on the computer.

The church had endowed Young with an expectation of privacy far beyond that which an average employee enjoys. Not only did the church install a special lock on the door, but it supplied only three keys to the door, two of which were in Young's sole possession. Additionally, Young had a recognized practice of allowing visitors into his office only with his permission or for limited purposes related to church business. Although Young's expectation of privacy would be more compelling if he had never allowed another person to use the office, such a condition would be unrealistic in any office setting. It is difficult to imagine circumstances within a realistic business setting which would give rise to a more legitimate expectation of privacy.

Young also had an objectively reasonable expectation of privacy in his office computer. Although the church owned the computer, Young was the sole regular user. Although the church administrator performed maintenance on the computer, there was no evidence that she or anyone other than Young stored personal files on the computer or used it for any purpose other than maintenance. The church had no written policy or disclaimer regarding the use of the computer. Specifically, there was no policy informing Young that others at the church could enter his office and view the contents of his computer. The fact that Young's computer was not networked to any other computers further heightens the reasonableness of his expectation of privacy in its files. The only way to access the computer to view its contents was to enter through the locked office door. It is clear under these circumstances that the church trusted Young to use the computer appropriately and that it gave no indication that the computer would be searched by anyone at the church. The fact that Young violated this trust does not detract from a proper analysis of whether he had a legitimate reason to expect that others would not enter his office and inspect the computer.

The district superintendent had authority to enter the office and inspect the computer under general provisions in the Book of Discipline, which gives district superintendents the responsibility to oversee pastors and local churches. While we do not doubt that the district superintendent had such authority, we observe that this general authority to supervise a pastor is distinguishable from an explicit policy indicating that a computer will be inspected periodically. All employees have supervisors, but many employees may still have a legitimate expectation that others will not examine their personal files, even if these files are brought into the workplace.

Notes

1. Who had the stronger privacy claim: Quon, Wolfe, or Young?

2. What are the relevant considerations? The barriers to obtaining the data in *Wolfe* were electronic: password protection; in *Young*, the court focused on physical barriers: locked doors; who had access to the room and to the computer. How should a court assess the relative weight of those factors?

3. Young was a private employee and Wolfe was a public employee. Should that make a difference?

4. The *Wolfe* court focused not on how the emails *could* have been found (*e.g.*, through routine maintenance) but how they were actually found. Does that make a difference in assessing the reasonableness of one's expectation of privacy?

§ 3.2 Private Searches and Seizures

1. In General

The Fourth Amendment is applicable only to governmental activity; hence, private searches and seizures are unregulated by it.[19] Case law has detailed three aspects of the private search doctrine that have significance when applied to searches of computers. They are: 1) determining who is a government agent; 2) ascertaining

---

19. *See, e.g.*, United States v. Jacobsen, 466 U.S. 109, 113 (1984).

what constitutes replication of a private search; and 3) determining under what circumstances the "context" of a private search destroys any reasonable expectation of privacy in objects not searched by the private party.

2. Who Is a Government Agent?

Whether a person is acting as an agent of the government "necessarily turns on the degree of the Government's participation in the private party's activities, [which] can only be resolved 'in light of all of the circumstances.'"[20] Nonetheless, two considerations for determining when a private party is a government agent are often the focus of the inquiry used by lower courts: (1) whether the government knew or acquiesced in the private party's conduct; and (2) whether the private party's purpose was to assist law enforcement efforts or to further his or her own ends.[21]

Although a variety of factual instances have been litigated,[22] a common situation involves repairmen who report their findings to the police. Courts have consistently held that observations by private computer technicians made during their examination of a computer given to them to repair do not implicate the Fourth Amendment.[23] For example, in *United States v. Grimes*, 244 F.3d 375 (5th Cir. 2001), a repairman, during the course of his examination of a computer brought to the computer store for repair by Grimes' wife, opened 17 files that he believed contained

---

20. Skinner v. Railway Labor Executives' Ass'n, 489 U.S. 602, 614–15 (1989).

21. *See, e.g.,* United States v. Soderstrand, 412 F.3d 1146 (10th Cir. 2005); United States v. Steiger, 318 F.3d 1039, 1045 (11th Cir. 2003); United States v. Grimes, 244 F.3d 375, 383 (5th Cir. 2001); Jarrett v. Commonwealth, 594 S.E.2d 295, 300–01 (Va. Ct. App. 2004). *See also* United States v. Jarrett, 338 F.3d 339, 344–45 (4th Cir. 2003) (viewing the two parts not as a "test" but as "factors").

22. *See, e.g.,* United States v. Ellyson, 326 F.3d 522 (4th Cir. 2003) (woman living in defendant's house was not government agent when she turned over to government computer disks containing child pornography); United States v. Poulsen, 41 F.3d 1330, 1335 (9th Cir. 1994) (manager of self-storage unit not acting as government agent when he entered defendant's unit and seized, *inter alia*, computer tapes); United States v. Nettles, 175 F. Supp. 2d 1089, 1091–92 (N.D. Ill. 2001) (Fourth Amendment inapplicable to hotel clerk's moving of computer equipment from hotel room to common storage area when actions were not at behest of government agents); United States v. Longo, 70 F. Supp. 2d 225, 258–60 (W.D.N.Y. 1999) (legal secretary's observations of defendant's computer files were within scope of employment and not a search); State v. Lasaga, 848 A.2d 1149 (Conn. 2004) (private university employee responsible for monitoring computer use not acting as government agent when he detected child pornography on school computer).

23. *See, e.g.,* United States v. Hall, 142 F.3d 988, 993 (7th Cir. 1998); United States v. Barth, 26 F. Supp. 2d 929, 932–35 (W.D. Tex. 1998) (Fourth Amendment inapplicable to computer repairman's examination of computer when performing repair work); People v. Emerson, 766 N.Y.S.2d 482, 486–87 (N.Y. Cty. Ct. 2003) (no reasonable expectation of privacy and hence, no search, when private computer repairman showed child pornography computer files to police that he had previously viewed); People v. Phillips, 831 N.E.2d 574 (Ill. 2005) (no search when police shown child pornography video on computer that had been previously viewed by computer repairman during course of repair efforts). *Cf.* Rogers v. State, 113 S.W.3d 452 (Tex. App. 2003) (finding no reasonable expectation of privacy in computer files that defendant had requested computer repairman to copy).

child pornography. After consultations with his supervisor, the technician called the police. An officer then came to the store and viewed the same 17 images. Without requesting the store employees to search the computer any further, the officer reported the findings to a FBI agent. The repairman's supervisor, meanwhile, copied the 17 images onto a floppy disk, which he gave to the police officer; the officer copied them before faxing the images to the FBI agent, who later seized the computer after obtaining a search warrant. Grimes claimed that the store's search went beyond the permission given by his wife, thereby invalidating any evidence that flowed from the search. The court found that the initial search, being private in nature, was not subject to Fourth Amendment applicability. It reasoned that the government was not involved in the discovery of the 17 images nor were the private parties acting with the intent to assist law enforcement officials. The court believed that the pre-warrant images viewed by the police officer and the FBI agent were "within the scope of the original private-party search" and "were in an area where Grimes no longer possessed a reasonable expectation of privacy."

On the other hand, it has been held that, when a repairman copied files based on a state trooper's request, a search within the meaning of the Amendment occurred.[24] Similarly, although a private computer repairman was acting in a private capacity when he observed the first file containing child pornography, after he related his observations to a FBI agent who asked him to copy the entire hard drive, his observations of additional files were as a government agent.[25]

Other common searches involve hackers. An anonymous computer hacker, known as "Unknownuser," generated several prosecutions for possession of child pornography stemming from his hacking activities.[26] Unknownuser obtained access to the computers via a Trojan horse program that he attached to a picture he posted to a news group frequented by persons interested in pornography. When the picture was downloaded, the Trojan horse program was also downloaded, allowing Unknownuser to gain access to the computers. After finding child pornography, Unknownuser reported those findings to law enforcement authorities.

---

24. United States v. Hall, 142 F.3d 988, 993 (7th Cir. 1998). *See also* United States v. Barth, 26 F. Supp. 2d 929, 936 (W.D. Tex. 1998) (computer repairman's first viewing of child pornography not a search but his later viewing of additional files after reporting his observation to police was as government agent).

25. United States v. Barth, 26 F. Supp. 2d 929, 935–36 (W.D. Tex. 1998). *But see* United States v. Peterson, 294 F. Supp. 2d 797, 800, 805 (D.S.C. 2003) (technician's observation of child pornography during repair of computer was not as agent of government, despite South Carolina statute requiring technician to report such observations and despite the fact that, after the technician's initial observations, he decided to open additional files because of that legal requirement).

26. *See* United States v. Jarrett, 338 F.3d 339 (4th Cir. 2003); United States v. Steiger, 318 F.3d 1039, 1042–46 (11th Cir. 2003) (no search when private hacker turned child pornography over to police that hacker found by accessing defendant's computer); Jarrett v. Commonwealth, 594 S.E.2d 295, 301–03 (Va. Ct. App. 2004) (same).

Although Unknownuser was truly unknown to law enforcement prior to his first report, thus making the conclusion that he was not a government agent an easy one, Unknownuser's subsequent efforts were preceded by an FBI agent's thanking him for his assistance in the first case and by the comment: "If you want to bring other information forward, I am available." Several months later, Unknownuser produced information about another child pornographer. Two different appellate courts subsequently rejected the claim that Unknownuser acted as a government agent based on the FBI agent's comments, reasoning that, although Unknownuser was motivated to aid law enforcement, the government did not involve itself in Unknownuser's search sufficiently to transform it into governmental action. Those courts asserted that mere acquiescence was insufficient; rather, the government must either participate in or affirmatively encourage the search. The mere expression of gratitude did not create an agency relationship; otherwise, as one court stated, "virtually any Government expression of gratitude for assistance well prior to an investigation would effectively transform any subsequent private search by the party into a Government search." The court noted that the government was under no affirmative obligation to discourage Unknownuser from hacking.

Subsequent to Unknownuser's providing the information that formed the basis of the second and third prosecutions, a FBI agent began a series of email exchanges with Unknownuser, which the Fourth Circuit described as the "proverbial 'wink and a nod;'" the agent informed Unknownuser that she could not ask him to search for additional child pornographers because that would make him an agent of the government and make the information he obtained unusable. The agent further advised that Unknownuser should feel free to send any additional information he obtained and that he would not be prosecuted for hacking. The Fourth Circuit viewed those exchanges as "probably" the type of government involvement that would create an agency relationship.

———————

United States v. Cameron

699 F.3d 621 (1st Cir. 2012)

[Cameron was convicted on 13 counts of crimes involving child pornography. He made a series of claims on appeal, including whether his motion to suppress was properly denied.]

During 2006 and 2007, Yahoo!, Inc. offered a service (which has since been discontinued) called "Yahoo! Photo" that allowed users to upload photographs to the Internet. Users could then share photographs with other Yahoo! Photo users. Each Yahoo! Photo album was linked to a particular Yahoo! "user" or "account." In turn, each "account" was designated by a "Login Name" (sometimes referred to as a "username" or "screen name"), such as "lilhottee00000," one of the screen names at issue in this case. A Yahoo! user might use multiple other Yahoo! services in addition to Yahoo! Photo, such as email.

Whenever a person created a Yahoo! account, Yahoo! recorded certain information, some of which was captured automatically and some of which was entered by the person who created the account. One piece of information that was automatically collected was the "Registration IP Address," which was the Internet Protocol address from which the account was created. Yahoo! also automatically recorded the date and time at which the account was created. Yahoo! recorded this information in an "Account Management Tool," which it maintained for the life of a Yahoo! account. Further, whenever a user logged into a Yahoo! account, Yahoo! automatically recorded the date and time of the login as well as the IP address from which the login occurred. Yahoo! stored this information in a "Login Tracker." The record indicates that, during the relevant time period, Yahoo! kept login records in its Login Tracker for sixty days.

During the same time period, Google, Inc. provided a service (also since discontinued) called "Google Hello." Google Hello allowed users to sign in with a username and then chat and trade photos with other users over the Internet. Google automatically maintained records indicating the times at which a user logged into and out of Google Hello, as well as the IP address from which the user accessed the service.

Businesses such as Google and Yahoo! had (and still have to this day) a duty to report any apparent violation of federal child pornography laws to the National Center for Missing and Exploited Children ("NCMEC"). *See* 42 U.S.C. § 13032(b)(1) (1998) (creating a reporting duty for any entity "engaged in providing an electronic communication service or a remote computing service to the public, through a facility or means of interstate or foreign commerce") (current version at 18 U.S.C. § 2258A(a)(1) (2012)). NCMEC is a non-profit organization that receives an annual grant from Congress to perform various functions related to preventing the exploitation of children. *See* 42 U.S.C. § 5773(b) (2012). Among these functions is the operation of a "cyber tipline to provide . . . electronic service providers an effective means of reporting" child pornography and other Internet-related crimes targeting children. *Id.* § 5773(b)(1)(P). NCMEC's "cyber tipline" is called the "CyberTipline." Once NCMEC receives a report of a possible child pornography crime via the CyberTipline, it determines "the appropriate international, Federal, State or local law enforcement agency for investigation" and forwards the report to that agency.

On March 15, 2007, Yahoo! received an anonymous report that child pornography images were contained in a Yahoo! Photo account belonging to a user with the username "lilhottyohh." The record does not indicate that Yahoo! knew, or ever attempted to find out, who made the anonymous report. In response to the anonymous tip, Yahoo! personnel searched the "lilhottyohh" account and discovered images that they believed to be child pornography. It is not known which Yahoo! employee conducted the search. Yahoo! had an established process for dealing with reports of child pornography. If Yahoo! learned of child pornography in an account, an employee in Yahoo!'s Customer Care Department temporarily removed the content from public view and reviewed it. If he or she determined that the account contained child pornography, Yahoo! deactivated the account and notified the Legal

Department. Meanwhile, the Customer Care Department created an archive of all the images associated with the account, including the date and time each image was uploaded and the IP address from which it was uploaded. If the Legal Department agreed that any images were child pornography, it then sent an electronic report to NCMEC via the CyberTipline. Each report listed a "Suspect Screen Name," a "Suspect Email Address," a "Suspect URL,"[n.2][27] and a "Suspect IP Address." The "Suspect IP Address" was the IP address that Yahoo! "associated" with the user.

Each CP Report also included a table listing the child pornography images being sent with the report. Yahoo! attached to each report the suspected child pornography images. For each child pornography image, Yahoo! listed the date and time at which the image was uploaded and the IP address from which it was uploaded. In addition, Yahoo attached data from the Account Management Tool and Login Tracker to each CP Report. Whenever Yahoo! sent a CP Report to NCMEC, Yahoo! automatically stored a receipt. The receipt included a unique number assigned to the report by NCMEC and a record of what Yahoo! reported to NCMEC, including the attachments to the CP Report.

In this case, Yahoo! sent a CP Report of the child pornography in the "lilhottyohh" account to NCMEC. Subsequently, Yahoo! sent additional CP Reports to NCMEC of child pornography found in the accounts of the users "lilhottee0000" and "harddude0000." All three CP Reports listed the same "Suspect IP Address": 76.179.26.185.

Cameron posits that Yahoo!'s search for child pornography in password-protected accounts violated the Fourth Amendment because Yahoo! acted as an agent of the government. Cameron further contends that, because the Yahoo! CP Reports to NCMEC were the result of Yahoo!'s search, and because NCMEC sent CyberTipline Reports to [law enforcement] after receiving Yahoo!'s reports, all subsequent searches executed by ICAC at Cameron's home or executed via search warrants served on Yahoo! and Google derived from Yahoo!'s original illegal searches. Thus, Cameron argues, all evidence obtained as a result of searches conducted during ICAC's investigation should have been suppressed.

A private search only implicates the Fourth Amendment if the private party acts as a "government agent." *United States v. Silva*, 554 F.3d 13, 18 (1st Cir. 2009). In *Silva*, we established that in determining whether a private party has acted as a government agent, courts must consider three factors: (1) "the extent of the government's role in instigating or participating in the search"; (2) "[the government's] intent and the degree of control it exercises over the search and the private party"; and (3) "the extent to which the private party aims primarily to help the government or to serve

---

27. [n.2] For the purposes of this case, we understand a Uniform Resource Locator ("URL") to be the string of characters that specifies the location of a document on the Internet. For example, the URL for the First Circuit's website (at the time of this writing) is "http://www.ca1.uscourts.gov". URLs are distinct from IP addresses. An IP address identifies a particular computer on the Internet, but that computer might host multiple documents, each of which might have their own URL.

its own interests." We will not find that a private party has acted as an agent of the government "simply because the government has a stake in the outcome of a search."

Here, as to the first *Silva* factor, there is no evidence that the government had any role in instigating or participating in the search. Yahoo! began searching Cameron's accounts after it received an anonymous tip regarding child pornography in the Yahoo! Photo album of user "lilhottyohh." There is no evidence that the person who sent this tip to Yahoo! was a government employee. Cameron contends that the Yahoo! employees who searched his accounts likely had "strong connections to law enforcement." However, this contention is rank speculation on Cameron's part, with no support in the record.

As to the second *Silva* factor, there is no evidence that the Government exercised any control over Yahoo! or over the search. As discussed above, Yahoo! employees conducted the search pursuant to Yahoo!'s own internal policy. Furthermore, there is no evidence that the Government compelled Yahoo! in any way to maintain such a policy. Cameron points to the fact that Yahoo had a duty under federal law to report child pornography to NCMEC in August of 2007. *See* 42 U.S.C. § 13032(b)(1) (repealed 2008). However, the statute did not impose any obligation to *search* for child pornography, merely an obligation to *report* child pornography of which Yahoo! became aware.

Finally, as to the third *Silva* factor, it is certainly the case that combating child pornography is a government interest. However, this does not mean that Yahoo! cannot voluntarily choose to have the same interest. As discussed above, there is no evidence that the government instigated the search, participated in the search, or coerced Yahoo! to conduct the search. Thus, if Yahoo! chose to implement a policy of searching for child pornography, it presumably did so for its own interests. The record does not reflect what Yahoo!'s interests might have been, but it is Cameron's burden to show that Yahoo! did what it did to further the government's interest, and he can point to no evidence to carry this burden.

Having applied the *Silva* factors, we conclude that Yahoo! was not acting as an agent of the government; therefore, its searches of Cameron's accounts did not violate the Fourth Amendment. [Reversed in part on other grounds and remanded.]

Notes

Are you persuaded by the *Cameron* court's analysis? Is NCMEC a government agent? What would be the result if NCMEC engaged in the search?

---

3. Replication and "Context" Issues: Defining the "Container"

A government search that merely replicates a previous private one is not a "search" within the meaning of the Fourth Amendment; rather, the Amendment applies only to the extent that the government has exceeded the scope of the private search.[28] The reasoning behind this rule, generally speaking, is that the original private party search extinguishes any reasonable expectation of privacy in the object searched.[29] What does it mean to "exceed" the private search?

There are also situations where the "context" in which an object is found may lead some courts to the conclusion that there is no legitimate expectation of privacy in that object. According to this view, due to the private search, there may not be any legitimate expectation of privacy remaining in aspects of the object that had not been examined during that private search. Under such circumstances, it might be concluded that the government expansion of the private intrusion does not invade any protected interest, which is to say that there is no search within the meaning of the Fourth Amendment. Frankly, the case law is less than clear whether this principle is firmly established — at least in Supreme Court jurisprudence.

The analysis of these principles begins with *Walter v. United States*, 447 U.S. 649 (1980). In that case, 12 packages were delivered to the wrong company. Employees opened the packages; inside the packages were 871 boxes of 8-millimeter film. On one side of each box "were suggestive drawings, and on the other were explicit descriptions of the contents."[30] One employee attempted to hold one or two of the films up to the light, but was unable to observe the content of the films. The recipients contacted federal agents, who viewed the films with a projector without first obtaining a warrant to search. Did that viewing via a projector violate the Fourth Amendment?

Although a majority of the Court concluded that the viewing of the films using a projector violated the Fourth Amendment, there was no majority opinion. In an opinion announcing the judgment of the Court, authored by Justice Stevens and joined by only one other Justice, Stevens asserted that the officers violated the Fourth Amendment because they exceeded the scope of the private search.[31] He reasoned that, because the private party had not actually viewed the films, projecting "the films was a significant expansion of the search that had been conducted previously by a private party and therefore must be characterized as a separate search." This was despite the fact that "the nature of the contents of these films was indicated by descriptive material on their individual containers." Stevens maintained:

---

28. United States v. Jacobsen, 466 U.S. 109, 115 (1984).

29. *Id.* at 120–21.

30. 447 U.S. at 652. The Supreme Court did not detail the information on the boxes. The lower court, however, stated that "[t]he top of each film box showed the name 'David's Boys' and a drawing of two nude males embracing and kissing; on the back of each were the title of the individual movie and a detailed description, in explicit terms, of the bizarre homosexual acts depicted in the film." United States v. Sanders, 592 F.2d 788, 792 (5th Cir. 1979).

31. Justice White, in a concurring opinion joined by Justice Brennan, believed the Fourth Amendment was violated because the agents had not obtained a warrant, regardless of whether the scope of the private search was exceeded. Justice Marshall concurred in the judgment but did not write an opinion.

[T]he labels on the film boxes gave [the federal agents] probable cause to believe that the films were obscene and that their shipment in interstate commerce had offended the federal criminal code. But the labels were not sufficient to support a conviction and were not mentioned in the indictment. Further investigation — that is to say, a search of the contents of the films — was necessary in order to obtain the evidence which was to be used at trial.

Stevens rejected the government's claim "that because the packages had been opened by a private party, thereby exposing the descriptive labels on the boxes, petitioners no longer had any reasonable expectation of privacy in the films." He believed that "[t]he private search merely frustrated that expectation in part. It did not simply strip the remaining unfrustrated portion of that expectation of all Fourth Amendment protection." In a curious footnote, however, Justice Stevens opined that "if a gun case is delivered to a carrier, there could then be no expectation that the contents would remain private, but if the gun case were enclosed in a locked suitcase, the shipper would surely expect that the privacy of its contents would be respected." The gun case example indicates that Stevens would hold that, in at least some circumstances where the objects inside the container can be ascertained by information outside the container, there is no reasonable expectation of privacy inside the container. Stevens, however, made no attempt to reconcile the gun case example with the facts or his analysis in *Walter*.[32]

The four dissenters in *Walter* believed that no legitimate expectation of privacy remained in the contents of the packages by the time the FBI received them because the private search had "clearly revealed the nature of their contents."[33] Accordingly, the viewing of the films by the FBI did not change the nature of the search and was not an additional search. The dissent also addressed Stevens' gun case hypothetical: "The films in question were in a state no different from Mr. Justice Stevens' hypothetical gun case when they reached the FBI. Their contents were obvious from 'the condition of the package,' and those contents had been exposed as a result of a purely private search that did not implicate the Fourth Amendment."

A perplexing question involving searches of computers, which has led to contradictory results, involves whether the scope of the private party search has been exceeded when law enforcement agents open additional files that had not been opened in the preceding private search. This question is similar to the one that so divided the Court in *Walter*. Some courts have held that the determinative inquiry

---

32. The gun case has been repeated several times to illustrate the situation where "the very nature" of the container "cannot support any reasonable expectation of privacy because [the] contents can be inferred from [the] outward appearance." Arkansas v. Sanders, 442 U.S. 753, 764–65 n.13 (1979). *See also Jacobsen*, 466 U.S. at 121.

33. *Walter*, 447 U.S. at 663 (Blackmun, J., dissenting).

is not the mere opening of additional files.[34] On the other hand, in *United States v. Barth*, 26 F. Supp. 2d 929 (W.D. Tex. 1998), the court rejected the government's contention that, once a private computer repairman opened a file containing an image of child pornography, Barth lost his reasonable expectation of privacy in the other files on the computer's hard drive, reasoning that the copying of the entire contents of the hard drive and the review of those files by law enforcement "far exceeded" the private viewings.

In this context, *United States v. Runyan*, 275 F.3d 449 (5th Cir. 2001), is particularly instructive. In that case, the defendant's estranged wife and her companions removed from Runyan's ranch various data storage devices and turned them over to the police. The private parties had examined only a randomly selected assortment of the floppy disks and CDs and they did not view any of the ZIP disks. The government agents examined every one of the floppy disks, ZIP disks, and CDs.

The *Runyan* court noted that there are two different analytical approaches to the problem posed by the facts. One line of authority holds that "a police search exceeds the scope of a prior private search when the police open a container that the private searchers did not open." A second line, according to the court, is reflected in *United States v. Bowman*, 907 F.2d 63 (8th Cir. 1990):

> In *Bowman*, an airline employee opened an unclaimed suitcase and found five identical bundles wrapped in towels and clothing. The employee opened one bundle and found a white powdery substance wrapped in plastic and duct tape. He contacted a federal narcotics agent, who identified the exposed bundle as a kilo brick of cocaine and then opened the other bundles, which also contained kilo bricks of cocaine. The court held that the agent did not act improperly in failing to secure a warrant to unwrap the remaining identical bundles, reasoning that the presence of the cocaine in the exposed bundle "'spoke volumes as to [the] contents [of the remaining bundles] — particularly to the trained eye of the officer.'"

Runyan attempted to harmonize the two approaches:

> [C]onfirmation of prior knowledge does not constitute exceeding the scope of a private search. In the context of a search involving a number of closed containers, this suggests that opening a container that was not opened by private searchers would not necessarily be problematic if the police knew with substantial certainty, based on the statements of the private searchers, their replication of the private search, and their expertise, what they would

---

34. *See, e.g.*, People v. Emerson, 766 N.Y.S.2d 482, 488 (N.Y. Cty. Ct. 2003) ("when an earlier, private search opens child pornography images on a hard drive in identified computer file folders which the private searcher found replete with file titles plainly suggesting images of like kind, defendant retains no reasonable expectation of privacy with respect to additional such image files in the same two computer file folders"). *Cf.* State v. Lasaga, 848 A.2d 1149 (Conn. 2004) (declining to determine if police exceeded scope of private search when they opened additional files because, even if those files were disregarded, warrant based on probable cause to search).

find inside. Such an "expansion" of the private search provides the police with no additional knowledge that they did not already obtain from the underlying private search and frustrates no expectation of privacy that has not already been frustrated.

Applying this guideline to the facts of the case before it, the *Runyan* court believed that the police's pre-warrant examination of the disks not opened by the private parties clearly exceeded the scope of the private search:

> The police could not have concluded with substantial certainty that all of the disks contained child pornography based on knowledge obtained from the private searchers, information in plain view, or their own expertise. There was nothing on the outside of any disk indicating its contents. . . . Indeed, [the private searchers] could not have known the contents of any of the ZIP disks, as [they] did not use hardware capable of reading these disks in their private search. The mere fact that the disks that [the private searchers] did not examine were found in the same location in Runyan's residence as the disks they did examine is insufficient to establish with substantial certainty that all of the storage media in question contained child pornography.

Turning to the question whether the police exceeded the scope of the private search because they opened more files on each of the disks than examined by the private searchers, while the record was not entirely clear whether the police actually did so, the court concluded that it would not have been constitutionally problematic for the police to have examined more files than did the private searchers. The court reasoned:

> [T]he police do not exceed the scope of a prior private search when they examine the same materials that were examined by the private searchers, but they examine these materials more thoroughly than did the private parties. In the context of a closed container search, this means that the police do not exceed the private search when they examine more items within a closed container than did the private searchers. . . . [A]n individual's expectation of privacy in the contents of a container has already been compromised if that container was opened and examined by private searchers[.] Thus, the police do not engage in a new "search" for Fourth Amendment purposes each time they examine a particular item found within the container.

––––––––––

Questions and Comments

1. What is the relevant "container"?

Runyan's approach is open to criticism.[35] One can take issue with the court's view of what the appropriate container is: should it be the computer; an individual

––––––––––

35. At least I think so. *See* THOMAS K. CLANCY, THE FOURTH AMENDMENT: ITS HISTORY AND INTERPRETATION §7.6.4. (3d ed. 2017); Thomas K. Clancy, *The Fourth Amendment Aspects of*

disk; the directory; the file folders; or each individual file? *Runyan* seems to point to each disk as the container and, hence, once that disk is opened by the private party, anything within it that the police examine is within the scope of the private search. The basis for the court's analysis is far from clear: why is not the entire hard drive of a computer the container and, once that container is opened by a private party, all data would be within that search's scope; on the other hand, why is not each data file a container, given that each must be separately "opened" to view the file's contents? Should a computer be viewed as a physical container with a series of electronic "containers"—that is, directories, folders, and files that must be each separately opened? Is each separate opening the examination of a new container?

One could draw an analogy to a filing cabinet in the physical world. Each filing cabinet may have one or more drawers and have a number of file folders in each drawer. For example, there may be a group of folders entitled tax records, each for a different year. If a private party opens "tax records 2004," under *Runyan* it would seem that the tax records for other years may be opened by government agents and not be labeled a search. Is that view correct? Nothing in previous Supreme Court case law supports viewing the entire filing cabinet as a container that permits wholesale searches of all the files therein once a private party opens one of them.[36] Is there a principled distinction between them and a metal filing cabinet when applying the private search doctrine? This is to say, do the rules regulating containers in the bricks and mortar world have equal applicability to computer searches?

2. Defeating a reasonable expectation of privacy in a container.

To the extent that *Runyan* grounds its analysis on the belief that the mere opening of additional files within a container already partially examined by a private party does not exceed the scope of that private search because the "container" no longer supports a reasonable expectation of privacy, there is little Supreme Court jurisprudence to support that view. Only in *United States v. Jacobsen*, 466 U.S. 109 (1984), has the Supreme Court held that the government activities were not a search, even though the government activity exceeded the private search. In that case, a Federal Express employee opened a damaged package and found several transparent plastic bags of white powder inside a closed tube wrapped in crumpled newspaper. The employee put the bags back in the tube, put the tube and the newspapers back in the box, and then summoned federal agents. The agent who responded opened the box, unpacked the bags of white powder, and performed a chemical field test confirming that the white powder was cocaine. Putting aside the chemical testing, which raised a separate issue, the Court found that the agent's actions did not implicate the Fourth Amendment because the agent's actions in removing the plastic bags from the tube and visually inspecting their contents "enabled the agent to learn

---

Computer Searches and Seizures: A Perspective and a Primer, 75 Miss. L.J. 193 (2005). *But see* Rann v. Atchison, 689 F.3d 832 (7th Cir. 2012) (following *Runyan*).

   36. *Cf.* United States v. Knoll, 16 F.3d 1313, 1321 (2d Cir. 1994) (viewing each closed opaque file folder as closed container).

nothing that had not previously been learned during the private search." Although the private party had not physically examined the contents of the package containing the white powder, the Court asserted that the package could no longer support a reasonable expectation of privacy. The Court concluded that the visual inspection was not a "search" because it did not infringe "any constitutionally protected privacy interest that had not already been frustrated as the result of private conduct."[37] By merely replicating the private party's actions, the agents in *Jacobsen* observed white powder in a *transparent* container. They learned nothing more from its mere removal, which is to say that no reasonable expectation of privacy was invaded by their actions. This is in marked contrast to *Runyan*, where the container did not disclose its contents prior to its opening and, as a result, the police did learn something new when the files were opened.

This leaves the difficult decision of *Walter* as possible support for the *Runyan* viewpoint. Clearly, the Court has changed since *Walter* and a majority might be willing to adopt the *Walter* dissent's view that context does sometimes destroy an expectation of privacy, even if the private party had not opened the same container as the governmental authorities. On the other hand, if Justice Stevens' view in *Walter* is adopted by a majority of the Court, it is difficult to envision a situation where the police could open a computer file unopened by the private party without exceeding the scope of that private search. The boxes in *Walter* certainly gave the police a high degree of confidence that they contained obscenity. So too would a private party search that opened some files with suggestive names that were in a folder with a series of other files. Thus, for example, if a private party opened files labeled "preteen.female9.rape", "preteen.female10.rape", and "preteen.female11. rape," and discovered images of young girls being raped, if there were additional files in the same folder labeled "preteen.female12.rape" and "preteen.female13.rape", most courts would easily conclude that the police had probable cause to believe that the "12" and "13" files also depicted images of child pornography. But under Stevens' view in *Walter*, mere probable cause—or even "substantial certainty"—does not eliminate Fourth Amendment applicability.

Which is the proper approach? Probable cause is the usual level of suspicion that justifies a search. Does moving to a higher level of suspicion, such as "substantial certainty," somehow make the Amendment inapplicable? That position would seem to hold that, the more certain the police are, the less applicable the Amendment becomes. Does that position confuse Fourth Amendment applicability with Fourth Amendment satisfaction? Underlying the private search doctrine is the view that the private party has already discovered what is in the container; in the Court's words, the private party has eliminated the owner's reasonable expectation of privacy in

---

37. *See also Jacobsen*, 466 U.S. at 143 (Brennan, J., dissenting) (observing that the "context in which the white powder was found" under his view of the facts "could not support a reasonable expectation of privacy" and that there was a "'virtual certainty'" that the DEA agent could identify it).

the contents of the container. Yet, when the governmental agent opens an opaque container that a private party has not opened, the agent does learn something that the private party did not learn. That is, the container does *in fact* hold a gun, drugs, or child pornography, or that the container *in fact* holds something else—despite all indications of what it held prior to its opening.

Finally, there remains the oft-stated gun case hypothetical. Is that situation different than the situation in *Jacobsen*, where the contents of the *transparent* package could be viewed without opening the container? The gun case hypothetical envisions a container that is specifically designed to hold a gun and whose exterior shape informs the observer that it is a gun case.[38] However, putting aside transparent gun cases, the shape of the case does not disclose what is inside; instead, it informs the observer that it is a case designed to hold guns and perhaps—or even probably—that there is a gun inside. The police will not *know* what is inside until they open the case or use other means, such as an x-ray, to examine its contents. The dissent in *Walter* was correct in asserting that the viewing of the films in that case and the gun case hypothetical presented identical scenarios. In my view, expressed elsewhere, in both situations, although the police may have had a high degree of confidence in what they would find when they opened the container, that confidence should not eliminate the applicability of the Amendment; instead, that confidence goes to the reasonableness of the police's actions.

People v. Joseph Michael Wilkinson

163 Cal. App. 4th 1554 (2008)

ROBIE, J.

After the denial of his motion to suppress evidence, defendant Joseph Michael Wilkinson pled no contest to a charge of burglary arising from his entry into the room belonging to his roommate, Jessica Schultze, to use her webcam to obtain computer images of her and her boyfriend, Harry Sadler.

Defendant and Schultze were sharing an apartment with a third person. Each of the three had his or her own room. In her room, Schultze had a computer with a webcam attached to it, which she used primarily for video conversations over the Internet. At that time, Sadler was either "spending a lot of time" at the apartment or had moved into Schultze's room.

On September 4, 2005, Sadler discovered a video file on Schultze's computer that showed defendant in Schultze's room. Suspicious that defendant was using the webcam to record them, Sadler conducted an investigation to determine "if things were

---

38. Gun cases come in many forms: some are mere rectangular hard-sided boxes; others are soft-sided and in the shape of a rifle or a shotgun. Rectangular boxes disclose nothing of the contents of the box. Instead, the gun case hypothetical refers to those containers that have the unique shape that says to the viewer that it is a container designed to hold a gun.

being changed on the computer while [he and Schultze] were away." Over the next several days, he determined that someone was deleting video files on the computer that the webcam had recorded and moving the webcam so that it pointed at the bed.

Officer James Walker responded to a complaint by Sadler and Schultze that defendant was using a webcam to record them. Following his conversation with Sadler and Schultze, Officer Walker took defendant to the jail for booking.

Sadler told the officer he intended to go into defendant's room to look for evidence and asked the officer if that would violate the law. The officer responded that Sadler could go anywhere in the apartment and pick up anything he found lying around anywhere in the apartment, which Sadler understood to include defendant's room.

After the officers left, Sadler and Schultze discussed what they should do, and Sadler decided to go into defendant's room to look for more evidence. He entered defendant's room and picked up about 15 to 20 compact discs he found strewn around the room. Some bore dates or words, but nothing indicating their contents. He took them to Schultze's room where he viewed three to five of them on Schultze's computer. On them he found images of Schultze's room and images of himself and Schultze "hanging out," "undressing," and "being naked," with some sexual content but no images of them having sexual intercourse. He went back to defendant's room, opened drawers, and took all the writable compact discs he could find.

Sadler returned to Schultze's computer and viewed about five to seven more of the discs. Every file showed a picture of the first image of the recording. Sadler opened files that seemed to have images of himself and Schultze naked or engaged in sexual conduct.

Meanwhile, at the police station, Officer Walker's sergeant "overruled" defendant's arrest. Officer Walker brought defendant home and left him in the patrol car while he explained to Sadler why defendant was no longer under arrest. Sadler told Officer Walker he had found evidence of defendant having taken images from Schultze's computer, put them on compact discs, and taken them back to his room. He also told Officer Walker about what was contained on some of the compact discs. Officer Walker and Sadler went to Schultze's room, where Sadler showed the officer images on two of the compact discs he had already viewed. Officer Walker told Sadler he would need to see more explicit images of Sadler and Schultze having sexual intercourse, and Sadler looked through 7 to 10 more discs to find the images the officer wanted.

Ultimately, Officer Walker took 36 compact discs Sadler had removed from defendant's room. At the police station, Detective Jimmy Vigon viewed images from "several" discs, which consisted of Sadler and Schultze "just sitting around watching TV to actually having sex."

Several searches potentially subject to the Fourth Amendment occurred in this case. First, Sadler (whom defendant claims acted as an agent for the police) searched defendant's room and the contents of some of the compact discs he took from defendant's room during Officer Walker's absence from the apartment. Second, when Officer Walker returned to the apartment, he viewed the contents of some of the compact discs that Sadler had viewed during his absence. Third, Sadler and Officer Walker together viewed additional images at Officer Walker's direction. Fourth, Detective Vigon viewed images at the police station.

Here, the evidence demonstrates that the police did not affirmatively encourage, instigate, or initiate Sadler's search of defendant's room, his seizure of the compact discs he found there, or his viewing of some of those discs during the time the officers had defendant out of the apartment. We reject defendant's argument that Officer Walker actively encouraged the search merely by telling Sadler (rightly or wrongly) he had the right to search. Moreover, as to Sadler's intent, there is substantial evidence that he and Schultze had the dual intent of helping the police investigation *and* getting the stolen images back from defendant. Sadler testified that after the officers left with defendant, he and Schultze talked about what they should do before he (and Schultze) entered defendant's room. In addition, Schultze testified that she would have gone into defendant's room even if Officer Walker had told her it was not okay because she wanted to get back any images of herself and Sadler that defendant had taken.

In sum, we conclude there was insufficient government participation in the search of defendant's room, the seizure of the compact discs, and the initial viewing of some of those discs to implicate the Fourth Amendment.

Defendant next argues that, even if Sadler's search was a private search, Officer Walker impermissibly expanded the scope of the private search by not limiting his viewing to the images Sadler had previously viewed. Defendant contends the discs were closed containers, the contents of which remained concealed from plain view at the time Officer Walker seized them, and the fact that Sadler had viewed some of the contents of the discs did not excuse Officer Walker from obtaining a warrant to search them. Defendant contends the evidence does not establish that the images on the first discs Sadler showed Officer Walker were the same images that Sadler had viewed already.

We agree with defendant's argument that the compact discs constituted closed containers, the contents of which were not apparent on their face. To the extent Officer Walker viewed images on the compact discs that Sadler had already viewed, his search was within the scope of the private search and did not implicate the Fourth Amendment.

Defendant contends it cannot be determined which images on which compact discs Sadler viewed before Officer Walker returned to the apartment and whether they were the same as the images and discs Sadler initially showed Officer Walker. Sadler testified that during Officer Walker's absence, he viewed a number of compact discs (not just two, as defendant asserts) containing images of himself and Schultze, and when Officer Walker returned, Sadler "showed him the images that I had already found and looked at." Moreover, although Sadler said he "picked a random one," we disagree with defendant's interpretation of this comment as suggesting it was a disc Sadler had not previously viewed. Even when Officer Walker expressed a need for something more (something with "the real thing on it because that's going to make or break everything"), Sadler responded: "I can do that. The one that we saw is right here."

We conclude Officer Walker's initial viewing of the compact discs—which disclosed sufficient evidence of a crime—was within the scope of the private search Sadler had previously conducted. We also conclude, however, that Officer Walker impermissibly exceeded the scope of the private search by directing Sadler to keep looking. When Sadler asked if he could "look through more of them to see if there's sexual [content]," Officer Walker replied, "Yeah, yeah, yeah." Sadler also testified that when Officer Walker "said that he would need more explicit images of [Schultze and him] having sexual intercourse," Sadler "looked through approximately probably seven to ten more CDs to find" images of Schultze and him having sexual intercourse, which he then showed to Officer Walker. According to Sadler, he showed Officer Walker "probably three to four of the" discs that contained "files of—of [Schultze] and [him] completely naked and doing sexual things."

The People argue there was no expansion of the private search because the additional images Officer Walker viewed were just "more evidence of the same crimes" and therefore did not harm defendant. However, neither the police (Officer Walker) nor the private searcher (Sadler) could have had a substantial certainty about the contents of any of the 36 compact discs taken from defendant's room. The discs on their face did not indicate their contents. The fact that the discs not previously viewed by Sadler were found in the same location (defendant's room) as the discs Sadler did examine was insufficient to establish the requisite substantial certainty.

As to any compact discs not viewed during the private search, Officer Walker's subsequent viewing of images on those discs, which Sadler showed Officer Walker at his direction, constituted a warrantless government search triggering the Fourth Amendment. The People offer no legal justification for that warrantless search. Accordingly, contrary to the trial court's conclusion, an illegal search did occur in this case.

Detective Vigon testified he viewed images from "several" discs, which consisted of Sadler and Schultze "just sitting around watching TV to actually having sex." There is no evidence in the record, however, as to exactly what discs he viewed or whether those discs were ones that Sadler had already viewed in his private search. As a result, it is impossible to determine whether Detective Vigon's viewing of the compact discs exceeded the scope of the private search. Because the People failed to show that Detective Vigon's viewing was limited to discs that had been previously viewed during the private search, we conclude that Detective Vigon's viewing of the discs was an illegal search also.

Note

Remedies. What are the consequences of an officer viewing more images than the private searcher had viewed? Consider *State v. Horton*, 962 So. 2d 459 (La. Ct. App. 2007), where a computer repairman at *Best Buy* viewed some images of child pornography and called the police. An officer looked at the same images but also viewed additional images. The police subsequently requested a warrant based solely on the images initially discovered by the private technician. The court ruled:

> Because the search warrant was apparently based on the same images inadvertently discovered by the *Best Buy* employees, we conclude that [the officer's] further exploration of additional images, while constituting an arguably unlawful search, did not taint the original warrantless viewing of the images upon which the search warrant was granted.

Chapter 4

Competing Views of the Nature of Digital Evidence Searches[1]

§ 4.1 Introduction

There are two principal approaches to measuring the reasonableness of searches involving electronic data stored on computers. One view asserts that a computer is a form of a container and that the data in electronic storage are mere forms of documents. As with all containers, they have the ability to hold physical evidence, including such items as wires, microchips, and hard drives. They also contain electronic evidence, that is, a series of digitally stored 0s and 1s that, when combined with a computer program, yield information that includes images, words, and spreadsheets. Accordingly, the traditional standards of the Fourth Amendment regulate obtaining the evidence in containers that happen to be computers. Perhaps the most significant consequence of that view results from the application of the plain view doctrine: in any legitimate search that permits looking at digital data, potentially all data can be examined to ascertain what it is.

A second view maintains that searches for data require a "special approach,"[2] requiring unique procedures and detailed justifications. Underlying that approach, in large part, is a concern for broad searches akin to the general searches that were condemned by the Framers of the Fourth Amendment. An essential postulate of the "special approach" is that computer technology is fundamentally different from anything in the past. This postulate has been articulated to include several interrelated premises. First, technology not only creates a vastly different system of storage, information, and privacy concerns, it also affords ways to minimize intrusions. Because such methods are available, so the reasoning goes, they must be used. Second, computer abilities are fundamentally different than anything previously known to humankind, mandating rejection of the plain view, document, and container doctrines that the Supreme Court has articulated to regulate those other types of searches. Third, because of the other premises, computer searches

---

1. An earlier version of the material in this section is in Thomas K. Clancy, *The Fourth Amendment Aspects of Computer Searches and Seizures: A Perspective and a Primer*, 75 Miss. L.J. 193 (2005).
2. This was the characterization of the court in *United States v. Carey*, 172 F.3d 1268 (10th Cir. 1999).

57

and seizures require the courts to create special search execution rules. Moreover, some courts see those special rules as having a limited shelf life:

> We realize that judicial decisions regarding the application of the Fourth Amendment to computer-related searches may be of limited longevity. Technology is rapidly evolving and the concept of what is reasonable for Fourth Amendment purposes will likewise have to evolve. . . . New technology may become readily accessible, for example, to enable more efficient or pinpointed searches of computer data, or to facilitate onsite searches. If so, we may be called upon to reexamine the technological rationales that underpin our Fourth Amendment jurisprudence in this technology-sensitive area of the law.[3]

To fully understand the competing approaches to digital searches and the consequences of each approach, traditional Fourth Amendment principles regulating the plain view doctrine and document searches must be understood. Those background principles are therefore discussed in this chapter and then applied to computer searches. Also examined are the premises of the special approach and whether traditional Fourth Amendment principles need to be—and can be—modified to regulate digital searches.

§ 4.2 Plain View Doctrine

Pursuant to the plain view doctrine, a police officer may seize evidence without a warrant if three requirements are met. (1) The officer observes an object from a vantage point that is reached by a prior valid intrusion or if the officer is otherwise legitimately at that location.[4] (2) The officer is in a location to seize the object lawfully. (3) The incriminating character of the object is immediately apparent,[5] which, the Court has clarified, means that the police have probable cause to believe the object is contraband or other evidence of criminal activity.[6]

---

3. United States v. Hill, 459 F.3d 966 (9th Cir. 2006).

4. A prior valid intrusion simply means that the search or seizure that put the police in the location to make the observation is reasonable within the meaning of the Fourth Amendment. That intrusion may be with or without a warrant, depending on the circumstances of the case. *See, e.g.,* Coolidge v. New Hampshire, 403 U.S. 443, 465 (1971) (plurality opinion) ("An example of the applicability of the 'plain view' doctrine is the situation in which the police have a warrant to search a given area for specified objects, and in the course of the search come across some other article of incriminating character. Where the initial intrusion that brings the police within plain view of such an article is supported, not by a warrant, but by one of the recognized exceptions to the warrant requirement, the seizure is also legitimate.").

5. Horton v. California, 496 U.S. 128, 136–37 (1990).

6. *E.g.,* Soldal v. Cook County, 506 U.S. 56, 66 (1992); Arizona v. Hicks, 480 U.S. 321 (1987).

This doctrine establishes that the observation of the object is not a *search*. Its main function is to permit the warrantless *seizure* of an object in such circumstances.[7] The warrantless seizure of the item is "deemed justified by the realization that resort to a neutral magistrate under such circumstances would often be impracticable and would do little to promote the objectives of the Fourth Amendment."[8] The essential rationale of the doctrine "is that if contraband is left in open view and observed by a police officer from a lawful vantage point, there has been no invasion of a legitimate expectation of privacy and thus no 'search' within the meaning of the Fourth Amendment—or at least no search independent of the initial intrusion that gave the officers their vantage point."[9]

In *Coolidge v. New Hampshire*, 403 U.S. 443 (1971), a plurality of the Court asserted that the discovery of the evidence also must be inadvertent. That element was never accepted by a majority of the Court and it was formally rejected in *Horton v. California*, 496 U.S. 128 (1990). Some states, based on their own constitutions, continue to require a showing of inadvertence.[10] The rationale for that requirement, as stated by the plurality in *Coolidge*, is that, if the police know in advance the location of the evidence, they should be required to get a warrant particularly describing the object in order to enforce the warrant preference model of reasonableness and the Warrant Clause's explicit mandate that objects to be seized must be particularly described. *Horton*, in rejecting the inadvertence requirement, although recognizing inadvertence as "a characteristic of most legitimate 'plain view' seizures," believed it was not a "necessary condition." *Horton* viewed the inadvertence requirement as inconsistent with the Court's employment of objective standards by which to measure reasonableness and that it did not further the values underlying the particularity requirement, given that the plain view doctrine does not permit officers to exceed the scope of an otherwise authorized search or seizure.

The scope of a permissible search is determined by the objects sought. If small objects (such as fibers or bullets) are the target of the search, law enforcement officials can look anywhere such an object may be hidden; if only large objects are sought, the officials can only look where that size of object can be concealed. In executing a search, it is not uncommon for the police to encounter objects that are incriminating or have evidentiary value for which they did not have prior authority to search or seize. So long as the police are within the permitted scope of the search when observing the objects, there has been no additional intrusion to get to the point where the object may be observed.[11]

---

7. *See* Soldal v. Cook County, 506 U.S. 56, 65–66 (1992).

8. Minnesota v. Dickerson, 508 U.S. 366, 375 (1993).

9. Minnesota v. Dickerson, 508 U.S. 366, 375 (1993). *See also* Horton v. California, 496 U.S. 128 (1990) (seizure of article in plain view invades owner's possessory interest not privacy interest).

10. *E.g.*, Commonwealth v. Balicki, 762 N.E.2d 290 (Mass. 2002).

11. *E.g.*, Horton v. California, 496 U.S. 128, 136–37 (1990) (during execution of warrant authorizing search for proceeds of robbery, weapons believed to be used in robbery properly seized).

Illustrative of this point is *Arizona v. Hicks*, 480 U.S. 321 (1987). In that case, the police lawfully entered Hicks' apartment after a bullet was fired through its floor, striking and injuring a man in the apartment below. During the course of a search for the shooter, other victims, and weapons, Officer Nelson observed stereo components that seemed out of place. Suspecting that the stereos were stolen, he moved some of the components so he could read the serial numbers. Thereafter, using the serial numbers, it was determined that the stereos had been taken in a robbery. Justice Scalia, writing for the Court, concluded that Nelson's moving of the equipment was "a 'search' separate and apart from the search for the shooter, victims, and weapons that were the lawful objective of his entry into the apartment." This is to say that the plain view doctrine had no application to justify the search because Nelson did not make the observation that resulted in probable cause to seize the items within the permissible scope of the search for the shooter, victims, and weapons. *Hicks* is thus a good illustration of what cannot be done; instead, only those objects that can be seen from the justified vantage point are within plain view.

The plain view doctrine differs from mere visual inspection from a lawful vantage point in that the officer is also in a lawful position to *seize* the object without an additional intrusion.[12] To illustrate, an officer standing outside a house may be in position to lawfully observe an object and recognize its incriminating character. Yet, absent exigent circumstances, he is usually not in a position where he may lawfully seize it; he must first obtain a warrant. To be entitled to a plain view seizure, the officer must not engage in any further unjustified search or seizure to get to the object.[13] For example, if an officer is validly in a house, pursuant to a warrant or otherwise, and observes contraband on a table next to where he is permitted to be, he may seize that item.[14]

Lower courts have had to address the permitted scope of the plain view doctrine to digitally produced evidence. Thus, in the context searches of computers for electronic evidence, if the police are otherwise validly in position to observe a computer screen, their observations of what is depicted on the screen have been considered to be in plain view.[15] As to observations of the contents of unopened files, what is

---

12. *E.g.*, Horton v. California, 496 U.S. 128 (1990) (officer must "have a lawful right of access to the object itself").

13. *E.g.*, Coolidge v. New Hampshire, 403 U.S. 443, 468 (1971) (plurality opinion):

[P]lain view alone is never enough to justify the warrantless seizure of evidence.... Incontrovertible testimony of the senses that an incriminating object is on premises belonging to a criminal suspect may establish the fullest possible measure of probable cause. But even where the object is contraband, this Court has repeatedly stated and enforced the basic rule that the police may not enter and make a warrantless seizure.

14. *See, e.g.*, Washington v. Chrisman, 455 U.S. 1, 12 (1982) (White, J., dissenting).

15. *See* United States v. Tanksley, 50 M.J. 609 (N-M. Ct. Crim. App. 1999) (observation of information on computer screen made during search of office was in plain view); People v. Blair, 748 N.E.2d 318, 323 (Ill. App. Ct. 2001) (when police observed "bookmarks with references to teenagers and so forth," they did not have probable cause to believe that the computer contained child

in plain view is often determined by whether the court accepts the view that data are mere types of document searches, and hence the official can look at all data to ascertain its value when executing a warrant to search for documents,[16] or whether the court takes a special approach to computer searches and imposes limitations on the search by, for example, file name or file type.[17] It also depends on how the court defines the relevant container.

———————

pornography); State v. One Pioneer CD-ROM Changer, 891 P.2d 600, 604–05 (Okla. Ct. App. 1994) (during execution of a search warrant based on allegations that the suspect was distributing pornographic material, police observations of computer monitor "displaying the words 'viewing' and/ or 'copying' with descriptions such as 'lesbian sex' and/or 'oral sex'" established that the equipment and its possible criminal use were in plain view). *Cf.* United States v. Turner, 169 F.3d 84, 88 (1st Cir. 1999) (observation of officer during consensual search of apartment of photograph of a nude woman on computer screen did not justify search of computer for other incriminating files); State v. Brown, 813 N.E.2d 956 (Ohio Ct. App. 2004) (incriminating nature of computers and their contents not immediately apparent based on mere observation of two computers in defendant's house, with no pornography displayed on the screen, when police merely knew that the pornographic material had been printed from some computer).

16. *See, e.g.*, United States v. Gray, 78 F. Supp. 2d 524, 531 n.11 (E.D. Va. 1999) (when an agent is engaged in a "systematic search" of computer files pursuant to a warrant, and, as long as he is searching for the items listed in the warrant, any evidence discovered in the course of that search could be seized under the "plain view" doctrine); Commonwealth v. Hinds, 768 N.E.2d 1067, 1072 (Mass. 2002) (police had right to open file that officer believed contained child pornography based on the file's name during valid search of computer for email; accordingly, child pornography was in plain view); State v. Schroeder, 613 N.W.2d 911, 916 (Wis. Ct. App. 2000) (rejecting limitations on a search based on file names and concluding that, during systematic search of all user-created files in executing a search warrant for evidence of online harassment and disorderly conduct, opening file containing child pornography in plain view); Frasier v. State, 794 N.E.2d 449, 462–66 (Ind. Ct. App. 2003) (rejecting limitations on a search based on file names and extensions, and concluding that the plain view doctrine applied when the police opened a file and observed child pornography during the execution of a warrant permitting the police to examine notes and records for evidence of drug trafficking). *Cf.* United States v. Wong, 334 F.3d 831, 838 (9th Cir. 2003) (under warrant permitting search of graphic files for evidence of murder, observations of files containing child pornography were in plain view); United States v. Tucker, 305 F.3d 1193, 1202–03 (10th Cir. 2002) (parole agreement authorized search of computer; upon viewing child pornography on it, plain view doctrine permitted warrantless seizure).

17. *E.g.*, United States v. Carey, 172 F.3d 1268, 1272–75 (10th Cir. 1999) (opening of files containing child pornography, at least after the first file was opened, during execution of search warrant for documentary evidence related to drug dealing, could not be justified by the plain view doctrine because files were "closed" and "unambiguously" named). *Cf.* United States v. Abbell, 914 F. Supp. 519, 520–21 (S.D. Fla. 1995) (in a criminal prosecution where a large volume of computer generated data was seized from the defendant's law office, a special master would determine whether documents and data were responsive to the search warrant or fell within an exception to the search warrant requirement such as the plain view doctrine); United States v. Maxwell, 45 M.J. 406, 422 (C.A.A.F. 1996) (where an officer used a personal computer to transport obscenity and child pornography, the plain view doctrine did not apply to the search of computer files under a screen name not listed in the warrant).

1. Distinguishing Merely Looking

United States v. Artem Bautista David

756 F. Supp. 1385 (D. Nev. 1991)

Lawrence R. Leavitt, United States Magistrate Judge.

[After his arrest on a charge of conspiracy to smuggle heroin into the United States, David entered into an agreement to cooperate with the government and met periodically with government agents to disclose his knowledge of drug trafficking activities.] The agreement was silent, however, on the subject of David providing the government with documents, records, receipts, and all like material which David had in his custody, or to which he had access. The agreement also provided that at the agents' direction, David would place consensually monitored telephone calls to his criminal associates. The telephone numbers of those associates were kept in David's computer memo book, access to which required the use of a password — "fortune" — which was known only to David.

During one such meeting in early May, 1990, David retrieved and disclosed certain information contained in the book. At the time, the agents were sitting across the table from him and were unable to see the password which David used or the information displayed on the book's screen. David did not volunteer the password to the agents, or offer to show them the book.

At the next meeting on May 7, 1990, David met with Customs Special Agent Eric Peterson and DEA Special Agent Don Ware. According to David's testimony, when he initially accessed the book at this meeting, Agent Peterson got up and stood directly behind him. David was aware that Peterson was looking over his shoulder, but did not feel that he could demand that Peterson move away. David did, however, try to position the book so as to minimize Peterson's view of it.

Agent Peterson's version of what occurred at the meeting is a little different. Peterson testified that on May 7, 1990, he first requested the access code from David, but David was unresponsive. Peterson admitted that he then stood behind David and observed David use the password "fortune" to access the book.

The Supreme Court has defined a *search* as an infringement of "an expectation of privacy that society is prepared to consider reasonable." Hence, a law enforcement officer who looks at something has not engaged in a "search" within the meaning of the Fourth Amendment unless someone else has a right to expect that the thing which is seen will remain private.

In evaluating the factual scenario described above, we begin by identifying those events which may have Fourth Amendment implications. The *first* such event occurred when Agent Peterson deliberately looked over David's shoulder to see the password to the book. David himself voluntarily accessed the book at a time when the agents were in close proximity to him. Agent Peterson was not required to stay seated across the table from David. Nor did David have a reasonable expectation that Peterson would not walk behind him, or remain outside of some imaginary zone of privacy within the enclosed room. It was Peterson's office, and he could move about in it wherever he pleased. The Court therefore finds that under the circumstances David had no reasonable expectation of privacy in the display that appeared on the screen, and accordingly concludes that Peterson's act of looking over David's shoulder to see the password did not constitute a search within the meaning of the Fourth Amendment. Hence, the Court need not reach the question whether the plain view doctrine would save the legality of the purported search.

---

2. "Immediately Apparent"

United States v. Devin C. Wilson

565 F.3d 1059 (8th Cir. 2009)

SHEPHERD, CIRCUIT JUDGE.

On the evening of September 2, 2006, members of the Caruthersville Police Department received a 911 emergency dispatch to 801 West Eighth Street in Caruthersville, Missouri to investigate a possible kidnapping. When the officers arrived at the residence, a 16-year old female was standing outside and got into the officers' police car. She told the officers that she had been kidnapped in Oklahoma City, Oklahoma. While the Victim was in the police car, Wilson drove up in his vehicle and the Victim told the officers that he was the person who had kidnapped her. She said that Wilson had forced her to work as a prostitute and exotic dancer and that he had ecstasy pills and crack cocaine in the house. She also said that her bags and clothing were still in the house. Based on this information, the officers arrested Wilson.

One of the arresting officers, Assistant Chief Tony Jones, then went to the prosecuting attorney's office to prepare an application and affidavit for a warrant to search Wilson's residence and vehicle. Officer Jones also directed Officer Tina Cook to interview the Victim. During this interview, the Victim told Officer Cook that Wilson had videotaped her engaging in various sexual acts using a video camera and his cellular phone. The Victim told Officer Cook that Wilson kept the video camera on the floor of the front room of his residence. She also told Officer Cook that Wilson kept drugs and a handgun in a closet on the first floor.

While Officer Cook was interviewing the Victim, Officer Jones was at the prosecuting attorney's office working on the warrant application. After the application and affidavit were typed, but before they were sworn to by Officer Jones, Officer Cook called prosecuting attorney Mike Hazel and informed him of what the Victim had said during her interview. Hazel added this information in handwriting to the warrant application.

Officer Jones obtained a warrant to search Wilson's residence and vehicle for controlled substances and the Victim's personal belongings. During the search, Officer Cook found a video camera on the floor of Wilson's front room, precisely where the

Victim said it would be. Officer Cook removed the video tape and left the camera at Wilson's residence. While searching Wilson's Cadillac, Officer Jones found a cellular phone with a built-in camera. Officer Jones eventually opened the phone and observed pornographic photographs stored on it.

Several months after the execution of the search warrant, Federal Bureau of Investigation Agent Herbert Stapleton went to Wilson's residence to execute a federal arrest warrant for the crime of being a felon in possession of a firearm. Agent Stapleton was aware of the Victim's child pornography allegations against Wilson. While executing the arrest, he recognized the video camera from photographs he had seen of the prior search. Because of his belief that the camera might be relevant to the child pornography accusations, Agent Stapleton seized the video camera. Federal agents later sought and obtained a search warrant to search the data stored on the cellular phone and videotape.

Wilson seeks suppression of the videotape, camera, and cellular phone on the grounds that they were not lawfully seized under the "plain view" exception to the warrant requirement. Wilson limits his appeal to whether the incriminating character of the seized items was immediately apparent. "Evidence is immediately apparent if there is probable cause to associate the property [seized] with criminal activity." "Probable cause demands not that an officer be sure or certain but only that the facts available to a reasonably cautious man would warrant a belief that certain items may be contraband or stolen property or useful as evidence of a crime." "In determining whether this requirement is met, we may consider the collective knowledge of the officers executing the searches."

The Victim informed Officer Cook that Wilson had used his cellular phone and a video camera to record her engaging in underage sexual activity. When Officer Cook discovered the video camera lying in the same location the Victim had described, she removed the tape. Furthermore, Officer Jones knew the details of Officer Cook's interview with the Victim before he seized the cellular phone. Finally, Agent Stapleton was familiar with the Victim's allegations and recognized the video camera from pictures of the earlier search when he seized the camera during Wilson's subsequent arrest on federal gun charges. Due to this information, probable cause existed, and the incriminating nature of each of the items was immediately apparent. Thus, the tape, video camera, and phone fall under the plain view exception, and the seizure of these items was proper.

————————

Notes

1. When Officer Jones opened the phone and observed the pictures, was that a separate search within the meaning of the Fourth Amendment?

2. **Contraband and Plain View.** In *Commonwealth v. Hinds*, 768 N.E.2d 1067 (Mass. 2002), during a consensual search of a computer for electronic mail, Officer McLean came across the "Chuck" directory.

McLean scrolled through the "Chuck" directory, looking for electronic mail files, i.e., file names with "EML" or similar default extensions. Although the "Chuck" directory did not on its face disclose any files related to electronic mail, McLean observed numerous file names with the extension "JPG," which indicated that the files contained graphic images. Many of the files had sexually explicit titles, some indicating that children were possibly the subjects, including files entitled "10YRSLUT, YNGSX15, KIDSEX1, TEENSEX, 10YOANAL, and 13YRSUCK," to name a few. Of particular concern to McLean was a file entitled "2BOYS.JPG." From a prior case, McLean recognized "2BOYS.JPG" as a file name for a specific child pornography image. McLean opened the file and confirmed that "2BOYS.JPG" was child pornography.

Were these files in plain view? Was it permissible for McLean to open the "2BOYS.JPG" file? The court ruled that the files were in plain view and added:

> McLean was not obligated to disregard files listed in plain view on the "Chuck" directory whose titles suggested contents that were contraband. Indeed, McLean testified that he opened the "2BOYS.JPG" file because he recognized it as a title for child pornography, not because he thought it might contain electronic mail.

> McLean had substantial experience with computer crimes and had worked for the Attorney General's "high tech squad." He had seen the "2BOYS.JPG" file in a prior computer case involving child pornography. The "2BOYS.JPG" file was listed in a directory littered with sexually explicit graphic file names indicating children as possible subjects. These facts, considered together, warranted McLean in believing that "2BOYS.JPG" was child pornography and that other files in the "Chuck" directory contained similar matter.

> [O]nce probable cause arose, McLean was warranted in opening the "2BOYS.JPG" on Thomas's computer and then on the defendant's to confirm that it was, indeed, child pornography and was located on the defendant's computer, as the defendant had no reasonable expectation of privacy in what was lawfully viewed and what appeared to be contraband.

3. Opening Closed Files: The Document Approach

United States v. Montgomery Johns Gray

78 F. Supp. 2d 524 (E.D. Va. 1999)

ELLIS, DISTRICT JUDGE.

On February 5, 1999, FBI agents executed a search warrant at defendant's home in Arlington, Virginia in connection with an investigation of unauthorized computer intrusions at the National Institute of Health's National Library of Medicine. Four computers belonging to defendant were seized and removed from defendant's home. At the FBI office, Special Agent Arthur Ehuan, of the Computer Analysis

Response Team made copies of the contents of the computers' electronic storage media, or hard drives. These copies, which Agent Ehuan made on magneto-optical disks, were in digital form. To translate the stored information into readable form, Agent Ehuan planned to make a series of CD-ROMs, so that the case agent, Special Agent Craig Sorum, could read and access defendant's files.

Agent Ehuan created, and gave to Agent Sorum, a separate CD-ROM containing a list of the directory structures of the hard drives on each of the four computers. Using this disc, Agent Sorum then performed a text string search of the file structures and identified which computers, of the four seized, appeared to contain the text strings most closely associated with the NLM items listed in the search warrant. Agent Sorum then asked Agent Ehuan to concentrate first on making readable CD-ROMs for this computer.

Before making the CD-ROMs, Agent Ehuan opened many of the directories and subdirectories on the targeted hard drive to determine the size of the files and to gauge how many directories would fit on a single CD-ROM, which can store only 650 megabytes, far less than the capacity of the magneto-optical disks. After determining which directories could be copied onto a particular CD-ROM, Agent Ehuan began the copying process. While information was being copied onto the CD-ROMs, a process that consumed approximately 45 minutes to an hour, Agent Ehuan, pursuant to CART routine practice, opened and looked briefly at each of the files contained in the directories and subdirectories being copied. CART agents routinely perform such preliminary reviews, opening files as they are being copied onto CD-ROMs to look for the materials listed in the search warrant in the hope that they might facilitate the case agent's search.

To open the directory files, Agent Ehuan used a program called CompuPic. When Agent Ehuan opened a file using CompuPic, thumbnail-sized images of all of the items contained within that file, pictures or text documents, would appear on the screen. This program enabled Agent Ehuan, upon opening a file, to see instantly the nature of the material contained within that file.

As Agent Ehuan was preparing to copy material onto the eighth CD-ROM, he opened a directory entitled "BBS," which is a common abbreviation for "Bulletin Board System/Service," in order to see the list of the individual files and subdirectories contained in that directory. In the course of opening the files in the BBS directory, Agent Ehuan opened a subdirectory entitled "Teen," which contained several files with the suffix ".jpg," which commonly denotes a picture file.[n.5][18] Like a number of others, this subdirectory contained pornographic pictures, but these,

---

18. [n.5] The NLM files that were the subject of the search were believed likely to be text files. Agent Ehuan nonetheless opened files that were labeled as picture files because computer files can be misleadingly labeled, particularly if the owner of those files is trying to conceal illegal materials. Indeed, in the course of this search, Agent Ehuan discovered some text files that were, in fact, mixed in with picture files. Moreover, Agent Ehuan did not believe that the warrant foreclosed the possibility that the NLM materials might include pictures.

Agent Ehuan thought, might also include images of minors in sexually explicit poses. Yet, he could not be certain, and, as the subdirectory did not contain any of the materials identified in the warrant, or other obvious evidence of a crime, Agent Ehuan continued his search of the BBS directory pursuant to the warrant. Thereafter, he saw a subdirectory entitled "Tiny Teen." The name of this subdirectory caused Agent Ehuan to wonder if the subdirectory contained child pornography. He testified, however, that he opened the "Tiny Teen" subdirectory not because he believed it might contain child pornography, but rather because it was the next subdirectory listed and he was opening all of the subdirectories as part of his routine search for the items listed in the warrant.

When he opened the "Tiny Teen" subdirectory, Agent Ehuan discovered yet another series of pornographic pictures, this time, however, he believed some of the pictures contained images of minors. He then asked another CART agent to view the pictures displayed on his computer screen. On doing so, this agent agreed the pictures appeared to be of minors. Agent Ehuan then notified Agent Sorum of his discovery, who after viewing the same images, also concluded that they contained child pornography. Agent Ehuan testified that, at that point, he may have returned to the subdirectory "Teen" to see if that directory indeed contained pornographic images of minors. After the brief return to the "Teen" subdirectory, however, Agent Ehuan ceased his search and he, based on what he had already discovered, obtained a second warrant authorizing a search of defendant's computer files for child pornography. This search disclosed additional images of child pornography, which, together with the images that triggered the application for the warrant, are the subject of defendant's motion to suppress.

The Fourth Amendment requires that a search warrant describe the things to be seized with sufficient particularity to prevent a general exploratory rummaging in a person's belongings. To prevent such rummaging, therefore, a "warrant must enable the executing officer to ascertain and identify with reasonable certainty those items that the magistrate has authorized him to seize." In some searches, however, it is not immediately apparent whether or not an object is within the scope of a search warrant; in such cases, an officer must examine the object simply to determine whether or not it is one that he is authorized to seize. Searches of records or documents present a variant of this principle, as documents, unlike illegal drugs or other contraband, may not appear incriminating on their face. As a result, in any search for records or documents, "innocuous records must be examined to determine whether they fall into the category of those papers covered by the search warrant." Although care must be taken to minimize the intrusion, records searches require that many, and often all, documents in the targeted location be searched because "few people keep documents of their criminal transactions in a folder marked 'crime records.'" Thus, agents authorized by warrant to search a home or office for documents containing certain specific information are entitled to examine all files located at the site to look for the specified information. So it is not surprising, then, that in the course of conducting a lawful search pursuant to a search warrant, law enforcement agents often discover evidence of criminal activity other than that which is the subject of the warrant. If an agent sees, in plain view, evidence of criminal activity other than that for which she is searching, this does not constitute an unreasonable search under the Fourth Amendment, for "[v]iewing an article that is already in plain view does not involve an invasion of privacy." These principles applied in the context of a document or record search means that, if an agent searching files pursuant to a search warrant discovers a document that contains evidence of another crime, that document can be seized under the "plain view" exception to the warrant requirement.

These principles are also dispositive of the instant case, as searches of computer files "present the same problem as document searches—the intermingling of relevant and irrelevant materials—but to a heightened degree" because of the massive storage capacity of modern computers. Thus, although care must be taken to ensure a computer search is not overbroad, searches of computer records "are no less constitutional than searches of physical records, where innocuous documents may be scanned to ascertain their relevancy."

It follows, then, that Agent Ehuan's search of the "Teen" and "Tiny Teen" subdirectories was not beyond the scope of the search warrant. In searching for the items listed in the warrant, Agent Ehuan was entitled to examine all of defendant's files to determine whether they contained items that fell within the scope of the warrant. In the course of doing so, he inadvertently discovered evidence of child pornography, which was clearly incriminating on its face. As Agent Ehuan was lawfully searching the "Teen" and "Tiny Teen" subdirectories pursuant to the first warrant when he saw the illegal pornography, viewing that evidence did not constitute an unreasonable search under the Fourth Amendment.

It is not persuasive to argue, as defendant does, that Agent Ehuan knew the two subdirectories did not contain NLM documents or hacker materials when he searched them because many of the files were tagged with the ".jpg" suffix, indicating a picture file, and none of the materials covered by the warrant were believed to be pictures. While the ".jpg" suffix generally denotes a picture file, there is no requirement that it do so, and, as a result, Agent Ehuan could not be certain that files with the ".jpg" suffix did not contain the materials for which he was authorized to search. Indeed, Agent Ehuan would have been remiss not to search files with a ".jpg" suffix simply because such files are generally pictures files, and he believed the NLM documents and hacker materials were more likely to be text files. He knew from his experience that computer hackers often intentionally mislabel files, or attempt to bury incriminating files within innocuously named directories. Indeed, in the course of his search of defendant's computer files, Agent Ehuan found some text files mixed in with picture files. This serves to underscore the soundness of the conclusion that Agent Ehuan was not required to accept as accurate any file name or suffix and limit his search accordingly.[n.8][19]

---

19. [n.8] The resolution of the motion to suppress does not turn on whether Agent Ehuan conducted the most technically advanced search possible, but on whether the search, as conducted

Defendant further argues that Agent Ehuan, having been alerted by the names of the "Teen" and "Tiny Teen" subdirectories, was looking for child pornography when he opened the two subdirectories. Agent Ehuan testified persuasively to the contrary; he stated that, while the names of the subdirectories were suspicious to him, he opened the "Teen" and "Tiny Teen" subdirectories in the course of a systematic search of the BBS directory. In other words, Agent Ehuan did not target those particular subdirectories because of their names, and, at all times, he was searching for the materials that were the subject of the search warrant.

In summary, the seized images of alleged child pornography may not be suppressed because the search was within the scope of the warrant, and reasonable under the Fourth Amendment.

––––––––––

Notes and Questions

The *Gray* court, in a footnote, stated:

> Not presented here is what result would obtain had Agent Ehuan not stopped his search and obtained a warrant after the initial discovery of the child pornography. Arguably, Agent Ehuan could have continued his systematic search of defendant's computer files pursuant to the first search warrant, and, as long as he was searching for the items listed in the warrant, any child pornography discovered in the course of that search could have been seized under the "plain view" doctrine.

What is the proper answer to that hypothetical?

4. Opening Closed Files: The Special Approach

A main goal of the special approach is to limit the amount of evidence that would otherwise be in plain view. In *United States v. Comprehensive Drug Testing, Inc.*,

––––––––––

was reasonable. Even assuming that the CompuPic program could have been modified to allow the searching agent to determine, without viewing the file, whether it contained pictures or text, Agent Ehuan's search was reasonable under the Fourth Amendment. First, although the FBI believed the files for which they were searching were more likely to be text than pictures, it was certainly possible that the stolen NLM materials might contain pictures, and so it would have been reasonable for Agent Ehuan to examine files containing pictures. Second, there is no evidence that Agent Ehuan, or CART, was aware that the program could be used in this manner, which is significant because, as computer technology changes so rapidly, it would be unreasonable to require the FBI to know of, and use, only the most advanced computer searching techniques. Finally, because he was conducting a records search, Agent Ehuan was entitled to look at all of defendant's files to determine whether or not they fell within the scope of the search warrant. And, as this search targeted computer files, there was a large amount of material to review. Under these circumstances, it was reasonable, within the meaning of the Fourth Amendment, for Agent Ehuan, in his routine preliminary file review, to use a computer program that enabled him to see instantly, upon opening a file, the general nature of the material contained within that file.

579 F.3d 989 (9th Cir. 2009), the initial *en banc* court issued a sweeping opinion purporting to ban the ability of the government to utilize plain view when seeking a warrant to search a computer or any other electronic storage medium. The court, through Judge Kozinski, asserted: "Magistrates should insist that the government waive reliance upon the plain view doctrine in digital evidence cases." The court, in part, reasoned:

> [The] pressing need of law enforcement for broad authorization to examine electronic records creates a serious risk that every warrant for electronic information will become, in effect, a general warrant, rendering the Fourth Amendment irrelevant. The problem can be stated very simply: There is no way to be sure exactly what an electronic file contains without somehow examining its contents—either by opening it and looking, using specialized forensic software, keyword searching or some other such technique. But electronic files are generally found on media that also contain thousands or millions of other files among which the sought-after data may be stored or concealed. By necessity, government efforts to locate particular files will require examining a great many other files to exclude the possibility that the sought-after data are concealed there.

> Once a file is examined, however, the government may claim that its contents are in plain view and, if incriminating, the government can keep it. Authorization to search *some* computer files therefore automatically becomes authorization to search all files in the same subdirectory, and all files in an enveloping directory, a neighboring hard drive, a nearby computer or nearby storage media. Where computers are not near each other, but are connected electronically, the original search might justify examining files in computers many miles away, on a theory that incriminating electronic data could have been shuttled and concealed there.

> We accept the reality that such over-seizing is an inherent part of the electronic search process and proceed on the assumption that, when it comes to the seizure of electronic records, this will be far more common than in the days of paper records. This calls for greater vigilance on the part of judicial officers in striking the right balance between the government's interest in law enforcement and the right of individuals to be free from unreasonable searches and seizures. The process of segregating electronic data that is seizable from that which is not must not become a vehicle for the government to gain access to data which it has no probable cause to collect.

The Ninth Circuit granted a rehearing en banc and vacated the opinion authored by Judge Kozinski in *Comprehensive Drug Testing*. That opinion is reproduced in section 4.4. Judge Kozinski had another opportunity to discuss the plain view doctrine in dissenting from an order denying a request that *United States v. Lemus*, 596 F.3d 512 (9th Cir. 2010), be heard *en banc*. Judge Kozinski observed:

Plain view is killing the Fourth Amendment. Because our plain-view case law is so favorable to the police, they have a strong incentive to maneuver into a position where they can find things in plain view, or close enough to lie about it. . . . Plain view encourages the police to find every possible loop-hole to get themselves into a place where they can take a good look around, discover some evidence and then get a warrant to seize what they already know is there. This tiresome two-step is the new dropsy evidence. As often as not, the chance of hitting the plain-view jackpot is what drives the police into a man's house, his doctor's office or his ISP. Carefully drawn limitations in a warrant and narrow justifications for exceptions to the warrant requirement are becoming after-thoughts. We should not abet such skirting of the Fourth Amendment by the police; it only encourages them to do worse.

5. Independent State Grounds: Inadvertence and File Names

Larry R. Frasier, Jr. v. State

794 N.E.2d 449 (Ind. Ct. App. 2003)

SULLIVAN, JUDGE.

On November 1, 2000, Brown County Sheriff's Department Detective Scott Southerland prepared an affidavit seeking a search warrant authorizing a search of Frasier's residence.

[Based on that affidavit, the police obtained a probable cause-based warrant,] which directed the police to enter Frasier's home and garage and to search for and seize the following:

> "Marijuana plants, processed marijuana, marijuana packaging materials and equipment, equipment used to grow marijuana, drug paraphernalia, notes and/or records related to the sale of marijuana, scales, safes and/or lock boxes used to store marijuana. . . ."

[The police had also sought authority to search for "pornographic images depicting persons believed to be children" but that request had been marked out by the issuing judge, and hence,] the search warrant did not authorize the search and seizure of such.

On November 1, 2001, Detective Southerland and other officers executed the warrant. When Southerland entered the Frasier residence, he went to the bedroom where a personal computer was located. Southerland first noticed an icon labeled "Smoke" located on the computer's "desktop." Upon opening this file to view it, Southerland discovered that it included a letter to a company which sold a product purporting to allow one to pass a urine drug screen. Southerland then began opening documents listed in the "Documents" sub-menu of the computer's "Start" menu. This sub-menu lists recently opened documents on the computer. The first document Southerland opened from this list contained an image of a young, nude female. Southerland believed that the image was evidence of child pornography and printed the image. He then opened "two or three more files," before he realized that the files listed in the "Documents" menu likely contained images. Southerland told another deputy what he had found and asked that deputy to seek a warrant to search for evidence of child pornography on the computer. Such a warrant was issued the following day.

Frasier contends that the discovery of the images on his computer was not inadvertent in that "it is undisputed that Southerland expected to find illegal pornography on the computer." Frasier bases this claim upon the fact that Southerland had originally sought authorization from the magistrate to search Frasier's computer for child pornography. Southerland had previously indicated that he was aware that it was an image file and that he was looking for images that might relate to marijuana. This testimony, although inconsistent, is not so incredibly dubious or inherently improbable that it runs counter to human experience. The trial court was within its discretion as the trier of fact to accept Southerland's testimony as true.

Frasier cites to *United States v. Carey*, 172 F.3d 1268 (10th Cir. 1999). The situation in *Carey* was similar to the one before us: the police had a warrant to search the defendant's computer for documentary evidence pertaining to the sale and distribution of controlled substances. While searching the computer for such information, a police officer noticed numerous files with sexually suggestive names which ended in the suffix ".jpg". After a search of text-based files proved unfruitful, the officer encountered files he was unable to view on the computer he was using. Therefore he copied the files to another computer where he was readily able to view a JPEG file which, upon opening for viewing, was discovered to contain child pornography. The officer proceeded to copy approximately 244 JPEG files, many of which also contained pornographic images of children.

The Tenth Circuit held that the plain view exception did not apply because, after viewing the first JPEG file, the executing officer's suspicion changed, and he had probable cause to believe the remaining JPEG files contained pornography. The court wrote:

> "it is plainly evident that each time he opened a subsequent JPG file, [the officer] expected to find child pornography and not material related to drugs. Armed with this knowledge, he still continued to open every JPG file to confirm his expectations. Under these circumstances, we cannot say the contents of each of those files were inadvertently discovered."[n.11][20]

---

20. [n.11] The *Carey* decision might be read in this regard as an attempt to resurrect the "inadvertence" requirement earlier discarded by the U.S. Supreme Court in *Horton v. California*. On the other hand, use of the word "inadvertently" in *Carey* may merely be recognition of the principle enunciated in *Horton* that although inadvertence is not a "necessary condition" it nevertheless is a "characteristic of most legitimate 'plain-view' seizures."

The court stated that, given the executing officer's inadvertent discovery of the first JPEG file during his search for documents relating to drug activity, its holding was limited to the "subsequent opening of numerous files the officer knew, or at least expected, would contain images of child pornography." Thus, the first image inadvertently opened by the officer was admissible pursuant to the plain view doctrine. Yet this image was also closed when the officer first stumbled across it while looking for other documents. Therefore, according to the *Carey* court, the fact that the document was closed cannot be the touchstone of whether the plain view doctrine is applicable; rather, it is whether the discovery was inadvertent.

Frasier's claim that the discovery of the first image file on his computer was advertent is simply an invitation for us to reweigh evidence and assess witness credibility. Southerland testified that he was unaware of what type of file he was opening when he first found an image containing suspected child pornography. Applying the logic of the *Carey* decision, this file was in plain view. As to the remaining files opened after it was learned that the first one contained pornography, we approach a situation similar to that in *Carey*, where the officer expected to find more child pornography when he opened the subsequent files. However, unlike the other images in *Carey*, which apparently were labeled with sexually suggestive titles, the subsequent files opened by Southerland were cryptically named. Only after a few such files were opened, and all contained pornographic images, did Southerland expect the rest of the files to likewise be pornographic. At this point, Southerland sought and received a search warrant before continuing the search—precisely what the officer in *Carey* failed to do.

> This is to be compared with the situation in *Carey*, where the court explicitly noted that:
>
>> "[t]his is not a case in which ambiguously labeled files were contained in the hard drive directory. It is not a case in which the officers had to open each file drawer before discovering its contents. Even if we employ the file cabinet theory, the testimony of Detective Lewis makes the analogy inapposite because he stated he knew, or at least had probable cause to know, each drawer was properly labeled and its contents were clearly described in the label."

The case before us *is* a case in which ambiguously labeled files were located on the hard drive and the officer had to "open" each file before discovering its contents.

We have our own concerns with the approach advocated by Frasier and suggested by the *Carey* court, which implies that the police must rely upon the label given to

---

Be that as it may, we are not here applying an inadvertence factor with regard to a federal Fourth Amendment analysis. Rather we are applying the inadvertence requirement pursuant to constitutional analysis under Article 1, Section 11 of the Indiana Constitution. The *Carey* case, therefore, provides useful guidance.

a file to determine its contents. A computer image file is not exactly the same as a physical photograph. An officer searching for physical documents relating to drugs can come across a photograph and see its contents without having to "open" the photograph. The situation with a computer image file containing a photograph is somewhat different. The image file must be "opened," i.e., read and interpreted by some program in order to render its contents into a humanly perceptible form, i.e., an image on the computer monitor. In this sense, a computer image file is akin to a photograph sealed in an envelope or folder. And the name given to the file is like a label stuck onto the envelope or folder. Although such a label might say "Tax Records," the photograph inside could be of a nude child. Likewise, a computer image file containing child pornography could easily be named "tax_records.xls," in an attempt to hide its actual contents. The approach suggested by Frasier would require the police to rely upon the name and file extension given to a file in order to determine its contents. As many have unfortunately found by way of email viruses, such identification methods are not always secure; a malicious executable program might easily be named "picture.jpg.exe" and appear to be a harmless image file. An officer searching for one type of record on a computer should not be forced to rely upon the name given to a file, which might very well hide its actual contents. In order to find out what is contained in the file, it must necessarily be "opened" in some way to ascertain its contents. The only sure way for Southerland to determine what was contained in any file on Frasier's computer, and whether this file was to be seized pursuant to the warrant, was for him to "open" it.

Because the image files found on Frasier's computer were inadvertently discovered in plain view while Southerland was executing a search warrant which he objectively believed to be valid, the plain view exception is applicable. Based upon these images, the police obtained a second search warrant which authorized a search for child pornography. Even if we follow the reasoning of the *Carey* court, and that of the trial court in the present case, at the very least the first image file opened by Southerland was inadvertent, and this was enough by itself to establish probable cause to support a warrant to search the rest of Frasier's computer for child pornography.

Questions

1. Compare *Gray, Carey,* and *Frasier.* In making that comparison, reconsider the question posed following the *Gray* case.

2. Note the importance of fact-finding by the motion court in *Frasier* regarding the officer's intent. Do you believe that the officer found the child pornography inadvertently? What is the relevance of the subjective intent of an officer in plain view cases? Should Fourth Amendment protections vary depending on the intent of the officer conducting the search? Why should only the first image in *Carey* be admissible but that all of the images in *Frasier* are admissible?

§ 4.3 Document Searches

In *Andresen v. Maryland*, 427 U.S. 463 (1976), the Supreme Court outlined the broad parameters of a permissible records search. In upholding the search of an office for documents that sought evidence of the crime of false pretenses by an attorney involved in real estate settlement activity, the Court asserted:

> Under investigation was a complex real estate scheme whose existence could be proved only by piecing together many bits of evidence. Like a jigsaw puzzle, the whole "picture" of petitioner's false-pretense scheme . . . could be shown only by placing in the proper place the many pieces of evidence that, taken singly, would show comparatively little. The complexity of an illegal scheme may not be used as a shield to avoid detection when the State has demonstrated probable cause to believe that a crime has been committed and probable cause to believe that evidence of this crime is in the suspect's possession.

Although authorizing a broad document search, the Court observed:

> We recognize that there are grave dangers inherent in executing a warrant authorizing a search and seizure of a person's papers that are not necessarily present in executing a warrant to search for physical objects whose relevance is more easily ascertainable. In searches for papers, it is certain that some innocuous documents will be examined, at least cursorily, in order to determine whether they are, in fact, among those papers authorized to be seized. Similar dangers, of course, are present in executing a warrant for the "seizure" of telephone conversations. In both kinds of searches, responsible officials, including judicial officials, must take care to assure that they are conducted in a manner that minimizes unwarranted intrusions upon privacy.

Several of the themes articulated by *Andresen* have been applied by lower courts to searches of computers for data. Those considerations include the complexity of the crime, whether innocuous files can be examined, and minimization procedures to reduce the intrusion upon the individual's protected interests. Antecedent to those themes, however, is the debate whether *Andresen's* framework for document searches is applicable to computer searches.

1. Data Are Forms of Records/Container Analogy

Many courts view data in computer storage as a form of a document. Hence, a warrant that authorizes a search for "writings" or "records" permits a search of computer files.[21] This is to say that the government need not know the exact "form

---

21. *See* United States v. Hunter, 13 F. Supp. 2d 574, 581 (D. Vt. 1998) (warrant authorizing search for "records" permitted search of "computers, disks, and similar property"); United States v.

that records may take."[22] Indeed, this view asserts that there is "no principled distinction between records kept electronically and those in paper form"[23] and, hence, there is "no justification for favoring those who are capable of storing their records on computer over those who keep hard copies of their records."[24] In both instances, consistent with *Andresen*, "innocuous documents may be scanned to ascertain their relevancy"[25] in "recognition of 'the reality that few people keep documents of their criminal transactions in a folder marked "[crime] records."'"[26]

Courts adopting this view have often analogized computers to filing cabinets or to containers:

> [The police] may search the location authorized by the warrant, including any containers at that location that are reasonably likely to contain items described in the warrant. . . . This container rationale is equally applicable to nontraditional, technological "containers" that are reasonably likely to hold information in less tangible forms. Similarly a warrant cannot be expected to anticipate every form an item or repository of information may take, and therefore courts have affirmed the seizure of things that are similar to, or the "functional equivalent" of, items enumerated in a warrant, as well as containers in which they are reasonably likely to be found.[27]

Musson, 650 F. Supp. 525, 531 (D. Colo. 1986) (seizure of computer diskettes approved under a warrant authorizing the seizure of "any records or writings of whatsoever nature showing any business or financial transactions"); Frasier v. State, 794 N.E.2d 449, 454, 460 (Ind. Ct. App. 2003) (warrant that authorized search of "notes and or records" of marijuana sales permitted police to examine computer files); People v. Gall, 30 P.3d 145, 153 (Colo. 2001) (when warrant authorized seizure of "written and printed material" indicating an intent to do physical harm to a person or building pursuant to an investigation of a conspiracy to murder and use explosives against a facility, seizure of computers permissible because they were "reasonably likely to serve as 'containers' for writings, or the functional equivalent of 'written or printed material'"); People v. Loorie, 630 N.Y.S.2d 483, 484–86 (N.Y. Cty. Ct. 1995) (warrant authorizing search for "records" permitted search of computer files). *Cf.* United States v. Triumph Capital Group, Inc., 211 F.R.D. 31 (D. Conn. 2002) (warrant authorizing search for "file records" included text, remnants, and fragments of deleted files); United States v. Harding, 273 F. Supp. 2d 411, 425 (S.D.N.Y. 2003) (because photographs may be taken by digital or film cameras and can be scanned if initially captured by film, a warrant authorizing the police to search for "photographs" allowed agents to open and inspect graphical image files on a zip disk).

22. United States v. Gawrysiak, 972 F. Supp. 853, 861 (D.N.J. 1997) (approving of warrant to search business office for evidence of fraud), *aff'd*, 178 F.3d 1281 (3d Cir. 1999). *Accord* United States v. Henson, 848 F.2d 1374, 1383 (6th Cir. 1988).

23. United States v. Lievertz, 247 F. Supp. 2d 1052, 1063 (S.D. Ind. 2002).

24. United States v. Hunter, 13 F. Supp. 2d 574, 583 (D. Vt. 1998).

25. *Id.* at 583. *Accord* Russo v. State, 228 S.W.3d 779 (Tex. Crim. App. 2007); United States v. Gray, 78 F. Supp. 2d 524, 528 (E.D. Va. 1999).

26. United States v. Hunter, 13 F. Supp. 2d 574, 583 (D. Vt. 1998), *quoting* United States v. Riley, 906 F.2d 841, 845 (2d Cir. 1990). *Accord* United States v. Maali M., 346 F. Supp. 2d 1226, 1265 (M.D. Fla. 2004).

27. People v. Gall, 30 P.3d 145, 153 (Colo. 2001). *See also* United States v. Al-Marri, 230 F. Supp. 2d 535, 541 (S.D.N.Y. 2002) (a computer is a form of a container); People v. Loorie, 630 N.Y.S.2d 483,

Following this view, computers have been said to be "reasonably likely to serve as 'containers' for writings, or the functional equivalent of 'written or printed material.'"[28] This is despite the recognition that computer file searches present "a heightened degree" of intermingling of relevant and irrelevant material: "[t]oday computers and computer disks store most of the records and data belonging to businesses and attorneys."[29]

Accepting this view does not mean that wholesale searches of data on computers are permitted. Instead, the courts look to traditional means to limit the scope of document searches, such as the nature of the criminal activity alleged[30] or the nature of the objects sought.[31] For example, searches of computers for evidence of

---

484–86 (N.Y. Cty. Ct. 1995) (same); United States v. Barth, 26 F. Supp. 2d 929, 936 (W.D. Tex. 1998) (same).

28. People v. Gall, 30 P.3d 145, 153 (Colo. 2001).

29. United States v. Hunter, 13 F. Supp. 2d 574, 581, 583 (D. Vt. 1998).

30. *See* Guest v. Leis, 255 F.3d 325, 336 (6th Cir. 2001) (warrants seeking subscriber information in obscenity investigation requiring that communications and computer records pertain to the listed offenses were as particular as circumstances permitted); United States v. Kow, 58 F.3d 423, 427 (9th Cir. 1995) (one way to make warrant particular is to specify suspected criminal conduct being investigated but warrant invalid when it authorized "the seizure of virtually every document and computer file" without indicating how items related to suspected crime); United States v. George, 975 F.2d 72, 76 (2d Cir. 1992) ("Mere reference to 'evidence' of a violation of a broad criminal statute or general criminal activity provides no readily ascertainable guidelines for the executing officers as to what items to seize."); In re Application of Lafayette Academy, Inc., 610 F.2d 1, 5–6 (5th Cir. 1979) (warrant that resulted in removal of four or five truckloads of documents and computer-related materials violated the particularity requirement when, *inter alia*, it did not specify type of fraud under investigation); United States v. Hunter, 13 F. Supp. 2d 574, 582–83 (D. Vt. 1998) (discussing limitations on scope search involving money laundering scheme); In re Search Warrant for K-Sports Imports, Inc., 163 F.R.D. 594, 597–98 (C.D. Cal. 1995) (warrant for "all computer records and data," without limiting to crime under investigation, violated particularity requirement); State v. Askham, 86 P.3d 1224, 1227 (Wash. Ct. App. 2004) (warrant sufficiently particular when it names crime under investigation or when it describes in "some detail" suspected criminal activity; hence, when accused suspected of using computer to make threats and false accusations and warrant details the type of text files and web sites to be searched that could have been used to conduct that activity, it was sufficient); United States v. Longo, 70 F. Supp. 2d 225, 251 (W.D.N.Y. 1999) (warrant that authorized search of hard drive and any data disks for "two documents, one a promissory note, entitled TGL-003, contained within the directory labeled MISC, and a purchase agreement entitled 911, contained in the directory entitled IMF" specifically described area to be searched); State v. Nuckolls, 617 So. 2d 724, 726, 728 (Fla. Ct. App. 1993) (warrant seeking records of used car business charged with forgery, odometer tampering, and other criminal violations sufficient when it authorized seizure of "[d]ata stored on computer, including, but not limited to, magnetic media or any other electronic form, hard disks, cassettes, diskettes, photo optical devices and file server magnetic backup tapes" because it left nothing to discretion of officers executing warrant).

31. *See* United States v. Thorn, 375 F.3d 679, 684–85 (8th Cir. 2004) (warrant that authorized search and seizure of electronic storage media containing images of minors engaged in sexual acts allowed examination of contents of various computer-related media); United States v. Wong, 334 F.3d 831, 837–38 (9th Cir. 2003) (warrant authorizing search of computer to "obtain data as it relates to this case" sufficiently particular when combined with warrant's list of items sought in house); State v. One Pioneer CD-ROM Changer, 891 P.2d 600, 604–05 (Okla. Ct. App. 1995)

child pornography and other sexual exploitation of children make up a shockingly large percentage of the decided cases; in response to particularity challenges in these cases, courts focus on the sufficiency of the allegations of criminal conduct[32] or the description of the objects[33] sought.

(seizure of computer system permissible under warrant authorizing seizure of "equipment" "pertaining to the distribution or display of pornographic material in violation of state obscenity laws"); Schalk v. State, 823 S.W.2d 633, 644, 651 (Tex. Crim. App. 1991) (in theft of trade secrets prosecution, "magnetic tapes" that contained or were reasonably believed to contain stolen data and/or files sufficiently described items to be seized).

32. *See* United States v. Meek, 366 F.3d 705, 714–15 (9th Cir. 2004) (warrant sufficient to search for crime involving use of Internet when it listed numerous items relating to seduction and sexual exploitation of children: sexually explicit material or paraphernalia used to lower inhibition of children, sex toys, photography equipment, child pornography, as well as material related to past molestation such as photographs, address ledgers including names of other pedophiles, journals of sexual encounters with children, computer equipment, information on digital and magnetic storage devices, computer printouts, computer software and manuals, and documentation regarding computer use); United States v. Hay, 231 F.3d 630, 637 (9th Cir. 2000) (upholding validity of search of computer equipment and files because warrant limited search to evidence of crimes involving sexual exploitation of children); United States v. Gleich, 293 F. Supp. 2d 1082, 1088 (D.N.D. 2003) (warrant authorizing search of computer for photographs, pictures, visual representations, or videos that included sexual conduct by minor, as defined by North Dakota statute, met particularity requirement), *aff'd*, 397 F.3d 608 (8th Cir. 2005); United States v. Hall, 142 F.3d 988, 996–97 (7th Cir. 1998) (when items listed in warrant qualified by phrases that items sought were related to child pornography, particularity requirement satisfied); United States v. Clough, 246 F. Supp. 2d 84, 87–88 (D. Me. 2003) (warrant in child pornography case authorizing search of "text documents" and "digital images" violated particularity requirement when there were "no restrictions on the search, no references to statutes, and no references to crimes or illegality"); State v. Wible, 51 P.3d 830, 837 (Wash Ct. App. 2002) (warrant particular when it limited search to images of children engaged in sexually explicit activity as defined by child pornography statute). *Cf.* United States v. Maxwell, 45 M.J. 406, 420 (C.A.A.F. 1996) (rejecting challenge to warrant that included persons who could have unknowingly received child pornography in their email mailboxes because to narrow the field to only those who had knowingly received images would have required advance search of mailboxes to ascertain if files had been opened).

33. *See* United States v. Gleich, 397 F.3d 608, 612 (8th Cir. 2005) (warrant authorizing search of home and personal computer for "photographs, pictures, visual representations or videos in any form that include sexual conduct by a minor" permitted search of all three computers in house); United States v. Thorn, 375 F.3d 679, 685 (8th Cir. 2004) (warrant that authorized search and seizure of electronic storage media containing images of minors engaged in sexual acts sufficed to provide authority to examine contents of various computer-related media); United States v. Campos, 221 F.3d 1143, 1147–48 (10th Cir. 2000) (warrant particular when it authorized, *inter alia*, seizure of computer equipment which may be used to depict or distribute child pornography); United States v. Upham, 168 F.3d 532, 535 (1st Cir. 1999) (upholding warrant issued for "[a]ny and all computer software and hardware, . . . computer disks, disk drives" in house of woman suspected of sending and receiving child pornography over Internet); Davis v. Gracey, 111 F.3d 1472, 1479 (10th Cir. 1997) ("equipment . . . pertaining to the distribution or display of pornographic material" was sufficiently precise to limit search to computer equipment connected with that criminal activity); United States v. Albert, 195 F. Supp. 2d 267, 275–76 (D. Mass. 2002) (warrant particular when it authorized search and seizure of computer, disks, software, and storage devices when there was probable cause to believe that the computer contained more than 1000 images of child pornography, given that the "search and seizure of the computer and its related storage equipment was the only practical way to obtain the images"); United States v. Allen, 53 M.J. 402 (C.A.A.F.

United States v. Curtis Robert Williams

592 F.3d 511 (4th Cir. 2010)

NIEMEYER, CIRCUIT JUDGE:

Based on evidence seized from his home during execution of a search warrant, Curtis Williams was convicted of possession of an unregistered machine gun and an unregistered silencer and possession of child pornography.

In September 2007, the Fairfax Baptist Temple in Fairfax Station, Virginia, began receiving threatening e-mail messages from an individual identifying himself as "Franklin Pugh." Similar and related e-mails were later received from several other e-mail accounts, registered in the names of children attending the Fairfax Baptist Temple School, who had been referred to in the earlier e-mails.

In an e-mail dated October 16, 2007, Pugh named several young boys who attended the Fairfax Baptist Temple School, describing their physical characteristics. He stated that he was a pedophile, that he could not face life without having sex with the boys, and that he could not attend the Fairfax Baptist Temple again unless he could give oral sex to a boy at the church whom he identified by name. At the end of the e-mail, he stated, "I know your boy's names. I know where they go for lunch after church. I know where they live. I know when they come and leave school. There's boys I'd love to sleep with right now. There is an endless supply. Boy dick is everywhere."

In an e-mail dated October 22, 2007, the sender, now identifying himself as one of the boys named in an earlier e-mail, wrote in the same vein as earlier e-mails. After sending several more e-mails, the sender announced that he would be getting a new account to send further messages. Nonetheless, several more e-mails were sent under this name, continuing to discuss molesting the boys at the Fairfax

---

2000) (warrant particular when it authorized search for computer files relating to nude photographs of juveniles, Internet locations of such material, or lists of such files); State v. Wible, 51 P.3d 830 (Wash. Ct. App. 2002) (warrant for child pornography satisfies particularity requirement if it limits seizable items by specifying type of material that qualifies as child pornography); State v. Maxwell, 825 A.2d 1224, 1234 (N.J. Super. Ct. Law Div. 2001) (in case involving use of telephone to call child victims of sexual assault, warrant that authorized search of computer for "computer address books" valid); State v. Patscheck, 6 P.3d 498, 499–500 (N.M. Ct. App. 2000) (in prosecution for sexual offenses against children, warrant that specified computer to be searched for "pornographic movies" valid); State v. Lehman, 736 A.2d 256, 260–61 (Me. 1999) (warrant not overbroad when it authorized seizure of all computer-related equipment in suspect's house when police knew only that the images of sexually exploited girls were taken by a digital camera and downloaded to a computer). *Cf.* United States v. Lamb, 945 F. Supp. 441, 457–59 (N.D.N.Y. 1996) (warrant satisfied particularity requirement in child pornography case seeking subscriber information and electronic mail messages sent to and received by 78 individuals from Internet service provider when messages were instrumentalities of crime used by child pornography traffickers to locate and communicate with persons of like mind).

Baptist Temple School, sacrificing them to God like Abraham and Isaac, and having sex with one of the boys post-sacrifice, unless "God makes me burn him."

Beginning on October 24, 2007, similar e-mails were received from an account registered under the name of the father of the pastor of Fairfax Baptist Temple. Again the messages discussed molesting the boys there.

Upon investigation, the Fairfax County Police determined that at least one of the e-mail accounts from which e-mails had been received had been accessed repeatedly by an Internet account registered to Karol Williams, in Clifton, Virginia, who is the wife of the defendant, Curtis Williams. Both Karol and Curtis were active members of the Fairfax Baptist Temple. Upon learning this, the police applied for a warrant to search Karol and Curtis Williams' home.

In the affidavit supporting the warrant application, Fairfax County Detective Craig Paul summarized the e-mails, detailed the police investigation to date, and stated that the evidence supported his belief that violations of state law had occurred, particularly § 18.2-60 of the Virginia Code, prohibiting any person from communicating threats to kill or do bodily harm to persons at elementary, middle, or secondary schools, and § 18.2-152.7:1, prohibiting harassment by computer by communicating "obscene, vulgar, profane, lewd, lascivious, or indecent language, or mak[ing] any suggestion or proposal of an obscene nature."

In addition to providing the factual basis for the violations, Detective Paul explained, "It has been your Affiant's training and experience that adults who are engaged in the sexual exploitation of children keep images and related documents with them. They also collect images and texts describing sexual interaction with minors and child erotica." The detective described the child pornography market, the use of computers and other recording devices, and the need to seize and search various types of electronic media to locate evidence of the threat crimes, including evidence properly characterized as child pornography.

Based on Detective Paul's affidavit, a Fairfax County magistrate issued a search warrant on October 25, 2007, that "commanded" officers to search for and seize from the home of Karol and Curtis Williams:

> Any and all computer systems and digital storage media, videotapes, video-tape recorders, documents, photographs, and Instrumentalities indicat[ive] of the offense of § 18.2-152.7:1 Harassment by Computer and § 18.2-60 Threats of death or bodily injury to a person or member of his family; threats to commit serious bodily harm to persons on school property, Code of Virginia (as amended).

Police, along with the FBI, executed the warrant the next day and seized several computers, CDs, DVDs, and other electronic media devices.

The FBI agents who had participated in the search of the Williams' house took the computers and electronic media and later searched their contents. During the course of that search, FBI Agent Michael French reported in an e-mail sent to the U.S. Attorney's Office in the Eastern District of Virginia that "we found many deleted images of young male erotica from September–October 2007. We also found [that] the ano-nymizer software TOR had been installed." He concluded by saying that he hoped to find Williams' "collection" on the laptop and USB thumbdrives the following week.

Sometime later during his search, Agent French opened a DVD that had been seized from the Williams' home, labeled with the words, "Virus Shield, Quarented Files, Destroy." Upon opening the DVD, he observed over a thousand images in "thumbnail view" of minor boys, some of which were sexually suggestive and some of which were sexually explicit. Of the total number of images, approximately 39 constituted child pornography.

Williams contends that the government's seizure of a DVD containing 39 images of child pornography violated his Fourth Amendment right against unreasonable searches and seizures. He asserts that the search warrant did not authorize a search of his computer and related digital media for child pornography. Rather, it only authorized a search for and seizure of evidence relating to two designated Virginia crimes involving threats of bodily harm and harassment by computer.

Reasoning that "[s]ince computers can hold so much information, touching on virtually every aspect of a person's life, the potential for invasion of privacy in a search of electronic evidence is significantly greater than in the context of a non-computer search," Williams argues that traditional Fourth Amendment rules can-not be successfully applied in this context. He specifically relies on an article by Professor Orin Kerr, in which Professor Kerr maintained that a new approach is needed for applying the Fourth Amendment to searches of computers and digital media. *See* Orin S. Kerr, *Searches and Seizures in a Digital World*, 119 Harv. L. Rev. 531 (2005). Professor Kerr explained:

> The new dynamics of computer searches and seizures teach important les-sons about the Fourth Amendment. For most of its first two centuries, the Fourth Amendment was used almost exclusively to regulate government searches of homes and containers. The mechanisms of home and con-tainer searches directed Fourth Amendment doctrine to focus primarily on the entrance to the home or container. In a world of physical barri-ers, actions that broke down those physical barriers became the focus of judicial attention. The world of digital search and seizure shows that this focus is contingent on the architecture of physical searches. As computer searches and seizures become more common in the future, we will begin to see twentieth-century Fourth Amendment doctrine as a contingent set of rules that achieves the foundational goals of the Fourth Amendment law given the dynamics of searching physical property. Those physical rules will be matched by a set of rules for digital searches and seizures that attempts to achieve the same purpose in a very different factual context.

Emphasizing the basic principle that a search warrant must not authorize general searches but must particularize the place and items to be searched, Williams argues that the warrant in this case must not be read to have authorized officers to view each file on the computer, but rather to have authorized a search of *only those files* in his computer that related to the designated state offenses. Applying this limitation to the search in this case, Williams argues that the authorization for the search of his computers and digital media was limited to files relating to the two Virginia crimes of threatening bodily harm and harassment by computer, and that the files relating to child pornography fell outside the scope of the warrant and therefore were seized without a warrant.

In addition, Williams argues that the search for and seizure of child pornography did not fall within any recognized exception to the Fourth Amendment's warrant requirement. To apply the plain-view exception in the context of computer searches would, Williams argues, "effectively read[] the warrant requirement out of the Fourth Amendment." Relying heavily on *United States v. Carey*, 172 F.3d 1268, 1273 (10th Cir. 1999), which held that child pornography discovered on a computer during the course of a search for evidence of drug transactions must be suppressed because it was not "inadvertently discovered," Williams argues that the plain-view exception cannot be applied in the context of computer searches unless the files sought to be seized pursuant to the exception are discovered "inadvertently." In this case, Williams observes that the officers suspected him of possessing child pornography from the outset of their investigation and that they used the warrant's authorization to search for such materials, which, he maintains, fell outside the scope of the warrant.

When a search requires review of a large collection of items, such as papers, "it is certain that some innocuous documents will be examined, at least cursorily, in order to determine whether they are, in fact, among those papers authorized to be seized." [*Andresen v. Maryland*, 427 U.S. 463, 482 n.11 (1976)]. If, in those circumstances, documents not covered by the warrant are improperly seized, the government should promptly return the documents or the trial judge should suppress them.

In this case, the warrant authorized a search for and seizure of "[a]ny and all computer systems and digital storage media, . . . documents, photographs, and Instrumentalities" indicative of the Virginia state law offenses stated in Va. Code Ann. §§ 18.2-152.7:1 (harassment by computer) and 18.2-60 (threats of death or bodily injury to a person or member of his family; threats to commit serious bodily harm to persons on school property). A violation of the referenced harassment by computer offense includes using a computer or computer network "to communicate obscene, vulgar, profane, lewd, lascivious, or indecent language, or to make any suggestion or proposal of an obscene nature, or threaten any illegal or immoral act."

While the warrant did not explicitly authorize a search for child pornography, it did authorize a search for instrumentalities of computer harassment and "photographs . . . indicati[ve] of" this offense, which involves communicating "obscene, vulgar, profane, lewd, lascivious, or indecent language," or making a "suggestion or proposal of an obscene nature," or threatening an "illegal or immoral act." Particularly in the context of the threats made in this case, which indicated that the person sending the e-mails to the church was a pedophile, pornographic images involving children were relevant to demonstrating the authorship and purpose of the e-mails.

The fact that the DVD containing child pornography might also have indicated crimes other than those described in the warrant does not preclude its seizure. "Courts have never held that a search is overbroad merely because it results in additional criminal charges." Thus, the fact that possession of child pornography is itself a crime does not render the seizure outside the scope of an investigation into the computer harassment crime. Whether seized evidence falls within the scope of a warrant's authorization must be assessed solely in light of the relation between the evidence and the terms of the warrant's authorization.

Even if we were to conclude that the warrant did not authorize a search for child pornography, we conclude alternatively that the seizure of the images portraying child pornography was, in any event, justified by the plain-view exception to the warrant requirement.

In this case, the warrant authorized a search of Williams' computers and digital media for evidence relating to the designated Virginia crimes of making threats and computer harassment. To conduct that search, the warrant impliedly authorized officers to open each file on the computer and view its contents, at least cursorily, to determine whether the file fell within the scope of the warrant's authorization — *i.e.*, whether it related to the designated Virginia crimes of making threats or computer harassment. To be effective, such a search could not be limited to reviewing only the files' designation or labeling, because the designation or labeling of files on a computer can easily be manipulated to hide their substance. Surely, the owner of a computer, who is engaged in criminal conduct on that computer, will not label his files to indicate their criminality.

Once it is accepted that a computer search must, by implication, authorize at least a cursory review of each file on the computer, then the criteria for applying the plain-view exception are readily satisfied. *First*, an officer who has legal possession of the computer and electronic media and a legal right to conduct a search of it is "lawfully present at the place from which evidence can be viewed," thus satisfying the first element of the plain-view exception. *Second*, the officer, who is authorized to search the computer and electronic media for evidence of a crime and who is therefore legally authorized to open and view all its files, at least cursorily, to determine whether any one falls within the terms of the warrant, has "a lawful right of access" to all files, albeit only momentarily. And *third*, when the officer then comes upon child pornography, it becomes "immediately apparent" that its possession by the computer's owner is illegal and incriminating. And so, in this case, any child pornography viewed on the computer or electronic media may be seized under the plain-view exception.

Williams, relying on the Tenth Circuit's opinion in *United States v. Carey*, advances an argument that the plain-view exception cannot apply to searches of computers and electronic media when the evidence indicates that it is the officer's *purpose* from the outset to use the authority of the warrant to search for unauthorized evidence because the unauthorized evidence would not then be uncovered "inadvertently."

This argument, however, cannot stand against the principle, well-established in Supreme Court jurisprudence, that the scope of a search conducted pursuant to a warrant is defined *objectively* by the terms of the warrant and the evidence sought, not by the *subjective* motivations of an officer. "The fact that an officer is interested in an [unauthorized] item of evidence and fully expects to find it in the course of a search should not invalidate its seizure if the search is confined in area and duration by the terms of a warrant or a valid exception to the warrant requirement." In [*Horton v. California*, 496 U.S. 128 (1990)], the Court *explicitly* rejected the very argument that Williams makes in this case, that unauthorized evidence must be suppressed because its discovery was not "inadvertent."

While Williams relies accurately on *Carey*, which effectively imposes an "inadvertence" requirement, such a conclusion is inconsistent with *Horton*. Inadvertence focuses incorrectly on the subjective motivations of the officer in conducting the search and not on the objective determination of whether the search is authorized by the warrant or a valid exception to the warrant requirement.

In this case, because the scope of the search authorized by the warrant included the authority to open and cursorily view each file, the observation of child pornography within several of these files did not involve an intrusion on Williams' protected privacy interests beyond that already authorized by the warrant, regardless of the officer's subjective motivations. And neither did the seizure of these photographs interfere with Williams' possessory interests, for once their nature as contraband became apparent, Williams' possessory interests were forfeited.

At bottom, we conclude that the sheer amount of information contained on a computer does not distinguish the authorized search of the computer from an analogous search of a file cabinet containing a large number of documents. As the Supreme Court recognized in *Andresen*, "[t]here are grave dangers inherent in executing a warrant authorizing a search and seizure of a person's papers that are not necessarily present in executing a warrant to search for physical objects whose relevance is more easily ascertainable." While that danger certainly counsels care and respect for privacy when executing a warrant, it does not prevent officers from lawfully searching the documents, nor should it undermine their authority to search a computer's files. We have applied these rules successfully in the context of warrants authorizing the search and seizure of non-electronic files and we see no reason to depart from them in the context of electronic files.

2. Rejection of the Document Search and Container Analogy: A "Special Approach"

Some authorities reject the container analogy and view searches for data on a computer much differently than paper document searches.[34] The leading case,

---

34. *See, e.g.*, Raphael Winick, *Searches and Seizures of Computers and Computer Data*, 8 HARV. J.L. & TECH. 75, 110 (1994) ("An analogy between a computer and a container oversimplifies a

United States v. Carey, 172 F.3d 1268 (10th Cir. 1999), espouses the view that law enforcement officers must take a "special approach" to the search of data contained on computers and that the "file cabinet analogy may be inadequate." This position is premised on the fact that "electronic storage is likely to contain a greater quantity and variety of information than any previous storage method."[35] As one judge has argued:

> A computer is fundamentally different from a writing, or a container of writings, because of its capacity to hold a vast array of information in many different forms, to sort, process, and transfer information in a database, to provide a means for communication via e-mail, and to connect any given user to the internet. A computer may be comprised of a wide variety of personal information, including but not limited to word processing documents, financial records, business records, electronic mail, internet access paths, and previously deleted materials. Because of these differences, the seizure of a computer raises many issues beyond those that might pertain to mere writings. . . .
>
> A "writing" is simply not particular enough to warrant a reasonable person to conclude that it includes a computer because a writing and a computer are two fundamentally different things, both in degree and in kind. . . . Moreover, Fourth Amendment analysis regarding the search and seizure of computers must be approached cautiously and narrowly because of the important privacy concerns inherent in the nature of computers, and because the technology in this area is rapidly growing and changing.[36]

Other arguments that searches of computers are different include the assertion that computers "present the tools to refine searches in ways that cannot be done with hard copy files. When confronting a file cabinet full of papers, there may be no way to determine what to seize without doing some level of review of everything in the cabinet"; in contrast, computer technology affords a variety of methods by which the government may tailor a search to focus on documents that evidence the alleged criminal activity.[37] Those methods, it has been asserted, include limiting

---

complex area of Fourth Amendment doctrine and ignores the realities of massive modern computer storage."). *See also* Susan W. Brenner & Barbara A. Frederiksen, *Computer Searches and Seizures: Some Unresolved Issues*, 8 Mich. Telecom. Tech. L. Rev. 39, 60–63, 81–82 (2002) (setting forth some of the differences between searches of "paper documents and computer-generated evidence" and maintaining that courts should impose restrictions on computer searches such as limiting the search by file types, by requiring a second warrant for intermingled files, and by imposing time frames for conducting the search).

35. Raphael Winick, *Searches and Seizures of Computers and Computer Data*, 8 Harv. J.L. & Tech. 75, 104 (1994). *See also In re* Search of: 3817 W. West End, 321 F. Supp. 2d 953, 958–59 (N.D. Ill. 2004) (asserting that searches of computers require "careful scrutiny of the particularity requirement" because, *inter alia*, of the "extraordinary volume of information that may be stored").

36. People v. Gall, 30 P.3d 145, 164–65 (Colo. 2001) (Martinez, J., dissenting).

37. *In re Search of: 3817 W. West End*, 321 F. Supp. 2d at 959.

searches by date range, doing key word searches, limiting searches by file type, and "focusing on certain software programs."[38]

Under this "special approach," courts have imposed several unique requirements: a search warrant seeking to seize computers or computer equipment must specify that it covers such items and the warrant must "include measures to direct the subsequent search of a computer."[39] Police officers may also have to limit the search by "observing files types and titles listed on the directory, doing a key word search for relevant terms, or reading portions of each file stored in the memory."[40] To restrict the scope of a search of a computer that contains intermingled documents, some authorities rejecting the premise that computer searches are just another form of a document search maintain that merely obtaining a warrant to search for specified items is insufficient. Instead,

> law enforcement must engage in the intermediate step of sorting various types of documents and then only search the ones specified in a warrant. Where officers come across relevant documents so intermingled with irrelevant documents that they cannot feasibly be sorted at the site, the officers may seal or hold the documents pending approval by a magistrate of the conditions and limitations on a further search through the documents. The magistrate should then require officers to specify in a warrant which type of files are sought.[41]

United States v. Michael Clay Payton
573 F.3d 859 (9th Cir. 2009)

CANBY, CIRCUIT JUDGE:

A California Superior Court judge issued a search warrant for a house in Merced County where Payton resided. Police believed that the occupants were selling

---

38. *Id.*

39. People v. Gall, 30 P.3d 145, 164–65 (Colo. 2001) (Martinez, J., dissenting). *See also In Re Search of: 3817 W. West End*, 321 F. Supp. 2d at 957 (maintaining that an issuing magistrate had authority to require government to follow "search protocol that attempts to ensure that the search will not exceed constitutional bounds").

40. United States v. Carey, 172 F.3d 1268 (10th Cir. 1999). *See also* People v. Carratu, 755 N.Y.S.2d 800, 807–09 (N.Y. Sup. Ct. 2003) (stating that police did or did not have right under warrant to open computer file folders based on name associated with that folder); *In re* Grand Jury Subpoena Duces Tecum Dated November 15, 1993, 846 F. Supp. 11, 13 (S.D.N.Y. 1994) (based on government's concession, asserting that key word search of information stored on computer would reveal information likely to be relevant to grand jury investigation); People v. Gall, 30 P.3d 145, 166 (Colo. 2001) (Martinez, J., dissenting) ("searches may be limited to avoid searching files not included in the warrant by 'observing files types and titles listed in the directory, doing a key word search for relevant terms, or reading portions of each file stored in the memory'").

41. *Carey*, 172 F.3d at 1275. *Accord* United States v. Walser, 275 F.3d 981, 986–87 (10th Cir. 2001); United States v. Campos, 221 F.3d 1143, 1148 (10th Cir. 2000).

drugs. The warrant directed officers to search for any item listed in "Attachment A," which included methamphetamine and materials used to cut and package it. Attachment A also included, among other things, "[s]ales ledgers showing narcotics transactions such as pay/owe sheets" and "[f]inancial records of the person(s) in control of the residence or premises, bank accounts, loan applications, [and] income and expense records." The warrant did not explicitly authorize the search of computers.

During the execution of the search, the officers found no evidence of drug sales. Officer Horn found a computer in Payton's bedroom with the screen saver activated. He moved the mouse, which removed the screen saver, and clicked open a file. It disclosed an image that he thought was child pornography. This and images like it eventually led to Payton's charge for possession of child pornography. Payton moved to suppress the evidence. He argued that the search of the computer exceeded the scope of the warrant.

We conclude that the search of Payton's computer exceeded the scope of the warrant and did not meet the Fourth Amendment standard of reasonableness. There is no question that computers are capable of storing immense amounts of information and often contain a great deal of private information. Searches of computers therefore often involve a degree of intrusiveness much greater in quantity, if not different in kind, from searches of other containers.

The search warrant did explicitly authorize a search of Payton's premises to find and seize, among other things, "[s]ales ledgers showing narcotics transactions such as pay/owe sheets," and "[f]inancial records of the person(s) in control of the premises." The crucial question is whether these provisions authorized the officers to look for such records on Payton's computer. We conclude that, under our recent and controlling precedent of *United States v. Giberson*, 527 F.3d 882 (9th Cir. 2008), as applied to the circumstances of this case, they did not.

In *Giberson*, officers discovered that Giberson had used false identification and was delinquent in his child support payments. They obtained a search warrant authorizing a search of his residence for, among other things, "'records, documents or correspondence . . . related to the use or attempted use' of other individual's identities." During the search, the officers discovered a computer on a desk in Giberson's bedroom; the computer was connected to a printer on a dresser. Next to the printer, the officers found a sheet of what appeared to be fake identification cards that were not of high quality and looked as if they could have been printed on the adjacent printer. In and on the desk, the officers found other documents evidencing the production of false identification, including fake Social Security cards and birth certificates. Acting on the advice of an Assistant U.S. Attorney who had been contacted, one of the officers secured the computer until the agents could obtain a second search warrant authorizing search of the computers for such documents. The computer was sent to a forensic laboratory, and a now authorized search for false identification documents revealed images of child pornography, for receipt and possession of which Giberson was later charged. He challenged the seizure of his computer in the initial search of his residence.

We stated the question that *Giberson* presented and our answer to it as follows:

> We have not yet had occasion to determine, in an opinion, whether computers are an exception to the general principle that a warrant authorizing the seizure of particular documents also authorizes the search of a container likely to contain those documents. We hold that, *in this case, where there was ample evidence that the documents in the warrant could be found on Giberson's computer*, the officers did not exceed the scope of the warrant when they seized the computer.

As we read this passage, it holds that *under certain circumstances*, computers are not an exception to the rule permitting searches of containers to find objects specified in a warrant. A reasonable negative inference is that, absent those circumstances, a search of a computer not expressly authorized by a warrant is not a reasonable search. Those circumstances are absent in the present case. The search of Payton's residence for evidence of drug sales produced none. There was nothing in the neighborhood of Payton's computer, or indeed in the entire residence, that suggested that evidence of drug sales or anything else specified in the warrant would be found on the computer in his bedroom. It is true, of course, that pay/owe sheets indicating drug sales were physically capable of being kept on Payton's computer. But a similar bare capability was present in *Giberson;* a computer is physically capable of containing false identification documents. In *Giberson*, we did not simply recite that fact and uphold the seizure; we relied quite specifically on the documents found next to the printer and the computer, in circumstances indicating a likelihood that they were created on and printed from the computer. It was the presence of those documents that rendered the search reasonable.

There was an additional factor that led us to conclude that the officers acted reasonably in *Giberson*. We stated:

> In the circumstances underlying this appeal, it was reasonable for the officers to believe that seizable items were stored on Giberson's computer, and to secure the computer and obtain a specific warrant and search it. . . . Their actions were particularly appropriate because the agents merely secured the computer while they waited to get a second warrant that would specifically authorize searching the computer's files. The seizure of the computer was therefore reasonable.

A seizure of a computer to await a second warrant is nevertheless a Fourth Amendment seizure, but it is far less intrusive than a search. In Payton's case, however, Officer Horn searched first and seized afterwards. When he first encountered the computer, he moved the mouse, inactivating the screen saver, and opened a file. In the absence of any circumstances supporting a reasonable belief that items specified in the warrant would be found on the computer, the search did not meet the Fourth Amendment standard of reasonableness.

We recognize that there are several statements in *Giberson* to the effect that no heightened Fourth Amendment standard should be applied to computers as opposed to other containers. For example, we stated that "[w]hile it is true that computers can store a large amount of material, there is no reason why officers should be permitted to search a room full of filing cabinets or even a person's library for documents listed in a warrant but should not be able to search a computer." We pointed out that, in *United States v. Gomez-Soto*, 723 F.2d 649 (9th Cir. 1984), we upheld a search of a cassette tape pursuant to a warrant that authorized a search for items that might be contained in it. If we permit such searches, "[t]here is no reason why material stored digitally on a computer should not also be searchable."

These and similar statements must be placed in context, however. They were made in response to Giberson's argument that computers could *never* be searched unless that authority was specifically granted in the search warrant. Indeed, Giberson conceded that it was reasonable for the officers to conclude that false identification documents might be found on his computer. He contended, however, that computers were sufficiently different from other containers that they were entitled to a bright-line categorical rule of heightened Fourth Amendment protection: no search is permissible without specific authorization in the warrant. Our opinion in *Giberson* rejected this contention, stating that the support for such an argument could not be "technology-specific" to computers alone.

Thus *Giberson* held that computers were not entitled to a special categorical protection of the Fourth Amendment. Instead, they remained subject to the Fourth Amendment's overall requirement that searches be constitutionally "reasonable." And, for the second time, *Giberson* stated its rule of reasonableness for the case before it:

> If it is reasonable to believe that a computer contains items enumerated in the warrant, officers may search it. Here, numerous documents related to the production of fake I.D.s were found in and around Giberson's computer and were arguably created on and printed from it. It was therefore reasonable for officers to believe that the items they were authorized to seize would be found in the computer, and they acted within the scope of the warrant when they secured the computer.

In Payton's case, however, the legitimating facts were absent. There was no comparable evidence pointing to the computer as a repository for the evidence sought in the search. The search of the computer preceded any attempt to secure the computer and seek a second warrant. We conclude that the search in those circumstances did not meet the Fourth Amendment requirement of reasonableness.

Our confidence in our conclusion is buttressed by contemplating the effect of a contrary decision. In order to uphold the search in this case, we would have to rule that, whenever a computer is found in a search for other items, if any of those items were *capable* of being stored in a computer, a search of the computer would be permissible. Such a ruling would eliminate any incentive for officers to seek explicit judicial authorization for searches of computers. But the nature of computers makes such searches so intrusive that affidavits seeking warrants for the search of computers often include a limiting search protocol, and judges issuing warrants may place conditions on the manner and extent of such searches, to protect privacy and other important constitutional interests. We believe that it is important to preserve the option of imposing such conditions when they are deemed warranted by judicial officers authorizing the search of computers. If unwarranted searches of computers are automatically authorized by upholding the search in Payton's case, that option will be lost. Indeed, the special considerations of reasonableness involved in the search of computers are reflected by the practice, exemplified in *Giberson*, of searching officers to stop and seek an explicit warrant when they encounter a computer that they have reason to believe should be searched.

For all of these reasons, we conclude that the search of Payton's computer without explicit authorization in the warrant exceeded the scope of that warrant and did not meet the Fourth Amendment standard of reasonableness illustrated by *Giberson*.

Should File Names or Types Limit the Scope of a Search?

Some authorities utilizing the "special approach" rely on the proposition that file name labels or extensions accurately indicate what the file contains. As one commentator has asserted:

> Computer programs store information in a wide variety of formats. For example, most financial spreadsheets store information in a completely different format than do word processing programs. Similarly, an investigator reasonably familiar with computers should be able to distinguish database programs, electronic mail files, telephone lists and stored visual or audio files from each other. Where a search warrant seeks only financial records, law enforcement officers should not be allowed to search through telephone lists or word processing files absent a showing of some reason to believe that these files contain the financial records sought.[42]

In *United States v. Carey*, 172 F.3d 1268 (10th Cir. 1999), the police had a warrant allowing them to search computer files for "names, telephone numbers, ledger receipts, addresses, and other documentary evidence pertaining to the sale and distribution of controlled substances." During the course of the search, Detective Lewis came across files with sexually suggestive titles and the extension "jpg." Upon

---

42. *See* Raphael Winick, *Searches and Seizures of Computers and Computer Data*, 8 Harv. J.L. & Tech. 75, 108–09 (1994). *See also* Amy Baron-Evans, *When the Government Seizes and Searches Your Client's Computer*, 27 Champion 18 (2003) ("Fortunately, the technical means exist to search computers for particular information without rummaging through private information not described in a warrant. For example, in a typical white collar case, relevant files can be isolated and irrelevant ones avoided through keyword searches. In a child pornography case, the government can search for picture files without the need to look at any text file.").

opening one of those files, Lewis observed child pornography. He subsequently downloaded numerous other "jpg" files and opened some of them, revealing additional child pornography. The "jpg" files featured sexually suggestive or obscene names, many including the word "teen" or "young." Lewis testified that, until he opened each file, he really did not know its contents. Lewis stated that image files could contain evidence pertinent to a drug investigation such as pictures of "a hydroponic growth system and how it's set up to operate" and that drug dealers often obscure or disguise evidence of their drug activity. He claimed: "I wasn't conducting a search for child pornography, that happened to be what these turned out to be." Although the trial court denied the motion without making any findings of fact, the appellate court reversed, asserting:

> [T]he case turns upon the fact that each of the files containing pornographic material was labeled "JPG" and most featured a sexually suggestive title. Certainly after opening the first file and seeing an image of child pornography, the searching officer was aware — in advance of opening the remaining files — what the label meant. When he opened the subsequent files, he knew he was not going to find items related to drug activity as specified in the warrant.

People v. Robert Carratu

194 Misc. 2d 595 (N.Y. Sup. Ct. 2003)

VICTOR M. ORT, J.

[Defendant, indicted for criminal possession of forgery devices, moved to suppress evidence.] Defendant's motion to suppress physical evidence raises the novel issue in this state of whether a warrant authorizing a search of the text files of a computer for documentary evidence pertaining to a specific crime will authorize a search of image files which appear to contain evidence of other criminal activity.

Det. Gerard Jetter of the Nassau County Police Department received information from Gary Lenz, an investigator for Cablevision, concerning the sale of illegal cable television access devices. In June, 1999 Lenz had seen an advertisement in Popular Mechanics magazine under the cable TV equipment section offering "Jerrold and Pioneer Wireless test units" for sale at $125 each. The ad gave a 24-hour "hotline" phone number of (516) 389-3536.

[The court then detailed a long investigation that ultimately led to the arrest of Carratu for selling the devices.]

Following the arrest of Mr. Carratu, Det. Jetter applied for search warrants for the entire premises located at 35 Stowe Place, Hempstead in Nassau County. The warrants were issued [and] authorized searches for devices capable of defeating the security and encryption system of a cable television operator; devices capable of de-scrambling telecommunications intended for use by cable television subscribers;

parts and equipment used for assembling and repairing such devices; records relating to the purchase, sale, and transportation of such devices; and financial records used in connection with the sale of such items. The warrant covering 35 Stowe Place also specifically authorized search for electronics manuals detailing the installation of devices capable of defeating cable TV security and encryption systems and de-scrambling telecommunications as well as computers and computer diskettes used in connection with the illegal activity.

Det. Jetter accompanied by various other detectives began the search of the house at 35 Stowe Place at around 4:40 p.m. In the dining room, the detectives found 59 wireless "supercubes" in cassette boxes, sixteen cable converter boxes, 34 cable de-scrambling devices, and assorted non-digital cubes. Cable converter boxes were removed from television sets in the living room and dining room and seized. Also found within the house was some PC board etching material and three boxes of assorted electronic parts.

In the computer room on the main floor, the detectives found items of identification in various names all but one of which showed the photograph of the defendant. Also found in the computer room was a copier, a Packard-Bell and a Sony Vaio computer, an Altima laptop computer, a computer monitor, a scanner, a printer, a paper cutter, a document shredder, a plastic box with assorted art supplies, and a plastic box with printing and software manuals. A Toshiba laptop computer was found on the kitchen counter.

The officers executing the search warrant were joined by Det. William Moylan, a computer forensic examiner for the Nassau County Police Department. After removing the power sources from Toshiba laptop, the Packard Bell, and the Sony Vaio, all three machines were taken to Crimes Against Property Squad office for further examination.

Between December 14, 2000 and September 11, 2001, Det. Moylan conducted forensic examination of the three computers. The initial procedure was to make a copy of the hard drive for each of the systems. Since the Toshiba laptop was protected by a password, it was necessary to remove the hard drive from the Toshiba and attach it to a separate computer in order to copy the hard drive. Then the directory for each of the hard drives was displayed, and the folders for each hard drive were listed alphabetically. Finally, the detective opened each folder and examined each user-generated file to determine whether it contained evidence pertaining to the illegal cable box operation. Within the folders themselves, Det. Moylan observed web pages downloaded from a website for cable boxes. In a folder labeled "Fake I.D." on the Sony hard drive, the detective observed image files of driver's licenses, social security cards, inspection stickers, and registration certificates. Another driver's license image was also found in a folder called "My Documents." In another folder labeled "customers" found in the Toshiba computer, the detective observed a file referring to Creative Alarms. In a folder labeled "DSS," the detective observed text files which appeared to relate to satellite television.

The substance of defendant's claim is that the search exceeded the scope of the warrant. Specifically, defendant claims that the officer conducting the search of his computer "made no effort to first examine those files or directories that by their name or nature might indicate some type of record or list . . . [nor did he] check if the nature of the file was graphic, data base, spread sheet or word processing."

In view of the Fourth Amendment's "particularity requirement," a warrant authorizing a search of the text files of a computer for documentary evidence pertaining to a specific crime will not authorize a search of image files containing evidence of other criminal activity.

The court concludes first that the web pages pertaining to the cable box website fall squarely within the terms of the warrant. Similarly, the folder labeled "customers" clearly pertained to the illegal cable box operation, and so Detective Moylan was entitled to open it. The folder labeled "DSS," which contained text files relating to satellite television, was ambiguously labeled. As a result, it was reasonable for Det. Moylan to open that file in search of documents pertaining to the illegal cable box operation. Accordingly, defendant's motion to suppress is denied as to the computer files relating to the cable box web site, the customer folder, and the DSS folder.

The court reaches a different conclusion with regard to the image files containing false identification documents. An examination of the supporting affidavit and the warrants themselves makes clear that the search warrants were issued to authorize a search of defendant's computers for documentary evidence relating to his illegal cable box operation. The court notes that the "Fake I.D." folder was not ambiguously labeled. To the contrary, the name of the folder clearly indicated that it likely contained false identification documents rather than documents or records concerning the sale of illegal cable boxes. Thus, from mere inspection of the folder name Det. Moylan had probable cause to seek a further warrant authorizing a search of the Sony computer for evidence of possession of forged instruments. And, since the file extension names on the files within the Fake I.D. folder indicated that they likely contained images, they appeared not to contain the type of text files which were akin to the items sought by the warrant.

When Det. Moylan opened the first image file in the Fake I.D. folder, he had reason to believe that it contained a phony identification document.

Because the My Documents folder was ambiguously labeled, if that folder had been opened first, Det. Moylan would have had no reason to suspect that it contained a file containing an image of a false identification document. However, the burden of proof as to the applicability of the plain view doctrine, as with all exceptions to the warrant requirement, is squarely on the prosecution. The People did not establish at the hearing which of the image files was opened first. Thus, there is no basis for the court to conclude that the image file in the My Documents folder was opened inadvertently. In these circumstances, defendant's motion to suppress is granted as to all computer files containing images of false identification documents. Defendant's motion to suppress physical evidence is in all other respects denied.

Notes and Questions

1. Other authorities reject the position that a search be restricted by file names or file types. Professional investigators recognize that computer users attempt to conceal criminal evidence by storing it "in random order with deceptive file names," thus requiring a search of all the stored data to determine whether it is included in the warrant.[43] Indeed, some authorities have asserted that "it is impossible to tell what a computer storage medium contains just by looking at it. Rather, one has to examine it electronically, using a computer that is running the appropriate operating system, hardware and software."[44] As one court has maintained:

> [Defendant] claims that the search should have been limited to certain files that are more likely to be associated with child pornography, such as those with a ".jpg" suffix (which usually identifies files containing images) or those containing the word "sex" or other key words.
>
> Defendant's proposed search methodology is unreasonable. "Computer records are extremely susceptible to tampering, hiding, or destruction, whether deliberate or inadvertent." Images can be hidden in all manner of files, even word processing documents and spreadsheets. Criminals will do all they can to conceal contraband, including the simple expedient of changing the names and extensions of files to disguise their content from the casual observer.
>
> Forcing police to limit their searches to files that the suspect has labeled in a particular way would be much like saying police may not seize a plastic bag containing a powdery white substance if it is labeled "flour" or "talcum powder." There is no way to know what is in a file without examining its contents, just as there is no sure way of separating talcum from cocaine except by testing it. The ease with which child pornography images can be disguised—whether by renaming sexyteenyboppersxxx.jpg as sundayschoollesson.doc,

---

43. United States v. Campos, 221 F.3d 1143, 1147 (10th Cir. 2000) (*quoting* affidavit). *See also* United States v. Maali M., 346 F. Supp. 2d 1226, 1265 (M.D. Fla. 2004) (expert explained that he could not rely on file names to determine what was responsive to warrant); Eoghan Casey, Digital Evidence and Computer Crime (2d Ed. 2004) (describing a methodical data filtering process that includes several different tools, *id*. at 632–43, and observing that digital evidence analysis requires examiners to employ filtering procedures to find potentially useful data and that "[l]ess methodical data reduction techniques, such as searching for specific keywords or extracting only certain file types may not only miss important clues but can still leave the examiners floundering in a sea of superfluous data," *id*. at 229–30).

44. United States v. Hill, 322 F. Supp. 2d 1081, 1088 (C.D. Cal. 2004), *aff'd*, 459 F.3d 966 (9th Cir. 2006).

or something more sophisticated—forecloses defendant's proposed search methodology.[45]

Similarly, in *United States v. Gray*, 78 F. Supp. 2d 524 (E.D. Va. 1999), the court rejected the argument that an agent could not search files tagged with the "jpg" extension, even though none of the materials covered by the warrant were believed to be pictures. The court reasoned:

> While the ".jpg" suffix generally denotes a picture file, there is no requirement that it do so, and, as a result, Agent Ehuan could not be certain that files with the ".jpg" suffix did not contain the materials for which he was authorized to search. Indeed, Agent Ehuan would have been remiss not to search files with a ".jpg" suffix simply because such files are generally pictures files, and he believed the NLM documents and hacker materials were more likely to be text files. He knew from his experience that computer hackers often intentionally mislabel files, or attempt to bury incriminating files within innocuously named directories. Indeed, in the course of his search of defendant's computer files, Agent Ehuan found some text files mixed in with picture files. This serves to underscore the soundness of the conclusion that Agent Ehuan was not required to accept as accurate any file name or suffix and limit his search accordingly.
>
> Defendant further argues that Agent Ehuan, having been alerted by the names of the "Teen" and "Tiny Teen" subdirectories, was looking for child pornography when he opened the two subdirectories. Agent Ehuan testified persuasively to the contrary; he stated that, while the names of the subdirectories were suspicious to him, he opened the "Teen" and "Tiny Teen" subdirectories in the course of a systematic search of the BBS directory. In other words, Agent Ehuan did not target those particular subdirectories because of their names, and, at all times, he was searching for the materials that were the subject of the search warrant.[46]

2. Do limitations on search authority based on file names or types comport with the ability of computer users to hide data in innocuously labeled files? Is the more sound approach to permit innocuous computer files to be scanned to ascertain their relevancy in "recognition of 'the reality that few people keep documents of their

---

45. *Id.* at 1090–91.

46. *See also* Guest v. Leis, 255 F.3d 325, 335 (6th Cir. 2001) (agents could legitimately check contents of directories to see if contents corresponded with labels placed on directories; otherwise suspects "would be able to shield evidence from a search simply by 'misfiling' it in directory labeled 'e-mail'"); State v. Schroeder, 613 N.W.2d 911, 916 (Wis. Ct. App. 2000) (rejecting limitations on search based on file names and concluding that, during systematic search of all user-created files in executing search warrant for evidence of online harassment and disorderly conduct, opening file containing child pornography in plain view); United States v. Abbell, 963 F. Supp. 1178, 1201 (S.D. Fla. 1997) (upholding seizure of computer disks despite fact that they did not contain responsive name because seizing agents "were not required to accept labels as indicative of the disks' contents").

criminal transactions in a [computer file] folder marked '[crime] records'"? *See United States v. Hunter*, 13 F. Supp. 2d 574, 583 (D. Vt. 1998).

Do Technological Search Programs Make the File Cabinet Analogy Inadequate?

Another premise of authorities rejecting the file cabinet analogy is that technological searches can be employed by the government to scan data held in electronic storage to reliably sort relevant information from information for which the government does not have probable cause to search. This is a technical question and not a legal one.

There are a variety of software programs that government investigators now routinely employ when searching for electronic evidence.[47] It has been recognized that "automated search techniques have inherent strengths and weaknesses:"

> The usefulness [of automated keyword searches] is limited to situations where there is some precise textual identifier that can be used as the search argument. Keyword searches are context insensitive, and cannot employ the discrimination used by a human investigator. If either the data encoding or the alleged criminal activity is complex in nature, human judgment will be required to determine the evidentiary value of specific electronic documents and whether the documents fall within the scope of the warrant.

> The benefits of electronic search techniques are that they are fast, accurate, and within the narrow scope of their capabilities. If the officers are searching for very specific information and know one or two exact phrases or words to search for, a comprehensive electronic search can be conducted in a matter of hours. For example, if the officers were searching for a copy of specific insurance claims or accounting records, and the officers knew with certainty that these records would contain specific phrases, numbers, or names, these records could be located very quickly. Once the appropriate electronic records were located, they could be copied on a file-by-file basis, in effect allowing seizure of only the files that fall within the scope of the warrant.

> By contrast, if the officers conducting the search do not have specific information (names, numbers, phrases) sufficient to allow an accurate identification of all relevant documents, electronic searches are far less useful. The use of common words or phrases as keywords may still help locate relevant evidence, but such searches yield a high number of false hits. False hits are documents that contain the searched—for term, but have no evidentiary value and are beyond the scope of the warrant.

----

47. One commonly used tool is Encase, designed by Guidance Software. *See* www.guidancesoftware.com.

The usefulness of keyword searches is further diminished by the fact that such searches are context insensitive. Computer data is encoded. Many computerized documents require specialized software to read or render their contents comprehensible. Such software provides the context required to interpret electronic data. For example, the medical records, accounting data, and medical appointment logs would most probably contain many abbreviations or coded values representing various medical procedures and associated charges. A record containing a patient's name, a numeric value of 1, a procedure code of 346 and a charge of 740000 might not seem suspicious. But if the numeric value 1 is a code that indicates that the patient is a male, and the medical procedure code of 346 identifies the operation as a hysterectomy, then the legitimacy of the $7400.00 charge is suspect. Without knowing the context of the numbers 1, 346, and 740000, the data represented cannot be evaluated for relevance.

The manner in which computer data is represented also limits the effective scope of automated search techniques. Many automated search tools are based on the detection of textual character strings embedded in documents. These techniques can only be applied to textual data, and not for pictures, diagrams, or scanned images. For example, a search for the word "submarine" would locate text that contained those characters, but it would fail to locate the scanned image of a submarine, a digital photo of the control tower, or even a scanned image or photo of the original document. The textual search would also fail to locate the desired document if it had been compressed, encrypted, or password protected. Depending on the software used for the search, it might or might not detect the word "submarine" in files that had been deleted.

Other types of searches depend on properly identifying documents by either document type or by file name. Searches by file name are unreliable because a user is free to name (or rename) files without regard to their content. Searches by file type, can be accomplished using specialized tools that identify files based on the "signature" associated with the program used to create the file. This technique can be used to identify or group files based on how data is represented. These tools can identify file format, but are not able to search content. Searches based on file type are not normally effective against files which have been encrypted, compressed, or password protected.[48]

---

48. Susan W. Brenner & Barbara A. Frederiksen, *Computer Searches and Seizures: Some Unresolved Issues*, 8 Mich. Telecom. Tech. L. Rev. 39, 60–62 (2002). Copyright © 2002, Susan W. Brenner, Barbara A. Frederiksen. All rights reserved. Reprinted by permission. *See also* Orin Kerr, *Digital Evidence and the New Criminal Procedure*, 105 Colum. L. Rev. 279, 303 (2005) ("Existing technology simply gives us no way to know ahead of time where inside a computer a particular file or piece of information may be located."); Eoghan Casey, Digital Evidence and Computer Crime (2d Ed. 2004) (describing a methodical data filtering process that includes several different

Notes and Questions

1. This passage merely describes the then current state of competition between criminal minds and government investigators. The ability to hide evidence in electronic storage constantly evolves and the government must keep pace or catch up.[49] There will always be a considerable amount of uncertainty at any given time whether any one search technique identifies with an acceptable degree of accuracy what a file contains without opening it.

2. A second question is a legal one: does the Fourth Amendment mandate that advanced technological search engines be used? If technology is constantly evolving—and it is, then the inquiry is a moving target. This is to say that law enforcement must always stay on the cutting edge of technological change and continually invest money and resources for new training and new equipment. The proper question for searches of data stored on a computer—as with all questions of reasonableness—is whether the means chosen by the government to execute the search are reasonably related to the purpose of the search. Does that inquiry mandate that the police utilize any specific technology or procedures at any given time, particularly where the state of technology creates uncertainty that the search would be effective if limited to certain means?

3. There is very little support in Supreme Court jurisprudence for the view that limits intrusions to a method that might permit evidence to go undetected once it is determined that the police have a warrant to search based on probable cause to believe that the place to be searched contains evidence of a crime. The Court has created a few unusual restrictions for probable-cause based intrusions due to heightened concerns for intrusions into the body and based on free-speech concerns. Is the search of a computer analogous to a forced surgical procedure to remove a bullet from a person's chest? *See Winston v. Lee*, 470 U.S. 753, 755 (1985). In contrast, the Court has held that a warrant based on probable cause is sufficient authority to search newspaper offices for evidence of a crime. *See Zurcher v. Stanford Daily*, 436 U.S. 547 (1978). Congress, in response to *Zurcher*, has imposed several statutory obligations on law enforcement when there is reason to believe that First Amendment materials are involved.

---

tools, *id.* at 632–43, and observing that digital evidence analysis requires examiners to employ filtering procedures to find potentially useful data and that "[l]ess methodical data reduction techniques, such as searching for specific keywords or extracting only certain file types may not only miss important clues but can still leave the examiners floundering in a sea of superfluous data," *id.* at 229–30).

49. *See, e.g.*, Eoghan Casey, Digital Evidence and Computer Crime 643 (2d Ed. 2004) (discussing the challenges to investigators of compressed files, encrypted files, e-mails, and email attachments, which require a "combination of tools with different features").

Does the Nature or Amount of Material Make Computers Different from Other Containers?

A fundamental premise of the "special approach" is the belief that "electronic storage is likely to contain a greater quantity and variety of information than any previous storage method."[50]

"Containers"

In the context of a search of an automobile, the Supreme Court stated that a container "denotes any object capable of holding another object. It thus includes closed or open glove compartments, consoles, or other receptacles located anywhere within the passenger compartment [of a vehicle], as well as luggage, boxes, bags, clothing, and the like."[51]

The Supreme Court at one point attempted to distinguish among types of containers in ranking expectations of privacy. Luggage had high expectations of privacy.[52] But other containers did not "deserve the full protection of the Fourth Amendment."[53] The bankruptcy of an analytical structure based on distinguishing between types of containers soon became evident, at least to a plurality of the Court in *Robbins v. California*, 453 U.S. 420, 426 (1981): it had no basis in the language of the Amendment, which "protects people and their effects, whether they are 'personal' or 'impersonal.'" Thus, the contents of closed footlockers or suitcases and opaque containers were immune from a warrantless search because the owners "reasonably 'manifested an expectation that the contents would remain free from public examination.'" Moreover, the plurality believed that it would be "impossible to perceive any objective criteria" to make any distinction between containers: "What one person may put into a suitcase, another may put into a paper bag." A majority of the Court later adopted the view that there was no distinction between "worthy" and "unworthy" containers:

> [T]he central purpose of the Fourth Amendment forecloses such a distinction. For just as the most frail cottage in the kingdom is absolutely entitled to the same guarantees of privacy as the most majestic mansion, so also may a traveler who carries a toothbrush and a few articles of clothing in a paper bag or knotted scarf claim an equal right to conceal his possessions

---

50. Raphael Winick, *Searches and Seizures of Computers and Computer Data*, 8 Harv. J.L. & Tech. 75, 104 (1994).

51. New York v. Belton, 453 U.S. 454, 460 n.4 (1981).

52. *See, e.g.*, United States v. Chadwick, 433 U.S. 1, 12–13 (1977) (contrasting reduced expectation of privacy surrounding an automobile with luggage and asserting: "Unlike an automobile, whose primary function is transportation, luggage is intended as a repository of personal effects. In sum, a person's expectations of privacy in personal luggage are substantially greater than in an automobile."). *Accord* Florida v. Jimeno, 500 U.S. 248, 253–54 (1991).

53. Arkansas v. Sanders, 442 U.S. 753, 764 n.13 (1979). Indeed, "some containers (for example a kit of burglar tools or a gun case) by their very nature [could not] support any reasonable expectation of privacy because their contents [could] be inferred from their outward appearance." *Id. Accord* Walter v. United States, 447 U.S. 649, 658 n.12 (1980).

from official inspection as the sophisticated executive with the locked atta-
che case.[54]

Notes and Questions

1. Will or should the Supreme Court reject a special rule for electronic evidence
containers? Are computers and other sophisticated digital devices that store data
"containers"? In *Riley v. California*, 573 U.S. ___, 134 S. Ct. 2473, 189 L. Ed. 2d 430
(2014), which is reproduced in Chapter 8, the Court commented on the claim that
cell phones should be viewed as a container:

> To further complicate the scope of the privacy interests at stake, the data a
> user views on many modern cell phones may not in fact be stored on the
> device itself. Treating a cell phone as a container whose contents may be
> searched incident to an arrest is a bit strained as an initial matter. See *New
> York v. Belton*, 453 U.S. 454, 460, n. 4 (1981) (describing a "container" as
> "any object capable of holding another object"). But the analogy crumbles
> entirely when a cell phone is used to access data located elsewhere, at the
> tap of a screen. That is what cell phones, with increasing frequency, are
> designed to do by taking advantage of "cloud computing." Cloud comput-
> ing is the capacity of Internet-connected devices to display data stored on
> remote servers rather than on the device itself. Cell phone users often may
> not know whether particular information is stored on the device or in the
> cloud, and it generally makes little difference. Moreover, the same type of
> data may be stored locally on the device for one user and in the cloud for
> another.

Did *Riley* embrace the special approach? If so, what does that mean going forward?
If not, how can you explain the special rule for the search of digital devices incident
to arrest set forth in that case?

2. Should there be separate rules for filing cabinets, diaries, books, floppy drives,
hard drives, paper bags, and other storage devices?

3. Given the pace of technological change, which permits ever greater storage of
information on ever smaller devices, are such distinctions illusory?

4. Does it matter that the evidence in electronic storage is intermingled with
other materials? Diaries may contain evidence unrelated to the crime; filing cabinets often hold not only files of business-related paper but also miscellaneous other

---

54. United States v. Ross, 456 U.S. 798, 822 (1982). *Accord* Florida v. Jimeno, 500 U.S. 248,
253–54 (1991). *See also* California v. Carney, 471 U.S. 386, 394 (1985) (rejecting distinction between
worthy and unworthy motor vehicles); New Jersey v. T.L.O., 469 U.S. 325, 337–39 (1985) (student
has protected privacy interest in her purse at school). *But cf.* California v. Greenwood, 486 U.S.
35, 40–41 (1988) (person leaving plastic trash bags for collection has no reasonable expectation of
privacy as to the contents of the bags).

documents, ranging from personal tax records to family photographs. Does the amount or method of intermingling with digital evidence make digital "containers" "special"?

§ 4.4 Limitations Based on Search Execution Procedures in Warrants

Does a warrant seeking digital evidence have to specify how the authorities will conduct the search or merely what the government is seeking? Some authorities require that the warrant set forth the police strategy for executing the search for electronic evidence.[55] In contrast, other courts have recognized that a warrant need not specify the methods of recovery of the data or the tests to be performed because "[t]he warrant process is primarily concerned with identifying *what* may be searched or seized—not how—and *whether* there is sufficient cause for the invasion of privacy thus entailed."[56]

1. Supreme Court Opinions on Execution Procedures

1. In *Andresen v. Maryland*, 427 U.S. 463 (1976), the Court stated that, for document searches, "responsible officials, including judicial officials, must take care to assure that they are conducted in a manner that minimizes unwarranted intrusions upon privacy." Nothing in that language suggests that the manner in which a search is to be conducted was subject to pre-authorization by the judiciary.

2. In *Dalia v. United States*, 441 U.S. 238 (1979), the Court stated that the Warrant Clause contains three requirements for a search warrant to issue: an oath or affirmation; probable cause to search; and a particular description of the place to be searched and the things to be seized. Grounded in that language, the *Dalia* Court rejected the claim that a warrant must specifically authorize a covert entry in order for such a manner of execution of a warrant to be legal. The Court reasoned:

> Nothing in the language of the Constitution or in this Court's decisions interpreting that language suggests that . . . warrants also must include a specification of the precise manner in which they are to be executed. On the contrary, it is generally left to the discretion of the executing officers to determine the details of how best to proceed with the performance of a search authorized by warrant—subject of course to the general Fourth Amendment protection "against unreasonable searches and seizures."
>
> It would extend the Warrant Clause to the extreme to require that, whenever it is reasonably likely that Fourth Amendment rights may be affected

---

55. *See, e.g., In re* Search of: 3817 W. West End, 321 F. Supp. 2d 953, 958–63 (N.D. Ill. 2004).
56. United States v. Upham, 168 F.3d 532, 537 (1st Cir. 1999).

in more than one way, the court must set forth precisely the procedures to be followed by the executing officers. Such an interpretation is unnecessary, as we have held . . . the manner in which a warrant is executed is subject to later judicial review as to its reasonableness.

3. *Dalia's* view was reaffirmed in *United States v. Grubbs*, 547 U.S. 90 (2006), which quoted *Dalia* at length and rejected creating unenumerated requirements for a warrant to issue. *See generally* Thomas K. Clancy, The Fourth Amendment: Its History and Interpretation § 12.2.2. (3d ed. 2017).

———————

2. Search Protocols — Digital Evidence Cases

a. Rejecting Protocol Requirement

United States v. Rebecca Christie

717 F.3d 1156 (10th Cir. 2013)

Gorsuch, Circuit Judge.

For Rebecca Christie, life must have seemed more virtual than real. She usually awoke around noon, settled in before her computer, and logged on to World of Warcraft for gaming sessions lasting well past midnight. There she assumed a new identity in a fantastical world filled with dragons and demons where players staged heroic adventures with and against other players. All the while back in the real world Ms. Christie ignored the needs of her three-year-old daughter. The neglect didn't prove fatal so long as Ms. Christie's husband was around to provide some care. But nine days after her husband left for an out-of-state deployment, the child was dead from dehydration.

Appealing second-degree murder and child abuse convictions, Ms. Christie raises significant questions about computer searches under the Fourth Amendment.

I

Ms. Christie's child began life a healthy baby girl. But by twenty-one months, something appeared badly wrong. She plummeted to the bottom fifth percentile in weight for her age and began suffering from chronic diarrhea. A pediatrician prescribed PediaSure, a nutritional drink that helps children gain weight. That seemed to do the trick: the diarrhea soon stopped and BW (the district court and parties refer to the child by her initials) began gaining weight. By all appearances, she had turned a corner.

But even the best cure won't work if it isn't administered. And it seems Ms. Christie and her then-husband Derek Wulf, himself a zealous gamer, weren't up to the job. For her part, Ms. Christie would put BW to bed each night around 10 p.m., shut BW's door, and failed to retrieve the child until noon or later the following day.

Because BW couldn't open the door herself, Ms. Christie effectively locked the child away without food or water for fourteen or more hours a day. Even when BW was free to seek food and water it appears little was available to her. Ms. Christie let slip to investigators that the child was always hungry and would sometimes try to eat the food she left out for the family cats. Ms. Christie's step-daughter (who visited on occasion) testified that Ms. Christie often wouldn't feed her or BW until noon and that BW's obvious hunger drove her to share her own food with BW.

Eventually, Mr. Wulf faced a deployment on the other side of the country. With the little care he provided BW now gone with him and the child's fate entirely in Ms. Christie's hands, the child was in trouble. Already badly malnourished, she succumbed to dehydration in nine days. An autopsy revealed that no inborn disorder was to blame. BW simply died from being ignored.

Medical experts testified that BW's desperate condition in the days before her death would have been blindingly clear. BW would have sought out water as a survival instinct. When that failed, she would have become lethargic and, on the day before her death, too weak to move. Her diapers wouldn't have needed changing. She would have had sticky saliva and then no saliva at all. She would have developed cracked lips, sunken eyes, and a sunken abdomen.

First responders confirmed that this is exactly what they saw when they found the child. They testified that BW's lips were cracked and blue, her eyes glassy, and her eyelids so dry they couldn't close. They said bones protruded from her body and her gums had turned black.

Because BW died on an Air Force base, federal authorities bore the responsibility to investigate and the power to prosecute. They proceeded against Ms. Christie and Mr. Wulf separately. In our proceeding, a federal jury found Ms. Christie guilty of second-degree murder, two assimilated state law homicide charges, as well as an assimilated child abuse charge. After trial, the district court dismissed the two assimilated homicide charges and entered a twenty-five year sentence on the remaining second-degree federal murder and the assimilated child abuse charge.

II

Much of the evidence presented at trial against Ms. Christie came from the computer she so prized. From their forensic analysis, FBI investigators learned that Ms. Christie's online activities usually kept her busy from noon to 3 a.m. with little pause. They learned that she was in a chat room only an hour before finding BW near death, and that she was back online soon afterwards. They learned from Ms. Christie's messages to other gamers that she was annoyed by her responsibilities as a mother and "want[ed] out of this house fast." When Mr. Wulf was slated for deployment, she announced to online friends that she would soon be free to "effing party."

Ms. Christie contends this evidence and more from her computer was uncovered in violation of her Fourth Amendment rights and the district court should have suppressed it from her trial. Because the court didn't, because it admitted the proof against her, Ms. Christie says a new trial is required. To be precise, Ms. Christie doesn't question whether the government's *seizure* of the computer satisfied the Fourth Amendment. The government took possession of the computer in May 2006 with Mr. Wulf's consent. Everyone accepts that he was at least a co-owner of the computer—it was a gift from his father—and everyone accepts he had at least apparent authority to relinquish its control. Instead, Ms. Christie attacks the propriety of the two *searches* the government undertook once it had control of the computer. To justify its searches the government does not seek to rely on Mr. Wulf's consent but points to a pair of warrants it sought and received, one for each search. It is these warrants Ms. Christie challenges, arguing they were issued in defiance of the Fourth Amendment.

A

The first warrant came in October 2006, some five months after authorities seized the computer. Ms. Christie argues this investigative delay—between seizure and search—was constitutionally impermissible, should have precluded any warrant from issuing, and itself requires the suppression of everything the government found. [Ed. The court rejected this argument.]

B

Next Ms. Christie attacks the validity of the second warrant, this one issued in May 2009, to conduct a more thorough search of her computer. She argues this warrant violated the Fourth Amendment's promise that "no Warrants shall issue" without "particularly describing the place to be searched, and the persons or things to be seized." The concern originally animating this so-called "particularity requirement" was a wish to prevent the sort of warrants English kings once favored, ones that proscribed few limits on the scope of the search to be conducted and included no explanation why they were issued. Even today the particularity requirement remains a vital guard against "wide-ranging exploratory searches," a promise that governmental searches will be "carefully tailored to [their] justifications." *Maryland v. Garrison*, 480 U.S. 79, 84 (1987). Probable cause to believe a suspect possesses a stolen car may justify issuing a warrant authorizing the search of her garage but not necessarily her attic, and probable cause to believe a gang member is hiding weapons may merit a warrant to conduct a search of his home but not necessarily his grandmother's. A warrant isn't ever supposed to be a license for just "a general . . . rummaging."

No doubt the particularity requirement and its underlying purposes are fully engaged when investigators seek to search a personal computer. Personal computers can and often do hold "much information touching on many different areas of a person's life." They can contain (or at least permit access to) our diaries, calendars, files, and correspondence—the very essence of the "papers and effects" the Fourth Amendment was designed to protect. In today's world, if any place or thing is especially vulnerable to a worrisome exploratory rummaging by the government, it may be our personal computers.

This court's efforts to apply the Fourth Amendment's particularity requirement to computer searches are still relatively new. But the parties seem to agree that our cases already draw at least one recognizable line. On the one hand, we have held invalid warrants purporting to authorize computer searches where we could discern no limiting principle: where, for example, the warrant permitted a search of "'any and all' information, data, devices, programs, and other materials," or "all computer and non-computer equipment and written materials in [a defendant's] house." On the other hand, we have said warrants may pass the particularity test if they limit their scope either "to evidence of specific federal crimes or [to] specific types of material."

The October 2009 warrant authorized a search of Ms. Christie's computer for

[a]ll records and information relating to the murder, neglect, and abuse of [BW] from June 19, 2002 (date of birth) to May 4, 2006, (date computer seized), including:

1. All photographs of [BW].

2. All correspondence and/or documents relating to [BW].

3. All records and information, including any diaries or calendars, showing the day-to-day activities of Rebecca Christie and/or [BW].

4. All addresses and/or contact information of friends, families, or acquaintances who may have had regular contact with Rebecca Christie and/or [BW].

According to Ms. Christie, paragraph 3 effectively permitted law enforcement to search any and all records and information on her computer for any and all purposes.

The government responds that all of its search efforts, including those authorized in paragraph 3, were restricted by the warrant's opening language.

We find it hard to fault the government's reasoning [based on prior case law in the Circuit].

Ms. Christie rejoins that if our current case law endorses the warrant in this case then our case law needs to be reexamined. In an age where computers permit access to most every "paper and effect" a person owns, she fears that merely restricting the government to a search topic or objective does little to prevent it from examining along the way virtually every bit and byte of our lives. Risking with it the possibility the government will claim to find "in plain view" evidence of crimes totally unrelated to the reasons spurring their search in the first place. The text of the Fourth Amendment says the government must identify with particularity "the place to be searched" and requiring it to describe that place tersely as "a computer" is to allow the government to traipse willy-nilly through an entire virtual world. To prevent that, Ms. Christie suggests a warrant must go further: it must specify limitations not just *what* the government may search for but *how* the government should go about its search.

In reply, the government argues that it's often difficult to know what search protocols might be reasonably required at the time of a warrant application, before the computer has been examined. Computer files can be misnamed by accident, disguised by intention, or hidden altogether, leaving investigators at a loss to know *ex ante* what sort of search will prove sufficient to ferret out the evidence they legitimately seek. Neither has the particularity requirement, the government points out, ever been understood to demand of a warrant "technical precision," or "elaborate detail," but only "practical" limitations, affording "reasonabl[e] specific[ity]." Though this court's efforts to apply the Fourth Amendment's particularity requirement to computer searches are still relatively new and our existing treatment is far from comprehensive, it also seems difficult to square Ms. Christie's demand for a how with our existing cases, all of which suggest a *what* may be particular enough. Indeed, we've gone so far as to suggest that it is "unrealistic to expect a warrant to prospectively restrict the scope of a search by directory, filename or extension or to attempt to structure search methods — that process must remain dynamic."

This isn't to say the Fourth Amendment has nothing to say on how a computer search should proceed. Even putting aside for the moment the question what limitations the Fourth Amendment's particularity requirement should or should not impose on the government *ex ante*, the Amendment's protection against "unreasonable" searches surely allows courts to assess the propriety of the government's search methods (the *how*) *ex post* in light of the specific circumstances of each case. So even if courts do not specify particular search protocols up front in the warrant application process, they retain the flexibility to assess the reasonableness of the search protocols the government actually employed in its search after the fact, when the case comes to court, and in light of the totality of the circumstances. Unlike an *ex ante* warrant application process in which the government usually appears alone before generalist judges who are not steeped in the art of computer forensics, this *ex post* review comes with the benefit, too, of the adversarial process where evidence and experts from both sides can be entertained and examined.

Whenever courts should review search protocols and whatever the scope of our authority to do so may be, one thing is certain. To undertake any meaningful assessment of the government's search techniques in this case (the *how*), we would need to understand what protocols the government used, what alternatives might have reasonably existed, and why the latter rather than the former might have been more appropriate. Unfortunately, however, that we do not have in this case. Though Ms. Christie bore the burden of proof in her suppression proceeding, she offered little evidence or argument suggesting how protocols the government followed in this case were unreasonable or insufficiently particular, especially when compared with possible alternatives. Without more help along these lines, we simply cannot assess rationally her challenge to the government's search procedures in this case and must leave the development of the law in this arena to future cases. * * * The judgment is affirmed.

b. Taint Teams and Special Masters

Donald F. Manno v. Christopher J. Christie

2008 U.S. Dist. LEXIS 65106 (D.N.J. 2008)

KUGLER, DISTRICT JUDGE:

Plaintiff Manno is a solo legal practitioner who maintains a law office at 601 Longwood Avenue, Cherry Hill, New Jersey. Manno has been in private practice for over twenty-five years, and he had approximately 100 active and open files in his office during the time at issue here, most of which were related to criminal defense matters. According to the Complaint, on May 7, 2008, the government applied for a search warrant to search Manno's law offices for "approximately sixteen broad categories of documents and things 'pertaining to' 43 listed individuals or entities from August 1, 2006 to the present" as part of an ongoing investigation into criminal activity. Magistrate Judge Ann Marie Donio authorized the warrant, which was executed on May 8. The search team will apparently have no further role in the investigation, and the case agents in charge of the investigation did not participate in the search.

In the course of executing the warrant, agents of the government inspected numerous files connected with clients other than the 43 enumerated individuals. FBI agents copied the hard drives of six computers in Manno's office and copied other external storage devices (including thumbdrives and CDs) as well. According to the Complaint, these electronic files include information on all the clients of the Manno firm for the past 15 years, including both open and closed matters. Manno alleges that Defendants did not try to first determine whether the hard drives and storage devices seized contained any information covered by the warrant; instead, they simply seized and copied all the electronic files. Some hard drives were copied at Manno's office; three laptops were taken from the office.

The government has not yet viewed the electronic material seized. The government's plan to review the material includes a preliminary review by FBI Special Agent Michael O'Brien to determine responsiveness to the warrant, with documents determined to be responsive to be next reviewed by AUSA Matt Smith to determine if they are protected by a privilege.

Manno claims the search and seizure violated the attorney-client privilege he holds with his clients and represents an impermissible seizure of his protected attorney work product. He does not challenge the probable cause determination underlying the warrant. He alleges that the seizure was overbroad and in violation of the Fourth Amendment.

Manno seeks an injunction barring the government from reproducing, disseminating, inspecting, or reading the electronic files seized; directing the government to immediately return the original hard drives and electronic media seizes as well as any copies made from them; and requiring the government to disclose the names or labels on all the files Defendants inspected. He also seeks damages for constitutional violations.

Plaintiff argues that the search and seizure was overbroad, because files on all clients and not just the 43 specifically mentioned in the warrant were "rifled" through and computer hard drives containing information on all clients were seized. The government contends that this broad preliminary seizure was necessary in order to discover material within the search warrant's authorization and that it was necessary to remove all the electronic media in order to have a computer technician be able to go through the media to locate all responsive materials.

The Court finds that Plaintiff has not shown that it is likely that he will succeed on his claims that the search was overbroad. Rather, the Court concludes that the search was likely reasonable.

In support of this broad search authorization, Defendants contend that seizure of all the electronic media was necessary to determine what pertained to the 43 clients listed in the warrant, and that it was necessary to take the computers off-site in order to review their contents. Defendant Special Agent Gilson, in his affidavit submitted in support of the search warrant application, attested that Manno was using computers in furtherance of alleged criminal activity. Gilson attested that to properly retrieve, analyze, document, and authenticate the data, a qualified computer specialists would need to go through the files, which would require seizure of all computer equipment and accessories.

The warrant in this case authorized a search and seizure that was broad but reasonable. If all of the material in Manno's office was in paper form, government agents could have done a brief review of each document to determine its responsiveness to the warrant. *Andresen v. Maryland*, 427 U.S. 463, 482 n.2 (1976) ("In searches for papers, it is certain that some innocuous documents will be examined, at least cursorily, in order to determine whether they are, in fact, among those papers authorized to be seized.") It is therefore reasonable for Agent O'Brien to briefly review each electronic document to determine if it is among the materials authorized by the warrant, just as he could if the search was only of paper files.

The government here has created a procedure to prevent undue disclosure of protected materials. They designated AUSA Matt Smith as the Privilege AUSA and FBI Special Agent Michael O'Brien as the Privilege Special Agent. In reviewing the material, Agent O'Brien will first go through and determine what items are within the scope of the search warrant. He will then pass along responsive items to AUSA Smith, who will review them for privilege. If he determines that the items are not privileged, he will turn them over to the prosecution team. If AUSA Smith finds that an item could be protected by a privilege, he will then determine whether a privilege exception such as the crime-fraud exception applies or whether the privilege has been waived. If AUSA Smith believes that material may be privileged but either the privilege has been waived or an exception applies, he will hold a "meet and confer" with Manno or any other individual who may have a claim of privilege in an attempt to work out a resolution. Then, if the parties cannot agree on a resolution, AUSA Smith will apply to the Court for a judicial determination on the privilege issue before turning anything over to the prosecution team. Any items found to be not within the scope of the warrant or covered by an effective privilege will be returned to Manno's office without being viewed by any other government agents.

Manno urges the Court to appoint a Special Master to conduct this review. Though the use of a Special Master or initial review by courts have been authorized in other cases, this Court finds that such measures are not required by the strictures of the Fourth Amendment or by the need to protect the attorney-client privilege. The Court concludes that government review procedures designed to prevent disclosure of privileged information are acceptable as long as the procedures involve judicial authorization before potentially privileged materials are disclosed. The privilege procedures proposed in this case represent a reasonable approach to balancing the need to review the material with the need to prevent disclosure of protected information, especially because there will be later opportunities to challenge the admissibility on privilege grounds of any evidence obtained by the government.

―――――――

c. The Special Approach

United States v. Comprehensive Drug Testing, Inc.

621 F.3d 1162 (9th Cir. 2010) (en banc)

PER CURIAM:

This case is about a federal investigation into steroid use by professional baseball players. More generally, however, it's about the procedures and safeguards that federal courts must observe in issuing and administering search warrants and subpoenas for electronically stored information.

In 2002, the federal government commenced an investigation into the Bay Area Lab Cooperative (Balco), which it suspected of providing steroids to professional baseball players. That year, the Major League Baseball Players Association also entered into a collective bargaining agreement with Major League Baseball providing for suspicionless drug testing of all players. Urine samples were to be collected during the first year of the agreement and each sample was to be tested for banned substances. The players were assured that the results would remain anonymous and confidential; the purpose of the testing was solely to determine whether more than five percent of players tested positive, in which case there would be additional testing in future seasons.

Comprehensive Drug Testing, Inc., an independent business, administered the program and collected the specimens from the players; the actual tests were performed by Quest Diagnostics, Inc., a laboratory. CDT maintained the list of players and their respective test results; Quest kept the actual specimens on which the tests were conducted.

During the Balco investigation, federal authorities learned of ten players who had tested positive in the CDT program. The government secured a grand jury subpoena in the Northern District of California seeking *all* "drug testing records and specimens" pertaining to Major League Baseball in CDT's possession. CDT and the Players tried to negotiate a compliance agreement with the government but, when negotiations failed, moved to quash the subpoena.

The day that the motion to quash was filed, the government obtained a warrant in the Central District of California authorizing the search of CDT's facilities in Long Beach. Unlike the subpoena, the warrant was limited to the records of the ten players as to whom the government had probable cause. When the warrant was executed, however, the government seized and promptly reviewed the drug testing records for hundreds of players in Major League Baseball (and a great many other people).

The government also obtained a warrant from the District of Nevada for the urine samples on which the drug tests had been performed. These were kept at Quest's facilities in Las Vegas. Subsequently, the government obtained additional warrants for records at CDT's facilities in Long Beach and Quest's lab in Las Vegas. Finally, the government served CDT and Quest with new subpoenas in the Northern District of California, demanding production of the same records it had just seized.

CDT and the Players moved in the Central District of California, pursuant to Federal Rule of Criminal Procedure 41(g), for return of the property seized there. Judge Cooper found that the government had failed to comply with the procedures specified in the warrant and, on that basis and others, ordered the property returned.

CDT and the Players subsequently moved in the District of Nevada, pursuant to Federal Rule of Criminal Procedure 41(g), for return of the property seized under the warrants issued by that court. The matter came before Judge Mahan, who granted the motion and ordered the government to return the property it had seized, with the exception of materials pertaining to the ten identified baseball players.

CDT and the Players finally moved in the Northern District of California, pursuant to Federal Rule of Criminal Procedure 17(c), to quash the latest round of subpoenas and the matter was heard by Judge Illston. In an oral ruling, Judge Illston quashed the subpoenas.

1. The Cooper Order

[The en banc court agreed that the government's appeal from the Cooper Order was untimely. As a result, under principles of issue preclusion,] once the Cooper Order became final, the government became bound by the factual determinations and issues resolved against it in that order. Specifically, Judge Cooper found that the government failed to comply with the conditions of the warrant designed to segregate information as to which the government had probable cause from that which was swept up only because the government didn't have the time or facilities to segregate it at the time and place of the seizure. Relatedly, Judge Cooper determined that the government failed to comply with the procedures outlined in our venerable precedent, *United States v. Tamura*, 694 F.2d 591 (9th Cir. 1982), which are designed to serve much the same purpose as the procedures outlined in the warrant. Finally,

Judge Cooper concluded that the government's actions displayed a callous disregard for the rights of third parties, viz., those players as to whom the government did not already have probable cause and who could suffer dire personal and professional consequences from a disclosure of their test results.

The affidavit supporting the first search warrant, the one that sought the drug testing records of the ten suspected baseball players, contains an extensive introduction that precedes any information specific to this case. The introduction seeks to justify a broad seizure of computer records from CDT by explaining the generic hazards of retrieving data that are stored electronically. In essence, the government explains, computer files can be disguised in any number of ingenious ways, the simplest of which is to give files a misleading name (pesto.recipe in lieu of blackmail. photos) or a false extension (.doc in lieu of .jpg or .gz). In addition, the data might be erased or hidden; there might be booby traps that "destroy or alter data if certain procedures are not scrupulously followed"; certain files and programs might not be accessible at all without the proper software, which may not be available on the computer that is being searched; there may simply be too much information to be examined at the site; or data might be encrypted or compressed, requiring passwords, keycards or other external devices to retrieve. The government also represented that "[s]earching computer systems requires the use of precise, scientific procedures which are designed to maintain the integrity of the evidence."

By reciting these hazards, the government made a strong case for off-site examination and segregation of the evidence seized. The government sought the authority to seize considerably more data than that for which it had probable cause, including various computers or computer hard drives and related storage media, and to have the information examined and segregated in a "controlled environment, such as a law enforcement laboratory." While the government did not point to any specific dangers associated with CDT, which is after all a legitimate business not suspected of any wrongdoing, it nevertheless made a strong generic case that the data in question could not be thoroughly examined or segregated on the spot.

Not surprisingly, the magistrate judge was persuaded by this showing and granted broad authority for seizure of data, including the right to remove pretty much any computer equipment found at CDT's Long Beach facility, along with any data storage devices, manuals, logs or related materials. The warrant also authorized government agents to examine all the data contained in the computer equipment and storage devices, and to attempt to recover or restore hidden or erased data. The magistrate judge, however, wisely made such broad seizure subject to certain procedural safeguards, roughly based on our *Tamura* opinion. Thus, the government was first required to examine the computer equipment and storage devices at CDT to determine whether information pertaining to the ten identified players "c[ould] be searched on-site in a reasonable amount of time and without jeopardizing the ability to preserve the data."

The warrant also contained significant restrictions on how the seized data were to be handled. These procedures were designed to ensure that data beyond the scope of the warrant would not fall into the hands of the investigating agents. Thus, the initial review and segregation of the data was not to be conducted by the investigating case agents but by "law enforcement personnel trained in searching and seizing computer data ('computer personnel')," whose job it would be to determine whether the data could be segregated on-site. These computer personnel—not the case agents—were specifically authorized to examine all the data on location to determine how much had to be seized to ensure the integrity of the search. Moreover, if the computer personnel determined that the data did not "fall within any of the items to be seized pursuant to this warrant or is not otherwise legally seized," the government was to return those items "within a reasonable period of time not to exceed 60 days from the date of the seizure unless further authorization [was] obtained from the Court." Subject to these representations and assurances, Magistrate Judge Johnson authorized the seizure.

Tamura, decided in 1982, just preceded the dawn of the information age, and all of the records there were on paper. The government was authorized to seize evidence of certain payments received by Tamura from among the records of Marubeni, his employer. To identify the materials pertaining to the payments involved a three step procedure: Examining computer printouts to identify a transaction; locating the voucher that pertained to that payment; and finding the check that corresponded to the voucher. The government agents soon realized that this process would take a long time unless they got help from the Marubeni employees who were present. The employees, however, steadfastly refused, so the agents seized several boxes and dozens of file drawers to be sorted out in their offices at their leisure.

We disapproved the wholesale seizure of the documents and particularly the government's failure to return the materials that were not the object of the search once they had been segregated. However, we saw no reason to suppress the properly seized materials just because the government had taken more than authorized by the warrant. For the future, though, we suggested that "[i]n the comparatively rare instances where documents are so intermingled that they cannot feasibly be sorted on site, ... the Government [should] seal[ ] and hold[ ] the documents pending approval by a magistrate of a further search." "If the need for transporting the documents is known to the officers prior to the search," we continued, "they may apply for specific authorization for large-scale removal of material, which should be granted by the magistrate issuing the warrant only where on-site sorting is infeasible and no other practical alternative exists."

No doubt in response to this suggestion in *Tamura*, the government here did seek advance authorization for sorting and segregating the seized materials off-site. But, as Judge Cooper found, "[o]nce the items were seized, the requirement of the Warrant that any seized items not covered by the warrant be first screened and segregated by computer personnel was completely ignored." Brushing aside an offer by on-site CDT personnel to provide all information pertaining to the ten identified baseball players, the government copied from CDT's computer what the parties have called the "Tracey Directory" which contained, in Judge Cooper's words, "information and test results involving hundreds of other baseball players and athletes engaged in other professional sports."

Counsel for CDT, contacted by phone, pleaded in vain that "all material not pertaining to the specific items listed in the warrant be reviewed and redacted by a Magistrate or Special Master before it was seen by the Government." Instead, the case agent "himself reviewed the seized computer data and used what he learned to obtain the subsequent search warrants issued in Northern California, Southern California, and Nevada." Judge Cooper also found that, in conducting the seizure in the manner it did, "[t]he Government demonstrated a callous disregard for the rights of those persons whose records were seized and searched outside the warrant."

The government also failed to appeal another ruling, by Judge Illston, that ordered return of the Tracey directory and all copies thereof. It held unlawful the government's failure to segregate data covered by the warrant from data not covered by it simply because both types were intermingled in the Tracey directory. In reaching this conclusion, Judge Illston necessarily rejected the argument about the scope of the warrant the government made before Judge Mahan. The Illston Order therefore has preclusive effect on the core legal questions resolved in the Mahan Order, viz., the government's failure to segregate intermingled data, as required by *Tamura*.

2. The Mahan Order

Judge Mahan determined that "[t]he government callously disregarded the affected players' constitutional rights." Judge Mahan also concluded that the government "unreasonab[ly] . . . refuse[d] to follow the procedures set forth in *United States v. Tamura* . . . upon learning that drug-testing records for the ten athletes named in the original April 8 warrants executed at Quest and at [CDT] were intermingled with records for other athletes not named in those warrants." We can and do uphold these findings based on the preclusive effect of the Cooper and Illston Orders. However, because the matter is important, and to avoid any quibble about the proper scope of preclusion, we also dispose of the government's contrary arguments.

A. Compliance with *Tamura*

The government argues that it *did* comply with the procedures articulated in *Tamura*, but was not required to return any data it found showing steroid use by other baseball players because that evidence was in plain view once government agents examined the Tracey Directory. The warrant even contemplated this eventuality, says the government, when it excluded from the obligation to return property any that was "otherwise legally seized."

The point of the *Tamura* procedures is to maintain the privacy of materials that are intermingled with seizable materials, and to avoid turning a limited search for particular information into a general search of office file systems and computer databases. If the government can't be sure whether data may be concealed, compressed, erased or booby-trapped without carefully examining the contents of every file—and we have no cavil with this general proposition—then everything the government chooses to seize will, under this theory, automatically come into plain view. Since the government agents ultimately decide how much to actually take, this will create a powerful incentive for them to seize more rather than less: Why stop at the list of all baseball players when you can seize the entire Tracey Directory? Why just that directory and not the entire hard drive? Why just this computer and not the one in the next room and the next room after that? Can't find the computer? Seize the Zip disks under the bed in the room where the computer once might have been. Let's take everything back to the lab, have a good look around and see what we might stumble upon.

This would make a mockery of *Tamura* and render the carefully crafted safeguards in the Central District warrant a nullity. One phrase in the warrant cannot be read as eviscerating the other parts, which would be the result if the "otherwise legally seized" language were read to permit the government to keep anything one of its agents happened to see while performing a forensic analysis of a hard drive. The phrase is more plausibly construed as referring to any evidence that the government is entitled to retain entirely independent of this seizure. The government had no such independent basis to retain the test results of other than the ten players specified in the warrant.

B. Initial Review by Computer Personnel

The government also failed to comply with another important procedure specified in the warrant, namely that "computer personnel" conduct the initial review of the seized data and segregate materials not the object of the warrant for return to their owner. The case agent immediately rooted out information pertaining to *all* professional baseball players and used it to generate additional warrants and subpoenas to advance the investigation. The record reflects no forensic lab analysis, no defusing of booby traps, no decryption, no cracking of passwords and certainly no effort by a dedicated computer specialist to separate data for which the government had probable cause from everything else in the Tracey Directory. Instead, as soon as the Tracey Directory was extracted from the CDT computers, the case agent assumed control over it, examined the list of all professional baseball players and extracted the names of those who had tested positive for steroids. Indeed, the government admitted at the hearing before Judge Mahan that "the idea behind taking [the copy of the Tracey Directory] was to take it and later on briefly peruse it to see if there was anything above and beyond that which was authorized for seizure in the initial warrant." The government agents obviously were counting on the search to bring constitutionally protected data into the plain view of the investigating agents.

But it was wholly unnecessary for the case agent to view any data for which the government did not already have probable cause because there was an agent at the scene who was specially trained in computer forensics. This agent did make an initial determination that the CDT computer containing the Tracey Directory could not be searched and segregated on-site, and that it would be safe to copy the Tracey Directory, rather than seizing the entire hard drive or computer. After that copy was made, however, it was turned over to the case agent, and the specialist did nothing further to segregate the target data from that which was swept up simply because it was nearby or commingled. The sequence of events supports the suspicion that representations in the warrant about the necessity for broad authority to seize materials were designed to give the government access to the full list of professional baseball players and their confidential drug testing records.

The government argues that it didn't violate the warrant protocol because the warrant didn't specify that *only* computer personnel could examine the seized files, and the case agent was therefore entitled to view them alongside the computer specialist. This, once again, is sophistry. It would make no sense to represent that computer personnel would be used to segregate data if investigatory personnel were also going to access all the data seized. What would be the point? The government doesn't need instruction from the court as to what kind of employees to use to serve its own purposes; the representation in the warrant that computer personnel would be used to examine and segregate the data was obviously designed to reassure the issuing magistrate that the government wouldn't sweep up large quantities of data in the hope of dredging up information it could not otherwise lawfully seize. This was an obvious case of deliberate overreaching by the government in an effort to seize data as to which it lacked probable cause.

C. Federal Rule of Criminal Procedure 41(g)

Judge Mahan cured this overreaching by ordering the government to return the illegally seized data. We have long held that Rule 41(g) empowers district courts to do just that.

We cannot see how Judge Mahan abused his discretion by concluding that "equitable considerations" required sequestration and the return of copies. The risk to the players associated with disclosure, and with that the ability of the Players Association to obtain voluntary compliance with drug testing from its members in the future, is very high. Indeed, some players appear to have already suffered this very harm as a result of the government's seizure.

3. The Illston Quashal

Judge Illston described the subpoena as "served after the government had obtained evidence . . . which has been determined now to have been illegally seized." Under the circumstances, Judge Illston regarded the subpoena as an unreasonable "insurance policy"—having seized materials unlawfully, the government then subpoenaed the very same materials in an attempt to moot any future proceedings for a return of property.

[In affirming Judge Illston's decision,] we emphasize that, while the government is free to pursue warrants, subpoenas and other investigatory tools, and may do so in whichever judicial district is appropriate in light of the location of the information sought, it must fully disclose to each judicial officer prior efforts in other judicial fora to obtain the same or related information, and what those efforts have achieved.

More than one of the judges involved in this case below commented that they felt misled or manipulated by the government's apparent strategy of moving from district to district and judicial officer to judicial officer in pursuit of the same information, and without fully disclosing its efforts elsewhere. The cause of justice will best be served if such judicial reactions to the government's conduct can be avoided in the future.

Concluding Thoughts

This case well illustrates both the challenges faced by modern law enforcement in retrieving information it needs to pursue and prosecute wrongdoers, and the threat to the privacy of innocent parties from a vigorous criminal investigation. At the time of *Tamura*, most individuals and enterprises kept records in their file cabinets or similar physical facilities. Today, the same kind of data is usually stored electronically, often far from the premises. Electronic storage facilities intermingle data, making them difficult to retrieve without a thorough understanding of the filing and classification systems used—something that can often only be determined by closely analyzing the data in a controlled environment. *Tamura* involved a few dozen boxes and was considered a broad seizure; but even inexpensive electronic storage media today can store the equivalent of millions of pages of information.

Wrongdoers and their collaborators have obvious incentives to make data difficult to find, but parties involved in lawful activities may also encrypt or compress data for entirely legitimate reasons: protection of privacy, preservation of privileged communications, warding off industrial espionage or preventing general mischief such as identity theft. Law enforcement today thus has a far more difficult, exacting and sensitive task in pursuing evidence of criminal activities than even in the relatively recent past. The legitimate need to scoop up large quantities of data, and sift through it carefully for concealed or disguised pieces of evidence, is one we've often recognized.

This pressing need of law enforcement for broad authorization to examine electronic records, so persuasively demonstrated in the introduction to the original warrant in this case creates a serious risk that every warrant for electronic information will become, in effect, a general warrant, rendering the Fourth Amendment irrelevant. The problem can be stated very simply: There is no way to be sure exactly what an electronic file contains without somehow examining its contents—either by opening it and looking, using specialized forensic software, keyword searching or some other such technique. But electronic files are generally found on media that also contain thousands or millions of other files among which the sought-after data may be stored or concealed. By necessity, government efforts to locate particular files will require examining a great many other files to exclude the possibility that the sought-after data are concealed there.

Once a file is examined, however, the government may claim (as it did in this case) that its contents are in plain view and, if incriminating, the government can keep it. Authorization to search *some* computer files therefore automatically becomes authorization to search all files in the same sub-directory, and all files in an enveloping directory, a neighboring hard drive, a nearby computer or nearby storage media.

Where computers are not near each other, but are connected electronically, the original search might justify examining files in computers many miles away, on a theory that incriminating electronic data could have been shuttled and concealed there.

The advent of fast, cheap networking has made it possible to store information at remote third-party locations, where it is intermingled with that of other users. For example, many people no longer keep their email primarily on their personal computer, and instead use a web-based email provider, which stores their messages along with billions of messages from and to millions of other people. Similar services exist for photographs, slide shows, computer code and many other types of data. As a result, people now have personal data that are stored with that of innumerable strangers. Seizure of, for example, Google's email servers to look for a few incriminating messages could jeopardize the privacy of millions.

It's no answer to suggest that people can avoid these hazards by not storing their data electronically. To begin with, the choice about how information is stored is often made by someone other than the individuals whose privacy would be invaded by the search. Most people have no idea whether their doctor, lawyer or accountant maintains records in paper or electronic format, whether they are stored on the premises or on a server farm in Rancho Cucamonga, whether they are commingled with those of many other professionals or kept entirely separate. Here, for example, the Tracey Directory contained a huge number of drug testing records, not only of the ten players for whom the government had probable cause but hundreds of other professional baseball players, thirteen other sports organizations, three unrelated sporting competitions, and a non-sports business entity—thousands of files in all, reflecting the test results of an unknown number of people, most having no relationship to professional baseball except that they had the bad luck of having their test results stored on the same computer as the baseball players.

Second, there are very important benefits to storing data electronically. Being able to back up the data and avoid the loss by fire, flood or earthquake is one of them. Ease of access from remote locations while traveling is another. The ability to swiftly share the data among professionals, such as sending MRIs for examination by a cancer specialist half-way around the world, can mean the difference between death and a full recovery. Electronic storage and transmission of data is no longer a peculiarity or a luxury of the very rich; it's a way of life. Government intrusions into large private databases thus have the potential to expose exceedingly sensitive information about countless individuals not implicated in any criminal activity, who might not even know that the information about them has been seized and thus can do nothing to protect their privacy.

It is not surprising, then, that all three of the district judges below were severely troubled by the government's conduct in this case. Judge Mahan, for example, asked "what ever happened to the Fourth Amendment? Was it . . . repealed somehow?" Judge Cooper referred to "the image of quickly and skillfully moving the cup so no one can find the pea." And Judge Illston regarded the government's tactics as "unreasonable" and found that they constituted "harassment." Judge Thomas, too, in his panel dissent, expressed frustration with the government's conduct and position, calling it a "breathtaking expansion of the 'plain view' doctrine, which clearly has no application to intermingled private electronic data."

Everyone's interests are best served if there are clear rules to follow that strike a fair balance between the legitimate needs of law enforcement and the right of individuals and enterprises to the privacy that is at the heart of the Fourth Amendment. *Tamura* has provided a workable framework for almost three decades, and might well have sufficed in this case had its teachings been followed. We have updated *Tamura* to apply to the daunting realities of electronic searches.

We recognize the reality that over-seizing is an inherent part of the electronic search process and proceed on the assumption that, when it comes to the seizure of electronic records, this will be far more common than in the days of paper records. This calls for greater vigilance on the part of judicial officers in striking the right balance between the government's interest in law enforcement and the right of individuals to be free from unreasonable searches and seizures. The process of segregating electronic data that is seizable from that which is not must not become a vehicle for the government to gain access to data which it has no probable cause to collect.

CHIEF JUDGE KOZINSKI, with whom JUDGES KLEINFELD, W. FLETCHER, PAEZ and M. SMITH join, concurring:

The opinion correctly disposes of the Fourth Amendment issues in this case, so I join it in full. I write separately because these issues are important and likely often to arise again. It would therefore be useful to provide guidance about how to deal with searches of electronically stored data in the future so that the public, the government and the courts of our circuit can be confident such searches and seizures are conducted lawfully. The guidance below offers the government a safe harbor, while protecting the people's right to privacy and property in their papers and effects. District and magistrate judges must exercise their independent judgment in every case, but heeding this guidance will significantly increase the likelihood that the searches and seizures of electronic storage that they authorize will be deemed reasonable and lawful.

When the government wishes to obtain a warrant to examine a computer hard drive or electronic storage medium to search for certain incriminating files, or when a search for evidence could result in the seizure of a computer, magistrate judges should insist that the government forswear reliance on the plain view doctrine. They should also require the government to forswear reliance on any similar doctrine that would allow retention of data obtained only because the government was required to segregate seizable from non-seizable data. This will ensure that future searches of electronic records do not "make a mockery of *Tamura*"—indeed, the Fourth Amendment—by turning all warrants for digital data into general warrants. If the government doesn't consent to such a waiver, the magistrate judge should order that the seizable and non-seizable data be separated by an independent third party under the supervision of the court, or deny the warrant altogether.

In addition, while it's perfectly appropriate for a warrant application to acquaint the issuing judicial officer with the theoretical risks of concealment and destruction of evidence, the government should also fairly disclose the *actual* degree of such risks in the case presented to the judicial officer. In this case, for example, the warrant application presented to Judge Johnson discussed the numerous theoretical risks that the data might be destroyed, but failed to mention that Comprehensive Drug Testing had agreed to keep the data intact until its motion to quash the subpoena could be ruled on by the Northern California district court, and that the United States Attorney's Office had accepted this representation. This omission created the false impression that, unless the data were seized at once, it would be lost. Such pledges of data retention are obviously highly relevant in determining whether a warrant is needed at all and, if so, what its scope should be. If the government believes such pledges to be unreliable, it may say so and explain why. But omitting such highly relevant information altogether is inconsistent with the government's duty of candor in presenting a warrant application. A lack of candor in this or any other aspect of the warrant application must bear heavily against the government in the calculus of any subsequent motion to return or suppress the seized data.

The process of sorting, segregating, decoding and otherwise separating seizable data (as defined by the warrant) from all other data should also be designed to achieve that purpose and that purpose only. Thus, if the government is allowed to seize information pertaining to ten names, the search protocol should be designed to discover data pertaining to those names only, not to others, and not those pertaining to other illegality. For example, the government has sophisticated hashing tools at its disposal that allow the identification of well-known illegal files (such as child pornography) without actually opening the files themselves. These and similar search tools should not be used without specific authorization in the warrant, and such permission should only be given if there is probable cause to believe that such files can be found on the electronic medium to be seized.

To that end, the warrant application should normally include, or the issuing judicial officer should insert, a protocol for preventing agents involved in the investigation from examining or retaining any data other than that for which probable cause is shown. The procedure might involve, as in this case, a requirement that the segregation be done by specially trained computer personnel who are not involved in the investigation. In that case, it should be made clear that *only* those personnel may examine and segregate the data. The government should also agree that such computer personnel will not communicate any information they learn during the segregation process absent further approval of the court.

At the discretion of the issuing judicial officer, and depending on the nature and sensitivity of the privacy interests involved, the computer personnel in question may be government employees or independent third parties not affiliated with the government. In a case such as this one, where the party subject to the warrant is not suspected of any crime, and where the privacy interests of numerous other parties who are not under suspicion of criminal wrongdoing are implicated by the search, the presumption should be that the segregation of the data will be conducted by an independent third party selected by the court. That third party should be prohibited from communicating any information learned during the search other than that covered by the warrant.

Once the data has been segregated (and, if necessary, redacted), the government agents involved in the investigation should be allowed to examine only the information covered by the terms of the warrant. Absent further judicial authorization, any remaining copies should be destroyed or, at least so long as they may be lawfully possessed by the party from whom they were seized, returned along with the actual physical medium that may have been seized (such as a hard drive or computer). The government should not retain copies of such returned data unless it obtains specific judicial authorization to do so.

Also, within a time specified in the warrant, which should be as soon as practicable, the government should provide the issuing officer with a return disclosing precisely what it has obtained as a consequence of the search, and what it has returned to the party from whom it was seized. The return should include a sworn certificate that the government has destroyed or returned all copies of data that it's not entitled to keep. If the government believes it's entitled to retain data as to which no probable cause was shown in the original warrant, it may seek a new warrant or justify the warrantless seizure by some means other than plain view.

This guidance can be summed up as follows:

1. Magistrate judges should insist that the government waive reliance upon the plain view doctrine in digital evidence cases.

2. Segregation and redaction of electronic data must be done either by specialized personnel or an independent third party. If the segregation is to be done by government computer personnel, the government must agree in the warrant application that the computer personnel will not disclose to the investigators any information other than that which is the target of the warrant.

3. Warrants and subpoenas must disclose the actual risks of destruction of information as well as prior efforts to seize that information in other judicial fora.

4. The government's search protocol must be designed to uncover only the information for which it has probable cause, and only that information may be examined by the case agents.

5. The government must destroy or, if the recipient may lawfully possess it, return non-responsive data, keeping the issuing magistrate informed about when it has done so and what it has kept.

This guidance is hardly revolutionary. It's essentially *Tamura's* solution to the problem of necessary over-seizing of evidence. Just as *Tamura* has served as a guidepost for decades, the procedures outlined above should prove a useful tool for the future. Nothing any appellate court could say, however, would substitute for the sound judgment that magistrate judges must and, I am confident will, exercise in striking this delicate balance.

CALLAHAN, CIRCUIT JUDGE, with whom IKUTA, CIRCUIT JUDGE, joins, concurring in part and dissenting in part from the en banc panel's per curiam opinion:

I initially express my concerns with the proposed guidelines for searches of electronically stored data that are set forth in the Chief Judge's concurring opinion. The concurrence is not joined by a majority of the en banc panel and accordingly the suggested guidelines are not Ninth Circuit law.

The breadth of the proposed guidelines for future digital evidence cases raises several serious concerns. Although I appreciate the desire to set forth a new framework with respect to searches of commingled electronic data, I remain wary of this prophylactic approach. The prescriptions go significantly beyond what is necessary to resolve this case.

Furthermore, the proffered "guidelines" are troubling because they are overbroad, unreasonably restrictive of how law enforcement personnel carry out their work, and unsupported by citations to legal authority. For example, the concurring opinion does not explain why it is now appropriate to grant heightened Fourth Amendment protections in the context of searches of computers based on the nature of the technology involved when we have previously cautioned just the opposite.

The concurring opinion also fails to acknowledge that its proffered guidance conflicts with the amendments to Federal Rule of Criminal Procedure 41(f)(1)(B), effective December 1, 2009. For instance, Rule 41(f)(1)(B) now states that in cases where an officer is seizing or copying electronically stored information, "[t]he officer may retain a copy of the electronically stored information that was seized or copied." This provision directly contradicts the suggestion that "[t]he government should not retain copies of such returned data." Similarly, Rule 41(f)(1)(B) now provides that "[i]n a case involving the seizure of electronic storage media or the seizure or copying of electronically stored information, the inventory may be limited to describing the physical storage media that were seized or copied." The concurring opinion, however, suggests that "the government should provide the issuing officer with a return disclosing precisely what it has obtained as a consequence of the search, and what it has returned to the party from whom it was seized." Presumably these suggestions are superseded by the detailed amendments to Rule 41, which provide comprehensive guidance in this area.

In addition, the suggested protocols essentially jettison the plain view doctrine in digital evidence cases, urging that magistrate judges "insist that the government waive reliance upon the plain view doctrine in digital evidence cases." This is put forth without explaining why the Supreme Court's case law or our case law dictates or even suggests that the plain view doctrine should be entirely abandoned in digital evidence cases. Instead of tailoring its analysis of the plain view doctrine to the facts of this case, the concurring opinion takes the bold, and unnecessary step of casting that doctrine aside. The more prudent course would be to allow the contours of the plain view doctrine to develop incrementally through the normal course of fact-based case adjudication. A measured approach based on the facts of a particular case is especially warranted in the case of computer-related technology, which is constantly and quickly evolving.

The concurring opinion offers no legal authority for its proposal requiring the segregation of computer data by specialized personnel or an independent third party. Also, the proposed *ex ante* restriction on law enforcement investigations raises practical, cost-related concerns. With respect to using an in-house computer specialist to segregate data, the suggestion essentially would require that law enforcement agencies keep a "walled-off," non-investigatory computer specialist on staff for use in searches of digital evidence. To comply, an agency would have to expand its personnel, likely at a significant cost, to include both computer specialists who could segregate data and forensic computer specialists who could assist in the subsequent investigation. The alternative would be to use an independent third party consultant, which no doubt carries its own significant expense. Both of these options would force law enforcement agencies to incur great expense, perhaps a crushing expense for a smaller police department that already faces tremendous budget pressures.

I interpret the majority's primary concern to be Agent Novitsky's search of the Tracey directory after it was removed from CDT's premises.[n.5][57] The majority focuses on statements made by Assistant United States Attorney Nedrow at the hearing before Judge Mahan that the idea behind taking the Tracey directory was to provide Agent Novitsky with an opportunity to "briefly peruse it to see if there was anything above and beyond that which was authorized for seizure in the initial warrant." Although Nedrow's language is troubling on its face, Agent Novitsky acted with the reasonable purpose of learning the location of the relevant material in the Tracey directory. Upon encountering other potentially incriminating material in the Tracey directory, he sought a subsequent warrant. We have previously found this approach acceptable. Therefore, the majority's determination that the government's actions in this case were inconsistent with *Tamura* is inconsistent with our case law.

In addition, the majority reads the warrant to state that the computer specialist, and only the computer specialist, was permitted to conduct the initial review of the

---

57. [n.5] I do not address here the government's argument that the plain view doctrine independently justified its search of the materials seized from CDT. I share some of the majority's concerns regarding broad application of the plain view doctrine to the search of computer data in this case. However, there are other contexts where application of the plain view doctrine might be more appropriate. *See, e.g., United States v. Wong*, 334 F.3d 831, 838 (9th Cir. 2003) (applying plain view doctrine to discovery of child pornography in the context of a valid search of a computer for evidence related to a murder investigation). I cannot subscribe to the generalized requirement set forth in Chief Judge Kozinski's "concurring opinion" that the government foreswear reliance on the plain view doctrine in digital evidence cases or that magistrate judges insist on such a waiver by the government.

commingled evidence seized from CDT. From this premise, the majority concludes that Agent Novitsky's involvement in that initial review of the seized materials constituted "deliberate over-reaching." But the warrant did not expressly limit the initial review to the computer specialist. It provided that the computer specialist would be involved in the determination of whether on-site review of the computer files was feasible and in the segregation process. It did not, however, by its terms exclude other case agents. The record does not indicate precisely why that language was included in the warrant. The computer specialist may have been included to facilitate the search and segregation efforts, to ensure that data would not be destroyed, to assist in the navigation through the computer files, or to uncover any mislabeled or hidden files. These purposes do not necessarily require exclusion of all other case agents.

Notes

1. Previous notes and materials pondered the question whether computers and other sophisticated digital devices that store data are "containers" or something "special" that require the creation of new rules. Those two views largely underpin the acceptance or rejection of search protocols. Assuming that search protocols are mandated by the Fourth Amendment in digital evidence cases, what should be the rules? Is the majority opinion in *Comprehensive Drug Testing* helpful in clarifying the proper procedures? Or is Judge Kozinski's list of five rules more helpful guidance?

2. What is the status of the plain view doctrine in the Ninth Circuit in digital evidence cases after *Comprehensive Drug Testing*? What is the constitutional basis for mandating elimination of the plain view doctrine in computer search cases?

3. Judge Kozinski, in his fifth guidance, asserts: "The government must destroy or, if the recipient may lawfully possess it, return non-responsive data, keeping the issuing magistrate informed about when it has done so and what it has kept." Is there any Supreme Court precedent for such a view? Is that view sound?

4. In *United States v. Schesso*, 730 F.3d 1040 (9th Cir. 2013), a panel of the Ninth Circuit interpreted the previous opinions in *United States v. Comprehensive Drug Testing, Inc.* ("*CDT III*"), 621 F.3d 1162, 1177 (9th Cir. 2010) (en banc) (per curiam) and an earlier en banc decision that was issued a year before in 2009. *United States v. Comprehensive Drug Testing, Inc.* ("*CDT II*"), 579 F.3d 989 (9th Cir. 2009) (en banc) (revised and superseded by *CDT III*). Judge McKeown, writing for the court in *Schesso* stated that the "precautionary search protocols," suggested as guidance in the concurring opinion in *CDT III* were not constitutionally based. He asserted that "the real concern animating the court in *CDT III* and *Tamura* [was] preventing the government from overseizing data and then using the process of identifying and segregating seizable electronic data 'to bring constitutionally protected data into . . . plain view.'" He added:

> *CDT II* laid out a number of procedural safeguards for future warrants as part of the majority opinion.

After *CDT II*, magistrate judges in the Western District of Washington took steps to implement the protocol, requiring the protocol for all warrants authorizing searches of electronically stored information. Because the government disagreed with this approach, ICE directed its agents not to agree to a waiver of plain view, for example, and adopted a practice of submitting its warrant applications to state judges rather than through the federal system.

Approximately a year later, the en banc court issued a new, amended opinion. The search protocol was no longer part of the majority opinion, but instead was moved to a concurring opinion and thus was no longer binding circuit precedent. By its own terms, the concurring opinion proposes the protocols not as constitutional requirements but as "guidance," which, when followed, "offers the government a safe harbor." *CDT III*, 621 F.3d at 1178 (Kozinski, C.J., concurring). Notably, there is no clear-cut rule: "District and magistrate judges must exercise their independent judgment in every case, but heeding this guidance will significantly increase the likelihood that the searches and seizures of electronic storage that they authorize will be deemed reasonable and lawful." *Id.*

Schesso's situation is unlike *CDT III* and *Tamura* in that the government properly executed the warrant, seizing only the devices covered by the warrant and for which it had shown probable cause. Based on the evidence that Schesso possessed and distributed a child pornography video on a peer-to-peer file-sharing network, law enforcement agents had probable cause to believe that Schesso was a child pornography collector and thus to search Schesso's computer system for any evidence of possession of or dealing in child pornography. In other words, Schesso's entire computer system and all his digital storage devices were suspect.

Tellingly, the search did not involve an over-seizure of data that could expose sensitive information about other individuals not implicated in any criminal activity—a key concern in both the per curiam and concurring opinions of *CDT III*—nor did it expose sensitive information about Schesso other than his possession of and dealing in child pornography. Indeed, inclusion of the search protocols recommended in the *CDT III* concurrence would have made little difference for Schesso. For example, the concurrence recommends that the government forswear reliance on the plain view doctrine, or have an independent third party segregate seizable from non-seizable data. Here, officers never relied on the plain view doctrine; they had probable cause to search for child pornography, and that is precisely what they found. The seized electronic data was reviewed by Investigator Holbrook, a specialized computer expert, rather than Detective Kennedy, the case agent, and Schesso does not assert that Holbrook disclosed to Kennedy "any information other than that which [was] the target of the warrant." Additionally, unlike the concern articulated in the concurrence in *CDT III*, which stated that the affidavit created the false impression that the data would be lost if not seized at once, here the affidavit explained that individuals who possess, distribute, or trade in child pornography "go to great lengths to conceal and protect from discovery their collection of sexually explicit images of minors."

Although we conclude that the exercise of "greater vigilance" did not require invoking the *CDT III* search protocols in Schesso's case, judges may consider such protocols or a variation on those protocols as appropriate in electronic searches. . . . Ultimately, the proper balance between the government's interest in law enforcement and the right of individuals to be free from unreasonable searches and seizures of electronic data must be determined on a case-by-case basis. The more scrupulous law enforcement agents and judicial officers are in applying for and issuing warrants, the less likely it is that those warrants will end up being scrutinized by the court of appeals.

Even if the warrant were deficient, the officers' reliance on it was objectively reasonable and the "good faith" exception to the exclusionary rule applies.

The affidavit included sufficient evidence connecting Schesso to the profile of a child pornography collector to justify the officers' reliance on the warrant. We have previously upheld comparably broad warrants based on similar evidence.

Our analysis is not affected by the officers' decision to seek a warrant from a Washington state court rather than the Western District of Washington. We recognize that the choice of forum was influenced by the Western District of Washington's policy at the time of requiring the search protocols outlined in *CDT II*. But evidence should be suppressed "only if it can be said that the law enforcement officer had knowledge, or may properly be charged with knowledge, that the search was unconstitutional under the Fourth Amendment." Because neither *CDT II* nor *CDT III* cast the search protocols in constitutional terms, state judicial officers cannot be faulted for not following protocols that were not binding on them, and law enforcement officers cannot be faulted for relying on a warrant that did not contain the non-binding protocols. Nothing prohibits the government from seeking a warrant from one forum over another where the government has the option to prosecute the case in state or federal court. The Fourth Amendment applies equally to state courts as to federal courts. The constitutionality of a warrant is not forum dependent.

If you were an attorney in the Ninth Circuit and were called on to give advice as to the current state of the law regarding search protocols in digital evidence searches, what would it be? Is *Schesso* a faithful interpretation of *CDT III*? Is it consistent?

Chapter 5

Warrants for Digital Evidence: Particularity Claims and Broad Seizures

§ 5.1 In General

The Fourth Amendment requires that a search warrant describe with particularity "the place to be searched, and the persons or things to be seized." The particularity requirement prevents a "general, exploratory rummaging in a person's belongings"[1] and the seizure of one thing under a warrant describing another.[2] It also "assures the individual whose property is searched or seized of the lawful authority of the executing officer, his need to search, and the limits of his power to search."[3] A warrant satisfies the particularity requirement if it enables the executing officer to identify with reasonable certainty those items that the issuing magistrate has authorized him to seize.[4] This is determined, *inter alia*, by the nature of the activity charged[5] and the nature of the objects to be seized.[6] For example, in Chapter 13, particularity claims related to allegations that the target of the search has "child pornography" are discussed. Without a sufficiently specific warrant, the search is considered warrantless.[7]

§ 5.2 Varieties of Computer Searches

There are two varieties of computer searches: one is to seize the equipment, that is, the computer hardware and software; the other is to obtain the data contained in the computer equipment, including on hard drives and various storage devices,

---

1. Coolidge v. New Hampshire, 403 U.S. 443, 467 (1971).

2. Marron v. United States, 275 U.S. 192, 196 (1927).

3. Groh v. Ramirez, 540 U.S. 551 (2004).

4. Maryland v. Garrison, 480 U.S. 79, 84 (1987).

5. *See, e.g.,* Andresen v. Maryland, 427 U.S. 463, 479–80 (1976) (phrase seeking all evidence was not general when modified by sentence referring to specific crime); United States v. Johnson, 541 F.2d 1311, 1314 (8th Cir. 1976); United States v. Abbell, 963 F. Supp. 1178, 1196 (S.D. Fla. 1997).

6. *See, e.g.,* State v. Wible, 51 P.3d 830, 836 (Wash. Ct. App. 2002) ("Courts evaluating alleged particularity violations distinguish between inherently innocuous items, such as [a] computer, and inherently illegal property, such as controlled dangerous substances. . . . Innocuous items require greater particularity.").

7. Groh v. Ramirez, 540 U.S. 551 (2004).

such as floppy disks. Helpful analysis in recognizing this distinction is contained in *In re Grand Jury Subpoena Duces Tecum Dated November 15, 1993*, 846 F. Supp. 11 (S.D.N.Y. 1994). Although decided under Federal Rule of Procedure 17(c) rather than under the Fourth Amendment, the court was presented with a subpoena that demanded that X Corporation provide the grand jury with the central processing unit, including the hard drive, of any computers supplied by the corporation to specified employees. The subpoena also demanded all computer-accessible data, including floppy diskettes created by those employees or their assistants. The court noted that, not only were corporate records within the scope of the subpoena, so were personal documents. The grand jury was investigating securities trading activities and obstruction of justice. The court observed:

> The subpoena at issue here is not framed in terms of categories of information. Rather, it demands specified information storage devices—namely, particular computer hard drives and floppy disks that contain data concededly irrelevant to the grand jury inquiry. . . . If the categories of materials properly are seen to be hard disk drives and floppy disks, then . . . it is highly probable that these devices will contain some relevant information. If, on the other hand, the categories of materials are seen to be the various types of documents contained on these devices, the subpoena would be unreasonably broad because there are easily separable categories of requested documents that undoubtedly contain no relevant information.

Concluding that the grand jury was actually seeking documents and not the devices that stored them, the court held that the subpoena was too broad. Similarly, under the Fourth Amendment, it must be determined whether the computer is a mere storage device for data[8] or whether the equipment[9] is the object sought.

1. Searches for Computer Equipment

In the context of warrants issued to seize computer software and hardware, the courts have often found fairly generic descriptions of the items to be seized to be sufficient.[10] For example, merely labeling the objects to be seized as evidence of, or

---

8. *See, e.g.*, United States v. Gawrysiak, 972 F. Supp. 853, 860–61 (D.N.J. 1997) (approving of warrant to search for documents related to wire fraud investigation, including records stored in magnetic or electronic forms), *aff'd*, 178 F.3d 1281 (3d Cir. 1999).

9. *See, e.g.*, Arkansas Chronicle v. Easley, 321 F. Supp. 2d 776, 793 (E.D. Va. 2004) (comparing seizure of computer equipment in child pornography cases, where those devices are considered instrumentalities of crime, with computers that are tools of journalist's trade that may or may not contain evidence); United States v. Hunter, 13 F. Supp. 2d 574, 584–85 (D. Vt. 1998) (warrant authorizing wholesale seizure of computers and related devices, without specifying crime for which computers were sought, violated particularity requirement).

10. *See, e.g.*, State v. Lehman, 736 A.2d 256, 260–61 (Me. 1999) (collecting cases).

an instrumentality[11] of, a crime as "computer equipment"[12] or even "equipment"[13] relating to a specific crime has sufficed. Of course, if computer equipment has been stolen and that specific equipment is the object of the search, it would have to be described with sufficient particularity to identify it.[14]

State v. Kenneth Stapleton

924 So. 2d 453 (La. Ct. App. 2006)

WILLIAMS, J.

Sgt. James Hart and Officer David Burton of the Vivian Police Department went to the defendant's trailer home to investigate a complaint of illegal drug activity. Upon the officers' arrival at the trailer, Sgt. Hart asked the defendant for permission to search the trailer. The defendant gave the officers oral permission and signed a written voluntary consent to search the trailer. The officers entered the trailer and immediately observed a bag containing what appeared to be marijuana seeds on a computer table located to the right of the door to the trailer. The officers noticed that the screen saver on the computer monitor was a picture of a marijuana field. The officers exited the trailer, advised the defendant of his *Miranda* rights and placed him under arrest. The defendant was placed in the patrol car. The officers then conducted a search of the trailer which revealed drug paraphernalia, including a pipe commonly used with illegal drugs, an "alien spaceman bong," forceps, vise grips and an "Indian style peace pipe" containing "tinfoil." Several hundred marijuana seeds were observed throughout the trailer. The officers also discovered items commonly used for cultivating and growing an indoor marijuana system, including fluorescent

---

11. *See, e.g.*, Arkansas Chronicle v. Easley, 321 F. Supp. 2d 776, 793 (E.D. Va. 2004) (comparing seizure of computer equipment in child pornography cases, where those devices are considered instrumentalities of crime, with computers that are tools of a journalist's trade).

12. *See* United States v. Lacy, 119 F.3d 742, 745–47 (9th Cir. 1997) (upholding warrant issued for search of "computer equipment and records" that resulted in seizure of computer, more than 100 computer disks, and documents when government knew that suspect had downloaded child pornography but did not know where the images had been stored, with the court concluding that "this type of generic classification is acceptable 'when a more precise description is not possible'"); United States v. Upham, 168 F.3d 532, 535 (1st Cir. 1999) (observing that warrant issued for "[a]ny and all computer software and hardware, . . . computer disks, disk drives" is easily administered by seizing officer based on objective criteria whether item is computer equipment).

13. Davis v. Gracey, 111 F.3d 1472, 1478–79 (10th Cir. 1997) (computers, monitors, keyboards, modems, CD-ROM drives, and changers were within the meaning of warrant that directed officers to search for "equipment . . . pertaining to the distribution or display of pornographic material").

14. *See, e.g.*, State v. Tanner, 534 So. 2d 535, 537 (La. Ct. App. 1988) (when defendant illegally copied software and other materials belonging to First Page Beeper Services, warrant not overbroad that authorized seizure of "all other computer related software" that bore the name "First Page Beepers"). *But cf.* State v. Wade, 544 So. 2d 1028, 1029–30 (Fla. Dist. Ct. App. 1989) (warrant, which resulted in seizure of 53 items, that authorized seizure of "computer equipment and business records" that had been stolen from Controlled Data Corporation was sufficiently particular when it incorporated by reference exhibit listing three specific items but was not limited to those items).

lighting, a timer, a water delivery system, plastic tubing, a five gallon bucket, Miracle Gro plant food, screening, potting soil and a tube of sealant.

While sitting in the patrol car, the defendant revealed to one of the police officers that he had obtained the instructions with regard to building a marijuana cultivating system by downloading the information from the internet onto his computer. As a result of this information, the officers seized the defendant's Gateway computer and twenty floppy disks.

A search warrant was issued to search the contents of the computer for "information concerning plans to build indoor marijuana cultivating devices." Subsequently, the computer and the floppy disks were taken to the Caddo Parish District Attorney's office for forensic analysis by Mark Fargerson, an investigator. During his perusal of the floppy disks, Fargerson came across images depicting under-aged males engaged in various sex acts. At that point, Fargerson stopped the search and sought a warrant to search the computer and floppy disks for evidence of child pornography.

The new search warrant was issued, authorizing Fargerson to search the computer and disks for "photographs and other visual reproductions depicting children under seventeen years of age engaged in sexual acts and/or sexual conduct." Pursuant to the warrant, Fargerson resumed his analysis of the images on the disks and discovered approximately 102 images of child pornography and an additional 69 images of child erotica.

The defendant contends because there was no search warrant for the floppy disks and no valid exception to the warrant requirement existed, the evidence was inadmissible. He notes that the original search warrant only extended to the computer and failed to mention any floppy disks.

A search warrant should describe with particularity the items to be seized. The warrant should be tested in a common sense and realistic manner without technical requirements of elaborate specificity.

Although the warrant authorizing the search of the computer did not mention the floppy disks, Fargerson extended his search of the computer's hard drive to include the accompanying disks. We conclude that Fargerson did not exceed the common sense scope of the warrant by checking the floppy disks. Indeed, he would have been remiss in his duties had he not extended his search to include the accompanying floppy disks.

Notes

1. In *State v. Hinahara*, 166 P.3d 1129 (N.M. Ct. App. 2007), the warrant authorized search for:

> computers, video tapes, computer diskettes, CDs, DVDs, photographs, and magazines containing child pornography.

When the police examined the hard drive, was the scope of the warrant violated? The court ruled that, based on a common sense reading of affidavit, the reference to computers and computer disks was sufficient to permit a search of the hard drive.

2. *United States v. Herndon*, 501 F.3d 683 (6th Cir. 2007), concerned a probation provision that permitted the authorities to check a "computer and any software at any time for Internet capacity and activity." Interpreting the scope of that provision, the court believed that the authorities could search all storage areas, including peripheral drives. It reasoned that a "computer" is "commonly understood to include the collection of components involved in computer's operation."

2. Searches for Data

As discussed elsewhere, there are two principal approaches to searches involving electronic data stored on computers, that is, whether a computer is a form of a container and the data in electronic storage mere forms of documents or whether such searches for data require a "special approach." A significant consequence of those competing views is in the application of the Fourth Amendment's particularity requirement. If data is considered a form of a document and the computer is just a container holding that document, the traditional limitations on document searches apply. On the other hand, if the court rejects such an analogy and adopts the "special approach" to searches of data on computers, then unique limitations are likely to be imposed.

§ 5.3 General Principles — Particularity

United States v. Loretta Otero

563 F.3d 1127 (10th Cir. 2009)

McCONNELL, CIRCUIT JUDGE.

While neither rain nor sleet nor snow could keep the residents along Postal Highway Contract Route 64 in Los Lunas, New Mexico from receiving their mail, the temptations of mail fraud and credit card theft were a different story. Loretta Otero, the assigned postal carrier for that route, was identified as the culprit and charged with a number of crimes arising out of her alleged theft. At trial, she moved to suppress two incriminating documents uncovered during a search of her computer on the grounds that the warrant authorizing the search lacked sufficient particularity. While we agree with the district court that the warrant was invalid for lack of particularity, we hold that the good faith exception to the exclusionary rule should apply.

In February 2001, a number of residents along Postal Highway Contract Route 64 began to lodge complaints that their mail was not being delivered. Specifically, they complained that they were missing credit cards, personal identification numbers, and billing statements. These residents had also noticed a number of unauthorized cash withdrawals from their accounts. Ms. Otero had been the assigned postal carrier on Postal Highway Contract Route 64 for more than thirteen years.

Understandably suspicious, Postal Inspector Stephanie Herman devised an investigation. On March 13, 2002, she prepared two test letters that appeared to be from credit card companies and were addressed to residents on Ms. Otero's route. Inspector Herman then conducted surveillance of Ms. Otero as she made her deliveries, confirming that the two test letters were never delivered. When Ms. Otero completed her route, returned to the Los Lunas Carrier Annex, gathered her personal belongings, and left the building, Inspector Herman stopped her in the parking lot and inspected her bags. Inside the bags Inspector Herman found not only the two test letters, but also six other pieces of First Class Mail, all addressed to residents on Ms. Otero's route and all from credit card companies. Ms. Otero was immediately placed on suspension and another carrier took over her route. Although Ms. Otero had been relieved of her delivery duties, residents reported that a week after her suspension she in fact continued making deliveries, though only of a very particular type of letter: credit card-related mail with outdated postmarks.

On March 27, 2002, Inspector Herman prepared a search warrant for Ms. Otero's residence. The key portion of the warrant outlining the scope of the search was Attachment B, which read in full:

ITEMS TO BE SEIZED:

1. Any and all mail matter addressed to residents of Highway Contract Route 064 in Los Lunas, New Mexico.

2. Any and all credit cards, credit card receipts and/or other records bearing names, addresses and/or credit card numbers of known victims and other residents from Highway Contract Route 064 in Los Lunas, New Mexico.

3. Any and all credit cards, credit card invoices, receipts, statements, affidavits of forgery, pre-approved offers, applications, correspondence, automatic teller machine (ATM) receipts and/or other records related to credit card or other accounts at financial institutions and/or businesses for individuals other than residents of 123 La Ladera Rd., Los Lunas, NM 87031 [Ms. Otero's address].

4. Any and all mail matter or correspondence addressed to individuals other than residents of 123 La Ladera Rd., Los Lunas, NM 87031.

5. Any and all materials including but not limited to letters, correspondence, journals, records, notes, data and computer logs bearing victim information and/or other information related to or pertaining to the theft of mail, the fraudulent credit cards, bank fraud and conspiracy including but not limited to credit card offers, receipts, credit card statements, financial statements, and financial transaction records.

COMPUTER ITEMS TO BE SEIZED

6. Any and all information and/or data stored in the form of magnetic or electronic coding on computer media or on media capable of being read

by a computer or with the aid of computer-related equipment. This media included floppy diskettes, fixed hard disks, removable hard disk cartridges, tapes, laser disks, video cassettes and other media which is capable of storing magnetic coding, as well as punch cards, and/or paper tapes and all printouts of stored data.

7. Any and all electronic devices which are capable of analyzing, creating, displaying, converting, or transmitting electronic or magnetic computer impulses or data. These devices include computers, computer components, computer peripherals, word processing equipment, modems, monitors, cables, printers, plotters, encryption circuit boards, optical scanners, external hard drives, external tape backup drives and other computer-related electronic devices.

8. Any and all instructions or programs stored in the form of magnetic or electronic media which are capable of being interpreted by a computer or related components. The items to be seized include operating systems, application software, utility programs, compilers, interpreters and other programs or software used to communicate with computer hardware or peripherals either directly or indirectly via telephone lines, radio or other means of transmission.

9. Any and all written or printed material which provides instructions or examples concerning the operation of the computer systems, computer software and/or any related device, and sign-on passwords, encryption codes or other information needed to access the computer system and/or software programs.

Inspector Herman attached an affidavit in which she stated that, in her experience, "people engaged in this type of criminal activity often keep records on the computers, including the hard drive and disks," and in which she explained the process for off-site recovery of such records and said that the search would "make every effort to review and copy only those programs, directories, files, and materials that are instrumentalities and/or evidence of the offenses described herein." That affidavit, however, was not explicitly incorporated into the warrant.

The magistrate judge signed the warrant and Inspector Herman executed it on March 28, 2002. She seized a computer hard drive, eighty-eight floppy disks, and two compact disks, all of which she sent to Robert Werbick, a forensic computer analyst with the Postal Inspection Service. Inspector Herman also sent a copy of the warrant, the application and affidavit in support of the warrant, and a cover letter explaining that the "search warrant was for items relating to the theft of credit cards and related correspondence from the mail on Highway Contract Route 064." The letter instructed Inspector Werbick to ascertain "[w]hether information described in Attachment B of the search warrant exists within the files on the hard drive, the floppy disks or the CDs." She also included a list of known victims and a list of the names and addresses of persons along the delivery route.

The government does not contest that a warrant authorizing a search of "any and all information and/or data" stored on a computer would be anything but the sort of wide-ranging search that fails to satisfy the particularity requirement. Its claim, rather, is that under a natural reading of the warrant the computer search is limited to uncovering only evidence of the mail and credit card theft along Ms. Otero's delivery route. In other words, paragraphs six, seven, eight, and nine, which fall under the heading "COMPUTER ITEMS TO BE SEIZED," are limited by paragraphs two, three, and five, which fall under the separate heading of "ITEMS TO BE SEIZED" and restrict the search to "information related to or pertaining to the theft of mail, the fraudulent credit cards, bank fraud and conspiracy."

It is true that "practical accuracy rather than technical precision controls the determination of whether a search warrant adequately describes the place to be searched." A warrant need not necessarily survive a hyper-technical sentence diagraming and comply with the best practices of *Strunk & White* to satisfy the particularity requirement. Nor is it beyond comprehension that the inspectors in this case would subjectively read the provisions pertaining to the computer search as being subject to the same limitations as the rest of the warrant, as the district court found they did. We agree with the district court, however, that the warrant describes the items to be seized with neither technical precision nor practical accuracy, and it therefore lacks sufficient particularity.

Attachment B is quite neatly divided into two subsections: "ITEMS TO BE SEIZED" and "COMPUTER ITEMS TO BE SEIZED." Each paragraph under the first section takes pains to limit the search to evidence of specific crimes or evidence pertaining to specific persons along Ms. Otero's delivery route. Each paragraph under the second section, in contrast, has no limiting instruction whatsoever. Read alone, they each authorize a search and seizure of "[a]ny and all" information, data, devices, programs, and other materials. There is no explicit or even implicit incorporation of the limitations of the first five paragraphs. The computer-related paragraphs do not even refer to the rest of the warrant. In fact, the presence of limitations in each of the first five paragraphs but absence in the second four suggests that the computer searches are *not* subject to those limitations. Even when read in the context of the overall warrant, therefore, the paragraphs authorizing the computer search were subject to no affirmative limitations.

The government contends that the warrant in this case is comparable to the warrant in *United States v. Brooks*, which we upheld. 427 F.3d 1246 (10th Cir. 2005). That warrant authorized officers to search for "evidence of child pornography," including "photographs, pictures, computer generated pictures or images, depicting partially nude or nude images of prepubescent males and or females engaged in sex acts," as well as "correspondence, including printed or handwritten letters, electronic text files, emails and instant messages." A technical reading of that warrant might suggest that the search of correspondence was wide-ranging and not limited to correspondence that related to child pornography. In context, however, we found that while "the language of the warrant may, on first glance, authorize a broad, unchanneled search through [the] document files, as a whole, its language more naturally instructs officers to search those files only for evidence related to child pornography." The warrant authorizing the search of Ms. Otero's computer, however, has significant structural differences from the warrant in *Brooks*. In *Brooks*, the portion authorizing the text search was not separated by paragraphs and headings from the portion authorizing the image search; the two portions were contained in a single paragraph, with no separation, and appeared under the same heading, namely, "evidence of child pornography." The structure of the warrant in *Brooks* thus suggested that the image and text searches were subject to the same limitations, whereas the structure of the warrant in this case, with its clearer divisions and stark contrasts between the two sections, suggests the opposite.

Differences such as subject headings and paragraph formation might seem insignificant, but if we are to follow our command of reading each part of the warrant in context, these structural indicators are useful tools. Affording the government a practical rather than a technical reading does not require us to indulge every possible interpretation. Though a reasonable person might be forgiven for reading the entire warrant as subject to limitations, we believe that the most practical reading authorizes a wide-ranging search of Ms. Otero's computer. The warrant as it pertained to the computer search was therefore invalid.

Finding that a warrant is invalid does not automatically require application of the exclusionary rule, and the motion to suppress should still be denied if the government can avail itself of *United States v. Leon*'s good faith exception. 468 U.S. 897 (1984). As the Supreme Court recently reemphasized, the exclusionary rule is a judicially-fashioned super-compensatory remedy whose focus is not on restoring the victim to his rightful position but rather on general deterrence. *See Herring v. United States*, 129 S. Ct. 695, 699–700 (2009). Because of this underlying purpose, "evidence should be suppressed 'only if it can be said that the law enforcement officer had knowledge, or may properly be charged with knowledge that the search was unconstitutional under the Fourth Amendment.'" In this case, the officers testified that they read the second half of the warrant as limited by the first, and the district court explicitly credited their testimony. They therefore did not have subjective "knowledge . . . that the search was unconstitutional."

Even if an officer lacks subjective knowledge that a warrant is legally deficient, however, pre-*Herring* precedent holds that "a warrant may be so facially deficient — *i.e.*, in failing to particularize the place to be searched or the things to be seized — that the executing officers cannot reasonably presume it to be valid." *Leon*, 468 U.S. at 923. The test is an objective one that asks "whether a reasonably well trained officer would have known that the search was illegal despite the magistrate's authorization." Not every deficient warrant, however, will be so deficient that an officer would lack an objectively reasonable basis for relying upon it. "Even if the court finds the warrant to be facially invalid . . . it 'must also review the text of the warrant and the circumstances of the search to ascertain whether the agents might have reasonably presumed it to be valid.'" We must "consider all of the circumstances," not only the text of the warrant, and we "assume that the executing officers have a reasonable knowledge of what the law prohibits."

In this case, Inspector Herman attempted to craft a warrant that would authorize a search for evidence of mail and credit card theft that had been hidden on Ms. Otero's computer. While the actual drafting did not accomplish her goals, one can see how a reasonable officer might have thought that the limitations in the first portion of Attachment B would be read to also apply to the second portion. Inspector Herman did not stop at her own understanding of the warrant, but sought the assistance of the Assistant United States Attorney, who ensured her that it satisfied the legal requirements. The magistrate judge then added his own approval. The affidavit that accompanied the warrant limited the computer search to those federal crimes for which there was probable cause. In enlisting Inspector Werbick's help in searching the disks and hard drive, Inspector Herman sent him not only the warrant but her affidavit, as well as instructions to search for items related to the theft of mail and credit card-related materials from Ms. Otero's mail route. She also provided him with information pertaining to known victims that would assist him in this search. Inspector Werbick understood his search as being limited to evidence of mail and credit card theft along Ms. Otero's route, and accordingly conducted a keyword search geared toward information about the known victims. Both Inspectors Herman and Werbick therefore had reason to believe that the warrant was subject to limitations, and they conducted their search accordingly. This is not the kind of "flagrant or deliberate violation of rights," *Herring*, 129 S. Ct. at 702, that the exclusionary rule was meant to deter.

Notes

Otero offers a good overview of particularity claims—and the difficulty for defendants to successfully challenge a warrant on those grounds. The standard for review to determine if a warrant satisfies the particularity requirement is not very demanding and, even if the standard has not been met, *Leon's* good faith exception (and now *Herring's*) will make suppression inappropriate in most circumstances. How would you draft the warrant in *Otero* to comply with the requirement of particularity?

---

1. Items to Be Seized: The Container Approach

People v. Kelli Marie Balint

138 Cal. App. 4th 200 (2006)

ARONSON, J.

A jury convicted Kelli Balint of receiving stolen property. She contends officers exceeded the scope of a search warrant for her residence when they confiscated an open laptop computer under a warrant clause authorizing seizure of "any items tending to show dominion and control" of the premises searched.

Erin Fouche's Compaq-brand laptop computer was stolen from her car in Irvine on October 30, 2002. Anaheim police officers executing a search warrant on November 25, 2002, found the computer on a living room sofa in Balint and John Stephens's Anaheim residence. The computer was open and turned on, and had been used repeatedly between October 30 and November 25. It contained data identifying Fouche as the owner.

Balint, who was not present during the search, telephoned police shortly after the search and asked an investigator whether they planned to arrest her. She claimed the Compaq computer belonged to her, explaining that she purchased it from a "girl" for $200. Asked if it was stolen, she admitted she "thought it was possible," but "didn't want to know if was stolen."

Balint argues investigating officers illegally seized the Compaq computer while executing the search warrant. She notes the warrant did not identify the Compaq computer, either in the "specifically enumerated" list of stolen property police could seize, or in the "encyclopedic list" of items demonstrating "dominion and control" of the residence. In other words, the seizure of the computer exceeded the scope of the warrant and amounted to a general search. We conclude investigators properly seized the computer pursuant to the warrant's dominion and control clause.

[The police obtained a search warrant to search for other stolen property and did not list the Compaq computer.] The warrant also authorized the search for "[a]ny items tending to show dominion and control of the location."[n.1][15]

Ten officers participated in the house search. Schmidt seized an open Compaq brand laptop computer that was "opened up and sitting on the sofa in the family room." He also seized other equipment and computers located on a shelf in a bedroom closet. Investigators seized other documents, including a September water bill in Balint's name.

The dominion and control clause at issue here is a standard feature in search warrant practice. Houses and vehicles ordinarily contain evidence identifying those individuals occupying or controlling them. Evidence identifying those in control of premises where stolen property is found tends to aid in conviction of the guilty

---

15. [n.1] The complete clause reads: "Any items tending to show dominion and control of the location, including delivered mail, whether inside the location or in the mail box, utility bills, phone bills, rent receipts, safe deposit box keys and receipts, keys and receipts for rental storage space, keys and receipts for post office box or mail drop rentals, ignition keys, car door and truck keys, recordation of voice transmissions on telephone answering machines, audio tapes and phone message receipts books, and written phone messages, and photographs tending to show occupation of residence and connection between co-conspirators, whether identified or unidentified. And any examples of handwriting including letters, address books, business records, cancelled checks, notes and/or lists."

party. Here, evidence connecting Balint to the residence where police located stolen property linked her to criminal behavior.

The scope of a warrant is determined by its language, reviewed under an objective standard without regard to the subjective intent of the issuing magistrate or the officers who secured or executed the warrant.

Here, the warrant authorized seizure of "*any* items tending to show dominion and control, including [list of items]." This language authorizes seizure of unenumerated items "tending to show dominion and control" of the premises. In other words, the itemized list following the word "including" may reasonably be interpreted as non-exclusive and merely descriptive of examples of items likely to show who occupied the residence.

This interpretation accounts for the different forms such evidence may take, while cabining the officers' search to the principle articulated in the warrant, namely, the items seized must be reasonably expected to show dominion and control of the residence. [*People v. Rogers*, 232 Cal. Rptr. 294 (Cal. Ct. App. 1986),] is instructive on this point. There the court concluded that officers requesting a warrant "could not be expected to divine in advance of their entry the precise nature of such evidence — whether mail, bills, checks, invoices, other documents, or keys. Nor could the officers be expected to know the precise location where such evidence would be located. To require such prescience from the officers would be patently unreasonable." Adoption of Balint's strict interpretation would not only ignore the ordinary meaning of the word "including," it would preclude seizure of unenumerated items that plainly demonstrate residency, such as bank statements, a box of checks, or a wallet with identification cards bearing the premise's address.

[*People v. Gall*, 30 P.3d 145 (Colo. 2001),] is particularly instructive concerning the seizure of laptop computers. In determining whether seizure of particular items exceeds the scope of the warrant, courts examine whether the items "are similar to, or the 'functional equivalent' of, items enumerated in the warrant, as well as containers in which they are reasonably likely to be found." *Gall* applied the "functional equivalency" test to the seizure of a laptop computer during the execution of a search warrant. There, the police obtained a warrant to investigate a possible conspiracy between the defendant and a coworker to murder their supervisors and use explosives during an attack at their workplace. The search warrant authorized seizure of "[a]ny and all" firearms, ammunition, and explosives, "written or printed material" that provided instructions or examples concerning the production or use of firearms and explosives, and "any documents or materials that show the occupier or possessor of the premises and vehicle." In addition to hundreds of written documents, the police seized two desktop computers and five laptop computers from a closet. As was done here, police later obtained additional warrants to search the hard drives of these computers for evidence of the suspected conspiracy. Investigators subsequently determined the laptop computers had been stolen.

The Colorado Supreme Court first noted that police officers may search the location authorized by the warrant, including any "containers" at that location that are reasonably likely to contain items described in the warrant. According to *Gall*, "[t]his container rationale is equally applicable to nontraditional, technological 'containers' that are reasonably likely to hold information in less tangible forms. Similarly a warrant cannot be expected to anticipate every form an item or repository of information may take, and therefore courts have affirmed the seizure of things that are similar to, or the 'functional equivalent' of, items enumerated in a warrant, as well as containers in which they are reasonably likely to be found."

Gall concluded the laptop computers were reasonably likely to serve as containers for writings, or the functional equivalent of "written or printed material" of a type enumerated in the warrant. The court further observed it was permissible to seize the computers rather than search them at the scene. Because the sorting of described items from intermingled, undescribed files would unduly prolong the officers' presence on the premises, the court concluded it would be less intrusive to transfer the computers to another location to complete the search. Also, such a search typically requires a degree of expertise beyond that of the executing officers, "not only to find the documents but to avoid destruction or oversearching."

Persuaded by the foregoing analysis, we conclude the open laptop computer at issue here amounts to an electronic container capable of storing data similar in kind to the documents stored in an ordinary filing cabinet, and thus potentially within the scope of the warrant. We perceive no reasonable basis to distinguish between records stored electronically on the laptop and documents placed in a filing cabinet or information stored in a microcassette.

Balint argues that the information on a laptop computer, in contrast to an immobile desktop computer, might reveal ownership of the computer but not information concerning ownership of the premises searched. We disagree. Many people use laptops as their primary computers and, in any event, a willingness to leave a mobile—and often expensive—device unattended in a residence suggests occupancy. Additionally, laptop computers are commonly used for personal correspondence, electronic payment of bills, and storing other information analogous to the examples listed in the warrant that are responsive to the dominion and control principle. Under the functional equivalency test, the fact these documents are in digital form does not bar officers from seizing the evidence. In particular, we note the police discovered the laptop computer in its "open" position, suggesting it was not merely stored on the premises. In sum, under the circumstances present here, we conclude an open laptop computer is likely to serve as a container of information tending to establish dominion and control of the residence in which it is found.

2. Items to Be Seized: The Special Approach

In *United States v. Payton*, 573 F.3d 859 (9th Cir. 2008), the authorities had a warrant to search for financial records in a drug case. The warrant did not explicitly authorize a search of computers. Rejecting the claim that records on a computer were within the scope of the warrant, the court maintained: "It is true . . . that pay/owe sheets indicating drug sales were physically capable of being kept on Payton's computer" but a contrary ruling "would eliminate any incentive for officers to seek explicit judicial authorization for searches of computers." *Payton* thus illustrates the view that computer searches and seizures require a special approach and that a warrant must generally authorize their search or seizure to comply with the particularity command of the Fourth Amendment.

3. Items to Be Seized: Social Media Accounts

United States v. Dontavious M. Blake, Tara Jo Moore
868 F.3d 960 (11th Cir. 2017)

Ed Carnes, Chief Judge:

After a nine-day trial, a jury found Dontavious Blake and Tara Jo Moore guilty of child sex trafficking for managing a prostitution ring involving at least two girls under the age of eighteen. Blake and Moore challenge numerous rulings the district court made before and during trial, and at sentencing.

Blake and Moore had a system for running their prostitution ring. One of them would post ads for prostitution services on the classifieds website Backpage. Moore would then take phone calls from potential customers who were responding to the ads. And Blake would give the prostitutes rides to their appointments and provide muscle. The money was split 50/50 between the working prostitute on the one hand and Blake and Moore on the other.

Through a variety of leads, the FBI discovered Blake and Moore's prostitution ring. It learned that the Backpage ads had been posted using an email address (hereafter the "S.B. email address"), which the FBI determined belonged to Moore. And it found out that at least two girls, known as T.H. and E.P., had been under the age of eighteen when they engaged in prostitution for Blake and Moore.

In the wake of those discoveries, the FBI arrested Blake and Moore. It continued the investigation, executing post-arrest search warrants relevant to this appeal. The second relevant search warrant the FBI executed directed Microsoft, which owns Hotmail, to turn over emails from two of Blake and Moore's email accounts, including the S.B. email account. The Microsoft warrant did not seek all emails in those two email accounts; instead, it was limited to certain categories of emails in them that were linked to the sex trafficking charges against Blake and Moore. For example, the warrant required Microsoft to turn over all "[e]mails, correspondence, and contact information for Backpage.com" and all "[e]mails and correspondence from online adult services websites" that were contained within the two email accounts.

Finally, the FBI also applied for and received two almost identical search warrants for Moore's Facebook account. Because that account was associated with the

S.B. email address and Moore's phone number, the FBI knew it belonged to her. At the time it executed the Facebook warrants, the FBI had extensive evidence linking Moore to the prostitution ring, including statements by T.H. inculpating her. And Moore's Facebook account was suggestive of criminal conduct: the publicly viewable version of the account listed Moore's occupation as "Boss Lady" at "Tricks R [U]s."

The two warrants required Facebook to "disclose" to the government virtually every type of data that could be located in a Facebook account, including every private instant message Moore had ever sent or received, every IP address she had ever logged in from, every photograph she had ever uploaded or been "tagged" in, every private or public group she had ever been a member of, every search on the website she had ever conducted, and every purchase she had ever made through "Facebook Marketplace," as well as her entire contact list. The disclosures were not limited to data from the period of time during which Moore managed the prostitution ring; one warrant asked for all data "from the period of the creation of the account" and the other did not specify what period of time was requested. The warrants did state that the only information that would be "seized," after all that data had been "disclosed" to the FBI, was data that "constitute[d] fruits, evidence and instrumentalities" of a specified crime.

Moore asserts that the Microsoft warrant and the Facebook warrants were so broad that they violated the Fourth Amendment's particularity requirement. The Fourth Amendment requires that "those searches deemed necessary should be as limited as possible." The "specific evil" that limitation targets "is not that of intrusion *per se*, but of a general, exploratory rummaging in a person's belongings." That type of rummaging was permitted during the colonial era by the "general warrant," an instrument "abhorred by the colonists." The Fourth Amendment is intended to preclude "general warrants" by "requiring a 'particular description' of the things to be seized."

Viewed against that constitutional history, the Microsoft warrant complied with the particularity requirement. It limited the emails to be turned over to the government, ensuring that only those that had the potential to contain incriminating evidence would be disclosed. Those limitations prevented "a general, exploratory rummaging" through Moore's email correspondence. The Microsoft warrant was okay.[16] [n.7]

The Facebook warrants are another matter. They required disclosure to the government of virtually every kind of data that could be found in a social media account. And unnecessarily so. With respect to private instant messages, for example, the

---

16. [n.7] It is somewhat troubling that the Microsoft warrant did not limit the emails sought to emails sent or received within the time period of Moore's suspected participation in the conspiracy. Nevertheless, the warrant was appropriately limited in scope because it sought only discrete categories of emails that were connected to the alleged crimes. As a result, the lack of a time limitation did not render the warrant unconstitutional.

warrants could have limited the request to messages sent to or from persons suspected at that time of being prostitutes or customers. And the warrants should have requested data only from the period of time during which Moore was suspected of taking part in the prostitution conspiracy. Disclosures consistent with those limitations might then have provided probable cause for a broader, although still targeted, search of Moore's Facebook account. That procedure would have undermined any claim that the Facebook warrants were the internet-era version of a "general warrant."

We are not convinced that the cases the government relies on, which involve seizing an entire hard drive located in the defendant's home and then later searching it at the government's offices, are applicable in the social media account context. *See, e.g.*, *United States v. Evers*, 669 F.3d 645, 652 (6th Cir. 2012); *United States v. Stabile*, 633 F.3d 219, 234 (3d Cir. 2011). The means of hiding evidence on a hard drive — obscure folders, misnamed files, encrypted data — are not currently possible in the context of a Facebook account. Hard drive searches require time-consuming electronic forensic investigation with special equipment, and conducting that kind of search in the defendant's home would be impractical, if not impossible. By contrast, when it comes to Facebook account searches, the government need only send a request with the specific data sought and Facebook will respond with precisely that data. *See generally* Information for Law Enforcement Authorities, Facebook, http://bit.ly/QkrAHX (last visited July 27, 2017). That procedure does not appear to be impractical for Facebook or for the government. Facebook produced data in response to over 9500 search warrants in the six-month period between July and December 2015. United States Law Enforcement Requests for Data, Facebook, http://bit.ly/2aICDHg (last visited July 27, 2017).

That said, we need not decide whether the Facebook warrants violated the Fourth Amendment because, even if they did, the district court did not err in allowing the government to use evidence gathered as a result of them. The Facebook warrants fall into the "good-faith exception" to the exclusionary rule established by *United States v. Leon*, 468 U.S. 897 (1984).

In *Leon* the Supreme Court held that "evidence obtained in objectively reasonable reliance on a subsequently invalidated search warrant" should generally not be excluded. The Court noted two circumstances that could justify exclusion in a case like this one: (1) if the warrant was based on an affidavit "so lacking in indicia of probable cause as to render official belief in its existence entirely unreasonable" or (2) if the warrant was "so facially deficient — i.e., in failing to particularize the place to be searched or the things to be seized — that the executing officers c[ould not have] reasonably presume[d] it to be valid."

The Facebook warrants do not fall within either category of excludable warrants. As we have already explained, probable cause supported issuance of the warrants. And while the warrants may have violated the particularity requirement, whether they did is not an open and shut matter; it is a close enough question that the warrants were not "so facially deficient" that the FBI agents who executed them could not have reasonably believed them to be valid. As a result, we affirm the district court's decision not to suppress the evidence gathered as a result of Microsoft warrant and the Facebook warrants.

AFFIRMED.

---

§ 5.4 A Warrant Exercise

Please review the following warrant and application and be prepared to discuss the following:

#1. Find text at #1.

Is it sufficient to list only "computer and electronic equipment" to describe the things to be seized or does the warrant have to also list the items listed in paragraphs a.–d.?

Assuming that the police are merely looking for data, why would the police *legitimately* want to seize the items listed in paragraph b.?

Under paragraph c., do the police have a legitimate reason to seize these items?

#2. Find at #2.

Under paragraph d., why do the police legitimately want to seize these items? Should such seizures be allowed routinely?

#3. Find at #3.

Is this broad seizure justified?

Is it necessary to specify in the warrant that the items will be examined off-site?

#4. Find text at #4.

The text sets out a lot of general information about computers. Is such information needed? Does it justify the broad seizures requested?

SEARCH WARRANT

STATE OF _____

To any lawful officer of _____

Upon reviewing the application and the accompanying affidavit of _____

_____,

(insert name and organization of the applicant/affiant)

which are made part of this Warrant and herein incorporated by reference, and having heard and considered evidence in support of the warrant from the affiant named therein, I find there is probable cause to believe that certain property subject to seizure under the laws of this State are located at:

_____ ,

(insert description and location of the place or person to be searched.
A photograph also may be inserted in this section)

including all approaches and appurtenances thereto and surrounding curtilage thereon.

That said things are particularly described as follows:

#1

Computer and Electronic Equipment, including the following:

a. Any and all information and/or data stored in the form of magnetic or electronic coding on computer media or on media capable of being read by a computer or with the aid of computer related equipment. This media includes network, servers, back-up tapes and diskettes, hard drives, floppy diskettes, fixed hard disks, removable hard disk cartridges, tapes, laser disks, video cassettes and other media which are capable of storing magnetic coding.

b. Any and all electronic devices which are capable of analyzing, creating, displaying, converting or transmitting electronic or magnetic computer impulses or data. These devices include computers, computer components, computer peripherals, word processing equipment, modems, monitors, printers, plotters, encryption circuit boards, optical scanners, external hard drives and other computer related devices.

c. Any and all instruction or programs stored in the form of electronic or magnetic media which are capable of being interpreted by a computer or related components. The items to be seized include operating systems, application software, utility programs, compilers, interpreters, and other programs or software used to communicate with computer hardware peripherals whether directly or indirectly via telephone lines, radio, or other means of transmission.

#2

d. Documents and other property related to computers and their operation, including manuals, and any devices to access computers, such as passwords and keys.

e. _____

(insert description of the items to be seized)

#3

THEREFORE, YOU ARE COMMANDED WITH THE NECESSARY AND PROPER ASSISTANTS TO SEARCH THE ABOVE-DESCRIBED PLACE OR PERSON FOR THE PROPERTY SPECIFIED. YOU ARE FURTHER COMMANDED

TO SEIZE THE ABOVE DESCRIBED PROPERTY IF FOUND. YOU ARE AUTHO-
RIZED TO REMOVE THE ITEMS SEIZED FROM THE PREMISES AND CON-
DUCT AN OFF-SITE EXAMINATION OF ALL ITEMS SEIZED, INCLUDING
THE CONTENTS OF ALL STORAGE MEDIA.

This Warrant may be served at any time of the day or night. After this Warrant is
served, this Warrant shall be returned to this Court, along with a written inventory
of the property seized.

WITNESS MY HAND, THIS THE DAY OF _____, 20_____.

_____   _____
Signature   Official Title

Application and Affidavit for Search Warrant
State of _____

To any lawful officer of _____

Whereas, _____ (affiant officer's name), known to me to be a
credible person, has this day made complaint on oath before me as follows:

1. That affiant has good reason to believe and does believe that certain things
described herein are now being concealed in or about the following place in this
County:

_____,

(insert description and location of the place or person to be searched.
A photograph also may be inserted in this section)

together with all approaches and appurtenances thereto and surrounding curtilage
thereon.

2. That said things are particularly described as follows:

Computer and Electronic Equipment, including the following:

**a. Any and all information and/or data stored in the form of magnetic or
electronic coding on computer media or on media capable of being read
by a computer or with the aid of computer related equipment. This media
includes network, servers, back-up tapes and diskettes, hard drives, floppy
diskettes, fixed hard disks, removable hard disk cartridges, tapes, laser
disks, video cassettes and other media which are capable of storing magnetic coding.**

**b. Any and all electronic devices which are capable of analyzing, creating,
displaying, converting or transmitting electronic or magnetic computer**

impulses or data. These devices include computers, computer components, computer peripherals, word processing equipment, modems, monitors, printers, plotters, encryption circuit boards, optical scanners, external hard drives and other computer related devices.

c. Any and all instruction or programs stored in the form of electronic or magnetic media which are capable of being interpreted by a computer or related components. The items to be seized include operating systems, application software, utility programs, compilers, interpreters, and other programs or software used to communicate with computer hardware peripherals whether directly or indirectly via telephone lines, radio, or other means of transmission.

d. Documents and other property related to computers and their operation, including manuals, and any devices to access computers, such as passwords and keys.

_____ ,

(insert description of the items to be seized)

3. The facts establishing the grounds for issuance of a Search Warrant are as follows:

part I: TRAINING, EDUCATION AND EXPERIENCE

I have been a law enforcement officer for _____ years. I am employed as a law enforcement officer by the _____ (insert organization and assignment) and have been so employed for _____ years. My law enforcement training and experience include the preparation, presentation, and service of criminal complaints, arrest, and search warrants, including _____ (insert number of search warrants obtained and number executed). In addition, _____ (insert specific training and experience relating to the particular crime that is the subject of this application).

part II. UNDERLYING FACTS AND CIRCUMSTANCES.

A. _____ (List all facts tending to establish probable cause for the search warrant to be issued in this particular case.)

#4

B. General information about computer related searches and seizures

the Role of the Computer — in general

Computer hardware, software and electronic files may be important to a criminal investigation in two distinct ways: (1) the objects themselves may be contraband, evidence, instrumentalities, or fruits of crime, and/or (2) the objects may be used as storage devices that contain contraband, evidence, instrumentalities, or fruits of crime in the form of electronic data. In the instant case, the warrant application requests permission to search the described items because the affiant believes that the computer was involved in the crime as detailed above.

Seizing Computer Equipment and Storage Devices & Conducting Subsequent Offsite Search

Based upon your affiant's knowledge, training, and experience, your affiant knows that searching and seizing information from computers often requires agents to seize most or all electronic storage devices (along with related peripherals) to be searched later by a qualified computer expert in a laboratory or other controlled environment. This is true because of the following:

A. <u>Volume and Location of Evidence</u>

Computer storage devices (such as hard disks, diskettes, etc.) can store millions of pages of data. A suspect may try to conceal criminal evidence, including storing it in random order with deceptive file names. This may require searching authorities to examine all the stored data to determine which particular files are evidence or instrumentalities of crime. This sorting process can take weeks, depending on the volume of data stored, and it is impractical, if not impossible, to attempt this kind of data search onsite. The alternative to extracting the items for analysis in a laboratory setting would be for law enforcement to occupy the premises for days, weeks, or months while the search and analysis proceeds. This alternative is far more invasive than an offsite search.

B. <u>Technical Requirements</u>

Searching computer systems for criminal evidence is a highly technical process requiring expert skill and a properly controlled environment. The vast array of computer hardware and software available requires even computer experts to specialize in some systems and applications, so it is difficult to know before a search which expert is qualified to analyze the system and its data. Also, data search protocols are exacting scientific procedures designed to protect the integrity of the evidence and to recover even "hidden," erased, compressed, password-protected, or encrypted files. Because computer evidence is vulnerable to inadvertent or intentional modification or destruction (both from external sources or from destructive code imbedded in the system as a "booby trap"), a controlled environment may be necessary to complete an accurate analysis. Further, such searches often require the seizure of most or all of a computer system's input/output peripheral devices, related software, documentation, and data security devices (including passwords) so that a qualified computer expert can accurately retrieve the system's data in a laboratory or other controlled environment. Proper examination of the items to be seized requires seizure of the entire computer system(s) and data.

Documents and Other Materials Related to Computer Operation

Affiant requests permission to seize any and all documents and other property related to computers and their operation, including manuals, and any devices to access computers, such as passwords and keys. This request is made because such materials contain information on how to run the computer and software programs and how to access data contained in storage devices and is needed to properly operate the system and to accurately obtain and copy the records and files authorized to be seized. This documentation may also assist in establishing the ownership and/or the operator of the computer system(s) being seized. Computer users sometimes employ passwords to protect their data files and records and a computer user will often write the password(s) in their system manuals, notebooks, on post-it notes, etc., and it is therefore necessary to seize all written material that is in close proximity of the computer system(s) being seized.

Use of Comprehensive Data Analysis Techniques by Experts

Searching a computer system for evidence may require a range of data analysis techniques. In some cases, it is possible for agents to conduct carefully targeted searches that can locate evidence without requiring a time-consuming manual search through unrelated materials that may be commingled with criminal evidence. In other cases, however, such techniques may not yield the evidence described in the warrant because criminals can mislabel or hide files and directories; encode communications to avoid using key words; attempt to delete files to evade detection; or take other steps designed to frustrate law enforcement searches for information. These steps may require agents to conduct extensive searches such as scanning areas of the disk not allocated to listed files, or opening every file and scanning its contents to determine whether it falls within the scope of the warrant. Thus, the search procedure for the electronic data contained in the computers or operating software or memory devices, computer hard drive and diskettes, is to be performed in a laboratory, or other controlled environment, and may include searches through all electronic storage devices and areas.

4. **WHEREFORE**, affiant requests that a search warrant issue directing a search of the above described place and seizure of the above described things.

_____
Affiant

Sworn to and Subscribed before me, the _____ day of _____, 20_____.

_____
Judge

Chapter 6

Search Execution Issues

Search execution issues address the manner in which law enforcement authorities execute a warrant or carry out a permissible warrantless search. Highlighted here are several unsettled areas of Fourth Amendment regulation related to computer and other digital evidence searches.

One issue is whether the manner in which the search is to be conducted needs to be preauthorized by an issuing magistrate. That issue is addressed in Chapter Four. Outside of the computer search context, the conventional view is that the Warrant Clause of the Fourth Amendment regulates the circumstances under which a warrant may issue but says nothing about the execution of a warrant. Instead, warrant execution issues are regulated by the Reasonableness Clause.[1] Hence, it has been often said: "Determining the reasonableness of any search involves a twofold inquiry: first, one must consider 'whether the . . . action was justified at its inception,' second, one must determine whether the search as actually conducted 'was reasonably related in scope to the circumstances which justified the interference in the first place.'"[2] Thus, even if the Fourth Amendment does not require preauthorization, the manner in which a search is conducted is still regulated by the fundamental command of the Amendment that the search be reasonable. The Court has stated that the "reasonable execution" of a search has to be "fleshed out" on a case-by-case basis.[3]

§6.1 Intermingled Documents and Proper Forensic Examinations

In *Nixon v. Administrator of General Services*, 433 U.S. 425 (1977), and *Andresen v. Maryland*, 427 U.S. 463 (1976), the Court gave government investigators broad ability to view documents intermingled with other documents to ascertain their relevancy under a search warrant for documentary evidence.[4]

---

1. *E.g.*, United States v. Grubbs, 547 U.S. 90 (2006); Dalia v. United States, 441 U.S. 238 (1979).
2. New Jersey v. T.L.O., 469 U.S. 325, 341 (1985).
3. United States v. Banks, 540 U.S. 31 (2003).
4. *Andresen* was a particularly sensitive situation involving a wide-ranging search of an attorney's office for documentary evidence. Presumably, privileged and otherwise confidential documents were in that office. *Cf.* United States v. Rayburn House Office Bldg., Room 2113, 497 F.3d 654

These cases recognized the government's ability to look for the proverbial needle in the haystack. Lower courts have confronted the problem of broad searches for documents and data in a variety of situations. Notwithstanding *Nixon* and *Andresen*, some courts require that, when a substantial number of documents are intermingled with documents that are not within the permissible scope of the search, the police must seal the documents seized and obtain a second warrant detailing the permissible scope of any further search.[5] Broad examinations of material in the course of looking for the evidence listed in the warrant is especially troublesome in computer data search cases. Some courts have raised these concerns in the computer context and created special rules to regulate such searches; others reject special rules. For more on this issue, see Chapter 4.

———————

United States v. Javier Perez

2015 WL 3498734 (E.D. Pa. 2015) (unreported),
aff'd, 217 WL 4679583 (3d Cir. Oct. 18, 2017) (unreported)

DuBois, District Judge.

Defendant Javier Perez is charged in the Indictment with two counts of distributing child pornography and one count of possessing child pornography. Perez has moved to preclude the Government from introducing at trial physical evidence obtained during a search of his computer. For the reasons that follow, Perez's Motion is denied.

On October 15 and October 23, 2013, an undercover Federal Bureau of Investigation agent downloaded two files containing visual depictions of child pornography shared by a computer signed on to the Ares network. An investigation of the Internet Protocol address which shared the downloaded files revealed that it was assigned to the home of Perez.

———————

(D.C. Cir. 2007) (FBI search of congressman's paper files in his congressional office violated Speech and Debate Clause; in contrast, copying his computer hard drives and other electronic data was constitutionally permissible because congressman had the opportunity to assert the privilege as to any data prior to viewing the materials by the executive).

5. *See* United States v. Comprehensive Drug Testing, Inc., 621 F.3d 1162 (9th Cir. 2010) (en banc) (discussing criteria for off-site computer search); United States v. Shilling, 826 F.2d 1365, 1369–70 (4th Cir. 1987) (although stating that "we cannot easily condone the wholesale removal of file cabinets and documents not covered by the warrant," concluding that there were legitimate practical concerns that prompted the removal of the file cabinets and observing that the seizure was not based on an intent to engage in a fishing expedition); United States v. Tamura, 694 F.2d 591 (9th Cir. 1982) (suggesting that when documents are so intermingled that sorting on-site is not feasible, Fourth Amendment violations can be avoided by sealing the documents and obtaining an additional search warrant). Other courts reject that requirement for document searches. *See, e.g.,* United States v. Hargus, 128 F.3d 1358, 1363 (10th Cir. 1997) (seizure of entire file cabinet permissible, including intermixed warrant-specified and unspecified documents).

On March 19, 2014, FBI Special Agent Laura Pagel submitted an affidavit and applied for a warrant to search Perez's house for items related to the possession and distribution of child pornography. A warrant authorizing the search for and seizure of, *inter alia,* all "visual depictions" of child pornography "on whatever medium," and documents, emails, records, notes, and other materials related to child pornography, was subsequently issued. On March 21, 2014, the warrant was executed, and agents seized one desktop computer and three thumbdrives from Perez's bedroom.

The Government employed the following search methodology to examine the seized items: The computer and thumbdrives were first delivered to the FBI's Computer Forensics Laboratory in Philadelphia. The first assigned case agent, Special Agent Andrea Manning, requested that the forensic examiner process the computer and thumbdrives for various types of evidence, including: graphic and video files, files which matched known child pornography images (CVIP files), internet history, internet favorites, and mobile syncs and data. The FBI examiner, after making an exact digital copy of the seized evidence, loaded the copy of the digital evidence into Forensic Toolkit ("FTK"), a forensic analysis tool. The FTK software then catalogued and segregated the requested files into a viewable format. At the May 1, 2015 hearing, FBI examiner Donald Justin Price explained that the software "scans the entire computer system. It looks at every file and folder and it identifies it based on the file type. So it'll categorize it as a document, a video, a graphic file, so on and so forth." The forensic software also compares the extension of each file with the source information of that file to identify if there is a mismatch. The program is thus able to identify and extract graphic images and video files, even if concealed in files with extensions that are not traditionally associated with those file types.

The examiner then reviewed the extracted data to filter out files that clearly fell outside the scope of the case agent's request, *e.g.,* generic application icons. The extracted data included CVIP hits, directory file listings, email, items from the recycle bin, graphic and video files, internet artifacts, and various "favorites." A digital copy of only the extracted evidence was provided to the case agent for further review.

In February 2015, Special Agent Manning asked the FBI examiner for additional information from Perez's computer and thumbdrives with respect to the Ares peer-to-peer program. The examiner followed the same protocol as was followed in the first examination, and subsequently provided Special Agent Manning with information concerning incomplete and complete Ares downloads, search terms, shared files, and the install date. The Government contends that the extracted files provided by the FBI examiner constituted only a limited portion of all the data on Perez's computer and thumbdrives.

Special Agent Manning, and subsequently Special Agent Schreier, reviewed the extracted files to determine whether they contained evidence related to the possession and distribution of child pornography. At the May 1, 2015 hearing, Special Agent Schreier testified that their examination of the extracted files consisted of the following: they viewed graphic images, including those attached to emails, in a thumbnail version, and only opened them when it was believed that they contained evidence related to child pornography; opened and played short portions of video files; opened emails without attachments only if the subject line or sender gave them reason to believe that they contained evidence of child pornography; and opened and cursorily examined other extracted file types, *e.g.* internet history, to determine whether those files contained evidence that fell within the scope of the warrant and to identify the internet user at particular times. The case agents determined that approximately ten files on the computer contained visual depictions of child pornography. They also found a list of search terms on the computer related to child pornography, which had been used to search the Ares network software, and determined that the computer had Ares network software. The evidence was recovered from Perez's computer hard drive.

Under the Fourth Amendment, a search pursuant to a warrant is limited to the scope of the warrant. "If the scope of the search exceeds that permitted by the terms of a validly issued warrant or the character of the relevant exception from the warrant requirement, the subsequent seizure is unconstitutional without more." "Whether evidence is within a search warrant's scope requires not a 'hypertechnical' analysis, but a 'common-sense, and realistic' one."

In his Motion to Suppress, Perez argues that the search of his computer and thumbdrives, which consisted, in part, of "[o]pening files in order to determine their contents," was not executed in accordance with the warrant's terms, but instead was a general rummaging in violation of the Fourth Amendment. At the May 1, 2015 hearing, counsel for defendant raised an additional argument—that the use of the FTK software to conduct the initial forensic examination of Perez's computer and thumbdrives exceeded the scope of the warrant in violation of the Fourth Amendment.

Perez's challenges to the Government's search methodology require the Court to reconcile two competing principles: "On one hand, it is clear that because criminals can—and often do—hide, mislabel, or manipulate files to conceal criminal activity, a broad, expansive search of the hard drive may be required. . . . On the other hand . . . granting the Government a *carte blanche* to search *every* file on the hard drive impermissibly transforms a limited search into a general one." *United States v. Stabile,* 633 F.3d 219, 237 (3d Cir.2011). Although the U.S. Court of Appeals for the Third Circuit has not yet adopted a particular method of addressing these competing principles, or reached the precise questions presented in this case, the Court is guided by the Third Circuit's decision in *Stabile* and the cases discussed therein, which address Fourth Amendment issues in the context of computer searches. The Court addresses each of Perez's arguments in turn.

i. The Government's Use of Forensic Analysis Software

Perez first argues that the Government's use of the FTK software exceeded the scope of the warrant in violation of the Fourth Amendment. The Court rejects this argument. Given the limited nature of the forensic software's examination, which consisted of cataloging and segregating files by file type into a viewable format, and the fact that Perez could have graphic and video files containing child pornography "virtually anywhere on his computer," the Court concludes that the Government did not exceed the scope of the warrant by using the FTK software.

Although the FTK software scanned Perez's computer hard drive and thumb-drives in their entirety to identify and segregate the requested files, the Court finds that this examination was permissible "to ensure that file names ha[d] not been manipulated to conceal their contents." *Stabile,* 633 F.3d at 241; *see United States v. Hill,* 459 F.3d 966, 978 (9th Cir.2006) ("[I]mages can be hidden in all manner of files, even word processing documents and spreadsheets. Criminals will do all they can to conceal contraband, including the simple expedient of changing the names and extensions of files to disguise their content from the casual observer."). Thus, the Government's use of the FTK software to extract particular files for further review did not violate the Fourth Amendment.

ii. The Case Agents' Search of Extracted Files

Perez next argues that the "[o]pening [of] files in order to determine their con-tents" by the case agents constituted a general rummaging in violation of the Fourth Amendment. The Court rejects this argument. Although, the Court is mindful of the risks associated with searches of electronic data, and agrees that a warrant to search a computer for specific evidence is not *"carte blanche* to search *every* file on the hard drive," "the essential watchword of the Fourth Amendment is reasonable-ness." The Court concludes that the Government's search of Perez's computer and thumbdrives was reasonable under the Fourth Amendment.

First, the search warrant did not limit the Government's search to particular file types, but rather broadly authorized the search for and seizure of evidence related to the possession and distribution of child pornography.[6][7] In light of this broad authorization, and "the particular difficulties in attempting to locate image files" on a computer, it was reasonable for the case agents to examine an array of file types, including the graphic, video, internet, and Ares files, which were the focus of their search.

Second, courts have upheld as reasonable more probing computer searches than the search at issue in this case. In particular, several circuit and district courts have upheld computer searches where law enforcement officials conducted a cursory review of *every* file on the computer by opening it or previewing it to determine each file's contents. *See United States v. Williams,* 592 F.3d 511, 521 (4th Cir.2010) (where warrant authorized search of defendant's computer and digital media for evidence

---

6. [n.7] The warrant authorized, *inter alia,* the search for and seizure of "[a]ll visual depictions of minors engaged in sexually explicit conduct (as defined in 18 U.S.C. §2256) produced using minors engaged in such conduct, on whatever medium (e.g., digital media. . . .)"; and all "corre-spondence, records, opened or unopened e-mails, chat logs, and internet history, pertaining to the possession, receipt, access to or distribution of child pornography."

related to computer harassment and threats, "the warrant impliedly authorized officers to open each file on the computer and view its contents, at least cursorily, to determine whether the file fell within the scope of the warrant's authorization").

In contrast to the above-cited cases, the record reveals that, in this case, the case agents previewed and/or opened a limited, filtered set of extracted files to determine whether they contained evidence of child pornography. Only the extracted graphic, video, and internet files in addition to those files related to the Ares application, were provided to the case agent for substantive review. At that point, the case agents viewed graphic images in a thumbnail version, and only opened them when it was believed that they contained evidence related to child pornography. They opened and played short portions of video files to determine whether they contained evidence related to the possession or distribution of child pornography as no thumbnail version was available; opened emails without attachments only if the subject line or sender gave them reason to believe that they contained evidence of child pornography; and opened and cursorily examined other extracted file types, *e.g.* internet history, to determine whether those files contained evidence that fell within the scope of the warrant and to identify the internet user at particular times. The record is devoid of evidence that at any point, the Government searched for evidence other than that which was authorized pursuant to the terms of the warrant. To the contrary, the previewing and/or opening of various files by the case agents was tailored to identifying evidence of child pornography, which was ultimately discovered, and which Perez's Motion seeks to suppress. *See United States v. Richards,* 659 F.3d 527, 540 (6th Cir.2011) ("[S]o long as the computer search is limited to a search for evidence explicitly authorized in the warrant, it is reasonable for the executing officers to open the various types of files located in the computer's hard drive in order to determine whether they contain such evidence.").

Finally, Perez has not presented any alternative search methodology that would have better "protect[ed] his legitimate interests and also permit[ted] a thorough search for evidence" of child pornography. For all these reasons, the Court concludes that the Government's search was reasonable.

United States v. Christopher Owen Schlingloff

901 F. Supp. 2d 1101 (C.D. Ill. 2012)

JAMES E. SHADID, CHIEF JUDGE.

On November 3, 2010, agents obtained a warrant to search the residence located at 1816 2nd Avenue, Rock Island, Illinois, for evidence of passport fraud and harboring an alien. The affidavit indicated that there was reason to believe that computer devices found in the residence would contain records related to these crimes due to the fact that one target of the investigation had used computer devices in the past to generate, store, and print documents used in the passport scheme. Schlingloff was not the target of the investigation but was present in the residence at the time the warrant was executed and informed agents that he was living there with the targets. Approximately 130 media devices were seized during the search, including a laptop and external storage device belonging to Schlingloff; these items were sent to the DSS Computer Investigations and Forensics Division office in Arlington, Virginia, for analysis.

In December 2010, Agent Scott McNamee, a computer forensic analyst, began to examine the seized devices. In doing so, McNamee used a computer software program known as Forensic Tool Kit or FTK to index/catalog all of the files on the devices into viewable formats. The Known File Filter or KFF in the software was enabled to flag and alert during processing to certain files that are identifiable from a library of known files previously submitted by law enforcement, such as contraband or child pornography. McNamee described enabling the KFF alert as his standard operating procedure. The KFF alert in this case identified to two video files entitled "Vicky" as child pornography. Based on his investigation of one to two dozen child pornography cases in the past, McNamee suspected that the files contained child pornography and briefly opened the files to confirm his belief. McNamee observed the image of a naked prepubescent girl and an adult male, closed the file, and stopped any further processing of both the laptop and the external storage device. He then notified Agent Michael Juni about his discovery.

Based on this information, Juni prepared an application for search warrant to search the laptop and external storage device for evidence of receipt and possession of child pornography. A search warrant issued on February 4, 2011, and a total of 33 video files containing known child pornography were found on these two devices. Files were also found indicating that Schlingloff was the owner and operator of the two devices.

On July 21, 2011, Schlingloff was interviewed by the police and admitted to downloading and viewing child pornography on the laptop in question. On August 17, 2011, Schlingloff was indicted on one count of possession of child pornography. Schlingloff moved to suppress the evidence found during the forensic examination of his laptop and external storage device. The Court initially denied the Motion to Suppress based in part on the mistaken belief that the filters in the FTK system had to be applied on an all or nothing basis and that the agent lacked the ability to disable the portion of the KFF specifically alerting to known child pornography or other contraband. Schlingloff then filed a Motion to Reconsider, bringing the factual error to the Court's attention and making it clear that the KFF alerts can be disabled or not affirmatively enabled as part of the processing with very little effort. Oral argument was held, and this Order follows.

Under the Fourth Amendment, search warrants must describe the things to be seized "with sufficient particularity to prevent a general exploratory rummaging through one's belongings." Schlingloff's argument is essentially that the use of the KFF filter in the FTK program to flag known files containing child pornography enabled the agents to unreasonably broaden a limited search for evidence of passport fraud into a general search for evidence of any illegal activity.

To the extent that Schlingloff suggests that the use of the FTK software in and of itself exceeded the scope of the warrant per se, his argument is unpersuasive. The Seventh Circuit has held that the use of the FTK filtering software to index and catalogue files into a viewable format does not, in and of itself, exceed the scope of a warrant based on the fact that digital evidence could be found virtually anywhere on a computer.

Schlingloff further argues that: (1) even if the use of the FTK software in and of itself is not problematic, enabling the KFF alerts in cases that do not involve suspected child pornography or some closely related cause of action necessarily broadens the scope of the search in an unconstitutional manner, and/or (2) the opening of the child pornography files by Agent McNamee takes the search beyond the scope of the warrant. These are the main issues addressed here.

McNamee concedes that despite his understanding that he was searching for evidence of passport fraud or identity theft, he consciously and affirmatively checked the box to include the KFF alerts for child pornography because that is his standard operating procedure.

> Q. (By Mr. Tasseff) [Y]ou wouldn't have received those alerts had you restricted your search for the objects of the warrant and clicked the hide button for KFF Alert, correct?
>
> A. (By Agent McNamee) I would not have clicked on the KFF.
>
> Q. You didn't in this instance, correct?
>
> A. No, I clicked to include the KFFs. . . .
>
> Q. You went ahead and did that because that's your standard operating procedure, isn't it?
>
> A. Yes.
>
> Q. The 30 some cases that you have done, you have done it every time, correct?
>
> A. Correct.
>
> Q. Does your agency investigate strictly child porn cases?
>
> A. No, it does not.
>
> Q. In fact, this child porn case is a rare exception to the general rule, isn't it?
>
> A. Yes. . . .
>
> Q. But you used the forensic tool that alerted you to the presence of child porn in a non-porn case, didn't you sir?
>
> A. Correct.

McNamee's testimony and the FTK User Guide reveal that the user can either choose to apply an existing, predefined filter or customize a filter based on the purposes of the search with relative ease by checking various boxes in the setup menu.

In doing so, the Court now understands that it is simple to make selections that allow the user to take advantage of the utility of the FTK program to categorize and sort out common known files such as program files, etc., without being required to flag the KFF alerts for child pornography files as part of the process.

The search here did not end with flagging the child pornography files during preprocessing, however. After the KFF alerted to the two files in question, McNamee believed that he recognized them to be part of the "Vicky" series of child pornography based on their hash values and his experience. Rather than stopping at this point to obtain a warrant to search for images of child pornography, McNamee briefly opened each file in order to confirm his suspicions before stopping any further processing and notifying Agent Juni. When the facts of this case are considered in their totality, the Court finds that suppression is required.

By opening the "Vicky" files flagged by the KFF alert, McNamee knew or should have known that those files would be outside the scope of the warrant to search for evidence of passport fraud or identity theft, particularly as the warrant did not specifically refer to evidence found in video files.

Additionally, in light of the admitted ability to confine the FTK search by not enabling the KFF filter for child pornography alerts, the Court finds that Agent McNamee took an affirmative additional step to enable the KFF alerts that would identify known child pornography files as part of his search for evidence of passport fraud or identity theft. In a case where the professed subject matter sought in the search bore no resemblance to child pornography, it is difficult to construe this as anything other than a deliberate expansion of the scope of the warrant, or at the very least, an affirmative step that effectively did so.

Given the ever increasing state of technology and consequently, technology related crimes, the Court finds that this issue is not going to go away, and in fact, will likely become more prevalent and finely contoured. Digital images or files can be located nearly anywhere on a computer and "may be manipulated to hide their true contents." Accordingly, more comprehensive and systematic searches have been found to be reasonable. Nevertheless, it is also important to note that there is normally no fear of degradation or dissipation of evidence or a rapidly evolving situation requiring the need to "shoot from the hip" in examining seized computer files without a proper warrant.

The promise of the Fourth Amendment to be free from unreasonable searches and seizures contemplates a warrant that sets forth with specificity the area to be searched and the subject matter of the search. So if a warrant authorizes an officer to look in all files on a computer, should the courts care how it is done? This Court believes so.

This caution seems particularly appropriate when considering the Government's proffered justification that the pornography files were in plain view or that they would have inevitably been discovered in a manual search. The plain view doctrine requires the officer to be where he has a right to be when he observes the evidence in plain view; the discovery must also be inadvertent.[7] The suggestion that the agent inadvertently came across a file when that same agent specifically set up the situation to find and highlight this type of file by "clicking" to enable the KFF alert is untenable.

The same follows with the argument that the files would have inevitably been discovered. The search request in this case was not limited solely to documents, but rather sought records, photographs, and evidence "in whatever form they may be kept" on the premises that would be relevant to the crimes of passport fraud or identity theft. Given that such evidence could have been stored electronically as document files, spreadsheets, photo files, or a variety of other file types, McNamee testified that procedure would have required him to examine every file on the laptop and external storage device either manually or with the assistance of the indexing and sorting software; it would have taken much longer and consumed more manpower resources to complete the task manually, but the file would have eventually been found, and the result would have been the same. To some degree, this argument misses the point, as the use of the filter did not require McNamee to look at all; the filter locates the files and brings them to the attention of the officer. Discovery is specifically targeted rather than the result of inadvertence.

All-encompassing manual searches may be theoretically possible, yet the availability of technology and lack of manpower resources make them impractical in the average case. This is supported by McNamee's testimony where he then qualified his response to concede that his department did not have the resources to perform full, manual searches of all seized electronic devices and that as a result, manual searches would hopelessly bog down his office to the point where the examinations could not get done within the constraints of the Speedy Trial Act.

The warrant as drafted in this case is not challenged as unconstitutional. The use of the KFF alerts alone may not move this case beyond the scope of the warrant; the alert on the Vicky files alone may not move this beyond the scope of the warrant. Under some circumstances, the act of briefly opening the files to confirm their contents may not move this beyond the scope of the warrant. But combine these with the additional facts of an agent affirmatively enabling the KFF filter to alert for child pornography in a non-pornography case that involves a search warrant seeking evidence of passport fraud and does not specifically refer to evidence in the form of videos, in conjunction with the agent opening the files once alerted to their presence, there can be no other conclusion than that the scope of the warrant was exceeded in this case.

For all these reasons, the Court agrees with Schlingloff that the scope of the warrant in this case was exceeded, thereby requiring the suppression of the opened child pornography files. Any other outcome would be contrary to the intent of the Fourth

---

7. [Editor: *But see* discussion of plain view doctrine in § 4.2.]

Amendment that search warrants must describe with particularity the things to be seized, so that a search for specified evidence does not devolve into a generalized search for something entirely different.

For the reasons set forth above, . . . Schlingloff's Motion to Suppress Evidence is GRANTED.

Notes

1. Compare *Perez* and *Schingloff.* Are they consistent?

2. Note that both cases involved the use of forensic software. FTL is used by federal authorities, and EnCase is commonly used by state and local authorities. *See* www .guidancesoftware.com (now called Opentext), which is a website worth exploring for more information. Each search was performed by a trained forensic examiner. As a prosecutor or defense counsel, familiarity with the software and how it was utilized by the examiner is now a crucial aspect of any challenge to search execution.

§ 6.2 On-Site vs. Off-Site Searches

One concern is whether the police must examine the objects on-site to ascertain their relevancy or whether they can broadly seize evidence and then examine it off-site to ascertain its importance. This often arises in the context of computer searches: may the government remove the computer, including its hard drive and discs, to the police station for detailed forensic examination? An example of a warrant seeking such authorization is in §5.4. {Note the language in the command clause and the affidavit in support of the warrant.} Answering this question, courts have fairly consistently held that, due to the intermingling of legitimate and illegitimate items, the technical difficulty of examination, and the volume of information seized, temporary seizures of the computer, the hard drive, and computer discs and removal off-site for examination are permitted.[8] Underlying the courts' views is the fundamental

---

8. *See, e.g.,* United States v. Walser, 275 F.3d 981, 985 (10th Cir. 2001) (observing that seizure is appropriate in a variety of circumstances, including "the impracticality of on-site sorting" and because "computer evidence is vulnerable to tampering or destruction"); Guest v. Leis, 255 F.3d 325, 335 (6th Cir. 2001) (due to the "technical difficulties of conducting a computer search in a suspect's home," permissible to seize the computers and their contents and remove to allow the police to locate the relevant data); United States v. Hay, 231 F.3d 630, 637 (9th Cir. 2000) (upholding, in a child pornography case, a warrant authorizing seizure of a defendant's entire computer system because the circumstances "justified taking the entire system off site because of the time, expertise, and controlled environment required for a proper analysis"); United States v. Upham, 168 F.3d 532, 535 (1st Cir. 1999) ("As a practical matter, the seizure and subsequent off-premises search of the computer and all available disks was about the narrowest definable search and seizure reasonably likely to obtain the images. A sufficient chance of finding some needles in the computer haystack was established by the probable-cause showing in the warrant application; and a search of a computer and co-located disks is not inherently more intrusive than the physical search of an entire house for a weapon or drugs."); United States v. Sissler, 966 F.2d 1455 (6th Cir. 1992) (police permitted to remove computers from defendant's residence to continue search off-site); Mahlberg v. Mentzer,

premise that "current technology does not permit proper on-site examination of computer files."[9] For example, in *United States v. Hill*,[10] Judge Kozinski sitting by designation in the District Court, concluded that the police were not required to bring with them equipment capable of reading computer storage media and an officer competent to operate it. He observed:

> Doing so would have posed significant technical problems and made the search more intrusive. . . . Because computers in common use run a variety of operating systems—various versions or flavors of Windows, Mac OS and Linux, to name only the most common—police would have had to bring with them a computer (or computers) equipped to read not only all of the major media types, but also files encoded by all major operating systems.

---

968 F.2d 772, 775 (8th Cir. 1992) (seizure of 160 computer disks permissible when searching for two computer files because of the possibility that the computer was "bobby-trapped" to erase itself and because it was unknown which disks contained the files); United States v. Schandl, 947 F.2d 462, 465–66 (11th Cir. 1991) (in tax evasion case, which requires "careful analysis and synthesis of a large number of documents," it might be more disruptive for the agents to conduct a thorough search of each individual document and computer disk before removing it; to insist on such a practice would substantially increase the time to conduct the search, thereby aggravating its intrusiveness); United States v. Leveto, 343 F. Supp. 2d 434, 449–50 (W.D. Pa. 2004) (in large tax fraud scheme, involving many documents and computer files, off-site inspection permissible); United States v. Albert, 195 F. Supp. 2d 267, 278–79 (D. Mass. 2002) (upholding an off-site search because "the mechanics of searching a hard drive by viewing all of the information it contains cannot be readily accomplished on site"); United States v. Hunter, 13 F. Supp. 2d 574, 583 (D. Vt. 1998) ("Often it is simply impractical to search a computer at the search site because of the time and expertise required to unlock all sources of information."); United States v. Yung, 786 F. Supp. 1561, 1569 (D. Kan. 1992) (computer files "clearly could not be individually reviewed prior to completion of the search"); People v. Gall, 30 P.3d 145, 154–55 (Colo. 2001) (seizure of computers and later search off-site upheld). *Cf.* United States v. Gawrysiak, 972 F. Supp. 853, 866 (D.N.J. 1997) ("A reasonable search of computer files may include copying those files on to a disk on the scene, for later time-consuming review of the index of documents to cull the relevant time periods and subject matters while returning the remainder.").

9. United States v. Al-Marri, 230 F. Supp. 2d 535, 541 n.3 (S.D.N.Y. 2002). *See also* United States v. Campos, 221 F.3d 1143 (10th Cir. 2000) (quoting FBI agent's explanation as to why it was not usually feasible to search for particular computer files in a person's home, which included the volume of information, user attempts to conceal criminal evidence, the need for an expert examiner, a controlled environment, the wide variety of computer hardware and software, and the vulnerably of the evidence to tampering or destruction); People v. Gall, 30 P.3d 145, 154–55 (Colo. 2001) ("In addition to the problems of volume and commingling, the sorting of technological documents may require a search to be performed at another location 'because that action requires a degree of expertise beyond that of the executing officers,' not only to find the documents but to avoid destruction or oversearching."). *Cf.* United States v. Greathouse, 297 F. Supp. 2d 1264, 1269, 1275 (D. Or. 2003) (although acknowledging that numerous cases have upheld the "wholesale seizure of computers and computer disks and records for later review for particular evidence as the only reasonable means of conducting a search," observing "that this may not always be true due to technological developments" and stating that, in the appropriate situation, "there may well be an obligation" to use a computer forensics program "to more narrowly tailor the search and seizure"); United States v. Hunter, 13 F. Supp. 2d 574, 583 (D. Vt. 1998) ("until technology and law enforcement expertise render on-site computer records searching both possible and practical, wholesale seizures, if adequately safeguarded, must occur").

10. 322 F. Supp. 2d 1081 (C.D. Cal. 2004), *aff'd*, 459 F.3d 966 (9th Cir. 2006).

Because operating systems, media types, file systems and file types are continually evolving, police departments would frequently have to modify their computers to keep them up-to-date. This would not be an insuperable obstacle for larger police departments and federal law enforcement agencies, but it would pose a significant burden on smaller agencies.

Even if the police were to bring with them a properly equipped computer, and someone competent to operate it, using it would pose two significant problems. First, there is a serious risk that the police might damage the storage medium or compromise the integrity of the evidence by attempting to access the data at the scene. As everyone who has accidentally erased a computer file knows, it is fairly easy to make mistakes when operating computer equipment, especially equipment one is not intimately familiar with. The risk that the officer trying to read the suspect's storage medium on the police laptop will make a wrong move and erase what is on the disk is not trivial. Even if the officer executes his task flawlessly, there might be a power failure or equipment malfunction that could affect the contents of the medium being searched. For that reason, experts will make a back-up copy of the medium before they start manipulating its contents. Various other technical problems might arise; without the necessary tools and expertise to deal with them, any effort to read computer files at the scene is fraught with difficulty and risk.

Second, the process of searching the files at the scene can take a long time. To be certain that the medium in question does *not* contain any seizable material, the officers would have to examine every one of what may be thousands of files on a disk—a process that could take many hours and perhaps days. Taking that much time to conduct the search would not only impose a significant and unjustified burden on police resources, it would also make the search more intrusive. Police would have to be present on the suspect's premises while the search was in progress, and this would necessarily interfere with the suspect's access to his home or business. If the search took hours or days, the intrusion would continue for that entire period, compromising the Fourth Amendment value of making police searches as brief and non-intrusive as possible.

Because of these considerations, the court concluded that the police were not required to examine the electronic storage media at the scene to determine which contained child pornography and which did not; the police were, instead, "entitled to seize all such media and take them to the police station for examination by an expert."

The Ninth Circuit,[11] which affirmed Judge Kozinski's opinion, nonetheless required the government to obtain pre-authorization in the warrant process and cautioned:

---

11. United States v. Hill, 459 F.3d 966, 975 (9th Cir. 2006).

Although computer technology may in theory justify blanket searches [for the reasons stated by Judge Kozinski], the government must still demonstrate to the magistrate *factually* why such a broad search and seizure is reasonable in the case at hand. There may well be situations where the government has no basis for believing that a computer search would involve the kind of technological problems that would make an immediate onsite search and selective removal of relevant evidence impracticable. Thus, there must be some threshold showing before the government may "seize the haystack to look for the needle."

Although the warrant in this case authorized a wholesale seizure, the supporting affidavit did not explain why such a seizure was necessary.

We do not approve of issuing warrants authorizing blanket removal of all computer storage media for later examination when there is no affidavit giving a reasonable explanation.[n.12][12] Without such individualized justification being presented to the magistrate, we cannot be sure that the judge was aware of the officers' intent and the technological limitations meriting the indiscriminate seizure — and thus was intelligently able to exercise the court's oversight function. An explanatory statement in the affidavit also assures us that the officers could not reasonably describe the objects of their search with more specificity. Accordingly, we hold that the warrant here was overbroad in authorizing a blanket seizure in the absence of an explanatory supporting affidavit, which would have documented the informed endorsement of the neutral magistrate.

Nonetheless, we conclude that suppression of the evidence of child pornography found on the defendant's seized zip disks is not an appropriate remedy. The pornographic images from the defendant's zip disks that he sought to exclude as evidence at trial was "seized and retained lawfully because described in and therefore taken pursuant to the valid search warrant." As we have discussed above, the officers' wholesale seizure was flawed here because they failed to justify it to the magistrate, not because they acted unreasonably or improperly in executing the warrant. Because the officers were "motivated by considerations of practicality rather than by a desire to engage in indiscriminate 'fishing,' we cannot say . . . that the officers so abused the warrant's authority that the otherwise valid warrant was transformed into a general one, thereby requiring all fruits to be suppressed."

---

12. [n.12] The magistrate must be made aware of what officers are contemplating and why they are doing so. For some people, computer files are the exclusive means of managing one's life — such as maintaining a calendar of appointments or paying bills. Thus, there may be significant collateral consequences resulting from a lengthy, indiscriminate seizure of all such files. However, in this case the district court granted the defendant the right to "mirror copies" of the seized storage media.

Therefore, we hold that the district court properly admitted the evidence of child pornography found on the defendant's computer storage media notwithstanding the lack of a sufficiently detailed supporting affidavit describing the need for wholesale seizure of such media.

Other courts have also expressed concerns about such wholesale seizures due to the disruption of a business, professional practice, and personal lives that such seizures entail.[13] Accordingly, courts have been cautious in their approval of such practices.[14] Some urge that the government copy the data and return the equipment as soon as possible.[15] In response to the uncertainty surrounding digital evidence searches, Federal Rule of Criminal Procedure 41 was modified as follows:

(e)(B) Warrant Seeking Electronically Stored Information.

A warrant under Rule 41(e)(2)(A) may authorize the seizure of electronic storage media or the seizure or copying of electronically stored information. Unless otherwise specified, the warrant authorizes a later review of the media or information consistent with the warrant. The time for executing the warrant in Rule 41(e)(2)(A) and (f)(1)(A) refers to the seizure or on-site copying of the media or information, and not to any later off-site copying or review.

In the Matter of the Search of Information Associated with [redacted]@mac.com that is Stored at Premises Controlled by Apple, Inc.

13 F. Supp. 3d 157 (D.C.D.C. 2014)

RICHARD W. ROBERTS, Chief Judge

The government challenges an order by Magistrate Judge John M. Facciola denying its second application for a search warrant under § 2703 of the Stored Communications Act, 18 U.S.C. §§ 2701–12. The magistrate judge denied the government's

---

13. United States v. Hunter, 13 F. Supp. 2d 574, 583 (D. Vt. 1998).

14. *See, e.g.*, United States v. Upham, 168 F.3d 532, 535 (1st Cir. 1999):
Of course, if the images themselves could have been easily obtained through an on-site inspection, there might have been no justification for allowing the seizure of *all* computer equipment, a category potentially including equipment that contained no images and had no connection to the crime. But it is no easy task to search a well-laden hard drive by going through all of the information it contains, let alone to search through it and the disks for information that may have been "deleted." The record shows that the mechanics of the search for images later performed off site could not readily have been done on the spot.

15. United States v. Hunter, 13 F. Supp. 2d 574, 583 (D. Vt. 1998). *Cf.* United States v. Leveto, 343 F. Supp. 2d 434, 441 (W.D. Pa. 2004) (in large tax fraud scheme, involving many documents and computer files, factually describing how executing officials took "considerable steps" to minimize the "upheaval" of veterinarian's business, including copying computer files rather than removing the computers).

application on the ground that the requested warrant amounted to an unconstitutional general warrant due, in large part, to the procedures set forth in the application for executing the requested warrant. Because the government's application complies with the Fourth Amendment and the specific procedures for executing the warrant are permissible under Federal Rule of Criminal Procedure 41 and controlling case law, the magistrate judge's order will be vacated, and the government's application for a search warrant will be granted.

BACKGROUND

On March 5, 2014, the government filed under 18 U.S.C. § 2703 of the Stored Communications Act, 18 U.S.C. §§ 2701–2712 a sealed application for a search warrant for electronic communications and other evidence stored on a computer.[16][1] The government's search warrant application related to a specific email account, [redacted]@mac.com, and involved alleged violations of 41 U.S.C. § 8702 (kickbacks) and 18 U.S.C. § 371 (conspiracy). The government's application included an affidavit in support of the search warrant providing factual information to support a finding of probable cause. In addition, the government's application included two attachments that set forth the place to be searched and the particular items that the government intended to seize, including specific information that the electronic service provider, Apple, Inc., would be required to disclose. The magistrate judge denied the government's application for a search warrant in part because the application failed to clearly indicate that Apple was required to disclose e-mails in particular, and because probable cause had not been established for all of the emails requested in the search warrant. In addition, the magistrate judge objected to the government's use of Rule 41(e)'s "two-step procedure"[17][3] for gathering evidence whereby Apple would first be required to disclose to the government all e-mails associated with the target e-mail account, and then, at a later point, the government would examine the e-mails at separate location to identify evidence specified in Attachment B to the government's application.

---

16. [n.1] Under the Stored Communications Act, an electronic communications provider is required to disclose contents, records, and other information of an electronic communication to a governmental entity, with or without notice to the subscriber, provided that the statutory requirements are met. 18 U.S.C. § 2703(a), (b), (c)(1)(A). To require an electronic service provider to disclose either the contents of electronic communications, or records and other information, the governmental entity must "obtain[] a warrant issued using the procedures described in the Federal Rules of Criminal Procedure . . . by a court of competent jurisdiction." *Id.* § 2703(b)(1)(A), (c)(1)(A).

17. [n.3] Federal Criminal Rule 41(e) sets forth the requirements for issuing a warrant, such as the information that must be contained in the warrant and the proper protocol for executing the warrant. Courts are permitted to issue warrants for the "seizure of electronic storage media or the seizure or copying of electronically stored information." Fed. R. Crim. P. 41(e)(2)(B). Included in that provision is authorization for subsequent off-site review of electronic information obtained in accordance with the search warrant. The rule expressly "authorizes a later review of the media or information consistent with the warrant[.]"

The government filed a second application for a search warrant on March 28, 2014. In the revised application, the government indicated that the warrant applied to the e-mail account for "[redacted]@mac.com," and that the warrant covered "information . . . dating from January 14, 2014, to the present, and stored at premises controlled by Apple Inc." Attachment B set forth further details on the particular items to be seized, which included the following records:

> All e-mails, including e-mail content, attachments, source and destination addresses, and time and date information, that constitute evidence and instrumentalities of violations of 41 U.S.C § 8702 (Solicitation and Receipt of Kickbacks) and 18 U.S.C. § 371 (Conspiracy), dated between January 14, 2014, to the present, including e-mails referring or relating to a government investigation involving any or all of the following: [individuals and entities have been redacted].

Attachment C to the government's revised application included the specific procedures for executing the search warrant wherein the government would first "conduct a search of the e-mails produced by the Provider and determine which are within the scope of the information to be seized specified in Attachment B," and then copy and retain those emails that are "within the scope of Attachment B." Law enforcement personnel would then "seal any information from Apple that does not fall within the scope of Attachment B," and would be prohibited from "further review [of] the information absent an order of the Court."

The magistrate judge rejected the government's revised application for a search warrant in a second memorandum opinion. Reiterating the rationale set forth in the first memorandum opinion, the magistrate judge again denied the government's application for a search warrant finding that it violated the Fourth Amendment because it amounted to an overly broad search warrant. In addition, the magistrate judge rejected the government's use of the two-step procedure under Rule 41(e), stating that the government was "'abusing the two-step procedure under Rule 41' by requiring Apple to disclose the entire contents of an e-mail account." To avoid issuing a general warrant that would permit the government to seize large amounts of data not supported by probable cause, the magistrate judge recommended that Apple perform the necessary search and turn over any relevant information to the government.

The government filed a challenge to the magistrate judge's order on April 21, 2014, seeking review of the magistrate judge's decision denying the application for a search warrant. In its challenge, the government argues that the application for search warrant complies with the Fourth Amendment. In addition, the government argues that the two-step procedure for executing the search warrant is permitted under Federal Rule of Criminal Procedure 41.

DISCUSSION

The magistrate judge rejected the government's application as an unconstitutional general warrant not because the government failed to provide sufficient facts to support a finding of probable cause for the particular e-mails sought, or because the government failed to specify with particularity the electronic records to be seized or the place to search for those records. Rather, in denying the government's application, the magistrate judge determined that the government was attempting to "seize large quantities of e-mails for which it ha[d] not established probable cause." Moreover, the magistrate judge rejected the government's manner for executing the warrant described in Attachment C to the government's search warrant application. Under those procedures Apple would be required to disclose to the government *all* e-mails and records related to the [redacted] @mac.com e-mail account. Upon receiving the relevant emails and records, the government would then examine the information obtained to determine what e-mails and other records are specified in the warrant as items to be seized. The magistrate judge determined that because "the two-step procedure is a narrow exception that requires an affirmative showing of need in the warrant application," the government's application was deficient because it "fail[ed] to provide *any* explanation for why the two-step procedure is necessary."

However, the government's warrant and the procedures for the warrant's execution appear to comport with the Constitution. First, the government's search warrant properly restricts law enforcement discretion to determine the location to be searched and the items to be seized. The government identifies the precise location to be searched — in this case, the [redacted]@mac.com e-mail account — and specifies in the attachments to its application the particular e-mails to be seized. In this way, law enforcement discretion is constrained and limited to the items to be seized that are specified in Attachment B to the warrant.

Second, the information contained in the affidavit accompanying the search warrant supports a finding of probable cause because there is a fair probability that the electronic communications and records that the government seeks, which are described in detail in the attachments to the government's search warrant application, will be found in the particular place to be searched. Moreover, the affidavit includes additional background information on the particular types of records that must be disclosed, the specific crimes for which the government seeks evidence, and the targeted entities and individuals. When read together with the affidavit, the government's application provides detailed information of the alleged criminal scheme and a thorough explanation for why evidence relevant to the investigation is likely to be found in e-mail records and other data related to the target email account.

Furthermore, the procedures the government adopts for executing the search warrant comply with the Fourth Amendment and are permissible under Rule 41. "The Federal Rules of Criminal Procedure are carefully tailored ground rules for fair and orderly procedures in administering criminal justice. Rule 41 embodies standards which conform with the requirements of the Fourth Amendment." Rule 41 expressly contemplates and authorizes the procedures the government adopts here to execute the search warrant:

> Computers and other electronic storage media commonly contain such large
> amounts of information that it is often impractical for law enforcement to

review all of the information during execution of the warrant at the search location. This rule acknowledges the need for a two-step process: officers may seize or copy the entire storage medium and review it later to determine what electronically stored information falls within the scope of the warrant.

Fed. R. Crim. P. 41(e)(2) advisory committee's note. Several courts have found the two-step procedure to be reasonable under the Fourth Amendment, provided that there is a valid warrant supported by probable cause. *See, e.g., United States v. Schesso,* 730 F.3d 1040, 1046 (9th Cir.2013) (upholding government's seizure of electronic data for a subsequent off-site search where there was a fair probability that evidence would be found on the defendant's personal computer and other electronic devices); *United States v. Evers,* 669 F.3d 645, 652 (6th Cir. 2012) ("The federal courts are in agreement that a warrant authorizing the seizure of a defendant's home computer equipment and digital media for a subsequent off-site electronic search is not unreasonable or overbroad, as long as the probable-cause showing in the warrant application and affidavit demonstrate a 'sufficient chance of finding some needles in the computer haystack.'").

In addition, because the government's proposed procedures comply with the Fourth Amendment and are authorized by Rule 41, there is no need for Apple to search through e-mails and electronic records related to the target account and determine which e-mails are responsive to the search warrant. Enlisting a service provider to execute the search warrant could also present nettlesome problems. As the government argues persuasively in its challenge, it would be unworkable and impractical to order Apple to cull the e-mails and related records in order to find evidence that is relevant to the government's investigation. To begin with, non-governmental employees untrained in the details of the criminal investigation likely lack the requisite skills and expertise to determine whether a document is relevant to the criminal investigation. Moreover, requiring the government to train the electronic service provider's employees on the process for identifying information that is responsive to the search warrant may prove time-consuming, increase the costs of the investigation, and expose the government to potential security breaches.

As the government argues in its challenge, law enforcement officers are provided with considerable discretion in determining how to execute a particular search warrant. The Supreme Court has explained that a search warrant's execution is "generally left to the discretion of the executing officers to determine the details of how best to proceed with the performance of a search authorized by warrant[.]" That said, although law enforcement officers are afforded wide discretion in executing search warrants, "the manner in which a warrant is executed is subject to later judicial review as to its reasonableness."

Finally, it should be noted that it is certainly true that searches for electronic data may present increased risks to the individual's right to privacy as technological advances enable law enforcement to monitor and collect large volumes of electronic communications and other data. At the same time, searches for electronic data present unique challenges for law enforcement officials tasked with prosecuting crimes and gathering evidence relevant to criminal investigations. Indeed, the practical realities of searches for electronic records may require the government to examine information outside the scope of the search warrant to determine whether specific information is relevant to the criminal investigation and falls within the scope of the warrant. Given these competing interests, courts must strike the proper balance between ensuring that the government's ability to effectively and efficiently investigate and prosecute crimes is implemented and assuring respect for individuals' Fourth Amendment rights. With these considerations in mind, and for the reasons articulated above, the government's second application for a search warrant will be granted.[18][10]

§ 6.3 Use of Experts

Because of the complicated nature of the evidence and equipment that computer-related searches give rise to, governmental authorities sometimes use civilian computer experts to facilitate the execution of a search warrant. Challenges to the use of such experts, although few, have been consistently rejected.[19] The civilian, of course, must be "serving a legitimate investigative function,"[20] including using his or her special expertise to identify "property of a technical nature not generally familiar to law enforcement officers."[21] Approval has even extended to situations where the private experts performed the search outside of the presence of law enforcement officials.[22]

§ 6.4 Deleted Files

When a computer user "deletes" a file, the data that was contained in that file may remain in the computer memory:

---

18. [n.10] The government also asserts that destroying or returning the evidence received from Apple could either expose the government to accusations that it "destroyed exculpatory evidence in violation of *Brady v. Maryland,* [373 U.S. 83 (1963),]" or hinder the government's "ability to lay a foundation for evidence and establish authenticity under Rule 901 and 1001–1006 of the Federal Rules of Evidence." The concerns presented by the government are valid and the procedures for executing the search warrant strike the appropriate balance between the government's interest in protecting the integrity of its investigation and the privacy interests at stake.

19. *See, e.g.,* Bellville v. Town of Northboro, 375 F.3d 25 (1st Cir. 2004) ("Federal constitutional law does not proscribe the use of civilians in searches."); United States v. Schwimmer, 692 F. Supp. 119, 126–27 (E.D.N.Y. 1988) (summarily rejecting challenge to use of computer expert).

20. Bellville v. Town of Northboro, 375 F.3d 25 (1st Cir. 2004).

21. State v. Wade, 544 So. 2d 1028, 1030–31 (Fla. Dist. Ct. App. 1989) (computer experts from company from which computer equipment was stolen assisted in identifying equipment). *Accord* Bellville v. Town of Northboro, 375 F.3d 25 (1st Cir. 2004).

22. *See* United States v. Bach, 310 F.3d 1063, 1066–68 (8th Cir. 2002) (private Internet service provider employees searched suspect's email).

Most word processing programs use some form of a recycle bin, into which documents are transferred when deleted. Thus, a computer is also like a wastebasket of discarded material. In order to attempt to permanently delete such documents, the recycle bin must be emptied. However, even emptying the recycle bin may not actually delete the document or file because the information may still remain on the computer's hard drive.

The intentional deletion of a file does not permanently erase the file. Instead, the computer internally marks the file as not needed, and clears space for storage of other files. The erasure of information only occurs when the computer overwrites the file with another file. Even then, fragments of information may be retrievable if the entire file is not overwritten. Furthermore, word processing programs may have saved portions or versions of documents regardless of whether the user intentionally saves the final version.

Thus, in general, a file or document may not be removed from the hard drive of a computer until it is reformatted. However, even then, it may be possible to partially recover documents or files removed from a hard drive, depending on how the drive was reformatted. Further, the potential for deleted material to be stored on a hard drive, with or without intentional saving by the user, is not limited to word processing documents, but applies to other programs and functions of a computer as well.[23]

Because technicians can often recover much of that data using electronic search technology, courts have confronted a variety of issues regarding the admissibility of such "deleted" data. Some courts have addressed—and rejected—the government claim that the files have been abandoned.[24] The analogy of deletion of a file to putting one's trash out in the street is flawed, according to one court, because in the latter situation, but not the former, every passerby can search the trash.[25]

On the other hand, defendants have claimed that the recovery of deleted files is outside the scope of a warrant;[26] the assertion is that a second warrant is required or the scope of the original warrant has been exceeded because the "deletion" of the documents creates a new and legally different expectation of privacy protected by the Amendment.[27] Rejecting such a claim, one court has reasoned that an "attempt to secrete evidence of a crime is not synonymous with a legally cognizable

---

23. People v. Gall, 30 P.3d 145, 161 (Colo. 2001) (Martinez, J., dissenting).

24. *See, e.g.,* United States v. Upham, 168 F.3d 532, 537 n.3 (1st Cir. 1999). *Cf.* United States v. Angevine, 281 F.3d 1130, 1135 (10th Cir. 2002) (when defendant did not have access to data he previously attempted to delete on university owned computer, he had no reasonable expectation of privacy in that data).

25. United States v. Upham, 168 F.3d 532, 537 n.3 (1st Cir. 1999).

26. *See, e.g., id.* at 537 (recovery of deleted files no different than "pasting together scraps of a torn-up ransom note").

27. Commonwealth v. Copenhefer, 587 A.2d 1353, 1356 (Pa. 1991).

expectation of privacy." The court analogized the situation to a paper tablet and a diary recorded in a private code, both of which may be subjected to scientific analysis after seizure pursuant to a warrant; the court concluded that no second warrant was required "before subjecting legally seized physical evidence to scientific testing and analysis to make it divulge its secrets."

§ 6.5 Time Periods for Warrants to Be Valid

Many jurisdictions require that a search warrant be executed within a designated period of time. For example, the federal rule requires that, except for tracking devices, the warrant must be executed within 14 days from the date the magistrate signed the warrant.[28] Execution of the warrant after that specified period of time has elapsed, and thus execution in violation of the governing statutory or procedural rules, could lead a court to find the warrant void.[29] If the warrant is invalid, the search would be considered warrantless and the standards applicable to a warrantless search or seizure would be applied. Hence, for example, if the place to be searched is a home and the warrant is invalid, it would be unreasonable unless the search fits within an exception to the warrant preference rule.

Other courts have a much different view, finding that, because the Fourth Amendment does not specify that a search warrant contain an expiration date,[30] the execution of a warrant in violation of a rule of procedure requires suppression of evidence only where "(1) there was 'prejudice' in the sense that the search might not have occurred or would not have been so abrasive if the rule had been followed, or (2) there is evidence of intentional and deliberate disregard of a provision in the Rule."[31] Probable cause can become stale and, for some courts, it may be conclusively presumed if the warrant is not executed within the time frame set by the applicable rule or statute.[32] On the other hand, merely executing the warrant within

---

28. Fed. R. Crim. P. 41(e)(2)(A)(I).

29. *E.g.*, State v. Miguel, 101 P.3d 214 (Ariz. Ct. App. 2004) (when statute set five day period to execute search warrant and warrant was not executed within that period, warrant became "void"); Spera v. State, 467 So. 2d 329 (Fla. Dist. Ct. App. 1985) (warrant not served within period specified by rule is void as stale). Presumably to avoid this result, some courts have adopted the reasonable continuation of a search warrant doctrine, which permits more than one entry at different times under a warrant, even if the latter entries are outside the statutory or rule-based time limit. *E.g.*, United States v. Keszthelyi, 308 F.3d 557, 568 (6th Cir. 2002) (collecting cases); United States v. Gerber, 994 F.2d 1556, 1559–60 (11th Cir. 1993) (collecting cases); People v. Superior Court, 151 Cal. App. 4th 85, 99–100 (2007) (completing search after statutory time limit expired results in no constitutional violation so long as probable cause to search still exists).

30. *See* State v. Miller, 429 N.W.2d 26, 34–35 (S.D. 1988).

31. Steffensen v. State, 900 P.2d 735, 739 (Alaska Ct. App. 1995) (collecting cases).

32. *E.g.*, State v. Miguel, 101 P.3d 214 (Ariz. Ct. App. 2004) (time period set by statute to execute warrant is legislative determination that probable cause will have dissipated; thus, when statute set five day period to execute search warrant and warrant was not executed within that period, the warrant was "void").

the time period specified by the rule or statute does not conclusively show that probable cause has not become stale.[33]

A few courts fail to distinguish between the period of time to execute a warrant, that is, the actual search of the location specified in the warrant, and the later examination of evidence seized from the location of the search.[34] In contrast, in *State v. Miller*, 429 N.W.2d 26 (S.D. 1988), the defendant challenged the examination of blood evidence found in his vehicle as a second search separate from the one where it had been recovered. The court rejected the contention that it was a search: "Once blood was found, in timely fashion, the vehicle could be seized as evidence of the crime committed. Subsequent examination of evidence to determine its evidentiary value does not constitute a search."

In *State v. Petrone*, 468 N.W.2d 676 (Wis. 1991), the court believed that the police could develop film that was properly seized under a warrant. The defendant had asserted that developing the film was "a second, separate search for which a warrant should have been obtained." Disagreeing with that claim, the court asserted: "A search warrant does not limit officers to naked-eye inspections of objects lawfully seized in the execution of a warrant." It reasoned:

> Developing the film is simply a method of examining a lawfully seized object. Law enforcement officers may employ various methods to examine objects lawfully seized in the execution of a warrant. For example, blood stains or substances gathered in a lawful search may be subjected to laboratory analysis. The defendant surely could not have objected had the deputies used a magnifying glass to examine lawfully seized documents or had enlarged a lawfully seized photograph in order to examine the photograph in greater detail. Developing the film made the information on the film accessible, just as laboratory tests expose what is already present in a substance but not visible with the naked eye. Developing the film did not constitute, as the defendant asserts, a separate, subsequent unauthorized search having an intrusive impact on the defendant's rights wholly independent of

---

33. *E.g.*, State v. Swift, 556 N.W.2d 243, 249 (Neb. 1996) (Although statute required that warrant be executed and returned within ten days of issuance, "it does not follow that compliance with the legislatively imposed time limit will in every instance result in a valid search." Whether a delay in executing a search warrant is unconstitutional depends on whether the probable cause set forth in the affidavit still exists at the time of the execution of the warrant.).

34. *See* United States v. Syphers, 426 F.3d 461, 468–69 (1st Cir. 2005) (although the computer was seized by the police in a timely manner, it was not forensically examined until almost five months later; although recognizing that Rule 41 did not apply because the warrant was issued by a state court, viewing the later examination of the computer as a delay in the execution of the warrant). *Cf.* Commonwealth v. Aviles, 790 N.E.2d 1103, 1106–07 (Mass. Ct. App. 2003) (recognizing that evidence lawfully obtained by police is subject to scientific testing). *But cf.* United States v. Brunette, 76 F. Supp. 2d 30 (D. Me. 1999) (imposing in the warrant a thirty day time limit for forensic analysis of the computer; when the analysis was not completed within the period specified and after granting an extension of time, suppressing the evidence recovered that was outside that time period), *aff'd*, 256 F.3d 14 (1st Cir. 2001).

the execution of the search warrant. The deputies simply used technological aids to assist them in determining whether items within the scope of the warrant were in fact evidence of the crime alleged. Because the undeveloped film was lawfully seized pursuant to the warrant, the deputies were justified in developing and viewing the film.

Moving from these more conventional forensic examinations of objects lawfully seized, some believe that digital evidence presents a different set of issues. Instead of the traditional search and seizure sequence, some commentators see the sequence as involving first a search, then a seizure (of the storage devices containing the digital evidence), followed by another search of those devices for the relevant digital evidence.[35] As a consequence, some commentators have proposed special rules to regulate digital evidence searches.[36] Of the few courts that have addressed the issue, however, most perceive that the federal rule and similar state rules regulate the initial time period for searching for and seizing the evidence and that the forensic examination of the digital evidence — like the forensic examination of other seized evidence — is not a new search.[37]

---

35. *See* Orin S. Kerr, *Search Warrants in an Era of Digital Evidence*, 75 Miss. L.J. 85, 86–87 (2005):

> The existing law governing the warrant process presumes single-step searches common to the collection of traditional physical evidence. The investigators enter the place to be searched, seize the property named in the warrant, and then leave. With computer searches, however, the one-step search process is replaced by a two-step search process. The investigators enter the place to be searched; seize the computer hardware; take the hardware off site; and then later search the equipment for the data it contains that may be evidence of crime. Two searches occur instead of one: the physical search comes first, and the electronic search comes second. Notably, in most cases the two searches are quite distinct: they occur at different times, in different places, and are performed by different people.

See also In re Search of 3817 W. West End, 321 F. Supp. 2d 953, 958 (N.D. Ill. 2004) ("It is frequently the case with computers that the normal sequence of 'search' and then selective 'seizure' is turned on its head. Because of the difficulties of conducting an on-site search of computers, the government frequently seeks (and, as here, obtains), authority to seize computers without any prior review of their contents."); Susan W. Brenner & Barbara A. Frederiksen, *Computer Searches and Seizures: Some Unresolved Issues*, 8 Mich. Telecomm. Tech. L. Rev. 39, 82 (2001–2002) ("In off-site computer searches, the execution of a warrant involves four stages, not two: a search designed to locate computer equipment; the seizure of that equipment and its removal to another location; a thorough search of the contents of the equipment which is conducted at that location; and a seizure of relevant evidence located in the course of that search.").

36. *See generally* Orin S. Kerr, *Search Warrants in an Era of Digital Evidence*, 75 Miss. L.J. 85 (2005).

37. *E.g.*, State v. Johnson, 831 N.W.2d 917 (Minn. Ct. App. 2013); United States v. Gorrell, 360 F. Supp. 2d 48, 55 n.5 (D.D.C. 2004); United States v. Hernandez, 183 F. Supp. 2d 468, 480 (D.P.R. 2002); State v. Grenning, 174 P.3d 706, 713–14 (Wash. Ct. App. 2008). *Cf.* People v. Shinohara, 872 N.E.2d 498 (Ill. Ct. App. 2007) (complex analysis of distinction between searching and seizing a computer and its forensic analysis and alternatively distinguishing between the forensic analysis and the initial search, that the rule regulating the time to search did not apply, and that any delay was not prejudicial).

State v. Keith R. Nadeau

1 A.3d 445 (Me. 2010)

LEVY, J.

[Nadeau's computer was lawfully seized by the police, who then sought a search warrant to examine its contents.] The search warrant was issued on December 11, 2007, and contained the following directive: "This warrant shall be executed between the hours of 7:00 A.M. and 9:00 P.M. and shall be returned, together with a written inventory, within 10 days of the issuance hereof, to the Maine District Court in Farmington." Nadeau argues that the completion of the forensic search of his computer on July 21, 2008, long exceeded the ten-day period specified by the warrant and was therefore unconstitutional because the warrant had expired. The State contends that the failure to complete the forensic examination of the computer within the ten-day period does not justify the exclusion of that evidence, arguing that "the complexity of computer searches require[s] more flexibility with regard to the manner in which the evidence is obtained."

Rule 41(d) of the Maine Rules of Criminal Procedure explicitly requires that warrants be executed and returned within ten days:

> The warrant may be executed and returned only within 10 days after its date. Upon the expiration of the 10 days, the warrant must be returned to the District Court designated in the warrant.

In *State v. Guthrie*, 90 Me. 448, 449, 38 A. 368, 368 (1897), we addressed the issue regarding the timing of the execution of a search warrant. In that case, we held that an unexplained three-day delay in executing a search warrant, once it had been issued, resulted in the warrant's expiration. We observed that search warrants are powerful investigative tools, the execution of which requires close judicial scrutiny and oversight: "[A search warrant] is a sharp and heavy police weapon to be used most carefully lest it wound the security or liberty of the citizen." To guard against the unlawful invasion of personal liberty, we concluded, "It is an integral principle in our system of law and government that ministerial officers assuming to execute a statute or process upon the property or person of a citizen shall execute it promptly, fully and precisely." Failure to execute a search warrant promptly rendered the warrant "functus officio."[n.9][38]

The execution of a search warrant is the act of lawfully searching for and taking possession of property as authorized by the warrant. Unlike *Guthrie*, where the police did not search for or take possession of the item that was described in the search warrant until after the warrant had expired, the officers in this case were

---

38. [n.9] Functus officio means "without further authority or legal competence because the duties and functions of the original commission have been fully accomplished."

already in possession of the computer at the time the warrant was issued. Thus, the warrant in the present case was effectively executed at the time it was issued, and there was no danger that a search for the computer conducted after the expiration of the ten-day period would result in a seizure based on stale probable cause. Further, once law enforcement officials are in lawful possession of an item, they need not obtain a search warrant each and every time they examine the item. *See United States v. Hernandez*, 183 F. Supp. 2d 468, 480 (D.P.R. 2002) ("The documents are seized within the time frame established in the warrant but examination of these documents may take a longer time, and extensions or additional warrants are not required."); *see also United States v. Triumph Capital Group, Inc.*, 211 F.R.D. 31, 65 (D. Conn. 2002) (holding that a special agent's subsequent searches of computer data, which was obtained from an initial search and seizure conducted pursuant to a warrant, were "not analogous to returning to a crime scene to search for additional evidence and do not establish an impermissible, warrantless second or continuing search"). Thus, the State's forensic examination of the computer after the ten-day return period specified in the warrant was neither unconstitutional nor a violation of M.R. Crim. P. 41(d).

Notes

In response to concerns about the execution of warrants for digital devices, Federal Rule of Criminal Procedure 41 was modified to provide:

(f) **Executing and Returning the Warrant.**

(1) **Warrant to Search for and Seize a Person or Property.**

(B) **Inventory.** An officer present during the execution of the warrant must prepare and verify an inventory of any property seized. The officer must do so in the presence of another officer and the person from whom, or from whose premises, the property was taken. If either one is not present, the officer must prepare and verify the inventory in the presence of at least one other credible person. In a case involving the seizure of electronic storage media or the seizure or copying of electronically stored information, the inventory may be limited to describing the physical storage media that were seized or copied. The officer may retain a copy of the electronically stored information that was seized or copied.

Chapter 7

Consent Searches; Compelling Disclosure of Passwords

This chapter addresses the validity of consent to search computers—a Fourth Amendment issue—and addresses compelling a suspect to disclose his password or encryption key—a Fifth Amendment issue.

§ 7.1 Consent—In General

The principles regulating the permissibility of a search or seizure based on a claim of consent do not change in the context of computer and other digital evidence searches.[1] However, computers and digital evidence searches present several challenges to the application of those principles.

Consent to search is a question of fact and is determined based on the totality of the circumstances.[2] The ultimate question turns on the voluntary nature of the consent.[3] A person may "delimit as he chooses the scope of the search to which he consents."[4] The government, in performing a search, cannot exceed the scope of the consent given. This is an objective inquiry: "what would the typical reasonable person have understood by the exchange between the officer and the suspect?"[5] Moreover, the scope of a consensual search is generally defined by its expressed object.[6]

---

1. *See, e.g.*, United States v. Mabe, 330 F. Supp. 2d 1234 (D. Utah 2004) (rejecting assertion that defendant consented to search of computer after police falsely stated that they had search warrant); People v. Yuruckso, 297 A.D.2d 299, 299–300 (N.Y. App. Div. 2002) (consent to search home computer valid, based on defendant's maturity, education, and other factors, even though police stated that, if he did not consent, they would obtain a search warrant and seize his work computer).

2. Ohio v. Robinette, 519 U.S. 33 (1996).

3. *See, e.g.*, Schneckloth v. Bustamonte, 412 U.S. 218, 219 (1973). Voluntariness—meaning the lack of coercion by the government agents—must be established. However, the consent need not be an informed one, which is to say that the person giving the consent need not know that he or she has the right to refuse, which is the essential holding of *Schneckloth*.

4. Florida v. Jimeno, 500 U.S. 248, 252 (1991). *Cf.* United States v. Lemmons, 282 F.3d 920, 924–25 (7th Cir. 2002) (although suspect gave limited consent initially, his later consent to search computer made search valid).

5. Florida v. Jimeno, 500 U.S. 248, 251 (1991).

6. *Id. See also* United States v. Raney, 342 F.3d 551, 558 (7th Cir. 2003) (seizure of "homemade" adult pornography within scope of consent to search for "'materials [that] are evidence in the nature of' child abuse, child erotica, or child exploitation" as it showed ability and intent

This is to say that consent "extends to the entire area in which the object of the search may be found and is not limited by the possibility that separate acts of entry or opening may be required to complete the search."[7]

For example, when a graduate student in computer science agreed to allow agents to search his entire home and to take his computer back to the FBI office for further examination, it was held that the student "would have realized that the examination of his computer would be more than superficial when the agents explained that they did not have the skills nor the time to perform the examination in his home."[8] Moreover, according to the court, "a graduate student in computer science would clearly understand the technological resources of the FBI and its ability to thoroughly examine his computer." Given the lack of limitations put on the search by the student, his cooperation, and his expertise, the court believed it was reasonable for the agents to conclude that they had unlimited access to the computer.

———————

§ 7.2 Consent — Scope Issues

People v. Robert S. Prinzing

907 N.E.2d 87 (Ill. App. Ct. 2009)

JUSTICE BOWMAN delivered the opinion of the court.

Robert S. Prinzing was convicted of possessing child pornography. He argues that, even if his consent was valid, the evidence should have been suppressed because the police exceeded the scope of his consent. We agree that the police exceeded the scope of the consent, and we reverse and remand.

The trial court held an evidentiary hearing on defendant's motion to suppress. Detective Smith testified as follows. He was employed with the Kane County sheriff's department and assigned to computer crimes and forensics. On October 29, 2003, he spoke with Ronald Wolfick, a special agent with Immigration and Customs Enforcement. Wolfick provided Detective Smith with information regarding

———————

to manufacture pornography depicting himself in sexual acts); United States v. Turner, 169 F.3d 84, 88–89 (1st Cir. 1999) (scope of defendant's permission to search apartment in connection with intruder's assault on neighbor exceeded when police accessed files on his computer because the police request would have been reasonably understood to be that they intended to search for physical evidence of the assault); State v. Brown, 813 N.E.2d 956, 960 (Ohio Ct. App. 2004) (scope of defendant's consent exceeded when police seized two computers from his home when he had merely given consent to look at computers).

7. United States v. Ross, 456 U.S. 798, 820–21 (1982). *See also* Florida v. Jimeno, 500 U.S. 248, 251 (1991) (consent to search car included closed paper bag on floor of car); Commonwealth v. Hinds, 768 N.E.2d 1067, 1071 (Mass. 2002) (when defendant consented to search of his computer for electronic mail, valid search not limited to specific directories or locations on computer).

8. United States v. Al-Marri, 230 F. Supp. 2d 535, 539–40 (S.D.N.Y. 2002).

online credit card purchases of child pornography and provided the credit card number used, which belonged to defendant. Detective Smith obtained a subpoena and contacted the bank that issued the credit card. The bank told Detective Smith that a fraudulent charge had been reported around the time that the card was used to purchase child pornography. The bank relayed that a new account number had been issued. On May 25, 2004, Detective Smith, along with Detective Grimes, went to defendant's residence. Detective Smith identified himself and stated that he was investigating fraud involving defendant's credit card. Detective Smith inquired "as to his card usage, the geographical area [in which] he might have used it, also if it was ever out of his control and through the course of the conversation trying to determine if he had lost control of that card where someone else could have acquired his credit card numbers." Defendant retrieved his credit card and gave it to Detective Smith. Detective Smith recognized the number as the one that had been used to purchase child pornography. Defendant told Detective Smith that he owned the credit card and maintained exclusive control over the card. Defendant stated that he used the card in the local area, when he went on trips, and occasionally for Internet purchases. Detective Smith asked defendant whether there had been any fraud reported on his credit card. Defendant stated that there had been an incident of fraud, his money was refunded, and he was issued a replacement card.

Detective Smith told defendant that if he used the card on the Internet, there was opportunity for others to steal his information. Detective Smith asked defendant if he still possessed the computer that he used to make Internet purchases. If there was any evidence of his system being compromised by unsafe Internet Web sites or a virus, it would likely be on the computer used to make Internet purchases. Defendant denied noticing any suspicious activity on his credit card. Defendant worked for Comcast and was very knowledgeable about computers, impressing Detective Smith. Defendant denied having any suspicion that the security on his computer had been compromised. Detective Smith testified that a virus could infect a computer when a person received a spam e-mail or visited a particular Web site embedded with the virus. He had an investigatory tool that allowed him to check for such viruses.

Detective Smith asked defendant if he could search his computer by using a special program, with the intent of trying to determine how his credit card information might have been stolen. Defendant consented. According to Detective Smith, he initially used a noninvasive tool to perform a "preview," which prevents any changes from happening to the computer when the system is turned off and on. The "preview" allows detectives to view the hard drive but prevents them from making any changes to any of its files. Normally, after the "preview" program, Detective Smith would use a program called "Image scan." The image scan looks for images related to Web pages to get a history of pages that the user has visited. The program brings up thumbnail images from Web pages. Depending upon what is found, he then would use a tool that would look for viruses or any key stroke loggers, which capture key strokes and send the information to a remote location. Detective Smith began the search of defendant's computer by using the image scan program. He was looking for thumbnails with the Visa logo, not for child pornography. Detective Smith testified that he did not inform defendant that he believed that his credit card information had been used to access child pornography Web sites, because "at this point [he] didn't feel that [defendant] still had been — was the offender. [Detective Smith] was curious as to how his information could have been compromised." He was concerned that defendant's credit card may have been compromised not once, but twice. Detective Smith explained that "when you visit a web site, if you go to make a purchase, you will see a Visa logo. That will be captured. Whatever the merchandise is being offered on that particular web page, it will have graphics that will show that." A Visa credit card number will not be captured. Detective Smith would have to click on the image to get to the vendor's Web site.

Detective Smith found several images that he suspected were child pornography. He found the images within 10 to 15 minutes after he began the scan. He denied that he was specifically looking for child pornography. Rather, he was looking for information related to defendant's credit card. He considered his investigation up to this point to be related to credit card fraud because there was evidence of only a few attempts to access the pornographic Web sites, whereas other investigations involved numerous attempts.

On cross-examination, Detective Smith admitted[, *inter alia*,] that he was specifically assigned to review cases that involved Internet child pornography [and that he was investigating the defendant for possession of child pornography].

Defendant testified. Around 5 p.m. on May 25, 2004, two detectives arrived at defendant's home. They told him that they were investigating a fraud case, which he thought was unusual considering that he did not have any complaints regarding any type of fraud. The detectives questioned him for approximately 10 or 15 minutes regarding his credit cards and credit card numbers. They asked if he had a particular credit card but did not inform him how they had acquired his credit card information. He produced all of the credit cards in his wallet. He told Detective Smith that he had a disputed charge at one time but that it had been resolved and he had been issued a new card. He thought that perhaps the credit card number that the detectives had was his old card number. His disputed charge took place sometime in June 2003. He had another disputed charge in August 2003, but a new card was not issued then. The detectives asked about his card usage and whether he was the sole user. They then asked to view his computer to check for viruses that could have stolen his credit card information. Defendant stated that "Detective Smith asked to view [the] computer to look for viruses, you know, signs that [a] hacker had been in [defendant's] computer, Trojan horses, worms, anything that might possibly capture key strokes that [he] was typing in to get [his] credit card information." He initially told the detectives that he did not feel it was necessary, because he had several firewalls in place and felt secure in his computer usage. Detective Smith insisted that it would be better for him to check defendant's computer because his programs were better than anything that is available commercially. After the third request, defendant agreed to allow Detective Smith to check his computer.

Detective Smith then produced a USB port cable and a couple of disks that he retrieved from his briefcase. He inserted a disk into defendant's computer, rebooted it, and then began looking at images that were on the computer. Defendant stated that it appeared that the program was creating files of pictures, because Detective Smith went to "a directory and [was] opening up different files, and every time he opened one up, it was populating with pictures from [the] computer." Defendant never saw any images with credit card logos; he saw only images that he had downloaded from the Internet or from his digital camera. Defendant was employed by Comcast, and he regularly checked systems for viruses. The programs he used to check for viruses never brought up images but only executable files. Viruses are not embedded in images but are executable programs. He thought it was odd that Detective Smith was looking only at pictures but defendant did not say anything. After about 15 to 20 minutes, Detective Smith stated that he was done looking at the computer and that he found an image that he felt was child pornography.

In its ruling, the trial court stated that it believed that Detective Smith's investigation of defendant initially related to child pornography, morphed into a credit card fraud investigation when he discovered that there was a disputed charge on defendant's card, and then, after he discovered child pornography on defendant's computer, morphed back to a child pornography investigation.

[After first determining] that defendant's consent was voluntary, we now examine whether the police exceeded the scope of the consent. In evaluating the scope of a defendant's consent, the court considers what a reasonable person would have understood by the exchange between the officer and the defendant. "[T]he parameters of a search are usually defined by the purpose of the search."

In this case, principles of law and technology collide. The court in *People v. Berry*, 731 N.E.2d 853 (Ill. App. 2000), addressed the scope of consent with respect to electronic devices, specifically a cellular phone. The *Berry* court stated that the lack of knowledge of what the officer is searching for does not change the effect of a "general" consent. If a consent to search is entirely open-ended, a reasonable person would have no cause to believe that the search will be limited in some way, and the consent would include consent to search the memory of electronic devices. The *Berry* court then considered the totality of the circumstances, which involved a detective asking to look at the defendant's cell phone and the defendant responding "'go right ahead.'" The officer, after receiving the defendant's response, opened the phone and retrieved the phone number of the phone by pressing a button. The defendant knew when the detective asked to search the phone that he was investigating a murder and that he was trying to determine whether the defendant owned the phone, and the defendant placed no explicit limitations on the scope of the search, either when he gave his general consent or while the officer examined the phone. Therefore, the court determined that, based on the totality of the circumstances, the detective did not exceed the scope of the defendant's general consent to search his phone when the detective activated the phone and retrieved the phone number.

Federal courts have also considered the scope of electronic device searches. In *United States v. Lemmons*, 282 F.3d 920, 925 (7th Cir. 2002), the court determined based on the totality of the circumstances that a police search did not exceed the defendant's general consent to search his computer. The police originally obtained consent to search for video recordings of the defendant's neighbor's bedroom. Once inside, the defendant showed police a sexually explicit photograph of his 17-year-old daughter. The police then asked whether there was anything on the defendant's computer that they should be aware of, and the defendant turned the computer on and invited the officers to look. The officers then opened images saved on the computer that were pornographic images of children. The court stated that the officers' search of the computer may have been illegal if the defendant had stuck to his original consent to search for a camera or recording device, or if he had limited his consent to search his computer to images of his neighbor, depending on the defendant's labeling system or other variables. Because the defendant did not limit the consent to search his computer, the police did not exceed the scope by searching random images.

In *United States v. Brooks*, 427 F.3d 1246, 1249 (10th Cir. 2005), the police requested to search the defendant's computer for child pornography by means of a "pre-search" disk. The police told the defendant that the pre-search disk would bring up all the images on the computer in a thumbnail format so that they could check for images of child pornography. Defendant asked if it would search text files and he was told that it would not. For some reason, the disk was not operating on the defendant's computer, so the officers performed a manual search of images. The defendant complained that the police exceeded the scope of his consent because they did not use the pre-search disk as he was told. The court disagreed, finding that the method in which the search was performed was irrelevant because the defendant knew that images would be searched and the officers searched only images and nothing more.

We find this case distinguishable from *Berry, Lemmons,* and *Brooks* because those cases dealt with general consents to search. Here, Detective Smith, by his own words, limited the scope of the intended computer search. Detective Smith specifically requested to search defendant's computer for viruses or key-logging programs to find out if defendant's credit card number had been stolen. The exchange between Detective Smith and defendant involved only an investigation of credit card fraud and the potential that someone had stolen defendant's credit card number by way of a computer virus. By Detective Smith's own description of the scanning programs that he normally used, the image scan disk searched images and Web site pages on the computer. According to Detective Smith's testimony, if an image came up with a Visa logo, Detective Smith could click on it and he would be brought to the Web page of the vendor. He did not testify that the vendor Web page would indicate whether defendant's credit card number was compromised. In fact, according to defendant, who worked for Comcast, no image would lead Detective Smith to discover a virus that could steal defendant's credit card number, as viruses and key-logging programs are executable files and not embedded in any image. Defendant consented to a search only for viruses, not images. Thus, we find that Detective Smith's search exceeded the scope of defendant's consent.

JUSTICE O'MALLEY, dissenting:

The . . . question is whether the police exceeded the scope of defendant's consent by viewing the images on his computer.

The principle to be drawn is not that an officer may have no purpose for a consent search ulterior to his stated purpose, but instead that a description of the purpose of a search can serve as an indicator of the scope of the contemplated search and thus can help define the scope of the consent. The restriction on the search comes not from the stated purpose of the search, but from what a reasonable person would have understood the extent of the consent to be—*i.e.*, what areas a reasonable person would have understood police had been granted authority to search. Courts say that the scope of a search generally is defined by its purpose because the stated purpose of a proposed search will often be the only explanation of the scope of the proposed search: the scope of a consent to a "search for drugs" without further explanation will be understood in those terms. Thus, police who describe a proposed automobile search by telling the suspect that they wish to search for liquor will have limited the scope of their search to places where liquor could be found, but any other contraband found in the course of that search may still lawfully be seized. Or, police who tell a suspect that they intend to search for weapons when they actually expect to find drugs may still seize drugs during their search, because "such a statement on the part of [law enforcement] could [not] affect the validity of [the suspect's] consent, the area to be searched being identical in either event."

It becomes very important to determine precisely how Smith and defendant described the requested search before defendant assented. The testimony is ambiguous on this point. It is true, as the majority and the parties note, that Smith told defendant that his purpose in searching the computer was to look for malware. However, the testimony does not include any description of how Smith described to defendant the process by which he would search the computer for malware. The majority seems to assume from this gap in the testimony that the only description given was that Smith would perform a "virus search," and the majority therefore repeats or implies several times that the scope of the consent was limited accordingly. I disagree with the majority's assumption.

Although the testimony does not directly state what Smith and defendant discussed prior to defendant's consent, it does provide clues. When asked to describe how he would search defendant's computer for malware, Smith described using an "image scan" program that boots the computer in a read-only mode and then calls up all of the images on the computer. The majority and the parties incorrectly imply that Smith testified that he examined the images themselves for signs of malware, but in his testimony Smith actually described differently the connection between the image scan and the search for malware. Smith said that he used the program to search for viruses because the program revealed the origin of each of the images, and, for those images originating from Web sites, Smith could ask defendant if he recalled visiting the sites. According to Smith, "[i]f someone [was] accessing his computer remotely unbeknownst to him, he [could] tell [Smith] then and there" that he had not visited the sites. Smith said that he focused his search on images portraying credit card logos, because such images often appear on Web pages that collect credit card numbers for purchases.

The efficacy of this "image viewing" technique as a virus search, especially when compared to the type of actual virus search Smith testified he forwent in order to do the image search, is questionable—a point with which the majority appears to agree. However, the issue here is not whether Smith pursued a search that would reveal viruses but, rather, whether he pursued a search consistent with the scope of the consent he had obtained, *i.e.*, consistent with what a reasonable person would have understood as the scope of the consent defendant granted. Smith's testimony contains the following passage:

> "Q. And when you asked him to view his—when you asked about his computer, was that your intent to try and use those programs?
>
> A. Yes, sir.
>
> Q. And did you, in fact, inform the defendant of that?
>
> A. Yes sir."

In the absence of testimony that directly relates how Smith described the program to defendant before defendant agreed to the search, Smith's description of the image scan program as a tool for detecting malware, convincing or not, gives us insight into the conversation referenced in his testimony.

Defendant's actions after the image search began provide added insight into what the two men discussed before defendant granted consent. Smith testified that defendant was in the room when Smith started the image scan program, watched as Smith conducted a review of the images on the computer, and continued to talk to Smith as Smith ran the program, yet never asked Smith to stop viewing the pictures. While it is true that a defendant's silence cannot be used to transform the original scope of the consent, it can provide an indication that the search was within the scope of the consent.

From the above, I infer that Smith discussed the image scan program with defendant before defendant granted consent, and, even if I were to conclude that Smith misled defendant as to the purpose of using the program, I would conclude that Smith's use of the program fell within the scope of the consent.

Notes

What is the permissible scope of a search of a computer for "viruses?" Is that a technical question? Is looking at logos within the scope of such a search? What evidence would you seek to introduce on this question?

——————

1. Scope: Does Consent to Search Include Forensic Exam?

United States v. Jonathan Luken

560 F.3d 741 (8th Cir. 2009)

MELLOY, CIRCUIT JUDGE.

An Immigration and Customs Enforcement investigation revealed that two credit card numbers believed to be Luken's were used in 2002 and 2003 to purchase child pornography from a website in Belarus. On July 25, 2006, three law-enforcement officers visited Luken at his place of employment. One of the officers, Agent Troy Boone of the South Dakota Department of Criminal Investigation, informed Luken that the officers believed Luken's credit card had been used to purchase child pornography. Boone told Luken that the officers wanted to speak with Luken privately about the matter and look at his home computer. Luken agreed to speak with them at his home and drove himself to his house to meet them.

Upon arriving at Luken's home, Luken allowed the officers to enter his house. Luken's wife was home, so Boone offered to speak with Luken privately in Boone's car. Luken agreed. Once inside the car, Boone informed Luken that Luken did not have to answer any questions, was not under arrest, and was free to leave. Luken nevertheless agreed to speak with Boone. Luken discussed the nature of his computer use and knowledge. He admitted to purchasing and downloading child pornography for several years. He also admitted to looking at child pornography within the previous month. He stated, however, that he believed he had no child pornography saved on his computer.

After Luken admitted to viewing child pornography, Boone asked Luken if officers could examine Luken's computer. Boone explained the nature of computer searches to Luken and told Luken that, even if files had been deleted, police often could recover them with special software. Boone asked Luken if a police search would reveal child pornography in Luken's deleted files. Luken stated that there might be "nature shots" on his computer, i.e., pictures of naked children not in sexually explicit positions, that he recently viewed for free. Boone then asked Luken to consent to a police search of Luken's computer, and Boone drafted a handwritten consent agreement stating, "On 7-25-06, I, Jon Luken, give law enforcement the permission to seize & view my Gateway computer." Luken signed and dated the agreement.

[The police seized the computer and Boone later] used forensic software to analyze it. Boone discovered approximately 200 pictures he considered child pornography.

The question before us is whether it was reasonable for Boone to consider Luken's consent to seize and "view" his computer to include consent to perform a forensic analysis on it. We believe it was.

Before Luken consented to police seizing and viewing his computer, Luken initially had told Boone that Luken believed there was no child pornography saved on his computer. Boone, however, explained to Luken that police could recover deleted files using special software. Boone then specifically asked Luken if such a search would reveal child pornography on Luken's computer. Luken responded that there probably would be such material on his computer and stated that police might find "nature shots" if they did such a search. At that point, Luken gave Boone permission to seize and view his computer without placing "any explicit limitation on the scope of the search."

Given the above-described exchange, we agree with the district court that a typical reasonable person would have understood that Luken gave Boone permission to forensically examine Luken's computer. Boone made it apparent to Luken that police intended to do more than merely turn on Luken's computer and open his easily accessible files. Boone explained that police possessed software to recover deleted files and asked Luken specifically if such software would reveal child pornography on Luken's computer. Luken responded by telling Boone that such a search would likely reveal some child pornography. He then gave Boone permission to seize and view the computer. In that context, a typical reasonable person would understand the scope of the search that was about to take place. Therefore, because we affirm the district court's finding that Luken consented to the search, we hold there were no Fourth Amendment violations.

---

2. Cell Phones: Scope of Consent

Jermaine L. Smith v. State

713 N.E.2d 338 (Ind. Ct. App. 1999)

Kirsch, Judge.

Smith appeals his conviction of theft, for using a "cloned" cellular telephone reprogrammed to have an internal electronic serial number ("ESN") different than its external ESN. Put in the vernacular, Smith was convicted of using an illegal cellular phone which had been modified such that, when in use, the charges would be billed to someone else's active cellular phone number.

Indiana State Police Sergeant David Henson pulled over a blue and white Oldsmobile driven by Steve Martin, in which Smith was a front seat passenger. Trooper Henson initiated the traffic stop because a computer check on the vehicle's license plate revealed the plate was registered to a yellow Oldsmobile rather than a blue and white one. Trooper Henson approached the vehicle and asked Martin for his license and registration. Following the arrival of Troopers Troy Sunier and Patrick Spellman, Martin and Smith were asked to exit the vehicle, separated, and questioned in an effort to determine if the car was stolen. The troopers' inquiries revealed that the car belonged to Smith, who had painted it a different color, which explained the apparently mismatched license plate.

During the course of this investigatory stop, Trooper Dean Wildauer arrived on the scene and asked Smith if he and Trooper Spellman could search the vehicle for guns, drugs, money, or illegal contraband. Smith consented to the search. While no guns, drugs, money, or illegal contraband were recovered as a result of the search, two cellular flip phones were retrieved from the front seat of Smith's car. One phone was found on the passenger's side of the vehicle where Smith had been sitting, and the other was found on the driver's side where Martin had been sitting. When asked whether the cellular phone found on the passenger's side was his, Smith stated that it was his girlfriend's; however, he could not recall the name of her service provider.

Trooper Wildauer then took both phones back to his police vehicle where he removed the batteries and performed a short-out technique on each device. The results of this field-test revealed that the cellular phones' internal ESNs did not match the external ESNs, indicating that the cellular phones had been illegally cloned, or reprogrammed such that, when in use, the charges would be billed to someone else's phone number. After discovering that the phones were cloned, Trooper Wildauer called a law enforcement hotline which informed him that the internal ESN of the cellular phone Smith claimed was his girlfriend's in fact belonged to GTE Mobilnet and was assigned to one of its legitimate service customers, Technology Marketing Corporation. Upon further questioning, Smith admitted that he had purchased the cloned phone on the street from an acquaintance and that he knew it was a clone.

Initially, we observe that Sergeant Henson's investigatory stop of Smith's vehicle was valid and supported by reasonable suspicion. There are no such indicators here that Smith's consent was in any way induced by fraud, fear, or intimidation. Under the totality of these circumstances, we conclude that Smith's consent to search his vehicle was voluntarily given.

Having held that Smith's consent to search was not constitutionally defective, we must then determine whether the troopers exceeded the scope of his consent. The standard for measuring the scope of a suspect's consent under the Fourth Amendment is that of objective reasonableness, in other words, "what would the typical reasonable person have understood by the exchange between the officer and the suspect?" In addition, the scope of a consensual search is generally defined by its expressed object.

Here, the expressed objects of the troopers' search were guns, drugs, money, or illegal contraband. When Smith gave the troopers permission to search his car for guns, drugs, money, or illegal contraband, a reasonable person would have understood Smith's consent to include permission to search any containers inside the vehicle which might reasonably contain those specified items. A cellular phone is a container capable of hiding such items as drugs or money. Therefore, it was proper for the troopers to seize the cellular phone long enough to determine whether it was truly an operating cellular phone or merely a pretense for hiding the expressed objects of their search.

Smith's consent did not authorize the troopers to access the computer memory of his cellular phone—an objectively reasonable person assessing in context Smith's verbal exchange with the troopers would have understood that the troopers intended to search only in places where Smith could have disposed of or hidden the specific items which they were looking for, namely, guns, drugs, money or other contraband. No objective person would believe that by performing a short-out technique on a cellular phone to retrieve its electronic contents, the troopers might reasonably find the expressed object of their search. Thus, where the troopers here obtained consent to search Smith's car for guns, drugs, money, or contraband, they had to limit their activity to that which was necessary to search for such items.

§7.3 Third Party Consent

The validity of third party consent depends on whether the person giving consent has either actual authority or apparent authority to consent.[9] In general, a third party may consent to a warrantless search when that party possesses "common authority over or other sufficient relationship to the premises or effects sought to be inspected."[10]

> Common authority is . . . not to be implied from the mere property interest a third party has in the property. The authority which justifies the third-party consent does not rest upon the law of property, with its attendant historical and legal refinements, but rests rather on mutual use of the property by persons generally having joint access or control for most purposes, so that it is reasonable to recognize that any of the co-inhabitants has the right to permit the inspection in his own right and that the others have assumed the risk that one of their number might permit the common area to be searched.[11]

The issue frequently arises in the context of shared computer use. The question, as with consent generally, turns on the person's access or control of the computer,

---

9. *See, e.g.*, United States v. Smith, 27 F. Supp. 2d 1111, 1115 (C.D. Ill. 1998).

10. United States v. Matlock, 415 U.S. 164, 171 (1974). *See also* Frazier v. Cupp, 394 U.S. 731, 740 (1969) (rejecting inquiry into "metaphysical subtleties" of argument that, because joint user of duffle bag only had actual permission to use one compartment, he could not consent to search of whole bag).

11. *Matlock*, 415 U.S. at 171 n.7.

regardless of whether the person is a spouse,[12] parent,[13] other family member,[14] house mate,[15] bailee,[16] systems administrator,[17] or other third party,[18] such as a computer repair person.[19]

1. Passwords and Encryption

The presence of password-protected files is an important consideration in assessing a third party's authority to consent. By creating password-protected files, the creator "affirmatively" intends to exclude the joint user and others from the files.[20] Under such circumstances, it has been reasoned, it cannot be said that the person has assumed the risk that the joint user would permit others to search the files.[21] On the other hand, the lack of passwords to protect files has been held to defeat a claim

---

12. *See* Walsh v. State, 512 S.E.2d 408, 411–12 (Ga. Ct. App. 1999) (defendant's wife had authority to consent to search of computer that she purchased and was available for use by family).

13. *See* People v. Blair, 748 N.E.2d 318, 324–25 (Ill. Ct. App. 2001) (father, who had no actual or apparent ownership of computer, could not validly consent to seizure of son's computer).

14. *See* State v. Guthrie, 627 N.W.2d 401 (S.D. 2001) (son-in-law possessed common authority over computer and could validly consent to its seizure when he had unconditional access and control over it).

15. *See* United States v. Smith, 27 F. Supp. 2d 1111, 1115–16 (C.D. Ill. 1998) (housemate had authority to consent to search of defendant's computer, to which she had joint access and which was located in common area of house; alternatively, government agents reasonably believed housemate could consent to search).

16. *See* United States v. James, 353 F.3d 606, 614–15 (8th Cir. 2003) (bailee, who agreed to store disks and who had been later directed to destroy them, did not have actual or apparent authority to permit police to take and examine them).

17. A systems administrator is the person "whose job is to keep [a computer] network running smoothly, monitor security, and repair the network when problems arise." U.S. Dep't of Justice, Searching and Seizing Computers and Electronic Evidence in Criminal Investigations 25 (3d ed. 2009). Those administrators "have 'root level' access to the systems they administer, which effectively grants them master keys to open any account and read any file on their systems." *Id.* Whether a systems administrator "may voluntarily consent to disclose information from or regarding a user's account varies based on whether the network belongs to a communications service provider, a private business, or a government entity." *Id.*

18. *See* United States v. Meek, 366 F.3d 705, 711 (9th Cir. 2004) ("Like private phone conversations, either party to a chat room exchange has the power to surrender each other's privacy interest to a third party.").

19. United States v. Barth, 26 F. Supp. 2d 929, 938 (W.D. Tex. 1998) (computer repair person did not have actual authority to consent to search of customer's hard drive, having "possession of the unit for the limited purpose of repair" and did not have apparent authority when police knew his status).

20. Trulock v. Freeh, 275 F.3d 391, 403 (4th Cir. 2001).

21. *Id. See also* United States v. Slanina, 283 F.3d 670, 676 (5th Cir.), *remanded on other grounds*, 537 U.S. 802 (2002), *on appeal after remand*, 359 F.3d 356 (5th Cir. 2004) (use of passwords and locking office doors to restrict employer's access to computer files is evidence of employee's subjective expectation of privacy in those files).

that the defendant had exclusive control of a computer and that his housemate did not have authority to consent to search.[22]

United States v. Ray Andrus
483 F.3d 711 (10th Cir. 2007)

Murphy, Circuit Judge.

Federal authorities first became interested in Ray Andrus during an investigation of Regpay, a third-party billing and credit card aggregating company that provided subscribers with access to websites containing child pornography. The investigation of Regpay led to an investigation of Regpay subscribers. One of the subscribers providing personal information and a credit card number to Regpay was an individual identifying himself as "Ray Andrus" at "3208 W. 81st Terr., Leawood, KS." The Andrus Regpay subscription was used to access a pornographic website called www.sunshineboys.com. Record checks with the drivers license bureau and post office indicated Ray Andrus, Bailey Andrus, and a third man, Richard Andrus, all used the West 81st Terrace address. The credit card number provided to Regpay was determined to belong to Ray Andrus. The email address provided to Regpay, "bandrus@kc.rr.com," was determined to be associated with Dr. Bailey Andrus.

Eight months into the investigation, agents believed they did not have enough information to obtain a search warrant for the Andrus residence. They, therefore, attempted to gather more information by doing a "knock and talk" interview with the hope of being able to conduct a consent search. ICE Special Agent Cheatham and Leawood Police Detective Woollen arrived at the Andrus house at approximately 8:45 a.m. on August 27, 2004. ICE Special Agent Kanatzar, a forensic computer expert, accompanied Cheatham and Woollen to the residence, but waited outside in his car for Cheatham's authorization to enter the premises.

Dr. Andrus, age ninety-one, answered the door in his pajamas. Dr. Andrus invited the officers into the residence and, according to the testimony of Cheatham and Woollen, the three sat in Dr. Andrus' living room, where the officers learned that Ray Andrus lived in the center bedroom in the residence. In response to the officers' questions, Dr. Andrus indicated Ray Andrus did not pay rent and lived in the home to help care for his aging parents. Cheatham testified he could see the door to Ray Andrus' bedroom was open and asked Dr. Andrus whether he had access to the bedroom. Dr. Andrus testified he answered "yes" and told the officers he felt free to enter the room when the door was open, but always knocked if the door was closed.

Cheatham asked Dr. Andrus for consent to search the house and any computers in it. Dr. Andrus signed a written consent form indicating his willingness to consent to a premises and computer search. He led Cheatham into Ray Andrus' bedroom

---

22. United States v. Smith, 27 F. Supp. 2d 1111, 1116 (C.D. Ill. 1998).

to show him where the computer was located. After Dr. Andrus signed the consent form, Cheatham went outside to summon Kanatzar into the residence. Kanatzar went straight into Andrus' bedroom and began assembling his forensic equipment. Kanatzar removed the cover from Andrus' computer and hooked his laptop and other equipment to it. Dr. Andrus testified he was present at the beginning of the search but left the bedroom shortly thereafter. Kanatzar testified it took about ten to fifteen minutes to connect his equipment before he started analyzing the computer. Kanatzar used EnCase forensic software to examine the contents of the computer's hard drive. The software allowed him direct access to the hard drive without first determining whether a user name or password were needed. He, therefore, did not determine whether the computer was protected by a user name or password prior to previewing the computer's contents. Only later, when he took the computer back to his office for further analysis, did he see Ray Andrus' user profile.[n.1]²³

Kanatzar testified he used EnCase to search for .jpg picture files. He explained that clicking on the images he retrieved allowed him to see the pathname for the image, tracing it to particular folders on the computer's hard drive. This process revealed folder and file names suggestive of child pornography. Kanatzar estimated it took five minutes to see depictions of child pornography. At that point, however, Cheatham came back into the room, told Kanatzar that Ray Andrus was on his way home, and asked Kanatzar to stop the search. Kanatzar testified he shut down his laptop computer.

The district court determined Dr. Andrus' consent was voluntary, but concluded Dr. Andrus lacked actual authority to consent to a computer search. The court based its actual authority ruling on its findings that Dr. Andrus did not know how to use the computer, had never used the computer, and did not know the user name that would have allowed him to access the computer.

The district court then proceeded to consider apparent authority. It indicated the resolution of the apparent authority claim in favor of the government was a "close call." The court concluded the agents' belief that Dr. Andrus had authority to consent to a search of the computer was reasonable up until the time they learned there was only one computer in the house. Because Cheatham instructed Kanatzar to suspend the search at that point, there was no Fourth Amendment violation.

Whether apparent authority exists is an objective, totality-of-the-circumstances inquiry into whether the facts available to the officers at the time they commenced the search would lead a reasonable officer to believe the third party had authority to consent to the search. When the property to be searched is an object or container, the relevant inquiry must address the third party's relationship to the object. The Supreme Court's most recent pronouncement on third party consent searches underscores that reasonableness calculations must be made in the context of social

---

23. [n.1] Kanatzar testified that someone without forensic equipment would need Ray Andrus' user name and password to access files stored within Andrus' user profile.

expectations about the particular item to be searched. The Court explained, "The constant element in assessing Fourth Amendment reasonableness in consent cases . . . is the great significance given to widely shared social expectations." For example, the Court said, "[W]hen it comes to searching through bureau drawers, there will be instances in which even a person clearly belonging on the premises as an occupant may lack any perceived authority to consent."

Courts considering the issue have attempted to analogize computers to other items more commonly seen in Fourth Amendment jurisprudence. Individuals' expectations of privacy in computers have been likened to their expectations of privacy in "a suitcase or briefcase." Password-protected files have been compared to a "locked footlocker inside the bedroom."

Because intimate information is commonly stored on computers, it seems natural that computers should fall into the same category as suitcases, footlockers, or other personal items that "command[] a high degree of privacy."

The inquiry into whether the owner of a highly personal object has indicated a subjective expectation of privacy traditionally focuses on whether the subject suitcase, footlocker, or other container is physically locked. Determining whether a computer is "locked," or whether a reasonable officer should know a computer may be locked, presents a challenge distinct from that associated with other types of closed containers. Unlike footlockers or suitcases, where the presence of a locking device is generally apparent by looking at the item, a "lock" on the data within a computer is not apparent from a visual inspection of the outside of the computer, especially when the computer is in the "off" position prior to the search. Data on an entire computer may be protected by a password, with the password functioning as a lock, or there may be multiple users of a computer, each of whom has an individual and personalized password-protected "user profile." *See* Oxford English Dictionary Online, http://dictionary.oed.com (last visited Dec. 22, 2006) (entry for "Password," definition 1.b.: defining "password" in the computing context as "[a] sequence of characters, known only to authorized persons, which must be keyed in to gain access to a particular computer, network, file, function, etc."). The presence of a password that limits access to the computer's contents may only be discovered by starting up the machine or attempting to access particular files on the computer as a normal user would.[n.5][24]

Courts addressing the issue of third party consent in the context of computers, therefore, have examined officers' knowledge about password protection as an indication of whether a computer is "locked" in the way a footlocker would be. For example, in *Trulock* [*v. Freeh*, 275 F.3d 391 (4th Cir. 2001)], the Fourth Circuit held a live-in girlfriend lacked actual authority to consent to a search of her boyfriend's

---

24. [n.5] The difficulty with seeing a "lock" on computer data is exacerbated by the forensic software sometimes used by law enforcement to conduct computer searches. The software, like the EnCase software used by Agent Kanatzar, allows user profiles and password protection to be bypassed.

computer files where the girlfriend told police she and her boyfriend shared the household computer but had separate password-protected files that were inaccessible to the other. The court in that case explained, "Although Conrad had authority to consent to a general search of the computer, her authority did not extend to Trulock's password-protected files." In *United States v. Morgan*, the Sixth Circuit viewed a wife's statement to police that she and her husband did not have individual usernames or passwords as a factor weighing in favor of the wife's apparent authority to consent to a search of the husband's computer. 435 F.3d 660, 663 (6th Cir. 2006). A critical issue in assessing a third party's apparent authority to consent to the search of a home computer, therefore, is whether law enforcement knows or should reasonably suspect because of surrounding circumstances that the computer is password protected.

In addition to password protection, courts also consider the location of the computer within the house and other indicia of household members' access to the computer in assessing third party authority. Third party apparent authority to consent to a search has generally been upheld when the computer is located in a common area of the home that is accessible to other family members under circumstances indicating the other family members were not excluded from using the computer. In contrast, where the third party has affirmatively disclaimed access to or control over the computer or a portion of the computer's files, even when the computer is located in a common area of the house, courts have been unwilling to find third party authority.

First, the officers knew Dr. Andrus owned the house and lived there with family members. Second, the officers knew Dr. Andrus' house had internet access and that Dr. Andrus paid the Time Warner internet and cable bill. Third, the officers knew the email address bandrus@kc.rr.com had been activated and used to register on a website that provided access to child pornography. Fourth, although the officers knew Ray Andrus lived in the center bedroom, they also knew that Dr. Andrus had access to the room at will. Fifth, the officers saw the computer in plain view on the desk in Andrus' room and it appeared available for use by other household members. Furthermore, the record indicates Dr. Andrus did not say or do anything to indicate his lack of ownership or control over the computer when Cheatham asked for his consent to conduct a computer search. It is uncontested that Dr. Andrus led the officers to the bedroom in which the computer was located, and, even after he saw Kanatzar begin to work on the computer, Dr. Andrus remained silent about any lack of authority he had over the computer. Even if Ray Andrus' computer was protected with a user name and password, there is no indication in the record that the officers knew or had reason to believe such protections were in place.

Andrus argues his computer's password protection indicated his computer was "locked" to third parties, a fact the officers would have known had they asked questions of Dr. Andrus prior to searching the computer. Under our case law, however, officers are not obligated to ask questions unless the circumstances are ambiguous. In essence, by suggesting the onus was on the officers to ask about password protection prior to searching the computer, Andrus necessarily submits there is inherent ambiguity whenever police want to search a household computer and a third party has not affirmatively provided information about his own use of the computer or about password protection. Andrus' argument presupposes, however, that password protection of home computers is so common that a reasonable officer ought to know password protection is likely. Andrus has neither made this argument directly nor proffered any evidence to demonstrate a high incidence of password protection among home computer users. The dissent, however, is critical of this court because it neither makes the argument for Andrus nor supplies the evidence to support the argument. The key aspect of the dissent is its criticism of the majority for refusing to "take judicial notice that password protection is a standard feature of operating systems." A judicially noticed fact is "one not subject to reasonable dispute in that it is either (1) generally known . . . or (2) capable of accurate and ready determination by resort to sources whose accuracy cannot reasonably be questioned." Fed. R. Evid. 201(b). Although judicial notice may be taken *sua sponte*, it would be particularly inappropriate for the court to wander undirected in search of evidence irrefutably establishing the facts necessary to support the dissent's conclusion regarding the absence of apparent authority: namely, that (a) password protection is a standard feature of most operating systems; (b) most users activate the standard password-protection feature; and (c) these are matters of such common knowledge that a reasonable officer would make further inquiry. Without a factual basis on which to proceed, we are unable to address the possibility that passwords create inherent ambiguities.[n.8][25]

Viewed under the requisite totality-of-the-circumstances analysis, the facts known to the officers at the time the computer search commenced created an objectively reasonable perception that Dr. Andrus was, at least, *one* user of the computer. That objectively reasonable belief would have been enough to give Dr. Andrus apparent authority to consent to a search. In this case, the district court found Agent Cheatham properly halted the search when further conversation with Dr. Andrus revealed he did not use the computer and that Andrus' computer was the only computer in the house. These later revelations, however, have no bearing on the reasonableness of the officers' belief in Dr. Andrus' authority at the outset of the computer search.

McKay, Circuit Judge, dissenting.

I take issue with the majority's implicit holding that law enforcement may use software deliberately designed to automatically bypass computer password protection based on third-party consent without the need to make a reasonable inquiry regarding the presence of password protection and the third party's access to that password.

---

25. [n.8] If the factual basis were provided, law enforcement's use of forensic software like EnCase, which overrides any password protection without ever indicating whether such protection exists, may well be subject to question. This, however, is not that case.

The development of computer password technology no doubt "presents a challenge distinct from that associated with other types of" *locked* containers. The unconstrained ability of law enforcement to use forensic software such as the EnCase program to bypass password protection without first determining whether such passwords have been enabled does not "exacerbate[ ]" this difficulty; rather, it avoids it altogether, simultaneously and dangerously sidestepping the Fourth Amendment in the process. Indeed, the majority concedes that if such protection were "shown to be commonplace, law enforcement's use of forensic software like EnCase . . . may well be subject to question." But the fact that a computer password "lock" may not be *immediately* visible does not render it unlocked. I appreciate that unlike the locked file cabinet, computers have no handle to pull. But, like the padlocked footlocker, computers do exhibit outward signs of password protection: they display boot password screens, username/password log-in screens, and/or screen-saver reactivation passwords.[n.3][26]

The fact remains that EnCase's ability to bypass security measures is well known to law enforcement. Here, ICE's forensic computer specialist found Defendant's computer turned off. Without turning it on, he hooked his laptop directly to the hard drive of Defendant's computer and ran the EnCase program. The agents made no effort to ascertain whether such security was enabled prior to initiating the search. The testimony makes clear that such protection was discovered during additional computer analysis conducted at the forensic specialist's office.

The burden on law enforcement to identify ownership of the computer was minimal. A simple question or two would have sufficed. Prior to the computer search, the agents questioned Dr. Andrus about Ray Andrus' status as a renter and Dr. Andrus' ability to enter his 51-year-old son's bedroom in order to determine Dr. Andrus' ability to consent to a search of the room, but the agents did not inquire whether Dr. Andrus used the computer, and if so, whether he had access to his son's password. At the suppression hearing, the agents testified that they were not immediately aware that Defendant's computer was the only one in the house, and they began to doubt Dr. Andrus' authority to consent when they learned this fact. The record reveals that, upon questioning, Dr. Andrus indicated that there was a computer in the house and led the agents to Defendant's room. The forensic specialist was then summoned. It took him approximately fifteen to twenty minutes to set up his equipment, yet, bizarrely, at no point during this period did the agents inquire about the presence of any other computers. The consent form, which Dr. Andrus signed prior to even showing the agents Defendant's computer, indicates that Dr. Andrus consented to the search of only a single "computer," rather than computers. In addition, the local police officer accompanying the ICE agents heard Dr. Andrus tell his wife that the agents wanted to search *Defendant's*

---

26. [n.3] I recognize that the ability of users to program automatic log-ins and the capability of operating systems to "memorize" passwords poses potential problems, since these only create the appearance of a restriction without actually blocking access.

computer, which would have caused a reasonable law enforcement official to question Dr. Andrus' ownership and use of the computer.

The record reflects that, even prior to the agent's arrival at the target home, the agents were cognizant of the ambiguity surrounding the search. The agents testified that they suspended their search due to doubts regarding Dr. Andrus' ability to consent only after they learned that the internet service used by Defendant came bundled with the cable television service and was paid by Dr. Andrus. The district court noted, however, that the agents were aware of this fact prior to the search, having subpoenaed the internet/cable records from the service provider prior to their "knock-and-talk." Given the inexcusable confusion in this case, the circumstantial evidence is simply not enough to justify the agents' use of EnCase software without making further inquiry.

Accordingly, in my view, given the case law indicating the importance of computer password protection, the common knowledge about the prevalence of password usage, and the design of EnCase or similar password bypass mechanisms, the Fourth Amendment and the reasonable inquiry rule, mandate that in consent-based, warrantless computer searches, law enforcement personnel inquire or otherwise check for the presence of password protection and, if a password is present, inquire about the consenter's knowledge of that password and joint access to the computer.

United States v. Frank Gary Buckner

473 F.3d 551 (4th Cir. 2007)

Diana Gribbon Motz, Circuit Judge.

This criminal investigation began when the Grottoes, Virginia police department received a series of complaints regarding online fraud committed by someone using AOL and eBay accounts opened in the name Michelle Buckner. On July 28, 2003, police officers went to the Buckner residence to speak with Michelle, but only Frank Buckner was at home. The officers then left, asking Frank to have Michelle contact them. A short while later, Frank Buckner himself called the police, seeking more information about why they wanted to speak with Michelle. The police responded that they wanted to talk with her about some computer transactions. That evening, Michelle Buckner went to the police station and told officers that she knew nothing about any illegal eBay transactions, but that she did have a home computer leased in her name. She further stated that she only used the home computer occasionally to play solitaire.

The next day, July 29, police returned to the Buckner residence to speak further with Michelle about the online fraud. Frank Buckner was not present. Michelle again cooperated fully, telling the officers "to take whatever [they] needed" and that she "want[ed] to be as cooperative as she could be." The computer Michelle had indicated was leased in her name was located on a table in the living room, just inside the front door of the residence. Pursuant to Michelle's oral consent, the officers seized the leased home computer.

At the time the officers seized the computer, it was turned on and running, with the screen visibly lit. The officers did not, at this time, open any files or look at any information on the computer. Instead, with Michelle's blessing, they shut down the computer and took its data—storage components for later forensic analysis. This analysis consisted of "mirroring"—that is, creating a copy of—the hard drive and looking at the computer's files on the mirrored copy.

At a suppression hearing, Frank Buckner offered the only affirmative evidence on the password issue, testifying that a password was required to use the computer. Buckner stated that he was the only person who could sign on to the computer and the only person who knew the password necessary to view files that he had created. Nothing in the record contradicts this testimony. Nor, however, is there any record evidence that the officers knew this information at the time they seized or searched the computer. Indeed, the evidence indicates that no officer, including the officer who conducted the search of the mirrored hard drive, ever found any indication of password protection. The Government's evidence was that its forensic analysis software would not necessarily detect user passwords.[n.1][27]

In *Trulock* [*v. Freeh*, 275 F.3d 391 (4th Cir. 2001)], we held that a co-resident of a home and co-user of a computer, who did not know the necessary password for her co-user's password-protected files, lacked the authority to consent to a warrantless search of those files. We likened these private files to a "locked box" within an area of common authority. Although common authority over a general area confers actual authority to consent to a search of that general area, it does not "automatically . . . extend to the interiors of every discrete enclosed space capable of search within the area."

The logic of *Trulock* applies equally here. "By using a password," Frank Buckner, like Trulock, "affirmatively intended to exclude . . . others from his personal files." For this reason, "it cannot be said that" Buckner "assumed the risk" that a joint user of the computer, not privy to password-protected files, "would permit others to search his files." Thus, Michelle Buckner did not have actual authority to consent to a search of her husband's password-protected files because she did not share "mutual use, general access or common authority" over those files.

Michelle's lack of actual authority, however, does not end our inquiry. Rather, it would be sufficient that Michelle had apparent authority to consent to the search at issue.

---

27. [n.1] The parties agree that none of Frank Buckner's files were encrypted. Nor is there any contention that the police officers *deliberately* used software that would avoid discovery of any existing passwords.

Frank Buckner contends that Michelle did not have common authority over his computer files — a fact that the officers must have known, according to Buckner, because Michelle had told them that she was not computer-savvy and that she only used the computer to play games.

Whether the officers reasonably believed that Michelle had authority to consent to a search of all the contents of the computer's hard drive, however, depends on viewing these facts in light of the *totality* of the circumstances known to the officers at the time of the search. At that time, the officers knew that the computer was located in a common living area of the Buckners' marital home, they observed that the computer was on and the screen lit despite the fact that Frank Buckner was not present, and they had been told that fraudulent activity had been conducted from that computer using accounts opened in *Michelle's* name. The officers also knew that the machine was leased solely in *Michelle's* name and that she had the ability to return the computer to the rental agency at any time, without Frank Buckner's knowledge or consent.

Furthermore, the officers did not have any indication from Michelle, or any of the attendant circumstances, that any files were password-protected. Even during the mirroring and forensic analysis processes, nothing the officers saw indicated that any computer files were encrypted or password-protected.[n.3][28] Despite Michelle's suggestion that she lacked deep familiarity with the computer, the totality of the circumstances provided the officers with the basis for an objectively reasonable belief that Michelle had authority to consent to a search of the computer's hard drive. Therefore, the police were justified in relying on Michelle's consent to search the computer and all of its files, such that no search warrant was required.

Note

EnCase is a software tool made by Guidance Software that is used by many computer forensic examiners. *See* www.guidancesoftware.com. It is very configurable. Should courts construe the Fourth Amendment to require investigators to determine the existence of password protection prior to examining a digital device? In all situations or only when there is reason to suspect that the device is used by more than one person? If password protection is discovered, what may an investigator then be permitted to do?

---

28. [n.3] We do not hold that the officers could rely upon apparent authority to search while simultaneously using mirroring or other technology to intentionally avoid discovery of password or encryption protection put in place by the user.

§ 7.4 Fifth Amendment Privilege: Requiring the Disclosure of Passwords, Decrypted Files

Does the Fifth Amendment prevent the government from forcing a person to provide a password or encryption key to permit it to access to digital files? The Fifth Amendment provides in part: "No person . . . shall be compelled in any criminal case to be a witness against himself. . . ." The history of the Amendment is complex. Under current doctrine, to qualify for the Fifth Amendment privilege, a communication "must be testimonial, incriminating, and compelled."[29] This section focuses on one aspect of the doctrine: what constitutes "testimony?" In the materials that follow, the other elements are assumed, that is, a subpoena is a form of compulsion and the data sought would be incriminating. In particular, the primary inquiry implicates the act of production doctrine, which regulates under what circumstances the government can compel a person to disclose documents. "Although the contents of a document may not be privileged, the act of producing the document may be."[30] Production itself acknowledges that the document exists, that it is in the possession or control of the producer, and that it is authentic.[31]

"Encryption involves the encoding of information, called 'plaintext,' into unreadable form, termed 'ciphertext.' The reverse process of transforming the ciphertext back into readable plaintext is called decryption. The purpose, of course, is to prevent anyone other than the user or intended recipient from reading private information."[32]

> Encryption has become pervasive in our modern, technologically oriented society. In the home, encryption technology can be found in a multitude of devices. DVD and Blu-ray players perform decryption of encrypted, copyrighted movies. Wireless routers utilize encryption for security over the air. Every time someone uses the Internet to pay bills or to make purchases online, that person uses encryption technology. Commercially, companies use encryption to protect their data and to allow employees to securely access company networks from home through a Virtual Private Network.
>
> Devices, both hardware and software, that utilize various encryption schemes are commonplace. Popular operating systems for computers, such as Microsoft Windows and Mac OS X, have some form of built-in encryption function that makes it easier for the public to use encryption technology. Commercial software is readily available to perform encryption of data and email. In addition to software-only solutions, hardware manufacturers

---

29. Hiibel v. Sixth Judicial Dist. Court of Nev., 542 U.S. 177, 189 (2004).

30. United States v. Doe, 465 U.S. 605, 612 (1984).

31. United States v. Hubbell, 530 U.S. 27, 36 (2000).

32. John Duong, Note, *The Intersection of the Fourth and Fifth Amendments in the Context of Encrypted Personal Data at the Border*, 2 Drexel L. Rev. 313, 324 (2009). Copyright © 2009, Drexel Law Review. All rights reserved. Reprinted by permission.

have even launched products that have built-in, automatic encryption, making it virtually transparent to the end user who need not understand the underlying encryption technology in order to use it. One thing is certain: encryption exists to protect information, whether commercial or private.

Today's encryption algorithms utilize complex mathematical routines to make it virtually impossible, given the computing power available today and in the foreseeable future, to "brute force" a passphrase. Even assuming that the government has the necessary computer processing power, there is still the question of whether it is even feasible given the resources necessary to perform the process of decryption. Without even knowing what the encrypted contents hold, it may be prohibitively expensive in time and cost to attempt decryption.[33]

In re Grand Jury Subpoena to Sebastien Boucher

2009 US. Dist. Lexis 13006 (D. Vt. Feb. 19, 2009)

WILLIAM K. SESSIONS, III, CHIEF JUDGE.

The Government appeals the United States Magistrate Judge's Opinion and Order granting defendant Sebastien Boucher's motion to quash a grand jury subpoena on the grounds that it violates his Fifth Amendment right against self-incrimination. The grand jury subpoena directs Boucher to

> provide all documents, whether in electronic or paper form, reflecting any passwords used or associated with the Alienware Notebook Computer, Model D9T, Serial No. NKD900TA5L00859, seized from Sebastien Boucher at the Port of Entry at Derby Line, Vermont on December 17, 2006.

In its submission on appeal, the Government stated that it does not in fact seek the password for the encrypted hard drive, but requires Boucher to produce the contents of his encrypted hard drive in an unencrypted format by opening the drive before the grand jury. The Government stated that it intends only to require Boucher to provide an unencrypted version of the drive to the grand jury.

On December 17, 2006, Boucher and his father crossed the Canadian border into the United States at Derby Line, Vermont. A Custom and Border Protection inspector directed Boucher's car into secondary inspection. The inspector conducting the secondary inspection observed a laptop computer in the back seat of Boucher's car, which Boucher acknowledged as his. The inspector searched the computer files and found approximately 40,000 images.

Based upon the file names, some of the files appeared to contain pornographic images, including child pornography. The inspector called in a Special Agent for

---

33. *Id.* at 324–28.

Immigration and Customs Enforcement with experience and training in recognizing child pornography. The agent examined the computer and file names and observed several images of adult pornography and animated child pornography. He clicked on a file labeled "2yo getting raped during diaper change," but was unable to open it. The "Properties" feature indicated that the file had last been opened on December 11, 2006.

After giving Boucher *Miranda* warnings, and obtaining a waiver from him, the agent asked Boucher about the inaccessible file. Boucher replied that he downloads many pornographic files from online newsgroups onto a desktop computer and transfers them to his laptop. He stated that he sometimes unknowingly downloads images that contain child pornography, but deletes them when he realizes their contents.

The agent asked Boucher to show him the files he downloads. Boucher navigated to drive "Z" of the laptop, and the agent began searching the Z drive. The agent located and examined several videos or images that appeared to meet the definition of child pornography.

The agent arrested Boucher, seized the laptop and shut it down. He applied for and obtained a search warrant for the laptop. In the course of creating a mirror image of the contents of the laptop, however, the government discovered that it could not find or open the Z drive because it is protected by encryption algorithms from the computer software "Pretty Good Protection," which requires a password to obtain access. The government is not able to open the encrypted files without knowing the password. In order to gain access to the Z drive, the government is using an automated system which attempts to guess the password, a process that could take years.

The Fifth Amendment to the United States Constitution protects "a person . . . against being incriminated by his own compelled testimonial communications." *Fisher v. United States*, 425 U.S. 391, 409 (1976). There is no question that the contents of the laptop were voluntarily prepared or compiled and are not testimonial, and therefore do not enjoy Fifth Amendment protection.

"Although the contents of a document may not be privileged, the act of producing the document may be." "'The act of production' itself may implicitly communicate 'statements of fact.' By 'producing documents in compliance with a subpoena, the witness would admit that the papers existed, were in his possession or control, and were authentic.'" *United States v. Hubbell*, 530 U.S. 27, 36 (2000). Thus, "the Fifth Amendment applies to acts that imply assertions of fact." It is "the attempt to force [an accused] to 'disclose the contents of his own mind' that implicates the Self-Incrimination Clause." Moreover, "[c]ompelled testimony that communicates information that may 'lead to incriminating evidence' is privileged even if the information itself is not inculpatory."

At issue is whether requiring Boucher to produce an unencrypted version of his laptop's Z drive would constitute compelled testimonial communication. *See In re Grand Jury Subpoena Duces Tecum Dated Oct. 29, 1992* (In re Grand Jury

Subpoena Duces Tecum Dated October 29, 1992, 1 F.3d 87, 93 (2d Cir. 1993) ("Self-incrimination analysis now focuses on whether the creation of the thing demanded was compelled and, if not, whether the act of producing it would constitute compelled testimonial communication . . . regardless of 'the contents or nature of the thing demanded.'").

The act of producing documents in response to a subpoena may communicate incriminating facts "in two situations: (1) 'if the existence and location of the subpoenaed papers are unknown to the government'; or (2) where production would 'implicitly authenticate' the documents."

Where the existence and location of the documents are known to the government, "no constitutional rights are touched," because these matters are a "foregone conclusion." The Magistrate Judge determined that the foregone conclusion rationale did not apply, because the government has not viewed most of the files on the Z drive, and therefore does not know whether most of the files on the Z drive contain incriminating material. Second Circuit precedent, however, does not require that the government be aware of the incriminatory *contents* of the files; it requires the government to demonstrate "with reasonable particularity that it knows of the existence and location of subpoenaed documents."

Thus, where the government, in possession of a photocopy of a grand jury target's daily calendar, moved to compel compliance with a subpoena for the original, the Second Circuit ruled that no act of production privilege applied. The existence and location of the calendar were foregone conclusions, because the target had produced a copy of the calendar and testified about his possession and use of it.

The target's production of the original calendar was also not necessary to authenticate it; the government could authenticate the calendar by establishing the target's prior production of the copy and allowing the trier of fact to compare the two.

Boucher accessed the Z drive of his laptop at the ICE agent's request. The ICE agent viewed the contents of some of the Z drive's files, and ascertained that they may consist of images or videos of child pornography. The Government thus knows of the existence and location of the Z drive and its files. Again providing access to the unencrypted Z drive "adds little or nothing to the sum total of the Government's information" about the existence and location of files that may contain incriminating information.

Boucher's act of producing an unencrypted version of the Z drive likewise is not necessary to authenticate it. He has already admitted to possession of the computer, and provided the Government with access to the Z drive. The Government has submitted that it can link Boucher with the files on his computer without making use of his production of an unencrypted version of the Z drive, and that it will not use his act of production as evidence of authentication.

Because Boucher has no act of production privilege to refuse to provide the grand jury with an unencrypted version of the Z drive of his computer, his motion to quash the subpoena (as modified by the Government) is denied. Boucher is directed to provide an unencrypted version of the Z drive viewed by the ICE agent. The Government may not make use of Boucher's act of production to authenticate the unencrypted Z drive or its contents either before the grand jury or a petit jury.

————————

In re Grand Jury Subpoena Duces Tecum Dated March 25, 2011.

United States v. John Doe

670 F.3d 1335 (11th Cir. 2012)

TJOFLAT, CIRCUIT JUDGE:

This is an appeal of a judgment of civil contempt. On April 7, 2011, John Doe was served with a subpoena duces tecum requiring him to appear before a Northern District of Florida grand jury and produce the unencrypted contents located on the hard drives of Doe's laptop computers and five external hard drives.[n.1][34] Doe informed the United States Attorney for the Northern District of Florida that, when he appeared before the grand jury, he would invoke his Fifth Amendment privilege against self-incrimination and refuse to comply with the subpoena. Because the Government considered Doe's compliance with the subpoena necessary to the public interest, the Attorney General, exercising his authority under 18 U.S.C. § 6003, authorized the U.S. Attorney to apply to the district court, pursuant to 18 U.S.C. §§ 6002 and 6003, for an order that would grant Doe immunity and require him to respond to the subpoena.

On April 19, 2011, the U.S. Attorney and Doe appeared before the district court. The U.S. Attorney requested that the court grant Doe immunity limited to "the use [of Doe's] act of production of the unencrypted contents" of the hard drives. That is, Doe's immunity would not extend to the Government's derivative use of contents of the drives as evidence against him in a criminal prosecution. The court accepted the U.S. Attorney's position regarding the scope of the immunity to give Doe and granted the requested order.

After the hearing adjourned, Doe appeared before the grand jury and refused to decrypt the hard drives. The U.S. Attorney immediately moved the district court for an order requiring Doe to show cause why Doe should not be held in civil contempt. The court issued the requested order, requiring Doe to show cause for his refusal to decrypt the hard drives. Doe, responding, explained that he invoked his Fifth Amendment privilege against self-incrimination because the Government's use of the decrypted contents of the hard drives would constitute derivative use of his immunized testimony, use not protected by the district court's grant of immunity. An alternative reason Doe gave as to why the court should not hold him in contempt

————————

34. [n.1] The contents of the drives were encrypted. The subpoena required Doe to decrypt and produce the contents.

was his inability to decrypt the drives. The court rejected Doe's alternative explanations, adjudged him in contempt of court, and ordered him incarcerated. Doe now appeals the court's judgment.

I.

This case began with the lawful seizure of seven pieces of digital media during the course of a child pornography investigation. In March 2010, law enforcement officials began an investigation of an individual using the YouTube.com account [redacted] whom the Government suspected of sharing explicit materials involving underage girls. During the course of their investigation, officers from the Santa Rosa County (Florida) Sheriff's office obtained several internet protocol ("IP") addresses from which [redacted] accessed the internet. Three of these IP addresses were then traced to hotels. Following a review of the hotels' guest registries, law enforcement officers found that the sole common hotel registrant during the relevant times was Doe.

In October 2010, law enforcement officers tracked Doe to a hotel in California and applied for a warrant to search his room. A judge granted the application and issued a search warrant, allowing the officers to seize all digital media, as well as any encryption devices or codes necessary to access such media. The officers seized seven pieces of digital media: two laptops — a 320-gigabyte ("GB") Dell Studio laptop and a 160 GB laptop; and five external hard drives — a 1.5-terabyte ("TB") Seagate external drive, a 1-TB Western Digital MyPassport external drive, a 1-TB external drive, a 500-GB Western Digital external drive, a 500-GB SimpleTech external drive. Federal Bureau of Investigation forensic examiners analyzed the digital media, but were unable to access certain portions of the hard drives.

The grand jury subpoena issued because the forensic examiners were unable to view the encrypted portions of the drives. The subpoena required Doe to produce the "unencrypted contents" of the digital media, and "any and all containers or folders thereon."

The focus of the motion to show cause hearing on April 19, 2011, was, in essence, whether the Fifth Amendment would bar the Government from establishing before a petit jury — say, if Doe were indicted for possession of child pornography in violation of 18 U.S.C. §2252 — that the decrypted contents (child pornography) were Doe's because (1) the hard drives belonged to Doe (which was not in dispute), and (2) contained child pornography. Doe contended that the establishment of point (2) would constitute the derivative use of his immunized grand jury testimony. That is, by decrypting the contents, he would be testifying that he, as opposed to some other person, placed the contents on the hard drive, encrypted the contents, and could retrieve and examine them whenever he wished.

The critical testimony during the show cause hearing came from forensic examiner Timothy McCrohan. McCrohan testified that he cloned over 5 TB of data from the digital media devices — an "enormous amount of data." He also testified that over a million pieces of data could be stored on a typical 320-GB hard drive.

McCrohan continued, "So when you're at five terabytes you're looking at 20 times that size. It could be in the multi-millions." Notably, McCrohan testified that the forensic examination indicated that the hard drives had been encrypted with a software program called "TrueCrypt." Essentially, TrueCrypt can make certain data inaccessible; in doing so, the program can create partitions within a hard drive so that even if one part of the hard drive is accessed, other parts of the hard drive remain secured. Because the hard drive was encrypted, the forensic examiners were unable to recover any data. Although they were unable to find any files, McCrohan testified that they believed that data existed on the still-encrypted parts of the hard drive. In support of this belief, the Government introduced an exhibit with nonsensical characters and numbers, which it argued revealed the encrypted form of data that it seeks.

In his testimony on cross-examination by Doe, however, McCrohan conceded that, although encrypted, it was possible that the hard drives contain nothing. Doe asked McCrohan, "So if a forensic examiner were to look at an external hard drive and just see encryption, does the possibility exist that there actually is nothing on there other than encryption? In other words, if the volume was mounted, all you would see is blank. Does that possibility exist?" McCrohan responded: "Well, you would see random characters, but you wouldn't know necessarily whether it was blank."[n.11][35]

When pressed by Doe to explain why investigators believed something may be hidden, McCrohan replied, "The scope of my examination didn't go that far." In response to further prodding, "What makes you think that there are still portions that have data[?]," McCrohan responded, "We couldn't get into them, so we can't make that call." Finally, when asked whether "random data is just random data," McCrohan concluded that "anything is possible."

II.

We hold that Doe's decryption and production of the hard drives' contents would trigger Fifth Amendment protection because it would be testimonial, and that such protection would extend to the Government's use of the drives' contents. The district court therefore erred in two respects. First, it erred in concluding that Doe's act of decryption and production would not constitute testimony. Second, in granting Doe immunity, it erred in limiting his immunity, under 18 U.S.C. §§ 6002 and 6003, to the Government's use of his act of decryption and production, but allowing the Government derivative use of the evidence such act disclosed.

---

35. [n.11] McCrohan's admission that blank space appears as random characters is supported by TrueCrypt's description on its website: "[F]ree space on any TrueCrypt volume is always filled with random data when the volume is created and no part of the (dismounted) hidden volume can be distinguished from random data." *Hidden Volume*, TrueCrypt, http://www.truecrypt.org/docs/?s=hidden-volume (last visited January 31, 2012).

A.

The Fifth Amendment provides . . . that no person "shall be compelled in any criminal case to be a witness against himself."

An individual must show three things to fall within the ambit of the Fifth Amendment: (1) compulsion, (2) a testimonial communication or act, and (3) incrimination. Here, the Government appears to concede, as it should, that the decryption and production are compelled and incriminatory.

The crux of the dispute here is whether the Government sought "testimony" within the meaning of the Fifth Amendment. The Government claims that it did not, that all it wanted Doe to do was merely to hand over pre-existing and voluntarily created files, not to testify. *See United States v. Hubbell*, 530 U.S. 27, 35–36 (2000) (noting that it is a "settled proposition that a person may be required to produce specific documents even though they contain incriminating assertions of fact or belief because the creation of those documents was not 'compelled' within the meaning of the privilege"). We agree—the files, if there are any at all in the hidden portions of the hard drives, are not themselves testimonial.

Whether the drives' contents are testimonial, however, is not the issue. What is at issue is whether the *act of production* may have some testimonial quality sufficient to trigger Fifth Amendment protection when the production explicitly or implicitly conveys some statement of fact. *See Fisher v. United States*, 425 U.S. 391, 410 (1976) ("The act of producing evidence in response to a subpoena nevertheless has communicative aspects of its own, wholly aside from the contents of the papers produced."). Thus, we focus on whether Doe's act of decryption and production would have been testimonial.

1.

Two seminal cases frame our analysis: *Fisher v. United States* and *United States v. Hubbell*. We start our discussion with this background.

In *Fisher*, the Court considered two Internal Revenue Service investigations, one in the Third Circuit and one in the Fifth Circuit, where the IRS sought to obtain voluntarily prepared documents the taxpayers had given to their attorneys. In each investigation, the IRS issued a summons requiring the taxpayer's attorney to hand over the documents, which included an accountant's work papers, copies of the taxpayer's returns, and copies of other reports and correspondence. When the attorney refused to comply with the summons on the ground that the documents were privileged and, moreover, protected by his Fifth Amendment privilege against self-incrimination, the IRS brought an enforcement action in district court. In both cases, the district court granted relief, ordering the attorney to comply with the summons, and its decision was appealed.

The Court treated the taxpayers as retaining possession of the documents. It then held that the taxpayers' act of production itself could qualify as testimonial if conceding the existence, possession and control, and authenticity of the documents tended to incriminate them. In the cases before it, though, the Court concluded that the act of producing the subpoenaed documents would not involve testimonial self-incrimination because the Government was in "no way relying on the truth telling of the taxpayer." This explanation became known as the "foregone conclusion" doctrine. The Court expressed it thusly:

> It is doubtful that implicitly admitting the existence and possession of the papers rises to the level of testimony within the protection of the Fifth Amendment. . . . Surely the Government is in no way relying on the "truth telling" of the taxpayer to prove the existence of or his access to the documents. The existence and location of the papers are a foregone conclusion and the taxpayer adds little or nothing to the sum total of the Government's information by conceding that he in fact has the papers. Under these circumstances by enforcement of the summons "no constitutional rights are touched. The question is not of testimony but of surrender."[n.19][36]

The Court reasoned that, in essence, the taxpayers' production of the subpoenaed documents would not be testimonial because the Government knew of the existence of the documents, knew that the taxpayers possessed the documents, and could show their authenticity not through the use of the taxpayers' mind, but rather through testimony from others. Where the location, existence, and authenticity of the purported evidence is known with reasonable particularity, the contents of the individual's mind are not used against him, and therefore no Fifth Amendment protection is available.

In *Hubbell*, a grand jury investigating the activities of Whitewater Development Corporation issued a subpoena duces tecum requiring Hubbell to provide eleven categories of documents. Hubbell invoked the Fifth Amendment privilege, so the Government obtained a district court order granting Hubbell §6002 immunity. Hubbell complied with the subpoena and turned over 13,120 pages of documents.

The grand jury subsequently returned a ten-count indictment charging Hubbell with several federal crimes. Asserting that the Government could not convict him without the immunized documents, Hubbell moved the district court to dismiss the indictment. The court held a hearing, found that the Government could not show that it had knowledge of the contents of the documents from a source

---

36. [n.19] The "foregone conclusion" doctrine is a method by which the Government can show that no testimony is at issue. This is related to, but distinct from, the Government's task in a criminal case brought against an individual given use and derivative-use immunity to show that evidence protected by the Fifth Amendment privilege is admissible because the Government could have obtained it from a "legitimate source, wholly independent of the compelled testimony." If in the case at hand, for example, the Government could prove that it had knowledge of the files encrypted on Doe's hard drives, that Doe possessed the files, and that they were authentic, it could compel Doe to produce the contents of the files even though it had no independent source from which it could obtain the files.

independent of the documents themselves, and dismissed the indictment. The Government appealed the dismissal.

The Supreme Court granted a writ of certiorari. The Court held that Hubbell's act of production was sufficiently testimonial to trigger Fifth Amendment protection, as knowledge of the implicit testimonial facts associated with his act of production was not a foregone conclusion. In so holding, the Court distinguished *Fisher*:

> Whatever the scope of this "foregone conclusion" rationale, the facts of this case plainly fall outside of it. While in *Fisher* the Government already knew that the documents were in the attorneys' possession and could independently confirm their existence and authenticity through the accountants who created them, here the Government has not shown that it had any prior knowledge of either the existence or the whereabouts of the 13,120 pages of documents ultimately produced by respondent. The Government cannot cure this deficiency through the overbroad argument that a businessman such as respondent will always possess general business and tax records that fall within the broad categories described in this subpoena.

In *Fisher*, therefore, the act of production was not testimonial because the Government had knowledge of each fact that had the potential of being testimonial. As a contrast, the Court in *Hubbell* found there was testimony in the production of the documents since the Government had no knowledge of the existence of documents, other than a suspicion that documents likely existed and, if they did exist, that they would fall within the broad categories requested.[n.22][37]

Drawing out the key principles from the Court's two decisions, an act of production can be testimonial when that act conveys some explicit or implicit statement of fact that certain materials exist, are in the subpoenaed individual's possession or control, or are authentic. The touchstone of whether an act of production is testimonial is whether the government compels the individual to use "the contents of his own mind" to explicitly or implicitly communicate some statement of fact.

Put another way, the Court has marked out two ways in which an act of production is *not testimonial*. First, the Fifth Amendment privilege is not triggered where the Government merely compels some physical act, i.e. where the individual is not called upon to make use of the contents of his or her mind. The most famous example is the key to the lock of a strongbox containing documents. Second, under the "foregone conclusion" doctrine, an act of production is not testimonial—even if

---

37. [n.22] The Court then held that, in light of the grant of immunity for the testimonial act of production, the Government could not introduce the contents of the documents in a later prosecution without showing "that the evidence it used in obtaining the indictment and proposed to use at trial was derived from legitimate sources 'wholly independent' of the testimonial aspect of respondent's immunized conduct in assembling and producing the documents described in the subpoena." Because the Government could not make that showing, the use of the documents derived directly or indirectly from the testimonial act of production violated the respondent's Fifth Amendment privilege. This aspect of the holding is relevant to part II.B, discussed *infra*.

the act conveys a fact regarding the existence or location, possession, or authenticity of the subpoenaed materials—if the Government can show with "reasonable particularity" that, at the time it sought to compel the act of production, it already knew of the materials, thereby making any testimonial aspect a "foregone conclusion."

2.

With this framework in hand, we turn to the facts of this case. We hold that the act of Doe's decryption and production of the contents of the hard drives would sufficiently implicate the Fifth Amendment privilege. We reach this holding by concluding that (1) Doe's decryption and production of the contents of the drives would be testimonial, not merely a physical act; and (2) the explicit and implicit factual communications associated with the decryption and production are not foregone conclusions.

First, the decryption and production of the hard drives would require the use of the contents of Doe's mind and could not be fairly characterized as a physical act that would be nontestimonial in nature. We conclude that the decryption and production would be tantamount to testimony by Doe of his knowledge of the existence and location of potentially incriminating files; of his possession, control, and access to the encrypted portions of the drives; and of his capability to decrypt the files.

We are unpersuaded by the Government's derivation of the key/combination analogy in arguing that Doe's production of the unencrypted files would be nothing more than a physical nontestimonial transfer. The Government attempts to avoid the analogy by arguing that it does not seek the combination or the key, but rather the contents. This argument badly misses the mark. In *Fisher*, where the analogy was born, and again in *Hubbell*, the Government never sought the "key" or the "combination" to the safe for its own sake; rather, the Government sought the files being withheld, just as the Government does here. Requiring Doe to use a decryption password is most certainly more akin to requiring the production of a combination because both demand the use of the contents of the mind, and the production is accompanied by the implied factual statements noted above that could prove to be incriminatory. Hence, we conclude that what the Government seeks to compel in this case, the decryption and production of the contents of the hard drives, is testimonial in character.

Moving to the second point, the question becomes whether the purported testimony is a "foregone conclusion." We think not. Nothing in the record before us reveals that the Government knows whether any files exist and are located on the hard drives; what's more, nothing in the record illustrates that the Government knows with reasonable particularity that Doe is even capable of accessing the encrypted portions of the drives.

To support its position, the Government points to McCrohan's testimony. It states in its answer brief that "[h]ere, the government knows of the 'existence' and 'whereabouts' of the decrypted records it has subpoenaed because the government *already physically* possesses those records." But McCrohan's testimony simply does not stretch as far as the Government wishes it would. As an initial matter, McCrohan admitted on cross-examination that he had no idea whether there was data on the encrypted drives. Responding to a question from Doe as to whether the random characters definitively indicated that encrypted data is present or instead could have indicated blank space, McCrohan conceded, "Well, you would see random characters, but you wouldn't know necessarily whether it was blank." Moreover, when pressed to answer why investigators believed data may be hidden, McCrohan replied, "The scope of my examination didn't go that far," and, "We couldn't get into them, so we can't make that call." Finally, when Doe posed the question of whether "random data is just random data," McCrohan concluded that "anything is possible."

To be fair, the Government has shown that the combined storage space of the drives *could* contain files that number well into the millions. And the Government has also shown that the drives are encrypted. The Government has not shown, however, that the drives *actually* contain any files, nor has it shown which of the estimated twenty million files the drives are capable of holding may prove useful. The Government has emphasized at every stage of the proceedings in this case that the forensic analysis showed random characters. But random characters are not files; because the TrueCrypt program displays random characters if there are files *and* if there is empty space, we simply do not know what, if anything, was hidden based on the facts before us. It is not enough for the Government to argue that the encrypted drives are *capable* of storing vast amounts of data, some of which *may* be incriminating. In short, the Government physically possesses the media devices, but it does not know what, if anything, is held on the encrypted drives.[n.25][38] Along the same lines, we are not persuaded by the suggestion that simply because the devices were encrypted necessarily means that Doe was trying to hide something. Just as a vault is capable of storing mountains of incriminating documents, that alone does not mean that it contains incriminating documents, or anything at all.

In sum, we think this case is far closer to the *Hubbell* end of the spectrum than it is to the *Fisher* end. As in *Hubbell*, "the Government has not shown that it had any prior knowledge of either the existence or the whereabouts of the [files]" that it seeks to compel Doe to produce. In *Fisher*, the Government knew exactly what documents it sought to be produced, knew that they were in the possession of the attorney, and knew that they were prepared by an accountant. Here, the Government has not shown that it possessed even a remotely similar level of knowledge as to the *files* on the hard drives at the time it attempted to compel production from Doe. Case law from the Supreme Court does not demand that the Government identify exactly the documents it seeks, but it does require some specificity in its requests—categorical

---

38. [n.25] This situation is no different than if the Government seized a locked strongbox. Physical possession of the entire lockbox is not the issue; whether the Government has the requisite knowledge of what is contained inside the strongbox is the critical question.

requests for documents the Government anticipates are likely to exist simply will not suffice.

The Government tries to analogize this case to *In re Boucher*, 2009 U.S. Dist. LEXIS 13006 (D. Vt. Feb. 19, 2009). The district court concluded that the "foregone conclusion" doctrine applied under those facts because any testimonial value derived from the act of production was already known to the Government and therefore added nothing to its case.

The Government correctly notes that *Boucher* did not turn on the fact that the Government knew the contents of the file it sought; *Fisher* and *Hubbell*, though, still require that the Government show its knowledge *that the files exist.* Thus, while in *Boucher* it was irrelevant that the Government knew what was contained in the file "2yo getting raped during diaper change," it was crucial that the Government knew that there existed a file under such a name. That is simply not the case here. We find no support in the record for the conclusion that the Government, at the time it sought to compel production, knew to any degree of particularity what, if anything, was hidden behind the encrypted wall.[n.28][39]

In short, we conclude that Doe would certainly use the contents of his mind to incriminate himself or lead the Government to evidence that would incriminate him if he complied with the district court's order. Moreover, the Government has failed to show any basis, let alone shown a basis with reasonable particularity, for its belief that encrypted files exist on the drives, that Doe has access to those files, or that he is capable of decrypting the files. The "foregone conclusion" doctrine does not apply under these facts.

B.

The district court still could have compelled Doe to turn over the unencrypted contents — and held him in contempt if he refused to do so — had the Government offered and the district court granted Doe constitutionally sufficient immunity.

In evaluating the immunity Doe received, we must look beyond the act-of-production label and ask this question: what conduct was actually immunized and what use would the Government make of the evidence derived from such conduct in a future prosecution? The Government stated that it would not use Doe's act of production against him in a future prosecution; but it would use the contents of the unencrypted drives against him. The district court incorporated the Government's position in its order granting immunity under 18 U.S.C. § 6002. The

---

39. [n.28] To be clear, the Government does not have to show that it knows specific file names. Knowledge of a file name, like the Government had in *Boucher*, would be an easy way for the Government to carry its burden of showing that the existence of the files it seeks is a "foregone conclusion." That said, if the Government is unaware of a particular file name, it still must show with some reasonable particularity that it seeks a certain file and is aware, based on other information, that (1) the file exists in some specified location, (2) the file is possessed by the target of the subpoena, and (3) the file is authentic.

act-of-production immunity, as the Government and the district court framed it, is not synonymous with use and derivative-use immunity.[n.31][40] More to the point, it is not the type of immunity mandated by 18 U.S.C. §6002. The question thus becomes, is the act-of-production immunity offered here sufficient to compel Doe to testify? We hold that the answer is most certainly, no.

[In] *Kastigar v. United States*, 406 U.S. 441, 449 (1972)[, the Court] held that §6002 "immunity from use and derivative use is coextensive with the scope of the [Fifth Amendment] privilege against self-incrimination." In so holding, the Court emphasized that such immunity "prohibits the prosecutorial authorities from using the compelled testimony in any respect."

Supreme Court precedent is clear: Use and derivative-use immunity establishes the critical threshold to overcome an individual's invocation of the Fifth Amendment privilege against self-incrimination. No more protection is necessary; no less protection is sufficient.[n.32][41]

The Government gave no such immunity in this case. In essence, the Government attempted to immunize the testimony itself, treating everything else as fair game. But for the reasons we just noted, the Government cannot obtain immunity only for the act of production and then seek to introduce the contents of the production, regardless of whether those contents are characterized as nontestimonial evidence, because doing so would allow the use of evidence *derived* from the original testimonial statement.

The Court in *Hubbell* expressly rejected the "manna from heaven" theory, which contended that if the Government omitted any description of how the documents were obtained, it would be as if they magically appeared on the courthouse steps and the Government could use the documents themselves.

To conclude, because Doe's act of production would have testimonial aspects to it, an order to compel him to produce the unencrypted contents of the drives would require immunity coextensive with the Fifth Amendment (and §6002). Immunity coextensive with the Fifth Amendment requires both use and derivative-use immunity. The Government's offer of act-of-production immunity clearly could not provide the requisite protection because it would allow the Government to use evidence

---

40. [n.31] The immunity statute, 18 U.S.C. §6002, clearly immunizes both the use of the testimony itself and any information derived from the testimony. The text of the statute provides in relevant part that

> no testimony or other information compelled under [an immunity] order (*or any information directly or indirectly derived from such testimony or other information*) may be used against the witness in any criminal case, except a prosecution for perjury, giving a false statement, or otherwise failing to comply with the order.

(emphasis added).

41. [n.32] The *Kastigar* Court concluded that transactional immunity—a prohibition on any future prosecution based on immunized testimony—exceeded the protections offered by the Fifth Amendment, but that immunity limited to the prohibition on the use of the testimonial evidence itself, not derivative evidence, offered too little protection to compel production.

derived from the immunized testimony. Thus, because the immunity offered here was not coextensive with the Fifth Amendment, Doe could not be compelled to decrypt the drives.

III.

We hold that Doe properly invoked the Fifth Amendment privilege. In response, the Government chose not to give him the immunity the Fifth Amendment and 18 U.S.C. §6002 mandate, and the district court acquiesced. Stripped of Fifth Amendment protection, Doe refused to produce the unencrypted contents of the hard drives. The refusal was justified, and the district court erred in adjudging him in civil contempt. The district court's judgment is accordingly REVERSED.

Notes

1. Compare the views expressed in John Duong, Note, *The Intersection of the Fourth and Fifth Amendments in the Context of Encrypted Personal Data at the Border*, 2 Drexel L. Rev. 313, 349–50 (2009):

> Unlike physical evidence, which exists independently from the person, there is no such separation between a person and his or her passphrase. The passphrase is inherently intertwined within the chasms of the mind of the individual. In other words, being compelled to produce a passphrase involves mining and extracting the contents of one's mind and that act itself inherently involves revealing the contents of that mind, which makes it a testimonial communication. This link simply cannot be conceptually severed.

2. Duong, in his Note, also argues:

> [T]he District Court [in *Boucher*] erred ... by claiming that the government already knew "of the existence and location of the Z drive and its files." This is precisely the kind of fishing expedition that the *Hubbell* Court rejected. In *Hubbell*, the Supreme Court stated that a broad-based belief of certain materials is not enough for application of the forgone conclusion doctrine. The government must be able to specify that it knew such materials existed and where they were located. In this case, the government only knew the existence and location of some of the child pornography files. Contrary to the District Court's assertion that the contents of the entire decrypted Z drive would not add much to the sum total of the government's knowledge, it could in fact add considerably if Boucher had many more incriminating files than were previously viewed by the Customs agents. The District Court should have performed the same analysis and held that Boucher must only produce the files of which the government already had prior knowledge.

Id. at 355 n.210.

In *Commonwealth v. Gelfgatt*, 11 N.E.3d 605 (Mass. 2014), the court applied the foregone conclusion doctrine to mandate that the accused be required to unlock his computers:

The investigation by the corruption, fraud, and computer crime division of the Attorney General's office uncovered detailed evidence that at least two mortgage assignments to Baylor Holdings were fraudulent. During his postarrest interview with State police Trooper Patrick M. Johnson, the defendant stated that he had performed real estate work for Baylor Holdings, which he understood to be a financial services company. He explained that his communications with this company, which purportedly was owned by Russian individuals, were highly encrypted because, according to the defendant, "[that] is how Russians do business." The defendant informed Trooper Johnson that he had more than one computer at his home, that the program for communicating with Baylor Holdings was installed on a laptop, and that "[e]verything is encrypted and no one is going to get to it." The defendant acknowledged that he was able to perform decryption. Further, and most significantly, the defendant said that because of encryption, the police were "not going to get to *any* of [his] computers," thereby implying that *all* of them were encrypted.

When considering the entirety of the defendant's interview with Trooper Johnson, it is apparent that the defendant was engaged in real estate transactions involving Baylor Holdings, that he used his computers to allegedly communicate with its purported owners, that the information on all of his computers pertaining to these transactions was encrypted, and that he had the ability to decrypt the files and documents. The facts that would be conveyed by the defendant through his act of decryption—his ownership and control of the computers and their contents, knowledge of the fact of encryption, and knowledge of the encryption key—already are known to the government and, thus, are a "foregone conclusion." The Commonwealth's motion to compel decryption does not violate the defendant's rights under the Fifth Amendment because the defendant is only telling the government what it already knows.

Based on *Boucher*, *In re Subpoena*, and *Gelfgatt*, what must the government know for the foregone conclusion doctrine to apply? Are the three cases consistent? If you were advising a client who was under investigation, what would you tell her about speaking with the police?

3. **An Ethical Quandary?** When faced with the order by the court in *Boucher*, as his attorney, what advice could you ethically provide? What are the consequences of refusing to comply with the court order vs. a possible conviction for child pornography charges?

4. The reasonableness of the search and seizure of computers at the International border is considered in Chapter 10.

5. **Biometrics.** What if the key to unlocking or decrypting the digital device is biometric? For example, the use of an index finger on a biometric reader. Is placing one's finger on the reader "testimonial" so that the Fifth Amendment privilege

would apply? Two lower court cases have examined the Fifth Amendment implications of the forced unlocking of a device by finger touch. *See State v. Diamond*, 890 N.W.2d 143 (Minn. Ct. App. 2017), *review granted* (Minn. 03/28/17); *Commonwealth v. Baust*, 89 Va. Cir. 267, 2014 WL 10355635 (Cir. Ct. Va. 2014). Both held that there was no Fifth Amendment protection for this compelled act. What about other physical characteristics, such as iris scans or facial recognition? The production of physical characteristics has generally not been found to implicate the Fifth Amendment. *E.g., United States v. Dionisio*, 410 U.S. 1 (1973) (suspect can be compelled to provide voice exemplar); *Schmerber v. Cal.*, 384 U.S. 757 (1966) (suspect may be compelled to give blood sample); *Gilbert v. Cal.*, 388 U.S. 263 (1967) (suspect may be compelled to provide handwriting exemplar). Which form of locking a computer offers more protection: passwords or a fingerprint?

6. **Facebook Passwords and Profiles.** Professor Caren Anderson sets out the issue:

> Does the Fifth Amendment privilege against self-incrimination shield someone who has posted incriminating information on his Facebook page from being forced to disclose his password or provide access to his profile? While in most cases, Facebook information is public, or law enforcement has sufficient identifying information about the account to subpoena the company directly, in rare situations a law-enforcement officer might find herself in the peculiar position of believing that incriminating information is posted on a Facebook page, but having no way to get to it without the suspect's cooperation.

Caren M. Morrison, *Passwords, Profiles, and the Privilege Against Self-Incrimination: Facebook and the Fifth Amendment*, 65 Ark. L. Rev. 133 (2012). As discussed in that article, the answer turns on how the act of production doctrine is construed, complicated by issues of authentication related to material posted on the account. *See also Juror Number One v. Superior Court*, 206 Cal. App. 4th 854 (2012) (to investigate possible misconduct of juror, upholding order compelling juror to execute consent form to Facebook to release for in camera review by trial court items juror posted during trial).

7. **Compelling Third Parties to Unlock Devices.** It has long been established that third parties can be forced by subpoena to appear before a grand jury or testify in court or otherwise assist law enforcement under the All Writs Act, first enacted in 1789. *E.g., United States v. Dionisio*, 410 U.S. 1 (1973) (noting "longstanding principle that 'the public has a right to every man's evidence'"). Can device manufacturers be compelled to assist in unlocking devices? Such compulsion can be seen as a direct conflict between the government's ability to obtain evidence and the company's own best interest, given that the purpose of encryption is to block third-party access.

Apple CEO Tim Cook condemned a request for such an order to force the company to unlock a phone as "dangerous" and said it would make Apple "hack [its] own users and undermine decades of security advancements that protect our customers—including tens of millions of American citizens—from sophisticated hackers and cybercriminals." Tim Cook, *A Message to Our Customers*, February 16, 2016, available at http://www.apple.com/customer-letter/. In ruling on the matter, the District Court concluded:

> In deciding this motion, I offer no opinion as to whether, in the circumstances of this case or others, the government's legitimate interest in ensuring that no door is too strong to resist lawful entry should prevail against the equally legitimate societal interests arrayed against it here. Those competing values extend beyond the individual's interest in vindicating reasonable expectations of privacy—which is not directly implicated where, as here, it must give way to the mandate of a lawful warrant. They include the commercial interest in conducting a lawful business as its owners deem most productive, free of potentially harmful government intrusion; and the far more fundamental and universal interest—important to individuals as a matter of safety, to businesses as a matter of competitive fairness, and to society as a whole as a matter of national security—in shielding sensitive electronically stored data from the myriad harms, great and small, that unauthorized access and misuse can cause.
>
> How best to balance those interests is a matter of critical importance to our society, and the need for an answer becomes more pressing daily, as the tide of technological advance flows ever farther past the boundaries of what seemed possible even a few decades ago. But that debate must happen today, and it must take place among legislators who are equipped to consider the technological and cultural realities of a world their predecessors could not begin to conceive. It would betray our constitutional heritage and our people's claim to democratic governance for a judge to pretend that our Founders already had that debate, and ended it, in 1789.
>
> Ultimately, the question to be answered in this matter, and in others like it across the country, is not whether the government should be able to force Apple to help it unlock a specific device; it is instead whether the All Writs Act resolves that issue and many others like it yet to come. For the reasons set forth above, I conclude that it does not. The government's motion is denied.

In re Apple, Inc., 149 F. Supp. 3d 341 (E.D.N.Y. 2016).

Chapter 8

Cell Phones, Other Mobile Digital Devices, and Traditional Fourth Amendment Doctrine Permitting Warrantless Searches

Mobile digital devices are everywhere and have wide-ranging capabilities. This chapter pays particular attention to one such device — the cell phone — and some of the circumstances where the police have searched the contents of those devices. The legal analysis is as complex as the modern technology that goes into a cell phone.

§ 8.1 Search Incident to Arrest

1. Basic Principles

The application of the search incident to arrest principle is one of the main consequences of an arrest. It involves a significant intrusion upon the person of the suspect, as well as the suspect's belongings within the area under the suspect's control. The evidentiary results of such searches often have a significant influence on the course of any subsequent criminal proceedings. Searches incident to arrest are a common form of search and, given the development of modern police forces and the statutory expansion of the number of crimes, such searches now apply to large numbers of criminal suspects. Given the ubiquity of portable digital devices carried on or about one's person in today's world, the search incident to arrest doctrine has potentially vast application.

Search incident to arrest principles have undergone significant evolution since the imposition of the exclusionary rule on federal authorities in *Weeks v. United States*, 232 U.S. 383 (1914), which itself recognized the propriety of a search incident to arrest. First, the nature of the justification for such searches have had several iterations. Many cases prior to *United States v. Robinson*, 414 U.S. 218 (1973), viewed searches incident to arrest in terms of an exception to the warrant requirement, which intimated an exigent circumstances rationale and, perhaps, a need to justify the search in each case. While not all of the United States Supreme Court's cases reflected that view, a dispositive doctrinal shift in the underlying justification for searches incident to arrest occurred in *Robinson*, where the Court stated:

> A custodial arrest of a suspect based on probable cause is a reasonable intrusion under the Fourth Amendment; that intrusion being lawful, a search incident to the arrest requires no additional justification. It is the fact of the lawful arrest which establishes the authority to search, and we hold that in the case of a lawful custodial arrest a full search of the person is not only an exception to the warrant requirement of the Fourth Amendment, but is also a "reasonable" search under that Amendment.

In *Robinson*, which involved the arrest of a person for driving after his license had been revoked, the Court adopted a "categorical" search incident to arrest rule: it applied to all arrests, regardless of the underlying factual circumstances. In so ruling, the Court rejected a case-by-case inquiry. *Robinson*'s view prevailed in subsequent decades[1] until *Arizona v. Gant*, 556 U.S. 332 (2009), changed the rule for vehicle searches and *Riley* (reproduced *infra*), changed the rule for cell phone searches.

A second consideration concerns the purpose of the search that is being authorized by the fact of the arrest. One aspect, always accepted, is that such searches serve to protect the safety of the officer by allowing the police to search for weapons and other objects that may be used to attack the officer. Thus, for example, in *Chimel v. California*, 395 U.S. 752 (1969), the Court observed: "When an arrest is made, it is reasonable for the arresting officer to search the person arrested in order to remove any weapons that the latter might seek to use in order to resist arrest or effect his escape. Otherwise, the officer's safety might well be endangered, and the arrest itself frustrated." The cases have also recognized a second purpose for a search incident to arrest: to recover evidence. It is here that much conflict, ambiguity, and changes of course permeate the case law.[2] One view is that the permissible search is for evidence of the crime committed. The broader view is that the search may be for any evidence of any crime. Depending on which view is adopted, the permitted scope of a search incident to arrest will vary.

2. Permissible Objects Sought

While older case law was somewhat unclear whether, other than weapons, the objects permissibly seized pursuant to the arrest had to relate to the offense for which the arrest was made,[3] modern Supreme Court jurisprudence, with few exceptions, does not impose any limits on the search based on the types of objects sought. *United States v. Robinson*, 414 U.S. 218 (1973), is the leading case. Robinson was arrested for operating a motor vehicle after his operator's permit had been revoked.

---

1. *E.g.*, Thornton v. United States, 541 U.S. 615 (2004); Michigan v. DeFillippo, 443 U.S. 31, 39 (1979). Some states reject the categorical federal rule on independent state grounds. *E.g.*, Pierce v. State, 171 P.3d 525 (Wyo. 2007) (rejecting per se rule of searches incident to all arrests under state constitution and requiring fact specific justification in each case).

2. *See generally* Thornton v. United States, 541 U.S. 615, 625 (2004) (Scalia, J., concurring).

3. *E.g.*, Marron v. United States, 275 U.S. 192, 198–99 (1927); United States v. Rabinowitz, 339 U.S. 56, 64 n.6 (1950).

The arresting officer subjected him to a full search. Upon feeling an object in one of Robinson's coat pockets, the officer removed it. The object was a "crumpled up cigarette package," which the officer opened, revealing gelatin capsules of white powder that, upon later analysis, proved to be heroin. The *Robinson* Court established bright-line authority to search, with no limitations based on the type of crime or the likelihood of finding additional evidence of that crime during the search. Subject to few exceptions, the effect of the Court's view is to afford complete discretion to the police as to the objects sought during the search. The ramifications are dramatic: all objects—from the clothing worn by the suspect[4] to the contents of wallets[5]—are subject to search.

3. Location of the Search

The scope of a search incident to arrest includes the location where the accused is arrested but the right to search does not extend to other places.[6] There is considerable fiction involved in fixing the place of search. The permissible location for searches incident to arrest is generally the spot where the police first detained the person, even if he or she has been moved some distance thereafter or is sitting handcuffed in a vehicle.[7] This result is widely criticized by commentators because, factually, there is usually no basis for believing that the suspect could obtain a weapon or destroy evidence in the area searched; yet, factual considerations are no longer the inquiry after *Robinson*, which substituted a categorical rule for any case-by-case analysis. The fictionalized area of control at least prevents the police from using the suspect as a "walking search warrant" by moving him into a house and from room to room to conduct a warrantless search of the house.[8]

The Court has often remarked that the search must be contemporaneous[9] or "substantially contemporaneous with the arrest" both as to time and place.[10] As with other features of the search incident to arrest rule, there is considerable debate

---

4. *E.g.*, Powell v. State, 796 So. 2d 404 (Ala. Ct. Crim. App. 1999), *aff'd*, 796 So. 2d 434 (Ala. 2001).

5. *E.g.*, United States v. Watson, 669 F.2d 1374 (11th Cir. 1982).

6. *E.g.*, Coolidge v. New Hampshire, 403 U.S. 443, 457 (1971).

7. *See generally* Myron Moskovitz, *A Rule in Search of a Reason: An Empirical Reexamination of* Chimel *and* Belton, 2002 Wis. L. Rev. 657.

8. Vale v. Louisiana, 399 U.S. 30, 33–34 (1970).

9. *E.g.*, Agnello v. United States, 269 U.S. 20, 29 (1925). *See generally* Edwin Butterfoss, *As Time Goes By: The Elimination of Contemporaneity and Brevity as Factors in Search and Seizure Cases*, 21 Harv. C.R. — C.L. L. Rev. 603, 620–35 (1986).

10. *E.g.*, Stoner v. California, 376 U.S. 483, 486 (1964) (invalidating warrantless search conducted two days before arrest). *Cf.* Preston v. State, 784 A.2d 601 (Md. Ct. Spec. App. 2001) (Collecting cases and observing: "Searches have been deemed to be 'essentially contemporaneous' with an arrest when made within a few minutes after the arrest even if the suspect, at the time of a search, has been placed in a police cruiser and handcuffed." Rejecting a delay of "at least two or three hours," the court added that "we have found none, where *any* court has held that a search that takes place two or more hours after an arrest is nevertheless 'essentially contemporaneous' with that arrest.").

as to the meanings of those requirements.[11] The Supreme Court seemed to abandon the contemporaneous limitation for searches of the *person* incident to a lawful arrest in *United States v. Edwards*, 415 U.S. 800 (1974), which involved the search of the defendant's clothing at the jail where he was incarcerated ten hours after he was arrested. The *Edwards* Court stated: "It is . . . plain that searches and seizures that could be made on the spot at the time of the arrest may legally be conducted later when the accused arrives at the place of detention." The Court broadly opined:

> [O]nce the accused is lawfully arrested and is in custody, the effects in his possession at the place of detention that were subject to search at the time and place of his arrest may lawfully be searched and seized without a warrant even though a substantial period of time has elapsed between the arrest and subsequent administrative processing, on the one hand, and the taking of the property for use as evidence, on the other. This is true where the clothing or effects are immediately seized upon arrival at the jail, held under the defendant's name in the "property room" of the jail, and at a later time searched and taken for use at the subsequent criminal trial. The result is the same where the property is not physically taken from the defendant until sometime after his incarceration.

Edwards' reasoning was a blend of various justifications for the permissibility of the search, including search incident to arrest, search incident to incarceration, inventory, and a probable cause-based analysis combined with the fact that Edwards and his property were rightfully in police custody. The *Edwards* Court "perceived little difference" in a search at the scene of the arrest and at the police station, with "similar" justifications supporting a search at either place. The Court also justified the delayed search based on a factual analysis of the case:

> [T]he police had probable cause to believe that the articles of clothing [Edwards] wore were themselves material evidence of the crime for which he had been arrested. But it was late at night; no substitute clothing was then available for Edwards to wear, and it would certainly have been unreasonable for the police to have stripped respondent of his clothing and left him exposed in his cell throughout the night. When the substitutes were purchased the next morning, the clothing he had been wearing at the time of arrest was taken from him and subjected to laboratory analysis. This was no more than taking from respondent the effects in his immediate possession that constituted evidence of crime. This was and is a normal incident of a custodial arrest, and reasonable delay in effectuating it does not change the fact that Edwards was no more imposed upon than he could have been at the time and place of the arrest or immediately upon arrival at the place of detention. The police did no more . . . than they were entitled to do incident to the usual custodial arrest and incarceration.

---

11. United States v. Hrasky, 453 F.3d 1099 (8th Cir. 2006).

In *United States v. Chadwick*, 433 U.S. 1 (1977), which did not involve the search incident to arrest doctrine because the object searched—a footlocker located in the trunk of a vehicle—was outside the defined area of an arrestee's control, the Court nonetheless observed:

> [W]arrantless searches of luggage or other property seized at the time of an arrest cannot be justified as incident to that arrest either if the "search is remote in time or place from the arrest," or no exigency exists. Once law enforcement officers have reduced luggage or other personal property not immediately associated with the person of the arrestee to their exclusive control, and there is no longer any danger that the arrestee might gain access to the property to seize a weapon or destroy evidence, a search of that property is no longer an incident of the arrest.

> Here the search was conducted more than an hour after federal agents had gained exclusive control of the footlocker and long after respondents were securely in custody; the search therefore cannot be viewed as incidental to the arrest or as justified by any other exigency.

In a footnote, the *Chadwick* Court sought to distinguish *Edwards:* "Unlike searches of the person, searches of possessions within an arrestee's immediate control cannot be justified by any reduced expectations of privacy caused by the arrest."

Given the mixture of rationales supporting the *Edwards* decision, combined with *Chadwick's* interpretation of that case and the lack of any guidance in subsequent Supreme Court case law, it is not surprising that the lower court decisions are in conflict. What appears clear after *Edwards* is that, using any of its alternative rationales, a full search of an arrestee at the police station is permitted. But what about other objects seized at the time of the arrest and transported to the station? Under current Supreme Court doctrine, many objects may be searched under the inventory search doctrine.[12] Some courts ask whether the administrative processes incident to arrest are still continuing at the time the search occurs.[13] Putting those considerations aside, lower courts have grappled with the impact of the *Edwards* and *Chadwick* "contemporaneous" requirement for a search incident to arrest. "Cases decided subsequent to *Chadwick* have distinguished between searches of items 'closely associated with the arrestee' made at the police station and searches of luggage and other articles of personal property not immediately associated with the person of the arrestee. The former may be searched long after the arrest, while the latter may be searched only incident to the suspect's arrest."[14] There has arisen a dubious jurisprudence of

---

12. *See* Thomas K. Clancy, The Fourth Amendment: Its History and Interpretation § 10.8. (3d ed. 2017.

13. *E.g.,* United States v. Finley, 477 F.3d 250, 260 n.7 (5th Cir. 2007); United States v. Ruigomez, 702 F.2d 61, 66 (5th Cir. 1983).

14. Preston v. State, 784 A.2d 601 (Md. Ct. Spec. App. 2001) (collecting cases). *See* United States v. Finley, 477 F.3d 250, 260 (5th Cir. 2007) ("Finley's cell phone does not fit into the category of

containers,[15] with fine distinctions between types of containers and their closeness of association with the person. Thus, cases have determined whether searches of wallets,[16] purses,[17] luggage,[18] and backpacks[19] are permissible.

4. Cell Phone Searches Incident to Arrest

May the digital contents of cell phones and similar devices be searched incident to arrest?

David Leon Riley v. California
134 S. Ct. 2473 (2014)[n.*][20]

CHIEF JUSTICE ROBERTS delivered the opinion of the Court.

These two cases raise a common question: whether the police may, without a warrant, search digital information on a cell phone seized from an individual who has been arrested.

I

A

In the first case, petitioner David Riley was stopped by a police officer for driving with expired registration tags. In the course of the stop, the officer also learned that Riley's license had been suspended. The officer impounded Riley's car, pursuant to department policy, and another officer conducted an inventory search of the car. Riley was arrested for possession of concealed and loaded firearms when that search turned up two handguns under the car's hood. An officer searched Riley incident to the arrest and found items associated with the "Bloods" street gang. He also seized a cell phone from Riley's pants pocket. According to Riley's uncontradicted assertion, the phone was a "smart phone," a cell phone with a broad range of other functions

---

'property not immediately associated with [his] person' because it was on his person at the time of his arrest.").

15. The Court, in other aspects of Fourth Amendment jurisprudence, had at one time attempted to create a distinction between containers but ultimately rejected that view as without logical support. *See* THOMAS K. CLANCY, THE FOURTH AMENDMENT: ITS HISTORY AND INTERPRETATION §4.6.1. (3d ed. 2017).

16. United States v. Phillips, 607 F.2d 808, 809–10 (8th Cir. 1979) (search of defendant's wallet at police station "substantial period of time" after arrest was valid search incident to arrest).

17. Curd v. City Court of Judsonia, 141 F.3d 839 (8th Cir. 1998) (plaintiff's purse permissibly searched at police station fifteen minutes after arrest).

18. United States v. $639,558 in U.S. Currency, 955 F.2d 712, 715–16 (D.C. Cir. 1992) (luggage search half an hour after arrest not contemporaneous); State v. Calegar, 661 P.2d 311, 315–16 (Idaho 1983) (suitcase seized from automobile in which defendant was arrested permissibly searched at police station).

19. People v. Boff, 766 P.2d 646, 650–51 (Colo. 1988).

20. [n.*] Together with No. 13-212, *United States v. Wurie*, on certiorari to the United States Court of Appeals for the First Circuit.

based on advanced computing capability, large storage capacity, and Internet connectivity. The officer accessed information on the phone and noticed that some words (presumably in text messages or a contacts list) were preceded by the letters "CK"—a label that, he believed, stood for "Crip Killers," a slang term for members of the Bloods gang.

At the police station about two hours after the arrest, a detective specializing in gangs further examined the contents of the phone. The detective testified that he "went through" Riley's phone "looking for evidence, because . . . gang members will often video themselves with guns or take pictures of themselves with the guns." Although there was "a lot of stuff" on the phone, particular files that "caught [the detective's] eye" included videos of young men sparring while someone yelled encouragement using the moniker "Blood." The police also found photographs of Riley standing in front of a car they suspected had been involved in a shooting a few weeks earlier.

Riley was ultimately charged, in connection with that earlier shooting, with firing at an occupied vehicle, assault with a semiautomatic firearm, and attempted murder. The State alleged that Riley had committed those crimes for the benefit of a criminal street gang, an aggravating factor that carries an enhanced sentence. Prior to trial, Riley moved to suppress all evidence that the police had obtained from his cell phone. He contended that the searches of his phone violated the Fourth Amendment, because they had been performed without a warrant and were not otherwise justified by exigent circumstances. The trial court rejected that argument. At Riley's trial, police officers testified about the photographs and videos found on the phone, and some of the photographs were admitted into evidence. Riley was convicted on all three counts and received an enhanced sentence of 15 years to life in prison.

B

In the second case, a police officer performing routine surveillance observed respondent Brima Wurie make an apparent drug sale from a car. Officers subsequently arrested Wurie and took him to the police station. At the station, the officers seized two cell phones from Wurie's person. The one at issue here was a "flip phone," a kind of phone that is flipped open for use and that generally has a smaller range of features than a smart phone. Five to ten minutes after arriving at the station, the officers noticed that the phone was repeatedly receiving calls from a source identified as "my house" on the phone's external screen. A few minutes later, they opened the phone and saw a photograph of a woman and a baby set as the phone's wallpaper. They pressed one button on the phone to access its call log, then another button to determine the phone number associated with the "my house" label. They next used an online phone directory to trace that phone number to an apartment building. When the officers went to the building, they saw Wurie's name on a mailbox and observed through a window a woman who resembled the woman in the photograph on Wurie's phone. They secured the apartment while obtaining a search warrant and, upon later executing the warrant, found and seized 215 grams of crack cocaine, marijuana, drug paraphernalia, a firearm and ammunition, and cash.

Wurie was charged with distributing crack cocaine, possessing crack cocaine with intent to distribute, and being a felon in possession of a firearm and ammunition. He moved to suppress the evidence obtained from the search of the apartment, arguing that it was the fruit of an unconstitutional search of his cell phone. The District Court denied the motion. Wurie was convicted on all three counts and sentenced to 262 months in prison.

II

As the text makes clear, "the ultimate touchstone of the Fourth Amendment is 'reasonableness.'" Our cases have determined that "[w]here a search is undertaken by law enforcement officials to discover evidence of criminal wrongdoing, . . . reasonableness generally requires the obtaining of a judicial warrant." *Vernonia School Dist. 47J v. Acton*, 515 U.S. 646, 653 (1995). Such a warrant ensures that the inferences to support a search are "drawn by a neutral and detached magistrate instead of being judged by the officer engaged in the often competitive enterprise of ferreting out crime." In the absence of a warrant, a search is reasonable only if it falls within a specific exception to the warrant requirement.

The two cases before us concern the reasonableness of a warrantless search incident to a lawful arrest. In 1914, this Court first acknowledged in dictum "the right on the part of the Government, always recognized under English and American law, to search the person of the accused when legally arrested to discover and seize the fruits or evidences of crime." Since that time, it has been well accepted that such a search constitutes an exception to the warrant requirement. Indeed, the label "exception" is something of a misnomer in this context, as warrantless searches incident to arrest occur with far greater frequency than searches conducted pursuant to a warrant.

Although the existence of the exception for such searches has been recognized for a century, its scope has been debated for nearly as long. That debate has focused on the extent to which officers may search property found on or near the arrestee. Three related precedents set forth the rules governing such searches:

The first, *Chimel v. California*, 395 U.S. 752 (1969), laid the groundwork for most of the existing search incident to arrest doctrine. Police officers in that case arrested Chimel inside his home and proceeded to search his entire three-bedroom house, including the attic and garage. In particular rooms, they also looked through the contents of drawers.

The Court crafted the following rule for assessing the reasonableness of a search incident to arrest:

> "When an arrest is made, it is reasonable for the arresting officer to search the person arrested in order to remove any weapons that the latter might seek to use in order to resist arrest or effect his escape. Otherwise, the officer's safety might well be endangered, and the arrest itself frustrated. In addition, it is entirely reasonable for the arresting officer to search for and seize any evidence on the arrestee's person in order to prevent its concealment or

destruction. . . . There is ample justification, therefore, for a search of the arrestee's person and the area 'within his immediate control'—construing that phrase to mean the area from within which he might gain possession of a weapon or destructible evidence."

The extensive warrantless search of Chimel's home did not fit within this exception, because it was not needed to protect officer safety or to preserve evidence.

Four years later, in *United States v. Robinson*, 414 U.S. 218 (1973), the Court applied the *Chimel* analysis in the context of a search of the arrestee's person. A police officer had arrested Robinson for driving with a revoked license. The officer conducted a patdown search and felt an object that he could not identify in Robinson's coat pocket. He removed the object, which turned out to be a crumpled cigarette package, and opened it. Inside were 14 capsules of heroin.

The Court of Appeals concluded that the search was unreasonable because Robinson was unlikely to have evidence of the crime of arrest on his person, and because it believed that extracting the cigarette package and opening it could not be justified as part of a protective search for weapons. This Court reversed, rejecting the notion that "case-by-case adjudication" was required to determine "whether or not there was present one of the reasons supporting the authority for a search of the person incident to a lawful arrest." As the Court explained, "[t]he authority to search the person incident to a lawful custodial arrest, while based upon the need to disarm and to discover evidence, does not depend on what a court may later decide was the probability in a particular arrest situation that weapons or evidence would in fact be found upon the person of the suspect." Instead, a "custodial arrest of a suspect based on probable cause is a reasonable intrusion under the Fourth Amendment; that intrusion being lawful, a search incident to the arrest requires no additional justification."

The Court thus concluded that the search of Robinson was reasonable even though there was no concern about the loss of evidence, and the arresting officer had no specific concern that Robinson might be armed. In doing so, the Court did not draw a line between a search of Robinson's person and a further examination of the cigarette pack found during that search. It merely noted that, "[h]aving in the course of a lawful search come upon the crumpled package of cigarettes, [the officer] was entitled to inspect it." A few years later, the Court clarified that this exception was limited to "personal property . . . immediately associated with the person of the arrestee." *United States v. Chadwick*, 433 U.S. 1, 15 (1977) (200-pound, locked footlocker could not be searched incident to arrest), abrogated on other grounds by *California v. Acevedo*, 500 U.S. 565 (1991).

The search incident to arrest trilogy concludes with *Gant*, which analyzed searches of an arrestee's vehicle. [*Arizona v.*] *Gant*, [556 U.S. 332 (2009),] like *Robinson*, recognized that the *Chimel* concerns for officer safety and evidence preservation underlie the search incident to arrest exception. As a result, the Court concluded that *Chimel* could authorize police to search a vehicle "only when the arrestee is unsecured and within reaching distance of the passenger compartment at the time of the search." *Gant* added, however, an independent exception for a warrantless search of a vehicle's passenger compartment "when it is 'reasonable to believe evidence relevant to the crime of arrest might be found in the vehicle.'" (quoting *Thornton v. United States*, 541 U.S. 615, 632 (2004) (SCALIA, J., concurring in judgment)). That exception stems not from *Chimel*, the Court explained, but from "circumstances unique to the vehicle context."

III

These cases require us to decide how the search incident to arrest doctrine applies to modern cell phones, which are now such a pervasive and insistent part of daily life that the proverbial visitor from Mars might conclude they were an important feature of human anatomy. A smart phone of the sort taken from Riley was unheard of ten years ago; a significant majority of American adults now own such phones. Even less sophisticated phones like Wurie's, which have already faded in popularity since Wurie was arrested in 2007, have been around for less than 15 years. Both phones are based on technology nearly inconceivable just a few decades ago, when *Chimel* and *Robinson* were decided. Absent more precise guidance from the founding era, we generally determine whether to exempt a given type of search from the warrant requirement "by assessing, on the one hand, the degree to which it intrudes upon an individual's privacy and, on the other, the degree to which it is needed for the promotion of legitimate governmental interests." Such a balancing of interests supported the search incident to arrest exception in *Robinson*, and a mechanical application of *Robinson* might well support the warrantless searches at issue here.

But while *Robinson*'s categorical rule strikes the appropriate balance in the context of physical objects, neither of its rationales has much force with respect to digital content on cell phones. On the government interest side, *Robinson* concluded that the two risks identified in *Chimel*—harm to officers and destruction of evidence—are present in all custodial arrests. There are no comparable risks when the search is of digital data. In addition, *Robinson* regarded any privacy interests retained by an individual after arrest as significantly diminished by the fact of the arrest itself. Cell phones, however, place vast quantities of personal information literally in the hands of individuals. A search of the information on a cell phone bears little resemblance to the type of brief physical search considered in *Robinson*.

We therefore decline to extend *Robinson* to searches of data on cell phones, and hold instead that officers must generally secure a warrant before conducting such a search.

A

We first consider each *Chimel* concern in turn. In doing so, we do not overlook *Robinson*'s admonition that searches of a person incident to arrest, "while based upon the need to disarm and to discover evidence," are reasonable regardless of "the probability in a particular arrest situation that weapons or evidence would in fact be found." Rather than requiring the "case-by-case adjudication" that *Robinson* rejected, we ask instead whether application of the search incident to arrest doctrine to this particular category of effects would "untether the rule from the justifications underlying the *Chimel* exception."

1

Digital data stored on a cell phone cannot itself be used as a weapon to harm an arresting officer or to effectuate the arrestee's escape. Law enforcement officers remain free to examine the physical aspects of a phone to ensure that it will not be used as a weapon — say, to determine whether there is a razor blade hidden between the phone and its case. Once an officer has secured a phone and eliminated any potential physical threats, however, data on the phone can endanger no one. Perhaps the same might have been said of the cigarette pack seized from Robinson's pocket. Once an officer gained control of the pack, it was unlikely that Robinson could have accessed the pack's contents. But unknown physical objects may always pose risks, no matter how slight, during the tense atmosphere of a custodial arrest. The officer in *Robinson* testified that he could not identify the objects in the cigarette pack but knew they were not cigarettes. Given that, a further search was a reasonable protective measure. No such unknowns exist with respect to digital data. As the First Circuit explained, the officers who searched Wurie's cell phone "knew exactly what they would find therein: data. They also knew that the data could not harm them."

The United States and California both suggest that a search of cell phone data might help ensure officer safety in more indirect ways, for example by alerting officers that confederates of the arrestee are headed to the scene. There is undoubtedly a strong government interest in warning officers about such possibilities, but neither the United States nor California offers evidence to suggest that their concerns are based on actual experience. The proposed consideration would also represent a broadening of *Chimel*'s concern that an *arrestee himself* might grab a weapon and use it against an officer "to resist arrest or effect his escape." And any such threats from outside the arrest scene do not "lurk[] in all custodial arrests." Accordingly, the interest in protecting officer safety does not justify dispensing with the warrant requirement across the board. To the extent dangers to arresting officers may be implicated in a particular way in a particular case, they are better addressed through consideration of case-specific exceptions to the warrant requirement, such as the one for exigent circumstances.

2

The United States and California focus primarily on the second *Chimel* rationale: preventing the destruction of evidence. Both Riley and Wurie concede that officers could have seized and secured their cell phones to prevent destruction of evidence while seeking a warrant. That is a sensible concession. See *Illinois v. McArthur*, 531 U.S. 326, 331–333 (2001). And once law enforcement officers have secured a cell phone, there is no longer any risk that the arrestee himself will be able to delete incriminating data from the phone.

The United States and California argue that information on a cell phone may nevertheless be vulnerable to two types of evidence destruction unique to digital data—remote wiping and data encryption. Remote wiping occurs when a phone, connected to a wireless network, receives a signal that erases stored data. This can happen when a third party sends a remote signal or when a phone is preprogrammed to delete data upon entering or leaving certain geographic areas (so-called "geofencing"). Encryption is a security feature that some modern cell phones use in addition to password protection. When such phones lock, data becomes protected by sophisticated encryption that renders a phone all but "unbreakable" unless police know the password.

As an initial matter, these broader concerns about the loss of evidence are distinct from *Chimel*'s focus on a defendant who responds to arrest by trying to conceal or destroy evidence within his reach. With respect to remote wiping, the Government's primary concern turns on the actions of third parties who are not present at the scene of arrest. And data encryption is even further afield. There, the Government focuses on the ordinary operation of a phone's security features, apart from *any* active attempt by a defendant or his associates to conceal or destroy evidence upon arrest.

We have also been given little reason to believe that either problem is prevalent. The briefing reveals only a couple of anecdotal examples of remote wiping triggered by an arrest. Similarly, the opportunities for officers to search a password-protected phone before data becomes encrypted are quite limited. Law enforcement officers are very unlikely to come upon such a phone in an unlocked state because most phones lock at the touch of a button or, as a default, after some very short period of inactivity. This may explain why the encryption argument was not made until the merits stage in this Court, and has never been considered by the Courts of Appeals.

Moreover, in situations in which an arrest might trigger a remote-wipe attempt or an officer discovers an unlocked phone, it is not clear that the ability to conduct a warrantless search would make much of a difference. The need to effect the arrest, secure the scene, and tend to other pressing matters means that law enforcement officers may well not be able to turn their attention to a cell phone right away. Cell phone data would be vulnerable to remote wiping from the time an individual anticipates arrest to the time any eventual search of the phone is completed, which might be at the station house hours later. Likewise, an officer who seizes a phone in an unlocked state might not be able to begin his search in the short time remaining before the phone locks and data becomes encrypted.

In any event, as to remote wiping, law enforcement is not without specific means to address the threat. Remote wiping can be fully prevented by disconnecting a phone from the network. There are at least two simple ways to do this: First, law enforcement officers can turn the phone off or remove its battery. Second, if they are concerned about encryption or other potential problems, they can leave a phone powered on and place it in an enclosure that isolates the phone from radio waves. Such devices are commonly called "Faraday bags," after the English scientist Michael Faraday. They are essentially sandwich bags made of aluminum foil: cheap, lightweight, and easy to use. They may not be a complete answer to the problem, but at least for now they provide a reasonable response. In fact, a number of law enforcement agencies around the country already encourage the use of Faraday bags.

To the extent that law enforcement still has specific concerns about the potential loss of evidence in a particular case, there remain more targeted ways to address those concerns. If "the police are truly confronted with a 'now or never' situation,"—for example, circumstances suggesting that a defendant's phone will be the target of an imminent remote-wipe attempt—they may be able to rely on exigent circumstances to search the phone immediately. Or, if officers happen to seize a phone in an unlocked state, they may be able to disable a phone's automatic-lock feature in order to prevent the phone from locking and encrypting data. Such a preventive measure could be analyzed under the principles set forth in our decision in *McArthur*, which approved officers' reasonable steps to secure a scene to preserve evidence while they awaited a warrant.

B

The search incident to arrest exception rests not only on the heightened government interests at stake in a volatile arrest situation, but also on an arrestee's reduced privacy interests upon being taken into police custody. *Robinson* focused primarily on the first of those rationales. But it also quoted with approval then-Judge Cardozo's account of the historical basis for the search incident to arrest exception: "Search of the person becomes lawful when grounds for arrest and accusation have been discovered, and the law is in the act of subjecting the body of the accused to its physical dominion." (quoting *People v. Chiagles*, 237 N.Y. 193, 197, 142 N.E. 583, 584 (1923)). Put simply, a patdown of Robinson's clothing and an inspection of the cigarette pack found in his pocket constituted only minor additional intrusions compared to the substantial government authority exercised in taking Robinson into custody. The fact that an arrestee has diminished privacy interests does not mean that the Fourth Amendment falls out of the picture entirely. Not every search "is acceptable solely because a person is in custody." To the contrary, when "privacy-related concerns are weighty enough" a "search may require a warrant, notwithstanding the diminished expectations of privacy of the arrestee." One such example, of course, is *Chimel*. *Chimel* refused to "characteriz[e] the invasion of privacy that results from a top-to-bottom search of a man's house as 'minor.'" Because a search of the arrestee's entire house was a substantial invasion beyond the arrest itself, the Court concluded that a warrant was required.

Robinson is the only decision from this Court applying *Chimel* to a search of the contents of an item found on an arrestee's person. In an earlier case, this Court had approved a search of a zipper bag carried by an arrestee, but the Court analyzed only the validity of the arrest itself. Lower courts applying *Robinson* and *Chimel*, however, have approved searches of a variety of personal items carried by an arrestee.

The United States asserts that a search of all data stored on a cell phone is "materially indistinguishable" from searches of these sorts of physical items. That is like saying a ride on horseback is materially indistinguishable from a flight to the moon. Both are ways of getting from point A to point B, but little else justifies lumping them together. Modern cell phones, as a category, implicate privacy concerns far beyond those implicated by the search of a cigarette pack, a wallet, or a purse. A conclusion that inspecting the contents of an arrestee's pockets works no substantial additional intrusion on privacy beyond the arrest itself may make sense as applied to physical items, but any extension of that reasoning to digital data has to rest on its own bottom.

1

Cell phones differ in both a quantitative and a qualitative sense from other objects that might be kept on an arrestee's person. The term "cell phone" is itself misleading shorthand; many of these devices are in fact minicomputers that also happen to have the capacity to be used as a telephone. They could just as easily be called cameras, video players, rolodexes, calendars, tape recorders, libraries, diaries, albums, televisions, maps, or newspapers. One of the most notable distinguishing features of modern cell phones is their immense storage capacity. Before cell phones, a search of a person was limited by physical realities and tended as a general matter to constitute only a narrow intrusion on privacy. Most people cannot lug around every piece of mail they have received for the past several months, every picture they have taken, or every book or article they have read—nor would they have any reason to attempt to do so. And if they did, they would have to drag behind them a trunk of the sort held to require a search warrant in *Chadwick*, rather than a container the size of the cigarette package in *Robinson*.

But the possible intrusion on privacy is not physically limited in the same way when it comes to cell phones. The current top-selling smart phone has a standard capacity of 16 gigabytes (and is available with up to 64 gigabytes). Sixteen gigabytes translates to millions of pages of text, thousands of pictures, or hundreds of videos. Cell phones couple that capacity with the ability to store many different types of information: Even the most basic phones that sell for less than $20 might hold photographs, picture messages, text messages, Internet browsing history, a calendar, a thousand-entry phone book, and so on. We expect that the gulf between physical practicability and digital capacity will only continue to widen in the future.

The storage capacity of cell phones has several interrelated consequences for privacy. First, a cell phone collects in one place many distinct types of information—an address, a note, a prescription, a bank statement, a video—that reveal much more in combination than any isolated record. Second, a cell phone's capacity allows even just one type of information to convey far more than previously possible. The sum of an individual's private life can be reconstructed through a thousand photographs labeled with dates, locations, and descriptions; the same cannot be said of a photograph or two of loved ones tucked into a wallet. Third, the data on a phone can date back to the purchase of the phone, or even earlier. A person might carry in his pocket a slip of paper reminding him to call Mr. Jones; he would not carry a record of all his communications with Mr. Jones for the past several months, as would routinely be kept on a phone.[n.1][21]

Finally, there is an element of pervasiveness that characterizes cell phones but not physical records. Prior to the digital age, people did not typically carry a cache of sensitive personal information with them as they went about their day. Now it is the person who is not carrying a cell phone, with all that it contains, who is the exception. According to one poll, nearly three-quarters of smart phone users report being within five feet of their phones most of the time, with 12% admitting that they even use their phones in the shower. A decade ago police officers searching an arrestee might have occasionally stumbled across a highly personal item such as a diary. But those discoveries were likely to be few and far between. Today, by contrast, it is no exaggeration to say that many of the more than 90% of American adults who own a cell phone keep on their person a digital record of nearly every aspect of their lives—from the mundane to the intimate. See *Ontario v. Quon*, 560 U.S. 746, 760 (2010). Allowing the police to scrutinize such records on a routine basis is quite different from allowing them to search a personal item or two in the occasional case.

Although the data stored on a cell phone is distinguished from physical records by quantity alone, certain types of data are also qualitatively different. An Internet search and browsing history, for example, can be found on an Internet-enabled phone and could reveal an individual's private interests or concerns—perhaps a search for certain symptoms of disease, coupled with frequent visits to WebMD. Data on a cell phone can also reveal where a person has been. Historic location information is a standard feature on many smart phones and can reconstruct someone's specific movements down to the minute, not only around town but also within a particular building. See *United States v. Jones*, 565 U.S. ——, —— (2012) (SOTO-MAYOR, J., concurring) ("GPS monitoring generates a precise, comprehensive record of a person's public movements that reflects a wealth of detail about her familial, political, professional, religious, and sexual associations.").

Mobile application software on a cell phone, or "apps," offer a range of tools for managing detailed information about all aspects of a person's life. There are apps for Democratic Party news and Republican Party news; apps for alcohol, drug, and gambling addictions; apps for sharing prayer requests; apps for tracking pregnancy symptoms; apps for planning your budget; apps for every conceivable hobby or pastime; apps for improving your romantic life. There are popular apps for buying or selling just about anything, and the records of such transactions may be accessible on the phone indefinitely. There are over a million apps available in each of the two major app stores; the phrase "there's an app for that" is now part of the popular

---

21. [n.1] Because the United States and California agree that these cases involve *searches* incident to arrest, these cases do not implicate the question whether the collection or inspection of aggregated digital information amounts to a search under other circumstances.

lexicon. The average smart phone user has installed 33 apps, which together can form a revealing montage of the user's life.

In 1926, Learned Hand observed (in an opinion later quoted in *Chimel*) that it is "a totally different thing to search a man's pockets and use against him what they contain, from ransacking his house for everything which may incriminate him." If his pockets contain a cell phone, however, that is no longer true. Indeed, a cell phone search would typically expose to the government far *more* than the most exhaustive search of a house: A phone not only contains in digital form many sensitive records previously found in the home; it also contains a broad array of private information never found in a home in any form—unless the phone is.

2

To further complicate the scope of the privacy interests at stake, the data a user views on many modern cell phones may not in fact be stored on the device itself. Treating a cell phone as a container whose contents may be searched incident to an arrest is a bit strained as an initial matter. See *New York v. Belton*, 453 U.S. 454, 460, n. 4 (1981) (describing a "container" as "any object capable of holding another object"). But the analogy crumbles entirely when a cell phone is used to access data located elsewhere, at the tap of a screen. That is what cell phones, with increasing frequency, are designed to do by taking advantage of "cloud computing." Cloud computing is the capacity of Internet-connected devices to display data stored on remote servers rather than on the device itself. Cell phone users often may not know whether particular information is stored on the device or in the cloud, and it generally makes little difference. Moreover, the same type of data may be stored locally on the device for one user and in the cloud for another. The United States concedes that the search incident to arrest exception may not be stretched to cover a search of files accessed remotely—that is, a search of files stored in the cloud. Such a search would be like finding a key in a suspect's pocket and arguing that it allowed law enforcement to unlock and search a house. But officers searching a phone's data would not typically know whether the information they are viewing was stored locally at the time of the arrest or has been pulled from the cloud.

Although the Government recognizes the problem, its proposed solutions are unclear. It suggests that officers could disconnect a phone from the network before searching the device—the very solution whose feasibility it contested with respect to the threat of remote wiping. Alternatively, the Government proposes that law enforcement agencies "develop protocols to address" concerns raised by cloud computing. Probably a good idea, but the Founders did not fight a revolution to gain the right to government agency protocols. The possibility that a search might extend well beyond papers and effects in the physical proximity of an arrestee is yet another reason that the privacy interests here dwarf those in *Robinson*.

C

Apart from their arguments for a direct extension of *Robinson*, the United States and California offer various fallback options for permitting warrantless cell phone searches under certain circumstances. Each of the proposals is flawed and contravenes our general preference to provide clear guidance to law enforcement through categorical rules. "[I]f police are to have workable rules, the balancing of the competing interests . . . 'must in large part be done on a categorical basis—not in an ad hoc, case-by-case fashion by individual police officers.'" The United States first proposes that the *Gant* standard be imported from the vehicle context, allowing a warrantless search of an arrestee's cell phone whenever it is reasonable to believe that the phone contains evidence of the crime of arrest. But *Gant* relied on "circumstances unique to the vehicle context" to endorse a search solely for the purpose of gathering evidence. Justice SCALIA'S *Thornton* opinion, on which *Gant* was based, explained that those unique circumstances are "a reduced expectation of privacy" and "heightened law enforcement needs" when it comes to motor vehicles. For reasons that we have explained, cell phone searches bear neither of those characteristics.

At any rate, a *Gant* standard would prove no practical limit at all when it comes to cell phone searches. In the vehicle context, *Gant* generally protects against searches for evidence of past crimes. In the cell phone context, however, it is reasonable to expect that incriminating information will be found on a phone regardless of when the crime occurred. Similarly, in the vehicle context *Gant* restricts broad searches resulting from minor crimes such as traffic violations. That would not necessarily be true for cell phones. It would be a particularly inexperienced or unimaginative law enforcement officer who could not come up with several reasons to suppose evidence of just about any crime could be found on a cell phone. Even an individual pulled over for something as basic as speeding might well have locational data dispositive of guilt on his phone. An individual pulled over for reckless driving might have evidence on the phone that shows whether he was texting while driving. The sources of potential pertinent information are virtually unlimited, so applying the *Gant* standard to cell phones would in effect give "police officers unbridled discretion to rummage at will among a person's private effects."

The United States also proposes a rule that would restrict the scope of a cell phone search to those areas of the phone where an officer reasonably believes that information relevant to the crime, the arrestee's identity, or officer safety will be discovered. This approach would again impose few meaningful constraints on officers. The proposed categories would sweep in a great deal of information, and officers would not always be able to discern in advance what information would be found where.

We also reject the United States' final suggestion that officers should always be able to search a phone's call log, as they did in Wurie's case. The Government relies on *Smith v. Maryland*, 442 U.S. 735 (1979), which held that no warrant was required to use a pen register at telephone company premises to identify numbers dialed by a particular caller. The Court in that case, however, concluded that the use of a pen register was not a "search" at all under the Fourth Amendment. There is no dispute here that the officers engaged in a search of Wurie's cell phone. Moreover, call logs typically contain more than just phone numbers; they include any identifying information that an individual might add, such as the label "my house" in Wurie's case.

Finally, at oral argument California suggested a different limiting principle, under which officers could search cell phone data if they could have obtained the same information from a pre-digital counterpart. But the fact that a search in the pre-digital era could have turned up a photograph or two in a wallet does not justify a search of thousands of photos in a digital gallery. The fact that someone could have tucked a paper bank statement in a pocket does not justify a search of every bank statement from the last five years. And to make matters worse, such an analogue test would allow law enforcement to search a range of items contained on a phone, even though people would be unlikely to carry such a variety of information in physical form. In Riley's case, for example, it is implausible that he would have strolled around with video tapes, photo albums, and an address book all crammed into his pockets. But because each of those items has a pre-digital analogue, police under California's proposal would be able to search a phone for all of those items — a significant diminution of privacy.

In addition, an analogue test would launch courts on a difficult line-drawing expedition to determine which digital files are comparable to physical records. Is an e-mail equivalent to a letter? Is a voicemail equivalent to a phone message slip? It is not clear how officers could make these kinds of decisions before conducting a search, or how courts would apply the proposed rule after the fact. An analogue test would "keep defendants and judges guessing for years to come."

IV

We cannot deny that our decision today will have an impact on the ability of law enforcement to combat crime. Cell phones have become important tools in facilitating coordination and communication among members of criminal enterprises, and can provide valuable incriminating information about dangerous criminals. Privacy comes at a cost. Our holding, of course, is not that the information on a cell phone is immune from search; it is instead that a warrant is generally required before such a search, even when a cell phone is seized incident to arrest. Our cases have historically recognized that the warrant requirement is "an important working part of our machinery of government," not merely "an inconvenience to be somehow 'weighed' against the claims of police efficiency." Recent technological advances similar to those discussed here have, in addition, made the process of obtaining a warrant itself more efficient.

Moreover, even though the search incident to arrest exception does not apply to cell phones, other case-specific exceptions may still justify a warrantless search of a particular phone. "One well-recognized exception applies when '"the exigencies of the situation" make the needs of law enforcement so compelling that [a] warrantless search is objectively reasonable under the Fourth Amendment.'" Such exigencies could include the need to prevent the imminent destruction of evidence in individual cases, to pursue a fleeing suspect, and to assist persons who are seriously injured or are threatened with imminent injury. In *Chadwick*, for example, the Court held that the exception for searches incident to arrest did not justify a search of the trunk at issue, but noted that "if officers have reason to believe that luggage contains some immediately dangerous instrumentality, such as explosives, it would be foolhardy to transport it to the station house without opening the luggage."

In light of the availability of the exigent circumstances exception, there is no reason to believe that law enforcement officers will not be able to address some of the more extreme hypotheticals that have been suggested: a suspect texting an accomplice who, it is feared, is preparing to detonate a bomb, or a child abductor who may have information about the child's location on his cell phone. The defendants here recognize—indeed, they stress—that such fact-specific threats may justify a warrantless search of cell phone data. The critical point is that, unlike the search incident to arrest exception, the exigent circumstances exception requires a court to examine whether an emergency justified a warrantless search in each particular case.[n.2][22]

Our cases have recognized that the Fourth Amendment was the founding generation's response to the reviled "general warrants" and "writs of assistance" of the colonial era, which allowed British officers to rummage through homes in an unrestrained search for evidence of criminal activity. Opposition to such searches was in fact one of the driving forces behind the Revolution itself. In 1761, the patriot James Otis delivered a speech in Boston denouncing the use of writs of assistance. A young John Adams was there, and he would later write that "[e]very man of a crowded audience appeared to me to go away, as I did, ready to take arms against writs of assistance." According to Adams, Otis's speech was "the first scene of the first act of opposition to the arbitrary claims of Great Britain. Then and there the child Independence was born." Modern cell phones are not just another technological convenience. With all they contain and all they may reveal, they hold for many Americans "the privacies of life." The fact that technology now allows an individual to carry such information in his hand does not make the information any less worthy of the protection for which the Founders fought. Our answer to the question of what police must do before searching a cell phone seized incident to an arrest is accordingly simple—get a warrant.

JUSTICE ALITO, concurring in part and concurring in the judgment.

I agree with the Court that law enforcement officers, in conducting a lawful search incident to arrest, must generally obtain a warrant before searching information stored or accessible on a cell phone. I write separately to address two points.

I

A

First, I am not convinced at this time that the ancient rule on searches incident to arrest is based exclusively (or even primarily) on the need to protect the safety

---

22. [n.2] In Wurie's case, for example, the dissenting First Circuit judge argued that exigent circumstances could have justified a search of Wurie's phone. See 728 F.3d 1, 17 (2013) (opinion of Howard, J.) (discussing the repeated unanswered calls from "my house," the suspected location of a drug stash). But the majority concluded that the Government had not made an exigent circumstances argument. The Government acknowledges the same in this Court.

of arresting officers and the need to prevent the destruction of evidence. This rule antedates the adoption of the Fourth Amendment by at least a century. See T. Clancy, *The Fourth Amendment: Its History and Interpretation* 340 (2008). In *Weeks v. United States*, 232 U.S. 383, 392 (1914), we held that the Fourth Amendment did not disturb this rule. And neither in *Weeks* nor in any of the authorities discussing the old common-law rule have I found any suggestion that it was based exclusively or primarily on the need to protect arresting officers or to prevent the destruction of evidence. On the contrary, when pre-*Weeks* authorities discussed the basis for the rule, what was mentioned was the need to obtain probative evidence.

What ultimately convinces me that the rule is not closely linked to the need for officer safety and evidence preservation is that these rationales fail to explain the rule's well-recognized scope. It has long been accepted that written items found on the person of an arrestee may be examined and used at trial. But once these items are taken away from an arrestee (something that obviously must be done before the items are read), there is no risk that the arrestee will destroy them. Nor is there any risk that leaving these items unread will endanger the arresting officers.

The idea that officer safety and the preservation of evidence are the sole reasons for allowing a warrantless search incident to arrest appears to derive from the Court's reasoning in *Chimel v. California*, 395 U.S. 752 (1969), a case that involved the lawfulness of a search of the scene of an arrest, not the person of an arrestee. As I have explained, *Chimel*'s reasoning is questionable, see *Arizona v. Gant*, 556 U.S. 332, 361–363 (2009) (Alito, J., dissenting), and I think it is a mistake to allow that reasoning to affect cases like these that concern the search of the person of arrestees.

B

Despite my view on the point discussed above, I agree that we should not mechanically apply the rule used in the predigital era to the search of a cell phone. Many cell phones now in use are capable of storing and accessing a quantity of information, some highly personal, that no person would ever have had on his person in hard-copy form. This calls for a new balancing of law enforcement and privacy interests. The Court strikes this balance in favor of privacy interests with respect to all cell phones and all information found in them, and this approach leads to anomalies. For example, the Court's broad holding favors information in digital form over information in hard-copy form. Suppose that two suspects are arrested. Suspect number one has in his pocket a monthly bill for his land-line phone, and the bill lists an incriminating call to a long-distance number. He also has in his a wallet a few snapshots, and one of these is incriminating. Suspect number two has in his pocket a cell phone, the call log of which shows a call to the same incriminating number. In addition, a number of photos are stored in the memory of the cell phone, and one of these is incriminating. Under established law, the police may seize and examine the phone bill and the snapshots in the wallet without obtaining a warrant, but under the Court's holding today, the information stored in the cell phone is out.

While the Court's approach leads to anomalies, I do not see a workable alternative. Law enforcement officers need clear rules regarding searches incident to arrest, and it would take many cases and many years for the courts to develop more nuanced rules. And during that time, the nature of the electronic devices that ordinary Americans carry on their persons would continue to change.

II

This brings me to my second point. While I agree with the holding of the Court, I would reconsider the question presented here if either Congress or state legislatures, after assessing the legitimate needs of law enforcement and the privacy interests of cell phone owners, enact legislation that draws reasonable distinctions based on categories of information or perhaps other variables. The regulation of electronic surveillance provides an instructive example. After this Court held that electronic surveillance constitutes a search even when no property interest is invaded, Congress responded by enacting Title III of the Omnibus Crime Control and Safe Streets Act of 1968, 82 Stat. 211. See also 18 U.S.C. § 2510 *et seq.* Since that time, electronic surveillance has been governed primarily, not by decisions of this Court, but by the statute, which authorizes but imposes detailed restrictions on electronic surveillance.

Modern cell phones are of great value for both lawful and unlawful purposes. They can be used in committing many serious crimes, and they present new and difficult law enforcement problems. At the same time, because of the role that these devices have come to play in contemporary life, searching their contents implicates very sensitive privacy interests that this Court is poorly positioned to understand and evaluate. Many forms of modern technology are making it easier and easier for both government and private entities to amass a wealth of information about the lives of ordinary Americans, and at the same time, many ordinary Americans are choosing to make public much information that was seldom revealed to outsiders just a few decades ago.

In light of these developments, it would be very unfortunate if privacy protection in the 21st century were left primarily to the federal courts using the blunt instrument of the Fourth Amendment. Legislatures, elected by the people, are in a better position than we are to assess and respond to the changes that have already occurred and those that almost certainly will take place in the future.

Questions

1. What ramifications do these new rules have on a search incident to arrest for other digital evidence devices?

2. How broad and important is *Riley*? Can it be put into the category of those courts adopting a "special approach" to digital searches and seizures? It clearly creates a unique rule for searches of cell phones incident to arrest. Does it have broader application for Fourth Amendment satisfaction issues?

3. Note the breadth of the language in *Riley* suggesting that a cell phone search "would typically expose to the government far *more* than the most exhaustive search of a home." Yet, the home has always been afforded the most Fourth Amendment protection? What does that language portend?

4. Note also the apparent rejection of the "container" analogy and the rejection of physical analogues by the Court. What framework should courts use?

5. Alito's concurring opinion notes anomalies. Should the police have different rules for searches of physical objects and digital devices? Or how about this rule: after the initial determination that the object does not pose a danger to the officer, the officer must get a warrant to search any object?

6. Alito indicates that Congress is better situated to develop appropriate rules. Do you agree? What rule would you draft?

7. After *Riley*, what advice would you give to police officers when they recover a digital device on a person incident to that person's arrest?

§ 8.2 Additional Theories to Justify a Search and the Scope of a Permissible Search of Cell Phones

1. Exigent Circumstances

"Exigent circumstances"[23] is a long-standing but nebulous doctrine that serves to excuse compliance with otherwise applicable Fourth Amendment reasonableness standards. The doctrine has traditionally been categorized as an exception to the warrant preference rule.[24] There is no finite—or definitive—list of exigent circumstances. *Kentucky v. King*[25] recently provided a list:

> Under the "emergency aid" exception, for example, "officers may enter a home without a warrant to render emergency assistance to an injured occupant or to protect an occupant from imminent injury." Police officers may enter premises without a warrant when they are in hot pursuit of a fleeing suspect. And . . . the need "to prevent the imminent destruction of evidence" has long been recognized as a sufficient justification for a warrantless search. More generally, the exigent circumstances doctrine is often applied.

Recognized exigent circumstances in other cases have included preventing imminent destruction of evidence,[26] and the discovery of dangerous items, such as explosives.[27]

---

23. Warden v. Hayden, 387 U.S. 294 (1967).

24. *E.g.*, Missouri v. McNeely, 133 S. Ct. 1552, 185 L. Ed. 2d 696 (2013); Brigham City v. Stuart, 547 U.S. 398 (2006).

25. 563 U.S. 452 (2011).

26. *E.g.*, Brigham City v. Stuart, 547 U.S. 398 (2006) (stating rule); United States v. Santana, 427 U.S. 38, 43 (1976) (drugs and money); Ker v. California, 374 U.S. 23, 40 (1963) (marijuana).

27. *E.g.*, United States v. Boettger, 71 F.3d 1410 (8th Cir. 1995) (explosive devices).

The essential rationale for the doctrine is in the meaning of exigency: there is an immediate, urgent, and compelling need for police action.[28] As the Supreme Court recognized in a case in which the police had responded to a report of an armed robbery and learned that the robber had entered the house minutes before the police arrived: "Speed here was essential."[29] The government bears the burden of proving that exigent circumstances justified the police actions.[30] The standard for exigent circumstances is an objective one, focusing on what a reasonable police officer would believe in the circumstances presented.[31]

The permissible scope of the intrusion is "as broad as may reasonably be necessary to prevent the dangers" that the exigency presents.[32] Hence, if the police are looking for an armed robber in a house, they can look not only where the robber may be found but also where the weapon may be hidden.[33] By comparison, the police may only need to freeze a situation pending the issuance of a warrant. Thus, for example, the proper course of action presented by an exigent circumstance may be to prevent a resident from entering his home while the police seek a warrant to search the home. In *Illinois v. McArthur*,[34] the Court upheld the exclusion of McArthur from his home, pending the issuance of a warrant to search. The police were outside the house to keep the peace while McArthur's wife removed her belongings. As the wife left, she informed the police that McArthur had marijuana in the house. After McArthur denied the police permission to search, the officers barred him from reentering unless an officer accompanied him. The Court viewed those actions as a seizure of the home. The Court stated:

> In the circumstances of the case before us, we cannot say that the warrantless seizure was *per se* unreasonable. It involves a plausible claim of specially pressing or urgent law enforcement need, *i.e.,* "exigent circumstances." Moreover, the restraint at issue was tailored to that need, being limited in time and scope, and avoiding significant intrusion into the home itself[.] Consequently, rather than employing a *per se* rule of unreasonableness, we balance the privacy-related and law enforcement-related concerns to determine if the intrusion was reasonable.

———————

28. *E.g.,* Michigan v. Tyler, 436 U.S. 499, 509 (1978) (exigent circumstances are compelling need and no time to get a warrant).

29. Warden v. Hayden, 387 U.S. 294 (1967).

30. Welsh v. Wisconsin, 466 U.S. 740, 750 (1984).

31. Brigham City v. Stuart, 547 U.S. 398 (2006).

32. Warden v. Hayden, 387 U.S. 294, 299 (1967).

33. *Id.* at 299–300.

34. 531 U.S. 326, 333–34 (2001).

State v. Jermichael James Carroll

778 N.W.2d 1 (Wis. 2010)

N. Patrick Crooks, J.

The defendant, Jermichael James Carroll, was charged with possession of a firearm by a felon [and subsequently convicted. The sole basis for that charge was an image that Carroll stored in his cellphone. The question before the court was whether the police legally obtained that image].

Detective Belsha of the Milwaukee police department and his partner were conducting surveillance on a residence as part of an armed robbery investigation. They observed a white Ford Escort leave that residence, slow down as it passed their squad car, and speed away.

The officers attempted to catch the vehicle, which reached speeds of 60 miles per hour on residential streets with speed limits no higher than 25 miles per hour. According to Belsha's testimony, the driver, Carroll, eventually pulled the car to "an abrupt stop" in a gas station lot and quickly got out of the car while holding an object in his hands. The officers could not identify what Carroll was holding, so Belsha drew his weapon and ordered Carroll to drop the object and get on the ground, which Carroll did. The officers then handcuffed Carroll behind his back.

After handcuffing Carroll, Belsha retrieved the dropped object, which was a flip-style cell phone. The cell phone was lying open on the ground and displayed an image of Carroll smoking a long, thin, brown cigarlike object ("the marijuana image"). Belsha, a member of the High Intensity Drug Trafficking Area Drug and Gang Task Force, testified that he recognized the object as a marijuana blunt.

When the officers asked Carroll for identification, Carroll did not have any with him but gave the officers his name. The officers ran a "routine check" and learned that he was driving with a suspended license. Carroll also had a record of being adjudicated delinquent for a drug-related felony two years earlier as a juvenile.

Belsha placed Carroll in the back seat of the squad car and sat in the front seat with the cell phone, where he activated the menus, opened the image gallery, scrolled through it, and saw images showing illegal drugs, firearms, and large amounts of U.S. currency. Specifically, Belsha testified that he saw an image of Carroll with what appeared to be a gallon-size bag of marijuana held in his teeth, and "several photos depicting firearms," including one showing Carroll holding a semiautomatic firearm ("the firearm image").

While Belsha continued to possess Carroll's cell phone, it rang several times and Belsha answered one of those calls, pretending to be Carroll. The caller asked for "four of those things; four and a split." Based on his training, Belsha recognized that the caller was attempting to purchase four and a half ounces of cocaine.

Two days later, Belsha sought a search warrant for the cell phone. After obtaining the warrant, the police downloaded the data on the cell phone, including the firearm image. Detective McQuown, who was trained in the handling of digital evidence, testified at a preliminary hearing that each image on the phone had attached "metadata," which he described as information indicating the date and time at which the image was created. He also testified that the metadata is based on the date and time updates regularly provided through cell phone towers. The metadata indicated that the firearm image had been created on May 22, 2006. Carroll was charged with possession of a firearm by a felon based on photographic evidence downloaded from the cell phone.

A. Constitutional Permissibility of the Warrantless Searches

1. Belsha's Initial Seizure of the Cell Phone

Carroll led officers on a high-speed chase in a car that the officers had been observing in connection with an armed robbery investigation, and exited his car quickly while holding an unknown object. Given that behavior, the officers would have been justified—based on the objective belief that Carroll could have been holding a weapon—in conducting a frisk or pat-down, which would have resulted in Belsha's legal possession of the cell phone. Hence, Belsha's order for Carroll to drop the object and his subsequent retrieval of it were reasonable actions, and accordingly, his initial seizure of the phone was justified.

After Belsha legally seized the open phone, his viewing of the marijuana image also was legitimate because that image was in plain view. Under Wisconsin case law, a warrantless seizure is justified under the plain view doctrine where the object is in plain view of an officer lawfully in a position to see it, the officer's discovery is inadvertent, and the seized object, either in itself or in context with facts known to the officer at the time of the seizure, supplies probable cause to believe that the object is connected to or used for criminal activity.

Here, Belsha was in legal possession of the phone and thus in a lawful position to view the display screen, which, according to Belsha's uncontroverted testimony, was open and displayed the marijuana image. Further, Belsha testified that based on his experience, he recognized the object Carroll was smoking in the image as a marijuana blunt. That, taken in context with other facts known to Belsha at the time, namely, that individuals involved in drug trafficking often personalize their phones with such images, provided sufficient probable cause to believe that the phone was an instrument of criminal activity and contained evidence linked to that activity. Under the circumstances, Belsha had probable cause to seize the cell phone.

2. Belsha's Continued Possession of the Cell Phone

After Belsha seized the phone with the marijuana image displayed, he continued to maintain possession of the phone after he had placed Carroll in the squad car. We conclude that that continued possession was justified. The Court in *United States v. Place*, 462 U.S. 696 (1983), addressed the ability of law enforcement agents to seize and detain a person's luggage based on reasonable suspicion that the luggage contained narcotics and under circumstances where that owner was not in custody or under arrest. The Court went on to hold that the agents had narrow authority to detain temporarily a container in such circumstances though the agents in that case exceeded their authority to do so. However, in reaching its conclusion, the Court explained,

> Where law enforcement authorities have probable cause to believe that a container holds contraband or evidence of a crime, but have not secured a warrant, the Court has interpreted the [Fourth] Amendment to permit seizure of the property, pending issuance of a warrant to examine its contents, if the exigencies of the circumstances demand it or some other recognized exception to the warrant requirement is present.

In other words, law enforcement agents are justified in seizing and continuing to hold a container if (1) there is probable cause to believe that it contains evidence of a crime, and (2) if exigencies of the circumstances demand it.

Although the "containers" discussed in *Place* were pieces of luggage, it is reasonable to analogize the cell phone in this case to the luggage in *Place*. The underlying concern with the agents' detention of the luggage in *Place* was that Place had a reasonable expectation of privacy in the contents of his bags. So, too, here, the concern is protecting a person's reasonable expectation of privacy in the contents of his or her cell phone. Other courts, in assessing the validity of a search without a warrant, have likened a person's privacy expectations in cell phones and electronic devices to that of closed containers in his or her possession. Accordingly, in this situation, the analogy to a closed container appears to be appropriate.

To establish probable cause to search, the evidence must indicate a "fair probability" that the particular place contains evidence of a crime. An officer's knowledge, training, and experience are germane to the court's assessment of probable cause.

Here, Belsha legally viewed the marijuana image; we consider that fact along with his testimony that he knew, based on his training and experience, that drug traffickers frequently personalize their cell phones with images of themselves with items acquired through drug activity. Furthermore, it is those personalized cell phones on which drug traffickers commonly make many of their transactions. We are satisfied, under all of the circumstances here, that that information, taken as a whole, gave Belsha probable cause to believe that the phone contained evidence of illegal drug activity.

Given that Belsha had probable cause to believe that a search of the phone would produce evidence of illegal drug activity, his continued possession of the phone while he sought a warrant was permissible. The same reasons that permitted Belsha to seize the phone in the first instance permitted him to continue to possess it in the short time after Carroll was secured. Exigent circumstances further justify that continued possession. Had Belsha returned the phone to Carroll and released him, Carroll could have deleted incriminating images and data, such as phone numbers and calling records stored in the phone.

3. Belsha's Browsing Through the Image Gallery and Answering the Incoming Call

Next, two things happened as Belsha continued to possess the phone legally. First, he opened and browsed through the cell phone's image gallery. Second, he answered an incoming call. As an initial matter, the image gallery search clearly seems to be contrary to the holding in *Place* because there were no exigent circumstances at the time requiring him to review the gallery or other data stored in the phone. We are satisfied that that search was indeed improper and that the evidence obtained from that search at that time was tainted.

However, Belsha's answering the incoming call was justified. We again apply the standard from *Place*, which requires that the officer had probable cause to believe that the device contains evidence of a crime and that exigent circumstances justify a warrantless search. Here, Belsha had probable cause to believe that the cell phone was a tool used in drug trafficking based on the plain view of the marijuana image and his knowledge that such images are typically found on drug traffickers' phones. That evidence shows more than a fair probability that an incoming call to such a phone would contain evidence of illegal drug activity.

Moreover, exigent circumstances permitted Belsha's answering the call. The test for whether exigent circumstances are present focuses on whether the officer reasonably believes that the delay necessary to obtain a warrant, under the circumstances, threatens the destruction of evidence. Several federal cases address whether an officer may, based on exigent circumstances, access data or answer incoming calls on an electronic device that the officer had legally seized.

In the foundational case, *United States v. Ortiz*, [84 F.3d 977 (7th Cir. 1996),] officers seized an electronic pager incident to Ortiz's arrest for distribution of heroin. While continuing to search Ortiz and his vehicle for evidence, one of the agents pushed a button on the pager that revealed the numeric codes that the pager previously had received. The district court denied Ortiz's motion to suppress that evidence. The Seventh Circuit Court of Appeals affirmed that denial based on the risk that the data would be destroyed or lost if agents were required to first obtain a warrant:

> Because of the finite nature of a pager's electronic memory, incoming pages may destroy currently stored telephone numbers in a pager's memory. . . . Thus, it is imperative that law enforcement officers have the authority to immediately "search" or retrieve, incident to a valid arrest, information from a pager in order to prevent its destruction as evidence.

In subsequent cases, other courts have adopted that rationale when evaluating an officer's ability to search a seized cell phone incident to arrest, and have permitted law enforcement to conduct a warrantless search of a phone's stored data, such as records of calls received and made, so long as the other requirements of the search incident to arrest exception were satisfied.

To be sure, cell phones and pagers are not interchangeable. Indeed, the court in *United States v. Wall*, 2008 U.S. Dist. LEXIS 103058 (S.D. Fla. 2008), observed that while exigent circumstances could justify a warrantless search of a cell phone,

> [t]he differences in technology between pagers and cell phones cut to the heart of this issue [of whether an officer's reading of stored text messages

within a cell phone was justified based on exigent circumstances]. The technological developments that have occurred in the last decade, since *Ortiz* was decided, are significant. Previously, there was legitimate concern that by waiting minutes or even seconds to check the numbers stored inside a pager an officer ran the risk that another page may come in and destroy the oldest number being stored. This was based on a platform of first-in-first-out storage of numbers used for pagers. Text messages on cell phones are not stored in the same manner.... [I]f a text message is not deleted by the user, the phone will store it.

In *Wall*, the court concluded that the government failed to demonstrate an exigency justifying the agent's search of the defendant's text messages. There, the government put forth no evidence of the danger of the text messages being destroyed; to the contrary, it acknowledged that such messages generally remain stored in the phone unless a user actively deletes them. Given that, the court concluded that the officers' review of the text messages was purely investigatory and evidence obtained from that review was therefore tainted.

Significantly, at least one court has concluded that when a government agent lawfully possesses a phone and there is probable cause to believe it is used in illegal drug activity, the agent can answer incoming calls if the calls arrive in a period when it is impracticable for the agent to obtain a warrant first. *See United States v. De La Paz*, 43 F. Supp. 2d 370, 375 (S.D.N.Y. 1999). In *De La Paz*, agents had lawfully seized a cell phone incident to an arrest. While the agents were processing the defendant's arrest, the defendant's phone rang nine times and the agents answered it each time. The court concluded that it was reasonable under the circumstances for the agents to answer the cell phone of a suspected drug dealer in the time between the arrest and arraignment, given both the impossibility of timely obtaining a warrant allowing agents to answer incoming calls and the risk of losing evidence by leaving those calls unanswered.

The consistent approach taken in these cases is that the courts scrutinized the nature of the evidence obtained, i.e., numeric codes on a pager, stored text messages, and incoming phone calls, and balanced that with an inquiry into whether the agent reasonably believed that the situation required a search to avoid lost evidence. Based on that assessment, it appears that the courts then reserved the exigent circumstances exception for searches directed at the type of evidence that is truly in danger of being lost or destroyed if not immediately seized.

Hence, we are satisfied that exigent circumstances justified Belsha's answering Carroll's cell phone. The fleeting nature of a phone call is apparent; if it is not picked up, the opportunity to gather evidence is likely to be lost, as there is no guarantee — or likelihood — that the caller would leave a voice mail or otherwise preserve the evidence. Given these narrow circumstances, Belsha had a reasonable belief that he was in danger of losing potential evidence if he ignored the call. Thus, the evidence obtained as a result of answering that phone call was untainted.

B. Independent Source Doctrine

Having determined that the warrantless seizure and subsequent viewing of the image gallery on Carroll's phone produced tainted evidence, we turn our attention to the question of whether the resulting warrant is nonetheless valid. We conclude . . . that the phone call Belsha answered is an untainted independent source of evidence to support the search warrant, that the untainted evidence, which is combined with the officer's knowledge of drug traffickers and Carroll's juvenile record, provides sufficient probable cause to issue the warrant, and that as a result, the warrant is valid. [Based on the warrant, the search that resulted in the recovery of the firearm image was valid.]

Notes

1. Does *Carroll* survive *Riley*?

2. In *Riley*, reproduced in the previous section, the Supreme Court gave a variety of examples of exigent circumstances. What are they? Which would apply to digital devices?

3. *Riley* rejected the possibility of remote wiping as a basis for searching a cell phone incident to arrest. What would have to be shown to establish an exigent circumstance when the government claims that a third party could remotely wipe a phone?

4. *Riley* viewed the ability to use Faraday bags as illuminating the lack of a need to search a cell phone incident to arrest. Another court, in a pre-*Riley* case, observed:

> Of course, that means the constable must carry one more piece of equipment: a supply of Faraday bags, perhaps of different sizes. And even that may not work. Two new phone makers recently announced cell phones specifically designed to secure their user's data from all others.[n.3][35] One appears to be designed to self-destruct if tampered with.[n.4][36]
>
> Consequently, preventing the swift destruction of cell phone evidence, *i.e.,* the exigency exception, is an interest that could conceivably swallow

----

35. [n.3] The "Blackphone." "Blackphone offers a full suite of applications giving worldwide users unprecedented control over privacy and security." *See* www.blackphone.ch/press-releases/.The "Privacy Phone." "FreedomPop, a Los Angeles-based mobile startup, announced what it's nicknamed the 'Snowden Phone' after the notorious whistle blower. The Privacy Phone comes with Private WiFi, a built-in commercial VPN service that encrypts all of the data coming to and from the phone by default." C. Farivar, *New "Snowden Phone,"* http://arstechnica.com/informationtechnology/2014/03/new-snowden-phone-likely-not-quite-up-to-snowden-levelstandards/, Mar. 5, 2014.

36. [n.4] Boeing's "Black." "This android phone will self-destruct. . . . Any attempt to break open the casing of the device would trigger functions that would delete the data and software contained within the device and make the device inoperable." S. Gallagher, *Update: Boeing's Black— This Android Phone Will Self-Destruct,* http://arstechnica.com/information-technology/2014/02/boeings-black-this-android-phone, Feb. 26, 2014.

the search warrant rule. With the emergence of simpler techniques to secure and encrypt the data on one's electronic device, the issue of cell phone search warrants may be short lived, regardless of the how the Supreme Court rules.

United States v. Michael Lustig, 3 F. Supp. 3d 808 (S.D. Cal.), *aff'd in part and rev'd in part on other grounds*, 830 F.3d 1075 (9th Cir. 2016). Is that view correct and what are the consequences of that view?

5. In *State v. Smith*, 920 N.E.2d 949 (Ohio 2009), the court rejected the legality of a search of a cell phone incident to arrest. The state also argued that the search of the cell phone was proper based on exigent circumstances, that is, "that cell phones store a finite number of calls in their memory and that once these records have been deleted, they cannot be recovered." The court concluded that the issue was not properly before it, reasoning:

> At the suppression hearing, the state offered no evidence or argument to support its claim that the search was justified by the need to preserve evidence. Additionally, even if one accepts the premise that the call records on Smith's phone were subject to imminent permanent deletion, the state failed to show that it would be unable to obtain call records from the cell phone service provider, which might possibly maintain such records as part of its normal operating procedures.

What advice would you give to police officers who are validly in possession of a ringing cell phone?

2. Inventory

United States v. Michael Lustig

3 F. Supp. 3d 808 (S.D. Cal.), *aff'd in part and rev'd in part on other grounds*,
830 F.3d 1075 (9th Cir. 2016)

ROGER T. BENITEZ, District Judge.

In June 2012, Lustig was arrested by San Diego County Sheriff deputies at a hotel for soliciting prostitution. . . . After Lustig was arrested inside a hotel, deputies located his car in the hotel parking lot. When they searched his person, deputies found car keys in Lustig's pockets. Deputies decided to impound the car and performed an inventory search prior to towing. Five additional phones were found in the car and their contents were searched. Lustig moves to suppress any evidence discovered during the search of the phones found in his car.

Although the search of Lustig's vehicle is not justified by the search-incident-to-arrest exception, police officers may perform a warrantless search according to an established policy when a vehicle is lawfully impounded. This is known as an inventory search. Under the community caretaking exception, law enforcement officers may tow and impound a vehicle that jeopardizes public safety. "Once a vehicle has been legally impounded, the police may conduct an inventory search, as long as it conforms to the standard procedures of the local police department."

Here, a deputy impounded Lustig's vehicle. The arrest report details the deputy's reasoning. "To prevent the vehicle from being vandalized or stolen, the vehicle was towed pursuant to [California Vehicle Code]. . . . Prior to the vehicle being towed, an inventory search was conducted." Defense counsel argued at the hearing that, "there is no authority . . . for towing a car from private property because the officers claim that they feared it was going to be stolen or vandalized. That doesn't pass the blush test."

However, that was the precisely the case in *Ramirez v. City of Buena Park*, 560 F.3d 1012 (9th Cir. 2009). Ramirez was found inside his car *in a drugstore parking lot* and arrested for being under the influence of a controlled substance. The car was then impounded. The impound was challenged as violating the Fourth Amendment. The Ninth Circuit observed, "[l]eaving Ramirez's car in the drugstore parking lot would have made it an easy target for vandalism or theft." "Therefore, we conclude that the officers' impoundment of Ramirez's car for its 'safekeeping' was reasonable under the community caretaking doctrine." In view of the fact that the deputy's stated reason for impounding Lustig's car was "to prevent the vehicle from being vandalized or stolen," the impounding was a permissible warrantless seizure under the vehicle impound doctrine. And because the impound was lawful, the inventory search was lawful. The discovery of the five cell phones in the center armrest of Lustig's vehicle during the inventory search was also lawful.

The more vexing problem here is that the deputies went beyond solely searching for and seizing the phones. According to the arrest report, the deputy conducted "a brief search of the phones result[ing] in additional text messages regarding prostitution." He then "downloaded the information contained in four of the six phones which had information which I believed [sic] was involved with prostitution." The deputy also "photographed some of the text messages from the inside of the other five phones as well as their phone number listed inside the phone."

There are three reasons why a warrantless inventory search is permitted when a vehicle is impounded: (1) for the protection of the vehicle owner's property; (2) for the protection of the police from claims by the owner; and (3) for the protection of the police from potential danger. *South Dakota v. Opperman*, 428 U.S. 364, 369 (1976). Under *Opperman*, the car phone search must be conducted according to an established policy of the law enforcement agency (in this case, the San Diego Sheriff's Office). If a search is conducted according to policy, as opposed to a general rummaging for evidence, then no warrant is necessary. There has been no evidence offered on this point from either party.

The government conducted the warrantless search, consequently, it is the government that bears the burden of demonstrating its search fits the inventory search exception. To carry its burden, the government must show that the search was performed according to "standardized criteria" or "established routine." This is because an inventory search "must not be a ruse for a general rummaging in order to discover evidence." *Florida v. Wells*, 495 U.S. 1, 4 (1990).

Without evidence that the vehicle was inventory searched according to department policy or routine, the warrantless search cannot be justified. Moreover, even if there was a policy or established routine that was followed, it is hard to imagine how a policy that instructs law enforcement to search the digital contents of a cell phone found during the inventory search, is designed to foster the approved aims of protecting the owner against loss and protecting deputies against suit or physical danger. As the Court explains, "[t]he policy or practice governing inventory searches should be designed to produce an inventory." *Wells*, 495 U.S. at 4. Searching a phone's contents does not produce an inventory of property and undermines the lawfulness of the search. On the record as it is, it appears that evidence discovered from Lustig's five car phones was not discovered lawfully as it has not been shown to be the fruit of a valid impound and inventory search.

Chapter 9

Seizures of Digital Evidence

§ 9.1 Intangible Property and Digital Evidence

The Court has stated that a seizure implicates the person's interest in retaining possession of his or her property.[1] It has often repeated the following definition: a "'seizure' of property occurs when there is some meaningful interference with an individual's possessory interests in that property."[2] The Court has sometimes also stated that a seizure "deprives the individual of dominion over his or her property."[3] One could question whether such definitions adequately convey the full nature of the individual's interests implicated by a seizure. Nonetheless, the Court's inquiry has focused on possession and lower court opinions relentlessly reflect that focus.

The Court has addressed numerous situations where a seizure of personal property has been claimed. Many of the property seizure cases are obvious and require little or no analysis: the police officer physically takes possession of an object. Perhaps the best known example is *United States v. Place*, 462 U.S. 696 (1983). In that case, law enforcement agents confronted Place at La Guardia Airport in New York after he aroused suspicions that he might be transporting drugs. Place refused to consent to a search of his luggage, which he had already retrieved upon arriving on his flight from Miami. An officer told Place that he was going to take the luggage to a judge to obtain a warrant. Thereafter, the luggage was taken to Kennedy Airport, where a trained narcotics detention dog sniffed its exterior and alerted to the presence of drugs. This was approximately ninety minutes after an officer had taken the luggage from Place. The Court found that there was "no doubt" that a seizure had occurred at the point when Place was told by the agent that the luggage would be taken to a judge.

On the other hand, some transfers of possession are not considered seizures. For example, in *Maryland v. Macon*, 472 U.S. 463 (1985), an undercover officer purchased items offered for sale at an adult bookstore. That purchase was not a seizure, according to the Court, because the sales clerk who sold the magazines "voluntarily transferred any possessory interest he may have had in the magazines to the

---

1. *E.g.*, Horton v. California, 496 U.S. 128, 132 (1990); United States v. Jacobsen, 466 U.S. 109, 113 (1984); United States v. Place, 462 U.S. 696, 705–07 (1983).
2. United States v. Jacobsen, 466 U.S. 109, 114 (1984).
3. Horton v. California, 496 U.S. 128, 133 (1990).

purchaser upon receipt of the funds." The *Macon* Court added that the officer "did not 'interfere' with any interest of the seller."

Also, merely handling an object is not considered a seizure. In *Arizona v. Hicks*, 480 U.S. 321 (1987), the police lawfully entered Hicks' apartment after a bullet fired through its floor struck and injured a man in the apartment below. During the course of a search for the shooter, other victims, and weapons, one of the officers noticed some stereo equipment and had a hunch that the equipment had been stolen. He moved some of the components so that he could read the serial numbers. Thereafter, using the serial numbers, it was determined that the stereo equipment had been taken in a robbery. The Court found that the government's initial actions of handling the equipment and the recording of the serial numbers did not amount to a seizure. Justice Scalia, for the majority, reasoned:

> We agree that the mere recording of the serial numbers did not constitute a seizure. To be sure, that was the first step in a process by which [Hicks] was eventually deprived of the stereo equipment. In and of itself, however, it did not "meaningfully interfere" with [Hicks'] possessory interest in either the serial numbers or the equipment, and therefore did not amount to a seizure.

Although the mere handling of an object might not be a seizure, it might be a search. Hence, the officer's act of turning over the stereo in *Hicks* to expose the serial numbers was considered a search. Similarly, in *Bond v. United States*, 529 U.S. 334 (2000), the Court was confronted with the question "whether a law enforcement officer's physical manipulation of a bus passenger's carry-on luggage" was a search. In that case, border patrol agent Cesar Cantu entered a bus stopped at a checkpoint. As Cantu walked through the bus, "he squeezed the soft luggage which passengers had placed in the overhead storage space above the seats." In the compartment above Bond's seat, Cantu "squeezed a green canvas bag and noticed that it contained a 'brick-like' object." Bond admitted that the bag was his and allowed Cantu to open it. "Upon opening the bag, Agent Cantu discovered a 'brick' of methamphetamine [which] had been wrapped in duct tape until it was oval-shaped and then rolled in a pair of pants." Chief Justice Rehnquist, writing for the Court, found that the agent's actions constituted a search. The Chief Justice first recognized that the luggage was "clearly an 'effect' protected by the Amendment" and that Bond "possessed a privacy interest in his bag." The government contended that by exposing his bag to the public, Bond had lost his reasonable expectation that his bag would not be physically manipulated. The *Bond* majority rejected that claim:

> Our Fourth Amendment analysis embraces two questions. First, we ask whether the individual, by his conduct, has exhibited an actual expectation of privacy; that is, whether he has shown that "he [sought] to preserve [something] as private." Here, petitioner sought to preserve privacy by using an opaque bag and placing that bag directly above his seat. Second, we inquire whether the individual's expectation of privacy is "one that society is prepared to recognize as reasonable." When a bus passenger places a bag

in an overhead bin, he expects that other passengers or bus employees may move it for one reason or another. Thus, a bus passenger clearly expects that his bag may be handled. He does not expect that other passengers or bus employees will, as a matter of course, feel the bag in an exploratory manner. But this is exactly what the agent did here. We therefore hold that the agent's physical manipulation of petitioner's bag violated the Fourth Amendment.

Bond and *Hicks* demonstrate that when government agents engage in physical manipulation, the Court will readily conclude that a search has occurred so long as that manipulation infringes upon a protected interest. As discussed below, some courts have imported a similar expectations analysis into the question whether a seizure of an effect has occurred.

Focusing on the intrusion aspect of the seizure analysis, there are only two significant Supreme Court cases where the issue was disputed, and the result was not obvious.[4] In *United States v. Van Leeuwen*, 397 U.S. 249 (1970), the Court addressed the possessory interest potentially implicated by detention of mail. The language in that case is at best "equivocal."[5] In *Van Leeuwen*, two packages mailed from Washington state were diverted by customs officials from the stream of the mail and detained for twenty-nine hours. During that time, the authorities sought to establish probable cause to search each package and obtain a warrant. Reviewing the detention, the Court held that "[n]o interest protected by the Fourth Amendment was invaded by forwarding the packages the following day rather than the day when they were deposited." It explained that, "[t]heoretically—and it is theory only that respondent has on his side—detention of mail could at some point become an unreasonable seizure . . . within the meaning of the Fourth Amendment." The Court added that, based on the circumstances of the case, the "29-hour delay between the mailings and the service of the warrant cannot be said to be 'unreasonable' within the meaning of the Fourth Amendment."

The Court in *Place* later characterized *Van Leeuwen* as "[e]xpressly limiting its holding to the facts of the case." *Place* also quoted Professor LaFave: "'*Van Leeuwen* was an easy case for the Court because the defendant was unable to show that the invasion intruded upon either a privacy interest in the contents of the packages or a possessory interest in the packages themselves.' 3 W. LaFave, Search and Seizure § 9.6, p. 60 (1982 Supp.)."

---

4. *See also* California v. Hodari D., 499 U.S. 621, 624 (1991). Although *Hodari D.* involved the question when a seizure of a person occurred, the Court observed:

From the time of the founding to the present, the word "seizure" has meant a "taking possession[.]" For most purposes at common law, the word connoted not merely grasping, or applying physical force to, the animate or inanimate object in question, but actually bringing it within physical control. A ship still fleeing, even though under attack, would not be considered to have been seized as a war prize. A res capable of manual delivery was not seized until "tak[en] into custody."

5. United States v. Hoang, 486 F.3d 1156, 1161 (9th Cir. 2007).

Many courts have viewed *Van Leeuwen* as involving a seizure—albeit a reasonable one that was based on articulable suspicion.[6] But *Place*'s citation to LaFave treated *Van Leeuwen*, as did some language in *Van Leeuwen* itself, as not affecting possessory interests; this is to say that no seizure occurred.

The second case is *United States v. Jacobsen*, 466 U.S. 109 (1984), where employees of a private freight carrier, Federal Express, observed a package that had been damaged during shipment. They opened the package pursuant to the company's insurance claim policy. The container was a cardboard box wrapped in brown paper. Inside the box were five or six pieces of crumpled paper covering a tube made of duct tape. A supervisor cut open the tube and observed clear plastic bags that contained white powder. The employees called the Drug Enforcement Administration and repackaged everything before a DEA agent arrived. Upon arrival, the DEA agent removed the packaging and observed the white powder inside the plastic bags.

One of the questions before the *Jacobsen* Court was whether there was a seizure within the meaning of the Amendment. Given that the Amendment only applies to governmental actions and does not apply to mere replication of private actions by government agents, the initial actions by the law enforcement agents in *Jacobsen* that replicated the actions of the private party did not implicate the Amendment. Putting those actions aside, the Court did find that a seizure had occurred. The Court adopted the following test: A "'seizure' of property occurs when there is some meaningful interference with an individual's possessory interests in that property." The Court found that one occurred when the "agents took custody of the package from Federal Express after they arrived." It did not further identify that point other than by stating: "Although respondents had entrusted possession of the items to Federal Express, the decision by governmental authorities to exert dominion and control over the package for their own purposes clearly constituted a 'seizure,' though not necessarily an unreasonable one."[7]

There are two questions in light of *Van Leeuwen* and *Jacobsen*. First, does the phrase "possessory interests" properly describe the scope of a person's protected interest in personal property? Second, did *Jacobsen* announce one test for seizure or two different ones? As to the first question, which has been little noted by courts and is discussed more fully elsewhere,[8] a fundamental problem is that *Jacobsen*'s definition of a seizure focuses on interference with a person's possessory interests. For goods in transit not accompanied by their owner, the owner has substantially—if not completely—temporarily given up that interest to send the property to another

---

6. *E.g.*, State v. Ochadleus, 110 P.3d 448, 452–55 (Mont. 2005) (collecting cases).

7. The agents also field tested some of the white powder, destroying some of it in the process. The Court found that the test was not a search and concluded that, while the test converted a temporary "deprivation of possessory interests into a permanent one," the field test had only a "*de minimis* impact on any property interest."

8. *See* Thomas K. Clancy, The Fourth Amendment: Its History and Interpretation §§ 3.4.3.–3.4.4., 5.2.5. (3d ed. 2017).

location. So, when law enforcement delay that transit, move the goods, or permit a dog to examine the goods, is it proper to view the concept of "seizure" in terms of "possession"?

As to the second question, some argue that the "meaningful interference" test is distinct from the concept of "dominion and control."[9] The disparity in results based on the two views is most acute in the context of temporary interferences with effects that are in transit in situations where the owner is not accompanying the goods. A few courts maintain that the government seizes property when it asserts dominion and control over goods during the time that the carrier was supposed to be transporting them to their destination.[10] Others have attempted to reconcile *Jacobsen*'s two statements:

> We do not believe the [*Jacobsen*] Court meant to express two different standards—*i.e.*, meaningful interference with a person's possessory interests and dominion and control—when instructing courts how to apply Fourth Amendment seizure principles. Instead, we believe the Court referenced dominion and control when applying the seizure standard. That is, we believe the Court concluded law enforcement's exertion of dominion and control over the package for its own purposes—and in contravention to Federal Express's custody of the package—constituted a seizure under the Fourth Amendment because it constituted some meaningful interference with a person's possessory interests. Thus, the seizure standard prohibits the government's conversion of an individual's private property, as opposed to the mere technical trespass to an individual's private property. . . . Because we do not believe *Jacobsen* enunciated separate standards for seizure cases, we will not concern ourselves with trying to apply "both" standards. Instead, we will focus on whether the [police's] conduct constituted some meaningful interference with [the defendant's] possessory interests in his checked luggage.[11]

Following that view, many courts use the "meaningful interference" with "possessory interests" standard to resolve whether a seizure has occurred. The key inquiry has been interpretation of the phrase "meaningful interference." Unfortunately, that phrase has never been defined by the Court. Lower courts have typically not interpreted that phrase in an expansive manner. Instead, the courts have examined

---

9. *See, e.g.*, Eric R. Carpenter, *Seizures Without Searches: Defining Property Seizures and Developing a Property Seizure Model*, 42 Gonz. L. Rev. 173 (2006–07).

10. *E.g.*, State v. Ressler, 701 N.W.2d 915 (N.D. 2005) (shipping company employee discovered a large amount of currency in a suspicious package and called the police, who took the package to a law enforcement center for a canine sniff); People v. Ortega, 34 P.3d 986, 991–92 (Colo. 2001) (seizure when, after dog alert, bag taken to bus station garage where defendant questioned); People v. McPhee, 628 N.E.2d 523, 529–30 (Ill. App. Ct. 1993) (seizure when police detective removed envelope from Federal Express facility and locked it in his police car for twenty minutes pending a dog sniff because police exercised dominion and control over it for police purposes).

11. United States v. Va Lerie, 424 F.3d 694 (8th Cir. 2005).

the question in the broader context of the transport of the luggage, packages, or other effects by the common carrier. Generally speaking, if law enforcement does not retain the goods beyond the time that the goods would have been in the custody of the carrier, many courts do not consider the actions to be a seizure. The reasoning behind this result varies somewhat. Some courts perform an expectations analysis: since the person has conveyed the package to a common carrier, he has given up actual possession and does not expect to regain possession until the time that the goods are scheduled to arrive; hence any interference with the person's possessory interest is seen as minimal.[12] This is sometimes viewed as a contractually-based inquiry; if the shipping company promises to deliver the goods by noon the next day, the government "seizure" begins at noon if the goods are detained beyond that time.[13]

Americans have come to expect a significant amount of inquiry into effects in transit. This has proved to be a significant part of the analysis for some courts. For example, in *United States v. Ward*, 144 F.3d 1024 (7th Cir. 1998), Ward purchased a ticket to travel by bus to Indianapolis. He checked his bag but did not accompany it on the bus trip. During a stop before reaching Indianapolis, a police officer determined that the bag was unaccompanied and removed it from the bus and set it on the ground so a dog could sniff it; after the dog alerted to the presence of drugs, the police obtained a search warrant, resulting in the recovery of a gun and drugs. The court stated: "Pragmatically speaking, Ward had no cognizable interest in repossessing his bag until the bus arrived in Indianapolis" and, by that time, "the temporary detention of his bag for investigatory purposes had long since concluded." The court observed:

> [Ward] could reasonably have foreseen that the bag would be handled, moved around, and even taken off the bus, whether at intermediate stops when the driver might need to remove the bag to sort and/or gain access to other luggage, or at a hub like St. Louis where the bag would have been transferred to another bus. He could have no reasonable expectation, in other words, that the bag would not be touched, handled, or even removed from the bus prior to the bag's arrival in Indianapolis. . . . Having surrendered custody of his bag to Greyhound for transport in the common luggage compartment of the bus, Ward could expect a significantly greater degree of handling by strangers than would a passenger who carried a bag with her onto the bus. Consequently, [the police] did not "seize" Ward's bag merely by touching and then removing it from the luggage compartment.

---

12. *E.g.*, United States v. Hoang, 486 F.3d 1156 (9th Cir. 2007) ("[A]n addressee's possessory interest is in the timely delivery of a package, not in 'having his package routed on a particular conveyor belt, sorted in a particular area, or stored in any particular sorting bin for a particular amount of time.'").

13. United States v. LaFrance, 879 F.2d 1, 7 (1st Cir. 1989) ("On this record, the only possessory interest at stake before Thursday noon was the contract-based expectancy that the package would be delivered [on time]. . . . Thus, detention of the parcel did not, indeed could not on these facts, intrude on appellees' possessory interest until the appointed hour, noon, had come and gone.").

Handling the bag to that limited extent did not impinge on any of the rights that the Fourth Amendment protects.

Other courts have applied similar reasoning to find that a person does not have a protected possessory interest infringed by some physical handling by the police that serves to facilitate an investigation:

Today police, airport security personnel, and travelers must all be concerned not only that drugs may be transported but that explosives, incendiary devices, and other items that threaten the safety of those on the airplane may be stored in luggage in the airplane's baggage compartment. Travelers today expect and want luggage X-rayed, sniffed, felt, and handled in a manner that is as non-intrusive as possible but consistent with ensuring that the checked luggage does not contain items that threaten their safety. Brief, non-intrusive detention of checked luggage for such examination no longer invades the traveler's reasonable expectation of privacy, does not unduly interfere with possessory rights, and is not a seizure under the Fourth Amendment.[14]

There are two bases to question this reasoning. First, it confuses Fourth Amendment applicability with satisfaction: the government may have weighty interests in certain contexts that justify a search or seizure; those interests do not eliminate the applicability of the Amendment. Hence, it is a search when one has to go through a metal detector at an airport; it may be justified due to the concerns with, *inter alia*, hijacking and terrorism. Second, one should seriously question a person's expectations when she checks a bag or mails a package. As one commentator has observed: "The idea that passengers expect the common carrier to handle their baggage only in furtherance of getting the baggage to its destination is essential in understanding the relationship between the possessory interest and government detainment."[15] There is more weighty support; in *Bond*, as previously discussed, the majority rejected the claim that a search did not occur when a police officer squeezed the sides of bags as he walked along the aisle of a bus:

When a bus passenger places a bag in an overhead bin, he expects that other passengers or bus employees may move it for one reason or another. Thus, a bus passenger clearly expects that his bag may be handled. He does not expect that other passengers or bus employees will, as a matter of course, feel the bag in an exploratory manner. But this is exactly what the agent

---

14. State v. Peters, 941 P.2d 228, 231 (Ariz. 1997) (en banc) (holding that the "warrantless detention [of checked luggage at an airport] for examination without reasonable suspicion is not a seizure and is permissible if made in such a manner that neither the traveler nor his luggage is unreasonably delayed").

15. Jonathan B. Strom, Note, *Checking Reasonableness at the Ticket Counter: The Eighth Circuit's Flawed Approach to Seizures of Checked Baggage in* United States v. Va Lerie, 92 Cornell L. Rev. 157 (2006).

did here. We therefore hold that the agent's physical manipulation of petitioner's bag violated the Fourth Amendment.[16]

Consistent with *Bond*, is it fair to say that persons who mail or check packages
expect that they will be moved to permit law enforcement to investigate the contents of the package? If *Bond* stands for the proposition that a search occurs when
government agents engage in physical manipulation to ascertain something about
the contents of the container, should movement and detention of an effect be considered a seizure if the police, and not the carrier, engage in the procedure to permit
them to learn something about the contents of the container?[17]

§ 9.2 Seizures of Digital Evidence

It has long been clear that intangible interests are protected by the Fourth Amendment and can be the target of a search and seizure; that was an essential lesson of
Katz, which found that a conversation could be seized.[18] Determining the point at
which a seizure occurs seems increasingly important in light of the revelations of
the Federal government's vast data copying and retention programs associated with
national security concerns.

Only a few cases address the question in the context of digital evidence and they
concern the copying of data. "Computer technologies often require investigators to
obtain a copy first and then search it later. Nearly every case begins with copying
data that will later be searched, and government investigators often will prefer to
copy more rather than less if the Fourth Amendment allows it."[19]

> If copying data is not a seizure, then copying cannot logically be regarded
> as a search and it does not violate an expectation of privacy. It is possible to
> copy files without examining the files. Therefore, if copying is not a seizure,
> it is outside the scope of the Fourth Amendment's reasonableness require-
> ments and is an activity which can be conducted at will, requiring neither
> the justification of a warrant nor an exception to the warrant requirement.[20]

---

16. Bond v. United States, 529 U.S. 334 (2000).

17. *Cf.* United States v. Lovell, 849 F.2d 910, 916 (5th Cir. 1988) (finding no seizure when border
patrol agents removed the luggage of airline passenger from the baggage conveyor belt, compressed
the bags' sides and smelled marijuana, detained the bags until a positive alert by a drug detection
canine, and then obtained a search warrant; the court reasoned that Lovell had surrendered his
luggage to a common carrier, with the expectation that he could reclaim his bags at his destination and that, in the absence of any delay in his travel or in the expected delivery of the suitcase,
the "momentary delay occasioned by the bags' removal from the conveyor belt was insufficient to
constitute a meaningful interference with [defendant's] possessory interest in his bags").

18. Katz v. United States, 389 U.S. 347 (1967).

19. Orin Kerr, *Fourth Amendment Seizures of Computer Data*, 119 YALE L.J. 700 (2010).

20. Susan W. Brenner & Barbara A. Frederiksen, *Computer Searches and Seizures: Some Unresolved Issues*, 8 MICH. TELECOMM. TECH. L. REV. 39, 113 (2001–2002).

In *United States v. Gorshkov*, 2001 U.S. Dist. LEXIS 26306 (W.D. Wash. May 23, 2001), FBI agents downloaded a file from a server located in Russia and held the copy of the file until a warrant was obtained. The district court concluded that the Fourth Amendment did not apply based on Supreme Court precedent declining to apply the Amendment outside the borders of the United States. The court also offered a second reason:

> [T]he agents' act of copying the data on the Russian computers was not a seizure under the Fourth Amendment because it did not interfere with Defendant's or anyone else's possessory interest in the data. The data remained intact and unaltered. It remained accessible to Defendant and any co-conspirators or partners with whom he had shared access. The copying of the data had absolutely no impact on his possessory rights.

In *In the Matter of the Application of the United States of America for a Search Warrant for Contents of Electronic Mail*, 665 F. Supp. 2d 1210 (D. Or. 2009), the court had a similar concept of what interests are implicated by a seizure. In that case, the issue before the court was whether a subscriber of an e-mail account was entitled to notice under Rule 41 when the government obtained copies of e-mails stored on the server of the Internet service provider. The court ruled that the account holder was not entitled to notice, reasoning in part, that in the case of electronic information,

> no property is actually taken or seized as that term is used in the Fourth Amendment context. The Supreme Court has stated that "[a] 'seizure' of property occurs when there is some meaningful interference with an individual's possessory interests in that property." Here, there was no such meaningful interference due to the nature of electronic information, which can be accessed from multiple locations, by multiple people, simultaneously. More specifically for the purposes of Rule 41, if no property was taken, there is no person from whom, or from whose premises, the property was taken.

The following case reflects a much different view:

———————

United States v. Howard Wesley Cotterman

2009 U.S. Dist. LEXIS 14300 (D. Ariz. Feb. 23, 2009)[21]

CHARLES R. PYLE, UNITED STATES MAGISTRATE JUDGE.

Howard and Maureen Cotterman entered the Lukeville Port of Entry seeking admission to the United States on April 6, 2007 at 9:57 a.m. A Treasury Enforcement

———————

21. The District Court's opinion in *Cotterman* was reversed on appeal on other grounds. *See* United States v. Cotterman, 709 F.3d 952 (9th Cir. 2013) (en banc).

Communication System hit was observed based on Mr. Cotterman's convictions for child sex crimes in 1992. Based on the TECS hit, the Cottermans were referred to secondary. At secondary, the Cottermans were told to exit the car, leave all their belongings in the car and they were not to touch those belongings until they were allowed to leave.

Two border inspectors searched the contents of the Cotterman's car for one and a half to two hours. Among other things, they found three cameras and two laptop computers which they turned over to Agent Alvarado for inspection. Agent Alvarez examined the cameras and laptops, but was unable to discover any contraband. However, on one of the computers, certain files were password protected.

The TECS hit was referred through the ICE chain of command and finally assigned to Sells duty agent Mina Riley. Agent Riley and her supervisor, Agent Craig Brisbine, traveled to Lukeville, arriving about 3:30 p.m. At Lukeville, Ms. Riley interviewed Mr. and Mrs. Cotterman separately. Mr. Cotterman offered to assist in accessing his computer, but Agent Riley declined due to concerns that Mr. Cotterman might be able to sabotage the computer.

Two computers and one camera were seized. Agent Brisbine drove the laptop computers and camera to Tucson, arriving between 10:30 p.m. and 11:00 p.m. He turned the equipment over to John Owen for forensic evaluation, which Owen began immediately. The Cottermans were finally allowed to leave Lukeville at approximately 6:00 p.m.

Owen continued the forensic examination on Saturday and Sunday. On Saturday he determined there was no contraband on the camera, and it was returned that day to the Cottermans. On Sunday it was determined that there was no contraband on Mrs. Cotterman's laptop. However, 75 images of child pornography were found on Mr. Cotterman's laptop in unallocated space. Mrs. Cotterman's laptop was returned Monday morning. However, a copy of the laptop was made by Owen and is still in his file, even though nothing illicit was found on her computer.

The Government's disregard of the Fourth Amendment in connection with border searches of electronic media is emphasized by the Government's continued possession of a copy of Mrs. Cotterman's hard drive. If there is probative information on the hard drive, seventeen months is more than enough time to determine that. The Government apparently believes that returning Mrs. Cotterman's laptop eliminates the intrusion on her privacy. Obviously, keeping a copy of the hard drive with no viable basis does violate Mrs. Cotterman's privacy interests as well as the field guidelines directive that the electronic media seized "shall not be retained by ICE longer than is necessary to determine its relevance to furthering the law enforcement mission of ICE." At this point in time, any incriminating evidence found now on the copy of Mrs. Cotterman's hard drive would be inadmissible because that hard drive was not subject to seizure for containing contraband.

———————

1. Revocation of Consent After the Mirror Image Is Made

United States v. Youssef Samir Megahed

2009 U.S. Dist. LEXIS 24441 (M.D. Fla. Mar. 18, 2009)

Steven D. Merryday, District Judge.

[Defendant sought to] suppress certain internet history recovered from a desktop computer seized from the Megahed family residence by agents of the Federal Bureau of Investigation on August 6, 2007.

First, the FBI possessed a valid and voluntary third-party consent to remove and search the computer hard drive.

Second, the seizure and search of the computer hard drive fell within the scope of a valid third-party consent. In short, a reasonable person assessing the exchange between Special Agent Palenzuela and Samir Megahed would have concluded that the FBI agents intended a complete search of the Megahed residence for (among other things) explosives, explosive materials, and evidence relating to explosives and bomb-making and that "items which [FBI agents] determine may be related to their investigation" would not exclude information stored on a home computer. Further, when requesting on August 7, 2007, that the computer be returned after the FBI copied the hard drive, Samir Megahed expressed no objection either to the removal of the computer or to the copying. Additionally, on the following day, Samir Megahed voluntarily authorized a complete search of the computer by executing a "consent to search computer."

Third, the October, 2007, revocation of consent by the defendant and the defendant's parents does not require suppression of the internet history. After agents searched the Megahed residence, seized the computer, captured a mirror image copy of the hard drive, and returned the hard drive to Samir Megahed, the evidence was discovered in the course of an examination of the FBI mirror image copy. In October, 2008, neither the defendant nor Samir Megahed retained a reasonable expectation of privacy in the mirror image copy that the FBI had obtained already with Samir Megahed's consent and had begun already to search. The revocation did not operate retroactively to nullify this history. *See United States v. Ponder*, 444 F.2d 816, 818 (5th Cir. 1971) ("[A] valid consent to a search . . . carries with it the right to examine and photocopy."); *Mason v. Pulliam*, 557 F.2d 426, 429 (5th Cir. 1977) (affirming an order that directed the return of original records and documents voluntarily provided to an IRS agent after withdrawal of consent but agreeing that the taxpayer's "withdrawal and reinvocation does not affect the validity of [the agent's] actions prior to the time he received notice that his right to retain Mason's papers was gone. The district court correctly refused to require the return of *copies* made prior to the demand by Mason's attorney."); *United States v. Ward*, 576 F.2d 243, 244–45 (9th Cir. 1978) (adopting the reasoning of *Mason* as to the use of records following revocation but concluding that "any evidence gathered or *copies made* from the records [before revocation] should not be suppressed.").

Notes

Cotterman and *Megahed* offer less than fully formed views regarding a person's interest in a copy of his or her data possessed by the government. Are the views consistent? Can the cases be distinguished on the ground that the "seizure" of the original data in *Cotterman* was non-consensual but that the "seizure" in *Megahed* was not? More broadly, what interest—if any—does a person have in a copy of her data when the original has been returned to her?

2. Digital Seizures: Seeking a Workable Definition

Several commentators believe that conceptual difficulty lurks in analyzing the search and seizure of digital evidence in electronic storage.[22] The issue turns on whether the mere copying of the data is a seizure. Thus, for example, two commentators argue:

> Copying has an effect upon the "ownership" rights of the party whose information is copied. For policy reasons, the copying of data should be defined as a seizure. Doing so does not prohibit law enforcement from copying files; it merely ensures that officers comply with the standards of reasonableness set out in the Fourth Amendment.[23]

In contrast, Orin Kerr proposes a complex definition of a seizure: "copying data 'seizes' it under the Fourth Amendment when copying occurs without human observation and interrupts the course of the data's possession or transmission."[24] Hence, according to Kerr, "copying is neither never nor always a seizure. Whether copying amounts to a seizure depends both on whether it is pre-observation or post-observation and on whether it interrupts the intended transmission or use of the data." Kerr explains the two limitations on his proposal. First, "only copying

---

22. *See, e.g.,* Orin S. Kerr, *Digital Evidence and the New Criminal Procedure*, 105 COLUM. L. REV. 279, 301 (2005) ("Detectives no longer need to impose a meaningful interference on a possessory interest to obtain digital evidence. Because police can create a perfect copy of the evidence without depriving the suspect of property, the new facts unhinge the [definition of a seizure] from its traditional function of limiting police investigations."); Paul Ohm, *The Olmsteadian Seizure Clause: The Fourth Amendment and the Seizure of Intangible Property*, 2008 STAN. TECH. L. REV. 2 (arguing that courts have interpreted the concept of seizure to exclude protection for intangible property such as computer data); Paul Ohm, *The Fourth Amendment Right to Delete*, 119 HARV. L. REV. 10 (2005) (contending that the Fourth Amendment should be read as implying a "the right to delete," that is, the right to control what happens to one's property, including copies). *But see* Randolph S. Sergent, *A Fourth Amendment Model for Computer Networks and Data Privacy*, 81 VA. L. REV. 1181, 1186 (1995) (arguing that copying computer files is a seizure because the possessory interest in a computer file includes the ability to control the dissemination and use of the information contained in that file).

23. Susan W. Brenner & Barbara A. Frederiksen, *Computer Searches and Seizures: Some Unresolved Issues*, 8 MICH. TELECOMM. & TECH. L. REV. 39, 113 (2001–2002).

24. Orin Kerr, *Fourth Amendment Seizures of Computer Data*, 119 YALE L.J. 700 (2010).

of data that has not been exposed to human observation by a government agent amounts to a seizure, because only that copying involves freezing the scene and adding to the information in the government's possession." He explains:

> The power to record what has been observed is designed to minimize loss; government agents use tools to avoid forgetting what they have learned. In contrast, the power to freeze the scene adds to what the government controls. Government agents take some evidence that was beyond the government's control and bring it within the government's control. The power to freeze the scene thus provides the opportunity for the government to use its search powers to collect evidence and then use it against a suspect. The power to preserve observations does not add to the government's power to collect evidence; it merely provides a way to retain information already collected.

Second, "copying data as part of its usual course of transmission or storage does not seize anything, because its intended path or timing has not been interrupted." On the other hand, Kerr asserts that "a government request to an ISP to make a copy of a suspect's remotely stored files and to hold the copy while the government obtains a warrant would . . . constitute a seizure" because the government's action "changes the path of the communication of contents that would have occurred in the ordinary course of business." It "freezes the scene at the government's request." He adds that a "government request to an ISP not to delete contents of communications that would have been deleted in the ordinary course of business would also be considered a seizure."

3. Is There a Need for Special Rules for Digital Evidence?

When government agents enter[25] a home or any other location where a person has a reasonable expectation of privacy to look for data on computers or other digital evidence, a search occurs.[26] Does a seizure occur when those records are located and copied? Can it be said that what is seized in such circumstances is the same as what is seized when the police seize a conversation, that is, an intangible protected interest? The act of seizing would be the copying of the data, just as the act of seizing a conversation is the recording of the conversation.

On the other hand, is there a need to precisely determine the point when the seizure occurs? Is it an abstract question with no practical consequences in the absence of the *use* of the data obtained? Is it sufficient to acknowledge that the use of a copy is the fruit of a prior seizure when the government had previously copied the data from a location where the individual had a recognized protected Fourth Amendment

---

25. That entrance may be physical or technological. *See, e.g.,* United States v. Heckenkamp, 482 F.3d 1142 (9th Cir. 2007) (remote search of computer files).

26. *E.g.,* Sabin v. Miller, 423 F. Supp. 2d 943 (S.D. Iowa 2006) (rejecting argument that no search occurred when state investigator entered home to retrieve computer records from personal home computer).

interest? Is the use of such information or a copy any different from that which confronted the Court many years ago in *Silverthorne Lumber Co. v. United States*, 251 U.S. 385 (1920), where federal officials illegally raided a company's offices and seized all of its books, records, and papers? The material records were photographed or copied. Although the district court ordered the originals returned to the company, it impounded the photographs and copies. After subpoenas were issued for the originals, the district court found the company in contempt for failing to comply. Upon review of that order, Justice Holmes, writing for the Supreme Court, asserted:

> The proposition could not be presented more nakedly. It is that although of course its seizure was an outrage which the Government now regrets, it may study the papers before it returns them, copy them, and then may use the knowledge that it has gained to call upon the owners in a more regular form to produce them; that the protection of the Constitution covers the physical possession but not any advantages that the Government can gain over the object of its pursuit by doing the forbidden act. *Weeks* [*v. United States*, 232 U.S. 383 (1914)], to be sure, had established that laying the papers directly before the grand jury was unwarranted, but it is taken to mean only that two steps are required instead of one. In our opinion such is not the law. It reduces the Fourth Amendment to a form of words. The essence of a provision forbidding the acquisition of evidence in a certain way is that not merely evidence so acquired shall not be used before the Court but that it shall not be used at all. Of course this does not mean that the facts thus obtained become sacred and inaccessible. If knowledge of them is gained from an independent source they may be proved like any others, but the knowledge gained by the Government's own wrong cannot be used by it in the way proposed.

Hence, in *Silverthorne*, the copies were considered the fruit of a prior illegal seizure. Regardless of whether the copy is considered a direct seizure or a fruit of a seizure of the original, the Fourth Amendment applies. It is the prohibited use of the copies, in any way, that is the central lesson of *Silverthorne*.

More recently, in *United States v. Jefferson*, 571 F. Supp. 2d 696 (E.D. Va. 2008), the FBI obtained a warrant to search a Congressman's home for evidence of fraud and bribery. During the course of the search, agents took photographs of 13 documents. The court viewed the question as "whether taking photographs . . . constitutes a meaningful interference with an individual's possessory privacy interest in the property seized." Recognizing that the Supreme Court has extended the Fourth Amendment's protections to intangible as well as tangible possessory interests, the district court viewed that precedent as standing

> for the proposition that the Fourth Amendment protects an individual's possessory interest in information itself, and not simply in the medium in which it exists. In essence these cases recognize that the Fourth Amendment privacy interest extends not just to the paper on which the information is written or the disc on which it is recorded but also to the information on

the paper or disc itself. It follows from this that recording the information by photograph or otherwise interferes with this possessory privacy interest even if the document or disc is not itself seized.

Summarizing, the court believed that those precedents

> support the proposition that individuals possess a constitutionally protected right to preserve the privacy of information recorded in books and documents against government attempts to photograph, transcribe, or otherwise copy the information. This conclusion is convincingly confirmed by recognizing that a contrary rule would significantly degrade the right to privacy protected by the Fourth Amendment. Thus, if Fourth Amendment protection did not extend to the information reflected in books and documents, then there would be no constitutional bar to police entering an individual's home pursuant to a lawful warrant and then evading the warrant's limits by recording every detail of the premises and its contents by way of high-resolution photographs and notes, all in a search for evidence of crimes unrelated to the matter giving rise to the warrant. To put this point more concretely, failure to recognize that photographing or taking notes of private information, without seizing the medium on which the information exists, constitutes a seizure under the Fourth Amendment would allow the government to ignore a narrowly circumscribed warrant in searching a premises containing volumes of documents by simply photographing the documents without removing them, and then reviewing the documents at length back at the station house.

The court accordingly held that the taking of the high-resolution photographs of documents was "both a search and a seizure of the information contained in those documents for Fourth Amendment purposes."

United States v. Stavros M. Ganias

755 F.3d 125 (2d Cir. 2014)

CHIN, CIRCUIT JUDGE:

In this case, Stavros M. Ganias appeals from a judgment convicting him, following a jury trial, of tax evasion. He challenges the conviction on the grounds that his Fourth Amendment rights were violated when the Government copied three of his computer hard drives pursuant to a search warrant and then retained files beyond the scope of the warrant for more than two-and-a-half years. We hold that the Government's retention of the computer records was unreasonable. Accordingly, we vacate the conviction and remand for further proceedings.

A. *The Facts*

In the 1980s, after working for the Internal Revenue Service for some fourteen years, Ganias started his own accounting business in Wallingford, Connecticut. He provided tax and accounting services to individuals and small businesses. In 1998, he began providing services to James McCarthy and two of McCarthy's businesses, American Boiler and Industrial Property Management. IPM had been hired by the Army to provide maintenance and security at a vacant Army facility in Stratford, Connecticut.

In August 2003, the Criminal Investigative Command of the Army received a tip from a confidential source that individuals affiliated with IPM were engaging in improper conduct, including stealing copper wire and other items from the Army facility and billing the Army for work that IPM employees performed for American Boiler. The source alleged that evidence of the wrongdoing could be found at the offices of American Boiler and IPM, as well as at the offices of "Steve Gainis [sic]," who "perform[ed] accounting work for IPM and American Boiler."

Based on this information, the Army commenced an investigation. Army investigators obtained several search warrants, including one to search the offices of Ganias's accounting business. The warrant, issued by the United States District Court for the District of Connecticut and dated November 17, 2003, authorized the seizure from Ganias's offices of:

> All books, records, documents, materials, computer hardware and software and computer associated data relating to the business, financial and accounting operations of [IPM] and American Boiler. . . .

The warrant was executed two days later. Army computer specialists accompanied investigators to Ganias's offices and helped gather the electronic evidence. The agents did not seize Ganias's computers; instead, the computer specialists made identical copies, or forensic mirror images, of the hard drives of all three of Ganias's computers. As a consequence, the investigators copied every file on all three computers—including files beyond the scope of the warrant, such as files containing Ganias's personal financial records. Ganias was present as the investigators collected the evidence, and he expressed concern about the scope of the seizure. In response, one agent "assured" Ganias that the Army was only looking for files "related to American Boiler and IPM." Everything else, the agent explained, "would be purged once they completed their search" for relevant files.

Back in their offices, the Army computer specialist copied the data taken from Ganias's computers (as well as data obtained from the searches of the offices of IPM and American Boiler) onto "two sets of 19 DVDs," which were "maintained as evidence." Some eight months later, the Army Criminal Investigation Lab finally began to review the files.

In the meantime, while reviewing the paper documents retrieved from Ganias's offices, the Army discovered suspicious payments made by IPM to an unregistered business, which was allegedly owned by an individual who had not reported any income from that business. Based on this evidence, in May 2004, the Army invited the IRS to "join the investigation" of IPM and American Boiler and gave copies of the imaged hard drives to the IRS so that it could conduct its own review and analysis. The Army and the IRS proceeded, separately, to search the imaged hard drives for files that appeared to be within the scope of the warrant and to extract them for further review.

By December 2004, some thirteen months after the seizure, the Army and IRS investigators had isolated and extracted the computer files that were relevant to IPM and American Boiler and thus covered by the search warrant. The investigators were aware that, because of the constraints of the warrant, they were not permitted to review any other computer records. Indeed, the investigators were careful, at least until later, to review only data covered by the November 2003 warrant.

They did not, however, purge or delete the non-responsive files. To the contrary, the investigators retained the files because they "viewed the data as the government's property, not Mr. Ganias's property." Their view was that while items seized from an owner will be returned after an investigation closes, all of the electronic data here were evidence that were to be protected and preserved. As one agent testified, "[W]e would not routinely go into DVDs to delete data, as we're altering the original data that was seized. And you never know what data you may need in the future. . . . I don't normally go into electronic data and start deleting evidence off of DVDs stored in my evidence room." The computer specialists were never asked to delete (or even to try to delete) those files that did not relate to IPM or American Boiler.

In late 2004, IRS investigators discovered accounting irregularities regarding transactions between IPM and American Boiler in the paper documents taken from Ganias's office. After subpoenaing and reviewing the relevant bank records in 2005, they began to suspect that Ganias was not properly reporting American Boiler's income. Accordingly, on July 28, 2005, some twenty months after the seizure of his computer files, the Government officially expanded its investigation to include possible tax violations by Ganias. Further investigation in 2005 and early 2006 indicated that Ganias had been improperly reporting income for both of his clients, leading the Government to suspect that he also might have been underreporting his own income.

At that point, the IRS case agent wanted to review Ganias's personal financial records and she knew, from her review of the seized computer records, that they were among the files in the DVDs copied from Ganias's hard drives. The case agent was aware, however, that Ganias's personal financial records were beyond the scope of the November 2003 warrant, and consequently she did not believe that she could review the non-responsive files, even though they were already in the Government's possession.

In February 2006, the Government asked Ganias and his counsel for permission to access certain of his personal files that were contained in the materials seized in November 2003. Ganias did not respond, and thus, on April 24, 2006, the Government obtained another warrant to search the preserved images of Ganias's personal financial records taken in 2003. At that point, the images had been in the Government's possession for almost two-and-a-half years. Because Ganias had altered the original files shortly after the Army executed the 2003 warrant, the evidence obtained in 2006 would not have existed but for the Government's retention of those images.

B. *Procedural History*

1. *The Indictment*

In October 2008, a grand jury indicted Ganias and McCarthy for conspiracy and tax evasion. The grand jury returned a superseding indictment in December 2009, containing certain counts relating to McCarthy's taxes and two counts relating to Ganias's personal taxes.

2. *The Motion to Suppress*

In February 2010, Ganias moved to suppress the computer files that are the subject of this appeal. In April 2010, the district court held a two-day hearing and, on April 14, 2010, it denied the motion, with an indication that a written decision would follow. On June 24, 2011, the district court filed its written decision explaining the denial of Ganias's motion to suppress.

DISCUSSION

B. *The Seizure and Retention of Ganias's Computer Records*

1. *Applicable Law*

The Fourth Amendment protects the rights of individuals "to be secure in their persons, houses, papers, and effects, against unreasonable searches and seizures." A search occurs when the Government acquires information by either "physically intruding on persons, houses, papers, or effects," or otherwise invading an area in which the individual has a reasonable expectation of privacy. A seizure occurs when the Government interferes in some meaningful way with the individual's possession of property.

Like 18th Century "papers," computer files may contain intimate details regarding an individual's thoughts, beliefs, and lifestyle, and they should be similarly guarded against unwarranted Government intrusion. If anything, even greater protection is warranted.

Not surprisingly, the ability of computers to store massive volumes of information presents logistical problems in the execution of search warrants. It is "comparatively" commonplace for files on a computer hard drive to be "so intermingled that they cannot feasibly be sorted on site." As evidenced by this case, forensic analysis of electronic data may take months to complete. It would be impractical for agents to occupy an individual's home or office, or seize an individual's computer, for such long periods of time. It is now also unnecessary. Today, advancements in technology enable the Government to create a mirror image of an individual's hard drive, which can be searched as if it were the actual hard drive but without interfering with the individual's use of his home, computer, or files.

In light of the significant burdens on-site review would place on both the individual and the Government, the creation of mirror images for offsite review is constitutionally permissible in most instances, even if wholesale removal of tangible papers would not be. Indeed, the 2009 amendments to the Federal Rules of Criminal Procedure, which added Rule 41(e)(2)(B), clearly contemplated off-site review of computer hard drives in certain circumstances.[n.10][27] Although Rule 41(e)(2)(B) was not in effect in 2003, when the warrant was executed with respect to Ganias's computers, case law both before and after the rule's adoption has recognized that off-site review of seized electronic files may be necessary and reasonable.

The off-site review of these mirror images, however, is still subject to the rule of reasonableness. The advisory committee's notes to the 2009 amendment of the Federal Rules of Criminal Procedure shed some light on what is "reasonable" in this context. Specifically, the committee rejected "a presumptive national or uniform time period within which any subsequent off-site copying or review of the media or electronically stored information would take place." Fed. R. Crim. P. 41(e)(2)(B) advisory committee's notes to the 2009 Amendments. The committee noted that several variables—storage capacity of media, difficulties created by encryption or electronic booby traps, and computer-lab workload—influence the duration of a forensic analysis and counsel against a "one size fits all" time period. In combination, these factors might justify an off-site review lasting for a significant period of time. They do not, however, provide an "independent basis" for retaining any electronic data "other than [those] specified in the warrant." *United States v. Comprehensive Drug Testing, Inc.*, 621 F.3d 1162, 1171 (9th Cir. 2010) (en banc).

2. Analysis

This case presents a host of challenging issues, but we need not address them all. The parties agree that the personal financial records at issue in this appeal were not covered by the 2003 warrant, and that they had been segregated from the responsive files by December 2004, before the Government began to suspect that Ganias was personally involved in any criminal activity. Furthermore, on appeal, Ganias does not directly challenge the Government's practice of making mirror images of computer hard drives when searching for electronic data, but rather challenges the reasonableness of its off-site review. Accordingly, we need not address whether: (1) the description of the computer files to be seized in the 2003 warrant was stated with sufficient particularity; (2) the 2003 warrant authorized the Government to make a

---

27. [n.10] Rule 41(e)(2)(B) provides:

> **Warrant Seeking Electronically Stored Information.** A warrant under Rule 41(e)(2)(A) may authorize the seizure of electronic storage media or the seizure or copying of electronically stored information. Unless otherwise specified, the warrant authorizes a later review of the media or information consistent with the warrant. The time for executing the warrant in Rule 41(e)(2)(A) and (f)(1)(A) refers to the seizure or on-site copying of the media or information, and not to any later off-site copying or review.

mirror image of the entire hard drive so it could search for relevant files off-site; or (3) the resulting off-site sorting process was unreasonably long.

Instead, we consider a more limited question: whether the Fourth Amendment permits officials executing a warrant for the seizure of particular data on a computer to seize and indefinitely retain every file on that computer for use in future criminal investigations. We hold that it does not.

If the 2003 warrant authorized the Government to retain all the data on Ganias's computers on the off-chance the information would become relevant to a subsequent criminal investigation, it would be the equivalent of a general warrant. The Government's retention of copies of Ganias's personal computer records for two-and-a-half years deprived him of exclusive control over those files for an unreasonable amount of time. This combination of circumstances enabled the Government to possess indefinitely personal records of Ganias that were beyond the scope of the warrant while it looked for other evidence to give it probable cause to search the files. This was a meaningful interference with Ganias's possessory rights in those files and constituted a seizure within the meaning of the Fourth Amendment. *See United States v. Place*, 462 U.S. 696, 708 (1983) (detaining a traveler's luggage while awaiting the arrival of a drug-sniffing dog constituted a seizure); *see also Soldal v. Cook Cnty.*, 506 U.S. 56, 62–64 (1992) (explaining that a seizure occurs when one's property rights are violated, even if the property is never searched and the owner's privacy was never violated); *Loretto v. Teleprompter Manhattan CATV Corp.*, 458 U.S. 419, 435 (1982) ("The power to exclude has traditionally been considered one of the most treasured strands in an owner's bundle of property rights.").

We conclude that the unauthorized seizure and retention of these documents was unreasonable. The Government had no warrant authorizing the seizure of Ganias's personal records in 2003. By December 2004, these documents had been separated from those relevant to the investigation of American Boiler and IPM. Nevertheless, the Government continued to retain them for another year-and-a-half until it finally developed probable cause to search and seize them in 2006. Without some independent basis for its retention of those documents in the interim, the Government clearly violated Ganias's Fourth Amendment rights by retaining the files for a prolonged period of time and then using them in a future criminal investigation.

The Government offers several arguments to justify its actions, but none provides any legal authorization for its continued and prolonged possession of the non-responsive files. First, it argues that it must be allowed to make the mirror image copies as a matter of practical necessity and, according to the Government's investigators, those mirror images were "the government's property." As explained above, practical considerations may well justify a reasonable accommodation in the manner of executing a search warrant, such as making mirror images of hard drives and permitting off-site review, but these considerations do not justify the indefinite retention of non-responsive documents. Without a warrant authorizing seizure of Ganias's personal financial records, the copies of those documents could not become *ipso facto* "the government's property" without running afoul of the Fourth Amendment.

Second, the Government asserts that by obtaining the 2006 search warrant, it cured any defect in its search of the wrongfully retained files. But this argument "reduces the Fourth Amendment to a form of words." If the Government could seize and retain non-responsive electronic records indefinitely, so it could search them whenever it later developed probable cause, every warrant to search for particular electronic data would become, in essence, a general warrant.

Third, the Government argues that it must be permitted to search the mirror images in its possession because the evidence no longer existed on Ganias's computers. But the ends, however, do not justify the means. The loss of the personal records is irrelevant in this case because the Government concedes that it never considered performing a new search of Ganias's computers and did not know that the files no longer existed when it searched the mirror images in its possession. And even if it were relevant, the Fourth Amendment clearly embodies a judgment that some evidence of criminal activity may be lost for the sake of protecting property and privacy rights.

Fourth, the Government contends that returning or destroying the non-responsive files is "entirely impractical" because doing so would compromise the remaining data that was responsive to the warrant, making it impossible to authenticate or use it in a criminal prosecution. We are not convinced that there is no other way to preserve the evidentiary chain of custody. But even if we assumed it were necessary to maintain a complete copy of the hard drive solely to authenticate evidence responsive to the original warrant, that does not provide a basis for using the mirror image for any other purpose.

Because the Government has demonstrated no legal basis for retaining the non-responsive documents, its retention and subsequent search of those documents were unconstitutional. The Fourth Amendment was intended to prevent the Government from entering individuals' homes and indiscriminately seizing all their papers in the hopes of discovering evidence about previously unknown crimes. Yet this is exactly what the Government claims it may do when it executes a warrant calling for the seizure of particular electronic data relevant to a different crime. Perhaps the "wholesale removal" of intermingled computer records is permissible where off-site sorting is necessary and reasonable, but this accommodation does not somehow authorize the Government to retain all non-responsive documents indefinitely, for possible use in future criminal investigations.

[Ed.: The appellate court granted rehearing *en banc* and later concluded (1) that there was good faith justified reliance on the warrant and that the exclusionary rule did not apply and (2) in light of that conclusion, it did not decide "whether retention of the forensic mirrors violated the Fourth Amendment." *United States v. Ganias*, 824 F.3d 199 (2d Cir. 2016).]

———

Notes and Questions

1. What are a person's interests in data?

2. Does "meaningful interference with a person's possessory interest" sufficiently describe that right as to papers and effects?

3. An underlying common theme that the Amendment protects the right to exclude has appeared often in the Court's opinions. Is the ability to exclude the essence of the right to be secure? I have argued elsewhere that the exclusionary function of the Amendment is so bound up with the right to be secure as to be equivalent to it: There is no security if one cannot exclude the government from intruding.[28] Indeed, the right to exclude has long been considered an essential attribute of the ownership of private property.[29] This right has been most consistently recognized in the context of physical invasions of the home.[30] As to personal effects, Justice Stevens observed in *Karo*: "The owner of property . . . has a right to exclude from it all the world, including the Government, and a concomitant right to use it exclusively for his own purposes."[31] The *Ganias* court seemed to have that view. How helpful is that view to determine when a seizure of digital evidence occurs?

4. Justice Brennan has asserted:

> Because the requirements of the Fourth Amendment apply only to "searches" and "seizures," an investigative technique that falls within neither category need not be reasonable and may be employed without a warrant and without probable cause, regardless of the circumstances surrounding its use. The prohibitions of the Fourth Amendment are not, however, limited to any preconceived conceptions of what constitutes a search or a seizure; instead we must apply the constitutional language to modern developments according to the fundamental principles that the Fourth Amendment embodies. Before excluding a class of surveillance techniques from the reach of the Fourth Amendment, therefore, we must be certain that none of the techniques so excluded threatens the areas of personal security and privacy that the Amendment is intended to protect.

United States v. Jacobsen, 466 U.S. 109, 136–37 (1984) (Brennan, J., dissenting). Is that view informative when applied to the question of when a seizure of digital data occurs?

---

28. Thomas K. Clancy, The Fourth Amendment: Its History and Interpretation § 3.4. (3d ed. 2017).

29. *E.g.*, Dolan v. City of Tigard, 512 U.S. 374, 384 (1994); Yee v. Escondido, 503 U.S. 519, 528 (1992); Loretto v. Teleprompter Manhattan CATV Corp., 458 U.S. 419, 435 (1982); Kaiser Aetna v. United States, 444 U.S. 164, 179–80 (1979).

30. *E.g.*, Alderman v. United States, 394 U.S. 165, 176–78 (1969).

31. United States v. Karo, 468 U.S. 705, 729 (1984) (Stevens, J., concurring in part and dissenting in part).

5. The court in *State v. Ressler*, 701 N.W.2d 915 (N.D. 2005), rejected the "meaningful interference" test in favor of a "dominion and control" analysis, believing that the latter provided "some mechanism to check what would otherwise be a nearly unrestrained power of government to temporarily confiscate any shipped package." Is that framework helpful to measure a person's interest in digital data? *Cf.* Paul Ohm, *The Olmsteadian Seizure Clause: The Fourth Amendment and the Seizure of Intangible Property*, 2008 STAN. TECH. L. REV. 2 ("While the meaningful interference conception of seizure focuses on the deprivation of the property owner, the dominion and control class focuses on the usurpation by the state of the property. With physical property, these competing emphases are two sides of the same coin: by exerting dominion and control, the police meaningfully interfere with the owner's possessory interests. This is not so with nonrivalrous property [such as digital data], over which the police can exert dominion and control with no interference to traditional possessory interests.").

6. When did the "seizure" of Ganias' personal data unrelated to the original investigation occur? At what point did it become unreasonable? Assuming that the government can seize on-site all data to search off-site, based on the panel decision in *Ganias*, what would you advise regarding what to do with data that is unresponsive to the initial off-site forensic examination?

§ 9.3 The Reasonableness of Warrantless Seizures of Digital Devices

Once it is established that a seizure has occurred, it must be justified as reasonable. Consistent with the treatment of seizures of persons, the Court has distinguished between temporary detentions, justified by articulable suspicion, and longer detentions, for which probable cause and a warrant may be needed.[32]

1. Warrantless Seizures

Commonwealth v. Charles Hinds, Jr.

768 N.E.2d 1067 (Mass. 2002)

SPINA, J.

[During a consensual search of a computer for electronic mail, Officer McLean found child pornography on the defendant's home computer. The court determined

---

32. *E.g.*, United States v. Place, 462 U.S. 696 (1983) (adopting two levels of justification for seizures of effects); United States v. Hoang, 486 F.3d 1156 (9th Cir. 2007) (collecting cases on justification for temporary detentions of mailed packages).

that the defendant voluntarily consented to the search and that the search performed was within the scope of the consent.]

McLean seized the defendant's computer and later obtained a search warrant. A subsequent search revealed thousands of images of child pornography stored on the defendant's computer. Having discovered illegal files on the defendant's computer, it was reasonable for McLean to seize the computer prior to obtaining a warrant because, by nature, computer data are not readily separable from the hard drive and McLean was faced with the prospect of their destruction. The alternative, posting an officer at the defendant's computer while a warrant was secured, would have been more intrusive to the defendant's and his family's privacy rights than simply to secure the defendant's hard drive and keyboard. The risk that computer data could be easily deleted and thus lost justified seizing the defendant's hard drive until such time as McLean could obtain a warrant.

Commonwealth v. Harold Kaupp

899 N.E.2d 809 (Mass. 2009)

Spina, J.

[School administrators at the Northeast Metropolitan Vocational High School in Wakefield became aware of several unauthorized computers connected to the high school's network. A network specialist investigated and accessed some open share files on the unauthorized computers. She found hacking tools, games, and pirated movies. The police joined in seeking to find the location of the computers. During the course of the investigation, several movies, including "Spiderman," were located.] Detective James concluded that the copy of "Spiderman" was unauthorized, as the movie had been released in theaters only recently. Detective James also found a motion picture file titled, "Beautiful Lolita Sandra Masturbates," showing what appeared to be a young girl masturbating.

[Eventually, a computer named "Sinister" was located] in the defendant's office, which was adjacent to the electronics shop.

[The] observation of the then recently released movie "Spiderman" on Sinister's open share furnished probable cause to believe that Sinister contained pirated movies, prompting Detective James to impound Sinister. Detective James refrained from searching Sinister's contents until the search warrant issued. The impoundment of an object pending the issuance of a search warrant violates the Fourth Amendment to the United States Constitution . . . only if it is unreasonable. Reasonableness necessarily turns on the facts of each case, requiring courts to "balanc[e] the need to search or seize against the invasion that the search or seizure entails." Given the ease with which computer files may be accessed and deleted, and the disruption that would have been created by posting an officer in the defendant's office and preventing students from entering pending the issuance of a search warrant, we conclude that the seizure was reasonable.[n.7][33]

2. Delays to Obtain a Warrant After a Warrantless Seizure

United States v. Peter J. Mitchell

565 F.3d 1347 (8th Cir. 2009)

PER CURIAM:

Sometime in 2005, Immigration and Customs Enforcement agents in New Jersey began an investigation of individuals engaged in distributing and receiving child pornography via the internet. In October 2005, an ICE agent located a commercial website whose banner page proclaimed "NOW YOU ARE [A] FEW MINUTES AWAY FROM THE BEST CHILDREN PORN SITE ON THE NET!" and which displayed more than a dozen images of minors engaged in sexual acts. After using his credit card on October 26, 2005 to purchase access to the website in an undercover capacity, the ICE agent's credit card statement displayed a $79.99 charge to "AdSoft," a bill payment service. Upon entry to the website, the ICE agent discovered it contained thousands of images of child pornography. Through the use of search warrants and wiretaps, agents were able to identify hundreds of individuals who had visited the website between October 2005 and February 2006.

The defendant, Peter Mitchell, was identified as a possible target of this investigation because information obtained from the issuer of his credit card reflected two charges of $79.99 to AdSoft on October 14, 2005 and June 14, 2006.

On February 22, 2007, ICE Special Agent Thomas West and FBI Special Agent Josh Hayes went to Mitchell's residence to conduct a "knock and talk." When Mitchell answered the front door, Agents West and Hayes asked if they could come inside and speak with him about an ongoing investigation, to which Mitchell gave his consent. Agents West and Hayes explained that they were conducting a child pornography investigation, and asked Mitchell whether he had purchased subscriptions to any pornography websites. Mitchell told them that he had purchased subscriptions to two pornography websites. After Mitchell told the agents that there were two personal computers in his residence—a laptop upstairs used primarily by his wife, and a desktop computer downstairs used primarily by Mitchell—the agents asked

---

33. [n.7] The potential destruction or loss of evidence on Sinister created an exigency justifying the warrantless *seizure* of Sinister. However, the Commonwealth maintains that the police did not need a warrant to *search* Sinister's contents because they seized Sinister pursuant to the exigent circumstances exception to the warrant requirement. We disagree. As we have noted, "an officer's authority to possess a package is distinct from his authority to examine its contents." The exigency necessitating Sinister's seizure dissipated once the computer had been secured, requiring the police to seek a search warrant to conduct a forensic analysis of Sinister's contents.

Mitchell whether either of the computers contained "illegal contraband." Mitchell responded "yes, probably." Agent West then asked Mitchell whether either of the computers contained any child pornography, to which Mitchell again responded "yes, probably."

Mitchell consented to a search of the upstairs laptop computer but refused to allow the agents to search the downstairs desktop computer. After Agent West performed a brief forensic examination of the laptop, he asked Mitchell if he could see the desktop computer. Mitchell assented, and brought the agents to the downstairs office where the computer was located. Upon viewing the desktop computer, Agent West asked Mitchell if that was the computer that contained the child pornography, and Mitchell stated that it was. Agent West then opened the computer's central processing unit, the casing which contains all the internal parts of the computer, and removed the computer's hard drive from the CPU. The agents departed from Mitchell's residence at approximately 12:00 p.m. with only the hard drive.

The following Sunday, February 25, 2007, West traveled to Virginia to attend a two-week ICE training course. On March 15, 2007, three days after his return to Savannah and twenty-one days after the initial seizure of Mitchell's hard drive, an application for a search warrant was presented to a United States magistrate judge, who issued it the same day. Acting pursuant to the warrant, Agent West accessed the materials stored on Mitchell's hard drive for the first time, and discovered electronic images of child pornography.

While the initial seizure of the hard drive was permissible, even "a seizure lawful at its inception can nevertheless violate the Fourth Amendment because its manner of execution unreasonably infringes possessory interests protected by the Fourth Amendment's prohibition on 'unreasonable searches.'" Thus, "even a seizure based on probable cause is unconstitutional if the police act with unreasonable delay in securing a warrant." The reasonableness of the delay is determined "in light of all the facts and circumstances," and "on a case-by-case basis." "[T]he reasonableness determination will reflect a 'careful balancing of governmental and private interests.'"

Computers are relied upon heavily for personal and business use. Individuals may store personal letters, e-mails, financial information, passwords, family photos, and countless other items of a personal nature in electronic form on their computer hard drives. Thus, the detention of the hard drive for over three weeks before a warrant was sought constitutes a significant interference with Mitchell's possessory interest. Nor was that interference eliminated by admissions Mitchell made that provided probable cause for the seizure. As the United States magistrate judge observed: "A defendant's possessory interest in his computer is diminished but not altogether eliminated by such an admission for two reasons: (1) a home computer's hard drive is likely to contain other, non-contraband information of exceptional value to its owner, and (2) until an agent examines the hard drive's contents, he cannot be certain that it actually contains child pornography, for a defendant who admits that his computer contains such images could be lying, factually mistaken, or wrong as a matter of law (by assuming that some image on the computer is unlawful when in fact it is not)."

While the possessory interest at stake here was substantial, there was no compelling justification for the delay. The hard drive was seized at noon on Thursday, February 25, 2007. Although Agent West testified that he was scheduled to depart for a two-week training program in West Virginia on February 28, 2007, this still left two and one-half days after seizing the hard drive before his scheduled departure. Indeed, the twenty-three-page supporting affidavit was largely composed of boiler plate language, and contained less than three double-spaced pages of original content. Moreover, although Agent West departed Savannah on February 28, 2007, the FBI agent who accompanied Agent West to Mitchell's residence could have secured a warrant during Agent West's absence.

The only reason Agent West gave for the twenty-one-day delay in applying for a search warrant was that he "didn't see any urgency of the fact that there needed to be a search warrant during the two weeks that [he] was gone," and that he "felt there was no need to get a search warrant for the content of the hard drive until [he] returned back from training." Subsequently, he explained that any sense of urgency was eliminated by Mitchell's admission that the hard drive contained child pornography.

The United States Attorney argues that Agent "West was the only agent in the Southern District of Georgia, and Savannah specifically, trained to conduct a forensic examination of the computer for child pornography." Because he was away until March 12, 2007, the search of the computer could not have been undertaken before then, even if a warrant had been obtained earlier. Thus, the argument continues, the delay "had no practical effect upon Mitchell's rights, for his possessory interest would not have been restored prior to" the issuance of the search warrant. Moreover, the United States magistrate judge suggested that "even if Agent West had secured a warrant on the day of the hard drive's seizure, his evaluation of that hard drive would not have been completed prior to his departure for the two-week training program, for given the thousands upon thousands of images and the numerous video files stored on Mitchell's hard drive, it took Agent West two weeks to complete his evaluation of only *some* of the images."

We find these arguments unpersuasive because they are predicated on the premise that Agent West's attendance at the training session would have provided an excuse for the delay in applying for the warrant and, if a warrant had been obtained, it would have justified a delay in commencing the search of the hard drive until three weeks after its seizure. We reject this premise.

"The purpose of securing a search warrant soon after a suspect is dispossessed of a closed container reasonably believed to contain contraband is to ensure its prompt return should the search reveal no such incriminating evidence, for in that event the government would be obligated to return the container (unless it had some other evidentiary value). In the ordinary case, the sooner the warrant issues, the sooner the property owner's possessory rights can be restored if the search reveals nothing incriminating." If anything, this consideration applies with even greater force to the hard drive of a computer, which "is the digital equivalent of its owner's home, capable of holding a universe of private information."

Under these circumstances, the excuse offered for the three-week delay in applying for a warrant is insufficient. If Agent West's attendance at the training seminar could not have been postponed to a later date, an issue as to which no evidence was offered, there is no reason why another agent involved in this nationwide investigation, who possessed qualifications similar to that of Agent West, could not have been assigned the task of conducting the forensic search of the hard drive. The fact that Agent West did all of the forensic examinations in Savannah does not provide a basis for undermining the significant Fourth Amendment interests at stake here.

While we conclude that the delay in obtaining a warrant here was not justified, we emphasize again that we are applying a rule of reasonableness that is dependent on all of the circumstances. So for example, if the assistance of another law enforcement officer had been sought, we would have been sympathetic to an argument that some delay in obtaining that assistance was reasonable. The same would be true if some overriding circumstances arose, necessitating the diversion of law enforcement personnel to another case. We also recognize that there may be occasions where the resources of law enforcement are simply overwhelmed by the nature of a particular investigation, so that a delay that might otherwise be unduly long would be regarded as reasonable. The circumstances in *United States v. Dass*, 849 F.2d 414 (9th Cir. 1988), are illustrative. There the government seized over 1000 packages from ten selected post offices in Hawaii as part of a joint state/federal task force assembled to slow the flow of drugs mailed from Hawaii. Within two days of their seizure, the packages were transported to a police station and exposed to drug-sniffing dogs. Officials proceeded to seek search warrants for "441 packages—an unanticipated flood of packages which were alerted by the dog." After mobilizing available resources, they began preparing warrant applications at the rate of seventy-five per week, a rate of one warrant every seventy-five minutes. Nevertheless, despite this effort, there were delays of between seven and twenty-three days between the seizures and issuance of warrants. While a split panel of the Ninth Circuit concluded that the delays were unreasonable, we agree with the dissenting judge that the evidence in the case demonstrated "legitimate and practical reasons for the delay in processing the flood of warrants to search the suspicious packages seized."

By contrast, the present case involved the seizure of a single hard drive. No effort was made to obtain a warrant within a reasonable time because law enforcement officers simply believed that there was no rush. Under these circumstances, the twenty-one-day delay was unreasonable. Because we conclude that the motion to suppress should have been granted, we reverse the judgment of conviction and remand the case to the district court for further proceedings consistent with this opinion.

———————

People v. Yoshiaki Shinohara

872 N.E.2d 498 (Ill. App. Ct. 2007)

JUSTICE FROSSARD delivered the opinion of the court:

Although defendant's computer was seized and inventoried on August 24, 2001, Detective Ciccola did not notify the Illinois State Police forensic crime unit of the facts of the investigation until October 29, 2001. On that date, Detective Ciccola contacted State Police Sergeant James Murray, head of the cyber crime unit. On November 7, 2001, the police obtained a search warrant for the computer, and on that same day Detective Ciccola delivered the computer to State Police Trooper Kaiton Bullock at the State Police crime lab. The search warrant had a return date of November 9, 2001, and specifically authorized the police to search defendant's "homemade mini tower computer" and seize "pictures of child pornography whether they are photographs and/or computer-generated images stored in the computer hard drive."

Trooper Bullock completed his forensic examination of the images recovered from defendant's computer on January 10, 2002. Detective Ciccola viewed the subject images on January 24, 2002, and the assistant State's Attorney concluded on January 29, 2002, that some of the images depicted child pornography.

[The court concluded that the defendant voluntarily consented to have the police look at the images on his computer and that, after viewing the images, the police had probable cause to seize defendant's computer.] Defendant contends that even if there had been probable cause to seize his computer, "[his] right to be free from unreasonable searches and seizures was still violated because the police did not obtain a search warrant in a reasonably diligent manner." Defendant notes that "Ciccola first seized [his] computer on August 24, 2001, but he did not obtain a search warrant until November 7, 2001 (75 days later)."

Defendant does not cite any legal authority which provides that delay in obtaining a warrant, in and of itself, transforms an initially lawful seizure supported by probable cause into an unlawful seizure requiring suppression of the item seized.

The detectives did have probable cause to seize defendant's computer at the time they took possession of it and inventoried it on August 24, 2001, because they had personally viewed images on it which reasonably justified their belief that defendant committed the crime of child pornography. We recognize that the police did not obtain a warrant to search the computer until November 7, 2001; however, this delay did not operate to transform the initially reasonable seizure of defendant's computer into an unreasonable seizure under the fourth amendment.

We recognize that delay in obtaining a search warrant could render a search unreasonable when the facts supporting the underlying probable cause may have grown stale or the item or place to be searched is subject to change. In the instant case, however, defendant has not argued that the condition or contents of his computer changed between the time the computer was seized and the search warrant was obtained. Moreover, the record reflects no such change. Accordingly, we conclude that the passage of approximately 75 days between the seizure by the police of defendant's computer and the issuance of a warrant authorizing the police to search that computer did not violate defendant's right under the fourth amendment to be free from unreasonable search and seizure and thus did not require suppression of the images recovered from that computer.

———————

Notes

1. Is *Shinohara* consistent with *Mitchell* and with *United States v. Place*, 462 U.S. 696, 705–07 (1983)? In *Place*, the Court found unreasonable a ninety minute detention of the suspect's luggage so a drug dog could be brought to the scene and sniff it for the presence of narcotics because the police had failed to "diligently pursue their investigation." The detention occurred after Place arrived at La Guardia Airport in New York on a flight from Miami. Prior to boarding that flight, Place had been stopped in the Miami airport by Drug Enforcement Administration authorities, who developed suspicion that he was a drug courier. They permitted him to board the plane and then called authorities in New York, who accosted Place and detained his luggage after his arrival. The agents then took the bags to Kennedy Airport to obtain a "sniff test" by a trained narcotics dog, which alerted to the presence of drugs. The Court stated that the "New York agents knew the time of Place's scheduled arrival at La Guardia, had ample time to arrange their additional investigation at that location, and thereby could have minimized the intrusion." Because they did not, the extended detention of the luggage violated the Fourth Amendment and the evidence later found inside the luggage was suppressed.

2. Why should suppression be the remedy if the only violation of the Fourth Amendment is that the police waited too long to get a warrant after legally seizing a digital device?

Chapter 10

Searches at the International Border

§ 10.1 Overview of the International Border Doctrine[1]

Every day more than a million people cross American borders, from the physical borders with Mexico and Canada to functional borders at airports such as Los Angeles (LAX), Honolulu (HNL), New York (JFK, LGA), and Chicago (ORD, MDW). As denizens of a digital world, they carry with them laptop computers, iPhones, iPads, iPods, Kindles, Nooks, Surfaces, tablets, Blackberries, cell phones, digital cameras, and more. These devices often contain private and sensitive information ranging from personal, financial, and medical data to corporate trade secrets.[2]

Travelers, their baggage, goods, and other items crossing the international border of the United States are subject to search. This *sui generis* power is grounded on national sovereignty, that is, the federal government has both the right and obligation to protect the nation's borders from legally excludable persons and things.[3] There is language in the cases speaking of that power in absolutist terms:

> Border searches ... from before the adoption of the Fourth Amendment, have been considered to be "reasonable" by the single fact that the person or item in question had entered into our country from outside. There has never been any additional requirement that the reasonableness of a border search depended on the existence of probable cause. This longstanding recognition that searches at our borders without probable cause and without a warrant are nonetheless "reasonable" has a history as old as the Fourth Amendment itself.[4]

---

1. *See* Thomas K. Clancy, THE FOURTH AMENDMENT: ITS HISTORY AND INTERPRETATION § 10.2. (3d ed. 2017).

2. United States v. Cotterman, 709 F.3d 952 (9th Cir. 2013) (en banc).

3. *E.g.*, United States v. Montoya de Hernandez, 473 U.S. 531, 538–39 (1985) (emphasizing sovereignty interests at the border); Almeida-Sanchez v. United States, 413 U.S. 266, 291 (1973) (White, J., dissenting) ("Jurisdiction over its own territory ... is an incident of every independent nation."); Carroll v. United States, 267 U.S. 132, 154 (1925) (speaking of the power of "national self protection"). "At the border, customs officials have more than merely an investigative law enforcement role. They are also charged, along with immigration officials, with protecting this Nation from entrants who may bring anything harmful into this country, whether that be communicable diseases, narcotics, or explosives." *Montoya de Hernandez*, 473 U.S. at 544.

4. United States v. Ramsey, 431 U.S. 606, 619 (1977).

Most recently, the Court has stated:

> Time and again, we have stated that "searches made at the border, pursuant to the long-standing right of the sovereign to protect itself by stopping and examining persons and property crossing into this country, are reasonable simply by virtue of the fact that they occur at the border."[5]

The Supreme Court has never invalidated a search or seizure at the border. Obscuring the clarity of that fact and the underlying border doctrine principles are two aspects of the Court's cases. First, as balancing became prevalent in the latter part of the twentieth century, that test began to insinuate itself into the Court's opinions, even as the Court has noted that "the Fourth Amendment's balance of reasonableness is qualitatively different at the international border."[6] Second, some of the Court's opinions have stated that, for intrusions beyond the scope of "routine" customs searches and inspections, the individual liberty interest protected by the Fourth Amendment is not outweighed by mere assertions of sovereignty and, in the balance of interests, individualized suspicion of illegal activity becomes necessary.[7] Hence, in *United States v. Montoya de Hernandez*, 473 U.S. 531 (1985), the Court upheld the sixteen hour detention of a person reasonably suspected to be a "balloon swallower," which is a method of smuggling narcotics into the country by hiding them in the person's alimentary canal. In contrast to "[r]outine searches of persons and effects of entrants," which are not "subject to any requirement of reasonable suspicion, probable cause or warrant," the detention in *Montoya de Hernandez* was viewed as nonroutine, but was nevertheless upheld, with the Court applying the balancing test:

> We hold that the detention of a traveler at the border, beyond the scope of a routine customs search and inspection, is justified at its inception if customs agents, considering all the facts surrounding the traveler and her trip, reasonably suspect that the traveler is smuggling contraband in her alimentary canal.

In *Montoya de Hernandez*, the Court noted that it was expressing no view "on what level of suspicion, if any, is required for nonroutine border searches such as strip, body cavity, or involuntary x-ray searches." In contrast, Justice Stevens, in his concurring opinion, believed that customs agents could "require that a nonpregnant person reasonably suspected of this kind of smuggling submit to an x-ray examination as an incident to a border search." Justice Brennan, dissenting, believed that travelers at the border could be routinely "subjected to questioning, patdowns, and thorough searches of their belongings." He believed that "body-cavity searches, x-ray searches, and stomach pumping" were "highly intrusive investigative techniques" that must be authorized by a judicial officer.

---

5. United States v. Flores-Montano, 541 U.S. 149, 152–53 (2004).

6. United States v. Montoya de Hernandez, 473 U.S. 531, 538 (1985).

7. *See, e.g., id.* at 541.

Lower courts and commentators have used variations of the balancing test and the distinction between routine and nonroutine intrusions to evaluate border searches and seizures. There are two issues here: the distinction between routine and nonroutine intrusions; and the needed level of suspicion to justify those intrusions. As to the first, a vague and somewhat complex jurisprudence[8] attempting to distinguish between the two types of intrusions had developed prior to *United States v. Flores-Montano*, 541 U.S. 149 (2004), with the courts creating lists of routine and nonroutine searches.[9] For example, patdowns[10] and shoe checks[11] were generally considered routine but body cavity[12] or strip searches[13] were not.

As to the level of suspicion needed, several decades of development created some unusual standards of reasonableness. For example, a "real suspicion" was said to justify a strip search,[14] a "clear indication" that a suspect was carrying contraband in a body cavity justified that examination,[15] but only a "minimal showing of suspicion" was needed for a patdown.[16] However, in the context of a border seizure, the Court explicitly stated in *United States v. Montoya de Hernandez* that it was rejecting reasonableness standards of individualized suspicion beyond reasonable suspicion and probable cause. Nonetheless, lower courts continue to use language suggesting different measures of reasonableness, albeit some have attempted to retrofit their jurisprudence to be consistent with Supreme Court case law.[17] Currently, the prevailing view appears to be that, for intrusive searches and seizures at the border, reasonable suspicion is needed.[18]

So how viable is the distinction between routine and nonroutine intrusions? In *United States v. Flores-Montano*,[19] the Court addressed the question whether customs officers at the international border must have reasonable suspicion to remove, disassemble, and search a vehicle's fuel tank for contraband. The district court had granted suppression on the basis of Ninth Circuit precedent requiring reasonable suspicion for "nonroutine" border searches and the appellate court had summarily affirmed.

---

8. *See, e.g.*, United States v. Molina-Tarazon, 279 F.3d 709, 713 (9th Cir. 2002) (border "searches of handbags, luggage, shoes, pockets and the passenger compartments of cars are clearly routine" and may be conducted without reasonable suspicion and the distinction between "'routine' and 'nonroutine' turns on the level of intrusiveness of the search").

9. *E.g.*, Tabbaa v. Chertoff, 509 F.3d 89, 98 (2d Cir. 2007).

10. *E.g.*, Kaniff v. United States, 351 F.3d 780, 784–88 (7th Cir. 2003) (collecting cases).

11. *E.g.*, United States v. Ramos-Saenz, 36 F.3d 59, 61 (9th Cir. 1994).

12. *E.g.*, United States v. Des Jardins, 747 F.2d 499, 505 (9th Cir. 1984).

13. *E.g.*, United States v. Irving, 452 F.3d 110, 123 (2d Cir. 2006).

14. United States v. Guadalupe-Garza, 421 F.2d 876, 879 (9th Cir. 1970).

15. United States v. Des Jardins, 747 F.2d 499, 505 (9th Cir. 1984).

16. United States v. Vance, 62 F.3d 1152, 1156 (9th Cir. 1995).

17. *E.g.*, United States v. Oyekan, 786 F.2d 832, 837 (8th Cir. 1986) (equating "real suspicion" with articulable suspicion, which justifies a strip search).

18. *E.g.*, United States v. Irving, 452 F.3d 110, 123 (2d Cir. 2006); Kaniff v. United States, 351 F.3d 780, 784–88 (7th Cir. 2003).

19. 541 U.S. 149 (2004).

Flores-Montano arrived at a border crossing in a station wagon and, although the facts suggested that there was reasonable suspicion of criminal activity, the federal government declined to argue the point because it wanted to test the Ninth Circuit precedent. A customs inspector, after brief questioning and tapping of the gas tank of the vehicle, referred Flores-Montano to a secondary station. After more tapping, a mechanic was called, who arrived 20 to 30 minutes later. The car was raised on a lift, the gas tank removed and disassembled, and marijuana recovered from inside of it. That process took about 15 to 25 minutes.

The Supreme Court unanimously found that the search was reasonable, with the Court maintaining that customs authorities have plenary authority to conduct such a search. The Court grounded its view on the belief that border searches are intrinsic to sovereignty, that there was significant historical support for such searches, that Congress had consistently authorized border intrusions, and that the government had a "paramount interest in protecting the border." Addressing the viability of the distinction between "routine" and "nonroutine border searches," the Court asserted:

> [T]he reasons that might support a requirement of some level of suspicion in the case of highly intrusive searches of the person—dignity and privacy interests of the person being searched—simply do not carry over to vehicles. Complex balancing tests to determine what is a "routine" search of a vehicle, as opposed to a more "intrusive" search of a person, have no place in border searches of vehicles.

Keeping open the possibility that some intrusions may be unreasonable, *Flores-Montano* specifically referenced drilling into vehicles and expressed no view on "'whether, and under what circumstances, a border search might be deemed unreasonable because of the particularly offensive manner it is carried out.'" The Court did not, however, repeat the routine-nonroutine distinction of previous cases.

In light of *Flores-Montano*, lower court opinions set aside the routine-nonroutine distinction, as applied to searches of objects, and instead focused on the manner in which the search was conducted.[20] Hence, in *United States v. Hernandez*, 424 F.3d 1056 (9th Cir. 2005), the Ninth Circuit observed that the "routine/non-routine analytical framework has been denounced by the Supreme Court insofar as searches of property are concerned." The *Hernandez* court applied *Flores-Montano* to the situation in which customs officials removed a door panel on a vehicle:

> [T]he initial search—which involved removal of the interior door panels in "an easy way, [so] that if we [don't] find anything [we] can put it back together without damage. Very gently"—caused no significant damage to, or destruction of, the vehicle. Nor did it undermine the safety of the vehicle, or present any potentially harmful effects to the health of the motorist. . . .

---

20. *See* United States v. Romm, 455 F.3d 990, 997 n.11 (9th Cir. 2006) (interpreting *Flores-Montano* to suggest "that the search of a traveler's property at the border will always be routine").

[T]he damage involved through the removal of the door panel in this case was minimal. In short, the gentle removal of the door panel was not "so destructive as to require a different result." . . . Neither can it be said that the search was conducted in a particularly offensive manner. . . . Therefore, reasonable suspicion was not required prior to conducting the search.

§ 10.2 Letters as Targets

In *United States v. Ramsey*, 431 U.S. 606 (1977), the Court was confronted with a situation in which a customs official, based on reasonable suspicion, opened letters mailed from Bangkok, Thailand, to addresses in Washington, D.C. Congress and applicable postal regulations had authorized the opening of an envelope if there was "reasonable cause to suspect" that there was merchandise imported contrary to the law. The Court upheld the inspection, which uncovered heroin in each of the envelopes. Addressing the "fear that '[i]f the Government is allowed to exercise the power it claims, the door will be open to the wholesale, secret examination of all incoming international letter mail,'" the Court concluded that that concern was not present in the case before it:

> Here envelopes are opened at the border only when the customs officers have reason to believe they contain other than correspondence, while the reading of any correspondence inside the envelopes is forbidden. Any "chill" that might exist under these circumstances may fairly be considered not only "minimal," but also wholly subjective.

Although reasonable suspicion was present, and the Court found the search justified on that ground, much of the opinion takes a much broader view of governmental authority at the border. The Court rejected the view that letter envelopes should be treated differently than other packages or wrappers:

> It is clear that there is nothing in the rationale behind the border-search exception which suggests that the mode of entry will be critical. It was conceded at oral argument that customs officials could search, without probable cause and without a warrant, envelopes carried by an entering traveler, whether in his luggage or on his person. Surely no different constitutional standard should apply simply because the envelopes were mailed not carried. The critical fact is that the envelopes cross the border and enter this country, not that they are brought in by one mode of transportation rather than another. It is their entry into this country from without it that makes a resulting search "reasonable."

The *Ramsey* Court continued:

> Almost a century ago this Court rejected such a distinction in construing a protocol to the Treaty of Berne, 19 Stat. 604, which prohibited the importation of letters which might contain dutiable items. Condemning the

unsoundness of any distinction between entry by mail and entry by other means, Mr. Justice Miller, on behalf of a unanimous Court, wrote:

> "Of what avail would it be that every passenger, citizen and foreigner, without distinction of country or sex, is compelled to sign a declaration before landing, either that his trunks and satchels in hand contain nothing liable to duty, or if they do, to state what it is, and even the person may be subjected to a rigid examination, if the mail is to be left unwatched, and all its sealed contents, even after delivery to the person to whom addressed, are to be exempt from seizure, though laces, jewels, and other dutiable matter of great value may thus be introduced from foreign countries."

The historically recognized scope of the border-search doctrine, suggests no distinction in constitutional doctrine stemming from the mode of transportation across our borders.

Accordingly, *Ramsey* rejected the dissent's view that Congress had shown heightened respect for "the individual's interest in private communication," finding that "no such support may be garnered from the history of the Fourth Amendment insofar as border searches are concerned." The majority also rejected any distinction "between letters mailed into the country and letters carried on the traveler's person."

§ 10.3 Data as Targets

There are several significant intimations in *Ramsey*, given the migration of so much information to digital form and the ability to send it anywhere in the world where there is an Internet connection. First, what about searches that examine digital data on computers and other storage devices at the border? Given that computers and other electronic devices can hold legally excludable information, do federal agents have the right to examine devices that could store such information? *Ramsey* clearly permits reasonable suspicion-based searches if it is accepted that data on a computer are the functional equivalent of a writing and that a computer file is the electronic equivalent of an envelope. But are suspicionless searches permitted? Here, one may seek to distinguish between mail, which is regulated by statutory and postal regulations, and digital data, which is not. *Ramsey*, however, rejected such a distinction.[21] Nonetheless, First Amendment and privacy concerns seem to lurk.

In *United States v. Arnold*,[22] the district court asserted that reasonable suspicion was required to conduct searches of laptop computers at the border. The court concluded:

---

21. *Cf.* California Bankers Ass'n v. Shultz, 416 U.S. 21, 62–63 (1974) (upholding regulations requiring banks to report commercial transactions that "take place across national boundaries" against a Fourth Amendment challenge based in part on the border doctrine).

22. 454 F. Supp. 2d 999 (C.D. Cal. 2006), *rev'd*, 523 F.3d 941 (9th Cir. 2008).

Fourth Amendment protection extends to the search of this type of personal and private information at the border. While not physically intrusive as in the case of a strip or body cavity search, the search of one's private and valuable personal information stored on a hard drive or other electronic storage device can be just as much, if not more, of an intrusion into the dignity and privacy interests of a person. This is because electronic storage devices function as an extension of our own memory. They are capable of storing our thoughts, ranging from the most whimsical to the most profound. Therefore, government intrusions into the mind — specifically those that would cause fear or apprehension in a reasonable person — are no less deserving of Fourth Amendment scrutiny than intrusions that are physical in nature.

Arnold is difficult to reconcile with the broad searches approved of at the border by Supreme Court cases, which make no distinction based on the objects sought (so long as it is not a search of a person) and the methods employed (so long as they are not particularly destructive). The Ninth Circuit reversed the lower court's decision in *Arnold*:

United States v. Michael Timothy Arnold

523 F.3d 941 (9th Cir. 2008)

O'Scannlain, Circuit Judge:

On July 17, 2005, forty-three-year-old Michael Arnold arrived at Los Angeles International Airport after a nearly twenty-hour flight from the Philippines. U.S. Customs and Border Patrol Officer Laura Peng first saw Arnold while he was in line waiting to go through the checkpoint and selected him for secondary questioning. She asked Arnold where he had traveled, the purpose of his travel, and the length of his trip. Arnold stated that he had been on vacation for three weeks visiting friends in the Philippines.

Peng then inspected Arnold's luggage, which contained his laptop computer, a separate hard drive, a computer memory stick (also called a flash drive or USB drive), and six compact discs. Peng instructed Arnold to turn on the computer so she could see if it was functioning. While the computer was booting up, Peng turned it over to her colleague, CBP Officer John Roberts, and continued to inspect Arnold's luggage.

When the computer had booted up, its desktop displayed numerous icons and folders. Two folders were entitled "Kodak Pictures" and one was entitled "Kodak Memories." Peng and Roberts clicked on the Kodak folders, opened the files, and viewed the photos on Arnold's computer including one that depicted two nude women. Roberts called in supervisors, who in turn called in special agents with the United States Department of Homeland Security, Immigration and Customs Enforcement. The ICE agents questioned Arnold about the contents of his computer and detained him for several hours. They examined the computer equipment and found numerous images depicting what they believed to be child pornography. The officers seized the computer and storage devices but released Arnold. Two weeks later, federal agents obtained a warrant.

Courts have long held that searches of closed containers and their contents can be conducted at the border without particularized suspicion under the Fourth Amendment. Searches of the following specific items have been upheld without particularized suspicion: (1) the contents of a traveler's briefcase and luggage; (2) a traveler's "purse, wallet, or pockets"; (3) papers found in containers such as pockets; and (4) pictures, films and other graphic materials.

Nevertheless, the Supreme Court has drawn some limits on the border search power. Specifically, the Supreme Court has held that reasonable suspicion is required to search a traveler's "alimentary canal," *United States v. Montoya de Hernandez*, 473 U.S. 531, 541 (1985), because "'[t]he interests in human dignity and privacy which the Fourth Amendment protects forbid any such intrusion [beyond the body's surface] on the mere chance that desired evidence might be obtained.'" However, it has expressly declined to decide "what level of suspicion, *if any*, is required for non-routine border searches such as strip, body cavity, or involuntary x-ray searches." Furthermore, the Supreme Court has rejected creating a balancing test based on a "routine" and "non-routine" search framework, and has treated the terms as purely descriptive.

Other than when "intrusive searches of *the person*" are at issue, the Supreme Court has held open the possibility "that some searches of *property* are so destructive as to require" particularized suspicion. Indeed, the Supreme Court has left open the question of "'whether, and under what circumstances, a border search might be deemed 'unreasonable' because of the particularly offensive manner in which it is carried out.'"

In any event, the district court's holding that particularized suspicion is required to search a laptop, based on cases involving the search of the person, was erroneous. The Supreme Court has stated that "[c]omplex balancing tests to determine what is a 'routine' search of a vehicle, as opposed to a more 'intrusive' search of a person, have no place in border searches of vehicles." Arnold argues that the district court was correct to apply an intrusiveness analysis to a laptop search despite the Supreme Court's holding in *Flores-Montano*, by distinguishing between one's privacy interest in a vehicle compared to a laptop. However, this attempt to distinguish *Flores-Montano* is off the mark. The Supreme Court's analysis determining what protection to give a vehicle was not based on the unique characteristics of vehicles with respect to other property, but was based on the fact that a vehicle, as a piece of property, simply does not implicate the same "dignity and privacy" concerns as "highly intrusive searches of the person."

We are satisfied that reasonable suspicion is not needed for customs officials to search a laptop or other personal electronic storage devices at the border.

Arnold has never claimed that the government's search of his laptop damaged it in any way; therefore, we need not consider whether "exceptional damage to property" applies. Arnold does raise the "particularly offensive manner" exception to the government's broad border search powers. But, there is nothing in the record to indicate that the manner in which the CBP officers conducted the search was "particularly offensive" in comparison with other lawful border searches. According to Arnold, the CBP officers simply "had me boot [the laptop] up, and looked at what I had inside. . . ."

Whatever "particularly offensive manner" might mean, this search certainly does not meet that test. Arnold has failed to distinguish how the search of his laptop and its electronic contents is logically any different from the suspicionless border searches of travelers' luggage that the Supreme Court and we have allowed.

With respect to these searches, the Supreme Court has refused to draw distinctions between containers of information and contraband with respect to their quality or nature for purposes of determining the appropriate level of Fourth Amendment protection. Arnold's analogy to a search of a home based on a laptop's storage capacity is without merit. The Supreme Court has expressly rejected applying the Fourth Amendment protections afforded to homes to property which is "*capable of functioning as a home*" simply due to its size, or, distinguishing between "worthy and 'unworthy' containers." *California v. Carney*, 471 U.S. 386, 393–94 (1985).

In *Carney*, the Supreme Court rejected the argument that evidence obtained from a warrantless search of a mobile home should be suppressed because it was "*capable of functioning as a home.*" The Supreme Court refused to treat a mobile home differently from other vehicles just because it could be used as a home. The two main reasons that the Court gave in support of its holding, were: (1) that a mobile home is "readily movable," and (2) that "the expectation [of privacy] with respect to one's automobile is significantly less than that relating to one's home or office."

Here, beyond the simple fact that one cannot live in a laptop, *Carney* militates against the proposition that a laptop is a home. First, a laptop goes with the person, and, therefore is "readily mobile." Second, one's "expectation of privacy [at the border] . . . is significantly less than that relating to one's home or office." Moreover, case law does not support a finding that a search which occurs in an otherwise ordinary manner, is "particularly offensive" simply due to the storage capacity of the object being searched. Because there is no basis in the record to support the contention that the manner in which the search occurred was "particularly offensive" in light of other searches allowed by the Supreme Court and our precedents, the district court's judgment cannot be sustained.

———————

The Ninth Circuit subsequently modified its view in the following case. The court adhered to *Arnold*'s view that an initial examination of a computer at the border required no suspicion but concluded that a forensic examination of a computer requires reasonable suspicion. That circuit has been a leader in exposing the "special approach" to computer searches and seizures. *Cotterman* reflects the same premises that courts use to create other, special procedures to search digital devices.

United States v. Howard Wesley Cotterman

709 F.3d 952 (9th Cir. 2013) (en banc)

The reasonableness of a search or seizure depends on the totality of the circumstances, including the scope and duration of the deprivation.

The legitimacy of the initial search of Cotterman's electronic devices at the border is not in doubt. Officer Alvarado turned on the devices and opened and viewed image files while the Cottermans waited to enter the country. It was, in principle, akin to the search in *United States v. Seljan*, 547 F.3d 993 (9th Cir. 2008) (en banc), where we concluded that a suspicionless cursory scan of a package in international transit was not unreasonable. Similarly, we have approved a quick look and unintrusive search of laptops. *United States v. Arnold*, 533 F.3d 1003, 1009 (9th Cir. 2008).[n.6][23] Had the search of Cotterman's laptop ended with Officer Alvarado, we would be inclined to conclude it was reasonable even without particularized suspicion. But the search here transformed into something far different. The difficult question we confront is the reasonableness, without a warrant, of the forensic examination that comprehensively analyzed the hard drive of the computer.

It is the comprehensive and intrusive nature of a forensic examination—not the location of the examination—that is the key factor triggering the requirement of reasonable suspicion here. To carry out the examination of Cotterman's laptop, Agent Owen used computer forensic software to copy the hard drive and then analyze it in its entirety, including data that ostensibly had been deleted. This painstaking analysis is akin to reading a diary line by line looking for mention of criminal activity—plus looking at everything the writer may have erased.[n.9][24]

Notwithstanding a traveler's diminished expectation of privacy at the border, the search is still measured against the Fourth Amendment's reasonableness requirement, which considers the nature and scope of the search. Significantly, the Supreme Court has recognized that the "dignity and privacy interests of the person being searched" at the border will on occasion demand "some level of suspicion in the case of highly intrusive searches of the person." [*United States v.*] *Flores-Montano*, 541 U.S. [149,] 152 [(2004)]. Likewise, the Court has explained that "some searches of property are so destructive," "particularly offensive," or overly intrusive in the manner in which they are carried out as to require particularized suspicion.

---

23. [n.6] Although the *Arnold* decision expressed its conclusion in broad terms, stating that, "reasonable suspicion is not needed for customs officials to search a laptop or other personal electronic storage devices at the border," the facts do not support such an unbounded holding. As an en banc court, we narrow *Arnold* to approve only the relatively simple search at issue in that case, not to countenance suspicionless forensic examinations.

24. [n.9] Agent Owen used a software program called EnCase that exhibited the distinctive features of computer forensic examination. The program copied, analyzed, and preserved the data stored on the hard drive and gave the examiner access to far more data, including password-protected, hidden or encrypted, and deleted files, than a manual user could access.

We are now presented with a case directly implicating substantial personal privacy interests. The private information individuals store on digital devices—their personal "papers" in the words of the Constitution—stands in stark contrast to the generic and impersonal contents of a gas tank.

The amount of private information carried by international travelers was traditionally circumscribed by the size of the traveler's luggage or automobile. That is no longer the case. Electronic devices are capable of storing warehouses full of information.

The nature of the contents of electronic devices differs from that of luggage as well. Laptop computers, iPads and the like are simultaneously offices and personal diaries. They contain the most intimate details of our lives: financial records, confidential business documents, medical records and private emails. This type of material implicates the Fourth Amendment's specific guarantee of the people's right to be secure in their "papers." The express listing of papers "reflects the Founders' deep concern with safeguarding the privacy of thoughts and ideas—what we might call freedom of conscience—from invasion by the government." These records are expected to be kept private and this expectation is "one that society is prepared to recognize as 'reasonable.'"

Electronic devices often retain sensitive and confidential information far beyond the perceived point of erasure, notably in the form of browsing histories and records of deleted files. This quality makes it impractical, if not impossible, for individuals to make meaningful decisions regarding what digital content to expose to the scrutiny that accompanies international travel. A person's digital life ought not be hijacked simply by crossing a border. When packing traditional luggage, one is accustomed to deciding what papers to take and what to leave behind. When carrying a laptop, tablet or other device, however, removing files unnecessary to an impending trip is an impractical solution given the volume and often intermingled nature of the files. It is also a time-consuming task that may not even effectively erase the files.

The present case illustrates this unique aspect of electronic data. Agents found incriminating files in the unallocated space of Cotterman's laptop, the space where the computer stores files that the user ostensibly deleted and maintains other "deleted" files retrieved from web sites the user has visited. Notwithstanding the attempted erasure of material or the transient nature of a visit to a web site, computer forensic examination was able to restore the files. It is as if a search of a person's suitcase could reveal not only what the bag contained on the current trip, but everything it had ever carried.

With the ubiquity of cloud computing, the government's reach into private data becomes even more problematic. In the "cloud," a user's data, including the same kind of highly sensitive data one would have in "papers" at home, is held on remote servers rather than on the device itself. The digital device is a conduit to retrieving information from the cloud, akin to the key to a safe deposit box. Notably, although the virtual "safe deposit box" does not itself cross the border, it may appear as a seamless part of the digital device when presented at the border. With access to the cloud through forensic examination, a traveler's cache is just a click away from the government.

This is not to say that simply because electronic devices house sensitive, private information they are off limits at the border. The relevant inquiry, as always, is one of reasonableness. But that reasonableness determination must account for differences in property. Unlike searches involving a reassembled gas tank or small hole in the bed of a pickup truck, which have minimal or no impact beyond the search itself—and little implication for an individual's dignity and privacy interests—the exposure of confidential and personal information has permanence. It cannot be undone. Accordingly, the uniquely sensitive nature of data on electronic devices carries with it a significant expectation of privacy and thus renders an exhaustive exploratory search more intrusive than with other forms of property.

After their initial search at the border, customs agents made copies of the hard drives and performed forensic evaluations of the computers that took days to turn up contraband. It was essentially a computer strip search. An exhaustive forensic search of a copied laptop hard drive intrudes upon privacy and dignity interests to a far greater degree than a cursory search at the border. It is little comfort to assume that the government—for now—does not have the time or resources to seize and search the millions of devices that accompany the millions of travelers who cross our borders. It is the potential unfettered dragnet effect that is troublesome.

We recognize the important security concerns that prevail at the border. The government's authority to protect the nation from contraband is well established and may be "heightened" by "national cris[e]s," such as the smuggling of illicit narcotics, the current threat of international terrorism and future threats yet to take shape. But even in the face of heightened concerns, we must account for the Fourth Amendments rights of travelers.

The effort to interdict child pornography is also a legitimate one. But legitimate concerns about child pornography do not justify unfettered crime-fighting searches or an unregulated assault on citizens' private information. Reasonable suspicion is a modest, workable standard that is already applied in the extended border search, *Terry* stop, and other contexts. Its application to the forensic examination here will not impede law enforcement's ability to monitor and secure our borders or to conduct appropriate searches of electronic devices.

Nor does applying this standard impede the deterrent effect of suspicionless searches, which the dissent contends is critical to thwarting savvy terrorists and other criminals. The Supreme Court has never endorsed the proposition that the goal of deterring illegal contraband at the border suffices to justify any manner of intrusive search. Rather, reasonableness remains the touchstone and the Court has expressed support for the deterrence value of suspicionless searches of a routine nature, such as vehicle checkpoints near the border. In practical terms, suspicionless searches of the type approved in *Arnold* will continue; border officials will conduct further, forensic examinations where their suspicions are aroused by what they find or by other factors. Reasonable suspicion leaves ample room for agents to draw on their expertise and experience to pick up on subtle cues that criminal activity may be afoot.

We have confidence in the ability of law enforcement to distinguish a review of computer files from a forensic examination. Determining whether reasonable suspicion is required does not necessitate a "complex legal determination[]" to be made on a "moment-by-moment basis." Rather, it requires that officers make a common-sense differentiation between a manual review of files on an electronic device and application of computer software to analyze a hard drive, and utilize the latter only when they possess a "particularized and objective basis for suspecting the person stopped of criminal activity."

International travelers certainly expect that their property will be searched at the border. What they do not expect is that, absent some particularized suspicion, agents will mine every last piece of data on their devices or deprive them of their most personal property for days (or perhaps weeks or even months, depending on how long the search takes). Such a thorough and detailed search of the most intimate details of one's life is a substantial intrusion upon personal privacy and dignity. We therefore hold that the forensic examination of Cotterman's computer required a showing of reasonable suspicion, a modest requirement in light of the Fourth Amendment.

———————

Notes and Questions

1. Judge Callahan's concurring and dissenting opinion in *Cotterman* reflected the other side of the digital search and seizure debate. He observed: "The majority's opinion turns primarily on the notion that electronic devices deserve special consideration because they are ubiquitous and can store vast quantities of personal information. That idea is fallacious and has no place in the border search context."

2. In 2018, the Department of Homeland Security adopted a new policy for forensic searches of digital devices: it requires reasonable suspicion of activity that violates the customs laws or in cases raising national security concerns. U.S. Customs and Border Prot., CBP Directive No. 3340-049A, Border Search of Electronic Devices 5 (2018).

3. Are there any limitations on searches of digital devices at the border? Are you comfortable with courts deferring to "the trained observations of customs officials" or agencies creating their own rules to regulate searches at the border? On the other hand, does *Cotterman*'s distinction between an initial examination and a forensic examination offer a workable standard? Is it consistent with Supreme Court precedent on the border doctrine? Does it satisfy legitimate sovereignty concerns?

§ 10.4 Defining the Border

A difficult question presented by today's world is how to define the border. Some argue that new rules must govern the Internet, which should be distinct from the "current territorially based legal systems."[25] On the other hand, Jack L. Goldsmith has asserted "that regulation of cyberspace is feasible and legitimate from the perspective of jurisdiction and choice of law."[26] Goldsmith cites examples of nation-states regulating content on the Internet within their borders:

> A government can choose to have no Internet links whatsoever and to regulate telephone and other communication lines to access providers in other countries. China, Singapore, and the United Arab Emirates have taken the somewhat less severe steps of (i) regulating access to the Net through centralized filtered servers, and (ii) requiring filters for in-state Internet service providers and end-users. . . . Germany has chosen to hold liable Internet access providers who have knowledge of illegal content and fail to use "technically possible and reasonable" means to filter it.

He also notes that "Cyberspace information can only appear in a geographical jurisdiction by virtue of hardware and software physically present in the jurisdiction. Available technology already permits governments and private entities to regulate the design and function of hardware and software to facilitate discrimination of cyberspace information flows along a variety of dimensions, including geography, network, and content." Whether it is permissible under the United States Constitution to restrict access to the Internet is not the question here; it is whether the sovereign power permits the government to search and seize data that violates the laws of the United States or is otherwise excludable. Goldsmith's article indicates that foreign governments recognize that the international border may be digital in nature.

Harvey Rishikof has maintained: "A political order with international penetrating and expansive technology for counterintelligence purposes will come at the expense of privacy, personal autonomy, and sovereignty as borders and transportation become increasingly transparent. This new political order will be very different from the classic 19th century liberal state, which for the last 200 years has been the ideal model of personal autonomy."[27]

The Supreme Court's cases all concern the physical border or its functional—but still physical—equivalent. Hence, a person at the border with a laptop is still at the border. Instead, imagine a person, while in a foreign country, who emails child pornography images to his home computer, which is located in the United States. If a letter can be searched coming into the country, what about emails, their

---

25. David R. Johnson & David Post, *Law and Borders — the Rise of Law in Cyberspace*, 48 Stan. L. Rev. 1367, 1401 (1996).

26. Jack L. Goldsmith, *Against Cyberanarchy*, 65 U. Chi. L. Rev. 1199, 1201 (1998).

27. Harvey Rishikof, *Long Wars of Political Order — Sovereignty and Choice: The Fourth Amendment and the Modern Trilemma*, 15 Cornell J.L. & Pub. Pol'y 587, 618 (2006).

attachments, or other forms of electronic communications? If they cannot be examined, what is to stop the wholesale creation of offshore businesses specializing in child pornography, illegal gambling, or copyright violations? What is to stop the digital transfer of terrorist plans? On the other hand, in today's world, the most routine in-state phone call may be routed to a satellite; an email to someone in the United States from someone in the United States may pass anywhere over the Internet. Are such communications now permissibly examined as border searches? One possible solution to such a quandary is to find the border search doctrine inapplicable, based on the wholly intra-national nature of the origin and destination of the communication, ignoring the technical means by which the communication is achieved. Does this functional approach satisfy the sovereignty concerns underlying the border search doctrine?[28]

Note and Question

In a letter to Senator Wyden on June 20, 2017, the then-acting director of the Customs and Border Service stated that the border service's authority to conduct border searches extended to "all merchandise entering or departing the United States, including information that is physically resident on an electronic device transported by an international traveler" but that the authority to search did "not extend to information that is located solely on remote servers." Does that policy satisfy the purpose of the border search doctrine?

---

28. *See generally* Symposium, *The Fourth Amendment at the International Border*, 78 Miss. L.J. 241 (2008).

Chapter 11

Fourth Amendment Applicability to Networks and the Internet

§ 11.1 Introduction — "Outside the Box"

This chapter examines Fourth Amendment considerations "outside the box." As noted in Chapter 2, this book uses some informal terms to distinguish between two situations. Issues involving the propriety of obtaining data on a computer or stored on any other digital device are referred to as *Inside the Box* issues. As to the proper methods to obtain data in transit and at its intended destination, such issues are referred to as *Outside the Box* considerations. The perspective from which this informal framework is measured is the individual user. She has her own device and may store data on that device — inside her box. She may also click send and transmit data somewhere else — outside her box. The distinction between *inside the box* and *outside the box* is solely designed to emphasize that much different legal regimes have been construed to predominate in each of those situations as it relates to the individual user's ability to object to governmental acquisition of the data.

From the perspective of the individual user, the Fourth Amendment clearly regulates the acquisition of data stored on that individual's computers and other digital devices — data inside her box. What is less clear is her ability to claim a protected interest so as to object to the acquisition of data in networks, in transit, or recovered from a third party. Broadly generalizing, the regulation of government acquisition of data on the Internet and in networks has been primarily regulated by statute. Those statutory requirements have been seen as more stringent than what the Fourth Amendment has been construed to require, resulting in statutory analysis often superseding Fourth Amendment analysis. Those statutes are considered in the next chapter. This chapter addresses Fourth Amendment issues. The 2018 decision by the Supreme Court in *Carpenter v. United States*, 585 U.S. __ (2018), has at the least unsettled many perceptions about primacy of statutory analysis and may be the vanguard of a new understanding of a broader role for the Fourth Amendment in regulating *outside the box*. This Chapter examines *Carpenter* in depth.

There are several considerations that influence Fourth Amendment analysis of network and Internet investigations. The fundamental one is whether a person has a protected interest — defined by the Supreme Court as a reasonable expectation of privacy in the data sought. There are several variables that need to be considered, including:

- What type of data is being sought;
- What steps the person has taken to protect his or her privacy; and
- Whether the data is obtained from a third party.

§ 11.2 Types of Information Sought: Content vs. Non-Content

1. Background Principles

Michael Lee Smith v. State of Maryland

442 U.S. 735 (1979)

Mr. Justice Blackmun delivered the opinion of the Court.

This case presents the question whether the installation and use of a pen register[n.1][1] constitutes a "search" within the meaning of the Fourth Amendment.

On March 5, 1976, in Baltimore, Md., Patricia McDonough was robbed. She gave the police a description of the robber and of a 1975 Monte Carlo automobile she had observed near the scene of the crime. After the robbery, McDonough began receiving threatening and obscene phone calls from a man identifying himself as the robber. On one occasion, the caller asked that she step out on her front porch; she did so, and saw the 1975 Monte Carlo she had earlier described to police moving slowly past her home. On March 16, police spotted a man who met McDonough's description driving a 1975 Monte Carlo in her neighborhood. By tracing the license plate number, police learned that the car was registered in the name of petitioner, Michael Lee Smith.

The next day, the telephone company, at police request, installed a pen register at its central offices to record the numbers dialed from the telephone at petitioner's home. The police did not get a warrant or court order before having the pen register installed. The register revealed that on March 17 a call was placed from petitioner's home to McDonough's phone. On the basis of this and other evidence, the police obtained a warrant to search petitioner's residence. The search revealed that a page in petitioner's phone book was turned down to the name and number of Patricia McDonough; the phone book was seized. Petitioner was arrested, and a six-man lineup was held on March 19. McDonough identified petitioner as the man who had robbed her.

---

1. [n.1] "A pen register is a mechanical device that records the numbers dialed on a telephone by monitoring the electrical impulses caused when the dial on the telephone is released. It does not overhear oral communications and does not indicate whether calls are actually completed." A pen register is "usually installed at a central telephone facility [and] records on a paper tape all numbers dialed from [the] line" to which it is attached.

By pretrial motion, he sought to suppress "all fruits derived from the pen register" on the ground that the police had failed to secure a warrant prior to its installation. The trial court denied the suppression motion, holding that the warrantless installation of the pen register did not violate the Fourth Amendment. Petitioner then waived a jury, and the case was submitted to the court on an agreed statement of facts. The pen register tape (evidencing the fact that a phone call had been made from petitioner's phone to McDonough's phone) and the phone book seized in the search of petitioner's residence were admitted into evidence against him. Petitioner was convicted and was sentenced to six years.

In determining whether a particular form of government-initiated electronic surveillance is a "search" within the meaning of the Fourth Amendment,[n.4][2] our lodestar is *Katz v. United States*, 389 U.S. 347 (1967). In *Katz*, Government agents had intercepted the contents of a telephone conversation by attaching an electronic listening device to the outside of a public phone booth. The Court rejected the argument that a "search" can occur only when there has been a "physical intrusion" into a "constitutionally protected area," noting that the Fourth Amendment "protects people, not places." Because the Government's monitoring of Katz' conversation "violated the privacy upon which he justifiably relied while using the telephone booth," the Court held that it "constituted a 'search and seizure' within the meaning of the Fourth Amendment."

Consistently with *Katz*, this Court uniformly has held that the application of the Fourth Amendment depends on whether the person invoking its protection can claim a "justifiable," a "reasonable," or a "legitimate expectation of privacy" that has been invaded by government action. This inquiry, as Mr. Justice Harlan aptly noted in his *Katz* concurrence, normally embraces two discrete questions. The first is whether the individual, by his conduct, has "exhibited an actual (subjective) expectation of privacy,"—whether, in the words of the *Katz* majority, the individual has shown that "he seeks to preserve [something] as private." The second question is whether the individual's subjective expectation of privacy is "one that society is prepared to recognize as 'reasonable,'"—whether, in the words of the *Katz* majority, the individual's expectation, viewed objectively, is "justifiable" under the circumstances.[n.5][3]

---

2. [n.4] In this case, the pen register was installed, and the numbers dialed were recorded, by the telephone company. The telephone company, however, acted at police request. In view of this, respondent appears to concede that the company is to be deemed an "agent" of the police for purposes of this case, so as to render the installation and use of the pen register "state action" under the Fourth and Fourteenth Amendments. We may assume that "state action" was present here.

3. [n.5] Situations can be imagined, of course, in which *Katz*' two-pronged inquiry would provide an inadequate index of Fourth Amendment protection. For example, if the Government were suddenly to announce on nationwide television that all homes henceforth would be subject to warrantless entry, individuals thereafter might not in fact entertain any actual expectation of privacy regarding their homes, papers, and effects. Similarly, if a refugee from a totalitarian country, unaware of this Nation's traditions, erroneously assumed that police were continuously monitoring his telephone conversations, a subjective expectation of privacy regarding the contents of his

[A] pen register differs significantly from the listening device employed in *Katz*, for pen registers do not acquire the *contents* of communications. This Court recently noted:

> "Indeed, a law enforcement official could not even determine from the use of a pen register whether a communication existed. These devices do not hear sound. They disclose only the telephone numbers that have been dialed — a means of establishing communication. Neither the purport of any communication between the caller and the recipient of the call, their identities, nor whether the call was even completed is disclosed by pen registers."

Given a pen register's limited capabilities, therefore, petitioner's argument that its installation and use constituted a "search" necessarily rests upon a claim that he had a "legitimate expectation of privacy" regarding the numbers he dialed on his phone.

This claim must be rejected. First, we doubt that people in general entertain any actual expectation of privacy in the numbers they dial. All telephone users realize that they must "convey" phone numbers to the telephone company, since it is through telephone company switching equipment that their calls are completed. All subscribers realize, moreover, that the phone company has facilities for making permanent records of the numbers they dial, for they see a list of their long-distance (toll) calls on their monthly bills. In fact, pen registers and similar devices are routinely used by telephone companies "for the purposes of checking billing operations, detecting fraud and preventing violations of law." Electronic equipment is used not only to keep billing records of toll calls, but also "to keep a record of all calls dialed from a telephone which is subject to a special rate structure." Pen registers are regularly employed "to determine whether a home phone is being used to conduct a business, to check for a defective dial, or to check for overbilling." Although most people may be oblivious to a pen register's esoteric functions, they presumably have some awareness of one common use: to aid in the identification of persons making annoying or obscene calls. Most phone books tell subscribers, on a page entitled "Consumer Information," that the company "can frequently help in identifying to the authorities the origin of unwelcome and troublesome calls." Telephone users, in sum, typically know that they must convey numerical information to the phone company; that the phone company has facilities for recording this information; and that the phone company does in fact record this information for a variety of legitimate business purposes. Although subjective expectations cannot be scientifically gauged, it is too much to believe that telephone subscribers, under these circumstances, harbor any general expectation that the numbers they dial will remain secret.

---

calls might be lacking as well. In such circumstances, where an individual's subjective expectations had been "conditioned" by influences alien to well-recognized Fourth Amendment freedoms, those subjective expectations obviously could play no meaningful role in ascertaining what the scope of Fourth Amendment protection was. In determining whether a "legitimate expectation of privacy" existed in such cases, a normative inquiry would be proper.

Petitioner argues, however, that, whatever the expectations of telephone users in general, he demonstrated an expectation of privacy by his own conduct here, since he "us[ed] the telephone *in his house* to the exclusion of all others." But the site of the call is immaterial for purposes of analysis in this case. Although petitioner's conduct may have been calculated to keep the *contents* of his conversation private, his conduct was not and could not have been calculated to preserve the privacy of the number he dialed. Regardless of his location, petitioner had to convey that number to the telephone company in precisely the same way if he wished to complete his call. The fact that he dialed the number on his home phone rather than on some other phone could make no conceivable difference, nor could any subscriber rationally think that it would.

Second, even if petitioner did harbor some subjective expectation that the phone numbers he dialed would remain private, this expectation is not "one that society is prepared to recognize as 'reasonable.'" This Court consistently has held that a person has no legitimate expectation of privacy in information he voluntarily turns over to third parties. *E.g., United States v. Miller*, 425 U.S. 435 (1976). In *Miller*, for example, the Court held that a bank depositor has no "legitimate 'expectation of privacy'" in financial information "voluntarily conveyed to . . . banks and exposed to their employees in the ordinary course of business." The Court explained:

> "The depositor takes the risk, in revealing his affairs to another, that the information will be conveyed by that person to the Government. . . . This Court has held repeatedly that the Fourth Amendment does not prohibit the obtaining of information revealed to a third party and conveyed by him to Government authorities, even if the information is revealed on the assumption that it will be used only for a limited purpose and the confidence placed in the third party will not be betrayed."

Because the depositor "assumed the risk" of disclosure, the Court held that it would be unreasonable for him to expect his financial records to remain private.

This analysis dictates that petitioner can claim no legitimate expectation of privacy here. When he used his phone, petitioner voluntarily conveyed numerical information to the telephone company and "exposed" that information to its equipment in the ordinary course of business. In so doing, petitioner assumed the risk that the company would reveal to police the numbers he dialed. The switching equipment that processed those numbers is merely the modern counterpart of the operator who, in an earlier day, personally completed calls for the subscriber. Petitioner concedes that if he had placed his calls through an operator, he could claim no legitimate expectation of privacy. We are not inclined to hold that a different constitutional result is required because the telephone company has decided to automate.

Petitioner argues, however, that automatic switching equipment differs from a live operator in one pertinent respect. An operator, in theory at least, is capable of remembering every number that is conveyed to him by callers. Electronic equipment, by contrast can "remember" only those numbers it is programmed to record, and telephone companies, in view of their present billing practices, usually do not record local calls. Since petitioner, in calling McDonough, was making a local call, his expectation of privacy as to her number, on this theory, would be "legitimate."

This argument does not withstand scrutiny. The fortuity of whether or not the phone company in fact elects to make a quasi-permanent record of a particular number dialed does not in our view, make any constitutional difference. Regardless of the phone company's election, petitioner voluntarily conveyed to it information that it had facilities for recording and that it was free to record. In these circumstances, petitioner assumed the risk that the information would be divulged to police. Under petitioner's theory, Fourth Amendment protection would exist, or not, depending on how the telephone company chose to define local-dialing zones, and depending on how it chose to bill its customers for local calls. Calls placed across town, or dialed directly, would be protected; calls placed across the river, or dialed with operator assistance, might not be. We are not inclined to make a crazy quilt of the Fourth Amendment, especially in circumstances where (as here) the pattern of protection would be dictated by billing practices of a private corporation.

We therefore conclude that petitioner in all probability entertained no actual expectation of privacy in the phone numbers he dialed, and that, even if he did, his expectation was not "legitimate." The installation and use of a pen register, consequently, was not a "search," and no warrant was required.

Mr. Justice Stewart, with whom Mr. Justice Brennan joins, dissenting.

It seems clear to me that information obtained by pen register surveillance of a private telephone is information in which the telephone subscriber has a legitimate expectation of privacy. The information captured by such surveillance emanates from private conduct within a person's home or office—locations that without question are entitled to Fourth and Fourteenth Amendment protection. Further, that information is an integral part of the telephonic communication that under *Katz* is entitled to constitutional protection.

The numbers dialed from a private telephone—although certainly more prosaic than the conversation itself—are not without "content." Most private telephone subscribers may have their own numbers listed in a publicly distributed directory, but I doubt there are any who would be happy to have broadcast to the world a list of the local or long distance numbers they have called. This is not because such a list might in some sense be incriminating, but because it easily could reveal the identities of the persons and the places called, and thus reveal the most intimate details of a person's life.

Mr. Justice Marshall, with whom Mr. Justice Brennan joins, dissenting.

Privacy is not a discrete commodity, possessed absolutely or not at all. Those who disclose certain facts to a bank or phone company for a limited business purpose need not assume that this information will be released to other persons for other purposes.

The crux of the Court's holding, however, is that whatever expectation of privacy petitioner may in fact have entertained regarding his calls, it is not one "society is prepared to recognize as 'reasonable.'" In so ruling, the Court determines that individuals who convey information to third parties have "assumed the risk" of disclosure to the government. This analysis is misconceived in two critical respects.

Implicit in the concept of assumption of risk is some notion of choice. At least in the third-party consensual surveillance cases, which first incorporated risk analysis into Fourth Amendment doctrine, the defendant presumably had exercised some discretion in deciding who should enjoy his confidential communications. By contrast here, unless a person is prepared to forgo use of what for many has become a personal or professional necessity, he cannot help but accept the risk of surveillance. It is idle to speak of "assuming" risks in contexts where, as a practical matter, individuals have no realistic alternative.

More fundamentally, to make risk analysis dispositive in assessing the reasonableness of privacy expectations would allow the government to define the scope of Fourth Amendment protections. For example, law enforcement officials, simply by announcing their intent to monitor the content of random samples of first-class mail or private phone conversations, could put the public on notice of the risks they would thereafter assume in such communications. Yet, although acknowledging this implication of its analysis, the Court is willing to concede only that, in some circumstances, a further "normative inquiry would be proper." No meaningful effort is made to explain what those circumstances might be, or why this case is not among them.

In my view, whether privacy expectations are legitimate within the meaning of *Katz* depends not on the risks an individual can be presumed to accept when imparting information to third parties, but on the risks he should be forced to assume in a free and open society. By its terms, the constitutional prohibition of unreasonable searches and seizures assigns to the judiciary some prescriptive responsibility. As Mr. Justice Harlan, who formulated the standard the Court applies today, himself recognized: "[s]ince it is the task of the law to form and project, as well as mirror and reflect, we should not . . . merely recite . . . risks without examining the desirability of saddling them upon society." In making this assessment, courts must evaluate the "intrinsic character" of investigative practices with reference to the basic values underlying the Fourth Amendment. And for those "extensive intrusions that significantly jeopardize [individuals'] sense of security . . . , more than self-restraint by law enforcement officials is required."

The use of pen registers, I believe, constitutes such an extensive intrusion. To hold otherwise ignores the vital role telephonic communication plays in our personal and professional relationships, as well as the First and Fourth Amendment interests implicated by unfettered official surveillance. Privacy in placing calls is of value not only to those engaged in criminal activity. The prospect of unregulated governmental monitoring will undoubtedly prove disturbing even to those with nothing illicit to hide. Many individuals, including members of unpopular political organizations or journalists with confidential sources, may legitimately wish to avoid disclosure of their personal contacts. Permitting governmental access to telephone records on less than probable cause may thus impede certain forms of political affiliation and journalistic endeavor that are the hallmark of a truly free society.

Just as one who enters a public telephone booth is "entitled to assume that the words he utters into the mouthpiece will not be broadcast to the world," so too, he should be entitled to assume that the numbers he dials in the privacy of his home will be recorded, if at all, solely for the phone company's business purposes. Accordingly, I would require law enforcement officials to obtain a warrant before they enlist telephone companies to secure information otherwise beyond the government's reach.

2. Content vs. Non-Content Defined

Matthew J. Tokson[4] has written a helpful description of the types of information that may be obtained as a result of network surveillance:

> For over one hundred years, the Supreme Court has held that the Fourth Amendment protects mailed letters and packages from inspection by postal authorities or other government agents. Yet from the start, the Court has distinguished between the content of a letter and the noncontent information disclosed on its envelope. Whereas noncontent envelope information is exposed and can be examined by anyone, the content of a letter is "as fully guarded from examination and inspection" as it would be if the party mailing the letter had retained it in his or her own home.
>
> The content/noncontent distinction remains important in the constitutional and statutory law governing the inspection of private communications, even as new technologies have dramatically altered the nature of communication itself.
>
> As a general semantic matter, the definition of "content" (and "contents") has remained largely the same since before *Smith* was decided. Indeed, according to the Oxford English Dictionary, it has remained largely the same since the early sixteenth century. Commonly, the first meaning of "content" is "that which is contained" in something; the second meaning is the "subject-matter" of a speech or piece of writing; and the third meaning is the "sum or substance of what is contained in a document; tenor, purport." As we can see, content is generally defined as not only the actual written words of a document, but also the general subject matter of the document and the purport of its message. Applied to the email context, a very narrow definition of "contents" might refer to only the actual letters contained in

---

4. Matthew J. Tokson, *The Content/Envelope Distinction in Internet Law*, 50 WILLIAM AND MARY L. REV. 2105 (2009). Copyright © 2009, Matthew J. Tokson, William and Mary Law Review. All rights reserved. Reprinted by permission.

the body of the email; a more expansive definition would include the overall gist of the message contained, or even the general subject matter discussed.

A. The Body of Email Messages

Emails are transmitted in "packets" of digitized information that travel through the Internet's infrastructure, and these packets may contain both email address ("header") and body text information. When the email reaches its destination server, the server reassembles the information into the header and the body of the email. Yet, nothing about this transmission process implicates the content status of the body itself in semantics or in constitutional law (or under the ECPA). Setting aside questions of whether certain email body information is protected by the Fourth Amendment, the "message in the body of the email itself," like a letter or a phone conversation, clearly constitutes the content of a communication.

B. Email To/From Information

Email to/from routing information is contained in the header portion of the email packet, and generally consists of email addresses, IP addresses, packet information, and information about servers that are transmitting the email message. Though this sort of information is used exclusively for directing emails and seems to be directly analogous to noncontent phone number information, some writers and privacy advocates have argued that it reveals more personal information than do phone numbers, and therefore should receive greater legal protection. Email addresses may, for instance, indicate the identity of the communicators with more specificity than phone numbers, which might be used by anyone in a household. Depending on the domain name of the address, email addresses may also reveal the communicator's workplace or university affiliation. Certainly, the marginal increase in specificity and the disclosure of a communicator's work or school affiliation might represent a tiny increase in the invasiveness of email pen registers relative to telephone pen registers. But none of the information disclosed by an email address concerns the actual content of any emails.

To be sure, government investigators might be able to make educated guesses as to the purpose of an email (or a phone call) between two parties, for example, a known drug addict and a known drug dealer. But one cannot argue that such to/from information actually reveals the contents of communications. Of course, observing the addressing information very likely reveals the identities of the communicators. But even that information does not reveal the details (or even the purpose or subject) of the communication itself—two people might talk about any subject.

D. Email Size and Text Length

The government's pen register information collection software—formerly called "Carnivore" and now called "DCS-1000," does not collect an email's subject line, but it does replace the text in the subject line with Xs, allowing a viewer to know how many letters were used in the subject. The government's pen register surveillance programs may also collect information about the total size of email transmissions. To be sure, the length of an email or email subject line (or a phone call, to which the same argument would apply) can tell an observer something about the email itself. The size of an email might also indicate that a file of that size has been attached to the email. Conceivably, authorities investigating a child pornographer might guess that he was sending child pornography images in captured emails of a certain size. But the size of the file does not actually indicate or rule out any specific content; it does not reveal whether a file exists or whether the file is an image or a similarly sized file of another type, and it certainly does not reveal anything about the content of the hypothetical image. Neither does the length of a line of text reveal the content of the text, nor its subject matter or purport. Guessing the content of even a three-letter subject heading would be impossible to do with any accuracy; not counting acronyms or punctuation (for example, "hi!"), there are still hundreds of distinct three-letter words.

E. Email Subject Headers

The subject line of an email cannot be directly compared to any feature of regular mail. It contains communicative writing and does not contain any routing information, but it is transmitted in the header portion of email packets. As such, it would probably not qualify as content under the very narrowest definition of the "contents" of a message. It appears on the external header portion of the email; only the body of the email is "contained" in the packaging that is the email header. Nonetheless, both the Department of Justice and the one district court to have commented on the matter have concluded that the subject header, despite its location in an email transmission, should be treated as content.

The House Report on the USA PATRIOT Act and the PATRIOT Act's amendments to the ECPA, state that subject lines are "clearly content." Likely as a result, the Department of Justice's policy is to treat email subject lines as content. Neither the Department's policy nor the House's legislative history give a reason for their interpretation; they simply consider email subject lines to be "letter" information despite their location. Under this rationale, the subject line would be just another form of email body text. This rationale is sound, and it provides an attractive bright line rule. Any information that is not used in routing a communication, and which itself may contain communicative text (for example, "The White Sox won"), is "letter" content, regardless of its location in the packet of data actually transferred between ISPs.

Email subject lines might also be considered contents to the extent that they obviously disclose the subject and purport of the body of the communication. In a recent district court case involving a pen register application, the magistrate judge found that, while the subject line was contained in the email header, the "information contained in the 'subject' would reveal the contents of the communication and would not be properly disclosed pursuant to a pen register or trap and trace device" under the ECPA.

III. Separating Content from Noncontent in Web Browsing Communications

Like emails, the transmission of website data on the Internet occurs via packets of digitized information. When an Internet user types in or navigates to a URL, the URL's domain name (for example "www.nytimes.com") is translated during transmission into the IP address of the target website. Specific website routing information, like the individual page URL, is generally placed inside the packet transmitted to the target's IP address, just as email to/from address information is generally placed inside packets, along with body text. The packet is sent to a website host computer's IP address. The host computer processes the URL information in this packet and uses it to select the web page requested. It then sends the website data to the user's computer.

This relatively simple process gives rise to many complex legal and semantic questions as to whether courts should consider any or all Internet communication information content, and further, whether courts should protect this information under the Fourth Amendment. The first of these questions is whether communications between a person and a website host computer should be considered communications at all.

The question is essentially confined to constitutional law because the extremely broad definition of "electronic communications," which the ECPA defines as "any transfer of signs, signals, writing, . . . data, or intelligence of any nature," appears to encompass web surfing activities. As for the constitutional issue, it appears that web surfing transmissions will similarly be treated as a form of communication, analogous in constitutional law to telephone conversations. Communicative data (such as website content, personal information, and blog comments) is transferred back and forth between Internet users and automated website hosts. Current law provides no reason to believe that the constitutional protection for the content of communications is diminished because one part of the communication is automated or available to the public. Courts have already implicitly treated telephone calls to an automated, voice recognition-based service as communications in which callers may have a reasonable expectation of privacy as to the content of their calls. In other words, there is no indication that websites sent to users are not considered communications just because they are transmitted by automated processes rather than other human beings—after all, a living person wrote them and posted them at some point. Accordingly, the one court to have addressed the issue has applied the Fourth Amendment "communications" framework of *Smith* to web surfing activities. A number of scholars have also considered web surfing activity to be a communication for the purposes of constitutional law. Still, a far more difficult question remains: which parts of this communication are content and which are not?

A. Website Text and Other Data Sent to Users; Data Input by Users and Sent to the Web Host

The question of whether website text transmitted to an Internet user or an Internet user's input data transmitted to a web host computer represents "content" is essentially answered once the transmissions are recognized as communications. As with email communications, the "body" of a web surfing communication is the nonrouting information contained in the digitized packets transferred over the Internet. Data that is input by users, including search terms typed into a search "box" on a web page, has been recognized by courts as content, at least as that term is defined in the ECPA. Because website transmissions are communications, the text and other information sent by websites to users is very likely to be treated as the contents of a communication for the purposes of statutory and constitutional law. As even proponents of a narrow reading of "content" have acknowledged, the nonrouting information in Internet packets represents Internet communications content.

B. URLs Containing Search Terms

When a user types search terms into a box on a search engine's website, the user is not actually searching the entire Internet. Instead, the user is directed to a page displaying the results of a search of the website's database. This occurs when the user's Internet browser adds the search terms into the URL sent to the website, which sends back the requested results page based on the URL. Indeed, typing the URL containing the search terms directly into an Internet browser takes one to the same results page.

As in the case of email subject lines, the arguments that search terms embedded in a URL are content could take two forms, one reflecting a very narrow definition of content, and the other reflecting the broad definition used in the ECPA. First, one could argue that the terms in the URL are actually the body text of a communication contained by the rest of the URL. Yet the terms in the URL are placed on the "envelope" of the Internet communication, and are not technically typed by the user (they are placed in the URL by the browser, which copies the text typed into the web page form). They are used for website routing just like any other URL information. It would be difficult to argue that the search terms in a URL are literally contained like the text of a letter.

Instead, both courts and scholars have focused on the argument that URLs containing search terms reveal the content of the user's input to the website, thus exposing that input and the subject and purpose of the entire communication. In one recent district court ruling, the magistrate held that URLs containing search terms had the potential to reveal the subject and purpose of communications, and therefore such URLs must be treated as contents under the broader definition used in the ECPA. Otherwise, pen registers could capture all of a user's search term information simply by capturing the URLs sent from his IP address. * * *

As an example, imagine that Alice Sebold's recent bestseller The Lovely Bones was not a novel, but rather the manifesto of a subversive political group disfavored by the government. Suppose that a user under investigation by the government for her political activities searched for the book and then clicked on the book's web page in order to see its publication details or to purchase it. Government investigators (or hackers) obtaining a URL with search terms sent to Amazon.com would know that the user was looking for "lovely bones" and would be able to visit the book's page by clicking on it in the Amazon results page that the following URL directs them to: http://www.amazon.com/s/ref=nb_ss_gw?url=search-alias%3Daps&field-keywords=lovely+bones.

Imagine that the search term URL could not be obtained for technical or legal reasons. Investigators or hackers obtaining only the URL of the book's page at Amazon.com would also know from reading the URL that the user was looking for the novel "lovely bones," and would be able to visit the book's page once they obtained the URL: http://www.amazon.com/Lovely-Bones-Novel-Alice-Sebold/dp/0316666343.

By contrast, Barnes and Noble's book page for The Lovely Bones does not provide the name of the book in the URL. Nonetheless, investigators or hackers would easily be able to ascertain which book the user was looking for by visiting the book's web page at its URL: http://search.barnesandnoble.com/booksearch/isbninquiry.asp?ean=0316666343.

The text in the three URLs differs; but, search terms or not, the three URLs all reveal to any observer with Internet access the same information: the user has requested and accessed the web page of The Lovely Bones. Only by blinding oneself to the realities of how URLs work could one argue that one of these URLs is meaningfully different from another in practice. Of course, this practical conclusion is not the end of the content inquiry under the law. The law may emphasize the form of communications over their function, and thereby require us to treat routing information as noncontent even when it reveals the entirety of a communication.

D. Website IP Addresses

An IP address can often be used to determine the domain name of the website contacted, either by simply entering the IP address into a web browser like a URL or by looking it up in an IP address database. As with

URLs, observation of the IP addresses contacted by an Internet user might be used to determine the website viewed regardless of whether the IP address information is obtained contemporaneously or in records of past web surfing communications. On the other hand, IP addresses reveal significantly less about the content of web surfing communications than do URLs; they do not point to a specific page on a website, but instead may refer to any one of a number of pages. They do not even necessarily reveal that a user has viewed the main page of a website, as the user's computer would communicate with the same IP address even if she jumped immediately to a specific page from the web host's database (perhaps directed there by a search engine). Further, multiple websites may share the same IP address. It is generally difficult to determine whether a given website shares its IP address with another website, at least without directly contacting the web host. Thus, in most cases, IP addresses will not reveal the underlying content or even subject matter of Internet communications with anything approaching the certainty of URLs.

Still, in cases in which a single website uses a single IP address, and when that website is either small enough or subject-specific enough, mere knowledge of the IP address contacted by the user could inevitably reveal the contents of the underlying communication.

For example, some websites, especially personal websites, may only contain one or two pages. If such websites happened to have their own IP addresses, they would reveal as much or nearly as much about the content of the underlying web surfing communication as would URLs. Of course, smaller websites like these are also likely to share an IP address with multiple other sites. IP addresses assigned to larger websites might also reveal the subject matter and purpose of the underlying Internet communications.

E. Size of Information Accessed or Files Downloaded from Websites

The government's pen register software can and likely does collect information about the amount of data transferred between an Internet user and a host website. Indeed, this may have occurred in *Forrester* [*see infra*], when the government's pen register captured the "total volume of information sent to or from [the defendant's] account." This might refer to the total volume of the defendant's web surfing activity, but, given the function of the government's pen register software, more likely refers to the total volume of information sent to and from each website. If so, the court erred when it approved this capture as "constitutionally indistinguishable from the use of a [telephone] pen register." Unlike the volume of data information that a pen register collects from email transmissions, volume information for individual websites may reveal the contents of web surfing communications, perhaps just as clearly as URLs do. Of course, for complex websites with many pages and/or many downloadable files, such total volume information is unlikely to yield much information beyond that already revealed by the IP address. However, for smaller, simpler websites, such information allows for a complete reconstruction of the content viewed and downloaded.

For instance, imagine that a simple website consisting of only four web pages and minimal text (constituting roughly 100 kb of data in total) allows users to download three files: a pdf of the Gettysburg Address (500 kb), a pdf of the Constitution (1000 kb), and a pdf of the long, rambling manifesto of a subversive political group (10,000 kb). If the user downloads any of the files, capturing the total volume of website activity tells an observer where the user surfed and which documents he downloaded (and in all probability, read: 600 kb of total activity means the user downloaded the Gettysburg Address; 1100 kb the Constitution; 1600 kb, both; 10,100 kb, the manifesto; and so on). In such situations, the argument that total volume data that reveals the content of web surfing communications should be treated as content for the purposes of constitutional law tracks exactly the argument about URLs made above.

———————————

United States v. Mark Stephen Forrester

512 F.3d 500 (9th Cir. 2008)

FISHER, CIRCUIT JUDGE:

Alba challenges the validity of computer surveillance that enabled the government to learn the to/from addresses of his e-mail messages, the Internet protocol addresses of the websites that he visited and the total volume of information transmitted to or from his account. We conclude that this surveillance was analogous to the use of a pen register that the Supreme Court held in *Smith v. Maryland*, 442 U.S. 735 (1979), did not constitute a search for Fourth Amendment purposes.

Following a lengthy government investigation, Forrester and Alba were indicted on October 26, 2001, and arraigned shortly thereafter. Forrester was charged with one count of conspiracy to manufacture and distribute "Ecstasy." Alba was also charged with that offense, as well as with engaging in a continuing criminal enterprise, conspiracy to transfer funds outside the United States in promotion of an illegal activity, and conspiracy to conduct financial transactions involving the proceeds of an illegal activity.

During its investigation of Forrester and Alba's Ecstasy-manufacturing operation, the government employed various computer surveillance techniques to monitor Alba's e-mail and Internet activity. The surveillance began in May 2001 after the government applied for and received court permission to install a pen register analogue known as a "mirror port" on Alba's account with PacBell Internet. The mirror port was installed at PacBell's connection facility in San Diego, and enabled the government to learn the to/from addresses of Alba's e-mail messages, the IP addresses of the websites that Alba visited and the total volume of information sent to or from his account. Later, the government obtained a warrant authorizing it to employ imaging and keystroke monitoring techniques, but Alba does not challenge on appeal those techniques' legality or the government's application to use them.

At trial, the government introduced extensive evidence showing that they and their associates built and operated a major Ecstasy laboratory. Witnesses described the lab as "very, very large," and seized documents show that it was intended to produce approximately 440 kilograms of Ecstasy (and $10 million in profit) per month. The government also presented evidence that Alba purchased precursor chemicals for Ecstasy, that Forrester met with a Swedish chemist in Stockholm to learn about manufacturing Ecstasy, that the defendants first tried to construct the lab in two other locations before settling on Escondido, California and that the Escondido lab was located inside an insulated sea/land container and contained an array of devices and chemicals used to make Ecstasy.

The jury convicted Forrester and Alba on all counts. The district court sentenced them each to 360 months in prison and six years of supervised release. Both defendants timely appealed. [The appeals court reversed Forester's conviction based on an inadequate waiver of counsel.]

We conclude that the surveillance techniques the government employed here are constitutionally indistinguishable from the use of a pen register that the Court approved in *Smith*. First, e-mail and Internet users, like the telephone users in *Smith*, rely on third-party equipment in order to engage in communication. *Smith* based its holding that telephone users have no expectation of privacy in the numbers they dial on the users' imputed knowledge that their calls are completed through telephone company switching equipment. Analogously, e-mail and Internet users have no expectation of privacy in the to/from addresses of their messages or the IP addresses of the websites they visit because they should know that this information is provided to and used by Internet service providers for the specific purpose of directing the routing of information. Like telephone numbers, which provide instructions to the "switching equipment that processed those numbers," e-mail to/from addresses and IP addresses are not merely passively conveyed through third party equipment, but rather are voluntarily turned over in order to direct the third party's servers.

Second, e-mail to/from addresses and IP addresses constitute addressing information and do not necessarily reveal any more about the underlying contents of communication than do phone numbers. When the government obtains the to/from addresses of a person's e-mails or the IP addresses of websites visited, it does not find out the contents of the messages or know the particular pages on the websites the person viewed. At best, the government may make educated guesses about what was said in the messages or viewed on the websites based on its knowledge of the e-mail to/from addresses and IP addresses—but this is no different from speculation about the contents of a phone conversation on the basis of the identity of the person or entity that was dialed. Like IP addresses, certain phone numbers may strongly indicate the underlying contents of the communication; for example, the government would know that a person who dialed the phone number of a chemicals company or a gun shop was likely seeking information about chemicals or firearms. Further, when an individual dials a pre-recorded information or subject-specific line, such as sports scores, lottery results or phone sex lines, the phone number may even show that the caller had access to specific content information. Nonetheless, the Court in *Smith* and *Katz* drew a clear line between unprotected addressing information and protected content information that the government did not cross here.[n.6][5]

The government's surveillance of e-mail addresses also may be technologically sophisticated, but it is conceptually indistinguishable from government surveillance of physical mail. In a line of cases dating back to the nineteenth century, the Supreme Court has held that the government cannot engage in a warrantless search of the contents of sealed mail, but can observe whatever information people put on the outside of mail, because that information is voluntarily transmitted to third parties. E-mail, like physical mail, has an outside address "visible" to the third-party carriers that transmit it to its intended location, and also a package of content that the sender presumes will be read only by the intended recipient. The privacy interests in these two forms of communication are identical. The contents may deserve Fourth Amendment protection, but the address and size of the package do not.

Finally, the pen register in *Smith* was able to disclose not only the phone numbers dialed but also the number of calls made. There is no difference of constitutional magnitude between this aspect of the pen register and the government's monitoring here of the total volume of data transmitted to or from Alba's account. Devices that obtain addressing information also inevitably reveal the amount of information coming and going, and do not thereby breach the line between mere addressing and more content-rich information.

We therefore hold that the computer surveillance techniques that Alba challenges are not Fourth Amendment searches. However, our holding extends only to these particular techniques and does not imply that more intrusive techniques or techniques that reveal more content information are also constitutionally identical to the use of a pen register.

———————

5. [n.6] Surveillance techniques that enable the government to determine not only the IP addresses that a person accesses but also the uniform resource locators ("URL") of the pages visited might be more constitutionally problematic. A URL, unlike an IP address, identifies the particular document within a website that a person views and thus reveals much more information about the person's Internet activity. For instance, a surveillance technique that captures IP addresses would show only that a person visited the New York Times' website at http://www.nytimes.com, whereas a technique that captures URLs would also divulge the particular articles the person viewed.

An Alternative View — Independent State Grounds

State v. Shirley Reid

945 A.2d 26 (N.J. 2008)

CHIEF JUSTICE RABNER delivered the opinion of the Court.

Modern technology has raised a number of questions that are intertwined in this case: To what extent can private individuals "surf" the "Web" anonymously? Do Internet subscribers have a reasonable expectation of privacy in their identity while accessing Internet websites? And under what circumstances may the State learn the actual identity of Internet users?

Reid is now under indictment for second-degree computer theft. She successfully moved to suppress the subscriber information obtained via the municipal subpoena.

We now hold that citizens have a reasonable expectation of privacy, protected by Article I, Paragraph 7, of the New Jersey Constitution, in the subscriber information they provide to Internet service providers.

Some background information about computers and the Internet may assist in evaluating the issues presented. The Internet is a global network of computers that allows for the "sharing" or "networking" of information to and from remote locations. Users of the Internet can send electronic mail, share files, and explore or "surf" the World Wide Web, a graphical computer-based information network. While surfing the Web, a user can visit and interact with sites maintained by businesses, educational institutions, governments, and individuals, which cover almost every conceivable topic.

An individual customer must select an Internet Service Provider like Comcast, AOL, or Verizon, in order to connect to the Internet. To sign up for service, a customer must disclose personal information including one's name, billing information, phone number, and home address.

To interact with other computers also attached to the Internet, a computer must be assigned an Internet Protocol address, or IP address. An IP address is a string of up to twelve numbers separated by dots — for example, 123.45.67.89. In certain situations, a computer is assigned a permanent IP address, called a static IP address. Most often, when an individual connects to the Internet, his or her Internet Service Provider dynamically assigns an IP address to the computer, which can change every time the user accesses the Internet. In other words, the "dynamic" IP address assigned to the computer can be different for each Internet session.

The American Registry for Internet Numbers is in charge of assigning IP addresses within North America. *See* http://www.arin.net/index.shtml. Anyone acquiring an IP address must register and provide ARIN certain contact information, which ARIN makes publicly available. However, most Internet users do not obtain IP addresses directly from ARIN; they instead "lease" an IP address from a service provider like Comcast, which is the actual, named registrant.

When an Internet user surfs the Web, sends e-mail, or shares a file, any site the user connects to can collect certain information, including the user's IP address. However, the sites ordinarily cannot identify the name of an individual user. Only the ISP can match the name of the customer to a dynamic IP address.

Recently, IP Address Locator Websites have become available to the general public.[n.1][6] Such websites operate similarly to a reverse phone directory: they permit a person to type in an IP address and obtain the name and location of the registrant for that address. Once again, because most Internet users access the Internet via third-party service providers like AOL, Comcast, Yahoo, and others, Address Locator Websites typically reveal the name and location of the service provider—such as Comcast—but not information about the individual user.

Thus, even with the advent of IP Address Locator Websites, most users continue to enjoy relatively complete IP address anonymity when surfing the Web.

On August 27, 2004, Timothy Wilson, the owner of Jersey Diesel, reported to the Lower Township Police Department that someone had used a computer to change his company's shipping address and password for its suppliers. The shipping address was changed to a non-existent address.

Wilson explained that Shirley Reid, an employee who had been on disability leave, could have made the changes. Reid returned to work on the morning of August 24, had an argument with Wilson about her temporary light duty assignment, and left. According to Wilson, Reid was the only employee who knew the company's computer password and ID.

Wilson learned of the changes through one of his suppliers, Donaldson Company, Inc. Both the password and shipping address for Jersey Diesel had been changed on Donaldson's website on August 24, 2004. According to an information technology specialist at Donaldson, someone accessed their website and used Jersey Diesel's username and password to sign on at 9:57 a.m. The individual changed the password and Jersey Diesel's shipping address and then completed the requests at 10:07 a.m.

Donaldson's website captured the user's IP address, 68.32.145.220, which was registered to Comcast. When Wilson contacted Comcast and asked for subscriber information associated with that address—so that he could identify the person who made the unauthorized changes—Comcast declined to respond without a subpoena.

On September 7, 2004, a subpoena *duces tecum* issued by the Lower Township Municipal Court was served on Comcast. The subpoena sought "[a]ny and all information pertaining to IP Address information belonging to IP address: 68.32.145.220, which occurred on 08/24/04 between 8:00 a.m. and 11:00 a.m. EST."

---

6. [n.1] Websites providing this service include: GeoBytes IP Address Locator Tool, http://www.geobytes.com/IpLocator.htm; IP-address.com, http://www.ip-adress.com/ipaddresstolocation/; and IP Address Location, http://www.ipaddresslocation.org/.

Comcast responded on September 16, 2004 and identified Reid as the subscriber of the IP address. In addition, Comcast provided the following information: Reid's address, telephone number, type of service provided, IP assignment (dynamic), account number, e-mail address, and method of payment.

Both the Fourth Amendment to the United States Constitution and Article I, Paragraph 7, of the New Jersey Constitution protect, in nearly identical language, "the right of the people to be secure . . . against unreasonable searches and seizures."

Federal case law interpreting the Fourth Amendment has found no expectation of privacy in Internet subscriber information. Those decisions draw on settled federal law that a person has no reasonable expectation of privacy in information exposed to third parties, like a telephone company or bank. The logic of those precedents extends to subscriber information revealed to an ISP.

Our inquiry does not end there because "despite the congruity of the language," the search and seizure protections in the federal and New Jersey Constitutions "are not always coterminous." Indeed, on multiple occasions this Court has held that the New Jersey Constitution "affords our citizens greater protection against unreasonable searches and seizures" than the Fourth Amendment.

During the past twenty-five years, a series of New Jersey cases has expanded the privacy rights enjoyed by citizens of this state. In 1982, this Court concluded . . . that telephone toll billing records are "part of the privacy package." In language that resonates today on the subject of computers, the Court observed that "[t]he telephone has become an essential instrument in carrying on our personal affairs." Moreover, a list of telephone numbers dialed in the privacy of one's home "'could reveal the identities of the persons and the places called, and thus reveal the most intimate details of a person's life.'"

Finding that Article I, Paragraph 7, of the New Jersey Constitution provides more protection than federal law affords, this Court concluded that a person "is entitled to assume that the numbers he dials in the privacy of his home will be recorded solely for the telephone company's business purposes." The Court rejected the underpinnings of federal case law by explaining that

> [i]t is unrealistic to say that the cloak of privacy has been shed because the telephone company and some of its employees are aware of this information. . . . This disclosure has been necessitated because of the nature of the instrumentality, but more significantly the disclosure has been made for a limited business purpose and not for release to other persons for other reasons.

More recently, this Court held that the New Jersey Constitution provides bank account holders a reasonable expectation of privacy in their bank records. [T]he Court noted that bank accounts "have become an indispensable part of modern commerce" for our citizens. Like long distance billing records, bank records reveal a great deal about the personal affairs, opinions, habits, and associations of depositors. The Court also noted that, although bank customers voluntarily provide information to banks, "they do so with the understanding that it will remain confidential." The disclosure is done to facilitate financial transactions, not to enable banks to broadcast the affairs of their customers.

ISP records share much in common with long distance billing information and bank records. All are integrally connected to essential activities of today's society. Indeed, it is hard to overstate how important computers and the Internet have become to everyday, modern life. Citizens routinely access the Web for all manner of daily activities: to gather information, explore ideas, read, study, shop, and more.

Individuals need an ISP address in order to access the Internet. However, when users surf the Web from the privacy of their homes, they have reason to expect that their actions are confidential. Many are unaware that a numerical IP address can be captured by the websites they visit. More sophisticated users understand that that unique string of numbers, standing alone, reveals little if anything to the outside world. Only an Internet service provider can translate an IP address into a user's name.

In addition, while decoded IP addresses do not reveal the content of Internet communications, subscriber information alone can tell a great deal about a person. With a complete listing of IP addresses, one can track a person's Internet usage. "The government can learn the names of stores at which a person shops, the political organizations a person finds interesting, a person's . . . fantasies, her health concerns, and so on." Such information can reveal intimate details about one's personal affairs in the same way disclosure of telephone billing records does. Although the contents of Internet communications may be even more revealing, both types of information implicate privacy interests.

The State compares IP addresses to the return addresses found on the outside of envelopes, which carry no privacy protection. But there is an important difference: letter writers choose to include their address on an envelope. They may also opt for anonymity and list no return address. Internet users have no such choice because they must have an IP address to access a website. In addition, the string of numbers that comprises an IP address and can be collected by a website is both less revealing and less public than a name or street address posted on an envelope.

It is well-settled under New Jersey law that disclosure to a third-party provider, as an essential step to obtaining service altogether, does not upend the privacy interest at stake. In the world of the Internet, the nature of the technology requires individuals to obtain an IP address to access the Web. Users make disclosures to ISPs for the limited goal of using that technology and not to promote the release of personal information to others. Under our precedents, users are entitled to expect confidentiality under these circumstances.[n.2][7]

---

7. [n.2] Users, of course, may waive their expectation of confidentiality in any number of ways. People routinely identify themselves on a website when they make a purchase or complete a survey.

For all of those reasons, we find that Article I, Paragraph 7, of the New Jersey Constitution protects an individual's privacy interest in the subscriber information he or she provides to an Internet service provider.

The New Jersey Wiretapping and Electronic Surveillance Control Act offers additional support for concluding that internet users have a reasonable expectation of privacy in their own subscriber information kept by an ISP. The Wiretap Act provides for disclosure of subscriber information, including name, address, telephone number, and means of payment, *only* when a law enforcement agency obtains "a grand jury or trial subpoena or when the State Commission of Investigation issues a subpoena." The Legislature's decision to protect disclosure of ISP information absent a subpoena is consistent with the privacy protection we recognize today.

One additional point bears mention about the right to privacy in ISP subscriber information: the reasonableness of the privacy interest may change as technology evolves. A *reasonable* expectation of privacy is required to establish a protected privacy interest. Internet users today enjoy relatively complete IP address anonymity when surfing the Web. Given the current state of technology, the dynamic, temporarily assigned, numerical IP address cannot be matched to an individual user without the help of an ISP. Therefore, we accept as reasonable the expectation that one's identity will not be discovered through a string of numbers left behind on a website.

The availability of IP Address Locator Websites has not altered that expectation because they reveal the name and address of service providers but not individual users. Should that reality change over time, the reasonableness of the expectation of privacy in Internet subscriber information might change as well. For example, if one day new software allowed individuals to type IP addresses into a "reverse directory" and identify the name of a user — as is possible with reverse telephone directories — today's ruling might need to be reexamined.

[The court thereafter determined that the subpoena by which the government had obtained the information was defective but that, if a proper one was issued, the government could reacquire the same information.] Suppression under the circumstances present here does not mean that the evidence is lost in its entirety. Comcast's records existed independently of the faulty process the police followed. And unlike a confession coerced from a defendant in violation of her constitutional rights, the record does not suggest that police conduct in this case in any way affected the records Comcast kept. As a result, the records can be reliably reproduced and lawfully reacquired through a proper grand jury subpoena.

————————

Likewise, employees often waive any privacy interests in their use of work-related computers as a condition of employment. No such waiver occurred here.

Note

Subscriber Information. Numerous courts have held that there is no Fourth Amendment protection against the disclosure of subscriber information by Internet service providers. *See Guest v. Leis*, 255 F.3d 325, 336 (6th Cir. 2001) (noting that "computer users do not have a legitimate expectation of privacy in their subscriber information because they have conveyed it to another person—the system operator"); *United States v. Cox*, 190 F. Supp. 2d 330 (N.D.N.Y. 2002) (no reasonable expectation in subscriber information provided to Internet service provider); *United States v. Kennedy*, 81 F. Supp. 2d 1103, 1110 (D. Kan. 2000) (same); *United States v. Hambrick*, 55 F. Supp. 2d 504, 507–09 (W.D. Va. 1999) (individual has no reasonable expectation of privacy in his name, address, social security number, credit card number, screen name, and proof of Internet connection obtained from Internet service provider); *Hause v. Commonwealth*, 83 S.W.3d 1, 10–12 (Ky. Ct. App. 2001) (no standing of subscriber to challenge warrant that obtained his name, address, and screen name from Internet service provider).

§ 11.3 Voluntary Exposure/Assumption of Risk

1. Peer-to-Peer Distribution Schemes

Peer-to-Peer networks are widely used for a variety of illegal activities, including copyright violations involving movies and music. It is a primary distribution scheme for child pornographers. A person seeking to trade files can download software that permits him to configure his computer to join such networks and share files. For example, one file sharing program was *Limewire*. (That filesharing program has now been permanently shut down as a result of protracted litigation.[8]) It was described as follows:

> LimeWire is a file-sharing program that can be downloaded from the internet free of charge; it allows users to search for and share with one another various types of files, including movies and pictures, on the computers of other persons with LimeWire. Once a user downloads the program onto his computer, the user can click on an icon that connects his computer to others on the network. Users can input search terms and receive a list of responsive files available on other computers connected to the network.[9]

Law enforcement is well aware of such networks and task forces and police departments engage in operations to identify persons utilizing peer-to-peer technology to trade illicit images. Government agents join such networks, search for files, and determine which constitute child pornography. Government agencies have software tools available to them that permit searches of large numbers of computers on a P2P

---

8. *See* www.limewire.com.
9. United States v. Ganoe, 538 F.3d 1117, 1119 (9th Cir. 2008).

network and have the ability to catch thousands of offenders. The techniques, used for years and continually becoming more sophisticated, are now widely exploited by authorities and large numbers of offenders are being identified as a result. Once a file is located, there are a few steps that must be taken to identify the computer that holds the file;[10] agents thereafter employ a warrant, consent, or (hopefully) otherwise seek to comply with Fourth Amendment satisfaction standards to search the suspect's computer. The case law is uniform that persons who put files in a folder that others can access to share on peer-to-peer networks do not have a reasonable expectation of privacy in such files.

United States v. Charles A. Borowy

595 F.3d 1045 (9th Cir. 2010)

PER CURIAM:

Borowy argues that the evidence recovered by an FBI agent who accessed his shared files on the peer-to-peer file-sharing service LimeWire was unconstitutionally obtained and that the district court should have suppressed this evidence.

On May 3, 2007, Special Agent Byron Mitchell logged onto LimeWire, a publically available peer-to-peer file-sharing computer program, to monitor trafficking in child pornography. Agent Mitchell conducted a keyword search in LimeWire using the term "Lolitaguy," a term known to be associated with child pornography. From the list of results returned by this search, Agent Mitchell identified known images of child pornography using a software program that verifies the "hash marks" of files and displays a red flag next to known images of child pornography. At least one of these files was shared through what was later determined to be Borowy's IP address. Using the "browse host" feature of LimeWire, Agent Mitchell viewed a list of the names of all of the approximately 240 files being shared from Borowy's IP address, several of which were explicitly suggestive of child pornography and two of which were red-flagged. Agent Mitchell downloaded and viewed seven files from Borowy's IP address, four of which were child pornography. Prior to downloading the files, Agent Mitchell did not have access to the files' contents. Execution of a search warrant resulting from Agent Mitchell's investigation led to the seizure of Borowy's laptop computer, CDs, and floppy disks. Forensic examination of these items revealed more than six hundred images of child pornography, including seventy-five videos.

Borowy moved to suppress this evidence, arguing that Agent Mitchell's activities in locating and downloading the files from LimeWire constituted a warrantless search and seizure without probable cause that violated Borowy's Fourth Amendment rights. Borowy argued that because he had purchased and installed a version of LimeWire that allows the user to prevent others from downloading or viewing

---

10. *See, e.g.*, United States v. Craighead, 539 F.3d 1073 (9th Cir. 2008).

the names of files on his computer and because he attempted to engage this feature, he had a reasonable expectation of privacy in the files. However, for whatever reason, this feature was not engaged when Agent Mitchell downloaded the seven files from Borowy's computer, and there was no restriction on Agent Mitchell's accessing those files.

Government conduct qualifies as a search only if it violates a reasonable expectation of privacy. Whether Agent Mitchell engaged in an unconstitutional search and seizure is largely controlled by *United States v. Ganoe*, 538 F.3d 1117, 1127 (9th Cir. 2008), which held that the defendant's expectation of privacy in his personal computer could not "survive [his] decision to install and use file-sharing software, thereby opening his computer to anyone else with the same freely available program." This result is consistent with that of other circuits that have considered the issue.

Borowy argues that his case is distinguishable from *Ganoe* because of his ineffectual effort to prevent LimeWire from sharing his files. However, as in *Ganoe*, "[t]he crux of [Borowy's] argument is that he simply did not know that others would be able to access files stored on his own computer" and that, although Borowy intended to render the files private, his "technical savvy" failed him. Borowy, like Ganoe, was clearly aware that LimeWire was a file-sharing program that would allow the public at large to access files in his shared folder unless he took steps to avoid it. Despite his efforts, Borowy's files were still entirely exposed to public view; anyone with access to LimeWire could download and view his files without hindrance. Borowy's subjective intention not to share his files did not create an objectively reasonable expectation of privacy in the face of such widespread public access. Because Borowy lacked a reasonable expectation of privacy in the shared files, Agent Mitchell's use of a keyword search to locate these files did not violate the Fourth Amendment.

Borowy also argues that the use of a "forensic software program" that is unavailable to the general public to confirm that the files contained child pornography rendered Agent Mitchell's conduct an unlawful Fourth Amendment search. We disagree. Borowy had already exposed the entirety of the contents of his files to the public, negating any reasonable expectation of privacy in those files. Moreover, the hash-mark analysis appears to disclose only whether the files in the list that Agent Mitchell's keyword search returned were known child pornography. In this context, the hash-mark analysis functioned simply as a sorting mechanism to prevent the government from having to sift, one by one, through Borowy's already publically exposed files.[n.2][11]

---

11. [n.2] Because we decide only the case in front of us, we reject Borowy's argument that our decision will allow unrestricted government access to all internet communications. We do not rule on whether, if confronted with different facts—for example, where the information was not already exposed to the public at large, where the hash-mark analysis might reveal more than whether a file is known child pornography, or where the government "vacuumed" vast quantities of data indiscriminately—we might find a Fourth Amendment violation. Here we are presented only with the limited case of a targeted search of publicly exposed information for known items of contraband.

Note

P2P and local networks. The same principles of voluntary exposure and assumption of risk have been applied to P2P activities on local networks. *See, e.g., United States v. King*, 509 F.3d 1338 (11th Cir. 2007):

> King resided in a dormitory at the Prince Sultan Air Base in Saudi Arabia. During his stay in the dormitory, King kept his personal laptop computer in his room and connected it to the base network. King understood that as a user of the base network, his activities on the network were subject to monitoring. King also believed that he had secured his computer so that others could not access the contents of its hard drive.
>
> On February 23, 2003, an enlisted airman was searching the base network for music files when he came across King's computer on the network. The airman was able to access King's hard drive because it was a "shared" drive. In addition to finding music files on King's computer, the airman also discovered a pornographic movie and text files "of a pornographic nature." The airman reported his discovery to a military investigator who in turn referred the matter to a computer specialist. This specialist located King's computer and hard drive on the base network and verified the presence of pornographic videos and explicit text files on the computer. She also discovered a folder on the hard drive labeled "pedophilia." The folder, however, contained no files. The computer specialist did not employ any "special means" to access King's computer because "everybody on the entire network" could obtain the same access.
>
> The computer specialist then filed a report with the investigator detailing what she had found, and the investigator obtained a search warrant for King's room. During a search of his room, military officials seized King's computer and also found CDs containing child pornography.

Rejecting King's claim that he had a reasonable expectation of privacy in the P2P files, the court reasoned in part:

> It is undisputed that King's files were "shared" over the entire base network, and that everyone on the network had access to all of his files and could observe them in exactly the same manner as the computer specialist did. Rather than analyzing the military official's actions as a search of King's personal computer in his private dorm room, it is more accurate to say that the authorities conducted a search of the military network, and King's computer files were a part of that network. King's files were exposed to thousands of individuals with network access, and the military authorities encountered the files without employing any special means or intruding into any area which King could reasonably expect would remain private. The contents of his computer's hard drive were akin to items stored in the unsecured

common areas of a multi-unit apartment building or put in a dumpster accessible to the public.

―――――――

2. Email Received and Chatroom Communications

Other preferred ways to use the Internet to trade and distribute child pornography include websites designed for that purpose and chat rooms, which are used to establish contacts and followed by transmission or trading of images. *See, e.g.,* *United States v. Hay*, 231 F.3d 630, 636 (9th Cir. 2000). Such forms of communication are, of course, used by millions of others for legal and illegal activities.

―――――――

Commonwealth v. Robert D. Proetto
771 A.2d 823 (Pa. Super. Ct. 2001)

DEL SOLE, J.:

Appellant, while a police officer, was arrested for criminal solicitation, dissemination of obscene materials and corruption of minors. These charges stemmed from his communications with a 15-year-old girl over the Internet.

The 15-year-old complainant, "E.E.," was connected to the Internet and while on the Internet was using the screen name "Ellynn." She was in a public chat room when she began receiving private chat messages from Appellant, who was using the screen name "CR907." While in this public chat room, E.E. was invited to enter a private chat room and converse "real time" with the person using the name "CR907." Appellant informed E.E. that he was a police officer working for the Colonial Regional Police Department and e-mailed her a picture of him in police uniform, telling her 907 was his badge number. E.E. informed Appellant that she was 15 years of age. Logs, printed hard copies of their on-line conversations, reflect that Appellant asked E.E. to videotape herself in the nude masturbating with her legs spread. Appellant also expressed interest in performing numerous sexual acts with her. While making these comments, Appellant stated that he had to be careful because E.E. was only 15 years old. Subsequently, Appellant transmitted to E.E. via e-mail a file containing a photograph of his erect penis.

During the next week, E.E. and Appellant chatted several more times. During these chats, Appellant made explicit remarks and repeatedly expressed his desire to talk on the telephone, meet, and engage in sexual acts with this 15-year-old girl. After each chat with CR907, E.E. logged, or saved, the Internet chat messages.

Shortly thereafter, E.E. reported these incidents to the Bristol Borough Police Department. Detective Randy Morris was assigned to investigate the charges. E.E. gave Detective Morris a diskette containing logs of the chat dialogues, e-mail messages and the two photographs Appellant had e-mailed to her. Detective Morris instructed E.E. to cease all communication with Appellant, but to page him the next time that Appellant was observed on-line.

A few days later, E.E. contacted Detective Morris when she saw CR907 in another public chat room. Detective Morris entered the chat room using the screen name "Kelly15F" and initiated conversation with Appellant. During that chat, Appellant wrote to Kelly15F that he would not mind kissing a 15-year-old as long as she would not tell anybody. He also suggested she make a nude videotape of herself in exchange for his sending her nude photographs of himself. Detective Morris made a log of the chat. The next day the matter was referred to the Bucks County District Attorney's Office and Appellant was subsequently arrested.

[Appellant sought to suppress evidence of the emails and chatroom conversations he had with E.E.]

As another court addressing this issue noted:

> E-mail transmissions are not unlike other forms of modern communication. . . . For example, if a sender of first-class mail seals an envelope and addresses it to another person, the sender can reasonably expect the contents to remain private and free from the eyes of the police absent a search warrant founded upon probable cause. However, once the letter is received and opened, the destiny of the letter then lies in the control of the recipient of the letter, not the sender, absent some legal privilege. . . . Thus an e-mail message, like a letter, cannot be afforded a reasonable expectation of privacy once that message is received.

Because E.E. received the e-mail messages and could forward them to anyone, Appellant had no reasonable expectation of privacy in them. Accordingly, there was no violation of his constitutional rights.

Moreover, Appellant could not have a reasonable expectation of privacy in his chat-room communications. When Appellant engaged in chat-room conversations, he did not know to whom he was speaking. Oftentimes individuals engaging in chat-room conversations pretend to be someone other than who they are. Appellant could not have a reasonable expectation of privacy in engaging in chat-room conversations.

Accordingly, the court did not err in failing to suppress the electronic communications first received by E.E. on the grounds that they were obtained in violation of Appellant's constitutional rights.

———————

People v. David Gariano

852 N.E.2d 344 (Ill. App. Ct. 2006)

Justice Sheila M. O'Brien delivered the opinion of the court:

Investigator Daniel K. Everett of the Chicago police department testified that in September 2001 he was assigned to the special investigations unit of the Youth Division where he investigated crimes against children committed over the Internet.

He created a "profile," a personal history associated with an AOL screen name that includes information such as gender, marital status, hobbies, and location, and used the "screen name" BrianN118. Nothing in Everett's "profile" indicated BrianN118's age. Everett testified that he was posing as an underage teenage boy under the screen name BrianN118.

Everett testified he monitored AOL chat rooms daily, entered the chat room to see who else was in the chat room, and waited to see if he was contacted by anyone using AOL's instant messaging.

The Unit supplied Everett with "power tools," a computer software program that enabled him to record, save, and print verbatim the words transmitted by defendant to Everett while using AOL's instant messaging. Everett testified that power tools transcribed instant messages on an immediate basis, similar to a court reporter.

AOL instant messaging is a private, one-on-one, in-time, electronic conversation between the sender and receiver, like a telephone call. Only the sender and receiver have access to instant messages.

On September 5, 2001, and September 6, 11, 17, 18, 19 and 21, 2001, Everett corresponded with defendant using instant messages. Everett activated the power tools program to automatically transcribe all of their messages. Defendant's AOL screen names were "Clncutexec" and "Ddgariano." Everett testified that he did not obtain defendant's consent to transcribe the instant messages. Everett used power tools to transcribe 23 pages of instant message conversations he had with defendant during these seven days.

Everett testified that he never intended that his instant message communications with defendant would be private.

Defendant called Jerry Saperstein, an expert in computer forensics and AOL protocols, as his witness. Saperstein testified, *inter alia*, to the four different methods of communication on AOL and testified that only a third party, like a hacker, deliberately attempting to intercept an instant message would be privy to the text in instant messages.

Saperstein concluded his testimony by testifying that instant messaging is one-on-one, real-time, private communication across a network. Instant messaging is a specific protocol that can only involve two people.

Everett, as BrianN118, had several instant message conversations with defendant, under either his Clncutexec or Ddgariano screen names. The parties discussed sex during the instant message conversations, and Everett retained all of defendant's instant messages by activating his power tools software.

Everett testified that on September 21, 2001, he and defendant agreed by instant message to meet at the corner of Illinois and State Streets on September 24, 2001, and to go to defendant's apartment to engage in sex. Defendant gave BrianN118 his telephone number, and on September 24, 2001, one of Everett's fellow officers spoke with defendant by phone, and the parties made the final meeting arrangements and discussed the clothing that each man would be wearing. Police officers observed defendant waiting at the prearranged meeting location, wearing the clothing he described on the telephone, and arrested him.

The instant message transcripts were read into the record [at the trial].

United States v. White, 401 U.S. 745 (1971), is dispositive. In *White*, the United States Supreme Court held:

> "[A] police agent who conceals his police connections may write down for official use his conversations with a defendant and testify concerning them, without a warrant authorizing his encounters with the defendant and without otherwise violating the latter's Fourth Amendment rights. For constitutional purposes, no different result is required if the agent instead of immediately reporting and transcribing his conversations with defendant, either (1) simultaneously records them with electronic equipment which he is carrying on his person; (2) or carries radio equipment which simultaneously transmits the conversations either to recording equipment located elsewhere or to other agents monitoring the transmitting frequency. If the conduct and revelations of an agent operating without electronic equipment do not invade the defendant's constitutionally justifiable expectations of privacy, neither does a simultaneous recording of the same conversations made by the agent or by others from transmissions received from the agent to whom the defendant is talking and whose trustworthiness the defendant necessarily risks."

Notes

The Fourth Amendment risk analysis has been uniformly applied to statements made in Internet chat rooms. *See Guest v. Leis*, 255 F.3d 325, 333 (6th Cir. 2001) (no expectation of privacy in material posted on bulletin board system that had disclaimer that personal communications were not private); *State v. Evers*, 815 A.2d 432, 439–40 (N.J. 2003) (person had no reasonable expectation of privacy in "pornographic material he unloosed into the electronic stream of commerce when he e-mailed two photographs . . . to fifty-one chat-room subscribers"). As one court has stated: "Clearly, when Defendant engaged in chat room conversations, he ran the risk of speaking with an undercover agent." *United States v. Charbonneau*, 979 F. Supp. 1177, 1185 (S.D. Ohio 1997).

§ 11.4 Information Obtained from Third Parties and from the Cloud

Carpenter is a big case — not only for digital evidence but for Fourth Amendment analysis broadly. It is also big for another reason — a combined 119 printed pages — and to do justice to it, large parts are reproduced here. This Chapter's treatment of *Carpenter* is divided into two parts. Part I: The majority worked within the *Katz*-reasonable expectation of privacy framework and ignored much of the dissents to the extent that each of them criticized *Katz* and sought to create alternatives to it to ground Fourth Amendment rights. Taking the majority opinion in isolation and working within that framework, there are many questions about the majority's opinion and the government's ability to obtain various types of digital evidence based on that opinion. Questions specifically addressed to the majority opinion are raised in the notes that follow it. Part II: The second part follows the notes and questions regarding the majority opinion. That part utilizes substantial sections of the dissents' alternative views of what the Amendment protects and its role in regulating the acquisition of digital evidence. It offers an opportunity for a broader discussion of Fourth Amendment theory.

Chapter 2 of this book introduced the fundamental framework of the Fourth Amendment, and two of those fundamentals are on full display in *Carpenter*: What does the Amendment protect? When is it satisfied? The *Carpenter* majority modestly stated that its opinion was a "narrow" one, but dissenting Justice Alito called it "revolutionary." Which is it?

1. The *Carpenter* Majority Opinion

Timothy Ivory Carpenter v. United States

585 U.S. ___, 138 S. Ct. 2206 (2018)

ROBERTS, C.J., delivered the opinion of the Court, in which GINSBURG, BREYER, SOTOMAYOR, and KAGAN, JJ., joined. KENNEDY, J., filed a dissenting opinion, in which THOMAS and ALITO, JJ., joined. THOMAS, J., filed a dissenting opinion. ALITO, J., filed a dissenting opinion, in which THOMAS, J., joined. GORSUCH, J., filed a dissenting opinion.

Chief Justice ROBERTS delivered the opinion of the Court.

This case presents the question whether the Government conducts a search under the Fourth Amendment when it accesses historical cell phone records that provide a comprehensive chronicle of the user's past movements.

I

There are 396 million cell phone service accounts in the United States — for a Nation of 326 million people. Cell phones perform their wide and growing variety of functions by connecting to a set of radio antennas called "cell sites." Although cell sites are usually mounted on a tower, they can also be found on light posts, flagpoles, church steeples, or the sides of buildings. Cell sites typically have several directional antennas that divide the covered area into sectors.

Cell phones continuously scan their environment looking for the best signal, which generally comes from the closest cell site. Most modern devices, such as smartphones, tap into the wireless network several times a minute whenever their signal is on, even if the owner is not using one of the phone's features. Each time the phone connects to a cell site, it generates a time-stamped record known as cell-site location information (CSLI). The precision of this information depends on the size of the geographic area covered by the cell site. The greater the concentration of cell sites, the smaller the coverage area. As data usage from cell phones has increased, wireless carriers have installed more cell sites to handle the traffic. That has led to increasingly compact coverage areas, especially in urban areas.

Wireless carriers collect and store CSLI for their own business purposes, including finding weak spots in their network and applying "roaming" charges when another carrier routes data through their cell sites. In addition, wireless carriers often sell aggregated location records to data brokers, without individual identifying information of the sort at issue here. While carriers have long retained CSLI for the start and end of incoming calls, in recent years phone companies have also collected location information from the transmission of text messages and routine data connections. Accordingly, modern cell phones generate increasingly vast amounts of increasingly precise CSLI.

In 2011, police officers arrested four men suspected of robbing a series of Radio Shack and (ironically enough) T-Mobile stores in Detroit. One of the men confessed that, over the previous four months, the group (along with a rotating cast of getaway drivers and lookouts) had robbed nine different stores in Michigan and Ohio. The suspect identified 15 accomplices who had participated in the heists and gave the FBI some of their cell phone numbers; the FBI then reviewed his call records to identify additional numbers that he had called around the time of the robberies.

Based on that information, the prosecutors applied for court orders under the Stored Communications Act to obtain cell phone records for petitioner Timothy Carpenter and several other suspects. That statute, as amended in 1994, permits the Government to compel the disclosure of certain telecommunications records when it "offers specific and articulable facts showing that there are reasonable grounds to believe" that the records sought "are relevant and material to an ongoing criminal investigation." 18 U.S.C. § 2703(d). Federal Magistrate Judges issued two orders directing Carpenter's wireless carriers — MetroPCS and Sprint — to disclose "cell/site sector [information] for [Carpenter's] telephone[] at call origination and at call termination for incoming and outgoing calls" during the four-month period when the string of robberies occurred. The first order sought 152 days of cell-site records from MetroPCS, which produced records spanning 127 days. The second order requested seven days of CSLI from Sprint, which produced two days of records covering the period when Carpenter's phone was "roaming" in northeastern Ohio. Altogether the Government obtained 12,898 location points cataloging Carpenter's movements — an average of 101 data points per day.

Carpenter was charged with six counts of robbery and an additional six counts of carrying a firearm during a federal crime of violence. Prior to trial, Carpenter moved to suppress the cell-site data provided by the wireless carriers. He argued that the

Government's seizure of the records violated the Fourth Amendment because they had been obtained without a warrant supported by probable cause. The District Court denied the motion. At trial, seven of Carpenter's confederates pegged him as the leader of the operation. In addition, FBI agent Christopher Hess offered expert testimony about the cell-site data. Hess explained that each time a cell phone taps into the wireless network, the carrier logs a time-stamped record of the cell site and particular sector that were used. With this information, Hess produced maps that placed Carpenter's phone near four of the charged robberies. In the Government's view, the location records clinched the case: They confirmed that Carpenter was "right where the . . . robbery was at the exact time of the robbery." Carpenter was convicted on all but one of the firearm counts and sentenced to more than 100 years in prison.

II

A

The Fourth Amendment protects "[t]he right of the people to be secure in their persons, houses, papers, and effects, against unreasonable searches and seizures." The "basic purpose of this Amendment," our cases have recognized, "is to safeguard the privacy and security of individuals against arbitrary invasions by governmental officials."

For much of our history, Fourth Amendment search doctrine was "tied to common-law trespass" and focused on whether the Government "obtains information by physically intruding on a constitutionally protected area." *United States v. Jones,* 565 U.S. 400 (2012). More recently, the Court has recognized that "property rights are not the sole measure of Fourth Amendment violations." In *Katz v. United States,* 389 U.S. 347, 351 (1967), we established that "the Fourth Amendment protects people, not places," and expanded our conception of the Amendment to protect certain expectations of privacy as well. When an individual "seeks to preserve something as private," and his expectation of privacy is "one that society is prepared to recognize as reasonable," we have held that official intrusion into that private sphere generally qualifies as a search and requires a warrant supported by probable cause.

Although no single rubric definitively resolves which expectations of privacy are entitled to protection, the analysis is informed by historical understandings "of what was deemed an unreasonable search and seizure when [the Fourth Amendment] was adopted." On this score, our cases have recognized some basic guideposts. First, that the Amendment seeks to secure "the privacies of life" against "arbitrary power." *Boyd v. United States,* 116 U.S. 616, 630 (1886). Second, and relatedly, that a central aim of the Framers was "to place obstacles in the way of a too permeating police surveillance."

We have kept this attention to Founding-era understandings in mind when applying the Fourth Amendment to innovations in surveillance tools. As technology has enhanced the Government's capacity to encroach upon areas normally guarded from inquisitive eyes, this Court has sought to "assure[] preservation of that degree of privacy against government that existed when the Fourth Amendment was adopted." *Kyllo v. United States,* 533 U.S. 27, 34 (2001). For that reason, we rejected in *Kyllo* a "mechanical interpretation" of the Fourth Amendment and held that use of a thermal imager to detect heat radiating from the side of the defendant's home was a search. Because any other conclusion would leave homeowners "at the mercy of advancing technology," we determined that the Government—absent a warrant—could not capitalize on such new sense-enhancing technology to explore what was happening within the home.

Likewise in *Riley v. California,* 573 U.S.—(2014), the Court recognized the "immense storage capacity" of modern cell phones in holding that police officers must generally obtain a warrant before searching the contents of a phone. We explained that while the general rule allowing warrantless searches incident to arrest "strikes the appropriate balance in the context of physical objects, neither of its rationales has much force with respect to" the vast store of sensitive information on a cell phone.

B

The case before us involves the Government's acquisition of wireless carrier cell-site records revealing the location of Carpenter's cell phone whenever it made or received calls. This sort of digital data—personal location information maintained by a third party—does not fit neatly under existing precedents. Instead, requests for cell-site records lie at the intersection of two lines of cases, both of which inform our understanding of the privacy interests at stake.

The first set of cases addresses a person's expectation of privacy in his physical location and movements. In *United States v. Knotts,* 460 U.S. 276 (1983), we considered the Government's use of a "beeper" to aid in tracking a vehicle through traffic. Police officers in that case planted a beeper in a container of chloroform before it was purchased by one of Knotts's co-conspirators. The officers (with intermittent aerial assistance) then followed the automobile carrying the container from Minneapolis to Knotts's cabin in Wisconsin, relying on the beeper's signal to help keep the vehicle in view. The Court concluded that the "augment[ed]" visual surveillance did not constitute a search because "[a] person traveling in an automobile on public thoroughfares has no reasonable expectation of privacy in his movements from one place to another." Since the movements of the vehicle and its final destination had been "voluntarily conveyed to anyone who wanted to look," Knotts could not assert a privacy interest in the information obtained.

This Court in *Knotts,* however, was careful to distinguish between the rudimentary tracking facilitated by the beeper and more sweeping modes of surveillance. The Court emphasized the "limited use which the government made of the signals from this particular beeper" during a discrete "automotive journey." Significantly, the Court reserved the question whether "different constitutional principles may be applicable" if "twenty-four hour surveillance of any citizen of this country [were] possible."

Three decades later, the Court considered more sophisticated surveillance of the sort envisioned in *Knotts* and found that different principles did indeed apply. In *United States v. Jones,* [565 U.S. 400 (2012),] FBI agents installed a GPS tracking device on Jones's vehicle and remotely monitored the vehicle's movements for 28 days. The Court decided the case based on the Government's physical trespass of the vehicle. At the same time, five Justices agreed that related privacy concerns would be raised by, for example, "surreptitiously activating a stolen vehicle detection system" in Jones's car to track Jones himself, or conducting GPS tracking of his cell phone. Since GPS monitoring of a vehicle tracks "every movement" a person makes in that vehicle, the concurring Justices concluded that "longer term GPS monitoring in investigations of most offenses impinges on expectations of privacy"—regardless whether those movements were disclosed to the public at large.[n.2][12]

In a second set of decisions, the Court has drawn a line between what a person keeps to himself and what he shares with others. We have previously held that "a person has no legitimate expectation of privacy in information he voluntarily turns over to third parties." *Smith v. Maryland*, 442 U.S. 735 (1979). That remains true "even if the information is revealed on the assumption that it will be used only for a limited purpose." *United States v. Miller*, 425 U.S. 435 (1976). As a result, the Government is typically free to obtain such information from the recipient without triggering Fourth Amendment protections.

This third-party doctrine largely traces its roots to *Miller*. While investigating Miller for tax evasion, the Government subpoenaed his banks, seeking several months of canceled checks, deposit slips, and monthly statements. The Court rejected a Fourth Amendment challenge to the records collection. For one, Miller could "assert neither ownership nor possession" of the documents; they were "business records of the banks." For another, the nature of those records confirmed Miller's limited expectation of privacy, because the checks were "not confidential communications but negotiable instruments to be used in commercial transactions," and the bank statements contained information "exposed to [bank] employees in the ordinary course of business." The Court thus concluded that Miller had "take[n] the risk, in revealing his affairs to another, that the information [would] be conveyed by that person to the Government."

Three years later, *Smith* applied the same principles in the context of information conveyed to a telephone company. The Court ruled that the Government's use of a pen register—a device that recorded the outgoing phone numbers dialed on a landline telephone—was not a search. Noting the pen register's "limited capabilities,"

---

12. [n.2] Justice Kennedy argues that this case is in a different category from *Jones* and the dragnet-type practices posited in *Knotts* because the disclosure of the cell-site records was subject to "judicial authorization." That line of argument conflates the threshold question whether a "search" has occurred with the separate matter of whether the search was reasonable. The subpoena process set forth in the Stored Communications Act does not determine a target's expectation of privacy.

the Court "doubt[ed] that people in general entertain any actual expectation of privacy in the numbers they dial." Telephone subscribers know, after all, that the numbers are used by the telephone company "for a variety of legitimate business purposes," including routing calls. And at any rate, the Court explained, such an expectation "is not one that society is prepared to recognize as reasonable." When Smith placed a call, he "voluntarily conveyed" the dialed numbers to the phone company by "expos[ing] that information to its equipment in the ordinary course of business." Once again, we held that the defendant "assumed the risk" that the company's records "would be divulged to police."

III

The question we confront today is how to apply the Fourth Amendment to a new phenomenon: the ability to chronicle a person's past movements through the record of his cell phone signals. Such tracking partakes of many of the qualities of the GPS monitoring we considered in *Jones*. Much like GPS tracking of a vehicle, cell phone location information is detailed, encyclopedic, and effortlessly compiled.

At the same time, the fact that the individual continuously reveals his location to his wireless carrier implicates the third-party principle of *Smith* and *Miller*. But while the third-party doctrine applies to telephone numbers and bank records, it is not clear whether its logic extends to the qualitatively different category of cell-site records. After all, when *Smith* was decided in 1979, few could have imagined a society in which a phone goes wherever its owner goes, conveying to the wireless carrier not just dialed digits, but a detailed and comprehensive record of the person's movements.

We decline to extend *Smith* and *Miller* to cover these novel circumstances. Given the unique nature of cell phone location records, the fact that the information is held by a third party does not by itself overcome the user's claim to Fourth Amendment protection. Whether the Government employs its own surveillance technology as in *Jones* or leverages the technology of a wireless carrier, we hold that an individual maintains a legitimate expectation of privacy in the record of his physical movements as captured through CSLI. The location information obtained from Carpenter's wireless carriers was the product of a search.[n.3][13]

A

A person does not surrender all Fourth Amendment protection by venturing into the public sphere. A majority of this Court has already recognized that individuals

---

13. [n.3] The parties suggest as an alternative to their primary submissions that the acquisition of CSLI becomes a search only if it extends beyond a limited period. As part of its argument, the Government treats the seven days of CSLI requested from Sprint as the pertinent period, even though Sprint produced only two days of records. Contrary to Justice Kennedy's assertion, we need not decide whether there is a limited period for which the Government may obtain an individual's historical CSLI free from Fourth Amendment scrutiny, and if so, how long that period might be. It is sufficient for our purposes today to hold that accessing seven days of CSLI constitutes a Fourth Amendment search.

have a reasonable expectation of privacy in the whole of their physical movements. Prior to the digital age, law enforcement might have pursued a suspect for a brief stretch, but doing so "for any extended period of time was difficult and costly and therefore rarely undertaken." For that reason, "society's expectation has been that law enforcement agents and others would not—and indeed, in the main, simply could not—secretly monitor and catalogue every single movement of an individual's car for a very long period."

Allowing government access to cell-site records contravenes that expectation. Although such records are generated for commercial purposes, that distinction does not negate Carpenter's anticipation of privacy in his physical location. Mapping a cell phone's location over the course of 127 days provides an all-encompassing record of the holder's whereabouts. As with GPS information, the time-stamped data provides an intimate window into a person's life, revealing not only his particular movements, but through them his "familial, political, professional, religious, and sexual associations." These location records "hold for many Americans the 'privacies of life.'" And like GPS monitoring, cell phone tracking is remarkably easy, cheap, and efficient compared to traditional investigative tools. With just the click of a button, the Government can access each carrier's deep repository of historical location information at practically no expense.

In fact, historical cell-site records present even greater privacy concerns than the GPS monitoring of a vehicle we considered in *Jones.* Unlike the bugged container in *Knotts* or the car in *Jones,* a cell phone—almost a "feature of human anatomy"—tracks nearly exactly the movements of its owner. While individuals regularly leave their vehicles, they compulsively carry cell phones with them all the time. A cell phone faithfully follows its owner beyond public thoroughfares and into private residences, doctor's offices, political headquarters, and other potentially revealing locales. Accordingly, when the Government tracks the location of a cell phone it achieves near perfect surveillance, as if it had attached an ankle monitor to the phone's user.

Moreover, the retrospective quality of the data here gives police access to a category of information otherwise unknowable. In the past, attempts to reconstruct a person's movements were limited by a dearth of records and the frailties of recollection. With access to CSLI, the Government can now travel back in time to retrace a person's whereabouts, subject only to the retention polices of the wireless carriers, which currently maintain records for up to five years. Critically, because location information is continually logged for all of the 400 million devices in the United States—not just those belonging to persons who might happen to come under investigation—this newfound tracking capacity runs against everyone. Unlike with the GPS device in *Jones,* police need not even know in advance whether they want to follow a particular individual, or when.

Whoever the suspect turns out to be, he has effectively been tailed every moment of every day for five years, and the police may—in the Government's view—call upon the results of that surveillance without regard to the constraints of the Fourth

Amendment. Only the few without cell phones could escape this tireless and absolute surveillance.

The Government and Justice Kennedy contend, however, that the collection of CSLI should be permitted because the data is less precise than GPS information. Not to worry, they maintain, because the location records did "not on their own suffice to place [Carpenter] at the crime scene"; they placed him within a wedge-shaped sector ranging from one-eighth to four square miles. Yet the Court has already rejected the proposition that "inference insulates a search." From the 127 days of location data it received, the Government could, in combination with other information, deduce a detailed log of Carpenter's movements, including when he was at the site of the robberies. And the Government thought the CSLI accurate enough to highlight it during the closing argument of his trial.

At any rate, the rule the Court adopts "must take account of more sophisticated systems that are already in use or in development." While the records in this case reflect the state of technology at the start of the decade, the accuracy of CSLI is rapidly approaching GPS-level precision. As the number of cell sites has proliferated, the geographic area covered by each cell sector has shrunk, particularly in urban areas. In addition, with new technology measuring the time and angle of signals hitting their towers, wireless carriers already have the capability to pinpoint a phone's location within 50 meters.

Accordingly, when the Government accessed CSLI from the wireless carriers, it invaded Carpenter's reasonable expectation of privacy in the whole of his physical movements.

B

The Government's primary contention to the contrary is that the third-party doctrine governs this case. In its view, cell-site records are fair game because they are "business records" created and maintained by the wireless carriers. The Government (along with Justice Kennedy) recognizes that this case features new technology, but asserts that the legal question nonetheless turns on a garden-variety request for information from a third-party witness.

The Government's position fails to contend with the seismic shifts in digital technology that made possible the tracking of not only Carpenter's location but also everyone else's, not for a short period but for years and years. Sprint Corporation and its competitors are not your typical witnesses. Unlike the nosy neighbor who keeps an eye on comings and goings, they are ever alert, and their memory is nearly infallible. There is a world of difference between the limited types of personal information addressed in *Smith* and *Miller* and the exhaustive chronicle of location information casually collected by wireless carriers today. The Government thus is not asking for a straightforward application of the third-party doctrine, but instead a significant extension of it to a distinct category of information.

The third-party doctrine partly stems from the notion that an individual has a reduced expectation of privacy in information knowingly shared with another. But the fact of "diminished privacy interests does not mean that the Fourth Amendment falls out of the picture entirely." *Smith* and *Miller,* after all, did not rely solely on the act of sharing. Instead, they considered "the nature of the particular documents sought" to determine whether "there is a legitimate 'expectation of privacy' concerning their contents." *Smith* pointed out the limited capabilities of a pen register; as explained in *Riley,* telephone call logs reveal little in the way of "identifying information." *Miller* likewise noted that checks were "not confidential communications but negotiable instruments to be used in commercial transactions." In mechanically applying the third-party doctrine to this case, the Government fails to appreciate that there are no comparable limitations on the revealing nature of CSLI.

The Court has in fact already shown special solicitude for location information in the third-party context. In *Knotts,* the Court relied on *Smith* to hold that an individual has no reasonable expectation of privacy in public movements that he "voluntarily conveyed to anyone who wanted to look." But when confronted with more pervasive tracking, five Justices agreed that longer term GPS monitoring of even a vehicle traveling on public streets constitutes a search. *Jones,* 565 U.S., at 430 (Alito, J., concurring in judgment); *id.,* at 415 (Sotomayor, J., concurring). Yet this case is not about "using a phone" or a person's movement at a particular time. It is about a detailed chronicle of a person's physical presence compiled every day, every moment, over several years. Such a chronicle implicates privacy concerns far beyond those considered in *Smith* and *Miller.*

Neither does the second rationale underlying the third-party doctrine—voluntary exposure—hold up when it comes to CSLI. Cell phone location information is not truly "shared" as one normally understands the term. In the first place, cell phones and the services they provide are "such a pervasive and insistent part of daily life" that carrying one is indispensable to participation in modern society. Second, a cell phone logs a cell-site record by dint of its operation, without any affirmative act on the part of the user beyond powering up. Virtually any activity on the phone generates CSLI, including incoming calls, texts, or e-mails and countless other data connections that a phone automatically makes when checking for news, weather, or social media updates. Apart from disconnecting the phone from the network, there is no way to avoid leaving behind a trail of location data. As a result, in no meaningful sense does the user voluntarily "assume[] the risk" of turning over a comprehensive dossier of his physical movements.

We therefore decline to extend *Smith* and *Miller* to the collection of CSLI. Given the unique nature of cell phone location information, the fact that the Government obtained the information from a third party does not overcome Carpenter's claim to Fourth Amendment protection. The Government's acquisition of the cell-site records was a search within the meaning of the Fourth Amendment.

* * *

Our decision today is a narrow one. We do not express a view on matters not before us: real-time CSLI or "tower dumps" (a download of information on all the devices that connected to a particular cell site during a particular interval). We do not disturb the application of *Smith* and *Miller* or call into question conventional surveillance techniques and tools, such as security cameras. Nor do we address other business records that might incidentally reveal location information. Further, our opinion does not consider other collection techniques involving foreign affairs or national security. As Justice Frankfurter noted when considering new innovations in airplanes and radios, the Court must tread carefully in such cases, to ensure that we do not "embarrass the future."

IV

Having found that the acquisition of Carpenter's CSLI was a search, we also conclude that the Government must generally obtain a warrant supported by probable cause before acquiring such records. Although the "ultimate measure of the constitutionality of a governmental search is 'reasonableness,'" our cases establish that warrantless searches are typically unreasonable where "a search is undertaken by law enforcement officials to discover evidence of criminal wrongdoing." Thus, "[i]n the absence of a warrant, a search is reasonable only if it falls within a specific exception to the warrant requirement."

The Government acquired the cell-site records pursuant to a court order issued under the Stored Communications Act, which required the Government to show "reasonable grounds" for believing that the records were "relevant and material to an ongoing investigation." 18 U.S.C. § 2703(d). That showing falls well short of the probable cause required for a warrant. The Court usually requires "some quantum of individualized suspicion" before a search or seizure may take place. Under the standard in the Stored Communications Act, however, law enforcement need only show that the cell-site evidence might be pertinent to an ongoing investigation—a "gigantic" departure from the probable cause rule. Consequently, an order issued under Section 2703(d) of the Act is not a permissible mechanism for accessing historical cell-site records. Before compelling a wireless carrier to turn over a subscriber's CSLI, the Government's obligation is a familiar one—get a warrant.

Justice Alito contends that the warrant requirement simply does not apply when the Government acquires records using compulsory process. Unlike an actual search, he says, subpoenas for documents do not involve the direct taking of evidence; they are at most a "constructive search" conducted by the target of the subpoena. Given this lesser intrusion on personal privacy, Justice Alito argues that the compulsory production of records is not held to the same probable cause standard. In his view, this Court's precedents set forth a categorical rule—separate and distinct from the third-party doctrine—subjecting subpoenas to lenient scrutiny without regard to the suspect's expectation of privacy in the records.

But this Court has never held that the Government may subpoena third parties for records in which the suspect has a reasonable expectation of privacy. Almost all of the examples Justice Alito cites contemplated requests for evidence implicating diminished privacy interests or for a corporation's own books. The lone exception, of course, is *Miller,* where the Court's analysis of the third-party subpoena merged with the application of the third-party doctrine.

Justice Alito overlooks the critical issue. At some point, the dissent should recognize that CSLI is an entirely different species of business record—something that implicates basic Fourth Amendment concerns about arbitrary government power much more directly than corporate tax or payroll ledgers. When confronting new concerns wrought by digital technology, this Court has been careful not to uncritically extend existing precedents.

If the choice to proceed by subpoena provided a categorical limitation on Fourth Amendment protection, no type of record would ever be protected by the warrant requirement. Under Justice Alito's view, private letters, digital contents of a cell phone—any personal information reduced to document form, in fact—may be collected by subpoena for no reason other than "official curiosity." Justice Kennedy declines to adopt the radical implications of this theory, leaving open the question whether the warrant requirement applies "when the Government obtains the modern-day equivalents of an individual's own 'paper' or 'effects,' even when those papers or effects are held by a third party." (citing *United States v. Warshak,* 631 F.3d 266, 283–288 (C.A.6 2010)). That would be a sensible exception, because it would prevent the subpoena doctrine from overcoming any reasonable expectation of privacy. If the third-party doctrine does not apply to the "modern-day equivalents of an individual's own 'papers' or 'effects,'" then the clear implication is that the documents should receive full Fourth Amendment protection. We simply think that such protection should extend as well to a detailed log of a person's movements over several years.

This is certainly not to say that all orders compelling the production of documents will require a showing of probable cause. The Government will be able to use subpoenas to acquire records in the overwhelming majority of investigations. We hold only that a warrant is required in the rare case where the suspect has a legitimate privacy interest in records held by a third party.

Further, even though the Government will generally need a warrant to access CSLI, case-specific exceptions may support a warrantless search of an individual's cell-site records under certain circumstances. "One well-recognized exception applies when '"the exigencies of the situation" make the needs of law enforcement so compelling that [a] warrantless search is objectively reasonable under the Fourth Amendment.'" Such exigencies include the need to pursue a fleeing suspect, protect individuals who are threatened with imminent harm, or prevent the imminent destruction of evidence.

As a result, if law enforcement is confronted with an urgent situation, such fact-specific threats will likely justify the warrantless collection of CSLI. Lower courts, for instance, have approved warrantless searches related to bomb threats, active shootings, and child abductions. Our decision today does not call into doubt warrantless access to CSLI in such circumstances. While police must get a warrant when collecting CSLI to assist in the mine-run criminal investigation, the rule we set forth does not limit their ability to respond to an ongoing emergency.

* * *

As Justice Brandeis explained in his famous dissent, the Court is obligated—as "[s]ubtler and more far-reaching means of invading privacy have become available to the Government"—to ensure that the "progress of science" does not erode Fourth Amendment protections. *Olmstead v. United States,* 277 U.S. 438 (1928). Here the progress of science has afforded law enforcement a powerful new tool to carry out its important responsibilities. At the same time, this tool risks Government encroachment of the sort the Framers, "after consulting the lessons of history," drafted the Fourth Amendment to prevent.

We decline to grant the state unrestricted access to a wireless carrier's database of physical location information. In light of the deeply revealing nature of CSLI, its depth, breadth, and comprehensive reach, and the inescapable and automatic nature of its collection, the fact that such information is gathered by a third party does not make it any less deserving of Fourth Amendment protection.

The judgment of the Court of Appeals is reversed, and the case is remanded for further proceedings consistent with this opinion.

The Majority's Opinion—Notes and Questions

1. **Subjective expectations in CSLI.** Prior to *Carpenter,* did individuals have an actual expectation of privacy in CSLI regarding their phones? Quoting *Katz,* the *Carpenter* majority stated that a person must seek to preserve something in private for it to be so. What steps do people take to preserve privacy in CSLI? Is Justice Gorsuch, in dissent, correct when he stated:

> What's left of the Fourth Amendment? Today we use the Internet to do most everything. Smartphones make it easy to keep a calendar, correspond with friends, make calls, conduct banking, and even watch the game. Countless Internet companies maintain records about us and, increasingly, *for* us. Even our most private documents—those that, in other eras, we would have locked safely in a desk drawer or destroyed—now reside on third party servers. *Smith* and *Miller* teach that the police can review all of this material, on the theory that no one reasonably expects any of it will be kept private. But no one believes that, if they ever did.

> * * * Can the government demand a copy of all your e-mails from Google or Microsoft without implicating your Fourth Amendment rights? Can it secure your DNA from 23andMe without a warrant or probable cause? *Smith* and *Miller* say yes it can—at least without running afoul of *Katz.* But that result strikes most lawyers and judges today—me included—as pretty unlikely. In the years since its adoption, countless scholars, too, have come to conclude that the "third-party doctrine is not only wrong, but horribly wrong." The reasons are obvious. "As an empirical statement

about subjective expectations of privacy," the doctrine is "quite dubious." People often *do* reasonably expect that information they entrust to third parties, especially information subject to confidentiality agreements, will be kept private. Meanwhile, if the third party doctrine is supposed to represent a normative assessment of when a person should expect privacy, the notion that the answer might be "never" seems a pretty unattractive societal prescription.

2. **Why may companies simply purchase the records from the provider but the government needs a warrant?** Consider Justice Kennedy's dissent:

> Major cell phone service providers keep cell-site records for long periods of time. There is no law requiring them to do so. Instead, providers contract with their customers to collect and keep these records because they are valuable to the providers. Among other things, providers aggregate the records and sell them to third parties along with other information gleaned from cell phone usage. This data can be used, for example, to help a department store determine which of various prospective store locations is likely to get more foot traffic from middle-aged women who live in affluent zip codes. The market for cell phone data is now estimated to be in the billions of dollars.

3. **How private is a person's physical location?** Consider the views of Justice Kennedy's dissent in *Carpenter*:

> In concluding that the Government engaged in a search, the Court unhinges Fourth Amendment doctrine from the property-based concepts that have long grounded the analytic framework that pertains in these cases. In doing so it draws an unprincipled and unworkable line between cell-site records on the one hand and financial and telephonic records on the other. According to today's majority opinion, the Government can acquire a record of every credit card purchase and phone call a person makes over months or years without upsetting a legitimate expectation of privacy. But, in the Court's view, the Government crosses a constitutional line when it obtains a court's approval to issue a subpoena for more than six days of cell-site records in order to determine whether a person was within several hundred city blocks of a crime scene. That distinction is illogical and will frustrate principled application of the Fourth Amendment in many routine yet vital law enforcement operations.
>
> * * * The Court errs, in my submission, when it concludes that cell-site records implicate greater privacy interests—and thus deserve greater Fourth Amendment protection—than financial records and telephone records.
>
> Indeed, the opposite is true. A person's movements are not particularly private. As the Court recognized in *Knotts,* when the defendant there "traveled over the public streets he voluntarily conveyed to anyone who wanted to look the fact that he was traveling over particular roads in a particular

direction, the fact of whatever stops he made, and the fact of his final destination." Today expectations of privacy in one's location are, if anything, even less reasonable than when the Court decided *Knotts* over 30 years ago. Millions of Americans choose to share their location on a daily basis, whether by using a variety of location-based services on their phones, or by sharing their location with friends and the public at large via social media.

And cell-site records, as already discussed, disclose a person's location only in a general area. The records at issue here, for example, revealed Carpenter's location within an area covering between around a dozen and several hundred city blocks. "Areas of this scale might encompass bridal stores and Bass Pro Shops, gay bars and straight ones, a Methodist church and the local mosque." These records could not reveal where Carpenter lives and works, much less his "'familial, political, professional, religious, and sexual associations.'"

By contrast, financial records and telephone records do "'revea[l] . . . personal affairs, opinions, habits and associations.'" What persons purchase and to whom they talk might disclose how much money they make; the political and religious organizations to which they donate; whether they have visited a psychiatrist, plastic surgeon, abortion clinic, or AIDS treatment center; whether they go to gay bars or straight ones; and who are their closest friends and family members. The troves of intimate information the Government can and does obtain using financial records and telephone records dwarfs what can be gathered from cell-site records.

Still, the Court maintains, cell-site records are "unique" because they are "comprehensive" in their reach; allow for retrospective collection; are "easy, cheap, and efficient compared to traditional investigative tools"; and are not exposed to cell phone service providers in a meaningfully voluntary manner. But many other kinds of business records can be so described. Financial records are of vast scope. Banks and credit card companies keep a comprehensive account of almost every transaction an individual makes on a daily basis. "With just the click of a button, the Government can access each [company's] deep repository of historical [financial] information at practically no expense." And the decision whether to transact with banks and credit card companies is no more or less voluntary than the decision whether to use a cell phone. Today, just as when *Miller* was decided, "'it is impossible to participate in the economic life of contemporary society without maintaining a bank account.'" But this Court, nevertheless, has held that individuals do not have a reasonable expectation of privacy in financial records.

Perhaps recognizing the difficulty of drawing the constitutional line between cell-site records and financial and telephonic records, the Court posits that the accuracy of cell-site records "is rapidly approaching GPS-level precision." That is certainly plausible in the era of cyber technology, yet the privacy interests associated with location information, which is often disclosed to the public at large, still would not outweigh the privacy interests implicated by financial and telephonic records.

4. **How long is enough; how much information is enough?** How many days of CSLI is enough to trigger the protections of the Amendment? Here are some of the majority's characterizations regarding historical cell phone records:

- "The first order sought 152 days of cell-site records from MetroPCS, which produced records spanning 127 days. The second order requested seven days of CSLI from Sprint, which produced two days of records covering the period when Carpenter's phone was "roaming" in northeastern Ohio. Altogether the Government obtained 12,898 location points cataloging Carpenter's movements—an average of 101 data points per day."

- It is a "qualitatively different category."

- Footnote 3:

  The parties suggest as an alternative to their primary submissions that the acquisition of CSLI becomes a search only if it extends beyond a limited period. As part of its argument, the Government treats the seven days of CSLI requested from Sprint as the pertinent period, even though Sprint produced only two days of records. Contrary to Justice Kennedy's assertion, we need not decide whether there is a limited period for which the Government may obtain an individual's historical CSLI free from Fourth Amendment scrutiny, and if so, how long that period might be. It is sufficient for our purposes today to hold that accessing seven days of CSLI constitutes a Fourth Amendment search.

- "Mapping a cell phone's location over the course of 127 days provides an all-encompassing record of the holder's whereabouts. As with GPS information, the time-stamped data provides an intimate window into a person's life, revealing not only his particular movements, but through them his "familial, political, professional, religious, and sexual associations." These location records "hold for many Americans the 'privacies of life.'"

- It offers "near perfect surveillance" of a "category of information otherwise unknowable."

- CSLI is retained by companies for up to five years and, hence, a suspect is "effectively been tailed every moment of every day for five years."

- CSLI access invaded "the whole of his physical movements."

- "We simply think that [Fourth Amendment] protection should extend as well to a detailed log of a person's movements over several years."

In *United States v. Jones*, 565 U.S. 400 (2012), government agents installed a GPS device on the undercarriage of a Jeep while the vehicle was parked in a public parking lot and then monitored it for 28 days, tracking the vehicle's movements. The Court unanimously found that a search within the meaning of the Fourth

Amendment occurred.[14] Justice Scalia, for the majority, relied on the traditional property law framework that pre-dated *Katz*. Justice Scalia had no problem demonstrating that Jones had a protected interest—a vehicle is an "effect," one of the four objects explicitly listed as protected by the Amendment. He stated: "By attaching the device to the Jeep, officers encroached on a protected area." The trespassory attachment, by itself, was insufficient to implicate the Amendment. In addition, Justice Scalia alternatively indicated that, for a search to occur, the government must have attached the device with the purpose of obtaining information or that there had to be subsequent use of the device.

Justice Alito, in his concurring opinion in which three other Justices joined, believed "the Court's reasoning largely disregard[ed] what is really important (the *use* of a GPS for the purpose of long-term tracking)." Justice Alito believed that "relatively short-term monitoring of a person's movements on public streets" did not implicate the Amendment but that "longer term GPS monitoring in investigations of most offenses" did. He saw no need to "identify with precision the point at which the tracking of this vehicle became a search, for the line was surely crossed before the 4-week mark." Justice Alito reserved on the question of whether it would apply to "extraordinary offenses," because "long-term tracking might have been mounted using previously available techniques" in such cases.

Noting the "novelty" of Justice Alito's framework, Justice Scalia, in his majority opinion, observed:

> [I]t remains unexplained why a 4-week investigation is "surely" too long and why a drug-trafficking conspiracy involving substantial amounts of cash and narcotics is not an "extraordinary offens[e]" which may permit longer observation. What of a 2-day monitoring of a suspected purveyor of stolen electronics? Or of a 6-month monitoring of a suspected terrorist?

In light of *Jones* and *Carpenter*, would "short term" CSLI be accessible without a warrant? What would "short term" be? And why would it be permissible? Should there be a difference between short-term GPS monitoring and CSLI information?

5. **Content/Non-Content Distinction.** *Smith* was premised on two grounds: the third party doctrine; and the content/non-content distinction, with that latter ground standing for the proposition that the Amendment protects the content of a conversation but not such non-content as the numbers dialed. What is the status of that distinction after *Carpenter*? Is it that CSLI *is* content? Or is that distinction now dead and instead the quest is to determine a "qualitative" difference? The Stored Communication Act is discussed in Chapter 12. It codifies much of the content/non-content distinctions in the case law that predated *Carpenter* and created a hierarchy of types of process to obtain records based in part on those distinctions. *Carpenter* clearly impacts the use of that Act to obtain information. Do we now need to

---

14. The Court only determined that the Fourth Amendment was implicated; it did not decide whether the Amendment was satisfied.

create a new list of items that are now viewed as "content" or "non-content"? Or does *Carpenter* abandon that framework and instead look for a multifactor "qualitative" difference among data held by third parties? Based on *Carpenter*, in which of the following held by third parties does a person have a reasonable expectation of privacy:

- bank records
- telephone dialing records
- real time CSLI
- credit card statements
- tower dumps (a download of information on all the devices that connected to a particular cell site during a particular interval)
- email headers
- websites visited, including URLs and website IP addresses
- to/from addresses of emails

Do you understand the *Carpenter* majority standard, and can you apply it to the items on the list? Justice Gorsuch in his dissent described the majority's opinion as "multilayered inquiry that seems to be only *Katz*-squared." Is that true or are we back to square one with *Katz*?

Consider the views of Justice Kennedy's dissent in *Carpenter*:

> The Court's decision will have ramifications that extend beyond cell-site records to other kinds of information held by third parties, yet the Court fails "to provide clear guidance to law enforcement" and courts on key issues raised by its reinterpretation of *Miller* and *Smith*.
>
> *First,* the Court's holding is premised on cell-site records being a "distinct category of information" from other business records. But the Court does not explain what makes something a distinct category of information. Whether credit card records are distinct from bank records; whether payment records from digital wallet applications are distinct from either; whether the electronic bank records available today are distinct from the paper and microfilm records at issue in *Miller*; or whether cell-phone call records are distinct from the home-phone call records at issue in *Smith*, are just a few of the difficult questions that require answers under the Court's novel conception of *Miller* and *Smith*.
>
> *Second,* the majority opinion gives courts and law enforcement officers no indication how to determine whether any particular category of information falls on the financial-records side or the cell-site-records side of its newly conceived constitutional line. The Court's multifactor analysis — considering intimacy, comprehensiveness, expense, retrospectivity, and voluntariness — puts the law on a new and unstable foundation.
>
> *Third,* even if a distinct category of information is deemed to be more like cell-site records than financial records, courts and law enforcement

officers will have to guess how much of that information can be requested before a warrant is required. The Court suggests that less than seven days of location information may not require a warrant. But the Court does not explain why that is so, and nothing in its opinion even alludes to the considerations that should determine whether greater or lesser thresholds should apply to information like IP addresses or website browsing history.

Fourth, by invalidating the Government's use of court-approved compulsory process in this case, the Court calls into question the subpoena practices of federal and state grand juries, legislatures, and other investigative bodies, as Justice Alito's opinion explains. Yet the Court fails even to mention the serious consequences this will have for the proper administration of justice.

In short, the Court's new and uncharted course will inhibit law enforcement and "keep defendants and judges guessing for years to come."

And consider Justice Gorsuch's dissenting views:

The Court today says that judges should use *Katz*'s reasonable expectation of privacy test to decide what Fourth Amendment rights people have in cell-site location information, explaining that "no single rubric definitively resolves which expectations of privacy are entitled to protection." But then it offers a twist. Lower courts should be sure to add two special principles to their *Katz* calculus: the need to avoid "arbitrary power" and the importance of "plac[ing] obstacles in the way of a too permeating police surveillance." While surely laudable, these principles don't offer lower courts much guidance. The Court does not tell us, for example, how far to carry either principle or how to weigh them against the legitimate needs of law enforcement. At what point does access to electronic data amount to "arbitrary" authority? When does police surveillance become "too permeating"? And what sort of "obstacles" should judges "place" in law enforcement's path when it does? We simply do not know.

The Court's application of these principles supplies little more direction. The Court declines to say whether there is any sufficiently limited period of time "for which the Government may obtain an individual's historical [location information] free from Fourth Amendment scrutiny." But then it tells us that access to seven days' worth of information *does* trigger Fourth Amendment scrutiny—even though here the carrier "produced only two days of records." Why is the relevant fact the seven days of information the government *asked for* instead of the two days of information the government *actually saw*? Why seven days instead of ten or three or one? And in what possible sense did the government "search" five days' worth of location information it was never even sent? We do not know.

Later still, the Court adds that it can't say whether the Fourth Amendment is triggered when the government collects "real-time CSLI or 'tower dumps' (a download of information on all the devices that connected to a particular cell site during a particular interval)." But what distinguishes historical data from real-time data, or seven days of a single person's data from a download of *everyone*'s data over some indefinite period of time? Why isn't a tower dump the *paradigmatic* example of "too permeating police surveillance" and a dangerous tool of "arbitrary" authority—the touchstones of the majority's modified *Katz* analysis? On what possible basis could such mass data collection survive the Court's test while collecting a single person's data does not? Here again we are left to guess. At the same time, though, the Court offers some firm assurances. It tells us its decision does *not* "call into question conventional surveillance techniques and tools, such as security cameras." That, however, just raises more questions for lower courts to sort out about what techniques qualify as "conventional" and why those techniques would be okay *even if* they lead to "permeating police surveillance" or "arbitrary police power."

Nor is this the end of it. After finding a reasonable expectation of privacy, the Court says there's still more work to do. Courts must determine whether to "extend" *Smith* and *Miller* to the circumstances before them. So apparently *Smith* and *Miller* aren't quite left for dead; they just no longer have the clear reach they once did. How do we measure their new reach? The Court says courts now must conduct a *second Katz*-like balancing inquiry, asking whether the fact of disclosure to a third party outweighs privacy interests in the "category of information" so disclosed. But how are lower courts supposed to weigh these radically different interests? Or assign values to different categories of information? All we know is that historical cell-site location information (for seven days, anyway) escapes *Smith* and *Miller*'s shorn grasp, while a lifetime of bank or phone records does not. As to any other kind of information, lower courts will have to stay tuned.

In the end, our lower court colleagues are left with two amorphous balancing tests, a series of weighty and incommensurable principles to consider in them, and a few illustrative examples that seem little more than the product of judicial intuition. In the Court's defense, though, we have arrived at this strange place not because the Court has misunderstood *Katz*. Far from it. We have arrived here because this is where *Katz* inevitably leads.

6. **Protections for Email.** Are the contents of email protected after *Carpenter*? Several of the opinions in *Carpenter* chose to discuss the Fourth Amendment's role in protecting emails. Justice Kennedy in his dissent observed:

> *Miller* and *Smith* may not apply when the Government obtains the modern-day equivalents of an individual's own "papers" or "effects," even when those papers or effects are held by a third party. See *Ex parte Jackson*, 96 U.S. 727 (1878) (letters held by mail carrier); *United States v. Warshak*, 631 F.3d 266 (C.A.6 2010) (e-mails held by Internet service provider).

The majority agreed with Justice Kennedy: "That would be a sensible exception, because it would prevent the subpoena doctrine from overcoming any reasonable expectation of privacy. If the third-party doctrine does not apply to the 'modern-day equivalents of an individual's own "papers" or "effects,"' then the clear implication is that the documents should receive full Fourth Amendment protection." Justice Gorsuch, in his dissent (quoted *infra*), also cited *Warshak* for the proposition that emails are protected, based on a bailment theory. *Warshak* is one of a very few cases that have found that a person *does* have a protected interest when the government obtains that person's emails from that person's email provider. *Warshak* was premised on the view that Warshak's contract with his email provider limited the circumstances under which the provider could examine the messages. *Compare United States v. Warshak*, 631 F.3d 266 (6th Cir. 2010) (finding expectation of privacy in emails obtained from ISP), *with United States v. Warshak*, 532 F.3d 521 (6th Cir. 2008) (en banc) (cataloging varieties of ISP agreements and using a contract analysis to opine that a legitimate expectation of privacy varied with the terms of the agreement). Is a contract theory sound? After *Carpenter*, is it needed?

Are emails, once sent, always protected everywhere, and for all time? Once one sends an email, it passes through many service providers, most of which are not bound by the contractual agreement that one has with the person's Internet service provider. Hence, if an email is sent by X using ISP#1 to Y, who has a contract with ISP#2, ISP#2 is in no way bound by X's agreement with ISP#1. The government could acquire the email from ISP#2 without implicating X's contractual rights. *Cf. State v. Marcum*, 319 P.3d 681 (Okla. 2014) (no reasonable expectation of privacy of sender in records held by recipient's provider). Does the sender have a protected interest in the email recovered from the recipient's cellphone? *See, e.g., State v. Carle*, 337 P.3d 904 (Or. App. 2014) (no reasonable expectation of privacy of sender in text message on recipient's cell phone); *United States v. Charbonneau*, 979 F. Supp. 1177, 1184 (S.D. Ohio 1997) ("an email message, like a letter, cannot be afforded a reasonable expectation of privacy once that message is received"); *United States v. Maxwell*, 45 M.J. 406, 418–19 (C.A.A.F. 1996) (no reasonable expectation of privacy in emails after being received by another person); *Commonwealth v. Proetto*, 771 A.2d 823 (Pa. Super. Ct. 2001) (email from recipient). *But see State v. Hinton*, 319 P.3d 3 (Wash. 2014) (based on independent state grounds, reasonable expectation of privacy in text message recovered from recipient's cell phone). The Stored Communications Act, discussed in Chapter 12, provides for different levels of process, depending in part on how long the email is held by the provider.

2. Fourth Amendment Theory: The Dissents

a. What Does the Fourth Amendment Protect?

Each of the four dissents in *Carpenter* offered criticism of the *Katz* framework in general and the *Carpenter* majority's formulation of that framework, including its application to CSLI. Each of the dissents had textual and other criticisms. What are those views? What is offered as an alternative?

b. Justice Thomas' Dissent, Speaking for Only Himself, Offered the Most Comprehensive Attack on Katz

This case should not turn on "whether" a search occurred. It should turn, instead, on *whose* property was searched. The Fourth Amendment guarantees individuals the right to be secure from unreasonable searches of "*their* persons, houses, papers, and effects." In other words, "*each* person has the right to be secure against unreasonable searches . . . in *his own* person, house, papers, and effects." By obtaining the cell-site records of MetroPCS and Sprint, the Government did not search Carpenter's property. He did not create the records, he does not maintain them, he cannot control them, and he cannot destroy them. Neither the terms of his contracts nor any provision of law makes the records his. The records belong to MetroPCS and Sprint.

II

Under the *Katz* test, a "search" occurs whenever "government officers violate a person's 'reasonable expectation of privacy.'" The most glaring problem with this test is that it has "no plausible foundation in the text of the Fourth Amendment." The Fourth Amendment, as relevant here, protects "[t]he right of the people to be secure in their persons, houses, papers, and effects, against unreasonable searches." By defining "search" to mean "any violation of a reasonable expectation of privacy," the *Katz* test misconstrues virtually every one of these words.

A

The *Katz* test distorts the original meaning of "searc[h]"—the word in the Fourth Amendment that it purports to define. Under the *Katz* test, the government conducts a search anytime it violates someone's "reasonable expectation of privacy." At the founding, "search" did not mean a violation of someone's reasonable expectation of privacy. The word was probably not a term of art, as it does not appear in legal dictionaries from the era. And its ordinary meaning was the same as it is today: "'[t]o look over or through for the purpose of finding something; to explore; to examine by inspection; as, to *search* the house for a book; to *search* the wood for a thief.'"

B

The *Katz* test strays even further from the text by focusing on the concept of "privacy." The word "privacy" does not appear in the Fourth Amendment (or anywhere else in the Constitution for that matter). Instead, the Fourth Amendment references "[t]he right of the people to be secure." It then qualifies that right by limiting it to "persons" and three specific types of property: "houses, papers, and effects." By connecting the right to be secure to these four specific objects, "[t]he text of the Fourth Amendment reflects its close connection to property." "[P]rivacy," by contrast, "was not part of the political vocabulary of the [founding]. Instead, liberty and privacy rights were understood largely in terms of property rights."

Those who ratified the Fourth Amendment were quite familiar with the notion of security in property. Security in property was a prominent concept in English law. See, *e.g.,* 3 W. Blackstone, Commentaries on the Laws of England 288 (1768) ("[E]very man's house is looked upon by the law to be his castle"); 3 E. Coke, Institutes of Laws of England 162 (6th ed. 1680) ("[F]or a man[']s house is his Castle, & domus sua cuique est tutissimum refugium [each man's home is his safest refuge]"). The political philosophy of John Locke, moreover, "permeated the 18th-century political scene in America." For Locke, every individual had a property right "in his own person" and in anything he "removed from the common state [of] Nature" and "mixed his labour with." Second Treatise of Civil Government § 27 (1690).

The concept of security in property recognized by Locke and the English legal tradition appeared throughout the materials that inspired the Fourth Amendment. In *Entick v. Carrington,* 19 How. St. Tr. 1029 (C.P. 1765) — a heralded decision that the founding generation considered "the true and ultimate expression of constitutional law," *Boyd v. United States,* 116 U.S. 616, 626 (1886) — Lord Camden explained that "[t]he great end, for which men entered into society, was to secure their property." The American colonists echoed this reasoning in their "widespread hostility" to the Crown's writs of assistance — a practice that inspired the Revolution and became "[t]he driving force behind the adoption of the [Fourth] Amendment." Prominent colonists decried the writs as destroying "'domestic security'" by permitting broad searches of homes. John Otis, who argued the famous Writs of Assistance case, contended that the writs violated "'the fundamental Principl[e] of Law'" that "'[a] Man who is quiet, is as secure in his House, as a Prince in his Castle.'" John Adams attended Otis' argument and later drafted Article XIV of the Massachusetts Constitution, which served as a model for the Fourth Amendment. See Clancy, The Framers' Intent: John Adams, His Era, and the Fourth Amendment, 86 Ind. L.J. 979, 982 (2011). Adams agreed that "[p]roperty must be secured, or liberty cannot exist." Discourse on Davila, in 6 The Works of John Adams 280 (C. Adams ed. 1851). Of course, the founding generation understood that, by securing their property, the Fourth Amendment would often protect their privacy as well. But the Fourth Amendment's attendant protection of privacy does not justify *Katz*'s elevation of privacy as the *sine qua non* of the Amendment. See T. Clancy, The Fourth Amendment: Its History and Interpretation § 3.4.4, p. 78 (2008) ("[The *Katz* test] confuse[s] the reasons for exercising the protected right with the right itself. A purpose of exercising one's Fourth Amendment rights might be the desire for privacy, but the individual's motivation is not the right protected"). Justice Harlan's focus on privacy in his concurrence reflects privacy's status as the organizing constitutional idea of the 1960's and 1970's. The organizing constitutional idea of the founding era, by contrast, was property.

C

In shifting the focus of the Fourth Amendment from property to privacy, the *Katz* test also reads the words "persons, houses, papers, and effects" out of the text. At its broadest formulation, the *Katz* test would find a search "*wherever* an individual may harbor a reasonable 'expectation of privacy.'" The Court today, for example, does not ask whether cell-site location records are "persons, houses, papers, [or] effects" within the meaning of the Fourth Amendment. Yet "persons, houses, papers, and effects" cannot mean "anywhere" or "anything." *Katz*'s catchphrase that "the Fourth Amendment protects people, not places," is not a serious attempt to reconcile the constitutional text. The Fourth Amendment obviously protects people; "[t]he question . . . is what protection it affords to those people." The Founders decided to protect the people from unreasonable searches and seizures of four specific things — persons, houses, papers, and effects. They identified those four categories as "the objects of privacy protection to which the *Constitution* would extend, leaving further expansion to the good judgment . . . of the people through their representatives in the legislature."

D

Carpenter stipulated below that the cell-site records are the business records of Sprint and MetroPCS. He cites no property law in his briefs to this Court, and he does not explain how he has a property right in the companies' records under the law of any jurisdiction at any point in American history. If someone stole these records from Sprint or MetroPCS, Carpenter does not argue that he could recover in a traditional tort action. Nor do his contracts with Sprint and MetroPCS make the records his, even though such provisions could exist in the marketplace. Cf., *e.g.*, Google Terms of Service, https://policies.google.com/terms ("Some of our Services allow you to upload, submit, store, send or receive content. You retain ownership of any intellectual property rights that you hold in that content. In short, what belongs to you stays yours").

E

The Court holds that the Government unreasonably searched Carpenter by subpoenaing the cell-site records of Sprint and MetroPCS without a warrant. But the Founders would not recognize the Court's "warrant requirement." The common law required warrants for some types of searches and seizures, but not for many others. The relevant rule depended on context. In cases like this one, a subpoena for third-party documents was not a "search" to begin with, and the common law did not limit the government's authority to subpoena third parties. Suffice it to say, the Founders would be confused by this Court's transformation of their common-law protection of property into a "warrant requirement" and a vague inquiry into "reasonable expectations of privacy."

III

That the *Katz* test departs so far from the text of the Fourth Amendment is reason enough to reject it. But the *Katz* test also has proved unworkable in practice.

After 50 years, it is still unclear what question the *Katz* test is even asking. This Court has steadfastly declined to elaborate the relevant considerations or identify any meaningful constraints.

Justice Harlan's original formulation of the *Katz* test appears to ask a descriptive question: Whether a given expectation of privacy is "one that society is prepared to recognize as 'reasonable.'" As written, the *Katz* test turns on society's actual, current views about the reasonableness of various expectations of privacy.

But this descriptive understanding presents several problems. For starters, it is easily circumvented. If, for example, "the Government were suddenly to announce on nationwide television that all homes henceforth would be subject to warrantless entry," individuals could not realistically expect privacy in their homes. A purely descriptive understanding of the *Katz* test also risks "circular[ity]." While this Court is supposed to base its decisions on society's expectations of privacy, society's expectations of privacy are, in turn, shaped by this Court's decisions. But the Court's supposed reliance on "real or personal property law" rings hollow. The whole point of *Katz* was to "'discredi[t]'" the relationship between the Fourth Amendment and property law, and this Court has repeatedly downplayed the importance of property law under the *Katz* test. Today, for example, the Court makes no mention of property law, except to reject its relevance.

As for "understandings that are recognized or permitted in society," this Court has never answered even the most basic questions about what this means. For example, our precedents do not explain who is included in "society," how we know what they "recogniz[e] or permi[t]," and how much of society must agree before something constitutes an "understanding."

Here, for example, society might prefer a balanced regime that prohibits the Government from obtaining cell-site location information unless it can persuade a neutral magistrate that the information bears on an ongoing criminal investigation. That is precisely the regime Congress created under the Stored Communications Act and Telecommunications Act. See 47 U.S.C. §222(c)(1); 18 U.S.C. §§2703(c)(1)(B), (d). With no sense of irony, the Court invalidates this regime today—the one that society actually created "in the form of its elected representatives in Congress."

Truth be told, this Court does not treat the *Katz* test as a descriptive inquiry. Although the *Katz* test is phrased in descriptive terms about society's views, this Court treats it like a normative question—whether a particular practice *should* be considered a search under the Fourth Amendment. And a normative understanding is the only way to make sense of this Court's precedents, which bear the hallmarks of subjective policymaking instead of neutral legal decisionmaking. "[T]he only thing the past three decades have established about the *Katz* test" is that society's expectations of privacy "bear an uncanny resemblance to those expectations of privacy that this Court considers reasonable." Yet, "[t]hough we know ourselves to be eminently reasonable, self-awareness of eminent reasonableness is not really a substitute for democratic election."

Because the *Katz* test is a failed experiment, this Court is dutybound to reconsider it.

c. The Other Three Dissents Also Criticized Katz on Textual Grounds

Most succinctly, Justice Gorsuch in his dissent observed:

The Amendment's protections do not depend on the breach of some abstract "expectation of privacy" whose contours are left to the judicial imagination. Much more concretely, it protects your "person," and your "houses, papers, and effects." Nor does your right to bring a Fourth Amendment claim depend on whether a judge happens to agree that your subjective expectation to privacy is a "reasonable" one. Under its plain terms, the Amendment grants you the right to invoke its guarantees whenever one of your protected things (your person, your house, your papers, or your effects) is unreasonably searched or seized. Period.

d. Dissenting Justice Kennedy Did Not Seek to Abandon Katz But to Reform It by Emphasizing the Role That Property Analysis Plays

The concept of reasonable expectations of privacy, first announced in *Katz*, sought to look beyond the "arcane distinctions developed in property and tort law" in evaluating whether a person has a sufficient connection to the thing or place searched to assert Fourth Amendment interests in it. Yet "property concepts" are, nonetheless, fundamental "in determining the presence or absence of the privacy interests protected by that Amendment." This is so for at least two reasons. First, as a matter of settled expectations from the law of property, individuals often have greater expectations of privacy in things and places that belong to them, not to others. And second, the Fourth Amendment's protections must remain tethered to the text of that Amendment, which, again, protects only a person's own "persons, houses, papers, and effects."

Katz did not abandon reliance on property-based concepts. The Court in *Katz* analogized the phone booth used in that case to a friend's apartment, a taxicab, and a hotel room. So when the defendant "shu[t] the door behind him" and "pa[id] the toll," he had a temporary interest in the space and a legitimate expectation that others would not intrude, much like the interest a hotel guest has in a hotel room or an overnight guest has in a host's home. The Government intruded on that space when it attached a listening device to the phone booth.

* * *

The Court has twice held that individuals have no Fourth Amendment interests in business records which are possessed, owned, and controlled by a third party. This is true even when the records contain personal and sensitive information. So when the Government uses a subpoena to obtain, for example, bank records, telephone records, and credit card statements from the businesses that create and keep these records, the Government does not engage in a search of the business's customers within the meaning of the Fourth Amendment.

Cell-site records are no different from the many other kinds of business records the Government has a lawful right to obtain by compulsory process. Customers like petitioner do not own, possess, control, or use the records, and for that reason have no reasonable expectation that they cannot be disclosed pursuant to lawful compulsory process.

e. The Dissent of Justice Gorsuch — Positive Law Theory

The Fourth Amendment protects "the right of the people to be secure in their persons, houses, papers and effects, against unreasonable searches and seizures." True to those words and their original understanding, the traditional approach asked if a house, paper or effect was *yours* under law. No more was needed to trigger the Fourth Amendment.

Beyond its provenance in the text and original understanding of the Amendment, this traditional approach comes with other advantages. Judges are supposed to decide cases based on "democratically legitimate sources of law"—like positive law or analogies to items protected by the enacted Constitution—rather than "their own biases or personal policy preferences." A Fourth Amendment model based on positive legal rights "carves out significant room for legislative participation in the Fourth Amendment context," too, by asking judges to consult what the people's representatives have to say about their rights. Nor is this approach hobbled by *Smith* and *Miller,* for those cases are just *limitations* on *Katz,* addressing only the question whether individuals have a reasonable expectation of privacy in materials they share with third parties. Under this more traditional approach, Fourth Amendment protections for your papers and effects do not automatically disappear just because you share them with third parties.

But what kind of legal interest is sufficient to make something *yours*? And what source of law determines that? Current positive law? The common law at 1791, extended by analogy to modern times? Both? Much work is needed to revitalize this area and answer these questions. I do not begin to claim all the answers today, but (unlike with *Katz*) at least I have a pretty good idea what the questions *are*. And it seems to me a few things can be said.

First, the fact that a third party has access to or possession of your papers and effects does not necessarily eliminate your interest in them. Ever hand a private document to a friend to be returned? Toss your keys to a valet at a restaurant? Ask your neighbor to look after your dog while you travel? You would not expect the friend to share the document with others; the valet to lend your car to his buddy; or the neighbor to put Fido up for adoption. Entrusting your stuff to others is a *bailment*. A bailment is the "delivery of personal property by one person (the *bailor*) to another (the *bailee*) who holds the property for a certain purpose." A bailee normally owes a legal duty to keep the item safe, according to the terms of the parties' contract if they have one, and according to the "implication[s] from their conduct" if they don't. A bailee who uses the item in a different way than he's supposed to, or against the bailor's instructions, is liable for conversion.

Our Fourth Amendment jurisprudence already reflects this truth. In *Ex parte Jackson,* 96 U.S. 727 (1878), this Court held that sealed letters placed in the mail are "as fully guarded from examination and inspection, except as to their outward form and weight, as if they were retained by the parties forwarding them in their own domiciles." The reason, drawn from the Fourth Amendment's text, was that "[t]he constitutional guaranty of the right of the people to be secure in their papers against unreasonable searches and seizures extends to *their papers,* thus closed against inspection, *wherever they may be*." It did not matter that letters were bailed to a third party (the government, no less). The sender enjoyed the same Fourth Amendment protection as he does "when papers are subjected to search in one's own household."

These ancient principles may help us address modern data cases too. Just because you entrust your data—in some cases, your modern-day papers and effects—to a third party may not mean you lose any Fourth Amendment interest in its contents. Whatever may be left of *Smith* and *Miller,* few doubt that e-mail should be treated much like the traditional mail it has largely supplanted—as a bailment in which the owner retains a vital and protected legal interest.

Second, I doubt that complete ownership or exclusive control of property is always a necessary condition to the assertion of a Fourth Amendment right. Where houses are concerned, for example, individuals can enjoy Fourth Amendment protection without fee simple title. Both the text of the Amendment and the common law rule support that conclusion. "People call a house 'their' home when legal title is in the bank, when they rent it, and even when they merely occupy it rent free." That rule derives from the common law. That is why tenants and resident family members—though they have no legal title—have standing to complain about searches of the houses in which they live.

Another point seems equally true: just because you *have* to entrust a third party with your data doesn't necessarily mean you should lose all Fourth Amendment protections in it. Not infrequently one person comes into possession of someone else's property without the owner's consent. Think of the finder of lost goods or the policeman who impounds a car. The law recognizes that the goods and the car still belong to their true owners, for "where a person comes into lawful possession of the personal property of another, even though there is no formal agreement between the property's owner and its possessor, the possessor will become a constructive bailee when justice so requires." At least some of this Court's decisions have already suggested that use of technology is functionally compelled by the demands of modern life, and in that way the fact that we store data with third parties may amount to a sort of involuntary bailment too.

Third, positive law may help provide detailed guidance on evolving technologies without resort to judicial intuition. State (or sometimes federal) law often creates rights in both tangible and intangible things. In the context of the Takings Clause we often ask whether those state-created rights are sufficient to make something someone's property for constitutional purposes. A similar inquiry may be appropriate for the Fourth Amendment. Both the States and federal government are actively legislating in the area of third party data storage and the rights users enjoy. See, *e.g.,* Stored Communications Act, 18 U.S.C. § 2701 *et seq.*; Tex. Prop.Code Ann. § 111.004(12) (West 2017) (defining "[p]roperty" to include "property held in any digital or electronic medium"). State courts are busy expounding common law property principles in this area as well. *E.g., Ajemian v. Yahoo!, Inc.,* 478 Mass. 169, 170, 84 N.E.3d 766, 768 (2017) (e-mail account is a "form of property often referred to as a 'digital asset'"); *Eysoldt v. ProScan Imaging,* 194 Ohio App.3d 630, 638, 2011–Ohio–2359, 957 N.E.2d 780, 786 (2011) (permitting action for conversion of web account as intangible property). If state legislators or state courts say that a digital record has the attributes that normally make something property, that may supply a sounder basis for judicial decisionmaking than judicial guesswork about societal expectations.

Fourth, while positive law may help establish a person's Fourth Amendment interest there may be some circumstances where positive law cannot be used to defeat it. *Ex parte Jackson* reflects that understanding. There this Court said that "[n]o law of Congress" could authorize letter carriers "to invade the secrecy of letters." So the post office couldn't impose a regulation dictating that those mailing letters surrender all legal interests in them once they're deposited in a mailbox. If that is right, *Jackson* suggests the existence of a constitutional floor below which Fourth Amendment rights may not descend. Legislatures cannot pass laws declaring your house or papers to be your property except to the extent the police wish to search them without cause. As the Court has previously explained, "we must 'assur[e] preservation of that degree of privacy against government that existed when the Fourth Amendment was adopted.'" Nor does this mean protecting only the specific rights known at the founding; it means protecting their modern analogues too. So, for example, while thermal imaging was unknown in 1791, this Court has recognized that using that technology to look inside a home constitutes a Fourth Amendment "search" of that "home" no less than a physical inspection might.

Fifth, this constitutional floor may, in some instances, bar efforts to circumvent the Fourth Amendment's protection through the use of subpoenas. No one thinks the government can evade *Jackson*'s prohibition on opening sealed letters without a warrant simply by issuing a subpoena to a postmaster for "all letters sent by John Smith" or, worse, "all letters sent by John Smith concerning a particular transaction." So the question courts will confront will be this: What other kinds of records are sufficiently similar to letters in the mail that the same rule should apply?

What does all this mean for the case before us? I would look to a more traditional Fourth Amendment approach. Even if *Katz* may still supply one way to prove a Fourth Amendment interest, it has never been the only way. Neglecting more traditional approaches may mean failing to vindicate the full protections of the Fourth Amendment.

Our case offers a cautionary example. It seems to me entirely possible a person's cell-site data could qualify as *his* papers or effects under existing law. Yes, the telephone carrier holds the information. But 47 U.S.C. § 222 designates a customer's cell-site location information as "customer proprietary network information" (CPNI),

and gives customers certain rights to control use of and access to CPNI about themselves. The statute generally forbids a carrier to "use, disclose, or permit access to
individually identifiable" CPNI without the customer's consent, except as needed
to provide the customer's telecommunications services. It also requires the carrier
to disclose CPNI "upon affirmative written request by the customer, to any person
designated by the customer." Congress even afforded customers a private cause of
action for damages against carriers who violate the Act's terms. Plainly, customers
have substantial legal interests in this information, including at least some right to
include, exclude, and control its use. Those interests might even rise to the level of a
property right.

The problem is that we do not know anything more. Before the district court
and court of appeals, Mr. Carpenter pursued only a *Katz* "reasonable expectations"
argument. Even in his merits brief before this Court, Mr. Carpenter's discussion
of his positive law rights in cell-site data was cursory. He offered no analysis, for
example, of what rights state law might provide him in addition to those supplied
by §222. In these circumstances, I cannot help but conclude—reluctantly—that
Mr. Carpenter forfeited perhaps his most promising line of argument.

f. Responses to Justice Gorsuch's Theory

The majority, given its holding that *Katz* applied to establish Carpenter's protected interest in the CSLI, did not respond to Justice Gorsuch. The other dissenters
did, rejecting the view that 47 U.S.C. §222, the Telecommunications Act, served to
give Carpenter a protected interest. Justice Thomas flatly observed:

> To come within the text of the Fourth Amendment, Carpenter must prove
> that the cell-site records are *his*; positive law is potentially relevant only
> insofar as it answers that question. The text of the Fourth Amendment can-
> not plausibly be read to mean "any violation of positive law" any more than
> it can plausibly be read to mean "any violation of a reasonable expectation
> of privacy."

Thomas added: "Although §222 'protects the interests of individuals against wrongful uses or disclosures of personal data, the rationale for these legal protections has
not historically been grounded on a perception that people have property rights in
personal data as such.' Any property rights remain with the companies." Justice
Alito observed:

> A statutory disclosure requirement is hardly sufficient to give someone
> an ownership interest in the documents that must be copied and disclosed.
> Many statutes confer a right to obtain copies of documents without creat-
> ing any property right.
>
> Carpenter's argument is particularly hard to swallow because nothing in
> the Telecommunications Act precludes cell service providers from charg-
> ing customers a fee for accessing cell-site records. It would be very strange
> if the owner of records were required to pay in order to inspect his own

property. Nor does the Telecommunications Act give Carpenter a property right in the cell-site records simply because they are subject to confidentiality restrictions. Many federal statutes impose similar restrictions on private entities' use or dissemination of information in their own records without conferring a property right on third parties.

It would be especially strange to hold that the Telecommunication Act's confidentiality provision confers a property right when the Act creates an express exception for any disclosure of records that is "required by law." So not only does Carpenter lack "'the most essential and beneficial'" of the "'constituent elements'" of property,—*i.e.,* the right to use the property to the exclusion of others—but he cannot even exclude the party he would most like to keep out, namely, the Government.

Justice Kennedy, in his dissent, expressed views similar to Justices Alito and Thomas, stating that

§ 222 does not grant cell phone customers any meaningful interest in cell-site records. The statute's confidentiality protections may be overridden by the interests of the providers or the Government. The providers may disclose the records "to protect the[ir] rights or property" or to "initiate, render, bill, and collect for telecommunications services." They also may disclose the records "as required by law"—which, of course, is how they were disclosed in this case. Nor does the statute provide customers any practical control over the records. Customers do not create the records; they have no say in whether or for how long the records are stored; and they cannot require the records to be modified or destroyed. Even their right to request access to the records is limited, for the statute "does not preclude a carrier from being reimbursed by the customers . . . for the costs associated with making such disclosures." So in every legal and practical sense the "network information" regulated by § 222 is, under that statute, "proprietary" to the service providers, not Carpenter.

3. The Role of Subpoenas

Note that the Government used a subpoena issued pursuant to the Stored Communications Act in *Carpenter,* and the majority found that, instead, a warrant was needed to obtain the SCLI. Is this to say that the statute was unconstitutional as applied? (Chapter 12 discusses that Act in detail.)

a. Justice Kennedy, with Whom Justice Thomas and Justice Alito Joined, Dissenting

Based on *Miller* and *Smith* and the principles underlying those cases, it is well established that subpoenas may be used to obtain a wide variety of records held by businesses, even when the records contain private information. Credit cards are a prime example. State and federal law enforcement, for instance, often subpoena credit card statements to develop probable cause to prosecute crimes ranging from drug trafficking and distribution to healthcare fraud to tax evasion. Subpoenas also may be used to obtain vehicle registration records, hotel records, employment records, and records of utility usage, to name just a few other examples.

And law enforcement officers are not alone in their reliance on subpoenas to obtain business records for legitimate investigations. Subpoenas also are used for investigatory purposes by state and federal grand juries, state and federal administrative agencies, and state and federal legislative bodies.

b. Justice Alito, with Whom Justice Thomas Joined, Dissenting

Justice Alito wrote the most about the role of subpoenas in obtaining government records and that part of his opinion is premised on his belief that Carpenter did *not* have a protected interest and had no grounds to object to the acquisition of the records. He detailed that the Fourth Amendment was originally viewed as not regulating the use of subpoenas but that, over time, the Court brought them within the coverage of the Amendment. An extensive excerpt of his opinion is next:

Today the majority holds that a court order requiring the production of cell-site records may be issued only after the Government demonstrates probable cause. That is a serious and consequential mistake.

A subpoena *duces tecum* permits a subpoenaed individual to conduct the search for the relevant documents himself, without law enforcement officers entering his home or rooting through his papers and effects. As a result, subpoenas avoid the many incidental invasions of privacy that necessarily accompany any actual search. And it was *those* invasions of privacy — which, although incidental, could often be extremely intrusive and damaging — that led to the adoption of the Fourth Amendment.

[I]n *Hale v. Henkel,* 201 U.S. 43 (1906), the Court found it "quite clear" and "conclusive" that "the search and seizure clause of the Fourth Amendment was not intended to interfere with the power of courts to compel, through a *subpoena duces tecum,* the production, upon a trial in court, of documentary evidence." Without that writ, the Court recognized, "it would be 'utterly impossible to carry on the administration of justice.'"

Hale, however, did not entirely liberate subpoenas *duces tecum* from Fourth Amendment constraints. While refusing to treat such subpoenas as the equivalent of actual searches, *Hale* concluded that they must not be unreasonable. The *Hale* Court left two critical questions unanswered: Under the Fourth Amendment, what makes the compulsory production of documents "reasonable," and how does that standard differ from the one that governs actual searches and seizures?

The Court answered both of those questions definitively in *Oklahoma Press Publishing Co. v. Walling,* 327 U.S. 186 (1946), where we held that the Fourth Amendment regulates the compelled production of documents, but less stringently than it does full-blown searches and seizures. "The primary source of misconception concerning the Fourth Amendment's function" in this context, the Court explained, "lies perhaps in the identification of cases involving so-called 'figurative' or 'constructive' search with cases of actual search and seizure." But the Court held that "the basic distinction" between the compulsory production of documents on the one hand, and actual searches and seizures on the other, meant that two different standards had to be applied.

The Court then set forth the relevant Fourth Amendment standard for the former. When it comes to "the production of corporate or other business records," the Court held that the Fourth Amendment "at the most guards against abuse only by way of too much indefiniteness or breadth in the things required to be 'particularly described,' if also the inquiry is one the demanding agency is authorized by law to make and the materials specified are relevant." Notably, the Court held that a showing of probable cause was not necessary so long as "the investigation is authorized by Congress, is for a purpose Congress can order, and the documents sought are relevant to the inquiry."

Since *Oklahoma Press,* we have consistently hewed to that standard.

Today, however, the majority inexplicably ignores the settled rule of *Oklahoma Press*. That is mystifying. This should have been an easy case regardless of whether the Court looked to the original understanding of the Fourth Amendment or to our modern doctrine.

As a matter of original understanding, the Fourth Amendment does not regulate the compelled production of documents at all. Here the Government received the relevant cell-site records pursuant to a court order compelling Carpenter's cell service provider to turn them over. That process is thus immune from challenge under the original understanding of the Fourth Amendment.

As a matter of modern doctrine, this case is equally straightforward. As Justice Kennedy explains, no search or seizure of Carpenter or his property occurred in this case. But even if the majority were right that the Government "searched" Carpenter, it would at most be a "figurative or constructive search" governed by the *Oklahoma Press* standard, not an "actual search" controlled by the Fourth Amendment's warrant requirement.

And there is no doubt that the Government met the *Oklahoma Press* standard here. Under *Oklahoma Press,* a court order must "'be sufficiently limited in scope, relevant in purpose, and specific in directive so that compliance will not be unreasonably burdensome.'" Here, the type of order obtained by the Government almost necessarily satisfies that standard. The Stored Communications Act allows a court to issue the relevant type of order "only if the governmental entity offers specific and articulable facts showing that there are reasonable grounds to believe that . . . the records . . . sough[t] are relevant and material to an ongoing criminal investigation." 18 U.S.C. §2703(d). And the court "may quash or modify such order" if the provider objects that the "records requested are unusually voluminous in nature or compliance with such order otherwise would cause an undue burden on such provider." No such objection was made in this case, and Carpenter does not suggest that the orders contravened the *Oklahoma Press* standard in any other way.

That is what makes the majority's opinion so puzzling. It decides that a "search" of Carpenter occurred within the meaning of the Fourth Amendment, but then it leaps straight to imposing requirements that—until this point—have governed only *actual* searches and seizures. Lost in its race to the finish is any real recognition of the century's worth of precedent it jeopardizes. For the majority, this case is apparently no different from one in which Government agents raided Carpenter's home and removed records associated with his cell phone.

All that the Court can muster is the observation that "this Court has never held that the Government may subpoena third parties for records in which the suspect has a reasonable expectation of privacy." Frankly, I cannot imagine a concession more damning to the Court's argument than that. As the Court well knows, the reason that we have never seen such a case is because—until today—defendants categorically had no "reasonable expectation of privacy" and no property interest in records belonging to third parties. By implying otherwise, the Court tries the nice trick of seeking shelter under the cover of precedents that it simultaneously perforates.

Not only that, but even if the Fourth Amendment permitted someone to object to the subpoena of a third party's records, the Court cannot explain why that individual should be entitled to *greater* Fourth Amendment protection than the party actually being subpoenaed. When parties are subpoenaed to turn over their records, after all, they will at most receive the protection afforded by *Oklahoma Press* even though they will own and have a reasonable expectation of privacy in the records at issue. Under the Court's decision, however, the Fourth Amendment will extend greater protections to someone else who is not being subpoenaed and does not own the records. That outcome makes no sense, and the Court does not even attempt to defend it.

Although the majority announces its holding in the context of the Stored Communications Act, nothing stops its logic from sweeping much further. The Court has offered no meaningful limiting principle, and none is apparent.

Holding that subpoenas must meet the same standard as conventional searches will seriously damage, if not destroy, their utility. Even more so than at the founding, today the Government regularly uses subpoenas *duces tecum* and other forms of compulsory process to carry out its essential functions. Grand juries, for example, have long "compel[led] the production of evidence" in order to determine "*whether* there is probable cause to believe a crime has been committed." Almost by definition, then, grand juries will be unable at first to demonstrate "the probable cause required for a warrant." If they are required to do so, the effects are as predictable as they are alarming: Many investigations will sputter out at the start, and a host of criminals will be able to evade law enforcement's reach.

4. The Third Party Doctrine

What is the basis of the third party doctrine? The majority declined to "extend" it to CSLI, viewing the third party doctrine as created in the wake of, and because of, *Katz*, to put limits on the reasonable expectations of privacy doctrine. Justice Gorsuch, in his dissent, basically agreed with that view, seeing *Smith* and *Miller* as "doubtful" applications of that doctrine. The other three dissents saw the third party doctrine much differently, that is, it flowed directly from the text of the Amendment itself.

a. Justice Alito, with Whom Justice Thomas Joined, Dissenting

By allowing Carpenter to object to the search of a third party's property, the Court threatens to revolutionize a second and independent line of Fourth Amendment doctrine.

The Fourth Amendment does not confer rights with respect to the persons, houses, papers, and effects of others. Its language makes clear that "Fourth Amendment rights are personal," and as a result, this Court has long insisted that they "may not be asserted vicariously."

In this case, as Justice Kennedy cogently explains, the cell-site records obtained by the Government belong to Carpenter's cell service providers, not to Carpenter. Carpenter did not create the cell-site records. Nor did he have possession of them; at all relevant times, they were kept by the providers. Once Carpenter subscribed to his provider's service, he had no right to prevent the company from creating or keeping the information in its records. Carpenter also had no right to demand that the providers destroy the records, no right to prevent the providers from destroying the records, and, indeed, no right to modify the records in any way whatsoever (or to prevent the providers from modifying the records). Carpenter, in short, has no meaningful control over the cell-site records, which are created, maintained, altered, used, and eventually destroyed by his cell service providers.

In the days when this Court followed an exclusively property-based approach to the Fourth Amendment, the distinction between an individual's Fourth Amendment rights and those of a third party was clear cut. We first asked whether the object of the search—say, a house, papers, or effects—belonged to the defendant, and, if it did, whether the Government had committed a "trespass" in acquiring the evidence at issue.

When the Court held in *Katz* that "property rights are not the sole measure of Fourth Amendment violations," the sharp boundary between personal and third-party rights was tested. Under *Katz,* a party may invoke the Fourth Amendment whenever law enforcement officers violate the party's "justifiable" or "reasonable" expectation of privacy. Thus freed from the limitations imposed by property law, parties began to argue that they had a reasonable expectation of privacy in items owned by others. After all, if a trusted third party took care not to disclose information about the person in question, that person might well have a reasonable expectation that the information would not be revealed.

Efforts to claim Fourth Amendment protection against searches of the papers and effects of others came to a head in *Miller,* where the defendant sought the suppression of two banks' microfilm copies of his checks, deposit slips, and other records. The defendant did not claim that he owned these documents, but he nonetheless argued that "analysis of ownership, property rights and possessory interests in the determination of Fourth Amendment rights ha[d] been severely impeached" by *Katz* and other recent cases. Turning to *Katz,* he then argued that he had a reasonable expectation of privacy in the banks' records regarding his accounts.

Acceptance of this argument would have flown in the face of the Fourth Amendment's text, and the Court rejected that development. Because Miller gave up "dominion and control" of the relevant information to his bank, the Court ruled that he lost any protected Fourth Amendment interest in that information. Later, in *Smith*, the Court reached a similar conclusion regarding a telephone company's records of a customer's calls. As Justice Kennedy concludes, *Miller* and *Smith* are thus best understood as placing "necessary limits on the ability of individuals to assert Fourth Amendment interests in property to which they lack a 'requisite connection.'"

The same is true here, where Carpenter indisputably lacks any meaningful property-based connection to the cell-site records owned by his provider. Because the records are not Carpenter's in any sense, Carpenter may not seek to use the Fourth Amendment to exclude them.

The Court seems to think that *Miller* and *Smith* invented a new "doctrine"—"the third-party doctrine"—and the Court refuses to "extend" this product of the 1970's to a new age of digital communications. But the Court fundamentally misunderstands the role of *Miller* and *Smith*. Those decisions did not forge a new doctrine; instead, they rejected an argument that would have disregarded the clear text of the Fourth Amendment and a formidable body of precedent.

In the end, the Court never explains how its decision can be squared with the fact that the Fourth Amendment protects only "[t]he right of the people to be secure in *their* persons, houses, papers, and effects."

b. Justice Kennedy, with Whom Justice Thomas and Justice Alito Joined, Dissenting

Miller and *Smith* set forth an important and necessary limitation on the *Katz* framework. They rest upon the commonsense principle that the absence of property law analogues can be dispositive of privacy expectations. The defendants in those cases could expect that the third-party businesses could use the records the companies collected, stored, and classified as their own for any number of business and commercial purposes. The businesses were not bailees or custodians of the records, with a duty to hold the records for the defendants' use. The defendants could make no argument that the records were their own papers or effects. The records were the business entities' records, plain and simple. The defendants had no reason to believe the records were owned or controlled by them and so could not assert a reasonable expectation of privacy in the records.

* * * Cell-site records are created, kept, classified, owned, and controlled by cell phone service providers, which aggregate and sell this information to third parties. As in *Miller,* Carpenter can "assert neither ownership nor possession" of the records and has no control over them.

Because Carpenter lacks a requisite connection to the cell-site records, he also may not claim a reasonable expectation of privacy in them. He could expect that a third party—the cell phone service provider—could use the information it collected, stored, and classified as its own for a variety of business and commercial purposes.

* * * In my respectful view the majority opinion misreads this Court's precedents, old and recent, and transforms *Miller* and *Smith* into an unprincipled and unworkable doctrine. The Court's newly conceived constitutional standard will cause confusion; will undermine traditional and important law enforcement practices; and will allow the cell phone to become a protected medium that dangerous persons will use to commit serious crimes.

* * * The Court appears, in my respectful view, to read *Miller* and *Smith* to establish a balancing test. For each "qualitatively different category" of information, the Court suggests, the privacy interests at stake must be weighed against the fact that the information has been disclosed to a third party. When the privacy interests are weighty enough to "overcome" the third-party disclosure, the Fourth Amendment's protections apply.

That is an untenable reading of *Miller* and *Smith.* The fact that information was relinquished to a third party was the entire basis for concluding that the defendants in those cases lacked a reasonable expectation of privacy. *Miller* and *Smith* do not establish the kind of category-by-category balancing the Court today prescribes.

5. The Future Through the Words of the Dissent

a. Justice Alito, with whom Justice Thomas Joined, Dissenting

The Court's reasoning fractures two fundamental pillars of Fourth Amendment law, and in doing so, it guarantees a blizzard of litigation while threatening many legitimate and valuable investigative practices upon which law enforcement has rightfully come to rely.

First, the Court ignores the basic distinction between an actual search (dispatching law enforcement officers to enter private premises and root through private papers and effects) and an order merely requiring a party to look through its own records and produce specified documents. The former, which intrudes on personal privacy far more deeply, requires probable cause; the latter does not. Treating an order to produce like an actual search, as today's decision does, is revolutionary. It violates both the original understanding of the Fourth Amendment and more than a century of Supreme Court precedent. Unless it is somehow restricted to the particular situation in the present case, the Court's move will cause upheaval. Must every grand jury subpoena *duces tecum* be supported by probable cause? If so, investigations of terrorism, political corruption, white-collar crime, and many other offenses will be stymied. And what about subpoenas and other document-production orders issued by administrative agencies?

Second, the Court allows a defendant to object to the search of a third party's property. This also is revolutionary. The Fourth Amendment protects "[t]he right of the people to be secure in *their* persons, houses, papers, and effects", not the persons, houses, papers, and effects of others. Until today, we have been careful to heed this fundamental feature of the Amendment's text. This was true when the Fourth Amendment was tied to property law, and it remained true after *Katz*, broadened the Amendment's reach.

By departing dramatically from these fundamental principles, the Court destabilizes long-established Fourth Amendment doctrine. We will be making repairs—or picking up the pieces—for a long time to come.

* * *

Although the majority professes a desire not to "'embarrass the future,'" we can guess where today's decision will lead.

One possibility is that the broad principles that the Court seems to embrace will be applied across the board. All subpoenas *duces tecum* and all other orders compelling the production of documents will require a demonstration of probable cause, and individuals will be able to claim a protected Fourth Amendment interest in any sensitive personal information about them that is collected and owned by third parties. Those would be revolutionary developments indeed.

The other possibility is that this Court will face the embarrassment of explaining in case after case that the principles on which today's decision rests are subject to all sorts of qualifications and limitations that have not yet been discovered. If we take this latter course, we will inevitably end up "mak[ing] a crazy quilt of the Fourth Amendment."

All of this is unnecessary. In the Stored Communications Act, Congress addressed the specific problem at issue in this case. The Act restricts the misuse of cell-site records by cell service providers, something that the Fourth Amendment cannot do. The Act also goes beyond current Fourth Amendment case law in restricting access by law enforcement. It permits law enforcement officers to acquire cell-site records only if they meet a heightened standard and obtain a court order. If the American people now think that the Act is inadequate or needs updating, they can turn to their elected representatives to adopt more protective provisions. Because the collection and storage of cell-site records affects nearly every American, it is unlikely that the question whether the current law requires strengthening will escape Congress's notice.

Legislation is much preferable to the development of an entirely new body of Fourth Amendment caselaw for many reasons, including the enormous complexity of the subject, the need to respond to rapidly changing technology, and the Fourth Amendment's limited scope. The Fourth Amendment restricts the conduct of the Federal Government and the States; it does not apply to private actors. But today, some of the greatest threats to individual privacy may come from powerful private companies that collect and sometimes misuse vast quantities of data about the lives of ordinary Americans. If today's decision encourages the public to think that this Court can protect them from this looming threat to their privacy, the decision will mislead as well as disrupt. And if holding a provision of the Stored Communications Act to be unconstitutional dissuades Congress from further legislation in this field, the goal of protecting privacy will be greatly disserved.

The desire to make a statement about privacy in the digital age does not justify the consequences that today's decision is likely to produce.

b. Justice Kennedy, with Whom Justice Thomas and Justice Alito Joined, Dissenting

The new rule the Court seems to formulate puts needed, reasonable, accepted, lawful, and congressionally authorized criminal investigations at serious risk in serious cases, often when law enforcement seeks to prevent the threat of violent crimes. And it places undue restrictions on the lawful and necessary enforcement powers exercised not only by the Federal Government, but also by law enforcement in every State and locality throughout the Nation. Adherence to this Court's long-standing precedents and analytic framework would have been the proper and prudent way to resolve this case.

* * *

This case should be resolved by interpreting accepted property principles as the baseline for reasonable expectations of privacy. Here the Government did not search anything over which Carpenter could assert ownership or control. Instead, it issued a court-authorized subpoena to a third party to disclose information it alone owned and controlled. That should suffice to resolve this case.

Having concluded, however, that the Government searched Carpenter when it obtained cell-site records from his cell phone service providers, the proper resolution of this case should have been to remand for the Court of Appeals to determine in the first instance whether the search was reasonable. And the Court's reflexive imposition of the warrant requirement obscures important and difficult issues, such as the scope of Congress' power to authorize the Government to collect new forms of information using processes that deviate from traditional warrant procedures, and how the Fourth Amendment's reasonableness requirement should apply when the Government uses compulsory process instead of engaging in an actual, physical search.

6. Cloud Computing

"Cloud computing" is a term based on industry usage of the cloud "as a metaphor for the ethereal Internet." As elusive as this concept sounds, it has a concrete impact on many of our daily interactions—just think about Internet websites like Google (Gmail), Amazon and Facebook. A cloud platform is storage or software access that is "rented" or temporarily stored with a remote cloud service provider. Software-as-a-service, SaaS, allows people and companies alike to use messaging and storage services without the requirement of managing the underlying technology.

The National Institute of Standards and Technology defines cloud computing this way:

> "a model for enabling convenient, on-demand network access to a shared pool of configurable computing resources (e.g., networks, servers, storage, applications, and services) that can be rapidly provisioned and released with minimal management effort or service provider interaction."

Cloud service providers offer services beyond just storing and sharing data. They also offer database management and mining and web services, including processing complicated and large sets of data as well as managing and providing access to medical records.

Cloud computing services are used by both individuals and businesses, domestically and internationally. Individuals, through cloud providers like Google, have the ability to store, access and share information in quantities and capacities of great proportion. Likewise, companies use cloud computing services for similar needs.

The desire for a small firm or solo shop to use a cloud-based service is fairly straightforward. As opposed to the traditional desktop-and-server-based application, cloud computing offers more cost savings and greater accessibility. Typically, cloud-based services eliminate large up-front licensing and server costs and have lower consulting and installation fees. Furthermore, these systems are easier to use and work with both Windows and Mac operating systems.

Cloud computing can act as a force multiplier that allows smaller firms to compete with larger firms without having to pay the costs of maintaining and managing their cloud-based web services, leaving them with the resources to provide core services competitive with their larger counterparts.

Nevertheless, large firms receive similar cost benefits from cloud computing, such as reduced overhead and greater reach. Of course, the benefits will have to be weighed against the problems associated with relinquishing control, such as privacy breaches.

Although sixty-nine percent of people using the Internet use at least one cloud-based computing service, many on these platforms are not aware if and/or when they are using a cloud service. Even if they are aware, it is likely that even less people are aware of where their data is being stored at any given time.[15]

Notes and Questions

1. When does a person have a subjective expectation of privacy that society will recognize as reasonable in data she has stored in the cloud? What are the relevant considerations? Are those considerations the same or different from obtaining information from a person's ISP or cell service provider?

2. In *Riley v. California*, 134 S. Ct. 2473 (2014), which was reproduced in Chapter 8, the Court made these comments:

> [T]he data a user views on many modern cell phones may not in fact be stored on the device itself. Treating a cell phone as a container whose contents may be searched incident to an arrest is a bit strained as an initial matter. But the analogy crumbles entirely when a cell phone is used to access data located elsewhere, at the tap of a screen. That is what cell phones, with increasing frequency, are designed to do by taking advantage of "cloud computing." Cloud computing is the capacity of Internet-connected devices to display data stored on remote servers rather than on the device itself. Cell phone users often may not know whether particular information is stored on the device or in the cloud, and it generally makes little difference. Moreover, the same type of data may be stored locally on the device for one user and in the cloud for another.

What, if anything, do these comments suggest about reasonable expectations of privacy in data not on one's own device and the third party doctrine's viability? How would the majority in *Carpenter* analyze cloud computing? (Note that Chief Justice Roberts wrote the majority opinions in both cases.)

3. There is much uncertainty in this area. What do you think of my views:

> Generally speaking, a person has a Fourth Amendment protected interest when one has taken steps to exclude: close the door; close the drapes; seal the letter in an envelope; enter into a contract for a self storage locker or a safe deposit box. Thus, for example, Katz took steps to exclude the unwanted ear by closing the door to the telephone booth. Renters have a protected interest in storage lockers. The same should be true in the digital world: encrypt the

---

15. Peter Brown, *Who Has Jurisdiction over the Clouds? A Look into Cloud Computing and the Jurisdictional Issues Surrounding the Use of Its Shared Networks and Servers*, 1010 PLI/PAT 139 (Practicing Law Institute 2010). Copyright © 2010, Peter Brown. All rights reserved. Reprinted by permission.

body of the email; enter into a contractual relationship with a cloud computing service that offers privacy. The Internet is not structured to protect privacy; one must take steps to exclude. It is more like a shopping mall where there is no right to exclude (or have privacy). Indeed, unlike the relatively passive invitations to shop that stores offer in a mall, Internet service providers and websites are designed to obtain information about those using the services and to exploit that information. Like Katz, those seeking to prevent prying must take steps to do so. An encrypted email message is the same as a letter in a sealed envelope; surely the government could open that flimsy white envelope and it may now have the capacity to decrypt the email message. But in both situations, the person has taken steps that, normatively, society acknowledges as reasonable (to use privacy analysis) and to exclude (to use security analysis). An unencrypted email is not like a letter—its like a post card. There are now a variety of web-based services that offer remote storage and computing. These, in my view, are akin to a self-storage unit; the parties enter into a contract that, normatively, gives the individual a protected interest.

See Thomas K. Clancy, The Fourth Amendment: Its History and Interpretation § 3.5.1.1. (3d ed. 2017).

Chapter 12

Statutory Regulation of Obtaining Data

§ 12.1 Introduction

This chapter examines the basic structure of three significant Federal statutes that regulate obtaining digital evidence by the government. Those statutes, all of which are subsumed under provisions of the Electronic Communications Privacy Act (ECPA), are:

- Pen/Trap Statute, 18 U.S.C. §§ 3121–27
- Wiretap Statute, 18 U.S.C. §§ 2510–22
- Stored Communications Act, 18 U.S.C. §§ 2701–12

Each of these statutes have evolved over time and they have generated much litigation. The reach and importance of each statute is subject to debate. Indeed, one court has observed that the intersection of the latter two statutes "is a complex, often convoluted, area of the law."[1] That difficulty is "compounded by the fact that the ECPA was written prior to the advent of the Internet and the World Wide Web."[2] Moreover, in the wake of the *Carpenter* decision, there are aspects of that statute scheme that may violate the Fourth Amendment. That 2018 decision, discussed in Chapter 11, has added a great deal of uncertainty. Its full impact may be years in the making.

This chapter's goals are modest: it introduces the main concepts of the statutes and provides a broad overview of their function in obtaining digital evidence. To begin, the statutes make two crucial distinctions. The first is between content and noncontent. The second is between real-time surveillance and retrospective obtaining of data.

The distinction between content and noncontent information is critical in determining the level of statutory protection. ECPA offers much less protection to noncontent information than content information. The Wiretap Act governs the interception of communications content in transit and provides the most protection, including stringent requirements for a wiretap order to issue and a suppression

---

1. United States v. Smith, 155 F.3d 1051, 1055 (9th Cir. 1998).
2. Konop v. Hawaiian Airlines, 302 F.3d 868, 874 (9th Cir. 2002).

remedy. The Pen Register Act governs the interception of the noncontent associated with communications; it requires a very low threshold to obtain an order and does not have an exclusionary remedy. The Stored Communications Act, which is the most complicated of the three statutes, regulates retrospective access to both the content and noncontent of communications held in electronic storage by certain communications providers. It offers different levels of protection through a hierarchical structure of types of process, depending on several contingencies, including the type of communications provider that has the information, the type of information sought, and how long the information has been in storage.

§ 12.2 The Pen/Trap Statute, 18 U.S.C. §§ 3121–3127

The Pen Register Act was adopted in response to *Smith v. Maryland*, 442 U.S. 735 (1979), which is excerpted in Chapter 11. *Smith* rejected the view that a person had any reasonable expectation of privacy in the numbers dialed from his telephone, thus permitting law enforcement agencies to obtain that dialing information without complying with the Fourth Amendment. A pen register records digits dialed on a telephone and a trap and trace device shows what numbers call a specific telephone, that is, all incoming phone numbers. The Pen Register Act initially applied to devices that recorded outgoing and incoming telephone numbers. The USA PATRIOT Act amended the statutory definition of pen registers and trap and trace devices to include any "device or process" that records "dialing, routing, addressing, or signaling information," other than content information, associated with an electronic communication. The statute continues to express a general prohibition against the installation or use of a pen register without a court order. 18 U.S.C. § 3121(a).

Pen Register defined § 3127(3)

- "a device or process which records or decodes dialing, routing, addressing, or signaling information transmitted by an instrument or facility from which a wire or electronic communication is transmitted, provided, however, that such information shall not include the contents of any communication"
- *function*: records outgoing addressing information (*e.g.*, a number dialed from a telephone).

Trap and Trace Device defined § 3127(4)

- "a device or process which captures the incoming electronic or other impulses which identify the originating number or other dialing, routing, addressing, or signaling information reasonably likely to identify the source of a wire or electronic communication, provided, however that such information shall not include the contents of any communication"
- *function*: records incoming addressing information (*e.g.*, caller ID information).

How orders obtained § 3122(b)(2)

- A government attorney may apply for a court order authorizing installation of a pen register and/or trap and trace device if "the information likely to be obtained is relevant to an ongoing criminal investigation."

- The standard for obtaining a court order is far from burdensome. An attorney for the Government must make an application for authorization to install and use a pen register "in writing under oath or equivalent affirmation, to a court of competent jurisdiction." 18 U.S.C. § 3122(a)(1). Such an application need only contain: "(1) the identity of the attorney for the Government or the State law enforcement or investigative officer making the application and the identity of the law enforcement agency conducting the investigation; and (2) certification by the applicant that the information likely to be obtained is relevant to an ongoing criminal investigation being conducted by that agency." 18 U.S.C. § 3122(b). Upon a finding that this burden has been met, the court "shall enter" such an order.[3]

- "So long as an attorney for the Government applies for a 'pen register' or 'trap and trace device' and the court finds that the attorney certified that the information obtained using the devices is relevant to an ongoing criminal investigation, the court is mandated to enter an *ex parte* order authorizing the use of the devices."[4]

---

1. Application for Internet Communications

In the Matter of Application of the United States of America for an Order Authorizing the Installation and Use of a Pen Register and a Trap & Trace Device on E-Mail Account

416 F. Supp. 2d 13 (D.D.C. 2006)

Hogan, C.J.

A pen register and a trap and trace device may be a "process"[n.5][5] used to gather information relating to "electronic communication." As for the term "electronic communication," the statute points to the definition found in 18 U.S.C. § 2510. That

---

3. In the Matter of Applications of the United States of America for Orders (1) Authorizing the Use of Pen Registries and Trap and Trace Devices, 515 F. Supp. 2d 325 (E.D.N.Y. 2007).

4. In the Matter of Application of the United States of America for an Order Authorizing Installation and Use of a Pen Register and Trap and Trace Device on E-mail Account, 416 F. Supp. 2d 13 (D.D.C. 2006).

5. [n.5] The statute does not define the term "process," so the Court will give that term its ordinary meaning. Given the breadth of this term, the Court concludes that it covers software and hardware operations used to collect information.

statute defines the term "electronic communication" to mean "any transfer of signs, signals, writing, images, sounds, data, or intelligence of any nature transmitted in whole or in part by a wire, radio, electromagnetic, photoelectronic or photooptical system that affects interstate or foreign commerce...." 18 U.S.C. §2510(12). Given that the statute defines an electronic communication to be any "transfer of signals" of "any nature" by means of virtually any type of transmission system (*e.g.*, wire, electromagnetic, etc.), there can be no doubt it is broad enough to encompass e-mail communications and other similar signals transmitted over the Internet. It therefore follows that pen registers and trap and trace devices may be processes used to gather information about e-mail communications.

There is some concern that current technology, particularly the use of a software process to obtain the requested information, increases the risk that content will be impermissibly procured and disclosed to the Government. A perhaps oversimplified response to that concern is that the stricture to avoid the contents of e-mail communications should be easy to comply with so long as the pen register and trap and trace processes or devices exclude all information relating to the subject line and body of the communication. The better approach, however, may be to take heed of the fact that "pen registers" and "trap and trace devices" are statutorily defined as processes or devices that are prohibited from collecting "the contents of any communication." 18 U.S.C. §3127(3)–(4). Consequently, the argument could be made that any process or device that collects the *content* of an electronic communication is not, in fact, a pen register or trap and trace device but, instead, is an electronic intercepting device as defined in Title III of the Omnibus Crime Control and Safe Streets Act, codified at 18 U.S.C. §§2510–2520. Consequently, the unauthorized use of that process or device would be subject to the penalties set forth in that statute.

---

2. "Post-Cut-Through Dialed Digits"

In the Matter of Applications of the United States of America for Orders (1) Authorizing the Use of Pen Registers and Trap and Trace Devices ...

515 F. Supp. 2d 325 (E.D.N.Y. 2007)

Azrack, Magistrate Judge.

Telephone use has expanded rapidly since the constitutionality of pen registers was examined in 1979. Today, Americans regularly use their telephones not just to dial a phone number, but to manage bank accounts, refill prescriptions, check movie times, and so on.

Dialed digits can now be categorized in a number of ways. "Post-cut-through dialed digits" ("PCTDD"), the subject of the instant application, "are any numbers dialed from a telephone after the call is initially setup or 'cut-through.'" In most instances, any digit dialed after the first ten is a PCTDD. "Sometimes these digits transmit real information, such as bank account numbers, Social Security numbers, prescription numbers, and the like." In such circumstances, PCTDD contain the "contents of communication." At other times, PCTDD "are other telephone numbers, as when a party places a credit card call by first dialing the long distance carrier access number and then the phone number of the intended party," or when an extension number is dialed.

While individuals may not have a reasonable expectation of privacy in the numbers that they dial to connect a phone call, the content they communicate over a phone line in the form of PCTDD is different. Technology has transformed the way Americans use phone lines. Now, instead of a human operator, individuals are asked to relay information to a machine by way of PCTDD in order to process requests and obtain information. When this communication includes content, it is the functional equivalent of voice communication and is protected as such. Moreover, the information that is often transmitted via PCTDD is often sensitive and personal. Bank account numbers, pin numbers and passwords, prescription identification numbers, social security numbers, credit card numbers, and so on, all encompass the kind of information that an individual wants and reasonably expects to be kept private.

Courts have long struggled with issues concerning the application of the Fourth Amendment to new technologies. Here, modern technology in the form of automated telephone systems have changed the collection capabilities of pen registers. However, the change in technology does not alter the mandates of the Fourth Amendment. The content of private communications remains protected. To read the Constitution more narrowly is to ignore the role that PCTDD and automated telephone systems have come to play in private communication.

Despite the investigative benefit which would come from access to all PCTDD, the Government cannot bootstrap the content of communications, protected by the Fourth Amendment, into the grasp of a device authorized only to collect call-identifying information. [Accordingly, the court believed that a pen register could not be lawfully employed to collect PCTDD.]

In re Certified Question of Law
858 F.3d 591 (FISA Ct. Rev. 2016)
United States Foreign Intelligence Surveillance Court of Review

Per Curiam.

The Foreign Intelligence Surveillance Court ("FISC") certified the following question to us:

> Whether an order issued under 50 U.S.C. § 1842 may authorize the Government to obtain all post-cut-through digits, subject to a prohibition on the affirmative investigative use of any contents thereby acquired, when there is no technology reasonably available to the Government that would permit:

(1) a PR/TT [pen register/trap-and-trace] device to acquire post-cut-through digits that are non-content DRAS [dialing, routing, addressing, and signaling] information, while not acquiring post-cut-through digits that are contents of a communication; or

(2) the Government at the time it receives information acquired by a PR/TT device, to discard post-cut-through digits that are contents of a communication, while retaining those digits that are non-content DRAS information.

We conclude that section 1842 authorizes, and the Fourth Amendment to the Constitution of the United States does not prohibit, an order of the kind described in the certification. Read fairly and as a whole, the governing statutes evince Congress's understanding that pen registers and trap-and-trace devices will, under some circumstances, inevitably collect content information. Congress has addressed this difficulty by requiring the government to minimize the incidental collection of content through the employment of such technological measures as are reasonably available—not by barring entirely, as a form of prophylaxis, the use of pen registers and trap-and-trace devices simply because they might gather content incidentally.

Nor does an order authorizing such surveillance run afoul of the Fourth Amendment's guarantee against unreasonable searches and seizures. The warrant requirement is generally a tolerable proxy for "reasonableness" when the government is seeking to unearth evidence of criminal wrongdoing, but it fails properly to balance the interests at stake when the government is instead seeking to preserve and protect the nation's security from foreign threat. We therefore hold that surveillance of this type may be constitutionally reasonable even when it is not authorized by a probable-cause warrant. We further hold, on the facts presented here, that the order under review reasonably balances the investigative needs of the government and the privacy interests of the people.

I

On January 21, 2016, a judge of the FISC approved an Application for Pen Register and Trap and Trace Device(s) after finding that the application met the requirements for a pen register/trap-and-trace authorization order under the Foreign Intelligence Surveillance Act ("FISA"). The authorization provided for the installation and use of pen register/trap-and-trace devices on a cellular telephone number used by the subject of an ongoing investigation to protect against clandestine intelligence activities, with the assistance of the service provider for that number.

As requested by the government, the court's order granted "the authority to record and decode all post-cut-through digits."

II

The problem in this case is this: Under presently available technology, there is no way for a pen register to distinguish between dialing information and content information contained in post-cut-through digits so that it can be directed to intercept only the former and not the latter. Therefore, in the case of a pen register order that authorizes the interception of post-cut-through digits, there is some risk that content information will be intercepted along with dialing information.

A

The statute that governs the use of pen registers and trap-and-trace devices for foreign intelligence purposes is title IV of FISA, 50 U.S.C. §§ 1841–46. That statute provides that the government can obtain an order authorizing the installation and use of a pen register or trap-and-trace device upon a statutorily sufficient showing, made either to a judge of the FISC or to a properly authorized magistrate judge.

The definitional section of title IV of FISA, section 1841, provides that the terms pen register and trap-and-trace device have the same meanings that are given to those terms in section 3127 of the title 18.

B

The question whether title IV of FISA authorizes pen register orders to collect post-cut-through digits turns on the meaning of the definitional language in 18 U.S.C. § 3127(3), and in particular the "proviso" clause, which reads as follows: "provided, however, that such information shall not include the contents of any communication." It is clear that the statutory language is intended to prohibit the use of pen registers for the purpose of intercepting content communications, such as bank account numbers, social security numbers, and personal identification numbers. The statute expresses that intent in an unusual way, however, by making the prohibition against intercepting content information part of the definition of "pen register."

The most literal interpretation of section 3127(3), read in isolation, leads to a problem. If a device ceases to be a pen register whenever it intercepts post-cut-through content information, it is impossible to know in advance whether the device is a pen register (and thus whether its use may be authorized under title IV of FISA).

A pen register intercepts the digits that are dialed. It does not distinguish between dialing information, on the one hand, and dialed digits that constitute "the contents of any communication," on the other. With currently available technology, that distinction can be drawn only after the information collected by the pen register has been decoded. Defining a device as a pen register depending on the nature of the material it ultimately collects thus poses a dilemma for courts that are asked to authorize the collection of dialing information, and in particular post-cut-through digits. A court seeking to determine whether to authorize a pen register application that includes post-cut-through digits cannot know in advance whether the device will intercept some content information and therefore be ineligible for an authorization order.

One approach to resolving that problem is to conclude that if there is any chance that content information will be intercepted, a pen register order that authorizes the collection of post-cut-through digits may not be entered. Adopting that theory, several courts have held that the pen register statute does not authorize the collection of any post-cut-through digits.[n.6][6]

The theory adopted by those courts might lead to the conclusion that the collection of post-cut-through digits may be authorized in circumstances in which the government can assure the court that it is highly unlikely that content information will be intercepted along with dialing information. None of the above-cited decisions have drawn that distinction, however. Rather, they have flatly barred the government from relying on the pen register statutes to intercept post-cut-through digits.

We think the better approach is to interpret the definitional language of section 3127(3) to mean that a court may not authorize the use of a pen register to collect content information, and that any content information that is collected cannot be used for any investigative purposes. Under that interpretation, a court can authorize the use of a pen register to collect post-cut-through digits, as long as the collecting agency takes all reasonably available steps to minimize the collection of content information and is prohibited from making use of any content information that may be collected.

We conclude that the latter interpretation of section 3127(3) is more in line with the statutory text and the purpose the provision was intended to serve. In particular, we do not believe Congress intended to prohibit the use of pen registers whenever there was any risk that the intercepted digits would constitute content information. To the contrary, we believe the best interpretation of the related provisions of the pen register statutes is that Congress understood that content information might sometimes be intercepted by authorized pen registers, but intended that steps should be taken to minimize that risk to the extent reasonably possible. Both the text and the legislative history of the pen register statutes support this interpretation of section 3127(3).

1

It is clear from the text of the pen register provisions in title 18, read as a whole, that Congress understood that some content information might be intercepted in the

---

6. [n.6] One of the courts that has addressed this issue has concluded that all post-cut-through digits constitute content information. *In re Application of the United States,* No. 08 MC 0595, 2008 WL 5255815 (E.D.N.Y. Dec. 16, 2008). On that premise, the court declined to authorize the interception of post-cut-through digits. That premise, however, is flawed, as it is well understood that post-cut-through digits can include both dialing information and content information, and that they may often include only dialing information. The amicus curiae argues that all post-cut-through digits are content with respect to the service provider, and that the interception of post-cut-through digits should never be authorized. That argument is unconvincing, as the definition of "contents" for purposes of pen registers is "information concerning the substance, purport, or meaning of [a wire, oral, or electronic] communication." 18 U.S.C. § 2510(8). That definition does not include dialing information, whether viewed from the perspective of the individual or the provider. The fact that the provider is not the one who uses that information for dialing purposes does not alter the fact that the information is dialing information.

course of executing a valid pen register order. One of those provisions is 18 U.S.C. § 3121(c). The statute states:

> (c) Limitation. A government agency authorized to install and use a pen register or trap and trace device under this chapter or under State law shall use technology reasonably available to it that restricts the recording or decoding of electronic or other impulses to the dialing, routing, addressing, and signaling information utilized in the processing and transmitting of wire or electronic communications so as not to include the contents of any wire or electronic communications.

18 U.S.C. § 3121(c).

That language requires the government to use "reasonably available" technology to avoid recording content information. But the prohibition is conditional, requiring the government to use such restricting technology only if it is "reasonably available." Thus, by requiring the use of "technology reasonably available" to restrict recording and decoding of intercepted information to dialing information, Congress recognized that such technology might not be available or might not achieve the objective with perfect accuracy.

The plain import of the statutory language is that, absent such "reasonably available" technology, lawfully authorized pen registers will sometimes intercept and decode content information contained in dialed digits, in addition to information regarding dialing information. Thus, section 3121(c) strikes a compromise that allows the government to obtain the dialing information to which it is entitled, while requiring that all reasonably available measures be taken to avoid or minimize the collection of content information.

The amicus curiae takes the position that the definitional language of section 3127(3) — "provided, however, that such information shall not include the contents of any communication" — plainly forecloses the conclusion that a pen register may lawfully intercept content under any circumstances. And some courts, likewise seizing on the "provided" clause of section 3127(3), have dismissed section 3121(c) as a mere "added precaution to ensure that, the Government does not use an authorized pen register to collect contents."

We cannot agree with either position. Our duty is "to construe statutes, not isolated provisions," and to properly discharge that duty, "we must read the [statute's] words in their context and with a view to their place in the overall statutory scheme." Of particular salience here, we are to avoid interpreting one statutory provision in a manner that would render another provision superfluous.

If section 3127(3) barred courts from authorizing the collection of post-cut-through digits, there would be no need for technology to distinguish between dialing information and content information. The need for technology to distinguish between the two types of information arises only if the courts can authorize investigators to intercept signals that can sometimes contain content. Because only post-cut-through digits can contain content information, the limitation of section 3121(c) must necessarily be directed to post-cut-through digits. And because the limitation in section 3121(c) is conditional, not absolute, the two provisions can be read in harmony only by construing them to permit the interception of post-cut-through digits under appropriate circumstances.[n.7]7

2

[In 1994], Congress added the "limitation" provision, section 3121(c), to the pen register statutes. The enacted version of section 3121(c) stated:

> A government agency authorized to install and use a pen register under this chapter or under State law shall use technology reasonably available to it that restricts the recording or decoding of electronic or other impulses to the dialing and signaling information utilized in call processing.

18 U.S.C. § 3121(c) (1994).

That provision recognized that pen registers were capable of intercepting content information. Congress's solution to that problem was to direct agencies using pen registers to use technology that was "reasonably available" to restrict the recording or decoding of content information and limit the information obtained to "the dialing and signaling information utilized in call processing." In effect, Congress directed the agencies to do the best they reasonably could to limit the interception of content information, but it did not suggest that, in the absence of such reasonably available technology, a pen register could not be authorized if it posed the risk of intercepting content information.

Both the House and Senate Reports on the 1994 Act explained that the purpose of the amendment was not to prohibit the use of pen registers, but to "require [ ] law enforcement to use reasonably available technology to minimize information obtained through pen registers."[n.9]8 In particular, the reports explained that the new provision would require government agencies "to use, when reasonably available, technology that restricts the information captured by such device to the dialing or signaling information necessary to direct or process a call, excluding any

---

7. [n.7] The amicus curiae contends that if the government's argument were applied to Internet pen registers, the government could collect information generated by a wide variety of activities on the Internet, including searching, uploading documents, and drafting emails. Nonetheless, the amicus argues that the prospect of such collections indicates that the government's statutory construction must be wrong. We disagree. Even assuming that the government's statutory theory would apply in the same manner in that different technological setting, we would have to determine whether any technology is reasonably available to excise content. Moreover, the application of the government's theory in that setting, if it had the consequences argued by amicus curiae, might call for a different Fourth Amendment balancing of interests.

8. [n.9] The term "minimization" has a familiar meaning in the context of interceptions of electronic communications. Section 2518(5) of title 18 directs that electronic surveillance must "be conducted in such a way as to minimize the interception of communications not otherwise subject to interception." The requirement of minimization thus contemplates that some unauthorized interception will inevitably occur, but that the agency must take steps to keep that interception to a minimum.

further communication conducted through the use of dialed digits that would otherwise be captured."

Following the attacks against New York and Washington on September 11, 2001, Congress enacted the USA PATRIOT Act of 2001. Among many other provisions, Congress modified portions of the pen register/trap-and-trace statute. The changes made at that time are at the heart of the issue before the court today.

The principal change to the pen register/trap-and-trace provisions was to make those provisions applicable not just to telephony, but to all forms of wire and electronic communications. In so doing, Congress made four amendments that bear on the present issue.

First, Congress omitted the words "call processing" and added the words "routing" and "addressing" to section 3121(c) to cover technologies other than telephony.

Second, Congress modified section 3121(c) to state explicitly that the purpose of directing the government to use "reasonably available" technology to limit the collection of certain electronic signals was "so as not to include the contents of any wire or electronic communications."

Third, Congress amended the definition of "pen register" by expanding the definition to include "dialing, routing, addressing, or signaling information transmitted by an instrument or facility from which a wire or electronic communication is transmitted."

Fourth, Congress added the proviso in the definitions of pen register and trap-and-trace device that read: "provided, however, that such information shall not include the contents of any communication."

The changes to sections 3121(c) and 3127 were added in the Senate. In the absence of a committee report, Senator Leahy, the chairman of the Senate Judiciary Committee, presented a detailed summary of the changes on the day before the Act was passed. He explained that the language used in the pen register and trap-and-trace statutes was intended "to expressly exclude the use of pen-trap devices to intercept 'content' which is broadly defined in 18 U.S.C. 2510(8)." He added that the Act "requires the government to use reasonably available technology that limits the interceptions under the pen/trap device laws 'so as not to include the contents of any wire or electronic communications.'"

Importantly, Senator Leahy recognized that, notwithstanding the statutory directive to use reasonably available technology to avoid collecting content information, the "pen/trap devices in use today collect 'content.'" In particular, he recognized the risk of collecting content information from "[t]he impulses made after a phone call is connected." He explained that the amendment to section 3121(c) was intended to underscore the need to incentivize the development of better technology to limit the interception of content information, particularly in light of the fact that the USA PATRIOT Act made the pen register provisions applicable to a wide array of modem communications technologies, such as the Internet, and not simply traditional telephone lines.

Senator Leahy also noted that, in light of the known risk of collecting content information from post-cut-through digits, he would have preferred a requirement of somewhat heightened judicial review for pen register and trap-and-trace applications. But in the absence of such a requirement, he acknowledged that the statute continued to require only that the government "use reasonably available technology" to limit the collection of content information.

Senator Leahy's comments make clear that the new language added in the 2001 statute was intended to avoid expanding the type of information that could be intercepted, not to narrow it. In particular, nothing in his comments, or elsewhere in the legislative history, suggests that, in the absence of an effective technological solution, the amendments to the pen register/trap-and-trace statutes were intended to prohibit the collection of dialing information simply because there was some risk that content information might incidentally be collected as well.

We therefore conclude that a close analysis of the statutes that have authorized pen register orders starting in 1986 does not support the view that Congress sought to prohibit any authorized collection of dialing information whenever it posed some risk of additionally collecting content information. What Congress elected was a course of minimization, principally through the use of "reasonably available technology."

III

Our analysis of the pen register statutes requires us to consider whether those statutes, if construed to authorize the interception of post-cut-through digits, would run afoul of the Fourth Amendment.

It may be that if a pen register interception were directed at the acquisition and use of content information, it would be unlawful in the absence of a court order issued on a showing of probable cause. In the context of criminal investigations, that would certainly be the case for the interception of conversations through electronic surveillance, *Berger v. New York*, 388 U.S. 41 (1967), and it has been held that probable cause is required to authorize the disclosure and use of content information in email communications, *see Warshak v. United States*, 490 F.3d 455 (6th Cir.2007), *vacated*, 532 F.3d 521 (6th Cir.2008) (en banc). The same rule might apply to the use of a pen register for the purpose of intercepting content information.

The constitutional issue is not whether a probable cause warrant is required to use a pen register to obtain content information for investigative purposes. Rather, the question is whether the risk of incidental collection of content information renders the collection of dialing information in post-cut-through digits unreasonable in the absence of a probable cause warrant, even when the content information will not be used for any purpose. We think the answer to that question is no.

When law enforcement officials undertake a search to uncover evidence of criminal wrongdoing, the familiar requirement of a probable-cause warrant generally achieves an acceptable balance between the investigative needs of the government and the privacy interests of the people. But it has long been recognized that some searches occur in the service of "special needs, beyond the normal need for law enforcement," and that, when it comes to intrusions of this kind, the warrant requirement is sometimes a poor proxy for the textual command of reasonableness.

We conclude that, in the circumstances presented here, the incidental collection of content information during the collection of post-cut-through digits—assuming it constitutes a search in the first place—is constitutionally reasonable, even when done without a probable-cause warrant.

The idea that official intrusions calculated to preserve the nation's security against foreign threat might require special constitutional treatment is not a new one. In *Katz v. United States,* the first page in the modem chapter of our search-and-seizure jurisprudence, the Supreme Court paused to observe that the Fourth Amendment's usual strictures might require adjustment "in a situation involving national security." 389 U.S. 347, 358 n. 23 (1967). Five years later, in *United States v. United States District Court (Keith),* the Court rejected the argument that no warrant need be obtained whenever the government engages in domestic surveillance related to "internal security matters." 407 U.S. 297, 299 (1972). But it took care to emphasize that *Keith* "involve[d] only the domestic aspects of national security," not any "issues which may be involved with respect to activities of foreign powers or their agents," and it noted "the view that warrantless surveillance, though impermissible in domestic security cases, may be constitutional where foreign powers are involved."

Consistent with this counsel, in the decade following *Keith,* a number of federal appeals courts recognized a "foreign intelligence" exception to the warrant requirement.

We thus conclude that when the government, acting pursuant to a program of surveillance involving a legitimate objective that goes beyond everyday crime control, seeks to use a pen register directed at a person located in the United States who is reasonably believed to be engaged in clandestine intelligence activities on behalf of a foreign government, it may do so without obtaining a probable-cause warrant even if its monitoring of post-cut-through digits constitutes a search under the Fourth Amendment.

We now turn to the question of reasonableness, a question that requires us to balance against the degree of the government's intrusion on individual privacy the degree to which that intrusion furthers the government's legitimate interests. In the circumstances presented here, the scale tips in the government's favor. The search, assuming it is one, is reasonable. In particular, the factors that render the search reasonable are (1) the paramount interest in investigating possible threats to national security; (2) the investigative importance of having access to the dialing information provided by post-cut-through digits, (3) the incidental nature of the collection of content information from post-cut-through digits, (4) the relatively slight intrusion on privacy entailed by the acquisition of post-cut-through digits, (5) the prohibition against the use of any content information obtained from the pen register or trap-and-trace device, (6) the steps taken by the government to minimize the dissemination of post-cut-through digits; and (7) the fact that FISA pen register interceptions are conducted only with the approval and under the supervision of a neutral magistrate, in this case a FISC judge. We discuss each of those factors in more detail below.

First, the Supreme Court has stated that "no governmental interest is more compelling" than national security. Thus, the government's investigative interest in cases arising under FISA is at the highest level and weighs heavily in the constitutional balancing process.

Second, the dialing information in post-cut-through digits may be of critical investigative importance in certain cases in which pen register authorization is sought. If the subject of a pen register uses a calling service, a pen register that does not collect post-cut-through digits will disclose no information at all about the ultimate destination of the call. Because subjects of national security investigations seek to avoid detection of their activities, the loss of access to post-cut-through digits is likely to substantially undercut the value of a pen register in a significant number of cases.

Third, a pen register authorized in a FISA investigation is targeted at dialing information; the collection of any content information from post-cut-through digits is incidental to the purpose of the pen register. The incidental collection of constitutionally protected material does not render the authorized collection of unprotected material unlawful.

The application of that rule to searches of documents is particularly instructive here. The Supreme Court recognized in *Andresen v. Maryland*, 427 U.S. 463, 482 n. 11 (1976), that "[i]n searches for papers, it is certain that some innocuous documents will be examined, at least cursorily, in order to determine whether they are, in fact, among those papers authorized to be seized." The incidental examination of such documents to determine whether they are subject to authorized seizure is analogous to the examination of post-cut-through digits to determine if they contain content information; once it is determined that particular post-cut-through digits contain content information, that information is excluded from any investigative use.

Fourth, the content information found in some post-cut-through digits is likely to be of marginal privacy value. As the FISC judge explained in the certification order, post-cut-through digits that constitute contents "involve a narrow category of information from a subset of calls placed from a targeted phone number" and thus represent "a lesser intrusion than, for example, obtaining the full contents of all calls to or from a targeted phone number." For that reason, in balancing the seriousness of the invasion of the individual's personal privacy against the importance of the government's interest, the degree of the intrusion resulting from collecting post-cut-through digits will typically be modest.

Fifth, any content information that is collected as part of the interception of post-cut-through digits may not be used for any investigative purpose, absent an order from the court. That prohibition on use protects against the risk that an investigative agency might seek to obtain authorization to intercept post-cut-through digits in order to obtain access to the content information contained therein.

Sixth, minimization procedures are available, and are regularly employed, to limit the extent to which content information that is incidentally intercepted during the collection of post-cut-through digits is made available to, or used and disseminated by, government agents.

The Department of Justice has taken several steps to minimize access to post-cut-through digits and reduce the risk that content information will be intercepted or disclosed. The prohibition against targeting or using content information obtained from post-cut-through digits was set forth in a 2002 memorandum of the Deputy Attorney General, and the FBI's field offices have been instructed to implement procedures to ensure compliance with the policies in that memorandum.

Among those procedures is a measure that requires masking post-cut-through digits in investigative file materials. Only an analyst who has undergone special training may unmask the post-cut-through digits, and only after providing justification for doing so. In some circumstances, depending on the nature of the subscriber to the telephone that was initially contacted, even an analyst may not examine post-cut-through digits. For example, if the initial connection is to a financial institution, an analyst may not examine any post-cut-through digits because there is reason to believe that post-cut-through digits may contain content.

Minimization measures have been recognized as important to the lawfulness of investigative procedures in various settings. Most significantly, federal wiretap law recognizes that some conversations that were not intended to be intercepted will inevitably be overheard. The answer given by Congress and endorsed by the courts is to require minimization of such intrusions to the extent reasonably practicable.

The Supreme Court has applied the same principle to document searches, emphasizing the importance of minimization in both settings. And in other Fourth Amendment contexts as well, the Supreme Court has emphasized the importance of minimization steps employed to reduce the intrusiveness of the invasion in question.

Finally, an important aspect of the use of pen registers in FISA investigations is the role played by FISC judges in authorizing and supervising pen register interceptions. Although the court does not require a showing of probable cause to authorize pen register interceptions, it is responsible for supervising the execution of pen register orders. As noted above, title IV of FISA contains a provision authorizing FISC judges "to impose additional privacy or minimization procedures with regard to the installation or use of a pen register or trap and trace device." 50 U.S.C. § 1842(h)(2).

In appropriate circumstances, FISC judges can use that authority to ensure that the interception of content information through the collection of post-cut-through digits is kept to a minimum, consistent with the government's right to intercept dialing information. Besides requiring that the government use all reasonably available technology to minimize or eliminate the collection of content information, FISC judges can insist that the government assess the risk of intercepting content information in particular cases and can deny authorization for post-cut-through digits (or impose further restrictions) when that risk is deemed to be unacceptably high as, for example, in the case of a request to renew an application for a pen register that has previously intercepted a substantial amount of content information.

IV

For the reasons set forth above, we answer the certified question in this matter as follows: the FISC may authorize the collection and decoding of post-cut-through digits as long as the government is prohibited from making investigative or evidentiary use of any content information contained in that material, and as long as the court directs that appropriate procedures be used to minimize the collection of content information, including the use of any reasonably available technology that may be developed to restrict the recording and decoding of pen register or trap-and-trace information to dialing information.

---

3. Content Related to Internet Activity

In re Application of the United States of America for an Order Authorizing the Use of a Pen Register and Trap on [xxx] Internet Service Account/User Name

396 F. Supp. 2d 45 (D. Mass. 2005)

COLLINGS, MAGISTRATE JUDGE.

The problem in using a "pen register" and/or a "trap and trace device" on computers by which people are communicating over the internet is to insure that the information given to law enforcement ". . . not include the contents of any communication" as provided in section 3127(3)(4).

An obvious problem occurs when one considers e-mail. That portion of the "header" which contains the information placed in the header which reveals the e-mail addresses of the persons to whom the e-mail is sent, from whom the e-mail is sent and the e-mail address(es) of any person(s) "cc'd" on the e-mail would certainly be obtainable using a pen register and/or a trap and trace device. However, the information contained in the "subject" would reveal the contents of the communication and would not be properly disclosed pursuant to a pen register or trap and trace device. After all, "'contents', when used with respect to any wire, oral, or electronic communication, includes any information concerning the substance, purport or meaning of that communication." Title 18 U.S.C. § 2510(8).

The use of a pen register to obtain the internet addresses accessed by a person presents additional problems. The four applications presently before me seek the Internet Protocol addresses which are defined as a "unique numerical address identifying each computer on the internet." The internet service provider would be required to turn over to the government the incoming and outgoing IP addresses "used to determine web-sites visited" using the particular account which is the subject of the pen register.

If, indeed, the government is seeking only IP addresses of the web sites visited and nothing more, there is no problem. However, because there are a number of internet service providers and their receipt of orders authorizing pen registers and trap and trace devices may be somewhat of a new experience, the Court is concerned that the providers may not be as in tune to the distinction between "dialing, routing, addressing, or signaling information" and "content" as to provide to the government only that to which it is entitled and nothing more.

Some examples serve to make the point. As with the "post-cut through dialed digit extraction," a user could go to an internet site and then type in a bank account number or a credit card number in order to obtain certain information within the site. While this may be said to be "dialing, routing, addressing and signaling information," it also is "contents" of a communication not subject to disclosure to the government under an order authorizing a pen register or a trap and trace device.

Second, there is the issue of search terms. A user may visit the Google site. Presumably the pen register would capture the IP address for that site. However, if the user then enters a search phrase, that search phrase would appear in the URL after the first forward slash. This would reveal content—that is, it would reveal, in the words of the statute, "... information concerning the substance, purport or meaning of that communication." Title 18 U.S.C. § 2510(8). The "substance" and "meaning" of the communication is that the user is conducting a search for information on a particular topic.

United States v. John C. Saville

2013 WL 3270411, U.S. Dist. LEXIS 88428 (D. Mont. June 21, 2013)

Dana L. Christensen, Chief Judge.

United States Magistrate Judge Jeremiah C. Lynch issued findings and recommendations on May 20, 2013, recommending Defendant John Saville's motion to suppress be denied. For the reasons stated below, this Court adopts Judge Lynch's findings and recommendations in full.

Defendant's argument that the search for the term Gnutella itself revealed content of his communication in violation of the pen/trap statute fails. The search term Gnutella did not inform law enforcement about the substance, meaning or purpose of any of Defendant's electronic communications. Rather, it merely indicated Defendant was utilizing the peer-to-peer network. This fact alone did not inform them that Defendant was viewing or accessing child pornography. Detective McNeil could have used a search term that provided such content-revealing information, such as "preteen hardcore." He did not, and he therefore did not violate the pen/trap order.

This Court agrees with Judge Lynch's reasoning, and Defendant's motion to suppress will be denied.

IT IS ORDERED:

1. Judge Lynch's Findings and Recommendations are adopted in full.

2. Defendant's motion to suppress is DENIED.

———————

United States v. John C. Saville

2013 U.S. Dist. LEXIS 89281 (D. Mont. May 20, 2013)

FINDINGS & RECOMMENDATION

JEREMIAH C. LYNCH, UNITED STATES MAGISTRATE JUDGE.

The government has charged Defendant John Saville by indictment with one count of receipt of child pornography in violation of 18 U.S.C. § 2252A(a)(2). Saville claims that the government searched his computer without a warrant in violation of his Fourth Amendment rights, and has moved to suppress all evidence resulting from the search. For the reasons detailed below, it is recommended that the motion to suppress be denied.

The Court makes the following factual findings based on the evidence and testimony presented at the suppression hearing. In October 2011, Bozeman Montana Police Detective Dana McNeil conducted a standard review of information in the Bozeman Police Department Child Protection System. The system is an online database that includes information about internet protocol addresses that are known to be in possession of and/or distributing child pornography on internet-based file-sharing networks like Gnutella.[n.1][9] Detective McNeil observed that a computer using the IP address of 69.144.201.186 was seen giving query hit results for multiple files of known child pornography.

After reviewing the investigative history of the IP address, Detective McNeil learned that software at the IP address had been operating using five different Globally Unique Identifiers (GUID)s.[n.2][10] Detective McNeil also noted that the peer-to-peer software engaging in this activity was identified as Shareaza, which is a known Gnutella software client that allows users to access the network.

For the next month or so, Detective McNeil used a proprietary law enforcement computer program in an attempt to download child pornography files from the

————————

9. [n.1] Gnutella is an internet-based file sharing network that allows users who have downloaded peer-to-peer software to share files with other users. Gnutella is an open, unsecured network, which means that anyone with internet access can download Gnutella client software and join the network for the purpose of sharing files.

10. [n.2] A GUID is a unique, random string of numbers and letters created when peer-to-peer software is installed on a computer.

69.144.201.186 IP address. But because the unidentified user had apparently disabled the browsing/downloading capability of the files, Detective McNeil was not able to download any files even though information about the files was still being broadcast on the Gnutella network.

The subscriber information associated with the IP address ultimately came back to the Comfort Inn in Bozeman. Detective McNeil discovered that the Comfort Inn's wireless network was unsecured, which meant that anyone could connect to the various wireless access points and would then be operating from the 69.144.201.186 IP address. It thus appeared to Detective McNeil that some unidentified user was connecting to the Comfort Inn's unsecured network and using Gnutella to download child pornography.

As Detective McNeil knew from prior training, there are devices available to help law enforcement investigators in such situations by locating computer systems that are connected to unsecured networks. The Gatekeeper, for example, is a hand held device that can be covertly deployed to monitor wireless traffic on an unsecured network and watch for particular pieces of information or keywords to be broadcast. When the Gatekeeper notes a particular piece of information or keyword, it alerts the investigator with an email. That email includes the Media Access Control ("MAC") Addresses[n.3][11] of the wireless network adapters engaged in the communication, including the one that broadcast the information.

Once the investigator has learned the MAC address of the wireless network adapter making the broadcast, the investigator can then deploy a companion device called the Shadow to "home in" on the network adapter. This is a matter of configuring the Shadow to locate the MAC address extracted by the Gatekeeper. The Shadow measures changes in signal strength from the network adapter, which means that the investigator can then use the Shadow to find, and literally walk over to, the location of the network adapter.

Hoping to use the Gatekeeper and Shadow to further his investigation, Detective McNeil sought and obtained a state court order authorizing the installation and use of pen register and trap and trace devices pursuant to the federal Pen Register and Trap and Trace Statute, 18 U.S.C. §§ 3122 and 3123. The order provided that pen-trap devices could "be installed and used to record, decode, and/or capture dialing, routing, addressing, and signaling information associated with all communications between wireless devices and WAPs[n.6][12] that are transmitted in the vicinity of the Comfort Inn" in Bozeman. The order specified that "[t]his information will include, but is not limited to, the date, time, and duration of the communication, and the following, without geographic limit: IP addresses, MAC addresses, Port

---

11. [n.3] "A MAC address is a unique code identifier assigned to a network communication device, such as a wireless router or laptop computer, by its manufacturer."

12. [n.6] A WAP is a wireless access point.

numbers, [and] Packet headers." The stated purpose of capturing this informa-tion was to "enable the government to determine the physical location of the Target Wireless Device(s)."

On December 7, 2011, Detective McNeil rented a room at the Comfort Inn and configured the Gatekeeper to monitor traffic on the hotel's wireless network for portions of the five GUIDs identified earlier in his investigation. When that yielded no results, Detective McNeil deployed the Gatekeeper in a surveillance vehicle in the parking lot of the Comfort Inn.

For the next few days, Detective McNeil continued monitoring the network using the Gatekeeper in the surveillance vehicle. During this period, Detective McNeil configured the Gatekeeper to not only search for the GUIDs, but to also monitor the network using the search terms "Gnutella" and "Shareaza." Detective McNeil selected "Gnutella" and "Shareaza" as additional search terms because he knew based on his investigation that the unidentified user of the target wireless device was on the Gnutella network and was using the Gnutella software client Shareaza.

Detective McNeil's expanded search strategy ultimately proved successful. On December 11, 2011, he received email notification that the Gatekeeper had hit on the keyword "Gnutella." That notification actually consisted of ten separate emails, each of which contained a "packet" of information. Based on his review of the pack-ets, Detective McNeil was able to identify the two MAC addresses of the wireless network adapters involved in the communications. Detective McNeil then deployed the Shadow in an attempt to locate the MAC addresses.

Detective McNeil followed the Shadow signal associated with one of the MAC addresses to a Ford Windstar van parked on the north side of the Comfort Inn. As Detective McNeil approached, he saw that the van was unoccupied and there was a laptop computer running on the passenger seat. Based on all of the evidence he had gathered at that point in his investigation, Detective McNeil applied for and obtained a state court search warrant for the van.

Detectives executed the warrant that evening, and identified Saville as the occu-pant of the van. Saville agreed to accompany Detective McNeil to the police station for questioning, while law enforcement officers on the scene searched the van. After being advised of his Miranda rights, Saville admitted to downloading images and movies of children engaging in sexual conduct. During their search of the van, law enforcement officers found and seized two computers, three thumb drives, and an external hard drive. Those items were later found to contain more than 1,000 child pornography files. The indictment in this case followed.

Saville argues that the government's use of the Gatekeeper and Shadow devices constituted an unlawful, warrantless search under the Fourth Amendment, and moves to suppress all evidence obtained as a result of their use in the investigation.

A "Fourth Amendment search occurs when the government violates a subjec-tive expectation of privacy that society recognizes as reasonable." Thus, "[a]s a pre-requisite to establishing the illegality of a search under the Fourth Amendment, a defendant must show that he had a reasonable expectation of privacy in the place searched." A Fourth Amendment search also occurs when "the Government obtains information by physically intruding on a constitutionally protected area."

Saville takes the position that the Gatekeeper captured content when it hit on the search term "Gnutella." In doing so, Saville focuses on the ten emails the Gatekeeper delivered to Detective McNeil. Each email contained a "packet" of information, which was made up of two parts—a "header" and a "payload." Saville's computer expert, Ken Michael, testified that a packet header contains all of the routing and signaling information associated with a particular communication, including such things as the source and destination IP addresses, MAC addresses, transmission control protocol, and size of the entire packet in bytes. According to Michael, the content of a communication is found exclusively in the payload. As Michael explained it, anything that is contained in the packet payload is properly characterized as content. Because it is undisputed that the keyword "Gnutella" was found in the payload portion of the packets delivered by the Gatekeeper, Michael testified that it must necessarily be characterized as content. In other words, it was Michael's opinion that "Gnutella" must be considered content simply by virtue of the fact that it appeared in the payload.

While Michael's view of what constitutes content may be a legitimate one in some contexts, it is not the definition that controls here. As it applies to the use of pen registers, the term "content" has a specific meaning. "[C]ontent" of a wire, oral, or electronic communication is statutorily defined to include "any information concerning the substance, purport, or meaning of that communication." 18 U.S.C. § 2510(8). To be considered content, the term "Gnutella" as captured in the payload must have conveyed something about the substance, purport, or meaning of Saville's electronic communications. But Michael never considered this definition, and failed to explain how the term "Gnutella" as it appeared in the payload conveyed anything at all about the substance or meaning of Saville's communications.

Detective McNeil testified convincingly as to why it did not. He explained that all of information captured by the Gatekeeper related to what he described as the initial "handshake" that takes place between two computers as they negotiate a protocol for communicating and before any data is actually exchanged. Detective McNeil made clear that packets exchanged during this initial "handshake" contain nothing more than dialing, routing, and signaling information, even in the payload. The packets captured by the Gatekeeper fall into this category.

While Detective McNeil agreed that, in theory, the Gatekeeper could have alerted to the keyword "Gnutella" if Saville had entered it as a search query, he stated that did not happen here. Detective McNeil deliberately avoided searching for commonly used content-laden terms like "pthc" (an acronym for "preteen hardcore"), which might have been more likely to hit on the content of a search query or the secure hash algorithm (SHA) value of a known child pornography file. In doing so, Detective McNeil complied with his statutory duty to use the technology available to him "so as to not include the contents of any wire or electronic communications." 18 U.S.C. § 3121(c).

The term "Gnutella" as it appeared in the payload was automatically generated by Saville's computer before any exchange of information had taken place between his computer and any other computer using the Gnutella network. It said nothing about the substance, meaning, or purpose of any communication by Saville, and so cannot be considered "content" within the meaning of the Pen-Trap statute. *See In re iPhone Application Litigation*, 844 F. Supp. 2d 1040, 1061 (N.D. Cal. 2012) (data that is "generated automatically, rather than through the intent of the user" does not constitute content). Because the Gatekeeper did not capture anything more than the than the routing, addressing, and signaling information transmitted by Saville's computer, there was no Fourth Amendment search.

Saville nonetheless argues that certain inferences can be drawn from the fact that the Gatekeeper hit on the word "Gnutella." Because Gnutella is commonly associated with the transmission of child pornography, Saville maintains it can be inferred from the fact that his computer was seeking to communicate with another computer on the Gnutella network that he was attempting to use his computer to download child pornography, thereby saying something about the content of his electronic communications.

But the Ninth Circuit rejected much the same theory in *United States v. Forrester*, 512 F.3d 500 (9th Cir. 2008), when it held that surveillance techniques revealing "the to/from addresses of e-mail messages" and "the IP addresses of websites visited" were "constitutionally indistinguishable from the use of a pen-register. . . ." While *Forrester* recognized that the government might be able to "make educated guesses about what was said in the messages or viewed on the websites," the court found that was "no different from speculation about the contents of a phone conversation on the basis of the identity of the person or entity that was dialed."

Likewise, while it may have been possible to speculate that Saville was planning on connecting his computer to another on the Gnutella network for the purpose of downloading child pornography, that too would be like speculating about the contents of a phone conversation based on the identity of the person or entity dialed. Even if the term "Gnutella" could be said to "strongly indicate" that Saville was intent upon downloading child pornography, it was simply serving a routing and addressing function as Saville's computer was attempting to establish a protocol for communicating with other devices on the Gnutella network. The Gatekeeper did not capture the content of any electronic communication by Saville.

As in *Forrester*, the surveillance techniques employed by Detective McNeil were the constitutional equivalent of the pen-trap devices approved of by the United States Supreme Court in *Smith*. As he used those devices here, Detective McNeil was at all times acting within the scope of the admittedly valid pen register order. This means there was no Fourth Amendment search, for which a warrant would have been required. Because there was no search, Saville's motion to suppress should be denied.

4. Remedies Under the Pen Register Statute

United States v. Mark Stephen Forrester

512 F.3d 500 (9th Cir. 2008)

FISHER, CIRCUIT JUDGE:

[Alba challenged the validity of computer surveillance that enabled the government to learn the to/from addresses of his email messages, the Internet protocol addresses of the websites that he visited, and the total volume of information transmitted to or from his account. As discussed in Chapter 11, where the facts of the case are set out, the court concluded that the surveillance was analogous to the use of a pen register that the Supreme Court held in *Smith v. Maryland*, 442 U.S. 735 (1979), did not constitute a search for Fourth Amendment purposes. Alba also claimed that the government's computer surveillance was beyond the scope of the then-applicable pen register statute, 18 U.S.C. §§ 3121–27.]

Assuming the surveillance violated the statute, there is no mention of suppression of evidence in the statutory text. Instead, the only penalty specified is that "[w]hoever knowingly violates subsection (a)" by installing or using a pen register without first obtaining a court order "shall be fined under this title or imprisoned not more than one year, or both." 18 U.S.C. § 3121(d). Where the legislature has already specified a remedy for a statutory violation, here fines and imprisonment, "we would 'encroach upon the prerogatives' of Congress were we to authorize a remedy not provided for by statute."

Indeed, two circuits have explicitly held (and we have implied) that evidence obtained in violation of the pen register statute need not be suppressed. The statutory text, our general reluctance to require suppression in the absence of statutory authorization, other circuits' holdings and our own indirect precedent all therefore lead us to conclude that suppression is inappropriate even if the computer surveillance came within the scope of the then-applicable pen register statute.

Notes

1. *Use of Pen/Traps by Providers.* Providers of electronic or wire communication services may use pen/trap devices on their own networks without a court order if:

- it relates to operation, maintenance, and testing of the communication service or to the protection of the provider's rights or property, or to the protection of users of that service; or

- it's to record the fact that a wire or electronic communication was initiated or completed to protect the provider, another provider furnishing service toward the completion of the wire communication, or a user of that service, from fraudulent, unlawful or abusive use of service; or

- the user of that service has given consent.

18 U.S.C. § 3121(b).

2. How viable is the content/noncontent distinction of *Smith v. Maryland*, 442 U.S. 735 (1979), which is preserved in the Pen/Trap Statute, in light of modern communications in the wake of *Carpenter v. United States*, 585 U.S. __ (2018), which is discussed in Chapter 11? Does a person's expectation of privacy change at the point she completes dialing the phone number or typing the web address and then continues to enter additional numbers or characters to access additional services or provide information? What are the consequences of such a change in expectations within the constitutional and statutory frameworks?

§ 12.3 The Wiretap Statute, 18 U.S.C. §§ 2510–22

The Wiretap Act, often referred to as "Title III," regulates the interception of the contents of wire, oral, or electronic communications, that is, "real time" capture of the communications in transit.[13] The Act has been described as "complex" and "famous (if not infamous) for its lack of clarity."[14] To protect the privacy of communications, Congress made it a crime under certain circumstances to capture real-time the content of information. Thus, the Wiretap Act serves as an "option for prosecuting computer intrusions that include real-time capture of information."[15] This section focuses instead on other features of the Act that regulate governmental acquisition of the contents of electronic communications. The classic example of the application of the Act is wiretapping a person's phone but it now applies to many other modes of communication.

Subject to exceptions, section 2511(1)(a) sets out a general rule: it prohibits using an electronic, mechanical, or other device to intercept the contents of private wire, oral, or electronic communications between parties. The prohibition applies to everyone in the United States, including private parties and governmental entities. To understand the scope of the application of the Act, there are several important terms.

---

13. The original act only covered wire and oral communications but Congress amended it in 1986 to include electronic communications. *See, e.g.*, Brown v. Waddell, 50 F.3d 285, 289 (4th Cir. 1995).

14. Steve Jackson Games v. United States Secret Service, 36 F.3d 457, 461 (5th Cir. 1994).

15. Computer Crime and Intellectual Property Section, U.S. Dept. of Justice, Prosecuting Computer Crimes 55 (2009).

1. Definitions

First, it only applies to certain communications:

- **"Oral communication"** § 2510(2)
  - "any oral communication uttered by a person exhibiting an expectation that such communication is not subject to interception under circumstances justifying such expectation"
- **"Wire communication"** § 2510(1)
  - "any aural transfer . . . of communications by . . . aid of wire, cable, or other like connection . . . furnished or operated . . . for the transmission of interstate or foreign communications or communications affecting interstate or foreign commerce"
    - **"Aural transfer"** § 2510(18) is defined as any communication "containing the human voice at any point"

Although the definition of a wire communication is complex, the most important aspect is that the communication must include the human voice. For example, all voice telephone communications qualify as wire communications.

- **"Electronic communication"** § 2510(12)
- "any transfer of signs, signals, writing, images, sounds, data, or intelligence . . . by a wire, radio, electromagnetic, photoelectronic or photooptical system that affects interstate or foreign commerce, but . . . not (A) any wire or oral communication; (B) any communication made through a tone-only paging device; (C) any communication from a tracking device . . . ; or (D) electronic funds transfer information stored by a financial institution"

This definition applies to most Internet communications, including the body of an email.[16] In *Konop v. Hawaiian Airlines*, 302 F.3d 868 (9th Cir. 2002), the court provided another example:

> Website owners . . . transmit electronic documents to servers, where the documents are stored. If a user wishes to view the website, the user requests that the server transmit a copy of the document to the user's computer. When the server sends the document to the user's computer for viewing, a transfer of information from the website owner to the user has occurred. Although the website owner's document does not go directly or immediately to the user, once a user accesses a website, information is transferred from the website owner to the user via one of the specified mediums. We therefore conclude that Konop's website fits the definition of "electronic communication."

Second, the statute requires interception of a covered communication:

---

16. *E.g., In re* Application of the United States, 416 F. Supp. 2d 13, 16 (D.D.C. 2006) (§ 2510(12) "is broad enough to encompass email communications and other similar signals transmitted over the Internet").

- "Intercept" § 2510(4)
  - "the aural or other acquisition of the contents of any wire, electronic, or oral communication through the use of any electronic, mechanical, or other device"

This term creates the content/noncontent distinction that is a main feature of ECPA. Also, although the statute does not explicitly require that the interception be contemporaneous with the transmission of the communication, "a contemporaneous requirement is necessary to maintain the proper relationship" between the Wiretap Act and the Stored Communications Act.[17] Every Circuit that has considered the question has adopted that view. *See Fraser v. Nationwide Mutual Insurance*, 352 F.3d 107, 113 (3d Cir. 2004); *United States v. Steiger*, 318 F.3d 1039, 1049 (11th Cir. 2003). Hence, a person who accesses a stored copy of a communication does not "intercept" that communication. *E.g.*, *Steve Jackson Games, Inc. v. United States Secret Service*, 36 F.3d 457, 460–63 (5th Cir. 1994). Thus, in *Steiger*, the court observed that the effect of a contemporaneous requirement for an intercept means that

> very few seizures of electronic communications from computers will constitute "interceptions."
>
> [T]here is only a narrow window during which an E-mail interception may occur—the seconds or mili-seconds before which a newly composed message is saved to any temporary location following a send command. Therefore, unless some type of automatic routing software is used (for example, a duplicate of all of an employee's messages are automatically sent to the employee's boss), interception of E-mail within the prohibition of [the Wiretap Act] is virtually impossible.

For example, in *Steiger*, a computer hacker trolling the Internet used a Trojan Horse to gain access to Steiger's computer. He found child pornography files. In rejecting the claims that the hacker violated the Wiretap Act, the court stated:

> There is nothing to suggest that any of the information provided in the [hacker's] e-mails to the [government agents] was obtained through contemporaneous acquisition of electronic communications while in flight. Rather, the evidence shows that the source used a Trojan Horse virus that enabled him to access and download information stored on Steiger's personal computer. This conduct, while possibly tortious, does not constitute an interception of electronic communications in violation of the Wiretap Act.

There is, however, some disagreement among courts as to whether a communication is intercepted if acquired while in transient electronic storage. *See United States v. Councilman*, 418 F.3d 67 (1st Cir. 2005) (electronic communications can be

---

17. Computer Crime and Intellectual Property Section, U.S. Dept. of Justice, Prosecuting Computer Crimes 165 (2009).

intercepted even if they are in electronic storage so long as the communications are in transient electronic storage intrinsic to the communication process).

Third, the statute only applies to the interception of the contents of a communication:

- "Contents" § 2510(8)

  - "any information concerning the substance, purport, or meaning of that communication"

---

2. Wiretap Orders, 18 U.S.C. § 2518

Wiretapping pursuant to a court order is the iconic example of governmental surveillance of communications. Such orders have more stringent requirements to issue than a traditional warrant. A court may grant a wiretap order under 18 U.S.C. § 2518 for wire communications only to investigate specified predicate offenses or for electronic communications to investigate any federal felony.

- A federal court may issue a Wiretap Order "if it determines, on the basis of the facts submitted by the applicant, that there is probable cause to believe (1) that an individual was committing, had committed, or is about to commit a crime; (2) that communications concerning that crime will be obtained through the wiretap; and (3) that the premises to be wiretapped were being used for criminal purposes or are about to be used or owned by the target of the wiretap." *United States v. Diaz*, 176 F.3d 52, 110 (2d Cir. 1999) (citing 18 U.S.C. § 2518(1) (b)(i), (3)(a), (b), (d)). The applicable standard for probable cause is the same as the standard for a search warrant, which is established if the "totality-of-the-circumstances" indicates a probability of criminal activity.[18]

- The government must prove necessity by making "a full and complete statement as to whether or not other investigative procedures have been tried and failed or why they reasonably appear to be unlikely to succeed if tried or to be too dangerous. . . ." § 2518(1)(c). The issuing judge may approve the wiretap if the judge determines that "normal investigative procedures have been tried and have failed or reasonably appear to be unlikely to succeed if tried or to be too dangerous. . . ." § 2518(3)(c). These requirements ensure that "wiretapping is not resorted to in situations where traditional investigative techniques would suffice to expose the crime."[19]

---

18. In the Matter of Applications of the United States of America for Orders (1) Authorizing the Use of Pen Registers and Trap and Trace Devices, 515 F. Supp. 2d 325 (E.D.N.Y. 2007).
19. United States v. Reed, 575 F.3d 900 (9th Cir. 2009).

Notes

1. **Wiretap Applications.** In 2009, more than 2,370 wiretap applications were granted in state and federal courts, a 26 percent increase over the previous year, according to a report issued by the Administrative Office of the U.S. Courts. 86 percent of the applications targeted drug crimes, with homicide cases the second most prevalent. Federal authorities sought 663 applications, with the remainder being state applications. 71 percent of the state applications were granted in California, New York and New Jersey. No applications were denied. *See* http://www.uscourts.gov/statistics-reports/wiretap-report-2009. In comparison, in 2016, a total of 3,168 wiretaps were reported as authorized, with 1,551 authorized by federal judges and 1,617 authorized by state judges. Two wiretap applications were reported as denied in 2016.

Applications concentrated in six states (California, New York, Colorado, Nevada, Florida, and New Jersey) accounted for 82 percent of all state wiretap applications. Applications in California alone constituted 35 percent of all applications approved by state judges. http://www.uscourts.gov/statistics-reports/wiretap-report-2016.

2. **Oral, Wire, and Electronic Communications.** The Act distinguishes between oral and wire communications on the one hand and electronic communications on the other: What are the significant differences? Why would Congress make such distinctions?

---

3. Remedies for Violations of the Wiretap Statute

Violations of the Wiretap statute may give rise to criminal liability, *see* § 2511(4), and/or civil liability, *see* § 2520. The statute authorizes a suppression remedy, *see* § 2518(10)(a), but, as a general rule, it is only available for illegal wiretaps of *wire* or *oral* communications—not of *electronic* communications. *See United States v. Steiger*, 318 F.3d 1039 (11th Cir. 2003). To obtain suppression, the person must have been a party to the wire or oral communication, *see* § 2518(10)(a). There are other important qualifications to the scope of the suppression remedy not discussed here.[20]

4. Exceptions to the General Prohibition Against Wiretapping Include:

- Computer "trespasser" communications 18 U.S. C. § 2511(2)(i)
  - Law enforcement may intercept a trespasser's communications if all of these requirements are met:

---

20. *See* Searching and Seizing Computers and Obtaining Electronic Evidence 183–88 (Computer Crime and Intellectual Property Section, U.S. Dept. of Justice 2009).

1. The owner or operator of the protected computer must authorize the interception of the trespasser's communications.

2. The person who intercepts the communications must be "lawfully engaged in an investigation."

3. The person who intercepts the communications must have "reasonable grounds to believe that the contents of the computer trespasser's communications will be relevant to the investigation."

4. The interception must not acquire any communications other than those transmitted to or from the computer trespasser (unless others whose communications are also intercepted have given consent).

- "Computer trespasser" 18 U.S.C. § 2510(21) is a person who

   1. accesses a protected computer without authorization and, thus, has no reasonable expectation of privacy in any communication transmitted to, through, or from the protected computer, and

   2. has no existing contractual relationship with the owner or operator of the protected computer for access to the protected computer.

- Consent, either actual or implied, of either party. 18 U.S.C. § 2511(2)(c)–(d)

- Communications providers may use wiretaps if:
  - in the ordinary course of business 18 U.S.C. § 2510(5)(a)
  - as necessary to provision of service 18 U.S.C. § 2511(2)(a)(i)
  - to protect their rights or property 18 U.S.C. § 2511(2)(a)(i)
  - inadvertently obtained content pertaining to crime 18 U.S.C. § 2511(3)(b)(iv)

- Under the Foreign Intelligence Surveillance Act of 1978. *See* 50 U.S.C. § 1801.

----

§ 12.4 Stored Communications Act, 18 U.S.C. §§ 2701–12

The Stored Communications Act (SCA) regulates access to and disclosure of stored electronic communications or account records held by network service providers such as Internet service providers. It has no applicability to data in real time transit. Whenever investigators seek stored email, account records, or subscriber information from certain defined classes of service providers, they must comply with the SCA. The Act serves several purposes: it creates criminal penalties for unauthorized access to certain stored communications; it creates a procedure for compelled disclosure of stored information to federal and state law enforcement officials; and it sets out the circumstances under which network service providers many voluntarily disclose information. The SCA sets out a series of classifications, reflecting the drafters' belief that different types of information are more or less deserving of privacy protection. It is a complex statute and courts have differed on the meaning of several of its provisions.

While drafting the ECPA's amendments to the Wiretap Act, Congress also recognized that, with the rise of remote computing operations and large databanks of stored electronic communications, threats to individual privacy extended well beyond the bounds of the Wiretap Act's prohibition against the "interception" of communications. These types of stored communications—including stored e-mail messages—were not protected by the Wiretap Act. Therefore, Congress concluded that "the information [in these communications] may be open to possible wrongful use and public disclosure by law enforcement authorities as well as unauthorized private parties." S. Rep. No. 99-541, at 3 (1986), *reprinted in* 1986 U.S.C.C.A.N. 3555, 3557.

Congress added Title II to the ECPA to halt these potential intrusions on individual privacy. This title, commonly referred to as the Stored Communications Act, established new punishments for accessing, without (or in excess of) authorization, an electronic communications service facility and thereby obtaining access to a wire or electronic communication in electronic storage. 18 U.S.C. § 2701(a). Another provision bars electronic communications service providers from "divulg[ing] to any person or entity the contents of a communication while in electronic storage by that service." *Id.* § 2702(a)(1).[21]

––––––––––

1. Overview

In the Matter of the Application of the United States of America for a Search Warrant for Contents of Electronic Mail and for an Order Directing a Provider of Electronic Communication Services to Not Disclose the Existence of the Search Warrant

665 F. Supp. 2d 1210 (D. Or. 2009)

MOSMAN, DISTRICT JUDGE.

When a person uses the Internet, the user's actions are no longer in his or her physical home; in fact he or she is not truly acting in private space at all. The user is generally accessing the Internet with a network account and computer storage owned by an [internet service provider] like Comcast or NetZero. All materials stored online, whether they are e-mails or remotely stored documents, are physically stored on servers owned by an ISP. When we send an e-mail or instant message

––––––––––

21. United States v. Councilman, 418 F.3d 67 (1st Cir. 2005).

from the comfort of our own homes to a friend across town the message travels from our computer to computers owned by a third party, the ISP, before being delivered to the intended recipient. Thus, "private" information is actually being held by third-party private companies.

This feature of the Internet has profound implications for how the Fourth Amendment protects Internet communications—if it protects them at all. The law here remains unclear and commentators have noted that there are several reasons that the Fourth Amendment's privacy protections for the home may not apply to our "virtual homes" online. First, it is uncertain whether we have a reasonable expectation of privacy in information sent through or stored by ISPs because the Fourth Amendment does not protect information revealed to third parties. Second, the government may obtain a court order, such as a grand jury subpoena, without a showing of probable cause for materials belonging to the target of an investigation but held by a third party, like e-mails stored by an ISP. Third, most ISPs are private actors, therefore they can read all the files stored on their servers without violating the Fourth Amendment.

Congress responded to this uncertainty by enacting the Stored Communications Act as part of the Electronic Communications Privacy Act of 1986. The SCA gives network account holders statutory privacy rights against access to stored information held by ISPs. The statute also creates Fourth Amendment-like privacy protections regulating the methods by which government investigators may obtain users' private information in a service provider's possession. First, the SCA limits the government's ability to compel service providers to disclose information in their possession about their subscribers. *See* 18 U.S.C. § 2703. Second, it limits the service provider's ability to voluntarily disclose information about their subscribers to the government. *See id.* § 2702.

The SCA regulates two types of service providers, providers of electronic communication service ("ECS") and providers of remote computing service ("RCS"). Except as authorized by subsection (b), providers of ECS may not divulge the contents of communications in electronic storage. *Id.* § 2702(a)(1). Similarly, absent a statutory exception, providers of RCS may not divulge the contents of any communication carried or maintained on the service on behalf of a customer or subscriber for the purpose of providing storage or computer processing services to the customer or subscriber. *Id.* § 2702(a)(2).

A few definitions will help clarify exactly how the SCA protects electronic communications. The statute defines ECS as "any service which provides to users thereof the ability to send or receive wire or electronic communications." *Id.* § 2510(15) *incorporated by id.* § 2711(1). Electronic storage is "any temporary, intermediate storage of a wire or electronic communication incidental to the electronic transmission thereof; and any storage of such communication by an [ECS] for purposes of backup protection of such communication." *Id.* § 2510(17). An RCS is defined as "the provision to the public of computer storage or processing services by means of an electronic communications system." *Id.* § 2711(2). Finally, an electronic communication system is "any wire, radio, electromagnetic, photooptical or photoelectronic facilities for the transmission of wire or electronic communications, and any computer facilities or related electronic equipment for the electronic storage of such communications." *Id.* § 2510(14).

In passing the Electronic Communications Privacy Act in 1986, Congress expressed the need to expand the protections of the Fourth Amendment to new forms of communication and data storage. The legislative history indicates that Congress wished to encourage the development and use of these new methods of communication by ensuring that they were protected and private. Congress recognized that courts had struggled with the application of the Fourth Amendment to the seizure of intangibles, like telephone conversations. They therefore sought to strike a balance between the competing interests addressed by the Fourth Amendment in the world of electronic communications by "protect[ing] privacy interests in personal and proprietary information, while protecting the Government's legitimate law enforcement needs."

DEFINITIONS: Only stored electronic and wire communications are protected by the SCA

- **"Electronic communication"** is defined in § 2510(12):
  - "any transfer of signs, signals, writing, images, sounds, data, or intelligence . . . by a wire, radio, electromagnetic, photoelectronic or photooptical system that affects interstate or foreign commerce, but . . . not (A) any wire or oral communication; (B) any communication made through a tone-only paging device; (C) any communication from a tracking device . . . ; or (D) electronic funds transfer information stored by a financial institution"

- **"Wire communication"** is defined in section 2510(1):
  - "any aural transfer . . . of communications by . . . wire, cable, or other like connection . . . furnished or operated . . . for the transmission of interstate or foreign communications or communications affecting interstate or foreign commerce"
  - An **Aural transfer** is any "containing the human voice at any point." § 2510(18).

---

2. Framework to Analyze the SCA

The United States Department of Justice offers a helpful three step approach to understanding the SCA:

> Agents and prosecutors must apply the various classifications devised by the SCA's drafters to the facts of each case to figure out the proper

procedure for obtaining the information sought. First, they must classify the network service provider (e.g., does the provider provide "electronic communication service," "remote computing service," or neither). Next, they must classify the information sought (e.g., is the information content "in electronic storage," content held by a remote computing service, a non-content record pertaining to a subscriber, or other information enumerated by the SCA). Third, they must consider whether they are seeking to compel disclosure or seeking to accept information disclosed voluntarily by the provider. If they seek compelled disclosure, they need to determine whether they need a search warrant, a 2703(d) court order, or a subpoena to compel the disclosure. If they are seeking to accept information voluntarily disclosed, they must determine whether the statute permits the disclosure.[22]

STEP #1: CLASSIFICATION OF PROVIDERS

The SCA applies only to two types of network service providers: providers of an "electronic communication service" and providers of a "remote computing service." If a provider does not fit within these definitions, the SCA does not regulate disclosures of information by that provider. Whether a provider is in either of those two classes or neither class depends on the nature of the particular communication sought. A provider can simultaneously provide "electronic communication service" with respect to one communication and "remote computing service" with respect to another communication, or a public provider can consecutively provide such services with respect to the same communication. Into which category a provider falls is fundamental in determining what the provider may disclose voluntarily and the type of process needed to compel disclosure. Those different disclosure rules are discussed in Step #3.

- **"Electronic communication service"** (ECS) § 2510(15)
  - "any service which provides . . . users . . . the ability to send or receive wire or electronic communications"

NOTE: applies to both public and non-public ECS providers.

- **"Remote computing service"** (RCS) § 2711(2)
  - "the provision to the public of computer storage or processing services by means of an electronic communications system"

NOTE: A non-public RCS provider is not covered by the SCA.

---

22. *See* COMPUTER CRIME AND INTELLECTUAL PROPERTY SECTION, U.S. DEPT. OF JUSTICE, PROSECUTING COMPUTER CRIMES 116 (2009).

To the Public

Andersen Consulting LLP v. UOP and Bickel & Brewer

991 F. Supp. 1041 (N.D. Ill. 1998)

BUCKLO, DISTRICT JUDGE.

Plaintiff, Andersen Consulting LLP brought an eight count complaint against the defendants, UOP and its counsel, the law firm of Bickel & Brewer. In Count I, Andersen alleges that the defendants knowingly divulged, or caused to be divulged, the contents of Andersen's e-mail messages in violation of the Electronic Communications Privacy Act.

UOP hired Andersen to perform a systems integration project in 1992. During the project, Andersen employees had access to and used UOP's internal e-mail system to communicate with each other, with UOP, and with third parties.

Dissatisfied with Andersen's performance, UOP terminated the project in December 1993. Subsequently UOP hired Bickel and Brewer and brought suit in Connecticut state court charging Andersen with breach of contract, negligence, and fraud. Andersen countersued in two different suits for defamation.

While these three cases were pending, UOP and Bickel and Brewer divulged the contents of Andersen's e-mail messages on UOP's e-mail system to the *Wall Street Journal*. The *Journal* published an article on June 19, 1997 titled "E-Mail Trail Could Haunt Consultant in Court." The article excerpted some of Andersen's e-mail messages made during the course of its assignment at UOP. This disclosure of the e-mail messages and their subsequent publication is the basis of this suit.

18 U.S.C. § 2702(a)(1) states that "a person or entity providing an electronic communication service to the public shall not knowingly divulge to any person or entity the contents of a communication while in electronic storage by that service."

To be liable for the disclosure of Andersen's e-mail messages, UOP must fall under the purview of the Act: UOP must provide "electronic communication service to the public." The statute does not define "public." The word "public," however, is unambiguous. Public means the "aggregate of the citizens" or "everybody" or "the people at large" or "the community at large." *Black's Law Dictionary* 1227 (6th ed. 1990). Thus, the statute covers any entity that provides electronic communication service (e.g., e-mail) to the community at large.

Andersen attempts to render the phrase "to the public" superfluous by arguing that the statutory language indicates that the term "public" means something other than the community at large. It claims that if Congress wanted public to mean the community at large, it would have used the term "general public." However, the fact that Congress used both "public" and "general public" in the same statute does not lead to the conclusion that Congress intended public to have any other meaning than its commonly understood meaning.

Andersen argues that the legislative history indicates that a provider of electronic communication services is subject to Section 2702 even if that provider maintains the system primarily for its own use and does not provide services to the general public. This legislative history argument is misguided. "A court's starting point to determine the intent of Congress is the language of the statute itself." If the language is "clear and unambiguous," the court must give effect to the plain meaning of the statute. Since the meaning of "public" is clear, there is no need to resort to legislative history.

Even if the language was somehow ambiguous, the legislative history does not support Andersen's interpretation. The legislative history indicates that there is a distinction between public and proprietary. In describing "electronic mail," the legislative history stated that "[e]lectronic mail systems may be available for public use or may be proprietary, such as systems operated by private companies for internal correspondence." Thus, Andersen must show that UOP's electronic mail system was available for public use.

In its complaint, Andersen alleges that UOP "is a general partnership which licenses process technologies and supplies catalysts, specialty chemicals, and other products to the petroleum refining, petrochemical, and gas processing industries." UOP is not in the business of providing electronic communication services. It does, however, have an e-mail system for internal communication as e-mail is a necessary tool for almost any business today.

UOP hired Andersen to provide services in connection with the integration of certain computer systems. As part of the project, "UOP provided an electronic communication service for Andersen to use. That electronic communication service could be used, and was used by Andersen and UOP personnel, to electronically communicate with (*i.e.*, send e-mail messages to, and receive e-mail messages from) other Andersen personnel, UOP personnel, third-party vendors and other third-parties both in and outside of Illinois."

Based on these allegations, Andersen claims that UOP provides an electronic communication service to the public. However, giving Andersen access to its e-mail system is not equivalent to providing e-mail to the public. Andersen was hired by UOP to do a project and as such, was given access to UOP's e-mail system similar to UOP employees. Andersen was not any member of the community at large, but a hired contractor. Further, the fact that Andersen could communicate to third-parties over the internet and that third-parties could communicate with it did not mean that UOP provided an electronic communication service to the public. UOP's internal e-mail system is separate from the internet. UOP must purchase internet access from an electronic communication service provider like any other consumer; it does not independently provide internet services.

ECS or RCS?

"The key to determining whether the provider is an ECS or RCS is to ask what role the provider has played and is playing with respect to the communication in question."[23]

> Today, most ISPs provide both ECS and RCS; thus, the distinction serves to define the service that is being provided at a particular time (or as to a particular piece of electronic communication at a particular time), rather than to define the service provider itself. The distinction is still essential, however, because different services have different protections.[24]

———————

[Note: The Supreme Court opinion in *City of Ontario v. Quon*, 560 U.S. 746 (2010), excerpted elsewhere in this book, reverses the following opinion of the Ninth Circuit on other grounds.]

Jerilyn Quon v. Arch Wireless Operating Co.

529 F.3d 892 (9th Cir. 2008)

Wardlaw, Circuit Judge:

The SCA defines an ECS as "any service which provides to users thereof the ability to send or receive wire or electronic communications." [18 U.S.C.] § 2510(15). The SCA prohibits an ECS from "knowingly divulg[ing] to any person or entity the contents of a communication while in electronic storage by that service," unless, among other exceptions not relevant to this appeal, that person or entity is "an addressee or intended recipient of such communication." *Id.* § 2702(a)(1), (b)(1), (b)(3).

An RCS is defined as "the provision to the public of computer storage or processing services by means of an electronic communications system." *Id.* § 2711(2). Electronic communication system—which is simply the means by which an RCS provides computer storage or processing services and has no bearing on how we interpret the meaning of "RCS"—is defined as "any wire, radio, electromagnetic, photooptical or photoelectronic facilities for the transmission of wire or electronic communications, and any computer facilities or related electronic equipment for the electronic storage of such communications." *Id.* § 2510(14). The SCA prohibits an RCS from "knowingly divulg[ing] to any person or entity the contents of any communication which is carried or maintained on that service." Unlike an ECS, an RCS may release the contents of a communication with the lawful consent of a "subscriber." *Id.* § 2702(a)(2), (b)(3).

———————

23. *See* Computer Crime and Intellectual Property Section, U.S. Dept. of justice, Prosecuting Computer Crimes 120 (2009).

24. In the Matter of the Application of the United States of America for a Search Warrant for Contents of Electronic Mail and for an Order Directing a Provider of Electronic Communication Services to not Disclose the Existence of the Search Warrant, 665 F. Supp. 2d 1210 (D. Or. 2009).

An ECS is defined as "any service which provides to users thereof the ability to send or receive wire or electronic communications." 18 U.S.C. §2510(15). Contrast that definition with that for an RCS, which "means the provision to the public of computer storage or processing services by means of an electronic communications system." *Id.* §2711(2). Congress contemplated this exact function could be performed by an ECS as well, stating that an ECS would provide (A) temporary storage incidental to the communication; and (B) storage for backup protection. *Id.* §2510(17).

The Senate Report identifies two main services that providers performed in 1986: (1) data communication; and (2) data storage and processing. First, the report describes the means of communication of information:

> [W]e have large-scale electronic mail operations, computer-to-computer data transmissions, cellular and cordless telephones, paging devices, and video teleconferencing. . . . [M]any different companies, not just common carriers, offer a wide variety of telephone and other communications services.

S. Rep. No. 99-541, at 2–3 (1986), U.S. Code Cong. & Admin. News 1986, pp. 3555, 3556–3557. Second,

> [t]he Committee also recognizes that computers are used extensively today for the storage and processing of information. With the advent of computerized recordkeeping systems, Americans have lost the ability to lock away a great deal of personal and business information. For example, physicians and hospitals maintain medical files in offsite data banks, businesses of all sizes transmit their records to remote computers to obtain sophisticated data processing services. These services as well as the providers of electronic mail create electronic copies of private correspondence for later reference. This information is processed for the benefit of the user but often it is maintained for approximately 3 months to ensure system integrity.

Under the heading "Remote Computer Services," the Report further clarifies that term refers to the processing or storage of data by an off-site third party:

> In the age of rapid computerization, a basic choice has faced the users of computer technology. That is, whether to process data inhouse on the user's own computer or on someone else's equipment. Over the years, remote computer service companies have developed to provide sophisticated and convenient computing services to subscribers and customers from remote facilities. Today businesses of all sizes — hospitals, banks and many others — use remote computing services for computer processing. This processing can be done with the customer or subscriber using the facilities of the remote computing service in essentially a time-sharing arrangement, or it can be accomplished by the service provider on the basis of information supplied by the subscriber or customer. Data is most often transmitted between these services and their customers by means of electronic communications.

In the Senate Report, Congress made clear what it meant by "storage and processing of information." It provided the following example of storage: "physicians and hospitals maintain medical files in offsite data banks." Congress appeared to view "storage" as a virtual filing cabinet. The Senate Report also provided an example of "processing of information": "businesses of all sizes transmit their records to remote computers to obtain sophisticated data processing services." In light of the Report's elaboration upon what Congress intended by the term "Remote Computer Services," it is clear that, before the advent of advanced computer processing programs such as Microsoft Excel, businesses had to farm out sophisticated processing to a service that would process the information.

––––––––––

Or Neither an ECS nor RCS?

Kevin Low v. LinkedIn Corporation

900 F. Supp. 2d 1010 (N.D. Cal. 2012)

Lucy H. Koh, District Judge.

Plaintiffs Kevin Low and Alan Masand bring this putative class action against LinkedIn Corp. alleging that personal information of the putative class members, including "personally identifiable browsing histor[ies]," were allegedly disclosed by Defendant to third party advertising and marketing companies through the use of "cookies" or "beacons."

In the Amended Complaint, Plaintiffs allege violations of the Stored Communications Act, 18 U.S.C. § 2701 *et seq.* [and other causes of action.] For the foregoing reasons, the Defendant's motion to dismiss is DENIED in part and GRANTED in part.

Unless otherwise noted, the following allegations are taken from the Amended Complaint and are presumed true for purposes of ruling on Defendant's motion to dismiss. Plaintiffs bring this putative class action on behalf of all persons in the United States who registered for LinkedIn services after March 25, 2007. LinkedIn is a web-based social networking site that presents itself as an online community offering professionals ways to network. Plaintiffs allege that LinkedIn allows transmission of users' LinkedIn browsing history, as well as the user's LinkedIn ID, to third parties, including advertisers, marketing companies, data brokers, and web tracking companies. According to Plaintiffs, LinkedIn's practices allow these third parties to identify both the individual LinkedIn user, and the user's browsing history in violation of federal and state laws and in violation of LinkedIn's privacy policy.

The Amended Complaint sets forth allegations regarding LinkedIn's general policies and practices related to the transmission of users' information to third parties. First, LinkedIn assigns each registered user a unique user identification number. Second, when an internet user visits a LinkedIn user's profile page, LinkedIn sends a command to the Internet user's browser that designates a third party from which the browser should download advertisements and other content. This command requires the internet user's browser to transmit two components of information: (1) the third party tracking ID ("cookies") on the user's hard drive corresponding with the designated third party, as well as (2) the URL of the LinkedIn profile being viewed, which includes the viewed party's LinkedIn ID (a unique number generated by LinkedIn to identify individual users).

Plaintiffs allege that third parties can theoretically de-anonymize a user's LinkedIn ID number. Although Plaintiffs' allegations are somewhat unclear, Plaintiffs allege that third parties can associate a LinkedIn user ID and URL of the user's profile page with a user's cookies ID and thus determine a LinkedIn user's identity. For example, Plaintiffs allege that third parties can correlate a user's LinkedIn ID and profile page with the corresponding cookies ID because LinkedIn users generally view their page more than any other LinkedIn profile page. The information transmitted to third parties includes the LinkedIn ID and URL of the page being viewed as well as the cookies ID of the person viewing the LinkedIn page. Thus, third parties can determine that a LinkedIn user ID corresponds with a specific internet user because the LinkedIn user ID transmitted with the most frequency is likely the cookies ID owner's profile page. Similarly, Plaintiffs allege that when a LinkedIn user selects his or her own LinkedIn profile, a unique "View Profile" URL is generated and transmitted to third parties, which contains that user's LinkedIn ID. From this transmission a third party could associate a LinkedIn user's numeric identification and profile page with the cookie ID of the LinkedIn user.

Once a third party can associate a LinkedIn ID and profile page with a cookies ID, Plaintiffs allege that a third party can associate a de-anonymized LinkedIn user's identity with the user's browsing history. An internet user's cookies ID corresponds to a third party's records of Internet users' internet histories. Plaintiffs allege that third parties can view a LinkedIn user's browser history, including the other LinkedIn profiles with which a user has interacted as well as potentially sensitive information that may be gathered based on a user's prior Internet history.

Low and Masand allege that they are both registered users of LinkedIn. Although Low has not paid money for the services LinkedIn provides, Masand purchased a "Job Seeker Premium" subscription in November 2011, and his subscription remained active throughout the relevant time period. Both Low and Masand allege that LinkedIn transmitted their LinkedIn user ID to third parties, "linking [their personal identities] to [the third party's] secretly embedded tracking device that surreptitiously recorded Mr. Low's [and Mr. Masand's] internet browsing history." Plaintiffs allege that as a result of the allegations explained above, Plaintiffs suffered two types of harm. First, Plaintiffs allege that they were "embarrassed and humiliated by the disclosure of his personally identifiable browsing history." Second, Plaintiffs allege that their personally identifiable browsing histories are valuable personal property; and that they "relinquished [their] valuable personal property without the compensation to which [they were] due."

Plaintiffs' first cause of action alleges that LinkedIn violated the federal Stored Communications Act. The SCA creates criminal and civil liability for certain unauthorized access to stored communications and records. "The SCA was enacted because the advent of the Internet presented a host of potential privacy breaches that the Fourth Amendment does not address." Despite this purpose, the SCA has a narrow scope: "[t]he SCA is not a catch-all statute designed to protect the privacy of stored Internet communications;" instead "there are many problems of Internet privacy that the SCA does not address." Generally, the SCA prohibits providers from (1) "knowingly divulg[ing] to any person or entity the contents of a communication." 18 U.S.C. § 2702(a)(1)–(2); *see id.* § 2707 (creating a private right of action).

The SCA covers two types of entities: (1) "remote computing services" ("RCS"), and (2) "electronic communication services" ("ECS"). The non-disclosure obligations depend on the type of provider at issue. Plaintiffs contend in their opposition that LinkedIn is an RCS for the purposes of its SCA liability. The SCA prohibits an entity "providing remote computing service to the public" from "knowingly divulge[ing] to any person or entity the contents of any communication which is carried or maintained on that service." 18 U.S.C. § 2702(a)(2).

The SCA only creates liability for a provider that is an RCS or an ECS. A provider of email services is an ECS. On the other hand, under the SCA the term "remote computing service" means "the provision to the public of computer *storage or processing services* by means of an electronic communications system." 18 U.S.C. § 2711(2). A "remote computing service" refers to "the processing or storage of data by an offsite third party." In defining RCS, "Congress appeared to view 'storage' as a virtual filing cabinet." Indeed, the Ninth Circuit has explained that "[i]n light of the Report's elaboration upon what Congress intended by the term 'Remote Computer Services,' it is clear that, before the advent of advanced computer processing programs such as Microsoft Excel, businesses had to farm out sophisticated processing to a service that would process the information."

Whether an entity is acting as an RCS or an ECS (or neither) is context dependent, and depends, in part, on the information disclosed. *See In re U.S.*, 665 F. Supp. 2d 1210, 1214 (D. Or. 2009) ("Today, most ISPs provide both ECS and RCS; thus, the distinction serves to define the service that is being provided at a particular time (or as to a particular piece of electronic communication at a particular time), rather than to define the service provider itself. The distinction is still essential, however, because different services have different protections.").

Although many allegations within the Amended Complaint relate to information that third parties would be able to *infer*, the Amended Complaint limits the information LinkedIn allegedly disclosed to third parties. The Amended Complaint alleges that LinkedIn transmits to third parties the LinkedIn user ID and the URL of the LinkedIn profile page viewed by the internet user. Even taking Plaintiffs' allegations as true, it does not appear that LinkedIn was functioning as an RCS[n.1][25] when it disclosed the LinkedIn user ID and the URL of the profile pages the user had viewed to third parties. LinkedIn was not acting as a "remote computing service" with respect to the disclosed information because it was not "processing or stor[ing] [ ] data by an offsite third party [in this case LinkedIn]." LinkedIn IDs are numbers generated by LinkedIn and were not sent by the user for offsite storage or processing. *See* 18 U.S.C. § 2702(a)(2)(A). LinkedIn was not acting "as a virtual filing cabinet," or as an offsite processor of data with respect to the user IDs it created. Similarly, the URL addresses of viewed pages were not sent to LinkedIn by Plaintiffs for storage or processing. *See* 18 U.S.C. § 2702(a)(2)(A)–(B). LinkedIn was not functioning as either a "filing cabinet" or "an advanced computer processing program such as Microsoft Excel," that allows businesses to "farm out sophisticated processing to a service that would process the information," with respect to the LinkedIn user IDs or the URLs of users' profile pages.

At least one commentator has seriously doubted the conclusion that a website, such as LinkedIn, provides "processing services" for its customers, qualifying it as an RCS. This view is supported by the legislative history of the SCA. Congress established liability for "remote computing services" to include services that store and process information. S. Rep. No. 99-541, at 3 (1986), reprinted in 1986 U.S.C.C.A.N. 3555, 3557 ("[C]omputers are used extensively today for the storage and processing of information. With the advent of computerized recordkeeping systems, Americans have lost the ability to lock away a great deal of personal and business information. For example, physicians and hospitals maintain medical files in offsite data banks, businesses of all sizes transmit their records to remote computers to obtain sophisticated data processing services."). Therefore, the Court finds that Plaintiffs have not stated a claim for relief pursuant to the SCA because Plaintiffs have not established that LinkedIn was acting as an RCS when it disclosed LinkedIn IDs and URLs of viewed pages to third parties. Therefore, Defendants' motion to dismiss the SCA claim is GRANTED.

Step #2: Information Held by Service Providers

1. Types of information held: As step #3 demonstrates, the type of process needed varies with the type of information sought.

- **Basic Subscriber and Session Information** § 2703(c)(2) lists the following categories:

    (A) name;

    (B) address;

---

25. [n.1] Nor was LinkedIn an ECS under the SCA as the alleged disclosures did not include e-mail transmissions or relate to LinkedIn's functionality as an electronic communication service.

(C) local and long distance telephone connection records, or records of session times and durations;

(D) length of service (including start date) and types of service utilized;

(E) telephone or instrument number or other subscriber number or identity, including any temporarily assigned network address; and

(F) means and source of payment for such service (including any credit card or bank account number).

NOTE: This list is straight-forward information about the identity of the subscriber, his or her relationship to the service provider, and session connection records.

- **Records or Other Information Pertaining to a Customer or Subscriber** §2703(c)(1) defines this as:

  - "a record or other information pertaining to a subscriber to or customer of such service (not including the contents of communications)"

NOTE: This category is referred to as "transactional records" and *includes* basic subscriber information and the following examples:

- Logs that record detailed account usage
- Logs showing sites visited and browsing patterns
- Logs identifying email correspondents
- Buddy list information
- Cell-site data for wireless phone calls
- Anything else revealing on-line usage

Interpretation: The U.S. Department of Justice views this as a "catch-all category that includes all records that are not contents." COMPUTER CRIME AND INTELLECTUAL PROPERTY SECTION, U.S. DEPT. OF JUSTICE, PROSECUTING COMPUTER CRIMES 122 (2009). "According to the legislative history of the 1994 amendments to §2703(c), the purpose of separating the basic subscriber and session information from other non-content records was to distinguish basic subscriber and session information from more revealing transactional information that could contain a "'person's entire on-line profile.'" *Id.*, *quoting* H.R. Rep. No. 103–827, at 17, 31–32 (1994), reprinted in 1994 U.S.C.C.A.N. 3489, 3497, 3511–12.

- **Contents** §2510(8): "includes any information concerning the substance, purport, or meaning of that communication."

2. "Electronic storage" §2510(17) — Only two categories of electronic communications in electronic storage are protected by the SCA:

The statute defines the term "electronic storage":

(A) any temporary, intermediate storage of a wire or electronic communication incidental to the electronic transmission thereof; and

(B) any storage of such communication by an electronic communication service for purposes of backup protection of such communication.

18 U.S.C. § 2510(17); *id.* § 2711(a) (incorporating Wiretap Act definitions into Stored Communications Act). There are two conflicting interpretations of this definition:

1. *Conventional interpretation of* § 2510(17):

Temporary, Intermediate Storage. The first category refers to temporary storage, such as when a message sits in an e-mail user's mailbox after transmission but before the user has retrieved the message from the mail server. United States v. Council-man, 418 F.3d 67 (1st Cir. 2005). An email in post-transmission storage (*i.e.*, that has reached its intended destination) is no longer in "electronic storage" because the storage, whether on an end user's computer or as a copy left on a service provider's computer, is no longer "temporary" nor "incidental to . . . transmission." *See, e.g.,* Fraser v. Nationwide Mutual Insurance Co., 135 F. Supp. 2d 623, 633 (E.D. Pa. 2001). Hence, the SCA does not apply to post-transmission storage of communications. Under this view, once the communication reaches its destination, it is no longer in "temporary, intermediate storage."

Backups. These are copies made by an ISP to ensure the integrity of its system.

2. *Minority View: Theofel:* A message in post-transmission backup storage on the provider's system is still in "electronic storage."

———————

George Theofel v. Alwyn Farey-Jones

359 F.3d 1066 (9th Cir. 2004)

KOZINSKI, CIRCUIT JUDGE:

Plaintiffs Wolf and Buckingham, officers of Integrated Capital Associates, Inc., are embroiled in commercial litigation in New York against defendant Farey-Jones. In the course of discovery, Farey-Jones sought access to ICA's e-mail. He told his lawyer Iryna Kwasny to subpoena ICA's ISP, NetGate.

Under the Federal Rules, Kwasny was supposed to "take reasonable steps to avoid imposing undue burden or expense" on NetGate. Fed. R. Civ. P. 45(c)(1). One might have thought, then, that the subpoena would request only e-mail related to the subject matter of the litigation, or maybe messages sent during some relevant time period, or at the very least those sent to or from employees in some way connected to the litigation. But Kwasny ordered production of "[a]ll copies of e-mails sent or received by anyone" at ICA, with no limitation as to time or scope.

NetGate, which apparently was not represented by counsel, explained that the amount of e-mail covered by the subpoena was substantial. But defendants did not relent. NetGate then took what might be described as the "Baskin-Robbins" approach to subpoena compliance and offered defendants a "free sample" consisting of 339 messages. It posted copies of the messages to a NetGate website where, without noti-fying opposing counsel, Kwasny and Farey-Jones read them. Most were unrelated to the litigation, and many were privileged or personal.

When Wolf and Buckingham found out what had happened, they asked the court to quash the subpoena and award sanctions. Magistrate Judge Wayne Brazil soundly roasted Farey-Jones and Kwasny for their conduct, finding that "the subpoena, on its face, was massively overbroad" and "patently unlawful," that it "transparently and egregiously" violated the Federal Rules, and that defendants "acted in bad faith" and showed "at least gross negligence in the crafting of the subpoena." He granted the motion to quash and socked defendants with over $9000 in sanctions to cover Wolf and Buckingham's legal fees. Defendants did not appeal that award.

Wolf, Buckingham and other ICA employees whose e-mail was included in the sample also filed this civil suit against Farey-Jones and Kwasny. They claim defendants violated the Stored Communications Act, 18 U.S.C. § 2701 *et seq.*

The Stored Communications Act provides a cause of action against anyone who "intentionally accesses without authorization a facility through which an electronic communication service is provided ... and thereby obtains, alters, or prevents authorized access to a wire or electronic communication while it is in electronic storage." 18 U.S.C. §§ 2701(a)(1), 2707(a).

Defendants ask us to affirm on the ground that the messages they accessed were not in "electronic storage" and therefore fell outside the Stored Communications Act's coverage. The Act defines "electronic storage" as "(A) any temporary, intermediate storage of a wire or electronic communication incidental to the electronic transmission thereof; and (B) any storage of such communication by an electronic communication service for purposes of backup protection of such communication." *Id.* § 2510(17), *incorporated by id.* § 2711(1). Several courts have held that subsection (A) covers e-mail messages stored on an ISP's server pending delivery to the recipient. *See In re DoubleClick, Inc. Privacy Litig.*, 154 F. Supp. 2d 497, 511–12 (S.D.N.Y. 2001); *Fraser v. Nationwide Mut. Ins. Co.*, 135 F. Supp. 2d 623, 635–36 (E.D. Pa. 2001); *cf. Steve Jackson Games, Inc. v. U.S. Secret Serv.*, 36 F.3d 457, 461–62 (5th Cir. 1994) (messages stored on a BBS pending delivery). Because subsection (A) applies only to messages in "temporary, intermediate storage," however, these courts have limited that subsection's coverage to messages not yet delivered to their intended recipient.

Defendants point to these cases and argue that messages remaining on an ISP's server after delivery no longer fall within the Act's coverage. But, even if such messages are not within the purview of subsection (A), they do fit comfortably within subsection (B). The only issue is whether the messages are stored "for purposes of backup protection." We think that, within the ordinary meaning of those terms, they are.

An obvious purpose for storing a message on an ISP's server after delivery is to provide a second copy of the message in the event that the user needs to download it again—if, for example, the message is accidentally erased from the user's own computer. The ISP copy of the message functions as a "backup" for the user. Notably, nothing in the Act requires that the backup protection be for the benefit of the ISP rather than the user. Storage under these circumstances thus literally falls within the statutory definition.

One district court reached a contrary conclusion, holding that "backup protection" includes only temporary backup storage pending delivery, and not any form of "post-transmission storage." We reject this view as contrary to the plain language of the Act. In contrast to subsection (A), subsection (B) does not distinguish between intermediate and post-transmission storage. Indeed, [the contrary] interpretation renders subsection (B) essentially superfluous, since temporary backup storage pending transmission would already seem to qualify as "temporary, intermediate storage" within the meaning of subsection (A). By its plain terms, subsection (B) applies to backup storage regardless of whether it is intermediate or post-transmission.

The United States, as amicus curiae, disputes our interpretation. It first argues that, because subsection (B) refers to "any storage of *such* communication," it applies only to backup copies of messages that are themselves in temporary, intermediate storage under subsection (A). The text of the statute, however, does not support this reading. Subsection (A) identifies a type of communication ("a wire or electronic communication") and a type of storage ("temporary, intermediate storage . . . incidental to the electronic transmission thereof"). The phrase "such communication" in subsection (B) does not, as a matter of grammar, reference attributes of the type of storage defined in subsection (A). The government's argument would be correct if subsection (B) referred to "a communication in such storage," or if subsection (A) referred to a communication in temporary, intermediate storage rather than temporary, intermediate storage of a communication. However, as the statute is written, "such communication" is nothing more than shorthand for "a wire or electronic communication."

The government's contrary interpretation suffers from the same flaw as *Fraser*'s: It drains subsection (B) of independent content because virtually any backup of a subsection (A) message will itself qualify as a message in temporary, intermediate storage. The government counters that the statute requires only that the underlying message be temporary, not the backup. But the lifespan of a backup is necessarily tied to that of the underlying message. Where the underlying message has expired in the normal course, any copy is no longer performing any backup function. An ISP that kept permanent copies of temporary messages could not fairly be described as "backing up" those messages.

The United States also argues that we upset the structure of the Act by defining "electronic storage" so broadly as to be superfluous and by rendering irrelevant certain other provisions dealing with remote computing services. The first claim relies on the argument that any copy of a message necessarily serves as a backup to the user, the service or both. But the mere fact that a copy *could* serve as a backup does not mean it is stored for that purpose. We see many instances where an ISP could hold messages not in electronic storage—for example, e-mail sent to or from the

ISP's staff, or messages a user has flagged for deletion from the server. In both cases, the messages are not in temporary, intermediate storage, nor are they kept for any backup purpose.

Our interpretation also does not render irrelevant the more liberal access standards governing messages stored by remote computing services. *See* 18 U.S.C. §§ 2702(a)(2), 2703(b). The government's premise is that a message stored by a remote computing service "solely for the purpose of providing storage or computer processing services to [the] subscriber," *id.* §§ 2702(a)(2)(B), 2703(b)(2)(B), would also necessarily be stored for purposes of backup protection under section 2510(17)(B), and thus would be subject to the more stringent rules governing electronic storage. But not all remote computing services are also electronic communications services and, as to those that are not, section 2510(17)(B) is by its own terms inapplicable. The government notes that remote computing services and electronic communications services are "often the same entities," but "often" is not good enough to make the government's point. Even as to remote computing services that are also electronic communications services, not all storage covered by sections 2702(a)(2)(B) and 2703(b)(2)(B) is also covered by section 2510(17)(B). A remote computing service might be the only place a user stores his messages; in that case, the messages are not stored for backup purposes.

Finally, the government invokes legislative history. It cites a passage from a 1986 report indicating that a committee intended that messages stored by a remote computing service would "continue to be covered by section 2702(a)(2)" if left on the server after user access. H.R. Rep. No. 647, 99th Cong., at 65 (1986). The cited discussion addresses provisions relating to remote computing services. We do not read it to address whether the electronic storage provisions also apply. The committee's statement that section 2702(a)(2) would "continue" to cover e-mail upon access supports our reading. If section 2702(a)(2) applies to e-mail even before access, the committee could not have been identifying an exclusive source of protection, since even the government concedes that unopened e-mail is protected by the electronic storage provisions.

The government also points to a subsequent, rejected amendment that would have made explicit the electronic storage definition's coverage of opened e-mail. This sort of legislative history has very little probative value; Congress might have rejected the amendment precisely because it thought the definition already applied.

We acknowledge that our interpretation of the Act differs from the government's and do not lightly conclude that the government's reading is erroneous. Nonetheless, for the reasons above, we think that prior access is irrelevant to whether the messages at issue were in electronic storage. Because plaintiff's e-mail messages were in electronic storage regardless of whether they had been previously delivered, the district court's decision cannot be affirmed on this ground.

Ernest Flagg v. City of Detroit

252 F.R.D. 346 (E.D. Mich. 2008)

GERALD E. ROSEN, DISTRICT JUDGE.

The Defendant City of Detroit entered into a contract for text messaging services with non-party service provider SkyTel, Inc. Under this contract, SkyTel provided text messaging devices and corresponding services to various City officials and employees, including at least some of the individual Defendants in this case. Although the City discontinued its contract with SkyTel in 2004, the company evidently continues to maintain copies of at least some of the text messages sent and received by City officials during the period when SkyTel provided this service to the City.

Upon learning of SkyTel's apparent retention of such communications, Plaintiff issued two broad subpoenas to SkyTel in February of 2008, seeking the disclosure of (i) all text messages sent or received by 34 named individuals, including the individual Defendants, during a number of time periods spanning over 5 years, and (ii) all text messages sent or received by any City official or employee during a four-hour time period in the early morning hours of April 30, 2003, the date that Plaintiff's mother was killed.

As pertinent here, the SCA generally prohibits—subject to certain exceptions—a "person or entity providing an electronic communication service to the public" from "knowingly divulg[ing] to any person or entity the contents of a communication while in electronic storage by that service." 18 U.S.C. § 2702(a)(1). It further prohibits—again, subject to certain exceptions—a "person or entity providing remote computing service to the public" from "knowingly divulg[ing] to any person or entity the contents of any communication which is carried or maintained on that service." 18 U.S.C. § 2702(a)(2). [n.6][26]

As is evident from these provisions, the prohibitions set forth in § 2702(a) govern service providers to the extent that they offer either of two types of services: an "electronic communications service" or a "remote computing service."

The potential importance of distinguishing between an "ECS" and an "RCS" lies in the different criteria for establishing an exception to the general rule against disclosure. The provider of an RCS may divulge the contents of a communication with the "lawful consent" of the subscriber to the service, while the provider of an ECS may divulge such a communication only with the "lawful consent of the originator or an addressee or intended recipient of such communication." 18 U.S.C. § 2702(b)(3).

---

26. [n.6] The SCA also prohibits a service provider from divulging subscriber or customer information or records "to any governmental entity." 18 U.S.C. § 2702(a)(3). This provision is not applicable here, where any such subscriber or customer information is being sought by a private party, Plaintiff.

Defendants' challenge to Plaintiff's request for disclosure of the SkyTel text messages rests upon what they view as a straightforward reading of the terms of the SCA. In particular, they first point to the SCA provision that generally prohibits a service provider such as SkyTel from (i) "knowingly divulg[ing] to any person or entity the contents of a communication while in electronic storage by" an electronic communication service ("ECS"), 18 U.S.C. § 2702(a)(1), or (ii) "knowingly divulg[ing] to any person or entity the contents of any communication which is carried or maintained on" a remote computing service ("RCS"), 18 U.S.C. § 2702(a)(2). Next, while the SCA recognizes various exceptions to this general rule of non-disclosure, Defendants submit that the only relevant exception is disclosure "with the lawful consent of" the originator or intended recipient of a communication or (in the case of an RCS) the subscriber to the service, 18 U.S.C. § 2702(b)(3), and they state their unwillingness to give the requisite consent. It follows, in Defendants' view, that SkyTel may not produce any text messages in this case.

If the archive and retrieval service provided by SkyTel qualifies as an RCS, it is . . . doubtful that this sort of retrieval would run afoul of § 2702(a). Under the pertinent subsection of § 2702(a), a service provider that provides an RCS is prohibited from "divulg[ing]" the "contents of any communication which is carried or maintained on that service . . . on behalf of . . . a subscriber or customer" only *if* the service provider "is not authorized to access the contents of any such communications for purposes of providing any services other than storage or computer processing." 18 U.S.C. § 2702(a)(2). Yet, to the extent that the contracts between the City and SkyTel provide a mechanism for the City to request the retrieval of text messages from the archive maintained by SkyTel, such a request presumably would supply the necessary "authoriz[ation]" for SkyTel to "access" the communications in this archive "for purposes of providing a [ ] service[ ] other than storage or computer processing" — namely, the service of retrieval. It is not a foregone conclusion, then, that SkyTel necessarily would engage in any activity prohibited under § 2702(a) by fulfilling the City's demand to retrieve text messages from an archive maintained at the behest of this customer.

The Court finds that the Defendant City has both the ability and the obligation to secure any such consent that the SCA may require. As observed earlier, the consent that is needed to satisfy § 2702(b)(3) depends upon the sort of service being provided. If this service is deemed to be an RCS, then the consent of the "subscriber" is sufficient to permit the service provider to divulge the contents of a communication maintained on this service. 18 U.S.C. § 2702(b)(3).[n.26][27] In contrast, if a service is determined to be an ECS, then only the "lawful consent of the originator or an

---

27. [n.26] The parties agree that the City is the "subscriber" of SkyTel's text messaging services within the meaning of § 2702. Thus, if the relevant service provided by SkyTel to the City is properly characterized as an RCS, SkyTel need only secure the City's consent in order to divulge the contents of any communications it has archived under its contracts with the City.

addressee or intended recipient" of a communication will suffice to overcome the prohibition against divulging this communication. 18 U.S.C. § 2702(b)(3).

This distinction between an ECS and an RCS was central to the rulings of the district and appellate courts in *Quon*, with the district court initially determining that the service at issue in that case was an RCS.

[In *Quon*,] Arch Wireless moved for summary judgment in its favor on the plaintiffs' SCA claim, arguing that the service it provided was an RCS and that the city, by requesting the disclosure of text messages maintained on this service, had provided the subscriber consent necessary to permit these disclosures without violating the prohibitions set forth in § 2702(a). In addressing this question, the district court initially observed that Arch Wireless appeared to have provided a "computer storage" service that was characteristic of an RCS, as the messages it had provided to the city were retrieved from long-term storage after already having been delivered and read by their recipients. Nonetheless, the court acknowledged that the maintenance of the text message in storage was not enough, standing alone, to distinguish an RCS from an ECS, because the SCA expressly contemplates that an ECS also entails the "electronic storage" of communications. Moreover, while it was clear that Arch Wireless provided an ECS to the city by supplying text messaging devices and associated services that enabled city employees to send and receive electronic communications, the district court construed the SCA and its legislative history as eschewing an "all or nothing" approach to characterizing a service provider's activities, and as instead recognizing that a service provider such as Arch Wireless could provide *both* RCSs and ECSs to a single customer.

Thus, the key question before the district court was whether the specific service that gave rise to the plaintiffs' SCA claims—*i.e.*, Arch Wireless's retrieval of text messages from storage after they had been transmitted and read by their recipients—should be deemed to be an RCS or an ECS. This, in turn, required the court to distinguish between the "electronic storage" utilized by an ECS and the "computer storage" provided by an RCS. As to the former, the statute defines "electronic storage" as "any temporary, intermediate storage of a wire or electronic communication incidental to the electronic transmission thereof," or "any storage of such communication by an electronic communication service for purposes of backup protection of such communication." 18 U.S.C. § 2510(17). Because the text messages that Arch Wireless had retrieved from storage and forwarded to the city had already been transmitted and read in the past, their continued storage could not be construed as "temporary" or "incidental to" their transmission. Rather, the district court reasoned that the characterization of Arch Wireless's service as an ECS or an RCS turned upon whether the text messages had been stored "for purposes of backup protection."

The court concluded that this was not the purpose for which Arch Wireless had stored the text messages that it subsequently provided to the city. In so ruling, the court relied principally on the Ninth Circuit's observation in an earlier case that a service does not store messages "for backup purposes" if it is "the only place a user stores his messages." The district court reasoned that "Arch Wireless' service would meet this definition," where the storage it provided was "long-term" and was "apparently . . . the single place where text messages, after they have been read, are archived for a permanent record-keeping mechanism." Consequently, the court held that the service provided by Arch Wireless was an RCS, and that any disclosures of communications maintained on this service were permissibly made with the consent of the subscriber City of Ontario.

The Ninth Circuit reversed this aspect of the district court's ruling, and held that "Arch Wireless provided an 'electronic communication service' to the City." This decision appears to rest on the "all-or-nothing" approach rejected by the district court, with the Ninth Circuit broadly "categoriz[ing] Arch Wireless" as providing a service for sending and receiving electronic communications, as opposed to a "computer storage" service. While the court recognized that Arch Wireless did "archiv[e] . . . text messages on its server," it noted that both ECSs and RCSs entail some form of "storage," and it found that Arch Wireless did not provide the "virtual filing cabinet" function that was cited in the legislative history of the SCA as characteristic of an RCS.

The Ninth Circuit then explained that the district court's reliance on its *Theofel* decision was misplaced, and that this prior ruling, properly understood, actually led to the opposite conclusion. As observed in *Quon*, the court in *Theofel* held that an internet service provider had stored e-mail messages on its server "for purposes of backup protection," since "[a]n obvious purpose for storing a message on an ISP's server after delivery is to provide a second copy of the message in the event that the user needs to download it again — if, for example, the message is accidentally erased from the user's own computer." The court in *Quon* found that this ruling governed the case before it, where "[t]he service provided by [the ISP in *Theofel*] is closely analogous to Arch Wireless's storage of [the plaintiffs'] messages," and where it was "clear that the messages were archived for 'backup protection,' just as they were in *Theofel*."

Finally, the Ninth Circuit addressed certain language in *Theofel* that Arch Wireless (and the district court) viewed as supporting the conclusion that its storage of messages was *not* for "backup protection":. . . .

Thus, the court held that Arch Wireless provided an ECS to the city, and that it violated the SCA by disclosing transcripts of text messages to the city without first securing the consent of the originator, addressee, or intended recipient of each such communication.

Upon carefully reviewing the district and appellate court rulings in *Quon*, this Court finds the lower court's reasoning more persuasive, on a number of grounds. First, the Court reads the Ninth Circuit's decision in that case — and, to some extent, the court's prior ruling in *Theofel* — as resting on a unitary approach, under which service providers contract with their customers to provide either an ECS or an RCS, but not both. Yet, the prohibitions against disclosure set forth in §2702(a) focus on the specific type of service being provided (an ECS or an RCS) with regard to a particular communication, and do not turn upon the classification of the service provider or on broad notions of the service that this entity generally or predominantly provides. Thus, the Court is inclined to agree with the view of the district court in *Quon* that "Congress took a middle course" in enacting the SCA, under which a service provider such as SkyTel may be deemed to provide both an ECS and an RCS to the same customer.

In light of the SCA's functional, context-specific definitions of an ECS and an RCS, it is not dispositive that SkyTel indisputably did provide an ECS to the City of Detroit in the past, or that it presumably kept text messages in "electronic storage" at times in connection with the ECS that it provided. Rather, the ECS/RCS inquiry in this case turns upon the characterization of the service that SkyTel *presently* provides to the City, pursuant to which the company is being called upon to retrieve text messages from an archive of communications sent and received by City employees in years past using SkyTel text messaging devices. The resolution of this issue, in turn, depends upon whether SkyTel has maintained this archive "for purposes of backup protection," so that its contents may be deemed to be held in "electronic storage" by an ECS, or whether this archive is more properly viewed as "computer storage" offered by an RCS.

Whatever might be said about the reasoning through which the district and appellate courts in *Quon* determined that the archive of text messages in that case did or did not serve the purpose of "backup protection,"[n.29][28] the circumstances of this case are far clearer. SkyTel is no longer providing, and has long since ceased to provide, a text messaging service to the City of Detroit — the City, by its own admission, discontinued this service in 2004, and the text messaging devices issued by SkyTel are no longer in use. Consequently, any archive of text messages that SkyTel continues to maintain on the City's behalf constitutes the *only* available record of these communications, and cannot possibly serve as a "backup" copy of communications stored elsewhere. In this respect, this Court is in complete agreement with the Ninth Circuit's observations in *Theofel*, that a service provider "that kept permanent copies of temporary messages could not fairly be described as 'backing up' those messages," and that "messages are not stored for backup purposes" if a computer repository is "the only place" where they are stored. Regardless of whether these observations applied to the services at issue in *Theofel* and *Quon*, the Court concludes that they

---

28. [n.29] The Court confesses that it is puzzled by the Ninth Circuit's observation that there was "no indication in the record" in that case that "Arch Wireless retained a permanent copy of the text messages or stored them for the benefit of the City," and that the evidence "instead" showed "that copies of the messages are 'archived' on Arch Wireless's server." In this Court's view, an "archive" is commonly understood as a permanent record, and the district court in *Quon* characterized Arch Wireless's repository in that case as "the single place where text messages, after they have been read, are archived for a permanent record-keeping mechanism." Moreover, once a service provider has successfully delivered a given text message to its intended recipient and the message has been opened and read, it would appear that any retention of a copy of this message in an "archive" could only be intended "for the benefit of" the customer, because this practice would serve no apparent purpose, whether backup or otherwise, for the service provider in its role as ECS.

apply with full force here—the service provided by SkyTel may properly be characterized as a "virtual filing cabinet" of communications sent and received by City employees. The Court finds, therefore, that the archive maintained by SkyTel constitutes "computer storage," and that the company's maintenance of this archive on behalf of the City is a "remote computing service" as defined under the SCA.

It is only a short step from this finding to the conclusion that the Defendant City is both able and obligated to give its consent, as subscriber, to SkyTel's retrieval of text messages.

––––––––––

DOJ Illustration of the SCA Classifications:

An example illustrates how the SCA's categories work in practice outside the Ninth Circuit, where *Theofel* does not apply. Imagine that Joe sends an email from his account at work ("joe@goodcompany.com") to the personal account of his friend Jane ("jane@localisp.com"). The email will stream across the Internet until it reaches the servers of Jane's Internet service provider, here the fictional LocalISP. When the message first arrives at Local-ISP, LocalISP is a provider of ECS with respect to that message. Before Jane accesses LocalISP and retrieves the message, Joe's email is in "electronic storage." Once Jane retrieves Joe's email, she can either delete the message from LocalISP's server or else leave the message stored there. If Jane chooses to store the email with LocalISP, LocalISP is now a provider of RCS (and not ECS) with respect to the email sent by Joe. The role of LocalISP has changed from a transmitter of Joe's email to a storage facility for a file stored remotely for Jane by a provider of RCS.

Next imagine that Jane responds to Joe's email. Jane's return email to Joe will stream across the Internet to the servers of Joe's employer, Good Company. Before Joe retrieves the email from Good Company's servers, Good Company is a provider of ECS with respect to Jane's email (just like LocalISP was with respect to Joe's original email before Jane accessed it). When Joe accesses Jane's email message and the communication reaches its destination (Joe), Good Company ceases to be a provider of ECS with respect to that email (just as LocalISP ceased to be a provider of ECS with respect to Joe's original email when Jane accessed it). Unlike LocalISP, however, Good Company does not become a provider of RCS if Joe decides to store the opened email on Good Company's server. Rather, for purposes of this specific message, Good Company is a provider of neither ECS nor RCS. Good Company does not provide RCS because it does not provide services to the public. Because Good Company provides neither ECS nor RCS with respect to the opened email in Joe's account, the SCA no longer regulates access to this email, and such access is governed solely by the Fourth Amendment. Functionally speaking, the opened email in Joe's account drops out of the SCA.

Finally, consider the status of the other copies of the emails in this scenario: Jane has downloaded a copy of Joe's email from LocalISP's server to her personal computer at home, and Joe has downloaded a copy of Jane's email from Good Company's server to his office desktop computer at work. The SCA governs neither. Although these computers contain copies of emails, these copies are not stored on the server of a third-party provider of RCS or ECS, and therefore the SCA does not apply. Access to the copies of the communications stored in Jane's personal computer at home and Joe's office computer at work is governed solely by the Fourth Amendment.[29]

STEP #3: OBTAINING INFORMATION FROM PROVIDERS

There are two possible types of disclosure: voluntary and compelled.

Voluntary Disclosure by Providers: depends on the type of provider *See* § 2702

- Providers of services not available "to the public" may freely disclose both contents and other records relating to stored communications.

- Disclosure prohibitions applying to providers of RCS or ECS services to the public § 2702(a)

- Content—Cannot knowingly divulge to anybody communications that are stored by the RCS or by the ECS in electronic storage.

- Non-content—Cannot knowingly divulge to the government.

- Exceptions to **content** disclosure prohibitions § 2702(b)

  - Public provider of ECS or RCS may divulge communication contents

  - to addressee or intended recipient, or his/her agent.

  - as authorized under Wiretap Act or compelled under § 2703.

  - with consent of originator, addressee or intended recipient, or subscriber.

  - to forward the communication to its destination.

  - as necessary to provide service or protect the provider's rights or property.

  - to National Center for Missing and Exploited Children (NCMEC) if mandated report of child pornography.

  - to a law enforcement agency if inadvertently obtained and it appears to pertain to commission of a crime.

  - to a government entity if the provider believes, in good faith, that a related emergency involving danger of death or serious physical injury requires disclosure without delay.

---

29. COMPUTER CRIME AND INTELLECTUAL PROPERTY SECTION, U.S. DEPT. OF JUSTICE, PROSECUTING COMPUTER CRIMES 125–26 (2009).

- Exceptions to **non-content** disclosure prohibitions § 2702(c)
  - Public provider of ECS or RCS may divulge a subscriber or customer record or other Information
    - if served with appropriate legal process under § 2703.
    - with customer consent.
    - as necessary to provide service or protect the provider's rights or property.
    - to a government entity if provider believes, in good faith, that a related emergency involving danger of death or serious physical injury requires disclosure without delay.
    - to NCMEC if in connection with report of child pornography.
    - to any person other than a government entity, for any reason.

An Example — Emergency Disclosures

Michael Aaron Jayne v. Sprint PCS

2009 U.S. Dist. LEXIS 13080 (E.D. Cal. 2009)

Gregory G. Hollows, United States Magistrate Judge.

[Plaintiff Jayne was on parole and sued a variety of persons and Sprint. He alleged a series of illegal actions by parole agents. He also alleged the following:]

Miss Shanda (or Shonda) Kessler went to the Anderson police to file a restraining order against plaintiff, then maliciously contacted defendant Abney [a parole agent], bypassing plaintiff's assigned parole agent, so that Abney would go after plaintiff. Defendants Blunk, Collier and the defendant identified only as [Anderson Police] Dispatch, coerced Kessler into saying plaintiff had held her against her will for six hours. These defendant officers than sent an exigent circumstances request/demand to plaintiff's cell phone provider, saying that plaintiff was wanted for kidnapping and that the cell phone service was to provide plaintiff's cell phone records and GPS location. Plaintiff asserts that this request/demand was made "without a warrant or real cause," and claims that defendant Sprint PCS provided the cell phone records to the Anderson police "based on this false and illegal pretense."

Defendant Sprint identifies itself as a wireless communications company having customers in every state, including California, and acknowledges that plaintiff was one such customer. Further, defendant Sprint accepts as true plaintiff's allegation that Sprint provided plaintiff's cell phone records to defendants upon a demand/request by defendants Blunk, Collier and Anderson Police Dispatch predicated on exigent circumstances. Nor does defendant Sprint, which disclaims any knowledge of plaintiff's interaction with law enforcement, in any manner contest plaintiff's version of the facts with regard to the legitimacy of the basis for the defendants' request.

Sprint contends that under the Stored Communications Act at 18 U.S.C. § 2702(c)(4), service providers are permitted to disclose telephone records so long as they have a good faith belief that there is an emergency requiring authorization. Moreover, according to Sprint, the SCA affords complete immunity from suit against a carrier which discloses such information pursuant to statutory authority, citing 18 USC § 2703(e). Defendant Sprint seeks dismissal from this action with prejudice.

Under 18 U.S.C. § 2702(c)(4), a provider of an electronic communication service "may divulge a record or other information pertaining to a subscriber to or customer of such service (not including the contents of communications covered by subsection (a)(1) or (a)(2))":

> to a governmental entity, if the provider, in good faith, believes that an emergency involving danger of death or serious physical injury to any person requires disclosure without delay of information relating to the emergency;

Under 18 USC § 2703(e):

> **No cause of action against a provider disclosing information under this chapter.**-No cause of action shall lie in any court against any provider of wire or electronic communication service, its officers, employees, agents, or other specified persons for providing information, facilities, or assistance in accordance with the terms of a court order, warrant, subpoena, statutory authorization, or certification under this chapter.

It has been found that "a provider who discloses records or other information pursuant to the authorization contained in 18 U.S.C. § 2702(c)(4) in emergency circumstances has the same protection from lawsuits as a provider who discloses the records pursuant to a court order."

Moreover, a district court has declined "to speculate whether it would ever be appropriate, under exigent circumstances when it would not be feasible to get a signed warrant or comply with other legal process, for the government to notify the ISP of an emergency and receive subscriber information without conforming with the ECPA."

To the extent that defendant Sprint's actions came within the provision of § 18 U.S.C. § 2702(c)(4), on the face of it, under § 2703(e), Sprint should be dismissed with prejudice as a defendant.

3. Compelling Disclosure § 2703

When providers are not allowed or do not choose to voluntarily disclose content or records, the government can compel providers to disclose information through appropriate legal process, depending on the nature of the communication in storage. There are five different levels of process. The more "process" utilized yields more types of information.

> The standard for court orders differs according to the duration of electronic storage and whether the information obtained is content or non-content. At the highest level, ordering an ISP to turn over the contents

of electronic communications stored for 180 days or less requires a standard search warrant. Communications contents stored for more than 180 days can be obtained either with a standard warrant or a subpoena (or a § 2703(d) court order) that must be coupled in most cases with prior notice to the ISP subscriber. A subscriber who has been notified that his personal information has been subpoenaed would likely have the opportunity to challenge the subpoena on the grounds of irrelevance, improper purpose, or procedural flaws. Numerous courts have recently held that a privacy interest inherent in many personal records (such as credit card or employment personnel records) allows the subject of the records to challenge subpoenas issued to third parties.

At the lowest level, only a subpoena is required to compel an ISP to disclose basic noncontent subscriber information, including name, address, records of session times, length and type of subscription, telephone number or network address, and source of payment including credit card number. A somewhat higher level of protection is granted to "other" noncontent records pertaining to the subscriber, a category that generally covers all transactional information (such as phone usage records or records of email headers) other than basic subscriber information. For these records, the government must generally obtain a § 2703(d) court order, which can be issued only if the government applicant provides "specific and articulable facts" demonstrating "reasonable grounds to believe that the [records] are relevant and material to an ongoing criminal investigation." Ironically, this standard is significantly higher than the standard governing Pen Register Act intercept orders, which generally provides no judicial review and requires no showing of specific and articulable facts. The "reasonable grounds for relevance" standard is lower than probable cause (and is akin to the general relevance standard for subpoenas), but does provide some degree of judicial scrutiny for noncontent record requests. Still, the standards for obtaining content in the ECPA, even content stored for more than 180 days, are substantially higher than those for noncontent. The lowest standard for obtaining stored content still requires notice to the subscriber (and the corresponding opportunity to challenge the surveillance); on the other hand, the highest standard for noncontent information does not require notice to the subscriber whose records are being observed. The statutory protection afforded to electronic communication information depends in large part on whether the information is classified as content or noncontent information under the ECPA.[30]

---

30. Matthew J. Tokson, *The Content/Envelope Distinction in Internet Law*, 50 WILLIAM & MARY L. REV. 2105 (2009). Copyright © 2009, Matthew J. Tokson, William and Mary Law Review. All rights reserved. Reprinted by permission.

Types of Process and Information Obtainable

Except in the Sixth and Ninth Circuits (which has departed from this structure), the five levels of process the government may use are:

- **With Subpoena** (no prior notice required) the government can obtain

  - basic subscriber information

  - opened messages and other files in non-RCS storage (because the SCA does not apply to such storage by non-public providers)

- **With Subpoena with Prior Government Notice to Subscriber or Customer**

  - opened email from a public provider if the government complies with the notice provisions of §§ 2703(b)(1)(B) and 2705

  - basic subscriber information, contents in RCS storage, and contents in electronic storage more than 180 days

- **With § 2703(d) Order** (no prior notice)

  - basic subscriber information, transactional records

  - the government must state specific and articulable facts that there are reasonable grounds to believe the communications or records are relevant and material to a criminal investigation

NOTE: need at least a § 2703(d) court order to obtain most account logs and transactional records

- **With § 2703(d) Order with Prior Government Notice to Subscriber or Customer**

  - the government can obtain everything in an account except for unopened email or voicemail stored with a provider for 180 days or less

  - the government can obtain basic subscriber information, transactional records, contents in RCS storage, and contents in electronic storage more than 180 days

- **With Search Warrant**

  - can obtain all contents and non-contents of an account

4. Miscellaneous SCA Provisions

1. Preservation of Evidence Requests § 2703(f)

- The government may direct providers to preserve existing records pending issuance of compulsory legal process but such requests have no prospective effect.

- Records and evidence are to be retained for up to 90 days (plus another 90 days if the request is renewed).

2. Orders not to disclose existence of legal process § 2705(b)

- Permits application for court order directing the service provider not to disclose the existence of the legal process by which disclosure is compelled whenever the government itself has no legal duty to notify the customer or subscriber of the process.

3. Remedies

- No statutory suppression remedy.
- Criminal penalty (for unlawful access to stored communications) § 2701(b)
  - 5-year felony, or a 10-year felony for a repeat offense, if committed for "commercial advantage, malicious destruction or damage, or private commercial gain, or in furtherance of any criminal or tortious act."
  - Otherwise a misdemeanor, or a 5-year felony for a repeat offense.
- Civil penalties
  - For a civil action against a "person or entity, other than the United States," relief can include money damages of no less than $1,000 per person, equitable or declaratory relief, reasonable attorney fees, and other reasonable litigation costs.
  - Willful or intentional violations can also result in punitive damages.
  - Good faith reliance on a court order or warrant, grand jury subpoena, legislative authorization, or statutory authorization provides a complete defense to any civil (or criminal) action.
- Suits may be brought against the United States for willful violations of the SCA.
  - Employees of the United States may be subject to disciplinary action for willful or intentional violations.
  - Qualified immunity may be available.

Notes

1. At the beginning of this section, it was noted that the SCA is a complex statute and courts have differed on the meaning of several of its provisions. Based on the various contradictory interpretations from courts, any one court can take many different paths to reach very different results. Few aspects of the law can be stated categorically. Is the statutory framework unnecessarily complex?

2. *Carpenter v. United States*, 585 U.S. __ (2018), which is discussed in Chapter 11, clearly creates a great deal of uncertainty about the constitutional viability of the SCA's categories of types of information and the levels of process needed to obtain each type of information. Looking at the various categories of data set forth above, which ones now require a warrant?

Chapter 13

Obscenity and Child Pornography

§ 13.1 Obscenity

The examination of obscenity as a category of speech unprotected by the First Amendment is a large topic. This book focuses on two aspects of that topic that are of particular importance due to modern communications. First, is the decades old standard set forth in *Miller* still viable? In particular, is the community standard that *Miller* created still adequate in light of modern communications? In the readings, *Miller* is excerpted to articulate the current obscenity standard; it is followed by two cases that examine the community standards aspect of *Miller* in the context of Internet and email communications. Second, although obscenity may take many forms, the two concluding cases in the next section focus on its use as an alternative means of charging persons engaged in activities that do not meet the current definition of child pornography.

1. The *Miller* Standard

Marvin Miller v. California

413 U.S. 15 (1973)

Mr. Chief Justice Burger delivered the opinion of the Court.

Appellant conducted a mass mailing campaign to advertise the sale of illustrated books, euphemistically called "adult" material. After a jury trial, he was convicted of knowingly distributing obscene matter. Appellant's conviction was specifically based on his conduct in causing five unsolicited advertising brochures to be sent through the mail in an envelope addressed to a restaurant in Newport Beach, California. The envelope was opened by the manager of the restaurant and his mother. They had not requested the brochures; they complained to the police.

The brochures advertise four books entitled "Intercourse," "Man-Woman," "Sex Orgies Illustrated," and "An Illustrated History of Pornography," and a film entitled "Marital Intercourse." While the brochures contain some descriptive printed material, primarily they consist of pictures and drawings very explicitly depicting men and women in groups of two or more engaging in a variety of sexual activities, with genitals often prominently displayed.

This Court has recognized that the States have a legitimate interest in prohibiting dissemination or exhibition of obscene material[n.2][1] when the mode of dissemination carries with it a significant danger of offending the sensibilities of unwilling recipients or of exposure to juveniles. It is in this context that we are called on to define the standards which must be used to identify obscene material that a State may regulate without infringing on the First Amendment as applicable to the States through the Fourteenth Amendment.

In *Roth*, the Court sustained a conviction under a federal statute punishing the mailing of "obscene, lewd, lascivious or filthy . . ." materials. The key to that holding was the Court's rejection of the claim that obscene materials were protected by the First Amendment. Five Justices joined in the opinion stating:

> "All ideas having even the slightest redeeming social importance — unorthodox ideas, controversial ideas, even ideas hateful to the prevailing climate of opinion — have the full protection of the (First Amendment) guaranties, unless excludable because they encroach upon the limited area of more important interests. But implicit in the history of the First Amendment is the rejection of obscenity as utterly without redeeming social importance. . . . This is the same judgment expressed by this Court in *Chaplinsky v. New Hampshire*, 315 U.S. 568, 571–572:

> ". . . There are certain well-defined and narrowly limited classes of speech, the prevention and punishment of which have never been thought to raise any Constitutional problem. These include the lewd and obscene. . . . It has been well observed that such utterances are no essential part of any exposition of ideas, and are of such slight social value as a step to truth that any benefit that may be derived from them is clearly outweighed by the social interest in order and morality. . . ."

---

1. [n.2] This Court has defined "obscene material" as "material which deals with sex in a manner appealing to prurient interest," Roth v. United States, 354 U.S. 476 (1957), but the *Roth* definition does not reflect the precise meaning of "obscene" as traditionally used in the English language. Derived from the Latin obscaenus, ob, to, plus caenum, filth, "obscene" is defined in the Webster's Third New International Dictionary (Unabridged 1969) as "1a: disgusting to the senses . . . b: grossly repugnant to the generally accepted notions of what is appropriate . . . 2: offensive or revolting as countering or violating some ideal or principle." The Oxford English Dictionary (1933 ed.) gives a similar definition, "(o)ffensive to the senses, or to taste or refinement, disgusting, repulsive, filthy, foul, abominable, loathsome." The material we are discussing in this case is more accurately defined as "pornography" or "pornographic material." "Pornography" derives from the Greek (porne, harlot, and graphos, writing). The word now means "1: a description of prostitutes or prostitution 2: a depiction (as in writing or painting) of licentiousness or lewdness: a portrayal of erotic behavior designed to cause sexual excitement." Webster's Third New International Dictionary. Pornographic material which is obscene forms a subgroup of all "obscene" expression, but not the whole, at least as the word "obscene" is now used in our language. We note, therefore, that the words "obscene material," as used in this case, have a specific judicial meaning which derives from the *Roth* case, i.e., obscene material "which deals with sex."

This much has been categorically settled by the Court, that obscene material is unprotected by the First Amendment. "The First and Fourteenth Amendments have never been treated as absolutes." We acknowledge, however, the inherent dangers of undertaking to regulate any form of expression. State statutes designed to regulate obscene materials must be carefully limited. As a result, we now confine the permissible scope of such regulation to works which depict or describe sexual conduct. That conduct must be specifically defined by the applicable state law, as written or authoritatively construed. A state offense must also be limited to works which, taken as a whole, appeal to the prurient interest in sex, which portray sexual conduct in a patently offensive way, and which, taken as a whole, do not have serious literary, artistic, political, or scientific value.

The basic guidelines for the trier of fact must be: (a) whether "the average person, applying contemporary community standards" would find that the work, taken as a whole, appeals to the prurient interest; (b) whether the work depicts or describes, in a patently offensive way, sexual conduct specifically defined by the applicable state law; and (c) whether the work, taken as a whole, lacks serious literary, artistic, political, or scientific value.

It is possible to give a few plain examples of what a state statute could define for regulation under part (b) of the standard announced in this opinion:

(a) Patently offensive representations or descriptions of ultimate sexual acts, normal or perverted, actual or simulated.

(b) Patently offensive representation or descriptions of masturbation, excretory functions, and lewd exhibition of the genitals.

At a minimum, prurient, patently offensive depiction or description of sexual conduct must have serious literary, artistic, political, or scientific value to merit First Amendment protection. For example, medical books for the education of physicians and related personnel necessarily use graphic illustrations and descriptions of human anatomy. In resolving the inevitably sensitive questions of fact and law, we must continue to rely on the jury system, accompanied by the safeguards that judges, rules of evidence, presumption of innocence, and other protective features provide, as we do with rape, murder, and a host of other offenses against society and its individual members.[n.9][2]

Under a National Constitution, fundamental First Amendment limitations on the powers of the States do not vary from community to community, but this does not mean that there are, or should or can be, fixed, uniform national standards of precisely what appeals to the "prurient interest" or is "patently offensive." These are essentially questions of fact, and our Nation is simply too big and too diverse for this Court to reasonably expect that such standards could be articulated for all

---

2. [n.9] The mere fact juries may reach different conclusions as to the same material does not mean that constitutional rights are abridged. That is one of the consequences we accept under our jury system.

50 States in a single formulation, even assuming the prerequisite consensus exists. When triers of fact are asked to decide whether "the average person, applying contemporary community standards" would consider certain materials "prurient," it would be unrealistic to require that the answer be based on some abstract formulation. The adversary system, with lay jurors as the usual ultimate factfinders in criminal prosecutions, has historically permitted triers of fact to draw on the standards of their community, guided always by limiting instructions on the law. To require a State to structure obscenity proceedings around evidence of a national "community standard" would be an exercise in futility.

It is neither realistic nor constitutionally sound to read the First Amendment as requiring that the people of Maine or Mississippi accept public depiction of conduct found tolerable in Las Vegas, or New York City. People in different States vary in their tastes and attitudes, and this diversity is not to be strangled by the absolutism of imposed uniformity.

---

2. Community Standards

United States v. Robert Alan Thomas

74 F.3d 701 (6th Cir. 1996)

EDMUNDS, DISTRICT JUDGE.

Robert Thomas and his wife Carleen Thomas began operating the Amateur Action Computer Bulletin Board System ("AABBS") from their home in Milpitas, California in February 1991. The AABBS was a computer bulletin board system that operated by using telephones, modems, and personal computers. Its features included e-mail, chat lines, public messages, and files that members could access, transfer, and download to their own computers and printers.

Information loaded onto the bulletin board was first converted into binary code, i.e., 0's and 1's, through the use of a scanning device. After purchasing sexually-explicit magazines from public adult book stores in California, Defendant Robert Thomas used an electronic device called a scanner to convert pictures from the magazines into computer files called Graphic Interchange Format files or "GIF" files. The AABBS contained approximately 14,000 GIF files. Mr. Thomas also purchased, sold, and delivered sexually-explicit videotapes to AABBS members. Customers ordered the tapes by sending Robert Thomas an e-mail message, and Thomas typically delivered them by use of the United Parcel Service.

Persons calling the AABBS without a password could view the introductory screens of the system which contained brief, sexually-explicit descriptions of the GIF files and adult videotapes that were offered for sale. Access to the GIF files, however, was limited to members who were given a password after they paid a membership fee and submitted a signed application form that Defendant Robert Thomas reviewed.

The application form requested the applicant's age, address, and telephone number and required a signature.

Members accessed the GIF files by using a telephone, modem and personal computer. A modem located in the Defendants' home answered the calls. After they established membership by typing in a password, members could then select, retrieve, and instantly transport GIF files to their own computer. A caller could then view the GIF file on his computer screen and print the image out using his printer. The GIF files contained the AABBS name and access telephone number; many also had "Distribute Freely" printed on the image itself.

In July 1993, a United States Postal Inspector, Agent David Dirmeyer, received a complaint regarding the AABBS from an individual who resided in the Western District of Tennessee. Dirmeyer dialed the AABBS' telephone number. As a non-member, he viewed a screen that read "Welcome to AABBS, the Nastiest Place On Earth," and was able to select various "menus" and read graphic descriptions of the GIF files and videotapes that were offered for sale.

Subsequently, Dirmeyer used an assumed name and sent in $55 along with an executed application form to the AABBS. Defendant Robert Thomas called Dirmeyer at his undercover telephone number in Memphis, Tennessee, acknowledged receipt of his application, and authorized him to log-on with his personal password. Thereafter, Dirmeyer dialed the AABBS's telephone number, logged-on and, using his computer/modem in Memphis, downloaded the GIF files listed in counts 2-7 of the Defendants' indictments. These GIF files depicted images of bestiality, oral sex, incest, sado-masochistic abuse, and sex scenes involving urination. Dirmeyer also ordered six sexually-explicit videotapes from the AABBS and received them via U.P.S. at a Memphis, Tennessee address. Dirmeyer also had several e-mail and chat-mode conversations with Defendant Robert Thomas.

On January 10, 1994, a search warrant was issued [and the] AABBS' location was subsequently searched, and the Defendants' computer system was seized.

On January 25, 1994, a federal grand jury for the Western District of Tennessee returned a twelve-count indictment charging Defendants Robert and Carleen Thomas with the following criminal violations: one count under 18 U.S.C. § 371 for conspiracy to violate federal obscenity laws—18 U.S.C. §§ 1462, 1465, six counts under 18 U.S.C. § 1465 for knowingly using and causing to be used a facility and means of interstate commerce—a combined computer/telephone system—for the purpose of transporting obscene, computer-generated materials (the GIF files) in interstate commerce, three counts under 18 U.S.C. § 1462 for shipping obscene videotapes via U.P.S., one count of causing the transportation of materials depicting minors engaged in sexually explicit conduct in violation of 18 U.S.C. § 2252(a)(1) as to Mr. Thomas only, and one count of forfeiture under 18 U.S.C. § 1467.

Defendants challenge venue in the Western District of Tennessee for counts 2-7 of their indictments. They argue that even if venue was proper under count 1 (conspiracy) and counts 8-10 (videotapes sent via U.P.S.), counts 2-7 (GIF files) should have been severed and transferred to California because Defendants did not cause the GIF files to be transmitted to the Western District of Tennessee. Rather, Defendants assert, it was Dirmeyer, a government agent, who, without their knowledge, accessed and downloaded the GIF files and caused them to enter Tennessee. We disagree. To establish a Section 1465 violation, the Government must prove that a defendant knowingly used a facility or means of interstate commerce for the purpose of distributing obscene materials. Contrary to Defendants' position, Section 1465 does not require the Government to prove that Defendants had specific knowledge of the destination of each transmittal at the time it occurred.

"Venue lies in any district in which the offense was committed," and the Government is required to establish venue by a preponderance of the evidence. This court examines the propriety of venue by taking "'into account a number of factors—the site of the defendant's acts, the elements and nature of the crime, the locus of the effect of the criminal conduct, and the suitability of each district for accurate fact finding.'"

Section 1465 is an obscenity statute, and federal obscenity laws, by virtue of their inherent nexus to interstate and foreign commerce, generally involve acts in more than one jurisdiction or state. Furthermore, it is well-established that "there is no constitutional impediment to the government's power to prosecute pornography dealers in any district into which the material is sent."

Substantial evidence introduced at trial demonstrated that the AABBS was set up so members located in other jurisdictions could access and order GIF files which would then be instantaneously transmitted in interstate commerce. Moreover, AABBS materials were distributed to an approved AABBS member known to reside in the Western District of Tennessee. Specifically, Defendant Robert Thomas knew of, approved, and had conversed with an AABBS member in that judicial district who had his permission to access and copy GIF files that ultimately ended up there. Some of these GIF files were clearly marked "Distribute Freely." In light of the above, the effects of the Defendants' criminal conduct reached the Western District of Tennessee, and that district was suitable for accurate fact-finding. Accordingly, we conclude venue was proper in that judicial district.

Under the first prong of the *Miller* obscenity test, the jury is to apply "contemporary community standards." Defendants acknowledge the general principle that, in cases involving interstate transportation of obscene material, juries are properly instructed to apply the community standards of the geographic area where the materials are sent. Nonetheless, Defendants assert that this principle does not apply here for the same reasons they claim venue was improper. As demonstrated above, this argument cannot withstand scrutiny. The computer-generated images described in counts 2-7 were electronically transferred from Defendants' home in California to the Western District of Tennessee. Accordingly, the community standards of that judicial district were properly applied in this case.

Issues regarding which community's standards are to be applied are tied to those involving venue. It is well-established that:

> [v]enue for federal obscenity prosecutions lies "in any district from, through, or into which" the allegedly obscene material moves, according to 18 U.S.C. § 3237. This may result in prosecutions of persons in a community to which they have sent materials which is obscene under that community's standards though the community from which it is sent would tolerate the same material.

Prosecutions may be brought either in the district of dispatch or the district of receipt and obscenity is determined by the standards of the community where the trial takes place. Moreover, the federal courts have consistently recognized that it is not unconstitutional to subject interstate distributors of obscenity to varying community standards.

Defendants and *Amicus Curiae* appearing on their behalf argue that the computer technology used here requires a new definition of community, i.e., one that is based on the broad-ranging connections among people in cyberspace rather than the geographic locale of the federal judicial district of the criminal trial. Without a more flexible definition, they argue, there will be an impermissible chill on protected speech because BBS operators cannot select who gets the materials they make available on their bulletin boards. Therefore, they contend, BBS operators like Defendants will be forced to censor their materials so as not to run afoul of the standards of the community with the most restrictive standards.

Defendants' First Amendment issue, however, is not implicated by the facts of this case. This is not a situation where the bulletin board operator had no knowledge or control over the jurisdictions where materials were distributed for downloading or printing. Access to the Defendants' AABBS was limited. Membership was necessary and applications were submitted and screened before passwords were issued and materials were distributed. Thus, Defendants had in place methods to limit user access in jurisdictions where the risk of a finding of obscenity was greater than that in California. They knew they had a member in Memphis; the member's address and local phone number were provided on his application form. If Defendants did not wish to subject themselves to liability in jurisdictions with less tolerant standards for determining obscenity, they could have refused to give passwords to members in those districts, thus precluding the risk of liability.

This result is supported by the Supreme Court's decision in *Sable Communications of Cal., Inc. v. F.C.C.* where the Court rejected Sable's argument that it should not be compelled to tailor its dial-a-porn messages to the standards of the least tolerant community. 492 U.S. 115, 125–26 (1989). The Court recognized that distributors of allegedly obscene materials may be subjected to the standards of the varying communities where they transmit their materials, and further noted that Sable was "free to tailor its messages, on a selective basis, if it so chooses, to the communities it chooses to serve." The Court also found no constitutional impediment to forcing Sable to incur some costs in developing and implementing a method for screening a customer's location and "providing messages compatible with community standards."

Thus, under the facts of this case, there is no need for this court to adopt a new definition of "community" for use in obscenity prosecutions involving electronic bulletin boards. This court's decision is guided by one of the cardinal rules governing the federal courts, i.e., never reach constitutional questions not squarely presented by the facts of a case.

United States v. Jeffrey A. Kilbride

584 F.3d 1240 (9th Cir. 2009)

Betty B. Fletcher, Circuit Judge:

Defendants' convictions arose from conduct relating to their business of sending unsolicited bulk email, popularly known as "spam," advertising adult websites. The advertisements appearing in Defendants' emails included sexually explicit images, two of which formed the basis for the obscenity convictions.

Defendants were indicted for [a variety of offenses, including] interstate transportation of obscene materials in violation of 18 U.S.C. § 1462 (Counts 4 and 5), [and] interstate transportation of obscene materials for sale in violation of 18 U.S.C. § 1465 (Counts 6 and 7). Defendants were convicted on all counts following a three-week jury trial. The two sexually explicit images forming the basis of the obscenity charges were introduced. Evidence was presented at trial as to the obscenity of the two images. The Government called eight witnesses from various parts of the country who had complained to the Federal Trade Commission about Defendants' emails. These witnesses testified to the circumstances under which they received Defendants' emails, their reactions to and attitude towards the images sent by Defendants, and their views on pornography generally. Some of the witnesses did not specifically recall receiving the two images at issue. The Government also presented evidence of over 662,000 complaints received by the FTC from around the country concerning Defendants' emails, including the text of some of the complaints.

Defendants' challenge to the adequacy of the jury instructions' definition of obscenity focuses on the instructions' explication of the meaning of the term "contemporary community standards." The application of contemporary community standards in defining obscenity is intended to ensure that "so far as material is not aimed at a deviant group, it will be judged by its impact on an average person, rather than a particularly susceptible or sensitive person—or indeed a totally insensitive one." The Court, in line with this view, has held, in a case involving obscenity disseminated via the regular mails, that for purposes of federal obscenity statutes no "precise geographical area" need be applied in defining "contemporary community standards." [*Hamling v. United States*, 418 U.S. 87 (1974)]. As a result, in federal obscenity prosecutions, a juror may simply "draw on knowledge of the community or vicinage from which he comes" in determining contemporary community standards.

Defendants raise alternative arguments as to why the district court improperly instructed the jury about the meaning of "contemporary community standards."

Defendants assert first that the jury instructions failed to comply with the prevailing definition of contemporary community standards for purposes of federal obscenity prosecutions outlined in *Hamling*. Defendants object specifically to various phrases in the district court's Jury Instruction defining obscenity, claiming they impermissibly allowed the jurors to rely on standards outside their own community or on some broad global standard in determining contemporary community standards. [This court] conclude[s that] the district court's instruction on the meaning of contemporary community standards was not prejudicial error according to the prevailing definition of obscenity in federal prosecutions.

Defendants assert in the alternative that *Hamling*'s prevailing definition of contemporary community standards is not appropriate for speech disseminated via email. Because persons utilizing email to distribute possibly obscene works cannot control which geographic community their works will enter, Defendants argue that applying *Hamling*'s definition of contemporary community standards to works distributed via email unavoidably subjects such works to the standards of the least tolerant community in the country. This, Defendants assert, unacceptably burdens First Amendment protected speech. To avoid this constitutional problem, Defendants argue, obscenity disseminated via email must be defined according to a national community standard. Defendants, however, did not raise this argument in the district court. Accordingly, we review the district court's failure to instruct the jury to apply a national community standard for plain error. We agree with Defendants that the district court should have instructed the jury to apply a national community standard, but we do not conclude that the district court's failure to do so was plain error.

Defendants' argument is not an entirely novel one. In *Sable Communications of California, Inc. v. FCC*, 492 U.S. 115 (1989), the Court rejected in part a facial challenge to a federal statute criminalizing the interstate transmission of obscene commercial telephone recordings. The appellant there offered sexually oriented telephone recordings nationally through the Pacific Bell telephone network. The appellant argued in part that the federal obscenity legislation under which it was prosecuted "place[d] message senders in a 'double bind' by compelling them to tailor all their messages to the least tolerant community." The Court, relying on its previous holding in *Hamling*, reaffirmed that the relevant contemporary community standards for defining obscenity under federal laws were not that of the national community and that the burden thereby placed on distributors of complying with varying local standards did not violate the First Amendment. However, in so ruling, the Court noted that the appellant was "free to tailor its messages, on a selective basis, if it so chooses, to the communities it chooses to serve" and that if the appellant's "audience is comprised of different communities with different local standards, [the appellant] ultimately bears the burden of complying with the prohibition on obscene messages."

Defendants assert that speech disseminated via email is distinguishable from the speech disseminated via regular mails or telephone at issue in *Hamling* and *Sable* because there is no means to control where geographically their messages will be received. Hence, they cannot tailor their message to the specific communities into which they disseminate their speech and truly must comply with the standards of the least tolerant community in a manner the defendants in *Hamling* and *Sable* did not.

The Supreme Court has analogously recognized that the application of localized community standards to define regulated indecent and obscene Internet speech may generate constitutional concerns for exactly this reason. In *Reno v. ACLU*, 521 U.S. 844 (1997), the Supreme Court declared certain provisions of the Communications Decency Act facially overbroad in violation of the First Amendment. The CDA provisions at issue in *Reno* sought to regulate obscene or indecent expression on the Internet relying on contemporary community standards to define regulated speech. The Court listed as one among several issues of facial overbreadth in the CDA that "the 'community standards' criterion as applied to the Internet means that any communication available to a nation wide audience will be judged by the standards of the community most likely to be offended by the message." *Reno* did not address, however, Defendants' argument that the application of local community standards to regulate Internet obscenity by itself renders a statute fatally overbroad.

The Supreme Court's fractured decision in *Ashcroft v. ACLU*, 535 U.S. 564 (2002), most directly addresses Defendants' argument. In *Ashcroft*, the Court reviewed the constitutionality of the Child Online Privacy Act, the narrower successor law to the Communications Decency Act, which sought to regulate material "harmful to minors" transmitted via the World Wide Web "for commercial purposes." The Third Circuit concluded that COPA was facially overbroad on the narrow ground that it identified material "harmful to minors," utilizing a test that relied on contemporary community standards. *ACLU v. Reno*, 217 F.3d 162, 173–74 (3d Cir. 2000). The Third Circuit found that COPA's use of contemporary community standards was constitutionally problematic because "Web publishers are without any means to limit access to their sites based on the geographic location of particular Internet users." The Supreme Court vacated the Third Circuit judgment, holding that "COPA's reliance on community standards . . . does not *by itself* render the statute substantially overbroad for purposes of the First Amendment." However, the eight Justices concurring in the judgment applied divergent reasoning to justify the Court's holding.

Justice Thomas, joined by two other justices, recognized that, regardless of whether a national or local community standard was used for defining material harmful to minors under COPA, "the variance in community standards across the country could still cause juries in different locations to reach inconsistent conclusions as to whether a particular work is 'harmful to minors.'" Justice Thomas, nonetheless, did not find this variance in community standards constitutionally problematic because

COPA was, unlike the CDA, narrow in application. As a result, Justice Thomas found controlling the rulings of *Hamling* and *Sable* condoning variance in local community standards. Justice Thomas did not view as constitutionally significant that distributors of potentially obscene material via the Internet could not control where the material was read. Justice Thomas explained: "If a publisher wishes for its material to be judged only by the standards of particular communities, then it need only take the simple step of utilizing a medium that enables it to target the release of its material into those communities." Were Justice Thomas's opinion the opinion of the Court, we would likely be compelled to reject the Defendants' position. Justice Thomas's opinion both denies the utility of and need for applying a national community standard in defining Internet obscenity.

But Justice Thomas's blanket dismissal of the overbreadth problem identified by the Third Circuit was not joined by a majority of the Court. The remaining two Justices forming the majority were much less sanguine about the application of local community standards in defining Internet obscenity. Justice O'Connor, writing for herself, agreed with Justice Thomas that the respondents had failed to demonstrate on the record before the Court that any variance in local community standards supported a finding that COPA was facially overbroad. However, Justice O'Connor believed that "respondents' failure to prove substantial overbreadth on a facial challenge in this case still leaves open the possibility that the use of local community standards will cause problems for regulation of obscenity on the Internet, for adults as well as children, in future cases." In Justice O'Connor's view, "given Internet speakers' inability to control the geographic location of their audience, expecting them to bear the burden of controlling the recipients of their speech, as we did in *Hamling* and *Sable*, may be entirely too much to ask, and would potentially suppress an inordinate amount of expression." Justice O'Connor concluded that, by contrast, "the lesser degree of variation that would result" from application of a national community standard "does not necessarily pose a First Amendment problem." As a result, Justice O'Connor viewed the "adoption of a national standard [as] necessary . . . for any reasonable regulation of Internet obscenity."

Justice Breyer, also writing for himself, agreed with Justice O'Connor that

> [t]o read the statute as adopting the community standards of every locality in the United States would provide the most puritan of communities with a heckler's Internet veto affecting the rest of the Nation. The technical difficulties associated with efforts to confine Internet material to particular geographic areas make the problem particularly serious.

In order to avoid the serious constitutional issues raised by applying local community standards, Justice Breyer interpreted COPA as applying a national community standard. Justice O'Connor's and Justice Breyer's opinions both support Defendants' view that application of local standards in defining Internet obscenity raises a serious constitutional concern that can be alleviated through application of a national community standard.

The remaining justices in the majority joined Justice Kennedy's opinion. Justice Kennedy agreed with Justices O'Connor and Breyer that "[t]he national variation in community standards constitutes a particular burden on Internet speech." However, Justice Kennedy declared that "[w]e cannot know whether variation in community standards renders the Act substantially overbroad without first assessing the extent of the speech covered and the variations in community standards with respect to that speech," which the Third Circuit had failed to do. Justice Kennedy's opinion also disagreed with Justices Breyer and O'Connor that application of a national community standard would eliminate any potential First Amendment issue because "the actual standard applied is bound to vary by community nevertheless."

The lone dissenter, Justice Stevens would have held that the use of varying local community standards to define speech regulated by COPA rendered the law unconstitutionally overbroad for the reasons outlined by Justices O'Connor and Breyer regardless of how it was construed. Justice Stevens noted that reliance on a national community standard, even if it could be read into COPA, would not obviate any unconstitutional variances as "jurors instructed to apply a national, or adult, standard will reach widely different conclusions throughout the country."

The divergent reasoning of the justices in and out of the majority in *Ashcroft* leaves us with no explicit holding as to the appropriate geographic definition of contemporary community standards to be applied here. Nonetheless, we are able to derive guidance from the areas of agreement in the various opinions. "When a fragmented Court decides a case and no single rationale explaining the result enjoys the assent of five Justices, 'the holding of the Court may be viewed as that position taken by those Members who concurred in the judgments on the narrowest grounds.'" *Marks v. United States*, 430 U.S. 188, 193 (1977). Here, Justice Thomas's opinion held broadly that application of either a national community standard or local community standards to regulate Internet speech would pose no constitutional concerns by itself. None of the remaining justices, however, joined that broad holding. Justices O'Connor and Breyer held more narrowly that while application of a national community standard would not or may not create constitutional concern, application of local community standards likely would. Justice O'Connor's and Justice Breyer's opinions, therefore, agreed with a limited aspect of Justice Thomas's holding: that the variance inherent in application of a national community standard would likely not pose constitutional concerns by itself. They did not join his broader conclusion, however, that application of local community standards is similarly unproblematic. In this latter disagreement, Justices O'Connor and Breyer were joined by Justice Kennedy's opinion, as well as Justice Stevens's dissent. Accordingly, five Justices concurring in the judgment, as well as the dissenting Justice, viewed the application of local community standards in defining obscenity on the Internet as generating serious constitutional concerns. At the same time, five justices concurring in the judgment viewed the application of a national community standard as not or likely not posing the same concerns by itself. Accordingly, following *Marks*, we must view the distinction

Justices O'Connor and Breyer made between the constitutional concerns generated by application of a national and local community standards as controlling.

Accepting this distinction, in turn, persuades us to join Justices O'Connor and Breyer in holding that a national community standard must be applied in regulating obscene speech on the Internet, including obscenity disseminated via email. The constitutional problems identified by the five justices with applying local community standards to regulate Internet obscenity certainly generate grave constitutional doubts as to the use of such standards in applying §§ 1462 and 1465 to Defendants' activities. Furthermore, the Court has never held that a jury may in no case be instructed to apply a national community standard in finding obscenity. To "avoid[] the need to examine the serious First Amendment problem that would otherwise exist," we construe obscenity as regulated by §§ 1462 and 1465 as defined by reference to a national community standard when disseminated via the Internet.[n.8][3]

In light of our holding, the district court's jury instructions defining obscenity pursuant to *Hamling* was error. However, this error does not require reversal because the district court's error was far from plain. Prior to our holding here, the relevant law in this area was highly unsettled with the extremely fractured opinion in *Ashcroft* providing the best guidance. Hence, we conclude that the district committed no reversible error in its §§ 1462 and 1465 jury instructions.

§ 13.2 Evolution of Child Pornography Regulation as a Separate Category of Prohibited Speech

The expansion of the Internet has led to an explosion in the market for child pornography, making it easier to create, access, and distribute these images of abuse. While "child pornography" is the term commonly used by lawmakers, prosecutors, investigators, and the public to describe this form of sexual exploitation of children, that term largely fails to describe the true horror that is faced by hundreds of thousands of children every year. The child victims are first sexually assaulted in order to produce the vile, and often violent, images. They are then victimized again when these images of

---

3. [n.8] We recognize that Justice Kennedy's opinion, as well Justice Stevens's dissent, viewed a national community standard as not resolving the constitutional problem created by applying local community standards to define obscenity on the Internet. In their view, juries' application of a national community standard will inevitably vary based on their own communal understanding and, therefore, a national community standard will not produce actual uniformity. Justice O'Connor, as well, was not willing to wholly foreclose the possibility that a national community standard may still pose a constitutional problem. Our holding today does not preclude the possibility that a defendant could successfully challenge the application of a national community standard in defining Internet obscenity by demonstrating unconstitutional variance persists or on any other grounds.

their sexual assault are traded over the Internet in massive numbers by like-minded people across the globe.

The anonymity afforded by the Internet makes the offenders more difficult to locate, and makes them bolder in their actions. Investigations show that offenders often gather in communities over the Internet where trading of these images is just one component of a larger relationship that is premised on a shared sexual interest in children. This has the effect of eroding the shame that typically would accompany this behavior, and desensitizing those involved to the physical and psychological damage caused to the children involved. This self-reinforcing cycle is fueling ever greater demand in the market for these images. In the world of child pornography, this demand drives supply. The individual collector who methodically gathers one image after another has the effect of validating the production of the image, which leads only to more production. Because the Internet has blurred traditional notions of jurisdiction and sovereignty, this urgent crime problem is truly global in scope, and requires a coordinated national and international response.[4]

The following sections examine crimes that have been created to address the wide-ranging practice of producing, distributing, and possessing child pornography. These crimes are among the most common of all crimes involving digital evidence.

Approximately twenty-six percent of all Internet pornography involves children. While it is difficult to obtain biographical information of the victims of this exploitation, teenagers are a significant portion of them. Of the juveniles identified as victims of crimes related to child pornography, fifty-nine percent are between the ages of twelve and seventeen, twenty-eight percent are between the ages of six and eleven, and thirteen percent are pre-school age.

Child pornography is a multi-billion dollar industry with estimates ranging up to twenty billion dollars profit annually. The percentage of victims who are teenagers indicates that there are hundreds of thousands of victimized teens. While a debate exists as to whether child sex crimes are decreasing, child pornography is clearly on the rise. Since 1988 the number of child pornography offenses has increased 1500%. Currently there are approximately fourteen million child pornography websites, some of them containing as many as one million images of child pornography per website.

[T]he reach of this industry expanded exponentially with the advent of the Internet. Over 20,000 child pornography images are posted on the Internet each week. The demand for such images is incessant. For example, there are 116,000 daily requests for child pornography on the file sharing

---

4. U.S. Department of Justice, The National Strategy for Child Exploitation Prevention and Interdiction: A Report to Congress 2–3 (2010).

service Gnutella alone. Accessibility is not the only negative aspect of the Internet. The Internet also provides unprecedented validation for offenders. In the past, an offender was not able to easily interact with other like minded people. The Internet itself, however, now "provides positive reinforcement for child pornographers in their beliefs encouraging further exploitation of children."[5]

This chapter utilizes federal statutes to examine the various crimes that have been created to address child pornography. The primary United States statute is Title 18 §2252A, which regulates several activities relating to material constituting or containing child pornography.[6] A person may be guilty of a crime if he or she:

(1) knowingly mails or transports or ships child pornography.

(2) knowingly receives or distributes (A) any child pornography or (B) any material that contains child pornography.

(3) knowingly (A) reproduces any child pornography or (B) advertises, promotes, presents, distributes, or solicits any material or purported material in a manner that reflects the belief, or that is intended to cause another to believe, that the material or purported material is, or contains—

(i) an obscene visual depiction of a minor engaging in sexually explicit conduct; or

(ii) a visual depiction of an actual minor engaging in sexually explicit conduct.

(4) knowingly sells or possesses with the intent to sell any child pornography.

(5) knowingly possesses, or knowingly accesses with intent to view, any book, magazine, periodical, film, videotape, computer disk, or any other material that contains an image of child pornography.

(6) knowingly distributes, offers, sends, or provides to a minor any visual depiction, including any photograph, film, video, picture, or computer generated image or picture, whether made or produced by electronic, mechanical, or other means, where such visual depiction is, or appears to be, of a minor engaging in sexually explicit conduct for purposes of inducing or persuading a minor to participate in any activity that is illegal.

(7) knowingly produces with intent to distribute, or distributes child pornography that is an adapted or modified depiction of an identifiable minor.

---

5. Mary Graw Leary, *Self-Produced Child Pornography: the Appropriate Societal Response to Juvenile Self-Sexual Exploitation*, 15 Va. J. Soc. Policy & L. 1 (2007). Copyright © 2007, Mary Graw Leary, Virginia Journal of Social Policy & Law. All rights reserved. Reprinted by permission.

6. To have federal jurisdiction, it is generally required that the activity occur in or affect interstate or foreign commerce by any means, including by computer, or occur within certain territorial areas subject to federal jurisdiction. This chapter does not address jurisdictional issues.

This chapter examines the main features of those crimes and looks at several problems of proof, such as establishing that the activity depicted is criminal and establishing the age of the person depicted. Preliminarily, the evolution of the First Amendment treatment of child pornography is examined, including its distinction from obscenity. Congress has recognized three different categories of child pornography—virtual, morphed, and depictions of real children; the First Amendment considerations of each category have been addressed by courts.

The following three cases each address the underlying justification for child pornography as a separate category or prohibited speech. It is important to examine how the rationale for that category was evolved beginning with *Ferber*, continuing with *Osborne*, and concluding with *Free Speech Coalition*. How has that rationale changed? What are the consequences of that change?

New York v. Paul Ira Ferber

458 U.S. 747 (1982)

Justice White delivered the opinion of the Court.

At issue in this case is the constitutionality of a New York criminal statute which prohibits persons from knowingly promoting sexual performances by children under the age of 16 by distributing material which depicts such performances.

This case arose when Paul Ferber, the proprietor of a Manhattan bookstore specializing in sexually oriented products, sold two films to an undercover police officer. The films are devoted almost exclusively to depicting young boys masturbating.

This case constitutes our first examination of a statute directed at and limited to depictions of sexual activity involving children. We believe our inquiry should begin with the question of whether a State has somewhat more freedom in proscribing works which portray sexual acts or lewd exhibitions of genitalia by children.

The *Miller* standard was an accommodation between the State's interests in protecting the "sensibilities of unwilling recipients" from exposure to pornographic material and the dangers of censorship inherent in unabashedly content-based laws. Like obscenity statutes, laws directed at the dissemination of child pornography run the risk of suppressing protected expression by allowing the hand of the censor to become unduly heavy. For the following reasons, however, we are persuaded that the States are entitled to greater leeway in the regulation of pornographic depictions of children.

First. It is evident beyond the need for elaboration that a State's interest in "safeguarding the physical and psychological well-being of a minor" is "compelling." "A democratic society rests, for its continuance, upon the healthy, well-rounded growth of young people into full maturity as citizens." Accordingly, we have sustained legislation aimed at protecting the physical and emotional well-being of youth even when the laws have operated in the sensitive area of constitutionally protected rights.

The prevention of sexual exploitation and abuse of children constitutes a government objective of surpassing importance. The legislative findings accompanying passage of the New York laws reflect this concern:

"[T]here has been a proliferation of exploitation of children as subjects in sexual performances. The care of children is a sacred trust and should not be abused by those who seek to profit through a commercial network based upon the exploitation of children. The public policy of the state demands the protection of children from exploitation through sexual performances."

Suffice it to say that virtually all of the States and the United States have passed legislation proscribing the production of or otherwise combating "child pornography." The legislative judgment, as well as the judgment found in the relevant literature, is that the use of children as subjects of pornographic materials is harmful to the physiological, emotional, and mental health of the child.[n.9][7] That judgment, we think, easily passes muster under the First Amendment.

Second. The distribution of photographs and films depicting sexual activity by juveniles is intrinsically related to the sexual abuse of children in at least two ways. First, the materials produced are a permanent record of the children's participation and the harm to the child is exacerbated by their circulation. Second, the distribution network for child pornography must be closed if the production of material which requires the sexual exploitation of children is to be effectively controlled. Indeed, there is no serious contention that the legislature was unjustified in believing that it is difficult, if not impossible, to halt the exploitation of children by pursuing only those who produce the photographs and movies. While the production of pornographic materials is a low-profile, clandestine industry, the need to market the resulting products requires a visible apparatus of distribution. The most expeditious if not the only practical method of law enforcement may be to dry up the market for this material by imposing severe criminal penalties on persons selling, advertising, or otherwise promoting the product. Thirty-five States and Congress have concluded that restraints on the distribution of pornographic materials are required in order to effectively combat the problem, and there is a body of literature and testimony to support these legislative conclusions.

The *Miller* standard does not reflect the State's particular and more compelling interest in prosecuting those who promote the sexual exploitation of children. Thus, the question under the *Miller* test of whether a work, taken as a whole, appeals to the prurient interest of the average person bears no connection to the issue of whether a child has been physically or psychologically harmed in the production of

---

7. [n.9] "[T]he use of children as . . . subjects of pornographic materials is very harmful to both the children and the society as a whole." It has been found that sexually exploited children are unable to develop healthy affectionate relationships in later life, have sexual dysfunctions, and have a tendency to become sexual abusers as adults. Sexual molestation by adults is often involved in the production of child sexual performances. When such performances are recorded and distributed, the child's privacy interests are also invaded.

the work. Similarly, a sexually explicit depiction need not be "patently offensive" in order to have required the sexual exploitation of a child for its production. In addition, a work which, taken on the whole, contains serious literary, artistic, political, or scientific value may nevertheless embody the hardest core of child pornography. "It is irrelevant to the child [who has been abused] whether or not the material . . . has a literary, artistic, political or social value." We therefore cannot conclude that the *Miller* standard is a satisfactory solution to the child pornography problem.

Third. The advertising and selling of child pornography provide an economic motive for and are thus an integral part of the production of such materials, an activity illegal throughout the Nation. "It rarely has been suggested that the constitutional freedom for speech and press extends its immunity to speech or writing used as an integral part of conduct in violation of a valid criminal statute." We note that were the statutes outlawing the employment of children in these films and photographs fully effective, and the constitutionality of these laws has not been questioned, the First Amendment implications would be no greater than that presented by laws against distribution: enforceable production laws would leave no child pornography to be marketed.

Fourth. The value of permitting live performances and photographic reproductions of children engaged in lewd sexual conduct is exceedingly modest, if not *de minimis.* We consider it unlikely that visual depictions of children performing sexual acts or lewdly exhibiting their genitals would often constitute an important and necessary part of a literary performance or scientific or educational work. If it were necessary for literary or artistic value, a person over the statutory age who perhaps looked younger could be utilized. Simulation outside of the prohibition of the statute could provide another alternative. Nor is there any question here of censoring a particular literary theme or portrayal of sexual activity. The First Amendment interest is limited to that of rendering the portrayal somewhat more "realistic" by utilizing or photographing children.

Fifth. Recognizing and classifying child pornography as a category of material outside the protection of the First Amendment is not incompatible with our earlier decisions. "The question whether speech is, or is not protected by the First Amendment often depends on the content of the speech." Thus, it is not rare that a content-based classification of speech has been accepted because it may be appropriately generalized that within the confines of the given classification, the evil to be restricted so overwhelmingly outweighs the expressive interests, if any, at stake, that no process of case-by-case adjudication is required. When a definable class of material bears so heavily and pervasively on the welfare of children engaged in its production, we think the balance of competing interests is clearly struck and that it is permissible to consider these materials as without the protection of the First Amendment.

There are, of course, limits on the category of child pornography which, like obscenity, is unprotected by the First Amendment. As with all legislation in this sensitive area, the conduct to be prohibited must be adequately defined by the applicable state law, as written or authoritatively construed. Here the nature of the harm to be combated requires that the state offense be limited to works that *visually* depict sexual conduct by children below a specified age. The category of "sexual conduct" proscribed must also be suitably limited and described.

The test for child pornography is separate from the obscenity standard enunciated in *Miller*, but may be compared to it for the purpose of clarity. The *Miller* formulation is adjusted in the following respects: A trier of fact need not find that the material appeals to the prurient interest of the average person; it is not required that sexual conduct portrayed be done so in a patently offensive manner; and the material at issue need not be considered as a whole. We note that the distribution of descriptions or other depictions of sexual conduct, not otherwise obscene, which do not involve live performance or photographic or other visual reproduction of live performances, retains First Amendment protection. As with obscenity laws, criminal responsibility may not be imposed without some element of scienter on the part of the defendant.

[The New York statute] incorporates a definition of sexual conduct that comports with the above-stated principles. The forbidden acts to be depicted are listed with sufficient precision and represent the kind of conduct that, if it were the theme of a work, could render it legally obscene: "actual or simulated sexual intercourse, deviate sexual intercourse, sexual bestiality, masturbation, sado-masochistic abuse, or lewd exhibition of the genitals." The term "lewd exhibition of the genitals" is not unknown in this area and, indeed, was given in *Miller* as an example of a permissible regulation. A performance is defined only to include live or visual depictions: "any play, motion picture, photograph or dance . . . [or] other visual representation exhibited before an audience." [The statute] expressly includes a scienter requirement.

We hold that [the statute] sufficiently describes a category of material the production and distribution of which is not entitled to First Amendment protection.

JUSTICE BRENNAN, with whom JUSTICE MARSHALL joins, concurring in the judgment.

The State has a special interest in protecting the well-being of its youth. This special and compelling interest, and the particular vulnerability of children, afford the State the leeway to regulate pornographic material, the promotion of which is harmful to children, even though the State does not have such leeway when it seeks only to protect consenting adults from exposure to such material. I also agree with the Court that the "tiny fraction" of material of serious artistic, scientific, or educational value that could conceivably fall within the reach of the statute is insufficient to justify striking the statute on the grounds of overbreadth.

But in my view application of [the New York statute] or any similar statute to depictions of children that in themselves do have serious literary, artistic, scientific, or medical value, would violate the First Amendment. The limited classes of speech, the suppression of which does not raise serious First Amendment concerns, have two attributes. They are of exceedingly "slight social value," and the State has a compelling interest in their regulation. The First Amendment value of depictions of children that are in themselves serious contributions to art, literature, or science, is, by definition, simply not "*de minimis.*" At the same time, the State's interest in suppression of such materials is likely to be far less compelling. For the Court's assumption of harm to the child resulting from the "permanent record" and "circulation" of the child's "participation," lacks much of its force where the depiction is a serious contribution to art or science. The production of materials of serious value is not the "low-profile, clandestine industry" that according to the Court produces purely pornographic materials. In short, it is inconceivable how a depiction of a child that is itself a serious contribution to the world of art or literature or science can be deemed "material outside the protection of the First Amendment."

———————

1. Possession of Child Pornography

Clyde Osborne v. Ohio

495 U.S. 103 (1990)

JUSTICE WHITE delivered the opinion of the Court.

In order to combat child pornography, Ohio enacted Rev.Code Ann. § 2907.323(A) (3), which provides in pertinent part:

"(A) No person shall do any of the following:

"(3) Possess or view any material or performance that shows a minor who is not the person's child or ward in a state of nudity, unless one of the following applies:

"(a) The material or performance is sold, disseminated, displayed, possessed, controlled, brought or caused to be brought into this state, or presented for a bona fide artistic, medical, scientific, educational, religious, governmental, judicial, or other proper purpose, by or to a physician, psychologist, sociologist, scientist, teacher, person pursuing bona fide studies or research, librarian, clergyman, prosecutor, judge, or other person having a proper interest in the material or performance.

"(b) The person knows that the parents, guardian, or custodian has consented in writing to the photographing or use of the minor in a state of nudity and to the manner in which the material or performance is used or transferred."

Osborne was convicted of violating this statute and sentenced to six months in prison, after the Columbus, Ohio, police, pursuant to a valid search, found four photographs in Osborne's home. Each photograph depicts a nude male adolescent posed in a sexually explicit position.

The threshold question in this case is whether Ohio may constitutionally proscribe the possession and viewing of child pornography or whether our decision in

Stanley v. Georgia, 394 U.S. 557 (1969), compels the contrary result. In *Stanley*, we struck down a Georgia law outlawing the private possession of obscene material. We recognized that the statute impinged upon Stanley's right to receive information in the privacy of his home, and we found Georgia's justifications for its law inadequate.

Assuming, for the sake of argument, that Osborne has a First Amendment interest in viewing and possessing child pornography, we nonetheless find this case distinct from *Stanley* because the interests underlying child pornography prohibitions far exceed the interests justifying the Georgia law at issue in *Stanley*.

In *Stanley*, Georgia primarily sought to proscribe the private possession of obscenity because it was concerned that obscenity would poison the minds of its viewers. We responded that "[w]hatever the power of the state to control public dissemination of ideas inimical to the public morality, it cannot constitutionally premise legislation on the desirability of controlling a person's private thoughts." The difference here is obvious: The State does not rely on a paternalistic interest in regulating Osborne's mind. Rather, Ohio has enacted § 2907.323(A)(3) in order to protect the victims of child pornography; it hopes to destroy a market for the exploitative use of children.

It is surely reasonable for the State to conclude that it will decrease the production of child pornography if it penalizes those who possess and view the product, thereby decreasing demand. In *Ferber*, where we upheld a New York statute outlawing the distribution of child pornography, we found a similar argument persuasive: "[T]he advertising and selling of child pornography provide an economic motive for and are thus an integral part of the production of such materials, an activity illegal throughout the Nation. 'It rarely has been suggested that the constitutional freedom for speech and press extends its immunity to speech or writing used as an integral part of conduct in violation of a valid criminal statute.'"

Given the importance of the State's interest in protecting the victims of child pornography, we cannot fault Ohio for attempting to stamp out this vice at all levels in the distribution chain. According to the State, since the time of our decision in *Ferber*, much of the child pornography market has been driven underground; as a result, it is now difficult, if not impossible, to solve the child pornography problem by only attacking production and distribution. Indeed, 19 States have found it necessary to proscribe the possession of this material.

Other interests also support the Ohio law. First, as *Ferber* recognized, the materials produced by child pornographers permanently record the victim's abuse. The pornography's continued existence causes the child victims continuing harm by haunting the children in years to come. The State's ban on possession and viewing encourages the possessors of these materials to destroy them. Second, encouraging the destruction of these materials is also desirable because evidence suggests that pedophiles use child pornography to seduce other children into sexual activity.[n.7][8]

---

8. [n.7] The Attorney General's Commission on Pornography, for example, states: "Child pornography is often used as part of a method of seducing child victims. A child who is reluctant to

Given the gravity of the State's interests in this context, we find that Ohio may constitutionally proscribe the possession and viewing of child pornography.

The Ohio statute, on its face, purports to prohibit the possession of "nude" photographs of minors. We have stated that depictions of nudity, without more, constitute protected expression. Relying on this observation, Osborne argues that the statute as written is substantially overbroad. We are skeptical of this claim because, in light of the statute's exemptions and "proper purposes" provisions, the statute may not be substantially overbroad under our cases. However that may be, Osborne's overbreadth challenge, in any event, fails because the statute, as construed by the Ohio Supreme Court on Osborne's direct appeal, plainly survives overbreadth scrutiny. Under the Ohio Supreme Court reading, the statute prohibits "the possession or viewing of material or performance of a minor who is in a state of nudity, where such nudity constitutes a lewd exhibition or involves a graphic focus on the genitals, and where the person depicted is neither the child nor the ward of the person charged." By limiting the statute's operation in this manner, the Ohio Supreme Court avoided penalizing persons for viewing or possessing innocuous photographs of naked children.

The Ohio Supreme Court also concluded that the State had to establish scienter in order to prove a violation of §2907.323(A)(3) based on the Ohio default statute specifying that recklessness applies when another statutory provision lacks an intent specification. The statute on its face lacks a *mens rea* requirement, but that omission brings into play and is cured by another law that plainly satisfies the requirement laid down in *Ferber* that prohibitions on child pornography include some element of scienter.

---

2. Virtual Child Pornography

John D. Ashcroft v. The Free Speech Coalition
535 U.S. 234 (2002)

JUSTICE KENNEDY delivered the opinion of the Court.

We consider whether the Child Pornography Prevention Act of 1996 (CPPA), 18 U.S.C. §2251 *et seq.*, abridges the freedom of speech. The CPPA extends the federal prohibition against child pornography to sexually explicit images that appear to depict minors but were produced without using any real children. The statute prohibits, in specific circumstances, possessing or distributing these images, which may be created by using adults who look like minors or by using computer imaging. The new technology, according to Congress, makes it possible to create realistic images of children who do not exist.

---

engage in sexual activity with an adult or to pose for sexually explicit photos can sometimes be convinced by viewing other children having 'fun' participating in the activity."

By prohibiting child pornography that does not depict an actual child, the statute goes beyond *Ferber*, which distinguished child pornography from other sexually explicit speech because of the State's interest in protecting the children exploited by the production process. As a general rule, pornography can be banned only if obscene, but under *Ferber*, pornography showing minors can be proscribed whether or not the images are obscene under the definition set forth in *Miller*.

The principal question to be resolved is whether the CPPA is constitutional where it proscribes a significant universe of speech that is neither obscene under *Miller* nor child pornography under *Ferber*.

Before 1996, Congress defined child pornography as the type of depictions at issue in *Ferber*, images made using actual minors. The CPPA retains that prohibition at 18 U.S.C. §2256(8)(A) and adds . . . Section 2256(8)(B), [which] prohibits "any visual depiction, including any photograph, film, video, picture, or computer or computer-generated image or picture," that "is, or appears to be, of a minor engaging in sexually explicit conduct." The prohibition on "any visual depiction" does not depend at all on how the image is produced. The section captures a range of depictions, sometimes called "virtual child pornography," which include computer-generated images, as well as images produced by more traditional means. For instance, the literal terms of the statute embrace a Renaissance painting depicting a scene from classical mythology, a "picture" that "appears to be, of a minor engaging in sexually explicit conduct." The statute also prohibits Hollywood movies, filmed without any child actors, if a jury believes an actor "appears to be" a minor engaging in "actual or simulated . . . sexual intercourse."

These images do not involve, let alone harm, any children in the production process; but Congress decided the materials threaten children in other, less direct, ways. Pedophiles might use the materials to encourage children to participate in sexual activity. "[A] child who is reluctant to engage in sexual activity with an adult, or to pose for sexually explicit photographs, can sometimes be convinced by viewing depictions of other children 'having fun' participating in such activity." Furthermore, pedophiles might "whet their own sexual appetites" with the pornographic images, "thereby increasing the creation and distribution of child pornography and the sexual abuse and exploitation of actual children." Under these rationales, harm flows from the content of the images, not from the means of their production. In addition, Congress identified another problem created by computer-generated images: Their existence can make it harder to prosecute pornographers who do use real minors. As imaging technology improves, Congress found, it becomes more difficult to prove that a particular picture was produced using actual children. To ensure that defendants possessing child pornography using real minors cannot evade prosecution, Congress extended the ban to virtual child pornography.

Fearing that the CPPA threatened the activities of its members, respondent Free Speech Coalition and others challenged the statute. The Coalition, a California trade association for the adult-entertainment industry, alleged that its members did not use minors in their sexually explicit works, but they believed some of these materials might fall within the CPPA's expanded definition of child pornography. The other respondents are Bold Type, Inc., the publisher of a book advocating the nudist lifestyle; Jim Gingerich, a painter of nudes; and Ron Raffaelli, a photographer specializing in erotic images. Respondents alleged that the "appears to be" and "conveys the impression" provisions are overbroad and vague, chilling them from producing works protected by the First Amendment.

The sexual abuse of a child is a most serious crime and an act repugnant to the moral instincts of a decent people. In its legislative findings, Congress recognized that there are subcultures of persons who harbor illicit desires for children and commit criminal acts to gratify the impulses. Congress also found that surrounding the serious offenders are those who flirt with these impulses and trade pictures and written accounts of sexual activity with young children.

As a general principle, the First Amendment bars the government from dictating what we see or read or speak or hear. The freedom of speech has its limits; it does not embrace certain categories of speech, including defamation, incitement, obscenity, and pornography produced with real children. While these categories may be prohibited without violating the First Amendment, none of them includes the speech prohibited by the CPPA. In his dissent from the opinion of the Court of Appeals, Judge Ferguson recognized this to be the law and proposed that virtual child pornography should be regarded as an additional category of unprotected speech. It would be necessary for us to take this step to uphold the statute.

Under *Miller*, the Government must prove that the work, taken as a whole, appeals to the prurient interest, is patently offensive in light of community standards, and lacks serious literary, artistic, political, or scientific value. The CPPA, however, extends to images that appear to depict a minor engaging in sexually explicit activity without regard to the *Miller* requirements. The materials need not appeal to the prurient interest. Any depiction of sexually explicit activity, no matter how it is presented, is proscribed. The CPPA applies to a picture in a psychology manual, as well as a movie depicting the horrors of sexual abuse. It is not necessary, moreover, that the image be patently offensive. Pictures of what appear to be 17-year-olds engaging in sexually explicit activity do not in every case contravene community standards.

The CPPA prohibits speech despite its serious literary, artistic, political, or scientific value. The statute proscribes the visual depiction of an idea—that of teenagers engaging in sexual activity—that is a fact of modern society and has been a theme in art and literature throughout the ages. Under the CPPA, images are prohibited so long as the persons appear to be under 18 years of age. This is higher than the legal age for marriage in many States, as well as the age at which persons may consent to sexual relations. It is, of course, undeniable that some youths engage in sexual activity before the legal age, either on their own inclination or because they are victims of sexual abuse.

Both themes—teenage sexual activity and the sexual abuse of children—have inspired countless literary works. William Shakespeare created the most famous pair of teenage lovers, one of whom is just 13 years of age. See Romeo and Juliet, act I, sc. 2, l. 9 ("She hath not seen the change of fourteen years"). In the drama, Shakespeare portrays the relationship as something splendid and innocent, but not juvenile. The work has inspired no less than 40 motion pictures, some of which suggest that the teenagers consummated their relationship. Shakespeare may not have written sexually explicit scenes for the Elizabethan audience, but were modern directors to adopt a less conventional approach, that fact alone would not compel the conclusion that the work was obscene.

Contemporary movies pursue similar themes. Last year's Academy Awards featured the movie, Traffic, which was nominated for Best Picture. The film portrays a teenager, identified as a 16-year-old, who becomes addicted to drugs. The viewer sees the degradation of her addiction, which in the end leads her to a filthy room to trade sex for drugs. The year before, American Beauty won the Academy Award for Best Picture. In the course of the movie, a teenage girl engages in sexual relations with her teenage boyfriend, and another yields herself to the gratification of a middle-aged man. The film also contains a scene where, although the movie audience understands the act is not taking place, one character believes he is watching a teenage boy performing a sexual act on an older man.

Our society, like other cultures, has empathy and enduring fascination with the lives and destinies of the young. Art and literature express the vital interest we all have in the formative years we ourselves once knew, when wounds can be so grievous, disappointment so profound, and mistaken choices so tragic, but when moral acts and self-fulfillment are still in reach. Whether or not the films we mention violate the CPPA, they explore themes within the wide sweep of the statute's prohibitions. If these films, or hundreds of others of lesser note that explore those subjects, contain a single graphic depiction of sexual activity within the statutory definition, the possessor of the film would be subject to severe punishment without inquiry into the work's redeeming value. This is inconsistent with an essential First Amendment rule: The artistic merit of a work does not depend on the presence of a single explicit scene. Under *Miller*, the First Amendment requires that redeeming value be judged by considering the work as a whole. Where the scene is part of the narrative, the work itself does not for this reason become obscene, even though the scene in isolation might be offensive. For this reason, and the others we have noted, the CPPA cannot be read to prohibit obscenity, because it lacks the required link between its prohibitions and the affront to community standards prohibited by the definition of obscenity.

The Government seeks to address this deficiency by arguing that speech prohibited by the CPPA is virtually indistinguishable from child pornography, which may be banned without regard to whether it depicts works of value. Where the images are themselves the product of child sexual abuse, *Ferber* recognized that the State had an interest in stamping it out without regard to any judgment about its content. The production of the work, not its content, was the target of the statute. The fact that a work contained serious literary, artistic, or other value did not excuse the harm it caused to its child participants. It was simply "unrealistic to equate a community's toleration for sexually oriented materials with the permissible scope of legislation aimed at protecting children from sexual exploitation."

Ferber upheld a prohibition on the distribution and sale of child pornography, as well as its production, because these acts were "intrinsically related" to the sexual abuse of children in two ways. First, as a permanent record of a child's abuse, the continued circulation itself would harm the child who had participated. Like a defamatory statement, each new publication of the speech would cause new injury to the child's reputation and emotional well-being. Second, because the traffic in child pornography was an economic motive for its production, the State had an interest in closing the distribution network. "The most expeditious if not the only practical method of law enforcement may be to dry up the market for this material by imposing severe criminal penalties on persons selling, advertising, or otherwise promoting the product." Under either rationale, the speech had what the Court in effect held was a proximate link to the crime from which it came.

Later, in *Osborne*, the Court ruled that these same interests justified a ban on the possession of pornography produced by using children. "Given the importance of the State's interest in protecting the victims of child pornography," the State was justified in "attempting to stamp out this vice at all levels in the distribution chain." *Osborne* also noted the State's interest in preventing child pornography from being used as an aid in the solicitation of minors. The Court, however, anchored its holding in the concern for the participants, those whom it called the "victims of child pornography." It did not suggest that, absent this concern, other governmental interests would suffice.

In contrast to the speech in *Ferber*, speech that itself is the record of sexual abuse, the CPPA prohibits speech that records no crime and creates no victims by its production. Virtual child pornography is not "intrinsically related" to the sexual abuse of children, as were the materials in *Ferber*. While the Government asserts that the images can lead to actual instances of child abuse, the causal link is contingent and indirect. The harm does not necessarily follow from the speech, but depends upon some unquantified potential for subsequent criminal acts.

The Government says these indirect harms are sufficient because, as *Ferber* acknowledged, child pornography rarely can be valuable speech. This argument, however, suffers from two flaws. First, *Ferber's* judgment about child pornography was based upon how it was made, not on what it communicated. The case reaffirmed that where the speech is neither obscene nor the product of sexual abuse, it does not fall outside the protection of the First Amendment.

The second flaw in the Government's position is that *Ferber* did not hold that child pornography is by definition without value. On the contrary, the Court recognized some works in this category might have significant value, but relied on virtual images—the very images prohibited by the CPPA—as an alternative and permissible means of expression: *Ferber*, then, not only referred to the distinction between actual and virtual child pornography, it relied on it as a reason supporting its holding. *Ferber* provides no support for a statute that eliminates the distinction and makes the alternative mode criminal as well.

The Government seeks to justify its prohibitions in other ways. It argues that the CPPA is necessary because pedophiles may use virtual child pornography to seduce children. There are many things innocent in themselves, however, such as cartoons, video games, and candy, that might be used for immoral purposes, yet we would not expect those to be prohibited because they can be misused. The Government, of course, may punish adults who provide unsuitable materials to children, and it may enforce criminal penalties for unlawful solicitation. The precedents establish, however, that speech within the rights of adults to hear may not be silenced completely in an attempt to shield children from it.

Here, the Government wants to keep speech from children not to protect them from its content but to protect them from those who would commit other crimes. The principle, however, remains the same: The Government cannot ban speech fit for adults simply because it may fall into the hands of children. The evil in question depends upon the actor's unlawful conduct, conduct defined as criminal quite apart from any link to the speech in question. This establishes that the speech ban is not narrowly drawn. The objective is to prohibit illegal conduct, but this restriction goes well beyond that interest by restricting the speech available to law-abiding adults.

The Government submits further that virtual child pornography whets the appetites of pedophiles and encourages them to engage in illegal conduct. The mere tendency of speech to encourage unlawful acts is not a sufficient reason for banning it. First Amendment freedoms are most in danger when the government seeks to control thought or to justify its laws for that impermissible end. The right to think is the beginning of freedom, and speech must be protected from the government because speech is the beginning of thought.

To preserve these freedoms, and to protect speech for its own sake, the Court's First Amendment cases draw vital distinctions between words and deeds, between ideas and conduct. The government may not prohibit speech because it increases the chance an unlawful act will be committed "at some indefinite future time." There is here no attempt, incitement, solicitation, or conspiracy. The Government has shown no more than a remote connection between speech that might encourage thoughts or impulses and any resulting child abuse. Without a significantly stronger, more direct connection, the Government may not prohibit speech on the ground that it may encourage pedophiles to engage in illegal conduct.

The Government next argues that its objective of eliminating the market for pornography produced using real children necessitates a prohibition on virtual images as well. Virtual images, the Government contends, are indistinguishable from real ones; they are part of the same market and are often exchanged. In this way, it is said, virtual images promote the trafficking in works produced through the exploitation of real children. The hypothesis is somewhat implausible. If virtual images were identical to illegal child pornography, the illegal images would be driven from the market by the indistinguishable substitutes. Few pornographers would risk prosecution by abusing real children if fictional, computerized images would suffice.

In the case of the material covered by *Ferber*, the creation of the speech is itself the crime of child abuse; the prohibition deters the crime by removing the profit motive. Even where there is an underlying crime, however, the Court has not allowed the suppression of speech in all cases. We need not consider where to strike the balance in this case, because here, there is no underlying crime at all. Even if the Government's market deterrence theory were persuasive in some contexts, it would not justify this statute.

Finally, the Government says that the possibility of producing images by using computer imaging makes it very difficult for it to prosecute those who produce pornography by using real children. Experts, we are told, may have difficulty in saying whether the pictures were made by using real children or by using computer imaging. The necessary solution, the argument runs, is to prohibit both kinds of images. The argument, in essence, is that protected speech may be banned as a means to ban unprotected speech. This analysis turns the First Amendment upside down.

In sum, § 2256(8)(B) covers materials beyond the categories recognized in *Ferber* and *Miller*, and the reasons the Government offers in support of limiting the freedom of speech have no justification in our precedents or in the law of the First Amendment. The provision abridges the freedom to engage in a substantial amount of lawful speech. For this reason, it is overbroad and unconstitutional.

JUSTICE THOMAS, concurring in the judgment.

The Government's most persuasive asserted interest in support of the Child Pornography Prevention Act of 1996 is the prosecution rationale—that persons who possess and disseminate pornographic images of real children may escape conviction by claiming that the images are computer generated, thereby raising a reasonable doubt as to their guilt. At this time, however, the Government asserts only that defendants *raise* such defenses, not that they have done so successfully. In fact, the Government points to no case in which a defendant has been acquitted based on a "computer-generated images" defense. While this speculative interest cannot support the broad reach of the CPPA, technology may evolve to the point where it becomes impossible to enforce actual child pornography laws because the Government cannot prove that certain pornographic images are of real children. In the event this occurs, the Government should not be foreclosed from enacting a regulation of virtual child pornography that contains an appropriate affirmative defense or some other narrowly drawn restriction.

The Court suggests that the Government's interest in enforcing prohibitions against real child pornography cannot justify prohibitions on virtual child pornography. But if technological advances thwart prosecution of "unlawful speech," the Government may well have a compelling interest in barring or otherwise regulating some narrow category of "lawful speech" in order to enforce effectively laws against pornography made through the abuse of real children. The Court does leave open the possibility that a more complete affirmative defense could save a statute's constitutionality, implicitly accepting that some regulation of virtual child pornography might be constitutional. I would not prejudge, however, whether a more complete affirmative defense is the only way to narrowly tailor a criminal statute that prohibits the possession and dissemination of virtual child pornography.

Justice O'Connor, with whom The Chief Justice and Justice Scalia join as to Part II, concurring in the judgment in part and dissenting in part.

II.

The Court has long recognized that the Government has a compelling interest in protecting our Nation's children. This interest is promoted by efforts directed against sexual offenders and actual child pornography. These efforts, in turn, are supported by the CPPA's ban on virtual child pornography. Such images whet the appetites of child molesters, who may use the images to seduce young children. Of even more serious concern is the prospect that defendants indicted for the production, distribution, or possession of actual child pornography may evade liability by claiming that the images attributed to them are in fact computer-generated. Respondents may be correct that no defendant has successfully employed this tactic. But, given the rapid pace of advances in computer-graphics technology, the Government's concern is reasonable. This Court's cases do not require Congress to wait for harm to occur before it can legislate against it.

Respondents argue that, even if the Government has a compelling interest to justify banning virtual child pornography, the "appears to be . . . of a minor" language is not narrowly tailored to serve that interest. They assert that the CPPA would capture even cartoon sketches or statues of children that were sexually suggestive. Such images surely could not be used, for instance, to seduce children. I agree. A better interpretation of "appears to be . . . of" is "virtually indistinguishable from"—an interpretation that would not cover the examples respondents provide. Not only does the text of the statute comfortably bear this narrowing interpretation, the interpretation comports with the language that Congress repeatedly used in its findings of fact. Finally, to the extent that the phrase "appears to be . . . of" is ambiguous, the narrowing interpretation avoids constitutional problems such as overbreadth and lack of narrow tailoring.

Reading the statute only to bar images that are virtually indistinguishable from actual children would not only assure that the ban on virtual child pornography is narrowly tailored, but would also assuage any fears that the "appears to be . . . of a minor" language is vague.

Although a content-based regulation may serve a compelling state interest, and be as narrowly tailored as possible while substantially serving that interest, the regulation may unintentionally ensnare speech that has serious literary, artistic, political, or scientific value or that does not threaten the harms sought to be combated by the Government. If so, litigants may challenge the regulation on its face as overbroad, but in doing so they bear the heavy burden of demonstrating that the regulation forbids a substantial amount of valuable or harmless speech. Respondents have not made such a demonstration. Respondents provide no examples of films or other materials that are wholly computer generated and contain images that "appea[r] to be . . . of minors" engaging in indecent conduct, but that have serious value or do not facilitate child abuse. Their overbreadth challenge therefore fails.

III.

Although in my view the CPPA's ban on youthful adult pornography appears to violate the First Amendment, the ban on virtual child pornography does not. It is true that both bans are authorized by the same text: The statute's definition of child pornography to include depictions that "appea[r] to be" of children in sexually explicit poses. Invalidating a statute due to overbreadth, however, is an extreme remedy, one that should be employed "sparingly and only as a last resort."

Heeding this caution, I would strike the "appears to be" provision only insofar as it is applied to the subset of cases involving youthful adult pornography.

CHIEF JUSTICE REHNQUIST, with whom JUSTICE SCALIA joins in part, dissenting.

Congress has a compelling interest in ensuring the ability to enforce prohibitions of actual child pornography, and we should defer to its findings that rapidly advancing technology soon will make it all but impossible to do so.

Other than computer-generated images that are virtually indistinguishable from real children engaged in sexually explicit conduct, the CPPA can be limited so as not to reach any material that was not already unprotected before the CPPA. The CPPA's definition of "sexually explicit conduct" is quite explicit in this regard. It makes clear that the statute only reaches "visual depictions" of:

> "[A]ctual or simulated . . . sexual intercourse, including genital-genital, oral-genital, anal-genital, or oral-anal, whether between persons of the same or opposite sex; . . . bestiality; . . . masturbation; . . . sadistic or masochistic abuse; or . . . lascivious exhibition of the genitals or pubic area of any person." 18 U.S.C. § 2256(2).

The Court and Justice O'Connor suggest that this very graphic definition reaches the depiction of youthful looking adult actors engaged in suggestive sexual activity, presumably because the definition extends to "simulated" intercourse. Read as a whole, however, I think the definition reaches only the sort of "hard core of child pornography" that we found without protection in *Ferber*. So construed, the CPPA bans visual depictions of youthful looking adult actors engaged in *actual* sexual activity; mere *suggestions* of sexual activity, such as youthful looking adult actors squirming under a blanket, are more akin to written descriptions than visual depictions, and thus fall outside the purview of the statute.

The reference to "simulated" has been part of the definition of "sexually explicit conduct" since the statute was first passed. But the inclusion of "simulated" conduct, alongside "actual" conduct, does not change the "hard core" nature of the image banned. The reference to "simulated" conduct simply brings within the statute's reach depictions of hardcore pornography that are "made to look genuine,"—including the main target of the CPPA, computer-generated images virtually indistinguishable from real children engaged in sexually explicit conduct. Neither actual conduct nor simulated conduct, however, is properly construed to reach depictions such as those in a film portrayal of Romeo and Juliet, which are far removed from the hardcore pornographic depictions that Congress intended to reach.

This narrow reading of "sexually explicit conduct" not only accords with the text of the CPPA and the intentions of Congress; it is exactly how the phrase was understood prior to the broadening gloss the Court gives it today. Indeed, had "sexually explicit conduct" been thought to reach the sort of material the Court says it does, then films such as Traffic and American Beauty would not have been made the way they were. Traffic won its Academy Award in 2001. American Beauty won its Academy Award in 2000. But the CPPA has been on the books, and has been enforced, since 1996. The chill felt by the Court has apparently never been felt by those who actually make movies.

In sum, while potentially impermissible applications of the CPPA may exist, I doubt that they would be "substantial . . . in relation to the statute's plainly legitimate sweep." The aim of ensuring the enforceability of our Nation's child pornography laws is a compelling one. The CPPA is targeted to this aim by extending the definition of child pornography to reach computer-generated images that are virtually indistinguishable from real children engaged in sexually explicit conduct. The statute need not be read to do any more than precisely this, which is not offensive to the First Amendment.

———————

3. Pandering

Free Speech Coalition, in a section of the opinion not reproduced here, struck down the "pandering" provision. In response, Congress adopted Title 18 § 2252A(a) (3)(B), which provides that a person may be guilty of a crime if he or she:

> (3) knowingly . . . (B) advertises, promotes, presents, distributes, or solicits any material or purported material in a manner that reflects the belief, or that is intended to cause another to believe, that the material or purported material is, or contains—(i) an obscene visual depiction of a minor engaging in sexually explicit conduct; or (ii) a visual depiction of an actual minor engaging in sexually explicit conduct[.]

———————

United States v. Michael Williams

553 U.S. 285 (2008)

JUSTICE SCALIA delivered the opinion of the Court.

Michael Williams, using a sexually explicit screen name, signed in to a public Internet chat room. A Secret Service agent had also signed in to the chat room under the moniker "Lisa n Miami." The agent noticed that Williams had posted a message that read: "Dad of toddler has 'good' pics of her an [sic] me for swap of your toddler pics, or live cam." The agent struck up a conversation with Williams, leading to an electronic exchange of nonpornographic pictures of children. (The agent's picture was in fact a doctored photograph of an adult.) Soon thereafter, Williams messaged that he had photographs of men molesting his 4-year-old daughter. Suspicious that "Lisa n Miami" was a law-enforcement agent, before proceeding further Williams demanded that the agent produce additional pictures. When he did not, Williams posted the following public message in the chat room: "HERE ROOM; I CAN PUT UPLINK CUZ IM FOR REAL—SHE CANT." Appended to this declaration was a hyperlink that, when clicked, led to seven pictures of actual children, aged approximately 5 to 15, engaging in sexually explicit conduct and displaying their genitals. The Secret Service then obtained a search warrant for Williams's home, where agents seized two hard drives containing at least 22 images of real children engaged in sexually explicit conduct, some of it sadomasochistic.

Williams was charged with one count of pandering child pornography under § 2252A(a)(3)(B) and one count of possessing child pornography under § 2252A(a)(5)(B). He pleaded guilty to both counts but reserved the right to challenge the constitutionality of the pandering conviction.

Generally speaking, § 2252A(a)(3)(B) prohibits offers to provide and requests to obtain child pornography. The statute does not require the actual existence of child pornography. In this respect, it differs from the statutes in *Ferber, Osborne*, and *Free Speech Coalition*, which prohibited the possession or distribution of child pornography. Rather than targeting the underlying material, this statute bans the collateral speech that introduces such material into the child-pornography distribution network. Thus, an Internet user who solicits child pornography from an undercover agent violates the statute, even if the officer possesses no child pornography. Likewise, a person who advertises virtual child pornography as depicting actual children also falls within the reach of the statute.

The statute's definition of the material or purported material that may not be pandered or solicited precisely tracks the material held constitutionally proscribable in *Ferber* and *Miller:* obscene material depicting (actual or virtual) children engaged in sexually explicit conduct, and any other material depicting actual children engaged in sexually explicit conduct.

A number of features of the statute are important to our analysis:

First, the statute includes a scienter requirement. The first word of § 2252A(a) (3) — "knowingly" — applies to . . . the new § 2252A(a)(3)(B) at issue here.

Second, the statute's string of operative verbs — "advertises, promotes, presents, distributes, or solicits" — is reasonably read to have a transactional connotation. That is to say, the statute penalizes speech that accompanies or seeks to induce a transfer of child pornography — via reproduction or physical delivery — from one person to another. For three of the verbs, this is obvious: advertising, distributing, and soliciting are steps taken in the course of an actual or proposed transfer of a product, typically but not exclusively in a commercial market. When taken in isolation, the two remaining verbs — "promotes" and "presents" — are susceptible of multiple and wide-ranging meanings. In context, however, those meanings are narrowed by the commonsense canon of *noscitur a sociis* — which counsels that a word is given more precise content by the neighboring words with which it is associated. Similarly, "presents," in the context of the other verbs with which it is associated, means showing or offering the child pornography to another person with a view to his acquisition.

To be clear, our conclusion that all the words in this list relate to transactions is not to say that they relate to *commercial* transactions. One could certainly "distribute" child pornography without expecting payment in return. Indeed, in much Internet file sharing of child pornography each participant makes his files available for free to other participants — as Williams did in this case. To run afoul of the statute, the speech need only accompany or seek to induce the transfer of child pornography from one person to another.

Third, the phrase "in a manner that reflects the belief" includes both subjective and objective components. "[A] manner that reflects the belief" is quite different from "a manner that would give one cause to believe." The first formulation suggests that the defendant must actually have held the subjective "belief" that the material or purported material was child pornography. Thus, a misdescription that leads the listener to believe the defendant is offering child pornography, when the defendant in fact does not believe the material is child pornography, does not violate this prong of the statute. (It may, however, violate the "manner . . . that is intended to cause another to believe" prong if the misdescription is intentional.) There is also an objective component to the phrase "manner that reflects the belief." The statement or action must objectively manifest a belief that the material is child pornography; a mere belief, without an accompanying statement or action that would lead a reasonable person to understand that the defendant holds that belief, is insufficient.

Fourth, the other key phrase, "in a manner . . . that is intended to cause another to believe," contains only a subjective element: The defendant must "intend" that the listener believe the material to be child pornography, and must select a manner of "advertising, promoting, presenting, distributing, or soliciting" the material that *he* thinks will engender that belief — whether or not a reasonable person would think the same. (Of course in the ordinary case the proof of the defendant's intent will be the fact that, as an objective matter, the manner of "advertising, promoting, presenting, distributing, or soliciting" plainly sought to convey that the material was child pornography.)

Fifth, the definition of "sexually explicit conduct" is very similar to the definition of "sexual conduct" in the New York statute we upheld against an overbreadth challenge in *Ferber*. If anything, the fact that the defined term here is "sexually *explicit* conduct," rather than (as in *Ferber*) merely "sexual conduct," renders the definition more immune from facial constitutional attack. "[S]imulated sexual intercourse" (a phrase found in the *Ferber* definition as well) is even less susceptible here of application to the sorts of sex scenes found in R-rated movies—which suggest that intercourse is taking place without explicitly depicting it, and without causing viewers to believe that the actors are actually engaging in intercourse. "Sexually *explicit* conduct" connotes actual depiction of the sex act rather than merely the suggestion that it is occurring. And "simulated" sexual intercourse is not sexual intercourse that is merely suggested, but rather sexual intercourse that is explicitly portrayed, even though (through camera tricks or otherwise) it may not actually have occurred. The portrayal must cause a reasonable viewer to believe that the actors actually engaged in that conduct on camera. Critically, § 2252A(a)(3)(B)(ii)'s requirement of a "visual depiction of an actual minor" makes clear that, although the sexual intercourse may be simulated, it must involve actual children (unless it is obscene). This change eliminates any possibility that virtual child pornography or sex between youthful-looking adult actors might be covered by the term "simulated sexual intercourse."

Offers to engage in illegal transactions are categorically excluded from First Amendment protection. One would think that this principle resolves the present case, since the statute criminalizes only offers to provide or requests to obtain contraband—child obscenity and child pornography involving actual children, both of which are proscribed, and the proscription of which is constitutional. The Eleventh Circuit, however, believed that the exclusion of First Amendment protection extended only to *commercial* offers to provide or receive contraband.

This mistakes the rationale for the categorical exclusion. It is based not on the less privileged First Amendment status of commercial speech but on the principle that offers to give or receive what it is unlawful to possess have no social value and thus, like obscenity, enjoy no First Amendment protection. Many long established criminal proscriptions—such as laws against conspiracy, incitement, and solicitation—criminalize speech (commercial or not) that is intended to induce or commence illegal activities. Offers to provide or requests to obtain unlawful material, whether as part of a commercial exchange or not, are similarly undeserving of First Amendment protection. It would be an odd constitutional principle that permitted the government to prohibit offers to sell illegal drugs, but not offers to give them away for free.

The Act before us does not prohibit advocacy of child pornography, but only offers to provide or requests to obtain it. There is no doubt that this prohibition falls well within constitutional bounds.

In sum, we hold that offers to provide or requests to obtain child pornography are categorically excluded from the First Amendment.

JUSTICE SOUTER, with whom JUSTICE GINSBURG joins, dissenting.

No one doubts the dealer may validly be convicted of an attempted drug sale even if he didn't know it was baking powder he was selling. Yet selling baking powder is no more criminal than selling virtual child pornography.

This response does not suffice, however, because it overlooks a difference between the lawfulness of selling baking powder and the lawful character of virtual child pornography. Powder sales are lawful but not constitutionally privileged. Any justification within the bounds of rationality would suffice for limiting baking powder transactions, just as it would for regulating the discharge of blanks from a pistol. Virtual pornography, however, has been held to fall within the First Amendment speech privilege, and thus is affirmatively protected, not merely allowed as a matter of course.

No one can seriously assume that after today's decision the Government will go on prosecuting defendants for selling child pornography (requiring a showing that a real child is pictured, under *Free Speech Coalition*); it will prosecute for merely proposing a pornography transaction manifesting or inducing the belief that a photo is real child pornography, free of any need to demonstrate that any extant underlying photo does show a real child. If the Act can be enforced, it will function just as it was meant to do, by merging the whole subject of child pornography into the offense of proposing a transaction, dispensing with the real-child element in the underlying subject. And eliminating the need to prove a real child will be a loss of some consequence. This is so not because there will possibly be less pornography available owing to the greater ease of prosecuting, but simply because there must be a line between what the Government may suppress and what it may not, and a segment of that line will be gone. This Court went to great pains to draw it in *Ferber* and *Free Speech Coalition*; it was worth drawing and it is worth respecting now in facing the attempt to end-run that line through the provisions of the Act.

If the deluded drug dealer is held liable for an attempt crime there is no risk of eliminating baking powder from trade in lawful commodities. But if the Act can effectively eliminate the real-child requirement when a proposal relates to extant material, a class of protected speech will disappear. True, what will be lost is short on merit, but intrinsic value is not the reason for protecting unpopular expression.

Notes

Is the dissent correct in asserting that *Williams* undermines *Free Speech Coalition*? Is *Williams* just a consumer protection case in that persons advertising a "product" must truthfully represent what that product is?

———————

4. Morphed Images

United States v. Dale Robert Bach
400 F.3d 622 (8th Cir. 2005)

MURPHY, CIRCUIT JUDGE.

[Following a series of investigative steps, police obtained a search warrant for Bach's Yahoo! account.]

One email in Bach's account had been received from Fabio Marco in Italy; that transmission is the basis for Bach's conviction for receiving child pornography. Marco's email to Bach had an attached photograph which showed a young nude boy sitting in a tree, grinning, with his pelvis tilted upward, his legs opened wide, and a full erection. Below the image was the name of AC, a well known child entertainer. Evidence at trial showed that a photograph of AC's head had been skillfully inserted onto the photograph of the nude boy so that the resulting image appeared to be a nude picture of AC posing in the tree.

Count 6 charged Bach with receiving child pornography in interstate or foreign commerce (the picture with AC's face), in violation of 18 U.S.C. §2252A(a)(2). [Bach was convicted of Count 6 and three other counts] and the district court imposed concurrent sentences of 121 months for counts 1, 4, and 6 and 180 months for count 7.

The district court instructed the jury that it could find Bach guilty of violating §2252A(a)(2) if it found that he knowingly received a visual depiction that "involves the use of a minor engaging in sexually explicit conduct" or "has been created, adapted, or modified to appear that an identifiable minor is engaging in sexually explicit conduct."

Bach argues that his conviction is invalid because the definition of child pornography in §2256(8)(C) violates the First Amendment. He contends that the definition covers images that only appear to depict an identifiable minor and that the definitions found unconstitutional in [*Ashcroft v. Free Speech Coalition*, 535 U.S. 234 (2002),] used similar language. He argues virtual pornography was protected by the Court in *Free Speech Coalition* because it did not involve the abuse of a real minor and there was no evidence that a real minor was used to produce the image with AC's head.

The government responds that morphed images such as the one in count 6 involve real children with consequential mental harm. It asserts that a morphed image may victimize several children at once because it may contain an underlying picture of real children being abused and exploited, as well as the face of an identifiable child whose own mental health and reputation may suffer. The government also argues that if the definition of child pornography in §2256(8)(C) were held unconstitutional, pornographers could avoid prosecution by simply pasting the heads of young stars over the faces of their victimized real children.

Section 2256(8)(C), the definition applied in Bach's prosecution for receiving the image with AC's face, covers any visual depiction that "has been created, adapted, or modified to appear that an identifiable minor is engaging in sexually explicit conduct." The definition in subsection (C) was intended by Congress to prevent harm to minors resulting from the use of "identifiable images . . . in pornographic depictions, even where the identifiable minor is not directly involved in sexually explicit activities." The definition in subsection (C) targets harm to an identifiable minor.

In *Ferber*, the Supreme Court recognized a compelling government interest in preventing the sexual exploitation and abuse of children. The distribution of child pornography is "intrinsically related" to the sexual abuse of children because it creates a "permanent record of the children's participation and the harm to the child is exacerbated by [its] circulation," and the production of pornography requiring the sexual exploitation of children cannot be "effectively controlled" unless that network is closed. In *Free Speech Coalition* the Court again focused on these harms, stating that "[l]ike a defamatory statement, each new publication . . . would cause new injury to the child's reputation and emotional well-being."

[In *Free Speech Coalition*, the Court] explicitly stated that it was not addressing the constitutionality of subsection (C). It differentiated the definition in (C), noting that it

> prohibits a more common and lower tech means of creating visual images, known as computer morphing. Rather than creating original images, pornographers can alter innocent pictures of real children so that the children appear to be engaged in sexual activity. Although morphed images may fall within the definition of virtual child pornography, they implicate the interests of real children and are in that sense closer to the images in *Ferber*.

Unlike the virtual pornography protected by the Supreme Court in *Free Speech Coalition*, the picture with AC's face implicates the interests of a real child and does record a crime. The picture depicts a young nude boy who is grinning and sitting in a tree in a lascivious pose with a full erection, his legs spread, and his pelvis tilted upward. The jury could find from looking at the picture that it is an image of an identifiable minor, and that the interests of a real child were implicated by being posed in such a way. This is not the typical morphing case in which an innocent picture of a child has been altered to appear that the child is engaging in sexually explicit conduct, for the lasciviously posed body is that of a child. *See* S. Rep. No. 108-002, at n. 2 (2003) ("[T]he morphing provision is explicitly aimed at the creation of a sexually explicit image using an innocent image of a child.").

Evidence in the record indicates that a photograph of the head of a well known juvenile, AC, was skillfully inserted onto the body of the nude boy so that the resulting depiction appears to be a picture of AC engaging in sexually explicit conduct with a knowing grin. Although there is no contention that the nude body actually is that of AC or that he was involved in the production of the image, a lasting record has been created of AC, an identifiable minor child, seemingly engaged in sexually explicit activity. He is thus victimized every time the picture is displayed. Unlike the virtual pornography or the pornography using youthful looking adults, as discussed in *Free Speech Coalition*, this image created an identifiable child victim of sexual exploitation. In *Free Speech Coalition* the Supreme Court continued to recognize the government's compelling interest in protecting a minor's physical and psychological well being, building on its decision in *Ferber*, pointing out the harm arising from pornography which is "intrinsically related" to the sexual abuse of children.

Although there may well be instances in which the application of § 2256(8)(C) violates the First Amendment, this is not such a case. The interests of real children are implicated in the image received by Bach showing a boy with the identifiable face of AC in a lascivious pose. This image involves the type of harm which can constitutionally be prosecuted under *Free Speech Coalition* and *Ferber*.

HEANEY, CIRCUIT JUDGE, concurring.

Bach contends that this conviction is constitutionally infirm because it rests on a definition of child pornography, contained in 18 U.S.C. § 2256(8)(C), which he claims violates the First Amendment. Had Bach challenged this statute on the ground that it was facially overbroad, as did the respondents in *Free Speech Coalition*, he may well have prevailed on his claim. In my view, the reasoning behind the Supreme Court's decision in *Free Speech Coalition* applies with equal force to subsection (C). The record reveals, however, that Bach only challenged the statute as it was applied to him. I agree with the majority that the statute survives scrutiny as applied, and therefore concur.

Notes

1. The *Bach* court seemed to limit its holding to the situation where there were two real children involved in the morphing and that AC was an identifiable child. What should be the result if the body of the person was that of an adult and AC's head was morphed onto it? Would the result change if only AC's head was that of a real child and the remainder of the image was virtual?

2. In *State v. Zidel*, 940 A.2d 255 (N.H. 2008), the Court held that the possession of morphed images violated the First Amendment when the children depicted did not actually engage in the sexual activity. The court limited its holding to "mere possession of morphed images that depicted heads and necks of identifiable minor females superimposed upon naked female bodies, and the naked bodies do not depict body parts of actual children engaging in sexual activity." The court reasoned that the First Amendment category of child pornography as prohibited speech was premised on the child being sexually abused.

Zidel seems to be an outlier. *See United States v. Hotaling*, 599 F. Supp. 2d 306 (N.D.N.Y. 2008) (upholding prosecution for morphed images where the child was not actually engaged in the sexual activity and observing that *Zidel* is at odds with "every other federal and state court" and finding that the use of children, regardless of their role in the image, was harmful to the physiological, emotional, and mental health of the children). Affirming the district court's decision in *Hotaling*, see 634 F.3d 725 (2d Cir. 2011), the appellate court observed:

> We agree with the Eighth Circuit [in *Bach*] that the interests of actual minors are implicated when their faces are used in creating morphed images that make it appear that they are performing sexually explicit acts. In this case, even though the bodies in the images belonged to adult females, they had been digitally altered such that the only recognizable persons were the minors. Furthermore, the actual names of the minors were added to many of the photographs, making it easier to identify them and bolstering the connection between the actual minor and the sexually explicit conduct. Unlike the computer generated images in *Free Speech Coalition*, where no actual person's image and reputation were implicated, here we have six identifiable minor females who were at risk of reputational harm and suffered the psychological harm of knowing that their images were exploited and prepared for distribution by a trusted adult.

3. The Eighth Circuit revisited *Bach* in *United States v. Anderson*, 759 F.3d 891 (8th Cir. 2014), where the court affirmed the denial of Anderson's motion to dismiss one count of distributing child pornography. Anderson took an image that originally depicted an adult male and adult female engaged in sexual intercourse and digitally superimposed a minor's face over the face of the female. He then transmitted the image to the minor's account with a caption that essentially said: "This is what we will do." The Eighth Circuit concluded that the image did *not* fit within the category of nonprotected speech:

> The government argues that because the morphed image in this case creates a lasting record of M.A., an identifiable minor, seemingly engaged in sexually explicit activity, it is analogous to the image in *Bach* and not protected by the First Amendment. There is an important distinction, however, between the morphed image in *Bach* and the morphed image in this case. Whereas the image in *Bach* recorded the sexual abuse of the nude minor who was posed in the original image, Anderson's morphed image superimposed M.A.'s face onto an image of two adults. No minor was sexually abused in the production of Anderson's image. [T]his difference is significant enough to distinguish Anderson's image from the unprotected speech in *Bach*—unless the Court were to conclude that morphed images like Anderson's come within a category of speech that has been historically unprotected but not yet specifically identified in the case law.

Nonetheless, the Eighth Circuit affirmed the denial of the motion to dismiss on the ground that the child pornography statutes, as applied to Anderson, satisfied strict scrutiny under the First Amendment:

Where a statute prohibits constitutionally protected speech based on its content, the government must demonstrate that the prohibition is "justified by a compelling interest and is narrowly drawn to serve that interest."

The Supreme Court has long recognized as "compelling" the government's "interest in safeguarding the physical and psychological well-being of a minor." In *Free Speech Coalition*, the Court continued to recognize this interest as compelling, and noted in *dicta* that "morphed images . . . implicate the interests of real children and are in that sense closer to the images in *Ferber*."

The morphed image at issue here implicates the government's interest in protecting minors, and a portion of our reasoning in *Bach* is on point. Even though "there is no contention that the nude body actually is that of [M.A.], . . . a lasting record has been created of [her] . . . seemingly engaged in sexually explicit activity. [She] is thus victimized every time the picture is displayed." Although subjects of morphed images like M.A. do not suffer the direct physical and psychological effects of sexual abuse that accompany the production of traditional child pornography, the morphed images' "continued existence causes the child victims continuing harm by haunting the children in years to come." "[M]orphed images are like traditional child pornography in that they are records of the harmful sexual exploitation of children. The children, who are identifiable in the images, are violated by being falsely portrayed as engaging in sexual activity."

"The First Amendment requires that the Government's chosen restriction on the speech at issue be 'actually necessary' to achieve its interest." Anderson argues that the law as applied here is not narrowly tailored because it encompasses an image that clearly depicts adult bodies and because it punishes "private" distribution of a morphed image. But the harm a child suffers from appearing as the purported subject of pornography in a digital image that is distributed via the Internet can implicate a compelling government interest regardless of the image's verisimilitude or the initial size of its audience. Anderson's distribution targeted M.A. through her Facebook account, and the image suggested her involvement in sexual intercourse as an eleven-year-old child. There was no less restrictive means for the government effectively to protect this child from the exploitation and psychological harm resulting from the distribution of the morphed image than to prohibit Anderson from disseminating it.

What is the difference between labeling morphed images non-protected speech versus protected speech that the government has the right to criminalize based on a compelling governmental interest? Does the latter depend on the distribution of the images or would mere possession be punishable?

———————

5. Obscene Cartoons Featuring Children

United States v. Christopher S. Handley

564 F. Supp. 2d 996 (S.D. Iowa 2008)

JAMES E. GRITZNER, DISTRICT JUDGE.

The Grand Jury returned a superseding indictment, charging Defendant with receipt of obscene visual representations of the sexual abuse of children in violation of 18 U.S.C. § 1466A(a), [and] possession of obscene visual representations of the sexual abuse of children in violation of 18 U.S.C. § 1466A(b).

The superseding indictment describes the images at issue in counts one through four as follows:

> one or more drawings or cartoons, that depict a minor engaging in sexually explicit conduct, and is obscene, and depicts an image that is, or appears to be, of a minor engaging in graphic bestiality, sadistic or masochistic abuse, or sexual intercourse, including genital-genital, oral-genital, anal-genital, or oral-anal, whether between person of the same or opposite sex, which lacks serious literary, artistic, political, or scientific value.

The superseding indictment describes the images at issue in count five as "a copy of a book containing visual depictions, namely drawings and cartoons, that depicted graphic bestiality, including sexual intercourse, between human beings and animals such as pigs, monkeys, and others." Defendant states all of the images at issue in counts one through five are drawings from Japanese anime comic books that were produced either by hand or by computer, and the drawings depict fictional characters. Defendant states there is no indication the drawings represent or refer to any actual persons, either minor or adult, and the drawings are purely a product of the artist's imagination.

Count one charges a violation of 18 U.S.C. § 1466A(a), which states,

> Any person who, in a circumstance described in subsection (d), knowingly produces, distributes, receives, or possesses with intent to distribute, a visual depiction of any kind, including a drawing, cartoon, sculpture, or painting, that—(1)(A) depicts a minor engaging in sexually explicit conduct; and (B) is obscene; or (2)(A) depicts an image that is, or appears to be, of a minor engaging in graphic bestiality, sadistic or masochistic abuse, or sexual intercourse, including genital-genital, oral-genital, anal-genital, or oral-anal, whether between persons of the same or opposite sex; and (B) lacks serious literary, artistic, political, or scientific value; or attempts or conspires to do so, shall be subject to the penalties provided in section 2252A(b)(1), including the penalties provided for cases involving a prior conviction.

Counts two through four charge a violation of 18 U.S.C. § 1466A(b), which states,

> Any person who, in a circumstance described in subsection (d), knowingly possesses a visual depiction of any kind, including a drawing, cartoon,

sculpture, or painting, that—(1)(A) depicts a minor engaging in sexually explicit conduct; and (B) is obscene; or (2)(A) depicts an image that is, or appears to be, of a minor engaging in graphic bestiality, sadistic or masochistic abuse, or sexual intercourse, including genital-genital, oral-genital, anal-genital, or oral-anal, whether between persons of the same or opposite sex; and (B) lacks serious literary, artistic, political, or scientific value; or attempts or conspires to do so, shall be subject to the penalties provided in section 2252A(b)(2), including the penalties provided for cases involving a prior conviction.

Section 1466A(a) criminalizes production, distribution, receipt, or possession with intent to distribute, whereas section 1466A(b) criminalizes simple possession. "The term 'sexually explicit conduct' has the meaning given the term in section 2256(2)(A) or 2256(2)(B)."

Defendant argues counts one through four of the superseding indictment should be dismissed because private possession of obscene materials is a right protected by the First Amendment. The Constitution prohibits "making mere private possession of obscene material a crime." *Stanley v. Georgia*, 394 U.S. 557, 568 (1969). The limited right to possess obscene materials in the privacy of one's own home recognized in *Stanley* depended not on First Amendment grounds, but on the right to privacy in the home found in the Fourth Amendment.

While mere possession of obscene materials within the privacy of an individual's own home is a right protected by the Fourth Amendment, the zone of privacy recognized in *Stanley* is not unlimited.

> We are not disposed to extend the precise, carefully limited holding of *Stanley* to permit importation of admittedly obscene materials simply because it is imported for private use only. To allow such a claim would be not unlike compelling the Government to permit importation of prohibited or controlled drugs for private consumption as long as such drugs are not for public distribution or sale. We have already indicated that the protected right to possess obscene material in the privacy of one's home does not give rise to a correlative right to have someone sell or give it to others. Nor is there any correlative right to transport obscene material in interstate commerce.

[*United States v. 12 200-Foot Reels of Super 8mm. Film*, 413 U.S. 123, 128 (1973).] Thus, while an individual has a limited right to possess obscene materials in the privacy of his own home, there exists no right to receive or possess obscene materials that have been moved in interstate commerce, and that is the illegal conduct with which Defendant is charged.

Defendant argues that [*Ashcroft v. Free Speech Coalition*, 535 U.S. 234 (2002),] gave constitutional legitimacy to pornography in which no real children are used. The Court disagrees. *Free Speech Coalition* dealt with whether the Child Pornography Prevention Act of 1996 abridged the freedom of speech. Section 2256(8)(B) banned child pornography that appeared to depict minors but was produced without using any actual children. Because the statute criminalized material that was neither child pornography involving actual children nor obscenity, the Supreme Court concluded the CPPA sought to reach beyond obscene material, and the statute was struck down as overbroad and unconstitutional.

Section 1466A (a)(1) and (b)(1) do not suffer from the same defect as those found in the CPPA in *Free Speech Coalition*. Sections 1466A(a)(1) and (b)(1) specifically include as an element of each offense that the material must be obscene.

Defendant argues even if the materials are deemed obscene, he has a constitutional right to possess them. Again, Defendant has not been charged with mere possession of obscenity in the privacy of his own home. Counts one through four charge Defendant with conduct that extends beyond the limited right recognized by *Stanley*, receipt of obscene visual depictions that were transported in interstate commerce and possession of obscene images that were transported in interstate commerce.

United States v. Dwight Edwin Whorley
550 F.3d 326 (4th Cir. 2008)

NIEMEYER, CIRCUIT JUDGE:

Dwight Whorley was convicted of knowingly receiving on a computer 20 obscene Japanese anime cartoons depicting minors engaging in sexually explicit conduct, in violation of 18 U.S.C. § 1462[.]

The Virginia Employment Commission maintains a public resource room in Richmond, Virginia, where job seekers may use Commission copiers, computers, and printers for employment-related purposes.

On March 30, 2004, a woman in the resource room informed a Commission employee that Dwight Whorley was viewing what appeared to be child pornography on a Commission computer. In response, the office manager and two supervisors went to the resource room and saw Whorley standing in front of the printer with papers in his hand. Upon request, Whorley showed the supervisor the documents, which depicted Japanese anime-style cartoons of children engaged in explicit sexual conduct with adults. Determining that the documents were an inappropriate use of state computer equipment, the manager banned Whorley from using the Commission's computers and escorted him from the premises.

Returning to the computer that Whorley had been using, the Commission employees found that his YAHOO! e-mail account was still open, and they also found several more copies of anime-style cartoons by the computer. After printing off several e-mails from that account and taking the computer out of service, the manager called his supervisor and the state police. Later, the FBI obtained more information from YAHOO! about Whorley's e-mail account.

[18 U.S.C. § 1462] provides:

> Whoever brings into the United States . . . or knowingly uses any express company or other common carrier or interactive computer service . . . for carriage in interstate or foreign commerce—
>
> (a) any obscene, lewd, lascivious, or filthy book, pamphlet, picture, motion-picture film, paper, letter, writing, print, or other matter of indecent character; or
>
> * * *
>
> Whoever knowingly takes or receives, from such express company or other common carrier or interactive computer service . . . any matter or thing the carriage or importation of which is herein made unlawful—
>
> Shall be fined under this title or imprisoned not more than five years. . . .

The focus of the statute's prohibition is on the movement of obscene matter in interstate commerce, not its possession in the home. This is manifested by the statute's prohibition of receiving obscene material from any "express company," "common carrier," or "interactive computer service."

Whorley contends that § 1462 is facially unconstitutional because its use of the word "receives" in prohibiting the receipt of obscene matter using instruments of interstate commerce makes the prohibition impermissibly vague in the context of receiving obscene matter from an interactive computer service. He maintains that "receives" is so broad that the statute ensnares the unwitting recipient of obscenity, such as one who innocently receives an "obscene textual message [sent] to a person's e-mail account" from a malicious third party, or finds to his dismay that an obscene image appears "as a 'pop-up ad' or as part of a paid sponsor's rotating advertisement." Consequently, he argues that "§ 1462 fails to give notice to the average person of when criminal liability attaches."

"A statute is impermissibly vague if it either (1) 'fails to provide people of ordinary intelligence a reasonable opportunity to understand what conduct it prohibits' or (2) 'authorizes or even encourages arbitrary and discriminatory enforcement.'"

In this case, Whorley's argument in fact suggests no vagueness or misunderstanding about the scope of the word "receives." Giving that term its ordinary meaning, his argument assumes that "receives" means to "come into possession of," to "acquire," or "to have delivered or brought to one." To be sure, one can "receive" obscene materials intentionally and knowingly, or negligently, or by mistake or accident. Section 1462, however, does not criminalize every receipt of obscene materials, but only the "knowing" receipt of them. It is thus apparent that in making his argument that "receives" is too vague, Whorley actually confuses *mens rea* with the question of whether the word "receives" itself is without sufficient meaning to be readily understood.

Whorley is probably correct in observing that evolving computer technology will constantly change the ways in which a person's computer may be used to "receive" obscene material from an interactive computer service and that those changes might, depending on the technology, present serious questions as to whether such material can be said to have been "received." But no such question exists here where Whorley actively used a computer to solicit obscene material through numerous and repetitive searches and ultimately succeeded in obtaining the materials he sought. Moreover, while the facts of each case will require a jury to determine whether an individual has, in fact, "knowingly received" obscene matter, the need for such a determination by the jury does not suggest that a statute is too vague.

§ 13.3 Elements of Child Pornography Offenses

1. Distribution

United States v. Joshua P. Navrestad

66 M.J. 262 (C.A.A.F. 2008)

JUDGE ERDMANN delivered the opinion of the court.

Specialist Joshua P. Navrestad was charged with distributing and possessing child pornography in violation of the Child Pornography Prevention Act of 1996. We granted this case to determine: whether sending a hyperlink to a Yahoo! Briefcase during an Internet chat session, where that Briefcase contained child pornography images, is legally sufficient to constitute distribution of child pornography. We hold, under the facts of this case, that Navrestad's actions did not constitute distribution of child pornography.

Navrestad had an account at an Internet café in a United States Army morale, welfare and recreation center in Vilseck, Germany. He would pay for a set amount of time and then use a kiosk-style computer terminal to access the Internet. While at the café, Navrestad had Internet chat sessions over the course of several days with someone who identified himself as "Adam." Navrestad believed "Adam" was a fifteen-year-old boy from New Hampshire while actually "Adam" was Detective James F. McLaughlin, a New Hampshire police officer.

During the course of several chat sessions, Navrestad made requests for phone sex and encouraged "Adam" to engage in sex acts with "Adam's" younger brother and a friend of "Adam's" who was also a minor. During these sessions "Adam" made inquiries about seeking pictures, often in response to Navrestad's requests for phone sex. Eventually, "Adam" made a specific request for pictures of "guys 10-13."

In response to "Adam's" request, Navrestad sought out child pornography on the Internet using the Internet café computer and located links to several Yahoo! Briefcases[n.4][9] that contained child pornography. While at the Internet café,

---

9. [n.4] Yahoo! Briefcase is an online service that allows users to store files on the Yahoo! servers. Users may or may not make the contents of their Briefcases public.

Navrestad opened and viewed the Briefcases to confirm the contents and then sent a hyperlink to one of the Briefcases that contained child pornography to "Adam."

The issue in this case centers on what was actually distributed when Navrestad sent the hyperlink to "Adam." Navrestad argues he did not distribute child pornography because a hyperlink does not contain "data . . . capable of conversion into a visual image" of child pornography. He argues that the hyperlink only contained data that is convertible to an address which, in this case, did not even take users directly to the prohibited images. The Government responds that this court should uphold the lower court because a hyperlink meets the definition of a "visual depiction" set forth in the 18 U.S.C. § 2256(5).

The initial inquiry is whether this hyperlink contains "data stored . . . by electronic means which is capable of conversion into a visual image[.]" Commencing our inquiry with a basic dictionary definition, we find that "hyperlink" is defined as "an electronic link providing direct access from one distinctively marked place in a hypertext or hypermedia document to another in the same or a different document." *Webster's Third New International Dictionary Unabridged* (2002). This definition centers on a hyperlink as an electronic link which provides access.[n.7][10]

David Hardinge, a senior systems administrator whose responsibilities include providing technical support for the Internet café at Vilseck, testified for the Government. During cross-examination, he defined a hyperlink as an address or a "way that you can display a web site," which the recipient can click on to go to the particular site. Hardinge agreed that a hyperlink is a shortcut to typing in the website address manually and that clicking on it does not move any documents on the user's computer.[n.8][11] He also agreed that it was an accurate analogy to say that sending a hyperlink is like sending someone an address of a store or of a location of a building.

Hardinge further agreed that sending an individual file as an attachment to an e-mail takes longer than sending a hyperlink because, with an attachment, the user is sending a file that is moving onto someone else's computer. He admitted that a picture is not sent to the recipient when a hyperlink is sent "[b]ecause a hyperlink is nothing more than . . . just a shortcut to get somewhere."

Unlike an e-mail attachment, the sending of a hyperlink in a chat session does not move a file or document from one location to another. As such, the data contained in the hyperlink is an electronic address that allows the recipient to direct his browser to the new location without having to type in the website of that location. The data contained in the hyperlink is not capable of conversion into any type of visual image. Rather, the data provides the recipient with the path to a website on a server distinct

---

10. [n.7] A "link" has been defined as "something in a document like an email, usually highlighted or underlined, that sends users who click on it directly to a new location—usually an internet address or a program of some sort."

11. [n.8] We note that while clicking on a hyperlink may create a file in the recipient's temporary Internet file folder, clicking this hyperlink does not move images or documents from the sender's computer to the recipient's computer.

from Navrestad's own computer. It is this separate server that contained the visual images of child pornography, not the hyperlink Navrestad sent. In contrast, a file received as an e-mailed attachment is self-contained and capable of conversion into an image independent of other factors. The difference between a hyperlink and a file that is sent as an e-mailed attachment is significant because the attached picture or graphics file is a complete image that is just not opened yet. When that complete image is received, it is housed on the recipient's computer.

Since the hyperlink sent by Navrestad was a path or address to a website and not a file that contains data that is "capable of being converted" into visual images, this case is distinguishable from circuit court cases that involved GIF files. In those cases, the defendants argued that GIF files were not visual depictions because the file itself was binary code and not images. Both courts, however, concluded that GIF files are included in the statutory definition of child pornography because "[t]he visual image transported in binary form starts and ends pornographically." In contrast, the hyperlink here did not start or end as pornography, but was simply a shortcut to a particular web address.[n.10][12]

The Government also argued that once the hyperlink was sent, the recipient was "just a click away" from the child pornography images. Here the Government confuses the manner of the alleged distribution with what is allegedly being distributed. Navrestad does not dispute that he sent the hyperlink to "Adam." His position is that the hyperlink did not contain child pornography as that term is defined in the CPPA and therefore cannot constitute the distribution of child pornography. We agree. However, even if the number of clicks were a factor in determining whether the hyperlink contained child pornography, the hyperlink in this case did not take the recipient directly to any child pornography images. When McLaughlin clicked on the link, he was taken to a directory of files and had to click on an individual file name in order to view the image.

We note that the United States Court of Appeals for the Eleventh Circuit has addressed a similar issue in an unpublished case where the defendant sent a hyperlink to his own Briefcase which contained child pornography. *United States v. Hair*, 178 Fed. Appx. 879 (11th Cir. 2006). That court determined the defendant was properly convicted of attempting to transport, and transporting child pornography in

---

12. [n.10] We have no quarrel with the hyperlink discussion in *Universal City Studios v. Corley*, which is consistent with the majority opinion. 273 F.3d 429, 455–457 (2d Cir. 2001) ("[H]yperlinks . . . facilitate instantaneous . . . access. . . ."). In relying on *Corley*, however, the dissent completely ignores the language of 18 U.S.C. §2256(5) and (8) which specifically prohibit the distribution of data which is "capable of conversion into" child pornography. The language in *Corley* upon which the dissent relies stands for the limited proposition that a hyperlink "facilitates" access to another Internet site. *Corley*, a civil case, does not suggest, let alone hold, that a hyperlink sends or distributes data that "is capable of conversion," into child pornography, as the criminal statute in this case requires for the offense of distribution. While the language relied upon by the dissent may be pertinent in a case in which an accused is charged with aiding and abetting the distribution of child pornography that is not the offense at issue in this case.

violation of 18 U.S.C. § 2252A(1). *Hair* is distinguishable from the instant case on several grounds: Hair was charged with both attempted transportation and transportation of child pornography; Navrestad was not charged with attempted distribution but only distribution of child pornography; the government in *Hair* also presented the transportation charge under an aiding and abetting theory, arguing that by sending the hyperlink, Hair had assisted Yahoo! in transporting child pornography; the Government did not present an aiding and abetting theory on Navrestad's distribution charge; the hyperlink Hair sent was to his own Briefcase over which he exercised dominion and control; the hyperlink Navrestad sent was to a public Briefcase over which he exercised no dominion or control.

Effron, Chief Judge, with whom Stucky, Judge, joins (dissenting):

The term "child pornography," which is not limited to images or pictures, includes "data stored on computer disk or by electronic means which is capable of conversion into a visual image."

According to Appellant, the hyperlink in the present case was not capable of conversion into child pornography because the recipient could not access the pornography through a one-step click on the hyperlink. Appellant relies on the fact that the recipient of the hyperlink had to take two steps to view the pornography: first, click on the briefcase to access the briefcase, and second, click on a specific file in the briefcase to view the child pornography.

The United States Court of Appeals for the Second Circuit, in *Universal City Studios, Inc. v. Corley*, 273 F.3d 429, 456 (2d Cir. 2001), encountered a similar objection when addressing the issue of improper trafficking of copyrighted material. In *Corley*, the district court issued an injunction prohibiting a company from posting software on its website that facilitated improper access to copyrighted materials through pirating software. The company also posted hyperlinks to other websites where the pirating software could be found.

In affirming the injunction against a variety of challenges, the Second Circuit offered the following description of the manner in which a hyperlink permits distribution of restricted information:

A hyperlink is a cross-reference (in a distinctive font or color) appearing on one web page that, when activated by the point-and-click of a mouse, brings onto the computer screen another web page. The hyperlink can appear on a screen (window) as text, such as the Internet address ("URL") of the web page being called up or a word or phrase that identifies the web page to be called up, for example, "DeCSS web site." Or the hyperlink can appear as an image, for example, an icon depicting a person sitting at a computer watching a DVD movie and text stating "click here to access DeCSS and see DVD movies for free!" The code for the web page containing the hyperlink includes a computer instruction that associates the link with the URL of the web page to be accessed, such that clicking on the hyperlink instructs the computer to enter the URL of the desired web page and thereby access that page. With a hyperlink on a web page, the linked web site is just one click away.

The Second Circuit agreed with the district court's conclusion that the DMCA, including statutory prohibitions against trafficking, should apply to hyperlinks because of the "functional capability" of the hyperlink even though the hyperlink was merely a path rather than an actual version of the pirating software. Although the hyperlink did not literally contain the pirating software, the Second Circuit observed, "[a hyperlink] conveys information, the Internet address of the linked web page, and has the functional capacity to bring the content of the linked web page to the user's computer screen."

As in the present case, the appellants in *Corley* contended that a hyperlink should be treated as merely publication of an address at which a third party might obtain prohibited material. The Second Circuit rejected the analogy, stating:

> Appellants ignore the reality of the functional capacity of . . . hyperlinks to facilitate instantaneous unauthorized access to copyrighted materials by anyone anywhere in the world. . . . [T]he injunction's linking prohibition validly regulates the Appellant's opportunity instantly to enable anyone anywhere to gain unauthorized access to copyrighted movies on DVDs.

The Second Circuit emphasized that hyperlinks take one "'almost instantaneously to the desired destination.'" Unlike a website address printed in the newspaper describing where to find child pornography, a hyperlink provides a means to transmit the content of the website to the user's computer. The recipient's ability to access and use images transmitted by hyperlink is functionally indistinguishable from the ability to access and use images transmitted as individually saved files.

In that context, the Second Circuit also rejected the company's suggestion that providing a hyperlink to a website should be analogized to a newspaper publishing the address of a bookstore that carries obscene materials. Focusing on the instantaneous distribution that occurs when a website is accessed via a hyperlink:

> Like many analogies posited to illuminate legal issues, the bookstore analogy is helpful primarily in identifying characteristics that *distinguish* it from the context of the pending dispute. If a bookstore proprietor is knowingly selling obscene materials, the evil of distributing such materials can be prevented by injunctive relief against the unlawful distribution (and similar distribution by others can be deterred by punishment of the distributor). And if others publish the location of the bookstore, preventive relief against a distributor can be effective before any significant distribution of the prohibited materials has occurred. The digital world, however, creates a very different problem. If obscene materials are posted on one web site and other sites post hyperlinks to the first site, the materials are available for instantaneous worldwide distribution before any preventive measures can be effectively taken.

The Second Circuit's functional treatment of distribution of information via hyperlinks in the context of the highly sensitive First Amendment considerations applicable to copyright litigation is consistent with the testimony developed during Appellant's trial. Witnesses for the Government established that a hyperlink provided an efficient means of distributing photographic images. One witness testified that although images can be distributed numerous ways, use of a hyperlink is "streamlined." One click on the hyperlink brought the recipient directly to the website, along with access to any files and digital images located at that website. Through the hyperlink, Appellant distributed child pornography by electronic means capable of conversion into images within the meaning of the statute, 10 U.S.C. § 2256(5), (8), and accomplished his distribution in a manner far more expeditious and efficient than if he had done so through traditional mail or by attaching individual files to an e-mail.

United States v. William Ralph Dodd

598 F.3d 449 (8th Cir. 2010)

Loken, Chief Judge.

William Ralph Dodd pleaded guilty to knowingly receiving and possessing child pornography. The presentence investigation report recommended that his base offense level be increased by two levels because the offenses involved distribution of child pornography. Dodd appeals, arguing that the court committed procedural error by imposing the enhancements.

Investigating internet distribution of child pornography, a law enforcement officer logged onto LimeWire, a peer-to-peer file sharing network, and conducted a search using the term "preteen." He connected to a responding internet address, reviewed the list of files that user was sharing, and confirmed that at least two of the files contained child pornography. The user was identified as Dodd. A warrant search of Dodd's home uncovered seventeen videos on his computer that contained child pornography. He was charged with knowingly distributing, receiving, and possessing child pornography. He pleaded guilty to knowing receipt and possession. The distribution count was dismissed.

The guidelines for child pornography offenses increase the base offense level by different amounts for specified types of distribution, providing, for example, five-level increases for distribution "for pecuniary gain" or "for the receipt . . . of a thing of value." U.S.S.G. § 2G2.2(b)(3)(A)–(B). The two-level increase here at issue applies if the offense involved distribution "other than distribution described in subdivisions (A) through (E)." § 2G2.2(b)(3)(F).

Dodd's PSR explained that peer-to-peer file sharing programs "allow internet users to share files on their computers with others utilizing the same program. A user can obtain files from other users' computers and allow other users to obtain files from his/her computer. In order to share one's files, the user must place them in a folder which is 'shared' with others." In this case, an investigator connected to Dodd's internet address by using this software to search the term "preteen," and determined that at least two of the files the user made available for downloading by other users of the program contained child pornography. The PSR recommended a two-level increase "[b]ecause the defendant distributed the material to another person."

Dodd argued, as he does on appeal, that the distribution enhancement is inappropriate when "there is absolutely no evidence that the defendant was aware that files downloaded to his saved file are available automatically to others." The government argued that LimeWire "is set up for the sole purpose of sharing files," and "affirmative steps must be taken in setting up that . . . system" to make the files in the shared folder available to others. "It doesn't happen by mistake and it doesn't happen by accident."

The leading Eighth Circuit case on this issue is *United States v. Griffin*, 482 F.3d 1008 (8th Cir. 2007). We concluded that the defendant in *Griffin* "was engaged in the distribution of child pornography" because his "use of the peer-to-peer file-sharing network made the child pornography files in his shared folder available to be searched and downloaded by other Kazaa users as evidenced by the partially downloaded file recovered by Danish authorities." Dodd urges us to distinguish *Griffin* because the defendant in that case admitted "he downloaded child pornography files from Kazaa, knew that Kazaa was a file-sharing network, and knew that, by using Kazaa, other Kazaa users could download files from him," whereas Dodd made no such admissions.

We conclude that the district court properly applied *Griffin* to the two-level distribution increase here at issue for two reasons. First, this is a fact-intensive inquiry. Thus, the issue is whether the district court clearly erred in finding by a preponderance of the evidence that Dodd distributed child pornography. In the plea agreement, Dodd admitted that he "knowingly and intentionally downloaded [child pornography] from the internet and stored these visual depictions on the hard drive of his computer." It is undisputed that he stored the downloaded material in a LimeWire folder shared with others. One can hypothesize that even a defendant who pleaded guilty to knowing receipt and possession might have no knowledge that his computer was equipped to distribute. But the purpose of a file sharing program is to share, in other words, to distribute. Absent concrete *evidence* of ignorance—evidence that is needed because ignorance is entirely counterintuitive—a fact-finder may reasonably infer that the defendant knowingly employed a file sharing program for its intended purpose. As the Tenth Circuit said in *United States v. Shaffer*, 472 F.3d 1219, 1223–24 (10th Cir. 2007):

> We have little difficulty in concluding that Mr. Shaffer distributed child pornography in the sense of having "delivered," "transferred," "dispersed," or "dispensed" it to others. He may not have actively pushed pornography on Kazaa users, but he freely allowed them access to his computerized stash of images and videos and openly invited them to take, or download, those items. It is something akin to the owner of a self-serve gas station. The owner

may not be present at the station, and there may be no attendant present at all. . . . But the owner has a roadside sign letting all passersby know that, if they choose, they can stop and fill their cars for themselves. . . . So, too, a reasonable jury could find that Mr. Shaffer welcomed people to his computer and was quite happy to let them take child pornography from it.

Second, the district court's ruling is consistent with the plain language of § 2G2.2, which broadly defines the term "distribution" as "any act, including possession with intent to distribute, production, advertisement, and transportation, related to the transfer of material involving the sexual exploitation of a minor." Effective November 1, 2009, the Commission added a clarifying sentence to this definition: "Accordingly, distribution includes posting material involving the sexual exploitation of a minor on a website for public viewing but does not include the mere solicitation of such material by a defendant." The Microsoft Computer Dictionary defines "post" as meaning, "To place a file on a server on a network or on a Web site." "Network" is defined as, "A group of computers . . . connected by communications facilities." "Server" is defined as, "On the Internet . . . a computer or program that responds to commands from a client." These definitions confirm that distribution as defined in § 2G2.2 includes operating a file sharing program that enables other participating users to access and download files placed in a shared folder, and then placing child pornography files in that folder.

Notes

Compare Navrestad's actions with those of Dodd. Are they distinguishable? Are the two men equally culpable in a moral sense? Should either be considered distributors in a legal sense?

2. Possession; Access with Intent to View

Some Preliminary Concepts

1. Downloading and Viewing

As the term is generally used, downloading an image requires a positive effort by the viewer to make a copy of the image in his hard drive. The person must instruct the computer to save or download the image and designate where it should store the image. Case law reveals that child pornography consumers use a wide variety of methods to download images. Users can use a web browser to download images directly off the websites. File sharing programs such as Kazaa and BearShare allow users to share files by downloading them from another user's computer. Images can also be transferred between computer users through Internet chat groups or newsgroups. Finally, images can be obtained, copied, or transferred by the use of removable storage such as CDs, floppy disks, or flash drives.

Once saved to the computer's hard drive, the saved image becomes part of the data on the computer and can be accessed at any time without an Internet connection. At this point, the user controls the image's destiny: The user can enlarge it, zoom in, zoom out, rotate it, print it, share it, edit it, and delete it. In fact, even if the user decides not to look at an image ever again, the image will remain on the computer until the user takes affirmative steps to delete it.

The user may choose to view the images on the Internet without downloading them onto the hard drive. Websites featuring child pornography include thumbnails that the viewer can enlarge. While the image is on the viewer's screen, the user is in control of the image. The viewer can undertake largely the same actions as if the image had been downloaded: He can enlarge it, zoom in or out, rotate it, print it, copy it to his computer, and show it to others.[13]

2. Cache and Temporary Internet Files

To speed up repeat viewing of a previously visited website, computers automatically make a copy of the data from visited websites in the form of "temporary Internet files" and store the data in what is called the "cache." Therefore, the first time a user visits a website two simultaneous processes occur: (1) the computer opens the website and shows it on the screen, and (2) the computer creates a copy of all the data on that website and stores it in the cache. When the user revisits the website, the computer compares the date on the website to the date on the previously stored temporary file; if unchanged, the computer displays the cached file on the screen, but, if the website has been updated, the computer displays the data from the website.

This process occurs automatically, without any prompting by the user, any time an Internet user visits any website; thus, it is generally outside the control of Internet users. In fact, since there is no indication to the user that this process is occurring, a computer user could take full advantage of the Internet-surfing capabilities of his computer without ever learning what is happening behind the scenes. Although it is possible to deactivate the cache function of a computer, the average computer user does not know how or why the process works. Even users that have a general idea of the process's function and operation might not know how to prevent it. A user needs advanced computer skills to directly access files in the cache while the computer is offline. Once properly accessed from inside the computer, however, temporary files are, for all relevant purposes, real files that contain images

---

13. Giannina Marin, Note, *Possession of Child Pornography: Should You Be Convicted When the Computer Cache Does the Saving for You?*, 60 Fla. L. Rev. 1205 (2008). Copyright © 2008, Florida Law Review. All rights reserved. Reprinted by permission.

that can be managed and manipulated like any other file, independent of an Internet connection. Finally, the cache can be easily deleted through the web browser without any special knowledge, or it can be deleted as part of routine computer maintenance.[14]

United States v. Stuart Romm

455 F.3d 990 (9th Cir. 2006)

BEA, CIRCUIT JUDGE:

Stuart Romm connected to the internet from a Las Vegas hotel room and visited websites containing images of child pornography. As Romm viewed the images online and enlarged them on his screen, his computer automatically saved copies of the images to his "internet cache." Based on 40 images deleted from his internet cache and two images deleted from another part of his hard drive, Romm was convicted of knowingly receiving and knowingly possessing child pornography in violation of 18 U.S.C. § 2252A(a)(2), (a)(5)(B).

Romm challenges the sufficiency of the evidence supporting each of his convictions, arguing he cannot be found guilty of possessing or receiving child pornography, when he merely viewed child pornography without "downloading" any of it to his hard drive.

From January 23, 2004 to February 1, 2004, Romm attended a training seminar held by his new employer in Las Vegas, Nevada. When the training seminar ended on February 1, 2004, Romm flew from Las Vegas, Nevada to Kelowna, British Columbia on business.

At the British Columbia airport, Canada's Border Services Agency discovered that Romm had a criminal history and stopped him for questioning. Romm admitted he had a criminal record and was currently on probation. Agent Keith Brown then asked Romm to turn on his laptop and briefly examined it. When Brown saw several child pornography websites in Romm's "internet history," Brown asked Romm if he had violated the terms of his probation by visiting these websites. Romm answered "Yes," and also said, "That's it. My life's over."

Meanwhile, Canada's immigration service had decided not to admit Romm into the country. Romm withdrew his application for entry and was placed under detention until the next flight to Seattle. Agent Brown then informed U.S. Customs in Seattle that Romm had been denied entry and possibly had illegal images on his computer. On February 2, 2004, Romm returned to Seattle. At the Seattle-Tacoma airport, Romm was interviewed by Agents Macho and Swenson of Immigration and Customs Enforcement. The agents told Romm they needed to search his laptop for

---

14. *Id.*

illegal images, and could arrange for the examination to be completed that night. Romm agreed. He told the agents he had been in sole possession of the laptop for the previous six to eight weeks. He also told the agents he had "drifted" away from his "therapy," and experienced "occasional lapses" during which he would view child pornography. But Romm repeatedly denied having any child pornography on his laptop.

ICE conducted a preliminary forensic analysis of the hard drive in Romm's laptop. When the preliminary analysis revealed ten images of child pornography, Agent Macho confronted Romm with this information and asked Romm why he had lied about having images on his computer. Romm looked down, adopted a "confessional mode," made little eye contact with his interrogators, and said that "he knew [the agents] were gonna find something on the computer." He also stated the agents had every right to arrest him and would probably do so.

Romm then described to the agents how he used Google to search for child pornography websites. When he found pictures he liked, Romm would keep them on his screen for five minutes and then delete them. Romm used the terms "save" and "download" to describe this operation. While staying in his hotel room in Las Vegas, Romm viewed child pornography and masturbated twice, while or shortly after viewing the child pornography; he claimed to have then deleted such images. In all, Romm used the internet for approximately six-and-a-half hours during his week-long stay in Las Vegas.

At trial, the government called three witnesses to testify about the forensic analysis of the hard drive in Romm's laptop. First, Agent Camille Sugrue described the preliminary analysis that she conducted with software called "EnCase." With EnCase, it is possible to recover deleted files, as well as information showing when the files were created, accessed, or modified. In conducting the preliminary analysis, Sugrue found ten images of child pornography. All of the images she found had been deleted from Romm's hard drive.

Second, Detective Timothy Luckie testified to the results of the full forensic analysis of Romm's hard drive. Luckie confirmed that all of the child pornography on Romm's computer had been deleted. The vast majority of the images Luckie found had been deleted from Romm's internet cache. EnCase did not reveal when the files had been deleted. Luckie's analysis also showed that Romm had enlarged a few smaller "thumbnail"[n.9][15] images in the internet cache.

Luckie next explained how files in the internet cache are deleted. First, on the default setting, the web browser automatically empties the internet cache when it reaches a given size. Second, the user can instruct the browser to empty the internet cache. Third, users who know where the internet cache is located can go into the cache and manually delete the files, rather than effect the deletions automatically

---

15. [n.9] The term "thumbnail," which derives from an artist's thumbnail sketch, refers to "a small image of a graphics file displayed in order to help you identify it."

through the web browser's default setting. EnCase did not reveal the settings on Romm's web browser, or how his internet cache had been emptied. Luckie opined "through experience and training," however, that Romm either had instructed his browser to empty the cache or had deleted the files manually. Luckie also noted Romm had erased his internet history at 2:25 p.m. on February 2, 2004, the same afternoon that Canada's Border Services Agency placed Romm on a flight back to Seattle.

Finally, Luckie testified that files in the internet cache are accessible, albeit "system-protected." A user who knows how to find the internet cache can view the images stored there. Once the user views the image, the user "can print, rename, [or] save [it] elsewhere, the same thing you can do with any other file."

The government's third expert witness, Darryl Cosme, exhibited to the jury 42 images of child pornography recovered from Romm's hard drive. He told the jury the provenance of some images, when each image was saved to the cache, and whether that image was a thumbnail or a full-sized picture. Cosme identified several websites in the internet history as related to child pornography.

Romm's expert witness, Thomas Keller, testified how the internet cache is "system-protected." According to Keller, "system-protection" blocks any user from accessing the cache, except by means of "system-commands." If, however, the user executes a system-command notwithstanding the computer's warning, he can copy the cached image to another location on the hard drive or view the image by copying it into an open program. Keller also testified that people delete their internet history and internet cache for legitimate reasons. Finally, Keller testified he found no evidence Romm ever went into the internet cache, or accessed the files there.

"There is sufficient evidence to support a conviction if, 'viewing the evidence in the light most favorable to the prosecution, any rational trier of fact could have found the essential elements of the crime beyond a reasonable doubt.'" Romm concedes there was sufficient evidence for the jury to find he acted with the requisite mental state of "knowingly," but rather contends that the act he committed was merely the viewing of child pornography, not the possession or receipt of it. We disagree. In the electronic context, a person can receive and possess child pornography without downloading it, if he or she seeks it out and exercises dominion and control over it. Here, we hold Romm exercised dominion and control over the images in his cache by enlarging them on his screen, and saving them there for five minutes before deleting them. While the images were displayed on Romm's screen and simultaneously stored to his laptop's hard drive, he had the ability to copy, print, or email the images to others. Thus, this evidence of control was sufficient for the jury to find that Romm possessed and received the images in his cache.

As we explain below, whether Romm "received" the images in his cache depends on whether he knowingly took possession of them. Thus, we begin by analyzing his conviction for knowingly possessing child pornography. It is a federal crime to "knowingly possess[] any book, magazine, periodical, film, videotape, computer disk, or any other material that contains an image of child pornography. . . ." 18 U.S.C. § 2252A(a)(5)(B).

Romm challenges the sufficiency of evidence of his control over the images in the internet cache. We interpret the term "knowing possession" according to its plain meaning, and presume Congress intended to apply traditional concepts of possession. "Possession" is "[t]he fact of having or holding property in one's power; the exercise of dominion over property." Thus, to establish possession, "'[t]he government must prove a sufficient connection between the defendant and the contraband to support the inference that the defendant exercised dominion and control over [it].'"

It is true that the images possessed by the defendant must be "contain[ed]" on a "computer disk or other [tangible] material." It is also true that "a defendant may be convicted [of possessing child pornography] only upon a showing that he knew that the [disks] contained an unlawful visual depiction." Therefore, to possess the images in the cache, the defendant must, at a minimum, know that the unlawful images are stored on a disk or other tangible material in his possession.

Romm exercised control over the cached images while they were contemporaneously saved to his cache and displayed on his screen. At that moment, as the expert testimony here established, Romm could print the images, enlarge them, copy them, or email them to others. No doubt, images could be saved to the cache when a defendant accidentally views the images, as through the occurrence of a "pop-up,"[n.14][16] for instance. But that is not the case here.

By his own admission to ICE, Romm repeatedly sought out child pornography over the internet. When he found images he "liked," he would "view them, save them to his computer, look at them for about five minutes[] and then delete them." Either while viewing the images or shortly thereafter, Romm twice masturbated. He described his activities as the "saving" and "downloading" of the images. While the images were displayed on screen and simultaneously stored to his cache, Romm could print them, email them, or save them as copies elsewhere. Romm could destroy the copy of the images that his browser stored to his cache. And according to detective Luckie, Romm did just that, either manually, or by instructing his browser to do so. Forensic evidence showed that Romm had enlarged several thumbnail images for better viewing. In short, given the indicia that Romm exercised control over the images in his cache, there was sufficient evidence for the jury to find that Romm committed the act of knowing possession.

————————

————————

16. [n.14] As an expert testified at trial, a "pop-up" is an unsolicited advertisement that will appear in a window that "pops up" unwanted in the user's web browser.

State v. Benjamin W. Mercer

782 N.W.2d 125 (Wis. Ct. App. 2010)

BROWN, C.J.

The issue in this case is whether individuals who purposely *view* digital images of child pornography on the Internet, even though the images are not found in the person's computer hard drive, nonetheless *knowingly possess* those images in violation of WIS. STAT. §948.12(1m) (2007–08). In the last decade, courts across the country have repeatedly decided that data recovered from a defendant's computer hard drive is evidence of possession. The evidence against Benjamin W. Mercer, however, comes from monitoring software that tracked his Internet browsing; there is no evidence that the contraband was in his computer hard drive. Mercer argues that this difference is significant because he interprets past cases as requiring evidence of an image in his computer hard drive in a place he knew could be accessed later, as well as further evidence that he manipulated the image. We disagree that the past cases present some kind of threshold regarding the evidence which must exist in order for the government to prove that a person knowingly possessed child pornography. Rather, those past cases merely chronicle the facts found in those cases, with the bottom line being that the defendant in each case affirmatively reached out for and obtained images of child pornography and had the ability to control those images. Since the monitoring software showed that Mercer repeatedly searched for and navigated within websites to click on images of child pornography and that Mercer had the ability to control those images, there was sufficient evidence for a jury to find knowing possession.

Mercer was the human resources director for the city of Fond du Lac, which, in December 2002, installed on its employees' work computers (including Mercer's) Sergeant Laboratories monitoring software. Mercer did not know about the monitoring software. Every time he logged in to his computer, the software collected information about what he did on his computer. The software tracked general information about computer use: the computer being used, which user was logged into that computer at any particular time, the amount of time the computer was used each day, and the program(s) being used. The city originally used the software to decide which computers to upgrade.

In 2004, the city found out that the software also had an alert function which would send an e-mail alert to the city whenever a user typed in an offensive or inappropriate word. The city activated the alert function and used the software's built-in dictionary. Then, if someone typed the keys spelling a word in the dictionary, the software would pick it up as questionable and send an e-mail alert to the city's information systems employees. The e-mail alert included information about which computer was the subject of the alert, the user's identity, the word that was typed, and the program that was being used. The software was capable of alerting on this information because, in addition to the general information mentioned above, the software kept a log of more specific information: every mouse click or keyboard stroke; if a keyboard stroke, which key was hit; the words in the title bar[n.2][17] of the program at the moment of that click or keystroke; and the time that action took place.

After the city started using the alert function, the information systems employees regularly received alerts regarding Mercer's computer use. The alerts suggested a pattern of Mercer surfing the Internet for, among other subjects, possible adult pornographic websites and pornographic websites involving children.

One of the city's information systems employees met with a police officer to review and recreate the content in the software logs for Mercer's computer use. The employee and officer reviewed the logs for Mercer's Internet Explorer use from June 2004 back through part of March 2004. They learned that Mercer had typed words such as "preteens," "preteen super models," "preteen hardcore," "lolita," and "lolidus" into the Yahoo!, Google, and MSN search engines and hit the enter key or clicked enter to get search results for those words. Based on the information from the title bar at each click, which was sometimes the actual web address, the information systems employees were able to use Internet Explorer to view the same websites that Mercer visited. The content of those websites included stories about children engaged in sexual acts and images of children in sexual situations. Then they expanded the time period to December 2002 through July 1, 2004, and reviewed what Mercer searched for with search engines like Yahoo!, Google, and MSN from December 2002 to July 1, 2004. They found that on fifty different days Mercer had performed numerous searches for "preteen," "lolita," and "lolidus," among other variations of those words, and clicked on links in the search results.

The State charged Mercer with fourteen counts of possession of child pornography in violation of WIS. STAT. § 948.12(1m). These charges stemmed from the use of his work computer on May 28, 2004. The State's case was, to a large extent, based on the testimony of the software's cofounder.

From this evidence, we relate the facts as follows: The computer user (Mercer) started at Yahoo!, then navigated to Perverts-R-Us (which, like Yahoo!, is a web portal to help a person navigate to and find other websites). Then the user clicked to enter "LOLITA NEWS: The Best Lolitas Here!" Lolita News contained a series of Internet magazines that people could click on and view. From there the user clicked to enter the magazine "Lolita LS-Flash," which showed up on the log as "Lolita-news .info/ls-flash.html." Then there was a click somewhere on LS-Flash that led the user to "Flash-005b.jpg," one of the charged images, and once the image was displayed the user clicked two more times within "Flash-005b.jpg." The next entry was back to LS-Flash, and then back to Lolita News. Next the user clicked to enter "LS-BARBIE" and clicked again to view "lsbar-007b-044.jpg," went back to "LS-BARBIE" to view another image, "Barbie-008a.jpg," and then to another one of the charged images. The user clicked four times while on the "Barbie-008a.jpg" image.

---

17. [n.2] The title bar is the horizontal bar that is generally displayed at the top of a computer program window. It bears the name of the program and a description of the contents displayed.

We will not repeat the entire log because the subsequent entries are similar. The software's cofounder testified that the clicks recorded in the log "indicate that the person is at each one of [the] particular magazines [linked to the Lolita-News website]; [the person is] going into the magazine and backing out; going in and backing out." They show the user going back to Lolita News and then clicking on one of the magazines and, once at the magazine, clicking back and forth to view images within each magazine before returning to Lolita News to choose a different magazine, like "LS-FANTASY," "LITTLE GUESTS" and "LS-LAND." Over the course of Mercer's web browsing that day, he returned to Yahoo! three times before returning to "LOLITA NEWS" and again clicking through the various magazines. The record also shows that Mercer navigated from Yahoo! to other nonpornographic websites, to other pornographic websites with lolita in the title, such as http://www.pornololita.info/cgi-bin/scj/out.cgi?link=lolita_bbs_pics, and to "Alt.Sex.Stories Text Repository."

The printout of the Lolita News homepage shows that the website states "The Best Lolita Portal" at the top, talks about how it has "24 Lolita Sites" with girls aged fourteen or younger, and then lists the lolita sites. The sites are the magazines Mercer visited (LS Dream, LS-Land, Touch-It, and so on), and Lolita News lists the sites on its homepage with a title, textual description, and a picture of young girls in various states of undress.

The jury also heard from a forensic expert that Mercer took steps to delete the place on his computer hard drive where the computer would automatically download any viewed images to (the "cache"). He had searched for the programs Evidence Eliminator and Window Washer, both of which are designed to delete Internet history (including the cache) and privacy information. And he searched the Windows Help Center for how to delete files associated with one's Internet browsing.

Mercer challenges the sufficiency of the evidence that he knowingly possessed the charged images. But the main theory driving Mercer's sufficiency of the evidence challenge does not depend on whether the historical facts supporting the verdict lacked the probative value and force sufficient to meet every essential element of the charged crime. Rather, the issue he raises is one of law — the application of a statute to a particular set of facts.

We start by examining the definition of the essential element at issue, knowing possession. *See* Wis. Stat. § 948.12(1m)(a); Wis JI— Criminal 2146A (May 2007). The statute states that: "Whoever possesses any undeveloped film, photographic negative, photograph, motion picture, videotape, or other recording of a child engaged in sexually explicit conduct under all of the following circumstances [is guilty of a class D felony]: (a) The person knows that he or she possesses the material." And the pattern jury instruction explains "possessed" as when "the defendant knowingly had actual physical control of the recording."

Cases sometimes refer to [the] concept [of] "constructive possession," which describes "circumstances that are sufficient to support an inference that the person exercised control over, or intended to possess, the item in question."

We previously addressed the meaning of knowing possession under Wis. Stat. § 948.12(1m) in *State v. Lindgren*, 275 Wis.2d 851, 687 N.W.2d 60, 2004 WI App. 159. Numerous other courts have also confronted this question in recent years. But in *Lindgren* and *all* of the other cases that we have found, the digital images were recovered from the defendant's hard drive. There is no forensic evidence in this case that the images were in Mercer's hard drive. And Mercer asserts that the lack of hard drive evidence makes all the difference because one cannot possess a digital image that is not in the hard drive. Mercer even has a name for the issue at hand. He characterizes this case as a "pure view" case.

We disagree with Mercer that this case falls so far on the viewing end of the possession-viewing spectrum that it represents a "pure view" case. The following hypothetical, advanced by a commentator in a legal journal, aptly describes what comes to our minds when we think of a "pure view" case. The same hypothetical also neatly contrasts "pure view" from what we ultimately believe is the situation in this case:

> Patrick Pedophile logs onto his computer and opens his web browser. He goes to a common search engine, like Google or Lycos, and types in several search terms including "lolita," "preteen nude pics," and "underage sex kittens." Upon receiving his search results, Patrick clicks on a particular website, which contains thumbnail images of child pornography. He then clicks on several of the thumbnail images to enlarge them and views them at his desk. As he is doing so, Patrick's coworker, Ian Innocent, happens to walk by Patrick's desk, where he stops to chat for a moment. When Ian arrives, he looks directly at Patrick's computer screen and views the precise same image that Patrick is viewing for several seconds.

> The distinction between Patrick and Ian's conduct is clear. Regardless of Ian's intent or knowledge about the images on Patrick's computer screen, Ian did not possess them. He had no control or dominion over them. He could not guide those images' destinies. He had no ability to move, alter, save, destroy, or choose the images. Ian merely viewed them. Contrast Ian's conduct with Patrick's conduct. Unlike Ian, Patrick sought the images out and affirmatively placed them on his computer screen. He had the ability . . . to move, alter, copy, save, destroy, and otherwise manipulate the image. Patrick had total ability to control and guide the image. In every sense, Patrick possessed the image at that time—and his possession was captured "on videotape" by his computer's cache file.

Ty E. Howard, *Don't Cache Out Your Case: Prosecuting Child Pornography Possession Laws Based on Images Located in Temporary Internet Files*, 19 Berkeley Tech. L.J. 1227, 1267–68 (2004). We do not consider Mercer to be in the same shoes as the fictional Ian. This is not a "pure view" case.

We also disagree with Mercer's assertion that, if the images were not found in his hard drive, he could not have possessed it as a matter of law. Mercer looks to past cases where the images *were* found in the computer hard drive and posits that in order to "possess" child pornography, the evidence *must* show that the image or images were found in the hard drive.

First, none of the cases have explicitly held that hard drive evidence is the sine qua non of a knowing possession case. Rather, some of the cases discuss possession in terms of what a user can do to control images in the hard drive, and some of the cases refer to what a user can do with images displayed on a computer screen from the Internet.

Legal commentators have also commented on the dangers of relying on cache evidence because of the automation of caching and the variation of knowledge among computer users about caching.

But computer forensic examiners, who specialize in the use of computer-related media for evidence, generally can recover the contents of a computer's cache and, with it, information about the user's browsing history. This browsing history includes the particular websites visited, the number of times visited, the degree of manipulation (such as enlarging, cutting, or pasting an image), and any downloading activity.

It seems to us that the facts and inferences derived from cache evidence is not all that different than that derived from the monitoring software employed by the city of Fond du Lac in this case. Both show which websites were visited and how often. Both show what the user searched for and how the user got to the website. Both record the computer user's web browsing activity. The only difference is that the evidence from the monitoring software device was instantly reviewable by system administrators without having to physically possess the computer.

Our impression of [the previously decided cases dealing with cache] is that courts are more concerned with how the defendants got to the website showing child pornography, than what the defendants actually did with the images. In all of the cases, the defendant *reached out* for the images. This fits with the definition of constructive possession: the user could save, print or take some other action to control the images, and the user affirmatively reached out for and obtained the images knowing that the images would be child pornography as shown by the pattern of web browsing. This may occur whether there is cache evidence or not. And that is the main point to be made here.

At oral argument, the State provided the following explanation of how viewing images and web browsing can constitute reaching out for images by describing the difference between "push technology" and "pull technology." In push technology, the receiver does not request the materials. The cyber equivalent is spam. The real world equivalent would be like walking on a route, which you cannot change, that has a newsstand displaying risqué magazines for passersby. As the State explained, people confronted with push technology "are not asking to see it, but it's there to view." In contrast, pull technology is where the receiver is asking for the materials. The cyber equivalent is clicking on a button and asking something to come to you.

Similarly, the real world equivalent would be like writing to a company and asking it to send you its marketing literature.

This distinction makes sense to us, because in pull technology the user knows what he or she is looking for and is making a request to obtain that material. So we conclude that an individual knowingly possesses child pornography when he or she affirmatively pulls up images of child pornography on the Internet and views those images knowing that they contain child pornography. Whether the proof is hard drive evidence or something else, such as the monitoring software here, should not matter because both capture a "videotape" of the same behavior. And images in either place can be controlled by taking actions like printing or copying the images.

Here, the evidence supporting the verdict tended to show, and the jury could find from it, that Mercer had a habit of surfing the Internet for pornography. He searched with terms associated with child pornography and looked at images and text stories. And his searches were not an isolated instance. He had searched using those terms on at least fifty different days. He was able to navigate directly to a web portal specific to sex. Moreover, on the day in question, he did not click on a website, see a child pornography image, and exit the website (indicating a mistake)—he clicked to look at a magazine and its images, had the image on his screen until he clicked back, at which point he looked at another magazine and its images and another and another and another. Then he left, did something else, and returned to look at still more magazines and images. And each time he pulled an image from the Internet onto his screen he controlled how long it was displayed on his screen and he had the ability to and knew how to print, save, or copy it. Moreover, the jury heard evidence from which it could infer that Mercer deleted the files where the forensic examiners would have found the child pornography stored in his hard drive. We conclude that there was sufficient evidence of knowing possession as a matter of law.

At the end of the day, the common thread underlying Mercer's arguments is the hypothesis that computers are only knowable to the technically savvy and he—not being of that ilk—could not have had the technical know-how necessary to "possess" pornography. For example, he contends that he has no real expertise in the caching process. But, while it is true that some computer-related issues may require expertise, that simply is not the case in many situations. People do not cower and sit in a corner every time the word "computer" is mentioned. Computers are becoming more and more a fact of everyday life. Technology issues aside, the facts before the jury were very clear and easy to understand. The jury could infer that an individual, who searches for a term associated with child pornography on *repeated* occasions, should be aware that he or she is controlling the request that child pornography be sent to him or her. And when that individual sees that the selected website shows images of child pornography and continues browsing through that website with the ability to control those images, a jury could conclude that the individual knowingly possessed the material. In this case, Mercer's *repetitive* searches for and navigation within child pornography websites show that this was not a person doing a search for a benign topic who just happened to mistakenly click on a website featuring child pornography. The evidence is sufficient to show knowing possession.

People v. James D. Kent

970 N.E.2d 833 (N.Y. 2012)

CIPARICK, J.

The question presented for our review is whether the evidence proffered at defendant's trial was legally sufficient to support his convictions for promoting a sexual performance by a child (Penal Law § 263.15) and possessing a sexual performance by a child (Penal Law § 263.16). We must consider, among other issues, the evidentiary significance of "cache files," or temporary Internet files automatically created and stored on a defendant's hard drive, and the defendant's awareness of the presence of such files. We conclude that where the evidence fails to show that defendant had such awareness, the People have not met their burden of demonstrating defendant's knowing procurement or possession of those files. We further conclude that merely viewing Web images of child pornography does not, absent other proof, constitute either possession or procurement within the meaning of our Penal Law.

The following evidence was adduced at defendant's trial. On May 26, 2005, defendant James D. Kent, a professor of public administration at a Dutchess County college, received a new office computer through a campus-wide technology upgrade. The files stored on the hard drive of the old computer were transferred to the new computer. On April 5, 2007, a student employee of the college's information technology department went to defendant's office in response to his complaints that his computer was malfunctioning. While running a virus scan of the computer's hard drive, the employee discovered a work folder containing numerous ".jpg" or picture files, displayed as "thumbnails," of scantily clad, prepubescent girls in provocative poses. When the virus scan failed to correct the computer's unresponsiveness, the employee removed defendant's hard drive and took it back to the IT office, where supervisors learned of the images. College administrators informed defendant that these images had been found on his computer, but defendant denied any knowledge of them. Approximately two weeks later, the college submitted defendant's hard drive to the Town of Poughkeepsie Police Department with a "Consent to Search" form signed by a college administrator.

Barry Friedman, an investigator in the computer forensic lab of the New York State Police, conducted a forensic analysis of defendant's hard drive using EnCase Software. Investigator Friedman explained that EnCase searches both allocated space, which contains data (including saved items or items sent to the "recycle bin") that is readily accessible to a user, and unallocated space, which contains material deleted from the allocated space and is inaccessible to a user. Defendant's computer contained Real Player, a downloadable media program used to play videos and music that maintains a "play" history. The computer also had two Internet browsers:

Internet Explorer and Mozilla Firefox. In addition to the default profile provided by Mozilla Firefox, a second profile under the name of "Jim" had been created.

The allocated space under the Jim profile on Mozilla Firefox contained a temporary Internet file known as a Web "cache." A cache contains images or portions of a Web page that are automatically stored when that page is visited and displayed on the computer screen; if the user visits the Web page again at a later date, the images are recalled from the cache rather than being pulled from the Internet, allowing the page to load more quickly. The cache under the Jim profile contained a .jpg image of a child pornography Web site called "School Backyard" that depicted children engaged in sexual intercourse with adults.

According to the EnCase software, the "School Backyard" page had been accessed on the morning of February 21, 2007. Within minutes of accessing "School Backyard," three other pages were accessed—two images of a young girl sitting in the front seat of her car with her wrists bound and a Web page labeled "Pedoland"—which were also stored in the Web cache. The cache contained several other Web pages labeled, among other things, "Best CP Sites Portal, the Best Lolita CP Sites," that provided links to child pornography Web sites. Additionally, the Real Player history included links to numerous videos with file names indicating that they contained child pornography that were accessed, some on multiple occasions, between 2005 and 2007. There was no evidence that defendant was aware either of the cache function of his computer or that any of these files were stored in the cache.

The allocated space on defendant's hard drive also contained a "My Documents" folder with subfolders labeled "cdocs" and another labeled "work," and an additional folder labeled "JK." The "cdocs" subfolder contained approximately 13,000 saved images of female children, whom Investigator Friedman estimated to be eight or nine years old, dressed in lingerie or bathing suits and many with their legs spread open. The "work" subfolder contained an additional 17,000 saved images of female children, some organized into further subfolders named for a particular child. The JK folder held a file labeled "porndef.pb," which contained a document that included the text of four messages dated between June 1999 and July 2000 and directed to the unidentified recipient "P.B." The messages apparently relate to a potential research project on the regulation of child pornography and include comments such as "sooner or later someone at this college is going to wonder why I keep looking at porno sites." A final message dated July 11, 2001 states:

> "Well, this last batch pretty much tears it. While, as somebody's father, I'm pretty appalled by this stuff, I also don't want to get arrested for having it. So let's do this—if this is a legitimate research project, let's write it up and tell the deans (and preferably also the cops) what we're doing and why. Otherwise, let's drop it in the most pronto possible fashion.

> "I don't even think I can mail the disk to you, or anyone else, without committing a separate crime. So I'll probably just go ahead and wipe them. You have the URLs if you want to pursue it.

"See you sooner or later, no doubt. Kent."

From the unallocated space on the computer, EnCase retrieved a video containing child pornography that had previously been downloaded and saved to the allocated space under the file name "Arina." EnCase also discovered over 130 .jpg images depicting children engaged in oral sex and sexual intercourse with dogs, adults and other children, children being penetrated by objects, and the lewd exhibition of the exposed genitals of female children. Like the "Arina" video, each of these images had been downloaded and stored in the allocated space of defendant's computer at some point between May 26, 2005 (the date that data was transferred from defendant's old computer to his new computer) and April 5, 2007 (the date the IT employee removed the hard drive) before the user deleted them, sending them to unallocated space. There was no evidence that defendant ever paid for access to any of the child pornography found on his computer.

Defendant was indicted on two counts of promoting a sexual performance by a child and 141 counts of possessing a sexual performance by a child. Counts 1 and 142 related, respectively, to defendant's alleged procurement and possession of the "School Backyard" Web page; counts 2 and 143 related, respectively, to defendant's alleged procurement and possession of the "Arina" video; counts 3 through 141 charged defendant with possession of the .jpg images recovered from the unallocated space of the hard drive. County Court found defendant guilty of both procurement counts (1 and 2) and 134 of the 141 possession counts, including counts 142 and 143. Defendant was sentenced to concurrent indeterminate prison terms of 1 to 3 years. The Appellate Division affirmed County Court's judgment.

Recognizing that "[t]he public policy of the state demands the protection of children from exploitation through sexual performances," the Legislature enacted article 263 of the Penal Law "to eradicate the social evil of child pornography." Penal Law § 263.15 provides that "[a] person is guilty of promoting a sexual performance by a child when, knowing the character and content thereof, he produces, directs or promotes any performance which includes sexual conduct by a child less than seventeen years of age." To "promote" means, among other things, "to procure," itself defined as "obtain, acquire . . . to get possession of by particular care or effort." Thus, "the term 'procure' . . . defines 'promote' for the purposes of Penal Law § 263.15 as simply the acquisition of child pornography, whether for personal consumption or for distribution to others." Penal Law § 263.16 provides that "[a] person is guilty of possessing a sexual performance by a child when, knowing the character and content thereof, he knowingly has in his possession or control any performance which includes sexual conduct by a child less than sixteen years of age."

For purposes of both the promotion and possession statutes, "performance" is defined as "any play, motion picture, photograph or dance." Furthermore, both crimes require that the defendant acted knowingly. The exercise of "[d]ominion or control is necessarily knowing, and such 'constructive possession' may qualify as knowing possession."

Defendant argues that merely "accessing and displaying" Web images of child pornography does not constitute procurement for purposes of Penal Law § 263.15. Defendant further contends that his possession convictions are invalid because Penal Law § 263.16 criminalizes the possession of tangible items only and that, absent proof that defendant was aware of his computer's cache function, he could not have knowingly possessed any item stored in the cache. For the reasons that follow, we agree with defendant's first proposition. We also agree that where a promotion or possession conviction is premised on cached images or files as contraband, the People must prove, at a minimum, that the defendant was aware of the presence of those items in the cache. We hold, however, that regardless of a defendant's awareness of his computer's cache function, the files stored in the cache may constitute evidence of images that were previously viewed; to possess those images, however, the defendant's conduct must exceed mere viewing to encompass more affirmative acts of control such as printing, downloading or saving.

Federal courts have held that for digital images to constitute evidence of knowing possession of child pornography, such images must be connected to something tangible (e.g., the hard drive), as they are when stored in a cache, and that the defendant must be aware of that connection.

The rule espoused by several other states and by the Appellate Division—that defendant's awareness of the automatic cache function is immaterial because it is not the cached files that constitute the contraband but the images previously displayed—is conceptually distinct as it does not rely on the tangibility of the image (i.e., its permanent placement on the defendant's hard drive and his ability to access it later) but on the fact that the image was, at one time, knowingly accessed and viewed.[n.4][18]

Like the federal courts to address the issue, we agree that where no evidence shows defendant was aware of the presence of the cached files, such files cannot underlie a prosecution for promotion or possession. This is necessarily so because a defendant cannot knowingly acquire or possess that which he or she does not know exists.

However, cached images can serve as evidence of defendant's prior viewing of images that were, at one time, resident on his computer screen. Such evidence, like a pattern of browsing for child pornography, is relevant to the mens rea of both crimes by showing that a defendant did not inadvertently access an illicit image or site or was not mistaken as to its content.

––––––––––––

18. [n.4] One legal commentator has described the distinction between these two approaches, deemed respectively, the "Present Possession" approach and "the Evidence Of" approach, as follows: "The first approach places legal significance on the images found in a cache . . . The second, alternative approach places legal significance on the images that the computer user sought out and placed on his computer screen. This approach holds that the copies of the images found in a cache constitute evidence of some prior (but no less real) knowing possession" (Ty E. Howard, *Don't Cache Out Your Case: Prosecuting Child Pornography Possession Laws Based on Images Located in Temporary Internet Files*, 19 BERKELEY TECH. L.J. 1227, 1254, 1255 [Fall 2004]).

Nonetheless, that such images were simply viewed, and that defendant had the theoretical capacity to exercise control over them during the time they were resident on the screen, is not enough to constitute their procurement or possession. We do not agree that "purposefully making [child pornography] appear on the computer screen—for however long the defendant elects to view the image—itself constitutes knowing control." Rather, some affirmative act is required (printing, saving, downloading, etc.) to show that defendant in fact exercised dominion and control over the images that were on his screen. To hold otherwise, would extend the reach of article 263 to conduct—viewing—that our Legislature has not deemed criminal.

The federal statute regulating conduct related to child pornography, 18 USC §2252A, provides a useful contrast. Section 2252A was amended in 2008 to provide that any person who either "knowingly possesses, *or knowingly accesses with intent to view*, any book, magazine, periodical, film, videotape, computer disk, or any other material that contains an image of child pornography" is subject to a fine and imprisonment. Neither provision of the Penal Law at issue here contains comparable language targeted toward the "pull technology" by which one accesses and views Internet images. The words that are employed—"procures" and "possesses"—would not, in ordinary speech, encompass the act of viewing.

Here, the "School Backyard" Web page was automatically stored in the cache in allocated space that was accessible to defendant. The People did not demonstrate that defendant knew that the page, or any other, for that matter, had been cached. While the cached page provided evidence that defendant previously viewed the site, the People presented no evidence that defendant downloaded, saved, printed or otherwise manipulated or controlled the image while it was on his screen. That defendant accessed and displayed the site, without more, is not enough. Thus, the evidence was insufficient to show that defendant knowingly possessed the "School Backyard" Web page, either in the form of the cached file or as an image on his screen. It follows, therefore, that there was not sufficient evidence that defendant procured the "School Backyard" page; defendant did not "get possession of [the page] by particular care or effort" as by downloading it. Thus, defendant's convictions under counts 1 and 142 should be reversed.

We agree with the Appellate Division, however, that defendant was properly convicted of promotion and possession of the "Arina" video, and possession of 132 images of child pornography recovered from the unallocated space on his computer. Investigator Friedman's testimony established that at some point defendant downloaded and/or saved the video and the images, thereby committing them to the allocated space of his computer, prior to deleting them. Thus, viewing the evidence in the light most favorable to the People, a rational factfinder could conclude that defendant acquired the video and exercised control over it and the images. That defendant did so knowingly was conclusively established by, among other things, copious evidence of his persistent pattern of browsing for child pornography sites; his meticulous cataloguing of thumbnail images of young, provocatively dressed girls; his deletion of illegal images and retention of legal ones; and defendant's messages to "P.B." discussing the pornographic content of the images and sites defendant perused.

Accordingly, the order of the Appellate Division should be modified by dismissing counts 1 and 142 of the indictment and remitting to County Court for resentencing and, as so modified, affirmed.

GRAFFEO, J. (concurring in result only).

Although it is not necessary for our Court to address these issues to resolve this case,[n.2][19] the majority has decided to consider whether the statutory bans on acquiring and possessing embrace the viewing of images of child pornography that are accessed on the Internet. The majority answers this question in the negative without engaging in an examination of the statutory text or purpose. Instead, it declares that viewing child pornography on the Internet is permissible and that "some affirmative act is required (printing, saving, downloading, etc.) to show that [the] defendant in fact exercised dominion and control over the images that were on his screen."

The result of the majority's analysis is that the purposeful viewing of child pornography on the Internet is now legal in New York. A person can view hundreds of these images, or watch hours of real-time videos of children subjected to sexual encounters, and as long as those images are not downloaded, printed or further distributed, such conduct is not proscribed. I am compelled to disagree because I believe that our Penal Law outlaws this purposeful activity.

Penal Law § 263.16 is directed at two distinct types of conduct: possession or control of child pornography. The word "possess" is restricted by language in another provision of the Penal Law to "tangible property." Since child pornography on the Internet is digital in format, it is intangible in nature and therefore cannot be "possessed" as that term is currently defined by the Penal Law. It goes without saying that in light of the majority's decision, the Legislature needs to revisit this definition if its intention has been to extend the scope of proscribed conduct to the intentional Internet viewing of child pornography.

But the breadth of the term "control" is not so limited by statutory definition. Consequently, this term should be interpreted in the manner that it is commonly understood. The usual meaning of "control" is to have power over or the ability to manage (*see e.g.* Webster's Third New International Dictionary, Unabridged

---

19. [n.2] Defendant was not charged with looking at the "School Backyard" images on the Internet. The theory of the prosecution was that he knowingly caused the images to be placed into the Internet cache (for count 1, charging promotion) and knowingly possessed them during a certain period of time that they were in the cache (for count 142, charging possession). The People introduced no proof at trial that defendant was aware of how caching worked, they conceded that it is an automatic process that most computer users are unfamiliar with, and the prosecutor told the judge that defendant did not, in fact, realize that the images were being saved in the cache. Based on those facts and the People's limited theory of the case, there is insufficient evidence that defendant knowingly procured or possessed the "School Backyard" images so I agree that counts 1 and 142 require dismissal.

[Merriam-Webster 2012], control, available at http://unabridged.merriam-webster
.com; Black's Law Dictionary 378 [9th ed 2009]). The question, then, is does a person
exercise power—that is, control—over child pornography when that person knowingly accesses and views such material on the Internet? In my view, this question can
be answered in the affirmative.

It is certainly possible to control something that is intangible—a fact that the
majority concedes in accepting that Penal Law § 263.16 applies to the saving or
downloading of child pornography onto a computer hard drive. When using the
Internet, a person must first decide to search for Web sites that contain child pornography and, once they are located, to choose a particular item to observe. Once
the desired image appears on the screen, the user must then engage in a variety of
decisions that exemplify control over the displayed depiction: continue looking at
the image or delete it; decide how long to view it; once the viewing is complete, to
keep the image in its own tab or browser window, or simply move on to some other
image or Web page; save the image to the hard drive or some other device; or print
it in a tangible format. Through this process, the viewer exercises power over the
image because he manages and controls what happens to it.

A few relatively common examples of control over Web pages illustrate this point.
When the Internet is used to conduct online banking, such as to transfer funds
between accounts, the user exercises control over the Web site displayed on the
screen by, for example, authorizing the transfer. The same is true about shopping on
the Internet—a person enters ordering and payment information and then approves
the transaction. Even when browsing news Web sites, the user controls the images
that appear on the screen by deciding whether to keep reading an article, click a
hyperlink, go to another site or exit the browser altogether.

Hence, the use of the term "control" in the statute can reasonably be interpreted
to cover precisely what the majority says it does not—consciously acquiring and
viewing child pornography on the Internet. If the majority's concern in adopting the
limited scope of "possession or control" is to prevent the prosecution of individuals
who inadvertently or unintentionally access such images on their computers, then it
is misplaced. I certainly share the concern—and there is no question that the Legislature did not intend that persons who view such material accidentally be prosecuted.

Under Penal Law § 263.16, the People must establish that defendant knowingly
possessed or controlled the images, "knowing the character and content thereof."
The People can prove this mens rea element through conduct such as that imported
by the majority into the control element—through storage, printing, forwarding
and the like. But this is not the only conduct that would support an inference that the
possession or control was "knowing." That images were intentionally accessed can be
inferred in any number of ways, such as evidence establishing the number of items
viewed on certain occasions, the frequency with which such images were viewed,
whether other images have been saved and the length of time spent browsing for
child pornography. This analysis regarding the consistency and quantity of viewings

will shield the inadvertent viewer of child pornography from prosecution. The more times a person accesses and views pornographic images of children, the less likely it is that the behavior was innocent or inadvertent. And, of course, the number of persons who have access to a certain computer and the availability of passwords or other personal information are also relevant inquiries. By adopting a narrow interpretation of the possession or control requirement, the majority has effectively conflated the mens rea element with the control element, resulting in a holding that explicitly legalizes the acquisition and viewing of child pornography over the Internet *even when that activity is clearly intentional.* This result is directly at odds with the relevant statutory language. When the promotion statutes were first created, the Legislature declared that the "public policy of the state demands the protection of children from exploitation through sexual performances" since the sale of child pornography was "abhorrent to the fabric of our society." It is beyond dispute that exploitation occurs regardless of whether child pornography is in a tangible format or on line, and an image does not become any less exploitive because it is viewed on a computer. The presence of an image on the Internet arguably exacerbates the harm inflicted on the child victim given its global availability and ease of access. And with the high quality of digital photography, the identity of children subjected to this sexual abuse is more apparent and may be preserved for their entire lives.

This is why in 1996—after the advent of widespread Internet usage and the digital transformation of society—the Legislature sought to ban the purposeful possession of child pornography. "Permitting the possession of child pornography is, in fact, extending permission to the sexual exploitation of children; after all, some child was indeed exploited in the production of such materials." Possession alone, without the conditions imposed by the majority, was seen as the scourge to be alleviated: "Someone who possesses child pornography does so at the expense of an exploited child, and society cannot hope to eradicate this evil unless the market for these perverse materials is destroyed."

It is important to note that a person need not purchase child pornography in order to violate the statutory ban. The protection of children was the impetus for the statutes and whether or not the viewer pays for an image does not lessen the emotional and physical damage experienced by the child. I concur with the broad consensus that a child is not just exploited when he or she is photographed or filmed while engaging in sexual activity. That child is violated each time the image is accessed and viewed simply because he or she never consented—and could not consent—to the dissemination of that image. Irreparable harm occurs even if no money changes hands.

I part company with the majority on this critical point. The market for child pornography enlarges with the knowing viewing of these images, regardless of whether a price has been paid by the viewer and regardless of whether the image is downloaded or printed, because the more frequent the images of children engaged in sexual conduct are accessed, the more the creators produce to satisfy the growing demand, which results in more children being coerced and groomed for the sex trade. And, perhaps most tragically, some children abused in this fashion become abusers themselves later in life, creating a vicious cycle of violence against children that the Internet helps to perpetuate.

Furthermore, there's no question that the purveyors of child pornography are experts at marketing their products. Electronic availability provides virtually instantaneous access to a wide array of child pornography in a relatively anonymous fashion—something that is presumably far easier, quicker and safer to the consumer than searching for a person or place that sells such material in a physical format. Images of children in sexually suggestive poses are made available at no cost on the Internet in hopes of whetting the appetite of viewers to move on to paid subscription Web sites that display more graphic portrayals of children having sex. From the viewpoint of these child victims, there is no such thing as a harmless viewing of their images. In addition, the expansion of the consumer pool eventually fuels the profit-making motive behind the distribution of child pornography and causes "an explosion in the market for child pornography, leading, in turn, to increased access, creation, and distribution of these abusive images" (US. Dept. of Justice, The National Strategy for Child Exploitation Prevention and Interdiction: A Report to Congress, at 138 [2010] [emphasis omitted]). The majority's decision to allow the knowing acquisition and viewing of child pornography will, unfortunately, lead to increased consumption of child pornography by luring new viewers who were previously dissuaded by the potential for criminal prosecution. I firmly believe that the Legislature recognized the pervasive nature of this criminal activity when it drafted the statutory text.

The facts of the case before us demonstrate why the Legislature believed that it was so important to criminalize this type of conduct. The "School Backyard" images were offered for free to viewers in order to entice Web visitors to pay to enter the site for access to additional child pornography. Although this case involves the defendant's viewing of no-fee pornographic images of children on the Internet, the majority does not—and cannot—dispute that the Legislature did not make a distinction between the intentional viewing of child pornography on the Internet that is paid for or viewed at no cost. I believe that the Legislature had ample justification for criminalizing all purposeful acquisition and consumption of child pornography irrespective of whether or not it was purchased. I therefore would hold that knowingly accessing and viewing child pornography on the Internet constitutes criminal conduct under our Penal Law.

Smith, J. (concurring).

I join Judge Ciparick's majority opinion, and add a few words to respond to Judge Graffeo's thoughtful concurrence. Judge Graffeo argues, in substance, that we can best effectuate the Legislature's intention by reading the statutes expansively, to include as many "consumers" as the statutory language can reasonably be interpreted to permit. I do not agree. Under Judge Graffeo's reading, someone who does no more than click on a link for the purpose of looking at a pornographic picture for free—someone who has never interacted with a child victim, has never copied, downloaded or saved a pornographic picture of a child, and has never put a penny in the pocket of a child pornographer — is subject to up to seven years in prison for a first offense. This is surely a stringent punishment for someone whom many would think more pathetic than evil. Nor can we safely assume that bringing as many consumers as possible within the reach of the law is the most effective way to lessen or eliminate the trade: A policy of draconian enforcement directed at the most minor and peripheral of users is perhaps no more likely to eliminate child pornography than a similar policy would be to eliminate illegal drugs.

———————

Notes

1. Knowing access with intent to view. In response to difficulties in proving possession for Internet related child pornography activities, Title 18 U.S.C. § 2252A(a) was amended to prohibit a person who:

> (5)(B) knowingly possesses, or *knowingly accesses with intent to view*, any book, magazine, periodical, film, videotape, computer disk, or any other material that contains an image of child pornography[.]

(Emphasis added). Most states, however, still only prohibit possession.

2. Possession vs. viewing child pornography: should there be a difference? Consider the following. In *Paroline v. United States*, 134 S. Ct. 1710 (2014), the Court considered the amount of restitution, if any, a person who pled guilty to possession of child pornography would be required to pay to one of the victims depicted in images he possessed. Paroline admitted to possessing between 150 and 300 images of child pornography, which included two that depicted the sexual exploitation of a young girl, now a young woman, who went by the pseudonym "Amy." The Court observed:

> The demand for child pornography harms children in part because it drives production, which involves child abuse. The harms caused by child pornography, however, are still more extensive because child pornography is "a permanent record" of the depicted child's abuse, and "the harm to the child is exacerbated by [its] circulation." Because child pornography is now traded with ease on the Internet, "the number of still images and videos memorializing the sexual assault and other sexual exploitation of children, many very young in age, has grown exponentially."

> One person whose story illustrates the devastating harm caused by child pornography is the respondent victim in this case. When she was eight and nine years old, she was sexually abused by her uncle in order to produce child pornography. Her uncle was prosecuted, required to pay about $6,000 in restitution, and sentenced to a lengthy prison term. The victim underwent an initial course of therapy beginning in 1998 and continuing into 1999. By the end of this period, her therapist's notes reported that she was "'back to normal'"; her involvement in dance and other age-appropriate activities, and the support of her family, justified an optimistic assessment. Her

functioning appeared to decline in her teenage years, however; and a major blow to her recovery came when, at the age of 17, she learned that images of her abuse were being trafficked on the Internet. The digital images were available nationwide and no doubt worldwide. Though the exact scale of the trade in her images is unknown, the possessors to date easily number in the thousands. The knowledge that her images were circulated far and wide renewed the victim's trauma and made it difficult for her to recover from her abuse. As she explained in a victim impact statement submitted to the District Court in this case:

> "Every day of my life I live in constant fear that someone will see my pictures and recognize me and that I will be humiliated all over again. It hurts me to know someone is looking at them — at me — when I was just a little girl being abused for the camera. I did not choose to be there, but now I am there forever in pictures that people are using to do sick things. I want it all erased. I want it all stopped. But I am powerless to stop it just like I was powerless to stop my uncle. . . . My life and my feelings are worse now because the crime has never really stopped and will never really stop. . . . It's like I am being abused over and over and over again."

> The victim says in her statement that her fear and trauma make it difficult for her to trust others or to feel that she has control over what happens to her.

The full extent of this victim's suffering is hard to grasp. Her abuser took away her childhood, her self-conception of her innocence, and her freedom from the kind of nightmares and memories that most others will never know. These crimes were compounded by the distribution of images of her abuser's horrific acts, which meant the wrongs inflicted upon her were in effect repeated; for she knew her humiliation and hurt were and would be renewed into the future as an ever-increasing number of wrongdoers witnessed the crimes committed against her.

§ 13.4 Proving at Trial That the Image Depicts a Real Child

United States v. Tom Vig

167 F.3d 443 (8th Cir. 1999)

BEAM, CIRCUIT JUDGE.

Tom Vig took his personal home computer to PC Doctor, a computer repair and service center, in Sioux Falls, South Dakota. Vig informed James Roby, service manager at PC Doctor, that the computer was not working properly because of something that had been downloaded off the Internet. While repairing the computer,

Roby came across computer images of children engaged in various forms of sexual activity.

A few days later, Matthew Miller, an FBI Special Agent met with Tom Vig concerning the allegation of child pornography on his computer. During the meeting, Tom Vig admitted to Miller that the computer was his and that he had seen and downloaded pictures of nude children out of curiosity. Miller requested and received Tom Vig's consent to seize and examine the computer. The following day, Miller examined the computer at PC Doctor and confirmed the existence of several images of children engaged in sexual activity on the computer's C and D hard drives. On February 24, Miller had a phone conversation with Tom Vig, during the course of which, Tom Vig explained to Miller that he used a special program to access and search various news groups on the Internet and that it was while he was in these news groups that he had seen and downloaded pictures of nude children onto the "C" drive. Miller also spoke with Tom Vig's son, Donovan Vig, who told Miller that he too accessed news groups where he had frequently seen pictures of nude children, some of whom appeared to be between five and six years old. According to Miller, but disputed by Donovan Vig at trial, Donovan Vig also admitted that he had downloaded such pictures but that he did not know why he did so.

Donovan Vig claims that the district court erred in denying his motion for judgment of acquittal because the government did not present sufficient evidence showing that the subjects of the visual depictions were real minors as required under the statute. *See* 18 U.S.C. § 2252(a)(4)(B)(i) & (ii).[n.10][20] In reviewing the sufficiency of the evidence, we consider it in the light most favorable to the jury verdict and accept all reasonable inferences from the evidence which tend to support the jury verdict. Vig's specific argument is that modern technology can create images so similar to a human being that it would be difficult to decipher what they are by just looking at them. Technology, he speculates, might create computer-generated images that look exactly like real children. He concludes that because the only evidence the government presented to show that the images were of real children were the images themselves, the government failed to meet its burden of proof. We disagree.

The images were viewed by the jury which was in a position to draw its own independent conclusion as to whether real children were depicted. Furthermore, the jury was aided in its observations by Dr. Rich Kaplan, an associate professor of pediatrics with a specialty in child maltreatment. Dr. Kaplan testified that at least one of the subjects from the image or images found in each of the thirteen files charged against Vig, except one, was a minor.

Vig, nevertheless, argues that although Dr. Kaplan may have testified that the subjects were minors, he failed to testify that they were real minors and not computer-generated images. We note, however, that the defense failed to cross-examine or in

---

20. [n.10] For purposes of this section, "minor" is defined as "any person under the age of eighteen years." 18 U.S.C. § 2256(1).

any way rebut the testimony elicited from Dr. Kaplan. Vig produced no expert evidence at trial to show that the images were computer generated or other than what they appeared to be. In essence, Vig's claim that the images may not have been of real children is purely speculative and we do not think that the government, as part of its affirmative case, was required to negate what is merely unsupported speculation. Proof beyond a reasonable doubt does not require the government to produce evidence which rules out every conceivable way the pictures could have been made without using real children. We think that the government presented sufficient evidence from which a jury could reasonably infer that the subjects of the visual depictions were actual minors engaging in sexually explicit conduct.

——————

United States v. Anthony Marchand

308 F. Supp. 2d 498 (D.N.J. 2004)

HOCHBERG, DISTRICT JUDGE.

Anthony Marchand is accused of possessing Child Pornography. The Defendant waived his right to a jury trial. Therefore, this Court is responsible for both findings of fact and conclusions of law. The issues for this Court are: 1) whether the images that the Defendant possessed depicted real minors and 2) whether the Defendant knew that the images he possessed depicted real minors.

Dr. Anthony Marchand was employed by Atlantic Health Systems as director of the pathology lab at Overlook Hospital in Summit, New Jersey. In October or November of 2000, the hospital experienced substantial problems with its computer network. During an investigation into the cause of these problems, a network engineer for the hospital noticed that Dr. Marchand's computer was accessing and downloading imagery from the internet, resulting in massive re-transmissions on the network. These re-transmissions would cause the network to crash. In April 2001, new firewall software was installed, due to the problems the hospital had experienced with the network. In addition, AHS installed a sniffer to monitor traffic through the AHS firewall in an effort to identify internet use that violated AHS' policy.

Dr. Marchand used a computer designated OBE, with the password "amarchand" in his office at Overlook. Between April and August 2001, the OBE computer generated sniffer alerts several times a week while being operated by Dr. Marchand. AHS then assigned a static IP address to Computer OBE to make it easier for the sniffer to trace information to and from Computer OBE and the Internet. Monitoring of the sniffer revealed that Dr. Marchand accessed a variety of web sites that appeared to display child pornography. For example, the sniffer program indicated that the web sites accessed by the OBE computer contained information such as "free illegal site," "free illegal kds," "illegal ki()s porno video," "illegally shocking 3-11y.o," and "_real_illegal_lolitas archive."

The Government conducted a search of Dr. Marchand's office and office computer. When Dr. Marchand was informed that a search warrant for child pornography was being executed in his office, he accompanied the FBI agents and hospital staff to another office where he answered questions. He also handed several computer disks to Special Agent William DeSa. Later in the interview, Agent DeSa stated that his use of the term child pornography referred to "actual kids engaging in sexual activity, either with children or with adults."

Dr. Marchand stated that he had additional images at home, and that he thought he had approximately 500 images of child pornography. Dr. Marchand then accompanied Agent DeSa and Special Agent Tanya Lamb DeSa to his home, where he turned over several additional CDs and a computer. Dr. Marchand told Agent Lamb that collecting these images ". . . was a hobby, that he didn't realize that it was illegal or improper for him to have for personal enjoyment." Dr. Marchand also explained to Agent Lamb "that some of the images . . . on the CDs . . . were images that he had morphed."[n.8][21]

The Government introduced into evidence 35 images from the total number seized. The evidence depicts prepubescent children engaged in sexually explicit conduct. The following is a description of a tiny sample of the images in evidence: 1) prepubescent female digitally manipulating an erect male penis; 2) prepubescent female being forced to perform fellatio on an adult male penis while the adult male is physically restraining her with his body; 3) prepubescent female being vaginally penetrated by an adult male penis; 4) prepubescent female and prepubescent male performing fellatio on adult male; 5) prepubescent female performing fellatio on an adult male; 5) prepubescent female being vaginally penetrated by an adult male while a second male stands behind her masturbating his erect male penis; 6) prepubescent female whose head is being held by the hair about to be forced to perform fellatio.

The children in each of the 35 images look real to the viewer. There is no indication in any of the pictures to alert the viewer that the image was created other than with the use of real children. The lighting in the images appears as it would in a photograph. The children's physical characteristics and their often highly expressive facial features are visible in great detail. A staple is visible in one of the images, indicating that the picture was taken from a compilation of multiple pages, such as a centerfold from a magazine. Some of the children are the subjects of a series[n.11][22] of pictures. In each of the pictures within one series, the child depicted has the same appearance, and other details of the images do not vary.

The children in the images range in age from three to fifteen. The Government's expert, Dr. Robert Johnson, estimated the age of the children by comparing the level of development of the children depicted in the images with the stages of sexual maturation designed by John Tanner ("the Tanner Scale"). The Tanner Scale shows pubic hair at specific stages and the age at which it is most likely to occur and the

---

21. [n.8] The Defendant used the term morphed to mean that he had in some way manipulated the images using the computer.
22. [n.11] A series refers to more than one picture of the same child.

breast development in females and the genitalia, penis, and testicle development in males.[n.12][23]

Eleven of the images introduced were earlier published as photographs in child pornography magazines that were printed prior to 1986, a date when computer technology to create realistic virtual images of human beings did not exist. Eight of the images introduced depict actual identified and named children from the United States, England, and Brazil, who had been the subject of investigations by law enforcement into the sexual abuse they suffered. Six of the images were part of two different series of photographs. Each of the images had a file name, and Dr. Marchand organized them into folders. He named the subdirectory containing these folders, "child."

The main thrust of the Defense was to show that technology exists to create realistic virtual images of child pornography that are indistinguishable from real images of child pornography, and that nothing in the bit structure of the digitized computer image would inform a diligent observer that the image was real rather than virtual. This defense was presented in order to rebut the Government's proofs that the images possessed by the Defendant were of real human children and to create reasonable doubt as to whether Dr. Marchand knew that the images were real rather than virtual from information available to him at the time he possessed the images.

Computer software such as POSER was presented by the Defense. POSER is a tool for artists to use in creating virtual images of people. Although the Defense did not submit any images that had been created using POSER, the Government introduced a limited number of virtual images of clothed adults as examples of what POSER can do. Two of these images were part of a recent contest held by POSER. No nude adults or children were adduced nor were any virtual images of sexually aroused body parts.

The degree to which the images created with POSER appear real and the accuracy of the details depend on the skill of the artist. For example, the software does not create details such as hair growth or vein visibility through skin, although POSER will adjust the size of each body part to be in proportion with the size of the overall human figure. Unlike images that are created by manipulating and "cutting and pasting" pre-existing images, images created with POSER will not contain internal inconsistencies in the background, known as artifacts, which indicate that the pictures are not real. However, when backgrounds other than those created by POSER are imported into the images, POSER will not automatically create proper lighting effects, leaving it to the artist to ensure that the lighting effects, such as shadows cast by one body upon an adjacent figure or upon the ground, appear realistic. The

---

23. [n.12] Some of the children were too young to be classified according to the Tanner scale. For these pictures, Dr. Johnson estimated the ages of the children depicted using his 30 years of experience in treating children.

pictures that the Defendant's expert characterized as indicative of pictures created with POSER do not appear at all realistic to the viewer.

The Government must also prove beyond a reasonable doubt that the Defendant knew that the images he possessed depicted real minors engaged in sexually explicit conduct. *U.S. v. X-Citement Video, Inc.*, 513 U.S. 64, 78 (1994). In *X-Citement Video*, the Court held that the term "knowingly" refers to the minority age of the persons depicted and the sexually explicit nature of the material. Thus, the Government [must] prove that the defendant knew the images he possessed depicted real children engaged in sexually explicit conduct.

The Government presented evidence that: 1) eleven of the images were taken from magazines created prior to the invention of computer technology that might make it possible to digitally create such images; 2) law enforcement agents from the U.S., England, and Brazil could positively identify by name the children in eight of the pictures as children whom they had met in person at a time not distant from the age that the child was when he or she was photographed; and 3) an opinion, from a qualified expert who reliably studied the images, that the physical development of the children depicted in the 35 images corresponds to the Tanner scale designed to show the level of physical development that children reach at different ages.

The Government linked the pre-1986 magazine photographs to the images that the Defendant downloaded from the internet. The Government's computer expert testified that one of the ways to determine whether an image depicts real children is to compare the image to those in the FBI's Child Exploitation and Obscenity Reference File. The Reference File contains approximately 10,000 images of scanned child pornography that were taken when computer technology was so primitive that a sound inference could be drawn that an image found in the Reference File depicts a real child. Eleven images possessed by Dr. Marchand matched the images in the Reference File and are found to be images of real minors engaged in sexually explicit conduct.

The Government also adduced proof in the form of direct witness identification of real children in eight of the images in evidence. These witnesses identified the children who appeared in the pictures, having met the children during law enforcement investigations into the abuse that these children had suffered.

Officer James Feehan of the Police Department in Peoria, Illinois positively identified the child in G122 as Melissa, who was between nine and ten years old when her father took pornographic pictures of her and distributed them over the internet. During his investigation, Officer Feehan met Melissa when she was fifteen years old. He testified that Melissa looked nearly the same at that age as she had looked five or six years earlier when the pornographic pictures were taken.

Special Agent John Brunell of the Kansas City Division of the FBI positively identified Chelsea as the child portrayed in G118. Agent Brunell met Chelsea when she was fifteen years old, while he was investigating the abuse she had suffered. The photographs of Chelsea that he seized during this investigation portray the same child who is depicted in G118. The title of the file containing Chelsea's image is "11yoposing13. jpg," suggesting to the Defendant that Chelsea was eleven years old when this photograph was taken.

Dr. Helio Sant'Anna e Silva, Jr., the Chief of Federal Police in the State of Santa Caterina, Brazil, identified the children in G115, G116, and G117. These images depict real children S.R.O.V., A.D.S.N., and W.R.O., who were ten, fourteen, and twelve years old, respectively when the pictures were taken. Dr. Silva was able to positively identify these children because he met them in the course of his work.

G113, G125, and G128 depict a family of child victims from the United Kingdom, including Helen and Gavin. Officer Sharon Girling of the National Crime Squad in London positively identified these children in the images, having met the children during the investigation of their abuse. Helen was approximately nine years old when the photographs were taken, and Gavin was under the age of eleven.

This evidence leaves no reasonable doubt that the images depict real children.

The Court has reviewed evidence regarding: 1) the appearance of the images; 2) the number of images; 3) the number and identity of web sites the Defendant accessed; 4) the language used in the web sites; 5) the mode and manner by which the Defendant viewed and stored the images; 6) the Defendant's state of mind; and 7) the available computer technology and manual skill required to create realistic virtual images, including a small sample of such images posted on the internet and created with the software most frequently discussed by the Defense. From this evidence, this Court must determine whether there is sufficient evidence from which an inference can be drawn beyond a reasonable doubt that the Defendant knew that the images he possessed were of real children engaged in sexually explicit conduct.

The knowledge element can be proven through direct and/or circumstantial evidence of actual knowledge and through a finding of willful blindness. "The Government may prove that a person acted knowingly by proving beyond a reasonable doubt that that person deliberately closed his eyes to what otherwise would have been obvious to him. One cannot avoid responsibility for an offense by deliberately ignoring what is obvious." To find knowledge based on willful blindness, it is not enough that a reasonable person would have been aware of the high probability of the truth. The Defendant himself must have been aware of the high probability that the images depicted real children. The Defendant's stupidity or negligence in not knowing is not sufficient to support a finding of knowledge based on willful blindness.

The Defendant argues that the application of willful blindness is not appropriate in this case because a computer can create virtual images of children that appear realistic. While the Court allowed the Defendant to introduce a Congressional Finding and the Solicitor General's argument in *Free Speech Coalition*, both of which suggested that the technology exists to create virtual images that are difficult to distinguish from real children, Congress also found that the technology will remain prohibitively expensive for the foreseeable future. Moreover, to determine the proper weight to give these findings, this Court must consider the context in which they were made and their lack of specificity. These were general conclusory statements by speakers unaware of the facts of this case. The Court does, however, consider the Congressional Finding and the Solicitor General's argument in determining whether reasonable doubt exists as to this Defendant's state of knowledge that his images portrayed real children in sexually explicit conduct.

This Court has viewed the images itself in considering whether reasonable doubt exists as to Dr. Marchand's knowledge that the children depicted in the images were real. All of the children in the 35 images look utterly real. The level of detail of the children's features in all of the images contrasts startlingly with the sample of POSER virtual images adduced as evidence of the best examples of what virtual-image technology can do. A staple is visible in the center seam of one of the images, which clearly indicated that the image was of a photograph previously stapled into printed matter. Some of the children were depicted in series. Such accurate series would be extremely difficult to create virtually without error. The sexual development of each child corresponded correctly to the age of each child, as evidenced by Dr. Johnson's testimony. The features and traits of the children in the images can be matched to a particular age range. For example, the level of breast development in images of a prepubescent girl corresponds appropriately to the level of pubic hair depicted. It is difficult enough for an artist working with virtual technology to accomplish this feat as to one image, let alone to repeat such mastery each time a child at a different age of prepubescence is created. This feat would be difficult to achieve even if the artist had the training and expertise of Dr. Johnson to know how much pubic development to show in order to correspond to the age of the child depicted in each of the images. Dr. Marchand, a trained medical professional, would have seen how accurate the level of sexual development was in the prepubescent nudes he saw.

The multiplicity of images and the fact that the Defendant downloaded them from different web sites also supports a finding that Dr. Marchand knew that at least one of the images depicted a real child. Could the Defendant have thought that each of the 35 images, downloaded from many unrelated web sites, was each digitally created by an artist who was skillful enough to complete the task so extraordinarily realistically? It is not as though Dr. Marchand confined himself to one web site which he believed was dedicated to virtual images. Is there reasonable doubt that this Defendant knew that in surfing the web for diverse child pornography sites, he would find at least one picture of a real child engaged in sexually explicit conduct?

In addition to the 35 images themselves, the Government also presented direct evidence regarding the Defendant's state of mind. Dr. Marchand defended himself in his interview with Agent Lamb by saying, *inter alia*, that he did not know it was illegal to possess the images and that some of the images were morphed (digitally manipulated using parts of different real children) on the CDs that he created. By distinguishing between pictures that were morphed and those that were not, the Defendant certainly implied that he believed that the "un-morphed" images depicted real children. Dr. Marchand attempted to exculpate his conduct by claiming that some images were morphed, but his effort at exculpation never claimed that some of the images were virtual. Moreover, the FBI agents told Dr. Marchand that they were interested in pictures of "actual kids engaging in sexual activity, either with children or with adults," and Dr. Marchand responded by saying that he had about 500 images of child pornography. This also sheds light on his state of mind. The Defendant's characterization of 500 of his images as child pornography, especially in light of his effort to distinguish between those that were morphed and those that were not, supports a strong inference that he knew that at least one depicted a real child.

The Defense did prove that software like POSER exists and can be used to create virtual images. In order to be persuaded by the Defendant's argument that the existence of POSER creates reasonable doubt, the fact finder must consider whether the Defendant believed that this virtual software was so widely used in 2002, with such consistent skill, that 35 different realistic action images of nude children and adults, including several in a single image, would appear on a wide range of child pornographic web sites. The Government introduced proof that POSER-created images do not look even remotely realistic. No POSER-created image was adduced of a single realistic-looking human, even fully clothed. No evidence of virtual, nude, sexually-aroused adults or virtual, nude, prepubescent children was adduced. No virtual action image was introduced. When asked whether the POSER images introduced into evidence were typical of the type of images that could be created using POSER, the Defendant's computer and internet technology expert testified that the images were indicative, though not necessarily typical, of the kind of images that could be created using POSER. Not one looked like a real person. Yet, every picture that the Defendant possessed appears absolutely real. Even the lighting and the shadows in each of the pictures is perfectly consistent with the various backgrounds contained in the images, a highly difficult feat to accomplish virtually. Even the Defendant's computer expert, when asked to point out those images that did not look like real photographs, could only point to one image, G121, and no others. Moreover, the expert conceded that when he looked at the pictures, he thought they were real.

Finally, this Court considers the testimony provided by Defendant's computer expert who testified that it is impossible to determine whether an image contains a picture of a real child or a virtually-created child, by examining the bit structure of the computer file. However, the bit structure for at least one of the Defendant's images did show that it was created by a digital camera, suggesting a photographic process rather than a virtual artistic process. Moreover, bit structure is a bit of a red herring. It is the appearance of the pictures themselves, the Defendant's own words, the lack of evidence that it is feasible to create large numbers of life-like, virtual, nude, prepubescent children with correct levels of sexual development, and the lack of evidence that it is feasible to create virtual, anatomic, sub-dural sexual arousal, the number of web sites which the Defendant visited, and the evidence presented regarding the Defendant's state of mind, that are most probative to a fact finder when assessing the Defendant's knowledge.

In this case, the evidence proves beyond a reasonable doubt that the Defendant knew that at least one of the pictures contained an image of a real child engaged in sexually explicit activity. The facts in this case also prove beyond a reasonable doubt that Dr. Marchand was aware of the high probability that the pictures depicted real minors and that he deliberately ignored the truth and was not merely foolish or negligent in failing to realize that the images portrayed real children. If the Defendant did not have actual knowledge that real children were portrayed, then he deliberately avoided knowing the truth.

———————

Notes

1. The National Center for Missing and Exploited Children has data bases of images of known children. *See* www.missingkids.com. The Center has experts and resources to help prosecutors, including providing names of persons (such as detectives) who are able to testify that the image is of a real child.

2. *Poser* is an example of a software that creates virtual images. A gallery of virtual (and nonpornographic) images using the software is available at: https://my .smithmicro.com/poser-photo-gallery.html#1.

3. Magazine images: it can be proven that an image is that of a real child by showing publication prior to computer image alteration/creation technology becoming commercially available. *See United States v. Guagliardo*, 278 F.3d 868 (9th Cir. 2002).

§ 13.5 Common Search and Seizure Issues in Child Pornography Cases

The advent of digital evidence is having a profound impact on Fourth Amendment principles and analysis: almost 70 percent of all reported appellate decisions involving the search or seizure of digital evidence are concerned with the recovery of child pornography. The alcohol prohibition era had a significant influence on Fourth Amendment analysis in the 1920s and 1930s. The drug wars of the last 50 years have also impacted the structure of search and seizure jurisprudence. Now, during the digital age, governmental investigations designed to locate child pornography are having a similar influence. This section accordingly reviews common Fourth Amendment issues related to the search and seizure of evidence related to child pornography.

A. Patrick Roberts has written about the role of a defense attorneys representing clients charged with such crimes. He observes:

> Because this area of the law is so closely tied to technological advances, counsel involved in Internet pornography defense must stay abreast of the law and technological developments to effectively represent their clients. Failure to fully understand how the Internet functions, how online communications continue to evolve, and how data is received, transmitted, and

stored could cause defense counsel to miss an opportunity to raise creative and novel arguments on behalf of their clients.[24]

Roberts noted that "search-and-seizure laws play a big role in the defense of Internet pornography charges" and that two of his biggest challenges revolve around his client's consenting to search and making statements to investigators prior to his being retained. Roberts continues:

> The first step is the client interview. This is crucial to developing a strategy, because the client is the most knowledgeable person regarding the facts and issues in the case. The client needs to explain how they obtained the images, which sites and user groups they visited, where they stored the images, and what steps they took, if any, to filter out unwanted images from the computer. If specific file-sharing software was used to obtain the images, the client needs to be specific about the source of that software and how it works, if known. Counsel also must find out how many people had access to the particular computer, and whether the files had any password protection.
>
> Immediately following this interview, counsel should seek to educate himself or herself about the software and hardware the client had at their disposal at the time the images were viewed. Counsel should determine which operating system the client used, the unique features of any file-sharing or file-storage software the client may have downloaded, and the extent to which the client has personal programming knowledge or a heightened technological savvy. Technological ignorance can be helpful, because a jury may find it easier to believe that files may have been downloaded inadvertently. It is also important to learn which search words were used to access potentially incriminating files.

1. Probable Cause to Believe a Person Possesses Child Pornography

To justify a search, a police officer must have probable cause to believe that the person, place, or thing to be searched has evidence of a crime. The probable cause standard is flexible, albeit seeking a significant amount of justification. In determining whether probable cause exists, the Court cautions, hypertechnical analysis divorced from the realities of everyday life has been rejected: "In dealing with probable cause . . . , as the name implies, we deal with probabilities. These are not technical; they are the factual and practical considerations of everyday life on which

---

24. A. Patrick Roberts, *Strategies for Defending Internet Pornography Cases Leading Lawyers on Analyzing Electronic Documents, Utilizing Expert Witnesses, and Explaining Technological Evidence*, ASPATORE, 2008 WL 5689427.

reasonable and prudent men, not legal technicians, act."[25] More precisely, the Court has said that probable cause is a "fair probability" that the person has committed the crime[26] or that contraband or evidence of a crime will be found.[27] It is more than "bare suspicion" but less than what would justify a conviction.[28] It does not require the fine tuning of evidence that even the "preponderance standard demands."[29] It not helpful to fix a "numerically precise degree of certainty" to the determination but it is clear that "only the probability, and not a prima facie showing, of criminal activity is the standard of probable cause."[30] Finally, a plurality has asserted that it is not a "more likely true than false" standard.[31]

As with other situations, probable cause determinations in the computer context are fact-bound.[32] The bulk of the case law concerns child pornographers and courts have been troubled by several questions: 1) as to subscribers of child pornography web sites, the amount of information needed in order to conclude that there is probable cause to search the subscriber's computer; 2) profile allegations; 3) staleness; and 4) establishing the location of the computer used to distribute or receive the materials.

a. Subscribers of Child Pornography Web Sites

There is a split of authority over the strength of the inference that can be drawn as to whether a person has child pornography on his computer based on membership in a child pornography web site. Some courts have indicated that mere membership

---

25. Brinegar v. United States, 338 U.S. 160, 175 (1949).

26. Michigan v. DeFillippo, 443 U.S. 31, 37 (1979).

27. United States v. Grubbs, 547 U.S. 90 (2006).

28. Brinegar v. United States, 338 U.S. 160 (1949).

29. Illinois v. Gates, 462 U.S. 213, 236 (1983).

30. *Id.*

31. Texas v. Brown, 460 U.S. 730, 742 (1983).

32. *See, e.g.,* Williford v. State, 127 S.W.3d 309, 313 (Tex. App. 2004) (probable cause to seize computer based on repairman's viewing of thumbnail picture of two naked boys on bed); Burnett v. State, 848 So. 2d 1170, 1173–75 (Fla. Dist. Ct. App. 2003) (no probable cause to support warrant to search computer for evidence of child pornography based on initial complaint that suspect had made lewd videotape of two children); State v. Staley, 548 S.E.2d 26, 28–29 (Ga. Ct. App. 2001) (although police had probable cause to believe that Staley had molested a specific child, that he had worked as a computer analyst, that he had been previously convicted of molesting a child and taking pictures of that child, and that the affiant detailed that pedophiles stored information relating to having sex with children, there was no nexus between either the crime of molesting that specific child or the propensities of child sex offenders and search of computer in Staley's apartment); Burke v. State, 27 S.W.3d 651, 653–56 (Tex. App. 2000) (fact-bound question whether there was probable cause to issue warrant in child pornography case).

in a child pornography site is sufficient.[33] Others have rejected that view.[34] To establish probable cause to search, many courts look for additional information—beyond membership in a child pornography site—that substantiates the person's sexual interest in children or in child pornography.[35] That additional information has included such factors as evidence of actual downloading[36]—as opposed to mere viewing,[37] automatic transmissions as part of the site's services,[38] use of suggestive

---

33. *See* United States v. Gourde, 440 F.3d 1065, 1070–72 (9th Cir. 2006) (en banc) (membership in Internet child pornography site for at least three months was sufficient to establish probable cause of downloading child pornography onto home computer); United States v. Martin, 426 F.3d 83 (2d Cir. 2005), *rehearing en banc denied*, 430 F.3d 73 (2d Cir. 2005); United States v. Wagers, 452 F.3d 534, 540 (6th Cir. 2006) (probable cause existed that suspect's home computer contained child pornography based on membership in child pornography website); United States v. Bailey, 272 F. Supp. 2d 822, 824–25 (D. Neb. 2003) (holding that "knowingly becoming a computer subscriber to a specialized Internet site that frequently, obviously, unquestionably and sometimes automatically distributes electronic images of child pornography to other computer subscribers alone establishes probable cause for a search of the target subscriber's computer even though it is conceivable that the person subscribing to the child pornography site did so for innocent purposes and even though there is no direct evidence that the target subscriber actually received child pornography on his or her computer"). *Cf.* United States v. Coreas, 419 F.3d 151 (2d Cir. 2005) (affirming on basis of precedent but asserting that mere membership should not be the basis for probable cause), *rehearing en banc denied*, 430 F.3d 73 (2d Cir. 2005).

34. *See* United States v. Perez, 247 F. Supp. 2d 459, 483–84 (S.D.N.Y. 2003) (subscription to known child pornography website created a "chance, but not a fair probability, that child pornography would be found").

35. *See, e.g.*, United States v. Froman, 355 F.3d 882, 884–91 (5th Cir. 2004) (upholding search warrant for member of group whose "singular goal . . . was to collect and distribute child pornography and sexually explicit images of children," when members could choose to automatically receive emails with attached images and Froman's interest in child pornography was shown by his chosen screen names, "Littlebuttsue" and "Littletitgirly"); State v. Schaefer, 668 N.W.2d 760, 770 (Wis. Ct. App. 2003) (because computer files are common way of storing photographs, reasonable inference that computer contained child pornography when suspect actively cultivated friendship of teenage boys by inviting them to use his home computer, used his computer to communicate with others interested in stories about adults sexually assaulting children, and visited Internet sites where child pornography was available for downloading).

36. *Perez*, 247 F. Supp. 2d at 483–84 (rejecting finding of probable cause and noting, *inter alia*, that, unlike other cases where there was evidence of downloading, the affidavit contained "nothing concrete to suggest that Perez had transmitted or received images of child pornography").

37. *See id.* at 483–84 n.12 ("The statute does not criminalize 'viewing' the images, and there remains the issue of whether images viewed on the internet and automatically stored in a browser's temporary file cache are knowingly 'possessed' or 'received.'"). *See also* United States v. Zimmerman, 277 F.3d 426, 435 (3d Cir. 2002) (without evidence that pornography was specifically downloaded and saved to defendant's computer, offending images "may well have been located in cyberspace, not in [the defendant's] home"); United States v. Tucker, 305 F.3d 1193, 1198 (10th Cir. 2002) (upholding conviction for possession of files automatically stored in browser cache because defendant's habit of manually deleting images from cache files established his control over them).

38. *See Perez*, 247 F. Supp. 2d at 485 (asserting that "the agents either had or could have had, before they requested the warrant, all the Yahoo logs, which provided extensive information—whether a subscriber was offered e-mail delivery options; whether he elected a delivery option; whether he uploaded or posted any images; when he subscribed; and whether he unsubscribed"). *Cf. Froman*, 355 F.3d at 884–91 (upholding search warrant for member of group whose "singular

names,[39] expert information on the retention habits of child pornography collectors (which often serves to dispel allegations of staleness and identifies the house as the place where the materials were viewed), and prior convictions involving sex offenses involving children or child pornography.[40]

Notes

Downloading vs. Viewing. The federal statute has been amended to prohibit mere access with intent to view child pornography images. *See* 18 U.S.C. § 2252A(a) (5)(A). This is to say that possession does not have to be the central inquiry and, for probable cause to search a computer, intentional access with intent to view would be a reasonable conclusion based on membership. Most states, however, still require possession. *See* Rebecca Michaels, Note, *Criminal Law — The Insufficiency of Possession in Prohibition of Child Pornography Statutes: Why Viewing a Crime Scene Should Be Criminal*, 30 W.N. ENG. L. REV. 817 (2008).

b. Retention Habits of Collectors

An explanation of child pornography collectors' retention habits was offered in *United States v. Lamb*, 945 F. Supp. 441, 460 (N.D.N.Y. 1996):

> Since the [child pornographic] materials are illegal to distribute and possess, initial collection is difficult. Having succeeded in obtaining images, collectors are unlikely to quickly destroy them. Because of their illegality and the imprimatur of severe social stigma such images carry, collectors will want to secret them in secure places, like a private residence. This proposition is not novel in either state or federal court: pedophiles, preferential child molesters, and child pornography collectors maintain their materials for significant periods of time.

---

goal . . . was to collect and distribute child pornography and sexually explicit images of children," when members could choose to automatically receive emails with attached images and Froman's interest in child pornography was shown by his chosen screen names, "Littlebuttsue" and "Littletitgirly").

39. *E.g.*, United States v. Shields, 458 F.3d 269, 279–80 (3d Cir. 2006) (maintaining that suggestive email address added to probable cause determination). A persistent question concerns the circumstances under which file names establish probable cause to search or seize a computer; a finding of probable cause often turns on the explicit nature of the names and the surrounding circumstances. *See, e.g.*, State v. Wible, 51 P.3d 830, 833–34 (Wash. Ct. App. 2002) (file names "8 year old Rape" and "8 year old Smile" gave context and meaning to repairman's tip that computer contained child pornography).

40. *See, e.g.*, United States v. Wagers, 452 F.3d 534 (6th Cir. 2006); United States v. Fisk, 255 F. Supp. 2d 694, 706 (E.D. Mich. 2003) (when the defendant had prior conviction for unlawful sexual involvement with a minor, had wired money to purveyor of child pornography, and when the purveyor sold that pornography over the Internet, there was probable cause to believe that computer contained child pornography).

Based on those habits, probable cause has often been found in child pornography cases when affiants, based on their training and experience, explain that collectors and distributors of child pornography typically store it in their homes.[41]

---

c. Pedophile Profiles

United States v. Edward S. Macomber

67 M.J. 214 (C.A.A.F. 2009)

Judge Baker delivered the opinion of the Court.

[Macomber was identified as a child pornography website subscriber. An investigation revealed that he was] a member of the Air Force stationed at Minot Air Force Base. [Special Agent Novlesky] contacted the Air Force Office of Special Investigation to share the information he had and to verify Appellant's identity and military status. SA Novlesky met with OSI Special Agent Patrick White to discuss options for proceeding with the investigation of Appellant, and the agents agreed to conduct a joint investigation. SA Novlesky recommended to OSI that Postal Inspector Rachel Griffin be contacted to send a target letter to Appellant offering him child pornography. OSI agreed and Inspector Griffin was contacted and brought in as part of the investigation team.

Inspector Griffin sent a letter and a "Sexual Interest Questionnaire" to Appellant from Eclipse Films, a fictional company purporting to specialize in illegal pornography. The correspondence stated that pornography offered by the film company was "illegal" and must be kept in the "strictest confidence." The correspondence was sent to Appellant's mailing address at Dorm 211 on Minot AFB. Appellant was on temporary duty to Guam at the time, so the letter was forwarded to him at his temporary duty location. Appellant completed the questionnaire listing "teen sex" and "pre-teen sex" among his sexual interests and indicated his interest in buying pornography from the company. He mailed the items back to Inspector Griffin at her undercover post office box. The letter was postmarked from Guam, but Appellant

---

41. *See, e.g.*, United States v. Lacy, 119 F.3d 742, 745 (9th Cir. 1997); United States v. Cox, 190 F. Supp. 2d 330, 333 (N.D.N.Y. 2002) (recognition of habits of child pornography collectors); State v. Lindgren, 687 N.W.2d 60, 64–65 (Wis. Ct. App. 2004) (when defendant took nude photographs of a 14 year old female employee at work, touched her vaginal area, and had allegedly taken pictures of other female employees, and affiant detailed habits and characteristics of child molesters, including, *inter alia*, that they collect sexually explicit materials, rarely dispose of them, and record diaries of their encounters on, *inter alia*, their computers, probable cause existed to search home computer for photographic evidence of underage children of sexually explicit nature); State v. Evers, 815 A.2d 432, 446, 448 (N.J. 2003) (probable cause to believe that pornographic images of children would be retained on computer due to retention habits of child pornographers). *But see* United States v. Greathouse, 297 F. Supp. 2d 1264, 1272 (D. Or. 2003) (even though agent indicated in affidavit that child pornography collectors routinely maintain their materials for long periods of time, rejecting that assertion as sufficient because it appeared "to be based upon a generalized sense developed through informal conversations with other agents").

indicated his return address on the envelope as "Dorm 211, Unit 503, Minot AFB, ND 58705." Inspector Griffin sent Appellant a letter thanking him for his interest list and describing the available videos fitting his stated sexual interests along with an order form pricing the videos at twenty dollars each.

On June 14, 2004, Inspector Griffin received a pre-stamped white business size envelope in the mail. The envelope was postmarked "Minot, ND June 8, 2004" with the return address listed as "Edward Macomber, Dorm 211, Unit 503, Minot AFB, ND 58705." The envelope contained a completed order form indicating Appellant's request to purchase two child pornography videos titled "IC-5 Mixed Sleepover" and "IN-9 Sweet Sixteen." A postal money order was enclosed for the amount of forty dollars payable to Eclipse Films. The purchaser was listed as "Ed Macomber, Dorm 211, Unit 503, Minot AFB, ND 58705."

SA White based the request for search authority on Appellant's actions prior to his receipt of the actual videos from Eclipse Films. Specifically, the request was based on Appellant's subscription to the "LustGallery.com" child pornography website using his dorm room address, his self-proclaimed interest in children engaged in sex, and his attempt to order movies containing child pornography. While the affidavit stated that SA White expected to find a parcel addressed to Appellant from Eclipse Films, this was not the basis for the search authority nor was it the reason the magistrate found probable cause.

The affidavit also included "pedophile profile information." This information was based on SA White's discussion with Inspector Griffin and included profile information relative to individuals interested in child pornography or those sexually interested in children. It was also based on SA White's training while attending the OSI Academy and the Federal Law Enforcement Training Center during which "typical behavior of child pornographers" was described. The affidavit stated:

> child pornographers and persons with a sexual attraction to children almost always maintain and possess child pornography materials such as: photographs, magazines, negatives, films, videotapes, graphic image files, correspondence, mailing lists, books, tapes, recordings and catalogs. These materials are stored in a secure but accessible location within their immediate control, such as in the privacy and security of their own homes, most often in their personal bedrooms.

Lt Col Harrold granted authority for the search of Dorm 211, Room 104, Minot AFB, ND 58705, and the search of Appellant's 2002 Mitsubishi Mirage.

The core legal question in the case is whether the military judge correctly ruled that the search authority had a substantial basis for determining that probable cause existed.

[Appellant argued that he did not fall] within the generic pedophile profile presented to the magistrate. In Appellant's view, without such an inference, there was no reason to believe pornography would be stored in his room. Appellant correctly points out that while SA White's affidavit presented a "pedophile profile," including and in particular the statement that pedophiles are likely to store pornography at their places of residence, it did not expressly conclude or state that Appellant fit the profile. Indeed, while courts have relied on such profiles to inform search determinations, clearly, a profile alone without specific nexus to the person concerned cannot provide the sort of articulable facts necessary to find probable cause to search.

But that is not this case. The stipulated facts reflect that Appellant had subscribed to an Internet child pornography web service in the past, and that he expressed an ongoing interest in child pornography in the present. He had recently filled out a questionnaire documenting this interest. Such facts may or may not place Appellant within a generic pedophile profile or a clinical pedophile profile but they certainly reflect an ongoing interest in child pornography. Based on common sense, law enforcement experience, and case law, the military judge reasonably concluded there was a fair probability that a person with an interest in child pornography, who has ordered child pornography in the past and in the present, is likely to store such pornography in some quantity at a secure and private location. For a service member residing on a military installation, that means his dormitory room, barracks, or vehicle.

RYAN, JUDGE (dissenting):

The affidavit's use of profile information related to "child pornographers and those with a sexual interest in children" cannot mitigate the scarcity of detail in the affidavit. Reliance on this profile is problematic, and I cannot agree that all the government ever need do to defeat nexus concerns is provide boilerplate language about the habits of the theoretical "collector."

In this case, nowhere does the affidavit specifically conclude that Appellant fits the "collector" profile because he possessed child pornography, is a "child pornographer," or a person "with a sexual interest in children." Admittedly, Appellant indicated an interest in viewing child pornography when he responded to the Eclipse Films survey and an interest in acquiring child pornography when he ordered two videos to be sent to him through the mail. But an express desire to have child pornography delivered to one's home in the future does not by itself support an inference that Appellant previously possessed child pornography in that home, or anywhere else. It is by no means axiomatic that a person who expresses an interest in owning something actually already has possessed it, particularly when that thing is contraband. While it is logical to infer that the website subscription gave Appellant access to child pornography, the affidavit neither informs the magistrate where the access occurred nor indicates that Appellant actually downloaded any images to possess in his room or elsewhere.

Although we have previously credited expert reference to "profile evidence" in cases involving child pornography, we have done so when there were "other factors" to "bolster the opinion as to where the child pornography might be found in appellant's home." In *United States v. Gallo*, 55 M.J. 418 (C.A.A.F. 2001), the affidavit supporting the request to search the appellant's home indicated that: (1) the appellant fit the profile of a pedophile; (2) the appellant had advertised for and solicited child pornography; (3) 262 pictures had been found on the appellant's work computer; and (4) the appellant had downloaded and uploaded child pornography from his work computer. Here, however, there were not sufficient "other factors" to allow the magistrate to rely on the profile.

Notes

1. **Linkage of Habits of Collectors to the Target of the Search.** In *Ellis v. State*, 971 A.2d 379 (Md. Ct. Spec. App. 2009), in reacting to the appellant's claim that there was no showing in the affidavit in support of the warrant that he was a collector, the court stated:

> Nowhere in the affidavit was appellant described as a child pornographer or preferential child molester. The boilerplate language described the known habits of child pornographers and preferential child molesters in general, without any reference to appellant. Although the implication of the boilerplate language being included in the affidavit was that the police suspected appellant of being a child pornographer or molester, such implication is clearly at odds with the stated facts of the investigation and the crimes charged. Therefore, the suppression court was eminently correct in striking the boilerplate language concerning child sex offenses and reviewing the affidavits on the remaining facts as they were set forth.

2. **How is That Linkage Made?** Consider *United States v. Lemon*, 590 F.3d 612 (8th Cir. 2010):

> Possession of child pornography is a crime that is continuing in nature, and the evidence in the warrant application established that Lemon was unlikely to have destroyed the illegal material. Although the last known exchange of child pornography occurred in December 2006, Officer Haider cited evidence that the IP address and [the] screen name [that Lemon used] were used in April 2008. These facts supported the inference that Lemon was still trading child pornography, particularly when coupled with Officer Haider's explanation that Lemon's behavior in November and December 2006 was indicative of a preferential collector who would maintain his collection for a long period of time.

3. **Is an assertion that the suspect is a child molester enough for a warrant to search for child pornography?** *See Dougherty v. City of Covina*, 654 F.3d 892 (9th Cir. 2011):

> Other circuits have split on the question of whether evidence of child molestation, alone, creates probable cause for a search warrant for child pornography. The Second Circuit has stated that a "crime allegedly involv[ing] the sexual abuse of a minor, [does] not relate to child pornography. . . . That the law criminalizes both child pornography and the

sexual abuse (or endangerment) of children cannot be enough." *United States v. Falso*, 544 F.3d 110, 123 (2d Cir. 2008). The Sixth Circuit agrees that, when probable cause is established "for one crime (child molestation) but [the warrant is] designed and requested [to] search for evidence of an entirely different crime (child pornography)," it is "beyond dispute that the warrant [i]s defective." *United States v. Hodson*, 543 F.3d 286, 292 (6th Cir. 2008). In fact, in *Hodson*, the evidence was much more related to viewing children in sex acts and to computers than the evidence in the affidavit here. There, in an internet chatroom, Hodson "confided that he . . . favored young boys, liked looking at his nine-and eleven-year-old sons naked, and had even had sex with his seven-year-old nephew. [Hodson] also expressed his desire to perform oral sex on the presumptive twelve-year-old boy . . . and his willingness to travel . . . to do so." Nonetheless, the Sixth Circuit firmly held that the warrant was "so lacking in indicia of probable cause that" not even the good-faith exception to unlawfully executed warrants could apply.

The Eighth Circuit, however, has rejected the reasoning of *Falso* and *Hodson*, stating "[t]here is an intuitive relationship between acts such as child molestation or enticement and possession of child pornography." *United States v. Colbert*, 605 F.3d 573, 578 (8th Cir. 2010). The affidavit in *Colbert*, however, did include evidence that the accused had enticed a child to come to his apartment.

Ultimately, the question of probable cause is "not readily, or even usefully, reduced to a neat set of legal rules." Thus, while the "totality of circumstances" could, in some instances, allow us to find probable cause to search for child pornography, Officer Bobkiewicz's conclusory statement [in this case] tying this "subject," alleged to have molested two children and looked inappropriately at others, to "having in [his] possession child pornography" is insufficient to create probable cause here.

d. Staleness

Staleness can occur when information relied on by the police to establish probable cause to search or seize has become outdated due to changed events or the passage of time. The question has been litigated often in lower courts. The typical methodology for the review of probable cause claims also applies to staleness inquiries. Hence, if a court is reviewing a warrantless search or seizure, the court would apply that standard of review;[42] if the search or seizure was based on a warrant, the good faith standard for the review of probable cause claims applies.[43] The Maryland Court

---

42. Most courts review the legal analysis *de novo*, both at the motion hearing and upon appellate review. *E.g.*, United States v. Khanani, 502 F.3d 1281, 1289 (8th Cir. 2007).

43. In *Connelly v. State*, 589 A.2d 958 (Md. 1991), the court collected relevant cases and observed:

of Appeals has summarized the principles that typically guide courts in assessing claims of staleness:

> In making an assessment of probable cause, one of the factors the warrant-issuing judge must consider is whether the "event[s] or circumstance[s] constituting probable cause, occurred at ... [a] time ... so remote from the date of the affidavit as to render it improbable that the alleged violation of law authorizing the search was extant at the time. ..." "There is no 'bright-line' rule for determining the 'staleness' of probable cause; rather, it depends upon the circumstances of each case, as related in the affidavit for the warrant." Factors used to determine staleness include: passage of time, the particular kind of criminal activity involved, the length of the activity, and the nature of the property to be seized. The Court of Special Appeals explained the general rule of stale probable cause in *Andresen v. State*, 24 Md. App. 128, 331 A.2d 78 (1975):

> The ultimate criterion in determining the degree of evaporation of probable cause, however, is not case law but reason. The likelihood that the evidence sought is still in place is a function not simply of watch and calendar but of variables that do not punch a clock: the character of the crime (chance encounter in the night or regenerating conspiracy?), of the criminal (nomadic or entrenched?), of the thing to be seized (perishable and easily transferable or of enduring utility to its holder?), of the place to be searched (mere criminal forum of convenience or secure operational base?), etc. The observation of a half-smoked marijuana cigarette in an ash-tray at a cocktail party may well be stale the day after the cleaning lady has been in; the observation of the burial of a corpse in a cellar may well not be stale three decades later. The hare and the tortoise do not disappear at the same rate of speed.

> The affidavit for a search warrant on probable cause, based on information and belief, should in some manner, by averment of date or otherwise, show that the event or circumstance constituting probable cause, occurred at the time not so remote from the date of the affidavit as to render it improbable that the alleged violation of law authorizing the search was extant at the time that application for the search warrant was made.

Addressing the question of good faith reliance, the *Connelly* court opined:

> Even though the warrant was found to be invalid by the intermediate appellate court on staleness grounds . . . , considerations of staleness of probable cause turn on the circumstances of each particular case, and reasonable minds may differ as to the correct determination. Accordingly, applying *Leon's* objective test in this case, we think that the officers, exercising professional judgment, could have reasonably believed that the averments of their affidavit related a present and continuing violation of law, not remote from the date of their affidavit, and that the evidence sought would likely be found at Connelly's store and at his residence.

Where the affidavit in a case "recites facts indicating activity of a protracted and continuous nature, or a course of conduct, the passage of time becomes less significant, so as not to vitiate the warrant."[44]

Staleness claims are common in child pornography cases but typically rejected due to the nature of digital evidence and the habits of collectors.[45] Even long periods of time between the initial report of the existence of child pornography and the execution of a subsequently issued warrant have not defeated the existence of probable cause.[46]

United States v. William David Burkhart

602 F.3d 1202 (10th Cir. 2010)

PAUL KELLY, JR., CIRCUIT JUDGE.

In the fall of 2006, the European Law Enforcement Organization investigated a child pornography ring and found an Italian national operating a web site that sold child pornography online. Europol searched the Italian's residence and found thousands of emails that he exchanged with customers. Europol sent the FBI about

----

44. Patterson v. State, 930 A.2d 348, 358–59 (Md. 2006). *See also* Gilbert v. State, 19 S.W.3d 595 (Ark. 2000) (discussing similar factors and holding that 46 day delay in executing warrant did not render probable cause stale).

45. *E.g.*, United States v. Lemon, 590 F.3d 612 (8th Cir. 2010); United States v. Paull, 551 F.3d 516 (6th Cir. 2009); United States v. Morales-Aldahondo, 524 F.3d 115 (5th Cir. 2008); Mehring v. State, 884 N.E. 2d 371, 377–80 (Ind. Ct. App. 2008); State v. Pickard, 631 S.E.2d 203 (N.C. Ct. App. 2006); State v. Felix, 942 So. 2d 5, 9–10 (Fla. Dist. Ct. App. 2006).

46. *E.g.*, United States v. Hay, 231 F.3d 630, 636 (9th Cir. 2000) (probable cause that computer in suspect's home contained child pornography was not stale, even though information was six months old, due to affiant's explanation that collectors and distributors rarely if ever dispose of it and store it in secure place); United States v. Lacy, 119 F.3d 742, 745 (9th Cir. 1997) (probable cause not stale in child pornography case when based on information 10 months old because affiant, based on her training and experience, explained that collectors and distributors of child pornography "rarely if ever" dispose of such material); United States v. Lamb, 945 F. Supp. 441, 460–61 (N.D.N.Y. 1996) (based, *inter alia*, on proposition that pedophiles, preferential child molesters, and child pornography collectors maintain their materials for significant period of time, five month delay from last transmission of child pornography to issuance of warrant did not render probable cause stale); Hause v. Commonwealth, 83 S.W.3d 1, 13–14 (Ky. Ct. App. 2002) (based on "hoarding" characteristics of child pornography collectors, information that was 178 days old not stale). *But cf.* United States v. Zimmerman, 277 F.3d 426, 433–34 (3rd Cir. 2002) (probable cause based on viewing of pornographic video file on defendant's computer six months prior to execution of search warrant was stale, absent evidence that defendant had downloaded the video clip and absent evidence of continuous criminal activity); United States v. Greathouse, 297 F. Supp. 2d 1264, 1269, 1272–73 (D. Or. 2003) ("Carefully considering all of the factors present in this case, including the limited incriminating evidence, the absence of any evidence of intervening criminal activity, the absence of any evidence that [the suspect] was a pedophile, and the fact that computer equipment becomes obsolete very quickly, I find that the thirteen month delay in this case is simply too long. If a line must be drawn in internet child pornography cases, I find that the line is one year absent evidence of ongoing or continuous criminal activity.").

10,000 emails between the Italian suspect and U.S. citizens. Among these emails with U.S. citizens, the FBI found forty-five messages between the Italian's email address and davidburkhart@sbcglobal.net. These emails verified purchases of various videos of a 13-year-old girl, the most recent message dated December 2, 2005. In April 2007, the FBI obtained from AT&T via an administrative subpoena the subscriber information for davidburkhart@sbcglobal.net. William David Burkhart, the subscriber, was listed as living at 1020 East Polk, Apartment 3, McAlester, Oklahoma. John Fitzer, an FBI agent, could not confirm that a William David Burkhart still lived at the East Polk address. Agent Fitzer found a William D. Burkhart in the Oklahoma Department of Motor Vehicles database with the same date of birth as William David Burkhart. William D. Burkhart had vehicles registered at two addresses in the McAlester area: 5490 Center Avenue and 5217 Carl Albert Road, which are located about a two-minute drive away from each other.

Agent Fitzer prepared separate applications and affidavits for separate search warrants for each address. The affidavits were identical in most respects: they set out Agent Fitzer's training and experience in law enforcement generally, and computer storage systems and child pornography investigations in particular. The affidavits related how the Europol investigation led to a William David Burkhart, the nature of the videos believed to be in Mr. Burkhart's possession, the characteristics of child pornography collectors, and descriptions of the places to be searched and the items to be seized. The affidavit for the Carl Albert Road address related a few links between a William D. Burkhart and that address: the DMV database listed a William D. Burkhart living at that address, a Jeep Cherokee was parked at that address and William D. Burkhart registered a Jeep Cherokee at that address, and the U.S. Postal Service confirmed that William D. Burkhart received mail there. Similarly, the affidavit for the Center Avenue address said that a Dodge pickup truck registered to a William D. Burkhart was parked there, that the mailbox had "Burkhart" on it, and that William D. Burkhart received mail there. Neither affidavit referred to the other one. Agent Fitzer presented both applications and affidavits to the magistrate judge at the same time on May 6, 2008. The magistrate took them into her office for a period of time, then returned, placed the agent under oath, took his statement that the affidavits were true and accurate, and signed the warrants in front of the agent.

Federal agents executed both warrants at the same time on May 8, 2008. At the 5490 Center Avenue address, Mr. Burkhart's ex-wife informed agents that he no longer lived there. Agents halted the execution of this warrant and returned it unserved. At 5217 Carl Albert Road, agents found William David Burkhart, the Defendant, as well as more than 400 DVDs with images of child pornography.

Generally, "probable cause to search cannot be based on stale information that no longer suggests that the items sought will be found in the place to be searched." "[W]hether information is too stale to establish probable cause depends on the nature of the criminal activity, the length of the activity, and the nature of the property to be seized."

When federal agents executed the warrant for Mr. Burkhart's home in April 2008, about two years and four months had passed since December 2, 2005, the date of the most recent email between the Italian child porn distributor and davidburkhart@ sbcglobal.net. Mr. Burkhart argues that this passage of time, combined with the lack of additional emails after the December 2005 email and the fact that he no longer lived at the mailing address provided to his email service provider, indicated that he voluntarily ceased attempts to obtain the child pornography.

Although the amount of time between the most recent email and the search gives us some pause, the "passage of time alone" cannot demonstrate staleness. In child pornography cases, the nature of the criminal activity and the nature of the property to be seized are especially relevant factors. Mr. Burkhart was charged with *possession* of child pornography, not acquiring it. His offense did not cease with his last purchase, but continued as long as he possessed the videos. His emails supported the magistrate's probable cause determination because they conclusively showed that he bought the videos. From that fact, one could reasonably infer that he likely still possessed the videos. The most recent evidence of Mr. Burkhart's possession, the December 2005 email, occurred well within the five-year statute of limitations. The volume of Mr. Burkhart's emails with the porn distributor as well as his enthusiasm supported Agent Fitzer's theory that Mr. Burkhart collected the videos. *See* 1 R. 78–79 ("I can't wait to watch her again," "Thank you for the N26, she was great as always, maybe a little better in this one! . . . She has to be the most beautiful girl in the world, and you are a very lucky fellow to have her model for you."). These facts, combined with Agent Fitzer's observation that collectors "typically retain [the materials] for many years," formed a substantial basis for the magistrate to determine that a fair probability existed that the videos would be found in Mr. Burkhart's home.

This court has repeatedly endorsed the "view that possessors of child pornography are likely to hoard their materials and maintain them for significant periods of time." The *Riccardi* court explained that such a view

> is supported by common sense and the cases. Since the materials are illegal to distribute and possess, initial collection is difficult. Having succeeded in obtaining images, collectors are unlikely to destroy them. Because of their illegality and the imprimatur of severe social stigma such images carry, collectors will want to secret them in secure places, like a private residence.

[*United States v. Riccardi*, 405 F.3d 852 (10th Cir. 2005)]. Mr. Burkhart acknowledges these cases, but claims that they are based on the outdated realities of regular mail, rather than the relative ease of anonymous collection through the Internet.

We are not persuaded. Admittedly, the Internet's speed, anonymity, and burgeoning porn market have lowered some practical barriers for any collector with a few hours, a high speed connection, and a credit card. But child pornography is still illegal to distribute and possess, and still carries severe social stigma, whether the possessor receives it by regular mail, email, or over the Internet. The illegality and social stigma may also complicate resale or disposal. Moreover, acquiring pornography is rarely free. Given the nature of the evidence to be seized, the Internet context may mitigate *against* staleness: information that a person received electronic images of child pornography is less likely than information about drugs, for example, to go stale because the electronic images are not subject to spoilage or consumption. Instead, electronic files "can have an infinite life span." We fail to see how even "on demand" Internet availability removes the incentive to hoard what has been collected. No facts negate the fair probability that the videos would be found in Mr. Burkhart's home. Mr. Burkhart points to the period between the last email with the Italian porn distributor in December 2005 and Europol's search in the fall of 2006 as evidence that he voluntarily quit trying to obtain pornography and, therefore, "the hoarding assumption is due little or no weight." However, the cessation of efforts to procure the videos is not inconsistent with the theory that Mr. Burkhart was hoarding the videos: a person may very well keep hoarding long after he stops acquiring.

_____

Notes

Deleted Files. In *Smith v. State*, 887 A.2d 470 (Del. 2005), where the affidavit described forensic analysis protocols "designed to protect the integrity of the evidence and to recover even 'hidden', erased, compressed pass-word protected, or encrypted files," the Court asserted:

> The affidavit alleged that Smith had used the same laptop computer for three years and that he was very protective of it. Data protocols were described by which investigators could recover computer files even after deletion. Unlike a gun or drugs, which may be disposed of quickly, computers and computer files can exist long after the commission of a crime. Federal courts have upheld search warrants for computer data issued months after the alleged acts took place, because the computer data continues to exist.

Based on the ability of the government to forensically recover images and the profiling of offenders, when does probable cause dissipate?

e. Locating the Computer: IP Addresses; Screen Names; Nexus Questions

IP ADDRESSES

Another significant question is ascertaining the location of the computer that has distributed or received the child pornography. This difficulty arises because many individuals use computers in a variety of locations, including in an office and at home.[47] Computers accessing the Internet are assigned an Internet Protocol number, which does "*not directly* reflect the geographic street address of the office, residence,

_____

47. *See, e.g.*, State v. Evers, 815 A.2d 432, 446 (N.J. 2003) ("Computers are in use in both homes and businesses, and, with the advent of the laptop, in almost every other conceivable place. Business

or building from which an individual accesses his email and/or the internet."[48] As a result, "law enforcement officials must conduct research and rely upon the addresses and data provided by internet providers, . . . as well as billing addresses for those service providers and/or credit card companies."[49] Many courts will infer that the computer is located in the home from the Internet Protocol address assigned to the user's account.[50] For example, in *United States v. Wagers*,[51] the court reasoned that, while the account holder

> had access to the internet from *many* locations, . . . his residence and business locations are certainly the most likely and suspect locations through which he would have accessed the internet. The question, then, is not whether he did or did not access child pornography through the suspect sites from those physical addresses, but, rather, giving the Magistrate Judge's decision great deference, whether there is a "fair probability" that evidence or fruits of criminal wrongdoing would be found.

Commonwealth v. Adalberto Martinez
71 N.E.3d 105 (Mass. 2017)

Botsford, J.

The defendant, Adalberto Martinez, appeals from his conviction of possessing child pornography. He challenges the denial of his motion to suppress computer evidence obtained pursuant to a search warrant. The gravamen of the defendant's claim is that the police needed to do more to link the defendant to the place searched and the items seized before a warrant could validly issue. We affirm the denial of the motion to suppress and the conviction.

Background.

1. IP addresses.

All computers that connect to the Internet identify each other through a unique string of numbers known as an Internet protocol address (IP address). In general,

---

people and students leave their homes with laptops, use them at other locations, and return home with them.").

48. United States v. Wagers, 339 F. Supp. 2d 934 (E.D. Ky. 2004), *aff'd*, 452 F.3d 534 (6th Cir. 2006).

49. United States v. Wagers, 339 F. Supp. 2d 934 (E.D. Ky. 2004), *aff'd*, 452 F.3d 534 (6th Cir. 2006).

50. *E.g.*, United States v. Renigar, 613 F.3d 990 (10th Cir. 2010); United States v. Vosburgh, 602 F.3d 512, 526–27 (3rd Cir. 2010); State v. Felix, 942 So. 2d 5 (Fla. Dist. Ct. App. 2006); State v. Brennan, 674 N.W.2d 200 (Minn. Ct. App. 2004). *See also* Ellis v. State, 971 A.2d 379, 389 (Md. Ct. Spec. App. 2009) (finding reasonable inference that defendant used his home computer from the circumstances); State v. Byrne, 972 A.2d 633, 637–42 (R.I. 2009) (in video voyeurism case, analogizing to child pornography cases to find nexus between taking pictures with a digital camera and the home); State v. Samson, 916 A.2d 977, 981–83 (Me. 2007) (finding reasonable nexus between home and digital child pornography pictures taken by defendant).

51. 339 F. Supp. 2d 934 (E.D. Ky. 2004), *aff'd*, 452 F.3d 534 (6th Cir. 2006).

when a subscriber purchases Internet service from an Internet service provider (ISP), the ISP selects from a roster of IP addresses under its control and assigns a unique IP address to the subscriber at a particular physical address. The IP address assigned to a particular subscriber may change over time, but the ISP keeps a log of which IP address is assigned to each subscriber at any given moment in time.

In the early days of the Internet, when a residential Internet subscriber went online using only a home computer connected to a hard-wired Internet connection, there was a very strong correlation between an IP address assigned to a subscriber and a particular computer. Now, however, many subscribers use a wireless Internet router, which allows multiple devices within the range of the router to connect to the Internet simultaneously. To the outside world, all of these devices will share a single public IP address—the one that the ISP has assigned to its subscriber. But internally, the router will identify each connected device by the device's own identifying number in order to channel data to and from the appropriate device. As a result, the correlation between an Internet subscriber's assigned IP address and any one particular Internet-enabled device may often be weaker than it once was. However, the correlation between an IP address and a physical address can still be strong, at least when the ISP has verified its assignment of a particular IP address to a subscriber at a specific physical address at a specific point in time.

2. Search warrant affidavit.

The affidavit in support of the contested search warrant and related materials aver the following. On March 9, 2012, State police Sergeant Michael Hill was investigating the use of "peer-to-peer" file sharing programs to possess and distribute child pornography. One such file-sharing program, Ares, allows a user to connect to another user's computer via the Internet and then download digital files that are stored locally on the other user's computer. Ares is an open-source software that any person can download for free via the Internet. There is a special version of the Ares program for law enforcement agencies that allows them to monitor and investigate individuals suspected of using Ares to share digital files of child pornography. Using the law enforcement version of Ares to download a file from another Ares user, investigators can determine (1) the user's IP address, (2) whether the user possesses and is sharing a particular file, (3) the "hash value" associated with a particular file, (4) the user's Ares username, and (5) the version of Ares software that the user's computer is operating. Because the law enforcement version of Ares displays both the IP addresses of Ares users and the hash values of files being shared, when police identify a file as one that contains child pornography, police can determine with a high degree of confidence when that child pornography file is being shared through a specific IP address.

In this case, Hill discovered that a computer using the IP address 65.96.142.191 and displaying the username "datflypapi@Ares" was sharing suspected child pornography via the Ares network. Through an online mapping tool (several of which exist on publicly accessible Web sites), Hill determined that this IP address was likely associated with a computer in Massachusetts. The computer using this IP address was sharing a total of ten files via the network. Hill found that a majority of these files had names containing terms commonly associated with child pornography. Over approximately thirty minutes, Hill downloaded and viewed four video files from the suspect computer and concluded that these files were child pornography. While downloading the files, Hill used another program that confirmed that a computer associated with the IP address 65.96.142.191 was connected to his computer.

By conducting an Internet search, Hill determined that the IP address in question was associated with Comcast Cable (Comcast), a major cable company and ISP. Based on the above information, the district attorney for the Berkshire district issued an administrative subpoena to Comcast asking to whom the IP address 65.96.142.191 was assigned during the thirty-minute period on March 9, 2012, during which Hill downloaded the four suspected child pornography video files from datflypapi@Ares. Comcast responded to the subpoena on March 15, 2012, and provided information that the IP address was assigned to a subscriber named "Angel Martinez" at a certain address in Fall River (apartment). Hill then referred the investigation to Detective Steven Washington of the Fall River police department. On April 2, 2012, Washington went to the apartment, which is part of a housing development. Washington discovered that Maria Avilez leased the apartment. On April 3, 2012, Washington sought and received, from the Fall River Division of the District Court, a warrant to search the apartment for computers and related items connected to the suspected possession and distribution of child pornography.

3. Execution of the search warrant.

Washington and two other officers executed the warrant on April 5, 2012. According to Washington's trial testimony, when the officers first knocked on the door of the apartment, no one answered. Washington then heard someone say, "Hey, he just ran out that way," and saw a "large male" running down a side street away from the apartment. The officers eventually entered the apartment. Inside they encountered the defendant's girl friend, Ruth Pereira, holding her infant child. Both Avilez and Angel Martinez, the defendant's cousin, arrived at the apartment while officers were conducting the search, but the defendant was not present.

During the search, Washington noticed two laptop computers underneath a basket of laundry. After some initial testing (which was not described in detail in the trial record), the officers seized the two computers and brought them back to the police station. Upon further inspection at the station, officers discovered five video files of child pornography on one of the defendant's laptop computers. It is not clear from the record whether any of these video files were among those observed by Hill during his Ares surveillance on March 9, 2012.

Discussion.

The sole issue on appeal is the validity of the search warrant issued for the apartment. Detective Washington's affidavit in support of the search warrant averred that a particular IP address was used to share child pornography and that this IP address had been assigned at the time in question to an Internet subscriber at the specific physical address to be searched. The central question is whether these averments were sufficient to establish probable cause for the search, even though the named subscriber was neither listed as, nor confirmed to be, living in the unit, and even though police had no information before the search linking the defendant to the residence. We conclude that the affidavit in this case did establish probable cause to search the apartment for computer evidence related to the suspected possession or distribution of child pornography.

"Under the Fourth Amendment and art. 14 [of the Massachusetts Declaration of Rights], a search warrant may issue only on a showing of probable cause." "The probable cause necessary to support the issuance of a search warrant does not require definitive proof of criminal activity." Rather, a warrant may issue if a magistrate finds "a substantial basis on which to conclude that the articles or activity described are probably present or occurring at the place to be searched." For probable cause to arise, the facts contained in an affidavit, plus the reasonable inferences that may be drawn from them, must allow the magistrate to determine that "the items sought are related to the criminal activity under investigation, and that they reasonably may be expected to be located in the place to be searched at the time the search warrant issues."

The probable cause inquiry in this case asks whether the facts averred in Washington's affidavit showed a sufficient nexus between the suspected criminal activity (possessing or distributing child pornography), the items sought (computers and related materials), and the place to be searched (the apartment). To that end, the nexus between the suspected criminal activity, the items sought, and the place to be searched may be based on, among other things, the type of crime, the extent of the suspect's opportunity for concealment, and normal inferences about where a criminal would be likely to hide evidence of the suspected crime.

Here, the affidavit described how Sergeant Hill had observed a computer associated with the IP address 65.96.142.191 that contained, and was sharing, child pornography via the Ares network. An Internet search revealed that this IP address had been issued to Comcast, the ISP. The district attorney for the Berkshire district then issued a subpoena to the ISP, which revealed that the IP address in question had been assigned during the relevant time period to a subscriber at the physical address of the apartment. The temporal and geographical links between the target IP address and the physical address to be searched provided a substantial basis for concluding that evidence sought (computers and related items) was connected to the suspected crime (possessing or sharing child pornography) and likely would be found at the specified premises (the apartment), and therefore gave rise to a sufficient nexus between the suspected criminal activity and the residence.

Of course, the ISP also provided a name associated with the service address and officers took subsequent steps to determine who actually lived at the apartment. In many cases, those pieces of information can serve a useful confirmatory role. But in the present case, we conclude that there was probable cause to search for evidence related to sharing child pornography based on the information police obtained through their Ares surveillance and the administrative subpoena, independent of whose name was on the Internet account or in the housing development's records. The probable cause showing necessary for issuance of a search warrant is "only a fair probability that evidence of such a crime would be found in particular locations," not "a prima facie showing that the defendant possessed child pornography." Police met that threshold here.

The defendant advances, in essence, three arguments about why investigators needed to do more to establish probable cause. We address each in turn.

First, he points out that before applying for the search warrant, the police were unable to verify that the subscriber named by the ISP—Angel Martinez—lived at the apartment, and also were unable to rule out the possibility that someone other than the named subscriber was responsible for using the IP address assigned to the apartment at the time in question. Therefore, the defendant argues, it was possible that a new (and innocent) person had moved into the apartment while Angel Martinez, living at a different address altogether, continued to pay the Internet bill, or that a new occupant merely took over the Internet payments without changing the name on the account.

It is true that investigators had no direct information that Angel Martinez personally had used, was using, or would ever use the IP address in question. However, in this particular case, the name of the Internet account holder did not defeat probable cause. The question before the magistrate was whether the apartment located at a certain address likely contained evidence of criminal activity—period. The question was *not* whether that address likely contained evidence of criminal activity *on the part of Angel Martinez* (or on the part of Avilez for that matter).

To that end, Detective Washington's supporting search warrant affidavit spelled out a relatively direct link between (1) the downloading and sharing of child pornography video files, (2) a specific IP address, and (3) a specific physical address to which that IP address had been assigned. From a technological standpoint, an IP address can be assigned to only one service address at any given point in time. Taken together, these facts gave rise to a reasonable inference that evidence related to possession or distribution of child pornography via the Internet likely would be found at the apartment—the one place, according to the ISP's records, to which the IP address in question was assigned during the relevant time period.

Once this nexus was established, the name of the account holder was essentially incidental. Although information showing that the named subscriber was also the person suspected of possessing or sharing the child pornography might have increased the likelihood that the sought-after evidence would be located at the service address, the lack of such information does not necessarily defeat probable cause. This is so precisely because an IP address can be assigned to only one service address at any given time—regardless of whose name is on the account.

Second, the defendant points out that investigators did not determine whether the Internet connection at the apartment used a wireless router and, if so, whether the wireless network required a password. This left open the possibility that someone other than the subscriber, located at a different physical address, was "joyriding" on an unsecured wireless network based out of the apartment. The defendant argues that this concern is especially acute in the present case because investigators knew that the apartment was part of a housing development, in which multiple residences were in close proximity to the target physical address.

The defendant's argument is misdirected. A showing of probable cause to search a place (as opposed to arrest a person) need not identify a specific criminal suspect—although frequently it does. Indeed, "[t]he critical element in a reasonable search is not that the owner of the property is suspected of crime but that there is reasonable cause to believe that the specific 'things' to be searched for and seized are located on the property to which entry is sought." In other words, police need only demonstrate a sufficient nexus between the criminal activity under investigation, the items sought, and a place to be searched where the items may reasonably be expected to be located—independent of whether they have identified a specific criminal suspect.[n.8][52] Certainly police may have an easier time demonstrating a sufficient nexus if they can link a specific suspect (e.g., the named Internet account holder) to the criminal activity. However, such a link is not always required.

The search warrant affidavit in this case demonstrated that child pornography was being shared via the Internet from a specific IP address. This IP address, in turn, had been assigned to a specific physical address during the time when the child pornography was being shared. These facts provided a substantial basis from which to conclude that evidence of downloading and sharing child pornography via the Internet would be located at the apartment, even if it turned out that an unauthorized user was "joyriding" using the targeted IP address.

The defendant is correct, from a technological standpoint, that if an Internet subscriber at the apartment set up an unsecured wireless Internet network, a computer outside of this physical address (in a neighboring unit, perhaps) could have used the targeted IP address to access the Internet and share child pornography.[n.10][53]

---

52. [n.8] To this point, the prosecutor and Detective Steven Washington had the following colloquy at trial:

Q.: "Now when you execute a warrant like this . . . are you conducting . . . [the search] for a person or for a device?"

A.: "A device."

Q.: "Okay. And why is that?"

A.: "Because I have no clue who is behind that device."

53. [n.10] Notably, there was no evidence, either at the suppression stage or at trial, that the apartment was home to an unsecured wireless Internet connection or that anyone other than the defendant used the Internet connection there. Nor was there any evidence that the defendant did not connect his laptop computers to the Internet through the IP address assigned to the apartment. However, even if we accept the defendant's hypothetical scenario of "joyriding," and it turned out that none of the defendant's devices contained child pornography, police still would have had probable cause to seize and search any Internet modems or routers in order to determine which devices were connected to the targeted IP address at the time when police witnessed child pornography being shared via the targeted IP address.

This point misses the mark, because probable cause does not require investigators to "establish to a certainty that the items to be seized will be found in the specified location," nor does it require them to "exclude any and all possibility that the items might be found elsewhere."

Finally, the defendant argues that, in a case like this, probable cause cannot arise until police show one of three things: (1) that the target IP address has not been linked to a wireless Internet service; (2) that the target IP address is linked to a wireless Internet service, but it is a secure connection requiring a password; or (3) that no one outside the target physical address could be accessing the network. The defendant urges that, without these showings, the likelihood of someone outside the target physical address using the target IP address is substantial enough to defeat probable cause. By and large, these proposals simply restate the defendant's arguments urging that the police, in order to show probable cause, should have been required to rule out the possibility that persons outside of the apartment may have been "joyriding" on the IP address assigned to that location at the time in question. To the extent that is the case, we reject these proposals for the reasons already mentioned.

Moreover, it is not clear whether it would be technologically feasible for investigators to do what the defendant asks. With respect to the first proposal, there is nothing in the record showing that a third party (like an ISP, for instance) would be able to determine whether a subscriber's connection to the Internet is through a hard-wired or wireless connection at any given point in time. With respect to the second, in the case of a subscriber who uses a wireless router, it is not clear how investigators would be able to ascertain whether the network is password-protected without first learning the name of that subscriber's wireless network. And regarding the third proposal, even assuming investigators knew that a target IP address was associated with an unprotected wireless network that had been accessed by devices not belonging to the subscriber, these considerations would not necessarily change the fact that, given the Ares surveillance conducted in this case, there remained a fair probability that any computers located at the apartment would contain evidence related to the possession or distribution of child pornography. The defendant's proposals merely illustrate that different hypothetical scenarios <u>could</u> lead to a different conclusion regarding probable cause. But those potentialities do not <u>necessarily</u> defeat probable cause, especially when they lack any factual underpinning. Instead, the fundamental question is whether there was a substantial basis from which to conclude that the items described in the application were <u>probably</u> present at the place to be searched. For all of these reasons, we affirm the denial of the defendant's motion to suppress.

We end with a cautionary note. Our decision today should not be read to mean that probable cause always exists any time investigators link illegal computer activity to an IP address and then link that IP address to a physical address. For one, police should (as they did in this case) connect the IP address with a physical address through a reliable method, such as an administrative subpoena to the ISP, rather than relying solely on a potentially unreliable method, such as certain IP address mapping services. Additionally, technologies that apparently were not at issue in this case may further erode the connection between an IP address and a physical address.

At the very least, certain cases may require police to disclose in a search warrant affidavit the possibility that one of these technologies is, or may be, in play based on facts known or reasonably knowable to investigators at the time. If such technologies become more common, it is entirely possible that we would require police to proceed in multiple steps, obtaining subpoenas related to each intermediary IP address or warrants to search each location hosting those IP addresses. Alternatively, some cases may require the police to examine forensically a wireless router to determine which devices were connected to it, and when, before they search particular computers. Such possibilities demonstrate why the probable cause analysis rarely, if ever, lends itself to bright-line rules.

<u>Conclusion.</u>

The order denying the motion to suppress and the defendant's conviction are affirmed.

––––––––––

Notes

In *State v. Brennan*, 674 N.W.2d 200 (Minn. Ct. App. 2004), although the suspect admittedly used his work laptop to view and store child pornography, the court found that there was a substantial basis for the magistrate's determination that probable cause existed to search the suspect's home computer based on the training and expertise of the affiant, who asserted that persons with an interest in child pornography tend to view it in their home. The court reasoned, in part, that "viewing and possessing child pornography is, by its nature, a solitary and secretive crime." It accordingly believed that a "court could reasonably draw an inference that the suspect would keep the illicit images in a place considered safe and secret, like the home." The court also relied on the transportable nature of laptops and stated that it was reasonable to infer "that the illicit images found on the laptop would also be found on [the suspect's] home computer."

Screen Names

Screen names help to identify who the person is. A "screen name" is an identity created by a user and may or may not have any correlation with the user's real name; an individual typically gains access to a screen name by supplying a password that is associated with that screen name.[54] Some courts will find probable cause to search the billing address associated with the screen name.[55] As one court has reasoned:

––––––––––

54. United States v. Grant, 218 F.3d 72, 73 n.1 (1st Cir. 2000).

55. *See, e.g.*, State v. Evers, 815 A.2d 432, 446 (N.J. 2003) ("the billing address of the Internet screen name—a screen name that had e-mailed photographs of child pornography—was the

> The billing address of an account tied to a computer screen name may not be an absolute guarantee that the holder of the computer screen name used the computer at the billing address to commit criminal activity, but there is a fair and logical inference that the computer will *probably* be found at that address and, if not, at least evidence of the identity of the holder of the screen name will be found there.[56]

Nonetheless, the court cautioned that it would prefer that law enforcement officials take additional steps to verify that the computer from which offending images were sent is located in the defendant's residence.[57]

Other courts have rejected the view that a registered screen name is sufficient to establish probable cause to search the subscriber's computer.[58] Instead, it has been suggested that additional information is needed, such as the fact that the suspect maintained a computer or computer-related equipment at the place to be searched that was capable of transmitting child pornography, the screen name required a particular password, the transmission of child pornography was to a unique Internet or ethernet address assigned to a particular computer at the location to be searched, or the person occupying the place to be searched had an "extreme" interest in young children or had access to Internet sites operated by entities that required those having access to maintain Internet-accessible child pornography.[59] Also relevant to the probable cause determination would be the habits of child pornography collectors, their propensity to collect child pornography and maintain the collection at home, and whether the suspect was a pedophile.

––––––––––––

---

logical place to search for evidence of the identity of the holder of the screen name and evidence of the crime").

56. State v. Evers, 815 A.2d 432, 446 (N.J. 2003). *See also* United States v. Campos, 221 F.3d 1143, 1145 (10th Cir. 2000) (upholding validity of search warrant for defendant's residence after "[l]aw enforcement agents determined that AOL subscriber who used the name 'IAMZEUS' was [defendant]"); Hause v. Commonwealth, 83 S.W.3d 1, 4–5, 11–12 (Ky. Ct. App. 2001) (upholding validity of search warrant for residence that was supported by subscriber information obtained from Internet service provider through California search warrant and verification of address by Kentucky law enforcement officials).

57. State v. Evers, 815 A.2d 432, 446 (N.J. 2003).

58. *See, e.g.,* Taylor v. State, 54 S.W.3d 21 (Tex. Ct. App. 2001) (no probable cause to search computer for child pornography in Taylor's home when affidavit merely alleged that one image of child pornography sent over the Internet had been traced to screen name registered to Taylor).

59. *See, e.g.,* Taylor v. State, 54 S.W.3d 21, 25–26 (Tex. Ct. App. 2001) (collecting cases). *See also* United States v. Bach, 400 F.3d 622, 627–28 (8th Cir. 2005) (probable cause existed to search defendant's home computer, even in absence of cross references of IP addresses provided by the ISP and his telephone records based, *inter alia,* on the fact that the user name employed to correspond to the minor was registered to defendant at his address); United States v. Grant, 218 F.3d 72, 75 (1st Cir. 2000) (because use of password-protected account requires that user know password associated with account, fair probability that person using account is registrant).

second photograph was sufficient to establish probable cause, however, because the photograph "involves an image in one of the first four categories (*i.e.*, sexual intercourse)" of sexually explicit conduct.

The Court now turns to the application of the foregoing principles to the magistrate's determination of probable cause based on Special Agent Tortorella's affidavit.

The affidavit presented to the issuing magistrate here suffers from [the] same problems described in the foregoing cases. The affidavit does not append, or provide *any* description of, the particular videos referenced in the e-mail correspondence between Mr. Genin and the YVM Operator. Notably, the affidavit does not describe which particular videos the unnamed IIU analyst reviewed or identify which of the five categories of sexually explicit conduct these videos allegedly fell into. The unnamed analyst's conclusory description—"child pornography"—covers *both* the first four categories of sexually explicit conduct, which courts have held are "clearly defined and easily recognized," as well as the last category—lasciviousness—which "calls into play [the] imprecise value judgments" of the unnamed IIU analyst[n.7][60] who determined that the videos depicted lascivious exhibition of the genitals or pubic area.

The e-mails themselves do not resolve this ambiguity. Although the statements contained in the e-mails undoubtedly establish probable cause to believe that the videos depict minors, the e-mails themselves do not describe behavior that falls within the first four categories of sexually explicit conduct. Nor do the e-mails contain any descriptions of the videos from which a magistrate could independently conclude that they depicted lascivious exhibition of the genitals or pubic area. In one of the e-mails to the YVM Operator, for example, Mr. Genin states that one of the videos shows a minor "applying lotion to that beautiful blonde's firm, athletic stomach," and, while describing another video, he claims to "love their tiny outfits and the way they pose." Assuredly, such descriptions of minors are sordid. Standing alone, however, they do not create probable cause to believe that the videos depict "lascivious exhibition of the genitals or pubic area."

The question, then, becomes whether the magistrate could have determined, based on the other videos discussed in the affidavit, that the particular videos referenced in the e-mail correspondence between Mr. Genin and the YVM Operator

---

60. [n.7] This problem was compounded in this case because the FBI agent who signed the warrant affidavit was not the individual who reviewed the videos and came to the conclusion that they contained child pornography. To be sure, the Supreme Court in *United States v. Ventresca* held that "[o]bservations of fellow officers of the Government engaged in a common investigation are plainly a reliable basis for a warrant applied for by one of their number." 380 U.S. 102, 111 (1965). Here, however, if the magistrate judge had wanted to question the Government as to the basis for its conclusion that the videos contained child pornography—one of the key legal determinations upon which the issuance of the warrant hinged—the affiant appearing before the magistrate would have been unable to offer any assistance.

fall within the lasciviousness category. Although this is a very close issue, the Court believes not. With respect to the videos peddled on the YVM websites, for example, the affidavit indicates that "some of the videos" contain behavior that falls within the first four categories of sexually explicit behavior, *i.e.*, sexual intercourse or acts. It also states that "many of the videos" depict minors "dressed in 'string' lingerie or . . . completely nude, and . . . pos[ing] such that their genitals are the focus of the image," behavior that most likely falls within the lasciviousness category. The affidavit, however, does not delineate whether these two categories of videos overlap and, if so, to what degree. That is, it is entirely possible that the YVM websites contained videos that fall outside the applicable definitions of child pornography. Similarly problematic is the absence of information linking the particular videos referenced in the e-mail correspondence to the videos that the affidavit describes as depicting sexually explicit conduct and as appearing on the YVM websites.

Accordingly, because the affidavit did not provide sufficient information for the magistrate to make an independent determination that the videos referenced in Mr. Genin's e-mails to the YVM Operator contained sexually explicit conduct, this Court holds that the magistrate lacked a substantial basis for issuing the search warrant.

The Court turns to whether the good-faith exception to the exclusionary rule applies under these circumstances.

The Supreme Court has held that the "marginal or nonexistent benefits produced by suppressing evidence obtained in objectively reasonable reliance on a subsequently invalidated search warrant cannot justify the substantial costs of exclusion." *United States v. Leon*, 468 U.S. 897, 922 (1984). The so-called good-faith exception asks "whether a reasonably well trained officer would have known that the search was illegal despite the magistrate's authorization."

Mr. Genin submits that the warrant affidavit was so lacking in indicia of probable cause that reliance on it was unreasonable. He notes that the affidavit did not describe or attach the alleged child pornography, but instead merely stated summarily that an unknown analyst of unstated qualifications and experience had determined that the videos contained child pornography.

The Court cannot agree that the affidavit was so lacking in indicia of probable cause that reliance upon it was objectively unreasonable. As discussed above, the requirement that, in the lasciviousness context, law enforcement officials append to the warrant affidavit, or include therein a reasonably detailed description of, the allegedly proscribed material is relatively new and, at least within the Second Circuit, "unclear." Finally, although probable cause in this case was lacking, the Court believes that it was a close issue and "certainly an issue upon which reasonable minds can differ." Therefore, the authorities' reliance on the issuing magistrate's probable cause determination was objectively reasonable.

Consequently, the physical evidence seized in this case shall not be suppressed.

Notes

1. Is an allegation in an affidavit that the image depicts "child sex" without further detailing the activity sufficient to satisfy the particularity requirement? *See State v. Reep*, 167 P.3d 1156 (Wash. 2007).

2. Is an allegation in an affidavit that the image depicts "child pornography" without further detailing the activity sufficient to satisfy the particularity requirement? *See State v. Perrone*, 834 P.2d 611 (Wash. 1992) (finding description insufficient).

§ 13.6 Self-Produced Child Pornography and Sexting

This chapter concludes with an excerpt from a law journal article on sexting and litigation on the proper societal responses to self-produced child pornography. What should be the proper societal response to sexting?

State v. Eric D. Gray

402 P.3d 254 (Wash. 2017)

Owens, J.

When he was 17 years old, Eric D. Gray electronically sent an unsolicited picture of his erect penis to an adult woman. The woman contacted the police, and Gray was charged with and convicted of one count of second degree dealing in depictions of a minor engaged in sexually explicit conduct under RCW 9.68A.050. He appealed, claiming the plain language of the statute does not anticipate minors who take and transmit sexually explicit images of themselves.

RCW 9.68A.050 prohibits developing or disseminating sexually explicit images of minors. On its face, this prohibition extends to any person who disseminates an image of any minor, even if the minor is disseminating a self-produced image. Because the statute is unambiguous, we take it on its face and find that Gray's actions are included under the statute.

In 2013, T.R., a 22-year-old woman, went to the Spokane County Sheriff's Office to report a series of harassing phone calls she had received over the past year. She stated that the caller used a restricted number and would not provide a name, but that she believed the caller was male. She also stated that she believed the caller was Gray.

T.R. also reported that she had received two text messages the day before. The first contained a photograph of an erect penis and the words "(Eric Gray) picture message sent from Pinger." The second message read, "'Do u like it babe? It's for you [T.R.]. And for Your daughter babe-Sent From TextFree!'" Using the phone number associated with the messages and additional information from the user's Pinger account, the Spokane County Sheriff's Office confirmed the messages came from Gray.

About two weeks later, the deputy who took T.R.'s report went to Gray's house to question him. Gray was 17 at the time and lived with his parents. He had been diagnosed with Asperger's syndrome and had a prior adjudication requiring him to register as a sex offender. Though initially composed during questioning and believing the sheriff had come to talk with him about his sex offender registration, Gray's demeanor quickly became agitated when he learned the deputy's actual purpose. He admitted that he had been calling T.R. for the past year and had sent the text messages. He stated that T.R. used to work for his mother, that he retrieved T.R.'s phone number from his mother's business records, and that he was attracted to T.R. He also admitted that it was his erect penis in the photograph.

The State charged Gray in juvenile court with one count of second degree dealing in depictions of a minor engaged in sexually explicit conduct under RCW 9.68A.050. It also charged him with one count of telephone harassment under RCW 9.61.230. Gray moved to dismiss both charges for insufficient evidence, which the trial court denied. In a stipulated facts trial, the court found Gray guilty of the second degree dealing in depictions of a minor charge. He was sentenced to 150 hours of community service, 30 days of confinement, and fees, before being released with credit for time served. He was again ordered to register as a sex offender.

The first issue here is whether the statute on its face applies to Gray. This court's duty is to "give effect to the Legislature's intent." The clearest indication of legislative intent is the language enacted by the legislature itself. Therefore, "if the meaning of a statute is plain on its face, we 'give effect to that plain meaning.'" However, we will not read a statute in isolation; we determine its plain meaning by taking into account "the context of the entire act" as well as other related statutes.

Here, the statute is unambiguous and we give it its plain meaning. RCW 9.68A.050 prohibits dealing in depictions of a minor engaged in sexually explicit conduct. In relevant part, it states that "[a] person commits the crime of dealing in depictions of a minor engaged in sexually explicit conduct in the second degree when he or she . . . [k]nowingly develops, . . . publishes, . . . [or] disseminate[s] . . . any visual or printed matter that depicts a minor engaged in an act of sexually explicit conduct. . . ." RCW 9.68A.050(2)(a). "Sexually explicit conduct" is a depiction "of the genitals or unclothed pubic or rectal areas of any minor . . . for the purpose of sexual stimulation of the viewer." RCW 9.68A.011(4)(f). A "minor" is "any person under eighteen years of age." RCW 9.68A.011(5). Finally, a "person" is any "natural person," whether an adult or a minor. RCW 9A.04.110(17), .090. Therefore, when any person, including a juvenile, develops, publishes, or disseminates a visual depiction of any minor engaged in sexual conduct, that person's actions fall under this statute's provisions.

Under this statute, the State properly charged Gray for his actions. When he was 17, Gray took a photo of his erect penis and sent it, unsolicited, to another person. Gray is a "natural person" and therefore a person for purposes of the statute. He was also under the age of 18, making him a minor under the statute as well. He stated he was attracted to T.R., and when he sent the picture he included the phrase "Do u like it, babe?," indicating an attempt to arouse the recipient. The picture he transmitted was, therefore, a visual depiction of a minor engaged in sexually explicit conduct because it was a picture of a minor's genitals designed to sexually stimulate the viewer. This falls squarely within the statute's plain meaning.

Gray argues that he cannot be charged under this statute because the "person" and the "minor" must be two different people. He states that had the legislature intended to include the depicted minor under the definition of "person," it would have explicitly done so. We disagree.

As noted above, a "person" is any natural person and a "minor" is merely a person who is not yet 18. Under this statute, there is nothing to indicate the "minor" cannot also be the "person." Contrary to Gray's arguments, we find that had the legislature intended to *exclude* the depicted minor from the definition of "person," it would have done so as it has in other sections in this chapter. *See* RCW 9.68A.101(3)(a) (specifically excluding minors receiving compensation for sexual conduct from the definition of a "person" guilty of promoting commercial sexual abuse of a minor). Because the legislature has not excluded minors from the definition of "person" here, Gray was properly charged under this statute.

Both Gray and amici urge that if we determine a minor can be charged under this statute for taking and disseminating sexually explicit pictures of himself, it could have dire consequences for other minors engaging in "sexting." They argue that the legislature never intended to criminalize teenagers consensually exchanging sexually explicit photographs, opining that doing so would be an impermissible infringement of those teenagers' First Amendment freedom of expression.

Though both parties and amici have briefed the issue, those are not the facts before us. We understand the concern over teenagers being prosecuted for consensually sending sexually explicit pictures to each other. We also understand the worry caused by a well-meaning law failing to adapt to changing technology. But our duty is to interpret the law as written and, if unambiguous, apply its plain meaning to the facts before us. Gray's actions fall within the statute's plain meaning. Because he was not a minor sending sexually explicit images to another consenting minor, we decline to analyze such a situation.

The statute here is unambiguous. A "person" is any person, including a minor. Images of a "minor" are images of any minor. Nothing in the statute indicates that the "person" and the "minor" are necessarily different entities. Therefore, the photographer or distributor may also be the minor in the photograph. Because of this, Gray was properly charged with taking and disseminating sexually explicit images of a minor.

The legislative findings support our plain reading. As noted above, our paramount duty is to effectuate the legislature's intent. We will diverge from a plain reading only if a "'contrary legislative intent is indicated.'"

Gray argues that the legislature intended to focus on adult purveyors of child pornography, not juveniles who voluntarily take photographs of their own bodies.

He cites to the legislative findings, stating that when the legislature "drafted the statute it was concerned about holding individuals who engage in the sexual abuse of children for their own commercial gain criminally accountable." We agree that this statute was undoubtedly intended to address the sexual abuse and exploitation of children by adults. However, the scope of this statute is larger than what Gray presents.

The legislature intended to destroy the blight of child pornography everywhere, from production of the images to commercial gain. As Gray notes, the State has a compelling interest in "protecting children from those who sexually exploit them." However, "this interest extends to stamping out the vice of child pornography at all levels in the distribution chain." This includes at its inception. It is our duty to effectuate the legislature's intent, not rewrite the words the legislature used. If the legislature intended to exclude children, it could do so by amending the statute. Because the statute was intended to curtail production of child pornography at all levels in the distribution chain, the statute prohibits Gray's actions.

Similarly, the dissent contends that there is a "long-standing and well-accepted rule" that when a legislature enacts a criminal law to protect a specific class, we cannot interpret the law to permit prosecution of a member of that protected class "unless the legislature explicitly says so." But the dissent overgeneralizes, relying on cases that deal with coconspirator/accomplice/aider and abettor liability and factual scenarios entirely different from this one.

The cases cited by the dissent deal largely with accomplice or coconspirator liability, rather than an individual acting alone. For example, in *Gebardi v. United States,* 287 U.S. 112 (1932), which the dissent discusses in detail, the Supreme Court addressed whether a woman who was trafficked for the purpose of prostitution could be held criminally liable for conspiring with the trafficker. Additionally, in *City of Auburn v. Hedlund*, 165 Wash.2d 645, 652, 201 P.3d 315 (2009), the only Washington case cited by the dissent, we addressed accomplice liability: whether a passenger and sole survivor in a car accident could be charged as an accomplice to driving under the influence. But here, Gray was not acting as an accomplice, aider and abettor, or coconspirator; he acted on his own.

We acknowledge that an exception for victims may apply in other contexts: for example, for children involved in the *manufacture* of child pornography. Indeed, "[w]hen a crime inherently requires 'two to tango,' but the statute is not intended to punish the victim of the crime—as is the case in prostitution or the manufacture of pornography—federal courts regularly apply a common-law exception to conspiratorial or accomplice liability." But this case is not about the manufacture of child pornography. It is about one individual's *distribution* of a sexually explicit image to an unwilling recipient. Contrary to the dissent's view, this court has not adopted a general presumption that all statutes designed to protect a particular class are presumed to exempt all members of that class from criminal liability, no matter the circumstances. The dissent paints with too broad a brush.

RCW 9.68A.050 is unambiguous and anticipates Gray's actions. The statute prohibits any person from developing or disseminating a sexually explicit image of any minor. Here, Gray sent a sexually explicit picture of himself to an adult woman. Because Gray is a person and because he sent a sexually explicit picture of himself while he was a minor, he was properly charged under the statute. Therefore, we affirm the Court of Appeals.

GORDON MCCLOUD, J. (dissenting)

For more than 80 years, the United States Supreme Court, federal courts, and Washington courts have held that when the legislature enacts a statute designed for the protection of one class—here, children depicted in sexually explicit conduct—it shows the legislature's intent to protect members of that class from criminal liability for their own depiction in such conduct. *E.g., Gebardi v. United States*, 287 U.S. 112, 119 (1932); *City of Auburn v. Hedlund*, 165 Wash.2d 645, 652, 201 P.3d 315 (2009). RCW 9.68A.050 was enacted against that historical backdrop. It was specifically intended to protect children depicted in pornography. Since the legislature enacted RCW 9.68A.050 to protect those children, it necessarily follows that those children who are depicted and hence exploited are exempt from prosecution under RCW 9.68A.050 for such depictions of themselves.

Indeed, if the legislature wanted us to apply a different rule of statutory interpretation—one that would permit members of the protected class to be charged, prosecuted, convicted, and imprisoned for up to 10 years for sexually explicit, exploitative depictions of their own bodies—it was the legislature's duty to explicitly say that they were departing from the general rule of statutory interpretation. The legislature did not say so here. Its silence must be construed as an endorsement of the general rule.

The majority's contrary interpretation of the statutory language produces absurd results. The majority's interpretation punishes children who text sexually explicit depictions of their own bodies to adults far more harshly that it punishes adults who do the same thing. It punishes children who text such depictions of their own bodies to adults even more harshly than adults who text such sexually explicit photos to children. It even punishes the child who is groomed and led into taking such photos and forwarding them to the grooming adult! In short, the majority's interpretation punishes the most vulnerable participant—the depicted child—no matter what personal pressures or personal struggles (Gray suffers from Asperger's syndrome) compelled the child to do it.

That cannot be what the legislature intended. I therefore respectfully dissent.

As the majority notes, "This court's duty is to 'give effect to the legislature's intent.'" To determine that intent, we begin with the language of the statute. The statute under which Eric Gray was convicted, RCW 9.68A.050(2)(a), provides in relevant part:

> *A person* commits the crime of dealing in depictions of a minor engaged in sexually explicit conduct in the second degree when he or she:

(i) Knowingly develops, duplicates, publishes, prints, disseminates, exchanges, finances, attempts to finance, or sells any visual or printed matter that depicts a minor engaged in an act of sexually explicit conduct as defined in RCW 9.68A.011(4) (f) or (g). . . .

(Emphasis added.) As the majority correctly notes, this statute lacks an explicit textual limit on what "person" may be prosecuted for exploiting "a minor."

But we do not stop with statutory language. Our duty is to figure out the legislature's intent, so we read that language in context to determine its meaning. And we presume that the legislature is familiar with existing rules of statutory interpretation.

Here, the statutory context shows that RCW 9.68A.050(2)(a) was enacted to protect "minor[s]" from sexual exploitation via depiction in pornography. Chapter 9.68A RCW is titled "Sexual Exploitation of Children." RCW 9.68A.001 explicitly states that legislative intent: "the prevention of sexual exploitation and abuse of children" and "the protection of children from sexual exploitation." It focuses on prosecuting those who gain from exploiting such depicted children: it is intended "to hold those who pay to engage in the sexual abuse of children accountable for the trauma they inflict on children." RCW 9.68A.001. That "Legislative findings, intent" section further clarifies that "[t]he state has a compelling interest in protecting children from those who sexually exploit them. . . ." RCW 9.68A.001(2). The majority agrees: "We agree that this statute was undoubtedly intended to address the sexual abuse and exploitation of children by adults." So, while the legislature also intended to "'stamp[] out the vice of child pornography at all levels in the distribution chain,'" the tool it chose was a statute that protects a particular class: minors vulnerable to sexual exploitation by their depiction in sexually explicit conduct. Gray is a member of that protected class. The legislature wrote this statute to protect him. Yet he was prosecuted because of his status as a member of that class—that is, because he himself was depicted while engaged in sexually explicit conduct.

As discussed above, the general rule is that a statute designed for the protection of a particular class is presumed to exempt that protected class from criminal liability for their own harm—even when a protected individual was a necessary and willing participant in his or her own exploitation or harm by the perpetrator.

In *Gebardi*, the foundational case for this principle, the Supreme Court addressed whether a woman who was trafficked for the purpose of prostitution could be held criminally liable for conspiring with the trafficker to accomplish her own prostitution. The statute barring such trafficking read, in relevant part,

> "*Any person* who shall knowingly transport . . . *any woman or girl* for the purpose of prostitution or debauchery, or for any other immoral purpose . . . [shall be deemed guilty of a felony]."

(quoting former 18 U.S.C. § 398 (1910)). This statute, like RCW 9.68A.050, is silent about whether the "person" subject to prosecution was meant to include the "woman or girl" who was trafficked. The Court, however, applied the rule that when Congress legislates to protect a particular class—there, the women or girls transported for prostitution—Congress is presumed to have protected members of that class from prosecution under the protective statute. Specifically, the *Gebardi* Court reasoned that the "failure of the Mann Act to condemn the woman's participation in those transportations which are effected with her mere consent" was "evidence of an affirmative legislative policy to leave her acquiescence unpunished." It therefore concluded that Congress's "affirmative legislative policy" was to *protect* the woman—to "immuni[ze]" her from criminal liability—and that to subject her to any form of criminal punishment for her participation in her own exploitation "would contravene that policy."

To be sure, as the majority notes, the specific holding of *Gebardi* is that the government could not prosecute the woman-victim as a *coconspirator* in the substantive Mann Act crime. But that holding was a corollary of the *Gebardi* Court's far less controversial conclusion that the government could not prosecute the woman-victim as a *principal*. And the *Gebardi* Court came to that decision—that the government could not prosecute the woman-victim whom the legislation was designed to protect as a principal in her own exploitation—despite the fact that the Mann Act allowed conviction of "any person," essentially the same language at issue in this case. In fact, the government did not even dispute this common sense conclusion that the victim could not be prosecuted for the crime as a principal in *Gebardi*; as that Court said, "[T]his conclusion [that the victim-woman cannot be prosecuted as a principal] is not disputed by the Government here, which contends only that the conspiracy charge will lie though the woman could not commit the substantive offense."

The majority's focus on the fact that *Gebardi* holds that the government cannot prosecute a member of the class that the legislature intended to protect as a conspirator thus undermines, rather than supports, its argument. The inference that the government is barred from prosecuting a member of the protected victim class, whom the legislation was designed to protect, as a *conspirator* flows directly from the rule that the government is barred from prosecuting a member of the protected victim class, whom the legislation was designed to protect, as a *principal.*

Gray is being prosecuted as a principal in his own exploitation in this case. The rule that a criminal statute designed for the protection of a particular class cannot be used to prosecute a member of that protected class for his or her own victimization (absent specific legislative authorization) thus applies with even greater force here than it would in the vicarious conspiratorial liability situation.

RCW 9.68A.050 is identical to the statute interpreted in *Gebardi* in all relevant aspects. Both use different words to describe the "person" subject to prosecution, on the one hand, and the "woman or girl" (in the federal statute) or "minor" (in the state statute) subject to protection from sexual exploitation, on the other. Both are designed for the protection of the vulnerable class—"woman or girl" transported for immoral purposes (in the federal statute) and "minor" depicted in pornography (in our state statute). And both are silent about whether members of the protected class can be prosecuted under that statute.

Gebardi held that in this situation, the legislature's silence cannot be read as an intent to prosecute members of the protected class for their own victimization. Instead, such silence must be read to exempt members of the protected class from such prosecution. In other words, it shows "an affirmative legislative policy" to leave the protected person who participates — here, Gray — "unpunished."

The majority's contrary interpretation will produce absurd results. It means that a child who texts explicit depictions of himself or herself can be punished more harshly than an adult who does exactly the same thing. I can't believe the legislature intended that result. It means that a 12-year-old girl who is groomed or lured into taking and then texting explicit depictions of herself to an adult can be prosecuted for succumbing to that grooming. I can't believe the legislature intended that result.

Indeed, the majority's interpretation conflicts with what advances in adolescent behavioral and neuroscience research inform us: that such a punitive approach to behavior modification in juveniles is not effective in preventing future offenses. Gray, diagnosed with Asperger's syndrome, is a prime example of someone who would benefit more from treatment and specialized services regarding appropriate social behavior than from incarceration or the social isolation of registering as a sex offender. The majority, however, holds that the statute takes the punitive approach to the depicted, vulnerable victim child. I can't believe the legislature intended that absurdity, either.

In fact, our court is required to interpret statutes to avoid such "'unlikely, absurd, or strained consequences.'" It is no answer to say, as the majority essentially does, that those are all different cases. When we interpret a statute, we have to consider how that interpretation will affect other cases and whether it will produce absurd results. RCW 9.68A.050 criminalizes "develop[ing]" or "disseminat[ing]," etc., the minor's sexual depiction, no matter who receives it. Unless we interpret the statute to exempt the exploited minor from liability for his or her own exploitation, we are subjecting all children in all the examples listed above — as well as the consensual sexting example that the majority tries to distinguish — to felony prosecution.

I respectfully dissent.

Mary Graw Leary, *Self-Produced Child Pornography: The Appropriate Societal Response to Juvenile Self-Sexual Exploitation*

15 Va. J. Social Policy and L. 1 (2007)[61]

Four percent of online American youths have been asked to send a sexually explicit photo of themselves on line. While a seemingly small number, with

---

61. Copyright © 2007, Mary Graw Leary, Virginia Journal of Social Policy & Law. All rights reserved. Reprinted by permission.

twenty-one million juveniles on line, and ten percent of children believing it is acceptable to post pictures of themselves on the Internet, this translates into hundreds of thousands of youth.

The National Center for Missing and Exploited Children reports that 5.4% of the images of child pornography observed on the Internet appear to be self-produced. With "in excess of 20,000 child pornography images [] posted on the Internet each week," this figure represents hundreds of thousands of images. Moreover, Dr. Kimberly Mitchell, author of the 2006 Youth Internet study, notes that those "numbers might even be higher today with the availability of camera phones or other photo-capturing gadgets." In a recent study of child pornography victims, fourteen percent of the images viewed were produced by juveniles.

Initially, one might conclude that these instances are all the result of grooming by adult predators. Research suggests otherwise, as the request to create images is more likely to occur when youths are with friends. "A lot of kids are using the Internet in groups. . . . When they are with friends, maybe they are egging each other on to do something they wouldn't normally do." Yet, when doing so they are producing, distributing, and possessing child pornography which is a violation of state and local laws with significant penalties.

The challenge for society is to determine the appropriate response. This activity is a crime for which there is no statutory defense of minority. The specific question facing justice systems is whether the arsenal for combating child pornography should include juvenile prosecution for minors who commit such crimes.

The importance of this question cannot be underestimated. As stated by the National Child Exploitation Coordination Centre (in the context of juveniles producing child pornography images of each other), "[t]he way in which law enforcement . . . deal[s] with these cases is very important. . . . The sexual development of both youth (victims and offenders) is underway and if these incidents are not handled appropriately both . . . may be harmed [] developmentally." Because this governmental intervention implicates the sexual and emotional development of young people, whatever the government response is should be multidisciplinary, including input from mental health professionals, child protective services, and social workers, as well as law enforcement, and the judiciary.

Governmental intervention is compelled by both the doctrine of parens patriae as well as governmental police powers. With regard to children and the state, the government has two main doctrinal bases for interference in children's lives. The first is the doctrine of parens patriae. This doctrine originated in Great Britain and gave the crown the right and responsibility to protect persons deemed incapable of caring for themselves. American jurisprudence retained this doctrine as the basis for government intervention in the lives of children who were exposed to danger because of the failure of those responsible for the children's safety to protect them. This doctrine formed a basis of the child protection movement as well as the juvenile court system. The second source of governmental regulation of juvenile behavior is the police powers. This source encompasses the state's power to promote public health, safety, and general welfare.

Under parens patriae, child pornography clearly calls the state to protect these children even from themselves. Because of the social harm child pornography poses to other children, it also is an issue of promoting safety and the general welfare, thus it can be based in the police powers as well.

When a child engages in criminal activity the government can respond in a number of ways, including through juvenile adjudication or through the civil child protection system. When this behavior is self-destructive, the government may or may not choose juvenile adjudication.

[The child pornography model] supports the option of juvenile prosecution. It recognizes the multiple social harms of child pornography and demands aggressive prosecution of all those who possess, share in any way, or create images of children engaged in sexually explicit conduct.

Because we as a society have acknowledged child pornography's harm extends beyond those children depicted, we cannot ignore this harm when the producer is a juvenile. Thus, our child pornography jurisprudence supports juvenile prosecution as an option to stem its proliferation.

[The example of] Justin Berry whose participation in self-exploitation was the subject of Congressional Testimony and a New York Times series [supports the view that prosecution should be an option].

Mr. Berry was a seemingly successful California high school student. President of his class, he lived with his mother, his parents having divorced years earlier. At thirteen, he received a web camera and went on line with the intent of "meeting girls" and making new friends. However, while online he was immediately exposed to people claiming friendship, but actually requesting him to engage in certain acts on his web camera. What began as seemingly innocuous requests for Mr. Berry to remove his shirt eventually evolved to his performing sexual acts. He received so much income and enjoyed both the attention and the funding, that soon he expanded his activity. It eventually grew to a series of websites which he created and performed the starring role. People paid forty-five dollars a month to join his fan base and additional fees of up to three hundred dollars to observe certain acts. In the final stages of his business, Mr. Berry engaged in live broadcasts of sexual acts with prostitutes and was bringing other minors into his productions. He made thousands of dollars and also turned eighteen years of age during the process. While it is clear that Mr. Berry began his activity as a misguided minor, he ended it as a highly commercialized entrepreneur who exploited other minors both as a juvenile and as an adult. Although he ultimately received immunity for his action, this was not without controversy and only after he provided the Department of Justice with approximately one thousand names and credit card numbers of adults who paid him for sexual performances over the Internet on his many websites.

This history illustrates the ripple effect of a juvenile's self-exploitive actions. Such activity increased the market for child pornography, validated his customers' actions, and increased the sexualization and eroticization of children. Moreover, while there are elements of misguided youth, there are also elements of criminality. Precisely because these crimes and these offenders are so complex, society must have a protocol to address this type of crime and juvenile prosecution must be included in that protocol.

When teens exploit themselves it is tragic. However, we must resist the temptation to regard this problem as purely one for parental intervention. The Berry case demonstrates that one cannot do so. While there are components of immaturity and victimization in this activity, there are also components of profit, exploitation of others, and the creating of child pornography which harms other children.

Indeed these aspects of child pornography, the harm to others and to self, compel society and the government to intervene in a mandatory way. Phrased another way, the social harm these actions cause, as well as the very purpose of the juvenile court system, demand that prosecution be included as a societal tool to combat this societal ill.

The harm the child does herself cannot be minimized. One might argue that, because these images are not a product of a forceful sexual assault, the social harm of these images is less. However, the Supreme Court rather insightfully articulated one harm of child pornography as the creation of a "permanent record of [the child's] participation." The use of the word "participation" is significant. That word includes both voluntary and involuntary participation. That a minor lacks the understanding of the destructiveness of her actions at the time of the crime does not mean she forfeits the harm she will more tangibly experience when she realizes the permanency of her actions.

With coerced images the immediate harm to the child may be more violent because the child is sexually assaulted in production. However, that does not justify the government failing to prosecute a self-exploiting juvenile. "Not prosecuting the child would do nothing to further society's interests [in protecting children from sexual exploitation]. Prosecution enables the state to prevent further illegal exploitation by supporting and providing any necessary counseling to the child." Moreover, the child is victimized not only at the time of production, but also throughout life as the images are repeatedly viewed. Later in life a minor becomes aware of that continued exploitation and deserves the same protection from further victimization. Indeed, to treat the possession of these images so differently than that of non-self-produced images would suggest these victims are less worthy of societal protection.

The way molesters use this contraband to harm other children further compels juvenile prosecution being considered. Child molesters use these images for their sexual gratification; as a tool to groom children to participate in sexual conduct; to affirm the notion that abusive relationships are acceptable; to lower the inhibitions of potential victims, and to obtain money and profit. "[C]hild pornography offending is a valid diagnostic indicator of pedophilia. Child pornography offenders were significantly more likely to show a pedophilic pattern of sexual arousal during phallometric testing than were comparison groups of offenders against adults or general sexology patients . . . [or] a combined group of offenders against children."

Finally, juvenile producers cause the exposure of other children to these images which has several deleterious effects. In addition to encouraging a societal perception of children as sexual objects, "[e]xposure to the sex industry . . . [including] live sex shows . . . may introduce such industries as viable employment options for some youth." The consequences of producing images, i.e. their use by child molesters, and their exposure to children are equally as devastating when the source is self-exploitive or assaultive. As a society, we talk of the sexual objectification of children seriously, we must act seriously and consistently, notwithstanding the age of the creator.

An important doctrinal underpinning in criminal justice is deterrence. Juveniles predisposed to reckless activity without regard for long term consequences have often been deterred by understanding the penalty for such actions. If juveniles understood that this activity is criminal behavior, presumably some would be deterred.

Sex offender treatment is critical to the juvenile's success. The importance of offenders actually taking responsibility for their actions cannot be underestimated. This often can only occur in a court setting which mandates treatment and monitoring. For many juveniles this may be the only path toward treatment and rehabilitation. Failure to do so will also eliminate the deterrent effect of the law.

States should develop policies which clearly allow for juvenile prosecution but also include [several] factors to consider. These fall into offender specific factors and crime specific factors. Regarding the offender specific factors, the state should assess the cause behind the juvenile engaging in this activity, the age of the juvenile, the presence or absence of a support network to prevent re-offending, the juvenile's amenability to rehabilitation, the frequency of exploitation, and the likelihood of rehabilitative success. Regarding the crime itself, the prosecutor should look to the circumstances surrounding the exploitation, whether the offender involved other juveniles, the role of this juvenile in the production, whether the production was commercial, whether it was for profit, the extent of the dissemination, the theme of the images, and the severity of the content.

Such a system will accomplish many important social functions. First, it will send a clear deterrent message to all people, even juveniles, that self-exploitation is the creation of child pornography and, therefore, is illegal and prosecutable. It will also recognize the severe social harm caused by the creation of such images and their circulation throughout the world. Finally, it will allow the state to have an array of alternative responses to this significant social ill, thus affording the state the discretion to determine if prosecution is required [or] another remedy is more appropriate.

———————

Maryjo Miller v. Jeff Mitchell in His Official Capacity as District Attorney of Wyoming County, Pennsylvania

598 F.3d 139 (3d Cir. 2010)

AMBRO, CIRCUIT JUDGE.

In 2008, the District Attorney of Wyoming County in Pennsylvania presented teens suspected of "sexting" with a choice: either attend an education program designed by the District Attorney in conjunction with two other agencies or face felony child pornography charges. Plaintiffs brought suit to enjoin the District Attorney from bringing criminal charges in retaliation for their refusal to attend the education program—an act they allege is constitutionally protected—and immediately filed a motion for preliminary injunctive relief. The District Court granted their motion. While the case was on appeal, the District Attorney determined that he would not file criminal charges against two of the three plaintiff minors. As to the remaining minor, Nancy Doe, and her mother, Jane Doe, we agree with the District Court that they have shown a likelihood of success on the merits of their constitutional retaliation claims, and therefore they are entitled to preliminary injunctive relief. Accordingly, we affirm.

"Sexting," as defined by plaintiffs, is "the practice of sending or posting sexually suggestive text messages and images, including nude or semi-nude photographs, via cellular telephones or over the Internet." In October 2008, school officials in the Tunkhannock, Pennsylvania, School District discovered photographs of semi-nude and nude teenage girls, many of whom were enrolled in their district, on several students' cell phones. The officials learned that male students had been trading these images over their cell phones, and turned the phones over to the Wyoming County District Attorney's Office. George Skumanick, then District Attorney, began an investigation.

In November 2008, Skumanick stated publicly to local newspaper reporters and an assembly at Tunkhannock High School that students possessing "inappropriate images of minors" could be prosecuted under Pennsylvania law for possession or distribution of child pornography, 18 Pa. Cons.Stat. §6312,[n.3][62] or criminal use of a communication facility, 18 Pa. Cons. Stat. §7512.[n.4][63] A few months later, Skumanick sent a letter to the parents of between 16 and 20 students—students on whose cell phones the pictures were stored and students appearing in the photographs—threatening to bring charges against those who did not participate in what has been referred to as an "education program":

---

62. [n.3] Section 6312, titled "[s]exual abuse of children," makes it a crime to "cause[ ] or knowingly permit[ ] a child under the age of 18 years to engage in a prohibited sexual act . . . if such person knows, has reason to know or intends that such act may be photographed, videotaped, depicted on computer or filmed."

63. Section 7512 prohibits the use of a communication facility "to commit, cause or facilitate the commission or the attempt thereof of any crime which constitutes a felony. . . ."

[Child's Name] has been identified in a police investigation involving the possession and/or dissemination of child pornography. In consultation with the Victims Resource Center and the Juvenile Probation Department, we have developed a six to nine month program which focuses on education and counseling. If you[r] son/daughter successfully completes this program[,] no charges will be filed and no record of his/her involvement will be maintained.

We have scheduled a meeting with all of the identified juveniles and their parents to discuss the program in more detail and to answer your questions. Following the meeting you will be asked to participate in the program. Participation in the program is voluntary. Please note, however, charges will be filed against those that do not participate or those that do not successfully complete the program.

The education program was divided into a Female Group and Male Group. The "Female Group" syllabus lists among its objectives that the participants "gain an understanding of what it means to be a girl in today's society, both advantages and disadvantages."

In the first session, students are assigned to write "a report explaining why you are here," "[w]hat you did," "[w]hy it was wrong," "[d]id you create a victim? If so, who?," and how their actions "affect[ed] the victim[,] [t]he school[, and] the community." The first two sessions focus on sexual violence, and the third on sexual harassment. The fourth session is titled "Gender identity-Gender strengths," and the fifth "Self Concept," which includes a "Gender Advantages and Disadvantages" exercise.

At the group meeting scheduled by the letter, held on February 12, 2009, Skumanick repeated his threat to bring felony charges unless the children submitted to probation, paid a $100 program fee, and completed the education program successfully. One parent, whose daughter had appeared in a photo wearing a bathing suit, asked how his child could be charged with child pornography based on that picture. Skumanick responded that she was posing "provocatively." When plaintiff Marissa Miller's father asked Skumanick who decided what "provocative" meant, Skumanick refused to answer and reminded his audience he could charge all of the minors with felonies, but instead was offering the education program. He told Mr. Miller, "[T]hese are the rules[. I]f you don't like them, too bad."

He then asked the parents to sign an agreement assigning the minors to probation and to participation in the program. Only one parent did so. Skumanick gave the other parents one week to sign.

Before the meeting, Skumanick had shown plaintiff MaryJo Miller and her ex-husband the two-year-old photograph of their daughter, in which Marissa Miller and Grace Kelly, 12 or 13-years-old at the time, are shown from the waist up wearing white, opaque bras. Marissa was speaking on the phone, while Grace was making a peace sign. Despite Ms. Miller's protests that her daughter and friend were merely being "goof balls" and were not naked, Skumanick claimed the image constituted child pornography because they were posed "provocatively." He promised to prosecute them on felony child pornography charges if they did not agree to his conditions and attend the proposed program.

After the meeting, Skumanick showed Jane Doe the photograph of her daughter Nancy, taken about a year earlier. In the photograph, Nancy is wrapped in a white, opaque towel, just below her breasts, appearing as if she just had emerged from the shower.

Eleven days later, on February 23, an administrator from Juvenile Court Services wrote the parents to inform them of an appointment scheduled for the following Saturday, February 28, at the Wyoming County Courthouse, "to finalize the paperwork for the informal adjustment." All of the parents and minors, except plaintiffs in this case, agreed to the conditions.

Plaintiffs filed suit on March 25, 2009, and immediately sought a temporary restraining order enjoining the District Attorney from initiating criminal charges against plaintiffs for the photographs. The District Court granted the requested relief on March 30, 2009, and the District Attorney timely filed an interlocutory appeal.

While this case was on appeal, Skumanick was defeated by Jeff Mitchell in the November 2009 election. Mitchell took office in January 2010. We refer to Skumanick when detailing the events underlying the lawsuit.

A party seeking a preliminary injunction must satisfy the traditional four-factor test: (1) a likelihood of success on the merits; (2) he or she will suffer irreparable harm if the injunction is denied; (3) granting relief will not result in even greater harm to the nonmoving party; and (4) the public interest favors such relief.

We agree with the District Court's analysis of irreparable harm, harm to the nonmoving party, and the public interest, and therefore focus our discussion, as did the parties, on the first factor, likelihood of success on the merits. At this stage, we "generally do[ ] not go into the merits any farther than is necessary to determine whether the moving party established a likelihood of success."

To state a claim under § 1983, plaintiffs must show that the defendant, under the color of state law, deprived them of a federal constitutional or statutory right. Plaintiffs base their claims on retaliation for the exercise of constitutionally protected rights, which "is itself a violation of rights secured by the Constitution actionable under section 1983." To prevail on a retaliation claim, a plaintiff must prove "(1) that he engaged in constitutionally-protected activity; (2) that the government responded with retaliation; and (3) that the protected activity caused the retaliation."

Plaintiffs have shown a reasonable likelihood of establishing that coercing Doe's participation in the education program violated (a) Jane Doe's Fourteenth Amendment right to parental autonomy and (b) Nancy Doe's First Amendment right against compelled speech.

Parents have a Fourteenth Amendment substantive due process right "to raise their children without undue state interference." "Choices about marriage, family life, and the upbringing of children are among associational rights this Court has ranked as of basic importance in our society, rights sheltered by the Fourteenth Amendment against the State's unwarranted usurpation, disregard, or disrespect." Indeed, the "interest of parents in the care, custody, and control of their children[ ] is perhaps the oldest of the fundamental liberty interests," and is well-established by long-standing Supreme Court precedent.

Here, Jane Doe objects to the education program's lessons in why the minors' actions were wrong, what it means to be a girl in today's society, and non-traditional societal and job roles. She particularly opposes these value lessons from a District Attorney who has "stated publicly that a teen[ ]age girl who voluntarily posed for a photo wearing a swimsuit violated Pennsylvania's child pornography statute." The program's teachings that the minors' actions were morally "wrong" and created a victim contradict the beliefs she wishes to instill in her daughter.

We agree that an individual District Attorney may not coerce parents into permitting him to impose on their children his ideas of morality and gender roles. An essential component of Jane Doe's right to raise her daughter—the "responsibility to inculcate moral standards, religious beliefs, and elements of good citizenship,"—was interfered with by the District Attorney's actions. While it may have been constitutionally permissible for the District Attorney to offer this education voluntarily (that is, free of consequences for not attending), he was not free to coerce attendance by threatening prosecution.

Government action that requires stating a particular message favored by the government violates the First Amendment right to refrain from speaking. A violation of the First Amendment right against compelled speech occurs "only in the context of actual compulsion," although that compulsion need not be a direct threat.

According to plaintiffs, the compelled speech arises from the program's requirement that the minors write a homework paper explaining "how [their] actions were wrong." Jane and Nancy Doe do not agree that appearing in the photograph was wrong, and they assert that requiring Nancy Doe to write an essay to that effect "invades the sphere of intellect and spirit which it is the purpose of the First Amendment to our Constitution to reserve from all official control." The compulsion here takes the form of the District Attorney's promise to prosecute Doe if she does not satisfactorily complete the education program.

We agree that Nancy Doe likely can show that the education program would violate her First Amendment freedom against compelled speech. She would be required to explain why her actions were wrong (presumably as a *moral*, not a *legal*, matter) in the context of a program that purports to teach, as Mitchell's counsel described at oral argument, "[w]hat it means to be a girl; sexual self-respect, [and] sexual identity." "[W]hat it means to be a girl in today's society," while an important sociological concern, in this case is a disconnect with the criminal and juvenile justice systems. This mismatch is all the more troubling given the age of the program's participants. Minors often are more susceptible to external influences, and while this susceptibility may weigh in favor of certain educational or rehabilitative programs, it also cautions against allowing actors in the juvenile and criminal justice systems to venture outside the realm of their elected authority.

Plaintiffs must show the Government responded with a retaliatory act. The test in our Circuit for determining whether an action is treated as retaliation is whether it is "sufficient to deter a person of ordinary firmness from exercising his constitutional rights." There is no doubt a prosecution meets this test, and the District Attorney does not argue otherwise.

There must be a causal link between the protected activity (the first element) and the retaliatory act (the second element). Plaintiffs allege that there is no probable cause to prosecute Doe, and the District Attorney's only motive for bringing a prosecution is to retaliate against her for refusing to attend the education program. We agree that plaintiffs have shown a likelihood of success on the causation prong of their retaliation claim, given the District Attorney's explicit statement that he will respond to (that is, retaliate for) Nancy Doe's failure to attend the education program, or not completing that program if she starts, by prosecuting her.

That the District Attorney's motive in bringing a prosecution is likely retaliatory is supported by the lack of evidence of probable cause. Assuming that the sexual abuse of children law applies to a minor depicted in the allegedly pornographic photograph, and that the photo in question could constitute a "prohibited sexual act"[n.16][64] (issues on which we need not opine), we discern no indication from this record that the District Attorney had any evidence that Doe ever possessed or distributed the photo. When asked at oral argument the basis for probable cause to charge Doe with possession or distribution of child pornography, Mitchell's counsel answered that it was "[t]he existence of that photograph . . . [,] the presence of that photograph on the cell phones of one or more of her . . . classmates." But appearing in a photograph provides no evidence as to whether that person possessed or transmitted the photo. Mitchell's counsel could not make a representation to us as to whether the District Attorney had, at the time of the TRO hearing, any evidence of her transmission of the photo. Despite ample opportunity, the District Attorney has failed to present any semblance of probable cause.

In sum, absent an injunction, the Does would have to choose either to assert their constitutional rights and face a prosecution of Nancy Doe based not on probable cause but as punishment for exercising their constitutional rights, or forgo

---

64. [n.16] "Prohibited sexual act" is defined as "sexual intercourse . . . , masturbation, sadism, masochism, bestiality, fellatio, cunnilingus, lewd exhibition of the genitals or nudity if such nudity is depicted for the purpose of sexual stimulation or gratification of any person who might view such depiction." The photograph of Doe could only fall under the last category—"nudity . . . depicted for the purpose of sexual stimulation or gratification of any person who might view such depiction."

those rights and avoid prosecution. On the facts before us, this Hobson's Choice is unconstitutional.

————————

Notes

Professor Leary, in the article excerpted, did not advocate prosecution of juveniles involved in production of child pornography as the preferred result but does argue that society should have a comprehensive multi-disciplinary response, including the option to involve juvenile courts if necessary in the most egregious of cases. She wrote a follow-up article detailing that prosecutors, together with members of other disciplines, should create a protocol using a variety of factors, including the nature of the offense, characteristics of the offender, and availability of other resources, to determine whether a juvenile court prosecution should be initiated. *See* Mary Graw Leary, *Sexting or Self-Produced Child Pornography? The Dialog Continues-Structured Prosecutorial Discretion Within a Multidisciplinary Response*, 17 Va. J. Soc. Pol'y & L. 486 (2010).

For a different point of view than proposed in Professor Leary' article, *see* Stephen F. Smith, *Jail for Juvenile Child Pornographers?: a Reply to Professor Leary*, 15 Va. J. Soc. Pol'y & L. 505 (2008) Professor Smith argues:

> In my view, children who produce and distribute pornographic images of themselves ordinarily should not be regarded as proper objects of punishment. In this context, child protective services, backed up if necessary by the threat of criminal prosecution, is a much more appropriate way of reforming minors and protecting them against the serious dangers to which they expose themselves by creating and distributing pornographic images of themselves. A prosecution-based response, though essential for sexual predators and others involved in the sexual exploitation of minors, would create far more problems than it would solve for minors who make the mistake of creating and distributing pornographic images of themselves.

Professor Leary, Professor Smith, and the litigation in *Gray* and *Miller* offer different perspectives on the problem of sexting. What is the proper societal response to sexting by children? Should it make a difference for criminal liability that the intended recipient was another juvenile (as compared to the adult in *Gray*) or whether the activity occurred in a school context? Are minors a protected class and not subject at all to prosecution?

Chapter 14

Policing the Internet for Crimes Involving Exploitation of Children

In response to the victimization of children through the use of computers and the Internet, law enforcement, legislatures, and private actors have responded in diverse ways to police the Internet. This chapter addresses some of those responses. It also examines the defense of entrapment and limitations on the liability of social networking sites for activity occurring on those sites.

§ 14.1 Traveler Cases

Child predators often use the internet to identify, and then coerce, their victims to engage in illegal sex acts. These criminals will lurk in chat rooms or on bulletin board websites that are popular with children and teenagers. They will gain the child's confidence and trust, and will then direct the conversation to sexual topics. Sometimes they send the child sexually explicit images of themselves, or they may request that the child send them pornographic images of themselves. Often, the defendants plan a face-to-face for the purpose of engaging in sex acts.[1]

From 2004 through 2008, [Internet Crimes Against Children] task force officers processed 20,562 documented online enticement complaints, including 7,879 documented complaints of suspected *travelers* — aggressive and dangerous online child predators who travel to the location of a child for the purpose of establishing physical contact.[2]

The next case, *Zahursky*, exemplifies the activities of two actors: persons interested in finding children on the Internet and sting operations set up by government agents to identify and arrest those persons. When reading the case, note the details of the conversation: Is the government agent doing or saying anything that you would consider improper? The two cases following *Zahursky* discuss when a person is entrapped by the government. Note the items that Zahursky brought with him at the time he was arrested; those are typical items that the police look for in

---

1. U.S. Dep't of Justice, The National Strategy for Child Exploitation Prevention and Interdiction: A Report to Congress 3 (2010).
2. *Id.* at 29.

traveler cases. The case addresses whether the seizure of those items was proper. As with many individuals who have a sexual interest in children, Zahursky had other encounters with children and the government produced evidence to that effect at his trial. Zahursky's challenge to that evidence is also a common claim.

United States v. Erik D. Zahursky
580 F.3d 515 (7th Cir. 2009)

Tinder, Circuit Judge.

A jury convicted Erik D. Zahursky of attempting to coerce or entice a minor under the age of eighteen to engage in sexual activity in violation of 18 U.S.C. § 2422(b).

On June 2, 2006, someone using the screen name "Gracepace101" contacted "Sad-Shelly200" in an adult internet chat room in *Yahoo!*. Shelly was the screen name of a fictitious fourteen-year-old girl created by Special Agent Ryan Moore, a member of the Electronic Crime Squad of the United States Secret Service. Shelly's *Yahoo!* profile which could be viewed by other persons in the chat room included a photo of a young girl. Moore checked the *Yahoo!* profile for Gracepace and learned that Gracepace's real name was Erik D. Zahursky.

In the first chat session, Zahursky initiated contact with "ur a cutie — [b]ummer i am old enough to be ur daddy." Shelly asked Zahursky how old he was, and he answered "34." He said that he was looking for ladies, but most were too far away, taken, too old or too young, but added that "i have [d]one a 14 year ol[d]." Zahursky asked Shelly if she was sexually active and whether she liked "older men." He stated that she was "lil young to be intimate with" unless she didn't mind. Zahursky asked Shelly where she lived and offered to meet with her to engage in sexual activity, saying: "woul[d] u like to [h]ave sex wit[h] me?" Shelly asked about his previous sexual encounters and whether the women were "like me?" Zahursky responded, "One was, s[h]e is now 18." The chat session continued for almost two hours with Zahursky explaining what he wanted them to do to each other sexually. About midway through the chat session, Zahursky suggested that he and Shelly meet and "play at [yo]ur house w[h]ile mommy is at work?" He cautioned that they would have to be discreet "because of society's view of age." Shelly asked about "the other girl like me." Zahursky reiterated that she was eighteen years old and said the last time he saw her she was fifteen. A few minutes later, Zahursky emailed Shelly, stating that "to initiate [yo]u into womanhoo[d] would be an honor." He also expressed an interest in a threesome involving two ladies.

Moore, posing as Shelly, had numerous chats and email communications with Zahursky almost daily from June 2 to June 21, 2006. In their chats and emails, Zahursky gave detailed descriptions of the sexual activities in which he wanted to engage with Shelly. His sexual intentions were clear. On June 10, Zahursky emailed Shelly that he would try to visit her the last two weeks of July.

On June 13, Zahursky emailed Shelly about having a threesome with two girls. He said that he was on the internet a few days before and "found another 14-year-old lady who might be interested in a 3-some." He discussed the sexual activities that the three of them could do together. Shelly wrote back to Zahursky, stating that she had figured out how they could get together — she would tell her mom that she was staying over with her friend Lindsey. In an instant message later that evening, Shelly asked Zahursky if he really wanted to be with her since she was inexperienced, and he said, "yes — we can experience each other — want to be with an old man? Another girl your age?" Shelly wrote, "sure, but I'm only 14, are you sure you still want me?" Zahursky replied, "the other girl is 14." He added that "Holly" was asking whether Shelly liked her. The next day, Zahursky emailed Shelly that the other fourteen-year-old was "Holly1989cutie."

Subsequently, he emailed Shelly that he hoped they could get together and that Holly could join them. He also suggested that Shelly's friend Lindsey might like to join them for "a sleep over for a week." Shelly emailed Zahursky on June 18 indicating that Lindsey was interested in joining them but would be away in July, so they had to meet in June. In another chat session, Shelly told Zahursky that Lindsey wanted to know if he had "any experience with girls our age, because she wants to know if you know how to treat us so it won't hurt." Zahursky wrote back "I won't hurt you. I have had one at 14." Shelly questioned, "For real?" and Zahursky replied, "Yes."

Zahursky and Shelly arranged to meet on June 21 at a Starbucks in Valparaiso, Indiana. He told her that he drove a gold Mercury Sable and described the clothing he would be wearing to their meeting. When Zahursky said he did not have enough money for a hotel room, Shelly suggested that they stay with Lindsey in her sister's dorm room. Subsequent emails and chats disclose that Zahursky and Shelly agreed to spend a few days together in the dorm room.

On June 19, Zahursky sent an email to Lindsey, using Shelly's email account, discussing his sexual intentions for the three of them. He asked whether he should bring condoms. Later that afternoon in a conversation about their meeting, Zahursky asked Shelly, "u want me to bring con[d]oms?" Shelly asked about hooking up "with the other girl that you met." Zahursky said that the other girl's screen name was "Holly1989cutie." Later he mentioned Holly again, saying that he was trying "to get a meet" for the three of them. Shelly asked if Zahursky was going to bring the K-Y stuff since it was her first time and she didn't want it to hurt. He said that he would check a pharmacy for K-Y warming lube. In a June 20 instant message, Shelly again asked if Zahursky was going to bring the K-Y. He responded that he had to check the pharmacy and that he would have the lube.

On June 21, Zahursky drove from his home in Lexington, Illinois, across state lines to the Starbucks in Valparaiso. He was driving a Mercury Sable and wearing the clothing he had described to Shelly. When he arrived at Starbucks, he went inside where he was approached by Moore and other agents who asked him to step outside. The agents took Zahursky into custody, patted him down, and handcuffed him in the parking lot. Moore knew from Zahursky's conversations with Shelly that

Zahursky had discussed the use of condoms and had said that he would bring some form of K-Y warming lubricant to his meeting with Shelly. However, no condoms or K-Y lubricant were found on Zahursky's person.

Meanwhile, Secret Service Agent Richard Bardwell had begun to search Zahursky's vehicle located outside of Starbucks. In the glove box, Bardwell found a coin purse that contained three condoms. From the trunk, he recovered a duffel bag that contained lubricant and more condoms. The agents searching the vehicle also found a printed copy of directions from Zahursky's residence in Illinois to the Starbucks in Valparaiso and a printed email message between Zahursky and Shelly.

Then the agents transported Zahursky to the Valparaiso police station where he was interviewed by Moore and another agent. Prior to any questioning about the offense, the agents advised Zahursky of his *Miranda* rights. Zahursky waived them and gave a recorded statement. During the interview, Zahursky stated that he was in Valparaiso to meet Shelly and Lindsey, two fourteen-year-old girls with whom he had on-line correspondence and with whom he intended to engage in sex.

Zahursky was tried by a jury. The district court, over the defendant's objection, admitted three pieces of evidence under Rule 404(b). The first was testimony by a young lady (who we will refer to as "SS") that she had sexual intercourse with Zahursky on two occasions five years earlier when she was fourteen or fifteen years old. The second piece of evidence was an internet chat on June 14, 2006, between someone using the Gracepace screen name and someone with the screen name "Xanthery." The person using the Gracepace name asked Xanthery if she would "ever consi[d]er [h]aving sex with an ol[d]er guy—like maybe me?" Xanthery's response was, "would you ever have sex with someone my age? ?" The reply was, "i have—14."

The third piece of Rule 404(b) evidence was several internet chats from June 11 through 15, 2006, between Zahursky and someone with the screen name "Holly1989cutie." On June 11 Holly identified herself as a fourteen-year-old female and asked if Zahursky liked younger girls. He said yes and offered to teach Holly how to have sexual intercourse and receive oral sex. Holly asked Zahursky if he had been with girls her age, and he answered yes, a fourteen-year-old. He suggested that while Holly's mom was at work, they could have a few sessions and continue at a hotel. He described the sexual things he wanted them to do to each other. Later that day, he sent Holly a message, saying that he couldn't wait to touch her all over. On June 13, Zahursky sent Holly an instant message, stating that he may have found another fourteen-year-old girl who would like to join them in a threesome. He said he wanted the three of them to get together for a few days and get acquainted sexually. Zahursky sent a similar message a few hours later, this time indicating that the other fourteen-year-old's screen name was "Sad_Shelly200." On June 15, he sent Holly a message saying that he could come over while her mom was at work so they could get to know each other and that she could spend the night or a couple of days with him "playing naughty."

Following the admission of the Rule 404(b) evidence, the district court gave the jury limiting instructions. The court instructed that SS's testimony and the chats between Gracepace101 and Holly1989cutie could be considered "only on the question of intent, motive, absence of mistake and modus operandi" and "only for this limited purpose." The court also instructed the jury that the evidence of the chat between Gracepace101 and Xanthery could be considered "only on the question of intent, motive and absence of mistake" and only for such limited purpose.

Zahursky testified at trial. He claimed that he talked to minors in adult chat rooms to use "reverse psychology" to get them to leave the chat rooms. He alleged that he was about to cut off the chats with Shelly when he suspected she was a cop, which made him curious, so he went to meet her to confirm his suspicions. He denied that he was going to the Starbucks to meet Shelly and have sex with her.

Zahursky contends that the district court erred in denying his motion to suppress the evidence found during the search of his vehicle.

A warrantless search is per se unreasonable under the Fourth Amendment subject to a few well-established exceptions. One of the exceptions is the automobile exception first recognized in *Carroll v. United States*, 267 U.S. 132 (1925). Under this exception, where there is probable cause to believe that a vehicle contains contraband or evidence of a crime, law enforcement may conduct a warrantless search of the vehicle.

"Probable cause" exists where based on a totality of the circumstances "there is a fair probability that contraband or evidence of a crime will be found in a particular place." It requires a probability, not absolute certainty, that contraband or evidence of a crime will be found.

The record establishes probable cause to search the vehicle. The agents knew from the internet chats and email messages with Shelly that Zahursky planned to bring condoms and lubricant with him. Thus, they had probable cause, based on Zahursky's own statements, to believe that Zahursky had these items, which would be evidence of a crime, with him when he met Shelly on June 21.

Furthermore, it was reasonable to believe that Zahursky would have left these items in his car instead of taking them into Starbucks. He surely wasn't going to use the condoms and lubricant inside Starbucks. Zahursky and Shelly had planned only to meet at the Starbucks before going to Lindsey's sister's dorm room where they planned to engage in sexual activity. It seems just as probable, if not more probable, that Zahursky would leave these items safely in his car until he reached his end destination rather than carrying them—needlessly—into a public coffee shop. Perhaps he would have a condom or two and some lubricant on his person. But based on his chats and emails with Shelly, it was reasonable to believe that Zahursky would have a collection of condoms and lubricant with him. He did, after all, anticipate repeated and continuous sexual activity with Shelly (and Lindsey) rather than one, brief sexual encounter. So, even if incriminating evidence had been found on his person, that would not negate the probability that more of the same would be found in his car.

Moreover, the agents had probable cause to search the car for evidence of the crime other than condoms and lubricant. They could search, for example, for evidence of Zahursky's trip from Lexington, Illinois, to Valparaiso, Indiana. Using a "means of interstate . . . commerce" is an element of the offense. There was a fair probability that the agents would find some evidence of Zahursky's interstate travel in his car—perhaps a map and/or directions, or a toll or gas receipt. These types of things likely would be found in a vehicle that had been driven some distance (150 miles based on Zahursky's testimony) and across state lines. And, as we know, the agents did find a printout of directions from Zahursky's house in Illinois to the Starbucks in Valparaiso.

Where law enforcement agents have probable cause to search a vehicle, they may search all areas in the vehicle in which contraband or evidence of criminal activity might be found, including closed containers, packages, compartments, and trunks. Therefore, the agents could lawfully search the glove compartment and trunk. It was reasonable to believe that condoms might be found in the coin purse and duffel bag; thus, upon finding the purse and bag, the agents could lawfully search those items as well. It also was reasonable to believe that lubricant might be found in the duffel bag which likely contained Zahursky's clothes and personal effects for his overnight visit with Shelly.

Zahursky's second challenge on appeal is to the trial court's admission of evidence under Rule 404(b). The court admitted evidence of Zahursky's internet chats with Xanthery and Holly and allowed SS to testify. We review the admission of Rule 404(b) evidence for an abuse of discretion. Evidence is admissible under Rule 404(b) if:

(1) the evidence is directed toward establishing a matter in issue other than the defendant's propensity to commit the crime charged;

(2) the evidence shows that the other act is similar enough and close enough in time to be relevant to the matter in issue;

(3) the evidence is sufficient to support a jury finding that the defendant committed the similar act; and

(4) the probative value of the evidence is not substantially outweighed by the danger of unfair prejudice.

Zahursky claims that segments of the Holly and Xanthery chats were not probative of his motive, intent, or lack of mistake but gave unnecessary, shocking, repulsive and sexually explicit details. Zahursky's knowledge and intent were at issue. "Prior instances of sexual misconduct with a child victim may establish a defendant's sexual interest in children and thereby serve as evidence of the defendant's motive to commit a charged offense involving the sexual exploitation of children." In both the Holly and Xanthery chats, Zahursky admitted to having had sex with a fourteen-year-old. And, in the Holly chats Zahursky clearly expressed his sexual interest in fourteen-year-old girls. Zahursky's admission to having had sex with a fourteen-year-old and the sexually explicit nature of the Xanthery and Holly chats make them probative as to his intent and motive in chatting with Shelly and then meeting her at Starbucks.

The revelations of the girls' ages in the chats make the chat evidence probative as to Zahursky's knowledge and absence of mistake. Holly told Zahursky that she was fourteen. Zahursky wrote Holly that he may have found another fourteen-year-old girl who might join them in a threesome and later identified the girl to Holly as none other than Shelly. Thus, this chat evidence is probative of Zahursky's knowledge that his target for sexual activity was a minor under the age of eighteen. The evidence is also probative as to the absence of any mistake on Zahursky's part regarding Shelly's age.

Zahursky next argues that the probative value of the Holly and Xanthery chats was substantially outweighed by excessively prejudicial details. He claims that the chats were cumulative evidence of his character. That evidence may be highly prejudicial does not compel its exclusion; the evidence must be *unfairly* prejudicial. "Evidence is unfairly prejudicial only if it will induce the jury to decide the case on an improper basis, commonly an emotional one, rather than on the evidence presented."

Zahursky has not shown that the district court erred in its implicit determination that the probative value of the chat evidence was not substantially outweighed by the danger of unfair prejudice or its cumulative nature. Zahursky denied going to meet Shelly with the intent to have sex with a minor. Without question, the chats were sexually explicit and detailed. In the chats with Holly, Zahursky wrote openly and graphically about his sexual fantasies and instructed Holly about sex and pleasuring men. The sexually explicit nature of the chat transcripts; Zahursky's open, graphic, and detailed discussions of his sexual fantasies; and his instructions to Holly about how to please men made this evidence highly probative. We see no reason to second-guess the district court's assessment that the "prejudicial" details were not unfairly prejudicial.

Lastly, Zahursky submits that SS's testimony was highly prejudicial because it was cumulative of information in the Shelly, Holly, and Xanthery chats; his confessions which were introduced into evidence; and his testimony on cross-examination. He also claims that SS's testimony inflamed the jury's emotions. However, SS's testimony was not merely cumulative; it came from a victim of Zahursky. Thus, SS's testimony was highly probative of Zahursky's intent and motive in chatting with and meeting Shelly. SS's testimony also showed that Zahursky intended to follow through with his plan to engage Shelly in sexual activities with him. Finally, it corroborated the accuracy of some of the critical vouching of his experience with an underage girl contained in the Shelly and Holly chats, thus further identifying Zahursky as the participant in those chats.

The Holly chats, Xanthery chats, and SS's testimony were admissible to rebut Zahursky's claims at trial as to why he chatted with Shelly about sex—to get minors to leave adult chat rooms; and why he drove to the Starbucks—not for coffee and not to meet Shelly for sex, but out of curiosity as to whether she was a college student or cop. This evidence also was admissible to rebut Zahursky's denial that he intended to have sex with a minor. Accordingly, this evidence was admissible to prove Zahursky's motive, intent, knowledge, and absence of mistake.

While this Rule 404(b) evidence might appeal to the jury's emotions (and surely didn't give anyone a favorable impression of Zahursky), the district court gave a limiting instruction, both after the jury heard the Rule 404(b) evidence and then again in the final jury instructions. "Absent any showing that the jury could not follow the court's limiting instruction, we presume that the jury limited its consideration of the testimony in accordance with the court's instruction." Zahursky has not shown that the jury could not follow the court's limiting instruction. We therefore can assume that this instruction removed any unfair prejudice from the admission of the Rule 404(b) evidence.

---

§ 14.2 Using a Computer to Entice a Child; Entrapment

State v. James R. Pischel

762 N.W.2d 595 (Neb. 2009)

MILLER-LERMAN, J.

James R. Pischel appeals his conviction for use of a computer to entice a child or a peace officer believed to be a child for sexual purposes, a violation of Neb. Rev. Stat. § 28-320.02.

Edward Sexton, an officer with the Lincoln Police Department, was assigned as an investigator in the technical investigations unit. As part of his investigative duties, Sexton would go into online chat rooms posing as a person under the age of 16. In February 2007, Sexton created a fictional profile with the screen name "ljb92." The profile for "ljb92" indicated that the user was a female located in Lincoln. The "Age" section of the profile was left blank, but in a miscellaneous section of the profile, it was stated that "92 is the year i was born."

Sexton testified that as "ljb92," on March 7, 2007, he had an online communication in a Nebraska chat room with a person using the screen name "lincolnpietaster." During the March 7 conversation, Sexton stated that "ljb92" was a 15-year-old female and "lincolnpietaster" responded by stating that "ljb92" was too young for him. Sexton testified at trial that after "lincolnpietaster" stated on March 7 that "ljb92" was too young for him, Sexton as "ljb92" responded, "Whatever." The conversation ended.

On June 1, 2007, Sexton was online under the "ljb92" screen name when he was contacted via instant messaging by a person using the screen name "lincolnpietaster."

Sexton believed that the screen name contained a sexual innuendo referring to oral sex. Pischel admitted at trial that he had communicated with "ljb92" using the screen name "lincolnpietaster" and that the name had a sexual innuendo that indicated he would like to perform oral sex on a woman.

The June 1, 2007, instant messaging conversation between Sexton as "ljb92" and Pischel as "lincolnpietaster" lasted approximately 3 hours, from shortly after noon until shortly before 3 p.m. While we would have preferred to paraphrase certain portions of such communications, the text of the communications is critical to the crime charged and to our analysis, and we therefore recite herein the actual words used by the parties to the communications, including grammatical errors.

Early in the conversation, "ljb92" sent a message asking, "asl?" which Sexton testified meant a request for the other person's age, sex, and location. Pischel identified himself as being "25 m," meaning a 25-year-old male. Sexton as "ljb92" responded with "15 f," indicating a 15-year-old female. Pischel asked "ljb92" for a picture, to which "ljb92" responded "u first." Pischel sent a picture of himself to "ljb92." Sexton sent Pischel pictures of a female officer from when she was 15 years old or younger.

The first part of the conversation involved general topics, but eventually Pischel asked "ljb92" whether she had any plans for the day and what she would like to do. Pischel told "ljb92" to "let me know if your ever looking for some fun" and "I'm always looking for pussy to eat." Sexton as "ljb92" responded "u really offering?" and Pischel responded "yeah, as long as your not a cop trying to bust me for sex with a minor." Sexton as "ljb92" denied being a police officer, and the conversation continued in this vein, with Pischel later stating, "but yeah if you want your pussy eaten, or more I'm offering" and "oh I'm cool if thats all you want . . . but I'll do anything else you want me to." Pischel asked "ljb92" "do you want to have sex, or do you want to give me oral, or do you just want to jack me off"; "ljb92" responded "how bout first 2."

Pischel then asked "so would you like me to come over?" and "ljb92" responded "not here," but asked whether he had a place to meet. Pischel proposed meeting at a restaurant; "ljb92" instead proposed meeting at Tierra Park near 27th Street and Highway 2. Pischel told "ljb92" that he would be driving "a green ford contour." The two made tentative plans to meet that day, but Pischel later decided it would not work and said that another day might work better. The two exchanged telephone numbers; Sexton as "ljb92" gave Pischel a number that belonged to the Lincoln Police Department. After Pischel determined that a meeting would not work on June 1, 2007, Sexton as "ljb92" told Pischel "I'm kinna let down," "feel like i been stood up," and "i close to being pissed" and sent Pischel an emoticon expressing anger. We note that in *U.S. v. Cochran*, 534 F.3d 631, 632 n. 1 (7th Cir. 2008), the court quoted a dictionary definition of "'emoticon'" as being "'a group of keyboard characters . . . that typically represents a facial expression or suggests an attitude or emotion and that is used especially in computerized communications (as e-mail).'" The conversation, continued for some time with graphic sexual talk, and during the conversation, Pischel told "ljb92" that his name was "James" and that he lived near 14th Street and Old Cheney Road. The two eventually ended the conversation by making plans for another online chat the next Monday, June 4.

At approximately 9:40 a.m. on June 4, 2007, "lincolnpietaster" initiated an instant messaging conversation with "ljb92." The conversation began with general topics but after 20 minutes, Pischel as "lincolnpietaster" said "maybe you should invite me over to eat you." Sexton as "ljb92" agreed that they could meet at the park they had discussed in the earlier conversation. Pischel stated he could meet "ljb92" at the park in 10 minutes and would be in a green car. Pischel ended the conversation at approximately 10:40 a.m., stating "see you soon."

During the June 4, 2007, conversation, Sexton realized a meeting was being set up and began making arrangements to have officers at Tierra Park. Between the June 1 and 4 conversations, Sexton and fellow investigators had discovered information about Pischel. Using the telephone number and other information Pischel gave in the June 1 conversation, investigators determined where Pischel lived. Investigators identified Pischel by comparing the picture he sent to "ljb92" to his driver's license photograph obtained from the Department of Motor Vehicles. Investigators also matched the description Pischel gave of his car to motor vehicle records for a car owned by Pischel.

An officer was observing Pischel's residence on the morning of June 4, 2007, and at approximately 10:45 a.m., the officer informed investigators stationed near Tierra Park that Pischel had left his residence and was headed toward the park. Officers observed Pischel's vehicle arrive and briefly park on a street adjacent to Tierra Park. Pischel began to drive away from the park but then turned back toward the park. Investigators asked an officer in a marked police cruiser to make a traffic stop of Pischel's vehicle. After stopping the vehicle, officers removed Pischel from the vehicle, arrested him, placed him in handcuffs, and placed him in the back of the police cruiser. Officers conducted a search of Pischel's vehicle and found two condoms in the console between the driver's seat and the passenger seat.

Sexton arrived at the scene after the officers had begun searching Pischel's vehicle. Pischel consented to a search of his home, and Sexton conducted the search. Sexton found a computer in the home and brought it to the police department for a search, which uncovered copies of the photographs that "ljb92" had sent to "lincolnpietaster" and information which indicated that the photograph files had been created on June 1, 2007, and accessed on June 4. The search also revealed a copy of the profile Sexton had created for "ljb92" and a copy of the photograph that Pischel had sent to "ljb92."

At trial, over Pischel's objection, the court admitted into evidence the condoms found in the search.

At trial, the court admitted into evidence printed transcripts of the two online conversations between "ljb92" and "lincolnpietaster" that occurred on June 1 and 4, 2007.

Pischel testified in his own defense. He admitted that he took part in the online chats with "ljb92" and that "ljb92" claimed to be a 15-year-old female; however, he testified that he did not believe that "ljb92" was under 16 years of age, because of various things the two had discussed and because the June 1, 2007, chat took place at a time when a 15-year-old would have been in school. Pischel testified that he thought "ljb92" was a woman in her late teens or early twenties who was merely interested in role-playing as a 15-year-old and that he did not question her age because he did not want "to break that role-play and risk not talking to her again."

Pischel testified that during the chats, he had lied about his own age, saying he was 25 when he was actually 30. Pischel testified that he was not interested in having sexual relations with a girl under 18 and that he had no interest in child pornography. He stated that he went to the park on June 4, 2007, hoping to meet a woman over the age of 18.

On cross-examination, Pischel admitted that he initiated the online conversations with "ljb92" on June 1 and 4, 2007; that he initiated the discussions of sexual behavior; that when he wrote to "ljb92" stating, "'I'm always looking for pussy to eat,'" it was not in response to any solicitation for sex on the part of "ljb92"; and that his intent in arranging times and places with "ljb92" was to meet "ljb92" and to engage in the sexual acts he had offered.

The jury found Pischel guilty of violating § 28-320.02. The district court thereafter sentenced Pischel to imprisonment for 1 to 2 years.

Pischel asserts that there was not sufficient evidence to support his conviction.

When reviewing a criminal conviction for sufficiency of the evidence to sustain the conviction, the relevant question for an appellate court is whether, after viewing the evidence in the light most favorable to the prosecution, any rational trier of fact could have found the essential elements of the crime beyond a reasonable doubt. An appellate court does not resolve conflicts in the evidence, pass on the credibility of witnesses, or reweigh the evidence. Such matters are for the finder of fact.

Pischel was charged under § 28-320.02 which provides:

> No person shall knowingly solicit, coax, entice, or lure (a) a child sixteen years of age or younger or (b) a peace officer who is believed by such person to be a child sixteen years of age or younger, by means of a computer . . . to engage in an act which would be in violation of section 28-319. . . .

The main pieces of evidence supporting Pischel's conviction were the transcripts of the online conversations between Pischel and Sexton posing as "ljb92." Such transcripts provided evidence that Pischel used a computer to communicate with a person using the screen name "ljb92," who Pischel was told was a 15-year-old girl. The transcripts further showed that Pischel offered to perform cunnilingus on "ljb92," asked whether "ljb92" wanted to have sexual intercourse with him and perform fellatio on him, suggested that the two meet to engage in such activities, and made arrangements to meet with "ljb92." In order to prove that Pischel was the person using the screen name "lincolnpietaster" to communicate with "ljb92," the State presented evidence that Pischel arrived at the time and location arranged for a meeting between "lincolnpietaster" and "ljb92." In addition to the evidence presented by the State, in his testimony offered in his defense, Pischel admitted that he took part in online conversations with "ljb92" using the screen name "lincolnpietaster," that he initiated such conversations, and that he initiated discussions of sexual behavior.

From such evidence the jury, as a rational trier of facts, could have found that Pischel used a computer to communicate with a police officer posing as a child 16 years of age or younger and that during such conversation Pischel solicited, coaxed, enticed, or lured such person to engage in acts of cunnilingus, fellatio, and sexual intercourse and that such acts, when performed with a person less than 16 years of age, would have been in violation of § 28-319.

Pischel argues that the evidence was insufficient to establish that he actually believed that "ljb92" was a 15-year-old girl. In this regard, he refers us to his testimony at trial that he did not believe "ljb92" was really a 15-year-old girl and that instead, he believed that "ljb92" was an adult woman who was role-playing as a 15-year-old. He also refers us to the online conversations where he points out that although he was offering to have sexual relations with "ljb92," he also indicated he did not want to meet if "ljb92" was "a cop trying to bust me for sex with a minor."

In contrast, the State notes that there was evidence that during the conversations, "ljb92" stated that "she" was 15 years old, that "ljb92" sent Pischel a picture of a girl who was 15 years old or younger and told Pischel that it was a picture of "ljb92," and that Pischel's computer contained the profile created for "ljb92" which indicated that "ljb92" was born in 1992. It is for the jury to assess the credibility of witnesses and the evidence noted by the State was sufficient to give the jury a basis to find that, contrary to Pischel's testimony, Pischel actually believed that "ljb92" was a child 16 years of age or younger.

Pischel next asserts that the district court erred by refusing his requested instruction on entrapment. We conclude that there was no evidence to raise the defense and that therefore, the court did not err in refusing the instruction.

When a defendant raises the defense of entrapment, the trial court must determine, as a matter of law, whether the defendant has presented sufficient evidence to warrant a jury instruction on entrapment. In Nebraska, entrapment is an affirmative defense consisting of two elements: (1) the government induced the defendant to commit the offense charged and (2) the defendant's predisposition to commit the criminal act was such that the defendant was not otherwise ready and willing to commit the offense. The burden of going forward with evidence of government inducement is on the defendant. In assessing whether the defendant has satisfied this burden, the initial duty of the court is to determine whether there is sufficient evidence that the government has induced the defendant to commit a crime. This determination is made as a matter of law, and the defendant's evidence of inducement need be only more than a scintilla to satisfy his or her initial burden.

A defendant need not present evidence of entrapment; he or she can point to such evidence in the government's case in chief or extract it from the cross-examination of the government's witnesses.

Inducement can be any government conduct creating a substantial risk that an otherwise law-abiding citizen would commit an offense, including persuasion, fraudulent representation, threats, coercive tactics, harassment, promise of reward, or pleas based on need, sympathy, or friendship. Inducement requires something more than that a government agent or informant suggested the crime and provided the occasion for it. Inducement consists of an opportunity plus something else, such as excessive pressure by the government upon the defendant or the government's taking advantage of an alternative, noncriminal type of motive.

The evidence presented by the State and Pischel's own admissions during his testimony indicate that the online conversations between Pischel and "ljb92" were initiated by Pischel and that discussions of sexual activity were initiated by Pischel. The evidence indicates that it was Pischel who first proposed the possibility of the two engaging in sexual activity and that he initiated discussions to arrange a time and place for the two to meet. The evidence of activity by agents of the State in this case was that Sexton merely created a profile, was present in a chat room, and responded to communications—including sexual communications initiated by Pischel. The communications by Sexton as "ljb92," including the associated emoticons, did not legally amount to inducement. The State merely created the opportunity for Pischel to communicate with a person described as a 15-year-old girl and to take such communication in a sexual direction.

Pischel argues that agents of the State played on his emotions and refers us to the end of the March 7 and June 1, 2007, conversations. On March 7, Pischel ended the brief online conversation with "ljb92" after being told that "ljb92" was less than 16 years of age. There was evidence that at the end of the March conversation, "ljb92" merely indicated "Whatever" and did not thereafter attempt to revive the conversation. The two did not converse again until June, and such conversation was initiated by Pischel.

With respect to the June 1, 2007, exchange, the evidence shows that after Pischel indicated to "ljb92" that it would not work for the two to meet that day, "ljb92" replied that "she" was "kinna let down" and was "close to being pissed" and sent an emoticon expressing anger. We note that although "ljb92" expressed some disappointment, such expressions were not persistent and that it was Pischel, not "ljb92," who initiated plans for the two to meet on June 4. We determine that such evidence does not indicate that the State was playing on Pischel's emotions to induce him into criminal activity and that the district court did not err as a matter of law when it concluded there was "not more than a scintilla of evidence" of inducement.

———————

United States v. Mark Douglas Poehlman

217 F.3d 692 (9th Cir. 2000)

KOZINSKI, CIRCUIT JUDGE.

Mark Poehlman, a cross-dresser and foot-fetishist, sought the company of like-minded adults on the Internet. What he found, instead, were federal agents looking to catch child molesters. We consider whether the government's actions amount to entrapment.

After graduating from high school, Mark Poehlman joined the Air Force, where he remained for nearly 17 years. Eventually, he got married and had two children. When Poehlman admitted to his wife that he couldn't control his compulsion to cross-dress, she divorced him. So did the Air Force, which forced him into early retirement, albeit with an honorable discharge.

These events left Poehlman lonely and depressed. He began trawling Internet "alternative lifestyle" discussion groups in an effort to find a suitable companion. Unfortunately, the women who frequented these groups were less accepting than he had hoped. After they learned of Poehlman's proclivities, several retorted with strong rebukes. One even recommended that Poehlman kill himself. Evidently, life in the HOV lane of the information superhighway is not as fast as one might have suspected.

Eventually, Poehlman got a positive reaction from a woman named Sharon. Poehlman started his correspondence with Sharon when he responded to an ad in which she indicated that she was looking for someone who understood her family's "unique needs" and preferred servicemen. Poehlman answered the ad and indicated that he "was looking for a long-term relationship leading to marriage," "didn't mind children," and "had unique needs too."

Sharon responded positively to Poehlman's e-mail. She said she had three children and was "looking for someone who understands us and does not let society's views stand in the way." She confessed that there were "some things I'm just not equipped to teach [the children]" and indicated that she wanted "someone to help with their special education."

In his next e-mail, Poehlman disclosed the specifics of his "unique needs." He also explained that he has strong family values and would treat Sharon's children as his own. Sharon's next e-mail focused on the children, explaining to Poehlman that she was looking for a "special man teacher" for them but not for herself. She closed her e-mail with the valediction, "If you understand and are interested, please write back. If you don't share my views I understand. Thanks again for your last letter."

Poehlman replied by expressing uncertainty as to what Sharon meant by special man teacher. He noted that he would teach the children "proper morals and give support to them where it is needed," and he reiterated his interest in Sharon.

Sharon again rebuffed Poehlman's interest in her: "One thing I should make really clear though, is that there can't be anything between me and my sweethearts special teacher." She then asked Poehlman for a description of what he would teach her children as a first lesson, promising "not to get mad or upset at anything written. If I disagree with something I'll just say so. I do like to watch, though. I hope you don't think I'm too weird."

Poehlman finally got the hint and expressed his willingness to play sex instructor to Sharon's children. In later e-mails, Poehlman graphically detailed his ideas to Sharon, usually at her prompting. Among these ideas were oral sex, anal sex and various acts too tasteless to mention. The correspondence blossomed to include a phone call from Sharon and hand written notes from one of her children. Poehlman made decorative belts for all the girls and shipped the gifts to them for Christmas.

Poehlman and Sharon eventually made plans for him to travel to California from his Florida home. After arriving in California, Poehlman proceeded to a hotel room where he met Sharon in person. She offered him some pornographic magazines featuring children, which he accepted and examined. He commented that he had always looked at little girls. Sharon also showed Poehlman photos of her children: Karen, aged 7, Bonnie, aged 10, and Abby, aged 12. She then directed Poehlman to the adjoining room, where he was to meet the children, presumably to give them their first lesson under their mother's protective supervision. Upon entering the room however, Poehlman was greeted by Naval Criminal Investigation Special Agents, FBI agents and Los Angeles County Sheriff's Deputies.

Poehlman was arrested and charged with attempted lewd acts with a minor in violation of California law. He was tried, convicted and sentenced to a year in state prison. Two years after his release, Poehlman was again arrested and charged with federal crimes arising from the same incident. A jury convicted him of crossing state lines for the purpose of engaging in sex acts with a minor in violation of 18 U.S.C. § 2423(b). He was sentenced to 121 months. Poehlman challenges the conviction on the grounds that it violates double jeopardy and that he was entrapped. Because we find there was entrapment, we need not address double jeopardy.

"In their zeal to enforce the law . . . Government agents may not originate a criminal design, implant in an innocent person's mind the disposition to commit a criminal act, and then induce commission of the crime so that the Government may prosecute." *Jacobson v. United States*, 503 U.S. 540, 548 (1992). On the other hand, "the fact that officers or employees of the Government merely afford opportunity or facilities for the commission of the offense does not defeat the prosecution. Artifice and stratagem may be employed to catch those engaged in criminal enterprises." The defense of entrapment seeks to reconcile these two, somewhat contradictory, principles.

When entrapment is properly raised, the trier of fact must answer two related questions: First, did government agents induce the defendant to commit the crime? And, second, was the defendant predisposed? Even if the government induces the crime, however, defendant can still be convicted if the trier of fact determines that he was predisposed to commit the offense. Predisposition is the defendant's willingness to commit the offense *prior* to being contacted by government agents, coupled with the wherewithal to do so. While our cases treat inducement and pre-disposition as separate inquiries, the two are obviously related: If a defendant is predisposed to commit the offense, he will require little or no inducement to do so; conversely, if the government must work hard to induce a defendant to commit the offense, it is far less likely that he was predisposed.

To raise entrapment, defendant need only point to evidence from which a ratio-nal jury could find that he was induced to commit the crime but was not otherwise predisposed to do so. The burden then shifts to the government to prove beyond a reasonable doubt that defendant was *not* entrapped.

The district court properly determined that the government was required to prove that Poehlman was not entrapped and gave an appropriate instruction. The jury nonetheless convicted Poehlman, which means that either it did not find that the government induced him, or did find that Poehlman was predisposed to com-mit the crime. Poehlman argues that he was entrapped as a matter of law. To suc-ceed, he must persuade us that, viewing the evidence in the light most favorable to the government, no reasonable jury could have found in favor of the government as to inducement or lack of predisposition.

"Inducement can be any government conduct creating a substantial risk that an otherwise law-abiding citizen would commit an offense, including persua-sion, fraudulent representations, threats, coercive tactics, harassment, promises of reward, or pleas based on need, sympathy or friendship." Poehlman argues that he was induced by government agents who used friendship, sympathy and psychologi-cal pressure to "beguile[] him into committing crimes which he otherwise would not have attempted."

According to Poehlman, before he started corresponding with Sharon, he was harmlessly cruising the Internet looking for an adult relationship; the idea of sex with children had not entered his mind. When he answered Sharon's ad, he clearly expressed an interest in "a long-term relationship leading to marriage." His only reference to children was that he "didn't mind" them. Even after Sharon gave him an opening by hinting about "not let[ting] society's views stand in the way," Poehl-man continued to focus his sexual attentions on the mother and not the daughters: "[I]f you don't mind me wearing your hose and licking your toes then I am open for anything."

It was Sharon who first suggested that Poehlman develop a relationship with her daughters: "I've had to be both mother and father to my sweethearts, but there are some things I'm just not equipped to teach them. I'm looking for someone to help with their special education." Poehlman's response to this ambiguous invitation was perfectly appropriate: "[A]s far as your children are concerned I will treat them as my own (as I would treat my boys if I had them with me) I have huge family values and like kids and they seem to like me alright too." Even when Sharon, in her next e-mail, became more insistent about having Poehlman be a special man teacher to her daughters, he betrayed no interest in a sexual relationship with them: "I am interested in being this special teasher, but in all honesty I really don't know exactly what you expect me to teach them other than proper morals and give support to them where it is needed."

In the same e-mail, Poehlman expressed a continued interest in an adult relationship with Sharon: "I have to be honest and tell you I would hope you would support and enjoy me sexually as well as in company and hopefully love and the sexual relations that go with it." It was only after Sharon made it clear that agreeing to serve as sexual mentor to her daughters was a condition to any further communications between her and Poehlman that he agreed to play the role Sharon had in mind for him.

The government argues that it did not induce Poehlman because Sharon did not, in so many words, suggest he have sex with her daughters. But this is far too narrow a view of the matter. The clear implication of Sharon's messages is that this is precisely what she had in mind. Contributing to this impression is repeated use of the phrases "special teacher" and "man teacher," and her categorical rejection of Poehlman's suggestion that he would treat her daughters as his own children and teach them proper morals with a curt, "I don't think you understand."

Sharon also salted her correspondence with details that clearly carried sexual innuendo. In her second e-mail to Poehlman, she explained that she had "discussed finding a special man teacher with my sweethearts and you should see the look of joy and excitement on their faces. They are very excited about the prospect of finding such a teacher." To round out the point, Sharon further explained that "I want my sweethearts to have the same special memories I have. . . . I've told them about my special teacher and the memories I have. I still get goosebumps thinking about it." From Sharon's account, one does not get the impression that her own special teacher had given her lessons in basket weaving or croquet. Finally, Sharon's third e-mail to Poehlman clearly adds to the suggestion of a sexual encounter between him and her daughters when she states: "I do like to watch, though. I hope you don't think I'm too weird." In light of Sharon's earlier statements, it's hard to escape the voyeuristic implications of this statement. After all, there would be nothing weird about having Sharon watch Poehlman engaged in normal father-daughter activities.

Sharon did not merely invite Poehlman to have a sexual relationship with her minor daughters, she made it a condition of her own continued interest in him. Sharon, moreover, pressured Poehlman to be explicit about his plans for teaching the girls: "Tell me more about how their first lesson will go. This will help me make my decision as to who their teacher will be." The implication is that unless Poehlman came up with lesson plans that were sufficiently creative, Sharon would discard Poehlman and select a different mentor for her daughters.

Sharon eventually drew Poehlman into a protracted e-mail exchange which became increasingly intimate and sexually explicit. Approximately three weeks into the correspondence, Poehlman started signing off as Nancy, the name he adopts when dressing in women's clothes. Sharon promptly started using that name, offering an important symbol of acceptance and friendship. In the same e-mail, Sharon complained that Poehlman had neglected to discuss the education of her two younger girls. "I thought it curious that you did not mention Bonnie or Karen. Are they too young to start their educations? I don't want them to feel left out, but at the same time If you aren't comfortable with them please say so."

Sharon also pushed Poehlman to be more explicit about his plans for the oldest daughter: "Abby is very curious (but excited) about what you expect her to do and I haven't been able to answer all her questions. Hope to hear from you soon." Poehlman responded to Sharon's goading: "Bonnie and Karen being younger need to learn how to please, before they can be taught how to be pleased. they will start be exploring each others body together as well as mine and yours, they will learn how to please both men and women and they will be pleasein Abby as well."

Over six months and scores of e-mails, Sharon persistently urged Poehlman to articulate his fantasies concerning the girls. Meanwhile Poehlman continued his efforts to establish a relationship with Sharon. For example, Poehlman twice proposed marriage, but this drew a sharp rebuke from Sharon:

> Nancy, I'm not interested in marriage or any type of relationship with my darlings' teacher. My quest as their mother is to find them the right teacher so that they get the same education I was fortunate enough to get at their ages. You need to understand this. This is not for me, but for them. I don't mean to sound harsh, but you can't imagine the number of people just looking for a wife or girlfriend online. I have to look past all this and concentrate on finding my darlings' special man teacher.

Poehlman nevertheless continued to seek a familial relationship with Sharon and her daughters, expressing himself ready to quit his job and move across the country to be with them.

As Justice Frankfurter noted in his concurrence in *Sherman*,

> Of course in every case of this kind the intention that the particular crime be committed originates with the police, and without their inducement the crime would not have occurred. But it is perfectly clear [that] ... where the police in effect simply furnished the opportunity for the commission of the crime, that this is not enough to enable the defendant to escape conviction.

Sherman v. United States, 356 U.S. 369, 382 (1958) (Frankfurter, J., concurring). Whether the police did more than provide an opportunity—whether they actually induced the crime, as that term is used in our entrapment jurisprudence—depends on whether they employed some form of suasion that materially affected what Justice Frankfurter called the "self-struggle [to] resist ordinary temptations."

Where government agents merely make themselves available to participate in a criminal transaction, such as standing ready to buy or sell illegal drugs, they do not induce commission of the crime. "An improper 'inducement' . . . goes beyond providing an ordinary 'opportunity to commit a crime.' An 'inducement' consists of an 'opportunity' *plus* something else—typically, excessive pressure by the government upon the defendant or the government's taking advantage of an alternative, non-criminal type of motive."

There is no doubt that the government induced Poehlman to commit the crime here. Had Sharon merely responded enthusiastically to a hint from Poehlman that he wanted to serve as her daughters' sexual mentor, there certainly would have been no inducement. But Sharon did much more. Throughout the correspondence with Poehlman, Sharon made it clear that she had made a firm decision about her children's sexual education, and that she believed that having Poehlman serve as their sexual mentor would be in their best interest. She made repeated references to her own sexual mentor, explaining that he could have mentored her daughters, had he not died in a car crash in 1985. While parental consent is not a defense to statutory rape, it nevertheless can have an effect on the "self-struggle [to] resist ordinary temptations." This is particularly so where the parent does not merely consent but casts the activity as an act of parental responsibility and the selection of a sexual mentor as an expression of friendship and confidence. Not only did this diminish the risk of detection, it also allayed fears defendant might have had that the activities would be harmful, distasteful or inappropriate, particularly since Sharon claimed to have herself benefitted from such experiences.

It is clear, moreover, that Poehlman continued to long for an adult relationship with Sharon, as well as a father-like relationship with the girls. He offered marriage; talked about quitting his job and moving to California; discussed traveling with Sharon and the girls; even offered his military health insurance benefits as an inducement. While refusing to give Poehlman hope of a sexual relationship with her, Sharon encouraged these fantasies; she went so far as to check out Poehlman's job prospects in California. The government thus played on Poehlman's obvious need for an adult relationship, for acceptance of his sexual proclivities and for a family, to draw him ever deeper into a sexual fantasy world involving these imaginary girls.

The jury could, nevertheless, have found Poehlman guilty if it found that he was predisposed to commit the offense. Quite obviously, by the time a defendant actually commits the crime, he will have become disposed to do so. However, the relevant time frame for assessing a defendant's disposition comes before he has any contact with government agents, which is doubtless why it's called *pre* disposition. In our case, the question is whether there is evidence to support a finding that Poehlman was disposed to have sex with minors prior to opening his correspondence with Sharon.

The fact that Poehlman willingly crossed state lines to have sex with minors after his prolonged and steamy correspondence with Sharon cannot, alone, support a finding of predisposition. It is possible, after all, that it was the government's inducement that brought Poehlman to the point where he became willing to break the law. We must consider what evidence there is as to Poehlman's state of mind *prior* to his contact with Sharon.

On this score, the record is sparse indeed; it is easier to say what the record does not contain than what it does. The government produced no e-mails or chat room postings where Poehlman expressed an interest in sex with children, or even the view that sex with children should be legalized. Nor did the government produce any notes, tapes, magazines, photographs, letters or similar items which disclosed an interest in sex with children, despite a thorough search of Poehlman's home. There was no testimony from the playmates of Poehlman's children, his ex-wife or anyone else indicating that Poehlman had behaved inappropriately toward children or otherwise manifested a sexual interest in them. Sharon's ad, to which Poehlman responded, does not clearly suggest that sex with children was to be the object of the relationship: "Divorced mother of 3 looking for someone who understands my family's unique needs. Servicemen preferred. Please E-mail me at Darlings3@aol.com." While one might presume that one or more of the children are minors, the phrase "unique needs" could, just as easily, connote children with physical disabilities, or merely the plight of a single mother of three.

Poehlman does not appear to have responded to her ad because it mentions children or their special needs. During the crucial first few exchanges, when Sharon focused Poehlman's attention on those special needs, he expressed confusion as to what she had in mind. Instead of exploiting the ambiguity in Sharon's messages to suggest the possibility of sex with her daughters, Poehlman pushed the conversation in the opposite direction, offering to act as a father figure to the girls and teach them "proper morals." While Poehlman's reluctance might have been borne of caution — the way a drug dealer might demur when he is unsure whether a prospective buyer is a government agent — the fact remains that Poehlman's earliest messages (which would be most indicative of his pre-existing state of mind) provide no support for the government's case on predisposition. To the contrary, Poehlman's reluctance forced Sharon to become more aggressive in her suggestions, augmenting the defendant's case for inducement.

Poehlman's enthusiastic, protracted and extreme descriptions of the sexual acts he would perform with Sharon's daughters are, according to the government, its strongest evidence of Poehlman's predisposition. Indeed, once he got the idea of what Sharon had in mind, Poehlman expressed few concerns about the morality, legality or appropriateness of serving as the girls' sexual mentor. But Poehlman was not convicted of writing smutty e-mails; he was convicted of crossing state lines, some six months later, to have sex with minors. The problem with using Poehlman's e-mails as evidence of predisposition is that they were all in response to specific, pointed suggestions by Sharon. The e-mails thus tell us what Poehlman's disposition was once the government had implanted in his mind the idea of sex with Sharon's children, but not whether Poehlman would have engaged in such conduct had he not been pushed in that direction by the government.

It is entirely plausible to infer that it was the government's graduated response—including e-mail correspondence, handwritten letters from the girls and Sharon, the use of intimate names, a photograph of Poehlman sent to Sharon, Poehlman handcrafting gifts for the girls and Sharon's willingness to help Poehlman look for a job in Southern California—that brought Poehlman to the point where he was willing to cross state lines for the purpose of having sex with the three young girls. Since the government has the burden of proof as to predisposition, materials like these e-mails, which do not demonstrate any preexisting propensity to engage in the criminal conduct at issue, simply cannot carry that burden.

This is not to say that statements made after the government's inducement can never be evidence of predisposition. If, after the government begins inducing a defendant, he makes it clear that he would have committed the offense even without the inducement, that would be evidence of predisposition. But only those statements that indicate a state of mind untainted by the inducement are relevant to show predisposition. Poehlman's protracted correspondence with Sharon, in fact, undermines the view that he was predisposed to commit the offense. Even as his e-mails became more intimate and explicit—usually in response to Sharon's constant hectoring for more details about Poehlman's lesson plans—he never gave any indication that being a sexual mentor to the girls in any way fulfilled his preexisting fantasies. To the contrary, Poehlman repeatedly tried to integrate Sharon's expectations of him into his own fantasies by insisting that the girls (and Sharon) parade around the house in nylons and high-heeled pumps ("as high of a heel as they can handle,")—as Poehlman himself apparently does.

The only indication in the record of any preexisting interest in children is Poehlman's statement in the hotel room that he has "always looked at little girls." But this is hardly an indication that he was prone to engage in sexual relations with minors. Having carefully combed the record for any evidence that Poehlman was predisposed to commit the offense of which he was convicted, we find none. To the extent the jury might have found that Poehlman was predisposed to commit the offense, that finding cannot be sustained.

"When the Government's quest for convictions leads to the apprehension of an otherwise law-abiding citizen who, if left to his own devices, likely would have never run afoul of the law, the courts should intervene." So far as this record discloses, Poehlman is such a citizen. Prior to his unfortunate encounter with Sharon, he was on a quest for an adult relationship with a woman who would understand and accept his proclivities, which did not include sex with children. There is surely enough real crime in our society that it is unnecessary for our law enforcement officials to spend months luring an obviously lonely and confused individual to cross the line between fantasy and criminality. The judgment of conviction is **REVERSED** on grounds of insufficiency of the evidence and the case is **REMANDED** with instructions that defendant be released forthwith.

———————

Notes

Pischel and *Poehlman* illustrate the fact the police agencies are using undercover identities to develop criminal cases against persons using the Internet. The two cases represent very different police tactics. Or is this really true? What police tactics, if any, to hide the officer's identity and seek to get individuals to incriminate themselves on the Internet should be allowed?

§ 14.3 Liability of Social Networking Sites

Julie Doe II, a Minor v. Myspace Incorporated

175 Cal. App. 4th 561 (2009)

BIGELOW, J.

The question posed by this appeal is: Can an internet Web server such as MySpace Incorporated, be held liable when a minor is sexually assaulted by an adult she met on its Web site? The answer hinges on our interpretation of section 230 of the Communications Decency Act. We hold section 230 immunizes MySpace from liability.

This appeal consolidates four cases involving similar facts and essentially identical legal allegations. In each case, one or more "Julie Does"—girls aged 13 to 15—were sexually assaulted by men they met through the internet social networking site, MySpace.com. The Julie Does, through their parents or guardians, have sued MySpace for negligence, gross negligence, and strict product liability.

MySpace.com is a social networking Web site founded in July 2003 that is popular with adults and teenagers. As of July 11, 2006, MySpace was the world's most visited domain on the internet for American users. MySpace membership is only open to users aged 14 and over. However, an underaged user can easily gain access simply by entering a false birth date to appear older.

MySpace users typically create profiles which include personal information on such topics as age, gender, interests, personality, background, lifestyle, and schools. Other MySpace users are then able to search and view profiles that fulfill specific criteria, such as gender, age range, body type, or school. MySpace channels information based on members' answers to various questions, allows members to search only the profiles of members with comparable preferences, and sends email notifications to its members. Although profiles are automatically set to allow public access, users can adjust the levels of privacy on their profile when they navigate to a specific webpage on the site and select a setting of "public" or "private." MySpace automatically sets to "private" all accounts for 14 and 15 year olds and does not allow searching or browsing of those accounts.

In its Terms of Use Agreement, users are prohibited from soliciting personal information from anyone under 18. MySpace also lists safety tips to new users which, among other things, cautions:

"• Don't post anything you wouldn't want the world to know (e.g., your phone number, address, IM screens name, or specific whereabouts). Avoid posting anything that would make it easy for a stranger to find you, such as where you hang out every day after school[;]

"• People aren't always who they say they are. Be careful about adding strangers to your friends list[;]

"• Don't mislead people into thinking that you're older or younger."

Similar cautionary advice is provided to parents in the "Tips for Parents" page.

Then 15-year-old Julie Doe II created a MySpace profile in 2005. In 2006, she met a 22-year-old man through MySpace and was sexually assaulted by him at an in-person meeting. As a result, he is currently serving 10 years in prison. Julie Doe III was also 15 when she created a MySpace profile. She subsequently met a 25-year-old man on MySpace, who "lured Julie Doe from her home, heavily drugged her, and brutally sexually assaulted her." Julie Doe III's attacker pled guilty to charges stemming from the incident and is currently serving 10 years in prison. Julie Doe IV was 13 years old when she created a MySpace profile. In 2006, she turned 14 years old and met an 18-year-old MySpace user. He and his adult friend met Julie Doe IV, drugged her and took turns sexually assaulting her. As of August 2007, the 18-year-old user is awaiting trial while his friend pled guilty to second degree felony rape and was sentenced to 4 and one-half years in prison. In 2006, 14-year-old Julie Doe V and 15-year-old Julie Doe VI each met 18-year-old and 19-year-old men on MySpace and were later sexually assaulted by the men at in-person meetings. As of August 2007, both men were awaiting trial.

The appellants each bring substantially identical causes of action against MySpace for negligence, gross negligence, and strict product liability. In summary, they complain that "MySpace has made a decision to not implement reasonable, basic safety precautions with regard to protecting young children from sexual predators[.] [¶] MySpace is aware of the dangers that it poses to underaged minors using [its Web site]. MySpace is aware that its Web site poses a danger to children, facilitating an astounding number of attempted and actual sexual assaults. . . ." They more specifically allege that MySpace should have implemented "readily available and practicable age-verification software" or set the default security setting on the Julie Does' accounts to "private."

[Demurrers of the complaints were sustained by the trial court on the ground that the claims were barred by section 230 and the plaintiffs appealed.]

A demurrer tests the sufficiency of the complaint; that is, whether it states facts sufficient to constitute a cause of action. To make this determination, the trial court may consider all material facts pleaded in the complaint and matters of which it may take judicial notice; it may not consider contentions, deductions or conclusions of fact or law. "Where the complaint's allegations or judicially noticeable facts reveal the existence of an affirmative defense, the 'plaintiff must "plead around" the defense, by alleging specific facts that would avoid the apparent defense. Absent such allegations, the complaint is subject to demurrer for failure to state a cause of action. . . .'"

Relevant portions of section 230 of the CDA provide as follows:

"(b) Policy

"It is the policy of the United States—

"(1) to promote the continued development of the Internet and other interactive computer services and other interactive media;

"(2) to preserve the vibrant and competitive free market that presently exists for the Internet and other interactive computer services, unfettered by Federal or State regulation;

"(3) to encourage the development of technologies which maximize user control over what information is received by individuals, families, and schools who use the Internet and other interactive computer services;

"(4) to remove disincentives for the development and utilization of blocking and filtering technologies that empower parents to restrict their children's access to objectionable or inappropriate online material; and

"(5) to ensure vigorous enforcement of Federal criminal laws to deter and punish trafficking in obscenity, stalking, and harassment by means of computer.

"(c) Protection for 'good samaritan' blocking and screening of offensive material

"(1) Treatment of publisher or speaker

"No provider or user of an interactive computer service shall be treated as the publisher or speaker of any information provided by another information content provider.

"(2) Civil liability

"No provider or user of an interactive computer service shall be held liable on account of—

"(A) any action voluntarily taken in good faith to restrict access to or availability of material that the provider or user considers to be obscene, lewd, lascivious, filthy, excessively violent, harassing, or otherwise objectionable, whether or not such material is constitutionally protected; or

"(B) any action taken to enable or make available to information content providers or others the technical means to restrict access to material described in paragraph (1). [subparagraph (A)].

"(d) Obligations of interactive computer service

"A provider of interactive computer service shall, at the time of entering an agreement with a customer for the provision of interactive computer service and in a manner deemed appropriate by the provider, notify such customer that parental control protections (such as computer hardware, software, or filtering services) are commercially available that may assist the customer in limiting access to material that is harmful to minors. Such notice shall identify, or provide the customer with access to information identifying, current providers of such protections.

"(e) Effect on other laws [¶] . . . [¶]

"(3) State law

"Nothing in this section shall be construed to prevent any State from enforcing any State law that is consistent with this section. No cause of action may be brought and no liability may be imposed under any State or local law that is inconsistent with this section."

The legislative history demonstrates Congress intended to extend immunity to all civil claims: "This section provides 'Good Samaritan' protections from civil liability for providers or users of an interactive computer service for actions to restrict or to enable restriction of access to objectionable online material." (142 Cong. Rec. H1130 (Jan. 31, 1996).)

Immunity under section 230 requires proof of three elements: (1) MySpace is an interactive computer services provider, (2) MySpace is not an information content provider[n.4][3] with respect to the disputed activity, and (3) appellants seek to hold MySpace liable for information originating with a third party user of its service. Appellants appear to take issue with the second and third elements required for immunity, arguing that they view MySpace as an information content provider and do not hold it liable for the communications between the Julie Does and their assailants, but rather, for MySpace's failure to institute reasonable security measures.

We first examine appellants' main argument: that their complaint does not treat MySpace as a publisher, which would trigger section 230 immunity, but instead alleges "a breach of a legal duty to provide reasonable safety measures to ensure that sexual predators did not gain otherwise unavailable access to minors through the use of the MySpace.com website. . . ." To circumvent section 230's immunity provisions, appellants narrowly construe section 230 to extend only to claims "stemming from harms caused by the defendant's republication of inherently offensive or harmful content." That is, appellants contend that the words themselves have to be tortious, such as in the case of a defamatory statement.

The leading case on immunity protection under section 230 is Zeran [v. America Online, Inc., 129 F.3d 327 (4th Cir. 1997)]. There, the plaintiff discovered that someone had falsely advertised on American Online that he was selling T-shirts

---

3. [n.4] The CDA defines information service provider as "any person or entity that is responsible, in whole or in part, for the creation or development of information provided through the Internet or any other interactive computer service." (§ 230(f)(3).)

containing tasteless slogans about the 1995 bombing of the Oklahoma City Federal Building. The plaintiff complained that America Online failed to remove the postings immediately, failed to notify other subscribers of the message's false nature and failed to effectively screen future defamatory material. The trial court granted America Online's motion for judgment on the pleadings and the Fourth Circuit affirmed, holding that immunity is extended even when a provider is notified of objectionable content on its site. The court reasoned:

> "Congress' purpose in providing the § 230 immunity was thus evident. Interactive computer services have millions of users. The amount of information communicated via interactive computer services is therefore staggering. The specter of tort liability in an area of such prolific speech would have an obvious chilling effect. It would be impossible for service providers to screen each of their millions of postings for possible problems. Faced with potential liability for each message republished by their services, interactive computer service providers might choose to severely restrict the number and type of messages posted. Congress considered the weight of the speech interests implicated and chose to immunize service providers to avoid any such restrictive effect."

Appellants' same argument was recently addressed by the Fifth Circuit in *Doe v. MySpace, Inc.*[, 528 F.3d 413 (5th Cir. 2008)]. There, a 13-year-old girl represented that she was 18 when she created a MySpace profile. As a result, her profile was automatically set to "public" and she met a 19-year-old man on MySpace a year later, when she was 14. The two spoke offline several times after exchanging phone numbers, and he sexually assaulted her when they met in person. The girl and her mother filed suit in an attempt to hold MySpace liable for failing to implement basic safety measures to protect minors from adult predators whom they meet on MySpace.

The Fifth Circuit interpreted the statute to provide broad immunity extending to cases arising from the publication of user-generated content.

It first considered the policy reasons underlying section 230's enactment, emphasizing Congress' intent "to remove disincentives for the development and utilization of blocking and filtering technologies that empower parents to restrict their children's access to objectionable or inappropriate online material." (§ 230(b)(4).) Further, cases from other circuit courts had broadly construed section 230, including one in which the service provider was notified of objectionable content on its site. As a result, the Fifth Circuit found the plaintiffs' "allegations are merely another way of claiming that MySpace was liable for publishing the communications and they speak to MySpace's role as a publisher of online third-party-generated content." The court further noted, "Parties complaining that they were harmed by a Web site's publication of user-generated content have recourse; they may sue the third party user who generated the content, but not the interactive computer service that enabled them to publish the content online."

In a different context, the Ninth Circuit extended section 230 immunity to an online dating service, finding it was not liable when an unidentified party posted a false online profile of an actress, which resulted in harassing phone calls, letters, and faxes to her home. [*Carafano v. Metrosplash.com, Inc.*, 339 F.3d 1119, 1122 (9th Cir. 2003)]. The *Carafano* court held that "[u]nder §230(c), . . . so long as a third party willingly provides the essential published content, the interactive service provider receives full immunity regardless of the specific editing or selection process."

Similarly, an Ohio district court extended section 230 immunity to an online dating service where the plaintiff had relied on another member's claim on her profile that she was 18 years old when he had sex with her. He was subsequently arrested for unlawful sexual conduct with a minor because, in fact, she was only 14. [*Doe v. SexSearch.com*, 502 F. Supp. 2d 719 (N.D. Ohio 2007), *aff'd*, 551 F.3d 412 (6th Cir. 2008).] The plaintiff asserted multiple causes of action, most of which were based on the allegation that the dating service had an obligation to, but failed, to discover the minor lied about her age. The defendant's motion to dismiss was granted on the ground that the complaint attempted to hold the dating service liable for its publication of content provided by the minor.

[We] conclude that section 230 immunity shields MySpace in this case. That appellants characterize their complaint as one for failure to adopt reasonable safety measures does not avoid the immunity granted by section 230. It is undeniable that appellants seek to hold MySpace responsible for the communications between the Julie Does and their assailants. At its core, appellants want MySpace to regulate what appears on its Web site. Appellants argue they do not "allege liability on account of MySpace's exercise of a publisher's traditional editorial functions, such as editing, altering, or deciding whether or not to publish certain material, which is the test for whether a claim treats a website as a publisher." But that is precisely what they allege; that is, they want MySpace to ensure that sexual predators do not gain access to (i.e., communicate with) minors on its Web site. That type of activity — to restrict or make available certain material — is expressly covered by section 230.

Appellants also contend MySpace is an information content provider and thus is not immunized by section 230. According to appellants, "MySpace acted as a content provider when it collaborated with the Does and their eventual attackers to create and then flesh out their MySpace profiles. . . . MySpace also acted as a content provider when it allowed the attackers to channel information in profiles, search and browse profiles for particular characteristics and then use the results of those queries to locate, contact, and eventually sexually assault the Julie Does."

Appellants rely on *Fair Housing Coun., San Fernando v. Roommates.com.*[, 521 F.3d 1157 (9th Cir. 2008),] to support their argument. There, the defendant ran a Web site to match people renting out spare rooms with people looking for a place to live. Before a subscriber can search listings or post housing opportunities on the Web site, he or she was required to answer a series of questions about his or her sex, sexual orientation, and whether he or she would bring children to a household. The site also encouraged subscribers to provide "additional comments" describing themselves and their desired roommate in an open-ended essay. Subscribers also received periodic emails, informing them of potential housing opportunities that matched their preferences. The plaintiffs complained that Roommates.com's business violated the federal Fair Housing Act and California's fair housing law, both of which prohibit discrimination on the basis of race, familial status or national origin.

The district court granted Roommates.com summary judgment, holding that it was entitled to immunity under section 230. The Ninth Circuit reversed in part, finding that Roommates.com was an information content provider as to the questions because it created the discriminatory questions, presented a limited choice of answers and designed its search and email systems to limit listings based on sex, sexual orientation, and presence of children. Further, Roommates.com forced subscribers to answer these questions as a condition of using its services. Immunity was extended, however, with regard to the additional comments section because it published the comments as written, did not provide guidance or urge subscribers to input discriminatory preferences.

Roommates.Com. presents us with two ends of the spectrum with respect to how much discretion a third party user has in the content he posts on the site. A subscriber writing in the additional comments section is given almost unfettered discretion as to content. On the other hand, the subscriber must select one answer from a limited number of choices in the question and answer profile section. Our situation falls somewhere in between. MySpace members are not allowed unfettered discretion as to what they put in their profile. Instead, it is alleged that MySpace users are urged to follow the on-screen prompts to enter a name, email address, gender, postal code, and date of birth. Users are also "encouraged" to enter personal information such as schools, interests and personality and background and lifestyle. This information is organized by the site and is searchable by other users. Unlike the questions and answers in *Roommates.Com.*, however, Appellants do not allege that MySpace's profile questions are discriminatory or otherwise illegal. Neither do they allege that MySpace requires its members to answer the profile questions as a condition of using the site.

The facts here align more closely with those in *Carafano*. There, the online dating service provided neutral tools which the anonymous poster used to publish the libelous content. The dating service did nothing to encourage the posting of such content and in fact, the posting was contrary to its express policies. As more fully explained in *Roommates.Com.*, "[t]he salient fact in *Carafano* was that the website's classifications of user characteristics did absolutely nothing to enhance the defamatory sting of the message, to encourage defamation or to make defamation easier: The site provided neutral tools specifically designed to match romantic partners depending on their voluntary inputs. By sharp contrast, Roommate's website is designed to force subscribers to divulge protected characteristics and discriminatory preferences, and to match those who have rooms with those who are looking for rooms based on criteria that appear to be prohibited by the [Fair Housing Act]." In light of the cases above, we find MySpace was not an information content provider subject to liability under section 230.

Notes

In 2018, Congress passed the following act to "Allow States and Victims to Fight Online Sex Trafficking Act of 2017" (FOSTA). The law provides:

18 U.S.C. § 2421A

§ 2421A. Promotion or facilitation of prostitution and reckless disregard of sex trafficking

(a) In general.—Whoever, using a facility or means of interstate or foreign commerce or in or affecting interstate or foreign commerce, owns, manages, or operates an interactive computer service (as such term is defined in defined in1 section 230(f) the Communications Act of 1934 (47 U.S.C. 230(f))), or conspires or attempts to do so, with the intent to promote or facilitate the prostitution of another person shall be fined under this title, imprisoned for not more than 10 years, or both.

(b) Aggravated violation.—Whoever, using a facility or means of interstate or foreign commerce or in or affecting interstate or foreign commerce, owns, manages, or operates an interactive computer service (as such term is defined in defined in1 section 230(f) the Communications Act of 1934 (47 U.S.C. 230(f))), or conspires or attempts to do so, with the intent to promote or facilitate the prostitution of another person and—

(1) promotes or facilitates the prostitution of 5 or more persons; or

(2) acts in reckless disregard of the fact that such conduct contributed to sex trafficking, in violation of 1591(a),

shall be fined under this title, imprisoned for not more than 25 years, or both.

(c) Civil recovery.—Any person injured by reason of a violation of section 2421A(b) may recover damages and reasonable attorneys' fees in an action before any appropriate United States district court.

(d) Mandatory restitution.—Notwithstanding sections 3663 or 3663A3 and in addition to any other civil or criminal penalties authorized by law, the court shall order restitution for any violation of subsection (b)(2). The scope and nature of such restitution shall be consistent with section 2327(b).

(e) Affirmative defense.—It shall be an affirmative defense to a charge of violating subsection (a), or subsection (b)(1) where the defendant proves, by a preponderance of the evidence, that the promotion or facilitation of prostitution is legal in the jurisdiction where the promotion or facilitation was targeted.

The preamble to the new statute stated:

It is the sense of Congress that—

(1) section 230 of the Communications Act of 1934 (47 U.S.C. 230; commonly known as the "Communications Decency Act of 1996") was never intended to provide legal protection to websites that unlawfully promote and facilitate prostitution and websites that facilitate traffickers in advertising the sale of unlawful sex acts with sex trafficking victims;

(2) websites that promote and facilitate prostitution have been reckless in allowing the sale of sex trafficking victims and have done nothing to prevent the trafficking of children and victims of force, fraud, and coercion; and

(3) clarification of such section is warranted to ensure that such section does not provide such protection to such websites.

Chapter 15

Property Crimes and Computer Misuse

§ 15.1 Introduction

Is there a need for new computer-specific crimes? One could ask that question in every context where criminal law regulates human behavior. This chapter examines the question in the context of property crimes.[1] First, consider a sampling of the many views:

- [L]egislatures can respond more effectively to most computer-related crimes by modifying existing criminal statutes, rather than by enacting new computer-specific laws. Computers are not so unique that the criminal law must be rewritten to account for them; indeed, most "computer crimes" correspond quite closely to older crimes, notably trespass or larceny. Simply by redefining "property," or broadening other statutory language, legislatures can bring "computer crimes" under those existing statutory prohibitions. Enacting wholly new statutes, aimed solely at crimes committed with the aid of electronic technology, too often produces unnecessary and ineffective legislation. Moreover, a legislative focus on the computer, rather than on the harm caused by conduct, can lead to the misconceived conclusion that conduct undertaken by means of a computer amounts to a crime, even though analogous conduct undertaken by other, less high-tech means does not. With few exceptions, legislatures should focus on results, rather than on the means employed. If the result warrants a criminal penalty, then a penalty should be imposed. To a great extent, traditional criminal statutes will achieve that result. If the result does not warrant a criminal penalty, then the involvement of a computer should not transform innocent activity into criminal conduct.[2]

    • Theoretical debates about how best to address cybercrime have their place, but, in the real world, companies and individuals face new harmful criminal

---

1. *See generally* Orin S. Kerr, *Cybercrime's Scope: Interpreting "Access" and "Authorization" in Computer Misuse Statutes*, 78 N.Y.U. L. Rev. 1596 (2003) (offering an overview of the application of property law concepts to cyber crime and the evolution of statutory responses to the rise of cyber crime).

2. Joseph M. Olivenbaum, *Ctrl-Alt-Delete: Rethinking Federal Computer Crime Legislation*, 27 Seton Hall L. Rev. 574 (1997). Copyright © 1997, Joseph M. Olivenbaum, Seton Hall Law Review. All rights reserved. Reprinted by permission.

activity that poses unique technical and investigatory challenges. There is nothing virtual about the real damage on-line crime can inflict off-line to victims. At the same time, technology is inviting uses that may result in significant, though sometimes inadvert, criminal and civil liability. The law is not always crystal clear about whether specific conduct is a crime, or about which tools investigators may use to collect evidence identifying the scope of the criminal activity and the perpetrator.

[S]pecific laws directed to specific problems are important for two main reasons. First, they serve to guide law enforcement as to how investigations may be conducted with appropriate respect for civil liberties and privacy. Second, specific laws make clear to people the boundary of legally permissible conduct.

Does this require endless effort to update the laws to keep pace with technology? Yes, but Congress returns every year with the job of making new laws. Will the pace of legal changes always be behind technological developments? Yes, but in my view the correct pace is a slow one. By the time a proposal has gone through the legislative process, the problem it seeks to address will have become more defined. Policy-makers are better able to craft a narrow and circumscribed law to address a clearly defined problem, and thus, minimize the risk of an overly expansive law that could chill innovation and technological development.[3]

The next section offers perspectives on this debate. It examines the application of two traditional crimes—larceny and trespass—to computers and sets out the challenges that courts face in applying those ancient principles to computers and digital data. The next chapter utilizes the Computer Fraud and Abuse Act (CFAA) to illustrate legislative responses to the complexity of modern forms of criminal behavior. The CFAA has broad applicability to most computers—indeed, any computer connected to the Internet—and regulates a variety of forms of abuse that can be characterized broadly as involving property crimes.

§ 15.2 Traditional Property Crimes

The crimes of trespass and larceny provide useful illustrations of the problems posed by computer technology. Typical criminal statutes define trespass as the unlawful entry onto another's property. Larceny is typically defined as the taking of another's property with the intent to deprive. Central to the definition of both crimes is the idea of property. With trespass, the property is geographical. A person commits trespass by physically moving into a specified geographical space. The paradigm of trespass,

---

3. Beryl A. Howell, *Real World Problems of Virtual Crime*, 7 Yale J. L. & Tech. 103 (2004–05). Copyright © 2004, Beryl A. Howell, Yale Journal of Law and Technology. All rights reserved. Reprinted by permission.

descended from centuries-old common law, is the unlawful entry onto real estate. Larceny too has traditionally been defined in terms of tangible property. The simplest conception of larceny, again springing from old common law and the social circumstances from which it arose, is the unlawful seizing and carrying off of one's neighbor's sheep. Both of these ancient crimes rest on the notion of property as physical property: property one can grab and walk off with, property one can stand on, property that can be fenced off or tied down.

Computers—the machines themselves—are, of course, tangible property that exists in the familiar physical world. But the interactions that the machines make possible do not involve tangible property and do not take place in the familiar physical world. Computer interactions occur, instead, in "cyberspace," the same "place" in which telephone conversations occur. The notion of geographical place is irrelevant to those interactions. They do not occur "in" a machine, but rather only by means of the machine. The geographical location of the persons involved in the interaction is irrelevant: the same operations can be executed on, or from, any similarly-equipped machine regardless of place. The notion of physical property is similarly irrelevant. Interactions in cyberspace consist of electromagnetic impulses, which may be "matter" as understood by a physicist, but do not easily correspond to "property" in the ordinary sense or as defined by the law.

Perhaps the simplest example of a computer crime is the unauthorized accessing of a computer, and the manipulation or copying of information stored on that computer. Does such an occurrence involve a trespass? In some sense, of course, there has been an unlawful entry onto the property of another. But "property" is precisely where the application of the law of trespass becomes problematic. The electronic intruder has not entered the property of anyone, certainly not in the old common-law sense of entry onto real estate. If the intruder copies or downloads information without authorization, has a larceny occurred? The old notion of larceny does not easily fit the situation. If the original data remain stored on the accessed machine, nothing has been "taken" from the owner: the owner still has exactly what she had prior to the "entry." And even if our intruder copies the information and then deletes the original, exactly what has been taken? The intruder has simply caused the reproduction of a series of electronic impulses—digital ones and zeroes—that can be read and then displayed by another machine. Such a description is far from the idea of property as typified by a neighbor's livestock.[4]

---

4. Joseph M. Olivenbaum, *Ctrl-Alt-Delete: Rethinking Federal Computer Crime Legislation*, 27 SEATON HALL L. REV. 574 (1997).

1. Larceny and Theft

Larceny is a common law crime dating to the early feudal era in England. It has traditionally required a showing of a "tresspassory taking and carrying away of the personal property of another with the intent to permanently deprive the possessor of the property."[5] Each those elements, over the centuries, came to have fixed — and highly technical — meanings, with common law courts generally declining to expand the crime to include new forms of appropriation of tangible or intangible things of value. Legislative bodies typically filled in some gaps in the common law to address some of the new forms of criminal activity, with statutory fixes dating back hundreds of years. The Twentieth Century was characterized by most states adopting new comprehensive theft statutes that were designed to eliminate hyper-technical distinctions between types of theft.

---

2. Applying Traditional Views

Charles Walter Lund v. Commonwealth

232 S.E.2d 745 (Va. 1977)

I'Anson, Chief Justice.

Lund was charged in an indictment with the theft of keys, computer cards, computer printouts and using "without authority computer operation time and services of Computer Center Personnel at Virginia Polytechnic Institute and State University . . . with intent to defraud, such property and services having a value of one hundred dollars or more." Code §§ 18.1-100 and 18.1-118 were referred to in the indictment as the applicable statutes. Defendant pleaded not guilty and waived trial by jury. He was found guilty of grand larceny[.]

Defendant was a graduate student in statistics and a candidate for a Ph.D. degree at V.P.I. The preparation of his dissertation on the subject assigned to him by his faculty advisor required the use of computer operation time and services of the computer center personnel at the University. His faculty advisor neglected to arrange for defendant's use of the computer, but defendant used it without obtaining the proper authorization.

The computer used by the defendant was leased on an annual basis by V.P.I. from the IBM Corporation. The rental was paid by V.P.I. which allocates the cost of the computer center to various departments within the University by charging it to the budget of that department. This is a bookkeeping entry, and no money actually changes hands. The departments are allocated "computer credits (in dollars) back for their use (on) a proportional basis of their (budgetary) allotments." Each

---

5. Joshua Dressler, Understanding Criminal Law 554 (5th ed. 2009).

department manager receives a monthly statement showing the allotments used and the running balance in each account of his department.

An account is established when a duly authorized administrator or "department head" fills out a form allocating funds to a department of the University and an individual. When such form is received, the computer center assigns an account number to this allocation and provides a key to a locked post office box which is also numbered to the authorized individual and department. The account number and the post office box number are the access code which must be provided with each request before the computer will process a "deck of cards" prepared by the user and delivered to computer center personnel. The computer print-outs are usually returned to the locked post office box. When the product is too large for the box, a "check" is placed in the box, and it is used to receive the print-outs at the "computer center main window."

Defendant came under surveillance on October 12, 1974, because of complaints from various departments that unauthorized charges were being made to one or more of their accounts. When confronted by the University's investigator, defendant initially denied that he had used the computer service, but later admitted that he had. He gave to the investigator seven keys for boxes assigned to other persons. One of these keys was secreted in his sock. He told the investigating officer he had been given the keys by another student. A large number of computer cards and print-outs were taken from defendant's apartment.

The director of the computer center testified that the unauthorized sum spent out of the accounts associated with the seven post office box keys, amounted to $5,065. He estimated that on the basis of the computer cards and print-outs obtained from the defendant, as much as $26,384.16 in unauthorized computer time had been used by the defendant. He said, however, that the value of the cards and print-outs obtained from the defendant was "whatever scrap paper is worth."

Defendant testified that he used the computer without specific authority. He stated that he knew he was a large computer user, but, because he was doing work on his doctoral dissertation, he did not consider this use excessive or that "he was doing anything wrong."

Four faculty members testified in defendant's behalf. They all agreed that computer time "probably would have been" or "would have been" assigned to defendant if properly requested. Dr. Hinkleman, who replaced defendant's first advisor, testified that the computer time was essential for the defendant to carry out his assignment. He assumed that a sufficient number of computer hours had been arranged by Lund's prior faculty advisor.

The head of the statistics department, at the time of the trial, agreed with the testimony of the faculty members that Lund would have been assigned computer time if properly requested. He also testified that the committee which recommended the awarding of degrees was aware of the charges pending against defendant when he was awarded his doctorate by the University.

The defendant contends that his conviction of grand larceny of the keys, computer cards, and computer print-outs cannot be upheld under the provisions of Code § 18.1-100 because (1) there was no evidence that the articles were stolen, or that they had a value of $100 or more, and (2) computer time and services are not the subject of larceny under the provisions of Code § 18.1-100 or 18.1-118.

Code § 18.1-100 provides as follows:

"Any person who: (1) Commits larceny from the person of another of money or other thing of value of five dollars or more, or

(2) Commits simple larceny not from the person of another of goods and chattels of the value of one hundred dollars or more, shall be deemed guilty of grand larceny. . . ."

Section 18.1-118 provides as follows:

"If any person obtain, by any false pretense or token, from any person, with intent to defraud, money or other property which may be the subject of larceny, he shall be deemed guilty of larceny thereof; . . . ."

The Commonwealth concedes that the defendant could not be convicted of grand larceny of the keys and computer cards because there was no evidence that those articles were stolen and that they had a market value of $100 or more. The Commonwealth argues, however, that the evidence shows the defendant violated the provisions of § 18.1-118 when he obtained by false pretense or token, with intent to defraud, the computer print-outs which had a value of over $5,000.

Under the provisions of Code § 18.1-118, for one to be guilty of the crime of larceny by false pretense, he must make a false representation of an existing fact with knowledge of its falsity and, on that basis, obtain from another person money or other property which may be the subject of larceny, with the intent to defraud.

At common law, larceny is the taking and carrying away of the goods and chattels of another with intent to deprive the owner of the possession thereof permanently. Code § 18.1-100 defines grand larceny as a taking from the person of another money or other thing of value of five dollars or more, or the taking not from the person of another goods and chattels of the value of $100 or more. The phrase "goods and chattels" cannot be interpreted to include computer time and services in light of the often repeated mandate that criminal statutes must be strictly construed.

At common law, labor or services could not be the subject of the crime of false pretense because neither time nor services may be taken and carried away. It has been generally held that, in the absence of a clearly expressed legislative intent, labor or services could not be the subject of the statutory crime of false pretense. Some jurisdictions have amended their criminal codes specifically to make it a crime to obtain labor or services by means of false pretense. We have no such provision in our statutes.

Furthermore, the unauthorized use of the computer is not the subject of larceny. Nowhere in Code § 18.1-100 or 18.1-118 do we find the word "use." The language of the statutes connotes more than just the unauthorized use of the property of another. It refers to a taking and carrying away of a certain concrete article of personal property. [For example,] the unauthorized use of machinery and spinning facilities of another to process wool did not constitute larceny under New York's false pretense statute.

We hold that labor and services and the unauthorized use of the University's computer cannot be construed to be subject of larceny under the provisions of Code §§ 18.1-100 and 18.1-118.

The Commonwealth argues that even though the computer print-outs had no market value, their value can be determined by the cost of the labor and services that produced them. We do not agree.

The cost of producing the print-outs is not the proper criterion of value for the purpose here. Where there is no market value of an article that has been stolen, the better rule is that its actual value should be proved.

Here the evidence shows that the print-outs had no ascertainable monetary value to the University or the computer center. Indeed, the director of the computer center stated that the print-outs had no more value than scrap paper. Nor is there any evidence of their value to the defendant, and the value to him could only be based on pure speculation and surmise. Hence, the evidence was insufficient to convict the defendant of grand larceny under either Code § 18.1-100 or 18.1-118.

For the reasons stated, the judgment of the trial court is reversed, and the indictment is quashed.

State v. Michael McGraw

480 N.E.2d 552 (Ind. 1985)

PRENTICE, JUSTICE.

Defendant was charged with nine counts of theft under Ind. Code § 35-43-4-2, by information alleging that he knowingly exerted "unauthorized control over the property of the City of Indianapolis, Indiana, to-wit: the use of computers and computer services with intent to deprive the City of Indianapolis, * * *." He was convicted upon two counts.

Defendant was employed by the City of Indianapolis, as a computer operator. The City leased computer services on a fixed charge or flat rate basis, hence the expense to it was not varied by the extent to which it was used. Defendant was provided with a terminal at his desk and was assigned a portion of the computer's information storage capacity, called a "private library," for his utilization in performing his duties.

Defendant became involved in a private sales venture and began soliciting his co-workers and using a small portion of his assigned library to maintain records associated with the venture. He was reprimanded several times for selling his products in the office and on "office time," and he was eventually discharged for unsatisfactory job performance and for continuing his personal business activities during office hours.

Defendant, at the time of his being hired by the City, received a handbook, as do all new employees, which discloses the general prohibition against the unauthorized use of city property.

He requested a former fellow employee to obtain a "print-out" of his business data and then to erase it from what had been his library. Instead, the "print-out" was turned over to Defendant's former supervisor and became the basis for the criminal charges.

Assuming that Defendant's use of the computer was unauthorized and that such use is a "property" under the theft statute, there remains an element of the offense missing under the evidence. The act provides: "A person who knowingly or intentionally exerts unauthorized control over property of another person with *intent* to deprive the other of any part of its value or use, commits theft, a class D felony." It is immediately apparent that the res of the statute, the harm sought to be prevented, is a deprivation to one of his property or its use—not a benefit to one which, although a windfall to him, harmed nobody.

Our question is, "Who was deprived of what?"

Not only was there no evidence that the City was ever deprived of any part of the value or the use of the computer by reason of Defendant's conduct, the uncontradicted evidence was to the contrary. The computer was utilized for City business by means of terminals assigned to various employee-operators, including Defendant. The computer processed the data from the various terminals simultaneously, and the limit of its capacity was never reached or likely to have been. The computer service was leased to the City at a fixed charge, and the tapes or discs upon which the imparted data was stored were erasable and reusable. Defendant's unauthorized use cost the City nothing and did not interfere with its use by others. He extracted from the system only such information as he had previously put into it. He did not, for his own benefit, withdraw City data intended for its exclusive use or for sale. Thus, Defendant did not deprive the City of the "use of computers and computer services" as the information alleged that he intended to do. We find no distinction between Defendant's use of the City's computer and the use, by a mechanic, of the employer's hammer or a stenographer's use of the employer's typewriter, for other than the employer's purposes. Under traditional concepts, the transgression is in the nature of a trespass, a civil matter—and a *de minimis* one, at that. Defendant has likened his conduct to the use of an employer's vacant bookshelf, for the temporary storage of one's personal items, and to the use of an employer's telephone facilities for toll-free calls. The analogies appear to us to be appropriate.

We have written innumerable times that intent is a mental function and, absent an admission, it must be determined by courts and juries from a consideration of the conduct and natural and usual consequences of such conduct. It follows that when the natural and usual consequences of the conduct charged and proved are not such as would effect the wrong which the statute seeks to prevent, the intent to effect that wrong is not so inferrable. No deprivation to the City resulted from Defendant's use of the computer, and a deprivation to it was not a result to be expected from such use, hence not a natural and usual consequence. There was no evidence presented from which the intent to deprive, an essential element of the crime, could be inferred.

PIVARNIK, JUSTICE, dissenting.

I must dissent from the majority opinion wherein the majority finds that Defendant did not take property of the City "with intent to deprive the owner of said property." In the first place, intent is clearly shown in that Defendant used the City computer system for his personal business, well knowing that he was doing so and well knowing that it was unauthorized. I think the Court of Appeals properly focused upon Defendant's unauthorized use of the computer for monetary gain and upon the definition of property as used in the statute and as defined by Ind. Code § 35-41-1-2. Time and use are at the very core of the value of a computer system. To say that only the information stored in the computer plus the tapes and discs and perhaps the machinery involved in the computer system, are the only elements that can be measured as the value or property feature of that system, is incorrect.

I think it is irrelevant that the computer processed the data from various terminals simultaneously and the limit of its capacity was never reached by any or all of the stations, including the defendant's. It is also irrelevant that the computer service was leased to the City at a fixed charge and that the tapes or discs upon which the imparted data was stored were erasable and reusable. The fact is the City owned the computer system of all the stations including the defendant's. The time and use of that equipment at that station belonged to the City. Thus, when the defendant used the computer system, putting on data from his private business and taking it out on printouts, he was taking that which was property of the City and converting it to his own use, thereby depriving the City of its use and value. The majority says: "Thus, Defendant did not deprive the City of the 'use of computers and computer services' as the information alleged that he intended to do." I disagree. I feel that is exactly what he did.

––––––––––

3. Expanding the Concepts of "Property" and "Taking"

State v. Randal Lee Schwartz

21 P.3d 1128 (Or. Ct. App. 2001)

DEITS, C.J.

Defendant worked as an independent contractor for Intel Corporation beginning in the late 1980s. Defendant's tasks included programming, system maintenance, installing new systems and software, and resolving problems for computer users.

In late 1991 or early 1992, defendant began working in Intel's Supercomputer Systems Division (SSD). SSD creates large computer systems that can cost millions of dollars and are used for applications such as nuclear weapons safety. Intel considers the information stored on its SSD computers to be secret and valuable. Each person using SSD computers must use a unique password in order to gain access to electronic information stored there. Passwords are stored in computer files in an encrypted or coded fashion.

In the spring of 1992, defendant and Poelitz, an Intel systems administrator, had a disagreement about how defendant had handled a problem with SSD's e-mail system. The problem was ultimately resolved in an alternative manner suggested by Poelitz, which upset defendant and made him believe that any future decisions he made would be overridden. Accordingly, defendant decided to terminate his SSD contract with Intel. As defendant himself put it, he "hadn't left SSD on the best of terms." At that time, his personal passwords onto all but one SSD computer were disabled so that defendant would no longer have access to SSD computers. His password onto one SSD computer, Brillig, was inadvertently not disabled.

After defendant stopped working with SSD, he continued to work as an independent contractor with a different division of Intel. In March 1993, Brandewie, an Intel network programmer and systems administrator, noticed that defendant was running a "gate" program on an Intel computer called Mink, which allowed access to Mink from computers outside of Intel. "Gate" programs like the one defendant was running violate Intel security policy, because they breach the "firewall" that Intel has established to prevent access to Intel computers by anyone outside the company. Defendant was using the gate program to use his e-mail account with his publisher and to get access to his Intel e-mail when he was on the road. When Brandewie talked to defendant about his gate program, defendant acknowledged that he knew that allowing external access to Intel computers violated company policy. Even though defendant believed that precautions he had taken made his gate program secure, he agreed to alter his program.

In July 1993, Brandewie noticed that defendant was running another gate program on Mink. This program was similar to the earlier gate program and had the same effect of allowing external access to Intel computers. Defendant protested that changes he had made to the program made it secure, but Brandewie insisted that the program violated company policy. At that point, defendant decided that Mink was useless to him without a gate program, so he asked that his account on that computer be closed. Defendant then moved his gate program onto an Intel computer called Hermeis. Because that computer was too slow for him, defendant finally moved his gate program onto the SSD computer Brillig.

In the fall of 1993, defendant downloaded from the Internet a program called "Crack," which is a sophisticated password guessing program. Defendant began to run the Crack program on password files on various Intel computers. When defendant ran the Crack program on Brillig, he learned the password for "Ron B.," one of Brillig's authorized users. Although he knew he did not have the authority to do so, defendant then used Ron B.'s password to log onto Brillig. From Brillig, he copied the entire SSD password file onto another Intel computer, Wyeth. Once the SSD password file was on Wyeth, defendant ran the Crack program on that file and learned the passwords of more than 35 SSD users, including that of the general manager of SSD. Apparently, defendant believed that, if he could show that SSD's security had gone downhill since he had left, he could reestablish the respect he had lost when he left SSD. Once he had cracked the SSD passwords, however, defendant realized that, although he had obtained information that would be useful to SSD, he had done so surreptitiously and had "stepped out of my bounds." Instead of reporting what he had found to anyone at SSD, defendant did nothing and simply stored the information while he went to teach a class in California.

After he returned from California, defendant decided to run the Crack program again on the SSD password file, this time using a new, faster computer called "Snoopy." Defendant thought that, by running the Crack program on the SSD password file using Snoopy, he would have "the most interesting figures" to report to SSD security personnel. On October 28, 1993, Mark Morrissey, an Intel systems administrator, noticed that defendant was running the Crack program on Snoopy. At that point, Morrissey contacted Richard Cower, an Intel network security specialist, for advice about how to proceed. In investigating defendant's actions, Morrissey realized that defendant had been running a gate program on the SSD computer Brillig, even though defendant's access should have been canceled. On October 29, 1993, Cower, Morrissey, and others at Intel decided to contact police.

Defendant challenges the trial court's denial of his motion for judgment of acquittal on counts two and three of the indictment. In counts two and three, respectively, defendant was charged as follows:

> "That the above named defendant(s) on and between August 1, 1993 and November 1, 1993, in Washington County, Oregon, did unlawfully and knowingly access and use a computer and computer network for the purpose of committing theft of the Intel SSD's password file[.] * * *

> "That the above named defendant(s) on and between October 21, 1993 and October 25, 1993, in Washington County, Oregon, did unlawfully and knowingly access and use a computer and computer system for the purpose of committing theft of the Intel SSD individual user's passwords[.]"

At the close of the state's case, defendant moved for a judgment of acquittal on counts two and three. Defendant argued that, because the state's theory was that he acted with the purpose of committing theft, the state had to prove the elements of the theft statute, ORS 164.015. According to defendant the state had failed, first, to put on evidence that he had taken property and, second, to put on evidence that he had acted with the intent or purpose to commit theft.

The parties do not dispute that the state proved that defendant "knowingly accesse[d] * * * or use[d] * * * any computer, computer system, computer network or any part thereof" as required by ORS 164.377(2)(c). The parties dispute only whether the evidence was sufficient to establish that defendant did so "for the purpose of * * * [c]ommitting theft, including, but not limited to, theft of proprietary information."

ORS 164.377 does not define "theft." However, the legislature has defined "theft" in a related statute. ORS 164.015 provides, in part:

> "A person commits theft when, with intent to deprive another of property or to appropriate property to the person or to a third person, the person:
>
> "(1) Takes, appropriates, obtains or withholds such property from an owner thereof[.]"

"Property" includes "any * * * thing of value." ORS 164.005(5). The parties do not dispute that the password file and individual passwords have value, and there is evidence in the record to support that proposition. The parties dispute, however, whether defendant "t[ook], appropriate[d], obtain[ed] or withh[e]ld" the password file and individual passwords.

Defendant argues that he could not have "taken, appropriated, obtained or withheld" the password file and individual passwords because, even though he moved them to another computer and took them in the sense that he now had them on his computer, the file and passwords remained on Intel's computers after he ran the Crack program. The individual users whose passwords defendant had obtained could still use their passwords just as they had before. Intel continued to "have" everything it did before defendant ran the Crack program and, consequently, defendant reasons, he cannot be said to have "taken" anything away from Intel.

The state responds that, by copying the passwords, defendant stripped them of their value. The state contends that, like proprietary manufacturing formulas, passwords have value only so long as no one else knows what they are. Once defendant had copied them, the passwords were useless for their only purpose, protecting access to information in the SSD computers. The loss of exclusive possession of the passwords, according to the state, is sufficient to constitute theft.

Under ORS 164.015, theft occurs, among other ways, when a person "takes" the property of another. "Take" is a broad term with an extensive dictionary entry. *Webster's Third New Int'l Dictionary*, 2329–31. Some of the dictionary definitions undermine defendant's argument. The first definition of "take" is "to get into one's hands or into one's possession, power, or control by force or stratagem * * *." Another definition provides "to adopt or lay hold of for oneself or as one's own * * *." *Black's* defines "take" to include "[t]o obtain possession or control * * *." *Black's Law Dictionary*, 1466 (7th ed. 1999). Those definitions indicate that the term "take" might include more than just the transfer of exclusive possession that defendant proposes. For example, "take" could include obtaining control of property, as defendant did with respect to the passwords and password file by copying them.

Turning back to the text of the statute under which defendant was charged, we note that the legislature contemplated that "theft" as used in ORS 164.377(2)(c) could be exercised upon, among other things, "proprietary information." "Proprietary information" includes "scientific, technical or commercial information * * * that is known only to limited individuals within an organization * * *." ORS 164.377(1)(i). Proprietary information, like the passwords and password files at issue here, is not susceptible to exclusive possession; it is information that, by definition, can be known by more than one person. Nevertheless, the legislature indicated that it could be subject to "theft" under ORS 164.377(2)(c). We conclude that the state presented sufficient evidence to prove that, by copying the passwords and password file, defendant took property of another, namely Intel, and that his actions, therefore, were for the purpose of theft.

United States v. Bertram E. Seidlitz

589 F.2d 152 (4th Cir. 1978)

FIELD, SENIOR CIRCUIT JUDGE:

Bertram Seidlitz appeals from his conviction on two counts of fraud by wire in violation of 18 U.S.C. § 1343.[n.1][6] As grounds for reversal, he urges that the prosecution failed to establish certain material elements of the crime. Although advanced in a somewhat novel factual context, we find appellant's contentions to be without merit.

On January 1, 1975, defendant Seidlitz assumed the position of Deputy Project Director for Optimum Systems, Inc. (OSI), a computer service company which was under contract to install, maintain, and operate a computer facility at Rockville, Maryland, for use by the Federal Energy Administration. Under the arrangement between OSI and FEA, persons working for FEA in various parts of the country could use key boards at communications terminals in their offices to send instructions over telephone circuits to the large computers in Rockville, and the computers' responses would be returned and reflected on a CRT (cathode ray tube) terminal which is a typewriter-like device with a keyboard and display screen similar to a television screen upon which the information is displayed as it is sent and received. Mr. Seidlitz helped to prepare the software which was installed at the Rockville facility as part of the project, and he was also responsible for the security of the central computer system. During his tenure, he had full access to the computers and to a software system known as "WYLBUR" which resided within them. In June,

---

6. [n.1] The federal wire fraud statute, 18 U.S.C. § 1343, provides:

    Whoever, having devised or intending to devise any scheme or artifice to defraud, or for obtaining money or property by means of false or fraudulent pretenses, representations, or promises, transmits or causes to be transmitted by means of wire, radio, or television communication in interstate or foreign commerce, any writings, signs, signals, pictures, or sounds for the purpose of executing such scheme or artifice, shall be fined not more than $1,000 or imprisoned not more than five years, or both.

1975, Seidlitz resigned this job and returned to work at his own computer firm in Alexandria, Virginia.

William Coakley, a computer specialist employed by FEA, was assigned temporarily to the OSI facility. On December 30, 1975, in an attempt to locate a friend who might be using the OSI system, he had the computer display the initials of everyone who was then using the WYLBUR software. Among the initials displayed by the computer were those of his supervisor, who was standing nearby and who was not using the computer. Suspicious that an unauthorized "intruder" might be using these initials in order to gain access to the system, Coakley asked Mr. Ewing, an OSI employee, if Ewing could determine what was happening. Ewing instructed the computer to display for him the data it was about to transmit to the possible intruder, and it proved to be a portion of the "source code" of the WYLBUR software system. Using other data provided by the computer, Wack concluded that the connection was by telephone from outside the complex. At his request, the telephone company manually traced the call to the Alexandria office of the defendant.

The following day, OSI activated a special feature of the WYLBUR system known as the "Milten Spy Function," which automatically recorded . . . any requests made of the computer by the intruder. The "spy" also recorded, before they were sent out to the intruder over the telephone lines, the computer's responses to such requests. Mr. Wack again asked the telephone company to trace the line when it was suspected that the unauthorized person, employing the same initials, was using the computer to receive portions of the WYLBUR source code. This manual trace on December 31 led once more to the defendant's office in Virginia, although OSI was not so informed.

Advised by OSI of the events of December 30 and 31, the FBI on January 3, 1976, secured . . . a warrant to search the defendant's Alexandria office. [Later,] the FBI executed the warrant to search Seidlitz' Alexandria office, seizing, among other items, a copy of the user's guide to the OSI system and some 40 rolls of computer paper upon which were printed the WYLBUR source code. A warrant was then issued to search the Seidlitz residence in Lanham, where officers found a portable communications terminal which contained a teleprinter for receiving written messages from the computer, as well as a notebook containing information relating to access codes previously assigned to authorized users of the OSI computers.

The indictment charged that the defendant had, on December 30 and 31, transmitted telephone calls in interstate commerce as part of a scheme to defraud OSI of property consisting of information from the computer system. Viewed in the light most favorable to the government, there was sufficient evidence from which the jury could find that the WYLBUR system was "property" as defined in the instruction given by the trial judge which is not contested on appeal. Even though software systems similar to OSI's WYLBUR were in use at non-OSI facilities, the evidence that OSI invested substantial sums to modify the system to suit its peculiar needs, that OSI enjoyed a multi-million dollar competitive advantage because of WYLBUR, and that OSI took steps to prevent persons other than clients and employees from using the system permitted a finding that the pilfered data was the property of OSI and not, as the defendant contends, property in the public domain subject to appropriation by persons such as himself.

––––––––––

Notes

This Chapter ends with the question poscd at its beginning: Is there a need for computer-specific crimes? Examining that question within the context of the traditional property crimes of trespass and larceny requires one to consider additional questions: What is the nature of "property" in the context of digital devices? Is property a mere tangible thing? *Compare Lund* with both the majority and the dissent in *McGraw.* Is there an intangible component? Is it subject to "taking and carrying away?" *Compare Schwartz* and *Seidlitz.*

Chapter 16

Computer Specific Crimes: Obtaining Confidential Information, Unauthorized Access, Fraud, and Damage

§ 16.1 Overview: Computer Fraud and Abuse Act — 18 U.S.C. § 1030

The Computer Fraud and Abuse Act (CFAA) is the primary federal statute aimed at combating computer crime. It targets several different types of criminal activity in its various sections and, based on its amendments, now applies broadly to any computer connected to the Internet.

In the early 1980s law enforcement agencies faced the dawn of the computer age with growing concern about the lack of criminal laws available to fight the emerging computer crimes. Although the wire and mail fraud provisions of the federal criminal code were capable of addressing some types of computer-related criminal activity, neither of those statutes provided the full range of tools needed to combat these new crimes.

In response, Congress included in the Comprehensive Crime Control Act of 1984 provisions to address the unauthorized access and use of computers and computer networks. The legislative history indicates that Congress intended these provisions to provide "a clearer statement of proscribed activity" to "the law enforcement community, those who own and operate computers, as well as those who may be tempted to commit crimes by unauthorized access." Congress did this by making it a felony to access classified information in a computer without authorization, and a misdemeanor to access financial records or credit histories stored in a financial institution or to trespass into a government computer. In so doing, Congress opted not to add new provisions regarding computers to existing criminal laws, but rather to address federal computer-related offenses in a single, new statute, 18 U.S.C. § 1030.

Even after enacting section 1030, Congress continued to investigate problems associated with computer crime to determine whether federal criminal laws required further revision. Throughout 1985, both the House and the Senate held hearings on potential computer crime bills, continuing the efforts begun in the year before. These hearings culminated in the Computer Fraud and Abuse Act (CFAA), enacted by Congress in 1986, which amended 18 U.S.C. § 1030.

In the CFAA, Congress attempted to strike an "appropriate balance between the Federal Government's interest in computer crime and the interests and abilities of the States to proscribe and punish such offenses." Congress addressed federalism concerns in the CFAA by limiting federal jurisdiction to cases with a compelling federal interest — i.e., where computers of the federal government or certain financial institutions are involved, or where the crime itself is interstate in nature.

In addition to clarifying a number of the provisions in the original section 1030, the CFAA also criminalized additional computer-related acts. For example, Congress added a provision to penalize the theft of property via computer that occurs as a part of a scheme to defraud. Congress also added a provision to penalize those who intentionally alter, damage, or destroy data belonging to others. This latter provision was designed to cover such activities as the distribution of malicious code and denial of service attacks. Finally, Congress also included in the CFAA a provision criminalizing trafficking in passwords and similar items.

As computer crimes continued to grow in sophistication and as prosecutors gained experience with the CFAA, the CFAA required further amendment, which Congress did [several times in succeeding years.][1]

The CFAA's scope has been expanded over the years to protect broad classes of computers and to address a wider range of criminal activity. Because the statute has been frequently modified, case law interpreting it must be examined with care to determine if the provision analyzed in the case is current. Moreover, the frequent statutory modifications have resulted in stylistic changes, such as reorganization and renumbering of subsections.

The current version of 18 U.S.C. § 1030 addresses several types of criminal activity:

- *National Security.* Section 1030(a)(1) prohibits unauthorized access to and distribution of classified government information.

- *Confidential Information.* Section 1030(a)(2) prohibits obtaining, without authorization, information from financial institutions, the United States, or any protected computer.

---

1. Computer Crime and Intellectual Property Section, Criminal Division, United States Department of Justice, Prosecuting Computer Crimes 1–2 (2007).

- *Unauthorized Access.* Section 1030(a)(3) proscribes intentionally accessing, without authorization, a nonpublic computer of a United States department or agency.

- *Fraud.* Section 1030(a)(4) prohibits accessing a protected computer, without authorization, with the intent to defraud and obtain something of value.

- *Damage.* Section 1030(a)(5) creates categories of offenses based on who the person accessing the computer is and on the type of damage caused.

- *Passwords.* Section 1030(a)(6) prohibits trafficking in passwords that would either permit unauthorized access to a government computer or affect interstate or foreign commerce.

- *Extortion.* Section 1030(a)(7) makes it illegal to transmit in interstate or foreign commerce any threat to cause damage to a protected computer with intent to extort something of value.

This chapter focuses on the crimes defined in sections (a)(2) through (a)(5).

§ 16.2 Key Definitions of the CFAA

Several key terms must be understood to understand the scope of CFAA's applicability. To be criminally liable under the statute, it must be shown that a person intentionally accesses a protected computer without authorization or exceeds authorization. The following discusses those key building blocks:

1. Protected Computer

Section 1030 addresses crimes against "protected" computers.

- A *computer* is defined in subsection (e)(1):

[T]he term "computer" means an electronic, magnetic, optical, electrochemical, or other high speed data processing device performing logical, arithmetic, or storage functions, and includes any data storage facility or communications facility directly related to or operating in conjunction with such device, but such term does not include an automated typewriter or typesetter, a portable hand held calculator, or other similar device[.]

- A *protected* computer is defined in 18 U.S.C. § 1030(e)(2) to be any computer

(A) exclusively for the use of a financial institution or the United States Government, or, in the case of a computer not exclusively for such use, used by or for a financial institution or the United States Government and the conduct constituting the offense affects that use by or for the financial institution or the Government; or

(B) which is used in or affecting interstate or foreign commerce or communication, including a computer located outside the United States that is used in a manner that affects interstate or foreign commerce or communication of the United States[.]

a. Current Version of "Protected Computer"

_____

United States v. Chad A. Powers
2010 U.S. Dist. LEXIS 34007 (D. Neb. Mar. 4, 2010)

THOMAS D. THALKEN, UNITED STATES MAGISTRATE JUDGE.

On or about March 3, 2009, through March 14, 2009, approximately eight images of Shaunna M. Briles, partially nude and/or engaging in provocative poses, were sent via her America Online e-mail account and addressed to individuals in her account address book. Briles was an Omaha, Nebraska resident at the time of the incident. Additional e-mails were sent to e-mail addresses Briles did not recognize. Some e-mails were sent to recipients in Nebraska, including a coworker. Briles, the registered holder of the e-mail account, intentionally gave the authorization password to Powers. Powers used the password to gain access to the e-mail account. The images contained in the e-mails were taken in 2003, and Briles had previously e-mailed the images to someone on a previous occasion. With authorized access to Briles' e-mail account, Powers was able to gain access to past e-mail messages in the account, and could subsequently access the images by exceeding the purpose for which the password was given.

Briles contacted Federal Bureau of Investigation Special Agent Justin Kolenbrander regarding the computer intrusion. On or about March 18, 2009, Kolenbrander interviewed Briles about the e-mail messages and the images. Briles told Kolenbrander three of the e-mail messages were sent from her AOL e-mail account on March 3, 2009, March 4, 2009, and March 14, 2009. Briles stated she became aware of the sent e-mail messages on or about March 5, 2009, after she noticed copies of three e-mail messages in her AOL e-mail account.

The same day, after the interview, Briles telephoned Kolenbrander and stated her sister, Stacy Mueller, received one of the e-mail messages on her work account at the Iowa Department of Public Safety. Kolenbrander contacted Mueller's supervisor, Steven Ray, and requested copies of the e-mail message headers for March 4, 2009, and March 14, 2009. On or about March 25, 2009, Kolenbrander received a CD-ROM from Ray containing digital copies of the email messages and the attached images.

Analysis of the March 4, 2009, and March 14, 2009, e-mail messages included on the CD-ROM show the e-mail messages originated from the Internet Protocol Address 68.230.83.202. The IP Address obtained from the e-mail messages was registered to Cox Communications in Atlanta, Georgia. Pursuant to a subpoena, Cox Communications provided subscriber information to confirm the IP Address 68.230.83.202 belonged to Powers, 2811 W. Deer Valley Road, Apartment 1029, Phoenix, Arizona, from January 10, 2009, through March 18, 2009.

At the evidentiary hearing, [Theresa Hiner, employed by the Federal Public Defenders Office to manage computer and network systems,] testified regarding use and access to computers and e-mail accounts. Hiner stated a person is not required to have a home computer to have an e-mail account. An individual can use a public computer to access an e-mail account from anywhere. E-mail accounts such as AOL reside on a server. A server is a computer system that holds information. E-mail accounts physically store e-mail messages and attachments on servers. When an e-mail message is sent with an attachment, the person receiving the e-mail message would view the contents of the message and attachment from the server through their Internet browser. Accordingly, the images attached to the e-mails were located on the server as opposed to stored on the hard drive of Briles' computer.

Powers alleges 18 U.S.C. § 1030(a)(2)(C) was not enacted to protect personal computers. Instead, Powers argues, Congress intended the statute to protect financial and governmental institutions from intrusions by hackers seeking information or maliciously altering the computer systems.

While the term "protected computer" includes computers used in financial or government situations, the CFAA provides notice and extends coverage to computers used in or affecting interstate communication. Under the CFAA, the servers that hosted Briles' e-mail account or contained the compromising images qualify as "protected computers" because the servers can be used in interstate communication. E-mail servers are able to send and receive e-mail messages from anywhere in the United States, which ability constitutes interstate communication.

---

b. Evolution of the Types of Computers Protected

Shurgard Storage Centers, Inc. v. Safeguard Self Storage, Inc.

119 F. Supp. 2d 1121 (W.D. Wash. 2000)

ZILLY, DISTRICT JUDGE.

[Shurgard Storage Centers and Safeguard Self Storage were competitors in the self-storage business. Shurgard alleged that Safeguard embarked on a systematic scheme to hire away key employees to obtain the plaintiff's trade secrets and that some of those employees, while still working for Shurgard, used the Shurgard's computers to send trade secrets to Safeguard via e-mail. Shurgard alleged a variety of causes of action, including violations of the Computer Fraud and Abuse Act. Safeguard sought dismissal of that claim on a variety of grounds, including that the computers were not "protected computers" under the CFAA.]

The defendant's argument is that the CFAA was only intended to protect information in large businesses where information, if released or stolen, could affect the public. The defendant maintains that since information from the storage business is not of the type that the CFAA was intended to protect (as opposed to the transportation or power-supply industries), the CFAA does not apply.

Nowhere in language of § 1030(a)(2)(C) is the scope limited to entities with broad privacy repercussions. The statute simply prohibits the obtaining of information from "*any* protected computer if the conduct involved an interstate or foreign communication." According to the statute, a protected computer is a computer used in interstate or foreign commerce. *See* 18 U.S.C. § 1030(e)(2)(B). This language is unambiguous. There is no reasonable implication in any of these terms that suggests only the computers of certain industries are protected. Therefore, the defendant's argument on this issue is unpersuasive.

The core of the defendant's arguments concerning legislative intent is that the CFAA was not meant to apply to the kind of factual situation presented in this case. Instead, the defendant maintains the CFAA is limited to those industries whose computers contain vast amounts of information, which if released, could significantly affect privacy interests in the public at large.

The first version of the CFAA was passed in 1984. This first bill was directed at protecting classified information on government computers as well as protecting financial records and credit information on government and financial institution computers. In 1986, the CFAA was amended to "provide additional penalties for fraud and related activities in connection with access devices and computers." Specifically, the 1986 amendments added protection for "federal interest computers:"

> Throughout its consideration of computer crime, the Committee has been especially concerned about the appropriate scope of Federal jurisdiction in this area. It has been suggested that, because some States lack comprehensive computer crime statutes of their own, the Congress should enact as sweeping a Federal statute as possible so that no computer crime is left uncovered. The Committee rejects this approach and prefers instead to limit Federal jurisdiction over computer crime to those cases in which there is a compelling Federal interest, i.e., where computers of the Federal Government or certain financial institutions are involved, or where the crime itself is interstate in nature.

The CFAA was amended in 1996, and the phrase "protected computer" was added in place of "federal interest computer." The Senate Report on these amendments demonstrates the broad scope of this phrase. *See* S. Rep. No. 104-357, at 3 (1996) ("[The CFAA is strengthened] by closing gaps in the law to protect better the confidentiality, integrity, and security of computer data and networks."); *Id.* at 4; ("The privacy protection coverage of the statute has two significant gaps. First, omitted from the statute's coverage is information on *any civilian* or State and local government computers, since the prohibition on unauthorized computer access to obtain non classified information extends only to the Federal Government when the perpetrator is an outsider."); *Id.* at 5; ("[The CFAA] facilitates addressing in a single statute the problem of computer crime, rather than identifying and amending every potentially applicable statute affected by advances in computer technology. As computers continue to proliferate in businesses and homes, and new forms of computer crimes emerge, Congress must remain vigilant to ensure that the [CFAA] is up-to-date and provides law enforcement with the necessary legal framework to fight computer crime.") *Id.*

Finally, in what is dispositive of the scope of the CFAA, the report states:

> The proposed subsection 1030(a)(2)(C) is intended to protect against the interstate or foreign theft of information by computer. . . . This subsection would ensure that the theft of intangible information by the unauthorized use of a computer is prohibited in the same way theft of physical items are protected. *In instances where the information stolen is also copyrighted, the theft may implicate certain rights under the copyright laws. The crux of the offense under subsection 1030(a)(2)(C), however, is the abuse of a computer to obtain the information.*

> . . . Those who improperly use computers to obtain other types of information—such as financial records, nonclassified Government information, and information of nominal value *from private individuals or companies*—face only misdemeanor penalties, *unless the information is used for commercial advantage*, private financial gain or to commit any criminal *or tortious act.*

> For example, individuals who intentionally break into, *or abuse their authority to use*, a computer and thereby obtain information of minimal value of $5,000 or less, would be subject to a misdemeanor penalty. The crime becomes a felony if the offense was committed for *purposes of commercial advantage* or private financial gain, for the purposes of *committing any criminal or tortious act in violation* . . . of the laws of the United States or of any State, or if the value of the information obtained exceeds $5,000.

This legislative history demonstrates the broad meaning and intended scope of the terms "protected computer" and "without authorization" that are also used in the other relevant sections. In sum, this passage makes clear that the CFAA was intended to encompass actions such as those allegedly undertaken by the present defendant. The legislative history of the CFAA comports with the plain meaning of the statute.

---

2. Intentional Access

a. How to Restrict Access: Code-Based and Contract-Based Restrictions

Code-based protection is, in essence, technical barriers to access that the computer owner programs by code into the computer software. Typical code-based "gatekeepers" include password protection, or a routing system that directs every would-be user to a main login page. The privacy advantages of code-based protection are twofold. First, it puts exclusionary control of the site in the hands of the computer owner (she may set password access and then assign passwords to users as she deems appropriate). Second, the computer itself, through the technical measures imposed by the owner, takes affirmative steps to control access by excluding members of the public who do not meet the site's coded access criteria. Importantly, technical code-based protection measures "actually have to control access to some degree," as opposed to indicating the permissible limits of access to a computer or website. In other words, code-based protection is the digital equivalent of a locked safe—a physical barrier around information that the user intends to keep private.

In comparison, a computer owner may control access by contract: She posts terms and conditions to which a user must agree before he is "permitted" to use the computer or the website. Common examples are a "terms of use" statement on or linked from the main page of a website, or a "click-through" agreement that stipulates terms to which the prospective user must affirmatively agree before she is granted access. However, unlike code-based protection, contract-based protection is not coded into the computer system. Instead, contract-based protection works "on the honor system, or perhaps more accurately, the honor system backed by contract law remedies."[2]

———————

CREATING RESTRICTIONS

EF Cultural Travel BV v. Zefer Corporation

318 F.3d 58 (5th Cir. 2003)

BOUDIN, CHIEF JUDGE.

EF and Explorica are competitors in the student travel business. Explorica was started in the spring of 2000 by several former EF employees who aimed to compete in part by copying EF's prices from EF's website and setting Explorica's own prices slightly lower. EF's website permits a visitor to the site to search its tour database and view the prices for tours meeting specified criteria such as gateway (*e.g.*, departure) cities, destination cities, and tour duration. In June 2000, Explorica hired Zefer, which provides computer-related expertise, to build a scraper tool that could "scrape" the prices from EF's website and download them into an Excel spreadsheet.

A scraper, also called a "robot" or "bot," is nothing more than a computer program that accesses information contained in a succession of webpages stored on the accessed computer. Strictly speaking, the accessed information is not the graphical interface seen by the user but rather the HTML source code—available to anyone who views the site—that generates the graphical interface. This information is then downloaded to the user's computer. The scraper program used in this case was not designed to copy all of the information on the accessed pages (*e.g.*, the descriptions of the tours), but rather only the price for each tour through each possible gateway city.

———————

2. Nicholas R. Johnson, Recent Development, *"I Agree" to Criminal Liability: Lori Drew's Prosecution under § 1030(a)(2)(C) of the Computer Fraud and Abuse Act, and Why Every Internet User Should Care*, 2009 U. ILL. J.L. TECH. & POL'Y 561. Copyright © 2009, University of Illinois Journal of Law, Technology & Pol'y. All rights reserved. Reprinted by permission.

Zefer built a scraper tool that scraped two years of pricing data from EF's website. After receiving the pricing data from Zefer, Explorica set its own prices for the public, undercutting EF's prices an average of five percent. EF discovered Explorica's use of the scraper tool during discovery in an unrelated state-court action brought by Explorica's President against EF for back wages.

What appears to have happened is that Philip Gormley, Explorica's Chief Information Officer and EF's former Vice President of Information Strategy, e-mailed Zefer a description of how EF's website was structured and identified the information that Explorica wanted to have copied; this may have facilitated Zefer's development of the scraper tool, but there is no indication that the structural information was unavailable from perusal of the website or that Zefer would have known that it was information subject to a confidentiality agreement.

EF also claims that Gormley e-mailed Zefer the "codes" identifying in computer shorthand the names of EF's gateway and destination cities. These codes were used to direct the scraper tool to the specific pages on EF's website that contained EF's pricing information. But, again, it appears that the codes could be extracted more slowly by examining EF's webpages manually, so it is far from clear that Zefer would have had to know that they were confidential.

The issue is whether use of the scraper "exceed[ed] authorized access." A lack of authorization could be established by an explicit statement on the website restricting access. (Whether public policy might in turn limit certain restrictions is a separate issue.) Many webpages contain lengthy limiting conditions, including limitations on the use of scrapers.[n.3][3]

The district court thought that a lack of authorization could also be inferred from the circumstances, using "reasonable expectations" as the test; and it said that three such circumstances comprised such a warning in this case: the copyright notice on EF's homepage with a link directing users to contact the company with questions; EF's provision to Zefer of confidential information obtained in breach of the employee confidentiality agreements; and the fact that the website was configured to allow ordinary visitors to the site to view only one page at a time.

We agree with the district court that lack of authorization may be implicit, rather than explicit. After all, password protection itself normally limits authorization by implication (and technology), even without express terms. But we think that in general a reasonable expectations test is not the proper gloss on subsection (a)(4) and we reject it.

---

3. [n.3] For example, the "legal notices" on one familiar website state that "you may print or download one copy of the materials or content on this site on any single computer for your personal, non-commercial use, provided you keep intact all copyright and other proprietary notices. Systematic retrieval of data or other content from this site to create or compile, directly or indirectly, a collection, compilation, database or directory without written permission from America Online is prohibited." AOL Anywhere Terms and Conditions of Use, *at* http://www.aol.com/copyright.html (last visited Jan. 14, 2003).

Our basis for this view is not that there is a "presumption" of open access to Internet information. The CFAA, after all, is primarily a statute imposing limits on access and enhancing control by information providers. Instead, we think that the public website provider can easily spell out explicitly what is forbidden and, consonantly, that nothing justifies putting users at the mercy of a highly imprecise, litigation-spawning standard like "reasonable expectations." If EF wants to ban scrapers, let it say so on the webpage or a link clearly marked as containing restrictions.

This case itself illustrates the flaws in the "reasonable expectations" standard. Why should the copyright symbol, which arguably does not protect the substantive information anyway, or the provision of page-by-page access for that matter, be taken to suggest that downloading information at higher speed is forbidden. EF could easily include—indeed, by now probably has included—a sentence on its home page or in its terms of use stating that "no scrapers may be used," giving fair warning and avoiding time-consuming litigation about its private, albeit "reasonable," intentions.

———————

"Intentional"

United States v. Lori Drew

259 F.R.D. 449 (C.D. Cal. 2009)

George H. Wu, District Judge.

While "intentionally" is undefined, the legislative history of the CFAA clearly evinces Congress's purpose in its choice of that word. Prior to 1986, 18 U.S.C. § 1030(a)(2) utilized the phrase "knowingly accesses." In the 1986 amendments to the statute, the word "intentionally" was substituted for the word "knowingly." In Senate Report No. 99-432 at 5–6, it was stated that:

> Section 2(a)(1) amends 18 U.S.C. 1030(a)(2) to change the scienter requirement from "knowingly" to "intentionally," for two reasons. First, intentional acts of unauthorized access—rather than mistaken, inadvertent, or careless ones—are precisely what the Committee intends to proscribe. Second, the Committee is concerned that the "knowingly" standard in the existing statute might be inappropriate for cases involving computer technology.... The substitution of an "intentional" standard is designed to focus Federal criminal prosecutions on those whose conduct evinces a clear intent to enter, without proper authorization, computer files or data belonging to another. Again, this will comport with the Senate Report on the Criminal Code, which states that "'intentional' means more than that one voluntarily engaged in conduct or caused a result. Such conduct or the causing of the result must have been the person's conscious objective."

———————

"Access"

United States v. Lori Drew

259 F.R.D. 449 (C.D. Cal. 2009)

George H. Wu, District Judge.

As to the term "accesses a computer," one would think that the dictionary definition of verb transitive "access" would be sufficient. That definition is "to gain or have access to; to retrieve data from, or add data to, a database." *Webster's New World Dictionary, Third College Edition*, 7 (1988). Most courts that have actually considered the issue of the meaning of the word "access" in the CFAA have basically turned to the dictionary meaning. However, academic commentators have generally argued for a different interpretation of the word. For example, as stated in Patricia L. Bellia, *Defending Cyberproperty*, 79 N.Y.U. L. Rev. 2164, 2253–54 (2004):

> We can posit two possible readings of the term "access." First, it is possible to adopt a broad reading, under which "access" means any interaction between two computers. In other words, "accessing" a computer simply means transmitting electronic signals to a computer that the computer processes in some way. A narrower understanding of "access" would focus not merely on the successful exchange of electronic signals, but rather on conduct by which one is in a position to obtain privileges or information not available to the general public. The choice between these two meanings of "access" obviously affects what qualifies as unauthorized conduct. If we adopt the broader reading of access, and any successful interaction between computers qualifies, then breach of policies or contractual terms purporting to outline permissible uses of a system can constitute unauthorized access to the system. Under the narrower reading of access, however, only breach of a code-based restriction on the system would qualify.

Professor Bellia goes on to conclude that "[c]ourts would better serve both the statutory intent of the CFAA and public policy by limiting its application to unwanted uses only in connection with code-based controls on access." It is simply noted that, while defining "access" in terms of a code-based restriction might arguably be a preferable approach, no case has adopted it and the CFAA legislative history does not support it.

State v. Anthony A. Allen

917 P.2d 848 (Kan. 1996)

Larson, Justice:

We are presented with the question of whether a person's telephonic connections that prompt a computer owner to change its security systems constitute felony computer crime in violation of K.S.A. 21-3755(b).

The charges against Anthony A. Allen arose from several telephonic connections he made with Southwestern Bell Telephone Company's computers in early 1995. After preliminary hearing, the trial court dismissed the complaint, finding no probable cause existed to believe Allen had committed any crime.

We affirm the trial court.

Allen admitted to Detective Kent Willnauer that he had used his computer, equipped with a modem, to call various Southwestern Bell computer modems. The telephone numbers for the modems were obtained by random dialing. If one of Allen's calls were completed, his computer determined if it had been answered by voice or another computer. These were curiosity calls of short duration.

The State presented no evidence which showed that Allen ever had entered any Southwestern Bell computer system. Detective Willnauer was unable to state that Allen had altered any programs, added anything to the system, used it to perform any functions, or interfered with its operation. Willnauer specifically stated he had no evidence that the Southwestern Bell computer system had been damaged.

Ronald W. Knisley, Southwestern Bell's Regional Security Director, testified Allen had called two different types of Southwestern Bell computer equipment-SLC-96 system environmental controls and SMS-800 database systems.

The telephone numbers for the SLC-96 systems were thought to be known only to Southwestern Bell employees or agents on a need-to-know basis. Access to the SLC-96 systems required knowledge of a password. If one connected to the system it displayed "KEYWORD?" without any identification or warning. No evidence existed that Allen attempted to respond to the prompt.

Testimony confirmed Allen also called and connected 28 times with the SMS-800 systems at several different modem numbers. Each call but two was under 1 minute. Upon connection with this system, a person would see a log on request and a "banner." The banner identifies the system that has answered the incoming call and displays that it is Southwestern Bell property and that access is restricted. Entry into the system itself then requires both a user ID and a password which must agree with each other. No evidence indicated Allen went beyond this banner or even attempted to enter a user ID or password.

Knisley testified that if entry into an SMS-800 system were accomplished and proper commands were given, a PBX system could be located which would allow unlimited and nonchargeable long distance telephone calls. There was no evidence this occurred, nor was it shown that Allen had damaged, modified, destroyed, or copied any data.

James E. Robinson, Function Manager responsible for computer security, testified one call to an SMS-800 system lasted 6 minutes and 35 seconds. Although the system should have retained information about this call, it did not, leading to speculation the record-keeping system had been overridden. Robinson speculated Allen had gained entry into the system but admitted he had no evidence that Allen's computer had done anything more than sit idle for a few minutes after calling a Southwestern Bell modem number.

Robinson testified that Southwestern Bell was unable to document any damage to its computer equipment or software as a result of Allen's activities. However, as a result of its investigation, Southwestern Bell decided that prudence required it to upgrade its password security system to a more secure "token card" process. It was the cost of this investigation and upgrade that the State alleges comprises the damage caused by Allen's actions. Total investigative costs were estimated at $4,140. The cost of developing deterrents was estimated to be $1,656. The cost to distribute secure ID cards to employees [totaled] $18,000. Thus, the total estimated damage was $23,796.

In closing arguments, the State admitted Allen did not get into the computer system, nor did he modify, alter, destroy, copy, disclose, or take possession of anything. Instead, the State argued Allen's conduct in acquiring the unlisted numbers and calling them constituted an "approach" to the systems, within the meaning of K.S.A. 21-3755(a)(1), which questioned the integrity of the systems and resulted in the altered or added security precautions.

Allen was charged under K.S.A. 21-3755, which in applicable part provides:

"[(a)](1) 'Access' means to approach, instruct, communicate with, store data in, retrieve data from, or otherwise make use of any resources of a computer, computer system or computer network.

"(b) Computer crime is:

"(1) Intentionally and without authorization gaining or attempting to gain access to and damaging, modifying, altering, destroying, copying, disclosing or taking possession of a computer, computer system, computer network or any other property;. . . .

"(e) Criminal computer access is intentionally, fraudulently and without authorization gaining or attempting to gain access to any computer, computer system, computer network or to any computer software, program, documentation, data or property contained in any computer, computer system or computer network."

Allen was charged with a violation of K.S.A. 21-3755(b)(1), with the second amended complaint alleging that he

"did then and there intentionally and without authorization gain access and damage a computer, computer system, computer network or other computer property which caused a loss of the value of at least $500.00 but less than $25,000.00."

After finding the evidence showed Allen had done nothing more than use his computer to call unlisted telephone numbers, the trial court ruled there was insufficient evidence to show Allen had gained access to the computer systems. Although a telephone connection had been established, the evidence showed Allen had done nothing more. The trial court reasoned that unless and until Allen produced a password that permitted him to interact with the data in the computer system, he had not "gained access" as the complaint required.

The State argues the trial court's construction of the statute ignores the fact that "access" is defined in the statute, K.S.A. 21-3755(a)(1), as "to approach, instruct, communicate with, store data in, retrieve data from, or otherwise make use of any resources of a computer, computer system or computer network." By this definition, the State would lead us to believe that any kind of an "approach" is criminal behavior sufficient to satisfy a charge that Allen did in fact "gain access" to a computer system.

The problem with the State's analysis is that K.S.A. 21-3755(b)(1) does not criminalize "accessing" (and, thus, "approaching") but rather "gaining or attempting to gain access." If we were to read "access" in this context as the equivalent of "approach," the statute would criminalize the behavior of "attempting to gain approach" to a computer or computer system. This phrase is lacking in any common meaning such that an ordinary person would have great difficulty discerning what conduct was prohibited, leading to an effective argument that the statute was void for vagueness.

The United States Department of Justice has commented about the use of "approach" in a definition of "access" in this context: "The use of the word 'approach' in the definition of 'access,' if taken literally, could mean that any unauthorized physical proximity to a computer could constitute a crime." National Institute of Justice, Computer Crime: Criminal Justice Resource Manual, p. 84 (2d ed.1989).

We read certain conduct as outside a statute's scope rather than as proscribed by the statute if including it within the statute would render the statute unconstitutionally vague. Consequently, although K.S.A. 21-3755 defines "access," the plain and ordinary meaning should apply rather than a tortured translation of the definition that is provided.

Webster's defines "access" as "freedom or ability to obtain or make use of." Webster's New Collegiate Dictionary, p. 7 (1977). This is similar to the construction used by the trial court to find that no evidence showed that Allen had gained access to Southwestern Bell's computers. Until Allen proceeded beyond the initial banner and entered appropriate passwords, he could not be said to have had the ability to make use of Southwestern Bell's computers or obtain anything. Therefore, he cannot be said to have gained access to Southwestern Bell's computer systems as gaining access is commonly understood.

State v. Joseph N. Riley

846 P.2d 1365 (Wash. 1993)

Guy, Justice.

Northwest Telco Corporation is a company that provides long distance telephone service. Telco's customers dial a publicly available general access number, then enter an individualized 6-digit access code and the long distance number they wish to call. A computer at Telco's central location then places the call and charges it to the account corresponding to the entered 6-digit code.

On January 9, 1990, Cal Edwards, Director of Engineering at Telco, observed that Telco's general access number was being dialed at regular intervals of approximately 40 seconds. After each dialing, a different 6-digit number was entered, followed by a certain long distance number. Edwards observed similar activity on January 10, between 10 p.m. and 6 a.m. From his past experience, Edwards recognized this activity as characteristic of that of a "computer hacker" attempting to obtain the individualized 6-digit access codes of Telco's customers. Edwards surmised that the hacker was using a computer and modem to dial Telco's general access number, a randomly selected 6-digit number, and a long distance number. Then, by recording which 6-digit numbers enabled the long distance call to be put through successfully, the hacker was able to obtain the valid individual access codes of Telco's customers. The hacker could then use those codes fraudulently to make long distance calls that would be charged improperly to Telco's paying customers.

On January 11, Edwards contacted Toni Ames, a U.S. West security investigator, and requested her assistance in exposing the hacker. In response, Ames established a line trap, which is a device that traces telephone calls to their source. By 3 p.m., Ames had traced the repeated dialing to the home of Joseph Riley in Silverdale, Washington. The dialing continued until 6 a.m. on January 12.

Riley contends that his convictions of computer trespass against Telco must be reversed because his conduct — repeatedly dialing Telco's general access number and entering random 6-digit numbers in an attempt to discover access codes belonging to others — does not satisfy the statutory definition of computer trespass. We disagree.

RCW 9A.52.110 provides in relevant part that

> [a] person is guilty of computer trespass in the first degree if the person, without authorization, intentionally gains access to a computer system or electronic data base of another. . . .

Riley contends he is not guilty of computer trespass because he did not enter, read, insert, or copy data from the telephone system's computer switch.

RCW 9A.52.110 criminalizes the unauthorized, intentional "access" of a computer system. The term "access" is defined under RCW 9A.52.010(6) as "to approach . . . or otherwise make use of any resources of a computer, directly or by electronic means." Riley's repeated attempts to discover access codes by sequentially entering random 6-digit numbers constitute "approach[ing]" or "otherwise mak[ing] use of any resources of a computer." The switch is a computer. Long distance calls are processed through the switch. Riley was approaching the switch each time he entered the general access number, followed by a random 6-digit number representing a customer access code, and a destination number. Therefore, Riley's conduct satisfied the statutory definition of "access" and so was properly treated as computer trespass.[n.5]4

3. Without or in Excess of Authorization

- 18 U.S.C. § 1030(e)(6) defines exceeds authorized access:

[T]he term "exceeds authorized access" means to access a computer with authorization and to use such access to obtain or alter information in the computer that the accesser is not entitled so to obtain or alter[.]

- The purpose of the distinction:

The legislative history of the CFAA reflects an expectation by Congress that persons who exceed authorized access are likely to be insiders, whereas persons who act without authorization are likely to be outsiders. As a result, Congress restricted the circumstances under which an insider—a user with authorized access—could be held liable for violating section 1030. "[I]nsiders, who are authorized to access a computer, face criminal liability only if they intend to cause damage to the computer, not for recklessly or negligently causing damage. By contrast, outside intruders who break into a computer could be punished for any intentional, reckless, or other damage they cause by their trespass."

According to this view, outsiders are intruders with no rights to use a protected computer system, and, therefore, they should be subject to a wider range of criminal prohibitions. Those who act without authorization can be convicted under any of the access offenses contained in the CFAA. However, users who exceed authorized access have at least some authority to access the computer system. Such users are therefore subject to criminal liability under more narrow circumstances.

In sum, "without authorization" generally refers to intrusions by outsiders, but some courts have also applied the term to intrusions by insiders who access computers other than the computer they are authorized to use, intrusions by insiders acting as agents for outsiders, and intrusions by insiders who violate clearly defined access policies. Section 1030 imposes greater liability on outsiders because their very presence on the computer or network constitutes trespass. Thus, certain subsections criminalize actions based upon access without authorization, but do not impose the same liability if the access merely exceeds authorization.[5]

- views on how to make the distinction:

---

4. [n.5] This interpretation of the statute does not criminalize repeated dialing of a busy telephone number because a computer trespass conviction requires an "intent to commit another crime." It is not disputed that Riley had such an intent.

5. COMPUTER CRIME AND INTELLECTUAL PROPERTY SECTION, CRIMINAL DIVISION, U.S. DEP'T OF JUSTICE, PROSECUTING COMPUTER CRIMES 4–5, 10 (2007).

"Authorized" is a nebulous concept. The lack of authorization is most easily ascertained in the context of an outsider hacking into a system by breaking a code-based restriction on access. But lack of authorization has been found in less obvious cases as the following different views illustrate. The court in *United States v. Nosal*, 676 F.3d 854 (9th Cir. 2012) (en banc) (*Nosal I*), outlined what it viewed as the stakes to computer users and to those visiting websites as to how broadly the statute should be interpreted:

> Does an employee who violates such a policy commit a federal crime? How about someone who violates the terms of service of a social networking website? This depends on how broadly we read the Computer Fraud and Abuse Act (CFAA).
>
> Minds have wandered since the beginning of time and the computer gives employees new ways to procrastinate, by g-chatting with friends, playing games, shopping or watching sports highlights. Such activities are routinely prohibited by many computer-use policies, although employees are seldom disciplined for occasional use of work computers for personal purposes. Nevertheless, under the broad interpretation of the CFAA, such minor dalliances would become federal crimes. While it's unlikely that you'll be prosecuted for watching Reason.TV on your work computer, you *could* be. Employers wanting to rid themselves of troublesome employees without following proper procedures could threaten to report them to the FBI unless they quit. Ubiquitous, seldom-prosecuted crimes invite arbitrary and discriminatory enforcement.
>
> Consider the typical corporate policy that computers can be used only for business purposes. What exactly is a "nonbusiness purpose"? If you use the computer to check the weather report for a business trip? For the company softball game? For your vacation to Hawaii? And if minor personal uses are tolerated, how can an employee be on notice of what constitutes a violation sufficient to trigger criminal liability?
>
> Basing criminal liability on violations of private computer use polices can transform whole categories of otherwise innocuous behavior into federal crimes simply because a computer is involved. Employees who call family members from their work phones will become criminals if they send an email instead. Employees can sneak in the sports section of the *New York Times* to read at work, but they'd better not visit ESPN.com. And sudoku enthusiasts should stick to the printed puzzles, because visiting www .dailysudoku.com from their work computers might give them more than enough time to hone their sudoku skills behind bars.
>
> The effect this broad construction of the CFAA has on workplace conduct pales by comparison with its effect on everyone else who uses a computer, smart-phone, iPad, Kindle, Nook, X-box, Blu-Ray player or any other Internet-enabled device. The Internet is a means for communicating via

computers: Whenever we access a web page, commence a download, post a message on somebody's Facebook wall, shop on Amazon, bid on eBay, publish a blog, rate a movie on IMDb, read www.NYT.com, watch YouTube and do the thousands of other things we routinely do online, we are using one computer to send commands to other computers at remote locations. Our access to those remote computers is governed by a series of private agreements and policies that most people are only dimly aware of and virtually no one reads or understands.

For example, up until very recently, Google forbade minors from using its services. Adopting the government's interpretation would turn vast numbers of teens and pre-teens into juvenile delinquents—and their parents and teachers into delinquency contributors. Similarly, Facebook makes it a violation of the terms of service to let anyone log into your account. Yet it's very common for people to let close friends and relatives check their email or access their online accounts. Some may be aware that, if discovered, they may suffer a rebuke from the ISP or a loss of access, but few imagine they might be marched off to federal prison for doing so.

Or consider the numerous dating websites whose terms of use prohibit inaccurate or misleading information. Or eBay and Craigslist, where it's a violation of the terms of use to post items in an inappropriate category. Under the government's proposed interpretation of the CFAA, posting for sale an item prohibited by Craigslist's policy, or describing yourself as "tall, dark and handsome," when you're actually short and homely, will earn you a handsome orange jumpsuit.

Not only are the terms of service vague and generally unknown—unless you look real hard at the small print at the bottom of a webpage—but website owners retain the right to change the terms at any time and without notice.

———————

a. Distinguishing between unauthorized access and exceeding authorized access

Bell Aerospace Services, Inc. v. U.S. Aero Services, Inc.

690 F. Supp. 2d 1267 (M.D. Ala. 2010)

Myron H. Thompson, District Judge.

Bell Aerospace Services, Inc. filed this lawsuit claiming that defendants U.S. Aero Services, Inc., two U.S. Aero officers, and seven other U.S. Aero employees violated federal law by acquiring Bell Aerospace's confidential and proprietary information and trade secrets without authorization. Bell Aerospace charges the defendants with violating the Computer Fraud and Abuse Act.

Bell Aerospace is in the business of providing helicopter maintenance support to both government and non-government agencies in Ozark, Alabama. In June 2008, Vice President of Operations Hartwell Wilson, along with the President and the General Manager, was fired.

In late August 2008, Steve Matherly (who had sold helicopters and parts to Bell Aerospace) and Wilson founded U.S. Aero, with Matherly as President and Wilson as General Manager. U.S. Aero performs work similar to that done by Bell Aerospace. U.S. Aero's employees include, in addition to Wilson, seven former employees of Bell Aerospace: Joe Thomas, Mike Hall, Sean Taylor, Ron Donahue, Timberly Moore, Mark Robison, and Rilda Blaha. While at Bell Aerospace, they each had been permitted to use the company's computers and each had had an individualized login user-name and password to access the company's servers and computer network. The events surrounding the departure of these seven employees are at the heart of this litigation.

In early September 2008, Wilson contacted four Bell Aerospace employees (Thomas, Hall, Taylor, and Donahue) about joining U.S. Aero as its first employees. Donahue, in turn, informed two more Bell Aerospace employees (Moore and Robison) about the new company, and they each spoke with Wilson about the new opportunity. Soon after, Wilson and Matherly met with these six employees, made them offers of employment from U.S. Aero, asking them to begin work on September 24. On September 18, Robison and Moore resigned from Bell Aerospace, and Thomas, Hall, Taylor, and Donahue resigned the next day. On September 19, the seventh Bell Aerospace employee, Blaha, learned about the new company and was offered a position after speaking to Wilson; she immediately resigned from Bell Aerospace. Wilson and these other employees were not subject to any non-compete agreements with Bell Aerospace.

Faced with the surprise resignation of seven employees, Bell Aerospace chose to escort all those who quit from the Ozark facility, permanently ending their employment with the company. Other Bell Aerospace employees then reported that hard copies of the company's production materials, including a package of drawings, were missing. As a result of these reports, the company hired computer-forensics experts to investigate what, if anything, was taken or copied by the seven former employees. Wilson and the seven other employees had previously signed confidentiality agreements with Bell Aerospace promising "not [to] remove any Company records of any kind . . . or otherwise use or disclose Company Proprietary information, [except] . . . as required in the performance of [his/her] Company job function." In addition, Wilson told some of the other former employees that "they were not to acquire, provide, bring any data, regardless of what it was, when they left employment at Bell Aerospace."

Bell Aerospace claims that the defendants violated the CFAA by accessing its computers "without authorization" or in "excess" of their authority and, "as a result of such conduct, cause[d] damage and loss." 18 U.S.C. § 1030(a)(5).

Without Authorization: "[A]n employer gives an employee 'authorization' to access a company computer when the employer gives the employee permission to use it." *LVRC Holdings LLC v. Brekka*, 581 F.3d 1127, 1133 (9th Cir. 2009). The seven former Bell Aerospace accused of accessing the company computers without authorization were each employed at the company while accessing its computers and each had permission to do so; therefore, each had "authorization" to access the computers and the materials found on its server.

Bell Aerospace argues that, whenever an employee breaches her fiduciary duty of loyalty to an employer in accessing documents on the employer's protected computer, that employee acts "without authorization." The company reasons that an employee's "authorization to access the [protected computer] terminate[s] when, having already engaged in misconduct and decided to quit . . . , he . . . violat[es] [] the duty of loyalty that agency law imposes on an employee."

First, this reasoning ignores the plain language of the statute. The CFAA differentiates between "without authority" and "exceeds authorized access." A person who accesses a protected computer "without authority" does so with no permission at all, like hackers, whom this statute was originally written to ward against; whereas, a person who "[e]xceeds authorized access" is one who "accesses a computer with authorization and . . . use[es] such access to obtain or alter information in the computer that the accesser is not entitled so to obtain or alter." 18 U.S.C. § 1030(e)(6). Therefore, as the Ninth Circuit Court of Appeals has aptly observed in *Brekka*, a person who "exceeds authorized access, . . . accesses information on the computer that the person is not entitled to access." Bell Aerospace's reasoning would improperly remove all distinction between "without authorization" and "exceeds authorization."

Second, this reading of the CFAA is buoyed by the nature of the statute itself. The CFAA is primarily a criminal statute, and when a statute has "both criminal and noncriminal applications," courts must "interpret the statute consistently." It is imperative when dealing with a criminal statute that "defendants are on notice as to which acts are criminal." Thus, "ambiguity concerning the ambit of criminal statutes should be resolved in favor of lenity," which "requires courts to limit the reach of criminal statutes to the clear import of their text and construe any ambiguity against the government." While the plain language of the CFAA dictates reading "without authorization" to mean "without permission or access," a finding of ambiguity would necessarily lead to the same result.

Because the seven employees who resigned had valid permission to utilize the Bell Aerospace computers, they were acting with authorization when they accessed the computers up until the time they each were escorted from the facility.

Exceeds Authorization: "Exceeds authorized access" should not be confused with exceeds authorized use. Therefore, at issue here is only whether the former Bell Aerospace employees exceeded their authorized access, not whether they exceeded their authorized use.

There is no evidence in the record to suggest that these employees "exceed[ed]" authorized access." [I]ndeed, the employees were "permitted access to [Bell Aero's] network and any information on that network" under their individual user accounts. Because it appears that the CFAA is concerned with access, not use, whether these employees did not have permission to copy or subsequently misuse the accessed data by sharing them is another matter that may be circumscribed by a different statute and is not at issue here.

Because the seven employees who resigned had valid permission to utilize the Bell Aerospace computers while employed at the company and because there is no evidence that they exceeded that authorization, Bell Aerospace's CFAA claim, to the extent it is based on a theory of "exceeds authorization," must fail.

––––––––––

United States v. David Nosal (*Nosall II*)

844 F.3d 1024 (9th Cir. 2016)

McKEOWN, Circuit Judge:

This is the second time we consider the scope of the Computer Fraud and Abuse Act, 18 U.S.C. § 1030, with respect to David Nosal. The CFAA imposes criminal penalties on whoever "knowingly and with intent to defraud, *accesses a protected computer without authorization, or exceeds authorized access*, and by means of such conduct furthers the intended fraud and obtains anything of value." *Id.* § 1030(a)(4).

Only the first prong of the section is before us in this appeal: "knowingly and with intent to defraud" accessing a computer "without authorization." Embracing our earlier precedent and joining our sister circuits, we conclude that "without authorization" is an unambiguous, non-technical term that, given its plain and ordinary meaning, means accessing a protected computer without permission. Further, we have held that authorization is not pegged to website terms and conditions. This definition has a simple corollary: once authorization to access a computer has been affirmatively revoked, the user cannot sidestep the statute by going through the back door and accessing the computer through a third party. Unequivocal revocation of computer access closes both the front door and the back door. This provision, coupled with the requirement that access be "knowingly and with intent to defraud," means that the statute will not sweep in innocent conduct, such as family password sharing.

Nosal worked at the executive search firm Korn/Ferry International when he decided to launch a competitor along with a group of co-workers. Before leaving Korn/Ferry, Nosal's colleagues began downloading confidential information from a Korn/Ferry database to use at their new enterprise. Although they were authorized to access the database as current Korn/Ferry employees, their downloads on behalf of Nosal violated Korn/Ferry's confidentiality and computer use policies. In 2012, we addressed whether those employees "exceed[ed] authorized access" with intent to defraud under the CFAA. *United States v. Nosal (Nosal I)*, 676 F.3d 854 (9th Cir.

2012) (en banc). Distinguishing between access restrictions and use restrictions, we concluded that the "exceeds authorized access" prong of § 1030(a)(4) of the CFAA "does not extend to violations of [a company's] use restrictions." We affirmed the district court's dismissal of the five CFAA counts related to Nosal's aiding and abetting misuse of data accessed by his co-workers with their own passwords.

The remaining counts relate to statutory provisions that were not at issue in *Nosal I*: access to a protected computer "without authorization" under the CFAA. When Nosal left Korn/Ferry, the company revoked his computer access credentials, even though he remained for a time as a contractor. The company took the same precaution upon the departure of his accomplices, Becky Christian and Mark Jacobson. Nonetheless, they continued to access the database using the credentials of Nosal's former executive assistant, Jacqueline Froehlich–L'Heureaux ("FH"), who remained at Korn/Ferry at Nosal's request. The question we consider is whether the jury properly convicted Nosal of conspiracy to violate the "without authorization" provision of the CFAA for unauthorized access to, and downloads from, his former employer's database called Searcher. Put simply, we are asked to decide whether the "without authorization" prohibition of the CFAA extends to a former employee whose computer access credentials have been rescinded but who, disregarding the revocation, accesses the computer by other means.

We directly answered this question in *LVRC Holdings LLC v. Brekka*, 581 F.3d 1127 (9th Cir. 2009), and reiterate our holding here: "[A] person uses a computer 'without authorization' under [the CFAA] ... when the employer has rescinded permission to access the computer and the defendant uses the computer anyway." This straightforward principle embodies the common sense, ordinary meaning of the "without authorization" prohibition.

Nosal and various amici spin hypotheticals about the dire consequences of criminalizing password sharing. But these warnings miss the mark in this case. This appeal is not about password sharing. Nor is it about violating a company's internal computer-use policies. The conduct at issue is that of Nosal and his co-conspirators, which is covered by the plain language of the statute. Nosal is charged with conspiring with former Korn/Ferry employees whose user accounts had been terminated, but who nonetheless accessed trade secrets in a proprietary database through the back door when the front door had been firmly closed. Nosal knowingly and with intent to defraud Korn/Ferry blatantly circumvented the affirmative revocation of his computer system access. This access falls squarely within the CFAA's prohibition on "knowingly and with intent to defraud" accessing a computer "without authorization," and thus we affirm Nosal's conviction for violations of § 1030(a)(4) of the CFAA.

The dissent mistakenly focuses on FH's authority, sidestepping the authorization question for Christian and Jacobson. To begin, FH had no authority from Korn/Ferry to provide her password to former employees whose computer access had been revoked. Also, in collapsing the distinction between FH's authorization and that of Christian and Jacobson, the dissent would render meaningless the concept of authorization. And, pertinent here, it would remove from the scope of the CFAA any hacking conspiracy with an inside person. That surely was not Congress's intent.

Background

I. Factual Background

Nosal was a high-level regional director at the global executive search firm Korn/ Ferry International. Korn/Ferry's bread and butter was identifying and recommending potential candidates for corporate positions. In 2004, after being passed over for a promotion, Nosal announced his intention to leave Korn/Ferry. Negotiations ensued and Nosal agreed to stay on for an additional year as a contractor to finish a handful of open searches, subject to a blanket non-competition agreement. As he put it, Korn/Ferry was giving him "a lot of money" to "stay out of the market."

During this interim period, Nosal was very busy, secretly launching his own search firm along with other Korn/Ferry employees, including Christian, Jacobson and FH. As of December 8, 2004, Korn/Ferry revoked Nosal's access to its computers, although it permitted him to ask Korn/Ferry employees for research help on his remaining open assignments. In January 2005, Christian left Korn/Ferry and, under instructions from Nosal, set up an executive search firm—Christian & Associates—from which Nosal retained 80% of fees. Jacobson followed her a few months later. As Nosal, Christian and Jacobson began work for clients, Nosal used the name "David Nelson" to mask his identity when interviewing candidates.

The start-up company was missing Korn/Ferry's core asset: "Searcher," an internal database of information on over one million executives, including contact information, employment history, salaries, biographies and resumes, all compiled since 1995. Searcher was central to Korn/Ferry's work for clients. When launching a new search to fill an open executive position, Korn/Ferry teams started by compiling a "source list" of potential candidates. In constructing the list, the employees would run queries in Searcher to generate a list of candidates. To speed up the process, employees could look at old source lists in Searcher to see how a search for a similar position was constructed, or to identify suitable candidates. The resulting source list could include hundreds of names, but then was narrowed to a short list of candidates presented to the client. Korn/Ferry considered these source lists proprietary.

Searcher included data from a number of public and quasi-public sources like LinkedIn, corporate filings and Internet searches, and also included internal, nonpublic sources, such as personal connections, unsolicited resumes sent to Korn/ Ferry and data inputted directly by candidates via Korn/Ferry's website. The data was coded upon entry; as a result, employees could run targeted searches for candidates by criteria such as age, industry, experience or other data points. However, once the information became part of the Searcher system, it was integrated with other data and there was no way to identify the source of the data.

Searcher was hosted on the company's internal computer network and was considered confidential and for use only in Korn/Ferry business. Korn/Ferry issued each employee a unique username and password to its computer system; no separate password was required to access Searcher. Password sharing was prohibited by a confidentiality agreement that Korn/Ferry required each new employee to sign. When a user requested a custom report in Searcher, Searcher displayed a message which stated: "This product is intended to be used by Korn/Ferry employees for work on Korn/Ferry business only."

Nosal and his compatriots downloaded information and source lists from Searcher in preparation to launch the new competitor. Before leaving Korn/Ferry, they used their own usernames and passwords, compiling proprietary Korn/Ferry data in violation of Korn/Ferry's computer use policy. Those efforts were encompassed in the CFAA accounts appealed in *Nosal I*.

After Nosal became a contractor and Christian and Jacobson left Korn/Ferry, Korn/Ferry revoked each of their credentials to access Korn/Ferry's computer system. Not to be deterred, on three occasions Christian and Jacobson borrowed access credentials from FH, who stayed on at Korn/Ferry at Nosal's request. In April 2005, Nosal instructed Christian to obtain some source lists from Searcher to expedite their work for a new client. Thinking it would be difficult to explain the request to FH, Christian asked to borrow FH's access credentials, which Christian then used to log in to Korn/Ferry's computer system and run queries in Searcher. Christian sent the results of her searches to Nosal. In July 2005, Christian again logged in as FH to generate a custom report and search for information on three individuals. Later in July, Jacobson also logged in as FH, to download information on 2,400 executives. None of these searches related to any open searches that fell under Nosal's independent contractor agreement.

II. Procedural Background

The government filed a second superseding indictment in February 2013 with three CFAA counts, two trade secrets counts and one conspiracy count. Nosal's remaining CFAA counts were based on the three occasions when Christian and Jacobson accessed Korn/Ferry's system for their new clients using FH's login credentials. The district court denied Nosal's motion to dismiss the three remaining CFAA counts. A jury convicted Nosal on all counts. The district court sentenced Nosal to one year and one day in prison, three years of supervised release, a $60,000 fine, a $600 special assessment and approximately $828,000 in restitution to Korn/Ferry.

Analysis

I. Convictions Under the Computer Fraud and Abuse Act

The key section of the CFAA at issue is 18 U.S.C. § 1030(a)(4), which provides in relevant part:

> Whoever . . . knowingly and with intent to defraud, accesses a protected computer without authorization, or exceeds authorized access, and by means of such conduct furthers the intended fraud and obtains anything of value . . . shall be punished. . . .

A key element of the statute is the requirement that the access be "knowingly and with intent to defraud." Not surprisingly, this phrase is not defined in the CFAA as it is the bread and butter of many criminal statutes. This mens rea element of the statute is critical because imposing the "intent to defraud" element targets knowing and specific conduct and does not embrace the parade of hypotheticals generated by Nosal and amici.

The CFAA defines "exceeds authorized access" as "access [to] a computer with authorization and [using] such access to obtain or alter information in the computer that the accesser is not entitled so to obtain or alter." *Id.* § 1030(e)(6). The statute does not, however, define "without authorization." Both terms are used throughout § 1030. In construing the statute, we are cognizant of the need for congruence among these subsections.

The interpretive fireworks under § 1030(a)(4) of the CFAA have been reserved for its second prong, the meaning of "exceeds authorized access." Not surprisingly, there has been no division among the circuits on the straightforward "without authorization" prong of this section. We begin with the two Ninth Circuit cases that bind our interpretation of "without authorization" — *Brekka* and *Nosal I* — and then move on to address the cases from our sister circuits that are in accord with *Brekka*, agreeing that "without authorization" is an unambiguous term that should be given its ordinary meaning.

Brekka involved a former employee in circumstances remarkably similar to Nosal: he wanted to compete using confidential data from his former company. Christopher Brekka worked as an internet marketer with LVRC Holdings, LLC, a residential addiction treatment center. LVRC assigned him a computer and gave him access credentials to a third-party website that tracked traffic and other information for LVRC's website. When negotiations to become part owner of LVRC broke down, Brekka left the company. LVRC sued him, claiming that he violated the CFAA by emailing certain confidential company documents to his personal email account while an employee and also by continuing to access LVRC's account on the external website after he left the company.

In *Brekka* we analyzed both the "without authorization" and "exceeds authorization" provisions of the statute under §§ 1030(a)(2) and (4). Because the CFAA does not define the term "authorization," we looked to the ordinary, contemporaneous meaning of the term: "'permission or power granted by an authority.'" (quoting Random House Unabridged Dictionary 139 (2001)). In determining whether an employee has authorization, we stated that, consistent with "the plain language of the statute . . . 'authorization' [to use an employer's computer] depends on actions taken by the employer." We concluded that because Brekka had permission to use his employer's computer, "[t]he most straightforward interpretation of §§ 1030(a)(2) and (4) is that Brekka had authorization to use the computer" while an employee.

Brekka's access after LVRC terminated his employment presented a starkly different situation: "There is no dispute that if Brekka accessed LVRC's information on the [traffic monitoring] website after he left the company . . . , Brekka would have accessed a protected computer 'without authorization' for purposes of the CFAA." Stated differently, we held that "a person uses a computer 'without authorization' under §§ 1030(a)(2) and (4) . . . when the employer has rescinded permission to access the computer and the defendant uses the computer anyway." In Brekka's case, there was no genuine issue of material fact as to whether Brekka actually accessed the website, and thus we affirmed the district court's grant of summary judgment.

Not surprisingly, in *Nosal I* as in this appeal, both the government and Nosal cited *Brekka* extensively. The focus of Nosal's first appeal was whether the CFAA could be interpreted "broadly to cover violations of corporate computer use restrictions or violations of a duty of loyalty." We unequivocally said "no": "For our part, we continue to follow in the path blazed by *Brekka* and the growing number of courts that have reached the same conclusion. These courts recognize that the plain language of the CFAA 'target[s] the unauthorized procurement or alteration of information, not its misuse or misappropriation.'" In line with *Brekka*, we stated that "'[w]ithout authorization' would apply to *outside* hackers (individuals who have no authorized access to the computer at all) and 'exceeds authorization access' would apply to *inside* hackers (individuals whose initial access to a computer is authorized but who access unauthorized information or files)." Because Nosal's accomplices had authority to access the company computers, we affirmed the district court's dismissal of the CFAA counts related to the period when the accomplices were still employed at Korn/Ferry.

In *Nosal I*, authorization was not in doubt. The employees who accessed the Korn/Ferry computers unquestionably had authorization from the company to access the system; the question was whether they exceeded it. What *Nosal I* did not address was whether Nosal's access to Korn/Ferry computers *after* both Nosal and his co-conspirators had terminated their employment and Korn/Ferry revoked their permission to access the computers was "without authorization." *Brekka* is squarely on point on that issue: Nosal and his co-conspirators acted "without authorization" when they continued to access Searcher by other means after Korn/Ferry rescinded permission to access its computer system. As *Nosal I* made clear, the CFAA was not intended to cover unauthorized use of information. Such *use* is not at issue here. Rather, under § 1030(a)(4), Nosal is charged with unauthorized access—getting into the computer after categorically being barred from entry.

The text of the CFAA confirms *Brekka*'s approach. Employing classic statutory interpretation, we consider the plain and ordinary meaning of the words "without authorization." Under our analysis in *Brekka*, "authorization" means "'permission or power granted by an authority.'" (quoting Random House Unabridged Dictionary 139 (2001)). Other sources employ similar definitions. Black's Law Dictionary defines "authorization" as "[o]fficial permission to do something; sanction or warrant." The Oxford English Dictionary defines it as "the action of authorizing," which means to "give official permission for or approval to." That common sense meaning is not foreign to Congress or the courts: the terms "authorize," "authorized" or "authorization" are used without definition over 400 times in Title 18 of the United States Code. We conclude that given its ordinary meaning, access "without authorization" under the CFAA is not ambiguous.

That straightforward meaning is also unambiguous as applied to the facts of this case.[n.6][6] Nosal and his co-conspirators did exactly what *Brekka* prohibits—a conclusion that is not affected by the co-conspirators' use of FH's legitimate access credentials. Implicit in the definition of authorization is the notion that someone, including an entity, can grant or revoke that permission. Here, that entity was Korn/Ferry, and FH had no mantle or authority to override Korn/Ferry's authority to control access to its computers and confidential information by giving permission to former employees whose access had been categorically revoked by the company. Korn/Ferry owned and controlled access to its computers, including the Searcher database, and it retained exclusive discretion to issue or revoke access to the database. By revoking Nosal's login credentials on December 8, 2004, Korn/Ferry unequivocally conveyed to Nosal that he was an "outsider" who was no longer authorized to access Korn/Ferry computers and confidential information, including Searcher. Korn/Ferry also rescinded Christian and Jacobson's credentials after they left, at which point the three former employees were no longer "insiders" accessing company information. Rather, they had become "outsiders" with no authorization to access Korn/Ferry's computer system. One can certainly pose hypotheticals in which a less stark revocation is followed by more sympathetic access through an authorized third party. But the facts before us—in which Nosal received particularized notice of his revoked access following a prolonged negotiation—present no such difficulties, which can be reserved for another day.

Our analysis is consistent with that of our sister circuits, which have also determined that the term "without authorization" is unambiguous. Although the meaning of "exceeds authorized access" in the CFAA has been subject to much debate among the federal courts, the definition of "without authorization" has not engendered dispute. Indeed, Nosal provides no contrary authority that a former employee whose computer access has been revoked can access his former employer's computer system and be deemed to act with authorization.

Beginning in 1991, the Second Circuit recognized that "authorization" is a word "of common usage, without any technical or ambiguous meaning." *United States v. Morris*, 928 F.2d 504, 511 (2d Cir. 1991). The court reaffirmed this holding in 2015, citing *Brekka* and stating that "common usage of 'authorization' suggests that one

---

6. [n.6] We do not invoke the rule of lenity because "the touchstone of the rule of lenity is statutory ambiguity," and "[t]he rule comes into operation at the end of the process of construing what Congress has expressed, not at the beginning as an overriding consideration of being lenient to wrongdoers." Here, because the statute "unambiguously cover[s] the defendant's conduct, the rule does not come into play." That the CFAA might support a narrower interpretation, as the dissent argues, does not change our analysis.

'accesses a computer without authorization' if he accesses a computer without permission to do so at all." *United States v. Valle*, 807 F.3d 508, 524 (2d Cir. 2015).

The Fourth Circuit's analysis mirrors the conclusion that the "without authorization" language is unambiguous based on its ordinary meaning:

> Recognizing that the distinction between ["exceeds authorized access" and access "without authorization"] is arguably minute, we nevertheless conclude based on the ordinary, contemporary, common meaning of "authorization," that an employee is authorized to access a computer when his employer approves or sanctions his admission to that computer. Thus, he accesses a computer "without authorization" when he gains admission to a computer without approval. Similarly, we conclude that an employee "exceeds authorized access" when he has approval to access a computer, but uses his access to obtain or alter information that falls outside the bounds of his approved access.

WEC Carolina Energy Solutions LLC v. Miller, 687 F.3d 199, 204 (4th Cir. 2012).

Like the other courts, the Sixth Circuit noted that "[t]he plain meaning of 'authorization' is '[t]he conferment of legality; . . . sanction.' Commonly understood, then, a defendant who accesses a computer 'without authorization' does so without sanction or permission." *Pulte Homes, Inc. v. Laborers' Int'l Union of N. Am.*, 648 F.3d 295, 303–04 (6th Cir. 2011) (quoting 1 Oxford English Dictionary 798 (2d ed. 1989)). Based on ordinary usage, the Sixth Circuit similarly reasoned that "'a person who uses a computer 'without authorization' *has no rights, limited or otherwise*, to access the computer in question.'"

In the face of multiple circuits that agree with our plain meaning construction of the statute, the dissent would have us ignore common sense and turn the statute inside out. Indeed, the dissent frames the question upside down in assuming that permission from FH is at issue. Under this approach, ignoring reality and practice, an employee could undermine the company's ability to control access to its own computers by willy nilly giving out passwords to anyone outside the company—former employees whose access had been revoked, competitors, industrious hackers or bank robbers who find it less risky and more convenient to access accounts via the Internet rather than through armed robbery.

Our conclusion does nothing to expand the scope of violations under the CFAA beyond *Brekka*; nor does it rest on the grace of prosecutorial discretion. We are mindful of the examples noted in *Nosal I* that ill-defined terms may capture arguably innocuous conduct, such as password sharing among friends and family, inadvertently "mak[ing] criminals of large groups of people who would have little reason to suspect they are committing a federal crime." But these concerns are ill-founded because § 1030(a)(4) requires access be "knowingly and with intent to defraud" and further, we have held that violating use restrictions, like a website's terms of use, is insufficient without more to form the basis for liability under the CFAA. The circumstance here—former employees whose computer access was categorically revoked and who surreptitiously accessed data owned by their former employer—bears little resemblance to asking a spouse to log in to an email account to print a boarding pass. The charges at issue in this appeal do not stem from the ambiguous language of *Nosal I*—"exceeds authorized access"—or even an ambiguous application of the phrase "without authorization," but instead relate to the straightforward application of a common, unambiguous term to the facts and context at issue.

We therefore hold that Nosal, a former employee whose computer access credentials were affirmatively revoked by Korn/Ferry acted "without authorization" in violation of the CFAA when he or his former employee co-conspirators used the login credentials of a current employee to gain access to confidential computer data owned by the former employer and to circumvent Korn/Ferry's revocation of access.

C. Jury Instruction on "Without Authorization"

With respect to the meaning of "without authorization," the district court instructed the jury as follows:

> Whether a person is authorized to access the computers in this case depends on the actions taken by Korn/Ferry to grant or deny permission to that person to use the computer. A person uses a computer "without authorization" when the person has not received permission from Korn/Ferry to use the computer for any purpose (such as when a hacker accesses the computer without any permission), or when Korn/Ferry has rescinded permission to use the computer and the person uses the computer anyway.

The instruction is derived directly from our decision in *Brekka* and is a fair and accurate characterization of the plain meaning of "without authorization." Although the term "without authorization" is unambiguous, it does not mean that the facts don't matter; the source and scope of authorization may well be at issue. Here, it was not disputed that Korn/Ferry was the source of permission to grant authorization. The jury instruction left to the jury to determine whether such permission was given.

Nosal challenges the instruction on the basis that the CFAA only criminalizes access where the party circumvents a technological access barrier. Not only is such a requirement missing from the statutory language, but it would make little sense because some § 1030 offenses do not require access to a computer at all. For example, § (a)(6) imposes penalties for trafficking in passwords "through which a computer can be accessed without authorization. . . ."

In any event, Nosal's argument misses the mark on the technological access point. Even if he were correct, any instructional error was without consequence in light of the evidence. The password system adopted by Korn/Ferry is unquestionably a technological barrier designed to keep out those "without authorization." Had a thief stolen an employee's password and then used it to rifle through Searcher, without doubt, access would have been without authorization.

The same principle holds true here. A password requirement is designed to be a technological access barrier.

AFFIRMED, EXCEPT VACATED IN PART AND REMANDED WITH RESPECT TO THE RESTITUTION AWARD.

Reinhardt, Circuit Judge, dissenting:

This case is about password sharing. People frequently share their passwords, notwithstanding the fact that websites and employers have policies prohibiting it. In my view, the Computer Fraud and Abuse Act does not make the millions of people who engage in this ubiquitous, useful, and generally harmless conduct into unwitting federal criminals. Whatever other liability, criminal or civil, Nosal may have incurred in his improper attempt to compete with his former employer, he has not violated the CFAA.

At issue are three incidents of password sharing. On these occasions while FH was still employed at Korn/Ferry, she gave her password to Jacobson or Christian, who had left the company. Her former colleagues then used her password to download information from Searcher. FH was authorized to access Searcher, but she did not download the information herself because it was easier to let Jacobson or Christian do it than to have them explain to her how to find it. It would not have been a violation of the CFAA if they had simply given FH step-by-step directions, which she then followed. Thus the question is whether because Jacobson and Christian instead used FH's password with her permission, they are criminally liable for access "without authorization" under the Act.

The majority finds the answer is "yes," but in doing so commits the same error as the circuits whose views we rejected in *Nosal I*. My colleagues claim that they do not have to address the effect of their decision on the wider population because Nosal's infelicitous conduct "bears little resemblance" to everyday password sharing. Notably this is the exact argument the *dissent* made in *Nosal I*: "This case has nothing to do with playing sudoku, checking email, [or] fibbing on dating sites. . . . The role of the courts is neither to issue advisory opinions nor to declare rights in hypothetical cases." 676 F.3d at 864, 866 (Silverman, J., dissenting) (internal quotation and citation omitted).

We, of course, rejected the dissent's argument in *Nosal I*. We did so because we recognized that the government's theory made all violations of use restrictions criminal under the CFAA, whether the violation was innocuous, like checking your personal email at work, or more objectionable like that at issue here. Because the statute was susceptible to a narrower interpretation, we rejected the government's broader reading under which "millions of unsuspecting individuals would find that they are engaging in criminal conduct." The same is true here. The majority does not provide, nor do I see, a workable line which separates the consensual password sharing in this case from the consensual password sharing of millions of legitimate account holders, which may also be contrary to the policies of system owners. There simply is no limiting principle in the majority's world of lawful and unlawful password sharing.

I.

Subsection (a)(2)(C) criminalizes nearly all intentional access of a "protected computer" without authorization. A "'protected computer' is defined as a computer affected by or involved in interstate commerce—effectively all computers with Internet access." This means that nearly all desktops, laptops, servers, smartphones, as well as any "iPad, Kindle, Nook, X-box, Blu-Ray player or any other Internet-enabled device," including even some thermostats qualify as "protected." Thus § 1030(a)(2)(C) covers untold millions of Americans' interactions with these objects every day. Crucially, violating (a)(2)(C) does not require "any culpable intent." Therefore if we interpret "without authorization" in a way that includes common practices like password sharing, millions of our citizens would become potential federal criminals overnight.

II.

The majority is wrong to conclude that a person necessarily accesses a computer account "without authorization" if he does so without the permission of the system owner. Take the case of an office worker asking a friend to log onto his email in order to print a boarding pass, in violation of the system owner's access policy; or the case of one spouse asking the other to log into a bank website to pay a bill, in violation of the bank's password sharing prohibition. There are other examples that readily come to mind, such as logging onto a computer on behalf of a colleague who is out of the office, in violation of a corporate computer access policy, to send him a document he needs right away. "Facebook makes it a violation of the terms of service to let anyone log into your account," we noted in *Nosal I*, but "it's very common for people to let close friends and relatives check their email or access their online accounts."

Was access in these examples authorized? Most people would say "yes." Although the system owners' policies prohibit password sharing, a legitimate account holder "authorized" the access. Thus, the best reading of "without authorization" in the CFAA is a narrow one: a person accesses an account "without authorization" if he does so without having the permission of *either* the system owner *or* a legitimate account holder.

This narrower reading is more consistent with the purpose of the CFAA. The CFAA is essentially an anti-hacking statute, and Congress intended it as such. Under the preferable construction, the statute would cover only those whom we would colloquially think of as hackers: individuals who steal or guess passwords or otherwise force their way into computers without the consent of an authorized user, not persons who are given the right of access by those who themselves possess that right. There is no doubt that a typical hacker accesses an account "without authorization": the hacker gains access without permission—*either* from the system owner *or* a legitimate account holder. As the 1984 House Report on the CFAA explained, "it is noteworthy that Section 1030 deals with an unauthorized access concept of computer fraud rather than the mere use of a computer. Thus, the conduct prohibited is analogous to that of 'breaking and entering.'" We would not convict a man for breaking and entering if he had been invited in by a houseguest, even if the homeowner objected. Neither should we convict a man under the CFAA for accessing a computer account with a shared password with the consent of the password holder.

III.

The majority's (somewhat circular) dictionary definition of "authorization"—"permission conferred by an authority"—hardly clarifies the meaning of the text. While the majority reads the statute to criminalize access by those without "permission conferred by" the system owner, it is also proper (and in fact preferable) to read the text to criminalize access only by those without "permission conferred by" either a legitimate account holder or the system owner. The question that matters is not what authorization *is* but who is entitled to give it. As one scholar noted, "there are two parties that have plausible claims to [give] authorization: the owner/operator of the computer, and the legitimate computer account holder." Under a proper construction of the statute, either one can give authorization.

At worst, the text of the statute is ambiguous as to who may give authorization. The First Circuit concluded that the meaning of the term "without authorization" in the CFAA "has proven to be elusive," *EF Cultural Travel BV v. Explorica, Inc.*, 274 F.3d 577, 582 n.10 (1st Cir. 2001), and an unambiguous definition eludes the majority even now. In that circumstance, the rule of lenity requires us to adopt the narrower construction—exactly the construction that is appropriate in light of the CFAA's anti-hacking purpose and concern for the statute's effect on the innocent behavior of millions of citizens. The text provides no refuge for the majority.

As the Supreme Court has repeatedly held, "where there is ambiguity in a criminal statute, doubts are resolved in favor of the defendant." If a "choice has to be made between two readings of what conduct Congress has made a crime, it is appropriate, before we choose the harsher alternative, to require that Congress should have spoken in language that is clear and definite." We are therefore bound to adopt the construction of CFAA that criminalizes access only by those without permission from *either* an account holder *or* the system owner.

The "venerable" rule of lenity ensures that individuals are on notice when they act. It "vindicates the fundamental principle that no citizen should be held accountable for a violation of a statute whose commands are uncertain. . . ." We must, therefore, read the CFAA not just in the harsh light of the courtroom but also from the perspective of its potential violators. In the everyday situation that should concern us all, a friend or colleague accessing an account with a shared password would most certainly believe—and with good reason—that his access had been "authorized" by the account holder who shared his password with him. Such a person, accessing an account with the express authorization of its holder, would believe that he was acting not just lawfully but ethically. "It's very common for people to let close friends and relatives check their email or access their online accounts," we said in *Nosal I*. "Some may be aware that, if discovered, they may suffer a rebuke from the ISP or a loss of access, but few imagine they might be marched off to federal prison for doing so." The majority's construction thus conflicts with the natural interpretation its freshly minted CFAA violators would have given to "without authorization." That alone should defeat the majority's conclusion.

Worse, however, the majority's construction would base criminal liability on system owners' access policies. That is exactly what we rejected in *Nosal I*. Precisely because it is unacceptable in our legal system to impose criminal liability on actions that are not proscribed "plainly and unmistakably," it is also unacceptable to base "criminal liability on violations of private computer use policies." Not only are those policies "lengthy, opaque, subject to change and seldom read," they are also private — by definition not addressed and perhaps not even accessible to shared password recipients who are not official users themselves. Just as the rule of lenity ensures that Congress, not the judiciary, creates federal crimes, the rule also ensures that the clear (and public) words of Congress — not the obscure policies of system owners — delimit their scope.

IV.

In construing any statute, we must be wary of the risks of "selective or arbitrary enforcement." The majority's construction of the CFAA threatens exactly that. It criminalizes a broad category of common actions that nobody would expect to be federal crimes. Looking at the fallout from the majority opinion, it is clear that the decision will have "far-reaching effects unintended by Congress."

Simply put, the majority opinion contains no limiting principle. Although the majority disavows the effects of its decision aside from dealing with former employees, it may not by fiat order that the reasoning of its decision stop, like politics used to, "at the water's edge." The statute says nothing about employment. Similarly, *Nosal I* discussed use restrictions, whether imposed by an employer or a third-party website, all in the same way. It did not even hint that employment was somehow special.

It is impossible to discern from the majority opinion what principle distinguishes authorization in Nosal's case from one in which a bank has clearly told customers that no one but the customer may access the customer's account, but a husband nevertheless shares his password with his wife to allow her to pay a bill. So long as the wife knows that the bank does not give her permission to access its servers in any manner, she is in the same position as Nosal and his associates. It is not "advisory" to ask why the majority's opinion does not criminalize this under § 1030(a)(2)(C); yet, the majority suggests no answer to why it does not.

Even if the majority opinion could be limited solely to employment, the consequences would be equally untoward. Very often password sharing between a current and past employee serves the interest of the employer, even if the current employee is technically forbidden by a corporate policy from sharing his password. For example, if a current Korn/Ferry employee were looking for a source list for a pitch meeting which his former colleague had created before retirement, he might contact him to ask where the file had been saved. The former employee might say "it's too complicated to explain where it is; send me your password and I'll find it for you." When the current employee complied and the former employee located the file, both would become federal criminals under the majority's opinion. I am confident that such innocuous password sharing among current and former employees is more frequent than the improper password sharing at issue here.

V.

Nosal's case illustrates some of the special dangers inherent in criminal laws which are frequently violated in the commercial world, yet seldom enforced. To quote a recent comment by a justice of the Supreme Court with regard to a statute that similarly could be used to punish indiscriminately: "It puts at risk behavior that is common. That is a recipe for giving the Justice Department and prosecutors enormous power over [individuals]." Transcript of Oral Argument at 38, *McDonnell v. United States*, 136 S.Ct. 891 (2016) (No. 15–474) (Breyer, J.). Indeed, as this opinion is being filed, the Supreme Court has issued its decision in *McDonnell* and reiterated that "we cannot construe a criminal statute on the assumption that the Government will use it responsibly." *McDonnell v. United States*, 579 U.S.—, 136 S.Ct. 2355, 195 L.Ed.2d 639 (2016). Here it is far worse. Broadly interpreted, the CFAA is a recipe for giving large corporations undue power over their rivals, their employees, and ordinary citizens, as well as affording such indiscriminate power to the Justice Department, should we have a president or attorney general who desires to do so.

Nosal was a senior member of Korn/Ferry and intended to start a competing business. He was also due a million dollars from Korn/Ferry if he abided by his departure agreement. When Korn/Ferry began its investigation of Nosal's possible malfeasance, it brought on ex–FBI agents to search through Christian's garbage and follow Jacobson around. It also hired a leading international corporate law firm consisting of over 600 lawyers, O'Melveny and Myers, which charged up to $1,100 per hour for the time of some its partners. One of O'Melveny's lead attorneys had recently left the office of the United States Attorney who would prosecute any case against Nosal. She referred the case to her former colleagues personally. O'Melveny also told the prosecutor that the case was "time-sensitive" because Korn/Ferry would have to file its civil case shortly, but that it would provide the prosecutor with the facts necessary to "demonstrate the criminal culpability of those involved." The law firm also provided the government with the liability theories it believed necessary to convict Nosal under the CFAA. Less than a month after O'Melveny approached the government, the FBI searched the residences of Jacobson, Christian, and the offices of Nosal's new business. That same day Korn/Ferry filed its civil complaint. In total, Korn/Ferry sought almost a million dollars in attorneys' fees from Nosal to compensate it for the work O'Melveny did to "assist" with the criminal prosecution.

To be clear, I am not implying that there is any misconduct on the part of the prosecution in this case. Nevertheless, private assistance of such magnitude blurs the line between criminal and civil law. Courts have long held that "a private citizen lacks a judicially cognizable interest in the prosecution or nonprosecution of another." Korn/Ferry and its counsel's employment of their overwhelming resources to persuade prosecutors to bring charges against an economic competitor has unhealthy ramifications for the legal system. Civil suits ordinarily govern economic controversies. There, private parties may initiate any good-faith action at their own expense. In criminal cases, however, the prosecutor who "seeks truth and not victims, [and] who serves the law and not factional purposes" must decide which cases go forward and which do not. Robert H. Jackson, *The Federal Prosecutor*, Address Before Conference of U.S. Attorneys (April 1, 1940), *in* 24 J. Am. Judicature Soc'y 18, 20 (1940). These decisions are inevitably affected by a variety of factors including the severity of the crime and the amount of available resources that must be dedicated to a prosecution.

Prosecutors cannot help but be influenced by knowing that they can count on an interested private party to perform and finance much of the work required to convict a business rival. As the Supreme Court found recently: "Prosecutorial discretion involves carefully weighing the benefits of a prosecution against the evidence needed to convict, [and] the resources of the public fisc." The balance weighs differently when a major international corporate firm will bear much of the cost which would otherwise have to be borne by the prosecutor's office. Prosecutors will also be able to use the work product of the country's finest and most highly paid corporate litigators, rather than investing its meager human resources in developing a complex commercial case different in kind from the cases it is ordinarily used to preparing. Undertaking such third-party financed cases which a United States attorney might not have prosecuted otherwise gives the appearance of well-financed business interests obtaining the services of the prosecutorial branch of government to accomplish their own private purposes, influencing the vast discretion vested in our prosecutors, and causing the enforcement of broad and ill-defined criminal laws seldom enforced except at the behest of those who can afford it. Moreover, to the extent that decisions to pursue such cases are influenced by such extraneous concerns, and prosecutorial discretion is tilted toward their enforcement, other criminal cases that might otherwise be chosen for prosecution may well be neglected and the criminal justice system itself become distorted.

---

b. Agency Theory to Find Lack of Authorization

Shurgard Storage Centers, Inc. v. Safeguard Self Storage, Inc.

119 F. Supp. 2d 1121 (W.D. Wash. 2000)

ZILLY, DISTRICT JUDGE.

[Shurgard Storage Centers and Safeguard Self Storage were competitors in the self-storage business. Shurgard alleged that Safeguard embarked on a systematic scheme to hire away key employees from the plaintiff for the purpose of obtaining the plaintiff's trade secrets and that some of those employees, while still working for the Shurgard, used the Shurgard's computers to send trade secrets to Safeguard via e-mail. Shurgard alleged a variety of causes of action, including violations of the Computer Fraud and Abuse Act. Safeguard sought dismissal of that claim on a variety of grounds.]

The plaintiff is the industry leader in full and self-service storage facilities in both the United States and Europe. The plaintiff's growth in the last 25 years is primarily due to the development and construction of top-quality storage centers in "high barrier to entry" markets. Pursuant to this strategy, the plaintiff has developed a sophisticated system of creating market plans, identifying appropriate development sites, and evaluating whether a site will provide a high return on an investment. The plaintiff invests significant resources in creating a marketing team to carry out these tasks for each potential market. These teams become familiar with the market, identify potential acquisition sites, and develop relationships with brokers and sellers in the market so that the plaintiff has the best opportunity to acquire a preferred site.

In late 1999, the defendant approached Eric Leland, a Regional Development Manager for the plaintiff, and offered him employment with the defendant. Because of his position with the plaintiff, Mr. Leland had full access to the plaintiff's confidential business plans, expansion plans, and other trade secrets. While still employed by the plaintiff, but acting as an agent for the defendant, Mr. Leland sent e-mails to the defendant containing various trade secrets and proprietary information belonging to the plaintiff. Mr. Leland did this without the plaintiff's knowledge or approval. Mr. Leland was later hired by the defendant in October 1999, and he has continued to give the defendant proprietary information belonging to the plaintiff. The defendant has hired away other employees of the plaintiff who have intimate knowledge of the plaintiff's business models and practices, and the defendant continues to recruit employees of the plaintiff.

The defendant notes that the plaintiff alleged that Mr. Leland had full access to all the information allegedly transferred to the defendant. Accordingly, the defendant argues that the plaintiff cannot maintain an action under § 1030(a)(2)(C) because it has not alleged that anyone accessed its computers without authorization or exceeded authorized access to those computers.

The plaintiff responds by arguing that the authorization for its former employees ended when the employees began acting as agents for the defendant. The plaintiff cites to the Restatement (Second) of Agency § 112 (1958) and argues that when Mr. Leland or other former employees used the plaintiff's computers and information on those computers in an improper way they were "without authorization."

Under the Restatement (Second) of Agency:

> Unless otherwise agreed, the authority of an agent terminates if, without knowledge of the principal, he acquires adverse interests or if he is otherwise guilty of a serious breach of loyalty to the principal.

Restatement (Second) of Agency § 112 (1958). Under this rule, the authority of the plaintiff's former employees ended when they allegedly became agents of the defendant. Therefore, they lost their authorization and were "without authorization" when they allegedly obtained and sent the proprietary information to the defendant via e-mail. The plaintiff has stated a claim under 18 U.S.C. § 1030(a)(2)(C).

———————

c. Non-Intended Use as Basis

United States v. Dimetriace Eva-Lavon John

597 F.3d 263 (5th Cir. 2010)

Owen, Circuit Judge:

Dimetriace Eva-Lavon John was found guilty by a jury on all counts of a seven-count indictment arising out of her involvement in a scheme to incur fraudulent charges on accounts held by various Citigroup customers.

Dimetriace Eva-Lavon John was employed as an account manager at Citigroup for approximately three years. By virtue of her position, she had access to Citigroup's internal computer system and customer account information contained in it. In September 2005, John provided Leland Riley, her half-brother, with customer account information enabling Riley and other confederates to incur fraudulent charges.

John accessed and printed information pertaining to at least seventy-six corporate customer accounts and provided it to Riley. The information was in the form of either scanned images of checks written by the account holders or printouts of computer screens containing detailed account information. Before he was apprehended, Riley and cohorts used information John had provided to incur fraudulent charges on four different accounts.

Whether John's convictions on Counts 6 and 7 may be sustained depends on the proper interpretation of "exceeds authorized access" as used in § 1030(a)(2) and defined in § 1030(e)(6).

John argues that she was authorized to use Citigroup's computers and to view and print information regarding accounts in the course of her official duties. The evidence, she contends, reflects only that she was not permitted to use the information to which she had access to perpetrate a fraud, she could make changes to account information only in compliance with a customer's request, and she was not permitted to take material she printed regarding accounts from her office building. She asserts that her mental state or motive at the time she accessed or printed account information cannot determine whether she violated 18 U.S.C. § 1030(a)(2). Specifically, she argues that the statute does not prohibit unlawful *use* of material that she was authorized to access through authorized use of a computer. The statute only prohibits using authorized access to obtain information that she is not entitled to obtain or alter information that she is not entitled to alter, John contends.

The question before us is whether "authorized access" or "authorization" may encompass limits placed on *the use* of information obtained by permitted access to a computer system and data available on that system. We conclude that it may, at least when the user knows or reasonably should know that he or she is not authorized to access a computer and information obtainable from that access in furtherance of or to perpetrate a crime.

To give but one example, an employer may "authorize" employees to utilize computers for any lawful purpose but not for unlawful purposes and only in furtherance of the employer's business. An employee would "exceed [ ] authorized access" if he or she used that access to obtain or steal information as part of a criminal scheme.

In *United States v. Phillips*, [477 F.3d 215 (5th Cir. 2007),] this court analyzed whether a criminal defendant had accessed university computers "without authorization," as distinguished from "exceed[ing] authorized access," and we recognized that "[c]ourts have . . . typically analyzed the scope of a user's authorization to access a protected computer on the basis of the expected norms of intended use or the nature of the relationship established between the computer owner and the user." John's situation differs from that of the student in *Phillips* because John was authorized to view and print all of the information that she accessed and that she provided to Riley. However, John's use of Citigroup's computer system to perpetrate fraud was not an intended use of that system.

John's use of Citigroup's computer system to perpetrate a fraud was also contrary to Citigroup employee policies, of which she was aware. The First Circuit has held that an employment agreement can establish the parameters of "authorized" access. [*EF Cultural Travel BV v. Explorica, Inc.*, 274 F.3d 577 (1st Cir. 2001).]

While we do not necessarily agree that violating a confidentiality agreement under circumstances such as those in *EF Cultural Travel BV* would give rise to criminal culpability, we do agree with the First Circuit that the concept of "exceeds authorized access" may include exceeding the purposes for which access is "authorized." Access to a computer and data that can be obtained from that access may be exceeded if the purposes for which access has been given are exceeded. In other words, John's access to Citigroup's data was confined. She was not authorized to access that information for any and all purposes but for limited purposes.

In the present case, the Government demonstrated at trial that Citigroup's official policy, which was reiterated in training programs that John attended, prohibited misuse of the company's internal computer systems and confidential customer information. Despite being aware of these policies, John accessed account information for individuals whose accounts she did not manage, removed this highly sensitive and confidential information from Citigroup premises, and ultimately used this information to perpetrate fraud on Citigroup and its customers.

———————

d. Websites: Terms of Use and Technical Barriers
Facebook, Inc. v. Power Ventures, Inc.
844 F.3d 1058 (9th Cir. 2016)

GRABER, Circuit Judge:

One social networking company, Facebook, Inc., has sued another, Power Ventures, Inc., over a promotional campaign. Power accessed Facebook users' data and initiated form e-mails and other electronic messages promoting its website. Initially, Power had implied permission from Facebook. But Facebook sent Power a cease and desist letter and blocked Power's IP address; nevertheless Power continued its campaign. Facebook alleges that Power's actions violated[, *inter alia*,] the Computer Fraud and Abuse Act of 1986. We hold that Power violated the CFAA . . . only after it received Facebook's cease and desist letter and nonetheless continued to access Facebook's computers without permission.

BACKGROUND

Defendant Power Ventures, a corporation founded and directed by CEO Steven Vachani, who also is a defendant here, operated a social networking website, Power .com. The concept was simple. Individuals who already used other social networking websites could log on to Power.com and create an account. Power.com would then aggregate the user's social networking information. The individual, a "Power user," could see all contacts from many social networking sites on a single page. The Power user thus could keep track of a variety of social networking friends through a single program and could click through the central Power website to individual social networking sites. By 2008, the website had attracted a growing following.

Plaintiff Facebook also operates a social networking website, Facebook.com. Facebook users, who numbered more than 130 million during Power's promotional campaign, can create a personal profile — a web page within the site — and can connect with other users. Facebook requires each user to register before accessing the website and requires that each user assent to its terms of use. Once registered, a Facebook user can create and customize her profile by adding personal information, photographs, or other content. A user can establish connections with other Facebook users by "friending" them; the connected users are thus called "friends."

Facebook has tried to limit and control access to its website. A non-Facebook user generally may not use the website to send messages, post photographs, or otherwise contact Facebook users through their profiles. Instead, Facebook requires third-party developers or websites that wish to contact its users through its site to enroll in a program called Facebook Connect. It requires these third parties to register with Facebook and to agree to an additional Developer Terms of Use Agreement.

In December 2008, Power began a promotional campaign to attract more traffic to its website; it hoped that Facebook users would join its site. Power placed an icon on its website with a promotional message that read: "First 100 people who bring 100 new friends to Power.com win $100." The icon included various options for how a user could share Power with others. The user could "Share with friends through my photos," "Share with friends through events," or "Share with friends through status." A button on the icon included the words "Yes, I do!" If a user clicked the "Yes, I do!" button, Power would create an event, photo, or status on the user's Facebook profile.

In many instances, Power caused a message to be transmitted to the user's friends within the Facebook system. In other instances, depending on a Facebook user's settings, Facebook generated an e-mail message. If, for example, a Power user shared the promotion through an event, Facebook generated an e-mail message to an external e-mail account from the user to friends. The e-mail message gave the name and time of the event, listed Power as the host, and stated that the Power user was inviting the recipient to this event. The external e-mails were form e-mails, generated each time that a Facebook user invited others to an event. The "from" line in the e-mail stated that the message came from Facebook; the body was signed, "The Facebook Team."

On December 1, 2008, Facebook first became aware of Power's promotional campaign and, on that same date, Facebook sent a "cease and desist" letter to Power instructing Power to terminate its activities. Facebook tried to get Power to sign its Developer Terms of Use Agreement and enroll in Facebook Connect; Power resisted. Facebook instituted an Internet Protocol block in an effort to prevent Power from accessing the Facebook website from Power's IP address. Power responded by switching IP addresses to circumvent the Facebook block. Through this period, Power continued its promotion even though it acknowledged that it took, copied, or made use of data from Facebook.com without Facebook's permission.

Power's campaign lasted less than two months. On December 20, 2008, Facebook filed this action. Toward the end of January 2009, Power ended its campaign. In April 2011, Power ceased doing business altogether. In total, more than 60,000 external e-mails promoting Power were sent through the Facebook system. An unknown number of internal Facebook messages were also transmitted.

The CFAA prohibits acts of computer trespass by those who are not authorized users or who exceed authorized use. It creates criminal and civil liability for whoever "intentionally accesses a computer without authorization or exceeds authorized access, and thereby obtains . . . information from any protected computer." 18 U.S.C. § 1030(a)(2)(C). "The statute thus provides two ways of committing the crime of improperly accessing a protected computer: (1) obtaining access without authorization; and (2) obtaining access with authorization but then using that access improperly." The CFAA provides a private right of action for "[a]ny person who suffers damage or loss by reason of a violation of this section." 18 U.S.C. § 1030(g).

First, we hold that Facebook suffered a loss within the meaning of the CFAA. The statute permits a private right of action when a party has suffered a loss of at least $5,000 during a one-year period. *Id.* § 1030(c)(4)(A)(i)(I). The statute defines "loss" to mean "any reasonable cost to any victim, including the cost of responding to an offense, conducting a damage assessment, and restoring the data, program, system, or information to its condition prior to the offense, and any revenue lost, cost incurred, or other consequential damages incurred because of interruption of service." *Id.* § 1030(e)(11). It is undisputed that Facebook employees spent many hours, totaling more than $5,000 in costs, analyzing, investigating, and responding to Power's actions. Accordingly, Facebook suffered a loss under the CFAA.

We next consider whether Power accessed Facebook's computers knowing that it was not authorized to do so. We have previously considered whether a defendant has accessed a computer "without authorization" or in a manner that "exceeds authorized access" under the CFAA.

From [previous] cases, we distill two general rules in analyzing authorization under the CFAA. First, a defendant can run afoul of the CFAA when he or she has no permission to access a computer or when such permission has been revoked explicitly. Once permission has been revoked, technological gamesmanship or the enlisting of a third party to aid in access will not excuse liability. Second, a violation of the terms of use of a website — without more — cannot establish liability under the CFAA.[n.1][7]

Here, initially, Power users arguably gave Power permission to use Facebook's computers to disseminate messages. Power reasonably could have thought that consent from *Facebook users* to share the promotion was permission for Power to access *Facebook's* computers.[n.2][8] In clicking the "Yes, I do!" button, Power users took action akin to allowing a friend to use a computer or to log on to an e-mail account. Because Power had at least arguable permission to access Facebook's computers, it did not initially access Facebook's computers "without authorization" within the meaning of the CFAA.

But Facebook expressly rescinded that permission when Facebook issued its written cease and desist letter to Power on December 1, 2008. Facebook's cease and desist letter informed Power that it had violated Facebook's terms of use and demanded that Power stop soliciting Facebook users' information, using Facebook content, or otherwise interacting with Facebook through automated scripts.[n.3][9] Facebook then imposed IP blocks in an effort to prevent Power's continued access.

---

7. [N.1] One can imagine situations in which those two principles might be in tension — situations in which, for example, an automatic boilerplate revocation follows a violation of a website's terms of use — but we need not address or resolve such questions on the stark facts before us.

8. [N.2] Because, initially, Power users gave Power permission to use Facebook's computers to disseminate messages, we need not decide whether websites such as Facebook are presumptively open to all comers, unless and until permission is revoked expressly.

9. [N.3] The mention of the terms of use in the cease and desist letter is not dispositive. Violation of Facebook's terms of use, without more, would not be sufficient to impose liability. But, in addition to asserting a violation of Facebook's terms of use, the cease and desist letter warned Power that it may have violated federal and state law and plainly put Power on notice that it was no longer authorized to access Facebook's computers.

The record shows unequivocally that Power knew that it no longer had authorization to access Facebook's computers, but continued to do so anyway. In requests for admission propounded during the course of this litigation, Power admitted that, after receiving notice that its use of or access to Facebook was forbidden by Facebook, it "took, copied, or made use of data from the Facebook website *without Facebook's permission* to do so." Contemporaneously, too, soon after receiving the cease and desist letter, Power's CEO sent an e-mail stating: "[W]e need to be prepared for Facebook to try to block us and the [sic] turn this into a national battle that gets us huge attention." On December 4, 2008, a Power executive sent an e-mail agreeing that Power engaged in four "prohibited activities"[n.4][10]; acknowledging that Power may have "intentionally and without authorization interfered with [Facebook's] possessory interest in the computer system," while arguing that the "*unauthorized use*" did not cause damage to Facebook; and noting additional federal and state statutes that Power "may also be accused of violating," beyond those listed in Facebook's cease and desist letter. E-mails sent later in December 2008 discussed the IP blocks that Facebook had imposed and the measures that Power took to evade them. Nevertheless, Power continued to access Facebook's data and computers without Facebook's permission.

The consent that Power had received from Facebook users was not sufficient to grant continuing authorization to access Facebook's computers after Facebook's express revocation of permission. An analogy from the physical world may help to illustrate why this is so. Suppose that a person wants to borrow a friend's jewelry that is held in a safe deposit box at a bank. The friend gives permission for the person to access the safe deposit box and lends him a key. Upon receiving the key, though, the person decides to visit the bank while carrying a shotgun. The bank ejects the person from its premises and bans his reentry. The gun-toting jewelry borrower could not then reenter the bank, claiming that access to the safe deposit box gave him authority to stride about the bank's property while armed. In other words, to access the safe deposit box, the person needs permission *both* from his friend (who controls access to the safe) *and* from the bank (which controls access to its premises). Similarly, for Power to continue its campaign using Facebook's computers, it needed authorization both from individual Facebook users (who controlled their data and personal pages) and from Facebook (which stored this data on its physical servers). Permission from the users alone was not sufficient to constitute authorization after Facebook issued the cease and desist letter.

In sum, as it admitted, Power deliberately disregarded the cease and desist letter and accessed Facebook's computers without authorization to do so. It circumvented

---

10. [n.4] The activities were:
   "— Using a person's Facebook account without Facebook's authorization;
   — Using automated scripts to collect information from their site;
   — Incorporating Facebook's site in another database[; and]
   — Using Facebook's site for commercial purposes[.]"

IP barriers that further demonstrated that Facebook had rescinded permission for Power to access Facebook's computers.[n.5][11] We therefore hold that, after receiving written notification from Facebook on December 1, 2008, Power accessed Facebook's computers "without authorization" within the meaning of the CFAA and is liable under that statute.

Accordingly, we hold that, after receiving the cease and desist letter from Facebook, Power intentionally accessed Facebook's computers knowing that it was not authorized to do so, making Power liable under the CFAA. We therefore affirm in part the holding of the district court with respect to the CFAA.

REVERSED in part, VACATED in part, AFFIRMED in part, and REMANDED.

———————

United States v. Lori Drew

259 F.R.D. 449 (C.D. Cal. 2009)

George H. Wu, District Judge.

This case raises the issue of whether (and/or when will) violations of an Internet website's terms of service constitute a crime under the Computer Fraud and Abuse Act.

In the Indictment, Drew was charged with . . . three counts of violating a felony portion of the CFAA, *i.e.*, 18 U.S.C. §§ 1030(a)(2)(C) and 1030(c)(2)(B)(ii), which prohibit accessing a computer without authorization or in excess of authorization and obtaining information from a protected computer where the conduct involves an interstate or foreign communication and the offense is committed in furtherance of a crime or tortious act.

The Indictment included, *inter alia*, the following allegations (not all of which were established by the evidence at trial). Drew, a resident of O'Fallon, Missouri, entered into a conspiracy in which its members agreed to intentionally access a computer used in interstate commerce without (and/or in excess of) authorization in order to obtain information for the purpose of committing the tortious act of intentional infliction of emotional distress upon "M.T.M.," subsequently identified as Megan Meier. Megan was a 13 year old girl living in O'Fallon who had been a classmate of Drew's daughter Sarah. Pursuant to the conspiracy, on or about September 20, 2006, the conspirators registered and set up a profile for a fictitious 16 year old male juvenile named "Josh Evans" on the www.MySpace.com website, and posted a photograph of a boy without that boy's knowledge or consent. Such

———————

11. [n.5] Simply bypassing an IP address, without more, would not constitute unauthorized use. Because a blocked user does not receive notice that he has been blocked, he may never realize that the block was imposed and that authorization was revoked. Or, even if he does discover the block, he could conclude that it was triggered by misconduct by someone else who shares the same IP address, such as the user's roommate or co-worker.

conduct violated My Space's terms of service. The conspirators contacted Megan through the MySpace network (on which she had her own profile) using the Josh Evans pseudonym and began to flirt with her over a number of days. On or about October 7, 2006, the conspirators had "Josh" inform Megan that he was moving away. On or about October 16, 2006, the conspirators had "Josh" tell Megan that he no longer liked her and that "the world would be a better place without her in it." Later on that same day, after learning that Megan had killed herself, Drew caused the Josh Evans MySpace account to be deleted.

[The jury found Drew not guilty of the felony charges but] did find Defendant "guilty" "of [on the dates specified in the Indictment] accessing a computer involved in interstate or foreign communication without authorization or in excess of authorization to obtain information in violation of Title 18, United States Code, Section 1030(a)(2)(C) and (c)(2)(A), a misdemeanor."

MySpace is a "social networking" website where members can create "profiles" and interact with other members. Anyone with Internet access can go onto the MySpace website and view content which is open to the general public such as a music area, video section, and members' profiles which are not set as "private." However, to create a profile, upload and display photographs, communicate with persons on the site, write "blogs," and/or utilize other services or applications on the MySpace website, one must be a "member." Anyone can become a member of MySpace at no charge so long as they meet a minimum age requirement and register.

In 2006, to become a member, one had to go to the sign-up section of the MySpace website and register by filling in personal information (such as name, email address, date of birth, country/state/postal code, and gender) and creating a password. In addition, the individual had to check on the box indicating that "You agree to the MySpace Terms of Service and Privacy Policy." The terms of service did not appear on the same registration page that contained this "check box" for users to confirm their agreement to those provisions. In order to find the terms of service, one had (or would have had) to proceed to the bottom of the page where there were several "hyperlinks" including one entitled "Terms." Upon clicking the "Terms" hyperlink, the screen would display the terms of service section of the website. A person could become a MySpace member without ever reading or otherwise becoming aware of the provisions and conditions of the MySpace terms of service by merely clicking on the "check box" and then the "Sign Up" button without first accessing the "Terms" section.[n.8][12]

As used in its website, "terms of service" refers to the "MySpace.com Terms of Use Agreement" ("MSTOS"). The MSTOS in 2006 stated, *inter alia:*

---

12. [n.8] Certain websites endeavor to compel visitors to read their terms of service by requiring them to scroll down through such terms before being allowed to click on the sign-on box or by placing the box at the end of the "terms" section of the site. MySpace did not have such provisions in 2006.

This Terms of Use Agreement ("Agreement") sets forth the legally binding terms for your use of the Services. By using the Services, you agree to be bound by this Agreement, whether you are a "Visitor" (which means that you simply browse the Website) or you are a "Member" (which means that you have registered with MySpace.com). The term "User" refers to a Visitor or a Member. You are only authorized to use the Services (regardless of whether your access or use is intended) if you agree to abide by all applicable laws and to this Agreement. Please read this Agreement carefully and save it. If you do not agree with it, you should leave the Website and discontinue use of the Services immediately. If you wish to become a Member, communicate with other Members and make use of the Services, you must read this Agreement and indicate your acceptance at the end of this document before proceeding.

By using the Services, you represent and warrant that (a) all registration information you submit is truthful and accurate; (b) you will maintain the accuracy of such information; (c) you are 14 years of age or older; and (d) your use of the Services does not violate any applicable law or regulation.

The MSTOS prohibited the posting of a wide range of content on the website including (but not limited to) material that: a) "is potentially offensive and promotes racism, bigotry, hatred or physical harm of any kind against any group or individual"; b) "harasses or advocates harassment of another person"; c) "solicits personal information from anyone under 18"; d) "provides information that you know is false or misleading or promotes illegal activities or conduct that is abusive, threatening, obscene, defamatory or libelous"; e) "includes a photograph of another person that you have posted without that person's consent"; * * * * MySpace also reserved the right to take appropriate legal action (including reporting the violating conduct to law enforcement authorities) against persons who engaged in "prohibited activity" which was defined as including, *inter alia:* a) "criminal or tortious activity", b) "attempting to impersonate another Member or person", c) "using any information obtained from the Services in order to harass, abuse, or harm another person", d) "using the Service in a manner inconsistent with any and all applicable laws and regulations" * * * * MySpace.com assumes no responsibility or liability for this material." Further, MySpace was allowed to unilaterally modify the terms of service, with such modifications taking effect upon the posting of notice on its website. Thus, members would have to review the MSTOS each time they logged on to the website, to ensure that they were aware of any updates in order to avoid violating some new provision of the terms of service. Also, the MSTOS provided that "any dispute" between a visitor/member and MySpace "arising out of this Agreement must be settled by arbitration" if demanded by either party.

At one point, MySpace was receiving an estimated 230,000 new accounts per day and eventually the number of profiles exceeded 400 million with over 100 million unique visitors worldwide. "Generally speaking," MySpace would not monitor new accounts to determine if they complied with the terms of service except on a limited basis, mostly in regards to photographic content. Sung testified that there is no way to determine how many of the 400 million existing MySpace accounts were created in a way that violated the MSTOS.

During the relevant time period herein, the misdemeanor 18 U.S.C. § 1030(a)(2)(C) crime consisted of the following three elements:

> First, the defendant intentionally [accessed without authorization] [exceeded authorized access of] a computer;

> Second, the defendant's access of the computer involved an interstate or foreign communication; and

> Third, by [accessing without authorization] [exceeding authorized access to] a computer, the defendant obtained information from a computer ... [used in interstate or foreign commerce or communication].

In this case, a central question is whether a computer user's intentional violation of one or more provisions in an Internet website's terms of services (where those terms condition access to and/or use of the website's services upon agreement to and compliance with the terms) satisfies the first element of section 1030(a)(2)(C). If the answer to that question is "yes," then seemingly, any and every conscious violation of that website's terms of service will constitute a CFAA misdemeanor.

In this particular case, the only basis for finding that Drew intentionally accessed MySpace's computer/servers without authorization and/or in excess of authorization was her and/or her co-conspirator's violations of the MSTOS by deliberately creating the false Josh Evans profile, posting a photograph of a juvenile without his permission and pretending to be a sixteen year old O'Fallon resident for the purpose of communicating with Megan. Therefore, if conscious violations of the My Space terms of service were not sufficient to satisfy the first element of the CFAA misdemeanor violation, Drew's motion would have to be granted on that basis alone. However, this Court concludes that an intentional breach of the MSTOS can potentially constitute accessing the MySpace computer/server without authorization and/or in excess of authorization under the statute.

There is nothing in the way that the undefined words "authorization" and "authorized" are used in the CFAA (or from the CFAA's legislative history) which indicates that Congress intended for them to have specialized meanings. As delineated in *Webster's New World Dictionary* at 92, to "authorize" ordinarily means "to give official approval to or permission for."

It cannot be considered a stretch of the law to hold that the owner of an Internet website has the right to establish the extent to (and the conditions under) which members of the public will be allowed access to information, services and/or applications which are available on the website. Nor can it be doubted that the owner can relay and impose those limitations/restrictions/conditions by means of written notice such as terms of service or use provisions placed on the home page of the website. While issues might be raised in particular cases as to the sufficiency of the notice

and/or sufficiency of the user's assent to the terms, and while public policy considerations might in turn limit enforcement of particular restrictions, the vast majority of
the courts (that have considered the issue) have held that a website's terms of service/
use can define what is (and/or is not) authorized access vis-a-vis that website.

Here, the MSTOS defined "services" as including "the MySpace.com Website . . . ,
the MySpace.com instant messenger, and any other connection with the Website. . .
." It further notified the public that the MSTOS "sets forth the legally binding terms
for your use of the services." Visitors and members were informed that "you are only
authorized to use the Services . . . if you agree to abide by all applicable laws and to
this Agreement." Moreover, to become a MySpace member and thereby be allowed
to communicate with other members and fully utilize the MySpace Services, one
had to click on a box to confirm that the user had agreed to the MySpace Terms of
Service. Clearly, the MSTOS was capable of defining the scope of authorized access
of visitors, members and/or users to the website.[n.22][13]

Justice Holmes observed that, as to criminal statutes, there is a "fair warning"
requirement. As he stated in *McBoyle v. United States*, 283 U.S. 25, 27 (1931):

> Although it is not likely that a criminal will carefully consider the text of the
> law before he murders or steals, it is reasonable that a fair warning should
> be given to the world in language that the common world will understand,
> of what the law intends to do if a certain line is passed. To make the warn-
> ing fair, so far as possible the line should be clear.

As further elaborated by the Supreme Court in *United States v. Lanier*, 520 U.S.
259, 266 (1997):

> There are three related manifestations of the fair warning requirement.
> First, the vagueness doctrine bars enforcement of "a statute which either for-
> bids or requires the doing of an act in terms so vague that men of common

---

13. [n.22] MySpace utilizes what have become known as "browsewrap" and "clickwrap" agreements in regards to its terms of service. Browsewraps can take various forms but basically the
website will contain a notice that—by merely using the services of, obtaining information from, or
initiating applications within the website—the user is agreeing to and is bound by the site's terms
of service. "Courts considering browsewrap agreements have held that 'the validity of a browsewrap license turns on whether a website user has actual or constructive knowledge of a site's terms
and conditions prior to using the site.'"

  Clickwrap agreements require a user to affirmatively click a box on the website acknowledging awareness of and agreement to the terms of service before he or she is allowed to
  proceed with further utilization of the website. Clickwrap agreements "have been routinely upheld by circuit and district courts."

  As a "visitor" to the MySpace website and being initially limited to the public areas of
  the site, one is bound by MySpace's browsewrap agreement. If one wishes further access
  into the site for purposes of creating a profile and contacting MySpace members (as Drew
  and the co-conspirators did), one would have to affirmatively acknowledge and assent
  to the terms of service by checking the designated box, thereby triggering the clickwrap
  agreement. As stated in the MSTOS, "This Agreement is accepted upon your use of the
  Website or any of the Services and is further affirmed by you becoming a Member."

intelligence must necessarily guess at its meaning and differ as to its application." Second, as a sort of "Junior version of the vagueness doctrine," the canon of strict construction of criminal statutes, or rule of lenity, ensures fair warning by so resolving ambiguity in a criminal statute as to apply it only to conduct clearly covered. . . . Third, although clarity at the requisite level may be supplied by judicial gloss on an otherwise uncertain statute, . . . due process bars courts from applying a novel construction of a criminal statute to conduct that neither the statute nor any prior judicial decision has fairly disclosed to be within its scope. In each of these guises, the touchstone is whether the statute, either standing alone or as construed, made it reasonably clear at the relevant time that the defendant's conduct was criminal.

The void-for-vagueness doctrine has two prongs: 1) a definitional/notice sufficiency requirement and, more importantly, 2) a guideline setting element to govern law enforcement. In *Kolender v. Lawson*, 461 U.S. 352, 357–58 (1983), the Court explained that:

As generally stated, the void-for-vagueness doctrine requires that a penal statute define the criminal offense with sufficient definiteness that ordinary people can understand what conduct is prohibited and in a manner that does not encourage arbitrary and discriminatory enforcement. . . . Although the doctrine focuses both on actual notice to citizens and arbitrary enforcement, we have recognized recently that the more important aspect of the vagueness doctrine "is not actual notice, but the other principal element of the doctrine—the requirement that a legislature establish minimal guidelines to govern law enforcement." Where the legislature fails to provide such minimal guidelines, a criminal statute may permit "a standardless sweep [that] allows policemen, prosecutors, and juries to pursue their personal predilections."

To avoid contravening the void-for-vagueness doctrine, the criminal statute must contain "relatively clear guidelines as to prohibited conduct" and provide "objective criteria" to evaluate whether a crime has been committed.

The pivotal issue herein is whether basing a CFAA misdemeanor violation upon the conscious violation of a website's terms of service runs afoul of the void-for-vagueness doctrine. This Court concludes that it does primarily because of the absence of minimal guidelines to govern law enforcement, but also because of actual notice deficiencies.

Terms of service which are incorporated into a browsewrap or clickwrap agreement can, like any other type of contract, define the limits of authorized access as to a website and its concomitant computer/server(s). However, the question is whether individuals of "common intelligence" are on notice that a breach of a terms of service contract can become a crime under the CFAA. Arguably, they are not.

First, an initial inquiry is whether the statute, as it is written, provides sufficient notice. Here, the language of section 1030(a)(2)(C) does not explicitly state (nor does it implicitly suggest) that the CFAA has "criminalized breaches of contract" in the context of website terms of service. Normally, breaches of contract are not the subject of criminal prosecution. Thus, while "ordinary people" might expect to be exposed to civil liabilities for violating a contractual provision, they would not expect criminal penalties. This would especially be the case where the services provided by MySpace are in essence offered at no cost to the users and, hence, there is no specter of the users "defrauding" MySpace in any monetary sense.

Second, if a website's terms of service controls what is "authorized" and what is "exceeding authorization"—which in turn governs whether an individual's accessing information or services on the website is criminal or not, section 1030(a)(2)(C) would be unacceptably vague because it is unclear whether any or all violations of terms of service will render the access unauthorized, or whether only certain ones will. For example, in the present case, MySpace's terms of service prohibits a member from engaging in a multitude of activities on the website, including such conduct as "criminal or tortious activity," "gambling," "advertising to . . . any Member to buy or sell any products," "transmit[ting] any chain letters," "covering or obscuring the banner advertisements on your personal profile page," "disclosing your password to any third party," etc. The MSTOS does not specify which precise terms of service, when breached, will result in a termination of MySpace's authorization for the visitor/member to access the website. If *any* violation of *any* term of service is held to make the access unauthorized, that strategy would probably resolve this particular vagueness issue; but it would, in turn, render the statute incredibly overbroad and contravene the second prong of the void-for-vagueness doctrine as to setting guidelines to govern law enforcement.

Third, by utilizing violations of the terms of service as the basis for the section 1030(a)(2)(C) crime, that approach makes the website owner—in essence—the party who ultimately defines the criminal conduct. This will lead to further vagueness problems. The owner's description of a term of service might itself be so vague as to make the visitor or member reasonably unsure of what the term of service covers. For example, the MSTOS prohibits members from posting in "band and filmmaker profiles . . . sexually suggestive imagery or any other unfair . . . [c]ontent intended to draw traffic to the profile." It is unclear what "sexually suggestive imagery" and "unfair content" mean. Moreover, website owners can establish terms where either the scope or the application of the provision are to be decided by them *ad hoc* and/or pursuant to undelineated standards. For example, the MSTOS provides that what constitutes "prohibited content" on the website is determined "in the sole discretion of MySpace.com. . . ." Additionally, terms of service may allow the website owner to unilaterally amend and/or add to the terms with minimal notice to users.

Fourth, because terms of service are essentially a contractual means for setting the scope of authorized access, a level of indefiniteness arises from the necessary application of contract law in general and/or other contractual requirements within the applicable terms of service to any criminal prosecution. For example, the MSTOS has a provision wherein "any dispute" between MySpace and a visitor/member/

user arising out of the terms of service is subject to arbitration upon the demand of either party. Before a breach of a term of service can be found and/or the effect of that breach upon MySpace's ability to terminate the visitor/member/user's access to the site can be determined, the issue would be subject to arbitration. Thus, a question arises as to whether a finding of unauthorized access or in excess of authorized access can be made without arbitration.

Furthermore, under California law,[n.28][14] a material breach of the MSTOS by a user/member does not automatically discharge the contract, but merely "excuses the injured party's performance, and gives him or her the election of certain remedies." Those remedies include rescission and restitution, damages, specific performance, injunction, declaratory relief, *etc.* The contract can also specify particular remedies and consequences in the event of a breach which are in addition to or a substitution for those otherwise afforded by law. The MSTOS does provide that: "MySpace.com reserves the right, in its sole discretion . . . to restrict, suspend, or terminate your access to all or part of the services at any time, for any or no reason, with or without prior notice, and without liability." However, there is no provision which expressly states that a breach of the MSTOS automatically results in the termination of authorization to access the website. Indeed, the MSTOS cryptically states: "you are only authorized to use the Services . . . if you *agree to* abide by all applicable laws and to this Agreement."

Treating a violation of a website's terms of service, without more, to be sufficient to constitute "intentionally access[ing] a computer without authorization or exceed[ing] authorized access" would result in transforming section 1030(a)(2)(C) into an overwhelmingly overbroad enactment that would convert a multitude of otherwise innocent Internet users into misdemeanant criminals.

One need only look to the MSTOS terms of service to see the expansive and elaborate scope of such provisions whose breach engenders the potential for criminal prosecution. Obvious examples of such breadth would include: 1) the lonely-heart who submits intentionally inaccurate data about his or her age, height and/or physical appearance, which contravenes the MSTOS prohibition against providing "information that you know is false or misleading"; 2) the student who posts candid photographs of classmates without their permission, which breaches the MSTOS provision covering "a photograph of another person that you have posted without that person's consent"; and/or 3) the exasperated parent who sends out a group message to neighborhood friends entreating them to purchase his or her daughter's girl scout cookies, which transgresses the MSTOS rule against "advertising to, or solicitation of, any Member to buy or sell any products or services through the Services." However, one need not consider hypotheticals to demonstrate the problem. In this case, Megan (who was then 13 years old) had her own profile on MySpace,

---

14. [n.28] According to the MSTOS, "If there is any dispute about or involving the Services, you agree that the dispute shall be governed by the laws of the State of California without regard to conflict of law provisions."

which was in clear violation of the MSTOS which requires that users be "14 years of age or older." No one would seriously suggest that Megan's conduct was criminal or should be subject to criminal prosecution.

Section 1030(a)(2)(C) does not set forth "clear guidelines" or "objective criteria" as to the prohibited conduct in the Internet/website or similar contexts. For instance, section 1030(a)(2)(C) is not limited to instances where the website owner contacts law enforcement to complain about an individual's unauthorized access or exceeding permitted access on the site. Nor is there any requirement that there be any actual loss or damage suffered by the website or that there be a violation of privacy interests.

In sum, if any conscious breach of a website's terms of service is held to be sufficient by itself to constitute intentionally accessing a computer without authorization or in excess of authorization, the result will be that section 1030(a)(2)(C) becomes a law "that affords too much discretion to the police and too little notice to citizens who wish to use the [Internet]."

———————

Notes

The Building Blocks of § 1030 Liability. From the reading you should be able to assemble those elements:

1. What computers are protected?

2. What does it mean to intentionally access a protected computer? For this question, there are several considerations: how is access restricted; what *mens rea* must be shown; and what does it mean to access the computer? As to the concept of "access," note that there is a split of authority: compare the discussion in *Drew*, *Allen*, and *Riley*?

3. The elements become more murky when examining the question of whether the person who accessed the protected computer was without or exceeded authorization. A clear split of authority is illustrated by *Nosal I* and *II, Shurgard Storage*, *Bell Aerospace*, *John*, *Power Ventures*, and *Drew*. What are those views and which is the better view? Another way to view those cases is to examine the person potentially prosecuted under the CFAA. Which of those persons, in your view, should be prosecuted? Why? Are they insiders or outsiders? If some are insiders, how would you distinguish among insiders for the purpose of imposing criminal liability? The dissent in *Nosal II* argued that the majority's opinion had no limiting principle and criminalized mere password sharing. Is that true? (Hint, look at the elements of each of the statute's subsections.)

4. *The Rule of Lenity and Void for Vagueness.* In *United States v. Nosal*, 676 F.3d 854 (9th Cir. 2012) (en banc) (*Nosal I*), the court relied on the Rule of Lenity to narrow the scope of the statute's reach, which the court summarized as:

> We need not decide today whether Congress *could* base criminal liability on violations of a company or website's computer use restrictions. Instead, we hold that the phrase "exceeds authorized access" in the CFAA does not

extend to violations of use restrictions. If Congress wants to incorporate misappropriation liability into the CFAA, it must speak more clearly. The rule of lenity requires "penal laws . . . to be construed strictly." "[W]hen choice has to be made between two readings of what conduct Congress has made a crime, it is appropriate, before we choose the harsher alternative, to require that Congress should have spoken in language that is clear and definite."

The rule of lenity not only ensures that citizens will have fair notice of the criminal laws, but also that Congress will have fair notice of what conduct its laws criminalize. We construe criminal statutes narrowly so that Congress will not unintentionally turn ordinary citizens into criminals. "[B]ecause of the seriousness of criminal penalties, and because criminal punishment usually represents the moral condemnation of the community, legislatures and not courts should define criminal activity." "If there is any doubt about whether Congress intended [the CFAA] to prohibit the conduct in which [Nosal] engaged, then 'we must choose the interpretation least likely to impose penalties unintended by Congress.'"

Other courts, including *Drew,* have grounded their narrowing views of the scope of the CFAA on the void-for-vagueness doctrine. What is that doctrine and what is its relationship to the Rule of Lenity?

5. *Websites.* Should there be a distinction between persons who violate a website's terms of use and those persons who circumvent technical barriers? If so, is it for Congress or courts interpreting the CFAA to make that distinction? Based on *Power Ventures,* if you were advising a client in the Ninth Circuit who was seeking to utilize access to another company's website to further its business, what advice would you provide? If you were advising a client seeking to prevent another company from utilizing its website in a manner that would make the CFAA applicable to those unwanted activities, what would you advise?

6. Can or should Congress define the concepts of without authorization or exceeds authorization more precisely? Should adding content to those terms be developed through case law? Consider the crime of trespass onto land, which is typically not defined by the governing statute. When are entries legal or not? In *Florida v. Jardines,* 569 U.S. __, 133 S. Ct. 1409 (2013), the Supreme Court held that the use of a trained drug-sniffing dog that alerted to the presence of drugs while on the front porch of a house was an illegal search. The majority distinguished between permissible entries of a curtilage and those that are not permitted by asking "whether [the homeowner] had given his leave (even implicitly) for them to do so." It grounded that distinction on the common law concept of a license:

"A license may be implied from the habits of the country". . . . We have accordingly recognized that "the knocker on the front door is treated as an invitation or license to attempt an entry, justifying ingress to the home by solicitors, hawkers and peddlers of all kinds." This implicit license typically permits the visitor to approach the home by the front path, knock promptly, wait briefly to be received, and then (absent invitation to linger longer) leave. Complying with the terms of that traditional invitation does not require fine-grained legal knowledge; it is generally managed without incident by the Nation's Girl Scouts and trick-or-treaters. Thus, a police officer not armed with a warrant may approach a home and knock, precisely because that is "no more than any private citizen might do."

But introducing a trained police dog to explore the area around the home in hopes of discovering incriminating evidence is something else. There is no customary invitation to do *that*. An invitation to engage in canine forensic investigation assuredly does not inhere in the very act of hanging a knocker. To find a visitor knocking on the door is routine (even if sometimes unwelcome); to spot that same visitor exploring the front path with a metal detector, or marching his bloodhound into the garden before saying hello and asking permission, would inspire most of us to—well, call the police. The scope of a license—express or implied—is limited not only to a particular area but also to a specific purpose. Consent at a traffic stop to an officer's checking out an anonymous tip that there is a body in the trunk does not permit the officer to rummage through the trunk for narcotics. Here, the background social norms that invite a visitor to the front door do not invite him there to conduct a search.

Obviously, a burglar is not permitted entry at all—as would an outside hacker seeking access to a computer. A police officer can enter the curtilage based on an implied invitation, but that officer exceeds his authorized permission when he brings a drug dog to search. Are there similar "background social norms" that can be employed in the context of the CFAA that can or should be used to determine when a computer user is authorized or not or exceeds authorization?

§ 16.3 Specific Sub-Sections of § 1030

The crimes detailed in the various subsections of 18 U.S.C. § 1030(a) build on the critical concepts just discussed, adding *actus rea* and *mens rea* requirements to address specific forms of criminal activity. For each of the following subsections, the readings detail what those additional elements are.

1. Obtaining Confidential Information.

Section 1030(a)(2) prohibits obtaining, without authorization, information from financial institutions, the United States, or private computers that are used in interstate commerce. It provides:

(a) Whoever—

(2) intentionally accesses a computer without authorization or exceeds authorized access, and thereby obtains—

(A) information contained in a financial record of a financial institution, or of a card issuer as defined in section 1602(n) of title 15, or contained in a file of a consumer reporting agency on a consumer, as such terms are defined in the Fair Credit Reporting Act (15 U.S.C. 1681 et seq.);

(B) information from any department or agency of the United States; or

(C) information from any protected computer[.]

Summary of the elements of (a)(2):

- intentional access
- without authorization or exceeds authorized access
- must obtain information but the statute does not define "obtains" or "information"
  - Senate Report No. 104-357, at 7 (1996) states that "the term 'obtaining information' includes merely reading it."
  - "Obtain[ing] information from a computer" has been described as "'includ[ing] mere observation of the data. Actual aspiration . . . need not be proved in order to establish a violation.'" Thus, [this] element is satisfied whenever a person using a computer contacts an Internet website and reads any response from that site.[15]
- information must be from a computer and fit within one of the three categories listed in subsections (A), (B), or (C).

OBTAINING INFORMATION: CELL PHONES VS. WEB SITES

Brenda Czech v. Wall Street on Demand, Inc.

674 F. Supp. 2d 1102 (D. Minn. 2009)

DONOVAN W. FRANK, DISTRICT JUDGE.

[A cell phone owner brought a putative class action against the sender of unwanted text messages, asserting, among other claims, various violations of the CFAA. The defendant (WSOD) provided financial information via text messaging to wireless devices, such as cell phones. WSOD allegedly did not track recycled or cancelled telephone numbers and, as a result, text messages were sometimes sent to persons who had not subscribed to the WSOD service.]

To plead an "information claim" under the CFAA, Czech must first satisfactorily allege facts that WSOD "intentionally accesse[d]" Czech's cell phone "without authorization or" by exceeding "authorized access, and thereby obtain[ed] . . . information from" the cell phone. The Court will first address the element that WSOD obtained information from the cell phone.

---

15. *United States v. Lori Drew*, 259 F.R.D. 449 (C.D. Cal. 2009).

Czech, [quoting the 1986 Senate Report asserted that] "[t]he threshold for alleging that a person 'obtained information' under CFAA is minimal" because the legislative history clarifies that the obtaining of information for purposes of the CFAA "'includes mere observation of the data'" and does not require "'physically removing the data from its original location or transcribing the data.'"

But even assuming the CFAA thus applies to those who "merely read" information, Czech's Second Amended Complaint still fails to meet the standard for pleading an "information claim" under the CFAA based on the receipt of unwanted text messages. In support of her contention that merely viewing information satisfies the requirement under the CFAA that a violator obtain information, Czech relies on *United States v. Drew*, 259 F.R.D. 449 (C.D.Cal.2009), to draw an analogy between websites and text messages. In *Drew*, the court "noted that the latter two elements of the section 1030(a)(2)(C) crime"—that is, accessing a computer involved in interstate commerce and obtaining information by unauthorized access—"will always be met when an individual using a computer contacts or communicates with an Internet website."

But the Court notes that while the CFAA apparently applies to a broad range of "data processing devices," there is a fundamental difference between viewing websites and communicating with wireless devices such as cell phones by sending text messages. A website, by definition, offers information (text, data, images) to anyone wishing and able to view it, whereas a cell phone (or other comparable wireless device) in its reception mode only receives incoming audio calls or text messages. Thus while anyone accessing a website will "obtain information" in the sense of viewing the text, data, or images available on that website, there is no plausible basis to conclude that the sender of a text message to a cell phone will likewise "obtain information," even by merely viewing or reading it, from the cell phone to which it sent the text message. Accordingly, even accepting Czech's argument that the CFAA extends to merely viewing information, a CFAA action confined to cell phones and comparable wireless devices simply does not present the possibility of viewing information as would a CFAA action regarding websites such as that at issue in *Drew*.

In sum, the Court rejects Czech's contention that her allegations—that when sending text messages WSOD obtained information from her cell phone by merely viewing such information as would one who is viewing a website—state a claim for violating subsection 1030(a)(2)(C).

Czech argues that the transmission of a text message results in the sender receiving a response "that the wireless number is active, the general geographic area where the user is located (via the [recipient's area code]), and that future text messages can be sent to that active wireless number." Czech further contends that "[k]nowing that a particular wireless number is active" and the associated area code "allows the sender . . . to sell, license, or otherwise market that number to others," and allows senders "to evade restrictions" imposed by Do Not Call lists and other comparable opt-out mechanisms. Finally, she claims that WSOD also obtained information by "obtaining a portion of the finite permanent or hard drive memory storage capacity of the phone."

The Court previously rejected as insufficient allegations that WSOD obtained information either by "'obtaining operation and storage capacity, bandwidth, and memory from their wireless devices,'" or "by receiving a 'receipt or delivery notification' from the wireless devices after the text messages were sent." The relevant allegations of the Second Amended Complaint fail to plausibly allege that the sender of a text message thereby obtains information from the recipient's cell phone.

Where the "computer" at issue under the CFAA is a cell phone or other comparable wireless device, rather than what is commonly known as a personal computer used for word processing, databases, etc., simply sending a text message to such a cell phone does not involve anything comparable to gaining unauthorized access to another's personal computer or computer network and then viewing (much less copying or removing) a word processing document or a database file. In short, sending a text message is essentially a one-way communication that does not implicate the obtaining of information from the recipient's cell phone, as this Court understands the intent of Congress.[n.15][16]

2. Trespassing into a Government Computer 18 U.S.C. § 1030(a)(3).

Section 1030(a)(3) prohibits "trespasses" by outsiders into federal government computers. It provides:

> (a) Whoever—
>
> (3) intentionally, without authorization to access any nonpublic computer of a department or agency of the United States, accesses such a computer of that department or agency that is exclusively for the use of the Government of the United States or, in the case of a computer not exclusively for such use, is used by or for the Government of the United States and such conduct affects that use by or for the Government of the United States.

Summarized, the elements are:

- intentional access
- without authorization
- either a nonpublic computer of the United States or affects the United States' use of a computer that it does not exclusively use

"Nonpublic" includes most government computers, but not Internet servers that, by design, offer services to members of the general public. For

---

16. [n.15] There are no allegations that WSOD obtained, for example, credit card numbers or passwords from Czech's cell phone.

example, a government agency's database server is probably nonpublic, while the same agency's web servers and domain name servers are "public."

The computer must be "of"—meaning owned or controlled by—a department or agency of the United States.

The computer must also be either exclusively for the use of the United States, or at least used "by or for" the Government of the United States in some capacity. For example, if the United States has obtained an account on a private company's server, that server is used "by" the United States even though it is not owned by the United States.

Demonstrating that the attacked computer is affected by an intrusion should be simple. Almost any network intrusion will affect the government's use of its computers because any intrusion potentially affects the confidentiality and integrity of the government's network and often requires substantial measures to reconstitute the network.[17]

---

3. Accessing to Defraud and Obtain Value 18 U.S.C. § 1030(a)(4).

Section 1030(a)(4) provides:

(a) Whoever—

(4) knowingly and with intent to defraud, accesses a protected computer without authorization, or exceeds authorized access, and by means of such conduct furthers the intended fraud and obtains anything of value, unless the object of the fraud and the thing obtained consists only of the use of the computer and the value of such use is not more than $5,000 in any 1-year period[.]

Summarized, the elements are:

- knowing access

- without or in excess of authorization

- with intent to defraud

  The phrase "knowingly and with intent to defraud" is not defined by section 1030. Very little case law under section 1030 exists as to its meaning, leaving open the question of how broadly a court will interpret the phrase.[18]

- access must further the intended fraud

---

17. Computer Crime and Intellectual Property Section, Criminal Division, U.S. Dep't of Justice, Prosecuting Computer Crimes 20–21 (2007).

18. Computer Crime and Intellectual Property Section, Criminal Division, U.S. Dep't of Justice, Prosecuting Computer Crimes 23 (2007).

For example:

- This element is met if a defendant alters or deletes records on a computer, and then receives something of value from an individual who relied on the accuracy of those altered or deleted records. In *United States v. Butler*, 16 Fed. Appx. 99 (4th Cir. 2001) (unpublished disposition), the defendant altered a credit reporting agency's records to improve the credit ratings of his coconspirators, who then used their improved credit rating to make purchases. In *United States v. Sadolsky*, 234 F.3d 938 (6th Cir. 2000), the defendant used his employer's computer to credit amounts for returned merchandise to his personal credit card.

- This element is met if a defendant obtains information from a computer, and then later uses that information to commit fraud. For example, in *United States v. Lindsley*, 254 F.3d 71 (5th Cir. 2001) (unpublished), the defendant accessed a telephone company's computer without authorization, obtained calling card numbers, and then used those calling card numbers to make free long-distance telephone calls.

- This element is met if a defendant uses a computer to produce falsified documents which are later used to defraud. For example, in *United States v. Bae*, 250 F.3d 774 (D.C. Cir. 2001), the defendant used a lottery terminal to produce back-dated tickets with winning numbers, and then turned those tickets in to collect lottery prizes.[19]

- obtains anything of value

This element is easily met if the defendant obtained money, cash, or a good or service with measurable value. Two more difficult cases arise when the defendant obtains only the use of a computer and when the defendant obtains only information.

Use of the computer as a thing of value

The statute recognizes that the use of a computer can constitute a thing of value, but this element is satisfied only if the value of such use is greater than $5,000 in any one-year period.

This condition will be met only in rare cases. At the time the statute was written, it was common for owners of top-of-the-line supercomputers to rent the right to run programs on their computer by the hour. In 1986, for example, an hour of time on a Cray X-MP/48 supercomputer reportedly cost $1,000. Conceivably, repeated and sustained use of a very expensive modern computer could reach the statutory threshold within one year.

Data or information as a thing of value

Aside from the "computer use" exception, subsection (a)(4) has no minimum dollar amount. Still, the legislative history suggests that some computer data

---

19. *Id.* at 25.

or information, alone, is not valuable enough to qualify. See S. Rep. 99-432, at 9, reprinted in 1986 U.S.C.C.A.N. 2479, 2487) ("In intentionally trespassing into someone else's computer files, the offender obtains at the very least information as to how to break into that computer system. If that is all he obtains, the offense should properly be treated as a simple trespass."). In other words, if all that is obtained are the results of port scans, or the names and IP addresses of other servers, it may not count as something of value.[20]

"ANYTHING OF VALUE"

United States v. Richard W. Czubinski

106 F.3d 1069 (1st Cir. 1997)

TORRUELLA, CHIEF JUDGE.

Czubinski appeals his jury conviction on . . . four counts of computer fraud, 18 U.S.C. § 1030(a)(4). We reverse the conviction on the . . . ground that the trial evidence mustered by the government was insufficient to support a guilty verdict, and hold that the defendant's motion for judgment of acquittal should have been granted on all counts. Unauthorized browsing of taxpayer files, although certainly inappropriate conduct, cannot, without more, sustain this federal felony conviction.

Czubinski was employed as a Contact Representative in the Boston office of the Taxpayer Services Division of the Internal Revenue Service. To perform his official duties, which mainly involved answering questions from taxpayers regarding their returns, Czubinski routinely accessed information from one of the IRS's computer systems known as the Integrated Data Retrieval System ("IDRS"). Using a valid password given to Contact Representatives, certain search codes, and taxpayer social security numbers, Czubinski was able to retrieve, to his terminal screen in Boston, income tax return information regarding virtually any taxpayer-information that is permanently stored in the IDRS "master file" located in Martinsburg, West Virginia. In the period of Czubinski's employ, IRS rules plainly stated that employees with passwords and access codes were not permitted to access files on IDRS outside of the course of their official duties.

In 1992, Czubinski carried out numerous unauthorized searches of IDRS files. He knowingly disregarded IRS rules by looking at confidential information obtained by performing computer searches that were outside of the scope of his duties as a Contact Representative, including, but not limited to, the searches listed in the indictment. For example, Czubinski accessed information regarding: the tax returns of two individuals involved in the David Duke presidential campaign; the joint tax return of an assistant district attorney (who had been prosecuting Czubinski's father on an unrelated felony offense) and his wife; the tax return of Boston

---

20. *Id.* at 26.

City Counselor Jim Kelly's Campaign Committee (Kelly had defeated Czubinski in the previous election for the Counselor seat for District 2); the tax return of one of his brothers' instructors; the joint tax return of a Boston Housing Authority police officer, who was involved in a community organization with one of Czubinski's brothers, and the officer's wife; and the tax return of a woman Czubinski had dated a few times. Czubinski also accessed the files of various other social acquaintances by performing unauthorized searches.

Nothing in the record indicates that Czubinski did anything more than knowingly disregard IRS rules by observing the confidential information he accessed. No evidence suggests, nor does the government contend, that Czubinski disclosed the confidential information he accessed to any third parties. The government's only evidence demonstrating any intent to use the confidential information for nefarious ends was the trial testimony of William A. Murray, an acquaintance of Czubinski who briefly participated in Czubinski's local Invisible Knights of the Ku Klux Klan Chapter and worked with him on the David Duke campaign. Murray testified that Czubinski had once stated at a social gathering in "early 1992" that "he intended to use some of that information to build dossiers on people" involved in "the white supremacist movement." There is, however, no evidence that Czubinski created dossiers, took steps toward making dossiers (such as by printing out or recording the information he browsed), or shared any of the information he accessed in the years following the single comment to Murray. No other witness testified to having any knowledge of Czubinski's alleged intent to create "dossiers" on KKK members.

We must assume, on this appeal, that Czubinski did indeed make such a comment. Nevertheless, the fact that during the months following this remark — that is, during the period in which Czubinski made his unauthorized searches — he did not create dossiers (there was no evidence that he created dossiers either during or after the period of his unauthorized searches); given the fact that he did not even take steps toward creating dossiers, such as recording or printing out the information; given the fact that no other person testifying as to Czubinski's involvement in white supremacist organizations had any knowledge of Czubinski's alleged intent to create dossiers or use confidential information; and given the fact that not a single piece of evidence suggests that Czubinski ever shared taxpayer information with others, no rational jury could have found beyond a reasonable doubt that, when Czubinski was browsing taxpayer files, he was doing so in furtherance of a scheme to use the information he browsed for private purposes, be they nefarious or otherwise. In addition, there was no evidence that Czubinski disclosed, or used to his advantage, any information regarding political opponents or regarding the person prosecuting his father.

On appeal [Czubinski] argues that he did not obtain "anything of value." We agree, finding that his searches of taxpayer return information did not satisfy the statutory requirement that he obtain "anything of value." The value of information is relative to one's needs and objectives; here, the government had to show that the information was valuable to Czubinski in light of a fraudulent scheme. The government failed, however, to prove that Czubinski intended anything more than to satisfy idle curiosity.

The plain language of section 1030(a)(4) emphasizes that more than mere unauthorized use is required: the "thing obtained" may not merely be the unauthorized use. It is the showing of some additional end—to which the unauthorized access is a means—that is lacking here. The evidence did not show that Czubinski's end was anything more than to satisfy his curiosity by viewing information about friends, acquaintances, and political rivals. No evidence suggests that he printed out, recorded, or used the information he browsed. No rational jury could conclude beyond a reasonable doubt that Czubinski intended to use or disclose that information, and merely viewing information cannot be deemed the same as obtaining something of value for the purposes of this statute.[n.15][21]

The legislative history further supports our reading of the term "anything of value." Here, a Senate co-sponsor's comments suggest that Congress intended section 1030(a)(4) to punish attempts to steal valuable data, and did not wish to punish mere unauthorized access:

> The acts of fraud we are addressing in proposed section 1030(a)(4) are essentially thefts in which someone uses a federal interest computer to wrongly obtain something of value from another. . . . Proposed section 1030(a)(4) is intended to reflect the distinction between the theft of information, a felony, and mere unauthorized access, a misdemeanor.

132 Cong. Rec. 7128, 7129, 99th Cong., 2d. Sess. (1986). The Senate Committee Report further underscores the fact that this section should apply to those who steal information through unauthorized access as part of an illegal scheme:

> The Committee remains convinced that there must be a clear distinction between computer theft, punishable as a felony [under section 1030(a)(4)], and computer trespass, punishable in the first instance as a misdemeanor [under a different provision]. The element in the new paragraph (a)(4), requiring a showing of an intent to defraud, is meant to preserve that distinction, as is the requirement that the property wrongfully obtained via computer furthers the intended fraud.

S. Rep. No. 432, 99th Cong., 2d Sess., *reprinted in* 1986 U.S.C.C.A.N. 2479, 2488. We find that Czubinski has not obtained valuable information in furtherance of a fraudulent scheme for the purposes of section 1030(a)(4).

---

21. [n.15] The district court found that the indictment sufficiently alleged that the confidential taxpayer information was itself a "thing of value" to Czubinski, given his ends. The indictment, of course, alleged specific uses for the information, such as creating dossiers on KKK members, that were not proven at trial. In light of the trial evidence—which, as we have said, indicates that there was no recording, disclosure or further use of the confidential information—we find that Czubinski did not obtain "anything of value" through his unauthorized searches.

4. Damaging a Computer or Information 18 U.S.C. § 1030(a)(5)

Section (a)(5) is an anti-hacking/anti-cracking provision and creates categories of offenses, based on different *actus rea* and *mens rea* requirements.

> Criminals can cause harm to computers in a wide variety of ways. For example, an intruder who gains unauthorized access to a computer can send commands that delete files or shut the computer down. Alternatively, intruders can initiate a "denial of service attack" that floods the victim computer with useless information and prevents legitimate users from accessing it. In a similar way, a virus or worm can use up all of the available communications bandwidth on a corporate network, making it unavailable to employees. In addition, when a virus or worm penetrates a computer's security, it can delete files, crash the computer, install malicious software, or do other things that impair the computer's integrity. Prosecutors can use section 1030(a)(5) to charge all of these different kinds of acts.

> Section 1030(a)(5) criminalizes a variety of actions that cause computer systems to fail to operate as their owners would like them to operate. Damaging a computer can have far-reaching effects. For example, a business may not be able to operate if its computer system stops functioning or it may lose sales if it cannot retrieve the data in a database containing customer information. Similarly, if a computer that operates the phone system used by police and fire fighters stops functioning, people could be injured or die as a result of not receiving emergency services. Such damage to a computer can occur following a successful intrusion, but it may also occur in ways that do not involve the unauthorized access of a computer system.[22]

Section (a)(5) provides:

> (a) Whoever—

> (5)(A) knowingly causes the transmission of a program, information, code, or command, and as a result of such conduct, intentionally causes damage without authorization, to a protected computer;

> (B) intentionally accesses a protected computer without authorization, and as a result of such conduct, recklessly causes damage; or

> (C) intentionally accesses a protected computer without authorization, and as a result of such conduct, causes damage and loss.

Each of these three provisions creates a separate crime, with distinct elements.

---

22. Computer Crime and Intellectual Property Section, Criminal Division, U.S. Dep't of Justice, Prosecuting Computer Crimes 29–32 (2007).

Summary of elements of (5)(A):

- knowingly causes the transmission of a program, information, code, or command
- as a result of such conduct, intentionally causes damage without authorization, to a protected computer

Summary of elements of (5)(B):

- intentional access to a protected computer without authorization
- as a result of such conduct, recklessly causes damage

Summary of elements of (5)(C):

- intentional access to a protected computer without authorization
- as a result of such conduct, causes damage and loss

Subsections (B) and (C) require that the defendant intentionally "access" a computer without authorization but are distinguished by the type of harm caused and the mental state that must be shown when causing that harm. In contrast, subsection (A) requires proof of the knowing transmission of something to damage a computer without authorization. The government does not need to prove "access." For example, most worms and Trojans spread though self-replication and there is no need to show intentional access to the affected systems.

All three subsections require "damage" but only subsection (C) also requires "loss." The statute, under section 1030(e), defines those terms:

> (8) the term "damage" means any impairment to the integrity or availability of data, a program, a system, or information[.]

> (11) the term "loss" means any reasonable cost to any victim, including the cost of responding to an offense, conducting a damage assessment, and restoring the data, program, system, or information to its condition prior to the offense, and any revenue lost, cost incurred, or other consequential damages incurred because of interruption of service[.]

"Thus, while 'damage' pertains to a physical or operational impairment of the device, 'loss' concerns any pecuniary cost incurred by the device's owner."[23]

> First, "damage" occurs when an act impairs the "integrity" of data, a program, a system, or information. This part of the definition would apply, for example, where an act causes data or information to be deleted or changed, such as where an intruder accesses a computer system and deletes log files or changes entries in a bank database.

> Similarly, "damage" occurs when an intruder changes the way a computer is instructed to operate. For example, installing keylogger software on a home computer can constitute damage. Damage also occurs if an intruder alters the security software of a victim computer so that it fails to detect

---

23. Czech v. Wall Street on Demand, Inc., 674 F. Supp. 2d 1102, 1107–08 (D. Minn. 2009).

computer trespassers. For example, in United States v. Middleton, part of the damage consisted of a user increasing his permissions on a computer system without authorization. United States v. Middleton, 231 F.3d 1207, 1213–14 (9th Cir. 2000).

In addition to the impairment of the integrity of information or computer systems, the definition of damage also includes acts that simply make information or computers "unavailable." Intruders have devised ways to consume all of a computer's computational resources, effectively making it impossible for authorized users to make use of the computer even though none of the data or software has been modified. Similarly, a "denial of service attack" floods a computer's Internet connection with junk data, preventing legitimate users from sending or receiving any communications with that computer.

- In the computer network world, an intrusion—even a fairly noticeable one—can amount to a kind of trespass that causes no readily discoverable impairment to the computers intruded upon or the data accessed. Even so, such "trespass intrusions" often require that substantial time and attention be devoted to responding to them. In the wake of seemingly minor intrusions, the entire computer system is often audited, for instance, to ensure that viruses, back-doors, or other harmful codes have not been left behind or that data has not been altered or copied. Even adding false information to a computer can impair its integrity. In addition, holes exploited by the intruder are sometimes patched, and the network generally is resecured through a rigorous and time-consuming technical effort. This process can be costly and time-consuming.[24]

- mental state of the defendant when causing damage / type of harm caused

Each subsection requires a different *mens rea* that must be shown to establish liability for the damage caused: intentional under subsection (A); reckless under subsection (B); and strict liability under subsection (C). Consistent with traditional criminal law theories, the punishment under the statute is more severe for the more culpable mental states. *See* 18 U.S.C. § 1030(c)(4)(A). The punishment also varies in part based on the type of harm caused. For example, section 1030(C)(4)(A)(i) lists a series of circumstances that serve to enhance the penalty under subsection (a)(5)(B). In general, those circumstances are:

I. loss to 1 or more persons during any 1-year period (and, for purposes of an investigation, prosecution, or other proceeding brought by the United States only, loss resulting from a related course of conduct

---

24. Computer Crime and Intellectual Property Section, Criminal Division, U.S. Dep't of Justice, Prosecuting Computer Crimes 35–36 (2007).

affecting 1 or more other protected computers) aggregating at least $5,000 in value;

II. the modification or impairment, or potential modification or impairment, of the medical examination, diagnosis, treatment, or care of 1 or more individuals;

III. physical injury to any person;

IV. a threat to public health or safety;

V. damage affecting a computer used by or for an entity of the United States Government in furtherance of the administration of justice, national defense, or national security; or

VI. damage affecting 10 or more protected computers during any 1-year period[.]

The Classic Example of a Hacker Causing Damage
United States v. Robert Tappan Morris
928 F.2d 504 (2d Cir. 1991)

Jon O. Newman, Circuit Judge:

18 U.S.C. § 1030(a)(5)(A) (1988) punishes anyone who intentionally accesses without authorization a category of computers known as "[f]ederal interest computers" and damages or prevents authorized use of information in such computers, causing loss of $1,000 or more.

Morris released into INTERNET, a national computer network, a computer program known as a "worm"[n.1][25] that spread and multiplied, eventually causing computers at various educational institutions and military sites to "crash" or cease functioning.

We conclude that section 1030(a)(5)(A) does not require the Government to demonstrate that the defendant intentionally prevented authorized use and thereby caused loss. We also find that there was sufficient evidence for the jury to conclude that Morris acted "without authorization" within the meaning of section 1030(a)(5)(A). We therefore affirm.

In the fall of 1988, Morris was a first-year graduate student in Cornell University's computer science Ph.D. program. Through undergraduate work at Harvard and in various jobs he had acquired significant computer experience and expertise. When Morris entered Cornell, he was given an account on the computer at the Computer Science Division. This account gave him explicit authorization to use computers at

---

25. [n.1] A "worm" is a program that travels from one computer to another but does not attach itself to the operating system of the computer it "infects." It differs from a "virus," which is also a migrating program, but one that attaches itself to the operating system of any computer it enters and can infect any other computer that uses files from the infected computer.

Cornell. Morris engaged in various discussions with fellow graduate students about the security of computer networks and his ability to penetrate it.

In October 1988, Morris began work on a computer program, later known as the INTERNET "worm" or "virus." The goal of this program was to demonstrate the inadequacies of current security measures on computer networks by exploiting the security defects that Morris had discovered. The tactic he selected was release of a worm into network computers. Morris designed the program to spread across a national network of computers after being inserted at one computer location connected to the network. Morris released the worm into INTERNET, which is a group of national networks that connect university, governmental, and military computers around the country. The network permits communication and transfer of information between computers on the network.

Morris sought to program the INTERNET worm to spread widely without drawing attention to itself. The worm was supposed to occupy little computer operation time, and thus not interfere with normal use of the computers. Morris programmed the worm to make it difficult to detect and read, so that other programmers would not be able to "kill" the worm easily.

Morris also wanted to ensure that the worm did not copy itself onto a computer that already had a copy. Multiple copies of the worm on a computer would make the worm easier to detect and would bog down the system and ultimately cause the computer to crash. Therefore, Morris designed the worm to "ask" each computer whether it already had a copy of the worm. If it responded "no," then the worm would copy onto the computer; if it responded "yes," the worm would not duplicate. However, Morris was concerned that other programmers could kill the worm by programming their own computers to falsely respond "yes" to the question. To circumvent this protection, Morris programmed the worm to duplicate itself every seventh time it received a "yes" response. As it turned out, Morris underestimated the number of times a computer would be asked the question, and his one-out-of-seven ratio resulted in far more copying than he had anticipated. The worm was also designed so that it would be killed when a computer was shut down, an event that typically occurs once every week or two. This would have prevented the worm from accumulating on one computer, had Morris correctly estimated the likely rate of reinfection.

Morris identified four ways in which the worm could break into computers on the network:

(1) through a "hole" or "bug" (an error) in SEND MAIL, a computer program that transfers and receives electronic mail on a computer;

(2) through a bug in the "finger demon" program, a program that permits a person to obtain limited information about the users of another computer;

(3) through the "trusted hosts" feature, which permits a user with certain privileges on one computer to have equivalent privileges on another computer without using a password; and

(4) through a program of password guessing, whereby various combinations of letters are tried out in rapid sequence in the hope that one will be an authorized user's password, which is entered to permit whatever level of activity that user is authorized to perform.

On November 2, 1988, Morris released the worm from a computer at the Massachusetts Institute of Technology. MIT was selected to disguise the fact that the worm came from Morris at Cornell. Morris soon discovered that the worm was replicating and reinfecting machines at a much faster rate than he had anticipated. Ultimately, many machines at locations around the country either crashed or became "catatonic." When Morris realized what was happening, he contacted a friend at Harvard to discuss a solution. Eventually, they sent an anonymous message from Harvard over the network, instructing programmers how to kill the worm and prevent reinfection. However, because the network route was clogged, this message did not get through until it was too late. Computers were affected at numerous installations, including leading universities, military sites, and medical research facilities. The estimated cost of dealing with the worm at each installation ranged from $200 to more than $53,000.

Section 1030(a)(5)(A), covers anyone who

(5) *intentionally accesses* a Federal interest computer without authorization, *and* by means of one or more instances of such conduct alters, damages, or destroys information in any such Federal interest computer, or *prevents authorized use* of any such computer or information, *and thereby*

(A) *causes loss* to one or more others of a value aggregating $1,000 or more during any one year period.

Morris argues that the Government had to prove not only that he intended the unauthorized access of a federal interest computer, but also that he intended to prevent others from using it, and thus cause a loss. The adverb "intentionally," he contends, modifies both verb phrases of the section. The Government urges that since punctuation sets the "accesses" phrase off from the subsequent "damages" phrase, the provision unambiguously shows that "intentionally" modifies only "accesses." Absent textual ambiguity, the Government asserts that recourse to legislative history is not appropriate.

With some statutes, punctuation has been relied upon to indicate that a phrase set off by commas is independent of the language that followed. However, we have been advised that punctuation is not necessarily decisive in construing statutes, and with many statutes, a mental state adverb adjacent to initial words has been applied to phrases or clauses appearing later in the statute without regard to the punctuation or structure of the statute. In the present case, we do not believe the comma after "authorization" renders the text so clear as to preclude review of the legislative history.

Despite some isolated language in the legislative history that arguably suggests a scienter component for the "damages" phrase of section 1030(a)(5)(A), the wording, structure, and purpose of the subsection, examined in comparison with its departure from the format of its predecessor provision persuade us that the "intentionally" standard applies only to the "accesses" phrase of section 1030(a)(5)(A), and not to its "damages" phrase.

The evidence permitted the jury to conclude that Morris's use of the SEND MAIL and finger demon features constituted access without authorization. While a case might arise where the use of SEND MAIL or finger demon falls within a nebulous area in which the line between accessing without authorization and exceeding authorized access may not be clear, Morris's conduct here falls well within the area of unauthorized access. Morris did not use either of those features in any way related to their intended function. He did not send or read mail nor discover information about other users; instead he found holes in both programs that permitted him a special and unauthorized access route into other computers.

Moreover, the jury verdict need not be upheld solely on Morris's use of SEND MAIL and finger demon. As the District Court noted, in denying Morris' motion for acquittal,

> Although the evidence may have shown that defendant's initial insertion of the worm simply exceeded his authorized access, the evidence also demonstrated that the worm was designed to spread to other computers at which he had no account and no authority, express or implied, to unleash the worm program. Moreover, there was also evidence that the worm was designed to gain access to computers at which he had no account by guessing their passwords. Accordingly, the evidence did support the jury's conclusion that defendant accessed without authority as opposed to merely exceeding the scope of his authority.

In light of the reasonable conclusions that the jury could draw from Morris's use of SEND MAIL and finger demon, and from his use of the trusted hosts feature and password guessing, his challenge to the sufficiency of the evidence fails.

———————

Notes

Under what section of the current version of the statute would Morris be guilty?

———————

"TRANSMISSION"

International Airport Centers v. Jacob Citrin

440 F.3d 418 (7th Cir. 2006)

POSNER, CIRCUIT JUDGE.

This appeal from the dismissal of the plaintiffs' suit for failure to state a claim mainly requires us to interpret the word "transmission" in a key provision of the

Computer Fraud and Abuse Act. The complaint alleges the following facts, which for purposes of deciding the appeal we must take as true. The defendant, Citrin, was employed by the plaintiffs-affiliated companies engaged in the real estate business that we'll treat as one to simplify the opinion, and call "IAC"—to identify properties that IAC might want to acquire, and to assist in any ensuing acquisition. IAC lent Citrin a laptop to use to record data that he collected in the course of his work in identifying potential acquisition targets.

Citrin decided to quit IAC and go into business for himself, in breach of his employment contract. Before returning the laptop to IAC, he deleted all the data in it—not only the data that he had collected but also data that would have revealed to IAC improper conduct in which he had engaged before he decided to quit. Ordinarily, pressing the "delete" key on a computer (or using a mouse click to delete) does not affect the data sought to be deleted; it merely removes the index entry and pointers to the data file so that the file appears no longer to be there, and the space allocated to that file is made available for future write commands. Such "deleted" files are easily recoverable. But Citrin loaded into the laptop a secure-erasure program, designed, by writing over the deleted files, to prevent their recovery. IAC had no copies of the files that Citrin erased.

The provision of the Computer Fraud and Abuse Act on which IAC relies provides that whoever "knowingly causes the transmission of a program, information, code, or command, and as a result of such conduct, intentionally causes damage without authorization, to a protected computer [a defined term that includes the laptop that Citrin used]," violates the Act. 18 U.S.C. § 1030(a)(5)(A)(i). Citrin argues that merely erasing a file from a computer is not a "transmission." Pressing a delete or erase key in fact transmits a command, but it might be stretching the statute too far (especially since it provides criminal as well as civil sanctions for its violation) to consider any typing on a computer keyboard to be a form of "transmission" just because it transmits a command to the computer.

There is more here, however: the transmission of the secure-erasure program to the computer. We do not know whether the program was downloaded from the Internet or copied from a floppy disk (or the equivalent of a floppy disk, such as a CD) inserted into a disk drive that was either inside the computer or attached to it by a wire. Oddly, the complaint doesn't say; maybe IAC doesn't know—maybe all it knows is that when it got the computer back, the files in it had been erased. But we don't see what difference the precise mode of transmission can make. In either the Internet download or the disk insertion, a program intended to cause damage (not to the physical computer, of course, but to its files—but "damage" includes "any impairment to the integrity or availability of data, a program, a system, or information," 18 U.S.C. § 1030(e)(8)) is transmitted to the computer electronically. The only difference, so far as the mechanics of transmission are concerned, is that the disk is inserted manually before the program on it is transmitted electronically to the computer. The difference vanishes if the disk drive into which the disk is inserted is an external drive, connected to the computer by a wire, just as the computer is connected to the Internet by a telephone cable or a broadband cable or wirelessly.

There is the following contextual difference between the two modes of transmission, however: transmission via disk requires that the malefactor have physical access to the computer. By using the Internet, Citrin might have erased the laptop's files from afar by transmitting a virus. Such long-distance attacks can be more difficult to detect and thus to deter or punish than ones that can have been made only by someone with physical access, usually an employee. The inside attack, however, while easier to detect may also be easier to accomplish. Congress was concerned with both types of attack: attacks by virus and worm writers, on the one hand, which come mainly from the outside, and attacks by disgruntled programmers who decide to trash the employer's data system on the way out (or threaten to do so in order to extort payments), on the other. If the statute is to reach the disgruntled programmer, which Congress intended by providing that whoever "*intentionally accesses* a protected computer without authorization, and as a result of such conduct, recklessly causes damage" violates the Act, 18 U.S.C. § 1030(a)(5)(A)(ii), it can't make any difference that the destructive program comes on a physical medium, such as a floppy disk or CD.

"Intentionally Cause Damage"

United States v. Allan Carlson

209 Fed. Appx. 181, 2006 U.S. App. LEXIS 31740 (3d Cir. Dec. 22, 2006)

Irenas, Senior District Judge.

Prior to his arrest and conviction, Carlson was an avid Philadelphia Phillies fan living in California. He became savvy with internet use and technology in 1999, and in 2000 began posting messages on online bulletin boards devoted to the Philadelphia Phillies as a way to communicate with other Phillies fans.

Beginning in 2001, Carlson engaged in two types of e-mail activities that caused damage to other internet users: "direct attack" e-mailing, in which Carlson sent thousands of e-mails to one particular e-mail address,[n.3][26] and "indirect attack" e-mailing, where he sent one e-mail to many e-mail addresses.[n.4][27]

---

26. [n.3] The Government referred to such tactics as "direct attacks" on individual e-mail users, as the user's e-mail inbox would immediately flood with e-mails sent by Carlson through a third party's IP address.

27. [n.4] The Government referred to this as an "indirect attack," in that it did not flood any one e-mail user's account immediately, but rather would flood the sender's e-mail address when e-mails sent to invalid addresses were bounced back to the sender. Because Carlson sent e-mails from addresses of other internet users, e-mails would be bounced back to those inboxes, rather than the inbox of Carlson.

In employing the direct attack method, Carlson sent thousands of e-mails mainly to a few e-mail addresses at the Philadelphia Phillies. Although the "from" field indicated that the e-mails were sent from various e-mail addresses not his own,[n.5][28] such as the FBI and the Philadelphia Phillies, they were not sent from those individuals and entities, but rather by Carlson using the Internet Protocol addresses of other computers. Carlson claims that he sent these e-mails in an attempt to inform journalists and Phillies management about issues with the management of the Phillies that he considered problematic, and to start conversations among other internet users concerning such problems. The evidence produced at trial showed that while some e-mails concerned the Phillies, others did not.

Examples of Carlson's direct attacks are as follows. On November 7, 2001, Carlson sent 1,168 e-mails entitled "The Mariner's Didn't Trade A-Rod" from "*Special Prosecutor@ fbi. gov*," an e-mail address belonging to a Canadian internet user, to six writers at Philadelphia Newspapers, Inc. ("PNI"). On November 11, 2001, Carlson sent over 5,000 e-mails entitled "Sign JASON GIAMBI" to one address at the Phillies. On March 12, Carlson sent 1,800 e-mails to one address at the Phillies, and another 1,800 e-mails to another Phillies' address. On March 14, 2002, Carlson sent an e-mail entitled "The Color of Crime" about raced-based crimes to 5,514 employees of PNI. The e-mails appeared to be from either Lillian Swanson, Ombudsman of the Philadelphia Inquirer, or Walker Lundy, an editor of the Inquirer.

When employing the indirect attack method, Carlson would send spam e-mails from spoofed accounts to thousands of people whose addresses he collected primarily by using computer software.[n.6][29] For example, On November 16, 2001, Carlson used the e-mail address of Greg Dubrow, a man with whom he had disagreements in conversations on an internet bulletin board. Carlson sent over 5,000 e-mails from Dubrow's address to a Phillies address, as well as thousands of e-mails to other addresses, from which Dubrow received 6,000 returned e-mails. On November 19, 2001, Carlson spoofed the e-mail address of Paul Hagen, a sports writer at the Philadelphia Daily News, which caused 6,638 copies of this e-mail to be returned to Paul Hagen's e-mail inbox. On April 9, 2002, Carlson sent thousands of e-mails from an address of a man who he claimed "stalked" him on the internet, 7,000 of which were returned as undeliverable to the alleged stalker's inbox.

At trial, Carlson admitted to engaging in these activities, but denied that he knew that each time he employed the "indirect attack" method of e-mailing, it would result in a spoofed e-mailer's receipt of hundreds of returned e-mails.[n.7][30] He also

---

28. [n.5] This act is referred to as "spoofing."

29. [n.6] The collection of large lists of e-mail addresses for use in spam or bulk mailing is referred to as "harvesting."

30. [n.7] Carlson obtained many e-mail addresses from the unsecured networks of high school and college alumni websites. Because the e-mail addresses of students typically become invalid after they graduate, such websites contain a large number of invalid addresses. Carlson claims he did not consider this result.

denied intending to cause damage by sending thousands of e-mails to one e-mail address, which would clog the address, result in delays, and at times require the purging of all e-mails, causing valuable business-related e-mails to be permanently lost.

The present appeal centers around whether the jury's conviction of Mr. Carlson based upon the finding that he intended to cause damage when he sent e-mails, using both direct and indirect attacks, was supported by the evidence.

We must view the sufficiency of the evidence claim in the light most favorable to the Government and should sustain a verdict if "any rational trier of fact could have found the essential elements of the crime beyond a reasonable doubt."

The Computer Fraud and Abuse Act requires proof that a criminal defendant:

> knowingly cause[d] the transmission of a program, information, code, or command, and as a result of such conduct, *intentionally* cause[d] damage without authorization, to a protected computer.

18 U.S.C. § 1030(a)(5)(A)(I). Section 1030(e)(8) defines "damage" as "any impairment to the integrity or availability of data, a program, a system, or information." Although the statute itself does not define "intentionally," this Court has defined it in the criminal context as performing an act deliberately and not by accident. Accordingly, the Government was required to prove at trial that Carlson deliberately caused an impairment to the integrity or availability of data, a program, a system, or information.

The jury, after being properly charged as to both the elements of the crime and the definitions of relevant terms used therein, found that Carlson knowingly accessed a computer without authorization and intentionally caused damage thereto. Significantly, the District Court defined the meaning of intent as follows:

> A person acts intentionally when what happens was the defendant's conscious objective. To act intentionally means to do an act deliberately and not by accident. The ultimate fact of intent, though subjective, may be established by circumstantial evidence based upon a person's outward manifestations, his words, his conduct, his acts and all the surrounding circumstances disclosed by the evidence and the rational and logical inferences that may be drawn from them. To find the defendant guilty of Counts 1 through 26, you must find beyond a reasonable doubt that he intended to cause damage to the protected computer.

At trial, Carlson admitted that in using the direct e-mailing method and sending thousands of e-mails to one inbox, the targeted inbox would flood with e-mails and thus impair the user's ability to access his other "good" e-mails. Carlson argued, however, that he only believed the targeted e-mail user's ability to access his email would be impaired for a few minutes.

Carlson contended that, in employing the indirect e-mailing method, although he intentionally spoofed e-mail addresses from which he sent thousands of e-mails at a time, he did not intend that the consequence of this would be to flood the spoofed sender's mailboxes with mail that was returned to sender and with replies requesting that the sender not e-mail the recipient in the future.

The testimony reflected, however, that Carlson was a sophisticated internet and email user. Carlson himself admitted to extensive knowledge of use of the internet and software, including knowledge of how to harvest e-mail addresses from websites, to send mass mailings, to use proxy servers, and to spoof e-mail addresses. It is clear from the evidence that Carlson's level of internet savvy, combined with his actions, could rationally be used as circumstantial evidence to conclude that Carlson intended the consequences of his actions.

We hold that sufficient evidence was presented at trial such that a reasonable juror could have found that Carlson, who intentionally accessed a computer without authorization, also intended the resultant damage.

Measuring "Damages"

The amendments to 18 U.S.C. § 1030 enacted in the USA PATRIOT Act essentially adopted the *Middleton* court's definition of loss, which is the next case. *See* 18 U.S.C. § 1030(e)(11).

United States v. Nicholas Middleton

231 F.3d 1207 (9th Cir. 2000)

Graber, Circuit Judge:

Middleton challenges his conviction for intentionally causing damage to a "protected computer" without authorization, in violation of 18 U.S.C. § 1030(a)(5)(A). Defendant argues that the trial court incorrectly instructed the jury on the "damage" element of the offense and that the government presented insufficient evidence of the requisite amount of damage. We disagree with each of Defendant's contentions and, therefore, affirm the conviction.

Defendant worked as the personal computer administrator for Slip.net, an Internet service provider. His responsibilities included installing software and hardware on the company's computers and providing technical support to its employees. He had extensive knowledge of Slip.net's internal systems, including employee and computer program passwords. Dissatisfied with his job, Defendant quit. He then began to write threatening e-mails to his former employer.

Slip.net had allowed Defendant to retain an e-mail account as a paying customer after he left the company's employ. Defendant used this account to commit his first unauthorized act. After logging in to Slip.net's system, Defendant used a computer program called "Switch User" to switch his account to that of a Slip.net receptionist, Valerie Wilson. This subterfuge allowed Defendant to take advantage of the benefits and privileges associated with that employee's account, such as creating and deleting accounts and adding features to existing accounts.

Ted Glenwright, Slip.net's president, discovered this unauthorized action while looking through a "Switch User log," which records all attempts to use the Switch User program. Glenwright cross-checked the information with the company's "Radius Log," which records an outside user's attempt to dial in to the company's modem banks. The information established that Defendant had connected to Slip .net.'s computers and had then switched to Wilson's account. Glenwright immediately terminated Defendant's e-mail account.

Nevertheless, Defendant was able to continue his activities. Three days later, he obtained access to Slip.net's computers by logging in to a computer that contained a test account and then using that test account to gain access to the company's main computers. Once in Slip.net's main system, Defendant accessed the account of a sales representative and created two new accounts, which he called "TERPID" and "SANTOS." Defendant used TERPID and SANTOS to obtain access to a different computer that the company had named "Lemming." Slip.net used Lemming to perform internal administrative functions and to host customers' websites. Lemming also contained the software for a new billing system. After gaining access to the Lemming computer, Defendant changed all the administrative passwords, altered the computer's registry, deleted the entire billing system (including programs that ran the billing software), and deleted two internal databases.

Glenwright discovered the damage the next morning. He immediately contacted the company's system administrator, Bruno Connelly. Glenwright and Connelly spent an entire weekend repairing the damage that Defendant had caused to Slip .net's computers, including restoring access to the computer system, assigning new passwords, reloading the billing software, and recreating the deleted databases. They also spent many hours investigating the source and the extent of the damage. Glenwright estimated that he spent 93 hours repairing the damage; Connelly estimated that he spent 28 hours; and other employees estimated that they spent a total of 33 hours. Additionally, Slip.net bought new software to replace software that Defendant had deleted, and the company hired an outside consultant for technical support.

Defendant argues that the district court instructed the jury improperly on the definition of "damage." Defendant requested this instruction: "Damage does not include expenses relating to creating a better or making a more secure system than the one in existence prior to the impairment." The court refused the request and gave a different instruction. The court explained to the jury that "damage" is an impairment to Slip.net's computer system that caused a loss of at least $5,000. The court continued:

> The term "loss" means any monetary loss that Slip.net sustained as a result of any damage to Slip.net's computer data, program, system or information that you find occurred.

> And in considering whether the damage caused a loss less than or greater than $5,000, you may consider any loss that you find was a natural and foreseeable result of any damage that you find occurred.

> In determining the amount of losses, you may consider what measures were reasonably necessary to restore the data, program, system, or information that you find was damaged or what measures were reasonably necessary to resecure the data, program, system, or information from further damage.

"In reviewing jury instructions, the relevant inquiry is whether the instructions as a whole are misleading or inadequate to guide the jury's deliberation." In this case, the district court's instructions on "damage" and "loss" correctly stated the applicable law. Defendant concedes that "damage" includes any loss that was a foreseeable consequence of his criminal conduct, including those costs necessary to "resecure" Slip.net's computers. He does not argue, therefore, that the court misstated the law.

Defendant contends instead that the court's instruction might have led the jury to believe that it could consider the cost of creating a better or more secure system and that his proposed additional instruction was needed to avoid that possibility. The district court's instruction, when read in its entirety, adequately presented Defendant's theory. The court instructed the jury that it could consider only those costs that were a "natural and foreseeable result" of Defendant's conduct, only those costs that were "reasonably necessary," and only those costs that would "resecure" the computer to avoid "further damage." That instruction logically excludes any costs that the jury believed were excessive, as well as any costs that would merely create an improved computer system unrelated to preventing further damage resulting from Defendant's conduct. In particular, the term "resecure" implies making the system as secure as it was before, not making it more secure than it was before. We presume that the jury followed the court's instructions.

Defendant's final argument is that the government presented insufficient evidence of the requisite $5,000 in damage. The government computed the amount of damage that occurred by multiplying the number of hours that each employee spent in fixing the computer problems by their respective hourly rates (calculated using their annual salaries), then adding the cost of the consultant and the new software. The government estimated the total amount of damage to be $10,092. Defendant and the government agree that the cost of Glenwright's time made up the bulk of that total.

Defendant observes that Slip.net paid Glenwright a fixed salary and that Slip.net did not pay Glenwright anything extra to fix the problems caused by Defendant's conduct. There also is no evidence, says Defendant, that Glenwright was diverted from his other responsibilities or that such a diversion caused Slip.net a financial loss. Defendant argues that, unless Slip.net paid its salaried employees an extra $5,000 for the time spent fixing the computer system, or unless the company was prevented from making $5,000 that it otherwise would have made because of the employees' diversion, Slip.net has not suffered "damage" as defined in the statute. We disagree.

In *United States v. Sablan*, 92 F.3d 865, 869 (9th Cir. 1996), this court held that, under the Sentencing Guidelines for computer fraud, it was permissible for the district court to compute "loss" based on the hourly wage of the victim bank's employees. The court reasoned, in part, that the bank would have had to pay a similar amount had it hired an outside contractor to repair the damage. Analogous reasoning applies here. There is no basis to believe that Congress intended the element of "damage" to depend on a victim's choice whether to use hourly employees, outside contractors, or salaried employees to repair the same level of harm to a protected computer. Rather, whether the amount of time spent by the employees and their imputed hourly rates were reasonable for the repair tasks that they performed are questions to be answered by the trier of fact.

Our review of the record identifies sufficient evidence from which a rational trier of fact could have found that Slip.net suffered $5,000 or more in damage. Glenwright testified that he spent approximately 93 hours investigating and repairing the damage caused by Defendant. That total included 24 hours investigating the break-in, determining how to fix it, and taking temporary measures to prevent future break-ins. Glenwright testified that he spent 21 hours recreating deleted databases and 16 hours reloading and configuring the billing software and its related applications. Glenwright estimated that his time was worth $90 per hour, based on his salary of $180,000 per year. He also testified, among other things, that he did not hire an outside contractor to repair the damage because he believed that he, as a computer expert with a pre-existing knowledge of the customized features of his company's computers, could fix the problems more efficiently. It is worth noting that, because the jury had to find only $5,000 worth of damage, it could have discounted Glenwright's number of hours or his hourly rate considerably and still have found the requisite amount of damage.

Other Slip.net employees testified to the hours that they spent fixing the damage caused by Defendant, and to their respective salaries. The government then presented expert testimony from which a jury could determine that the time spent by the employees was reasonable. Defendant cross-examined the government's witnesses on these issues vigorously, and he presented contrary expert testimony. By the verdict, the jury found the government witnesses' testimony to be more credible, a finding that was within its power to make. We hold, on this record, that the conviction was not based on insufficient evidence.

Notes

1. **Federal Wire Fraud Statute.** 18 U.S.C. §§ 1341, 1434 which prohibits the use of interstate mail or wire transmissions to further a fraudulent scheme to obtain money or property, has application to some schemes. For example, the following acts has been found to violate it:

- posting a fraudulent solicitation for money on a classified ad website;[31]

---

31. United States v. Pirello, 255 F.3d 728, 732 (9th Cir. 2001).

- transferring funds fraudulently through a computer system;[32]

- altering computer clocks to "backdate" reports;[33] and

- using a computer program by a reseller of long distance phone service to add extra minutes to customer calls.[34]

2. Proliferation of Offenders:

The Internet's much-celebrated ability to lower transaction costs and provide greater connectivity to the outside world for businesses and consumers, and governments and citizens, also results in similar force multiplication for criminals. Violators can broaden the geographic reach of their targets, increase the volume of their activities through automation, and benefit from the reduced physical presence—and less exposure to physical intervention—that the Internet provides. As an example, in 2009, Albert Gonzalez, a former government informant, was indicted on charges of conspiracy to gain unauthorized access to computers, to commit fraud in connection with computers and to damage computers, in the process stealing 170 million credit and debit card numbers. [*United States v. Gonzalez*, 2009 U.S. Dist. LEXIS 50791 (D. Mass. May 26, 2009).] The case is believed to be the largest hacking and identity theft case ever prosecuted in the United States.[35]

3. For proposed solutions to some of the challenges facing prosecutors seeking to prosecute persons engaged in internet-facilitated fraud, *see* Patrick E. Corbett, *Prosecuting the Internet Fraud Case Without Going Broke*, 76 Miss. L.J. 841 (2007).

---

32. United States v. Briscoe, 65 F.3d 576, 580–81 (7th Cir. 1995).

33. United States v. Gaind, 31 F.3d 73, 75 (2d Cir. 1994).

34. Mid Atlantic Telcom, Inc. v. Long Distance Servs., Inc., 18 F.3d 260, 264 (4th Cir. 1994).

35. Salil K. Mehra, *Law and Cybercrime in the United States Today*, 58 Am. J. Comp. L. 659 (2010). Copyright © 2010, Salil K. Mehra, American Society of Comparative Law. All rights reserved. Reprinted by permission.

Chapter 17

Intellectual Property

This Chapter introduces the basics of copyright law. It also provides an opportunity to reflect on the current social attitudes toward infringement and the manner and scope of technology assisted intellectual property law violations.

§ 17.1 Copyright

Intellectual property theft, broadly conceived, can occur in a variety of ways.[1] This section introduces copyright infringement and focuses on the use of Internet technology to achieve the infringement. The Constitution grants Congress the power to legislate in the area of copyrights and it has done so since the birth of the Republic.[2] Copyright law protects all "original works of authorship fixed in any tangible medium of expression, now known or later developed, from which they can be perceived, reproduced, or otherwise communicated, either directly or with the aid of a machine or device." 17 U.S.C. § 102(a). Copyright protects only the creative expression of an idea — but not the idea itself.[3] Novel ideas, methods, and processes may be protected by patent or trade secret law but they are not copyrightable.

> The law of copyright is designed to foster the production of creative works and the free flow of ideas by providing legal protection for creative expression. Copyright provides protection against the infringement of certain exclusive rights in "original works of authorship fixed in any tangible medium of expression," including computer software; literary, musical, and dramatic works; motion pictures and sound recordings; and pictorial, sculptural, and architectural works. *See* 17 U.S.C. § 102(a).[4]

---

1. *See, e.g.*, John R. Grimm, Stephen F. Guzzi, & Kathleen Elizabeth Rupp, *Intellectual Property Crimes*, 47 Am. Crim. L. Rev. 741 (2010) (outlining numerous offenses addressing misappropriation of intellectual property).

2. U.S. Const. Art. I, § 8, cl. 8 ("The Congress shall have Power . . . [t]o promote the Progress of Science and useful Arts, by securing for limited Times to Authors and Inventors the exclusive Right to their respective Writings and Discoveries.").

3. *See* 17 U.S.C. § 102(b) ("In no case does copyright protection . . . extend to any idea, procedure, process, system, method of operation, concept, principle, or discovery").

4. U.S. Dep't of Justice, Prosecuting Intellectual Property Crimes 6 (4th ed. 2013).

Nonetheless, the Supreme Court has recognized that there must be a

> sound balance between the respective values of supporting creative pur-
> suits through copyright protection and promoting innovation in new com-
> munication technologies by limiting the incidence of liability for copyright
> infringement. The more artistic protection is favored, the more technologi-
> cal innovation may be discouraged; the administration of copyright law is
> an exercise in managing the trade-off.[5]

The Internet and digital technology have facilitated the creation of a vast market for
pirated intellectual property, including music, videos, software, and movies. The
economic consequences of such piracy are staggering:

> This interconnected global economy creates unprecedented business
> opportunities to market and sell intellectual property worldwide. Geo-
> graphical borders present no impediment to international distribution
> channels. Consumers enjoy near-immediate access to almost any product
> manufactured in the United States or abroad, and they are accustomed to
> using the international credit card system and online money brokers (such
> as PayPal) to make payment a virtually seamless process worldwide. If
> the product can not be immediately downloaded to a home PC, it can be
> shipped to arrive by next day air.

> However, the same technology that benefits rights-holders and consum-
> ers also benefits IP thieves seeking to make a fast, low-risk buck. Total global
> losses to United States companies from copyright piracy alone in 2005 were
> estimated to be $30–$35 billion, not counting significant losses due to
> Internet piracy, for which meaningful estimates were not yet available.

> Trafficking in counterfeit merchandise presents economic consequences
> no less severe. It has been estimated that between 5% and 7% of world trade
> is in counterfeit goods, which is equivalent to approximately $512 billion
> in global lost sales. Counterfeit products are not limited to bootleg DVDs
> or fake "designer" purses; they include prescription drugs, automobile and
> airline parts, food products, and insecticides. As a result, the trade in coun-
> terfeit merchandise threatens the health and safety of millions of Ameri-
> cans and costs manufacturers billions of dollars each year.

> Whether sold via the Internet or at sidewalk stands on New York's famous
> Canal Street, the harm to the U.S. economy from IP theft is substantial.
> Total losses suffered by U.S. industries due to their products being coun-
> terfeited is estimated at between $200 and $250 billion per year, costing
> 750,000 American jobs.[6]

---

5. MGM v. Grokster, 545 U.S. 913 (2005).

6. U.S. Dep't of Justice, Prosecuting Intellectual Property Crimes 2–3 (3rd ed. 2006).
The most recent version of this manual estimates that loses of $650 billion dollars in the G20

The materials in this section set forth the primary statute regulating copyright infringement, examine the elements needed to establish criminal liability, and then examine the evolution of file sharing technology and methods. "Criminal copyright prosecutions have remained rare in the United States despite attempts in the late 1990s to broaden the scope of prosecution as peer-to-peer file sharing took off."[7] In contrast, the music industry and other private actors have been aggressively policing the Internet for copyright violations.

1. 17 U.S.C. § 506(a) Provides:

(1) In general. Any person who willfully infringes a copyright shall be punished as provided under section 2319 of title 18, if the infringement was committed—

(A) for purposes of commercial advantage or private financial gain;

(B) by the reproduction or distribution, including by electronic means, during any 180-day period, of 1 or more copies or phonorecords of 1 or more copyrighted works, which have a total retail value of more than $1,000; or

(C) by the distribution of a work being prepared for commercial distribution, by making it available on a computer network accessible to members of the public, if such person knew or should have known that the work was intended for commercial distribution.

(2) Evidence. For purposes of this subsection, evidence of reproduction or distribution of a copyrighted work, by itself, shall not be sufficient to establish willful infringement of a copyright.

(3) Definition. In this subsection, the term "work being prepared for commercial distribution" means—

(A) a computer program, a musical work, a motion picture or other audiovisual work, or a sound recording, if, at the time of unauthorized distribution—

(i) the copyright owner has a reasonable expectation of commercial distribution; and

(ii) the copies or phonorecords of the work have not been commercially distributed; or

(B) a motion picture, if, at the time of unauthorized distribution, the motion picture—

(i) has been made available for viewing in a motion picture exhibition facility; and

---

countries in 2008 from counterfeit or pirated products and that figure was expected to double by 2015. *Id.* at 2–3 (4th ed. 2013).

7. Salil K. Mehra, *Law and Cybercrime in the United States Today*, 58 Am. J. Comp. L. 659 (2010).

(ii) has not been made available in copies for sale to the general public in the United States in a format intended to permit viewing outside a motion picture exhibition facility.

––––––––––

Analysis of the elements of a criminal prosecution for copyright infringement under 17 U.S.C. § 506(a):

- **A Valid Copyright**

A work is protected by copyright law from the moment it is created. *See* 17 U.S.C. §§ 101–102(a), 408(a).

- **Infringement**

Infringement is the threshold requirement for both criminal and civil copyright infringement cases. Copyright infringement can be proven by either direct or indirect evidence showing that the defendant had access to the copyrighted work and that the alleged copy is "substantially similar" in idea and in expression of idea. The copyright infringement element may be established even if the person distributing the infringing work did not personally produce the copies.

The substantial similarity test is a two step analysis that requires: (i) a showing of substantial similarity in the basic ideas involved, established by focusing on specific "extrinsic" criteria, such as the type of work involved, the materials used, the subject matter, and the setting for the subject; and (ii) a showing that the defendant's alleged copy expresses the same "intrinsic" substance and value as the original work.

Courts may also employ the "virtual identity" standard instead of the substantial similarity test, which allows the potentially infringing work to be broken down into protected and unprotected elements which are then compared to elements of the original work. The virtual identity test looks at the two works as a whole to determine if they are virtually identical.

It is not infringement for the owner of a copy of a computer program to make, or authorize the making of, a copy or adaptation, if such a step is deemed essential to using the program, or if the step is solely for archival purposes and the copy can be destroyed if necessary.[8]

- **Willfulness**

A majority of the courts have interpreted the term to mean that the government must show the defendant specifically intended to violate copyright law; however, the Second Circuit once took a different view, holding

––––––––––

8. John R. Grimm, Stephen F. Guzzi, & Kathleen Elizabeth Rupp, *Intellectual Property Crimes*, 47 Am. Crim. L. Rev. 741 (2010). Copyright © 2010, American Criminal Law Review. All rights reserved. Reprinted by permission.

that "willfulness" requires only an intent to copy, rather than an intent to infringe.[9] The majority rule in criminal copyright cases requiring a higher standard of willfulness is also consistent with civil copyright cases, which likewise hold that willfulness is not just an intent to copy, but rather an intent to infringe.[10]

· **Alternative Elements Regarding Financial Gain/Other Thresholds**

Subsections (A)–(C) list three alternative requirements: (A) The infringement must be for commercial advantage or private financial gain; (B) the infringer reproduced or distributed, during any 180-day period, one or more copies or phonorecords of one or more copyrighted works, with a total retail value of more than $1,000; or (C) distributing "a work being prepared for commercial distribution" by making it available on a publicly-accessible computer network, if the person knew or should have known that the work was intended for commercial distribution. Subsection (C) addresses pre-release infringement. The "willfulness" element must be shown for each of these three alternatives methods of committing a criminal copyright violation.

PENALTIES: 18 U.S.C. § 2319

Felony penalties attach when the violation consists of the reproduction or distribution of at least ten copies that are valued together at more than $2,500 in a 180-day period, or when the violation involves distribution of a work being prepared for commercial distribution over a publicly-accessible computer network. If the offense does not satisfy these alternative felony elements, it is a misdemeanor. *See* 18 U.S.C. § 2319(b)(3). A person found guilty of a misdemeanor may be sentenced to up to one year of imprisonment and a $100,000 fine or twice the monetary gain or loss. The sentences for felony convictions vary, depending upon whether it is a first-time felony conviction and upon the specific subsection violated. The sentences range from 3 to 10 years imprisonment and fines up to $250,000 for first time offenses.

2. Evolution of File Sharing

Sandra Leigh King, *While You Were Sleeping*,

11 S.M.U. Sci. & Tech. L. Rev. 291 (2008)[11]

I. Introduction

As of 2004, it was reported that software companies were facing piracy rates as high as forty percent. In 2005, the video game market was estimated at $28 billion,

---

9. *Id.*

10. U.S. Dep't of Justice, Prosecuting Intellectual Property Crimes 29 (4th ed. 2013).

11. Copyright © 2008 Sandra Leigh King, Southern Methodist University Science and Technology Law Review. All rights reserved. Reprinted by permission.

second only to the entertainment industry. However, approximately $2.4 billion has been lost to global piracy. Some reports estimated that the U.S. video game market was expected to grow to $15.3 billion by 2008, an indication that the amount that has been lost to global piracy may have been grossly underestimated. As of 2004, there were over 176 different file-sharing venues on the Internet.

Some experts have stated that illegal file sharing has contributed up to thirty percent of the overall decline in music sales. Further, reverse engineering only exacerbates the problem. It is also important to remember that, when the *Napster* case was decided, there were no portable MP3 players readily available like the iPod. Since *Napster*, the file sharing industries have been playing catch-up—always two steps behind and one step forward.

II. How Did All of This Happen After the *Napster* Decision? The Evolution of Illegal Video Game Sharing

A. Phase One: Centralized servers (or "brokers")

Napster is recognized as the most notorious file-sharing service. Napster was eventually held liable for vicarious and contributory copyright infringement. Vicarious infringement describes "[a] person's liability for an infringing act of someone else, even though the person has not directly committed an act of infringement. For example, a concert theater can be vicariously liable for an infringing performance of a hired band." Contributory infringement is defined as "[t]he act of participating in, or contributing to, the infringing acts of another person. The law imposes vicarious liability for contributory infringement." In particular concerning copyrights, contributory infringement involves "[t]he act of either (1) actively inducing, causing, or materially contributing to the infringing conduct of another person, or (2) providing the goods or means necessary to help another person infringe (as by making facilities available for an infringing performance)."

For those of us who remember, and perhaps used, the Napster system, it did not require a great amount of creativity to identify infringing material. Characters were rearranged, or perhaps just one or two left off of the end of a title. In the video game context, online infringers often will post the popular game "World of Warcraft" as "War of Worldcraft" in an attempt to avoid liability for copyright infringement.

B. Phase Two: De-Centralized Central Servers

Many cyber-pirates quickly realized that a Napster-like "centralized server" model would not go unnoticed as far as illegally downloading copyrighted materials were concerned. The centralized server then was morphed into a two-tier system called FastTrack. The Grokster website, among others, employed the FastTrack system. Unlike the centralized server used in Napster, Grokster employed the two-tiered FastTrack system, "in which the first tier consists of supernodes (powerful machines with fast connections)[n.26][12] and the second tier consists of the majority of machines, clusters of which connect to individual supernodes."

Like its predecessor Napster, Grokster suffered the same fate. The decision in the *Grokster* case, though, perhaps created more confusion than certainty concerning copyright law. On one hand, the Supreme Court said that peer-to-peer file sharing, when used for purposes such as copyright infringement, is *per se* illegal, but the Court left open the question of how to determine whether a company who posts peer-to-peer software on the internet is purposely inducing its users to violate the law.[n.28][13] Morpheus, an original FastTrack user, eventually switched to a Gnutella-based system, which has since become the de facto choice of online gamers.

Under FastTrack, "[c]onnections are initiated to the network by connecting to a central server and choosing a suitable supernode from there. Thanks to this two-tier approach, searches are many magnitudes faster compared to Gnutella-like networks. Once data has been located, downloading takes place in the same manner as Gnutella, by connecting directly to the remote host."

Unlike Napster, as of 2002, FastTrack supported a great variety of file formats, such as movies and software applications. Additionally, FastTrack differed from Napster because of its geographical location, and being "outside [the United States], makes it more difficult for U.S.-based copyright holders like RIAA [Recording Industry Association of America] to ban it." It was the most popular peer-to-peer network for file swapping over the Internet as of 2002. The Supreme Court's June 27, 2005 ruling against both Grokster and StreamCast Networks "created serious concern among advocates of file-sharing technology, along with some sighs of relief that the decision left room for future technological innovations."

Peer-to-peer software (whose genesis was FastTrack's decentralized server system) is designed to allow someone, after downloading the software, to search and download files directly from other online users without utilizing a central server. In some ways, peer-to-peer was designed to get around the problem of Napster-like liability by shifting liability to individual users. By allowing companies who distribute peer-to-peer software to turn a "blind eye" to legions of users who use the

---

12. [n.26] Supernodes are basically computers with broadband connectability that operate in a modified peer-to-peer network. As explained by the Kazaa website, "[a] computer using Kazaa can become a Supernode if they have a modern computer and are accessing the Internet with a broadband connection. Being a Supernode does not affect your PC's performance noticeably. If your computer is functioning as a Supernode, other Kazaa users in your neighborhood will automatically upload to your machine a small list of files they are sharing, whenever possible, using the same Internet Service Provider. When they search, they send the search request to you as a Supernode. The download will take place between the PC on which the file is shared and the PC that requested the file, not via the Supernode." Kazaa, Supernodes, http://kazaa.com/us/help/faq /supernodes.htm (last visited Aug. 13, 2008).

13. [n.28] *See* MGM Studios, Inc. v. Grokster, Ltd., 545 U.S. 913, 939–40 (2005).

software to illegally share copyrighted materials, these peer-to-peer networks could perhaps avoid Napster's fate.

III. And then There Was Gnutella

Gnutella allows sharing of anything as simple as your prize-winning chili recipe, to a copy of the video game your kids got for Christmas, to the latest version of Linux. Users of Gnutella can choose which files they want to share or can make their entire hard drive available. The wide variety and volume of materials being shared out in cyberspace obviously means that policing the Gnutella network users is problematic. Instead of focusing on one form of media (whether it be music, video, or games), there is a much deeper and wider pond to wade to find infringers.

Gnutella's model of file sharing does not involve a central server to keep track of all user files. Basically, here is how Gnutella works:

> [A] user starts with a networked computer, which we'll call "A," equipped with a Gnutella "servent" (so called because the program acts as a combination of a "server" and a "client"). Computer "A" will connect to another Gnutella-networked computer, "B." A will then announce that it is "alive" to B, which will in turn announce to all the computers that it is connected to, "C," "D," "E," and "F," that A is alive. The computers C, D, E, and F will then announce to all computers to which they are connected that A is alive; those computers will continue the pattern and announce to the computers they are connected to that computer A is alive.

This pattern continues like the old 1970s Prell Shampoo commercials where one friend tells another friend, and then that friend tells another, and so on. Thus, it is not hard to understand that the reach of the Gnutella network is geometric.

Modern examples of these peer-to-peer Gnutella-based systems include popular systems such as Lime Wire, BitTorrent, and eMule (which replaced eDonkey). Peer-to-peer software is designed to allow someone who has downloaded the software to search and download files directly from other online users without utilizing a central server.

IV. And then the Torrents Came . . .

Torrents are similar to an online ant colony in that they are a very complicated way of communicating information through the use of very tiny creatures, in this case bits or bytes.[n.58][14] Little ants pillage picnic baskets, just as bits or bytes are pillaged in a torrent program system. Each ant takes a small piece of the whole, but unlike the ant analogy, torrents allow the whole to be reconstructed in the end.

---

14. [n.58] Torrents, which vary in size, include tracker information, piece size, uncompressed file size, and comments. "A .torrent file is a file that contains the basic information about a file or set of files. This includes the file names, sizes, the date created and some other information." Track Trap, What is a Torrent?, http://www.tracktrap.com/whatis.php (last visited Aug. 1, 2008). These torrents are then uploaded to a popular peer-to-peer website by a hacker or group of hackers. *Id.*

BitTorrent,[n.59][15] unlike Napster, Grokster, iMesh, or other FastTrack programs, is a peer-to-peer program that is perhaps one of the cleverest ways to avoid Napster-like liability.

But exactly how does a torrent system work? The BitTorrent system, instead of making available an entire file of copyrighted material, makes only one part of the material available for sharing. The BitTorrent software allows users to download that specific part and then also does the user's "shopping" for the other parts of the whole work. The "shopper" then attaches in proper order the other parts (known as torrents) to complete an entire copyrighted file. This process is similar to making a quilt where the quilter gets a copy of a square, and then there is some magical quilting genie that goes out and gets all of the other squares needed to make a complete quilted blanket. Large torrents that take lots of time to download together are what are known as "warez." When a user links all of the torrents together, the user has a complete package of warez. Multiple pieces of software are called "warez." One "ware" (short for software) is equal to one piece of software (e.g., a video game, movie, television show, music recording, or some other form of electronic entertainment). "Warez web sites are [basically] Internet locations that offer software and other programs which have been illegally manipulated to defeat or bypass copyright protection programming." The term generally refers to illegal releases by organized groups of software that includes everything but the box and the manual.

In 2007, after much pressure from the Motion Picture Association of America, BitTorrent agreed to only allow sharing of non-pirated files. The service is a paid service but also allows for free downloads, similar to Apple's iTunes and what has become of the next generation of Napster. However, torrents are still alive and thriving. Furthermore, torrents are the preferred way for users to steal material off the Internet. Websites like Back 2 the Roots allow torrent downloads. In particular, Back 2 the Roots publishes old Amiga video games, and even though these Amiga games are no longer readily accessible, it is still illegal to publish copies of them.

IX. Non-Internet File Sharing, Copying and Other Illegal Mechanisms: Illegal Copies, Bootleg Copies, Emulators, Mod Chips, and Modified Game Consoles

Obviously, video game manufacturers create ways to secure their products, just like retail stores embed certain products with detectors that go off when a customer tries to take the product without paying for it. However, clever pirates have figured out multiple ways to circumvent embedded security measures put into place by video game companies. One particular circumvention technique is the use of modification chips. Mod chips are small electronic devices that are used to modify or disable built-in security restrictions on video game consoles and handheld devices. Basically, mod chips circumvent the embedded security system in the console and trick the device into thinking that the game in use is a legitimate, authorized copy.

---

15. [n.59] BitTorrent, www.bittorrent.com (last visited Aug. 1, 2008).

Another technique is the use of emulators. A gamer can use an emulator to play games on a platform other than the one for which the game was originally designed. One of the biggest threats to the intellectual property rights of video games developers is the ability of users to take advantage of these emulators. Such use weakens the value of developers' intellectual property. Furthermore, the repercussions of these emulators affect not only developers but the industry as a whole.

As of February 14, 2008, Nintendo estimated that it had lost nearly $1 billion in sales because of global piracy. In Japan, for example, the copyrights of both old and new video games have been infringed. Classic video games have been sold or used overseas without a license or permission, and some companies have even replaced the logos of the original publishers with their own logo, thereby claiming ownership of another's work.

Additionally, in Great Britain, thousands of gamers used the Internet "to get their hands on a video game banned because of its graphic scenes of torture and murder." The game being leaked, "Manhunt 2," originates from Great Britain and involves a violent killing spree in a mental institution. The British Board of Film Classification banned the game from being sold because of its extremely violent nature. However, once the game was leaked onto the Internet, savvy users with technical knowledge could download the game and play it on modified game consoles, thereby circumventing the BBFC's ruling.

Another significant problem involves video games with strikingly similar characters and plot lines. There are, however, some sites that walk the line of copyright infringement. One of these sites is GameTap.com, which, while not allowing exact copies of video games to be played by multiple users or shared on the Internet, allows users to play games that have similar characters and similar plots to other creative works of art. Further complicating the issue is that there are multiple layers of infringement: 1) the initial infringement of characters and plot lines stolen from other creative works, and 2) the illegal sharing of these materials on the Internet. Additionally, clever users can figure out a way to reverse engineer these programs and then create an entirely new (third level) of infringement. However, users must be careful regarding copycatting another game, or other copyrighted material, because "[t]he similarity between the two works need not be literal . . . substantial similarity may be found even if none of the words or brush strokes or musical notes are identical." Thus, video game authors (and those who reverse engineer and create "copycat" games) need to be very careful about infringing games that are already in circulation, including games that are no longer readily available.

X. Illegal Video Game Downloads—It's Not Just about the Game, but the Music Too

The heavy metal band Metallica is accusing that its song "One" is being illegally used in the popular game Guitar Hero III. Additionally, Motley Crue has recently become "the first band to release a new single exclusively through the popular video game 'Rock Band.'" Thus, there are several layers of infringement when dealing with video games. When the video game creator uses music without paying a license fee, the creator infringes on the artist's copyright-protected song(s). Furthermore, if the video game with the music (whether the music was licensed or not) is illegally downloaded, then the music incorporated into that video game is also illegally downloaded. Thus, it is plausible that a video game player could be liable for multiple counts of copyright infringement just for a single download. Further, some online superhero video games allow users to create characters, many of which infringe on established copyrighted characters.

XII. Ethical Considerations and Potential Liability for Universities and Colleges

It is important for parents and educators to explain to our children and students that it is perfectly legal (in fact, encouraged) to make one archival copy of the music, movies, etc. that you own. If you are like me and have children that treat DVDs and CDs as hockey pucks, you can appreciate the logic of this rule.

Many people do not intentionally violate copyright law when they download video games. Many times these individuals are fooled by language that states "This Product is 100% Legal." The problem is that while downloading the file-sharing software is in fact legal, the downloading and uploading of copyrighted material is illegal. Many youths (and adults) forget that it is just as illegal to allow people to upload from their computer as it is to download from another file sharer's computer/ server.

A lot of confusion exists among youth, college students, and adults concerning what can and cannot be copied, particularly when it pertains to vintage video games that children like me played in the 1980s on stand-alone arcade systems in the church's youth building or at the local arcade at the mall. Unfortunately for us, our only hope of obtaining that vintage version of Pong or Donkey Kong or Pac Man is searching Ebay, scouring flea markets, or finding a random game room that still has vintage stand alone game consoles. Under U.S. copyright laws, "copyrights owned by corporations are valid for 95 years from the date of first publication, [and b]ecause video and computer games have been around a little more than three decades, the copyrights of all video and computer programs will not expire for many decades to come."

XVII. Liability Goes Both Ways

It is important to remember that even if you do not actually download anything, you can still be liable for whatever copyright-protected material you put out there for others to copy and download. For example, you are not liable for downloading Gnutella-based software or other file-sharing software, but you are liable when you use Gnutella or other file-sharing software to download copyrighted materials without payment of a license fee. You need to be certain that, when you download Gnutella-based software like Lime Wire, you do not allow your copyright-protected material to be made accessible to others. Most of these websites have "check the box" formats where you can choose what you want to make available to others. If you fail to ensure the copyright protected material is not available to the outside world, then you can be subject to both vicarious and copyright infringement liability.

———————

Arista Records LLC v. Lime Group LLC
784 F. Supp. 2d 398 (S.D.N.Y. 2011)

KIMBA M. WOOD, DISTRICT JUDGE.

Plaintiffs are thirteen major record companies that collectively produce, manufacture, distribute, sell, and license "the vast majority of copyrighted sound recordings sold in the United States." Plaintiffs raise various federal and state law claims of secondary copyright infringement against Lime Wire LLC (LW); Mark Gorton, the Chairman and sole Director of LW; Lime Group LLC; and the M.J.G. Lime Wire Family Limited Partnership (collectively, "Defendants") for their role in distribution of the LimeWire software program. LimeWire permits users of the program to share digital files over the Internet. Plaintiffs allege that LimeWire users employ LimeWire to obtain and share unauthorized copies of Plaintiffs' sound recordings, and that Defendants facilitate this infringement by distributing and maintaining LimeWire.

Plaintiffs move for partial summary judgment [*inter alia*] on their claims of (1) inducement of infringement; [and] (2) contributory infringement. LW, Gorton, and Lime Group move for summary judgment on each of these claims, and on Plaintiffs' claim of vicarious copyright infringement.

A. *File-Sharing Programs*

Over the last several years, technologies have developed that make it inexpensive and easy to record, distribute, and share music via the Internet. Many artists now digitally record songs to sell through online music retailers. Individuals who purchase digital recordings often share them with others by using free or low-cost software or Internet programs, known as "file-sharing programs." File-sharing programs allow users to exchange digital files, including digital recordings, with each other through the Internet. Most digital recordings released in the United States, however, are copyright protected, and the copyright owners do not authorize sharing through file-sharing programs. A number of companies that have distributed file-sharing programs, including the distributors of the programs Napster, Kazaa, Morpheus, and Grokster, have faced liability for copyright infringement, on the ground that they facilitated infringement committed by users of their programs. *See e.g., A & M Records, Inc. v. Napster, Inc.*, 239 F.3d 1004 (9th Cir. 2001).[n.5][16]

———————

16. [n.5] Napster, Inc. was one of the first companies to develop a file-sharing program that permitted users to exchange digital recordings via the Internet. The vast majority of files that were shared through the Napster program were digital recordings protected by copyright, the sharing of which was not authorized. Napster was found liable of contributory and vicarious copyright infringement. The Napster program was shut down by a court-ordered injunction.

B. *Creation and Design of LimeWire*

LW was founded in June 2000. The company released LimeWire in August 2000. LimeWire is a file-sharing program that utilizes "peer-to-peer" technology. By employing P2P technology, LimeWire permits its users to share digital files via an Internet-based network known as the "Gnutella network." LimeWire users can share almost all files stored on their computers with other LimeWire users.[n.6][17] When a LimeWire user wishes to locate digital files available through the network, she enters search criteria into the search function on LimeWire's user interface. LimeWire then scans the computers of other LimeWire users, to locate files that match the search criteria. The LimeWire user can download any files that LimeWire locates. When the user downloads a file, LimeWire transfers a digital copy of the file from the computer on which it is located to the LimeWire user's computer.

C. *Plaintiffs' Copyrighted Recordings*

Plaintiffs sell and distribute the vast majority of all recorded music in the United States. They allege that they own the copyrights or exclusive rights to more than 3000 sound recordings, which are listed in exhibits to the First Amended Complaint. In this litigation, Plaintiffs have provided documentation establishing that they own the copyrights to thirty popular recordings. Plaintiffs allege that LimeWire users share and download unauthorized digital copies of the Recordings via LimeWire, and that Defendants are secondarily liable for this infringement because they distribute and maintain LimeWire.

V. *Infringement Claims Against LW*

A. *Direct Infringement*

Plaintiffs' infringement claims against LW are based on theories of secondary liability. To establish their secondary liability claims, Plaintiffs first must establish that LimeWire users directly infringed Plaintiffs' copyrights. There are no genuine issues of material fact as to direct infringement. The evidence in the record establishes that LimeWire users infringed Plaintiffs' copyrights by sharing unauthorized digital copies of the Recordings through LimeWire.

1. *Legal Standard*

Secondary liability for copyright infringement may be imposed on a party that has not directly infringed a copyright, but has played a significant role in direct infringement committed by others, for example by providing direct infringers with a product that enables infringement. *See Metro-Goldwyn-Mayer, Inc. v. Grokster*, 545 U.S. 913, 929–30 (2005); *Sony Corp. v. Universal City Studios*, 464 U.S. 417, 434–35 (1984). The rationale for secondary liability is that a party who distributes infringement-enabling products or services may facilitate direct infringement on a

---

17. [n.6] LimeWire recommends that "all LimeWire users share generously with one another." LimeWire's default settings make all files that a user downloads through LimeWire available to other LimeWire users for download.

massive scale, making it "impossible to enforce [copyright protection] effectively against all direct infringers." In such circumstances, "the only practical alternative is to go against the distributor of the copying device for secondary liability."[n.20][18]

To recover on a claim based on secondary liability, a plaintiff first must establish direct infringement by the relevant third party, *i.e.* the party that received the infringement-enabling device.

To establish direct infringement, a plaintiff must show that (1) the plaintiff owns the copyright or copyrights at issue; and (2) the third party infringed the copyrights by unauthorized copying or distribution.

2. *Application*

The evidence establishes that LimeWire users have infringed Plaintiffs' copyrights. First, Plaintiffs have proven that they own the copyrights for the Recordings. Second, the evidence demonstrates that LimeWire users employed LimeWire to share and download the Recordings without authorization. Plaintiffs have submitted documentation and electronic storage media data showing that LimeWire users share and download unauthorized digital copies of the Recordings through LimeWire. Plaintiffs have provided hard drives that contain digital copies of the Recordings, with electronic evidence that establishes that the Recordings were downloaded by LimeWire users without authorization.

The report from Plaintiffs' expert, Dr. Richard Waterman, also supports a finding of direct infringement. Dr. Waterman analyzed a random sample of files available on LimeWire, and determined that 93% of those files were protected or highly likely to be protected by copyright, and thus not authorized for free distribution through LimeWire. Dr. Waterman also analyzed the rate at which the sample files were requested for download by LimeWire users. Based on this analysis, he estimated that 98.8% of the files requested for download through LimeWire are copyright protected and not authorized for free distribution.

LW argues that statistical evidence of the "availability" of copyright-protected files and of download "requests" is insufficient to establish *actual* infringing activity by LimeWire users. Some courts have held that "request" evidence, on its own, does not suffice to establish direct infringement. Plaintiffs, however, do not rely solely on evidence of "requests" and "availability" of the Recordings. Rather, they have

---

18. [n.20] It is notable that major record companies, including Plaintiffs, have pursued legal action against individuals who commit direct copyright infringement, with considerable success. Plaintiffs have sued more than 6,000 LimeWire users for direct copyright infringement. They have obtained judgments against more than 700 users and settled claims against almost 4,000 users. The damage awards and other litigation costs imposed upon individual infringers and the publicity concerning such cases have arguably had some deterrent effect on Internet users' infringing activities through online networks. *See* Justin Hughes, *On the Logic of Suing One's Customers and the Dilemma of Infringement-Based Business Models*, 22 Cardozo Arts & Ent. L.J. 725, 731–35 (2005) (discussing the extent to which record companies' lawsuits against music consumers for P2P copyright infringement are increasing awareness of copyright law and deterring future infringement).

submitted substantial direct and circumstantial evidence showing infringement by LimeWire users. Dr. Waterman's report supports this evidence, and provides context as to the scope of infringement.

The Court therefore finds that LimeWire users have directly infringed Plaintiffs' copyrights. The Court turns to the merits of the parties' motions for summary judgment.

B. *Inducement of Copyright Infringement*

The evidence establishes that LW, by distributing and maintaining LimeWire, intentionally encouraged direct infringement by LimeWire users. Plaintiffs, therefore, are entitled to summary judgment on their claim against LW of inducement of copyright infringement.

1. *Legal Standard*

In *Grokster*, the Supreme Court confirmed that inducement of copyright infringement constitutes a distinct cause of action. The Court held that the *Grokster* defendants "induced" copyright infringement by distributing a device with the "object of promoting its use to infringe copyright, as shown by a clear expression or other affirmative steps taken to foster infringement."

To establish a claim for inducement, a plaintiff must show that the defendant (1) engaged in purposeful conduct that encouraged copyright infringement, with (2) the intent to encourage such infringement.

A defendant's intent to foster infringement can be established by evidence of the defendant's "clear expression" of such an intent, or of "affirmative steps [the defendant has] taken to foster infringement." Direct evidence of inducement is an "advertisement or solicitation that broadcasts a message designed to stimulate others to commit violations." Such evidence, however, is "not [the] exclusive way of" proving inducement liability. In *Grokster*, the Supreme Court found that three specific kinds of evidence, considered in the context of the record as a whole, supported a finding that the defendants intended to induce infringement: (1) defendants' internal communications and advertising efforts, which evidenced a clear intent to target users of Napster, a population well-known for committing copyright infringement through file-sharing programs; (2) defendants' failure to develop and implement filtering tools or other means of limiting infringement; and (3) defendants' reliance on infringing activity for the success of their business (including evidence that defendants' advertising revenue depended on Grokster having a high volume of users, which in turn depended overwhelmingly on users' ability to engage in infringing activities through the program). After making these findings, the Supreme Court remanded the case to the district court to determine whether to grant Plaintiffs' motion for summary judgment on the inducement claim.

On remand, the *Grokster* district court found that the evidence established defendants' unlawful intent as a matter of law, and granted plaintiffs' motion for summary judgment. The district court based its decision on evidence that: (1) the

Grokster file-sharing program was used "overwhelmingly for infringement"; (2) defendants marketed Grokster to Napster users (who were known for their infringing activities), as evidenced in defendants' internal communications and advertising and marketing efforts; (3) defendants provided technical assistance to users seeking to infringe; (4) defendants ensured that Grokster would be capable of infringing use; (5) defendants relied on revenue that depended on users' ability to commit infringement through the program; and (6) defendants failed to take meaningful affirmative steps to prevent or mitigate the infringement facilitated by Grokster.

2. *Application*

The evidence before the Court establishes that LW is liable for inducement of copyright infringement. First, there is overwhelming evidence that LW engaged in purposeful conduct that fostered infringement: LW created and distributes LimeWire, which users employ to commit a substantial amount of infringement. Second, the following factors, taken together, establish that LW *intended* to encourage infringement by distributing LimeWire: (1) LW's awareness of substantial infringement by users; (2) LW's efforts to attract infringing users; (3) LW's efforts to enable and assist users to commit infringement; (4) LW's dependence on infringing use for the success of its business; and (5) LW's failure to mitigate infringing activities.

a. *LW's awareness of substantial infringement by LimeWire users*

Plaintiffs have presented evidence showing that LimeWire is used overwhelmingly for infringement. Dr. Waterman's report establishes that nearly all of the files shared and downloaded by LimeWire users are copyrighted, and not authorized for free distribution through LimeWire. According to the report, the overwhelming majority of download requests through LimeWire are for copyright-protected files, which makes it nearly certain that most actual downloads involve unauthorized content.

Plaintiffs also have presented evidence establishing that LW was aware of the substantial infringement being committed by LimeWire users. In internal communications, LW regularly discussed the fact that LimeWire users downloaded copyrighted digital recordings through the program. For example, a draft of a LW Offering Memorandum, created in 2001, states that LimeWire "allows people to exchange *copyrighted* mp3 files." A September 2002 statement of LW's goals acknowledges that: "Currently, the most common use of the Gnutella Network is the sharing of music files, many of them copyrighted." Other LW documents state that "the only information being shared on peer networks are media files," a category composed primarily of copyrighted digital recordings, and that the "[s]haring [of] media files is bringing the initial user base" to LimeWire.

In 2006, LW developed a strategic plan to "convert" LimeWire users who were sharing unauthorized digital recordings into customers of LW's online music store, which would sell authorized music. In the Conversion Plan, LW openly acknowledged that the majority of LimeWire's users were infringers. The Plan stated that (1)

25% of LimeWire's users were "hardcore pirates;" (2) 25% of users were "morally persuadable;" (3) 20% of users were legally aware; and (4) 30% of users were "samplers and convenience users." The Plan provided that over time LW would introduce features to LimeWire to block users from downloading infringing recordings, and to direct them to LW's online store.

Further evidence that LW knew that LimeWire users were committing copyright infringement is contained in (1) emails sent to the company by LimeWire users; (2) a collection of articles maintained by LW employees in a file labeled "Knowledge of Infringement"; and (3) the numerous mainstream news articles about widespread infringing activities through LimeWire and similar peer-to-peer networking program.

The massive scale of infringement committed by LimeWire users, and LW's knowledge of that infringement, supports a finding that LW intended to induce infringement.

b. *LW's efforts to attract infringing users*

Plaintiffs have presented significant evidence showing that LW purposefully marketed LimeWire to individuals who were known to use file-sharing programs to share copyrighted recordings, or who expressed an interest in doing so.

In February 2001, a court-ordered injunction shut down Napster, after Napster Inc. (the company that distributed the Napster program) was found liable for copyright infringement on the ground that it had facilitated copyright infringement committed by Napster users. Following Napster's demise, LW announced that it expected thirty percent, "[w]ith possibly up to 100 percent," of Napster users to switch to using LimeWire and similar programs, such as Kazaa and Morpheus. LW developed plans to attract Napster users to LimeWire. Internal email correspondence, often involving LW's CEO and Director Mark Gorton, reveal that LW contemplated a number of strategies to promote LimeWire to Napster users, including initiating press campaigns on college campuses relating to "file-sharing and getting free MP3's"; hiring "campus reps" at "Napster-banned colleges"; running a "Napster Independence Day" promotion; and publicizing features of LimeWire that make "finding your favorite artist or album . . . easier."

From 2002 to 2006, LW conducted a marketing campaign through Google AdWords, whereby Google users who entered certain search queries, such as "replacement napster," "napster mp3," "napster download," "kazaa morpheus," "mp3 free download," and dozens of other phrases containing the words "napster," "kazaa," or "morpheus," would see an advertisement leading them to the LimeWire website. LW's Google advertisements promoted LimeWire with direct references to other infringement-fostering programs. For example, LW purchased banner advertisements for LimeWire that read "Join Millions of Morpheus users and download the best P2P file-sharing application for free. Free music downloads . . ."; "Outperforms Morpheus!"; and "Faster Downloads Than Kazaa!" In its promotional materials, LW touted user testimonials declaring that the LimeWire application is "excellent for downloading music files" and "[h]ands-down the best current mp3 search tool." LW also marketed LimeWire as "similar to the popular Napster service, in that [LimeWire] enables the sharing, searching, and downloading of MP3 music files." It is undisputed that the vast majority of "MP3 music files" are copyrighted and not authorized for free distribution through LimeWire.

The evidence that LW marketed LimeWire to users of Napster and similar programs, and promoted LimeWire's infringing capabilities supports the conclusion that LW intentionally induced infringement.

c. *LW's efforts to enable and assist users to commit infringement*

The evidence demonstrates that LW optimized LimeWire's features to ensure that users can download digital recordings, the majority of which are protected by copyright, and that LW assisted users in committing infringement.

LimeWire's search functions are designed to facilitate searches for copyrighted digital recordings. The program's user interface allows users to search for specific artists or albums, or to search for music by genre. A number of LimeWire's genre categories—including "Classic Rock," "SoundTrack," and "Top 40"—relate specifically to popular music and inevitably guide users to copyrighted recordings.

LW tested and sought to improve LimeWire's ability to search for and download unauthorized copies of digital recordings. For example, in August 2000, LW conducted a search for Sinead O'Connor's copyrighted song "Nothing Compares 2 U," which it considered a "definitive test" of LimeWire's file-sharing capabilities. The fact that LW tested LimeWire by searching for infringing content gives rise to a "particularly forceful" inference that LW intended to promote copyright infringement.

In addition to ensuring that users can obtain unauthorized copies of recordings through LimeWire, LW has actively assisted LimeWire users in committing infringement. The record reveals several online communications between LW employees and LimeWire users that plainly relate to unauthorized sharing of digital recordings through LimeWire. In many instances, LimeWire users requested assistance in sharing and downloading digital music files, most of which were copyrighted. In response, LW employees offered technical information about the system's functionality, thereby helping users obtain unauthorized copies of recordings.

Evidence that LW has ensured that LimeWire can be used to commit infringement, and that the company has actively assisted infringing users, supports a finding that LW "intended and encouraged" infringement.

d. *LW's dependence on infringement for success of its business*

From 2004 to 2006, LW's annual revenue grew from nearly $6 million to an estimated $20 million. Such growth has depended greatly on LimeWire users' ability to commit infringement through LimeWire.

Since 2000, LimeWire has developed an enormous user base. The program is widely available online, and can be downloaded for free. LW has estimated that

LimeWire was downloaded over three million times during its first year in existence. By 2003, LW boasted that around two million users accessed the program every month. At the time Plaintiffs filed this action, LW claimed that LimeWire had four million users per day. LW has acknowledged that the "[s]haring [of] media files," a category comprised mostly of copyrighted digital recordings, "[brought] the initial user base" to LimeWire. The company has continued to develop LimeWire's user base by promoting the program's infringing capabilities, and marketing it to users known to commit infringement.

LW's sources of revenue depend on LimeWire attracting the massive user population generated by its infringement-enabling features. From 2000 to 2004, LW earned revenue primarily by selling advertising space on LimeWire and LW's website, and by distributing software bundled with LimeWire. As LimeWire's user base expanded, LW's revenues from advertising and software distribution increased. In 2004, LW began selling LimeWire "Pro," an upgraded version of LimeWire that is available for purchase and makes file-sharing activities easier. In January 2008, LW obtained licenses to sell approximately half a million songs, and opened an online LimeWire Store offering authorized sales of digital music. LW markets LimeWire "Pro" and the LimeWire Store to LimeWire users. LW's commercial success, therefore, is derived largely from the high-volume use of LimeWire, most of which is infringing. This evidence supports a finding that LW intended to induce infringement.

e. *LW's failure to mitigate infringing activities*

The evidence reveals that LW has not implemented in a meaningful way any of the technological barriers and design choices that are available to diminish infringement through file-sharing programs, such as hash-based filtering, acoustic fingerprinting, filtering based on other digital metadata, and aggressive user education.

In May 2006, LW implemented an optional, hash-based content filter. A hash-based filter can identify a digital file that contains copyrighted content, and block a user from downloading the file.[n.28][19] The "default" setting of LimeWire's hash-based filter was "off," however, meaning that LimeWire users would have to affirmatively turn the filter "on" for it to have any effect on the transfer of digital recordings to or from their computers. LW could have made the hash-based content

---

19. [n.28] Hash-based filtering utilizes a digital file's "hash," which is a numeric representation of a file based on a complex algorithm, to identify and block infringing files. A hash-based content filter may compare files scheduled for online transfer against a database of digital files that are known to possess audio content protected by copyright. Where there is a match, transfer of the digital file may be blocked to prevent unauthorized transfer and copyright infringement. Two audio files may contain the same song recording but have different hashes as a result of different settings or "ripping" software that have been applied to the respective files. Because a digital audio file's hash will depend not only on its audio content but also on a number of other factors and settings, a hash-based filtering system cannot be expected to recognize and thwart *all* infringement on a file-sharing system. A hash-based filter system nevertheless has the capacity to substantially diminish unauthorized transfers through a file-sharing system.

filter mandatory for all LimeWire users, or made "on" the default setting, so that a user's file-sharing activities would be subject to the filtering process unless he affirmatively deactivated the filter. According to LW's expert Steven Gribble, LW chose to set the filter to "off" because it wished to provide users with "enough flexibility to enable, disable, or configure filtering." LW's decision was a conscious "design choice", the direct result of which was a failure to mitigate infringement.

LW considered, but failed to implement, several other plans to block the availability of infringing content through LimeWire. LW discussed a plan for a "hybrid" filtering system that would have combined hash-based filtering and acoustic fingerprinting.[n.30][20] The company also developed, but did not implement, its Conversion Plan, which would have included a user education campaign designed to inform users about the legal consequences of copyright infringement and to promote the purchase of authorized music through the LW online store. Under the Conversion Plan, LW eventually would have implemented hash-based filtering and acoustic fingerprinting to prevent users from downloading unauthorized files.

LW was aware of other filtering mechanisms that it could have used to mitigate infringing use. For example, LW could have used a keyword-based filter to block unauthorized recordings from appearing in LimeWire searches. LW already uses keyword-based filtering to allow users to limit their receipt of adult content: a LimeWire user can activate a keyword-based filter that prevents a search from bringing up files containing keyword terms that LW has identified as likely to contain pornographic content. LW also has implemented filters to prevent online sharing of personal document files and software program files.

Plaintiffs also note that LW does in fact employ active filtering technology, but only to prevent LimeWire users from sharing digital recordings purchased from the LimeWire online store. This selective filtering further demonstrates LW's knowledge of infringement-mitigating technologies and the company's intentional decision not to employ any such technologies in a way that meaningfully deters LimeWire users' infringing activities.

The only step LW has taken to address infringement is to post an electronic notice that appears when a user first downloads LimeWire. The notice states that "LimeWire Basic and LimeWire PRO are peer-to-peer programs for sharing authorized files only. Downloading either program does not constitute a license for obtaining or distributing unauthorized content." Before a user can initiate the download of the LimeWire software, he must choose from the following statements: (1) "I will not use LimeWire for copyright infringement," or (2) "I might use LimeWire for

---

20. [n.30] Acoustic fingerprinting can monitor the uploading or downloading of digital files. Two audio files that sound the same will have the same acoustic fingerprint. Digital files may be transmitted to a content recognition filter that compares the files against an existing database of unauthorized digital content. If the acoustic fingerprint of a particular file matches a copyright-protected file present in the existing database, the transfer of that file may be blocked. Content filtering software tools have been effectively implemented by other P2P file-sharing systems.

copyright infringement." If the user selects the second option, LimeWire will not download. The user may then change his response to "I will not use LimeWire for copyright infringement" in order to download the program. The notice and "statement of intent" requirement, on their own, do not constitute meaningful efforts to mitigate infringement.

LW chose not to implement any meaningful infringement-reduction strategies in part because it recognized that, "as long as there were other [P2P] applications that didn't filter," LimeWire users would respond to filtering by switching "to another [P2P application] that doesn't have that filtering behavior or that is less aggressive in making fewer files available."

Failure to utilize existing technology to create meaningful barriers against infringement is a strong indicator of intent to foster infringement.

In conclusion, the evidence shows LW has engaged in purposeful conduct that fostered infringement, with the intent to foster such infringement. LW distributes LimeWire, and (1) is aware that LimeWire's users commit a substantial amount of copyright infringement; (2) markets LimeWire to users predisposed to committing infringement; (3) ensures that LimeWire enables infringement and assists users committing infringement; (4) relies on the fact that LimeWire enables infringement for the success of its business; and (5) has not taken meaningful steps to mitigate infringement. Accordingly, the Court GRANTS Plaintiffs' motion for summary judgment on their claim of inducement of infringement against LW.

C. Contributory Copyright Infringement

Plaintiffs and LW cross-move for summary judgment on Plaintiffs' claim that LW is secondarily liable for copyright infringement because it "materially contributed" to infringement committed by LimeWire users. The Court finds that summary judgment is not warranted because the Court cannot determine, based on the record, whether LimeWire is capable of substantial noninfringing uses.

1. Legal Standard

A defendant may be held liable for contributory copyright infringement if, "with knowledge of the infringing activity," it "materially contributes to the infringing conduct of another." Unlike an inducement claim, a claim for contributory infringement *does not* require a showing that the defendant intended to foster infringement. *See Grokster*, 545 U.S. at 942 (Ginsburg, J., concurring) (noting that an inducement claim and a contributory infringement claim "capture different culpable behavior"). Rather, to establish a "material contribution" claim, a plaintiff must show that the defendant (1) had actual or constructive knowledge of the infringing activity, and (2) encouraged or assisted others' infringement, or provided machinery or goods that facilitated infringement.

A defendant's contribution to a third party's infringing activities must be "material" to give rise to a claim for contributory infringement. For example, a defendant who is peripherally involved in infringement, such as one who provides online payment services for transactions involving infringement, does not "materially contribute" to infringement. In contrast, where a "computer system operator learns of specific infringing material available on his system and fails to purge such material from the system," that party "knows of and contributes to direct infringement" and may be liable for contributory copyright infringement.

In *Sony Corp. v. Universal City Studios*, the Supreme Court established a rule, known as the *Sony-Betamax* rule, that shields some defendants from liability for contributory infringement. 464 U.S. at 442. Pursuant to the *Sony-Betamax* rule, a defendant who distributes a product that materially contributes to copyright infringement *will not* be liable for contributory infringement if the product also is "widely used for legitimate, unobjectionable purposes" or is "merely . . . capable of substantial noninfringing use." *Id.* (finding that the defendant was not liable for contributory infringement based on its distribution of the Betamax video recorder, because the recorder was "capable of a substantial non-infringing use," namely "time-shifting," i.e. permitting a user to record a television program to watch at a later time). The purpose of the *Sony-Betamax* rule is to "leave[ ] breathing room for innovation and a vigorous commerce." *Grokster*, 545 U.S. at 933.[n.32][21]

The plaintiffs in *Grokster* brought a claim for contributory infringement. The defendants argued that the Grokster P2P file-sharing program was capable of supporting substantial noninfringing uses, such that the *Sony-Betamax* rule precluded defendants' liability for contributory infringement. The defendants offered evidence that Grokster users employed the program to exchange some authorized files, including authorized digital recordings, digital files of public domain books, and authorized software files. The defendants also argued that, in the future, users would exchange even more authorized content through Grokster, including academic research, public domain files, and user-created audio and video files. The Ninth Circuit found that the defendants' evidence established that Grokster was "capable of substantial noninfringing" uses, and thus granted summary judgment in favor of defendants on the contributory infringement claim.

The plaintiffs appealed the Ninth Circuit's ruling regarding contributory infringement to the Supreme Court. On appeal, the Supreme Court did not decide whether the Ninth Circuit had been correct in granting summary judgment on the contributory infringement claim.[n.33][22] Rather, the Supreme Court issued two concurring opinions, which took differing positions on whether the Ninth Circuit

---

21. [n.32] The rule also stems from the recognition of the tension between artistic protection and technological innovation. The Supreme Court has noted that the "administration of copyright law is an exercise in managing the tradeoff." *Grokster*, 545 U.S. at 928; *see also Twentieth Century Music Corp. v. Aiken*, 422 U.S. 151, 156 (1975) ("[T]he ultimate aim [of copyright law] is . . . to stimulate artistic creativity for the public good. . . . When technological change has rendered its literal terms ambiguous, the Copyright Act must be construed in light of this basic purpose.").

22. [n.33] The Court's controlling opinion addressed only the plaintiffs' claim for inducement of infringement.

had been correct in holding, as a matter of law, that Grokster was capable of substantial non-infringing uses.

In her concurring opinion, Justice Ginsburg, joined by Chief Justice Rehnquist and Justice Kennedy, found that there was "at least a genuine issue of material fact" as to whether Grokster was capable of substantial noninfringing uses, and thus that the Ninth Circuit had erred in granting summary judgment in favor of defendants. Justice Ginsburg stated that, at the time of the lawsuit, Grokster was "overwhelmingly used to infringe." Given this, defendants' evidence of some non-infringing uses was insufficient, on summary judgment, to establish "a reasonable prospect that substantial or commercially significant noninfringing uses were likely to develop over time."

Justice Breyer, joined by Justice Stevens and Justice O'Connor, reached a different conclusion. In his concurring opinion, Justice Breyer agreed that the vast majority of Grokster users employed the program for infringing purposes. He concluded, however, that the defendants had established that Grokster was capable of significant non-infringing uses based on the evidence that (1) Grokster was already used for some noninfringing purposes; and (2) there was "a significant future market for noninfringing uses of [Grokster]." Accordingly, Justice Breyer stated, it was appropriate to grant summary judgment in defendants' favor on the contributory infringement claim.

2. Application

As previously discussed, Plaintiffs have established that LW has been aware of the prevalence of its users' infringing activities since the creation of LimeWire. LW "materially contributed" to the infringement by designing, distributing, supporting, and maintaining the program.

There exists a genuine issue of material fact, however, as to whether LimeWire is "capable of substantial noninfringing uses" such that liability should not be imposed pursuant to the *Sony-Betamax* rule. Currently, LimeWire is used overwhelmingly for infringement. LW, however, has presented evidence of some types of noninfringing content that users share and download through LimeWire, including: (1) electronic copies of books that are in the public domain or authorized for online distribution; (2) historical documents, archival films, and other public domain works; and (3) digital music recordings produced by musicians seeking to promote their work through free online distribution, including musicians who use LW's MagnetMix service (a service that assists musicians and other independent artists in distributing their works online, without the assistance or expense of a recording company). LW argues that additional non-infringing uses for LimeWire are likely to develop in the future.

In light of the evidence presented, the Court cannot determine, as a matter of law, whether LimeWire is capable of substantial non-infringing uses. The record before the Court is insufficient to permit the Court to assess the "technological feasibility or commercial viability" of LimeWire's potential non-infringing uses.

Summary judgment on Plaintiffs' contributory infringement claim, therefore, is not appropriate. Accordingly, the Court DENIES the parties' cross-motions for summary judgment.

D. *Vicarious Copyright Infringement*

LW moves for summary judgment on Plaintiffs' claim of vicarious copyright infringement. The Court denies LW's motion for summary judgment based on the evidence that LW (1) had the right and ability to supervise and control LimeWire users' infringing activities; and (2) possessed a direct financial interest in the infringing activity.

1. *Legal Standard*

A defendant is liable for vicarious copyright infringement if it "profit[s] from direct infringement while declining to exercise a right to stop or limit it." To establish liability, a plaintiff must show that the defendant "[1] had the right and ability to supervise the infringing activity and . . . [2] has a direct financial interest in such activities."

The first element of the test for vicarious liability is satisfied if the plaintiff proves that the defendant had the ability to supervise or control the third parties' infringing activity and failed to do so.

The second element of the vicarious infringement test requires showing a "causal relationship between the infringing activity and any financial benefit [the] defendant reaps." The financial benefit need not be tied directly to sales of the infringing goods. It may also be established by evidence showing that users are attracted to a defendant's product because it enables infringement, and that use of the product for infringement financially benefits the defendant.

2. *Application*

There is substantial evidence that LW had the right and ability to limit the use of its product for infringing purposes, including by (1) implementing filtering; (2) denying access; and (3) supervising and regulating users. LW has not exercised any meaningful supervisory control over LimeWire users' infringing activity, or provided a legitimate reason for its failure to do so.

The evidence establishes that LW possesses a direct financial interest in users' infringing activity. As discussed earlier, LimeWire users are drawn to LimeWire because the program permits infringement. LW has profited from its ability to attract infringing users, including through increased advertising revenue and increased sales of LimeWire Pro and authorized music.

LW contends that because LimeWire is capable of substantial non-infringing uses, LW cannot be liable for vicarious infringement. The Court, however, has found no case in which the *Sony-Betamax* rule was applied in the context of a vicarious infringement claim; some courts have explicitly rejected such an application. The Court, therefore, declines to extend the *Sony-Betamax* rule to Plaintiffs' vicarious liability claim. Moreover, even if the rule did apply, summary judgment in favor of LW would be unwarranted because the record does not support a finding that LimeWire is capable of substantial noninfringing uses.

Accordingly, the Court DENIES LW's motion for summary judgment as to Plaintiffs' claim of vicarious copyright infringement.

Notes

1. A permanent injunction against Lime Wire, shutting it down, was issued on October 26, 2010. *See* http://www.limewire.com.

2. Copyright violations extend to situations where there is vicarious liability. Hence, companies like Napster and Lime Wire may be responsible for the acts of users of their services. In contrast, as discussed in § 14.3, social networking sites, such as MySpace and Facebook, have broad immunity for materials posted on their sites by third parties. Which is the proper model for policing the Internet: imposing a burden on websites to police their own sites or how individuals use those sites or immunizing those websites from the acts of third parties?

––––––––––

3. Illegal "Warez" Organizations and Internet Piracy

The Computer Crime and Intellectual Property Section of the Department of Justice described these organizations in a release related to "Operation Buccaneer," involving a coordinated international effort (*see* https://web.archive.org/web/20110709085739/http://www.cybercrime.gov/ob/OBorg&pr.htm):

- In the early 1990s, groups of individuals working in underground networks organized themselves into competitive gangs that obtained software, "cracked," or "ripped" it (i.e. removed various forms of copy protections) and posted it on the Internet for other members of the group. This network of individuals and groups, numbering in the thousands, evolved into what is today loosely called the "warez scene" or community.

- At the top of the warez scene are a handful of "release" groups that specialize in being the first to obtain, crack (i.e., remove or circumvent copyright protections), and distribute or release the latest software, games, movies, or music to the warez scene. Frequently, these new "releases" reach the Internet days or weeks before the product is commercially available. Release groups compete against each other to attain a reputation as the fastest providers of the highest quality, free pirated software, including utility and application software, computer and console games, and movies.

- As technology has advanced, the top warez groups have become more technologically sophisticated and security conscious to avoid detection by law enforcement. Many of the elite groups communicate about warez business only through private e-mail servers, sometimes using encryption, and in closed, invitation-only IRC channels. Additionally, most members disguise their true IP addresses (and thus their true locations) when communicating in IRC by routing their communications through "virtual hosts" or bounce boxes. Finally, many warez groups protect their large FTP archive sites—which can contain tens of thousands of copies of software, games, music, and music for free downloading—through a combination of security measures that include bounce sites, automated programs for IP address and user password verification, and the use of non-standard ports for FTP traffic.

- The specific reasons that an individual becomes and remains involved in the top warez "release" or "courier" organizations may vary. However, it is almost always the case that a primary motivator is the desire to gain access to a virtually unlimited amount of free software, game, movie, and/or music titles available on the huge file storage and transfer sites (FTP sites) maintained by, or offering user privileges to, these elite warez groups. These computer sites not only offer a tremendous variety of quality copyrighted works, but they also generally have extremely fast Internet connections for rapid, efficient downloading and uploading. Other possible motivators or enticements for warez group members may include: (1) the thrill and social comraderie they obtain through clandestine participation in illegal activity; (2) the improved personal reputation or fame in the warez scene that comes with membership in the "top" groups, and in helping to keep those groups on top; and (3) financial profit, as some involved in the larger warez organizations take the pirated products and sell them for commercial gain.

- Today it is estimated that approximately 8–10 of the largest warez "release" groups in the world are responsible for the majority of the pirated software, games, and movies available on the Internet. These highly organized "release" groups specialize in being the first to release new pirated software, games, and movies to the warez community for unauthorized reproduction and further distribution worldwide. Individual groups generally specialize in "releasing" only certain types of copyrighted works; for instance, two of the oldest groups, DrinkOrDie and Razor1911, specialize in releasing application software and PC or console games, respectively. In addition to their release work, these warez groups also maintain large FTP archive (or "leech") sites for the benefit of their members and others engaged in Internet software piracy. An average FTP archive site may contain between 10,000 to 25,000 individual titles of software, games, movies, and music, all of which is made available for free downloading ("leeching") by group members and valued warez associates or contributors to the site.

- The top-level release groups are highly structured organizations with defined roles and leadership hierarchy. These organizations generally have a Leader, who oversees and directs all aspects of the group; three Council members or Senior Staff, who direct and manage the day-to-day operations of the group; 10 to 15 Staff, who frequently are the most active and skilled contributors to the group's day to day "release" work; and finally, the general membership, whose functions and involvement in the group vary. Members generally only interact via the Internet and know each other only by their screen nicknames, such as "bandido," "hackrat," "erupt," or "doodad."

- A pirated version of a software application, game, or movie is frequently available worldwide even before it is made commercially available to the public. In many instances, warez groups illegally obtain advanced copies of copyrighted products from company or industry insiders, then crack the copyright protections before distributing the pirated versions on the Internet to an ever-expanding web of FTP sites worldwide. Within hours of first being posted on the Internet, a pirated version of a copyrighted product can be found on thousands of Internet sites worldwide. Eventually, these pirated versions find their way onto pay-for-access websites from China to the U.S., where users are charged monthly or per-purchase fees for downloading the unauthorized copies.

- Additionally, these warez "releases" provide an unending supply of new product to counterfeit hard goods criminal organizations. For instance, almost every new PC and console game is "cracked" and available on warez sites either before or within 24 hours of their commercial release ("0-Day" releases). Hard good pirate syndicates in Asia and Russia (for example) will download a "warez" 0-Day game release and mass produce it at optical disc manufacturing facilities. These counterfeit hard goods are then illegally sold in foreign markets often weeks before the manufacturer ships the authentic goods for the official release date in those particular markets. This can cripple the market for the legitimate products.

The "Release" Process:

- Speed and efficiency are essential to the process for preparing and packaging new pirated software for release and distribution to the warez community. The process generally has four stages and can occur within a matter of hours:

- SUPPLY: First, a group member known as a supplier will post an original digital copy of new computer software to the group's Internet drop site, which is a computer where software is posted for retrieval by members of the group. Frequently, warez suppliers are company insiders who have access to final versions of the company's new software products before their public release date.

- CRACK: Once the new supply is posted to the drop site, another group member, known as a cracker, retrieves the software and removes or circumvents all embedded copyright protection controls (e.g., serial numbers, tags, duplication controls, dongle protections, security locks).

- TESTING and PACKING: Following a successful crack, the software must be tested to ensure that it is still fully operational. Following testing, the software is then "packed," or broken into file packets that are more easily distributed by other group members.

• PRE[-Release]/Courier: After the software has been cracked, tested and packed, it is returned to the drop site, where individuals who will transfer or distribute the pirated copy across the Internet are waiting for new arrivals. Once picked up by the "preers," the illegal product is distributed to warez locations around the world in a matter of minutes. In each instance, the new "release" will include an information file (aka ".nfo file") which, among other things, proclaims and attributes credit for the release to the originating warez group. These messages allow groups and their members to get the credit they crave and develop not only their own reputations within the scene, but also that of the group.

_____

Notes on Emerging Issues

1. **Internet Streaming.**

"Streaming" generally refers to the delivery of digital media content in real time, so that it may be watched, listened to, or played contemporaneously with the transfer of the media data to a recipient's device. Popular streaming media sites and services currently include YouTube, Hulu, Vimeo, Pandora, and Spotify. Netflix and Amazon, for instance, offer online streaming of movies in addition to offering copies of movies for sale or rental, and (in the case of Amazon) offering downloads of music files for a fee. There are also a large and growing number of Internet sites that offer infringing content via streaming, many of which derive substantial revenues through advertising or user subscription fees. In contrast to a "download" model, in which a recipient receives a complete and permanent copy of a media file, when media content is delivered solely for streaming, the recipient will generally not retain a complete or permanent copy of the media file on the receiving device (although pieces of the media file being received may be buffered or stored temporarily as part of the streaming process). Streaming is also comparatively resource intensive, as playing media files to many different users in real time, without pauses or gaps, requires powerful servers and significant amounts of Internet bandwidth. Widespread use of streaming has become an increasingly viable option to disseminate media content both legitimately and illegitimately as costs for data storage processing power and bandwidth have fallen significantly.[23]

As of 2013, the Department of Justice believed that existing criminal copyright laws were "not ideally suited to address serious cases of infringing streaming:"

[E]xisting criminal copyright law provides felony penalties only for infringements that involve the "reproduction" or "distribution" of a minimum number of copies above a threshold value. To the extent that streaming of

_____

23. U.S. Dep't of Justice, Prosecuting Intellectual Property Crimes 76 (4th ed. 2013).

copyrighted works does not involve creating or transferring complete or permanent copies of a work, it is generally viewed as implicating copyright's "public performance" and "public display" rights in a work, rather than the "reproduction" or "distribution" rights. Accordingly, an illegal streaming site that willfully infringes copyrighted works by streaming may not violate the reproduction or distribution rights to a sufficient degree to be eligible for felony copyright penalties.[24]

2. Online Storage Services.

[T]he past several years have witnessed a rapid rise in the use of a new generation of online file storage services, referred to generically by such terms as "cloud storage" or "web storage" services, "webhards," or "cyber-lockers." A wide range of sites and services fall into this category, including Amazon's Cloud Drive, Apple's iCloud, Microsoft's SkyDrive, Google Drive, Dropbox, Rapidshare, MediaFire, and Filesonic. The specific features, intended uses, and target markets for these services vary widely; some are designed and marketed primarily for data backup or for access to personal files while traveling, while some are focused more on facilitating transfers of large data files to others. Many provide substantial amounts of storage for free. The capability of cyberlocker services to disseminate large media files has led to their use in large scale piracy of movies, music, software, and other copyrighted works. Although the use of cyberlockers to infringe copyright is a relatively recent trend, the same principles apply to cyber-lockers as to other types of online infringement. Individual users of cyber-lockers who make use of cyberlockers to reproduce, distribute, or otherwise infringe copyright willfully may be prosecuted criminally, provided the other elements of the criminal copyright statute (e.g., minimum numeric and monetary thresholds; commercial advantage or private financial gain; online distribution of pre-release works) are met. Operators of cyberlock-ers may also be subject to prosecution for criminal copyright infringement where they willfully distribute or disseminate infringing content, or under theories of aiding and abetting or conspiracy to commit criminal copyright infringement. See 18 U.S.C. §§ 2, 371.

To the extent that cyberlockers are used to distribute large media files to a group or to the public, they function much like popular user-generated content ("UGC") sites like YouTube or Vimeo. However, a common feature that generally distinguishes cyberlockers from UGC sites is that cyberlock-ers are generally not designed to be searchable by outside users or the web-crawlers used by search engines to index publicly-available content on the Internet. On many cyberlocker sites, the only way to access a particular file is to know the specific URL or address where the file is located. Partly as a

---

24. *Id.* at 77.

result, an ecosystem of "linking sites" has developed that compile and categorize links to media files located on cyberlocker sites (as well as BitTorrent or other links to P2P networks), enabling users to search for and locate particular files, including pirated media content. Many of these linking sites are supported by advertising, and some may also receive affiliate commissions in exchange for driving traffic to a cyberlocker or other content-hosting site. The fact that a "pure" linking site does not host infringing content itself may present additional challenges to criminal prosecution. Most courts that have addressed the issue in civil cases have held that merely providing links to infringing content does not violate the distribution right or otherwise constitute direct copyright infringement (although such conduct may still result in secondary liability under a theory of contributory or vicarious infringement). The extent to which merely linking to infringing content hosted by other sites may constitute criminal copyright infringement under 17 U.S.C. § 506 has not been conclusively resolved by the courts. Regardless of whether linking itself amounts to a substantive violation of § 506, however, defendants who facilitate infringement by others by providing links to infringing material online may nevertheless by prosecuted under theories of aiding and abetting (18 U.S.C. § 2) or conspiracy (18 U.S.C. § 371), provided that the other requisite elements of criminal infringement (e.g., willfulness, numeric and monetary thresholds, online distribution of pre-release work) can be shown.[25]

§ 17.2 The Digital Millennium Copyright Act, 17 U.S.C. §§ 1201–05

A statute that has broad applicability to Internet activities is The Digital Millenium Copyright Act, 17 U.S.C. §§ 1201–05, which prohibits the use of computers and other digital devices to circumvent technological measures used to protect copyrighted works. In contrast to copyright law, which focuses on infringement of a copyrighted work, the DMCA focuses primarily on the facilitation of infringement through creation or trafficking in tools that circumvent access or copy control. A defendant who has violated the DMCA has not necessarily infringed on a copyrighted work under copyright law; instead, the DMCA "targets the circumvention of digital walls guarding copyrighted material (and trafficking in circumvention tools), [it] does not concern itself with the use of those materials after circumvention has occurred."[26]

With the advent of digital media and the Internet as a means to distribute such media, large-scale digital copying and distribution of copyrighted

---

25. *Id.* at 78–79.
26. Universal City Studios, Inc. v. Corley, 273 F.3d 429, 443 (2d Cir. 2001).

material became easy and inexpensive. In response to this development, and to prevent large-scale piracy of digital content over the Internet, in 1997 the World Intellectual Property Organization (WIPO) responded with two treaties, the Copyright Treaty, and the Performances and Phonograms Treaty, to prohibit pirates from defeating the digital locks that copyright owners use to protect their digital content from unauthorized access or copying. Specifically, Article 11 of the WIPO Copyright Treaty prescribes that contracting states

> shall provide adequate legal protection and effective legal remedies against the circumvention of effective technological measures that are used by authors in connection with the exercise of their rights under this Treaty or the Berne Convention and that restricts acts, in respect of their works, which are not authorized by the authors concerned or permitted by law.

The United States signed these treaties on April 12, 1997, and ratified them on October 21, 1998. To implement these treaties, Congress enacted Title I of the Digital Millennium Copyright Act (DMCA) on October 28, 1998, with the twin goals of protecting copyrighted works from piracy and promoting electronic commerce. Congress accomplished these goals by enacting prohibitions relating to the circumvention of copyright protection systems as set forth in 17 U.S.C. § 1201, and the integrity of copyright management information pursuant to 17 U.S.C. § 1202. Criminal enforcement has largely focused on violations of the anticircumvention and anti-trafficking prohibitions in 17 U.S.C. § 1201.[27]

Section 1201 has three prohibitions:[28]

- **Section 1201(a)(1) prohibits circumvention of access controls:**

No person shall circumvent a technological measure that effectively controls access to a work protected under this title.

- **Section 1201(a)(2) prohibits trafficking in technology designed to circumvent access controls:**

No person shall manufacture, import, offer to the public, provide, or otherwise traffic in any technology, product, service, device, component, or part thereof, that—

   (A) is primarily designed or produced for the purpose of circumventing a technological measure that effectively controls access to a work protected under this title;

---

27. U.S. Dep't of Justice, Prosecuting Intellectual Property Crimes 233–34 (4th ed. 2013).

28. Congress enacted specific provisions to protect certain uses, including exceptions for law enforcement, reverse engineering, encryption research, and security testing. 17 U.S.C. § 1201(e)–(g) and 1201(f).

(B) has only limited commercially significant purpose or use other than to circumvent a technological measure that effectively protects a right of a copyright owner under this title; or

(C) is marketed by that person or another acting in concert with that person with that person's knowledge for use in circumventing a technological measure that effectively controls access to a work protected under this title.

- **Section 1201(b)(1) prohibits trafficking in technology designed to circumvent copy controls:**

No person shall manufacture, import, offer to the public, provide, or otherwise traffic in any technology, product, service, device, component, or part thereof, that—

(A) is primarily designed or produced for the purpose of circumventing protection afforded by a technological measure that effectively protects a right of a copyright owner under this title in a work or a portion thereof;

(B) has only limited commercially significant purpose or use other than to circumvent protection afforded by a technological measure that effectively protects a right of a copyright owner under this title in a work or a portion thereof; or

(C) is marketed by that person or another acting in concert with that person with that person's knowledge for use in circumventing protection afforded by a technological measure that effectively protects a right of a copyright owner under this title in a work or a portion thereof.

United States v. Elcom Ltd.

203 F. Supp. 2d 1111 (N.D. Cal. 2002)

GARZA, JUDGE.

Through the DMCA, Congress sought to prohibit certain efforts to unlawfully circumvent protective technologies, while at the same time preserving users' rights of fair use. Some understanding of the interplay between copyright and fair use is essential to understanding the issues confronting Congress. In brief, copyright grants authors the exclusive right to make and distribute copies of their original works of authorship but the doctrine of fair use permits a certain amount of copying for limited purposes without infringing the copyright, notwithstanding the exclusive rights of the copyright owner.

As part of the balance Congress sought to strike in protecting the rights of copyright owners while preserving fair use, Congress enacted three new anti-circumvention prohibitions, Section 1201(a)(1), Section 1201(a)(2) and Section 1201(b). The first two provisions target circumvention of technological measures that effectively control *access* to a copyrighted work; the third targets circumvention of technological measures that impose limitations on the *use* of protected works. With regard to the first category, Congress banned both the act of circumventing access control restrictions as well as trafficking in and marketing of devices that are primarily designed for such circumvention.

The third prohibition, however, addresses a different circumvention, specifically, circumventing a technological measure that imposes limitations on the use of a copyrighted work, or in the words of the statute, that "effectively protects the right of a copyright owner." [In Section 1201(b)], Congress did *not* ban the act of circumventing the use restrictions. Instead, Congress banned only the trafficking in and marketing of devices primarily designed to circumvent the use restriction protective technologies. Congress did not prohibit the act of circumvention because it sought to preserve the fair use rights of persons who had lawfully acquired a work.

In fact, Congress expressly disclaimed any intent to impair any person's rights of fair use: "Nothing in this section shall affect rights, remedies, or defenses to copyright infringement, including fair use, under this title [17 U.S.C.A. § 1 et seq.]." Thus, circumventing use restrictions is not unlawful, but in order to protect the rights of copyright owners while maintaining fair use, Congress banned trafficking in devices that are primarily designed for the purpose of circumventing any technological measure that "effectively protects a right of a copyright owner," or that have limited commercially significant purposes other than circumventing use restrictions, or that are marketed for use in circumventing the use restrictions.

MDY Industries, LLC v. Blizzard Entertainment, Inc.

629 F.3d 928 (9th Cir. 2010)

CALLAHAN, CIRCUIT JUDGE:

Blizzard Entertainment, Inc. is the creator of World of Warcraft, a popular multiplayer online role-playing game in which players interact in a virtual world while advancing through the game's 70 levels. MDY Industries, LLC and its sole member Michael Donnelly developed and sold Glider, a software program that automatically plays the early levels of WoW for players.

MDY brought this action for a declaratory judgment to establish that its Glider sales do not infringe Blizzard's copyright or other rights, and Blizzard asserted counterclaims under the Digital Millennium Copyright Act ("DMCA"), 17 U.S.C. § 1201 *et seq.*, and for tortious interference with contract under Arizona law. The district court found MDY and Donnelly liable for secondary copyright infringement, violations of DMCA § 1201(a)(2) and (b)(1), and tortious interference with contract. We reverse the district court except as to MDY's liability for violation of DMCA § 1201(a)(2) and remand for trial on Blizzard's claim for tortious interference with contract.

I.

A. World of Warcraft

In November 2004, Blizzard created WoW, a "massively multiplayer online role-playing game" in which players interact in a virtual world. WoW has ten million subscribers, of which two and a half million are in North America. The WoW software has two components: (1) the game client software that a player installs on the computer; and (2) the game server software, which the player accesses on a subscription basis by connecting to WoW's online servers. WoW does not have single-player or offline modes.

WoW players roleplay different characters, such as humans, elves, and dwarves. A player's central objective is to advance the character through the game's 70 levels by participating in quests and engaging in battles with monsters. As a player advances, the character collects rewards such as in-game currency, weapons, and armor. WoW's virtual world has its own economy, in which characters use their virtual currency to buy and sell items directly from each other, through vendors, or using auction houses. Some players also utilize WoW's chat capabilities to interact with others.

B. Blizzard's use agreements

Each WoW player must read and accept Blizzard's End User License Agreement ("EULA") and Terms of Use ("ToU") on multiple occasions. The EULA pertains to the game client, so a player agrees to it both before installing the game client and upon first running it. The ToU pertains to the online service, so a player agrees to it both when creating an account and upon first connecting to the online service. Players who do not accept both the EULA and the ToU may return the game client for a refund.

C. Development of Glider and Warden

Donnelly is a WoW player and software programmer. In March 2005, he developed Glider, a software "bot" (short for robot) that automates play of WoW's early levels, for his personal use. A user need not be at the computer while Glider is running. As explained in the Frequently Asked Questions ("FAQ") on MDY's website for Glider:

> Glider . . . moves the mouse around and pushes keys on the keyboard. You tell it about your character, where you want to kill things, and when you want to kill. Then it kills for you, automatically. You can do something else, like eat dinner or go to a movie, and when you return, you'll have a lot more experience and loot.

Glider does not alter or copy WoW's game client software, does not allow a player to avoid paying monthly subscription dues to Blizzard, and has no commercial use independent of WoW. Glider was not initially designed to avoid detection by Blizzard.

The parties dispute Glider's impact on the WoW experience. Blizzard contends that Glider disrupts WoW's environment for non-Glider players by enabling Glider users to advance quickly and unfairly through the game and to amass additional game assets. MDY contends that Glider has a minimal effect on non-Glider players, enhances the WoW experience for Glider users, and facilitates disabled players' access to WoW by auto-playing the game for them.

In summer 2005, Donnelly began selling Glider through MDY's website for fifteen to twenty-five dollars per license. Prior to marketing Glider, Donnelly reviewed Blizzard's EULA and client-server manipulation policy. He reached the conclusion that Blizzard had not prohibited bots in those documents.

In September 2005, Blizzard launched Warden, a technology that it developed to prevent its players who use unauthorized third-party software, including bots, from connecting to WoW's servers. Warden was able to detect Glider, and Blizzard immediately used Warden to ban most Glider users. MDY responded by modifying Glider to avoid detection and promoting its new anti-detection features on its website's FAQ. It added a subscription service, Glider Elite, which offered "additional protection from game detection software" for five dollars a month.

Thus, by late 2005, MDY was aware that Blizzard was prohibiting bots. MDY modified its website to indicate that using Glider violated Blizzard's ToU. In November 2005, Donnelly wrote in an email interview, "Avoiding detection is rather exciting, to be sure. Since Blizzard does not want bots running at all, it's a violation to use them." Following MDY's anti-detection modifications, Warden only occasionally detected Glider. As of September 2008, MDY had gross revenues of $3.5 million based on 120,000 Glider license sales.

D. Financial and practical impact of Glider

Blizzard claims that from December 2004 to March 2008, it received 465,000 complaints about WoW bots, several thousand of which named Glider. Blizzard spends $940,000 annually to respond to these complaints, and the parties have stipulated that Glider is the principal bot used by WoW players. Blizzard introduced evidence that it may have lost monthly subscription fees from Glider users, who were able to reach WoW's highest levels in fewer weeks than players playing manually. Donnelly acknowledged in a November 2005 email that MDY's business strategy was to make Blizzard's anti-bot detection attempts financially prohibitive:

> The trick here is that Blizzard has a finite amount of development and test resources, so we want to make it bad business to spend that much time altering their detection code to find Glider, since Glider's negative effect on the game is debatable. . . . [W]e attack th[is] weakness and try to make it a bad idea or make their changes very risky, since they don't want to risk banning or crashing innocent customers.

II.

B. The Digital Millennium Copyright Act

The DMCA contains three provisions directed at the circumvention of copyright owners' technological measures. The Supreme Court has yet to construe these provisions, and they raise questions of first impression in this circuit. The first provision, 17 U.S.C. § 1201(a)(1)(A), is a general prohibition against "circumventing a technological measure that effectively controls access to a work protected under [the Copyright Act]." The second prohibits trafficking in technology that circumvents a technological measure that "effectively controls access" to a copyrighted work. 17 U.S.C. § 1201(a)(2). The third prohibits trafficking in technology that circumvents a technological measure that "effectively protects" a copyright owner's right. 17 U.S.C. § 1201(b)(1).

We turn to consider whether Glider violates DMCA § 1201(a)(2) and (b)(1) by allowing users to circumvent Warden to access WoW's various elements. MDY contends that Warden's scan.dll and resident components are separate, and only scan.dll should be considered as a potential access control measure under § 1201(a)(2). However, in our view, an access control measure can both (1) attempt to block initial access and (2) revoke access if a secondary check determines that access was unauthorized. Our analysis considers Warden's scan.dll and resident components together because the two components have the same purpose: to prevent players using detectable bots from continuing to access WoW software.

D. Construction of § 1201

We begin by considering the scope of DMCA § 1201's three operative provisions, §§ 1201(a)(1), 1201(a)(2), and 1201(b)(1). We consider them side-by-side, because "[w]e do not . . . construe statutory phrases in isolation; we read statutes as a whole. Thus, the [term to be construed] must be read in light of the immediately following phrase. . . ."

1. *Text of the operative provisions*

"We begin, as always, with the text of the statute." [Ed. The text of the statutes are reproduced at the beginning of this subsection.]

2. *Our harmonization of the DMCA's operative provisions*

For the reasons set forth below, we believe that § 1201 is best understood to create two distinct types of claims. First, § 1201(a) prohibits the circumvention of any technological measure that effectively controls access to a protected work and grants copyright owners the right to enforce that prohibition. Second, and in contrast to § 1201(a), § 1201(b)(1) prohibits trafficking in technologies that circumvent technological measures that effectively protect "a right of a copyright owner." Section 1201(b)(1)'s prohibition is thus aimed at circumventions of measures that protect the copyright itself: it entitles copyright owners to protect their existing exclusive rights under the Copyright Act. Those exclusive rights are reproduction, distribution, public performance, public display, and creation of derivative works. 17 U.S.C. § 106. Historically speaking, preventing "access" to a protected work in itself has not been a right of a copyright owner arising from the Copyright Act.

Our construction of § 1201 is compelled by the four significant textual differences between § 1201(a) and (b). First, § 1201(a)(2) prohibits the circumvention of a measure that "effectively controls access to *a work protected under this title*," whereas § 1201(b)(1) concerns a measure that "effectively protects *a right of a copyright owner under this title in a work or portion thereof.*" (emphasis added). We read § 1201(b)(1)'s language — "right of a copyright owner under this title" — to reinforce copyright owners' traditional exclusive rights under § 106 by granting them an additional cause of action against those who traffic in circumventing devices that facilitate infringement. Sections 1201(a)(1) and (a)(2), however, use the term "work protected under this title." Neither of these two subsections explicitly refers to traditional copyright infringement under § 106. Accordingly, we read this term as extending a new form of protection, i.e., the right to prevent circumvention of access controls, broadly to works protected under Title 17, i.e., copyrighted works.

Second, as used in § 1201(a), to "circumvent a technological measure" means "to descramble a scrambled work, to decrypt an encrypted work, or otherwise to avoid, bypass, remove, deactivate, or impair a technological measure, without the authority of the copyright owner." 17 U.S.C. § 1201(a)(3)(A). These two specific examples of unlawful circumvention under § 1201(a) — descrambling a scrambled work and decrypting an encrypted work — are acts that do not necessarily infringe or facilitate infringement of a copyright. Descrambling or decrypting only enables someone to watch or listen to a work without authorization, which is not necessarily an infringement of a copyright owner's traditional exclusive rights under § 106. Put differently, descrambling and decrypting do not necessarily result in someone's reproducing, distributing, publicly performing, or publicly displaying the copyrighted work, or creating derivative works based on the copyrighted work.

The third significant difference between the subsections is that § 1201(a)(1)(A) prohibits circumventing an effective access control measure, whereas § 1201(b) prohibits trafficking in circumventing devices, but does not prohibit circumvention itself because such conduct was already outlawed as copyright infringement. The Senate Judiciary Committee explained:

> This . . . is the reason there is no prohibition on conduct in 1201(b) akin to the prohibition on circumvention conduct in 1201(a)(1). The prohibition in 1201(a)(1) is necessary because prior to this Act, the conduct of circumvention was never before made unlawful. The device limitation on 1201(a)(2) enforces this new prohibition on conduct. The copyright law has long forbidden copyright infringements, so no new prohibition was necessary.

This difference reinforces our reading of § 1201(b) as strengthening copyright owners' traditional rights against copyright infringement and of § 1201(a) as granting copyright owners a new anti-circumvention right.

Fourth, in § 1201(a)(1)(B)–(D), Congress directs the Library of Congress to identify classes of copyrighted works for which "noninfringing uses by persons who are users of a copyrighted work are, or are likely to be, adversely affected, and the [anti-circumvention] prohibition contained in [§ 1201(a)(1)(A)] shall not apply to such users with respect to such classes of works for the ensuing 3-year period." There is no analogous provision in § 1201(b). We impute this lack of symmetry to Congress' need to balance copyright owners' new anti-circumvention right with the public's right to access the work. Sections 1201(a)(1)(B)–(D) thus promote the public's right to access by allowing the Library to exempt circumvention of effective access control measures in particular situations where it concludes that the public's right to access outweighs the owner's interest in restricting access. In limiting the owner's right to control access, the Library does not, and is not permitted to, authorize infringement of a copyright owner's traditional exclusive rights under the copyright. Rather, the Library is only entitled to moderate the new anti-circumvention right created by, and hence subject to the limitations in, DMCA § 1201(a)(1).[n.8][29]

Our reading of § 1201(a) and (b) ensures that neither section is rendered superfluous. A violation of § 1201(a)(1)(A), which prohibits circumvention itself, will not be a violation of § 1201(b), which does not contain an analogous prohibition on circumvention. A violation of § 1201(a)(2), which prohibits trafficking in devices that facilitate circumvention of *access* control measures, will not always be a violation of § 1201(b)(1), which prohibits trafficking in devices that facilitate circumvention of measures that protect against *copyright infringement*. Of course, if a copyright owner puts in place an effective measure that both (1) controls access and (2) protects against copyright infringement, a defendant who traffics in a device that circumvents that measure could be liable under both § 1201(a) and (b). Nonetheless, we read the differences in structure between § 1201(a) and (b) as reflecting Congress's intent to address distinct concerns by creating different rights with different elements.

3. *Our construction of the DMCA is consistent with the legislative history*

Although the text suffices to resolve the issues before us, we also consider the legislative history in order to address the parties' arguments concerning it. Our review of that history supports the view that Congress created a new anticircumvention right in § 1201(a)(2) independent of traditional copyright infringement and granted copyright owners a new weapon against copyright infringement in § 1201(b)(1). For instance, the Senate Judiciary Committee report explains that § 1201(a)(2) and (b)(1) are "not interchangeable": they were "designed to protect two distinct rights and to target two distinct classes of devices," and "many devices will be subject to challenge only under one of the subsections." That is, § 1201(a)(2) "is designed to protect access to a copyrighted work," while § 1201(b)(1) "is designed to protect the traditional copyright rights of the copyright owner." Thus, the Senate Judiciary Committee understood § 1201 to create the following regime:

---

29. [n.8] In addition to these four textual differences, we note that § 1201(a)(2) prohibits the circumvention of "a technological measure," and § 1201(b)(1) prohibits the circumvention "of protection afforded by a technological measure." In our view, these terms have the same meaning, given the presumption that a "legislative body generally uses a particular word with a consistent meaning in a given context."

> [I]f an effective technological protection measure does nothing to prevent access to the plain text of the work, but is designed to prevent that work from being copied, then a potential cause of action against the manufacturer of a device designed to circumvent the measure lies under § 1201(b)(1), but not under § 1201(a)(2). Conversely, if an effective technological protection measure limits access to the plain text of a work only to those with authorized access, but provides no additional protection against copying, displaying, performing or distributing the work, then a potential cause of action against the manufacturer of a device designed to circumvent the measure lies under § 1201(a)(2), but not under § 1201(b).

The Senate Judiciary Committee proffered an example of § 1201(a) liability with no nexus to infringement, stating that if an owner effectively protected access to a copyrighted work by use of a password, it would violate § 1201(a)(2)(A):

> [T]o defeat or bypass the password and to make the means to do so, as long as the primary purpose of the means was to perform this kind of act. This is roughly analogous to making it illegal to break into a house using a tool, the primary purpose of which is to break into houses.

The House Judiciary Committee similarly states of § 1201(a)(2), "The act of circumventing a technological protection measure put in place by a copyright owner to control access to a copyrighted work is the electronic equivalent of breaking into a locked room in order to obtain a copy of a book." We note that bypassing a password and breaking into a locked room in order to read or view a copyrighted work would not infringe on any of the copyright owner's exclusive rights under § 106.

We read this legislative history as confirming Congress's intent, in light of the current digital age, to grant copyright owners an independent right to enforce the prohibition against circumvention of effective technological access controls. In § 1201(a), Congress was particularly concerned with encouraging copyright owners to make their works available in digital formats such as "on-demand" or "pay-per-view," which allow consumers effectively to "borrow" a copy of the work for a limited time or a limited number of uses. As the House Commerce Committee explained:

> [A]n increasing number of intellectual property works are being distributed using a "client-server" model, where the work is effectively "borrowed" by the user (e.g., infrequent users of expensive software purchase a certain number of uses, or viewers watch a movie on a pay-per-view basis). To operate in this environment, content providers will need both the technology to make new uses possible and the legal framework to ensure they can protect their work from piracy.

Our review of the legislative history supports our reading of § 1201: that section (a) creates a new anticircumvention right distinct from copyright infringement, while section (b) strengthens the traditional prohibition against copyright infringement. We now review the decisions of the Federal Circuit that have interpreted § 1201 differently.

4. *The Federal Circuit's decisions*

The Federal Circuit has adopted a different approach to the DMCA. In essence, it requires § 1201(a) plaintiffs to demonstrate that the circumventing technology infringes or facilitates infringement of the plaintiff's copyright (an "infringement nexus requirement"). *See Chamberlain Group, Inc. v. Skylink Techs., Inc.*, 381 F.3d 1178, 1203 (Fed.Cir.2004); *Storage Tech. Corp. v. Custom Hardware Eng'g & Consulting, Inc.*, 421 F.3d 1307 (Fed. Cir. 2005).

The seminal decision is *Chamberlain*. In *Chamberlain*, the plaintiff sold garage door openers ("GDOs") with a "rolling code" security system that purportedly reduced the risk of crime by constantly changing the transmitter signal necessary to open the door. Customers used the GDOs' transmitters to send the changing signal, which in turn opened or closed their garage doors.

Plaintiff sued the defendant, who sold "universal" GDO transmitters for use with plaintiff's GDOs, under § 1201(a)(2). The plaintiff alleged that its GDOs and transmitters both contained copyrighted computer programs and that its rolling code security system was a technological measure that controlled access to those programs. Accordingly, plaintiff alleged that the defendant—by selling GDO transmitters that were compatible with plaintiff's GDOs—had trafficked in a technology that was primarily used for the circumvention of a technological measure (the rolling code security system) that effectively controlled access to plaintiff's copyrighted works.

The Federal Circuit rejected the plaintiff's claim, holding that the defendant did not violate § 1201(a)(2) because, *inter alia*, the defendant's universal GDO transmitters did not infringe or facilitate infringement of the plaintiff's copyrighted computer programs. The linchpin of the *Chamberlain* court's analysis is its conclusion that DMCA coverage is limited to a copyright owner's rights under the Copyright Act as set forth in § 106 of the Copyright Act. Thus, it held that § 1201(a) did not grant copyright owners a new anti-circumvention right, but instead, established new causes of action for a defendant's unauthorized access of copyrighted material when it infringes upon a copyright owner's rights under § 106. Accordingly, a § 1201(a)(2) plaintiff was required to demonstrate a nexus to infringement—i.e., that the defendant's trafficking in circumventing technology had a "reasonable relationship" to the protections that the Copyright Act affords copyright owners. The Federal Circuit explained:

> Defendants who traffic in devices that circumvent access controls in ways that facilitate infringement may be subject to liability under § 1201(a)(2). Defendants who use such devices may be subject to liability under § 1201(a)(1) whether they infringe or not. Because all defendants who traffic in devices that circumvent rights controls necessarily facilitate infringement, they may be subject to liability under § 1201(b). Defendants who use such devices may be subject to liability for copyright infringement. *And finally,*

> *defendants whose circumvention devices do not facilitate infringement are not*
> *subject to § 1201 liability.*

Chamberlain concluded that § 1201(a) created a new cause of action linked to copyright infringement, rather than a new anti-circumvention right separate from copyright infringement, for six reasons.

First, *Chamberlain* reasoned that Congress enacted the DMCA to balance the interests of copyright owners and information users, and an infringement nexus requirement was necessary to create an anti-circumvention right that truly achieved that balance. Second, *Chamberlain* feared that copyright owners could use an access control right to prohibit exclusively fair uses of their material even absent feared foul use. Third, *Chamberlain* feared that § 1201(a) would allow companies to leverage their sales into aftermarket monopolies, in potential violation of antitrust law and the doctrine of copyright misuse. Fourth, *Chamberlain* viewed an infringement nexus requirement as necessary to prevent "absurd and disastrous results," such as the existence of DMCA liability for disabling a burglary alarm to gain access to a home containing copyrighted materials.

Fifth, *Chamberlain* stated that an infringement nexus requirement might be necessary to render Congress's exercise of its Copyright Clause authority rational. The Copyright Clause gives Congress "the task of defining the scope of the limited monopoly that should be granted to authors . . . in order to give the public appropriate access to their work product." Without an infringement nexus requirement, Congress arguably would have allowed copyright owners in § 1201(a) to deny all access to the public by putting an effective access control measure in place that the public was not allowed to circumvent.

Finally, the *Chamberlain* court viewed an infringement nexus requirement as necessary for the Copyright Act to be internally consistent. It reasoned that § 1201(c)(1), enacted simultaneously, provides that "nothing in this section shall affect rights, remedies, limitations, or defenses to copyright infringement, including fair use, under this title." The *Chamberlain* court opined that if § 1201(a) creates liability for access without regard to the remainder of the Copyright Act, it "would clearly affect rights and limitations, if not remedies and defenses."

Accordingly, the Federal Circuit held that a DMCA § 1201(a)(2) action was foreclosed to the extent that the defendant trafficked in a device that did not facilitate copyright infringement.

5. *We decline to adopt an infringement nexus requirement*

While we appreciate the policy considerations expressed by the Federal Circuit in *Chamberlain*, we are unable to follow its approach because it is contrary to the plain language of the statute. In addition, the Federal Circuit failed to recognize the rationale for the statutory construction that we have proffered. Also, its approach is based on policy concerns that are best directed to Congress in the first instance, or for which there appear to be other reasons that do not require such a convoluted construction of the statute's language.

i. Statutory inconsistencies

Were we to follow *Chamberlain* in imposing an infringement nexus requirement, we would have to disregard the plain language of the statute. Moreover, there is significant textual evidence showing Congress's intent to create a new anticircumvention right in § 1201(a) distinct from infringement. As set forth *supra*, this evidence includes: (1) Congress's choice to link only § 1201(b)(1) explicitly to infringement; (2) Congress's provision in § 1201(a)(3)(A) that descrambling and decrypting devices can lead to § 1201(a) liability, even though descrambling and decrypting devices may only enable non-infringing access to a copyrighted work; and (3) Congress's creation of a mechanism in § 1201(a)(1)(B)–(D) to exempt certain non-infringing behavior from § 1201(a)(1) liability, a mechanism that would be unnecessary if an infringement nexus requirement existed.

Though unnecessary to our conclusion because of the clarity of the statute's text, we also note that the legislative history supports the conclusion that Congress intended to prohibit even non-infringing circumvention and trafficking in circumventing devices. Moreover, in mandating a § 1201(a) nexus to infringement, we would deprive copyright owners of the important enforcement tool that Congress granted them to make sure that they are compensated for valuable non-infringing access—for instance, copyright owners who make movies or music available online, protected by an access control measure, in exchange for direct or indirect payment.

The *Chamberlain* court reasoned that if § 1201(a) creates liability for access without regard to the remainder of the Copyright Act, it "would clearly affect rights and limitations, if not remedies and defenses." This perceived tension is relieved by our recognition that § 1201(a) creates a new anti-circumvention right distinct from the traditional exclusive rights of a copyright owner. It follows that § 1201(a) does not limit the traditional framework of exclusive rights created by § 106, or defenses to those rights such as fair use. We are thus unpersuaded by *Chamberlain's* reading of the DMCA's text and structure.

ii. Additional interpretive considerations

Though we need no further evidence of Congress's intent, the parties, citing *Chamberlain*, proffer several other arguments, which we review briefly in order to address the parties' contentions. *Chamberlain* relied heavily on policy considerations to support its reading of § 1201(a). As a threshold matter, we stress that such considerations cannot trump the statute's plain text and structure. Even were they permissible considerations in this case, however, they would not persuade us to adopt an infringement nexus requirement. *Chamberlain* feared that § 1201(a) would allow companies to leverage their sales into aftermarket monopolies, in tension with antitrust law and the doctrine of copyright misuse. Concerning antitrust law, we note that there is no clear issue of anti-competitive behavior in this case because Blizzard does not seek to put a direct competitor who offers a competing role-playing game out of business and the parties have not argued this issue. If a § 1201(a)(2) defendant in a future case claims that a plaintiff is attempting to enforce its DMCA anti-circumvention right in a manner that violates antitrust law, we will then consider the interplay between this new anti-circumvention right and antitrust law.

Chamberlain also viewed an infringement nexus requirement as necessary to prevent "absurd and disastrous results," such as the existence of DMCA liability for disabling a burglary alarm to gain access to a home containing copyrighted materials. In addition, the Federal Circuit was concerned that, without an infringement nexus requirement, § 1201(a) would allow copyright owners to deny all access to the public by putting an effective access control measure in place that the public is not allowed to circumvent. Both concerns appear to be overstated, but even accepting them, *arguendo*, as legitimate concerns, they do not permit reading the statute as requiring the imposition of an infringement nexus. As § 1201(a) creates a distinct right, it does not disturb the balance between public rights and the traditional rights of owners of copyright under the Copyright Act. Moreover, § 1201(a)(1)(B)–(D) allows the Library of Congress to create exceptions to the § 1201(a) anticircumvention right in the public's interest. If greater protection of the public's ability to access copyrighted works is required, Congress can provide such protection by amending the statute.

In sum, we conclude that a fair reading of the statute (supported by legislative history) indicates that Congress created a distinct anti-circumvention right under § 1201(a) without an infringement nexus requirement. Thus, even accepting the validity of the concerns expressed in *Chamberlain*, those concerns do not authorize us to override congressional intent and add a non-textual element to the statute. Accordingly, we reject the imposition of an infringement nexus requirement. We now consider whether MDY has violated § 1201(a)(2) and (b)(1).

E. Blizzard's § 1201(a)(2) claim

1. *WoW's literal elements and individual non-literal elements*

We agree with the district court that MDY's Glider does not violate DMCA § 1201(a)(2) with respect to WoW's literal elements and individual non-literal elements, because Warden does not effectively control access to these WoW elements. First, Warden does not control access to WoW's literal elements because these elements—the game client's software code—are available on a player's hard drive once the game client software is installed. Second, as the district court found:

> [WoW's] individual nonliteral components may be accessed by a user without signing on to the server. As was demonstrated during trial, an owner of the game client software may use independently purchased computer programs to call up the visual images or the recorded sounds within the game client software. For instance, a user may call up and listen to the roar a particular monster makes within the game. Or the user may call up a virtual image of that monster.

Since a player need not encounter Warden to access WoW's individual non-literal elements, Warden does not effectively control access to those elements. Our conclusion is in accord with the Sixth Circuit's decision in *Lexmark International v. Static Control Components*, 387 F.3d 522 (6th Cir. 2004). In *Lexmark*, the plaintiff sold laser printers equipped with an authentication sequence, verified by the printer's copyrighted software, that ensured that only plaintiff's own toner cartridges could be inserted into the printers. The defendant sold microchips capable of generating an authentication sequence that rendered other manufacturers' cartridges compatible with plaintiff's printers.

The Sixth Circuit held that plaintiff's § 1201(a)(2) claim failed because its authentication sequence did not effectively control access to its copyrighted computer program. Rather, the mere purchase of one of plaintiff's printers allowed "access" to the copyrighted program. Any purchaser could read the program code directly from the printer memory without encountering the authentication sequence. The authentication sequence thus blocked only one form of access: the ability to make use of the printer. However, it left intact another form of access: the review and use of the computer program's literal code. The Sixth Circuit explained:

> Just as one would not say that a lock on the back door of a house "controls access" to a house whose front door does not contain a lock and just as one would not say that a lock on any door of a house "controls access" to the house after its purchaser receives the key to the lock, it does not make sense to say that this provision of the DMCA applies to otherwise-readily-accessible copyrighted works. Add to this the fact that the DMCA not only requires the technological measure to "control access" but requires the measure to control that access "effectively," 17 U.S.C. § 1201(a)(2), and it seems clear that this provision does not naturally extend to a technological measure that restricts one form of access but leaves another route wide open.

Here, a player's purchase of the WoW game client allows access to the game's literal elements and individual non-literal elements. Warden blocks one form of access to these elements: the ability to access them while connected to a WoW server. However, analogously to the situation in *Lexmark*, Warden leaves open the ability to access these elements directly via the user's computer. We conclude that Warden is not an effective access control measure with respect to WoW's literal elements and individual non-literal elements, and therefore, that MDY does not violate § 1201(a)(2) with respect to these elements.

2. *WoW's dynamic non-literal elements*

We conclude that MDY meets each of the six textual elements for violating § 1201(a)(2) with respect to WoW's dynamic non-literal elements. That is, MDY (1) traffics in (2) a technology or part thereof (3) that is primarily designed, produced, or marketed for, or has limited commercially significant use other than (4) circumventing a technological measure (5) that effectively controls access (6) to a copyrighted work.

The first two elements are met because MDY "traffics in a technology or part thereof"—that is, it sells Glider. The third and fourth elements are met because Blizzard has established that MDY *markets* Glider for use in circumventing Warden, thus satisfying the requirement of § 1201(a)(2)(C).[n.16][30] Indeed, Glider has no function other than to facilitate the playing of WoW. The sixth element is met because, as the district court held, WoW's dynamic non-literal elements constitute a copyrighted work.

The fifth element is met because Warden is an effective access control measure. To "effectively control access to a work," a technological measure must "in the ordinary course of its operation, require[ ] the application of information, or a process or a treatment, with the authority of the copyright owner, to gain access to the work." 17 U.S.C. § 1201(a)(3)(B). Both of Warden's two components "require[ ] the application of information, or a process or a treatment . . . to gain access to the work." For a player to connect to Blizzard's servers which provide access to WoW's dynamic non-literal elements, scan.dll must scan the player's computer RAM and confirm the absence of any bots or cheats. The resident component also requires a "process" in order for the user to continue accessing the work: the user's computer must report portions of WoW code running in RAM to the server. Moreover, Warden's provisions were put into place by Blizzard, and thus, function "with the authority of the copyright owner." Accordingly, Warden effectively controls access to WoW's dynamic non-literal elements.[n.17][31] We hold that MDY is liable under § 1201(a)(2) with respect to WoW's dynamic non-literal elements. Accordingly, we affirm the district court's entry of a permanent injunction against MDY to prevent future § 1201(a)(2) violations.

---

30. [n.16] To "circumvent a technological measure" under § 1201(a) means to "descramble a scrambled work, to decrypt an encrypted work, or otherwise to avoid, bypass, remove, deactivate, or impair a technological measure, *without the authority of the copyright owner.*" A circuit split exists with respect to the meaning of the phrase "without the authority of the copyright owner." The Federal Circuit has concluded that this definition imposes an additional requirement on a § 1201(a)(2) plaintiff: to show that the defendant's circumventing device enables third parties to access the copyrighted work without the copyright owner's authorization. The Second Circuit has adopted a different view, explaining that § 1201(a)(3)(A) plainly exempts from § 1201(a) liability those whom a copyright owner authorizes to circumvent an access control measure, not those whom a copyright owner authorizes to access the work. We find the Second Circuit's view to be the sounder construction of the statute's language, and conclude that § 1201(a)(2) does not require a plaintiff to show that the accused device enables third parties to access the work without the copyright owner's authorization. Thus, Blizzard has satisfied the "circumvention" element of a § 1201(a)(2) claim, because Blizzard has demonstrated that it did not authorize MDY to circumvent Warden.

31. [n.17] The statutory definition of the phrase "effectively control access to a work" does not require that an access control measure be strong or circumvention-proof. Rather, it requires an access control measure to provide some degree of control over access to a copyrighted work. As one district court has observed, if the word "effectively" were read to mean that the statute protects "only successful or efficacious technological means of controlling access," it would "gut" DMCA § 1201(a)(2), because it would "limit the application of the statute to access control measures that thwart circumvention, but withhold protection for those measures that can be circumvented."

F. Blizzard's § 1201(b)(1) claim

Blizzard may prevail under § 1201(b)(1) only if Warden "effectively protect[s] a right" of Blizzard under the Copyright Act. Blizzard contends that Warden protects its reproduction right against unauthorized copying. We disagree.

First, although WoW players copy the software code into RAM while playing the game, Blizzard's EULA and ToU authorize all licensed WoW players to do so. We have explained that ToU § 4(B)'s bot prohibition is a license covenant rather than a condition. Thus, a Glider user who violates this covenant does not infringe by continuing to copy code into RAM. Accordingly, MDY does not violate § 1201(b)(1) by enabling Glider users to avoid Warden's interruption of their *authorized* copying into RAM.

Second, although WoW players can theoretically record game play by taking screen shots, there is no evidence that Warden detects or prevents such allegedly infringing copying. This is logical, because Warden was designed to reduce the presence of cheats and bots, not to protect WoW's dynamic non-literal elements against copying. We conclude that Warden does not effectively protect any of Blizzard's rights under the Copyright Act, and MDY is not liable under § 1201(b)(1) for Glider's circumvention of Warden.

Examples

EXAMPLE OF CIRCUMVENTING ACCESS CONTROLS

Congress intended Title I of the DMCA to apply to copyrighted works that are in digital format and thus could easily and inexpensively be accessed, reproduced, and distributed over the Internet without the copyright owner's authorization. The DMCA therefore applies to what one might call a "digital lock"—a technological measure that copyright owners use to control who may see, hear, or use copyrighted works stored in digital form. These digital locks are commonly called either "access controls" or "copy controls," depending on what function the digital lock is designed to control.

The DMCA states that a digital lock, or "technological measure" (as the DMCA refers to such locks), constitutes an access control "if the measure, in the ordinary course of its operation, requires the application of information, or a process or a treatment, with the authority of the copyright owner, to gain access to the work." 17 U.S.C. § 1201(a)(3)(B). For example, a technology that permits access to a newspaper article on an Internet Web site only by those who pay a fee or have a password would be considered an access control. In this example, the author (i.e., copyright owner) uses such fees or password requirements as access controls that allow the author to distinguish between those who have the author's permission to read the online article from those who do not. If a user does not pay the fee or enter the password, then the user cannot lawfully read the article or otherwise access it.

[C]ircumvention of an access control occurs when someone bypasses the technological measure's gatekeeping capacity, thereby precluding the copyright owner from determining which users have permission to access the digital copyrighted work and which do not.[32]

EXAMPLE OF TRAFFICKING

Universal City Studios, Inc. v. Eric Corley

273 F.3d 429 (2d Cir. 2001)

JON O. NEWMAN, CIRCUIT JUDGE.

[Corley and his company appealed from the judgment of the United States District Court for the Southern District of New York, enjoining] them from various actions concerning a decryption program known as "DeCSS." The injunction primarily bars the Appellants from posting DeCSS on their web site and from knowingly linking their web site to any other web site on which DeCSS is posted.

This appeal concerns the anti-trafficking provisions of the DMCA, which Congress enacted in 1998 to strengthen copyright protection in the digital age. Fearful that the ease with which pirates could copy and distribute a copyrightable work in digital form was overwhelming the capacity of conventional copyright enforcement to find and enjoin unlawfully copied material, Congress sought to combat copyright piracy in its earlier stages, before the work was even copied. The DMCA therefore backed with legal sanctions the efforts of copyright owners to protect their works from piracy behind digital walls such as encryption codes or password protections. In so doing, Congress targeted not only those pirates who would *circumvent* these digital walls (the "anti-circumvention provisions," contained in 17 U.S.C. § 1201(a)(1)), but also anyone who would *traffic* in a technology primarily designed to circumvent a digital wall (the "anti-trafficking provisions," contained in 17 U.S.C. § 1201(a)(2), (b)(1)).

Corley publishes a print magazine and maintains an affiliated web site geared towards "hackers," a digital-era term often applied to those interested in techniques for circumventing protections of computers and computer data from unauthorized access. The so-called hacker community includes serious computer-science scholars conducting research on protection techniques, computer buffs intrigued by the challenge of trying to circumvent access-limiting devices or perhaps hoping to promote security by exposing flaws in protection techniques, mischief-makers interested in disrupting computer operations, and thieves, including copyright infringers who want to acquire copyrighted material (for personal use or resale) without paying for it.

---

32. U.S. DEP'T OF JUSTICE, PROSECUTING INTELLECTUAL PROPERTY CRIMES 235, 243 (4th ed. 2013).

In November 1999, Corley posted a copy of the decryption computer program "DeCSS" on his web site, http://www.2600.com ("2600.com").[n.2][33] DeCSS is designed to circumvent "CSS," the encryption technology that motion picture studios place on DVDs to prevent the unauthorized viewing and copying of motion pictures. Corley also posted on his web site links to other web sites where DeCSS could be found.

Following a full non-jury trial, the District Court entered a permanent injunction barring Corley from posting DeCSS on his web site or from knowingly linking via a hyperlink to any other web site containing DeCSS.

For decades, motion picture studios have made movies available for viewing at home in what is called "analog" format. Movies in this format are placed on videotapes, which can be played on a video cassette recorder ("VCR"). In the early 1990s, the studios began to consider the possibility of distributing movies in digital form as well. Movies in digital form are placed on disks, known as DVDs, which can be played on a DVD player (either a stand-alone device or a component of a computer). DVDs offer advantages over analog tapes, such as improved visual and audio quality, larger data capacity, and greater durability. However, the improved quality of a movie in a digital format brings with it the risk that a virtually perfect copy, *i.e.*, one that will not lose perceptible quality in the copying process, can be readily made at the click of a computer control and instantly distributed to countless recipients throughout the world over the Internet. This case arises out of the movie industry's efforts to respond to this risk by invoking the anti-trafficking provisions of the DMCA.

The movie studios were reluctant to release movies in digital form until they were confident they had in place adequate safeguards against piracy of their copyrighted movies. The studios took several steps to minimize the piracy threat. First, they settled on the DVD as the standard digital medium for home distribution of movies. The studios then sought an encryption scheme to protect movies on DVDs. They enlisted the help of members of the consumer electronics and computer industries, who in mid-1996 developed the Content Scramble System ("CSS"). CSS is an encryption scheme that employs an algorithm configured by a set of "keys" to encrypt a DVD's contents. The algorithm is a type of mathematical formula for transforming the contents of the movie file into gibberish; the "keys" are in actuality strings of 0's and 1's that serve as values for the mathematical formula. Decryption in the case of CSS requires a set of "player keys" contained in compliant DVD

---

33. [n.2] "2600" has special significance to the hacker community. It is the hertz frequency ("a unit of frequency of a periodic process equal to one cycle per second," Webster's Third New International Dictionary 1061 (1993)) of a signal that some hackers formerly used to explore the entire telephone system from "operator mode," which was triggered by the transmission of a 2600 hertz tone across a telephone line, or to place telephone calls without incurring long-distance toll charges. One such user reportedly discovered that the sound of a toy whistle from a box of Cap'n Crunch cereal matched the telephone company's 2600 hertz tone perfectly.

players, as well as an understanding of the CSS encryption algorithm. Without the player keys and the algorithm, a DVD player cannot access the contents of a DVD. With the player keys and the algorithm, a DVD player can display the movie on a television or a computer screen, but does not give a viewer the ability to use the copy function of the computer to copy the movie or to manipulate the digital content of the DVD.

The studios developed a licensing scheme for distributing the technology to manufacturers of DVD players. Player keys and other information necessary to the CSS scheme were given to manufacturers of DVD players for an administrative fee. In exchange for the licenses, manufacturers were obliged to keep the player keys confidential. Manufacturers were also required in the licensing agreement to prevent the transmission of "CSS data" (a term undefined in the licensing agreement) from a DVD drive to any "internal recording device," including, presumably, a computer hard drive.

With encryption technology and licensing agreements in hand, the studios began releasing movies on DVDs in 1997, and DVDs quickly gained in popularity, becoming a significant source of studio revenue. In 1998, the studios secured added protection against DVD piracy when Congress passed the DMCA, which prohibits the development or use of technology designed to circumvent a technological protection measure, such as CSS.

In September 1999, Jon Johansen, a Norwegian teenager, collaborating with two unidentified individuals he met on the Internet, reverse-engineered a licensed DVD player designed to operate on the Microsoft operating system, and culled from it the player keys and other information necessary to decrypt CSS. The record suggests that Johansen was trying to develop a DVD player operable on Linux, an alternative operating system that did not support any licensed DVD players at that time. In order to accomplish this task, Johansen wrote a decryption program executable on Microsoft's operating system. That program was called, appropriately enough, "DeCSS."

If a user runs the DeCSS program (for example, by clicking on the DeCSS icon on a Microsoft operating system platform) with a DVD in the computer's disk drive, DeCSS will decrypt the DVD's CSS protection, allowing the user to copy the DVD's files and place the copy on the user's hard drive. The result is a very large computer file that can be played on a non-CSS-compliant player and copied, manipulated, and transferred just like any other computer file. DeCSS comes complete with a fairly user-friendly interface that helps the user select from among the DVD's files and assign the decrypted file a location on the user's hard drive. The quality of the resulting decrypted movie is "virtually identical" to that of the encrypted movie on the DVD. And the file produced by DeCSS, while large, can be compressed to a manageable size by a compression software called "DivX," available at no cost on the Internet. This compressed file can be copied onto a DVD, or transferred over the Internet (with some patience).

Johansen posted the executable object code, but not the source code, for DeCSS on his web site. The distinction between source code and object code is relevant to this case, so a brief explanation is warranted. A computer responds to electrical charges, the presence or absence of which is represented by strings of 1's and 0's. Strictly speaking, "object code" consists of those 1's and 0's. While some people can read and program in object code, "it would be inconvenient, inefficient and, for most people, probably impossible to do so." Computer languages have been written to facilitate program writing and reading. A program in such a computer language—BASIC, C, and Java are examples—is said to be written in "source code." Source code has the benefit of being much easier to read (by people) than object code, but as a general matter, it must be translated back to object code before it can be read by a computer. This task is usually performed by a program called a compiler. Since computer languages range in complexity, object code can be placed on one end of a spectrum, and different kinds of source code can be arrayed across the spectrum according to the ease with which they are read and understood by humans. Within months of its appearance in executable form on Johansen's web site, DeCSS was widely available on the Internet, in both object code and various forms of source code.

In November 1999, Corley wrote and placed on his web site, 2600.com, an article about the DeCSS phenomenon. His web site is an auxiliary to the print magazine, *2600: The Hacker Quarterly*, which Corley has been publishing since 1984. As the name suggests, the magazine is designed for "hackers," as is the web site. While the magazine and the web site cover some issues of general interest to computer users—such as threats to online privacy—the focus of the publications is on the vulnerability of computer security systems, and more specifically, how to exploit that vulnerability in order to circumvent the security systems. Representative articles explain how to steal an Internet domain name and how to break into the computer systems at Federal Express. Corley's article about DeCSS detailed how CSS was cracked, and described the movie industry's efforts to shut down web sites posting DeCSS. It also explained that DeCSS could be used to copy DVDs. At the end of the article, the Defendants posted copies of the object and source code of DeCSS. In Corley's words, he added the code to the story because "in a journalistic world, . . . [y]ou have to show your evidence . . . and particularly in the magazine that I work for, people want to see specifically what it is that we are referring to," including "what evidence . . . we have" that there is in fact technology that circumvents CSS. Writing about DeCSS without including the DeCSS code would have been, to Corley, "analogous to printing a story about a picture and not printing the picture." Corley also added to the article links that he explained would take the reader to other web sites where DeCSS could be found.

2600.com was only one of hundreds of web sites that began posting DeCSS near the end of 1999. The movie industry tried to stem the tide by sending cease-and-desist letters to many of these sites. These efforts met with only partial success; a number of sites refused to remove DeCSS. In January 2000, the studios filed this lawsuit.

[The DMCA] contains three provisions targeted at the circumvention of technological protections. The first is subsection 1201(a)(1)(A), the anti-circumvention provision. The second and third provisions are subsections 1201(a)(2) and 1201(b)(1), the "anti-trafficking provisions." To "circumvent a technological measure" is defined, in pertinent part, as "to descramble a scrambled work ... or otherwise to ... bypass ... a technological measure, without the authority of the copyright owner." *Id.* § 1201(a)(3)(A).

Subsection 1201(b)(1) is similar to subsection 1201(a)(2), except that subsection 1201(a)(2) covers those who traffic in technology that can circumvent "a technological measure *that effectively controls access* to a work protected under" Title 17, whereas subsection 1201(b)(1) covers those who traffic in technology that can circumvent "protection afforded by a technological measure *that effectively protects a right of a copyright owner* under" Title 17. *Id.* § 1201(a)(2), (b)(1). In other words, although both subsections prohibit trafficking in a circumvention technology, the focus of subsection 1201(a)(2) is circumvention of technologies designed to *prevent access* to a work, and the focus of subsection 1201(b)(1) is circumvention of technologies designed to *permit access* to a work but *prevent copying* of the work or some other act that infringes a copyright.

[The lower] Court concluded that an injunction was highly appropriate in this case. The Court observed that DeCSS was harming the Plaintiffs, not only because they were now exposed to the possibility of piracy and therefore were obliged to develop costly new safeguards for DVDs, but also because, even if there was only indirect evidence that DeCSS availability actually facilitated DVD piracy, the threat of piracy was very real, particularly as Internet transmission speeds continue to increase. Acknowledging that DeCSS was (and still is) widely available on the Internet, the Court expressed confidence in

> the likelihood ... that this decision will serve notice on others that "the strong right arm of equity" may be brought to bear against them absent a change in their conduct and thus contribute to a climate of appropriate respect for intellectual property rights in an age in which the excitement of ready access to untold quantities of information has blurred in some minds the fact that taking what is not yours and not freely offered to you is stealing.

The Court's injunction barred the Defendants from: "posting on any Internet web site" DeCSS; "in any other way ... offering to the public, providing, or otherwise trafficking in DeCSS"; violating the anti-trafficking provisions of the DMCA in any other manner, and finally "knowingly linking any Internet web site operated by them to any other web site containing DeCSS, or knowingly maintaining any such link, for the purpose of disseminating DeCSS."

The Appellants first argue that, because their constitutional arguments are at least substantial, we should interpret the statute narrowly so as to avoid constitutional problems. They identify three different instances of alleged ambiguity in the statute that they claim provide an opportunity for such a narrow interpretation.

First, they contend that subsection 1201(c)(1), which provides that "[n]othing in this section shall affect rights, remedies, limitations or defenses to copyright infringement, including fair use, under this title," can be read to allow the circumvention of encryption technology protecting copyrighted material when the material will be put to "fair uses" exempt from copyright liability. We disagree that subsection 1201(c)(1) permits such a reading. Instead, it simply clarifies that the DMCA targets the *circumvention* of digital walls guarding copyrighted material (and trafficking in circumvention tools), but does not concern itself with the *use* of those materials after circumvention has occurred. Subsection 1201(c)(1) ensures that the DMCA is not read to prohibit the "fair use" of information just because that information was obtained in a manner made illegal by the DMCA. The Appellants' much more expansive interpretation of subsection 1201(c)(1) is not only outside the range of plausible readings of the provision, but is also clearly refuted by the statute's legislative history.[n.13][34]

Second, the Appellants urge a narrow construction of the DMCA because of subsection 1201(c)(4), which provides that "[n]othing in this section shall enlarge or diminish any rights of free speech or the press for activities using consumer electronics, telecommunications, or computing products." This language is clearly precatory: Congress could not "diminish" constitutional rights of free speech even if it wished to, and the fact that Congress also expressed a reluctance to "enlarge" those rights cuts against the Appellants' effort to infer a narrowing construction of the Act from this provision.

Third, the Appellants argue that an individual who buys a DVD has the "authority of the copyright owner" to view the DVD, and therefore is exempted from the DMCA pursuant to subsection 1201(a)(3)(A) when the buyer circumvents an encryption technology in order to view the DVD on a competing platform (such as Linux). The basic flaw in this argument is that it misreads subsection 1201(a)(3)(A). That provision exempts from liability those who would "decrypt" an encrypted DVD with the authority of a copyright owner, not those who would "view" a DVD with the authority of a copyright owner. In any event, the Defendants offered no

---

34. [n.13] The legislative history of the enacted bill makes quite clear that Congress intended to adopt a "balanced" approach to accommodating both piracy and fair use concerns, eschewing the quick fix of simply exempting from the statute all circumventions for fair use. It sought to achieve this goal principally through the use of what it called a "fail-safe" provision in the statute, authorizing the Librarian of Congress to exempt certain users from the anti-circumvention provision when it becomes evident that in practice, the statute is adversely affecting certain kinds of fair use.

Congress also sought to implement a balanced approach through statutory provisions that leave limited areas of breathing space for fair use. A good example is subsection 1201(d), which allows a library or educational institution to circumvent a digital wall in order to determine whether it wishes legitimately to obtain the material behind the wall. It would be strange for Congress to open small, carefully limited windows for circumvention to permit fair use in subsection 1201(d) if it then meant to exempt in subsection 1201(c)(1) *any* circumvention necessary for fair use.

evidence that the Plaintiffs have either explicitly or implicitly authorized DVD buyers to circumvent encryption technology to support use on multiple platforms. [n.15][35]

We conclude that the anti-trafficking and anti-circumvention provisions of the DMCA are not susceptible to the narrow interpretations urged by the Appellants. We therefore proceed to consider the Appellants' constitutional claims. [The court upheld that Act despite numerous constitutional challenges and concluded] that they provide no basis for disturbing the District Court's judgment.

Notes

1. The DMCA creates civil remedies, 17 U.S.C. § 1203, and criminal sanctions, *id.* § 1204. It specifically authorizes a court to "grant temporary and permanent injunctions on such terms as it deems reasonable to prevent or restrain a violation." *Id.* § 1203(b)(1).

2. For more analysis of the DMCA, see U.S. Dep't of Justice, Prosecuting Intellectual Property Crimes Ch. v (4th ed. 2013). The Electronic Frontier Foundation has taken positions highly critical of the Act and its enforcement. *See* http://www.eff.org/wp/unintended-consequences-under-dmca.

---

35. [n.15] Even if the Defendants had been able to offer such evidence, and even if they could have demonstrated that DeCSS was "primarily designed . . . for the purpose of" playing DVDs on multiple platforms (and therefore not for the purpose of "circumventing a technological measure"), the Defendants would defeat liability only under subsection 1201(a)(2)(A). They would still be vulnerable to liability under subsection 1201(a)(2)(C), because they "marketed" DeCSS for the copying of DVDs, not just for the playing of DVDs on multiple platforms.

Chapter 18

Spyware, Adware, Malware; Phishing; Spam; and Identity-Related Crime

§ 18.1 Spyware, Adware, Malware

The types of software labeled spyware, adware, and malware, all of which have at least negative connotations associated with them, do not have precise definitions. Here is one effort:

> *"Spyware"* is a form of software that collects personal and confidential information about a person or organization without their proper knowledge or informed consent, and reports it to a third party. In its benign form, spyware technology may be used, for example, to facilitate the transmission of information about software updates to users. But spyware can also be used to improperly access and communicate sensitive and confidential information, and to facilitate the delivery of "pop-up" and "pop-over" messages to a user's computer (in which case the software may be referred to as *"adware"*). Adware may use data collected over the course of the user's Web browsing and searching to derive the user's interests and send targeted ads to be displayed to the user. *"Malware"* is a term used to refer to spyware-type technologies that alter or interfere with the operation of a local computer, by changing a browser home page or altering security settings, installing unwanted or malicious software that may improperly access personal or security information such as passwords and financial account information.[1]

These forms of software are tools to achieve some further end. Some of those goals are criminal, some are not. Those ends vary widely. For example, the purpose may be simply to collect information for commercial or other legal purposes. It may be employed to remotely control the computer, use it to facilitate botnet communications,[2] or to facilitate identity theft.

---

1. Jeffrey D. Neuburger, *New Media, Technology and the Law: a Summary of Key Legal Developments Affecting Technology and Emerging Business Models*, 1034 PLI/PAT 193 (2011). Copyright © 2011, Jeffrey D. Neuburger. All rights reserved. Reprinted by permission.

2. Federal Trade Commission v. Pricewert, 2010 U.S. Dist. LEXIS 12273 (N.D. Cal. Jan. 20, 2010). That court defined a botnet as "a network of computers that have been compromised by

Although malware has been around for a long time, it remains a "massive, chronic" problem that continues to evolve.[3] Symantec in 2013 reported some of the trends:

> One in 291 emails contained a virus in 2012, which is down from one in 239 in 2011. Of that email-borne malware, 23 percent of it contained URLs that pointed to malicious websites. This is also down from 2011, where 39 percent of email-borne malware contained a link to a malicious website. Much like the drop in spam and phishing rates, a drop in emails that contain viruses does not necessarily mean that attackers have stopped targeting users. Rather, it more likely points to a shift in tactics, targeting other online activities, such as social networking.[4]

Symantec's 2017 report further illustrates the continued evolution of the problems:

> While just over half of all emails (53 percent) are spam, a growing proportion of that spam contains malware. This increase in email-borne malware is driven largely by a professionalization of malware spamming operations. Malware authors can outsource their spam campaigns to specialized groups who conduct major spam campaigns. The sheer scale of email malware operations indicates that attackers are making considerable profits from these kinds of attacks and email is likely to continue to be one of the main avenues of attack in 2017.

The 2017 report noted that the overall malware rate increased in 2016 to one of every 131 emails.

Another example is ransomware, which "permanently locks people out of their computer unless they pay a swinging 'fine' to the perpetrators." That "malware is often quite sophisticated, difficult to remove, and in some cases it persists in safe mode, blocking attempts at remote support."[5] Symantec has also observed that Internet criminals are making money from malware that stays hidden on the victims' computers:

> Operating in botnets with many thousands of computers acting collectively, these stealthy programs send out spam or generate bogus clicks on website advertisements (which generate referral income for the site owners). These techniques don't generate rapid returns like ransomware; however, they are much less likely to be discovered and, thanks to clever coding, are more difficult to remove. Consequently, they can generate a constant stream of revenue over time.[6]

---

malicious code and surreptitiously programmed to follow instructions issued by a Botnet Command and Control Server."

3. SYMANTEC INTERNET SECURITY THREAT REPORT 2013, Vol. 18.
4. SYMANTEC INTERNET SECURITY THREAT REPORT 2013, Vol. 18.
5. *Id.* at 50.
6. *Id.* at 51.

The Federal Trade Commission has pursued numerous actions against entities that have distributed spyware.[7] Its position is that federal anti-spyware legislation is unnecessary because the agency has authority over the improper use of spyware technology under existing law.[8] Federal prosecutors have also instituted criminal prosecutions against distributors of spyware under the federal computer fraud and electronic communications privacy statutes, discussed elsewhere in this book. Individuals and others have sought to bring civil claims against companies who utilize spyware, with mixed results, using various theories of liability.[9] Numerous states have adopted antispyware laws, some with criminal penalties, but prosecutions are rare.[10] In sum, as a broad proposition, the criminal law litigation in this area usually results in the conviction of some other substantive crime that was the goal of using the software; the software was the means—or part of the means—by which that criminal activity occurred.

User Agreements

People v. Direct Revenue

19 Misc. 3d 1124(A) (N.Y. Sup. Ct. 2008) (unpublished)

Herman Cahn, J.

Petitioner Attorney General seeks injunctive and monetary relief against respondent Direct Revenue, LLC and its principals for allegedly deceptive and illegal practices relating to the installation of pop-up advertising software on consumers' computers. Respondents move to dismiss.

Direct Revenue is engaged in the business of advertising. Specifically, the company produces software, including software that delivers advertisements to consumers' computer screens through the Internet. Although the petition characterizes its products as "spyware," at oral argument petitioner conceded that the software at issue does not collect consumer computer usage information for publication to third parties. Rather, the parties agree that the software merely generates pop-up ads geared to a consumer's Internet usage.

Direct Revenue does not charge fees to consumers. Instead, it receives compensation from the companies whose products and services it advertises. To induce

---

7. *E.g.*, Federal Trade Commission v. Pricewert, 2010 U.S. Dist. LEXIS 12273 (N.D. Cal. Jan. 20, 2010).

8. Jeffrey D. Neuburger, *New Media, Technology and the Law: A Summary of Key Legal Developments Affecting Technology and Emerging Business Models*, 1034 PLI/PAT 193 (2011).

9. *E.g.*, Zango, Inc. v. PC Tools PTY Ltd., 494 F. Supp. 2d 1189 (W.D. Wash. 2007); Sotelo v. DirectRevenue, 384 F. Supp. 2d 1219 (N.D. Ill. 2005). *See generally* Daniel B. Garrie, Yoav Griver, Mari Joller, *Regulating Spyware: Challenges and Solutions*, 13 J. Internet L. 3 (2010) (discussing civil remedies consumers can pursue).

10. Jessica L. McCurdy, *Computer Crimes*, 47 Am. Crim. L. Rev. 287, 325 (2010).

consumers to view the ads, the company offers them popular software applications, such as screensavers or games, free. When the free application is downloaded by the consumer, the applications install another piece of software from Direct Revenue known as an "advertising client," which generates the pop-up ads. The ads may be discarded by clicking on an "X" in the upper right-hand corner of the box in which they appear.

In many cases, Direct Revenue contracts with third-party distributors to disseminate the "advertising client." Those distributors, in turn, contract with subdistributors to assist in the process. The third parties bundle Direct Revenue's advertising client software along with their own software programs which they offer to internet users. The distributors leave a "stub" file on consumers' computer, which sends a message to Direct Revenue's servers to facilitate installation and updating of the advertising software.

In response to consumers who complained that Direct Revenue's ad-generating software was being installed on their computers without notice or consent, the Attorney General commenced an investigation in November 2004. Between November 2004 and March 2006, AG investigators conducted 29 tests of websites which distributed Direct Revenue's advertising client. The transactions were conducted over the Internet from computers located in New York City.

Seven of the 29 transactions were conducted directly with Direct Revenue, either through a Direct Revenue website, or a Direct Revenue advertisement appearing at a website operated by a third party. In each of the seven cases, the investigator was presented with a computer hyperlink which specifically referred to Direct Revenue's end-user license agreement ("EULA"). A dialog box labeled "Security Warning" appeared each time, offering the user the option of accepting the terms of the EULA by clicking "Yes" or declining it by clicking "No." The accompanying message explained that by clicking on "Yes," the user acknowledged that he or she had read the EULA and agreed to be bound by its terms.

The pertinent provisions of the EULA are as follows:

Section 1 ("Acceptance of Agreement")

The Software will collect information about websites you access and will use that information to display advertising on your computer.

By clicking Yes, 'install' or downloading, installing or using the Software, you acknowledge that you have read and understood this Agreement, agree to be bound by its terms, and represent that you have the necessary rights and permissions to install the Software on the computer being used. If you do not agree to be bound by the terms of this Agreement . . . you may not download or use the software.

Section 2 ("Functionality"):

This Software delivers advertising and various information and promotional messages to your computer screen while you view Internet web pages.

By installing the Software, you understand and agree that the Software may, without further notice to you, automatically perform the following: display advertisements of advertisers who pay a fee to [Direct Revenue], in the form of pop-up ads, interstitial ads and various other ad formats . . . automatically update the Software and install added features or functionality or additional software.

Section 3 ("Uninstall and Remove Software"):

You may uninstall the Software at any time by visiting www.mypctuneup .com.

Section 11 ("Disclaimer of Warranty"):

[Respondent] DISCLAIM ALL WARRANTIES OF ANY KIND, EXPRESS OR IMPLIED.

Section 12 ("Limitation of Liability"):

[Respondent shall not] BE LIABLE TO YOU OR TO ANY THIRD-PARTY FOR ANY DIRECT, INDIRECT INCIDENTAL, CONSEQUENTIAL, SPECIAL PUNITIVE OR OTHER DAMAGES.

In six of the seven cases involving transactions with Direct Revenue, the AG investigator clicked "Yes" and downloaded the free software. In one case, the investigator declined to accept it and no software was installed on the computer.

The remaining 22 of the 29 transactions were conducted with websites or advertisements of third party distributors. [In a section of the opinion not reproduced, the court dismissed claims relating to the 22 transactions involving third party distributors.]

In addition to the specific instances identified in the course of the AG's investigation, petitioner alleges that Direct Revenue's software has been installed 150 million times in computers all over the world. The petition asserts five causes of action, alleging deceptive acts and practices under General Business Law § 349 (Count I), false advertising under GBL § 350 (Count II), negligent supervision (Count III), trespass to chattels (Count IV) and computer tampering in the fourth degree as defined by Penal Law § 156.20 (Court V). In addition to injunctive relief against respondents' allegedly unlawful advertising and installation practices, petitioner seeks disgorgement of revenues under a theory of unjust enrichment, a monetary penalty of $500 per deceptive or unlawful action under GBL § 350-d and a judgment of $2,000 against each respondent under CPLR § 8303(a)(6).

The petition is dismissed. Petitioner has not established any deceptive conduct or false advertising in connection with the seven specifically identified transactions with Direct Revenue, insofar as all of the completed installations were authorized by the AG investigators in accordance with the terms of the EULA. Furthermore, no recovery is available against respondent for the alleged millions of other consumer transactions because petitioner has failed to provide meaningful notice of how those transactions were deceptive or whether they took place in New York.

Finally, petition's demand for disgorgement fails because there is no allegation that respondent improperly took anything of value from a consumer, and petitioner has no statutory authority to seek such damages on its own behalf.

In each case that the AG's investigators successfully installed respondents' advertising client, they first clicked on the "Yes" button on a dialog box to assent to the terms of the EULA. This conduct created a binding "click-wrap" agreement which bars any claim for deceptive or unlawful conduct. Under New York law, such contracts are enforced so long as the consumer is given a sufficient opportunity to read the EULA, and assents thereto after being provided with an unambiguous method of accepting or declining the offer. Claims that a consumer was not aware of the agreement or did not actually read it must be disregarded where, as here, it is undisputed that the agreement was acknowledged and accepted by clicking on the relevant icon. It is not necessary that it be made impossible for the consumer to signal assent or proceed to installation without being first forced to read the EULA; rather, it is sufficient that a separate hyperlink leading to the agreement is available.

Given the disclosures made in the EULA regarding the pop-up ads and respondents' relevant policies, no GBL § 349 for a deceptive practice may be asserted. Petitioner does not identify anything in the EULA that is false, deceptive or misleading. Furthermore, the clear disclaimers and waivers of liabilities bar any remedy. There is no allegation that respondents made prior or other representations to consumers that contradicted the terms of the EULA.

Acceptance of the EULA also bars the common law claim of trespass to chattel. Such a cause of action requires that the interference with the plaintiff's property occur without consent. Although consent may be found invalid where procured by affirmative fraudulent misrepresentations, no such deception is alleged here. For similar reasons, the claim for computer tampering under Penal Law § 156.20 fails because consent is a defense under the statute.

The false advertising claim must also be dismissed. There is no dispute that four of the six completed installations were not preceded by any advertisement at all. The advertisements for the remaining two merely described Direct Revenue's software as "free," and it is conceded that no consumer was ever charged for it. To the extent that the obligation to receive the advertising client can be construed as a qualification on the word "free," respondent did disclose that condition by reference to the EULA as permitted by the Federal Trade Commission guidelines regarding the use of the word (see, FTC Guide § 251.1[c]). Under GBL § 350-d, "it is a complete defense that the advertisement is subject to and complies with the rules and regulations of, and the statues administered by the Federal Trade Commission."

Finally, petitioner does not dispute that no recovery may be sought for the remaining transaction with respondent which did not conclude with the installation of the allegedly offensive advertising client.

The petition must be dismissed as to the remaining millions of unidentified consumer transactions. CPLR § 3013 provides that "[s]tatements in a pleading shall be sufficiently particular to give the court and parties notice of the transactions, occurrences, or series of transactions or occurrences, intended to be proved and the material elements of each cause of action. . . ." Merely identifying a transaction without supplying facts indicating how it gives rise to claim is insufficient. Although petitioner is seeking a $500 penalty per transaction—and thus billions of dollars in damages—the pleadings fail to identify anything about the additional transactions other than that they involved installations of respondents' advertising client. Petitioner fails to specify which transactions were deceptive, which advertisements were false, which were conducted with Direct Revenue, and which were conducted with third party distributors or subdistributors. Petitioner also fails to state where the transactions occurred, which is a fatal defect in notice because the alleged statutory violations are barred for transactions occurring outside of New York.

Petitioner relies primarily on the premise that the 29 identified transactions were representative of all other transactions. Insofar as the court has determined that respondent cannot be held liable for any fraud or deception with respect to the identified installations, no wrongfulness can be imputed to the larger, unspecified class. Furthermore, petitioner fails to identify the methodology by which it determined that the original transactions were representative of all others. Given that each transaction would present, inter alia, individualized issues of consent to the installation and reliance on the EULA, petitioner's blanket assumption regarding their similarity is untenable.

Notes

The concept of "user control" from click-of-the-button "consent" has been criticized by the Center for Democracy and Technology as too narrow a focus to protect the decisions that consumers make online:

> The current opt-in/opt-out consent paradigm at best only gives consumers control over their data at the point of collection. Long after data is collected, it lives in a Wild West of shared and sold personal profiles and databases that give consumers no control over how their identities will be tracked and used. An analysis of the FTC's 2009 settlement with Sears highlights the need to move beyond today's notice and consent regime. Between 2007 and 2008, Sears encouraged users to download tracking software on their computers. This software monitored consumers' activities for clues about both online and offline behavior, peering into online secure sessions and culling information from consumers' email subjects and recipients, online bank statements, drug prescription records, video rental records, and similar histories and accounts. Although Sears offered customers a $10 coupon to download the software, the Commission nonetheless brought a complaint, concluding that consumers are harmed by privacy invasions in and of themselves. Companies must be certain that consumers clearly understand when they are selling their privacy. The FTC's complaint focused on the fact that the extensive tracking undertaken

by the software was neither accurately represented nor adequately disclosed by language buried deep in the Privacy Statement and User License Agreement (PSULA). The complaint represents broader recognition that few consumers read or understand these kinds of disclosures about online data collection and use practices. In its guidance to Sears about how the company could legally encourage users to download tracking software, the FTC missed an opportunity to materially improve comprehensive privacy protections available to consumers. The Commission required that "if Sears advertises or disseminates any tracking software in the future, it must clearly and prominently disclose the types of data the software will monitor, record, or transmit" and "obtain express consent from the consumer to the download or installation of the Tracking Application." The disclosure, the FTC concluded, must occur separately from any general terms of service or user license agreement and, if data will be accessed by a third party, must include a notification that data will be available to a third party; consumer consent should involve clicking a button that is not pre-selected as a default.

With its decision to merely require that one ineffective form of disclosure and consent be replaced by a slightly improved version, the FTC failed to ensure holistic privacy protections for the future: even the clearest of disclosures cannot, on their own, protect consumers from privacy risks or return meaningful control back to the consumer. Despite the monumental privacy invasion involved in the Sears case, we would not be surprised to see the same practices used in the future by companies that track consumers just as insidiously but provide marginally clearer notification of their practices. Indeed, a company in similar circumstances may be able to sell consumers' personal information to others with no ability to revoke that information from the buyer if consumers later change their mind. Such a company would merely need to be a little more upfront about its intentions than Sears was in this case. This is the ultimate failure of the notice, consent and security regime.

On the other hand, had the FTC taken the opportunity to outline a multitiered privacy framework based on a full set of [Fair Information Practice (FIP)] principles that Sears and other companies must work within, the Commission would have taken a much more significant step toward meaningful protection of consumer privacy. Consider, instead, what might have transpired had Sears applied the FIPs principle of Transparency—which is often equated with "notice" but is indeed much broader—when developing its software. Transparency would require consumers have access to the personal information entities have been collecting about them. It is difficult to imagine that Sears would have collected and stored sensitive health and financial information if they then had to let consumers see the personal profiles being constructed about them (like the one registered Google and

BlueKai users can access). The Individual Participation and Data Quality and Integrity principles reinforce the need for this access, as they require that consumers have the tools to correct mistakes or challenge information reported in these profiles. After all, the best way to ensure that data is accurate is to provide consumers with access to review and correct it.

Ensuring data quality is imperative, for data collected by one entity is often shared or sold to third parties for secondary uses. Sharing or selling consumer data, or using it for price discrimination, employment decisions, or to make credit or insurance decisions, is a serious concern and often directly harmful to consumers; this data can be even more harmful when it is inaccurate. But profile access alone is not a strong enough check to protect consumers against secondary uses of personal data. Full implementation of the Data Minimization, Purpose Specification, and Use Limitation principles would help provide this check. The Data Minimization principle, for example requires that entities only collect data "that is directly relevant and necessary to accomplish the specified purpose(s) and only retain [that data] for as long as is necessary to fulfill the specified purpose(s)." It is hard to believe that consumer banking information is "directly relevant and necessary" to Sears' business model. And if such data were relevant, the Purpose Specification principle would have forced Sears to "specifically articulate" this relevance; we imagine that being required to publicly announce alarming data-use practices might act as a prophylactic for insidious tracking. The Use Limitation principle dovetails with Purpose Specification to protect against illegitimate uses of collected data. The data retention limits outlined within the Data Minimization principle provide an additional check: if data is deleted or aggregated then it cannot be used in a way that is harmful to the individual consumer. Of course, absent security measures to protect collected data and accountability measures put in place by individual companies, trade associations, the FTC, or Congress, all of these promises could prove empty. But with such measures firmly in place, these individual FIP principles can work in concert to buttress stronger privacy protections.[11]

What do you think of the current legal regime of "click-of-the-button consent," which *Direct Revenue* illustrates? Should it suffice to bar liability for deceptive practices relating to the installation of pop-up advertising? Is it sufficient to permit collecting information from the consumer's computer? Are the principles set forth by the Center for Democracy and Technology better? Why?

---

11. David Sohn, *Refocusing the FTC's Role in Privacy Protection, Comments of the Center for Democracy and Technology in Regards to the FTC Consumer Protection Roundtable*, Nov. 9, 2009 (http://www.cdt.org/pdfs/20091105 _ftc_paiv_comments.pdf), *reprinted in* 994 PLI/Pat 769 (2010). Copyright © 2009, Center for Democracy and Technology. All rights reserved. Reprinted by permission.

§ 18.2 Phishing

Phishing has no precise definition but is generally viewed as a tool to commit a substantive crime by obtaining "confidential information over the Internet under false pretenses in order to fraudulently obtain credit card numbers, passwords, or other personal data."[12] According to the Anti-Phishing Working Group, Phishing is defined as follows:

> Phishing is a criminal mechanism employing both social engineering and technical subterfuge to steal consumers' personal identity data and financial account credentials. Social-engineering schemes use spoofed e-mails purporting to be from legitimate businesses and agencies to lead consumers to counterfeit websites designed to trick recipients into divulging financial data such as usernames and passwords. Technical-subterfuge schemes plant crimeware onto PCs to steal credentials directly, often using systems to intercept consumers['] online account user names and passwords — and to corrupt local navigational infrastructures to misdirect consumers to counterfeit websites (or authentic websites through phisher-controlled proxies used to monitor and intercept consumers' keystrokes).[13]

United States v. Bogdan Boceanu

2013 U.S. Dist. LEXIS 15292 (D. Conn. Feb. 4, 2013)

Janet C. Hall, District Judge.

On December 11, 2012, a jury found the defendant, Bogdan Boceanu, guilty of conspiracy to commit bank fraud, in violation of 18 U.S.C. § 1349, and conspiracy to commit fraud in connection with access devices, in violation of 18 U.S.C. § 1029(b)(2). Boceanu is incarcerated and awaiting sentencing.

Before the court are Boceanu's Motion to Dismiss and Motion for a Judgment of Acquittal as to Count One of the Second Superseding Indictment: conspiracy to commit bank fraud. For the following reasons, Boceanu's Motions are denied.

A Second Superseding Indictment in this case charged Boceanu and others with conspiracy to commit bank fraud, conspiracy to commit fraud in connection with access devices, *i.e.*, credit card fraud, and aggravated identity theft. Boceanu, who was tried alone, was convicted by a jury on both counts of conspiracy. The government dismissed the two counts of aggravated identity theft against Boceanu prior to trial.

During the three day trial in December 2012, the government presented evidence of a conspiracy to commit bank fraud and credit card fraud. At trial, the

---

12. The America Heritage Dictionary of the English Language (4th Ed. 2004).
13. www.antiphishing.org/reports/apwg_report_q2_2010.pdf.

evidence concerning the bank fraud conspiracy consisted of: (1) the testimony of Suzanne Novak, a former People's Bank customer, who received a phishing email targeting customers of People's Bank that had been sent around June 13, 2005; (2) the testimony of David Cracauer—on whose compromised computer the fake People's Bank website was hosted—that the information provided by customers duped into responding to the email was sent to the email address Vercartil@yahoo.com; (3) the testimony of cooperating witness Gabriel Sain that he engaged in the phishing scheme with others, including Boceanu; that Boceanu used the email address damnedasp@yahoo.com; and that Boceanu exchanged emails that contained stolen information, including names, addresses, Social Security numbers, credit card numbers, and bank identification numbers as well as a program for harvesting email addresses; (4) emails between damnedasp@yahoo.com and other members of the conspiracy, including an email sent to vercartil@yahoo.com in June 2005, asking for a list of credit numbers that were "good," *i.e.*, working, and an email in response containing a subset of the numbers contained in the original email; and (5) testimony from FBI Special Agent Martin McBride that co-defendant Ovidiu-Ionut Nicola Roman used the email address vercartil@yahoo.com.

On December 10, 2012, at the end of the government's case, Boceanu moved for a judgment of acquittal pursuant to Rule 29(a). The court reserved decision on the Motion pursuant to Rule 29(b). On December 11, 2012, the jury found Boceanu guilty of conspiracy to commit bank fraud and conspiracy to commit fraud in connection with access devices.

Rule 29(a) provides that district courts "must enter a judgment of acquittal of any offense for which the evidence is insufficient to sustain a conviction." In deciding whether to grant a motion pursuant to Rule 29, the court should "view the evidence in the light most favorable to the government, drawing all inferences in the government's favor and deferring to the jury's assessments of the witnesses' credibility." A jury verdict shall be sustained "so long as any rational trier of fact could have found the essential elements of the crime beyond a reasonable doubt." "[I]f the evidence viewed in the light most favorable to the prosecution gives equal or nearly equal circumstantial support to a theory of guilt and a theory of innocence, then a reasonable jury must necessarily entertain a reasonable doubt."

Boceanu argues that the evidence adduced at trial is insufficient to sustain his conviction for conspiracy to commit bank fraud because the only evidence connecting Boceanu to the conspiracy to commit bank fraud—as opposed to the conspiracy to commit credit card fraud—were the emails he exchanged with co-defendant Nicola-Roman around the same time that Nicola-Roman sent the People's Bank phishing email.

To prove a conspiracy to commit bank fraud, the Government must establish the following two elements: (1) that two or more persons entered into the alleged agreement to commit bank fraud, and (2) that the defendant knowingly and willfully joined in the agreement. The agreement to commit bank fraud must have been an agreement to engage in a scheme or artifice to defraud, or obtain money or property from, a federally-insured financial institution by means of materially false or fraudulent pretenses, representations, or promises. *See* 18 U.S.C. § 1344.

Boceanu does not challenge the sufficiency of the evidence related to the first element of the crime of conspiracy. An agreement existed to engage in bank fraud as evidenced by the phishing email directing recipients to a fake website for People's Bank, which is a federal-insured bank.

As to the second element, Boceanu argues that the only evidence introduced by the government connecting him to the bank fraud conspiracy were the emails containing credit card numbers that he exchanged with Nicola-Roman in June 2005. Those emails were sent within the same month that Nicola-Roman sent the People's Bank email. Boceanu argues that there is no evidence that those emails—and the credit card numbers contained therein—were related to the People's Bank scheme. Because the evidence related to the People's Bank scheme was the only evidence of a scheme to defraud a federally-insured bank, without connecting Boceanu to the People's Bank phishing scheme, Boceanu argues that he cannot be found guilty of conspiracy to commit bank fraud.

The government, however, did not ask the jury to make the inference that the emails exchanged between Boceanu and Nicola-Roman contained credit card information obtained from the People's Bank scheme. Rather, the government asked the jury to infer that Boceanu was involved with the People's Bank scheme because he worked "closely with Nicola-Roman and others as part of the conspiracy at a time when one of the targets of the conspiracy was People's Bank." Given the extensive evidence that Boceanu participated in a phishing scheme with his codefendants, that he obtained a program to extract email addresses, and that he worked closely with Nicola-Roman on the phishing scheme at the same time that Nicola-Roman was engaging in the People's Bank website scam, the court concludes that, taking the evidence in a light most favorable to the government, a reasonable jury could find that Boceanu knowingly and willfully joined the agreement to commit bank fraud against People's Bank.

For the foregoing reasons, Boceanu's Motion to Dismiss pursuant to Rule 29(a) and his Motion for Judgment of Acquittal pursuant to Rule 29(c) are DENIED.

Facebook, Inc. v. Jeremi Fisher

2009 U.S. Dist. LEXIS 122578 (N.D. Cal. Dec. 21, 2009) (unreported)

JEREMY FOGEL, DISTRICT JUDGE.

Plaintiff Facebook, Inc. alleges that Defendants Jeremi Fisher, Philip Porembski, and Ryan Shimeall, individually and through various affiliated corporate entities, have engaged in an ongoing phishing and spamming campaign against Facebook and its users in violation of (1) the Controlling the Assault of Non-Solicited

Pornography and Marketing Act ("CAN-SPAM"), 15 U.S.C. §7701 *et seq.*; (2) the Computer Fraud and Abuse Act ("CFAA"), 18 U.S.C. §1030 *et seq.*, (3) Cal.Penal Code §502; and (4) Cal. Bus. & Prof.Code §22948. Facebook also asserts a claim for breach of contract. Facebook seeks a temporary restraining order enjoining Defendants from engaging in the alleged phishing and spamming activities against Facebook and its users. For the reasons set forth below, the motion will be granted.

Facebook is a well-known social networking website with over 175 million users. Facebook users must register with the website and agree to Facebook's Terms of Use. Upon registration, users are given a unique username and password to access their own user profiles as well as the profiles of their "friends." Users may send messages to each other through the Facebook website, either by e-mail or by postings on a user's "wall." To preserve the integrity of its website, Facebook maintains strict policies against spam or any other form of unsolicited advertising. The Terms of Use prohibit any activity that would impair the operation of the website, including the use of data-mining "bots, robots, spiders, or scrapers" to gain access to users' login information, posting of unsolicited advertising or circulation of such advertising via e-mail, providing false personal information or falsely stating or otherwise misrepresenting oneself, or any use of another person's account without Facebook's prior authorization.

Facebook alleges that Defendants are registered Facebook users who are bound by the Terms of Use. Since November 2008, Defendants allegedly have engaged in a phishing and spamming scheme that has compromised the accounts of a substantial number of Facebook users. Defendants' activity allegedly has escalated substantially. The alleged scheme generally operates as follows: Defendants send emails to multiple Facebook users. The emails appear to be legitimate messages and ask the recipients to click on a link to another website. That website is a phishing site designed to trick users into divulging their Facebook login information. Once users divulge the information, Defendants then use it to send spam to the friends of the users, and as the cycle repeats the number of compromised Facebook accounts increases rapidly. Facebook also alleges that certain spam messages redirect users to websites that pay Defendants for each user visit. While Facebook has been reasonably successful in combating this scheme, the expanding scope of the operation has made it increasingly difficult to neutralize Defendants' activities.

The standard for issuing a TRO is the same as that for issuing a preliminary injunction. In the Ninth Circuit, a party seeking a preliminary injunction must show either (1) a likelihood of success on the merits and the possibility of irreparable injury, or (2) that serious questions are raised and the balance of the hardships tips in the movant's favor. These formulations represent two points on a sliding scale in which the required degree of irreparable harm increases as the probability of success decreases. In the instant case, Facebook engaged in substantial investigative activity before filing suit and has presented sufficient evidence in support of the instant motion to demonstrate a likelihood of success on the merits with respect to the claims asserted in the operative complaint. In addition, there is a clear possibility of irreparable injury with respect both to Facebook's reputation and to the personal privacy of Facebook users. Finally, the balance of hardships clearly favors Facebook because it has expended significant time and resources to combat Defendants' activities, which as noted above are expanding at a considerable rate. Likewise, Defendants will suffer little or no hardship if enjoined from their allegedly illegal scheme. Accordingly, Facebook is entitled to temporary injunctive relief.

ORDER

IT IS HEREBY ORDERED that: 1. Defendants Jeremi Fisher, Philip Porembski, Ryan Simeall, and Choko Systems LLC, Harm, Inc., PP Web Services LLC, and iMedia Online Services LLC, and all of their officers, agents, servants, employees and attorneys and persons in active concert or participation with them who receive actual notice of this Order are hereby enjoined from:

a. Initiating or procuring transmission of unsolicited commercial electronic messages on or through Facebook's computers, Facebook's website, Facebook's networks, or to Facebook users;

b. Accessing or attempting to access Facebook's website, networks, data, information, user information, profiles, computers, and/or computer systems;

c. Soliciting, requesting, or taking any action to induce Facebook users to provide identifying information or representing that such solicitation, request, or action is being done with Facebook's authorization or approval;

d. Retaining any copies, electronic or otherwise, of any Facebook information, including login information and/or passwords, obtained through illegitimate and/or unlawful actions;

e. Engaging in any activity that alters, damages, deletes, destroys, disrupts, diminishes the quality of, interferes with the performance of, or impairs the functionality of Facebook's computers, computer system computer network, data, website, or services;

f. Engaging in any unlawful activities alleged in the operative complaint;

g. Entering or accessing the physical premises or facilities of Facebook or its counsel; and

h. Engaging in any activity that violates, and/or encourages, induces or facilitates violations of the Terms of Use attached as Exhibit A to this Order.

2. This Order shall take effect immediately and shall remain in effect pending a hearing in this Court on Facebook's motion for a preliminary injunction.

Notes

1. Subsequently, the *Fisher* court permanently enjoined the defendants from accessing and abusing Facebook services. The court observed:

> As a result of Defendants' spam campaign, Facebook has received more than 8,000 user complaints, and more than 4,500 Facebook users have deactivated their accounts. Additionally, Facebook has expended large financial and professional resources to upgrade its security measures. Defendants have demonstrated a willingness to continue their activities without regard for Facebook's security measures or cease and desist requests. Thus, it is appropriate that Defendants be permanently enjoined from accessing and abusing Facebook services.

Facebook, Inc. v. Jeremi Fisher; 2011 U.S. Dist. LEXIS 9668 (N.D. Cal. Jan. 26, 2011) (unreported).

2. According to the 2017 Symantec Internet Security Report, phishing rates, which have been in decline for the several years, dropped again in 2016, falling from 1 in 1,846 emails to 1 in 2,596 emails. That report stated that targeted spear-phishing campaigns, instead of the mass-mailing phishing campaigns of old, are now favored by attackers. For more on phishing, *see, e.g.*, http://www.justice.gov/opa/report_on_phishing.pdf (U.S. and Canada joint report); www.apwg.org (Anti-Phishing Working Group website).

§ 18.3 Spam

> Generally, the public considers spam to be any unwanted, annoying e-mail message(s) received via computer. However, the federal statute and the preempted state statutory definitions served to narrow further the applicability of [that popular concept]. The statutory definitions refer to three characteristics, singly or in any combination. These characteristics concern whether the e-mail message is commercial in nature, whether it was unsolicited by the recipient, and whether it was sent to a single individual or sent in bulk to several individuals.[14]

By the first decade of the Twentieth Century, unsolicited commercial e-mail, commonly known as "spam," had become one of the most pervasive intrusions in the lives of Americans.[15]

> In 2008, spam comprised an estimated eighty percent of all e-mails sent worldwide. And according to at least one source, the United States generates more spam than any other country around the world.

---

14. John E. Brockhoeft, *Evaluating the Can-Spam Act of 2003*, 4 Loy. U. New Orleans Sch. L.—L. & Tech. Ann. 1 (2004).

15. Senate Report No. 102, 108th Cong., 1st Sess. 2003.

Spam often results in decreased employee productivity because of the necessity of sorting through the huge volumes of spam received every day for legitimate business e-mail. Additionally, though spam filters are now common, there is always the risk that a filter will block legitimate e-mail and, for a business, missing time sensitive e-mails can be extremely detrimental to customer relations. According to a study by Nucleus Research, Inc., spam costs U.S. businesses an estimated $71 billion in lost productivity, or approximately $712 per employee, per year. Though these figures are difficult to verify, and different sources often suggest widely different figures, it is clear that businesses pay a high price for the convenience of e-mail communication. Spamming has become so prevalent that there is now a plethora of sites devoted to calculating the cost of spam to individual businesses, as well as those offering protection from it.

Spam also has a huge impact on the environment. A recent study, published by McAffee, illustrates the staggering environmental costs of spam. According to the study, spam uses thirty-three billion kilowatt-hours per year, the equivalent of the electricity used in 2.4 million U.S. homes. Spam e-mailing also causes emissions of greenhouse gases at a rate equivalent to 3.1 million passenger cars using two billion gallons of gasoline.[16]

According to the 2017 Symantec Internet Security Report, spam rates remained steady at 53 percent of all emails in 2016 after declining in recent years. Congress passed legislation to address the problem of unsolicited commercial email, entitled the "Controlling the Assault of Non-Solicited Pornography and Marketing Act of 2003" (codified at 18 U.S.C. § 1037, 15 U.S.C. §§ 7701–7713), often referred to by the short title: "CAN-SPAM Act of 2003." This section focuses on the aspect of the legislation codified as 18 U.S.C. § 1037, creating criminal penalties for commercial spam. The Senate report asserted that the Act "aims to address the problem of spam by creating a Federal statutory regime that would give consumers the right to demand that a spammer cease sending them messages, while creating civil and criminal sanctions for the sending of spam meant to deceive recipients as to its source or content."[17] The report explained:

> The purposes of this legislation are to: (i) prohibit senders of electronic mail for primarily commercial advertisement or promotional purposes from deceiving intended recipients or Internet service providers as to the source or subject matter of their e-mail messages; (ii) require such e-mail senders to give recipients an opportunity to decline to receive future commercial e-mail from them and to honor such requests; (iii) require senders of unsolicited commercial e-mail (UCE) to also include a valid physical address in

---

16. Note, Ariella Mutchler, *Can-Spam Versus the European Union E-privacy Directive: Does Either Provide a Solution to the Problem of Spam?*, 43 Suffolk U.L. Rev. 957 (2010).

17. Senate Report No. 102, 108th Cong., 1st Sess. 2003.

the e-mail message and a clear notice that the message is an advertisement or solicitation; and (iv) prohibit businesses from knowingly promoting, or permitting the promotion of, their trade or business through e-mail transmitted with false or misleading sender or routing information.

The Senate report discussed the dimensions of the problem:

> In an April 2003 report entitled, False Claims in Spam, the Federal Trade Commission found that 66 percent of all spam contains some kind of false, fraudulent, or misleading information, either in the e-mail's routing information, its subject line, or the body of its message. The FTC also determined that most spam messages can generally be grouped into one of several major categories, such as those promoting: investment or get-rich-quick "opportunities" (20 percent); pornographic websites or adult-oriented material (18 percent); credit card or financial offers (17 percent); and health products and services (10 percent).
>
> One common method of collecting consumers' addresses, known as a "dictionary attack", involves rapid, short-burst communications with the target ISP's server (known as "pinging" the server) with automatically-generated, recipient e-mail addresses in alphabetical (or dictionary) order. In this attack, the spammer's software will record which addresses cause the server to respond positively that it is ready to accept e-mail for a tested recipient e-mail address. Each positive response from the server confirms a valid address at the target ISP, and the addresses are collected into a list that is used to send a block of spam to that server at a later time. Another common method of obtaining consumers' e-mail addresses is to capture them from websites where users post their addresses in order to communicate with other users of the website. This practice, known as e-mail address "harvesting", is often done by automated software robots that scour the Internet looking for and recording posted e-mail addresses.
>
> Additionally, many spam messages contain "web bugs" or other hidden technological mechanisms to immediately notify a spammer via the Internet when an unsolicited message has been opened. Far short of replying to a spam message, a consumer's mere act of opening a spam message containing a web bug may eventually cause that consumer to receive more spam as a result of confirming to the spammer his or her willingness or susceptibility to open unsolicited e-mail.
>
> In addition to false sender information, spammers often lure consumers to open their e-mail by adding appealing or misleading e-mail subject lines. The FTC reported that 42 percent of spam contains misleading subject lines that trick the recipient into thinking that the e-mail sender has a personal or business relationship with the recipient. Typical examples are subject lines such as "Hi, it's me" and "Your order has been filled". Moreover, e-mail messages with deceptive subject lines may still lead unsuspecting

consumers to websites promoting completely unrelated products or even scams, such as pornography or get-rich-quick pyramid schemes.

Compounding these problems is the fact that nearly all spam being sent today is considered untraceable back to its original source without extensive and costly investigation. Although many ISPs try to locate spammers in order to shut down their operations, spammers can rather easily disguise their whereabouts, quickly move to other ISPs, or set up websites at new domains in order to avoid being caught.

Consumers who buy products offered through spam face numerous risks, including the exposure and sharing of sensitive personal information over the Internet, and credit card or identity theft. In a recent example, the FTC filed a complaint against 30 Minute Mortgage Inc., which it claimed used an array of deceptions to lure consumers into sharing their personal financial data. According to the FTC, the company advertised itself as a national mortgage lender and used spam to urge potential customers to complete detailed online loan applications. The applications required consumers to supply sensitive personal information, such as their names, addresses, phone numbers, Social Security numbers, employment information, income, first and second mortgage payments, and asset account types and balances. The company assured consumers that when they submitted the loan applications, their sensitive information would be protected. Instead, the FTC alleges the company and its principals sold or offered to sell thousands of completed applications to nonaffiliated third parties.

Spam also is used to lure unwary users to websites that contain viruses, spyware, or other malicious computer code. Late last year, for instance, an Internet adult entertainment company created a "Trojan horse" program that was downloaded to unsuspecting users' computers. Users were tricked into accepting the program through a spam message that promised to deliver an electronic greeting card. The downloaded program, however, instead routed users to the company's pornography websites.

Pornographers, long on the cutting edge of technology, have taken to employing increasingly brazen techniques to sell their products and services. As mentioned above, the FTC estimates that 18 percent of all spam is pornographic or "adult-oriented" material. While not all of such spam contains images, spammers often do send graphic sexual images embedded in the body of spam so that simply upon opening the e-mail message, a user is assaulted with explicit photographs or video images. More frequently, though, spam contains HTML code and a JavaScript applet that together automatically load a pornographic web page as soon as the spam message is either opened or, in some cases, simply "previewed" in certain e-mail programs" preview panes.

———————

18 U.S.C. § 1037

(a) **In general.** — Whoever, in or affecting interstate or foreign commerce, knowingly —

(1) accesses a protected computer without authorization, and intentionally initiates the transmission of multiple commercial electronic mail messages from or through such computer,

(2) uses a protected computer to relay or retransmit multiple commercial electronic mail messages, with the intent to deceive or mislead recipients, or any Internet access service, as to the origin of such messages,

(3) materially falsifies header information in multiple commercial electronic mail messages and intentionally initiates the transmission of such messages,

(4) registers, using information that materially falsifies the identity of the actual registrant, for five or more electronic mail accounts or online user accounts or two or more domain names, and intentionally initiates the transmission of multiple commercial electronic mail messages from any combination of such accounts or domain names, or

(5) falsely represents oneself to be the registrant or the legitimate successor in interest to the registrant of 5 or more Internet Protocol addresses, and intentionally initiates the transmission of multiple commercial electronic mail messages from such addresses, or conspires to do so, shall be punished as provided in subsection (b).

(b) **Penalties.** — The punishment for an offense under subsection (a) is —

(1) a fine under this title, imprisonment for not more than 5 years, or both, if —

(A) the offense is committed in furtherance of any felony under the laws of the United States or of any State; or

(B) the defendant has previously been convicted under this section or section 1030, or under the law of any State for conduct involving the transmission of multiple commercial electronic mail messages or unauthorized access to a computer system;

(2) a fine under this title, imprisonment for not more than 3 years, or both, if —

(A) the offense is an offense under subsection (a)(1);

(B) the offense is an offense under subsection (a)(4) and involved 20 or more falsified electronic mail or online user account registrations, or 10 or more falsified domain name registrations;

(C) the volume of electronic mail messages transmitted in furtherance of the offense exceeded 2,500 during any 24-hour period, 25,000 during any 30-day period, or 250,000 during any 1-year period;

(**D**) the offense caused loss to one or more persons aggregating $5,000 or more in value during any 1-year period;

(**E**) as a result of the offense any individual committing the offense obtained anything of value aggregating $5,000 or more during any 1-year period; or

(**F**) the offense was undertaken by the defendant in concert with three or more other persons with respect to whom the defendant occupied a position of organizer or leader; and

(3) a fine under this title or imprisonment for not more than 1 year, or both, in any other case.

––––––––––

Section 1037 has three broad applicability requirements:

• *The spam must be commercial.*

The federal statute's applicability is limited to commercial e-mail messages. Those are messages "the primary purpose of which is the commercial advertisement or promotion of a commercial product or service (including content on an Internet website operated for a commercial purpose)." 15 U.S.C. § 7702(2)(A). The federal statute provides some limitations: "The inclusion of a reference to a commercial entity or a link to the website of a commercial entity in an electronic mail message does not, by itself, cause such message to be treated as a commercial electronic mail message for purposes of this title if the contents or circumstances of the message indicate a primary purpose other than commercial advertisement or promotion of a commercial product or service." 15 U.S.C. § 7702(2)(D).

• *The spam must be unsolicited.*

The statute "does not use the word 'unsolicited.'"[18] Instead, it excludes a "transactional or relationship message." 15 U.S.C. § 7702(2)(B). It defines such a message as an e-mail message the primary purpose of which is "to facilitate, complete, or confirm a commercial transaction that the recipient has previously agreed to enter into with the sender," 15 U.S.C. § 7702(17)(A)(i), "to provide warranty information, product recall information, or safety or security information with respect to a commercial product or service used or purchased by the recipient," 15 U.S.C. § 7702(17)(A)(ii), "and to provide notification concerning a change in the terms or features of; notification of a change in the recipient's standing or status with respect to; or at regular periodic intervals, account balance information or other type of account statement with respect to a subscription, membership, account, loan, or comparable ongoing commercial relationship involving

––––––––––

18. John E. Brockhoeft, *Evaluating the Can-Spam Act of 2003*, 4 Loy. U. New Orleans Sch. L.—L. & Tech. Ann. 1 (2004).

the ongoing purchase or use by the recipient of products or services offered by the sender," 15 U.S.C. § 7702(17)(A)(iii). A "transactional or relation-ship message" also includes a message designed "to provide information directly related to an employment relationship or related benefit plan in which the recipient is currently involved, participating, or enrolled," 15 U.S.C. § 7702(17)(A)(iv), or that delivers goods or services, including prod-uct updates or upgrades, that the recipient is entitled to receive under the terms of a transaction that the recipient had previously agreed to enter into with the sender, 15 U.S.C. § 7702(17)(A)(v).

"The statute's definition of 'transactional or relationship message' can be boiled down to two kinds of potentially unsolicited messages: (1) those sent by a sender with whom the recipient has conducted a commercial transac-tion or (2) those sent within an employment context."[19]

- *The spam is in bulk.*

Section 1037 requires the transmission of "multiple" e-mail messages and defines "multiple" to mean "more than 100 electronic mail messages dur-ing a 24-hour period, more than 1,000 electronic mail messages during a 30-day period, or more than 10,000 electronic mail messages during a 1-year period." 18 U.S.C. § 1037(d)(3).

United States v. Jeffrey A. Kilbride

584 F.3d 1240 (9th Cir. 2009)

BETTY B. FLETCHER, CIRCUIT JUDGE:

[Defendants' convictions arose from conduct relating to their business of send-ing unsolicited bulk email, advertising adult websites. Defendants challenged their convictions on a variety of grounds and the court's discussion of the First Amend-ment challenge to their obscenity convictions is reproduced in Chapter 13. They also claimed that 18 U.S.C. § 1037 was unconstitutionally vague.]

Defendants began their bulk email advertising business in 2003. They initially operated the business through an American corporation, using servers in Arizona. In response to new legislation regulating email communication, the Defendants shifted the operation of their business overseas, running it through Ganymede Marketing, a Mauritian company, and using servers located in the Netherlands. Although Defendants used a business structure preventing a direct link to Gany-mede, Defendants were its true owners and operators. If a recipient of Defendants' emails signed on to the advertised website and paid a fee, Defendants earned a com-mission from the entity promoted. The advertisements appearing in Defendants'

----

19. *Id.*

emails included sexually explicit images, two of which formed the basis for the obscenity convictions.

Defendants had their employees place fictitious information in the headers[n.1][20] of their bulk emails. Defendants' employee Jennifer Clason created nonsensical domain names and matched them with generic user names to generate a series of different email addresses that were almost certainly nonfunctional. These were placed in the "From" field of the headers of each email sent out.[n.2][21] Another employee of Defendants, Kirk Rogers, designed a program utilized by Defendants that generated non-functioning email addresses in the "From" field by combining the domain name used to send each email with the recipient of the email's user name. In addition, the email address appearing in the "From" field and "Return-Path" field of the headers of Defendants' emails differed, indicating at least one was false.

Defendants also falsified information appearing in the registration of the domain names they used. The registrant for each of the emails was listed as Ganymede Marketing. The correct physical address for Ganymede was listed, but the contact person and phone number listed were false. The email listed in the registration was never tested for functionality, though the evidence indicates that at some point it became invalid. A reverse look-up of the internet provider address appearing in the email headers came back to a different entity, Kobalt Networks, registered in the Netherlands.

Defendants challenge their convictions for violation of 18 U.S.C. § 1037 on the ground that § 1037 is unconstitutionally vague both on its face and as applied to Defendants' conduct. Defendants were convicted specifically under 18 U.S.C. § 1037(a)(3) and (a)(4). Section 1037(a)(3) provides:

> Whoever, in or affecting interstate or foreign commerce, knowingly . . . materially falsifies header information in multiple commercial electronic mail messages and intentionally initiates the transmission of such messages . . . shall be punished. . . .

Section 1037(a)(4) provides:

> Whoever, in or affecting interstate or foreign commerce, knowingly . . . registers, using information that materially falsifies the identity of the actual registrant, for five or more electronic mail accounts or online user accounts or two or more domain names, and intentionally initiates the transmission of multiple commercial electronic mail messages from any combination of such accounts or domain names . . . shall be punished. . . .

---

20. [n.1] A "header" is called "header information" in the relevant statute and defined as "the source, destination, and routing information attached to an electronic mail message, including the originating domain name and originating electronic mail address, and any other information that appears in the line identifying, or purporting to identify, a person initiating the message." 15 U.S.C. § 7702(8).

21. [n.2] In an email address, the user name is the portion appearing before the @ symbol, while the domain name is the portion appearing after the @.

"Initiates" is defined by statute as "to originate or transmit such message or to procure the origination or transmission of such message." 15 U.S.C. § 7702(9). The statute further provides that

> header information or registration information is materially falsified if it is altered or concealed in a manner that would impair the ability of a recipient of the message, an Internet access service processing the message on behalf of a recipient, a person alleging a violation of this section, or a law enforcement agency to identify, locate, or respond to a person who initiated the electronic mail message or to investigate the alleged violation.

18 U.S.C. § 1037(d)(2). Defendants argue that the terms "impair" and "altered or concealed" as used in the statute's definition of "materially falsified" are unconstitutionally vague. They also assert an as-applied vagueness challenge claiming these terms gave them insufficient notice that the conduct they committed was illegal under § 1037.

"Vagueness doctrine is an outgrowth not of the First Amendment, but of the Due Process Clause of the Fifth Amendment." "Vague statutes are invalidated for three reasons: (1) to avoid punishing people for behavior that they could not have known was illegal; (2) to avoid subjective enforcement of laws based on 'arbitrary and discriminatory enforcement' by government officers; and (3) to avoid any chilling effect on the exercise of First Amendment freedoms." A statute is unconstitutionally vague as applied if it failed to put a defendant on notice that his conduct was criminal. A statute is unconstitutionally vague on its face if it "fails to provide a person of ordinary intelligence fair notice of what is prohibited, or is so standardless that it authorizes or encourages seriously discriminatory enforcement." For statutes like § 1037 involving criminal sanctions "the requirement for clarity is enhanced." However, even applying this heightened requirement, "due process does not require impossible standards of clarity."

We conclude Defendants' as-applied vagueness challenge fails even applying a heightened requirement of clarity. They had clear notice their conduct was a violation of § 1037(a)(3) and (a)(4). Defendants assert that they lacked notice that their actions would constitute "material falsification" under the statute. The terms Defendants regard as vague in the definition of material falsification are "impair," "altered," and "concealed." "When Congress does not define a term in a statute, we construe that term according to its ordinary, contemporary, common meaning." "Impair" is defined as: "to make worse: diminish in quantity, value, excellence, or strength: do harm to." Webster's Third New International Dictionary Unabridged 1131 (Philip Babcock Gove et al. eds., 1993). "Alter" is defined as "to cause to become different in some particular characteristic . . . without changing into something else." *Id.* at 63. "Conceal" is defined as "to prevent disclosure or recognition of: avoid revelation of: refrain from revealing: withhold knowledge of: drawn attention from: treat so as to be unnoticed." *Id.* at 469. In the headers of their bulk emails, Defendants intentionally replaced the email addresses from which the emails were sent with fictitious addresses. It is quite obvious that this constituted intentionally causing to be different or preventing the disclosure of the actual header information in a manner diminishing the ability of recipients to identify, locate, or respond to Defendants or their agents in violation of § 1037(a)(3). Defendants also intentionally replaced the actual phone and contact person for Ganymede with fictitious information. Again, it should have been clear to the Defendants that this constituted intentionally causing to be different or preventing the disclosure of the actual domain name registration information in a manner diminishing the ability of a recipient to contact Defendants or their agents as the actual registrants of the domain name directly or through Ganymede.

Defendants sole concrete argument in support of their as-applied challenge is that, with regard to their conviction under § 1037(a)(4), there was no attempt made by the Government to determine whether the email listed in their domain registration was inaccurate. Defendants assert that they had no notice under the terms of the statute that the intentional placing of a false contact person and phone number in their registration would constitute intentional impairment when the email listed may have been accurate. This argument is unpersuasive. As an initial matter, evidence was presented at trial that the email listed in the domain name registrations at issue was invalid. Even were this not the case, "impair" clearly is not synonymous with "completely obstruct." To impair, according to its plain meaning, merely means to decrease. It should have been clear to Defendants that intentionally falsifying the identity of the contact person and phone number for the actual registrant constitutes intentionally decreasing the ability of a recipient to locate and contact the actual registrant, regardless of whether a recipient may still be left some avenue to do so. We therefore conclude Defendants had notice that their conduct violated § 1037.

Defendants' facial vagueness challenge is similarly unavailing. We have held that "ordinarily a plaintiff who engages in some conduct that is clearly proscribed cannot complain of the vagueness of the law as applied to the conduct of others." However, "we have relaxed that requirement in the First Amendment context, permitting plaintiffs to argue that a statute is overbroad because it is unclear whether it regulates a substantial amount of protected speech." We need not determine whether § 1037 regulates protected speech, thereby permitting Defendants' facial vagueness challenge, as in any case Defendants' challenge would be unsuccessful. In parallel to their as-applied challenge, Defendants' facial challenge rests on the claim that the term "impair" is so vague as to leave it to the complete discretion of police officers how the statute is enforced. We disagree. "Impair" is a broad term that potentially subjects a wide swath of conduct to regulation under § 1037. Nonetheless, as already discussed, it has a clear meaning that is not open to wholly subjective interpretation in the manner of other terms found to be unconstitutionally vague.[n.9][22]

---

22. [n.9] By itself, the statute's failure to define a baseline of ability a recipient should have for locating an initiator of an email or actual registrant of a domain name could render the meaning of "impair" imprecise. However, any vagueness concerns this failure creates are obviated by the

Defendants also argue that the definition of "material falsification" renders § 1037 unconstitutionally vague specifically as to whether it would criminalize private registration of a domain name. As testified to at trial, private registration is a service that allows registration of a domain name in a manner that conceals the actual registrant's identity from the public absent a subpoena. We fail to perceive any vagueness on this point. Based on the plain meaning of the relevant terms discussed above, private registration for the purpose of concealing the actual registrant's identity would constitute "material falsification." Defendants assert that many innocent people who privately register without the requisite intent may be subject to investigation for violation of § 1037 until their intent can be determined, allowing for abuse by enforcement authorities. This may be so, but it does not make the statute unconstitutionally vague. As we recently noted, "'[w]hat renders a statute vague is not the possibility that it will sometimes be difficult to determine whether the incriminating fact it establishes has been proved; but rather the indeterminacy of precisely what that fact is.'" While determining as a factual matter whether the requisite intent for culpability under § 1037 exists may prove difficult, this does not demonstrate that the concept of intent as used in the statute is an entirely indeterminate, subjective one. Hence, the problem Defendants identify is irrelevant to the vagueness inquiry.

United States v. Michael Steven Twombly

475 F. Supp. 2d 1019 (S.D. Cal. 2007)

BURNS, DISTRICT JUDGE.

[The defendants moved to dismiss the indictment.] The charges in this case stem from a large number of electronic messages sent between April and September, 2004. The Government alleges Defendant Twombly leased dedicated servers using an alias, including one server from Biznesshosting, Inc. According to the Government's allegations, within approximately two hours after Biznesshosting provided Twombly with logon credentials, it began receiving complaints regarding spam electronic mail messages originating from its network. Defendants allegedly sent approximately 1 million spam electronic mail messages, followed several days later by another 1.5 million. The spam messages allegedly contained advertising for computer software, and directed recipients to the website of a software company with an address in Canada. The Government alleges this website was falsely registered under the name of a non-existent business, and that the messages' routing information and "From" lines were falsified, preventing recipients, internet service providers, and law enforcement agencies from identifying, locating, or responding to the senders. Biznesshosting allegedly investigated the complaints, traced the spam to

---

statute's requirement that any impairment to the recipient's ability be intentional to result in culpability. By including this scienter requirement, the statute protects against arbitrary definition of what constitutes the baseline of ability from which impairment occurs.

the server leased by Defendant Twombly, and terminated his account. The Government alleges the traffic generated by Defendant Twombly's leased server led internet-based anti-spam services to blacklist Biznesshosting's network domain, resulting in both immediate and continuing financial loss to Biznesshosting.

The Government alleges a search by the FBI uncovered approximately twenty dedicated servers leased by Defendant Twombly using false credentials. Defendant Twombly allegedly leased the servers for a man known only as "Josh," and was paid $100 for each set of logon credentials he provided to "Josh." "Josh" was allegedly later determined to be Defendant Eveloff. The Government alleges both Defendants caused the spam messages to be sent.

The relevant sections of the statute under are as follows:

§ 1037. Fraud and related activity in connection with electronic mail

(a) In general.—Whoever, in or affecting interstate or foreign commerce, knowingly—

. . . .

(3) materially falsifies header information in multiple commercial electronic mail messages and intentionally initiates the transmission of such messages, [or]

(4) registers, using information that materially falsifies the identity of the actual registrant, for five or more electronic mail accounts or online user accounts or two or more domain names, and intentionally initiates the transmission of multiple commercial electronic mail messages from any combination of such accounts or domain names, . . . shall be punished as provided in subsection (b).

Section 1037(d)(2) explains in part the meaning of § 1037(a)(3) and (4):

(2) Materially.—For purposes of paragraphs (3) and (4) of subsection (a), header information or registration information is materially falsified if it is altered or concealed in a manner that would impair the ability of a recipient of the message, an Internet access service processing the message on behalf of a recipient, a person alleging a violation of this section, or a law enforcement agency to identify, locate, or respond to a person who initiated the electronic mail message or to investigate the alleged violation.

Defendants seek dismissal of the indictment because, they contend, it fails to allege *mens rea*, an essential element. Defendants argue that although the statute includes the *mens rea* "knowing," implicit in the statute is the element of intent to commit a criminal act. The Ninth Circuit construes criminal statutes "in light of the fundamental principle that a person is not criminally responsible unless 'an evil-meaning mind' accompanies 'an evil-doing hand.'"

Section (a)(3) includes two *mens rea* elements: a defendant must "knowingly" materially falsify header information, and then "intentionally" transmit it. Section (a)(4) likewise includes two *mens rea* requirements: a defendant must "knowingly" register for accounts using information that materially falsifies the registrant's identity, and "intentionally" send commercial emails from those accounts.

Depending on the context of the statute, different terms may be used to show criminal intent. Here, section (a)(3) requires a higher *mens rea* than general criminal intent; a defendant must "knowingly" falsify header information and "intentionally" transmit it. Thus, a defendant must at the very least know he is being deceptive while sending multiple commercial emails. [T]his satisfies the "evil-meaning mind" requirement.

Defendants ask the Court to consider online deception an innocent peccadillo or even a positive good,[n.3][23] that is not the view of this statute, which is particularly aimed at deception. Nor is it appropriate for reasons of policy. Deception, even where it is not criminal, is neither innocent nor worthy of any constitutional protection — particularly in the commercial context.

Section (a)(4) is open to two interpretations, depending on whether "knowingly" modifies only "registers" or whether it also modifies "using information that materially falsifies the registrant's identity." Although Defendants do not raise this, if the former interpretation is used, this section could potentially penalize innocent behavior, if an innocent agent were to register and send emails. The Court need not reach this hypothetical argument, however. While the Court acknowledges some potential ambiguity in section (a)(4), it has no application to the facts of this case.

The indictment largely tracks the language of the statute and thus refers to "knowing" and "intentional" acts without mentioning general criminal intent. The indictment does not end there, however. As part of Count 1 (section (a)(3)), the indictment specifically charges that the two Defendants conspired to lease servers using false names. It alleges also that Defendant Twombly leased servers using false identities, or fraudulently (alleging that Twombly "leased" or "fraudulently leased" dedicated servers "using the false identity" or "under the false identity" of various fictitious people, or "under a false name"). The indictment also alleges that Eveloff paid Twombly every time Twombly leased a server using a false name. The allegations therefore foreclose the possibility of innocent behavior being penalized in this case.

This motion [to dismiss] is therefore DENIED.

Notes

Kilbride and *Twombly* illustrate the types of offenders that § 1037 sought to address — bulk spammers engaged in deceptive practices. The two cases set out and

---

23. [n.3] Defendants raise this in the context of their overbreadth argument: "People have been using false information to sign up for e-mail accounts since the internet went public. Anonymity was one of the great things about the internet. As written, section (a)(4) criminalizes a large category of innocent conduct."

apply the elements of proof needed to be shown under subsections (3) and (4). What are those elements?

§ 18.4 Identity-Related Crime

"The terms 'identity theft' and 'identity fraud' refer to all types of crimes in which someone wrongfully obtains and uses another person's personal data in some way that involves fraud or deception, typically for economic or other gain, including immigration benefits."[24] In 2003, the Federal Trade Commission sampled households and determined that 4.6 % of survey participants were victims of some type of identity theft in the past year, suggesting "that almost 10 million Americans were the victims of some form of identity theft within [that] year."

> Identity-related crime can be defined as a cycle with five distinct phases: (1) unauthorized or illegal acquisition of identifying data or items (e.g., cards or documents); (2) transfer of the initially acquired identifying data or documents; (3) manipulation of the data or items (e.g., through alteration, compilation, or forgery/counterfeiting); (4) transfer of the manipulated data or items; and (5) use of the data or items for fraud or concealment of criminal identity.[25]

Digital devices as tools may be used in any of the five cycles and the theft of identity may itself be a tool to achieve some further criminal aim, such as fraud. In a recent report by the Attorney General of the United States and the Minister of Public Safety of Canada, the report noted that the "predominant reason that criminals engage in identity-related crime is to commit fraud: that is, to make use of others' true identities or synthetic identities for financial gain through the unlawful obtaining of goods, services, or benefits from the public or private sectors."[26] It listed a study that, in 2009, showed that, in the United States,

> identity thieves used victims' information to commit credit card fraud (76% percent), phone or utilities fraud (11 percent), bank fraud (14 percent), Internet service or payment accounts fraud (15 percent), loan fraud (7 percent), and other types of fraud, including government benefits, medical services, and employment-related fraud (4%).

The report also listed a variety of other purposes for identity-related crime, including concealment of identity, support for criminal organizations, and terrorism.

Every state has criminalized identity theft. "Most state identity theft statutes make it a crime to assume another person's identity or use 'personal identifying information

---

24. Cong. Record Vol. 150 (2004) House Report No. 108-528 (June 8, 2004).

25. IDENTITY-RELATED CRIME: A THREAT ASSESSMENT (REPORT OF THE ATTORNEY GENERAL OF THE UNITED STATES AND THE MINISTER OF PUBLIC SAFETY OF CANADA) (November 2010).

26. *Id.*

of that other person' to 'obtain goods, money, property or services or . . . credit in' that person's name. Some expansive state statutes follow the federal approach by also making it a crime to use another's personal identifying information to commit or to aid and abet the commission of other crimes."[27]

18 U.S.C. § 1028 prohibits a variety of activities in connection with identity-related crime. Those prohibitions include:

- knowing transfer, possession, or use of a means of identification to commit a crime;

- production, transfer, or possession (under certain circumstances) of false or illegally issued identification documents; and

- production, transfer, or possession of a "document-making implement," including computers, with the intent to use it in the production of a false identification document.

The joint report of the Attorney General of the United States and the Minister of Public Safety of Canada observed:

> All identity-related crime must begin, at some time, with the acquisition of valuable personal information by criminals. Their methods of doing so vary widely, depending on the technological skill and sophistication of the criminal and the manner in which those data are stored and accessible. Some criminals seek to target repositories of large amounts of personal data for unauthorized access, or to use methods enabling them to build their own data repositories for resale of those data or for criminal use. To do so, they may use technological skills to hack into databases or use malicious computer code to gain access, "social engineering" skills to trick members of the public into voluntarily disclosing their own data or to develop relationships with and compromise corporate or government insiders with access to large data repositories, or a combination of both. Other criminals, lacking those skills, may content themselves with low-skill methods of acquiring personal data, ranging from break-ins to pickpocketing to mail theft to persuading people to disclose data voluntarily.
>
> In many cases, the data, physical cards, or documents that identity thieves have acquired are not ready for immediate use. Depending on how the identity thief wants to profit from the unauthorized acquisition, he may need to gather the data or physical items so that they can be physically transferred elsewhere, or extract the relevant data from them so that they can be transmitted electronically. For example, in numerous phishing schemes, criminals download code onto targeted computers that not only

27. Susan W. Brenner and Megan Rehberg, *"Kiddie Crime"? The Utility of Criminal Law in Controlling Cyberbullying*, 8 First Amend. L. Rev. 1 (2009).

captures the keystrokes of greatest value (e.g., login names and passwords for online bank accounts) but causes those data to be emailed to an online address of the criminals' choosing.

———————

United States v. Vladimir Cabrera

208 F.3d 309 (5th Cir. 2000)

STAHL, CIRCUIT JUDGE.

Vladimir Cabrera appeals his conviction for possession of a document-making implement under 18 U.S.C. § 1028 (1994 & Supp. 1996). Specifically, he (a) asserts that under a proper interpretation of § 1028, the prosecution presented insufficient evidence upon which to ground a conviction. We affirm.

In early 1998, Cabrera and an accomplice, Joseph Medeiros, engaged in a scheme to produce counterfeit identification documents, including Massachusetts and Rhode Island driver's licenses, Massachusetts and Rhode Island state employee identification cards, Rhode Island and Puerto Rico birth certificates, U.S. Department of Health and Human Services Social Security cards, and U.S. Department of Justice Immigration and Naturalization Service Resident Alien cards.

The government's evidence supported the conclusions that Cabrera employed a computer, a document scanner, a printer, and commercial software that together could be used to scan, alter, and reproduce documents. When used in conjunction with this hardware and software, computer files containing previously scanned official documents stripped of all identifying material served as digitized "templates" from which forgeries could easily be fabricated. First, using the aforementioned equipment, Cabrera scanned genuine documents into his computer, saved the images on his computer hard drive and on floppy disks, removed or altered the identifying information and photographs on the documents, and then printed the documents on photographic paper. Medeiros then inserted new identifying information onto the documents, trimmed the counterfeits, and laminated them as appropriate. Cabrera kept the computer equipment at his home, while the equipment Medeiros used was stored in a suitcase that the two owned jointly. On June 10, 1998, U.S. Secret Service Agents searched Cabrera's apartment pursuant to a warrant. They found Cabrera's computer equipment, a board used for measuring and trimming documents, Microsoft's "Picture It!" software, which Cabrera apparently had used to create the counterfeit materials, the digitized templates, and sundry fake documents in various stages of completion.

A federal grand jury returned a two-count indictment, charging, inter alia, that Cabrera possessed document-making implements with the intent that such implements be used in the production of false identification documents, in violation of 18 U.S.C. § 1028(a)(5). At the relevant time period, the statute defined "document-making implement" to mean any implement or impression specially designed or primarily used for making an identification document, a false identification document, or another document-making implement.[n.1][28]

Count One was based on Cabrera's possession of the computer, printer, and scanner.

During Cabrera's trial, Secret Service Agent James Mooney testified for the government regarding the templates found on Cabrera's hard drive and on the diskettes. Agent Mooney also described the software installed on Cabrera's computer and how it could be used for scanning, altering and reproducing documents. On cross-examination, Agent Mooney acknowledged that computers were available to the public and that they had uses aside from those of which Cabrera stood accused. But when Cabrera's counsel then attempted to further examine him regarding the general uses to which anyone could put computer equipment, the court intervened, and the following sidebar exchange regarding the meaning of §1028's "primarily used" prong ensued:

THE COURT:

Congress might have been a little bit more precise in their definition, but as I read that definition in the context of this statute, I read it as referring to the possession and the intent of the possessor in putting it to use. So I think that the general use that anyone might put a computer to — in this case, a computer to, is not relevant.

> MR. McCORMICK [Cabrera's Counsel]: I wanted to ask generally if [computer equipment] was primarily used for the making of —
>
> THE COURT: No, because that primarily refers to the possession of this individual, not the general public.

At the trial's close, the district court instructed the jury only that:

> [a]s used in these instructions, the term "document making implement" means any implement or impression specially designed or primarily used for making an identification document, a false identification document or another document making implement.

The instructions did not specify any particular meaning for the terms "specially designed" or "primarily used." Although Cabrera's counsel did not object to these instructions, the government *did* object, stating that they did not adequately specify that the statute referred to Cabrera's primary use of the equipment rather than the general uses to which any computer user primarily would put such equipment.

---

28. [n.1] This language has since been amended and now defines "document-making implement" as "any implement, impression, electronic device, or computer hardware or software, that is specifically configured or primarily used for making an identification document, a false identification document, or another document-making implement." 18 U.S.C. §1028(d)(1) (1994 & Supp. 1998) (as amended).

Meanwhile, Cabrera had moved for judgment of acquittal on both counts, arguing that "on the evidence presented, it ha[d] not been shown that the computer, printer and scanner referred to in the indictment [we]re document making implements." The jury convicted Cabrera on Count One, and the district judge denied his motion for a judgment of acquittal on that count.

Cabrera argues first that his computer system was not proven to constitute a document-making implement within the meaning of the statute, because "there was no proof, either directly [sic] or by inference, that [it] was . . . specially designed or *generally* used to produce identification documents, false identification documents or other document making implements." To determine the sufficiency of the evidence, we "canvass the evidence (direct and circumstantial) in the light most agreeable to the prosecution and decide whether that evidence, including all plausible inferences extractable therefrom, enables a rational factfinder to conclude beyond a reasonable doubt that the defendant committed the charged crime."

We first find that Cabrera's computer system was "specially designed" for the production of identification documents. As an initial matter, we hold that the statute's text is unambiguous. It does not exclude from its reach implements that could have legitimate other uses if not altered by the perpetrator's modifications. Cabrera suggests that the "specially designed" prong refers not to a defendant's specific implements, but to implements that *as a class* are uniquely configured to fabricate false identification documents. His interpretation is not tenable. Neither the statute nor Cabrera provides any basis upon which a court could determine the proper level of generality at which to define the class. Should we look to the class of "computers fitted with scanners, printers, document-altering software and digitized templates"? The class of all "computers"? All "electronic implements"? All "implements" of any sort? Nothing in § 1028 requires such arbitrary classification. Rather, the statute unambiguously asks the fact-finder to consider whether the item *that the defendant is charged with possessing* was "specially designed" for producing forgeries. Asserting that the statute is ambiguous, Cabrera notes that courts may look to a statute's legislative history when its language itself is not conclusive and clear. But even if § 1028 were unclear (and we believe it is not) Cabrera's resort to its legislative history would be unavailing. The House Judiciary Committee's report on the False Identification Crime Control Act of 1982 — in which the disputed "specially designed" language was first introduced — stated that "the committee intend[ed] to exclude implements such as office photocopying machines, which are designed for more general and legitimate purposes." H.R. Rep. No. 97-802, at 11 (1982), *reprinted in* 1982 U.S.C.C.A.N. 3519, 3530. This language might support an argument that standard computer equipment, bereft of any special-purpose hardware or software, would fall beyond the statute's reach. Perhaps an offender could, it would seem, have used an ordinary word processor and an ordinary printer with ordinary paper to produce false documents, just as an offender could have used an office photocopier to do so, without having violated former § 1028. But Cabrera's computer arrangement, unlike a standard office photocopier, was specifically designed to facilitate counterfeiting. A modern computer is not analogous to an "office photocopying machine[ ]" circa 1982, which in Congress's view likely could not be altered or specialized, but rather to a modern photocopier fitted with software and hardware that render it uniquely suited to produce illicit materials. We have no reason to believe that such a device would escape § 1028's reach simply because both it and its 1982 analogue were called "photocopiers." A photocopier configured with special-purpose hardware or software may be "specially designed" for the fabrication of identifying documents, and so may a similarly configured computer.

In fact, the more relevant portion of the legislative history is that which precedes the language quoted above. The House committee report noted that the term "document-making implement" would include "text in a distinctive type face and layout that when reproduced [is] part of an identification document." This statement, of course, accurately describes the templates, which were merely computer files containing digital images of "text in a distinctive type face and layout." Alone, each template formed "part of an identification document" and together with the inserted data, each would constitute a *complete* document.

Cabrera contends that his system was not specially designed for the fabrication of false identification documents, emphasizing that the hardware at issue—namely, the computer, printer, and scanner—were not *uniquely* suited to such activity. However, the evidence adduced at trial permitted a jury to conclude that Cabrera's system also included software, such as the "Picture It!" program, which testimony indicated "could be used . . . to accept scann[ed] images and also to place those images onto computer-produced documents." Most tellingly, the system also included digitized templates of various official identification documents stored on Cabrera's hard drive and floppy disks. A jury viewing this paraphernalia as a whole could reasonably have deemed the system "specially designed . . . for making . . . a false identification document."

Cabrera urges that the "primarily used" prong of the "document-making implement" definition refers to an item's "general usage" rather than the particular use to which a defendant put it. The government acknowledges that if it was required to prove that as a *general matter*, computers, scanners, and printers are primarily used for making identification documents or false identification documents, Cabrera's conviction must be overturned because the court was presented with no evidence supporting that conclusion. The government contends, however, that the relevant inquiry focuses not on the uses of some hypothetical user, but on Cabrera's own primary use of the computer system. We share the government's view, and find that a jury reasonably could have found that Cabrera's equipment was "primarily used" for the fabrication of documents as that term is set forth in former § 1028.

First, as the government notes, Congress could have used a word such as "generally" in lieu of "primarily" if it intended the meaning that Cabrera proposes. Congress's choice not to use that term suggests that it did not intend the inquiry to focus on an item's typical use within society. Relatedly, the section's legislative history suggests that Congress fully expected § 1028 to cover implements that were "generally" used for purposes other than the fabrication of documents. The House Judiciary Committee report noted that "specialized paper or ink" could constitute document-making implements under the "primarily used" prong. H.R. Rep. No. 97-802, at 11, *reprinted in* 1982 U.S.C.C.A.N. at 3530. Paper and ink— even "specialized" paper and ink—are not "generally" used for the production of false identification documents, but could, in a given case, be "primarily used" in the service of such ends by a particular defendant. The committee's remarks, then, lend credence to the government's case-specific interpretation of the "primarily used" prong. Moreover, the treatment which former § 1028 has been accorded by the courts suggests that "primarily used" refers to the *defendant's* primary use of the item in question. While no court appears to have analyzed the meaning of this prong, it has been found to encompass an assortment of paraphernalia not "generally" used for illicit purposes, including laminating machines, plastic laminating pouches, packets of rub-on letters, erasers, tape, scissors, and small photographs.

Finally, as the government points out, at least one other statute with language similar to § 1028's has been treated in a manner consistent with the government's position here. The statute prohibiting fraud in connection with an "access device" addresses, inter alia, "device-making equipment," and defines that term to mean "any equipment, mechanism, or impression designed *or primarily used* for making an access device or a counterfeit access device." 18 U.S.C. § 1029(e)(6) (1994 & Supp. 1998) (emphasis added). The Eleventh Circuit, in applying this statute, examined whether a defendant's mobile phone was primarily used to make an access device or a counterfeit access device. Although the court ultimately found that it was primarily used by the defendant for making telephone calls and that it therefore did not fall within the ambit of § 1029(e)(6), the court's very pursuit of the inquiry reflected its belief that what mattered was the particular use to which the defendant put the device, not its "general" use within society.

The evidence showed that Cabrera repeatedly used his computer, scanner, printer, software, and digitized templates to create false identification documents. This system was used in conjunction with laminates, Exacto blades, a supply of photographic-quality paper, and genuine identification documents. There was no evidence to demonstrate that Cabrera used his system for any *other* purpose. The jury thus reasonably could have found that this equipment was "primarily used" for Cabrera's document production.

Notes

1. The Federal Trade Commission website offers a great deal of information about ID theft. The FTC hosts the Identity Theft Data Clearinghouse, which contains more than 815,000 complaints from victims. *See* www.ftc.gov/bcp/edu/microsites /idtheft/law-enforcement/investigations.html.

2. See also *Flores-Figueroa v. United States*, 129 S. Ct. 1886 (2009) (in prosecuting a defendant under the aggravated identity theft statute, the government must prove that the defendant knew that the "means of identification" that the defendant unlawfully transferred, possessed, or used, in fact belonged to another actual person).

Chapter 19

Other Crimes Against Persons: Cyberbullying, Threats, Stalking, Harassment, and Defamation

Cyberbullying is a popular—albeit nebulous—label that includes several forms of abusive activity.[1] Depending on the jurisdiction, the abusive activity may or may not fall into a variety of criminal statutes, including new crimes labeled cyberbullying or more traditional crimes such as harassment, threats, stalking, or defamation. Often, the lines between these crimes are not sharp and definitions vary from jurisdiction to jurisdiction. Indeed, to address perceived culpable cyberbullying behavior, prosecutors have sometimes taken novel approaches. Hence, for example, in the *Drew* case reproduced in Chapter 16, Lori Drew allegedly set up a profile as a young boy on MySpace and, pretending to be the boy, chatted with Megan Meier over a period of time. Putting aside the details of the alleged chats, Ms. Drew was charged under the Federal Computer Fraud and Abuse Act with intentionally and without authorization accessing a computer used in interstate commerce and, by means of an interstate communication, obtaining information from that computer to further a tortious act—the intentional infliction of emotional distress. A jury convicted her of three misdemeanor charges, but the federal district judge overturned the guilty verdicts and acquitted her.

§ 19.1 Cyberbullying

One commentator has observed that cyberbullying generally has four elements:

First, the cyberbullying behavior must be intentional, not incidental. Second, the bullying must be repeated and reoccurring, not an isolated incident. Third, there must be harm to a particular individual. Fourth, these actions must be carried out through electronic means, including cell phones and computers.[2]

---

1. *See, e.g.,* Patrick E. Corbett, *Cyberbullying and Other High-Tech Crimes Involving Teens*, 12 J. Internet L. 1 (2008).

2. Comment, Ashliegh Hammer, *An Age-Old Problem Poses New Constitutional Challenges in the Modern Digital Age: The Desperate need for Cyberbullying Reform in Texas*, 49 Tex. Tech L.

Excerpted in this section are two views of the scope of the "crime" of cyberbullying. Professor Patrick Corbett offers this hypothetical:

> Robert sends several instant messages to those on his email "buddy" list that state classmate Eric cheated on an exam (when Eric did not and Robert knew that he did not). He encourages them to hassle Eric for cheating. A few send nasty emails to Eric. Eric is so upset that he misses three days of school. A crime? What if this is posted to Robert's Facebook site?

> Michigan law criminalizes the posting of messages without consent. Under a law passed in 2001, individuals are prohibited from posting a message through the use of any medium of communication (including the Internet and high-tech communication devices) without the victim's consent, if:

> - "The person knows or has reason to know that posting the message could cause" multiple instances of "unconsented contact" with the victim;
> - "Posting the message is intended to cause conduct that would make the victim feel" frightened or harassed;
> - "Conduct arising from posting the message would cause a reasonable person to suffer emotional distress and to feel" frightened or harassed; and
> - "Conduct arising from posting the message causes the victim to suffer emotional distress and to feel" frightened or harassed. [Mich. Comp. Laws § 750.411s.]

> This offense is a felony punishable by up to two years imprisonment. Significantly, there is no requirement that the message that is posted be untruthful; the information could be entirely truthful and still be criminal if all other elements of the offense are met. Moreover, there appears to be no clear requirement that the "unconsented contact" actually occur as long as it "could" occur from the posting of the message.

> Assuming that the prosecutor chose to take the case, it appears that Robert could be facing a felony charge whether he sent instant messages or posted the information on his Facebook site. He posted the messages through a medium of communication; it appears that he intended that the posting would result in harassment to Eric in that he knew Eric did not cheat but he encouraged others to hassle him as if he had; the posting of the message would cause a reasonable person to feel harassed in that nobody enjoys being called a cheater (especially when it is not true); and Eric actually suffered emotional distress in that he missed three days of school.[3]

REV. 457 (2017).

3. Patrick E. Corbett, *Cyberbullying and Other High-Tech Crimes Involving Teens*, 12 J. INTERNET L. 1 (2008).

_____

Questions

1. What potential problems do you see with the scope of the Michigan statute?

2. The Michigan law excerpted in Professor Corbert's article is not limited to cyberbullying in the educational context. Should it be?

CYERBULLYING LIMITED TO THE EDUCATIONAL CONTEXT

Susan W. Brenner and Megan Rehberg offer this view:[4]

Cyberbullying has garnered a variety of definitions as it has gained notoriety. Since the definitions in common use tend to be imprecise, our first task is to define the phenomenon we intend to analyze. The primary problem we see with many of the current de facto definitions is that they do not differentiate between bullying in an educational context and bullying in a general societal context. It is necessary to distinguish adult-on-adult bullying from what has traditionally been considered bullying, i.e., student-on-student aggression that occurs in an educational context. This is essential because much of what constitutes adult bullying—and certainly the more serious types of adult bullying—can be addressed with existing criminal law.

For our purposes, therefore, we use a definition of cyberbullying that encompasses only that conduct which occurs in an educational context. We define cyberbullying as the repeated use of computer or other modern communications technology to engage in non-physical abuse of one or more individuals when the actors are all constituents of a common educational context. Two parts of this definition are significant. The first is the requirement that the contact be repeated; the second is that the conduct takes place within an educational context.

What do we mean by "educational context"? Does it only encompass students who have not yet attained a high school diploma? Or should it also encompass college, university, graduate, and even trade-school students? We could exclude the latter categories because of the premise noted earlier: that cyberbullying should be distinguished from simple adult-on-adult aggression. But while there are important empirical differences between K-12 students and adults who attend post-secondary educational institutions, every educational context can generate the dynamics that give rise to bullying and cyberbullying. We therefore do not limit the educational context element of our definition to the K-12 sector; our definition

_____

4. Susan W. Brenner & Megan Rehberg, *"Kiddie Crime"? The Utility of Criminal Law in Controlling Cyberbullying*, 8 FIRST AMEND. L. REV. 1 (2009). Copyright © 2009, Susan W. Brenner, Megan Rehberg, North Carolina Law Review Association. All rights reserved. Reprinted by permission.

encompasses cyberbullying in any educational institution, regardless of the age of those who attend. Our limitation of the education sector, however, distinguishes our definition from others that require, for example, only "willful and repeated harm." Our definition allows us to consider the possibility that traditional criminal law—which is generally adequate to deal with generic adult-on-adult cyberbullying—may not be adequate when the cyberbullying involves adults who are also students.

Brenner and Rehberg create a taxonomy of cyberbullying in the educational context, listing the categories as student-on-student, student-on-teacher, teacher-on-student, and teacher-on-teacher. They also distinguish between private versus public cyberbullying:

> We define public cyberbullying as involving any material that is posted in a public forum: YouTube, MySpace, Facebook, Twitter, blogs, or websites. This material can range from embarrassing pictures that the subject would rather not see posted, to harassing quotes posted to a Facebook wall, to the cyberbully's own social networking page. Also included in this definition would be any instances of "private" cyberbullying spread to a large number of people—e.g., a text sent to a large number of people, forwarding a private e-mail to a group of friends, or posting a status message on an instant messenger client such as Trillian or AOL Instant Messenger.

> A prime example of "public" cyberbullying is the rise of "sexting," the act of sending sexually charged material via cell phone text messages. While raising a host of child pornography issues, sexting itself is not cyberbullying, as it does not fit within our definition. The act moves into the realm of cyberbullying when the "sexts" are sent to those other than the intended recipients.

> In a tragic example, Jesse Logan, an eighteen-year-old from Cincinnati, Ohio, committed suicide after a nude picture she sent to her boyfriend was forwarded to other classmates at her school. The cyberbullying then crossed into more traditional forms of bullying as the classmates harassed her, calling her derogatory names and ultimately making attending school so traumatic that she began skipping school and ultimately hung herself in her closet.

> Private cyberbullying, on the other hand, tends to be between the cyberbully and the target. E-mails, instant messages, and private messages on social networking sites all fall into this category. This type of cyberbullying can cause just as much emotional harm as public cyberbullying, as seen in the Megan Meier case from Missouri. [T]he Meier case involved private cyberbullying carried out via MySpace and AOL Instant Messenger. That case ended just as tragically as the Logan case mentioned above—Meier committed suicide in her closet after receiving a private message that stated, "The world would be a better place without you."

They maintain:

> One of the characteristics that differentiate what we are calling "kiddie crime" from crime proper is the nature and impact of the harm inflicted by each. Crime is catholic and generic; the harms it encompasses are not limited to a particular segment of society. Thefts victimize rich and poor, individuals and artificial entities alike. The same is true of most other crimes. Some regulatory offenses encompass harm that is necessarily limited to a particular segment of society, but the harms encompassed by traditional crimes are pervasive and democratic in nature.
>
> Kiddie crime, on the other hand, inflicts harms that are peculiar to a particular context: schools (of whatever type). To the extent that conduct that would otherwise constitute kiddie crime inflicts a generic harm that has been addressed by the criminal law, it can be prosecuted as a crime. It is, as we have seen, the residual harms that constitute kiddie crime.
>
> The issue we, as a society, need to resolve is whether kiddie crime should be treated as a non-criminal phenomenon or whether the harms it inflicts should become the focus of new, kiddie crime-specific criminal statutes. We can create new crimes; the question in this instance is whether we should create new crimes that encompass the residual and consequently so-far unaddressed harms constituting kiddie crime.
>
> The answer to that question lies in two aspects of kiddie crime. One is the nature of the harms involved. The other is the fact that kiddie crime is unique to a specific social context.
>
> Modern criminal law addresses two types of harm: "hard harms" and "soft harms." Hard harms are the bedrock of criminal law. They involve the infliction of tangible, egregious injuries to persons or property and, as such, are the oldest and most persistent harms. Every society either must outlaw the infliction of a set of core physical harms (such as murder, assault, and rape) on individuals or descend into a state of chaos in which the strong exploit the weak.
>
> Unlike hard harms, which involve tangible injury to persons or property, soft harms are more difficult to define. Essentially, they involve the infliction of some type of injury to morality affectivity, or a systemic concern with the safety of individuals and the integrity of property. Kiddie crime encompasses the residuum of affective harms that have not already been criminalized, probably for good reason.
>
> Criminalizing the infliction of affective harm is a dicey undertaking. [I]n criminalizing the infliction of some soft harms, legislators worked to include elements that would prevent the statutes from being held void for vagueness and from predicating criminal liability on the subjective vagaries of potential victims. While we cannot say that the criminalization of soft harms has gone as far as it can without violating constitutional principles,

we believe it is wise to be cautious in expanding the use of the criminal sanction to deter the infliction of soft harms.

To create new crimes that target the so-far unaddressed soft harms that constitute kiddie crime, we would have to move much further into the territory of affective harms. To address the residual harm that cannot be prosecuted as stalking or harassment, we would have to predicate liability on a subset of the conduct criminalized by these statutes. We could therefore make it a (new) crime to commit a single act that caused the victim to suffer emotional distress; if we wanted to set the liability bar a little higher but still achieve essentially the same result, we could make it a crime (another new crime) (i) to engage in a course of conduct that caused the victim to suffer emotional distress, or (ii) to commit a single act that caused the victim to suffer substantial emotional distress. We might, in addition or instead, reduce the level of mens rea from purpose or intention to knowing or even to reckless conduct.

We could do this with stalking and harassment, and could probably do something similar with other relevant soft harm crimes (such as threats or invasion of privacy). We should not do it because lowering the bar further for the imposition of criminal liability on those who inflict soft harm is a very bad idea, even if we ignore the vagueness and other legal challenges that could be brought to the scaled-down offenses. It would trivialize the import and significance of the criminal law; the parsimonious use of criminal sanctions to discourage the infliction of egregious affective harm is a necessary step in a world in which soft harms assume a greater importance than in the past.

We cannot criminalize every instance in which people hurt each other's feelings; hurting other people's feelings, intentionally and inadvertently, is an unpleasant but unavoidable aspect of life. There are some things that are not, and should not become, crimes. As the drafters of the Restatement of Torts noted, law cannot take cognizance of

insults, indignities, threats, annoyances, petty oppressions, or other trivialities. The rough edges of our society are still in need of a good deal of filing down, and . . . [we] must . . . be hardened to . . . acts that are definitely inconsiderate and unkind. There is no occasion for the law to intervene in every case where someone's feelings are hurt. There must still be freedom to express an unflattering opinion, and some safety valve must be left through which irascible tempers may blow off relatively harmless steam. [RESTATEMENT (SECOND) OF TORTS § 46 cmt. d (1965).]

This is particularly true for cyberbullying because it takes place in a specific context and involves a more or less immature population that can be expected to have more rough edges than the general, primarily adult, population.

We believe kiddie crime is most appropriately addressed within the context from which it emerges—within the school the victim and perpetrator(s) attend. Having schools address kiddie crime is appropriate for several reasons. One, as we have seen, is that it is inappropriate to extend criminal liability to the very real but lesser levels of soft harm kiddie crime inflicts on its victims. Another reason is that addressing kiddie crime seems to fall within schools' educational mission; schools are, after all, responsible for filing down the rough edges of the students who are in their charge. Finally, educational institutions are also victims of kiddie crime; schools are concerned about cyberbullying because it can have a detrimental effect on their ability to carry out their educational mission.

When the soft harms inflicted by a cyberbully rise to the level of stalking, harassment, or [] other crimes, the bully can be prosecuted and sanctioned by the criminal justice system. This is appropriate because the harms the cyberbully inflicted are of a severity justifying the imposition of criminal liability; they transcend the context-specific harm involved in kiddie crime. If the soft harms inflicted by a cyberbully do not rise to this level, they fall into the residual category of kiddie crime; since the context-specific harms constituting kiddie crime are the product of the educational context and impact on that context, they should be addressed there.

Schools can deal more quickly and easily with "soft" harms caused by cyberbullying—detentions, suspensions, and expulsions can be meted out and finalized before a single complaint and answer could be filed. Further, those disciplinary procedures assure that the students can stay in school and continue the process of "filing down the edges." Criminalizing this behavior would unnecessarily punish students who are still in the throes of learning about appropriate behavior, online and off.

Additionally, schools can modify their codes of conduct easily to cover cyberbullying issues, giving themselves jurisdiction over any issues that may arise. While the schools still need to show a material disruption under *Tinker v. Des Moines Indep. Cmty. Sch. Dist.*[, 393 U.S. 503 (1969)], some argue that a victim being forced to attend school with his cyberbully and then go home to find more teasing online would be enough of a disruption for that particular student to rise to this standard.

Finally, if the individual students feel the harms rise to the level of necessitating some intervention in the legal system, he can always fall back on the gap-filler tort of intentional infliction of emotional distress and take his antagonist to court.

Notes

1. What do you think of the proposal of Brenner and Rehberg? At what point should cyberbullying be labeled "criminal"?

2. Many states that have passed cyber bullying laws have written them to protect students and school districts. *See* www.bullypolice.org. Some laws only apply if the student has been bullied by the use of a computer or electronic device belonging to the school or if the offense takes place on school grounds. Other statutes protect the student, even if the bullying occurs off-campus, if it can be proven that the bullying affects the student's ability to learn or is disruptive to the school.

§ 19.2 Threats

What is a threat?

A "threat" is similar to a promise: When A threatens B, he articulates an intention to do something harmful to B or to someone or something B cares about.[5]

Anthony Douglas Elonis v. United States

135 S. Ct. 2001 (2015)

Chief Justice ROBERTS delivered the opinion of the Court.

Federal law makes it a crime to transmit in interstate commerce "any communication containing any threat . . . to injure the person of another." 18 U.S.C. § 875(c). Petitioner was convicted of violating this provision under instructions that required the jury to find that he communicated what a reasonable person would regard as a threat. The question is whether the statute also requires that the defendant be aware of the threatening nature of the communication, and—if not—whether the First Amendment requires such a showing.

I

A

Anthony Douglas Elonis was an active user of the social networking Web site Facebook. Users of that Web site may post items on their Facebook page that are accessible to other users, including Facebook "friends" who are notified when new content is posted. In May 2010, Elonis's wife of nearly seven years left him, taking with her their two young children. Elonis began "listening to more violent music" and posting self-styled "rap" lyrics inspired by the music. Eventually, Elonis changed the user name on his Facebook page from his actual name to a rap-style nom de plume, "Tone Dougie," to distinguish himself from his "on-line persona." The lyrics Elonis posted as "Tone Dougie" included graphically violent language and imagery. This material was often interspersed with disclaimers that the lyrics were "fictitious,"

---

5. Susan W. Brenner & Megan Rehberg, *"Kiddie Crime"? The Utility of Criminal Law in Controlling Cyberbullying*, 8 FIRST AMEND. L. REV. 1 (2009).

with no intentional "resemblance to real persons." Elonis posted an explanation to another Facebook user that "I'm doing this for me. My writing is therapeutic."

Elonis's co-workers and friends viewed the posts in a different light. Around Halloween of 2010, Elonis posted a photograph of himself and a co-worker at a "Halloween Haunt" event at the amusement park where they worked. In the photograph, Elonis was holding a toy knife against his co-worker's neck, and in the caption Elonis wrote, "I wish." Elonis was not Facebook friends with the co-worker and did not "tag" her, a Facebook feature that would have alerted her to the posting. But the chief of park security was a Facebook "friend" of Elonis, saw the photograph, and fired him.

In response, Elonis posted a new entry on his Facebook page:

> "Moles! Didn't I tell y'all I had several? Y'all sayin' I had access to keys for all the f***in' gates. That I have sinister plans for all my friends and must have taken home a couple. Y'all think it's too dark and foggy to secure your facility from a man as mad as me? You see, even without a paycheck, I'm still the main attraction. Whoever thought the Halloween Haunt could be so f***in' scary?"

This post became the basis for Count One of Elonis's subsequent indictment, threatening park patrons and employees.

Elonis's posts frequently included crude, degrading, and violent material about his soon-to-be ex-wife. Shortly after he was fired, Elonis posted an adaptation of a satirical sketch that he and his wife had watched together. In the actual sketch, called "It's Illegal to Say . . . ," a comedian explains that it is illegal for a person to say he wishes to kill the President, but not illegal to explain that it is illegal for him to say that. When Elonis posted the script of the sketch, however, he substituted his wife for the President. The posting was part of the basis for Count Two of the indictment, threatening his wife:

> "Hi, I'm Tone Elonis.
>
> Did you know that it's illegal for me to say I want to kill my wife? . . .
>
> It's one of the only sentences that I'm not allowed to say. . . .
>
> Now it was okay for me to say it right then because I was just telling you that it's illegal for me to say I want to kill my wife. . . .
>
> Um, but what's interesting is that it's very illegal to say I really, really think someone out there should kill my wife. . . .
>
> But not illegal to say with a mortar launcher.
>
> Because that's its own sentence. . . .
>
> I also found out that it's incredibly illegal, extremely illegal to go on Facebook and say something like the best place to fire a mortar launcher at her house would be from the cornfield behind it because of easy access to a getaway road and you'd have a clear line of sight through the sun room. . . .

Yet even more illegal to show an illustrated diagram. [diagram of the house]. . . ."

The details about the home were accurate. At the bottom of the post, Elonis included a link to the video of the original skit, and wrote, "Art is about pushing limits. I'm willing to go to jail for my Constitutional rights. Are you?"

After viewing some of Elonis's posts, his wife felt "extremely afraid for [her] life." A state court granted her a three-year protection-from-abuse order against Elonis (essentially, a restraining order). Elonis referred to the order in another post on his "Tone Dougie" page, also included in Count Two of the indictment:

"Fold up your [protection-from-abuse order] and put it in your pocket

Is it thick enough to stop a bullet?

Try to enforce an Order

that was improperly granted in the first place

Me thinks the Judge needs an education

on true threat jurisprudence

And prison time'll add zeros to my settlement . . .

And if worse comes to worse

I've got enough explosives

to take care of the State Police and the Sheriff's Department."

At the bottom of this post was a link to the Wikipedia article on "Freedom of speech." Elonis's reference to the police was the basis for Count Three of his indictment, threatening law enforcement officers.

That same month, interspersed with posts about a movie Elonis liked and observations on a comedian's social commentary, Elonis posted an entry that gave rise to Count Four of his indictment:

"That's it, I've had about enough

I'm checking out and making a name for myself

Enough elementary schools in a ten mile radius to initiate the most heinous school shooting ever imagined

And hell hath no fury like a crazy man in a Kindergarten class

The only question is . . . which one?"

Meanwhile, park security had informed both local police and the Federal Bureau of Investigation about Elonis's posts, and FBI Agent Denise Stevens had created a Facebook account to monitor his online activity. After the post about a school shooting, Agent Stevens and her partner visited Elonis at his house. Following their visit, during which Elonis was polite but uncooperative, Elonis posted another entry on his Facebook page, called "Little Agent Lady," which led to Count Five:

"You know your s***'s ridiculous

when you have the FBI knockin' at yo' door

Little Agent lady stood so close

Took all the strength I had not to turn the b**** ghost

Pull my knife, flick my wrist, and slit her throat

Leave her bleedin' from her jugular in the arms of her partner

[laughter]

So the next time you knock, you best be serving a warrant

And bring yo' SWAT and an explosives expert while you're at it

Cause little did y'all know, I was strapped wit' a bomb

Why do you think it took me so long to get dressed with no shoes on?

I was jus' waitin' for y'all to handcuff me and pat me down

Touch the detonator in my pocket and we're all goin'

[BOOM!]

Are all the pieces comin' together?

S***, I'm just a crazy sociopath

    that gets off playin' you stupid f***s like a fiddle

And if y'all didn't hear, I'm gonna be famous

Cause I'm just an aspiring rapper who likes the attention

who happens to be under investigation for terrorism

cause y'all think I'm ready to turn the Valley into Fallujah

But I ain't gonna tell you which bridge is gonna fall

into which river or road

And if you really believe this s***

I'll have some bridge rubble to sell you tomorrow

[BOOM!][BOOM!][BOOM!]

B

A grand jury indicted Elonis for making threats to injure patrons and employees of the park, his estranged wife, police officers, a kindergarten class, and an FBI agent, all in violation of 18 U.S.C. §875(c). In the District Court, Elonis moved to dismiss the indictment for failing to allege that he had intended to threaten anyone. The District Court denied the motion, holding that Third Circuit precedent required only that Elonis "intentionally made the communication, not that he intended to make a threat." At trial, Elonis testified that his posts emulated the rap lyrics of the well-known performer Eminem, some of which involve fantasies about killing his ex-wife. In Elonis's view, he had posted "nothing . . . that hasn't been said already." The Government presented as witnesses Elonis's wife and co-workers, all of whom said they felt afraid and viewed Elonis's posts as serious threats.

Elonis requested a jury instruction that "the government must prove that he intended to communicate a true threat." The District Court denied that request. The jury instructions instead informed the jury that

> "A statement is a true threat when a defendant intentionally makes a statement in a context or under such circumstances wherein a reasonable person would foresee that the statement would be interpreted by those to whom the maker communicates the statement as a serious expression of an intention to inflict bodily injury or take the life of an individual."

The Government's closing argument emphasized that it was irrelevant whether Elonis intended the postings to be threats—"it doesn't matter what he thinks." A jury convicted Elonis on four of the five counts against him, acquitting only on the charge of threatening park patrons and employees. Elonis was sentenced to three years, eight months' imprisonment and three years' supervised release.

II

An individual who "transmits in interstate or foreign commerce any communication containing any threat to kidnap any person or any threat to injure the person of another" is guilty of a felony and faces up to five years' imprisonment. 18 U.S.C. § 875(c). This statute requires that a communication be transmitted and that the communication contain a threat. It does not specify that the defendant must have any mental state with respect to these elements. In particular, it does not indicate whether the defendant must intend that his communication contain a threat.

The fact that the statute does not specify any required mental state, however, does not mean that none exists. We have repeatedly held that "mere omission from a criminal enactment of any mention of criminal intent" should not be read "as dispensing with it." This rule of construction reflects the basic principle that "wrongdoing must be conscious to be criminal. As Justice Jackson explained, this principle is "as universal and persistent in mature systems of law as belief in freedom of the human will and a consequent ability and duty of the normal individual to choose between good and evil." The "central thought" is that a defendant must be "blameworthy in mind" before he can be found guilty, a concept courts have expressed over time through various terms such as *mens rea*, scienter, malice aforethought, guilty knowledge, and the like. Although there are exceptions, the "general rule" is that a guilty mind is "a necessary element in the indictment and proof of every crime." We therefore generally "interpret[] criminal statutes to include broadly applicable scienter requirements, even where the statute by its terms does not contain them."

This is not to say that a defendant must know that his conduct is illegal before he may be found guilty. The familiar maxim "ignorance of the law is no excuse" typically holds true. Instead, our cases have explained that a defendant generally must "know the facts that make his conduct fit the definition of the offense," even if he does not know that those facts give rise to a crime.

In *Liparota v. United States,* we considered a statute making it a crime to knowingly possess or use food stamps in an unauthorized manner. 471 U.S. 419 (1985). The

Government's argument, similar to its position in this case, was that a defendant's conviction could be upheld if he knowingly possessed or used the food stamps, and in fact his possession or use was unauthorized. But this Court rejected that interpretation of the statute, because it would have criminalized "a broad range of apparently innocent conduct" and swept in individuals who had no knowledge of the facts that made their conduct blameworthy. For example, the statute made it illegal to use food stamps at a store that charged higher prices to food stamp customers. Without a mental state requirement in the statute, an individual who unwittingly paid higher prices would be guilty under the Government's interpretation. The Court noted that Congress *could* have intended to cover such a "broad range of conduct," but declined "to adopt such a sweeping interpretation" in the absence of a clear indication that Congress intended that result. The Court instead construed the statute to require knowledge of the facts that made the use of the food stamps unauthorized.

To take another example, in *Posters 'N' Things, Ltd. v. United States,* this Court interpreted a federal statute prohibiting the sale of drug paraphernalia. 511 U.S. 513 (1994). Whether the items in question qualified as drug paraphernalia was an objective question that did not depend on the defendant's state of mind. But, we held, an individual could not be convicted of selling such paraphernalia unless he "knew that the items at issue [were] likely to be used with illegal drugs." Such a showing was necessary to establish the defendant's culpable state of mind.

C

Section 875(c), as noted, requires proof that a communication was transmitted and that it contained a threat. The "presumption in favor of a scienter requirement should apply to *each* of the statutory elements that criminalize otherwise innocent conduct." The parties agree that a defendant under Section 875(c) must know that he is transmitting a communication. But communicating *something* is not what makes the conduct "wrongful." Here "the crucial element separating legal innocence from wrongful conduct" is the threatening nature of the communication. The mental state requirement must therefore apply to the fact that the communication contains a threat.

Elonis's conviction, however, was premised solely on how his posts would be understood by a reasonable person. Such a "reasonable person" standard is a familiar feature of civil liability in tort law, but is inconsistent with "the conventional requirement for criminal conduct—*awareness* of some wrongdoing." Having liability turn on whether a "reasonable person" regards the communication as a threat—regardless of what the defendant thinks—"reduces culpability on the all-important element of the crime to negligence," and we "have long been reluctant to infer that a negligence standard was intended in criminal statutes." Under these principles, "what [Elonis] thinks" does matter.

In support of its position the Government relies most heavily on *Hamling v. United States,* 418 U.S. 87 (1974). In that case, the Court rejected the argument that individuals could be convicted of mailing obscene material only if they knew the "legal status of the materials" distributed. Absolving a defendant of liability because he lacked the knowledge that the materials were legally obscene "would permit the defendant to avoid prosecution by simply claiming that he had not brushed up on the law." It was instead enough for liability that "a defendant had knowledge of the contents of the materials he distributed, and that he knew the character and nature of the materials."

This holding does not help the Government. In fact, the Court in *Hamling* approved a state court's conclusion that requiring a defendant to know the character of the material incorporated a "vital element of scienter" so that "not innocent but *calculated purveyance* of filth . . . is exorcised." In this case, "calculated purveyance" of a threat would require that Elonis know the threatening nature of his communication. Put simply, the mental state requirement the Court approved in *Hamling* turns on whether a defendant knew the *character* of what was sent, not simply its contents and context.

In light of the foregoing, Elonis's conviction cannot stand. The jury was instructed that the Government need prove only that a reasonable person would regard Elonis's communications as threats, and that was error. Federal criminal liability generally does not turn solely on the results of an act without considering the defendant's mental state. That understanding "took deep and early root in American soil" and Congress left it intact here: Under Section 875(c), "wrongdoing must be conscious to be criminal."

There is no dispute that the mental state requirement in Section 875(c) is satisfied if the defendant transmits a communication for the purpose of issuing a threat, or with knowledge that the communication will be viewed as a threat. In response to a question at oral argument, Elonis stated that a finding of recklessness would not be sufficient. Neither Elonis nor the Government has briefed or argued that point, and we accordingly decline to address it. Given our disposition, it is not necessary to consider any First Amendment issues.

Our holding makes clear that negligence is not sufficient to support a conviction under Section 875(c), contrary to the view of nine Courts of Appeals. There was and is no circuit conflict over the question Justice Alito and Justice Thomas would have us decide—whether recklessness suffices for liability under Section 875(c). No Court of Appeals has even addressed that question. We think that is more than sufficient "justification," for us to decline to be the first appellate tribunal to do so.

The judgment of the United States Court of Appeals for the Third Circuit is reversed, and the case is remanded for further proceedings consistent with this opinion.

Justice Aʟɪᴛᴏ, concurring in part and dissenting in part.

In *Marbury v. Madison,* 1 Cranch 137, 177, 2 L.Ed. 60 (1803), the Court famously proclaimed: "It is emphatically the province and duty of the judicial department to say what the law is." Today, the Court announces: It is emphatically the prerogative of this Court to say only what the law is not.

The Court's disposition of this case is certain to cause confusion and serious problems. Attorneys and judges need to know which mental state is required for conviction under 18 U.S.C. § 875(c), an important criminal statute. This case squarely presents that issue, but the Court provides only a partial answer. The Court holds that the jury instructions in this case were defective because they required only negligence in conveying a threat. But the Court refuses to explain what type of intent was necessary. Did the jury need to find that Elonis had the *purpose* of conveying a true threat? Was it enough if he *knew* that his words conveyed such a threat? Would *recklessness* suffice? The Court declines to say. Attorneys and judges are left to guess.

This will have regrettable consequences. While this Court has the luxury of choosing its docket, lower courts and juries are not so fortunate. They must actually decide cases, and this means applying a standard. If purpose or knowledge is needed and a district court instructs the jury that recklessness suffices, a defendant may be wrongly convicted. On the other hand, if recklessness is enough, and the jury is told that conviction requires proof of more, a guilty defendant may go free. We granted review in this case to resolve a disagreement among the Circuits. But the Court has compounded—not clarified—the confusion.

Section 875(c) provides in relevant part:

> "Whoever transmits in interstate or foreign commerce any communication containing . . . any threat to injure the person of another, shall be fined under this title or imprisoned not more than five years, or both."

Thus, conviction under this provision requires proof that: (1) the defendant transmitted something, (2) the thing transmitted was a threat to injure the person of another, and (3) the transmission was in interstate or foreign commerce.

At issue in this case is the *mens rea* required with respect to the second element—that the thing transmitted was a threat to injure the person of another. This Court has not defined the meaning of the term "threat" in § 875(c), but in construing the same term in a related statute, the Court distinguished a "true 'threat'" from facetious or hyperbolic remarks. In my view, the term "threat" in § 875(c) can fairly be defined as a statement that is reasonably interpreted as "an expression of an intention to inflict evil, injury, or damage on another." Webster's Third New International Dictionary 2382 (1976). Conviction under § 875(c) demands proof that the defendant's transmission was in fact a threat, *i.e.*, that it is reasonable to interpret the transmission as an expression of an intent to harm another. In addition, it must be shown that the defendant was at least reckless as to whether the transmission met that requirement.

Why is recklessness enough? My analysis of the *mens rea* issue follows the same track as the Court's, as far as it goes. I agree with the Court that we should presume that criminal statutes require some sort of *mens rea* for conviction. To be sure, this presumption marks a departure from the way in which we generally interpret statutes. We "ordinarily resist reading words or elements into a statute that do not appear on its face." But this step is justified by a well-established pattern in our criminal laws. "For several centuries (at least since 1600) the different common law crimes have been so defined as to require, for guilt, that the defendant's acts or omissions be accompanied by one or more of the various types of fault (intention, knowledge, recklessness or—more rarely—negligence)." Based on these "background rules of the common law, in which the requirement of some *mens rea* for a crime is firmly embedded," we require "some indication of congressional intent, express or implied, . . . to dispense with *mens rea* as an element of a crime."

For a similar reason, I agree with the Court that we should presume that an offense like that created by § 875(c) requires more than negligence with respect to a critical element like the one at issue here. As the Court states, "[w]hen interpreting federal criminal statutes that are silent on the required mental state, we read into the statute 'only that *mens rea* which is necessary to separate wrongful conduct from "otherwise innocent conduct."'" Whether negligence is morally culpable is an interesting philosophical question, but the answer is at least sufficiently debatable to justify the presumption that a serious offense against the person that lacks any clear common-law counterpart should be presumed to require more.

Once we have passed negligence, however, no further presumptions are defensible. In the hierarchy of mental states that may be required as a condition for criminal liability, the *mens rea* just above negligence is recklessness. Negligence requires only that the defendant "should [have] be [en] aware of a substantial and unjustifiable risk," while recklessness exists "when a person disregards a risk of harm of which he is aware." And when Congress does not specify a *mens rea* in a criminal statute, we have no justification for inferring that anything more than recklessness is needed. It is quite unusual for us to interpret a statute to contain a requirement that is nowhere set out in the text. Once we have reached recklessness, we have gone as far as we can without stepping over the line that separates interpretation from amendment.

There can be no real dispute that recklessness regarding a risk of serious harm is wrongful conduct. In a wide variety of contexts, we have described reckless conduct as morally culpable. Indeed, this Court has held that "reckless disregard for human life" may justify the death penalty. Someone who acts recklessly with respect to conveying a threat necessarily grasps that he is not engaged in innocent conduct. He is not merely careless. He is aware that others could regard his statements as a threat, but he delivers them anyway.

Accordingly, I would hold that a defendant may be convicted under § 875(c) if he or she consciously disregards the risk that the communication transmitted will be interpreted as a true threat. Nothing in the Court's non-committal opinion prevents lower courts from adopting that standard.

II

There remains the question whether interpreting § 875(c) to require no more than recklessness with respect to the element at issue here would violate the First Amendment. Elonis contends that it would. I would reject that argument.

It is settled that the Constitution does not protect true threats. And there are good reasons for that rule: True threats inflict great harm and have little if any social value. A threat may cause serious emotional stress for the person threatened and those who care about that person, and a threat may lead to a violent confrontation. It is true that a communication containing a threat may include other statements that have value and are entitled to protection. But that does not justify constitutional protection for the threat itself.

Elonis argues that the First Amendment protects a threat if the person making the statement does not actually intend to cause harm. In his view, if a threat is made for a "'therapeutic'" purpose, "to 'deal with the pain' . . . of a wrenching event," or for "cathartic" reasons, the threat is protected. But whether or not the person making a threat intends to cause harm, the damage is the same. And the fact that making a threat may have a therapeutic or cathartic effect for the speaker is not sufficient to justify constitutional protection. Some people may experience a therapeutic or cathartic benefit only if they know that their words will cause harm or only if they actually plan to carry out the threat, but surely the First Amendment does not protect them.

Elonis also claims his threats were constitutionally protected works of art. Words like his, he contends, are shielded by the First Amendment because they are similar to words uttered by rappers and singers in public performances and recordings. To make this point, his brief includes a lengthy excerpt from the lyrics of a rap song in which a very well-compensated rapper imagines killing his ex-wife and dumping her body in a lake. If this celebrity can utter such words, Elonis pleads, amateurs like him should be able to post similar things on social media. But context matters. "Taken in context," lyrics in songs that are performed for an audience or sold in recorded form are unlikely to be interpreted as a real threat to a real person. Statements on social media that are pointedly directed at their victims, by contrast, are much more likely to be taken seriously. To hold otherwise would grant a license to anyone who is clever enough to dress up a real threat in the guise of rap lyrics, a parody, or something similar.

The facts of this case illustrate the point. Imagine the effect on Elonis's estranged wife when she read this: "'If I only knew then what I know now . . . I would have smothered your ass with a pillow, dumped your body in the back seat, dropped you off in Toad Creek and made it look like a rape and murder.'" Or this: "There's one way to love you but a thousand ways to kill you. I'm not going to rest until your body is a mess, soaked in blood and dying from all the little cuts." Or this: "Fold up your [protection from abuse order] and put it in your pocket[.] Is it thick enough to stop a bullet?"

There was evidence that Elonis made sure his wife saw his posts. And she testified that they made her feel "'extremely afraid'" and "'like [she] was being stalked.'" Considering the context, who could blame her? Threats of violence and intimidation are among the most favored weapons of domestic abusers, and the rise of social media has only made those tactics more commonplace. A fig leaf of artistic expression cannot convert such hurtful, valueless threats into protected speech.

It can be argued that § 875(c), if not limited to threats made with the intent to harm, will chill statements that do not qualify as true threats, *e.g.,* statements that may be literally threatening but are plainly not meant to be taken seriously. We have sometimes cautioned that it is necessary to "exten[d] a measure of strategic protection" to otherwise unprotected false statements of fact in order to ensure enough "'breathing space'" for protected speech. A similar argument might be made with respect to threats. But we have also held that the law provides adequate breathing space when it requires proof that false statements were made with reckless disregard of their falsity. Requiring proof of recklessness is similarly sufficient here.

Justice Thomas, dissenting.

Because the Court of Appeals properly applied the general-intent standard, and because the communications transmitted by Elonis were "true threats" unprotected by the First Amendment, I would affirm the judgment below.

I

A

Because § 875(c) criminalizes speech, the First Amendment requires that the term "threat" be limited to a narrow class of historically unprotected communications called "true threats." To qualify as a true threat, a communication must be a serious expression of an intention to commit unlawful physical violence, not merely "political hyperbole"; "vehement, caustic, and sometimes unpleasantly sharp attacks"; or "vituperative, abusive, and inexact" statements. It also cannot be determined solely by the reaction of the recipient, but must instead be "determined by the interpretation of a *reasonable* recipient familiar with the context of the communication," lest historically protected speech be suppressed at the will of an eggshell observer. There is thus no dispute that, at a minimum, § 875(c) requires an objective showing: The communication must be one that "a reasonable observer would construe as a true threat to another." And there is no dispute that the posts at issue here meet that objective standard.

The only dispute in this case is about the state of mind necessary to convict Elonis for making those posts. On its face, § 875(c) does not demand any particular mental state. As the Court correctly explains, the word "threat" does not itself contain a *mens rea* requirement. But because we read criminal statutes "in light of the background rules of the common law, in which the requirement of some *mens rea* for a crime is firmly embedded," we require "some indication of congressional intent, express or implied, . . . to dispense with *mens rea* as an element of a crime." Absent such indicia, we ordinarily apply the "presumption in favor of scienter" to require only "proof of *general intent*—that is, that the defendant [must] posses[s] knowledge with respect to the *actus reus* of the crime."

Under this "conventional *mens rea* element," "the defendant [must] know the facts that make his conduct illegal." But he need not know *that* those facts make his conduct illegal. It has long been settled that "the knowledge requisite to knowing violation of a statute is factual knowledge as distinguished from knowledge of the law."

Our default rule in favor of general intent applies with full force to criminal statutes addressing speech. . . . Decades before §875(c)'s enactment, courts took the same approach to the first federal threat statute, which prohibited threats against the President. In 1917, Congress enacted a law punishing anyone

> "who knowingly and willfully deposits or causes to be deposited for conveyance in the mail . . . any letter, paper, writing, print, missive, or document containing any threat to take the life of or to inflict bodily harm upon the President of the United States, or who knowingly and willfully otherwise makes any such threat against the President." Act of Feb. 14, 1917, ch. 64, 39 Stat. 919.

Courts applying this statute shortly after its enactment appeared to require proof of only general intent. In *Ragansky v. United States*, 253 F. 643 (C.A.7 1918), for instance, a Court of Appeals held that "[a] threat is knowingly made, if the maker of it comprehends the meaning of the words uttered by him," and "is willfully made, if in addition to comprehending the meaning of his words, the maker voluntarily and intentionally utters them as the declaration of an apparent determination to carry them into execution." The court consequently rejected the defendant's argument that he could not be convicted when his language "[c]oncededly . . . constituted such a threat" but was meant only "as a joke." Likewise, in *United States v. Stobo*, 251 F. 689 (Del.1918), a District Court rejected the defendant's objection that there was no allegation "of any facts . . . indicating any intention . . . on the part of the defendant . . . to menace the President of the United States." As it explained, the defendant "is punishable under the act whether he uses the words lightly or with a set purpose to kill," as "[t]he effect upon the minds of the hearers, who cannot read his inward thoughts, is precisely the same." At a minimum, there is no historical practice requiring more than general intent when a statute regulates speech.

B

Applying ordinary rules of statutory construction, I would read §875(c) to require proof of general intent. To "know the facts that make his conduct illegal" under §875(c), a defendant must know that he transmitted a communication in interstate or foreign commerce that contained a threat. Knowing that the communication contains a "threat"—a serious expression of an intention to engage in unlawful physical violence—does not, however, require knowing that a jury will conclude that the communication contains a threat as a matter of law. Instead, like one who mails an "obscene" publication and is prosecuted under the federal obscenity statute, a defendant prosecuted under §875(c) must know only the words used in that communication, along with their ordinary meaning in context.

General intent divides those who know the facts constituting the *actus reus* of this crime from those who do not. For example, someone who transmits a threat who does not know English — or who knows English, but perhaps does not know a threatening idiom — lacks the general intent required under §875(c). Likewise, the hapless mailman who delivers a threatening letter, ignorant of its contents, should not fear prosecution. A defendant like Elonis, however, who admits that he "knew that what [he] was saying was violent" but supposedly "just wanted to express [him]-self," acted with the general intent required under §875(c), even if he did not know that a jury would conclude that his communication constituted a "threat" as a matter of law.

Demanding evidence only of general intent also corresponds to §875(c)'s statutory backdrop. As previously discussed, before the enactment of §875(c), courts had read the Presidential threats statute to require proof only of general intent. Given Congress' presumptive awareness of this application of the Presidential threats statute — not to mention this Court's similar approach in the obscenity context — it is difficult to conclude that the Congress that enacted §875(c) in 1939 understood it to contain an implicit mental-state requirement apart from general intent. There is certainly no textual evidence to support this conclusion. If anything, the text supports the opposite inference, as §875(c), unlike the Presidential threats statute, contains no reference to knowledge or willfulness. Nothing in the statute suggests that Congress departed from the "conventional *mens rea* element" of general intent, I would not impose a higher mental-state requirement here.

C

Requiring general intent in this context is not the same as requiring mere negligence. General intent under §875(c) prevents a defendant from being convicted on the basis of any *fact* beyond his awareness. In other words, the defendant must *know* — not merely be reckless or negligent with respect to the fact — that he is committing the acts that constitute the *actus reus* of the offense.

But general intent requires *no* mental state (not even a negligent one) concerning the "fact" that certain words meet the *legal* definition of a threat. That approach is particularly appropriate where, as here, that legal status is determined by a jury's application of the legal standard of a "threat" to the contents of a communication. And convicting a defendant despite his ignorance of the legal — or objective — status of his conduct does not mean that he is being punished for negligent conduct. By way of example, a defendant who is convicted of murder despite claiming that he acted in self-defense has not been penalized under a negligence standard merely because he does not know that the jury will reject his argument that his "belief in the necessity of using force to prevent harm to himself [was] a reasonable one."

D

The majority today at least refrains from requiring an intent to threaten for §875(c) convictions, as Elonis asks us to do. Elonis contends that proof of a defendant's intent to put the recipient of a threat in fear is necessary for conviction, but that element cannot be found within the statutory text. "[W]e ordinarily resist reading words or elements into a statute that do not appear on its face," including elements similar to the one Elonis proposes. As the majority correctly explains, nothing in the text of §875(c) itself requires proof of an intent to threaten. The absence of such a requirement is significant, as Congress knows how to require a heightened *mens rea* in the context of threat offenses. See §875(b) (providing for the punishment of "[w]hoever, with intent to extort . . . , transmits in interstate or foreign commerce any communication containing any threat to kidnap any person or any threat to injure the person of another"); see also §119 (providing for the punishment of "[w]hoever knowingly makes restricted personal information about [certain officials] . . . publicly available . . . with the intent to threaten").

Elonis nonetheless suggests that an intent-to-threaten element is necessary in order to avoid the risk of punishing innocent conduct. But there is nothing absurd about punishing an individual who, with knowledge of the words he uses and their ordinary meaning in context, makes a threat. For instance, a high-school student who sends a letter to his principal stating that he will massacre his classmates with a machine gun, even if he intended the letter as a joke, cannot fairly be described as engaging in innocent conduct.

Elonis also insists that we read an intent-to-threaten element into §875(c) in light of the First Amendment. But our practice of construing statutes "to avoid constitutional questions . . . is not a license for the judiciary to rewrite language enacted by the legislature," and ordinary background principles of criminal law do not support rewriting §875(c) to include an intent-to-threaten requirement. We have not altered our traditional approach to *mens rea* for other constitutional provisions. The First Amendment should be treated no differently.

II

In light of my conclusion that Elonis was properly convicted under the requirements of §875(c), I must address his argument that his threatening posts were nevertheless protected by the First Amendment.

A

Elonis does not contend that threats are constitutionally protected speech, nor could he: "From 1791 to the present, . . . our society . . . has permitted restrictions upon the content of speech in a few limited areas," true threats being one of them. Instead, Elonis claims that only *intentional* threats fall within this particular historical exception.

If it were clear that intentional threats alone have been punished in our Nation since 1791, I would be inclined to agree. But that is the not the case. Although the Federal Government apparently did not get into the business of regulating threats until 1917, the States have been doing so since the late 18th and early 19th centuries. And that practice continued even after the States amended their constitutions to include speech protections similar to those in the First Amendment.

Shortly after the founding, several States and Territories enacted laws making it a crime to "knowingly send or deliver any letter or writing, with or without a name subscribed thereto, or signed with a fictitious name, . . . threatening to maim, wound, kill or murder any person, or to burn his or her [property], though no money, goods or chattels, or other valuable thing shall be demanded," *e.g.,* 1795 N.J. Laws §57, at 108; see also, *e.g.,* 1816 Ga. Laws p. 178; 1816 Mich. Territory Laws p. 128; 1827 Ill. Crim. Code §108; 1832 Fla. Laws, at 68–69. These laws appear to be the closest early analogue to §875(c), as they penalize transmitting a communication containing a threat without proof of a demand to extort something from the victim. Threat provisions explicitly requiring proof of a specific "intent to extort" appeared alongside these laws, but those provisions are simply the predecessors to §875(b) and §875(d), which likewise expressly contain an intent-to-extort requirement.

The laws without that extortion requirement were copies of a 1754 English threat statute subject to only a general-intent requirement. The statute made it a capital offense to "knowingly send any Letter without any Name subscribed thereto, or signed with a fictitious Name . . . threatening to kill or murder any of his Majesty's Subject or Subjects, or to burn their [property], though no Money or Venison or other valuable Thing shall be demanded." 27 Geo. II, ch. 15, in 7 Eng. Stat. at Large 61 (1754). Early English decisions applying this threat statute indicated that the appropriate mental state was general intent.

Unsurprisingly, these early English cases were well known in the legal world of the 19th century United States. And as this Court long ago recognized, "It is doubtless true . . . that where English statutes . . . have been adopted into our own legislation; the known and settled construction of those statutes by courts of law, has been considered as silently incorporated into the acts, or has been received with all the weight of authority." In short, there is good reason to believe that States bound by their own Constitutions to protect freedom of speech long ago enacted general-intent threat statutes.

B

Adopting Elonis' view would make threats one of the most protected categories of unprotected speech, thereby sowing tension throughout our First Amendment doctrine. We generally have not required a heightened mental state under the First Amendment for historically unprotected categories of speech. For instance, the Court has indicated that a legislature may constitutionally prohibit "'fighting words,' those personally abusive epithets which, when addressed to the ordinary citizen, are, as a matter of common knowledge, inherently likely to provoke violent reaction"—without proof of an intent to provoke a violent reaction. Because the definition of "fighting words" turns on how the "ordinary citizen" would react to the language, this Court has observed that a defendant may be guilty of a breach of the peace if he "makes statements likely to provoke violence and disturbance of good order, even though no such eventuality be intended," and that the punishment of such statements "as a criminal act would raise no question under [the Constitution]." The Court has similarly held that a defendant may be convicted of mailing obscenity under the First Amendment without proof that he knew the materials were legally obscene. And our precedents allow liability in tort for false statements about private persons on matters of private concern even if the speaker acted negligently with respect to the falsity of those statements. I see no reason why we should give threats pride of place among unprotected speech.

*   *   *

There is always a risk that a criminal threat statute may be deployed by the Government to suppress legitimate speech. But the proper response to that risk is to adhere to our traditional rule that only a narrow class of true threats, historically unprotected, may be constitutionally proscribed.

The solution is not to abandon a mental-state requirement compelled by text, history, and precedent. Not only does such a decision warp our traditional approach to *mens rea,* it results in an arbitrary distinction between threats and other forms of unprotected speech. Had Elonis mailed obscene materials to his wife and a kindergarten class, he could have been prosecuted irrespective of whether he intended to offend those recipients or recklessly disregarded that possibility. Yet when he threatened to kill his wife and a kindergarten class, his intent to terrify those recipients (or reckless disregard of that risk) suddenly becomes highly relevant. That need not — and should not — be the case.

Nor should it be the case that we cast aside the mental-state requirement compelled by our precedents yet offer nothing in its place. Our job is to decide questions, not create them. Given the majority's ostensible concern for protecting innocent actors, one would have expected it to announce a clear rule — any clear rule. Its failure to do so reveals the fractured foundation upon which today's decision rests.

I respectfully dissent.

Notes

1. **Hate on the Internet.** The Internet has generated a proliferation of web sites and other forums that are used to express bias, hate, and prejudice. The sites cover the range of possible hatreds, including targeting persons of different races, religions, sexual orientation, ethnicity, and gender. For one example of a web site that was held to have crossed over the line from free speech to prohibited activity, *see Planned Parenthood v. American Coalition of Life Activists*, 290 F.3d 1058 (9th Cir. 2002) (*en banc*) (finding that material on website constituted true threat of force against doctors who performed abortions). For an overview of the Supreme Court's treatment of threats and an argument that the rise in the use of the Internet merits a change in that approach, *see, e.g.*, Scott Hammack, Note, *The Internet Loophole: Why Threatening Speech On-Line Requires Modification of the Courts' Approach to True Threats and Incitement*, 36 Colum. J.L. & Soc. Probs. 65 (2002).

2. Were Elonis's posts "true threats" or some other crime? Was it protected speech? What, if anything, should or could be done to address communications such as his? What state of mind should suffice to criminalize communications such as his?

3. **Interstate Communications.** 18 U.S.C. §875 requires that the threat be an interstate communication. The Supreme Court in *Elonis* was not confronted with a challenge based on that ground, but the lower court was. In *United States v. Elonis*, 730 F.3d 321 (3d Cir. 2013), reversed on the other grounds just discussed by the Supreme Court, the court lower court stated:

> Elonis contends the jury instruction stating communications that travel over the internet necessarily travel in interstate commerce violated his due process rights because the government was required to prove interstate transmission as an element of the crime. The District Court instructed the jury: "Because of the interstate nature of the Internet, if you find beyond a reasonable doubt that the defendant used the Internet in communicating a threat, then that communication traveled in interstate commerce."

> In *United States v. MacEwan* we explained the difference between interstate transmission and interstate commerce. 445 F.3d 237, 243–44 (3d Cir.2006). The defendant in *MacEwan* contended the government failed to prove he received child pornography through interstate commerce because a Comcast witness testified it was impossible to know whether a particular transmission traveled through computer servers located entirely within Pennsylvania, or to any other server in the United States. "[W]e conclude[d] that because of the very interstate nature of the Internet, once a user submits a connection request to a website server or an image is transmitted from the website server back to [the] user, the data has traveled in interstate commerce." "Having concluded that the Internet is an instrumentality and channel of interstate commerce . . . [i]t is sufficient that MacEwan downloaded those images from the Internet, a system that is inexorably intertwined with interstate commerce."

> Elonis distinguishes *MacEwan* by stating that in that case the government presented evidence on how the internet worked. But the government's evidence in *MacEwan* did not show that any one of the defendant's internet transmissions traveled outside of Pennsylvania. We found that fact to be irrelevant to the question of interstate commerce because submitting data on the internet necessarily means the data travels in interstate commerce. Instead, we held "[i]t is sufficient that [the defendant] downloaded those images from the Internet." Based on our conclusion that proving internet transmission alone is sufficient to prove transmission through interstate commerce, the District Court did not err in instructing the jury.

§ 19.3 Stalking and Harassment

1. The Impact of Technology

Cindy Southworth and Sarah Tucker offer an overview of the impact of technology on stalking and harassment practices and victims:[6]

> The Digital Age is bringing many opportunities to survivors of abuse and their advocates. Across America, victims of domestic violence are using the revolutionary tool of the Internet to map roads to new lives by reaching out to shelters, researching restraining orders, and finding housing and employment opportunities. However, at the same time, advancements in technology are posing unique challenges to enhancing victim safety. Abusers regularly use a variety of technologies to stalk current and former intimate partners, ranging from phones to mapping to computer technologies. Some abusers install global positioning systems to stalk their victim's real-time locations with extraordinary accuracy, while others use telephones to leave hundreds of messages in a single day. Other stalkers use technologies like caller ID during a relationship to monitor their partner's calls, and to locate her after she has fled. Still others use online databases, electronic records, and web search engines to locate, track, and harass former partners. Regardless of the tool or technology used, perpetrators have the same primary goal: abusing power to gain and maintain control over their victims.

2. Criminalization of Stalking and Harassment

Susan W. Brenner & Megan Rehberg, *"Kiddie Crime"? The Utility of Criminal Law in Controlling Cyberbullying,*
8 First Amend. L. Rev. 1 (2009):[7]

The criminalization of harassment began about a century ago, when it became apparent that telephones could be used for less-than-legitimate reasons. The initial problem occurred when callers used "vulgar, profane, obscene or indecent language."

Concerned about the "harm" being done to the women and children who received such calls, states responded by adopting statutes that created the crime of "telephone harassment." While telephone harassment tended to focus only on obscene or threatening phone calls, some states broadened their harassment statutes to encompass more general conduct, such as "anonymous or repeated telephone calls that are

---

6. Cindy Southworth & Sarah Tucker, *Technology, Stalking and Domestic Violence Victims*, 76 Miss. L.J. 667 (2007).

7. Copyright © 2009, Susan W. Brenner, Megan Rehberg, North Carolina Law Review Association. All rights reserved. Reprinted by permission.

intended to harass or annoy." This approach to harassment still survives in the basic harassment statutes of many states.

The basic harassment statutes in effect until the last decade of the twentieth century generally failed to encompass more problematic conduct, such as touching someone, insulting them, or following them. That began to change in 1989, when actress Rebecca Schaeffer was stalked and killed by an obsessive fan. Shocked by the Schaeffer murder and five similar murders, California legislators passed the nation's first criminal stalking law in 1990. By 1993, forty-eight states had followed suit. In 1999, New York became the final state to adopt a criminal stalking statute.

Most of the state stalking statutes followed the California model, which essentially defines stalking as aggravated harassment:

> Any person who willfully, maliciously, and repeatedly follows or willfully and maliciously harasses another person and who makes a credible threat with the intent to place that person in reasonable fear for his or her safety, or the safety of his or her immediate family is guilty of the crime of stalking, punishable by imprisonment in a county jail for not more than one year, or by a fine of not more than one thousand dollars ($1,000), or by both that fine and imprisonment, or by imprisonment in the state prison. [Cal. Penal Code § 646.9(a) (West 1999).]

The California stalking statute has two actus reus elements: (i) repeatedly following or otherwise harassing the victim; and (ii) a credible threat to the victim or victim's family. It defines "harass[ment]" as engaging in a "course of conduct directed at a specific person that seriously alarms, annoys, torments, or terrorizes the person and that serves no legitimate purpose." The statute defines "credible threat" as a

> verbal or written threat, . . . or a threat implied by a pattern of conduct or a combination of verbal, written, or electronically communicated statements and conduct, made with the intent to place the person that is the target of the threat in reasonable fear for his or her safety or the safety of his or her family, and made with the apparent ability to carry out the threat so as to cause the person who is the target of the threat to reasonably fear for his or her safety or the safety of his or her family.

As society became more familiar with the nuances of the conduct involved in and "harm" inflicted by stalking, states began to expand the scope of their statutes. While contemporary stalking statutes still tend to target "credible threats" directed at the victim or victim's family, many also criminalize conduct that would cause a "'reasonable person' to . . . suffer severe emotional distress." Missouri's statute, for example, states that anyone "who purposely and repeatedly harasses . . . another person commits the crime of stalking," and defines "harasses" as engaging "in a course of conduct directed at a specific person that serves no legitimate purpose, that would cause a reasonable person to suffer substantial emotional distress, and that actually causes substantial emotional distress to that person."

The Missouri statute does not define "emotional distress," but other statutes do. The Michigan stalking statute defines it as "significant mental suffering or distress that may, but does not necessarily, require medical or other professional treatment or counseling."

A few states have included language in their statutes to make it clear that they apply to electronic stalking, or cyberstalking. Such language is probably not necessary because the essence of the crime of stalking is, as with other crimes, the perpetrator's engaging in activity that he or she knows will inflict certain "harm" upon the victim with the purpose of inflicting such "harm." As long as stalking statutes proscribe the infliction of the prohibited "harm," the means used to inflict it need not be set out in the statute.

It has been difficult, and arguably problematic, for criminal law to address the infliction of emotional "harm." The "emotional distress" stalking and harassment statutes represent a compromise: although they criminalize the infliction of affective "harm," they do not predicate the imposition of criminal liability purely on self-diagnosed psychic injury. Instead, they incorporate a "reasonable person" standard to ensure that the imposition of liability is based not on the idiosyncrasies of a particular individual, but on conduct that can be deemed to inflict an objectively ascertainable "harm."

Stalking has no generally accepted definition:

> While the federal government, all 50 states, the District of Columbia, and U.S. territories have enacted criminal laws to address stalking, the legal definition of stalking varies across jurisdictions. State laws vary regarding the element of victim fear and emotional distress, as well as the requisite intent of the stalker. Some state laws specify that the victim must have been frightened by the stalking, while others require only that the stalking would have caused a reasonable person to experience fear. In addition, states vary on what level of fear is required. Some state laws require prosecutors to establish fear of death or serious bodily harm, while others require only that prosecutors establish that the victim suffered emotional distress. Interstate stalking is defined by federal law [in] 18 U.S.C. § 2261A.

Stalking Victims in the United States-Revised, U.S. Department of Justice (2012), available at http://www.bjs.gov/content/pub/pdf/svus_rev.pdf. According to the report, which defined stalking as "a course of conduct directed at a specific person that would cause a reasonable person to feel fear," approximately 3.4 million people were victims of stalking during a 12-month period in 2005 and 2006. Of those victimized, more than one in four reported that the stalking occurred in the form of e-mail, instant messaging, blogs or bulletin boards, internet sites about the victim, or a chat room.

18 U.S.C. § 2261A provides:

Whoever—

(1) travels in interstate or foreign commerce or is present within the special maritime and territorial jurisdiction of the United States, or enters or leaves Indian country, with the intent to kill, injure, harass, intimidate, or place under surveillance with intent to kill, injure, harass, or intimidate another person, and in the course of, or as a result of, such travel or presence engages in conduct that—

(A) places that person in reasonable fear of the death of, or serious bodily injury to—

(i) that person;

(ii) an immediate family member (as defined in section 115) of that person; or

(iii) a spouse or intimate partner of that person; or

(B) causes, attempts to cause, or would be reasonably expected to cause substantial emotional distress to a person described in clause (i), (ii), or (iii) of subparagraph (A); or

(2) with the intent to kill, injure, harass, intimidate, or place under surveillance with intent to kill, injure, harass, or intimidate another person, uses the mail, any interactive computer service or electronic communication service or electronic communication system of interstate commerce, or any other facility of interstate or foreign commerce to engage in a course of conduct that—

(A) places that person in reasonable fear of the death of or serious bodily injury to a person described in clause (i), (ii), or (iii) of paragraph (1)(A); or

(B) causes, attempts to cause, or would be reasonably expected to cause substantial emotional distress to a person described in clause (i), (ii), or (iii) of paragraph (1)(A),

shall be punished as provided in section 2261 (b) of this title.

United States v. Jovica Petrovic

701 F.3d 849 (8th Cir. 2012)

RILEY, CHIEF JUDGE.

Jovica Petrovic was convicted of four counts of interstate stalking and two counts of interstate extortionate threat. The district court sentenced Petrovic to ninety-six months imprisonment. Petrovic appeals his convictions and sentence. We affirm.

I. BACKGROUND

Petrovic and the victim, M.B., began a relationship in 2006, married in 2009, and later divorced. During their relationship, Petrovic resided in Florida and M.B. resided in Missouri, where she and her ex-husband, R.B., shared custody of their two young children. Petrovic and M.B. often met in Florida or Missouri, and M.B. occasionally allowed Petrovic to take pictures of her in the nude or performing various sex acts. M.B. also confided in Petrovic, revealing private and intimate information in text messages, such as the sexual abuse M.B. suffered as a young girl, her suicidal thoughts and tendencies, family secrets, and self-doubts about her fitness as a mother. Petrovic saved thousands of these text messages.

During their relationship, Petrovic also accumulated other potentially embarrassing information about M.B. In July 2009, M.B. attempted suicide at Petrovic's home after finding evidence leading her to believe Petrovic was having an extramarital affair. After M.B. was taken to the hospital for treatment, Petrovic took pictures of the pool of blood that had formed on the floor. In December 2009, Petrovic took several trips to Missouri to see M.B. During these trips, Petrovic stayed at a local hotel and secretly filmed M.B. having sexual intercourse with him. Petrovic took steps to ensure that M.B. was identifiable in the videos. He refused to turn off the lights, removed the sheets from the bed, and directed M.B.'s face and exposed genitalia toward the concealed camera.

On December 28, 2009, M.B. informed Petrovic by text message that she was ending their relationship. In response, Petrovic sent M.B. text messages informing her that he had secretly recorded their recent sexual encounters and had saved all of the text messages M.B. previously sent him. Petrovic threatened to post this information on the internet so M.B.'s family could read the messages and see the videos, if M.B. did not continue their relationship. Petrovic stated he was not "blackmail[ing]" M.B. and was only saving the information for his own "protection," but told M.B. to "be smart." Petrovic informed M.B. she and her family could soon visit his new website, "www.[M.B.]slut.com." M.B. understood Petrovic intended to "ruin [her] life" if she did not "get back together with [Petrovic]," but M.B. nevertheless permanently ended the relationship.

Petrovic then began a campaign to carry out his threats. Over the course of the next few months, Petrovic mailed dozens of homemade postcards to addresses throughout M.B.'s community, including to M.B.'s workplace, M.B.'s family members, R.B.'s home, and local businesses like the neighborhood drugstore. The postcards typically portrayed a picture of a scantily clad M.B. along with abusive language (for example, "I am just a whore 4 sale") and directions to a website, "www.marriedto[M.B.].com." The postcards were viewed by M.B.'s children, other family members, and many acquaintances. News of the website spread throughout the community, and almost everyone M.B. knew became aware of the site.

The website was publicly accessible in March 2010. Petrovic reported his site was "huge," containing "20,000 or 30,000 pages" of material reflecting months of preparation by Petrovic, who began creating the site in August 2009. The site contained links to dozens of images of M.B. posing in the nude or engaging in sex acts with Petrovic, and included many from the tapes Petrovic secretly recorded. Visitors to the site could view scores of pictures of M.B.'s children and other family members by clicking on a link next to the pornographic material. Several photographs of

M.B. performing a sex act with Petrovic were repeatedly and prominently displayed throughout the website, including on the site's home page. Petrovic also posted thousands of pages of the text messages M.B. had sent him. The messages were color-coded by speaker and organized chronologically, with the most private and embarrassing messages given special pages to increase readership. Petrovic posted the pictures of the blood from M.B.'s suicide attempt, further highlighting her suicidal thoughts and history. Private information about M.B. and her family was also revealed, including M.B.'s contact information and the social security numbers of her children. M.B. did not authorize Petrovic to release any of this information. After learning of the website, M.B. "had a breakdown" and "wanted to die."

Besides the website and postcards, Petrovic sent several packages containing enlarged photographs of M.B. engaging in various sex acts with Petrovic to M.B. at her work, to M.B.'s boss, to M.B.'s family members, and to R.B.'s home, where M.B.'s seven-year-old child viewed the pornographic material. Petrovic also repeatedly made harassing phone calls to M.B's workplace, and physically intimidated M.B. on several occasions—on one such occasion, pursuing M.B. in a rental van at a high rate of speed while M.B. was on her way home from work.

In June 2010, M.B.'s sister was able to have Petrovic's website shut down for a few days. On June 20, 2010, Petrovic relaunched the site and posted a message stating, "Nobody can stop me to publish this website" and offering to shut down the site if M.B. gave him his "furniture, what she stoled [sic] from me, the wedding and engagement ring, . . . and $100,000." M.B. did not comply with Petrovic's demands, and the website remained operational. On July 19, 2010, Petrovic was arrested by United States Postal Inspectors.

II. DISCUSSION

A. First Amendment

Petrovic first argues 18 U.S.C. § 2261A(2)(A),[n.2][8] the interstate stalking statute, violates his right to freedom of speech under the First Amendment to the United States Constitution. Petrovic contends the statute is unconstitutional both facially and as applied to him.

1. As Applied Challenge

"[W]hen 'speech' and 'nonspeech' elements are combined in the same course of conduct, a sufficiently important governmental interest in regulating the nonspeech element can justify incidental limitations on First Amendment freedoms." *United States v. O'Brien*, 391 U.S. 367, 376 (1968). A governmental regulation satisfies this

---

8. [n.2] "Whoever . . . with the intent . . . to . . . injure, harass, or place under surveillance with intent to . . . injure, harass, or intimidate, or cause substantial emotional distress to a person in another State . . . uses the mail, any interactive computer service, or any facility of interstate or foreign commerce to engage in a course of conduct that causes substantial emotional distress to that person or places that person in reasonable fear of . . . serious bodily injury . . . shall be punished as provided in section 2261(b) of this title."

standard if (1) "it is within the constitutional power of the Government"; (2) "it furthers an important or substantial governmental interest"; (3) "the governmental interest is unrelated to the suppression of free expression"; and (4) "the incidental restriction on alleged First Amendment freedoms is no greater than is essential to the furtherance of that interest."

Petrovic contends § 2261A(2)(A) fails *O'Brien*'s four-pronged test in his case. However, we need not reach the merits of the *O'Brien* test if, as a preliminary matter, we determine the communications for which Petrovic was convicted under the statute are not protected by the First Amendment. Because we hold Petrovic's communications fall outside the First Amendment's protection, we do not reach the merits of the *O'Brien* test.

The First Amendment provides "Congress shall make no law . . . abridging the freedom of speech." While it generally "means that government has no power to restrict expression because of its message, its ideas, its subject matter, or its content," certain "well-defined and narrowly limited classes of speech" permit content-based restrictions on speech. One such category is "speech integral to criminal conduct."

The jury convicted Petrovic of two counts of interstate extortionate threat in violation of 18 U.S.C. § 875(d) for his December 28, 2009 and June 20, 2010 communications. The communications for which Petrovic was convicted under § 2261A(2)(A) were integral to this criminal conduct as they constituted the means of carrying out his extortionate threats. Petrovic threatened to destroy M.B.'s reputation if she terminated their sexual relationship. When M.B. ended the relationship, Petrovic carried out this threat. Petrovic also threatened to continue the humiliating communications unless M.B. paid him $100,000, and when M.B. did not comply, Petrovic carried out this threat for continuing harassment as well. Because Petrovic's harassing and distressing communications were integral to his criminal conduct of extortion under § 875(d), the communications were not protected by the First Amendment.

Furthermore, "where matters of purely private significance are at issue, First Amendment protections are often less rigorous . . . because restricting speech on purely private matters does not implicate the same constitutional concerns as limiting speech on matters of public interest." We previously have held that in "extreme case[s]" it is "constitutionally permissible for a governmental entity to regulate the public disclosure of facts about private individuals." "[A]bsent a compelling state interest," such speech

> can be regulated . . . because of its constitutionally proscribable content only if: (1) any such regulation is viewpoint-neutral; (2) the facts revealed are not already in the public domain; (3) the facts revealed about the otherwise private individual are not a legitimate subject of public interest; and (4) the facts revealed are highly offensive.

M.B. was a private individual, and Petrovic's communications revealed intensely private information about M.B. The interstate stalking statute is viewpoint neutral.

It proscribes stalking and harassing conduct without making the further content discrimination of proscribing only certain forms of that conduct. Second, the intimately private facts and photographs revealed by Petrovic were never in the public domain before Petrovic began his campaign to humiliate M.B. Third, the public has no legitimate interest in the private sexual activities of M.B. or in the embarrassing facts revealed about her life. Finally, the information Petrovic publicized to the community was highly offensive. The communications for which Petrovic was convicted under § 2261A(2)(A) may be proscribed consistent with the First Amendment. The statute is not unconstitutional as applied to Petrovic.

2. Facial Challenge

Petrovic also contends § 2261A(2)(A) is facially invalid. "In the First Amendment context . . . a law may be invalidated as overbroad if 'a substantial number of its applications are unconstitutional, judged in relation to the statute's plainly legitimate sweep.'"

An overbreadth challenge like Petrovic's will "[r]arely . . . succeed against a law or regulation that is not specifically addressed to speech or to conduct necessarily associated with speech (such as picketing or demonstrating)." Section 2261A(2)(A) is directed toward "course[s] of conduct," not speech, and the conduct it proscribes is not "necessarily associated with speech." Because the statute requires both malicious intent on the part of the defendant and substantial harm to the victim, see § 2261A(2)(A), "[i]t is difficult to imagine what constitutionally-protected . . . speech would fall under these statutory prohibitions. Most, if not all, of the [statute's] legal applications are to conduct that is not protected by the First Amendment." The rare application of the statute that offends the First Amendment "can still be remedied through as-applied litigation." Because a substantial number of the statute's applications will not be unconstitutional, we decline to use the "'strong medicine' of overbreadth to invalidate the entire [statute]."

C. "Sexual Relationship" as a "Thing of Value"

To be convicted under the interstate extortionate threat statute, Petrovic must have intended to extort from M.B. "any money or other thing of value." 18 U.S.C. § 875(d). The district court instructed the jury, over Petrovic's objection, that a "sexual relationship" could constitute a "thing of value" under § 875(d). Petrovic maintains this was error that caused him to be improperly convicted of one charge of violating § 875(d) for his December 28, 2009 communications in which Petrovic threatened to harm M.B.'s reputation if she ended their relationship.

"Congress'[s] frequent use of 'thing of value' in various criminal statutes has evolved the phrase into a term of art which the courts generally construe to envelop[ ] both tangibles and intangibles." Petrovic concedes a "thing of value" under § 875(d) includes intangible objectives. Numerous intangible objectives have been held to constitute things of value under a variety of other statutes, including romantic pursuits and sex-related consideration.

These holdings reflect the principle that value is a subjective, rather than objective, concept where "the focus of the . . . term is to be placed on the value which the defendant subjectively attaches" to what is sought to be received. Although these cases differ in procedural postures and involve different statutes than does the present case, we see no reason why a "thing of value" under § 875(d) is more narrow than what the broad term of art encompasses in other contexts. A defendant can attach value to a "sexual relationship" just as readily as to sexual intercourse or other sex-related considerations, and a "sexual relationship" may be an intangible "thing of value" one intends to extort under § 875(d). The district court did not err by instructing the jury that a "sexual relationship" could be a "thing of value" under § 875(d).

E. Sufficiency of the Evidence

Petrovic finally argues the jury lacked sufficient evidence to convict him under 18 U.S.C. § 2261A(2)(A). "We review de novo sufficiency of the evidence challenges" and will uphold the jury's verdict "if there is an interpretation of the evidence that would allow a reasonable jury to find [Petrovic] guilty beyond a reasonable doubt."

1. 18 U.S.C. § 2261A(2)(A)

Conviction under § 2261A(2)(A) requires a jury to find three basic elements beyond a reasonable doubt: (1) malicious intent by the defendant toward a victim in another jurisdiction; (2) a "course of conduct" making use of a facility of interstate commerce; and (3) substantial harm to the victim. Petrovic contends no reasonable jury could have found the first and third elements beyond a reasonable doubt based on the evidence adduced at trial.

With respect to the intent element, Petrovic alleges the evidence "did not prove that . . . Petrovic had any intention to harass [M.B.]" but instead only "showed an emotionally turbulent and disdainful marriage between . . . Petrovic and [M.B.]." We disagree. Ample evidence supported the jury's finding Petrovic intended to harass M.B. or cause M.B. substantial emotional distress, such as: (1) text messages in which Petrovic referenced the website and told M.B. to "[e]njoy [her] pain," and Petrovic wished M.B. a "painful and unhappy life," suggesting a "TANTRUM IN YOUR HEART," and a "TANTRUM ON YOUR SOUL"; (2) postcards sent by Petrovic to M.B.'s ex-husband, employer, family members, and local businesses referring readers to the website and displaying images of M.B. in sexually suggestive poses along with abusive language; and (3) the prominent disclosure of intensely intimate and private information about M.B. on the website, including the sexual abuse she suffered as a child and pictures of M.B. engaged in a variety of surreptitiously recorded sex acts. Based on the evidence adduced at trial, the jury reasonably found Petrovic had the requisite intent required by § 2261A(2)(A).

Petrovic also proposes no reasonable jury could find M.B. suffered "substantial emotional distress" as a result of Petrovic's conduct. He argues any emotional distress suffered by M.B. was not "conclusively tie[d]" to his conduct, but was instead caused by M.B.'s "long history of mental health problems." At trial, M.B. testified, as a result of Petrovic's conduct, she "had a breakdown," "fe[lt] like somebody [had] rip[ped her] entire inside out of [her]" which "was the worst feeling in [her] life," became estranged from family members, and was depressed and contemplated suicide. M.B.'s sister, former employer, and ex-husband all testified about the severe emotional toll Petrovic's actions took on M.B. The jury reasonably found M.B. suffered substantial emotional distress caused by Petrovic's conduct rather than any pre-existing mental health issues.

State v. Ellison

900 N.E.2d 228 (Ohio Ct. App. 2008)

CUNNINGHAM, JUDGE.

Ripley C. Ellison challenges her conviction for telecommunications harassment under R.C. 2917.21(B). We find merit to her appeal and reverse her conviction.

Ellison and Savannah Gerhard were childhood friends but had a falling out during seventh grade. According to Ellison, the fallout occurred when her younger brother accused Gerhard of molesting him. The Hamilton County Department of Job and Family Services [JFS] investigated the claim and determined that it did not have enough evidence to substantiate that the abuse had occurred.

As teenagers, Ellison and Gerhard attended the same high school. During the summer of 2007, Ellison posted on her Internet "MySpace" page a picture of Gerhard that was captioned "Molested a little boy," and she stated in her personal profile that she hated Gerhard. Ellison allowed for public, rather than private, viewing of her MySpace page.

After hearing about the posting from others, Gerhard used the Internet to view Ellison's MySpace page. Gerhard had previously observed a short remark by Ellison on a contemporary's MySpace page that also referred to the molestation accusation. But Ellison never directly communicated these postings to Gerhard, who also had a MySpace account.

Ellison was charged criminally for telecommunications harassment under R.C. 2917.21(B).

At a bench trial, Gerhard confirmed that Ellison had never directly communicated with her over the Internet and that she had sought out the postings. She added, however, that she had felt "harassed" by the postings and that she had overheard Ellison make a similar remark about her at school.

Ellison testified that she believed her brother's accusations against Gerhard were true. And she gave the following explanation for posting the offensive material: "I think that other people need to know how she is. And she denies everything, but a lot of people believe that she did it. And I was told that she did it. And so I think that other people have a right to know."

Subsequently, Ellison was convicted on one count of telecommunications harassment. In this appeal, she argues that her conviction was not supported by sufficient evidence and violated her free-speech rights under the federal and state constitutions. We hold that the evidence was not sufficient to support the conviction, and, therefore, we do not address Ellison's freedom-of-speech challenge.

The state prosecuted Ellison under R.C. 2917.21(B), which provides that "[n]o person shall make or cause to be made a telecommunication, or permit a telecommunication to be made from a telecommunications device under the person's control, with purpose to abuse, threaten, or harass another person." The state proceeded in this case under a theory that Ellison had posted a "rumor" on the Internet to harass Gerhard.

Ellison contends that the evidence was insufficient to establish that she had made a "telecommunication" where she did not directly contact Gerhard. She concedes, however, that a direct contact is not expressly required by the statutory definition of telecommunication: "the origination, emission, dissemination, transmission, or reception of data, images, signals, sounds, or other intelligence or equivalence of intelligence of any nature over any communication system by any method, including, but not limited to, a fiber optic, electronic, magnetic, optical, digital, or analog method."

And we find it significant that the legislature defined a telecommunication broadly, with words such as dissemination. For these reasons, we decline to hold that a direct contact is required to establish a telecommunication under the statute. In this case, the state presented sufficient evidence of a telecommunication, despite the lack of a direct contact.

Ellison contends also that the lack of a direct communication completely contradicted any assertion that she had intended to harass Gerhard when she made the telecommunication.

Harassment is not defined in the statute, but it is defined in Black's Law Dictionary as "[w]ords, conduct, or action (usu. repeated or persistent) that, being directed at a specific person, annoys, alarms, or causes substantial emotional distress in the person and serves no legitimate purpose." In 1999, the legislature deleted the word "annoy" from R.C. 2917.21(B). Thus, for conduct to rise to the level of criminal harassment under this section of the statute, the accused must have intended to alarm or to cause substantial emotional distress to the recipient, not just to annoy her.

Importantly, the statute creates a specific-intent crime: the state must prove the defendant's specific purpose to harass. The burden is not met by establishing only that the defendant knew or should have known that her conduct would probably cause harassment. The legislature has created this substantial burden to limit the statute's scope to criminal conduct, not the expression of offensive speech.

In this case, the state had the burden of establishing beyond a reasonable doubt that Ellison's specific purpose in making the telecommunication was to harass

Gerhard. The state argued that Ellison's posting of the "rumor" after JFS had found the allegation unsubstantiated showed a purpose to harass. But JFS's conclusion did not mean that dissemination of the allegation could not serve the legitimate purpose of warning others of what Ellison believed to be criminal behavior. Moreover, it was undisputed that Ellison never directed a telecommunication to Gerhard despite the opportunity to do so. These facts rendered the state's position untenable. No rational trier of fact, viewing the evidence in the light most favorable to the state, could have been convinced of Ellison's specific intent to harass Gerhard when she made the telecommunication.

Thus, we hold that the state failed to establish that Ellison had made a telecommunication with the purpose to harass, where she had a legitimate purpose for posting the accusation against Gerhard on the Internet, and where Ellison did not directly telecommunicate with Gerhard.

PAINTER, JUDGE, concurring.

It is a scary thought that someone could go to jail for posting a comment on the Internet. If so, we could not build jails fast enough.

The statute on telecommunications harassment is the successor to the former telephone-harassment law. It is designed to prohibit harassing or threatening calls. Of course the calls may now be made over a traditional phone line, a cellular phone, or the Internet. But posting an annoying—but nonthreatening—comment on a website is not a crime under this statute. It might well be a civil wrong, but it is not jailable. The First Amendment would not allow punishment for making a non-threatening comment on the Internet, just as it would not for writing a newspaper article, posting a sign, or speaking on the radio.

———————

A.B. v. State
885 N.E.2d 1223 (Ind. 2008)

DICKSON, JUSTICE.

A.B., a juvenile, appeals her adjudication as a delinquent child for her postings on the Internet site MySpace.com that, if committed by an adult, would constitute the criminal offense of Harassment. [We] reverse the trial court [because] the State failed to prove all of the statutory elements for the offense of Harassment.

MySpace is "an online community that lets you meet your friends' friends." Most aptly described as a social networking site, individuals can create "profiles" listing their interests in books, television, music, movies, and so forth, as well as posting pictures, music, and videos. MySpace allows its members to control who can view the entirety of their "profile." On all "profiles," certain information is displayed to other members and visitors that "allows our users to identify each other and expand their network of friends." MySpace users have a choice to make their "profiles" public or private. For example, if a member wishes to restrict public access to her "profile," she may make it viewable to only those that she has accepted as friends, but information such as the member's photo and first name are still displayed for public view. A "group" page differs from a "profile" in that "group" pages are sites where people of common interests can join and make postings. A "group" can be public or private at the discretion of its "moderator," or creator.

When the 2005–06 school year began, A.B. was a student at Greencastle Middle School, where Shawn Gobert had been principal for thirteen years. Sometime before February 2006, she transferred to a different school. In February 2006, Mr. Gobert learned from some of his students of a vulgar tirade posted on MySpace that apparently targeted his actions in enforcing a school policy. As appropriate for a responsible and prudent school administrator, Mr. Gobert investigated. With the assistance of others, including some students, he discovered that a "Mr. Gobert" "profile" had been created on a MySpace Internet web page, purportedly by him, and on which A.B. had posted a vulgarity-laced tirade directed against him. In fact, another juvenile, R.B., a friend of A.B. and at the time a student at Greencastle Middle School, had created this false "Mr. Gobert" MySpace private "profile" and allowed access to it by twenty-six designated "friends," one of whom was A.B. A.B. then made her posting about Mr. Gobert on this private "profile". Thereafter, however, A.B. created her own MySpace "group" page, accessible by the general public, and titled with a vulgar expletive directed against Mr. Gobert and Greencastle schools.

As a result, delinquency proceedings were initiated against A.B. The various surviving counts allege her use of a computer network to harass Mr. Gobert. Counts I and V allege that A.B. used a computer network to transmit the following:

> "hey you piece of greencastle s* *t. what the f* *k do you think of me know (sic) that you cant [sic] control me? huh? ha ha ha guess what ill [sic] wear my f* *king piercings all day long and to school and you cant [sic] do s* *t about it.! ha ha f* *king ha! stupid b* *tard![n.12][9]

Counts III and VII each allege Harassment based on A.B.'s transmission of "die . . . gobert . . . die;" and Counts IV and VIII are based on A.B.'s transmission of "F* *K MR. GOBERT AND GC SCHOOLS!"

The offense of Harassment in the Indiana Criminal Code, includes the following:

> A person who, with intent to harass, annoy, or alarm another person but with no intent of legitimate communication:
>
> (4) uses a computer network . . . or other form of electronic communication to
>
> (A) communicate with a person; or
>
> (B) transmit an obscene message or indecent or profane words to a person; commits harassment, a Class B misdemeanor.

---

9. [n.12] In this and other MySpace statements by A.B. quoted in this opinion, the vulgar expletives actually used are identified symbolically.

Indiana Code § 35-45-2-2(a)(4) (2004).

For a person to commit an act with the intent to harass, annoy, or alarm another person, common sense informs that the person must have a subjective expectation that the offending conduct will likely come to the attention of the person targeted for the harassment, annoyance, or alarm. In *J.T. v. State*, 718 N.E.2d 1119, 1124 (Ind. Ct. App. 1999), a delinquency adjudication was reversed when the Court of Appeals concluded that a student did not "know or have good reason to believe" that the alleged harassing information "would reach" the victim, and thus "did not have the requisite intent to commit harassment."

A.B. contends on appeal that the evidence failed to prove the requisite intent common to all the surviving counts: that she transmitted the messages with the intent to harass, annoy, or alarm Shawn Gobert but without any intent of legitimate communication.

In juvenile delinquency adjudication proceedings, the State must prove every element of the offense beyond a reasonable doubt.

The trial court's written findings referred to postings by A.B. on both her friend's private "profile" and on A.B.'s public "group." To the extent arguably related to the intent element, the court's order finding A.B. to be a delinquent child included these findings:

> Here, Mr. Gobert is the principal. The web site was accessible by other students and the public. It is obvious to the Court that such information, while not directly sent to Mr. Gobert, was going to end up with him, due to the job and standing within the juvenile community.

> While the court does not know exactly what [A.B.'s] intent was, from the common sense reading of the displayed message, the Court can not envision any other intent but to harass, annoy or alarm.

> [T]he Court can not envision when such communication could be labeled "legitimate."

The allegedly harassing communications by A.B. identified in Counts I, III, V, and VII were postings by A.B. on her friend's MySpace "private profile" site. This "profile" site, and A.B.'s comments posted on it, could not be seen by the general public except for those persons specifically accepted as "friends" by the creator of the "profile." This posting was not viewable by the general public, and Mr. Gobert was able to view it only because R.B., the student who created the "profile," eventually authorized him to access the "profile" during his investigation. At the fact-finding hearing, there was no evidence showing that A.B. expected that Mr. Gobert would see or learn about A.B.'s messages posted on the private "profile." We find no probative evidence or reasonable inferences to establish that A.B., when making her postings on her friend's private "profile," had a subjective expectation that her conduct would likely come to the attention of Mr. Gobert.

The analysis differs as to Counts IV and VIII, which refer to A.B.'s remarks on her MySpace "group" page. Because this site was publicly accessible, it may be reasonably inferred that A.B. had a subjective expectation that her words would likely reach Mr. Gobert. This alone, however, does not establish the intent element specified in the Harassment statute. To commit the offense of Harassment, a person must have "the intent to harass, annoy, or alarm another person *but with no intent of legitimate communication.*" While A.B. titled her "group" page with the vulgar expletive, her own posting on the page elaborated as follows:

> [R.B.] made a harmless joke profile for Mr. Gobert. and [sic] some retarded b* *ch printed it out and took it to the office. [R.B.] is expelled, has to go to court, might have to go to girl [sic] school, and has to take the 8th grade over again! that's [sic] just from the school, her paretns [sic] have grounded her, and took [sic] her computer, she cant [sic] be online untill [sic] 2007! GMS is full of over reacting idiots!

Other than the title and this posting on A.B.'s "group" page, there was no other evidence relevant to the issue of her intent as to Counts IV and VIII. And the content of the posting presents strong evidence that A.B. intended her "group" page as legitimate communication of her anger and criticism of the disciplinary action of Mr. Gobert and the Greencastle Middle School against her friend, the creator of the private "profile." This affirmative proof makes it impossible for the State to have carried its burden to prove "*no intent of legitimate communication.*"

Notwithstanding the trial court's observation that it could not "envision" any intent other than to harass, annoy, or alarm Mr. Gobert, we find this conclusion unsupported by the evidence, particularly the lack of knowledgeable testimony regarding the nature and operation of MySpace and the extent to which its "profiles" and "groups" are publicly accessible. We also observe that it is even more plausible that A.B., then fourteen-years old, merely intended to amuse and gain approval or notoriety from her friends, and/or to generally vent anger for her personal grievances. Reviewing the evidence presented at the fact-finding hearing, we conclude that there was insufficient substantial evidence of probative value to prove beyond a reasonable doubt that A.B. had the requisite intent to harass, annoy, or alarm Mr. Gobert when she made the postings.

Susan W. Brenner & Megan Rehberg, *"Kiddie Crime"? The Utility of Criminal Law in Controlling Cyberbullying,*
8 First Amend. L. Rev. 1 (2009):[10]

The *A.B.* court's holding is both correct and instructive. While it may not be impossible to convict someone who engages in indirect cyberbullying of

---

harassment, it is highly unlikely. When an indirect cyberbully posts ostensibly bullying messages on a website or other online resource the putative victim cannot access, it will be difficult to prove that his or her intention was to harass that person. [S]talking and harassment both assume conduct directed at the victim; they do so because that assumption is implicit in the essential dynamic of traditional, malum in se crimes. For such a crime to have been committed, there must have been a perpetrator, actual or contemplated harm, and a victim who was the target of that harm. In the physical world, the nexus between perpetrator, victim, and consequent harm is inevitably direct; there is no other way to inflict harm in the real world.

When cyberspace is the vector of activity—especially expressive activity—the existence of such a nexus becomes uncertain. We have all said things that could harm others in more or less serious ways, never intending that they reach the person in question. They usually do not because social mores inhibit most of us from telling A what B said about him. Additionally, our reliance on the presumptive confidentiality of the critiques we share with our friends and family would negate any inference of an intent to harass in the unlikely event we were prosecuted. The idea of prosecuting someone on the basis of such conduct seems absurd, yet it is functionally analogous to what happened to A.B.

The differentiating factor in *A.B.* (and similar cases) is that the presumptive confidentiality we assume in the real world becomes problematic online, at least when the actor posts comments on a site that is at least potentially accessible to the target of the comments. When we post "irritating or malicious gossip" online, we publish the comments to the world. However, if we post comments without considering whether the target is likely to see them, we do not engage in the premeditated, focused communications involved in direct cyberbullying.

How should we handle situations in which this malicious targeting is absent but the online circulation of gossip still inflicts harm on the person it concerns? Until Internet use became common in the 1990s, the publication of material (gossip, rumor, news, etc.) was controlled by the mainstream media. Corporations engaged in disseminating content via print, radio, and television signals. The material the mainstream media publish is limited by two factors. First, the cost involved in publication by traditional means acts as a de facto content filter; publishing material about matters of general public interest is likely to be more profitable than publishing material that will interest only a few people. Second, the possibility of being sued (for defamation, copyright infringement, invasion of privacy, etc.) causes mainstream media companies to rely on a cadre of professional editors, reporters, and other staff, whose collective purpose is to filter content and prevent the publication of actionable material.

As a result of potential liability, the mainstream media (i) publish gossip about people whose lives are likely to be of general public interest (celebrities) but (ii) do not publish gossip about non-celebrities, i.e., those whose lives will almost certainly not be of interest to the general public. This meant that prior to the Internet, non-celebrities bore little, if any, risk of having gossip about themselves circulated among a wider audience. Gossip stayed where it had always been—within the localized group comprising the individual's co-workers, acquaintances, friends, and family.

The Internet changed that. Now we all face the prospect of experiencing what was once the sole province of Hollywood celebrities. We can have our own paparazzi, whether we like it or not. Unlike professional paparazzi (who are motivated by profit), our paparazzo (or paparazzi) may be motivated by jealousy, insecurity, or boredom. And unlike those who have traditionally been the targets of paparazzi, we have done nothing to inject ourselves into the public arena. We expect celebrities to shrug off the more or less accurate (but usually embarrassing) gossip paparazzi generate about them; but those of us who are not celebrities are outraged when our own, freelance paparazzi do something similar to us.

Should criminal stalking and harassment laws be expanded to encompass online gossip about private citizens? Here, we are concerned with the general, non-targeted publication involved in indirect cyberbullying. If, as noted earlier, the publication of the material were targeted specifically at the victim, as in direct cyberbullying, it might be possible to prosecute under existing stalking and harassment laws. Indirect cyberbullying raises a different and much more difficult issue: the imposition of criminal liability for the general publication of non-defamatory gossip.

We seem to be left with two alternatives. One is to expand current criminal stalking or harassment laws so they encompass the generalized publication of gossip that constitutes indirect cyberbullying. The other is to accept our new-found, and perhaps unwelcome, status as "lower-case" public figures, i.e., as someone whose personality, appearance, activities, or predilections can become grist for an amateur online paparazzo (or paparazzi).

While some may find the first alternative appealing, it would be unworkable in practice and is almost certainly unconstitutional. It would be unworkable because the criminal justice system would be inundated with requests for prosecutions, most of which would be denied due to a lack of resources. Rejected requests might lead the original victim to retaliate in kind, which could lead to a consequent, also likely-to-be-rejected request for prosecution by the cyberbully-become-victim. While prosecutions might be brought in a few particularly egregious cases, they would probably do little to discourage determined cyberbullies. As to the constitutional issues, expanded stalking and harassment statutes criminalizing the circulation of simple gossip would likely violate the First Amendment because they would bar the publication of non-defamatory content and opinion. They would probably also be held void for vagueness due to the difficulty involved in articulating what was, and was not, permissible in online commentary about someone.

That leaves the second alternative, which is eminently feasible but more than a little unsatisfying. We would have to tolerate the aggravating attentions of those who choose to become our paparazzi. We would have to accept the proposition that has been bandied about for more than decade: cyberspace transforms everyone into a public figure, or more accurately, cyberspace has the potential to transform everyone into a public figure.

We find this alternative unsatisfying because we are used to a world in which we have been able to ignore what is said about us, at least for the most part. We know, at some level, that our friends, colleagues, and acquaintances gossip about us behind our backs, but as long as we do not know what they say, we can ignore it. When what they say migrates online, it becomes difficult—if not impossible—to ignore. Because we are the products of a real-world culture which dictates that gossip is not to reach the person it concerns, we are likely to be outraged and want the perpetrators sanctioned, somehow. But that reaction may be an historical artifact, the product of a non-networked culture. As one author noted:

> In a bygone era, members of a community would gather at the local soda fountain to "chew the fat"—discuss . . . local politics, share the latest gossip, or complain about the weather. These days, millions of people are engaged in the same conversations not over root beer floats at soda fountains, but over keyboards in online communities known as social-networking web sites.

As social networking becomes more pervasive, we are likely to become more accustomed to—and more comfortable with—the fact that "chewing the fat" has migrated online, and the attendant reality that gossip can easily leak into wider circulation. If it simply leaks, and is not deliberately directed at the person it concerns (direct cyberbullying), we may have to live with that. The pragmatic assumptions we tend to make about when gossip reaches its target in the real world will no longer be valid, which may make the notion of holding the leaker criminally liable for what he or she has done hopelessly problematic.

––––––––––

Notes

1. Are *Petrovic*, *A.B.*, and *Ellison* consistent? Distinguishable? Which of the three defendants in those cases should be viewed as criminal? Why? What *mens rea* should be sufficient to establish criminality? Should it matter that the acts performed be labeled direct or indirect harassment? Finally, do we now all have our own paparazzi—who may disseminate gossip or unpleasant private facts about us without fear of criminal prosecution?

2. **Cyber Gender Harassment.** Studies indicate that the majority of individuals targeted for cyber gender harassment are overwhelmingly female. *See* Danielle Keats Citron, *Law's Expressive Value in Combating Cyber Gender Harassment*, 108 Mich. L. Rev. 373, 378–79 (2009). Professor Citron, in her article, argues for a new approach:

> The notion that cyber harassment is trivial is both widespread and damaging. Because so many refuse to recognize cyber harassment as harmful,

women suffer in silence, often sacrificing their female identities and their online lives. A cyber civil rights agenda would change this by recognizing and naming cyber harassment as gender discrimination. By changing the social meaning of online harassment and recharacterizing it as a civil rights violation, we may be able to transform online behavior in a manner that permits women to claim the internet as equally their own.

§ 19.4 Defamation

Susan W. Brenner & Megan Rehberg, *"Kiddie Crime"? The Utility of Criminal Law in Controlling Cyberbullying,*

8 First Amend. L. Rev. 1 (2009):[11]

Defamation is a relatively new crime in Anglo-American law. In the early seventeenth century, the English Court of Star Chamber criminalized defamatory comments directed toward an individual on the theory that "they tend to create breaches of the peace when the defamed . . . undertake to revenge themselves on the defamer." The Court of Star Chamber used the Roman doctrine of libellis famosis to create the new offense, which is why it came to be known as libel. English colonists brought the offense with them when they came to America, and it eventually became part of the criminal law of the states.

Since it was meant to prevent dueling and other forms of physical conflict, criminal libel has traditionally been consigned to the category of "offenses against the public peace." The gravamen of the crime was publishing material that was likely "to cause disorder, riot or breach of the peace."

Though it was an established common law crime, criminal libel was rarely prosecuted in the United States in the nineteenth and twentieth centuries, which was one of the reasons the drafters of the Model Penal Code gave for not including it in their template of offenses. In their commentary on this issue, they said deciding "whether to penalize anything like libel" was "one of the hardest questions" they confronted. They began with the premise that "penal sanctions cannot be justified . . . by the fact that defamation is damaging to a person in ways that entitle him to maintain a civil suit." Noting that penal sanctions are only appropriate for "harmful behavior which exceptionally disturbs the community's sense of security," the drafters of the Model Penal Code considered whether libel falls into this category. They concluded that behavior "exceptionally disturbs the community's sense of security" for either of two reasons: the "harm" inflicted "is very grave, as in rape or murder, so that even the remote possibility of being . . . victimized terrifies us. Or our alarm may,

---

as in the case of petty theft or malicious mischief, derive from the higher likelihood that such lesser harms will be inflicted upon us."

The architects of the Model Penal Code found that "personal calumny falls in neither of these classes" and is "therefore inappropriate for penal control," which probably explained "the paucity of prosecutions" and "near desuetude of private criminal libel" laws in the United States. Accordingly, they did not include a libel provision in the final version of the Code. As a result, while libel is included in the criminal codes of some states, it tends to be a minor crime and is almost never prosecuted.

At least nineteen states criminalize general libel; three others criminalize specific types of libel. The general libel statutes fall into two categories: those that focus on causing a "breach of the peace" and those that focus on publishing a "statement or object tending to . . . impeach the honesty, integrity, virtue, or reputation or expose the natural defects [of someone] and thereby to expose him to public hatred, contempt, or ridicule." At common law, truth was not a defense in a criminal libel prosecution, but at least some of the state criminal libel statutes recognize truth as a defense. And while civil libel requires that the defamatory material have been communicated to someone other than the victim, criminal libel only requires that it have been communicated to "a person other than the publisher of the" material. The premise that publication to the victim suffices for criminal libel apparently derives from the historical concern with preventing breaches of the peace.

There is no federal criminal defamation provision.

———————

Thomas Mink v. Susan Knox

613 F.3d 995 (10th Cir. 2010)

Seymour, Circuit Judge.

Thomas Mink appeals the district court's dismissal of his 42 U.S.C. § 1983 complaint against Susan Knox, a deputy district attorney, on qualified immunity grounds. We reverse.

Mr. Mink, a student at the University of Northern Colorado ("UNC"), created a fictional character, "Junius Puke," for the editorial column of his internet-based journal, *The Howling Pig*. The editorial column displayed altered photographs of Junius Peake, a UNC professor, wearing dark sunglasses and a Hitler-like mustache. Junius Puke's editorial column addressed subjects on which Mr. Peake would be unlikely to write, in language he would be unlikely to use, asserting views that were diametrically opposed to Mr. Peake's.

Mr. Peake, who was not amused, contacted the Greeley police, who started investigating a potential violation of Colorado's criminal libel statute, Colo. Rev. Stat. § 18-13-105. [T]he detective in charge prepared a search warrant affidavit to submit to the office of the district attorney for legal review. The deputy district attorney, Susan Knox, reviewed and approved the search warrant affidavit, which was identical to the warrant with respect to the eleven paragraphs listing the items to be seized. The affidavit and warrant were presented to and approved by a magistrate judge. The Greeley police then searched the home where Mr. Mink lived with his mother and confiscated their personal computer, as well as written materials referencing The Howling Pig.

Mr. Mink and his mother subsequently filed suit in federal district court against the City of Greeley, Colorado, the district attorney, Detective Ken Warren, and a "John Doe" assistant district attorney, seeking damages for the search and seizure, among other things. The district court granted Mr. Mink's motion for a temporary restraining order and ordered the City of Greeley to return "to the Plaintiffs the computer, and all contents thereof, seized following the search of Plaintiffs' home." Thereafter, the district attorney issued a written "No File" decision, concluding that the statements contained in The Howling Pig could not be prosecuted under the Colorado criminal libel statute.

Mr. Mink then amended his complaint, removing his mother as a plaintiff and adding Ms. Knox as a defendant. The district court granted Ms. Knox's motion to dismiss the suit in its entirety, holding in part that Mr. Mink's constitutional claims against Ms. Knox were barred by absolute immunity. We reversed, determining that

> a prosecutor is entitled to absolute immunity for those actions that cast him in the role of an advocate initiating and presenting the government's case. Absolute immunity, however, does not extend to those actions that are investigative or administrative in nature, including the provision of legal advice outside the setting of a prosecution.

We concluded that Ms. Knox "was not wearing the hat of an advocate," when she reviewed the affidavit in support of the warrant, and "thus, is not entitled to absolute prosecutorial immunity." Nevertheless, we noted that Ms. Knox "may be entitled to qualified immunity if she reasonably concluded probable cause existed to support the warrant application, or that the application of the Supreme Court's First Amendment cases to the criminal libel statute was not clearly established under the circumstances here."

[On remand the district court concluded that Ms. Knox was entitled to qualified immunity. On appeal from that remand,] Mr. Mink asks us to decide whether the district court erred when it dismissed,

> on the basis of qualified immunity, Mr. Mink's claim alleging an unlawful search and seizure in violation of the Fourth Amendment, where the search lacked probable cause because clearly-established First Amendment law protected Mr. Mink's speech, and because the overbroad affidavit and warrant violated clearly-established Fourth Amendment law[.]

The first question is whether there was probable cause to believe that Mr. Mink's publication of The Howling Pig violated the Colorado criminal libel statute.

It goes without saying that a government official may not base her probable cause determination on an "unjustifiable standard," such as speech protected by the First

Amendment. We thus turn to whether Mr. Mink's speech was protected by the First Amendment.

For centuries, the common law has afforded a cause of action to a person whose reputation has been damaged by the publication of false and defamatory statements. *Milkovich v. Lorain Journal Co.*, 497 U.S. 1, 11–12 (1990). A passage from Shakespeare's Othello is often quoted in explanation.

> Who steals my purse steals trash . . .
>
> But he that filches from me my good name
>
> Robs me of that which not enriches him,
>
> And makes me poor indeed.

Id. (quoting Act III, scene 3).

Nevertheless, the Supreme Court has recognized a number of constitutional limits on various categories of speech which may be the subject of state defamation actions, in order to maintain a balance between the protection of one's individual reputation and the freedom of speech of another person. After all, "[w]hatever is added to the field of libel is taken from the field of free debate," *New York Times Co. v. Sullivan*, 376 U.S. 254, 272 (1964), as well as from "individual liberty" and "the common quest for truth and the vitality of society as a whole." *Hustler Magazine v. Falwell*, 485 U.S. 46, 51 (1988). Moreover,

> [t]he First Amendment is not limited to ideas, statements, or positions which are accepted; which are not outrageous; which are decent and popular; which are constructive or have some redeeming element; or which do not deviate from community standards and norms; or which are within prevailing religious or moral standards. . . . The First Amendment standards are not adjusted to a particular type of publication or particular subject matter.

Pring v. Penthouse Int'l, Ltd., 695 F.2d 438, 443 (10th Cir. 1982).

In balancing individual reputation and freedom of speech, the Court has identified various culpability requirements. *New York Times* recognized the need for "a federal rule that prohibits a public official from recovering damages for a defamatory falsehood relating to his official conduct unless he proves that the statement was made with 'actual malice'—that is, with knowledge that it was false or with reckless disregard of whether it was false or not." The Court extended the *New York Times* rule to "public figures" in *Curtis Publishing Co. v. Butts*, 388 U.S. 130 (1967). In *Gertz v. Robert Welch, Inc.*, 418 U.S. 323 (1974), the Court held that although "the *New York Times* malice standard was inappropriate for a private person attempting to prove he was defamed on matters of public interest," nevertheless states may not "impose liability without requiring some showing of fault," or "permit recovery of presumed or punitive damages on less than a showing of *New York Times* malice."

As to the "constitutional limits on the *type* of speech which may be the subject of state defamation actions," "the *Bresler-Letter Carriers-Falwell* line of cases provides protection for statements," such as parody, fantasy, rhetorical hyperbole, and imaginative expressions, "that cannot 'reasonably [be] interpreted as stating actual facts' about an individual." Because no reasonable person would take these types of speech as true, they simply cannot impair one's good name. "This provides assurance that public debate will not suffer for lack of 'imaginative expression' or the 'rhetorical hyperbole' which has traditionally added much to the discourse of our Nation."

To determine whether a statement purports to state actual facts about an individual, the Court scrutinizes the meaning of the statement in context. "Context is crucial and can turn what, out of context, appears to be a statement of fact into 'rhetorical hyperbole,' which is not actionable."

Even false statements of fact are protected from a defamation claim if any reasonable person would recognize the statements as parody. As the Court held in *Falwell*, an ad parody of the Reverend Jerry Falwell, in which he purportedly stated during an interview that his "first time" was during "a drunken incestuous rendezvous with his mother in an outhouse," constituted a caricature of him which no one reasonably would consider to be true, even though Reverend Falwell could have proved the assertion of an incestuous relationship with his mother to be absolutely false.

Although the Supreme Court has not yet squarely addressed whether fantasy, parody, rhetorical hyperbole, or imaginative expression is actionable in a case where a plaintiff is neither a public figure nor the speech on a matter of public concern, this circuit and at least one other circuit have done so. In *Levinsky's Inc. v. Wal-Mart Stores, Inc.*, 127 F.3d 122 (1st Cir. 1997), the court concluded that a portion of the statements claimed by a private person to be defamatory were constitutionally protected, stating:

> The First Amendment's shielding of figurative language reflects the reality that exaggeration and non-literal commentary have become an integral part of social discourse. For better or worse, our society has long since passed the stage at which the use of the word "bastard" would occasion an investigation into the target's lineage or the cry "you pig" would prompt a probe for a porcine pedigree. Hyperbole is very much the coin of the modern realm. In extending full constitutional protection to this category of speech, the *Milkovich* Court recognized the need to segregate casually used words, no matter how tastelessly couched, from fact-based accusations.

Applying this analysis, the court held that the word "trashy" was hyperbole and therefore shielded from defamation liability notwithstanding the court's inability to determine whether the context of the statement involved a matter of public concern.

Pring emphasized that in all cases involving fantasy, parody, rhetorical hyperbole, or imaginative expression, the constitutional inquiry in deciding whether a statement is actionable remains the same: whether the charged portions, in context, could be reasonably understood as describing actual facts about the plaintiff or actual events in which he participated. This makes sense because if a statement of fact is clearly a spoof, or satirical as in *Falwell*, it matters not if the outrageously stated facts are false because no one would believe them to be true.[n.9][12]

The test of what a particular statement could reasonably be understood to have asserted is what a *reasonable reader* would understand the author to be saying, considering the kind of language used and the context in which it is used.

Following this path, we held in *Pring:*

> The test is not whether the story is or is not characterized as "fiction," "humor," or anything else in the publication, but whether the charged portions in context could be reasonably understood as describing actual facts about the plaintiff or actual events in which she participated. If it could not be so understood, the charged portions could not be taken literally.

We also noted that whether a statement could be reasonably understood as fact is a question of law.

The dispositive question is whether a reasonable person would conclude that the statements in *The Howling Pig* were actual statements of fact about Mr. Peake, or attributable to him, rather than a satirical spoof. For the reasons stated below, we conclude that the answer is no.

The Howling Pig humorously altered Mr. Peake's photograph to create the character of Junius Puke, its "editor." Another photo was altered to depict Mr. Peake/Puke made up as a character in the rock band KISS. Junius Puke covered subjects and used language that Mr. Peake, a professor of finance, surely would not have. For example, the editorial said:

> This will be a regular bitch sheet that will speak truth to power, obscenities to clergy, and advice to all the stoners sitting around watching Scooby Doo.

> This will be a forum for the pissed off and disenfranchised in Northern Colorado, basically everybody.

> I made it to where I am through hard work, luck, and connections, all without a college degree.

> Dissatisfaction with a cushy do-nothing ornamental position led me to form this subversive little paper.

> I don't normally care much about the question of daycare since my kids are grown and other people's children give me the willies[.]

---

12. [n.9] Accordingly, if we determine that the charged portions of *The Howling Pig* would not have been reasonably believed to be true statements about Professor Peake, it is not relevant to our analysis whether Mr. Peake was a public figure or speaking on a matter of public concern. For purposes of the probable cause analysis in this case, therefore, our inquiry ends if we determine that the charged portions of *The Howling Pig* could not be libelous—that is, could not reasonably be taken as true.

Significantly, *The Howling Pig* editorials even contained an express disclaimer regarding the editor:

> The Howling Pig would like to make sure that there is no possible confusion between our editor Junius Puke and the Monfort Distinguished Professor of Finance, Mr. Junius "Jay" Peake. Mr. Peake is an upstanding member of the community as well as an asset to the Monfort School of Business where he teaches about microstructure. Peake is active in many community groups, married and a family man. He is nationally known for his work in the business world, and has consulted on questions of market structure. Junius Puke is none of those things and a loudmouth know-it-all to boot, but luckily he's frequently right and so is a true asset to this publication.

According to the search warrant affidavit itself:

> The picture [of Junius Peake] has been altered to include sunglasses, a smaller nose and a small moustache similar to that of Hitler's. The person in the photograph is identified on the website as Junius Puke. The picture is accompanied by a biography of Mr. Puke. According to the site, its purpose is to draw attention to issues rampant in Northern Colorado and Elsewhere [sic].

Balanced against all this, Detective Warren provided Mr. Peake's complaint to him as the sole basis of the alleged defamatory content articulated in the affidavit. Thus, the affidavit said that "[Mr. Peake] told Detective Warren that the statements made on the website about him are false." When asked to provide some examples, Mr. Peake cited the following:

1) The website uses his photograph and identifies him as the Editor in Chief Junius Puke.

2) The website states that he "gambled in tech stocks" in the 90's.

3) The website states: The dark glasses are to avoid being recognized since he fears the good natured ribbing of his colleagues on Wall Street where he managed to luck out and ride the tech bubble of the nineties like a $20 whore and make a fortune.

4) The website contains many opinions and articles about The University of Northern Colorado, the Greeley Community and Northern Colorado. As this is an "editorial" column, those statements are attributed to Mr. Puke, and therefore Mr. Peak [sic]. Mr. Peak [sic] feels that these opinions are not his but have been attributed to him.

The test is not how Mr. Peake would characterize *The Howling Pig's* editorial column, but how a reasonable person would understand those statements in that context. In our judgment, the district court reached the only possible conclusion in its January 9, 2004 order granting the temporary restraining order. "[W]hat's written in this case is satire. . . . [A]s written it is crass and vulgar, but that makes it no less protected by the First Amendment." "[T]his is the purest of speech which has been tolerated by all but tyrants and despots from ancient times." It is apparent from our review of the charged portions of the column on the editorial page of *The Howling Pig* that no reasonable reader would believe that the statements in that context were said by Professor Peake in the guise of Junius Puke, nor would any reasonable person believe they were statements of fact as opposed to hyperbole or parody. The comments asserted as defamation constituted satire in its classic sense. As such, they are protected speech under the First Amendment, and a state may not deem them to constitute libel, particularly criminal libel. The district attorney recognized as much when he concluded that *The Howling Pig* could not be prosecuted under the statute.

Because a reasonable person would not take the statements in the editorial column as statements of facts by or about Professor Peake, no reasonable prosecutor could believe it was probable that publishing such statements constituted a crime warranting search and seizure of Mr. Mink's property.

[The court also concluded that the warrant violated the particularity requirement and that the prosecutor was not entitled to qualified immunity.] In sum, we conclude the amended complaint plausibly alleged that Ms. Knox violated Mr. Mink's clearly established constitutional rights. Accordingly, we **REVERSE** the district court's decision granting Ms. Knox's motion to dismiss and **REMAND** for further proceedings consistent with this opinion.

GORSUCH, CIRCUIT JUDGE, concurring.

The question the court confronts is whether probable cause existed to think that Mr. Mink's column constituted "criminal libel." I agree with my colleagues that the answer to that question must be "no." I reach this conclusion for a simple and straightforward reason: this court has already said so. *Pring v. Penthouse International, Ltd.*, 695 F.2d 438 (10th Cir.1982), established in this circuit the rule that the First Amendment precludes defamation actions aimed at parody, even parody causing injury to individuals who are not public figures or involved in a public controversy. *Pring* is binding on us, answers the probable cause question at issue, and is thus the beginning and end of my inquiry on that question.

After noting *Pring* controls, the majority proceeds to offer a lengthy new defense of that decision. The majority may be right in all it says. But this isn't beyond peradventure. As the majority notes, the Supreme Court has yet to address how far the First Amendment goes in protecting parody. And reasonable minds can and do differ about the soundness of a rule that precludes private persons from recovering for reputational or emotional damage caused by parody about issues of private concern. One might argue, for example, that such a rule unnecessarily constitutionalizes limitations that state tort law already imposes. Or that such a rule may unjustly preclude private persons from recovering for intentionally inflicted emotional distress regarding private matters, in a way the First Amendment doesn't compel.

Respectfully, I would avoid these thickets. Whoever has the better path through them, it's better yet that we sidestep them altogether.

––––––––––

Notes

1. Is there a role for a criminal defamation statute to regulate content on the Internet?

2. What remedy, if any, should a person like Professor Junius Peake have against comments posted by persons like Mr. Mink?

3. **Immunity for providers of an interactive computer service.**

Common law created three categories of publishers for purposes of defamation and holds them to different standards of liability depending on which category they fall into. Primary publishers, such as book or newspaper publishers, are held to a standard of liability comparable to authors because they have actively cooperated in the publishing of the libelous material. Distributors, also referred to as secondary publishers, are held to a lower standard for liability and may only be considered liable for defamation if they knew or had reason to know that the material they distribute is defamatory. The last category of publishers, those referred to as conduits (such as a telephone companies), are rarely held liable since they lack any ability to screen or control third party speech.

Relying on these common law distinctions, the court in *Stratton Oakmont, Inc. v. Prodigy Services Co.*, [23 Media L. Rep. 1794 (N.Y. Sup. Ct. 1995),] held an ISP that hosted an online bulletin board liable for the statements posted by third parties, primarily because this ISP advertised that it would monitor and remove offensive content from its bulletin board. In response to this ruling, which Congress feared would significantly chill free speech and punish good faith efforts to monitor and remove offensive content from websites, Congress adopted § 230(c) of the Communications Decency Act of 1996 to immunize ISP's from such vicarious liability. Section 230(c) provides that "[n]o provider or user of an interactive computer service shall be treated as the publisher or speaker of any information provided by another information content provider." Information content provider is defined as anyone who is "responsible, in whole or in part, for the creation or development of information provided through the Internet or any other interactive computer service." Courts have interpreted this clause broadly and continually reject the argument that § 230(c) allows for distributor liability for ISP's.[13]

See § 14.3 for more on the immunity conferred by Congress in the Communications Decency Act, 47 U.S.C. § 230.

---

13. Salil K. Mehra, *Law and Cybercrime in the United States Today*, 58 Am. J. Comp. L. 659 (2010). Copyright © 2010, Salil K. Mehra, American Society of Comparative Law. All rights reserved. Reprinted by permission.

Chapter 20

Sentencing

Can or should our old rules and policies regarding sentencing and punishment apply? When we talk about investigating cyber crime, we frequently assert that constitutional rules of criminal procedure pertaining to traditional crime apply in the same manner to cyber crime, only with some nuances. But what about our sentencing purposes and procedures and our societal purposes of punishment? Those fundamental concepts for responding to criminal conduct may well be radically different with regard to cyber crime. For example, if a cyber criminal is not motivated by forces the same as or similar to those motivating a regular criminal, our traditional models aimed at deterrence might not work well, or not work at all. Likewise, when the fact or scope of Internet victimization is undiscovered or difficult to detect until long after the event, our traditional models of measuring harm might fail to adequately address the problem.

When we consider the so-called "traveler" cases involving attempted sexual exploitation of children and the varieties of Internet fraud, for example, I have to wonder to what extent we are hitting the mark with sentencing. Does the digital and Internet age challenge or require us to re-examine our notions of case disposition and punishment? What should we do differently? If our goals may be different with regard to cyber criminals, what should our primary sentencing goals be? Do we seek to impose punishment that approximately equals the harm done, or do we focus on deterrence? Do we seek to rehabilitate offenders, or should we focus on protecting the public through incapacitation? Should our sentencing practices and concerns focus more on the offender or on the harm caused to victims?[1]

§ 20.1 Federal Sentencing Guidelines — Enhancements

The United States Sentencing Guidelines have several specific offense characteristics and adjustments that are applicable to computer crimes. Two of them are considered here.

---

1. Donald R. Mason, *Sentencing Policy and Procedure as Applied to Cyber Crimes: A Call for Reconsideration and Dialogue*, 76 Miss. L.J. 903, 907 (2007). Copyright © 2007, Mississippi Law Journal. All rights reserved. Reprinted by permission.

1. Use of Computer

United States v. Neil Scott Kramer

631 F.3d 900 (8th Cir. 2010)

WOLLMAN, CIRCUIT JUDGE.

Steve Wozniak, co-founder of Apple Computer, recently mused: "Everything has a computer in it nowadays." But is an ordinary cellular phone—used only to place calls and send text messages—a computer? The district court, relying on the definition of "computer" found in 18 U.S.C. § 1030(e)(1), concluded that Neil Kramer's was, and imposed an enhanced prison sentence for its use in committing an offense. We affirm.

Neil Kramer pleaded guilty to transporting a minor in interstate commerce with the intent to engage in criminal sexual activity with her, a violation of 18 U.S.C. § 2423(a). He also acknowledged that he used his cellular telephone—a Motorola Motorazr V3—to make voice calls and send text messages to the victim for a six-month period leading up to the offense.

The district court—over Kramer's objection—concluded that the phone was a "computer," *see* 18 U.S.C. § 1030(e)(1), applied a two-level enhancement for its use to facilitate the offense, *see* U.S. Sentencing Guidelines Manual § 2G1.3(b)(3) (2009), and sentenced Kramer to 168 months' imprisonment. Although this sentence is within both the original and enhanced guidelines ranges, the district court acknowledged that without the enhancement it would have sentenced Kramer to 140 months' imprisonment.

Kramer argues (1) that application of the enhancement was procedural error because a cellular telephone, when used only to make voice calls and send text messages, cannot be a "computer" as defined in 18 U.S.C. § 1030(e)(1), and (2) that even if a phone could be a computer, the government's evidence was insufficient to show that his phone met that definition.

U.S. Sentencing Guidelines Manual § 2G1.3(b)(3) provides a two-level enhancement for "the use of a computer . . . to . . . persuade, induce, entice, coerce, or facilitate the travel of, the minor to engage in prohibited sexual conduct. . . ." "'Computer' has the meaning given that term in 18 U.S.C. § 1030(e)(1)," U.S. Sentencing Guidelines Manual § 2G1.3(b)(3) cmt. n.1 (2009), that is, it "means an electronic, magnetic, optical, electrochemical, or other high speed data processing device performing logical, arithmetic, or storage functions, and includes any data storage facility or communications facility directly related to or operating in conjunction with such device," 18 U.S.C. § 1030(e)(1). It does not, however, "include an automated typewriter or typesetter, a portable hand held calculator, or other similar device." 18 U.S.C. § 1030(e)(1).

Kramer first argues that the district court incorrectly interpreted the term "computer" to include a "basic cell phone" being used only to call and text message the victim. In his view, the enhancement should apply only when a device is used to access the Internet. We disagree.

The language of 18 U.S.C. § 1030(e)(1) is exceedingly broad. If a device is "an electronic . . . or other high speed data processing device performing logical, arithmetic, or storage functions,"[n.3][2] it is a computer. This definition captures any device that makes use of an electronic data processor, examples of which are legion. *Accord* Orin S. Kerr, *Vagueness Challenges to the Computer Fraud and Abuse Act*, 94 MINN. L.REV. 1561, 1577 (2010) ("Just think of the common household items that include microchips and electronic storage devices, and thus will satisfy the statutory definition of 'computer.' That category can include coffeemakers, microwave ovens, watches, telephones, children's toys, MP3 players, refrigerators, heating and air-conditioning units, radios, alarm clocks, televisions, and DVD players, in addition to more traditional computers like laptops or desktop computers."). Additionally, each time an electronic processor performs any task—from powering on, to receiving keypad input, to displaying information—it performs logical, arithmetic, or storage functions. These functions are the essence of its operation. *See* The New Oxford American Dictionary 277 (2d ed. 2005) (defining "central processing unit" as "the part of a computer in which operations are controlled and executed").

Furthermore, there is nothing in the statutory definition that purports to exclude devices because they lack a connection to the Internet. To be sure, the term computer "does not include an automated typewriter or typesetter, a portable hand held calculator, or other similar device." But this hardly excludes all non-Internet-enabled devices from the definition of "computer"—indeed, this phrasing would be an odd way to do it. Whatever makes an automated typewriter "similar" to a hand held calculator—the statute provides no further illumination—we find few similarities between those items and a modern cellular phone containing an electronic processor. Therefore we conclude that cellular phones are not excluded by this language.

Of course, the enhancement does not apply to every offender who happens to use a computer-controlled microwave or coffeemaker. Application note 4 to § 2G1.3(b)(3) limits application of the enhancement to those offenders who use a computer "to communicate directly with a minor or with a person who exercises custody, care, or supervisory control of the minor." Therefore, the note continues, the enhancement

---

2. [n.3] The parties disagree over the meaning of this language. Kramer argues that the word "electronic" modifies "high speed data processing device" and therefore the device must be both "electronic" and "high speed." The government argues that "electronic, magnetic, optical, [and] electrochemical" data processing devices are, by their nature, "high speed," and the language "other high speed" was included to expand the statute to cover additional types of high-speed devices that were not, or could not be, enumerated. We need not resolve this dispute because even if Kramer's reading of the statute is correct, a modern cellular phone can be a "high speed" electronic device. Indeed, modern cellular phones process data at comparable or faster rates than the desktop computers that existed when § 1030(e)(1) was enacted.

"would not apply to the use of a computer or an interactive computer service to obtain airline tickets for the minor from an airline's Internet site." This is a meaningful limitation on the applicability of the enhancement, but it is no help to Kramer.

We acknowledge that a "basic" cellular phone might not easily fit within the colloquial definition of "computer." We are bound, however, not by the common understanding of that word, but by the specific—if broad—definition set forth in § 1030(e)(1). Now it may be that neither the Sentencing Commission nor Congress anticipated that a cellular phone would be included in that definition.[3][n.5] As technology continues to develop, § 1030(e)(1) may come to capture still additional devices that few industry experts, much less the Commission or Congress, could foresee. But to the extent that such a sweeping definition was unintended or is now inappropriate, it is a matter for the Commission or Congress to correct. We cannot provide relief from plain statutory text. *See United States v. Mitra*, 405 F.3d 492, 495 (7th Cir. 2005) ("As more devices come to have built-in intelligence, the effective scope of [§ 1030(e)(1)] grows. This might prompt Congress to amend the statute but does not authorize the judiciary to give the existing version less coverage than its language portends.").

Kramer's second contention—that the government's evidence was insufficient to demonstrate that *his* cellular phone was a computer—also fails. "The government must prove the facts needed to support a sentencing enhancement by a preponderance of the evidence, and we review the district court's fact findings for clear error."

The government introduced the phone's user's manual and a printout from Motorola's website describing the phone's features. The government did not, however, offer any expert testimony regarding the phone's capabilities. Although doing so might have aided our review, the materials presented to the district court were sufficient to show by a preponderance of the evidence that Kramer's phone was an "electronic . . . or other high speed data processing device" that "perform[ed] logical, arithmetic, or storage functions" when Kramer used it to call and text message the victim.

The printout reveals that the phone is powered by a "680 mAh Li-ion" battery, has "5MB" of memory, is capable of running software, makes use of a "Graphic Accelerator" to run its color display screens, has a "User-customizable" main menu, and comes with "Preloaded" text messages. Also, the user's manual contains a "Software Copyright Notice" which warns that the phone "may include copyrighted Motorola and third-party software stored in semiconductor memories or other media." Together, these are sufficient to show that the phone makes use of an electronic data processor.

---

3. [n.5] Indeed the Commission, explaining its reasons for "expand[ing] the enhancement" found in guidelines § 2G2.2(b)(5) to include the use of an "interactive computer service," expressed its view that "the term 'computer' did not capture all types of Internet devices." Therefore, it continued, "the amendment expands the definition of 'computer' to include other devices that involve interactive computer services (*e.g.*, Web-Tv)."

Furthermore, that processor performs arithmetic, logical, and storage functions when the phone is used to place a call. The user's manual notes that the phone "keeps lists of incoming and outgoing calls, even for calls that did not connect," and "displays the phone number for incoming calls in [the] phone's external and internal displays." Additionally, the phone keeps track of the "Network connection time," which is "the elapsed time from the moment [the user] connect[s] to [the] service provider's network to the moment [the user] end[s] the call by pressing [the end key]." This counting function alone is sufficient to support a finding that the phone is performing logical and arithmetic operations when used to place calls.

The same is true when the phone is used to send text messages. Most fundamentally, the phone stores sets of characters that are available to a user when typing a message. As the user types, the phone keeps track of the user's past inputs and displays the "entered text," i.e., the message being composed. The user may also delete characters previously entered, either "one letter at a time" or all at once. In addition, the phone allows the users to "set different primary and secondary text entry modes, and easily switch between modes as needed when [they] enter data or compose a message," including "iTAP" mode which uses "software" to "predict[ ] each word" as it is entered. These capabilities all support the district court's finding that the phone performed arithmetic, logical, and storage functions when Kramer used it to send text messages to the victim.

For these reasons, we affirm Kramer's sentence.

United States v. Todd Franklin Lewis

605 F.3d 395 (6th Cir. 2010)

Kennedy, Circuit Judge.

Todd Franklin Lewis pleaded guilty to transporting a visual depiction of a minor engaged in sexually explicit conduct. At sentencing, Lewis unsuccessfully challenged the two-level guideline sentence enhancement the court imposed for his use of a computer in commission of the crime of conviction. Lewis now appeals the ruling of the court as to this enhancement.

On April 13, 2007, United States Secret Service Special Agent Eric Adams logged on to the Yahoo! Internet chat room "Fetishes." Using the undercover name "miamimisswith2," Agent Adams posed as a 35-year-old adult female with two young daughters ages 9 and 12. Another user with the screenname "sigmadogman" then initiated a conversation via instant messaging with Agent Adams. "Sigmadogman" indicated that he was a 42-year-old man from Michigan and used graphic language to indicate his interest in engaging in sexual acts with Agent Adams' fictional daughters. During this chat, "sigmadogman" also sent at least twenty different images to "miamimisswith2" that depicted various sexual acts. Agent Adams later sent these images to the National Center for Missing and Exploited Children, who determined that at least six of the images qualified as child pornography involving female minors ages 8 and 12.

On April 23, 2007, Agent Adams had another undercover conversation with "sigmadogman" about the prospect of him traveling to Miami to have sexual intercourse with the two fictional daughters of "miamimisswith2." In this conversation, "sigmadogman" indicated that he was willing to travel in May 2007 and would pay $1300 to be able to have sexual intercourse for an entire week with both daughters and with "miamimisswith2" herself.

Meanwhile, Agent Adams obtained a subpoena of Yahoo! Legal Compliance in order to procure customer and registration information for the user name "sigmadogman." On May 1, 2007, Yahoo! Legal Compliance responded to the subpoena and indicated that the user name was registered to Todd Lewis in Kalkaska, Michigan, and remained active. Yahoo! also provided the IP addresses that were used by "sigmadogman" on the days in question. Agent Adams then located and subpoenaed the Internet provider of these IP addresses, who eventually revealed that the addresses in question had been assigned to Todd Lewis on the days in which "sigmadogman" had "chatted" with Agent Adams.

[A] search warrant was [later] authorized and officers executed the warrant on December 11, 2007. Lewis was present during the search and was properly read his *Miranda* rights. Lewis waived his rights, however, and told officers that he possessed a large quantity of child pornography on his computer and had in fact chatted with "miamimisswith2" about traveling to Florida and paying for sexual intercourse with her and her children. Lewis's computer was seized, and a subsequent forensic examination of it revealed that it stored at least fifteen images of child pornography.

Lewis argues that the district court committed reversible error by applying a two-level sentence enhancement under U.S.S.G. § 2G2.2(b)(6) for his use of a computer to transmit the illicit images. Lewis claims that this enhancement amounts to impermissible double-counting in his case because use of a computer is already an inherent element of the crime of conviction itself. We disagree.

Lewis pleaded guilty to violating 18 U.S.C. § 2252(a)(1), which states the following:

(a) Any person who—

(1) knowingly transports or ships using any means or facility of interstate or foreign commerce or in or affecting interstate or foreign commerce *by any means including by computer or mails*, any visual depiction, if—

(A) the producing of such visual depiction involves the use of a minor engaging in sexually explicit conduct; and

(B) such visual depiction is of such conduct;

. . .

shall be punished as provided in subsection (b) of this section.

The sentencing guidelines, meanwhile, provide a two-point enhancement to a defendant's total offense level "[i]f the offense involved the use of a computer or an interactive computer service for the possession, transmission, receipt, or distribution of the material, or for accessing with intent to view the material." U.S.S.G. § 2G2.2(b)(6). Lewis points to the phrase "including by computer" in the text of 18 U.S.C. § 2252(a) and argues that use of a computer, at least in his case, was an element of the offense that the government had to prove. Therefore, he argues, it amounted to double-counting when the sentencing judge also gave Lewis a two-level enhancement under § 2G2.2(b)(6) for the same computer use.

Lewis mischaracterizes the elements of a § 2252(a) offense. The fact that the statute articulates computer use as *one* means of transporting the proscribed depictions does not mean that use of a computer is a required element of the crime. Lewis did not need to use a computer in order to violate the criminal statute in question. According to the statutory language, Lewis would have violated § 2252(a) had he transported the depiction "by any means" affecting interstate commerce. Admittedly, Lewis's use of a computer did serve to satisfy the jurisdictional element of § 2252(a) in this case. But because Lewis could have violated the statute without using a computer, we cannot say that computer use is an element of the crime. The fact that he did use a computer, then, may serve as an offense characteristic affecting the determination of his sentence, *see* U.S.S.G. § 1B1.3(a)(1) (including as relevant conduct all of defendant's acts that "occurred during the commission of the offense of conviction"), and which may result in an additional sentence enhancement.

This position is bolstered by the fact that the U.S.S.G. § 2G2.2(b)(6) enhancement for using a computer aims at punishing a distinct harm beyond the mere transmission of child pornography. Specifically, "[d]istributing child pornography through computers is particularly harmful because it can reach an almost limitless audience. Because of its wide dissemination and instantaneous transmission, computer-assisted trafficking is also more difficult for law enforcement officials to investigate and prosecute." As such, we cannot accept Lewis's position that enhancing his sentence for his use of a computer is double-counting when the enhancement is designed to address a distinct harm.

2. Special Skills

Section 3B1.3 of the Guidelines advises sentencing courts to increase a defendant's offense level by two "[i]f the defendant . . . used a special skill[] in a manner that significantly facilitated the commission or concealment of the offense." The commentary provides some guidance as to what qualifies as a special skill:

> "Special skill" refers to a skill not possessed by members of the general public and usually requiring substantial education, training or licensing. Examples would include pilots, lawyers, doctors, accountants, chemists, and demolition experts.

U.S.S.G. § 3B1.3, cmt. n.4. "A defendant does not need to have formal education or professional stature to have a special skill within the meaning of § 3B1.3[;] a special skill can be derived from experience or from self-tutelage." *United States v. Nelson-Rodriguez*, 319 F.3d 12, 58 (1st Cir. 2003).

United States v. Kent Aoki Lee

296 F.3d 792 (9th Cir. 2002)

KLEINFELD, CIRCUIT JUDGE.

The Honolulu Marathon Association has a web site at "www.honolulu-marathon .org." During the relevant time, U.S. residents could use the site to register for the Honolulu Marathon and pay the registration fee online. Although many Japanese enter the race, the site did not permit online registration from Japan, but told Japanese entrants to register through an office in Japan.

Lee lived in Honolulu, where he owned a video rental store. Lee came up with a scheme to sell marathon services to the marathon's Japanese market. Lee owned a computer server, which he kept on the premises of an internet service provider with whom he had a dial-up internet account. He registered the domain name "www .honolulu-marathon.com" and created a site almost identical to the official Honolulu Marathon site by copying its files onto his server. While the official site did not permit online registration from Japan, Lee's site contained an online registration form written in Japanese on which runners could enter personal information and credit card information. While the official registration fee was $65, Lee's site charged $165. The extra $100 over the registration fee covered a package including transportation to the race site, a meal, and a tour. Of course, none of this was legitimate, since Lee's web site and registration package were not authorized by the Honolulu Marathon Association. Seventeen people tried to register through Lee's site.

Lee's scheme was uncovered and he pleaded guilty to one count of wire fraud. The main issue at sentencing was whether the district court could impose the special skills adjustment based on Lee's use of computer skills in creating his phony site.

Lee created his phony site by copying the legitimate site's files onto his computer server. Web sites consist of multiple web pages, which consist of individual computer files written in "hypertext markup language," or "HTML." The HTML files constituting a web site are located through a directory on a computer server. A computer directory is like a card in an old-fashioned library catalog, that tells where to find a book on a shelf. However a site's HTML files are referenced, they are linked together in the directory to create the whole web site. These links reflect the specific location of individual files within the server's structure of directories and subdirectories. The graphics on a web page are actually individual computer files to which that page's HTML file links, causing them to appear when the web page is displayed. An individual graphic file may be in the same directory as the HTML file to which it's linked, or in a subdirectory, or on another computer server altogether, and the link reflects that specific location. To copy a web site onto another computer server, it's not enough to copy the HTML file and the graphics for each web page. The copier must also recreate the directory structure of the original site or edit the links in the HTML files to reflect the different directory structure.

The creator of the genuine Honolulu Marathon site testified that Lee could have copied most of the site without knowing much about its directory structure, by using off-the-shelf software such as Microsoft's *FrontPage 98*, aided by a general circulation book such as *Front Page 98 for Dummies.* She also testified that a program like *FrontPage* would have written a line of code into the fake site's HTML files, indicating that it had been used. There weren't any such lines of code in the HTML files on Lee's site, suggesting that he didn't use this easy approach to copying the site. The creator of the authorized web site also testified that Lee could have pirated the site, much more slowly and laboriously, by using a text editor to copy it page by page (there were 130 individual web pages) and recreating the original site's directory structure so that each web page would properly display graphics and link to the other pages on the site. The legitimate site had two features, databases containing entrants' registration information and a list of past race results, that Lee could not copy onto his phony site, so he linked to those features on the genuine site so that they would appear to be part of his fake web site.

Lee's phony site contained one feature that was not on the genuine site, the online entry form that allowed residents of Japan to sign up for the marathon and provide a credit card account number to be billed for payment of the entry fee. The information entered on this form was processed using a "script," which is a program written in "common gateway interface," or "CGI," a programming language. The CGI script used by Lee's phony site didn't directly charge credit cards. It just stored the credit card data in a file on Lee's server, so that Lee could manually charge the cards later. (This database file was password protected, which the government's witness testified would require some knowledge of the server's operating system.) An excerpt of *FrontPage 98 for Dummies* that was read into the record told readers that to do CGI scripts, they should get help from someone experienced with computer programming. The official site's creator testified that writing a CGI form-handling script from scratch would have required significant programming expertise, but that modifying an existing script would have been much easier. She also testified that CGI scripts could be downloaded from the internet, and that web sites could be found that advised how to modify scripts to suit particular online forms.

The district court did not make a finding as to whether Lee copied the web site the easy way, such as by using *FrontPage 98* and *Front Page 98 for Dummies* (and perhaps deleting the software's identifying code using a text editor), or the hard way, using a text editor to copy the web site's HTML files page by page and figuring out the original site's directory structure. Nor did the court make a finding as to whether Lee downloaded the CGI script for his online form from the internet or made it himself from scratch, and if so, whether he had any expert assistance.

Nor did the court make a finding as to whether Lee or his internet service provider maintained his server. The district court found that Lee "was skilled at accessing and manipulating computer systems" and imposed the special skills enhancement. The adjustment raised the guideline sentencing range from six to twelve months to ten to sixteen months. This increase deprived the district court of the sentencing option of imposing no imprisonment.

We said in another special skills adjustment case, *United States v. Petersen*, [98 F.3d 502 (9th Cir. 1996),] in dictum that we now adopt, that "[b]ecause a district court's determination that a defendant's particular abilities constitute a 'special skill' is essentially a matter of 'application of the guidelines to the facts,' ... an abuse of discretion standard should guide our review," except where "questions of law may arise in deciding whether a defendant used a special skill," for which review is non-deferential.

The special skill adjustment provides for a two-level increase "[i]f the defendant abused a position of public or private trust, or used a special skill, in a manner that significantly facilitated the commission or concealment of the offense." [U.S.S.G. § 3B1.3 (2000)] The application note defining "special skill" says that it is "a skill not possessed by members of the general public and usually requiring substantial education, training, or licensing. Examples would include pilots, lawyers, doctors, accountants, chemists, and demolition experts." [*Id.*, commentary, application note 3.]

The district court based its imposition of the adjustment on our decision in *Petersen*. The issue in the case at bar is whether Lee was more like the defendant in *Petersen*, or more like the defendant in another of our special skills cases, going the other way, *United States v. Green*[, 962 F.2d 938 (9th Cir. 1992)]. We conclude that the scope of discretion was not broad enough, in view of the limited findings, to treat this case like *Petersen*, and that it has to be put in the same class as *Green*, where we held that it was an abuse of discretion to impose the special skills adjustment. This conclusion keeps our circuit's law consistent with that of the Sixth Circuit, which held in *United States v. Godman*, [223 F.3d 320 (6th Cir. 2000),] that a level of computer expertise like Lee's did not justify imposition of the adjustment.

The defendant in *Petersen*, which upheld the adjustment, was an expert hacker. He hacked into a national credit reporting agency's computer system and stole personal information that he used to order fraudulent credit cards. Then he hacked into a telephone company's computers, seized control of the telephone lines to a radio station, and arranged for himself and his confederates to be the callers who "won" two Porsches, $40,000, and two trips to Hawaii in a radio call-in contest. Then he hacked into a national commercial lender's computer and got it to wire $150,000 to him through two other banks. This goes far beyond the computer skills of a clever high school youth or even many people who earn their livings as computer technicians and software engineers. The district court found that Petersen had "extraordinary knowledge of how computers work and how information is stored, how information is retrieved, and how the security of those systems can be preserved or invaded" and imposed the special skill adjustment. We affirmed, holding that "[d]espite Petersen's lack of formal training or licensing, his sophisticated computer skills reasonably can be equated to the skills possessed by pilots, lawyers, chemists, and demolition experts" for purposes of the special skills adjustment.

In a footnote, we went out of our way in *Petersen* to caution against routine application of the special skills enhancement to people with computer skills:

> We do not intend to suggest that the ability to use or access computers would support a "special skill" adjustment under all circumstances. Computer skills cover a wide spectrum of ability. Only where a defendant's computer skills are particularly sophisticated do they correspond to the Sentencing Commission's examples of "special skills"—lawyer, doctor, pilot, etc. Courts should be particularly cautious in imposing special skills adjustments where substantial education, training, or licensing is not involved.

This footnote distinguishes *Petersen* from the case at bar, because Lee's skills are not "particularly sophisticated" like Petersen's, and unlike Petersen's, don't "correspond to the Sentencing Commission's examples of 'special skills'—lawyer, doctor, pilot, etc." As we said in *Petersen*, "where substantial education, training or licensing is not involved," district courts must be especially cautious about imposing the adjustment.

Petersen distinguished *Green*, where we reversed a special skills adjustment. Green took graphic design classes, learned from an instructor about paper that could be used for currency and about how it could be properly cut, ordered the special paper from a paper company (which tipped off the Secret Service), and took numerous photographs of currency, in the course of his counterfeiting scheme. We held that the printing and photographic skills were not so "special" as to permit the district court to impose the adjustment, saying it's not enough that "the offense was difficult to commit or required a special skill to complete."

In *Godman*, the Sixth Circuit considered *Petersen* and quoted and followed our limiting footnote that we quote above. Like Green, Godman was a counterfeiter, but Godman used an off-the-shelf professional page publishing program, Adobe PageMaker, with a scanner and a color inkjet printer. He'd learned PageMaker in a week, and had specialized computer experience preparing and repeatedly updating a color catalog. *Godman* held that the special skills adjustment could not properly be imposed, because Godman's level of computer skills was not analogous to the level of skill possessed by the lawyers, doctors, pilots, etc. listed in the application note. The Sixth Circuit held that the district court erred by stressing "overmuch" that Godman's skills were not shared by the general public: "As the Application Note's reference to the substantial training of such professionals as doctors and accountants suggests, emphasis is better placed on the difficulty with which a particular skill is acquired." The Sixth Circuit emphasized that "[s]uch skills are acquired through months (or years) of training, or the equivalent in self-tutelage."

Our own cases have suggested factors that might make a skill "special" for purposes of this sentencing adjustment, including a "public trust" rationale, the level of sophistication, and special educational or licensing requirements. But this adjustment becomes open-ended to the point of meaninglessness if the phrase "special skill" is taken out of its context. There probably isn't an occupation on earth that doesn't involve some special skill not possessed by people outside it, and few of us who sit as judges would know how to do the work of most of the people who appear before us. So asking whether a skill is "special," in the sense of not being common among the adult population, like driving a car, doesn't get us very far toward deciding any cases.

And focusing much on the "specialness" of a skill is also hard to reconcile with our precedents. In *United States v. Harper,* [33 F.3d 1143 (9th Cir. 1994),] the defendant's skills were very special indeed. The robber had worked for both a bank and an ATM service company, and used the knowledge gained in both occupations to come up with a unique scheme to rob an ATM. At just the right time for the last service call of the day, when the ATM service office would empty out while the robbery was going on, she made a withdrawal from an ATM but didn't take the money. She knew that leaving the cash would cause the ATM to shut itself down and generate a service call, which would put technicians on the site, and that they would open the machine so that she and her confederates could rob it. As skills go, Harper's were quite special, but we reversed the sentence because they weren't like those of "pilots, lawyers, doctors, accountants, chemists and demolition experts."

Our cases are best reconciled, and this sentencing guideline is best read, as a two-part test. The test is not just whether the skill is "not possessed by members of the general public," but also, as a *sine qua non,* whether it is a skill "usually requiring substantial education, training, or licensing." The application note's reference to "pilots, lawyers, doctors, accountants, chemists, and demolition experts" requires reasoning by analogy, not just reference to dictionary definitions of "special" and "skill." The special skill adjustment falls within the same guideline as an adjustment for people who abuse a "position of public or private trust, or used a special skill." The application notes limit the position of trust adjustment to people with "professional or managerial discretion," analogous to attorneys who hold their clients' money in trust, physicians who treat patients, and "executives" (but not tellers) who manage a bank's loans. The application note for special skills parallels the application note for positions of trust in its reference to people trained or employed at a high level.

Lee was a video rental store operator who copied a web site. The findings don't establish whether he used off-the-shelf software or had to know more about programming, but it doesn't matter because either way, his level of sophistication was nothing like Petersen's. His skills were more like Green's or Godman's than Petersen's, and not in the class of "pilots, lawyers, doctors, accountants, chemists, and demolition experts." Thus, under our precedents and the guideline's application notes, the district court's imposition of the special skills adjustment was not supported by the findings. We therefore reverse and remand for resentencing.

Notes

This book and course have now gone full circle and the Use of a Computer and Special Skills guidelines once again underline a fundamental question: Are crimes committed with a computer "special" requiring enhanced treatment of offenders (or, as discussed earlier, requiring special rules for the search and seizure of digital devices)? The Use of Computer guideline, as construed in *Lewis*, maintains that persons who commit crimes using a computer will be treated as more culpable. Is that premise for enhanced sentencing valid? The Special Skills guideline, construed in *Lee*, focuses on the sophistication of the user. Who fits into that guideline? Is it a moving target, that is, what constitutes a special skill today becomes a common one tomorrow? Why should such a user be treated as more culpable?

————————

§ 20.2 Sentencing in Child Pornography Cases

United States v. Jerry Paull

551 F.3d 516 (6th Cir. 2009)

Boggs, Chief Judge.

Jerry Paull was convicted pursuant to a conditional plea agreement on four counts of knowing possession of child pornography under the Child Pornography Protection Act, 18 U.S.C. § 2252 *et seq.* and sentenced to imprisonment for 210 months. He appeals his sentence, claiming that the district court incorrectly calculated his guideline range and abused its discretion in failing to vary downward in light of his efforts at rehabilitation and his poor health. For the reasons discussed below we affirm Paull's conviction and his sentence.

[Special Agent Hagan obtained a search warrant for Paull's residence.] In the course of the search, officers found a garbage can in the garage with "a number of double and triple bagged bundles" in it. In those bundles "there were printed images of child pornography" and "a number of floppy disks, a number of CDs, videotapes, as well as a number of computer printouts of Mr. Paull's." The collection of child pornography totaled over 3,700 images, not including the video tapes. Agent Hagan took this evidence from the garage into the kitchen and laid it on the table in front of Paull, telling him that she no longer needed "to talk with [him] because . . . [she] had the evidence there" and then left the kitchen. Paull immediately requested to speak with her and she returned to the kitchen.

He proceeded to give an oral statement taking responsibility for "all the items that were in the garage [and admitting] that they contained child pornography." He subsequently provided a written statement that memorialized his confession and explained his history of involvement with child pornography. Paull entered a conditional plea of guilty on all four counts of the indictment, reserving his right to appeal his sentence. The agreement stipulated to an applicable offense level of 30, which included several enhancements based on the circumstances of the crime (enhancements of two levels for images containing a prepubescent minor, four levels for images portraying sadistic/masochistic conduct; two levels for the use of computer; and five levels for the possession of over 600 illegal images). The agreement also left open the possibility of additional reductions or enhancements to this agreed-upon offense level. To that end, the Pre-Sentence Investigation Report recommended two additional enhancements: two levels for obstruction of justice under U.S.S.G. § 3C1.1 and five levels for a pattern of activity involving the sexual abuse of a minor under U.S.S.G. § 2G2.2(b)(5). The report also recommended against a downward adjustment for acceptance of responsibility pursuant to U.S.S.G. § 3E1.1(a) because of Paull's obstruction of justice. The addition of these adjustments yielded an offense level of 37 and a guideline range of 210 to 262 months of imprisonment.

At the sentencing hearing, the district court made findings of fact and adopted the report's recommendations. First, the court held that Paull had not demonstrated sufficient acceptance of responsibility to support a reduction because he only cooperated when it was in his best interest and because his behavior supported an obstruction of justice enhancement.

Indeed, the court held that two courses of behavior supported the upward adjustment for obstruction of justice. The court's credibility determination at the suppression hearing supported a finding that Paull perjured himself in giving his version of events. The court also found Paull had consistently "wiped the computer for the reason . . . that he could be caught possessing this material."

The court held that the evidence supported the adjustment for a pattern of activity involving the sexual abuse of a minor. The court based this enhancement on allegations from Andrew Barry, a friend of Paull's son, that during the early and mid-80s, Paull molested him. The court relied on a letter sent from Barry to the United States Attorney's office and testimony from the probation officer assigned to the case that recounted telephone interviews with Barry and several of his family members and concluded the allegations were credible.

The district court then sentenced Paull to 210 months in prison, the bottom of the guideline range for an offense level of 37. In doing so, the court rejected Paull's argument for downward variances based on his poor health, his on-going rehabilitation, and his own history of child sexual abuse. The court explained that "your age, your health, your lack of a criminal history under [18 U.S.C. §] 3553 are factors that the Court must and I have considered. I also consider the fact that there's mandatory minimum sentences in this case that are required." But in addition, § 3553 requires "taking into consideration the information . . . about what happens to the victims. . . ." The court emphasized that Paull demonstrated no "empathy, emotion, sorrow, compassion for those children, those thousands of children that are put in this position by people in a place of trust." The court concluded that because the § 3553(a) factors point in opposite directions, "the only fair thing to do is to sentence you within the guidelines."

Paull claims that the sentence was substantively unreasonable. Our circuit takes a deferential approach to this type of substantive sentencing challenge. This is especially true in cases, like Paull's, where the district court agrees with the recommendations in the sentencing guidelines. In such cases "this court has embraced an appellate presumption of reasonableness" that the defendant must rebut.

Paull attempts to do so with two arguments. First, he alleges that the sentence is greater than necessary to serve the purposes of §3553(a). Second, he argues that the district court over-emphasized the impact on victims and inappropriately discounted factors that weighed for a downward variance. Taken in concert and at full face value these claims make at least a plausible argument that the presumption has been rebutted: Paull is an old and sick man who has been extraordinary in his attempts to rehabilitate himself and but for the district court's over-emphasis on the impact on the victims he should have received a lighter sentence. The record, however, also contains material that belies this characterization of the considerations relevant to Paull's sentencing. The district court's summary illustrates the competing factors:

> Now, I could vary up, and that's something I considered in this case due to the nature of the volume and the number of images you had and the extent of what you did, or I could vary down because of your age, your health, and your lack of criminal background and, in fact, the things that you've done since your arrest to try to prevent yourself from ever engaging in this type of conduct.

> But I want you to know I've taken all of that into consideration, and I think the only fair thing to do is sentence you within the guidelines.

Far from being impermissible or inadequate, this analysis of the considerations the court found most important—the defendant's circumstances and the seriousness of the crime—is just the sort of balancing a sentencing court should be doing. Indeed, this is what is meant by the "on-the-scene assessment of the competing considerations" to which we are to defer.

More broadly, we cannot say, in light of our deferential review, that the sentence of 210 months of imprisonment was unreasonable. It is at the lower end of the guidelines range and accurately reflects both the reasons to vary downward and the severity of Paull's offense. To be sure, there are reasons here—as in any sentencing case—to be sympathetic to the defendant. Paull is a former minister who has admirably worked with a sex addiction group at rehabilitating himself and others, and the combination of his age, his various health problems, and the length of his sentence mean he almost certainly will die in jail or shortly after his sentence expires. But our role as an appellate court is not "to impose sentences in the first instance or to second guess the individualized sentencing discretion when it appropriately relies on the §3553(a) factors. . . ." Indeed, we routinely uphold the sentences of sick defendants and the sentences of rehabilitated defendants over their appeals for a variance. This is because we are reviewing for unreasonable sentences, not sympathetic defendants. Defendants such as Paull are sentenced only after their crime, the *actual* possession of images of *actual* young children depicting *actual* sexual abuse has been proven or they, as in Paull's case, have admitted to guilt, pursuant to a constitutionally prescribed process designed to guard against erroneous conviction.

Under these circumstances, it seems to me that the dissent's suggestion that such convictions "border[] on" "the thousands of witchcraft trials and burnings conducted in Europe and here from the Thirteenth to the Eighteenth Centuries" cannot be maintained, without some risk of terminological inexactitude.

Merritt, Circuit Judge, dissenting.

As a recent October 23, 2008, *Wall Street Journal* article by Amir Efrati points out, our federal legal system has lost its bearings on the subject of computer-based child pornography. Our "social revulsion" against these "misfits" downloading these images is perhaps somewhat more rational than the thousands of witchcraft trials and burnings conducted in Europe and here from the Thirteenth to the Eighteenth Centuries, but it borders on the same thing. In 2008 alone the Department of Justice has brought 2,200 cases like this one in the federal courts. Some trial and appellate judges are sending these mentally ill defendants like Paull to federal prison for very long sentences. But the 17½ year sentence for Paull may be the longest yet. He is a 65-year-old, psychologically disabled, former minister with Type 1 diabetes with many complications. [n.1][4] How could this sentence be "not greater than necessary" to punish this crime?

[The dissent argued that the lower court relied on impermissible information in fashioning the sentence and] would, therefore, reverse the judgment of the district court and remand for re-sentencing based only on the facts corresponding to the defendant's guilty plea.

APPENDIX

The defendant married Donna Rankin in June 11, 1966, in Tuscarawas County, Ohio. Ms. Rankin is 62 years old and is a retired school teacher. The couple have two children: Katherine, who is 40 years old and resides in North Carolina; and Eric, who is 35 years old and resides in Tennessee. Mr. Paull indicated Katherine is not his biological daughter. Rather, she is the daughter of his brother, Phillip, whom the defendant and his wife obtained custody of when she was approximately 18 months old and eventually adopted when she was 5 years old. . . . According to information received from the defendant's physician, Mr. Paull has suffered from Type I diabetes for approximately 30 years, with complications resulting in retinopathy, neuropathy and frequent severe hypoglycemia and seizures. Mr. Paull also suffers from osteoporosis and Meniere's disease which results in severe vertigo. The defendant also

---

4. [n.1] *See* the portions of the pre-sentence report concerning Mr. Paull and his problems attached as an appendix.

suffers from hypercholesterolemia, and has a history of bronchiectasis. In 2007, the defendant was also diagnosed with coronary artery disease.

Since 1994, the defendant's diabetes has required him to use an insulin pump to help regulate his glucose. According to a diagnosis in 2004 by the defendant's physician, Dr. Sheehan, individuals with cardiac autonomic neuropathy similar to Mr. Paull can have a 50% 5 year mortality rate. The doctor also stated due to the defendant's Meniere's disease, he is at significant risk for acute vertigo and falls which, given his osteoporosis, could have disastrous consequences such as bone fractures. Mr. Paull is also prone to pneumonia based on having bronchiectasis.

Mr. Paull is currently prescribed Novalog, Insulin Pump, Plavis, Pravacol, Lisinopril, Actonel Tabs 4, Dyazide, Meclizine, Diazepam (Valium), Nitroquick, Ketoconazole Cream, Ambien CR, and Tiamcinolone Acetone Cream.

In 1991, the defendant did suffer a fall due to his Meniere disease in which he fractured his left shoulder and hip, requiring surgery to both. The defendant has also undergone Angioplasty and had two stents placed in his heart after suffering a heart attack in January 2007. Mr. Paull is currently participating in cardiovascular therapy. The defendant stated he as prone to episodes of vertigo regularly and was prescribed Valium to help reduce the frequency of the attacks. Mr. Paull stated it is unknown what triggers his episodes of vertigo and indicated he last experienced an episode in January 2007.

United States v. Justin K. Dorvee
616 F.3d 174 (2d Cir. 2010)

B.D. Parker, Jr., Circuit Judge:

Justin K. Dorvee pled guilty to one count of distribution of child pornography. He was sentenced by the United States District Court for the Northern District of New York to the statutory maximum of 240 months.

In his plea agreement, Dorvee admitted the following facts. On or about April 14, 2007, he began conversing online with someone he believed was a 14-year-old male named "Matt," but who in fact was an undercover officer for the Maryland Heights, Missouri Police Department. During this conversation, Dorvee discussed, among other things, his fetish for young boys' feet, and the fact that he had a "crush on males that are too young for him." Dorvee also sent Matt a number of computer images depicting boys between the ages of 11 and 15, which were not sexually explicit.

Between October and June 2007, Dorvee conversed online with someone he believed was a 14 year-old male named "Seth" but who, again, was an undercover officer, this time with the Warren County, New York Sheriff's Office. The two engaged in sexually explicit conversations and Dorvee also sent him videos and images via the internet, including videos of minors engaging in sexually explicit conduct, and of Dorvee masturbating. During their conversations, Dorvee indicated that he would like to meet, to photograph, and to engage in sexual conduct with Seth. On October 19, 2007, Dorvee arranged to meet Seth, and was arrested when he arrived for the meeting. At the time of his arrest, Dorvee had a camera in his back-pack that he said he intended to use to photograph Seth's feet and penis.

A search warrant executed at Dorvee's residence yielded computer disks and a computer containing several thousand still images and approximately 100 to 125 computer videos depicting minors engaged in sexually explicit conduct. Some of the images depicted prepubescent minors, and others depicted sadomasochistic conduct. Dorvee traded these videos and images on the internet with approximately 20 other individuals. The Presentence Investigation Report, prepared for the district court by the probation office, indicated that he admitted to taking approximately 300 non-explicit photographs of neighborhood children in public in an attempt to capture images of their feet.

The PSR initially calculated a Guidelines range of 262 to 327 months, based on a total offense level of 39 and a criminal history category of I. Importantly, however, the PSR noted that because the statutory maximum for the offense of conviction is twenty years of incarceration, "the Guideline range is 240 months." In reaching its preliminary calculation of 262 to 327 months, the PSR stated that the base offense level was 22, and applied the following sentencing enhancements: (1) a two-level increase pursuant to U.S.S.G. §2G2.2(b)(2) because "the material involved a prepubescent minor or a minor who had not attained the age of 12 years"; (2) a seven-level increase pursuant to §2G2.2(b)(3)(E) because the offense involved "[d]istribution to a minor that was intended to persuade, induce, entice, coerce, or facilitate the travel of, the minor to engage in prohibited sexual conduct"; (3) a four-level increase pursuant to §2G2.2(b)(4) because "the offense involved material that portrays sadistic or masochistic conduct or other depictions of violence"; (4) a two-level increase pursuant to §2G2.2(b)(6) because the offense "involved the use of a computer"; and (5) a five-level increase pursuant to §2G2.2(b)(7) because the offense involved 600 or more images. Pursuant to §3E1.1, the PSR subtracted three levels for acceptance of responsibility, resulting in a total offense level of 39. U.S.S.G. §2G2.2(b).

The [United States Sentencing] Commission has often openly opposed these Congressionally directed changes. In 1996, the Commission criticized the two-level computer enhancement (which is currently set forth at §2G2.2(b)(6) and was adopted pursuant to statutory direction) on the ground that it fails to distinguish serious commercial distributors of online pornography from more run-of-the-mill users.[n.8][5] Speaking broadly, the Commission has also noted that "specific direc-

---

5. [n.8] Congress directed that the Guidelines be amended to include a computer enhance-ment of *at least* two levels when it passed the Sex Crimes Against Children Prevention Act of 1995. The SCACPA also required the Commission to submit a report to Congress concerning offenses involving child pornography, and although the Commission criticized the enhancement in that statutorily-required report, Congress was not persuaded by the Commission's advice.

tives to the Commission to amend the guidelines make it difficult to gauge the effectiveness of any particular policy change, or to disentangle the influences of the Commission from those of Congress."

The § 2G2.2 sentencing enhancements cobbled together through this process routinely result in Guidelines projections near or exceeding the statutory maximum, even in run-of-the-mill cases. The base offense level for distribution of child pornography, which in 1991 was 13, has been gradually increased to 22 as the Commission has attempted to square the Guidelines with Congress's various directives. On top of that, many of the § 2G2.2 enhancements apply in nearly all cases. Of all sentences under § 2G2.2 in 2009, 94.8% involved an image of a prepubescent minor (qualifying for a two-level increase pursuant to § 2G2.2(b)(2)), 97.2% involved a computer (qualifying for a two-level increase pursuant to § 2G2.2(b)(6)), 73.4% involved an image depicting sadistic or masochistic conduct or other forms of violence (qualifying for a four-level enhancement pursuant to § 2G2.2(b)(4)), and 63.1% involved 600 or more images (qualifying for a five-level enhancement pursuant to § 2G2.2(b)(7)(D)).[n.9][6] In sum, these enhancements, which apply to the vast majority of defendants sentenced under § 2G2.2, add up to 13 levels, resulting in a typical total offense level of 35.

An ordinary first-time offender is therefore likely to qualify for a sentence of at least 168 to 210 months, rapidly approaching the statutory maximum, based solely on sentencing enhancements that are all but inherent to the crime of conviction. Consequently, adherence to the Guidelines results in virtually no distinction between the sentences for defendants like Dorvee, and the sentences for the most dangerous offenders who, for example, distribute child pornography for pecuniary gain and who fall in higher criminal history categories. This result is fundamentally incompatible with [18 U.S.C.] § 3553(a). By concentrating all offenders at or near the statutory maximum, § 2G2.2 eviscerates the fundamental statutory requirement in § 3553(a) that district courts consider "the nature and circumstances of the offense and the history and characteristics of the defendant" and violates the principle that courts must guard against unwarranted similarities among sentences for defendants who have been found guilty of dissimilar conduct.

The irrationality in § 2G2.2 is easily illustrated by two examples. Had Dorvee actually engaged in sexual conduct with a minor, his applicable Guidelines range could have been considerably lower. An adult who intentionally seeks out and contacts a twelve year-old on the internet, convinces the child to meet and to cross state lines for the meeting, and then engages in repeated sex with the child, would qualify for a total offense level of 34, resulting in a Guidelines range of 151 to 188 months in prison for an offender with a criminal history category of I. Dorvee, who never

---

6. [n.9] While this number may seem high, the large number of images possessed by individuals convicted of child pornography likely stems from the fact that the Guidelines count each video as 75 images. It is also worth noting that 96.6% of defendants received at least a two-level enhancement based on the number of images possessed.

had any contact with an actual minor, was sentenced by the district court to 233 months of incarceration. What is highly ironic is that the district court justified its 233-month sentence based on its fear that Dorvee *would* sexually assault a child in the future.

A defendant convicted under 18 U.S.C. § 2252A(a)(5) of possessing on his computer two nonviolent videos of seventeen-year-olds engaging in consensual sexual conduct qualifies for a base offense level of 18 under § 2G2.2(a)(1), a two-level enhancement for use of a computer under § 2G2.2(b)(6), and a three-level enhancement for number of images under § 2G2.2(b)(7)(B). Even with no criminal history, this individual's total offense level of 23 would result in a Guidelines sentence of 46 to 57 months. This is the same Guidelines sentence as that for an individual with prior criminal convictions placing him in a criminal history category of II, who has been convicted of an aggravated assault with a firearm that resulted in bodily injury.

The Sentencing Commission is, of course, an agency like any other. Because the Commission's Guidelines lack the force of law, sentencing courts are no longer bound to apply the Guidelines. But, in light of the Sentencing Commission's relative expertise, sentencing courts "must consult those Guidelines and take them into account when sentencing." This deference to the Guidelines is not absolute or even controlling; rather, like our review of many agency determinations, "[t]he weight of such a judgment in a particular case will depend upon the thoroughness evident in [the agency's] consideration, the validity of its reasoning, its consistency with earlier and later pronouncements, and all those factors which give it power to persuade, if lacking power to control." On a case-by-case basis, courts are to consider the "specialized experience and broader investigations and information available to the agency" as it compares to their own technical or other expertise at sentencing and, on that basis, determine the weight owed to the Commission's Guidelines.

In keeping with these principles, in *Kimbrough* [*v. United States*, 552 U.S. 85 (2007),] the Supreme Court held that it was not an abuse of discretion for a district court to conclude that the Guidelines' treatment of crack cocaine convictions typically yields a sentence "greater than necessary" to achieve the goals of § 3553(a), because those particular Guidelines "do not exemplify the Commission's exercise of its characteristic institutional role." As we have explained here, the same is true for the child pornography enhancements found at § 2G2.2. Following *Kimbrough*, we held that "a district court may vary from the Guidelines range based solely on a policy disagreement with the Guidelines, even where that disagreement applies to a wide class of offenders or offenses." That analysis applies with full force to § 2G2.2.

District judges are encouraged to take seriously the broad discretion they possess in fashioning sentences under § 2G2.2—ones that can range from non-custodial sentences to the statutory maximum—bearing in mind that they are dealing with an eccentric Guideline of highly unusual provenance which, unless carefully applied, can easily generate unreasonable results. While we recognize that enforcing federal prohibitions on child pornography is of the utmost importance, it would be manifestly unjust to let Dorvee's sentence stand. We conclude that Dorvee's sentence was substantively unreasonable and, accordingly, must be revisited by the district court on remand.

———————

§ 20.3 Restrictions on Internet Use or Using Computers

Lester Gerard Packingham v. North Carolina

137 S. Ct. 1730 (2017)

Justice KENNEDY delivered the opinion of the Court.

In 2008, North Carolina enacted a statute making it a felony for a registered sex offender to gain access to a number of websites, including commonplace social media websites like Facebook and Twitter. The question presented is whether that law is permissible under the First Amendment's Free Speech Clause, applicable to the States under the Due Process Clause of the Fourteenth Amendment.

I

A

North Carolina law makes it a felony for a registered sex offender "to access a commercial social networking Web site where the sex offender knows that the site permits minor children to become members or to create or maintain personal Web pages." N.C. Gen. Stat. Ann. §§ 14–202.5(a), (e) (2015). A "commercial social networking Web site" is defined as a website that meets four criteria. First, it "[i]s operated by a person who derives revenue from membership fees, advertising, or other sources related to the operation of the Web site." Second, it "[f]acilitates the social introduction between two or more persons for the purposes of friendship, meeting other persons, or information exchanges." Third, it "[a]llows users to create Web pages or personal profiles that contain information such as the name or nickname of the user, photographs placed on the personal Web page by the user, other personal information about the user, and links to other personal Web pages on the commercial social networking Web site of friends or associates of the user that may be accessed by other users or visitors to the Web site." And fourth, it "[p]rovides users or visitors . . . mechanisms to communicate with other users, such as a message board, chat room, electronic mail, or instant messenger."

The statute includes two express exemptions. The statutory bar does not extend to websites that "[p]rovid[e] only one of the following discrete services: photo-sharing, electronic mail, instant messenger, or chat room or message board platform." The law also does not encompass websites that have as their "primary purpose the facilitation of commercial transactions involving goods or services between [their] members or visitors."

According to sources cited to the Court, §14–202.5 applies to about 20,000 people in North Carolina and the State has prosecuted over 1,000 people for violating it.

B

In 2002, petitioner Lester Gerard Packingham—then a 21-year-old college student—had sex with a 13-year-old girl. He pleaded guilty to taking indecent liberties with a child. Because this crime qualifies as "an offense against a minor," petitioner was required to register as a sex offender—a status that can endure for 30 years or more. As a registered sex offender, petitioner was barred under §14–202.5 from gaining access to commercial social networking sites.

In 2010, a state court dismissed a traffic ticket against petitioner. In response, he logged on to Facebook.com and posted the following statement on his personal profile:

> "Man God is Good! How about I got so much favor they dismissed the ticket before court even started? No fine, no court cost, no nothing spent.. . . . . Praise be to GOD, WOW! Thanks JESUS!"

At the time, a member of the Durham Police Department was investigating registered sex offenders who were thought to be violating §14–202.5. The officer noticed that a "'J.R. Gerrard'" had posted the statement quoted above. By checking court records, the officer discovered that a traffic citation for petitioner had been dismissed around the time of the post. Evidence obtained by search warrant confirmed the officer's suspicions that petitioner was J.R. Gerrard.

Petitioner was indicted by a grand jury for violating §14–202.5. The trial court denied his motion to dismiss the indictment on the grounds that the charge against him violated the First Amendment. Petitioner was ultimately convicted and given a suspended prison sentence. At no point during trial or sentencing did the State allege that petitioner contacted a minor—or committed any other illicit act—on the Internet.

Petitioner appealed to the Court of Appeals of North Carolina. That court struck down §14–202.5 on First Amendment grounds, explaining that the law is not narrowly tailored to serve the State's legitimate interest in protecting minors from sexual abuse. The North Carolina Supreme Court reversed, concluding that the law is "constitutional in all respects." The Court granted certiorari and now reverses.

II

A fundamental principle of the First Amendment is that all persons have access to places where they can speak and listen, and then, after reflection, speak and listen once more. The Court has sought to protect the right to speak in this spatial context. A basic rule, for example, is that a street or a park is a quintessential forum for the exercise of First Amendment rights. Even in the modern era, these places are still essential venues for public gatherings to celebrate some views, to protest others, or simply to learn and inquire.

While in the past there may have been difficulty in identifying the most important places (in a spatial sense) for the exchange of views, today the answer is clear. It is cyberspace—the "vast democratic forums of the Internet" in general, and social media in particular. Seven in ten American adults use at least one Internet social networking service. One of the most popular of these sites is Facebook, the site used by petitioner leading to his conviction in this case. According to sources cited to the Court in this case, Facebook has 1.79 billion active users. This is about three times the population of North America.

Social media offers "relatively unlimited, low-cost capacity for communication of all kinds." On Facebook, for example, users can debate religion and politics with their friends and neighbors or share vacation photos. On LinkedIn, users can look for work, advertise for employees, or review tips on entrepreneurship. And on Twitter, users can petition their elected representatives and otherwise engage with them in a direct manner. Indeed, Governors in all 50 States and almost every Member of Congress have set up accounts for this purpose. In short, social media users employ these websites to engage in a wide array of protected First Amendment activity on topics "as diverse as human thought."

The nature of a revolution in thought can be that, in its early stages, even its participants may be unaware of it. And when awareness comes, they still may be unable to know or foresee where its changes lead. Cf. D. Hawke, Benjamin Rush: Revolutionary Gadfly 341 (1971) (quoting Rush as observing: "'The American war is over; but this is far from being the case with the American revolution. On the contrary, nothing but the first act of the great drama is closed'"). So too here. While we now may be coming to the realization that the Cyber Age is a revolution of historic proportions, we cannot appreciate yet its full dimensions and vast potential to alter how we think, express ourselves, and define who we want to be. The forces and directions of the Internet are so new, so protean, and so far reaching that courts must be conscious that what they say today might be obsolete tomorrow.

This case is one of the first this Court has taken to address the relationship between the First Amendment and the modern Internet. As a result, the Court must exercise extreme caution before suggesting that the First Amendment provides scant protection for access to vast networks in that medium.

III

This background informs the analysis of the North Carolina statute at issue. Even making the assumption that the statute is content neutral and thus subject to intermediate scrutiny, the provision cannot stand. In order to survive intermediate scrutiny, a law must be "narrowly tailored to serve a significant governmental interest." In other words, the law must not "burden substantially more speech than is necessary to further the government's legitimate interests."

For centuries now, inventions heralded as advances in human progress have been exploited by the criminal mind. New technologies, all too soon, can become instruments used to commit serious crimes. The railroad is one example and the telephone another. So it will be with the Internet and social media.

There is also no doubt that, as this Court has recognized, "[t]he sexual abuse of a child is a most serious crime and an act repugnant to the moral instincts of a decent people." *Ashcroft v. Free Speech Coalition,* 535 U.S. 234, 244 (2002). And it is clear that a legislature "may pass valid laws to protect children" and other victims of sexual assault "from abuse." The government, of course, need not simply stand by and allow these evils to occur. But the assertion of a valid governmental interest "cannot, in every context, be insulated from all constitutional protections."

It is necessary to make two assumptions to resolve this case. First, given the broad wording of the North Carolina statute at issue, it might well bar access not only to commonplace social media websites but also to websites as varied as Amazon.com, Washingtonpost.com, and Webmd.com. The Court need not decide the precise scope of the statute. It is enough to assume that the law applies (as the State concedes it does) to social networking sites "as commonly understood"—that is, websites like Facebook, LinkedIn, and Twitter.

Second, this opinion should not be interpreted as barring a State from enacting more specific laws than the one at issue. Specific criminal acts are not protected speech even if speech is the means for their commission. Though the issue is not before the Court, it can be assumed that the First Amendment permits a State to enact specific, narrowly tailored laws that prohibit a sex offender from engaging in conduct that often presages a sexual crime, like contacting a minor or using a website to gather information about a minor. Specific laws of that type must be the State's first resort to ward off the serious harm that sexual crimes inflict. (Of importance, the troubling fact that the law imposes severe restrictions on persons who already have served their sentence and are no longer subject to the supervision of the criminal justice system is also not an issue before the Court.)

Even with these assumptions about the scope of the law and the State's interest, the statute here enacts a prohibition unprecedented in the scope of First Amendment speech it burdens. Social media allows users to gain access to information and communicate with one another about it on any subject that might come to mind. By prohibiting sex offenders from using those websites, North Carolina with one broad stroke bars access to what for many are the principal sources for knowing current events, checking ads for employment, speaking and listening in the modern public square, and otherwise exploring the vast realms of human thought and knowledge. These websites can provide perhaps the most powerful mechanisms available to a private citizen to make his or her voice heard. They allow a person with an Internet connection to "become a town crier with a voice that resonates farther than it could from any soapbox."

In sum, to foreclose access to social media altogether is to prevent the user from engaging in the legitimate exercise of First Amendment rights. It is unsettling to suggest that only a limited set of websites can be used even by persons who have completed their sentences. Even convicted criminals—and in some instances espe-cially convicted criminals—might receive legitimate benefits from these means for access to the world of ideas, in particular if they seek to reform and to pursue lawful and rewarding lives.

IV

The primary response from the State is that the law must be this broad to serve its preventative purpose of keeping convicted sex offenders away from vulnerable victims. The State has not, however, met its burden to show that this sweeping law is necessary or legitimate to serve that purpose.

It is instructive that no case or holding of this Court has approved of a statute as broad in its reach. The closest analogy that the State has cited is *Burson v. Freeman,* 504 U.S. 191 (1992). There, the Court upheld a prohibition on campaigning within 100 feet of a polling place. That case gives little or no support to the State. The law in *Burson* was a limited restriction that, in a context consistent with constitutional tradition, was enacted to protect another fundamental right—the right to vote. The restrictions there were far less onerous than those the State seeks to impose here. The law in *Burson* meant only that the last few seconds before voters entered a poll-ing place were "their own, as free from interference as possible." And the Court noted that, were the buffer zone larger than 100 feet, it "could effectively become an impermissible burden" under the First Amendment.

The better analogy to this case is *Board of Airport Comm'rs of Los Angeles v. Jews for Jesus, Inc.,* 482 U.S. 569 (1987), where the Court struck down an ordinance pro-hibiting any "First Amendment activities" at Los Angeles International Airport because the ordinance covered all manner of protected, nondisruptive behavior including "talking and reading, or the wearing of campaign buttons or symbolic clothing." If a law prohibiting "all protected expression" at a single airport is not constitutional, it follows with even greater force that the State may not enact this complete bar to the exercise of First Amendment rights on websites integral to the fabric of our modern society and culture.

*   *   *

It is well established that, as a general rule, the Government "may not suppress lawful speech as the means to suppress unlawful speech." That is what North Caro-lina has done here. Its law must be held invalid.

The judgment of the North Carolina Supreme Court is reversed, and the case is remanded for further proceedings not inconsistent with this opinion.

Justice GORSUCH took no part in the consideration or decision of this case.

Justice ALITO, with whom THE CHIEF JUSTICE and Justice THOMAS join, concurring in the judgment.

The North Carolina statute at issue in this case was enacted to serve an interest of "surpassing importance"—but it has a staggering reach. It makes it a felony for a registered sex offender simply to visit a vast array of websites, including many that appear to provide no realistic opportunity for communications that could facilitate the abuse of children. Because of the law's extraordinary breadth, I agree with the Court that it violates the Free Speech Clause of the First Amendment.

I cannot join the opinion of the Court, however, because of its undisciplined dicta. The Court is unable to resist musings that seem to equate the entirety of the internet with public streets and parks. And this language is bound to be interpreted by some to mean that the States are largely powerless to restrict even the most dangerous sexual predators from visiting any internet sites, including, for example, teenage dating sites and sites designed to permit minors to discuss personal problems with their peers. I am troubled by the implications of the Court's unnecessary rhetoric.

I

A

The North Carolina law at issue makes it a felony for a registered sex offender "to access a commercial social networking Web site where the sex offender knows that the site permits minor children to become members or to create or maintain personal Web pages." And as I will explain, the statutory definition of a "commercial social networking Web site" is very broad.

B

A content-neutral "time, place, or manner" restriction must serve a "legitimate" government interest, and the North Carolina law easily satisfies this requirement. As we have frequently noted, "[t]he prevention of sexual exploitation and abuse of children constitutes a government objective of surpassing importance." "Sex offenders are a serious threat," and "the victims of sexual assault are most often juveniles." "[T]he . . . interest [of] safeguarding the physical and psychological well-being of a minor . . . is a compelling one," and "we have sustained legislation aimed at protecting the physical and emotional well-being of youth even when the laws have operated in the sensitive area of constitutionally protected rights."

Repeat sex offenders pose an especially grave risk to children. "When convicted sex offenders reenter society, they are much more likely than any other type of offender to be rearrested for a new rape or sexual assault."

The State's interest in protecting children from recidivist sex offenders plainly applies to internet use. Several factors make the internet a powerful tool for the would-be child abuser. First, children often use the internet in a way that gives offenders easy access to their personal information—by, for example, communicating with strangers and allowing sites to disclose their location. Second, the internet provides previously unavailable ways of communicating with, stalking, and ultimately abusing children. An abuser can create a false profile that misrepresents the abuser's age and gender. The abuser can lure the minor into engaging in sexual conversations, sending explicit photos, or even meeting in person. And an abuser can use a child's location posts on the internet to determine the pattern of the child's day-to-day activities—and even the child's location at a given moment. Such uses of the internet are already well documented, both in research and in reported decisions.[n.3][7]

Because protecting children from abuse is a compelling state interest and sex offenders can (and do) use the internet to engage in such abuse, it is legitimate and entirely reasonable for States to try to stop abuse from occurring before it happens.

C

1

It is not enough, however, that the law before us is designed to serve a compelling state interest; it also must not "burden substantially more speech than is necessary to further the government's legitimate interests." The North Carolina law fails this requirement.

A straightforward reading of the text of N.C. Gen. Stat. Ann. § 14–202.5 compels the conclusion that it prohibits sex offenders from accessing an enormous number of websites. The law defines a "commercial social networking Web site" as one with four characteristics. First, the website must be "operated by a person who derives revenue from membership fees, advertising, or other sources related to the operation of the Web site." Due to the prevalence of advertising on websites of all types, this requirement does little to limit the statute's reach.

Second, the website must "[f]acilitat[e] the social introduction between two or more persons for the purposes of friendship, meeting other persons, or information exchanges." The term "social introduction" easily encompasses any casual exchange, and the term "information exchanges" seems to apply to any site that provides an opportunity for a visitor to post a statement or comment that may be read by other visitors. Today, a great many websites include this feature.

Third, a website must "[a]llo[w] users to create Web pages or personal profiles that contain information *such as* the name or nickname of the user, photographs

---

7. [n.3] For example, in *State v. Gallo*, 275 Or. App. 868, 365 P.3d 1154 (2015), a 32-year-old defendant posing as a 15-year-old boy used a social networking site to contact and befriend a 16-year-old autistic girl. "He then arranged to meet the victim, took her to a park, and sexually abused her." In *United States v. Steele*, 664 Fed. Appx. 260 (C.A.3 2016), the defendant "began interacting with a minor [victim] on the gay social networking cell phone application 'Jack'd.'" He eventually met the 14-year-old victim and sexually abused him.. Sadly, these cases are not unique. See, *e.g.*, *Himko v. English*, 2016 WL 7645584 (N.D.Fla., Dec. 5, 2016) (a convicted rapist and registered sex offender "contacted a sixteen-year-old girl using . . . Facebook" and then exchanged explicit text messages and photographs with her), report and recommendation adopted, 2017 WL 54246 (Jan. 4, 2017); *Roberts v. United States*, 2015 WL 7424858 (S.D. Ohio, Nov. 23, 2015) (the defendant "met a then 14-year-old child online via a social networking website called vampirefreaks.com" and then enticed the child to his home and "coerced the child to perform oral sex on him"), report and recommendation adopted, 2016 WL 112647 (Jan. 8, 2016), certificate of appealability denied, No. 16–3050 (CA6 June 15, 2016); *State v. Murphy*, 2016–0901 (La. App. 1 Cir. 10/28/16), 206 So.3d 219, 224 (a defendant "initiated conversations" with his 12-year-old victim "on a social network chat site called 'Kik'" and later sent sexually graphic photographs of himself to the victim and received sexually graphic photos from her).

placed on the personal Web page by the user, other personal information about the user, and links to other personal Web pages on the commercial social networking Web site of friends or associates of the user that may be accessed by other users or visitors to the Web site." This definition covers websites that allow users to create anything that can be called a "personal profile," *i.e.*, a short description of the user. Contrary to the argument of the State, everything that follows the phrase "such as" is an illustration of features that a covered website or personal profile may (but need not) include.

Fourth, in order to fit within the statute, a website must "[p]rovid[e] users or visitors . . . mechanisms to communicate with other users, *such as* a message board, chat room, electronic mail, or instant messenger." This requirement seems to demand no more than that a website allow back-and-forth comments between users. And since a comment function is undoubtedly a "mechanis[m] to communicate with other users," it appears to follow that any website with such a function satisfies this requirement.

2

The fatal problem for § 14–202.5 is that its wide sweep precludes access to a large number of websites that are most unlikely to facilitate the commission of a sex crime against a child. A handful of examples illustrates this point.

Take, for example, the popular retail website Amazon.com, which allows minors to use its services and meets all four requirements of § 14–202.5's definition of a commercial social networking website. First, as a seller of products, Amazon unquestionably derives revenue from the operation of its website. Second, the Amazon site facilitates the social introduction of people for the purpose of information exchanges. When someone purchases a product on Amazon, the purchaser can review the product and upload photographs, and other buyers can then respond to the review. This information exchange about products that Amazon sells undoubtedly fits within the definition in § 14–202.5. It is the equivalent of passengers on a bus comparing notes about products they have purchased. Third, Amazon allows a user to create a personal profile, which is then associated with the product reviews that the user uploads. Such a profile can contain an assortment of information, including the user's name, e-mail address, and picture. And fourth, given its back-and-forth comment function, Amazon satisfies the final statutory requirement.

Many news websites are also covered by this definition. For example, the Washington Post's website gives minors access and satisfies the four elements that define a commercial social networking website. The website (1) derives revenue from ads and (2) facilitates social introductions for the purpose of information exchanges. Users of the site can comment on articles, reply to other users' comments, and recommend another user's comment. Users can also (3) create personal profiles that include a name or nickname and a photograph. The photograph and name will then appear next to every comment the user leaves on an article. Finally (4), the back-and-forth comment section is a mechanism for users to communicate among themselves. The site thus falls within § 14–202.5 and is accordingly off limits for registered sex offenders in North Carolina.

Or consider WebMD—a website that contains health-related resources, from tools that help users find a doctor to information on preventative care and the symptoms associated with particular medical problems. WebMD, too, allows children on the site. And it exhibits the four hallmarks of a "commercial social networking" website. It obtains revenue from advertisements. It facilitates information exchanges—via message boards that allow users to engage in public discussion of an assortment of health issues. It allows users to create basic profile pages: Users can upload a picture and some basic information about themselves, and other users can see their aggregated comments and "likes." WebMD also provides message boards, which are specifically mentioned in the statute as a "mechanis[m] to communicate with other users."

As these examples illustrate, the North Carolina law has a very broad reach and covers websites that are ill suited for use in stalking or abusing children. The focus of the discussion on these sites—shopping, news, health—does not provide a convenient jumping off point for conversations that may lead to abuse. In addition, the social exchanges facilitated by these websites occur in the open, and this reduces the possibility of a child being secretly lured into an abusive situation. These websites also give sex offenders little opportunity to gather personal details about a child; the information that can be listed in a profile is limited, and the profiles are brief. What is more, none of these websites make it easy to determine a child's precise location at a given moment. For example, they do not permit photo streams (at most, a child could upload a single profile photograph), and they do not include up-to-the-minute location services. Such websites would provide essentially no aid to a would-be child abuser.

Placing this set of websites categorically off limits from registered sex offenders prohibits them from receiving or engaging in speech that the First Amendment protects and does not appreciably advance the State's goal of protecting children from recidivist sex offenders. I am therefore compelled to conclude that, while the law before us addresses a critical problem, it sweeps far too broadly to satisfy the demands of the Free Speech Clause.[n.15][8]

II

While I thus agree with the Court that the particular law at issue in this case violates the First Amendment, I am troubled by the Court's loose rhetoric. After noting that "a street or a park is a quintessential forum for the exercise of First Amendment rights," the Court states that "cyberspace" and "social media in particular"

---

8. [n.15] I express no view on whether a law that does not reach the sort of sites discussed above would satisfy the First Amendment. Until such a law is before us, it is premature to address that question.

are now "the most important places (in a spatial sense) for the exchange of views." The Court declines to explain what this means with respect to free speech law, and the Court holds no more than that the North Carolina law fails the test for content-neutral "time, place, and manner" restrictions. But if the entirety of the internet or even just "social media" sites[n.16][9] are the 21st century equivalent of public streets and parks, then States may have little ability to restrict the sites that may be visited by even the most dangerous sex offenders. May a State preclude an adult previously convicted of molesting children from visiting a dating site for teenagers? Or a site where minors communicate with each other about personal problems? The Court should be more attentive to the implications of its rhetoric for, contrary to the Court's suggestion, there are important differences between cyberspace and the physical world.

I will mention a few that are relevant to internet use by sex offenders. First, it is easier for parents to monitor the physical locations that their children visit and the individuals with whom they speak in person than it is to monitor their internet use. Second, if a sex offender is seen approaching children or loitering in a place frequented by children, this conduct may be observed by parents, teachers, or others. Third, the internet offers an unprecedented degree of anonymity and easily permits a would-be molester to assume a false identity.

The Court is correct that we should be cautious in applying our free speech precedents to the internet. Cyberspace is different from the physical world, and if it is true, as the Court believes, that "we cannot appreciate yet" the "full dimensions and vast potential" of "the Cyber Age," we should proceed circumspectly, taking one step at a time. It is regrettable that the Court has not heeded its own admonition of caution.

United States v. Ronald Scott Paul

274 F.3d 155 (5th Cir. 2001)

KING, CHIEF JUDGE:

Paul took his personal computer to Electronic Services and Repair, a small computer repair business in Port Isabel, Texas. While working on the computer, a technician discovered child pornography on the hard drive and contacted the Federal Bureau of Investigations. The FBI's background check on Paul revealed a 1986 offense involving child pornography. After Paul had retrieved his computer from the repair technician, FBI agents searched Paul's residence pursuant to a valid warrant. The agents seized the computer, which contained a large number of files with images of child pornography that had been downloaded from the Internet. The agents also seized assorted photographs of children, magazines with nude photographs of children and adults, books with pictures of nude prepubescent boys,

---

9. [n.16] As the law at issue here shows, it is not easy to provide a precise definition of a "social media" site, and the Court makes no effort to do so. Thus, the scope of its dicta is obscure.

videotapes of random children filmed in public settings, a large bag of children's clothes, and several children's swimsuits covered with sand.

Additionally, the agents seized a medical bag containing basic medical supplies and Spanish-language flyers advertising lice removal for children. In the flyers, Paul informed parents that he would spray their children with a product that kills lice. The flyers also stated that Paul would conduct a complete physical examination on each child for "overall health," which necessarily required the child to completely undress. The agents also found between ten and twenty personal cameras in Paul's residence.

Further review of Paul's computer revealed electronic mail communications discussing sources of child pornography, including websites, chat rooms, and newsgroups that allowed both receiving and sending of pornographic images. In one of these e-mails, Paul discussed how easy it was to find "young friends" by scouting single, dysfunctional parents through Alcoholics Anonymous or local welfare offices and winning their friendship, thereby securing access to their young sons.

Paul pled guilty to one charge of knowingly possessing a computer hard drive with three or more images of child pornography that traveled through interstate commerce. The government offered four images as samples of the child pornography that Paul possessed. Paul admitted that these exhibits were images he received from the Internet and stored on his computer hard drive.

The court ordered the probation office to prepare a presentence report. [The court ultimately sentenced Paul to a period of incarceration, followed by three years of supervision after release from prison.] The district court imposed a number of special conditions on Paul's supervised release term [of three years, including] that Paul "shall not have[,] possess or have access to computers, the Internet, photographic equipment, audio/video equipment, or any item capable of producing a visual image."

Paul contends that a blanket prohibition on computer or Internet use is excessively broad and cannot be justified based solely on the fact that his offense involved a computer and the Internet. He points out that computers and Internet access have become indispensable communication tools in the modern world and that the restriction imposed by the district court would prohibit him from accessing computers and the Internet for legitimate purposes, such as word processing and research.

The supervised release condition at issue in the instant case is reasonably related to Paul's offense and to the need to prevent recidivism and protect the public. The record reveals that Paul has in the past used the Internet to encourage exploitation of children by seeking out fellow "boy lovers" and providing them with advice on how to find and obtain access to "young friends." Restricting his access to this communication medium clearly serves the dual statutory goals of protecting the public and preventing future criminal activity. While the condition at issue prohibits access to both computers and the Internet and it contains no proviso permitting

Paul to use these resources with the approval of his probation office, we cannot say that that the district court abused its discretion in determining that an absolute ban on computer and Internet use was reasonably necessary to protect the public and to prevent recidivism.

[W]e reject the . . . implication that an absolute prohibition on accessing computers or the Internet is *per se* an unacceptable condition of supervised release, simply because such a prohibition might prevent a defendant from using a computer at the library to "get a weather forecast" or to "read a newspaper online" during the supervised release term. We find that such a supervised release condition can be acceptable if it is reasonably necessary to serve the statutory goals outlined in 18 U.S.C. § 3583(d). In the instant case, the district court had strong evidentiary support for its determination that a strict ban on computer and Internet use was reasonably necessary. Moreover, Paul has articulated no specific objections to the computer and Internet ban suggesting how his occupational affairs or his expressive activities will be adversely impacted by the fact that he will be unable to "use a computer or the Internet at a library, cybercafe or . . . an airport" during the term of his supervised release.[n.17][10] We conclude that the district court did not abuse its discretion in imposing this condition of supervised release.

United States v. Mark Wayne Russell

600 F.3d 631 (D.C. Cir. 2010)

WILLIAMS, SENIOR CIRCUIT JUDGE:

Defendant Mark Russell pleaded guilty to one count of travel with intent to engage in illicit sexual conduct, in violation of 18 U.S.C. § 2423(b) (2006). The district court sentenced him to 46 months of imprisonment and 30 years of supervised release. A special condition of his supervised release specifies that Russell may not "possess or use a computer for any reason." We vacate the computer restriction and remand for resentencing.

In June 2006, using a computer at his home in Columbia, Maryland, Russell entered an internet chat room and initiated a conversation with an individual identifying herself as a 13-year old girl; "she" was actually a member of the District of Columbia Metropolitan Police Department. Three days later, Russell again engaged the "child" in an online chat. Over the course of their second chat, Russell performed a solo sex act live via webcam and invited the "child" to have sex with him. The purported child, in response, provided her address in Washington, D.C., and said that her mother would not be home until seven or eight that evening. Russell drove to the address, parked his car, and e-mailed the "child" to say he had

---

10. [n.17] The record reveals that Paul has primarily been employed in recent years as a truck driver.

arrived. After a period of waiting, he began to drive away, at which point he was arrested.

Russell was 46 when he was sentenced, and approximately 50 at the time of his release. He had worked as an applied systems engineer at Johns Hopkins University for ten years before becoming unemployed at the end of April 2006. Before this arrest, he had had no contact with the law. According to his wife of 23 years, the mother of their three children, he had been depressed in the period just before his arrest.

[The court found that the condition deprived the defendant of substantially more liberty than was "reasonably necessary," and vacated the condition.]

The computer restriction affirmatively and aggressively interferes with the goal of rehabilitation. It is hard to imagine white collar work in 2010 not requiring access to computers, just as white collar work 100 years ago would almost invariably have required the use of pens and pencils. In fact Russell's training and experience mark him not only as a white collar worker but as one at the most technically sophisticated end of the white collar distribution. He holds a Bachelors of Science degree in engineering and a Masters degree in Strategic Intelligence, and his 10 years as an applied systems engineer at Johns Hopkins suggest a work life fitted to the skills so acquired. Even a lot of blue collar work requires some computer use. Although we cannot rely on evidence developed since the sentence, it is totally unsurprising in the realities of the modern world that in his post-release search for employment Russell has evidently found that computer use is required for filling out most job applications, including those at McDonald's, as well as discharging the duties of even low tech occupations, such as keeping inventory at PETCO, and producing frames at A.C. Moore. Because the computer restriction prevents Russell from continuing in a field in which he has decades of accumulated academic and professional experience, it directly conflicts with the rehabilitative goal of sentencing. It also, of course, places a substantial burden on Russell's liberty, must be no greater than reasonably necessary to achieve the goals of deterrence as well as rehabilitation.

The district court's restriction is scheduled to elapse more than three decades after sentencing. A provision for modification by the probation department—a minimum change suitable on remand—would allow the restriction to adjust to ongoing developments in technology and to secure a reasonable balance between the statute's rehabilitative and deterrence goals. Given the ample room for adjusting the sentence to enable a better balance among those goals, the computer restriction in its current form is substantively unreasonable.

We have found only one case, *United States v. Paul*, 274 F.3d 155 (5th Cir. 2001), that upholds, against proper challenge, a categorical prohibition on computer possession or use without provision for probation office modification. Not only is *Paul* an outlier, but in key respects it represents a far stronger case for blanket restriction.

Most obviously, Paul's computer restriction was to last three years, or one tenth of the duration of Russell's—a difference that makes Paul's restriction both less burdensome and less likely to become a still poorer fit over time. Moreover, Paul had suggested no way in which the computer and internet ban would adversely affect his occupational prospects, whereas Russell made clear that his rehabilitation would depend at least in part on his ability to apply his professional training, which in turn would depend on his being able to access computers. Although Paul had pled guilty only to possessing child pornography that traveled through interstate commerce, the record showed that Paul had engaged in a sustained, extensive and sophisticated pattern of sexual predation over many years, continuously aided and magnified by the internet. And he had a prior child pornography conviction. Finally, of course, the computer and internet have permeated everyday life in ways that make a restriction on their use far more burdensome than when *Paul* was decided.

We have found no instance other than *Paul* where a court has upheld a prohibition on the defendant's use of computers or the internet that was not subject to relaxation by the probation office. Many cases have upheld restrictions subject to such relaxation. In several of these cases defendants' conduct was more egregious than Russell's—he had either completed sex acts with a child, or caused another to do so in order to obtain images of the conduct, or took more drastic steps toward completion of the acts than did Russell (defendant flew to site of intended rendezvous after developing a ruse to separate the minor from his or her mother for the weekend). In contrast, the courts have generated a large universe of decisions rejecting such unmodifiable restrictions, typically invoking (as here) the public interest in the defendant's rehabilitation through the productive use of his or her skills. In at least one such case, the defendant's conduct, unlike Russell's, manifested a course of completed child molestations.

KAREN LeCRAFT HENDERSON, CIRCUIT JUDGE, concurring:

I am unwilling to subscribe to the notion that a restriction (or ban) on a criminal defendant's computer use, at least where the computer enables the crime, constitutes "a substantial burden" on liberty. A defendant convicted of vehicular homicide can permanently lose his driving privilege and the resulting ban on his use of an automobile—which, like Russell's computer, enabled the crime—does not deprive him of his liberty. That Russell's white collar career may be adversely affected by the computer ban—a result the majority supports with anecdotal predictions—does not *ipso facto* translate into a deprivation of liberty. We can judicially note that millions of Americans every day perform jobs without using (or even seeing) a computer. If Russell cannot find a job, it is more likely because of his criminal record than the computer ban. While I do not believe the thirty-year computer ban implicates Russell's liberty, I nevertheless recognize that the weight of authority is to the contrary. For that reason, I join in the remand for the district court to again exercise its discretion in refining the computer ban condition of Russell's supervised release.

United States v. Arthur William Heckman

592 F.3d 400 (3d Cir. 2010)

Ambro, Circuit Judge.

Arthur William Heckman was indicted and pled guilty to one count of transporting child pornography. He was sentenced to 180 months' imprisonment, followed by a lifetime term of supervised release. On appeal, Heckman challenges[,*inter alia*, a lifetime] ban on Internet access.

Heckman emailed 18 pictures of minors engaging in sexually explicit conduct to a stranger in an Internet chat room. Though Heckman believed the recipient to be a person who shared his interest in child pornography, he was actually transmitting the images to an undercover special agent with the Federal Bureau of Investigation.

The following special conditions of lifetime supervised release are at issue in Heckman's appeal:

> The defendant is prohibited from access to any Internet service provider, bulletin board system, or any other public or private computer network.

He challenges this special condition as plain error. We agree. Since this is an area of law that requires a fact-specific analysis, we consider each of our relevant precedents in some detail. Throughout, we remain sensitive to three factors that have guided our prior holdings in this area: (1) the *length* and (2) *coverage* of the imposed ban; and, (3) the defendant's underlying *conduct*.

We first upheld a conditional ban on Internet access in *United States v. Crandon*, 173 F.3d 122 (3d Cir. 1999). There the defendant was a 30-year-old resident of New Jersey who met a 14-year-old girl from Minnesota on the Internet. After corresponding online for several months, Crandon traveled from New Jersey to Minnesota and engaged in sexual relations with the girl. The District Court imposed a three-year condition on Crandon's supervised release that directed him "not [to] 'possess, procure, purchase[,] or otherwise obtain access to any form of computer network, bulletin board, Internet, or exchange format involving computers *unless specifically approved by the United States Probation Office*.'" Therefore, Crandon's ban was both limited (to three years) and conditional (subject to exceptions approved by the Probation Office).[n.4][11]

---

11. [n.4] Even conditional bans raise concerns about the discretion they afford probation officers. As Judge Easterbrook cautions:

> Terms should be established by judges *ex ante*, not probation officers acting under broad delegations and subject to loose judicial review *ex post*. . . . Courts should do what they can to eliminate open-ended delegations, which create opportunities for arbitrary action—opportunities that are especially worrisome when the subject concerns what people may read. Is the probation officer to become a censor who determines that [the defendant] may read the *New York Times* online, but not the version of *Ulysses* at Bibliomania.com? Bureaucrats acting as guardians of morals offend the first amendment as well as the ideals behind our commitments to the rule of law.

On appeal, we held that the Internet access ban was justified, given Crandon's conduct—namely, that he "used the Internet as a means to develop an illegal sexual relationship with a young girl over a period of several months." With this underlying, directly exploitative conduct in mind, we concluded that the ban was "narrowly tailored and . . . directly related to deterring [the defendant] and protecting the public."

Four years later, we refused to uphold a more restrictive, five-year ban in *United States v. Freeman*, 316 F.3d 386 (3d Cir. 2003). There the defendant's offense did not include the direct exploitation of a minor. Instead, it involved the distribution of child pornography by a convicted child molester. The District Court imposed a special condition that was both lengthier (five years rather than three years) and more restrictive (adding a ban on computer equipment in the defendant's residence to a conditional Internet ban).

In spite of Freeman's prior criminal record as a child molester, we struck down this five-year ban as "overly broad," explaining that, since the defendant had not used the Internet to seduce a minor, there was no need to "cut off Freeman's access to email or benign [I]nternet usage," especially in light of the fact that "a more focused restriction, limited to pornography sites and images, can be enforced by unannounced inspections of material stored on Freeman's hard drive or removable disks." In this, we explicitly distinguished *Crandon*, explaining that "the defendant in *Crandon* used the [I]nternet to contact young children and solicit inappropriate sexual contact with them." Importantly, "[s]uch use of the [I]nternet is . . . more difficult to trace than simply using the [I]nternet to view pornographic web sites."

In 2007, we rejected a lifetime, unconditional ban on all computer access in [*United States v. Voelker*, 489 F.3d 139 (3rd Cir. 2007)]. There the defendant engaged in an Internet conversation during which he briefly exposed the buttocks of his three-year-old daughter over a webcam. It was later determined that Voelker, who had no criminal record, also possessed a stockpile of child pornography. The District Court imposed a special condition that was much lengthier (lifetime rather than three years) and more restrictive (an unconditional computer ban rather than a conditional Internet ban) than the one we upheld in *Crandon*.

On appeal, we struck down this ban as "the antithesis of a 'narrowly tailored' sanction." In so holding, we distinguished *Crandon*, noting the difference in duration of the special conditions imposed, as "Crandon's restrictions remained in place for three years," while "Voelker's restrictions will last as long as he does." We also determined Crandon's offense to be worse than Voelker's, as "Crandon used computers and the [I]nternet to actually seek out, and then communicate with, his victim." Finally, we contrasted the coverage of the two bans, as "Crandon was allowed to continue using standalone computers and computer equipment, and he retained the right to use the [I]nternet with the consent of the Probation Office. Voelker is

---

United States v. Scott, 316 F.3d 733, 736 (7th Cir. 2003) (Easterbrook, J.).

not afforded either of those options." In the end, we refused to approve "such an all-encompassing, severe, and *permanent* restriction."

Finally, we upheld a ten-year, conditional ban on Internet access in [*United States v. Thielemann*, 575 F.3d 265 (3rd Cir. 2009).] There the defendant pled guilty to one count of receiving child pornography, but this understated the magnitude of his conduct. Indeed, Thielemann was actively involved in not only distributing child pornography, but also in encouraging (successfully) the direct exploitation of minors.

The District Court sentenced Thielemann to the statutory maximum of 240 months in prison and 10 years of supervised release, including a conditional ban on Internet access. This is the lengthiest ban that we have upheld. In our analysis, we emphasized the relatively limited coverage of Thielemann's ban, noting that he could "own or use a *personal* computer as long as it is not connected to the [I]nternet; thus he is allowed to use word processing programs and other benign software." Further, we added that Thielemann "may seek permission from the Probation Office to use the [I]nternet during the term of his ten-year restriction, which is a far cry from the unyielding lifetime restriction in *Voelker*." Finally, we noted the importance of Thielemann's underlying conduct. He did more than "simply trade child pornography; he [used] [I]nternet communication technologies to facilitate, entice, and encourage the real-time molestation of a child." Given this conduct, we concluded that "[t]he restriction on computer and [I]nternet use [was closely related] to the goals of deterrence and protection of the public, and [did] not involve greater deprivation of liberty than is necessary."

If upheld, Heckman's ban would be the most restrictive Internet ban that we have permitted — both in terms of the length and coverage of the ban itself and the nature of the defendant's underlying conduct. Considering the ban's length, it is much longer than the three-year ban approved in *Crandon* and the ten-year ban recently approved in *Thielemann.* As for its coverage, it is more restrictive than the Internet bans upheld in *Crandon* and *Thielemann*, both of which included provisions allowing for access to the Internet on approval by the Probation Office. Finally, focusing on the conduct underlying Heckman's conviction, this would be the first time that we have upheld an Internet ban for a conviction involving the transmission of child pornography rather than the direct exploitation of children. In fact, considering these factors collectively, Heckman's special condition would be the broadest Internet ban upheld by any Circuit Court to date.

There is little doubt that Heckman's extensive history as a sex offender justifies appropriate restrictions whenever he is released from prison. To repeat, the District Court recognized that Heckman's criminal conduct was "almost unbroken from the time he was nineteen years old until today at age forty-eight." For this understandable reason, the Government argues that the "most significant" factor in this case is that "Heckman presents a record of sexual abuse of children which is not remotely matched in any of this Court's prior cases."

This record cannot be ignored. However, Heckman's criminal history alone does not justify the unprecedented ban on Internet access imposed by the District Court in this case. Indeed, we have long recognized the draconian nature of Internet bans—even in cases where we have upheld them. Furthermore, even when faced with a well-established sex offender, special conditions still must be tailored to the underlying conduct at issue in the given case, as well as any related actions in the defendant's criminal past.

Heckman is undoubtedly a serial offender. Yet he has never been convicted of criminal behavior that involved the use of the Internet either to lure a minor into direct sexual activity (such as Crandon) or to entice another to exploit a child directly (such as Thielemann). In cases upholding similar (though less restrictive) Internet bans, the predatory use of the Internet *in the act itself* was essential to our holding. In cases involving the straight transmission or possession of child pornography, such as *Freeman*, we rejected the ban. To uphold Heckman's ban under our precedent, we would have to make the inferential leap that, given his criminal history, it is likely that he will eventually use the Internet to exploit a minor directly (and do so late in his 70s)—not just distribute child pornography. Although such an inference may be plausible, there is no indication that Heckman has ever used the Internet for such a purpose. Furthermore, there are alternative, less restrictive, means of controlling Heckman's post-release behavior, including the computer monitoring condition already imposed by the District Court in this case.

We do not hold that limited Internet bans of shorter duration can never be imposed as conditions of supervised release for this type of conduct, but when placed within the context of related precedents, the unconditional, lifetime ban imposed by the District Court in this case is so broad and insufficiently tailored as to constitute "plain error." We thus hold that this ban involved a "greater deprivation of liberty than is reasonably necessary."

Notes

1. For cases upholding life time bans, *see United States v. Stults*, 575 F.3d 834 (8th Cir. 2009); *United States v. Boston*, 494 F.3d 660 (8th Cir. 2007); *United States v. Alvarez*, 478 F.3d 864 (8th Cir. 2007). *But see United States v. Duke*, 788 F.3d 392 (5th Cir. 2015):

> In sum, the district court abused its discretion by imposing a condition of supervised release that prohibited Duke from accessing computers or the Internet for the rest of his life. Such a condition is not narrowly tailored and therefore imposes a greater deprivation than reasonably necessary to prevent recidivism and protect the public, especially in light of the ubiquity and importance of the Internet.

What impact does *Packingham* have on such bans? Should a registered sex offender be treated differently than someone on probation or parole?

2. Because child pornography is so prevalent, and many cases are flowing through the federal and state courts, the debate as to what to do with the offenders—both the length of sentence—and post release controls on their behavior—is a continuing one. The following list presents some additional options. What should society's response be?

————————

OTHER OPTIONS FOR LIMITING COMPUTER USE

1. **Monitoring Software.** *See generally* Marc Harrold, *Computer Searches of Probationers*, 75 MISS. L.J. 273 (2005). Harrold offers an overview of the "four basic approaches" to monitoring software. Those four methods are: (1) filtering software, which blocks access to certain websites and logs a user's usage; (2) system resident software that can only be accessed by the probation agent while at the probationer's computer; (3) system resident software that sends email reports to the probation agent; and (4) "forced gateway" software that can be reviewed remotely. In *Heckman*, the court observed that a computer monitoring condition had been imposed by the District Court and that the condition provided for extensive computer monitoring, paid for by Heckman:

> The defendant shall submit to an initial inspection by the United States Probation Office and to any examinations during supervision of the defendant's computer and any devices, programs, or applications. The defendant shall allow the installation of any hardware or software systems which monitor or filter computer use. The defendant shall abide by the standard conditions of computer monitoring and filtering that will be approved by this Court. The defendant is to pay the cost of the computer monitoring not to exceed the monthly contractual rate, in accordance with the probation officer's discretion.

2. **Probation Searches.** In a concurring opinion in *United States v. Russell*, 600 F.3d 631 (D.C. Cir. 2010), Judge Henderson noted that, in exercising its discretion in refining a condition of Russell's supervised release upon remand, in the event the district court permitted some computer use, 18 U.S.C. § 3583(d) expressly provided:

> The court may order, as an explicit condition of supervised release . . . that [Russell] submit his . . . computer, other electronic communications or data storage devices or media, and effects to search at any time, with or without a warrant, by any law enforcement or probation officer with reasonable suspicion . . . and by any probation officer in the lawful discharge of the officer's supervision functions.

3. **Prohibitions on Websites/Filtering.** In *United States v. Holm*, 326 F.3d 872 (7th Cir. 2003), the court rejected a broad restriction on the defendant's computer and Internet use, stating that "[v]arious forms of monitored Internet use might provide a middle ground between the need to ensure that Holm never again uses the

Worldwide Web for illegal purposes and the need to allow him to function in the modern world." *See also* Emily Brant, Comment, *Sentencing "Cybersex Offenders": Individual Offenders Require Individualized Conditions When Courts Restrict Their Computer Use and Internet Access*, 58 Catholic U.L. Rev. 779 (2009):

> "[T]he software regulates content only on the computer in which it is installed, and none of the software presently available is completely effective." Even if these programs are completely effective in blocking desired websites, they nonetheless fail to prevent an offender from trafficking inappropriate material via e-mail and it is almost impossible for probation officers to ensure that these programs remain up-to-date, given the ever-increasing number of social networks. Even more troubling is the fact that software is also available that allows knowledgeable Internet users to delete the names of sites visited from the computer's hard drive.

Index